LABOR & EMPLOYMENT LAW

Text and Cases

LABOR & EMPLOYMENT LAW

Text and Cases

FOURTEENTH EDITION

DAVID P. TWOMEY

Professor of Law

Carroll School of Management, Boston College

Member of the Massachusetts and Florida Bars

SOUTH-WESTERN
CENGAGE Learning

Australia • Brazil • Canada • Mexico • Singapore • Spain • United Kingdom • United States

SOUTH-WESTERN
CENGAGE Learning™

Labor & Employment Law: Text & Cases, Fourteenth Edition

David P. Twomey

VP Editorial Director: Jack W. Calhoun

Editor-in-Chief: Rob Dewey

Acquisitions Editor: Vicky True

Development Editor: Krista Kellman

Media Editor: Kristen Meere

Content Project Manager: Patrick Franzen

Editorial Assistant: Krista Kellman

Marketing Manager: Jennifer Garamy

Marketing Coordinator: Heather McAuliffe

Marketing Communications Manager: Sarah Greber

Creative Director: Rob Hugel

Senior Art Director: Michelle Kunkler

Production Technology Analyst: Starratt Alexander

Manufacturing Buyer: Kevin Kluck

Permissions Editor: Margaret Chamberlain-Gaston

Production Service: Pre-Press PMG

Internal Designer: Juli Cook

Cover Designer: Tin Box Studio, Inc.

Cover Image: © Skip Nall/Photodisc, Inc.

Compositor: Pre-Press PMG

For product information and technology assistance, contact us at **Cengage Learning Academic Resource Center, 1-800-423-0563**

For permission to use material from this text or product, submit all requests online at **www.cengage.com/permissions**

Further permissions questions can be e-mailed to **permissionrequest@cengage.com**

Library of Congress Control Number: 2008942498

Student Edition:
ISBN-13: 978-0-324-59484-3

ISBN-10: 0-324-59484-4

South-Western Cengage Learning
5191 Natorp Boulevard
Mason, Ohio 45040
USA

Cengage Learning products are represented in Canada by Nelson Education, Ltd.

For your course and learning solutions, visit **academic.cengage.com.**

Purchase any of our products at your local college store or at our preferred online store **www.ichapters.com.**

Printed in the United States of America
1 2 3 4 5 6 7 13 12 11 10 09

Dedicated to:
David Leo, S.J., Joe Laughlin, S.J., and John Mandile, S.J., who had
such a wonderful impact on the lives of so many students at BC High;
and the extraordinary Bill McInnes, S.J. of Boston College.

———————

BRIEF CONTENTS

Contents

CHAPTER 10 | **Public Employment and Labor Law**   321

Section

CHAPTER 11 | **Occupational Safety and Health Law**   353

Section

CHAPTER 12 | **Discrimination Laws: Protected Classes under Title VII
and the Constitution**   387

Section

PREFACE

WHAT IS NEW IN THIS EDITION

The new edition of *Labor & Employment Law* continues to present a comprehensive treatment of labor and employment law topics. New text, cases, and case problems have been added throughout the book. However, the unprecedented number and scope of recent administrative and court decisions required many major revisions throughout the book to properly present current developments in the law.

NEW CHAPTER

The federal administrative agencies dealing with labor and employment law matters have issued many important and often controversial decisions since the last edition of this text. For example, the National Labor Relations Board (NLRB), which had a majority of Republican appointees since December 2002, came under heavy criticism concerning its decisions not only from union and opposition political leaders, but from academicians as well. A letter signed by 57 labor law professors was sent to Congress in December 2007 asserting in part that: "[b]y overturning precedent and establishing new rules ... the Board has regularly denied or impaired the very statutory rights it is charged with protecting ...." The then Chairman of the NLRB responded that the decisions were not politicized and that the complaints were politically motivated. In light of these developments, Chapter , a short new introductory chapter, presents an overview of basic administrative law principles and outlines the federal court system with a labor and employment law focus. Care has been taken to present both the majority and dissenting opinions of the controversial cases recently decided by administrative agencies so that the readers may determine for themselves the "correctness" of the decisions under administrative law principles. And, with an understanding of the federal court system, readers may follow the appropriate appellate review process, up to the Supreme Court in some cases, as labor and employment law precedents are established.

NEW CASES

Each chapter contains numerous court and agency cases relevant to the topic at hand. Reflecting the growing importance of labor and employment law cases in the federal court system, the U.S. Supreme Court decided an unusually large number of labor and employment law cases, eleven, during the 2007-2008 term. The cases are referenced or reported in this edition of the textbook, including two "retaliation" cases adding to the Court's landmark 2006 *BNSF v. White* "retaliation" decision, and a large number of other equal employment opportunity cases. Some cases were selected for their historical import, some for their particularly insightful discussion of the issues, and some because they represent turning points in the law. All have been carefully edited to remove extraneous discussion while preserving the integrity of the opinion.

Each decision is followed by case questions to guide the student through the opinion and assist in identification of the cogent issues and arguments.

At the end of each chapter is a selection of case problems. The case problems are derived from court and administrative agency decisions in real cases and offer students the opportunity to apply the legal principles in each chapter to real-life situations.

SIGNIFICANT REVISIONS

In Chapter 4, substantial coverage is devoted to the Labor Board's new definitions utilized to determine "supervisory" status of employees and their eligibility or exclusion from the coverage and rights of the National Labor Relations Act. The chapter also details union efforts to avoid the NLRB election process and the Board's *Dana Corp.* decision modifying the "recognition bar doctrine." The Board's *Register-Guard* decision is also presented, which involves discipline of a union officer for using company owned e-mail for union business, although the company permitted personal use of e-mail for a wide variety of nonbusiness purposes.

Chapter 5, involving protection of employee rights, includes a new section that applies the *Myers Industries* rule that the activities of a single employee acting with the purpose of furtherance of the goals of a group can be protected "concerted" activity under Section 7 of the NLRA. Chapter 6 presents, with new clarity, guidance for the murky statutory language of Section 8(b)(4) of the NLRA, which involves union secondary activity, including consumer picketing, handbilling, and bannering. The Board majority's recent precedent on "permanent replacement status" and the dissenting view is covered in Chapter 7. The new edition contains court decisions on ERISA and public sector union security clauses. It also contains new OSHA cases and a new section on "Violence in the Workplace," including employer obligations under the act's general duty clause to develop and implement workplace violence prevention plans.

Major revisions to the equal employment opportunity chapters reflect recent decisions by the Supreme Court and U.S. courts of appeals. These updates appear in Chapter 12 sections on "National Origin Discrimination and 'English Only' Rules" and "Protection Against Retaliation," which includes a subsection on "Employer Preventative Steps." Significant new developments in Age Discrimination Law adverse to employers are presented in Chapter 14, while text and a case demonstrate how difficult it is for a plaintiff to win an age discrimination case.

The Americans with Disabilities Act of 1990 was amended by the ADA Amendments Act of 2008, effective January 1, 2009. The major changes to the ADA are presented in Chapter 15 and new text also focuses on the increased importance of employers' obligations to provide "reasonable accommodations" under the ADA. Newly developing "whistleblower law" is presented in Chapter 16, including protection of public employee whistleblowers after *Garcetti* and whistleblower protection under the Sarbanes-Oxley Act. Chapter 17 presents text and a recent decision on employee privacy rights concerning text messaging. Chapter 18 provides new text and cases on overtime and immigration issues.

DETAILED FOOTNOTES

The detailed footnotes in each chapter are a hallmark feature of this text. The footnotes in this edition have been fully updated and new footnotes have been added throughout. The footnotes not only meticulously provide case citations for further research or assignments, but also provide interesting side-stories to help illustrate the legal concepts explored, offer historical or additional information, and give differing points of view to encourage critical thinking and discussion.

LABOR & EMPLOYMENT LAW INSTRUCTOR RESOURCES

INSTRUCTOR'S MANUAL

www.cengage.com/blaw/twomey

The Instructor's Manual for the new edition of *Labor & Employment Law* contains questions and answers for each of the cases reported in the text as well as answers to end-of-chapter questions and problems. Also helpful for the instructor, the manual includes Author's Comments, which offer suggestions for sparking classroom discussion while referencing specific cases, footnotes, and sections of the text.

TEXT COMPANION WEBSITE

www.cengage.com/blaw/twomey

The companion website for this edition of *Labor & Employment Law* has been greatly enhanced to streamline necessary resources. In addition to providing access to the Instructor's Manual and Court Case Updates, the website now also offers links to the following: important labor and employment law sites, labor and employment law blogs, legal forms and documents, free legal research sites (comprehensive and circuit-specific), help in the classroom, labor and employment law directories, departments, agencies, associations, and organizations. In addition, a list of recent labor and employment law cases with links directly to the excerpted versions is available on the website.

COURT CASE UPDATES

www.cengage.com/blaw/cases

South-Western's Court Case Updates provide monthly summaries of the most important legal cases happening around the country.

WESTLAW® ACCESS

www.westlaw.com

Westlaw®, West Group's vast online source of value-added legal and business information, contains over 15,000 databases of information spanning a variety of jurisdictions, practice areas, and disciplines. Qualified instructors may receive ten complimentary hours of Westlaw for their course (certain restrictions apply; contact your South-Western Legal Studies in Business representative for details).

BUSINESS LAW DIGITAL VIDEO LIBRARY

www.cengage.com/blaw/dvl

This dynamic online video library features over 60 video clips that spark class discussion and clarify core legal principles, including 14 videos that address employment law topics (such as employment at will, employment discrimination, employee privacy, etc). The library is organized into four series:

- *Legal Conflicts in Business* includes specific modern business and e-commerce scenarios.
- *Ask the Instructor* contains straightforward explanations of concepts for student review.
- *Drama of the Law* features classic business scenarios that spark classroom participation.
- *LawFlix* contains clips from many popular films, including *Bowfinger, The Money Pit, Midnight Run*, and *Casino*.

Access to the Business Law Digital Video Library is available as an optional package with each new student text at no additional charge. Contact your South-Western Legal Studies in Business representative for details

BUSINESS LAW COMMUNITY WEBSITE

www.cengage.com/community/blaw

Visit South-Western's Legal Studies in Business Community website for a wealth of resources to help you deliver the most effective course possible, including our "Great Ideas in Teaching Business Law" section. Our Community Website offers teaching tips and ideas for making the subject interesting and appealing to your students. Ideas include class presentations, discussion ideas, research projects and more.

TO THE INSTRUCTOR

The law of labor and employment relations was not created in the abstract but was developed out of the intense and often violent struggle between groups with widely divergent and conflicting interests. Both humanity and inhumanity played key roles in the unfolding drama, and the equitable resolution of conflicts was never so clear at the time as it always is with the benefit of hindsight. If you keep this thought in mind and communicate it to your classes, the subject matter of labor and employment law will have a vitality for your students that can rarely be appreciated by merely reading the pages in a book.

Many instructors set aside time each week to discuss current labor and employment law issues as they develop by requiring reports to the class from newspapers, periodicals, and current court decisions. By using the vehicle of current issues, you can put the struggle between management and labor in perspective, draw the students into the controversy, and thereby help them crystallize in their own minds the arguments on both sides, the conflicting interests, and the balance and compromise so necessary in our complex society.

This edition contains more material than previous editions, more than would normally be covered in a one-semester course. The intent is for instructors to select those materials that best fulfill their course objectives and the needs of their students.

TO THE STUDENT

Labor and employment law is widely considered to be a difficult subject; it is challenging and exciting, having a significant current impact on the lives of most Americans.

Part of the difficulty of the subject can be traced to the specialized vocabulary. This vocabulary plays an integral role in the discipline, and the student's task will be made easier by frequent and regular reference to the Glossary.

ACKNOWLEDGEMENTS

I wish to thank all those who have helped make this book possible, especially the reviewers of this and prior editions Christine Neylon O'Brien, *Boston College*; Michael K. Fee Esq. of Needham, Massachusetts; Len Bierman, *Texas A&M University*; Anne L. Draznin, *University of Illinois, Springfield*; Hank Findley, *Troy State University*; Brian Heshizer, *Georgia Southwestern State University*; Richard J. Hunter, Jr., *Seton Hall University*; Penelope R. Jennings, *California State University, Northridge*; Doug Kennedy, *University of Wisconsin, Stout* and *St. Mary's University of Minnesota*; Susan Mae McCabe, *Kellogg Community College*; William B. Read, *Husson College*; Judy N. Rudolf, *South College, Asheville*; Beth Anne Wolfson, *Bentley College*; Kiren Dosanjh Zucker, *California State University, Northridge*; and Bruce Zucker, *California State University, Northridge*. I am grateful for the research assistance and helpful comments of my colleague Margo E. K. Reder. Kathleen M. Kyratzoglou provided invaluable assistance in the preparation of the manuscript.

Suggestions for the improvement of this book will be cordially welcomed. Thanks to Neal Orkin of Drexel University for his suggestion.

David P. Twomey
Carroll School of Management,
Boston College
Chestnut Hill,
Massachusetts

ABOUT THE AUTHOR

David P. Twomey graduated from Boston College, earned his MBA at the University of Massachusetts at Amherst, and, after two years of business experience, entered Boston College Law School, where he earned his Juris Doctor degree.

While a law student, he began his teaching career as Lecturer in Finance and Marketing at Simmons College in Boston. He joined the faculty of the Boston College, Carroll School of Management in 1968 as an assistant professor and was promoted to the rank of professor in 1978. Professor Twomey has received numerous teaching and service awards at Boston College. He has written 32 editions of books and numerous articles on labor, employment, and business law topics. He has a special interest in curriculum development, serving four terms as chairman of his school's Educational Policy Committee. As chairman of the Business Law Department for over a decade, he served as a spokesperson for a strong legal and ethical component in both the undergraduate and graduate curriculum.

Professor Twomey is a nationally known labor arbitrator, having been selected by the parties as arbitrator in numerous disputes throughout the country in the private and public sectors. In the context of impending nationwide rail and airline strikes, his service includes appointments by Presidents Ronald Reagan, George H. W. Bush, William J. Clinton, and George W. Bush to eight Presidential Emergency Boards, whose recommendations served as basis for the resolution of these labor disputes. Professor Twomey is a member of the National Academy of Arbitrators. He is also a member of the Massachusetts, Florida, and federal bars.

OVERVIEW; EARLY DOCTRINES; CURRENT APPLICATIONS

CHAPTER **I**

SECTION 1: INTRODUCTION

Numerous federal statutes regulate the employment relationships of employees and employers in the United States. A number of the federal statutes affecting employment relations and covered in this book follow:

1. The Railway Labor Act of 1926 (RLA), which regulates the rights of workers to form unions and engage in collective bargaining in the railway and airline industries.
2. The National Labor Relations Act of 1935 (NLRA) and the Labor Management Relations Act of 1947 (LMRA), which govern the rights of workers in the private sector to form and join unions and engage in collective bargaining.
3. The Fair Labor Standards of 1938 (FLSA), which sets minimum wages and regulates overtime pay and child labor.

4. The Labor-Management Reporting and Disclosure Act of 1959 (LMRDA), which affects the conduct of unions regarding secondary boycotts and recognitional picketing and provides a bill of rights for union members.
5. Title VII of the Civil Rights Act of 1964 as amended in 1972 and 1991, which prohibits discrimination in employment on account of race, color, religion, national origin, or sex.
6. The Age Discrimination in Employment Act of 1967 as amended (ADEA), which prohibits discrimination in employment on account of age.
7. The Occupational Safety and Health Act of 1970 (OSHA), which seeks to assure all workers safe and healthful working conditions.
8. The Employee Retirement Income Security Act of 1974 (ERISA), which sets vesting rights, fiduciary and administrative standards, and reporting requirements for employee pension plans.
9. The Worker Adjustment and Retraining Notification Act of 1988 (WARN Act), which requires employers with 100 or more employees to give 60 days' notice of plant closings and layoffs.
10. The Americans with Disabilities Act of 1990 (ADA), which prohibits discrimination in employment on account of disability.
11. The Family and Medical Leave Act of 1993 (FMLA), which requires employers to provide unpaid leaves for certain family and medical reasons.
12. The Uniformed Services Employment and Reemployment Rights Act of 1994, which protects civilian job rights of individuals who leave their jobs for active military service.

The states also have a very important role in the regulation of employment relationships between employers and employees, administering unemployment compensation insurance programs and regulating workers' compensation programs, as well as setting the public policy regarding the termination of at-will employees and state and local government employee collective bargaining rights.

THE UNIONIZED WORKFORCE

The decline in the number of unionized workers in the United States is seen by some as a reason to deemphasize the study of labor relations law. It is true that since 1983, the first year for which comparable union data are available, the percentage of U.S. workers belonging to unions has shrunk from 20.1 percent of the nation's workforce to approximately 12.1 percent in 2007. The highly unionized blue-collar sectors of our economy, including manufacturing, mining, and transportation, have suffered employment declines, often due to improved laborsaving technology. This decline has adversely impacted the percentage of unionized workers in the United States. However, approximately 22.1 percent of our nation's transportation and utility workers continue to be represented by unions, with 11.3 percent of manufacturing and 13.9 percent of construction workers maintaining union membership. Some 35.9 percent of all employees in federal, state, and local government service are union members. Labor has not been very successful in organizing so-called white-collar workers such as clerical, professional, technical, sales, and other such employees. Musicians, actors, and professional athletes are highly unionized, and many college faculty members, engineers, physicians, and nurses are unionized. While about 15.7 million U.S. workers belonged to unions in 2007, some 1.6 million other workers are represented by unions even though they are not union members, and many other millions of U.S. workers receive wage and benefit adjustments comparable to or in excess of union wage rates and benefits because their employers track and pay differentials in order to avoid the unionization of their companies.[1]

IMPORTANCE AND COMPLEXITY OF LABOR LAWS

Labor relations laws do not just apply to unionized employers. *All* employers meeting appropriate jurisdictional requirements are subject to federal labor laws, and their employees have the right to form and join labor unions: the employers are obligated to bargain with the union representatives if a majority of the employees vote for such representation.

A narrow summary treatment of labor laws is of some informational value to students of management and economics. However, our labor laws are quite complex. Since 1926, with the enactment of the Railway Labor Act, to the present, the courts have been called on to resolve constantly developing and very difficult policy questions in labor relations law. Often labor law decisions involve the interaction of several laws, including antitrust, anti-injunction, and labor relations laws. However, considered category by category, case by case, the elements of complex legal doctrines become clear and understandable for students of management and economics.

Louis of Boston is one of that city's priciest clothing stores. The president of Louis decided to contract out the alteration work performed by in-house tailors. She believed that she had the legal right to outsource the work and lay off the employees at the expiration of the store's collective bargaining contract with the needle trades union. As will be seen in Chapter 5, labor law is not that simple, and an employer's bargaining obligation does not end at the expiration of the contract. After consulting with an employment law attorney and following 19 days of intermittent protests and adverse publicity, Louis of Boston issued an apology for not having followed the letter and spirit of the law and reinstated its nine tailors with back pay. And Wal-Mart, with all of its legal resources, had to be told by the Labor Board and ordered by the U.S. Court of Appeals, after eight years of litigation expenses, that although it did not have an obligation to bargain with the union representing 10 meat department employees as its Jacksonville, Texas store about its decision to convert its "boxed meat" operations there (which required specialized meat cutting skills) to selling only prepackaged case-ready meat, it did have an obligation to bargain with the union over the "effects" of this conversion decision. The Board found that Wal-Mart had therefore committed an unfair labor practice in violation of the National Labor Relations Act.[2]

The president of a nonunion electrical components manufacturing company, Electromation, Inc., of Elkhart, Indiana, set up action committees made up of employees and managers to deal with employee disaffection caused by the company's alteration of an employee bonus plan resulting from economic conditions. The company's president believed that further unilateral management action to resolve the problems the plan's alteration created with employees was not going to work, and he thus wanted to involve some of his 200 employees in reaching solutions to

---

[1] For the latest information on union membership see http://www.bls.gov/news.release/union2.toc.htm.

[2] *UFCW, Local 540 v. NLRB* 519 F.3d 490 (D.C. Cir. 2008).

the numerous problems affecting employees. The company was also aware that employee discontent would lead to a union-organizing campaign; and soon after the committees were formed, a union began an organizational drive at Electromation. The company believed that it had the legal and managerial right to form the action committees of managers and employees. However, Electromation was found to have violated the National Labor Relations Act (NLRA); the precedent cited was the very first case decided by the National Labor Relations Board in 1935, which prohibited the Greyhound Bus Co. from usurping from employees their legally protected rights under the NLRA to a bargaining representative of their own choosing. Employee and management cooperation is very important in today's global economy; and whether it is a nonunion or union company, intricate knowledge of labor relations law is essential in setting up lawful employee-management teams. The extent of management rights in this regard will be presented in Chapter 5.

APPLICATION OF DISCRIMINATION AND OTHER EMPLOYMENT LAW

When four white executives of Texaco, Inc., were caught on tape making racist statements about minority employees and discussing how to conceal evidence sought by plaintiffs in a racial discrimination lawsuit, no argument could be made that such conduct was either legal or acceptable. When Laura Zubulake filed a gender discrimination lawsuit against her employer, UBS Warburg LLC, instead of the employer's HR personnel making a diligent inquiry into her complaints, evidence found in e-mails subpoenaed in pretrial discovery indicated that senior management decided to "exit her ASAP." And, instead of helping her, her attorney believed that the company made every effort to build a file against her. Louis of Boston initially believed and argued that it had a right to outsource its work because the contract with the union had expired, and Electromation, Inc., believed and fervently argued that it had a right to form the joint employee-management committees. And Wal-Mart argued that it had no obligation to bargain with the union because technology changes made specialized skills unnecessary and that the bargaining unit was inappropriate. The conduct of the Texaco executives, however, was simply inexcusable and intolerable. Within two weeks of the release of the tape, Texaco agreed to settle for $176.1 million the underlying lawsuit that sparked the episode with the executives.[3] The jury hearing Ms. Zubulake's case awarded her $2,214,009 in back pay, $6,863,100 in front pay, and $20,169,081 in punitive damages.[4] Employment discrimination based on race, color, religion, national origin, sex, age, or disability is both unacceptable and illegal in our society. The applicable laws and the several narrow defenses are for the most part uncomplicated and straightforward. Certain complicated issues exist involving burdens of proof, disparate impact cases, and affirmative action. Most of the other employment laws

---

[3] David Thomas, "The Real Shame of the Texaco Case," *Boston Sunday Globe*, November 17, 1996, pp. D1 and D5.

[4] John Herzfeld, "Federal Jury Awards $29.2 Million to Fired UBS Equities Saleswoman," DLR No. 67 (April 8, 2005) p. 1. See also Randall Smith, "Salomon Is Told to Pay Broker $3.2 Million," *Wall Street Journal*, December 17, 2002, p. 1. The article reveals an estimate that Salomon Smith Barney and Merrill Lynch have paid out hundreds of millions of dollars to settle about 900 sexual harassment claims. The article also reveals the significant progress Salomon has made on gender issues since 1998.

covered in this book are also readily understandable and of significant importance to students of management and economics.

SECTION 2: HISTORICAL CONTEXT: THE CRIMINAL CONSPIRACY DOCTRINE

The first recorded American labor relations case took place in Philadelphia and involved a criminal proceeding in 1806 against eight members of a guild of boot-makers and shoemakers (cordwainers) who had gone on strike against their employers: *Commonwealth v. Pullis.* The employer group of masters asked the jury to establish the principle that the strike of the guild members was a criminal conspiracy in restraint of trade. The cordwainers were charged with (1) mutually agreeing to refuse to work for an employer who paid less than a fixed rate (which was higher than what had customarily been paid), (2) agreeing to try to prevent other craftsmen from working except at this rate, and (3) agreeing not to work for anyone who employed a cordwainer who had broken the guild's rules. The jury found the defendants guilty, and the court fined each defendant $8.

In the landmark 1842 decision *Commonwealth v. Hunt,* written by Chief Justice Lemuel Shaw of the Massachusetts Supreme Judicial Court, the court refuted, but did not squarely repudiate, the criminal conspiracy doctrine. Several members of the Boston Journeymen Bootmakers Society had been convicted of criminal conspiracy to withhold their services from an employer until such time as the employer discharged a journeyman named Jeremiah Horne, because Horne was not a member of the Bootmakers Society. The conviction was appealed, and the appeals court ruled that it was not an invalid purpose for the society to induce all those engaged in the same occupation to become members of the society. According to the court, the legality of unions depended on their purpose and the means by which the purpose was carried out.

| CASE 1.1 | COMMONWEALTH V. PULLIS (PHILADELPHIA CORDWAINERS' CASE OF 1806)
PHILADELPHIA MAYOR'S COURT, 3 COMMONS AND GILMORE. |

[From the judge's charge to the jury.] What is the case now before us?... A combination of workmen to raise their wages may be considered in a twofold point of view: one is to benefit themselves [and] the other is to injure those who do not join their society. The rule of law condemns both. If the rule be clear, we are bound to conform to it even though we do not comprehend the principle upon which it is founded. We are not to reject it because we do not see the reason of it. It is enough, that it is the will of the majority. It is law because it is their will—if it is law, there may be good reasons for it though we cannot find them out. But the rule in this case is pregnant with sound sense

and all the authorities are clear upon the subject. Hawkins, the greatest authority on the criminal law, has laid it down, that a combination to maintaining one another, carrying a particular object, whether true or false, is criminal....

In the profound system of law, (if we may compare small things with great) as in the profound systems of Providence ... there is often great reason for an institution, though a superficial observer may not be able to discover it. If obedience alone is required in the present case, the reason may be this. One man determines not to work under a certain price and it may be individually the opinion of all: in such a case

continued

it would be lawful in each to refuse to do so, for if each stands, alone, either may extract from his determination when he pleases. In the turnout of last fall, if each member of the body had stood alone, fettered by no promises to the rest, many of them might have changed their opinion as to the price of wages and gone to work; but it has been given to you in evidence, that they were bound down by their agreement, and pledged by mutual engagements, to persist in it, however contrary to their own judgment. The continuance in improper conduct may therefore well be attributed to the combination. The good sense of those individuals was prevented by this agreement, from having its free exercise.... Is it not restraining, instead of promoting, the spirit of '76 when men expected to have no law but the Constitution, and laws adopted by it or enacted by the legislature in conformity to it? Was it the spirit of '76, that either masters or journeymen, in regulating the prices of their commodities should set up a rule contrary to the law of their country? General and individual liberty was the spirit of '76. It is our first blessing. It has been obtained and will be maintained.... Though we acknowledge it is the hard hand of labour that promises the wealth of a nation, though we acknowledge the usefulness of such a large body of tradesmen and agree they should have every thing to which they are legally entitled; yet we conceive they ought to ask nothing more. They should neither be slaves nor the governors of the community.

The sentiments of the court, not an individual of which is connected either with the masters or journeymen; all stand independent of both parties ... are unanimous. They have given you the rule as they have found it in the book, and it is now for you to say, whether the defendants are guilty or not. The rule they consider as fixed, they cannot change it. It is now, therefore, left to you upon the law, and the evidence, to find the verdict. If you can reconcile it to your consciences, to find the defendants not guilty, you will do so; if not, the alternative that remains, is a verdict of guilty.

[The jury found the defendants guilty of combining and conspiring to raise their wages, and the penalty was a fine of eight dollars for each defendant.]

Case Questions

1. How did the court view the combination of workers with respect to their intent?
2. Did the court find the continuance of the withholding of labor attributable to a combination?

CASE 1.2

COMMONWEALTH V. HUNT
SUPREME JUDICIAL COURT OF MASSACHUSETTS, 4 METCALF 111, 38 AM. DEC. 346 (1842).

SHAW, C. J....

The general rule of the common law is that it is a criminal and indictable offense for two or more to confederate and combine together, by concerted means, to do that which is unlawful or criminal, to the injury of the public, or portions or classes of the community, or even to the rights of an individual. This rule of law may be equally in force as a rule of the common law, in England and in this commonwealth; and yet it must depend upon the local laws of each country to determine whether the purpose to be accomplished by the combination, or the concerted means of accomplishing it, be unlawful or criminal in the respective countries.... Without attempting to review and reconcile all the cases, we are of the opinion, that as a general description, though perhaps not a precise and accurate definition, a conspiracy must be a combination of two or more persons, by some concerted action, to accomplish some criminal or unlawful purpose, or to accomplish some purpose, not in itself criminal or unlawful, by criminal or unlawful means....

The averment is this: that the defendants and others formed themselves into a society and agreed not to work for any person who should employ any journeyman or other person not a member of such society after notice given him to discharge such workman.

The manifest intent of the association is to induce all those engaged in the same occupation to become members of it. Such a purpose is not unlawful. It would give them a power which might be exerted

continued

for useful and honorable purposes, or for dangerous and pernicious ones. If the latter were the real and actual object, and susceptible of proof, it should have been specially charged. Such an association might be used to afford each other assistance in times of poverty, sickness, and distress; or to raise their intellectual, moral, and social condition; or to make improvement in their art; or for other proper purposes. Or the association might be designed for purposes of oppression and injustice. But in order to charge all those who become members of an association with the guilt of criminal conspiracy, it must be averred and proved that the actual, if not the avowed object of the association was criminal. An association may be formed, the declared objects of which are innocent and laudable, and yet they may have secret articles, or an agreement communicated only to the members, by which they are banded together for purposes injurious to the peace of society or the rights of its members. Such would undoubtedly be a criminal conspiracy, on proof of the fact, however meritorious and praiseworthy the declared objects might be. The law is not to be hoodwinked by colorable pretenses. It looks at truth and reality, through whatever disguise it may assume. But to make such an association, ostensibly innocent, the subject of prosecution as a criminal conspiracy, the secret agreement which makes it so, is to be averred and proved as the gist of the offense. But when an association is formed for purposes actually innocent, and afterward its powers are abused by those who have the control and management of it, to purposes of oppression and injustice, it will be criminal in those who thus misuse it, or give consent thereto, but not in the other members of the association. In this case, no such secret agreement, varying the objects of the association from those avowed, is set forth in this count of the indictment.

Nor can we perceive that the objects of this association, whatever they may have been, were to be attained by criminal means. The means which they proposed to employ, as averred in this count, and which, as we are not to presume, were established by the proof, were, that they would not work for a person, who, after due notice, should employ a journeyman not a member of their society. Supposing the object of the association to be laudable and lawful, or at least not unlawful, are these means criminal? The case supposes that these persons are not bound by contract, but free to work for whom they please, or not to work, if they so prefer. In this state of things, we can not perceive that it is criminal for men to agree together to exercise their own acknowledged rights, in such a manner as best to subserve their own interests. One way to test this is to consider the effect of such an agreement, where the object of the association is acknowledged on all hands to be a laudable one. Suppose a class of workmen, impressed with the manifold evils of intemperance, should agree with each other not to work in a shop in which ardent spirit was furnished, or not to work in a shop in which any one used it, or not to work for an employer who should, after notice, employ a journeyman who habitually used it. The consequences might be the same. A workman who should still persist in the use of ardent spirit, would find it more difficult to get employment; a master employing such a one might at times, experience inconvenience in his work, in losing the services of a skillful but intemperate workman. Still it seems to us, that as the object would be lawful, and the means not unlawful, such an agreement could not be pronounced a criminal conspiracy....

We think, therefore, that associations may be entered into, the object of which is to adopt measures that may have a tendency to impoverish another, that is, to diminish his gains and profits, and yet so far from being criminal or unlawful, the object may be highly meritorious and public-spirited. The legality of such an association will therefore depend upon the means to be used for its accomplishment. If it is to be carried into effect by fair or honorable and lawful means, it is, to say the least, innocent; if by falsehood or force, it may be stamped with the character of conspiracy....

Several other exceptions were taken, and have been argued; but this decision on the main question has rendered it unnecessary to consider them.

It is so ordered.

Case Questions

1. What was the "manifest intent" of the labor organization in the case?
2. How does the court define a criminal conspiracy?
3. State the rule of law developed by the court.

SECTION 3: HISTORICAL CONTEXT: THE CONTRACTUAL INTERFERENCE DOCTRINE

The weapons used by organized labor in the 1870s, 1880s, and 1890s to obtain recognition and economic gains were picketing, strikes, and boycotts. Some employers responded with professional strikebreakers and blacklists. And employers turned to the courts and sought and obtained injunctions against picketing, boycotts, and strike activities. The *Vegelahn v. Guntner* decision, including the dissenting opinion of Justice Oliver Wendell Holmes, then on the Massachusetts Supreme Judicial Court, is presented in this section. In *Vegelahn*, the union engaged in picketing in front of the employer's business in order to try to persuade current employees and job applicants not to enter the business, and it sought to persuade individuals to break their employment contracts with the employer. The court enjoined this conduct.

With acceptance of the interference with contractual relations theory by the judiciary, employers often obtained a written pledge from each worker that in exchange for employment, the worker agreed not to join a union during the period of his or her employment. Such contracts were called **yellow-dog contracts** with connotations of animal servitude as opposed to human dignity. In the *Hitchman Coal and Coke v. Mitchell* case decided in 1917, the U.S. Supreme Court upheld an injunction against a union, prohibiting it from interfering with the yellow-dog contracts in effect at two coal mines. The *Hitchman* precedent served as a model for other employers at that time to adopt similar contractual relations with their employees as a means of union avoidance.

Yellow-dog contracts were outlawed by Section 2(5) of the Railway Labor Act of 1926 and Section 3 of the Norris-LaGuardia Act of 1932.

CASE 1.3 | VEGELAHN V. GUNTNER
SUPREME JUDICIAL COURT OF MASSACHUSETTS, 167 MASS. 92, 44 N.E. 1077 (1896).

ALLEN, J....

The principal question in this case is whether the defendants should be enjoined against maintaining the patrol. The report shows that, following upon a strike of the plaintiff's workmen, the defendants conspired to prevent him from getting workmen and thereby to prevent him from carrying on his business, unless and until he should adopt a certain schedule of prices. The means adopted were persuasion and social pressure, threats of personal injury or unlawful harm conveyed to persons employed or seeking employment, and a patrol of two men in front of the plaintiff's factory, maintained from half past 6 in the morning till half past 5 in the afternoon, on one of the busiest streets of Boston. The number of men was greater at times, and at times showed some little disposition to stop at the plaintiff's door.

The patrol proper at times went further than simple advice not obtruded beyond the point where the other person was willing to listen; and it was found that the patrol would probably be continued if not enjoined. There was also some evidence of persuasion to break existing contracts. The patrol was maintained as one of the means of carrying out the defendant's plan, and it was used in combination with social pressure, threats of personal injury or unlawful harm, and persuasion to break existing contracts. It was thus one means of intimidation, indirectly to the plaintiff, and directly to persons actually employed, or seeking to be employed, by the plaintiff, and of rendering such employment unpleasant and intolerable to such persons.

Such an act is an unlawful interference with the rights of both the employer and of the employed.

continued

An employer has a right to engage all persons who are willing to work for him, at such prices as may be mutually agreed upon, and persons employed or seeking employment have a corresponding right to enter into or remain in the employment of any person or corporation willing to employ them. These rights are secured by the [C]onstitution itself....

The defendants contend that these acts were justifiable because they were only seeking to secure better wages for themselves by compelling the plaintiff to accept their schedule of wages. This motive or purpose does not justify maintaining a patrol in front of the plaintiff's premises, as a means of carrying out their conspiracy. A combination among persons merely to regulate their own conduct is within allowable competition, and is lawful, although others may be indirectly affected thereby. But a combination to do injurious acts expressly directed to another, by way of intimidation or constraint, either of himself or of persons employed or seeking to be employed by him, is outside of allowable competition, and is unlawful.... We therefore think that the injunction should be in the form originally issued.

So ordered.

HOLMES, J. (dissenting) ...

One of the eternal conflicts out of which life is made up is that between the efforts of every man to get the most he can for his services, and that of society, disguised under the name of capital, to get his services for the least possible return. Combination on the one side is patent and powerful. Combination on the other is the necessary and desirable counterpart, if the battle is to be carried on in a fair and equal way....

If it be true that workingmen may combine with a view, among other things, to getting as much as they can for their labor, just as capital may combine with a view to getting the greatest possible return, it must be true that, when combined, they have the same liberty that combined capital has, to support their interest by argument, persuasion, and the bestowal or refusal of those advantages which they otherwise lawfully control. I can remember when many thought that, apart from violence or breach of contract, strikes were wicked, as organized refusals to work. I suppose that intelligent economists and legislators have given up that notion today. I feel pretty confident that they equally will abandon the idea that an organized refusal by workmen of social intercourse with a man who shall enter their antagonist's employ is unlawful, if it is disassociated from any threat of violence, and is made for the sole object of prevailing, if possible, in a contest with their employer about the rate of wages. The fact that the immediate object of the act by which the benefit to themselves is to be gained is to injure their antagonist does not necessarily make it unlawful, any more than when a great house lowers the price of goods for the purpose and with the effect of driving a smaller antagonist from the business....

Case Questions

1. Was the picketing peaceful or tainted with violence?
2. What was the scope of the court's injunction?
3. In his classic dissent, how does Justice Holmes justify the infliction of injury by a labor organization?

| CASE 1.4 | HITCHMAN COAL & COKE CO. V. MITCHELL
SUPREME COURT OF THE UNITED STATES, 245 U.S. 229 (1917). |

PITNEY, J....

This was a suit in equity, commenced October 24, 1907, in the United States Circuit (afterwards District) Court for the Northern District of West Virginia, by the Hitchman Coal & Coke Company, against certain officers of the United Mine Workers of America....

Plaintiff owns about 5,000 acres of coal lands situated at or near Benwood, in Marshall county, West Virginia, and within what is known as the "Panhandle District" of that state, and operates a coal mine thereon employing between 200 and 300 men, and having an annual output, in and before

continued

1907, of about 300,000 tons. At the time of filing of the bill, and for a considerable time before and ever since, it operated its mine "nonunion," under an agreement with its men to the effect that the mine should be run on a nonunion basis, that the employees should not become connected with the union while employed by plaintiff, and that if they joined it their employment with plaintiff should cease....

... The general object of the bill was to obtain an injunction to restrain defendants from interfering with the relations existing between plaintiff and its employees in order to compel plaintiff to "unionize" the mine....

... On April 15, 1906, defendant Zelenka, vice-president of the subdistrict, visited the mine, called a meeting of the miners, and addressed them in a foreign tongue, as a result of which they went on strike the next day, and the mine was shut down until the 12th of June, when it resumed as a "nonunion" mine, so far as relations with the U.M.W.A. were concerned.

During this strike plaintiff was subjected to heavy losses and extraordinary expenses with respect to its business, of the same kind that had befallen it during the previous strikes.

About the 1st of June a self-appointed committee of employees called upon plaintiff's president, stated in substance that they could not remain longer on strike because they were not receiving benefits from the union, and asked upon what terms they could return to work. They were told that they could come back, but not as members of the United Mine Workers of America; that thenceforward the mine would be run nonunion, and the company would deal with each man individually. They assented to this, and returned to work on a nonunion basis. Mr. Pickett, the mine superintendent, had charge of employing the men, then and afterwards, and to each one who applied for employment he explained the conditions which were that while the company paid the wages demanded by the union and as much as anybody else, the mine was run nonunion and would continue so to run; that the company would not recognize the United Mine Workers of America; that if any man wanted to become a member of that union he was at liberty to do so; but he could not be a member of it and remain in the employ of Hitchman Company; that if he worked for the company he would have to work

as a nonunion man. To this each man employed gave his assent, understanding that while he worked for the company he must keep out of the union.

Since January 1908 (after the commencement of the suit), in addition to having this verbal understanding, each man has been required to sign an employment card expressing in substance the same terms. This has neither enlarged nor diminished plaintiff's rights, the agreement not being such as is required by law to be in writing. Under this arrangement as to the terms of employment, plaintiff operated its mine from June 2, 1906, until the commencement of the suit in the fall of the following year.

During the same period a precisely similar method of employment obtained, at the Glendale mine, a property consisting of about 200 acres of coal land adjoining the Hitchman property on the south, and operated by a company having the same stockholders and the same management as the Hitchman mine; the office of the Glendale mine being at the Hitchman Coal & Coke Company's office. Another mine in the Panhandle, known as Richland, a few miles north of the Hitchman, likewise was run "nonunion."

In fact, all coal mines in the Panhandle and elsewhere in West Virginia, except in a small district known as the Kanawha field, were run "nonunion" while the entire industry in Ohio, Indiana, and Illinois was operated on the "closed shop" basis so that no man could hold a job about the mines unless he was a member of the United Mine Workers of America. Pennsylvania occupied a middle ground, only a part of it being under the jurisdiction of the union. Other states need not be particularly mentioned.

The unorganized condition of the mines in the Panhandle and some other districts was recognized as a serious interference with the purposes of the union in the Central Competitive Field, particularly as it tended to keep the cost of production low, and, through competition with coal produced in the organized field, rendered it more difficult for the operators there to maintain prices high enough to induce them to grant certain concessions demanded by the Union....

What are the legal consequences of the facts that have been detailed?

That the plaintiff was acting within its lawful rights in employing its men only upon terms of

continued

continuing nonmembership in the United Mine Workers of America is not open to question. Plaintiff's repeated costly experience of strikes and other interferences while attempting to "run union" were a sufficient explanation of its resolve to run "nonunion," if any were needed. But neither explanation nor justification is needed. Whatever may be the advantages of "collective bargaining," it is not bargaining at all, in any just sense, unless it is voluntary on both sides.... This court repeatedly has held that the employer is as free to make nonmembership in a union a condition of employment as the working man is free to join the union, and that this is part of the constitutional rights of personal liberty and private property, not to be taken away even by legislation, unless through some proper exercise of the paramount police power....

Defendants set up, by way of justification or excuse, the right of workingmen to form unions, and to enlarge their membership by inviting other workingmen to join. The right is freely conceded, provided the objects of the union be proper and legitimate, which we assume to be true, in a general sense, with respect to the union here in question. *Gompers v. Bucks Stove & Range Co.*, 221 U.S. 418, 439. The cardinal error of defendants' position lies in the assumption that the right is so absolute that it may be exercised under any circumstances and without any qualification; whereas in truth, like other rights that exist in civilized society, it must always be exercised with reasonable regard for the conflicting rights of others. *Brennan v. United Hatters*, 73 N.J. Law. 729, 749....

In any aspect of the matter, it cannot be said that defendants were pursuing their object by lawful means. The question of their intentions—of their bona fides—cannot be ignored. It enters into the question of malice. As Bowen, L. J., justly said, in the *Mogul Steamship Case*, 23 Q.B. Div. 613:

> Intentionally to do that which is calculated in the ordinary course of events to damage, and which does, in fact, damage another in that other person's property or trade, is actionable if done without just cause or excuse.

Another fundamental error in defendants' position consists in the assumption that all measures that may be resorted to are lawful if they are "peaceable"—that is, if they stop short of physical violence, or coercion through fear of it. In our opinion, any violation of plaintiff's legal rights contrived by defendants for the purpose of inflicting damage, or having that as its necessary effect, is as plainly inhibited by the law as if it involved a breach of the peace. A combination to procure concerted breaches of contract by plaintiff's employees constitutes such a violation....

Upon all the facts, we are constrained to hold that the purpose entertained by defendants to bring about a strike at plaintiff's mine in order to compel plaintiff, through fear of financial loss, to consent to the unionization of the mine as the lesser evil, was an unlawful purpose, and that the methods resorted to by Hughes—the inducing of employees to unite with the union in an effort to subvert the system of employment at the mine by concerted breaches of the contracts of employment known to be in force there, not to mention misrepresentation, deceptive statements, and threats of pecuniary loss communicated by Hughes to the men—were unlawful and malicious methods, and not to be justified as a fair exercise of the right to increase the membership of the union....

That the damage resulting from a strike would be irremediable at law is too plain for discussion.

As against the answering defendants, plaintiff's right to an injunction is clear; as to the others named as defendants, but not served with process, the decree is erroneous, as already stated....

The decree of the Circuit Court of Appeals is reversed, and the degree of the District Court is modified as above stated....

Case Questions

1. What agreement did the Hitchman Company ask its employees to abide by?
2. At the time of this case, what states were mining coal on a closed-shop basis?
3. What is a closed shop?
4. Were the organizing efforts of the UMWA peaceful? Was this a good defense?
5. Did the Court concede that workers had the right to form and join labor organizations?
6. Did the Court uphold the yellow-dog contract?

SECTION 4: HISTORICAL CONTEXT: EARLY APPLICATIONS OF THE SHERMAN ACT

Labor organizations were on the defensive in the 1910s and 1920s. Not only were they subject to injunctions by the courts, but the courts applied the antitrust laws to them. In the 1915 case of *Lawlor v. Loewe*, the U.S. Supreme Court ruled that a nationwide boycott by the hatters' union against a nonunion hat manufacturer, Dietrich Loewe, violated the antitrust laws. The Court ruled that Loewe was entitled to collect treble damages from the 248 members of the union. The Court applied Section 1 of the Sherman Act to include agreements between laborers to extend control over a labor market. Section 1 of the Act provides in part: "Every contract, combination in the form of trust or otherwise, or conspiracy, in restraint of trade or commerce among the several states … is declared to be illegal." Section 7 of the Sherman Act provided the statutory basis for the damages assessed against each of the union members.

CASE 1.5	LAWLOR V. LOEWE
	SUPREME COURT OF THE UNITED STATES, 235 U.S. 522 (1915).

HOLMES, J.…

The substance of the charge is that the plaintiffs were hat manufacturers who employed nonunion labor; that the defendants were members of the United Hatters of North America and also of the American Federation of Labor; that in pursuance of a general scheme to unionize the labor employed by manufacturers of fur hats (a purpose previously made effective against all but a few manufacturers), the defendants and other members of the United Hatters caused the American Federation of Labor to declare a boycott against the plaintiffs and against all hats sold by the plaintiffs to dealers in other States and against dealers who should deal in them; and that they carried out their plan with such success that they have restrained or destroyed the plaintiffs' commerce with other States. The case now has been tried, the plaintiffs have got a verdict and the judgment of the District Court has been affirmed by the Circuit Court of Appeals. 209 F. 721, 126 C.C.A. 445.

The grounds for discussion under the statute have been narrowed by the case of *Eastern States Retail Lumber Dealers' Ass'n v. United States*, 234 U.S. 600. Whatever may be the law otherwise, that case establishes that, irrespective of compulsion or even agreement to observe its intimation, the circulation of a list of "unfair dealers," manifestly intended to put the ban upon those whose names appear therein,

among an important body of possible customers combined with a point of view to joint action and in anticipation of such reports, is within the prohibitions of the Sherman Act if it is intended to restrain and restrains commerce among the States.

It requires more than the blindness of justice not to see that many branches of the United Hatters and the Federation of Labor, to both of which the defendants belonged, in pursuance of a plan emanating from headquarters made use of such lists, and of the primary and secondary boycott in their effort to subdue the plaintiffs to their demands. The union label was used and a strike of the plaintiffs' employees was ordered and carried out to the same end, and the purpose to break up the plaintiffs' commerce affected the quality of the acts. *Loewe v. Lawlor*, 208 U.S. 274, 299. We agree with the Circuit Court of Appeals that a combination and conspiracy forbidden by the statute were proved, and that the question is narrowed to the responsibility of the defendants for what was done by the sanction and procurement of the societies above named.

The court in substance instructed the jury that if these members paid their dues and continued to delegate authority to their officers unlawfully to interfere with the plaintiffs' interstate commerce in such circumstances that they know or ought to have known, and such officers were warranted in the belief that

continued

they were acting in the matters within their delegated authority, then such members were jointly liable, and no others. It seems to us that this instruction sufficiently guarded the defendants' rights, and that the defendants got all that they were entitled to ask in not being held chargeable with knowledge as a matter of law. It is a tax on credulity to ask any one to believe that members of labor unions at that time did not know that the primary and secondary boycott and the use of the "We don't patronize" or "Unfair" list were means expected to be employed in the effort to unionize shops. Very possibly they were thought to be lawful. See *Gompers v. United States*, 233 U.S. 604. By the Constitution of the United Hatters the directors are to use "all the means in their power" to bring shops "not under our jurisdiction" "into the trade." The bylaws provide a separate fund to be kept for strikes, lockouts, and agitation for the union label. Members are forbidden to sell nonunion hats. The Federation of Labor with which the Hatters were affiliated had organization of labor for one of its objects, helped affiliated unions in trade disputes, and to that end, before the present trouble, had provided in its Constitution for prosecuting and had prosecuted many what it called legal boycotts. Their conduct in this and former cases was made public especially among the members in every possible way. If the words of the documents on their face and without explanation did not authorize what was done, the evidence of what was done publicly

and habitually showed their meaning and how they were interpreted. The jury could not but find that by the usage of the unions the acts complained of were authorized, and authorized without regard to their interference with commerce among the States. We think it unnecessary to repeat the evidence of the publicity of this particular struggle in the common newspapers and union prints, evidence that made it almost inconceivable that the defendants, all living in the neighborhood of the plaintiffs, did not know what was done in the specific case. If they did not know that, they were bound to know the constitution of their societies, and at least well might be found to have known how the words of those constitutions had been construed in the act....

*Judgment affirmed.**

Case Questions

1. What purpose was pursued by the United Hatters?
2. What pressure methods did the American Federation of Labor and the United Hatters exert?
3. State the rule of the case.

---

*By Section 301(b) of the National Labor Relations Act of 1947, money judgments are enforceable only against the union as an entity "and shall not be enforceable against any individual member or his assets."

SECTION 5: INJUNCTIONS AND THE CLAYTON ACT

Understanding labor-related statutory and case materials requires familiarity with the injunctive process. An **injunction** is a mandatory or prohibitory order issued by a court of equity. An injunction is prohibitory if it orders the defendant to refrain from specified conduct; it is mandatory if it requires performance of an affirmative act. An injunction gives relief to an aggrieved party in those cases where the remedy of monetary damages is inadequate. A single injunction may have prohibitory and mandatory aspects at the same time, as when a union is concurrently ordered to refrain from violence in picketing and to bargain in good faith with the employer.

A **temporary restraining order** may be issued prior to a hearing on an injunction. It should be issued only in exceptional or urgent situations, its purpose being to maintain the status quo of the subject in dispute until a court hearing takes place. A **temporary injunction**, also called a preliminary injunction, is granted after a hearing (but before a full trial) and enjoins commission of the disputed acts while a court hears and studies the case on its merits. A **final injunction** is issued after a trial on the merits.

The earliest recorded issuance of a court injunction in a labor dispute dates from the 1880s. The case of *In re Debs*,[5] decided in 1895, popularized the usage of the injunction in labor cases in America. One authority has found records in state and federal courts, from 1890 to 1931, of 1,872 labor injunctions granted at employers' requests and 223 cases in which such applications for relief were denied.[6]

Courts have authority to enforce injunctions with their contempt powers, including the assessment of fines or imprisonment. Direct contempts that occur in a court's presence may be adjudged immediately and sanctioned summarily by the court. Except for serious criminal contempt, in which a jury is required, traditional distinctions between civil and criminal contempt proceedings do not pertain in direct contempt cases. A contempt fine assessed by a judge without a jury trial is considered "civil contempt" if it either coerces the defendant into compliance with a court's order or compensates for losses sustained. However, contempt involving out-of-court disobedience of complex injunctions often requires elaborate and reliable fact-finding and, under those circumstances, criminal procedural protections, such as the right to counsel and proof beyond a reasonable doubt. These protections are necessary and appropriate to protect the due process rights of the parties and to prevent the arbitrary exercise of judicial power.

As applied to trespasses by labor, the employer found the injunction a keen and effective tool for the following reasons:

1. Speed of action was secured, since affidavit proof (sworn statements in writing) was admitted to issue a preliminary injunction, as opposed to the live testimony of witnesses under oath and subject to cross-examination.
2. Delay between issuance of the preliminary and the final injunction was often so prolonged as to ensure defeat of the strikers or picketers, notwithstanding eventual victory of the union in securing dissolution of the restraining order.
3. The employer had a choice of tribunal to which to direct the plea and could select an antilabor forum, either federal or state.
4. Lack of a jury trial in equity reduced labor's chances of winning an injunction case.
5. Blanket and obscure language in the wording of some injunctions intimidated union members because of their inability to separate legal from illegal acts as well as their inability to determine exactly what conduct was permissible and what was forbidden.

In reaction to this situation, organized labor carried on a relentless lobbying effort in Congress to secure a narrowing of judicial injunctive power in labor cases. The first fruit of this campaign was the Clayton Antitrust Act of 1914. Congress here sought to substantially reenact the Sherman Antitrust Act of 1890. At the

---

[5] 158 U.S. 164 (1895).

[6] E. E. Witte, *The Government in Labor Disputes* (New York: McGraw-Hill Book Co., 1932), 64.

same time, it sought to withdraw the applicability of that Act to labor combinations and to divest the courts of their wide injunctive powers in labor dispute cases. Section 6 provided "that the labor of a human being is not a commodity or article of commerce … nor shall such (labor) organizations, or the members thereof, be held or construed to be illegal combinations or conspiracies in restraint of trade, under the antitrust laws."

Section 20 imposes a statutory restriction on injunctive relief by providing that no injunction would issue in a labor dispute between employers and employees unless irreparable injury to property and property rights was threatened for which the remedy at law (damages) was inadequate. Narrow Supreme Court interpretations of the Clayton Act weakened the mandates of Sections 6 and 20, as set forth in the *Duplex v. Deering*[7] and *American Steel Foundaries*[8] decisions of 1921. The courts found a path around the Act by making the exception the rule under various theories, among them that the Act did not change preexisting law, did not apply in boycott cases, did not protect "outsiders" such as union organizers, did not apply where the union objective was recognition, did not apply where yellow-dog contracts were in effect, and, finally, did not protect strikers since they were no longer employees.

Use of injunctions against unions was even more popular after passage of the Clayton Act, because an employer could now bring an action in a federal court as a party plaintiff. Under the Sherman Act, only the government had that power. Disappointed by the Supreme Court's adverse construction of the Clayton Act in the *Duplex* and *American Steel Foundaries* cases, organized labor intensified its political pressure at both state and federal levels, securing, in 1932, passage of the Federal Anti-Injunction Act (Norris-LaGuardia Act). This legislation effectively divested the federal courts of their equity power to issue injunctions at the behest of private parties in those situations where a bona fide labor dispute existed. The jurisdictional requirements set forth in Section 7 of the Act furnished an almost insurmountable barrier to injunctive action when coupled with Section 13 of the Act, which very broadly defined the term **labor dispute** as to include controversies without regard to whether the relation of employer and employee existed.

The enactment of the Norris-LaGuardia Act in the depths of the Great Depression of the 1930s during the last years of the Hoover administration placed employers in a difficult position, with both congressional and judicial tenor having taken a complete turnaround from favoring management. Employers turned for assistance to the state courts, only to find that many states had also barred the door with anti-injunction legislation patterned after the Norris-LaGuardia Act.

With the enactment of the Labor Management Relations Act of 1947 (Taft-Hartley Act) and the Labor-Management Reporting and Disclosure Act of 1959 (Landrum-Griffin Act) reflecting a public policy change, immunities from injunctive action afforded labor by the Anti-Injunction Act were substantially narrowed. Section 10(1) of the National Labor Relations Act allows the National Labor Relations Board to seek appropriate injunctive relief against unions in certain matters such as secondary boycotts and jurisdictional disputes.

---

[7] 254 U.S. 443 (1921).

[8] 257 U.S. 184 (1921).

SECTION 6: CONTINUING IMPACT OF ANTITRUST LAWS

The Labor Management Relations Act of 1947 embodies the congressional policy favoring bargaining as the best means of resolving disputes between employers and employees, thereby preserving economic stability and industrial peace. Labor law allows employees to form unions, which then act as the employees' exclusive bargaining representative. Unions and employers have a duty to bargain in good faith toward mutually acceptable agreements that cover wages, hours, and working conditions. Federal labor law also allows employers to band together with other employers in the same industry to form multiemployer bargaining units. Labor law, then, in facilitating the setting of the prices that groups of employers will pay for labor, would appear to be in conflict with the national antitrust policy favoring unrestricted economic competition and precluding the fixing of prices. To avoid this potential conflict, the Supreme Court has recognized a nonstatutory labor exemption that immunizes certain *results* of that bargaining process from antitrust attack. This nonstatutory exemption protects union-employer collective bargaining agreements dealing with wages, hours, and working conditions from being subject to antitrust law.

The nonstatutory exemption does not, however, exempt all agreements between unions and employers. In *United Mine Workers v. Pennington*[9] the Supreme Court made clear that unions continue to remain subject to federal antitrust laws to the extent that a union joins with an employer group to eliminate other employers from the industry and to the extent that a union agrees with one set of employers to impose specified wage scales on other employer bargaining units.

In *Brown v. Pro Football, Inc.*, presented in this section, the U.S. Supreme Court recognized that the nonstatutory antitrust exemption can be applied where needed to make the collective bargaining process work. And it applied the exemption to shield football team owners from an antitrust attack for agreeing together as a multiemployer bargaining group to impose a set weekly salary figure of $1,000 per week on its 235 developmental squad professional football players after the employer group could not reach agreement on this issue with the players union. If there was no existing bargaining relationship with a union, the employers would not be able to collectively set the rates they would pay for the developmental squad members, and a clear antitrust violation would have existed. Many agents of professional players would prefer that the football players union be decertified in order to destroy the nonstatutory exemption and bring about full free agency for players.

CASE 1.6	ANTHONY BROWN v. PRO FOOTBALL, INC. SUPREME COURT OF THE UNITED STATES, 116 S. CT. 2116 (1996).

[After their collective bargaining agreement expired, the National Football League (NFL) and the NFL Players Association, a labor union, began to negotiate a new contract. The NFL presented a plan that would permit each club to establish a "developmental squad" of substitute players, each of whom would be paid the same $1,000 weekly salary. The union disagreed, insisting that the 235 individual developmental squad

continued

---

[9] 381 U.S. 657 (1965).

members should be free to negotiate their own salary. When negotiations reached an impasse in June 1989, the NFL unilaterally implemented the plan. Anthony Brown of the Washington Redskins filed a class action antitrust suit, claiming that the employers' agreement to pay them $1,000 per week restrained trade in violation of the Sherman Act. A jury granted an award of $10 million to the class, which was trebled by the district court to a $30 million judgment for the players. The court of appeals reversed, holding that the owners were immune from antitrust liability under the federal labor laws. The matter was appealed to the U.S. Supreme Court.]

BREYER, J....

Labor law itself regulates directly, and considerably, the kind of behavior here at issue—the postimpasse imposition of a proposed employment term concerning a mandatory subject of bargaining. Both the Board and the courts have held that, after impasse, labor law permits employers unilaterally to implement changes in preexisting conditions, but only insofar as the new terms meet carefully circumscribed conditions. For example, the new terms must be "reasonably comprehended" within the employer's preimpasse proposals (typically the last rejected proposals), lest by imposing more or less favorable terms, the employer unfairly undermined the union's status.... The collective-bargaining proceeding itself must be free of any unfair labor practice, such as an employer's failure to have bargained in good faith. See *Akron Novelty Mfg. Co.,* 224 N.L.R.B. 998, 1002 (1976) (where employer has not bargained in good faith, it may not implement a term of employment); P. Hardin, The Developing Labor Law 697 (3rd ed. 1992) (same). These regulations reflect the fact that impasse and an accompanying implementation of proposals constitute an integral part of the bargaining process....

In these circumstances, to subject the practice to antitrust law is to require antitrust courts to answer a host of important practical questions about how collective bargaining over wages, hours and working conditions is to proceed—the very result that the implicit labor exemption seeks to avoid. And it is to place in jeopardy some of the potentially beneficial labor-related effects that multiemployer bargaining can achieve. That is because unlike labor law, which sometimes welcomes anti-competitive agreements conducive to industrial harmony, antitrust law forbids all agreements among competitors (such as competing employers) that unrea-

sonably lessen competition among or between them in virtually any respect whatsoever....

If the antitrust laws apply, what are employers to do once impasse is reached? If all impose terms similar to their last joint offer, they invite an antitrust action premised upon identical behavior (along with prior or accompanying conversations) as tending to show a common understanding or agreement. If any, or all, of them individually impose terms that differ significantly from that offer, they invite an unfair labor practice charge. Indeed, how can employers safely discuss their offers together even before a bargaining impasse occurs? A preimpasse discussion about, say, the practical advantages or disadvantages of a particular proposal, invites a later antitrust claim that they agreed to limit the kinds of action each would later take should an impasse occur.... All this is to say that to permit antitrust liability here threatens to introduce instability and uncertainty into the collective-bargaining process, for antitrust law often forbids or discourages the kinds of joint discussions and behavior that the collective-bargaining process invites or requires.... The judgment of the Court of Appeals is affirmed.

It is so ordered.

JUSTICE STEVENS, dissenting...

In his classic dissent in *Lochner v. New York,* 198 U.S. 45, 75 (1905), Justice Holmes reminded us that our disagreement with the economic theory embodied in legislation should not affect our judgment about its constitutionality. It is equally important, of course, to be faithful to the economic theory underlying broad statutory mandates when we are construing their impact on areas of the economy not specifically addressed by their texts. The unique features of this case lead me to conclude that the Court has reached a decision that conflicts with the basic purpose of both the antitrust laws and the national labor policy expressed in a series of congressional enactments....

Congress is free to act to exempt the anti-competitive employer conduct that we review today. In the absence of such action, I do not believe it is for us to stretch the limited exemption that we have fashioned to facilitate the express statutory exemption created for labor's benefit so that unions must strike in order to restore a prior practice of individually negotiating salaries. I therefore agree with the position that the District Court adopted below.

continued

Because the developmental squad salary provisions were a new concept and not a change in terms of the expired collective bargaining agreement, the policy behind continuing the non-statutory labor exemption for the terms of a collective bargaining agreement after expiration (to foster an atmosphere conducive to the negotiation of a new collective bargaining agreement) does not apply. To hold that the non-statutory labor exemption extends to shield the NFL from antitrust liability for imposing restraints never before agreed to by the union would ... infringe on the union's freedom to contract,...

Case Questions

1. Identify the "non-statutory labor exemption" and explain its significance.
2. Did the non-statutory labor exemption from the antitrust laws expire upon the parties reaching bargaining impasse?
3. If the NFL Players Association decertifies, may NFL players bring suit against NFL owners for antitrust violations for the league's salary cap and employer-imposed uniform salary rates for developmental squad players?

SECTION 7: THE EMPLOYMENT RELATIONSHIP

The relationship of an employer and an employee exists when, pursuant to an express or implied agreement of parties, one person, the employee, undertakes to perform services or to do work under the direction and control of another, the employer, for compensation. In older cases, this relationship was called the **master-servant relationship.**

An employee is hired to work under the control of the employer. An employee differs from an **agent**, who is authorized to negotiate or make contracts with third persons on behalf of, and under the control of, a principal. An employee differs from an **independent contractor**, who is to perform a contract independent of, or free from, control by the other party.

CREATION OF EMPLOYMENT RELATIONSHIP

The relationship of employer and employee can be created only with the consent of both parties. Generally, the agreement of the parties is a contract. It is therefore subject to all of the principles applicable to contracts. The contract will ordinarily be express, but it may be implied, such as when the employer accepts the rendering of services that a reasonable person would recognize as being rendered with the expectation of receiving compensation.

In the case of individual employment contracts, both parties must assent to the terms of the contract. Subject to statutory restrictions, the parties are free to make a contract on any terms they choose.

Collective bargaining contracts govern the rights and obligations of employers and employees subject to these contracts. Under collective bargaining, representatives of the employees bargain with a single employer or a group of employers for an agreement on wages, hours, and working conditions. The agreement worked out by the representatives of the employees, usually union officials, is generally subject to a ratification vote by the employees. Terms usually found in collective bargaining contracts are (1) identification of the work belonging exclusively to designated classes of employees; (2) wage and benefits clauses; (3) promotion and lay-off clauses, which are generally tied in part to seniority; (4) a management's rights clause; and (5) a grievance procedure. A grievance procedure provides a means by which persons claiming that the contract was violated or that they were disciplined or discharged without just cause may ultimately have their cases decided by impartial labor arbitrators.

TERMINATION OF EMPLOYMENT CONTRACTS

Ordinarily, a contract of employment may be terminated in the same manner as any other contract. If it is to run for a definite period of time, the employer cannot terminate the contract at an earlier date without justification. If the employment contract does not have a definite duration, it is terminable at will. Under the **employment-at-will doctrine**, the employer has historically been allowed to terminate the employment contract at any time for any reason or for no reason. Court decisions—and in some instances, statutes—have changed the rule in most states by limiting the power of the employer to discharge employees. Some courts have carved out exceptions to the employment-at-will doctrine when the discharge violated an established public policy. Other courts still follow the common law at-will doctrine, leaving the policy-making issue to the state's legislature.

An employer may be justified in discharging an employee because of the employee's (1) nonperformance of duties, (2) misrepresentation or fraud in obtaining the employment, (3) disobedience of proper direction, (4) disloyalty, (5) theft or other dishonesty, (6) possession or use of drugs or intoxicants, (7) misconduct, or (8) incompetence.

Employers generally have the right to lay off employees because of economic conditions, including lack of work. Such actions are sometimes referred to as **reductions in force (RIFs)**.

CHAPTER QUESTIONS AND PROBLEMS

1. What three early common law doctrines were applied to labor organizations?
2. What is the present status of the so-called yellow-dog contract?
3. May the National Labor Relations Board obtain injunctive relief against unions in light of the Federal Anti-Injunction Act?
4. The National Electrical Contractors' Association (NECA) is a national trade association composed of electrical contractors. NECA negotiates a nationwide collective bargaining agreement with the International Brotherhood of Electrical Workers (IBEW). The electrical contractors who belong to NECA pay annual dues and a service charge in exchange for the benefits of being an NECA member. One such benefit is the single NECA labor agreement that covers the IBEW members employed by the electrical contractors.

Approximately 50 percent of the electrical work in the United States is performed by NECA member companies, with the remainder being performed by non-NECA contractors who negotiate separately with the IBEW, employ members of other unions, or are nonunion.

NECA member companies realized that non-NECA companies had a competitive advantage over NECA contractors when they bid for jobs because they did not have to recover the cost of NECA membership in their quoted price. Therefore, IBEW and NECA placed a provision in their national agreement requiring that in any job involving a party to the agreement, the employer would pay 1 percent of its gross labor payroll into the National Electrical Industry Fund to be jointly administered by NECA and IBEW.

Because the agreement was binding on all IBEW locals, its effect was to force non-NECA contractors employing IBEW members to pay into the fund.

Non-NECA contractors brought an action claiming that the Industry Fund provision constituted price fixing by NECA and IBEW, an antitrust violation under the Sherman Act. They requested an injunction against IBEW and NECA's agreement. IBEW and NECA argued that no injunction could be issued.

May an injunction be issued by a court against the NECA-IBEW agreement? If so, should an injunction issue in this case? Decide. [*NECA, Inc. v. National Contractors' Association*, 110 LRRM 2385 (4th Cir.)]

5. United Mine Workers of America, District 28, engaged in a protracted labor dispute with the Clinchfield Coal Co. and Sea "B" Mining Co. over alleged unfair labor practices. In April 1989, the companies filed suit in Virginia to enjoin the union from conducting unlawful strike-related activities. The trial court entered an injunction that prohibited the union and its members from, among other things, obstructing ingress and egress to company facilities, throwing objects at and physically threatening company employees, placing tire-damaging "jackrocks" on roads used by company vehicles, and picketing with more than a specified number of people at designated sites. The court additionally ordered the union to take all steps necessary to ensure compliance with the injunction, to place supervisors at picket sites, and to report all violations to the court.

On May 16, 1989, the trial court held a contempt hearing and found that the union had committed 72 violations of the injunction. After fining the union $642,000 for its disobedience, the court announced that it would fine the union $100,000 for any future violent breach of the injunction and $20,000 for any future nonviolent infraction.

In seven subsequent contempt hearings held between June and December 1989, the court found the union in contempt for more than 400 separate violations of the injunction, many of them violent. Each contempt hearing was conducted as a civil proceeding before the trial judge, in which the parties conducted discovery, introduced evidence, and called and cross-examined witnesses. The trial court required that contumacious acts be proved beyond a reasonable doubt, but did not afford the union a right to jury trial.

The court levied $52 million in fines against the unions and directed that the money be paid to the state and two of its counties. The union contends that the fines were criminal and could not be imposed absent a criminal trial. The state contends that the fine schedule was intended to coerce compliance with the injunction and therefore the fines were civil and properly imposed in civil proceedings. Decide. [*United Mine Workers of America v. Bagwell*, 114 S.Ct. 2552]

6. When the Strand Theatre of Shreveport Corporation's collective bargaining agreement with its union expired, the theatre refused to bargain with the union over a new contract. Under basic contract law, when a contract expires, the parties are free to make or not make a new contract; and a new contract is not made unless there is assent to all terms by both parties. Was the theatre within its legal rights in choosing not to bargain with the union after the expiration of the collective bargaining agreement? Decide. [*NLRB v. Strand Theatre of Shreveport Corp.*, 493 F.3d 515 (5th Cir. 2007)]

7. On October 2, 2007, a federal district court jury awarded Anucha Browne Sanders, the former senior vice president of the New York Knicks basketball team, $11.6 million in punitive damages against the team's owner, Madison Square Garden; its chairman, James Dolan; and its president and head coach, Isiah Thomas. Browne Sanders was seeking an additional $9.6 million in compensatory damages at a subsequent trial stage. On December 10, 2007, the parties settled for

what news media reported to be $11.5 million.

Ms. Browne Sanders said:

> The jury's verdict in this case sent a powerful and enduring message that harassment and retaliation at Madison Square Garden will not be tolerated. It is my hope that all women will be able to work in an environment that is free of discrimination and harassment, and that any woman who stands up for her rights will be taken seriously by her employer rather than retaliated against.

Madison Square Garden officials stated that they "vehemently disagree with the jury's decision," but settled the matter under pressure from NBA Commissioner Stern. Isiah Thomas stated that he was "completely innocent." Google *Browne Sanders–Isiah Thomas sexual harassment trial* and read the reported testimony and commentary. Do you believe that "the law" against sexual harassment in the workplace and retaliation against the victim reporting misconduct is complicated? Did the notoriety of this case have a "teaching effect" on all employers that harassment and retaliation should not be tolerated because it is harmful to victims and costly to the employers who allow such misconduct to exist? ["Post-Verdict Settlement Reached Former Knicks Executive's Case," DLR No. 238, A-12 (Dec. 12, 2007)]

CONGRESS, ADMINISTRATIVE AGENCIES, AND THE COURTS

CHAPTER **2**

SECTION

SECTION 8: INTRODUCTION

A federal **administrative agency** is a government body charged with implementing and "administrating" legislation enacted by Congress. Administrative agencies commonly have broad rulemaking, enforcement, and adjudicatory powers. Federal administrative agencies dealing with labor and employment law issues include the National Mediation Board (NMB), the National Labor Relations Board (NLRB), the Equal Employment Opportunity Commission (EEOC), and numerous agencies within the Department of Labor (DOL). The structure and functions of each agency are governed by the statute or statutes it administers. Radical structural differences exist between agencies. For example, members of the EEOC do not "decide" individual cases under an administrative law system similar to the adjudicative procedures of the National Labor Relations Act (NLRA). The Occupational Safety & Health

Administration (OSHA) has the authority under its organic statute the Occupational Safety and Health Act to promulgate standards, conduct inspections, and seek enforcement for noncompliance with OSHA regulations. An independent agency, the Occupational Safety and Health Review Commission, adjudicates contested enforcement actions undertaken by OSHA, but has limited non-policy making adjudicatory powers. In contrast, the NLRB uses an adjudicatory model as opposed to rulemaking and makes policy decisions on a case-by-case basis. This short introductory chapter presents an overview of basic administrative law principles, discusses the standards for court review of agency determinations on law and policy, and identifies the federal courts available for the review of legal issues resulting from administrative agency action or inaction. Discussion of administrative procedures under specific federal labor and employment laws will be more fully presented in the chapters dealing with the law(s) in question.

SECTION 9: OPEN OPERATIONS OF ADMINISTRATIVE AGENCIES

The public has ready access to the activities of administrative agencies. That access comes in three ways: (1) open records, (2) open meetings, and (3) public announcement of agency guidelines. The actions and activities of most federal agencies that are not otherwise regulated are controlled by the Administrative Procedures Act.[1]

The *Freedom of Information Act*[2] (FOIA) provides that information contained in records of federal administrative agencies be available to citizens upon proper request. The primary purpose of this statute is "to ensure that government activities be opened to the sharp eye of public scrutiny."[3] To ensure that members of the public understand how to obtain records, the FOIA provides that "[e]ach agency shall ... publish in the *Federal Register* for the guidance of the public ... the methods whereby the public may obtain information, make submittals or requests, or obtain decisions."[4] There are exceptions to this right of public scrutiny. They prevent individuals and companies from obtaining information that is not necessary to their legitimate interests and might harm the person or company whose information is being sought.[5] FOIA exemptions include commercial and financial information not ordinarily made public by the person or company that supplies the information to the agency as part of the agency's enforcement role.[6]

SECTION 10: AGENCY "REGULATIONS" AS LAW

An agency may adopt regulations—the rulemaking function—within the scope of its authority. The power of an agency to carry out a congressional program "necessarily

---

[1] Administrative Procedures Act, 5 U.S.C. § 550 *et seq.*

[2] U.S.C. 552 *et seq.* The Electronic Freedom of Information Act Amendments of 1996 extend the public availability of information to electronically stored data.

[3] *Brady-Lunny v. Massey*, 185 F. Supp. 2d 928 (C.D. Ill. 2002).

[4] 5 U.S.C. § 552(a)(1)(a).

[5] Additional protection is provided by the Privacy Act of 1974, 5 U.S.C. § 552a(b); *Pilon v. U.S. Department of Justice*, 73 F.3d 1111 (D.C. Cir. 1996).

[6] *Sun-Sentinel Company v. U.S. Dept. of Homeland Security*, 431 F. Supp. 2d 1258 (S.D. Fla. 2006).

requires the formulation of policy and the making of rules to fill any gap left by Congress."[7] If the regulation is not authorized by the law creating the agency, anyone affected by it can challenge the regulation on the basis that the agency has exceeded its authority. However, when the agency establishes a rational basis for its rule, courts accept the rule and do not substitute their own judgment for the agency's rule.[8] The rulemaking steps follow.

1. *Congressional Enabling Act*: Before an agency can begin rulemaking proceedings, it must be given jurisdiction by congressional enactment in the form of a statute. For example, Congress has enacted broad statutes governing discrimination in employment practices and has given authority to the EEOC to establish definitions, rules, and guidelines for compliance with those laws. Sometimes an existing agency is assigned the responsibility for new legislation implementation and enforcement. For example, the Department of Labor has been assigned the responsibility to handle the whistleblower protection provisions of the Sarbanes-Oxley Act that provide protection against retaliation and/or termination to those who report financial improprieties at their companies. The Department of Labor has been in existence for almost a century, but it was assigned this new responsibility because of its expertise in handling other whistleblower statutes.

2. *Agency Research of the Problem*: After jurisdiction is established, the agency has the responsibility to research the issues and various avenues of regulation for implementing the statutory framework. As the agency does so, it determines the costs and benefits of the problems, issues, and solutions. The study may be done by the agency, or the study may be completed by someone hired by the agency.

3. *Proposed Regulations*: Following the study, the agency proposes regulations that must be published. To provide publicity for all regulations, the Federal Register Act[9] provides that proposed administrative regulations be published in the *Federal Register*. This government publication, published five days a week, lists all administrative regulations, all presidential proclamations and executive orders, and other documents and classes of documents that the president and Congress directs to be published.

4. *Public Comment Period*: Following the publication of the proposed rules, the public has the opportunity to provide input on them. Called the public comment period, this time must last at least 30 days (with certain emergency exceptions) and may consist simply of letters written by those affected that are filed with the agency or of hearings conducted by the agency in Washington, D.C., or at specified locations around the country.

5. *Options after Public Comment*: After receiving the public input on the proposed rule, an agency can decide to promulgate the rule. The agency can also decide to withdraw the rule. For example, the EEOC had proposed rules on

---

[7] *Virginia v. Browner*, 80 F.3d 869 (4th Cir. 1996).

[8] *Covad Communications Co. v. FCC*, 430 F.3d 528 (D.C. Cir. 2006).

[9] 44 U.S.C. § 1505 *et seq.*

handling religious discrimination in the workplace. The proposed rules that would have required employers to police those workers wearing a cross or another religious symbol met with so much public and employer protest that they were withdrawn. The agency can decide to modify the rule based on comments and then promulgate or, if the modifications are extensive or material, modify and put the proposed rule back out for public comment.

SECTION 11: THE ADJUDICATORY FUNCTION

While most federal administrative agencies "change" policy matters pursuant to the notice-and-comment procedures of the Administrative Procedures Act, the NLRB has chosen to make policy changes on a case-by-case basis.[10] This "adjudication" method of policy making, as is the custom of the Labor Board, utilizes a factual record developed before an administrative law judge (ALJ), the ALJ's recommended decision, and the proceedings before the Board members. The Board and the labor relations community are often able to identify novel cases, or cases ripe for policy reconsideration, and interested unions and employer-aligned groups not a party to the case are allowed to file **amicus briefs** for consideration by the Board.[11] The steps of the administrative adjudicatory functions of the NLRB are presented in detail in Chapter 4.

SECTION 12: EXHAUSTION OF ADMINISTRATIVE REMEDIES

All parties interacting with an agency must follow the procedures specified by the law. No appeal to a court is possible until the agency has acted on the party's matter before it. As a matter of policy, parties are required to exhaust administrative remedies before they may go to court or take an appeal.

Exceptions to the **exhaustion-of-administrative-remedies** requirement are that (1) available remedies provide no genuine opportunity for adequate relief, (2) irreparable injury may occur if immediate judicial relief is not provided, (3) an appeal to the administrative agency would be futile, or (4) a substantial constitutional question has been raised.

SECTION 13: COURT REVIEW OF AGENCY FINDINGS OF FACT

Appellate challenges in U.S. Courts of Appeals to agency final orders often are focused on the agency's findings of fact on which its conclusions of law are based.

---

[10] The NLRB nevertheless has broad rulemaking power under Section 6 of the NLRA, 29 U.S.C. § 156 (2000).

[11] In the Labor Board's *IBM Corp.* decision, 174 L.R.R.M 1537 (BNA 2004), which changed Board policy and ruled that nonunion employees do not have the right to have a coworker present during an investigatory interview, the Board granted the joint request of LPA, Inc., the Equal Employment Advisory Council, Associated Builders and Contractors, the Chamber of Commerce of the United States, the Society for Human Resource Management, the International Mass Retail Association, and the National Association of Manufacturers to file an amicus brief on behalf of the employer. The AFL-CIO did not file a brief in this case.

The Administrative Procedures Act directs that the reviewing court should set aside agency action "unsupported by substantial evidence." Regarding determinations of fact by the NLRB, which will be discussed in detail in Chapter 4, Section 10(e) of the Taft-Hartley Act states that "[t]he findings of the Board with respect to questions of fact if supported by substantial evidence on the record considered as a whole shall be conclusive."

SECTION 14: COURT REVIEW OF AGENCY DETERMINATIONS ON LAW AND POLICY: THE *CHEVRON* FRAMEWORK

The U.S. Supreme Court set forth the role of the federal judiciary in reviewing an administrative agency's application of its organic statute in *Chevron U.S.A. v. Natural Resources Defense Council, Inc.*[12] The *Chevron* Court designed a two-step analytical framework for the reviewing court on matters of law and policy. First, the court must ask whether Congress has spoken directly on the question at issue. If so, the reviewing court and the agency must give effect to this congressional intent as expressed in the statute. Second, if the statute is silent or ambiguous on the question at issue, the reviewing court then must ask whether the agency's interpretation is "based on a permissible construction of the statute."[13] The power of an agency to administer a congressionally created program necessarily requires the formulation of policy to fill gaps left implicitly or explicitly by Congress. If it is a reasonable policy choice, the agency's construction of the statute is controlling, even if the reviewing court would have chosen a different interpretation. The agency's interpretation is to be given "controlling weight unless [it is] arbitrary, capricious or manifestly contrary to statute."[14]

A reviewing court may, under the first *Chevron* step, conclude that the issue is one of law rather than one of delegated policy and reject the agency's decision or rule.

Under its second step, the *Chevron* Court noted that for "judicial purposes" in reconciling conflicting policies, the administrator's interpretation is entitled to deference as opposed to the reviewing judges, who are not experts in the field.[15] The Court stated in part:

> ...[A]n agency to which Congress has delegated policymaking responsibilities may, within the limits of that delegation, properly rely upon the incumbent administration's views of wise policy to inform its judgments. While agencies are not directly accountable to the people, the Chief Executive is, and it is entirely appropriate for this political branch of Government to make such policy choices—resolving the competing interests which Congress itself either inadvertently did not resolve, or intentionally left to be resolved by the agency charged with the administration of the statute in light of everyday realities.[16]

---

[12] 467 U.S. 837 (1984).

[13] *Id.* at 843.

[14] *Id.* at 844.

[15] *Chevron*, 467 U.S. at 865.

[16] *Id.* at 865, 866. *NLRB v. Curtain Matheson Scientific*, 494 U.S. 775, 786 (1990).

In addition to the general principles of administrative law discussed in the landmark *Chevron* decision, the U.S. Supreme Court has specifically emphasized that the NLRB has the primary responsibility for developing and applying national labor policy.[17] The Court has stated that it will uphold a Board rule as long as it is rational and consistent with the Act.[18] And the Court has stated that a Board rule is entitled to deference even if it represents a departure from the Board's prior policy.[19]

SECTION 15: THE FEDERAL COURT SYSTEM

A selective outline of the federal court system is helpful in understanding the travel of labor and employment law cases from administrative agencies to review or trial in an appropriate federal court.

FEDERAL DISTRICT COURTS

The district courts of the United States, commonly referred to as federal district courts, are the general trial courts of the federal court system. They are courts of original jurisdiction that hear both civil and criminal matters. Civil cases that can be brought in federal district courts include (1) civil suits in which the United States is a party, (2) cases between citizens of different states that involve damages of $75,000 or more, and (3) cases that arise under the U.S. Constitution or federal laws and treaties. Federal district courts are located in each of the states and territories of the United States.

Regarding labor laws, regional directors of the NLRB must ask a U.S. district court for a temporary restraining order in unlawful secondary boycott and strike cases under Section 10(k) of the NLRA. Regional directors may petition a U.S. district court for appropriate temporary injunctive relief or a restraining order in unfair labor practice proceedings to stay in effect until the Board makes the final disposition of the case. Section 301 of the Taft-Hartley Act grants federal district courts jurisdiction to resolve suits for violation of collective bargaining contracts, and Section 303 allows employers to sue unions for damages from secondary boycotts. A wide variety of motions involving labor-related laws are also heard before federal district courts. Cases are litigated by the parties themselves in the federal district courts after the procedures of the EEOC have been completed without a settlement and the agency has issued a right-to-sue letter. In unusual situations, the EEOC itself may litigate "pattern-or-practice" and precedent-establishing systemic cases.

U.S. COURTS OF APPEALS

The U.S. federal court system is clustered geographically into 12 judicial circuits, including one for the District of Columbia. A thirteenth Federal Circuit located in Washington D.C. is defined by subject matter such as patent and trademark

---

[17] *Fall River Dyeing & Finishing Corp. v. NLRB*, 482 U.S. 27, 42 (1987).

[18] *NLRB v. J. Weingarten, Inc.*, 420 U.S. 251, 265–266 (1975).

[19] *Id.*

FIGURE 2.1 | THE 13 FEDERAL JUDICIAL CIRCUITS

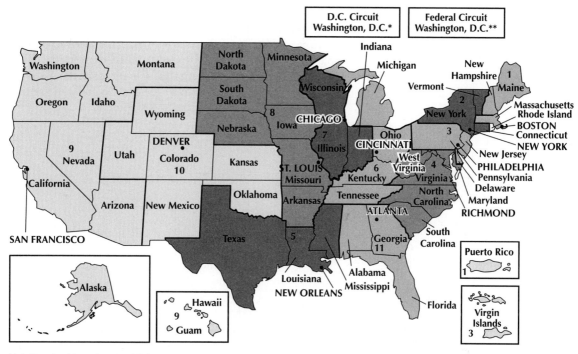

*A sizable portion of the caseload of the D.C. Circuit comes from the federal administrative agencies and offices located in Washington, D.C., such as the National Labor Relations Board and the Labor Department, as well as appeals from the U.S. District Court of the District of Columbia.

**Rather than being defined by geography like the regional courts of appeals, the Federal Circuit is defined by subject matter, having jurisdiction over such matters as patent infringement cases, appeals from the Court of Federal Claims and the Court of International Trade, and appeals from administrative rulings regarding subject matter such as unfair import practices and tariff schedule disputes.

appeals (see Figure 2.1). Persons or businesses who lose cases before the NLRB or the numerous agencies under the Department of Labor may obtain review of the final order of the agency in the U.S. Court of Appeals. Section 10(f) of the Taft-Hartley Act designates that such review take place in the circuit where the unfair labor practice is alleged to have taken place or where the person resides or transacts business or in the D.C. Circuit Court of Appeals. The Board has no authority to compel compliance with its final orders, and under Section 10(e) of the Act, it must apply to an appropriate U.S. Court of Appeals for enforcement of its final order. Generally, a panel of three judges reviews each case. However, some decisions, called **en banc decisions**, are made by the circuit's full panel of judges.

U.S. SUPREME COURT

From a labor and employment law perspective, the nine justices of the U.S. Supreme Court hear appeals from the U.S. Court of Appeals, using "judicial discretion" in selecting the issues of public importance that the Court will hear during each term from the hundreds of cases appealed to the Court. When the Court decides to hear a case, it issues a **writ of certiorari,** giving official notice that it will review the case. It is common for the Court to decide to review an issue when a U.S. Court of Appeals has rendered a decision in conflict with a decision of another U.S. Court of Appeals on the same matter—called a "conflict in the circuits." For example, in *Burlington Northern & Santa Fe Railway v. White,* the Third, Fourth, and Sixth Circuits had applied a different standard for the anti-retaliation provision of the Civil Rights Act than the District of Columbia Circuit and the Seventh Circuit applied. The Supreme Court was called upon to resolve the splits in the circuits in the *BNSF v. White* case. The case is presented in Chapter 12.

CHAPTER QUESTIONS AND PROBLEMS

1. In April 2002, Evelyn Coke, a domestic worker who provided "companionship services" to elderly and infirm men and women, brought a lawsuit against her former employer, Long Island Care at Home, Ltd. (LI Care), and its owner, Maryann Osborne. Ms. Coke alleged that LI Care failed to pay her the minimum wages and overtime wages to which she was entitled under the FLSA, and she sought a judgment for those unpaid wages. All parties assume for present purposes that the Fair Labor Standards Act (FLSA) entitles Coke to payment if, but only if, the statutory exemption for "companionship services" does not apply to companionship workers paid by third-party agencies such as Long Island Care. In 1974, Congress amended the FLSA to include many "domestic service" employees not previously subject to requirements of minimum wage and maximum hours. When doing so, Congress simultaneously created an exemption that excluded from FLSA coverage certain subsets of employees "employed in domestic service employment," including babysitters "employed on a casual basis" and companionship workers. The Department of Labor (DOL) then promulgated a set of regulations that included the following:

   > Interpretations, says that exempt companionship workers include those who are employed by an employer or agency other than the family or household using their services... [whether] such an employee [is assigned] to

more than one household or family in the same workweek.... 40 Fed. Reg. 7407 [codified at 29 CFR § 552. 109(a)].

   The FLSA does not define the statutory terms "domestic service employment" and "companionship services." It authorizes the Secretary of Labor "to prescribe necessary rules, regulation, and orders with regard to the 1974 amendments made by this Act." The DOL gave notice, it proposed regulations, it received public comment, and it issued final regulations in light of the public comment. The resulting regulation is quoted above. Does the second step of the *Chevron* framework apply to the facts of this case? Where large enterprise third-party employers like LI Care can avoid paying minimum wage and overtime rates to workers like Evelyn Coke, may reviewing judges find the regulation unwise and unenforceable? Decide. [*Long Island Care at Home, Ltd. v. Coke,* 127 S.Ct. 239 (2007)]

2. Section 7 of the National Labor Relations Act (NLRA) provides in part that employees shall have the right "to engage in ... concerted activities for the purpose of ... mutual aid or protection." In 1973, the Labor Board issued its *Weingarten* decision, which held that an employer violates Section 8(a)(1) of the NLRA when it denies an employee's request, based on Section 7 of the Act, for the presence of a union representative at an investigatory interview that the employee reasonably believes might result in

disciplinary action. The Board's decision was upheld by the Supreme Court, and the right of an employee to request and obtain the presence of a coworker at an investigatory interview was extended to nonunion workplaces by the Board's 1982 *Material Research Corp.* decision. Three years later, in 1985, the Reagan Board reversed this decision in the *Sears, Roebuck Co.* case, holding that *Weingarten* principles do not apply in nonunion settings. In the Clinton Board's year 2000 *Epilepsy Foundation of Northeast Ohio* decision, it reimposed the *Materials Research* holding, concluding that unrepresented employees have a right to have a coworker present during investigatory interviews. And three years later, with the changing composition of the Board, on June 9, 2004, in a 3-2 decision, the Bush II Board reversed the year 2000 decision in its *IBM Corp.* decision and ruled that nonunion employees do not have the right to have a coworker present during an investigatory interview. Read the edited version of the *IBM Corp.* case in Chapter 5, page 144.

Consider the merits of the policy considerations relied on by the majority. Remember that the Labor Board's custom is to follow an "adjudication" method of establishing policy precedents. Was the Board majority within the *Chevron* principles when it made the policy decision to divest more than 90 percent of all non-management workers employed in the U.S. private sector subject to the NLRA the right to have a coworker present at an investigatory interview that could lead to discipline or discharge? Decide. [*IBM Corp.* 174 LRRM 1537 (2004)]

Railway and Airline Labor Relations Law

CHAPTER 3

SECTION 16: HISTORY, PURPOSE, CONSTITUTIONALITY

Strikes in the early days of the railway industry had a crippling effect on our nation's economy. As a result, Congress enacted the Arbitration Act of 1888 as the first in a series of legislative attempts to promote the peaceful settlement of disputes in the industry. The 1888 Act provided for voluntary arbitration between the parties and for the creation of investigatory boards in work stoppage situations. However, these boards, which were appointed by the president as need arose, lacked power other than the power of publicity to enforce their conclusions upon the merits of a labor dispute. The arbitration provisions were rarely used, and the investigatory powers were invoked only in connection with the Pullman strike of 1894.

Congress decided to supplant the Arbitration Act of 1888 with the Erdman Act of 1898. This legislation strengthened the voluntary arbitration provisions of its predecessor, introduced federal mediation services to further peaceful settlement efforts, and made it illegal for an employer to discriminate against employees who belonged to a union. The Supreme Court, in *Adair v. United States*,[1] invalidated

---

[1] 208 U.S. 161 (1908).

the antidiscrimination portion of the Act, ruling that Congress could not stop employers from firing employees because they were union members.

Upon failure of hoped-for results from the Erdman Act, Congress passed the Newlands Act of 1913, which established a permanent three-member Board of Mediation but retained almost intact the voluntary arbitration features of the Erdman Act. The Newlands Act met its end in 1916 when four railroad brotherhoods initiated demands for the eight-hour day.[2] A strike loomed imminent as the Brotherhood of Locomotive Firemen and Enginemen flatly rejected arbitration of this issue. A strike was prevented only upon passage of the Adamson Act of 1916, which established the eight-hour day for railway employees.

During the years of World War I, railroads were operated by the federal government. A general order of the Director General of Railroads served to protect railway workers who sought to form and join labor organizations from discrimination for such activities. These war years were marked by a peaceful labor front and the flourishing of collective bargaining. The government entered into agreements with authorized bargaining agents, and any disputes arising from diverse interpretations of these agreements were required to be ultimately referred to boards of adjustment for final resolution. Strikes were implicitly outlawed by this mandatory settlement procedure.

As the railroads were returned to private operation, Congress enacted the Transportation Act of 1920. This Act created a Railway Labor Board of three members—the carriers, the employees, and the public securing one representative each. The Board was empowered to publish its decisions upon investigation of the facts of a dispute; sole reliance was to be placed upon the force of public opinion. While arbitration was fostered by the Transportation Act of 1920, mediation was completely neglected as being ineffective. The conspicuous failing of the Transportation Act was the inability of the Railway Labor Board to compel injunctive compliance on the part of the party adversely affected by an award. While public opinion did give rise to some pressure, generally it was not an effective force in the resolution of disputes.

In enacting the Railway Labor Act of 1926, Congress drew heavily upon the experience it had accumulated in railway labor legislation and disputes since 1888. The machinery for peaceful arbitration and mediation was strengthened, and emphasis continued to rest upon the voluntary settlement procedure rather than upon the compulsory provisions of the Act, although the latter were available if required.

The purpose of the Railway Labor Act was to avoid work stoppages by employees and lockouts by employers through establishing a legal basis for negotiation, mediation, and arbitration procedure. The principle of mediation, which had been discarded by the Transportation Act of 1920, was to play a principal role again. Major power of administration was vested in a nonpartisan Board of Mediation appointed by the president.

Section 2, Third, of the 1926 Act, which gives each party the right to designate representatives without the "interference, influence or coercion" of the other, was a

---

[2]Brotherhood of Locomotive Engineers, Brotherhood of Railway Conductors, Brotherhood of Locomotive Firemen and Enginemen, and the Brotherhood of Railway Trainmen.

prime area of controversy. In its *Texas & New Orleans*[3] decision, the Supreme Court ruled that the Act was a valid exercise of the federal commerce power and that the right of labor to organize without employer impediment could also be constitutionally protected. "As the carriers subjected to the Act have no constitutional right to interfere with the freedom of employees to make their selections, they cannot complain of the statute on constitutional grounds."

SECTION 17: EXPANDING COVERAGE

After observing the Railway Labor Act of 1926 in operation for eight years, Congress sought to solve problems that, by then, had become apparent. In 1934, 1936, 1951, and 1966, the Railway Labor Act was amended. Certain amendments are as follows:

1. Under the 1934 amendments, the duty to recognize and bargain with the designated representative of the employees was vastly strengthened by the addition of Section 2, Ninth, which provides a method for the designation of bargaining representatives by certification procedure.
2. The National Railroad Adjustment Board and the National Mediation Board were created by the 1934 amendments.
3. The 1936 amendment to the Railway Labor Act extended coverage of the Act to common air carriers in interstate or foreign commerce and the transportation of United States mail.
4. The original Act declared illegal any form of compulsory unionism, but Section 2, Eleventh, added in 1951, now permits rail and airline employees to bargain for certain security measures, namely, the **union shop** (where all workers must become union members) and the **checkoff** of dues, initiation fees, and assessments (a procedure whereby the employer deducts these amounts directly from the employees' pay and remits the amounts to the union). These provisions closely parallel those found in the amended National Labor Relations Act.

In *Virginian Railway Co. v. System Federation No. 40,*[4] the Supreme Court gave the 1934 amendments the vitality lacking in all its predecessors by permitting judicial enforcement of the statutory duty to make and maintain agreements concerning rates of pay, rules, and working conditions.

SECTION 18: ADMINISTRATION, REMEDY, ENFORCEMENT

Three major agencies are invoked by the Railway Labor Act to effect its administrative aspects—the Surface Transportation Board, which is the successor to the Interstate Commerce Commission (ICC); the National Mediation Board; and the National Railroad Adjustment Board.

---

[3] *Texas & New Orleans Railroad v. Brotherhood of Railroad Clerks*, 281 U.S. 548 (1930).
[4] 300 U.S. 515 (1937).

THE SURFACE TRANSPORTATION BOARD

The Surface Transportation Board created under the ICC Termination Act of 1995 has the responsibility to approve the consolidation, merger, or sale of any railroad properties.[5] Under the prior statute, the ICC had authority to require railroads seeking expedited approval of rail line acquisitions or mergers to provide economic protection for adversely affected employees. The ICC developed "New York Dock" conditions, which provided up to six years of income protection for terminated or displaced rail employees. The ICC Termination Act of 1995 contains specific statutory language that limits the Surface Transportation Board's authority regarding protection for midsized or Class II rail carriers. In the *Association of American Railroads v. Surface Transportation Board* case, the U.S. Court of Appeals for the D.C. Circuit reversed a Surface Transportation Board decision extending modified severance benefits to railroad workers who were "displaced"—that is, forced to transfer into lower-paying jobs—as a result of an acquisition. The court majority held that the statutory term **severance** applied only to employees whose employment was terminated.[6]

THE NATIONAL MEDIATION BOARD

The most important agency created by the Railway Labor Act is the National Mediation Board (NMB). It is composed of three impartial members appointed by the president, no more than two of whom can be of the same political party. Their terms extend for three years. The NMB's powers and duties may be classified into four categories:

1. Representation questions under Section 2, Ninth, of the Railway Labor Act (RLA).
2. Mediation questions under Section 5 of the Act. These concern the reconciliation of differences between the carrier and the labor organization at the time they are negotiating *new* agreements with reference to wages, hours, and working conditions. Note that the NMB has no power to dictate that conditions be incorporated or to require that new agreements be reached upon the expiration of existing agreements. It is merely an intermediary having the duty to bring the parties into negotiation.
3. Administrative support for the National Railroad Adjustment Board as well as for the Public Law (PL) Boards established under the 1966 amendments. The NMB maintains a panel of neutral referees for service on these and certain other boards.
4. Arbitration under Section 5, First, of the RLA. In some instances, labor disputes may reach a critical stage upon failure of negotiations between the parties. If mediation is unsuccessful, the NMB is bound to propose arbitration.

If arbitration is rejected, the NMB may, pursuant to Section 10 of the RLA, advise the president of the United States that the dispute threatens to deprive

---

[5] Pub. L 104–88 (1995). See also 49 USC § 5.
[6] 162 F.3d 101 (D.C. Cir. 1998).

sections of the country of essential transportation service. The president, then, has the discretionary power to issue an executive order creating a Presidential Emergency Board (PEB) to investigate and file a report concerning the dispute. The PEB, which ordinarily consists of three members, will then hold hearings and submit a report to the president within 30 days, setting forth recommendations for the fair and equitable resolution of the dispute. The disputants are required by law to maintain the status quo until the Emergency Board submits its report and for 30 days thereafter, wherein the parties again must try to reach an agreement based on the recommendations. At the expiration of a maximum of 60 days, if the parties still are at an impasse, they are free to engage in a strike or a lockout. The effect is to delay action on the part of the disputants in the hope that they will satisfactorily settle their dispute. Labor is not deprived of its right to strike under the Act, nor is the employer deprived of the lockout; however, these rights may be exercised only upon compliance with the purposely long and drawn-out procedures of the Act.

Congress has not allowed widespread work stoppages to occur in the railroad industry but has resolved disputes by enacting legislation binding the parties to the recommendations of the Presidential Emergency Boards or by imposing a form of "last best offer" arbitration.[7] Because Congress has the power to enforce Emergency Board recommendations, the recommendations have a very significant weight with the parties and may serve as the basis for the resolution of the disputes.[8] The *Burlington Northern v. BMWE* decision, which held that federal courts may not enjoin secondary picketing by railroad employees, contains a vivid example of the dispute resolution procedures of the RLA.

THE NATIONAL RAILROAD ADJUSTMENT BOARD

The National Railroad Adjustment Board (NRAB) was created by the 1934 amendment to interpret questions "growing out of grievances or out of the interpretation ... of [existing] agreements concerning rates of pay, rules, or working conditions," Section 3, First, (i).

---

[7] Congress resolved a one-day nationwide rail strike in 1991 by enacting Pub. L. 102–29, which had the effect of imposing most of the recommendations of PEB 219. On July 26, 1992, Congress enacted Pub. L. 102–306 to end a two-day nationwide strike/lockout, a law that mandated a form of last best offer arbitration subsequent to the recommendations of PEBs 220, 221, and 222. The use of Presidential Emergency Boards has not been common in the airline industry. However, in the context of a threatened airline strike planned for the holiday period of December 2001, which would have deprived the country of essential transportation services, PEB 236 was created on December 20, 2001, by President G. W. Bush to investigate and report on a dispute between United Airlines and the Machinists Union, Local 141-m. Subsequently, the parties were able to reach agreement without a work stoppage.

[8] For example, the recommendations of Presidential Emergency Board No. 211, August 14, 1986, served as the basis of the resolution of the multi-issued dispute between six railway unions representing 107,000 employees and most of the nation's Class 1 railroads concerning the renewal of their collective bargaining agreements. The 1996 round of PEBs led to the peaceful resolution of contract negotiations for most of the industry's carriers and unions. Section 9a of the RLA allows the parties to a labor dispute involving rail passenger service, or a governor of any state involved, to request the president to establish a PEB to investigate and issue a report and recommendations regarding the disputes See, for example, PEB 237 involving SEPTA and the United Transportation Union, report dated May 11, 2004.

BURLINGTON NORTHERN RAILROAD CO. V. BROTHERHOOD OF MAINTENANCE OF WAY EMPLOYEES
SUPREME COURT OF THE UNITED STATES, 481 U.S. 429 (1987).

[The Brotherhood of Maintenance of Way Employees (BMWE) expanded its strike against the Maine Central Railroad to other rail carriers that had no connection and were not substantially aligned with the struck railroad. A federal district court in Illinois issued a preliminary injunction against the union's picketing of any railroad other than those involved in the primary dispute. The court of appeals reversed the district court, holding that under the Norris-LaGuardia Act (the Federal Anti-Injunction Act), a federal court does not have jurisdiction to enjoin secondary picketing in railway labor disputes. The Supreme Court granted certiorari to decide whether a federal court has jurisdiction to issue such an injunction.]

BRENNAN, J....

[A]s this case illustrates, § 10 of the RLA provides a ready mechanism for the Executive Branch to intervene and interrupt any self-help measures by invoking an Emergency Board and thereby imposing at a minimum a 60-day cooling-off period. If the Board's recommendations are not initially accepted by the parties, Congress has the power to enforce the Board's recommendation by statute, as it has done here. Allowing secondary picketing in the self-help period is thus not inconsistent with the structure or purpose of the Act, and may in fact increase the likelihood of settlement prior to self-help. This is therefore not a case in which "the scheme of the Railway Labor Act could not begin to work without judicial

involvement." *Chicago & North Western, supra.* 402 U.S. at 595 (Brennan J., dissenting).

While opinions regarding the RLA's success in meeting its goals have varied over time, it does appear that under the RLA labor and management have been able to resolve most conflicts without resort to secondary picketing. We decline, at this advanced stage of the RLA's development, to find in it an implied limit on a union's resort to secondary activity. Instead, "if Congress should now find that abuses in the nature of secondary activities have arisen in the railroad industry ... it is for the Congress, and not the Courts, to strike the balance 'between the uncontrolled power of management and labor to further their respective interests.'" *Trainmen v. Jacksonville Terminal Co.,* 394 U.S., at 392....

... In the Norris-LaGuardia Act, Congress divested federal courts of the power to enjoin secondary picketing in railway labor disputes. Congress has not seen fit to restore that power. Accordingly, we affirm the decision of the Court of Appeals.

It is so ordered.

Case Questions

1. Do procedures exist for the executive branch to intervene in a railway labor dispute and interrupt any self-help measures that may be disrupting essential transportation services?
2. Does the Supreme Court have the power to enjoin secondary activity by rail unions?

The Railway Labor Act, as amended in 1966, provides that National Railroad Adjustment Board awards shall be final and binding on the parties to the dispute.[9] If a carrier does not comply with an NRAB order implementing an award, a proceeding for enforcement of the award may be brought in a U.S. District Court up to two years after noncompliance. Under the 1966 amendments, the losing party may also obtain court review of an adverse order of the NRAB, but the grounds for judicial review are the narrow grounds commonly provided for review of arbitration awards. Section 3, First, (p) and (q), provides that an order may be set

---

[9]The 1996 amendments eliminated an exception for money awards.

aside in either enforcement or review proceedings only on the three following grounds:

1. Failure of the NRAB to comply with the requirements of the RLA
2. Failure of the order to conform, or confine itself, to matters within the scope of the NRAB's jurisdiction
3. Fraud or corruption by a member of the NRAB

Unions have an obligation to provide fair representation for all persons in a bargaining unit, and an individual may bring a lawsuit on the theory that a union breached its duty of fair representation.[10]

OTHER BOARDS OF ADJUSTMENT

The 1966 amendments to the Railway Labor Act provide that unions or carriers may request the establishment of special boards of adjustment (called PL Boards by the National Mediation Board under Public Law 89–456) to resolve disputes that have been pending before the NRAB for a year or more. These boards consist of three members. The provision authorizing such special boards was added to the RLA to eliminate a large backlog of cases then pending before the NRAB and to build in a procedure for the expeditious handling of future cases. Even before the 1966 amendments, the RLA, Section 3, Second, authorized the establishment of system, group, or regional permanent adjustment boards by mutual consent of the parties for the local settlement of disputes otherwise referable to the NRAB for hearing at the NRAB's headquarters in Chicago, Illinois. The awards of special, system, group, or regional boards of adjustment have the same legal effect as an NRAB award.[11]

MAJOR AND MINOR DISPUTES

Railway management and railway labor commonly classify disputes between themselves as "major" and "minor." Railway management ordinarily cannot change the rates of pay, rules, or working conditions of its employees that are set forth in labor agreements except by following the lengthy process of bargaining and mediation required by the Railway Labor Act, particularly Section 6 of the Act.[12] Railway unions seeking better wages, hours, and working conditions also must follow the lengthy process of the RLA. Such disputes are considered **major disputes**.

In contrast, a **minor dispute** is a dispute between a carrier and a union over the meaning or application of a particular provision of an existing collective agreement.

---

[10] *Foust v. Electrical Workers*, 442 U.S. 42 (1979). See Section 78 of this book for a discussion of the law concerning a union's duty of fair representation.

[11] In *Cole v. Erie Lackawanna Railway Co.*, 541 F.2d 528 (6th Cir. 1976), the Sixth Circuit Court of Appeals found that federal district courts could exercise limited judicial review over determinations of PL Boards. The court of appeals agreed with the trial court that Section 3, First, (j), requires the board to serve formal notice of its proceedings on the aggrieved party so that the party would be in a position to make a determination as to whether the party wanted to be represented by the union, by counsel, or by self-representation. In *Ollman v. SBA No. 1063* 2005 WL 602386 (W.D.N.Y. Mar. 14, 2005), a federal district court held, however, that when an employee is represented by a union, the carrier need not give notice of an SBA hearing to the employee and that notice to the employee by the union is sufficient.

[12] 45 U.S.C. § 156.

A dispute may involve whether the carrier violated the discipline rule of the collective agreement by discharging an employee or disagreement over the proper application of a pay rule in the agreement. Minor disputes are resolved, after proper handling on the railroad property, by the NRAB or another adjustment board established by the carrier and the union under Section 3 of the RLA.[13] The *UTU and BNSF* arbitration award presented in this section is an example of a minor dispute resolved by a board of adjustment that consisted of a carrier official, a union official, and a neutral chairperson.

Railway management and labor often disagree over whether a dispute is a major or minor one. The courts look at whether a claim has been made where the terms of the existing agreement establish the right to take the disputed action. The dispute may thus be conclusively resolved by interpreting the existing agreement, making it a minor dispute. Other disputes are major disputes. In *Consolidated Rail Corp v. RLEA*,[14] the Supreme Court held that "[i]f an employer asserts a claim that the parties' agreement gives the employer the discretion to make a particular change in working conditions without prior negotiation, and if that claim is arguably justified by the terms of the parties' agreement (i.e., the claim is neither obviously insubstantial or frivolous, nor made in bad faith)," it is a minor dispute, and the employer may make the change and the courts must defer to the arbitral jurisdiction of the adjustment board. The *Airline Professionals Association, IBT v. ABX Air, Inc.* case is a recent example of the *Conrail* court's rule on "major" and "minor" disputes.

In *Hawaiian Airlines v. Norris*,[15] Grant Norris, an airplane mechanic, was terminated for insubordination for failure to sign a maintenance record for a plane he considered unsafe, and he reported the mechanical problem to the FAA. Norris filed suit in a state court under the Hawaii Whistleblower Protection Act, claiming he was wrongfully terminated in violation of the Whistleblower Act for reporting the mechanical problem. The airline contended that the termination was a minor dispute subject to the exclusive dispute resolution provisions of the RLA and that the state court theory was preempted by the RLA. The U.S. Supreme Court decided that Norris's whistle-blower claim was independent of the collective bargaining agreement and not preempted by the RLA.

AIRLINE BOARDS

The airlines are not subject to NRAB jurisdiction. The Railway Labor Act provides for air carriers and their employees to establish system boards of adjustment for the resolution of grievances. In *Machinists v. Central Airlines, Inc.*, the Supreme Court ruled that awards of air carrier system boards of adjustment are enforceable by federal law in federal courts.[16] Like NRAB procedures, the National Mediation Board aids in the designation of neutrals for service with air carrier system boards. However, neutrals are not compensated by the NMB as are the neutrals who serve with the NRAB. The parties are required to compensate the neutrals who serve with air carrier boards.

---

[13] 45 U.S.C. § 153.

[14] 491 U.S. 299 (1989).

[15] 512 U.S. 246 (1994).

[16] 372 U.S. 682 (1963).

CASE 3.2	BNSF RAILWAY AND UNITED TRANSPORTATION UNION
	115 LA 1319 (2001)

[Engineer S_ was suspended from work for one year for operating rules violations for his handling of his train's speed in the descent of the Cajon Pass east of San Bernardino, California, on March 8, 1998. The matter was appealed to a Public Law Board, whose binding decision was rendered on June 5, 2001.]

On the Cajon Subdivision trains are required to maintain certain speeds while descending the steep grade at Cajon Pass west of Summit depending on the tonnage of the train and braking capacity according to the requirements set forth in Division Time Table No. 2 in effect October 1, 1996. On March 8, 1998 Engineer S_ and Conductor Klatt operated [their train] from Barstow to Los Angeles. Some 10 days later,... they were contacted by Road Foreman of Engines Worcester who was investigating the speed of their train between Cajon and Baseline on March 8, 1998. Engineer S_ was held out of service soon after his discussions with Mr. Worcester.

The record reveals that the speed of westbound trains operating over the Cajon Pass are subject to strict scrutiny by the Carrier, and it is well known by all employees operating in this area that event recorders will be read for train speed by a Carrier official for *all* westbound trains operating over the Cajon Pass. Both Engineer S_ and Conductor Klatt testified that they used the Carrier rules and the paperwork given for their train in Barstow on March 8, 1998 to determine what speed to operate down the Cajon Pass. They both testified that they determined their train was a "15-30" train, meaning that their train travelling on the south track from Summit to Cajon was to operate at 15 mph, and from Cajon to Baseline the train was to operate at 30 mph. Were their train to be over 6,500 tons, under the speed regulations set forth in Division Timetable No. 2, they would be required to operate at 20 mph from Cajon to Baseline.

Conductor Klatt testified in part in response to questions from the Hearing Officer:

Q   There's been an awful lot of testimony here and many, many exhibits about this train and other trains and how the computer system works. And Mr. Martin, who I would consider an expert, said for the record that no information that he saw would tend to make myself or anyone

reading the transcript think that your train was less than 6,500 tons.

Is there anything that comes to your mind that would tend to—that needs to be entered in here today that would make me think otherwise?

A   The only thing that I could add is that, when I get there and do my signal awareness form what we qualify for in the back there, and I do fill those out and turn them in. As new as I am and as cautious as I am, I know I did it. And I haven't had one engineer yet that hasn't asked me "What did you get?"

And if there is a discrepancy between us two, then we go back and figure it out what it is before we even leave the lobby. And I know that S_ and I had done that.

Q   S_ is?

A   S_. I know S_ and I did that before we left the lobby. Even as we're going along before we go down the hill, I still open up my book to make sure what we are just because I'm new. I just want to make sure.

There is no question but that the crew believed that their train was a "15-30" train, not a "15-20" train. Indeed, Road Foreman of Engines J.L. Worcester testified in part that the crew had run the train as though they had a train under 6,500 tons as follows:

Q   Do you have the same list that the train crew had?

A   No, I do not.

Q   Did they operate that train between Summit and Baseline on the south track as if they had a train under 6,500 tons?

A   Yes

A fair and proper evaluation of whether or not Engineer S_ exceeded the proper speed in violation of the Carrier rules requires a review of the paperwork that Conductor and Engineer used on March 8, 1998 to determine the speed for the Cajon Pass....

The Hearing Officer questioned Engineer S_ as follows:

Q   Okay. And, again, besides Exhibit C, which is the list you're talking about, all the other exhibits, the AEI scanners, the archive, the files

continued

of train lists, the Train Event, is any of that information ever less than 6,500 tons?

A   I wouldn't know. I don't even know—I have never seen any of that information or how to obtain it before....

All of the other exhibits referred to by the Hearing Officer had no meaning to Engineer S_. A mountain of printouts cannot substitute for the critical documents that were not produced in this case—the train list with the train profile which the crew members used to determine the appropriate speed to descend the Cajon Pass. It may well be that the train in fact was over 6,500 tons. But the crew is only responsible for the Rules violations charged if the information provided them on the train list and train profile at Barstow on March 8, 1998 showed the train to be over 6,500 tons.

In the instant case Mr. Martin testified that there was no way to go back into the computer system and print out a copy of the list that would have been given the crew on March 8, 1998 in Barstow. And the record reveals that the crew members do not keep this paperwork in the ordinary course of their duties for the Carrier, nor has any requirement been shown that such paperwork should be turned into the Carrier. Conductor Klatt testified that he turned into the Carrier his Signal Awareness Form on which he recorded his figures in determining the speed for the train.... And Mr. Klatt testified that the figures from the train list to determine the speed was what he "input on my signal awareness form." Such a document would be relevant and material in this case, but it was not produced by the Carrier.

It is evident that compliance with speed regulations over the Cajon Pass is a most serious matter to the Carrier, for improper speed can lead to a catastrophe. And the matter of discipline for a speed violation to an employee is a most serious matter. In the instant case Engineer S_ was suspended from service without pay from March 16, 1998 through March 15, 1999, with a three year probation period. The stakes are high for the Carrier and the employee. All parties concerned are genuinely interested in the fairness of the disciplinary system.

As set forth initially the Carrier has the burden of proof. We find it has failed to meet that burden of proof in this case.

Award
Claim sustained. [Engineer reinstated to service with back pay.]

Case Questions

1.   Did the carrier produce evidence that the train was operating at an excessive speed considering the weight of the train? Did the Board find that the carrier met its burden of proof?

2.   If the train was operated 10 miles per hour over the speed limit from Cajon to Baseline in violation of company operating rules and the speed set forth in the division timetable, is a one-year suspension an appropriate penalty for the engineer? Give the carrier's view on this matter. State the union's view. What did the Board say about this matter?

CASE 3.3	AIRLINE PROFESSIONALS ASSOCIATION, IBT V. ABX AIR, INC.
	UNITED STATES COURT OF APPEALS, 400 F.3D 411 (6TH CIR. 2005)

[ABX operates as a common carrier, delivering packages and freight by air. From June 1997 through July 31, 2001, ABX and the Airline Professionals Association, IBT, were parties to a collective bargaining agreement, pursuant to which the Union was the collective bargaining representative of various employees, including pilots. At all times relevant to this matter, ABX and the union were engaged in contract negotiations for a successor agreement, each having served upon the other a Section 6 notice, the requisite notice of intent to seek modifications of

the 1997 CBA. In the fall of 1999, Byron Russell, a pilot employed by ABX, applied for disability and benefits after he was diagnosed by his physician as suffering from "stress and anxiety." Unwilling to rely solely on the diagnosis of Russell's doctor, ABX insisted that Russell undergo an independent medical examination (IME) with Dr. Joseph Westermeyer. Russell complied, and Dr. Westermeyer found that he was suffering from conditions more severe than mere stress and anxiety and was unfit to fly. Dr. Westermeyer provided a full report

continued

to ABX, and Russell began receiving disability benefits. He remained on disability leave until April 1, 2002, when he notified ABX of his readiness to return to work. Despite Russell's presenting a second-class medical certificate from the Federal Aviation Administration clearing him to fly, ABX's flight management had concerns about whether Russell was in fact fit to fly an airplane. ABX therefore directed him to attend another IME by Dr. Westermeyer, which Russell refused to do.

On April 25, 2002, the union filed a grievance on behalf of Russell, which complained that by requiring Russell to submit to an IME before returning to work, ABX violated the terms of the 1997 CBA between the parties. The union also sought injunctive relief in federal district court, claiming that ABX's action violated the RLA by imposing new working conditions not authorized by the parties' CBA. The district court held that the complaint raised a "major dispute" under the RLA, over which the court had jurisdiction, and granted summary judgment to the Union. ABX appealed.]

BATCHELDER, C. J....

One of the purposes of the RLA is "[t]o avoid any interruption to commerce or to the operation of any [air or rail] carrier engaged therein." 45 U.S.C. § 151a (1). To that end, the RLA provides mandatory procedures for resolving disputes between carriers and unions. 45 U.S.C. § 151a. For purposes of determining which of the RLA's procedures are to be followed in resolving such disputes, the courts have classified those disputes as either "major" or "minor." *See Elgin. J. & E. Ry.*

Co. v. Burley, 325 U.S. 711, 732, 65 S.Ct. 1282, 89 L.Ed. 1886 (1945). Major disputes are defined as disputes "over the formation of collective agreements or efforts to secure them. They arise where there is no such agreement or where it is sought to change the terms of one...." *Id.* at 723, 65 S.Ct. 1282; *see also ABX Air, Inc. v. Airline Professionals Assoc.*, 266 F.3d 392, 396 (6ᵗʰ Cir. 2001) ("*ABX I*") ("Major disputes involve disagreements over the creation of contractual rights during bargaining for a CBA or to change the terms of an existing agreement.") Minor disputes, on the other hand, can be resolved by interpreting the terms of the CBA. *Airline Professionals Assoc. v. ABX Air, Inc.*, 274 F.3d 1023, 1028 (6ᵗʰ Cir. 2001) ("*ABX II*"). Stated differently, major disputes seek to create contractual

rights; minor disputes seek to enforce them. *Elgin*, 325 U.S. at 723, 65 S.Ct. 1282.

When a major dispute occurs, the parties must engage in the lengthy process of bargaining and mediation set out in RLA §§ 5 and 6, 45 U.S.C. §§ 155 and 156. *Consolidated Rail Corp. v. Railway Labor Executives' Assoc. et al.*, 491 U.S. 299, 302 (1989) (hereinafter "*Conrail*"). During that process, the parties must maintain the "status quo," and the employer is prohibited from implementing the contested changes in working conditions. *Id.* at 302–3. The district courts have subject matter jurisdiction to enjoin a violation of the status quo pending the exhaustion of the required procedural remedies. *Id.* at 303.

Minor disputes, by contrast, must first be resolved through the normal grievance procedure. *Conrail*, 491 U.S. at 303. We held in *ABX I* that

> [i]f discussions fail to yield a solution, both parties are subject to compulsory and binding arbitration before an adjustment board under 45 U.S.C. § 152, Sixth and § 184. While the courts have no jurisdiction to resolve the substance of minor disputes, they can enjoin strikes over minor disputes in order to enforce compliance with the RLA's dispute resolution provisions.

ABX I, 266 F.3d at 396 (internal citations omitted).

The district court had jurisdiction over the Union's complaint only if the dispute over ABX's requirement that the pilot submit to an IME before returning from disability leave is a major dispute. We review de novo the district court's construction of the RLA regarding the scope of its subject matter jurisdiction. *ABX I*, 266 F.3d at 395.

ABX has the burden of demonstrating that this case involves a minor dispute under the RLA, but that burden is not heavy. As the *Conrail* Court explained,

> [I]f an employer asserts a claim that the parties' agreement gives the employer the discretion to make a particular change in working conditions without prior negotiation, and if that claim is arguably justified by the terms of the parties' agreement (i.e., the claim is neither obviously insubstantial or frivolous, nor made in bad faith), the employer may make the change and the courts must defer to the arbitral jurisdiction of the Board.

continued

491 U.S. at 310. Anticipating *Conrail*, the Seventh Circuit said in *Railway Labor Executives' Ass'n v. Norfolk & W. Ry. Co.*, "[b]ecause a major dispute can escalate into a strike, if there is any doubt as to whether a dispute is major or minor a court will construe the dispute to be minor." 833 F.2d 700, 705 (7th Cir. 1987).

ABX concedes that at the time Russell was asked to submit to an IME, the parties had served on each other the requisite Section 6 notices and were renegotiating the CBA, and that they were therefore involved in a major dispute. As a preliminary matter, we must decide whether every dispute arising under a CBA that is being renegotiated is a major dispute. Addressing this question, the D.C. Circuit has held that:

> The RLA was designed to provide mechanisms that would "facilitate the orderly and peaceful resolution of labor-management disputes." To that end, Congress devised one track, with a focus on arbitration, for minor disputes that center around the definition of rights already agreed upon, and another, with a focus on mediation (and potential presidential intervention), for major ones that raise broader issues likely in themselves to engender a strike. The expiration of the collective bargaining agreement tells us little or nothing about the track for which a dispute is suitable.... Accordingly, we reject the proposition that the expiration of the agreements and filing of § 6 notices automatically make the dispute a major one.
> *Air Line Pilots Assn. v. Eastern Air Lines, Inc.*, 863 F.2d 891, 899 (D.C. Cir. 1988).

The district court erred in determining that this dispute between ABX and the Union is a major dispute. The court's observation that the CBA does not explicitly permit ABX to require an IME before allowing a pilot to return to work after disability leave, while correct, does not, either alone or in conjunction with the court's findings on past practice and the availability of other methods to ensure safety, lead to the conclusion that ABX's position is not arguably justifiable.

Collective bargaining agreements may include both express and implied terms. *Conrail*, 491 U.S. at 311, 109 S.Ct. 2477. Implied terms are part of the CBA and may be used to justify the employer's challenged actions. *ABX II*, 274 F.3d at 1028. This Court found those implied terms in *ABX II*, a case involving the same parties and the same CBA before us today, holding that "management retains discretion with respect to the hiring, firing, promoting, supervising, planning,

and other management functions, except as limited by the collective bargaining agreement and public law." 274 F.3d at 1029. This principle "stems from the understanding that collective bargaining agreements... [cannot] expressly regulate every conceivable employment matter." *Id.* at 1031.

The Union argues that there is neither any implied term in the CBA nor any past history or practice that would permit ABX to impose the IME requirement, which the Union views as a change in working conditions. Rather, the Union contends, because Article 16.A of the CBA provides that "[t]he physical standards required of a crewmember shall be the standards established by [the FAA]," and because Russell had obtained a second class airman medical certificate from the FAA, only the FAA had the authority to determine Russell's fitness to fly and ABX had no right to require anything further before permitting Russell to return to work. ABX argues that while Article 16.A establishes that ABX's standards must be the same as those set by the FAA, neither the CBA nor anything in the applicable sections of the Code of Federal Regulations, 14 C.F.R. §§ 67.1 et seq., requires that the FAA is the sole determiner of whether those standards have been met....

We hold that ABX's claim that it has the right to require employees to submit to IMEs before returning from disability is neither "obviously insubstantial or frivolous, nor made in bad faith," *Conrail*, 491 U.S. at 310, 109 S.Ct. 2477, but rather, is arguably justified under the written and implied terms of the parties' 1997 CBA and the applicable law. Accordingly, we hold that this dispute is a minor one for the purposes of the RLA, over which the district court lacked jurisdiction. *See ABX II*, 274 F.3d at 1028 ("The adjustment board exercises exclusive jurisdiction over minor disputes.") Whether the terms of the 1997 CBA, in fact, allowed ABX to require Russell to submit to an IME must be determined by the System Board of Adjustment.

[Matter dismissed.]

Case Questions

1. Explain the procedures used to resolve major and minor disputes under the RLA.
2. Did the Court decide that ABX may require that a pilot who has obtained a second-class airman medical certificate from the FAA nevertheless must also submit to further medical evaluation by the Carrier's physician?

SECTION 19: BARGAINING REPRESENTATION

The National Mediation Board has original jurisdiction over representation issues. Section 2, Fourth, of the Railway Labor Act permits employees to "bargain collectively through representatives of their own choosing" and to be free from employer interference in their organizational efforts. The procedure for designation of representatives, elections, and certification is stated in Section 2, Ninth, of the RLA. The rules of the NMB prescribe a petition by those interested in securing bargaining agency rights, such petition to be supported by a substantial (35 percent) showing of interest. Following this, an election may be held, with certification accruing to the majority representative. Under NMB procedures, eligible employees are mailed ballots that are returned by mail to the NMB's offices in Washington, D.C., where they are held in a safe until a predetermined ballot count date.[17] However, the RLA permits certification without the necessity of a formal election; that is, the representative may prove its majority status by means of signature cards or by a consent election.[18]

SECTION 20: STRIKE INJUNCTIONS

As discussed in Section 18 of this chapter, the Railway Labor Act sets forth specific procedures that must be followed before employees may exercise their right to strike. Where employees strike without fulfilling the requirements of the Act, their employer may seek to obtain a court injunction against the strike. Ordinarily the use of a strike injunction is prohibited because of Section 4 of the Norris-LaGuardia Act. However, the Supreme Court held in *Chicago and North Western Railway Company v. United Transportation Union* that a strike injunction may be issued when such a remedy is the only practical and effective means of enforcing a union's duty to exert every reasonable effort to make and maintain agreements.[19]

SECTION 21: JURISDICTIONAL ISSUES: THE RLA AND THE NLRA

The federal Railway Labor Act is the law governing labor relations in the railroad and airline industries, while the National Labor Relations Act is the federal law governing most other private sector industries and the U.S. Postal Service. The National Mediation Board (NMB) is the agency with primary jurisdiction regarding establishing representation rights and providing mediation under the RLA. The National Labor Relations Act excludes from the definition of "employer," contained in Section 2(2) of the NLRA, "any person subject to the Railway Labor

---

[17] NMB No. 251 (1981). See *United States v. Trans World Airlines, Inc.*, 107 LRRM 2571 (D.D.C 1981), for an example of the NMB's compelling an air carrier to provide a list of names and addresses of employees in order to conduct a rerun representation election.

[18] In its *Burlington Northern Santa Fe Railway* decision, 32 NMB 163 (2005) certification was not extended to cover a voluntarily recognized acquired line.

[19] 402 U.S. 570 (1971). See also *Teamsters v. North American Airlines*, 2005 WL 2233915 (N.D. Cal. Sept. 14, 2005).

Act," The National Labor Relations Board (NLRB) usually declines jurisdiction over cases where the employer meets the definition of "carrier" as set forth in the RLA.[20] Normally, the NLRB defers to the NMB in the first instance, declining or accepting jurisdiction based on the opinion of the NMB. For example, in the NLRB's *Aircraft Services International Group* decision, it declined jurisdiction over a company that provided fueling services for airplanes, work traditionally done by air carriers, relying on the NMB decision to assert jurisdiction.[21]

In *BRT v. Jacksonville Terminal Co.*,[22] the U.S. Supreme Court set forth the standard for determining whether a labor dispute is governed by the RLA or the NLRA, stating "when the traditional railway labor organization acts on behalf of employees subject to the Railway Labor Act in a dispute with carriers subject to the Railway Labor Act, the organizations must be deemed, *pro tanto*, [as far as it goes] exempt from the National Labor Relations Act."[23]

In *Air Line Pilots Association (ABX Air, Inc.)*,[24] the NLRB ruled that an airline union was subject to the NLRA. The case resulted from complexities following a merger and restructuring of companies in the business of rapid pickup, sorting, and carriage of documents, small parcels, and other freight in both ground and air operations. One predecessor employer prior to the merger had a small number of pilots covered by the NLRA, but none of those employees were involved in the underlying dispute, which involved a traditional railway labor organization (ALPA) acting on behalf of employees subject to the Railway Labor Act (ASTAR pilots) and a carrier subject to the Railway Labor Act (ABX Air, Inc.). In its *ALPA v. NLRB (ABX Air, Inc.)* decision, the Ninth Circuit Court of Appeals ruled, utilizing the *Jacksonville Terminal* standard, that the NLRB had failed to apply the law correctly and did not have jurisdiction over a grievance filed by the union to enforce a collective bargaining agreement entered into by a carrier under the RLA.[25]

CHAPTER QUESTIONS AND PROBLEMS

1. Why did Congress first regulate disputes in the railway industry?

2. How did the 1926 RLA improve the prior situation? How did the 1934 amendments improve the RLA?

3. What rights of employers are protected by the RLA?

4. Why did the 1966 amendments to the RLA establish special boards of adjustment?

5. Does Section 4 of the Norris-LaGuardia Act prohibit the use of strike injunctions in cases arising under the RLA?

6. Flight attendants employed by Transamerica Airlines, Inc., and represented by the Teamsters Union went on strike over new contract terms. The Air Line Pilots Association (ALPA), the exclusive bargaining representative of Transamerica's pilots, decided to

---

[20] 45 U.S.C. § 151 (railroad), § 181 (air carrier).

[21] 175 LRRM 1395 (2004).

[22] 394 U.S. 369.

[23] *Id.* at 376, 377.

[24] 2005 NLRB LEXIS 451 (Aug. 27, 2005).

[25] 525 F.3d 862 (9th Cir. 2008).

honor Teamster picket lines, thereby grounding nearly all Transamerica's flights. After a month of supporting the flight attendants, ALPA negotiated a back-to-work agreement with Transamerica and returned to work. The agreement included a clause stating, "There shall be no reprisals or recriminations by either side as a result of activities during the strike." After the pilots returned to work, ALPA initiated union disciplinary action against pilots who had flown during the strike, ultimately fining them the amount of money they earned during the strike.

The fined pilots refused to pay and brought an action in federal district court claiming ALPA violated the "no reprisal" clause of the back-to-work agreement by fining them. ALPA sought to dismiss the federal court action by contending that the federal court did not have jurisdiction under the RLA to decide matters of contract interpretation.

Does the district court have jurisdiction? What forum resolves contract interpretation disputes between ALPA and the carrier? [*Frehtelkotter v. Air Line Pilots Association*, 111 LRRM 3065 (9th Cir.)]

7. The Transport Workers Union of America represented flight attendants for Eastern Airlines. The collective bargaining agreement in effect between the union and Eastern included a clause requiring that "any and all" flying performed for Eastern would be performed by flight attendants named on the current Eastern Airlines seniority list. Subsequently Eastern agreed to assume the Latin American service routes of the bankrupt Braniff Airways, Inc. Part of the agreement covering routes to eight Latin American countries included a provision requiring Eastern to hire approximately 310 flight attendants employed by Braniff who would reside in those countries to work the Latin American flights.

The union claimed Eastern had unilaterally ignored the language of the collective bargaining agreement by employing flight

attendants not listed on the seniority roster in violation of the RLA. The union sought a preliminary injunction restoring the flight attendant issue to the status quo pending a full trial. Eastern claimed the union was not entitled to an injunction under the RLA.

May the union obtain an injunction against Eastern under the Act? If so, should an injunction be issued? Decide. [*Local 553 v. Eastern Airlines*, 111 LRRM 2402 (E.D.N.Y.)]

8. The United Transportation Union (UTU), a representative of the employees of Burlington-Northern Railroad Company, notified the railroad of a new request governing the compensation of train crews. The union requested that road or yard crews working without a fireman receive extra compensation and that firemen working with a reduced train or yard crew receive extra compensation. The carrier characterized this request as improper and barred by a previous agreement with the union that imposed a moratorium on the change of payment for certain train crews. The union maintained its request was not barred by the moratorium provision and invoked mediation of the matter under the RLA. At mediation, the parties agreed to submit the issue of the moratorium clause to arbitration and, in the meantime, recess mediation. After the conference, however, the union asked if negotiations could be continued without submitting the moratorium issue to arbitration. The railroad understood the union request to mean that the issue would not be submitted to arbitration, provided the UTU did not strike on that issue. On April 1, the National Mediation Board acknowledged that mediation was recessed with agreement of the parties. On April 13, the UTU struck Burlington-Northern over the crew payments issue. On April 23, the railroad submitted the moratorium issue to arbitration.

Burlington-Northern sought an injunction prohibiting the union from striking over this issue. The UTU maintained its right to resort to a strike under the RLA.

What factors must be considered by the court before a strike injunction may be issued? Should an injunction be granted in this case? Decide. [*Burlington-Northern Railroad v. UTU*, 110 LRRM 2340 (N.D. Ill.)]

9. The International Association of Machinists filed a petition with the National Mediation Board calling for a Board investigation of a representation dispute among certain employees of British Airways. After eight days of hearings, the NMB found that among the employees in question, a craft or class of office-clerical employees existed that was distinct from a craft or class of fleet and passenger employees. Although the Machinists wanted to represent both classes of employees, the Board ruled they did not have sufficient support among the office class. The Board did rule that the fleet and passenger employees at British Airways were involved in a representation dispute and that they were entitled to an election. The Machinists were subsequently certified as the representatives of the fleet and passenger class.

The employer brought an action in U.S. District Court alleging that the NMB improperly designated the fleet and passenger employees as a class or craft under the RLA because the NMB ignored evidence offered by British Airways that would have prevented this determination. The union claimed that the court should not have scrutinized the NMB process of determining a craft or class of employees under the RLA and sought to dismiss the action.

What factors must the NMB consider in determining classes or crafts under the Act? May the court overrule the NMB's determination of a class or craft of employees for representation purposes under the RLA in this case? Decide. [*British Airways Board v. NMB*, 109 LRRM 2527 (E.D.N.Y.)]

10. The International Brotherhood of Teamsters was the certified representative of Western Airline's mechanics, stock clerks, and flight instructors. The Air Transport Employees'

Union represented Western's clerical, office, fleet, and passenger service employees. Collective bargaining agreements in effect between the unions and Western provided that they were binding on Western's successors. After negotiations in which both unions agreed to significant wage concessions, the unions and Western executed letter agreements. These agreements provided that in the event of Western's merger with or acquisition by another airline, Western would ensure that work performed by union employees would continue to be assigned to union employees and be covered by the collective bargaining agreements.

Two years later Delta Airlines and Western agreed to a merger. Under the agreement, Western would cease to exist on the following April 1. The agreement made no mention of whether Delta would recognize the unions or be bound by the collective bargaining agreements. Delta employees in the crafts covered by Western's collective bargaining agreements were nonunion.

Prior to the merger date, the unions filed grievances claiming that Western's agreement to merge violated the collective bargaining agreements. Pursuant to the collective bargaining agreements, both unions requested arbitration to determine whether the agreements had been breached. Western refused to submit to arbitration, stating that arbitration should not be the vehicle for deciding who would represent Delta employees after the merger. Western argued that because the issues involved the unions' representation status, they were not arbitral, but instead fell within the exclusive jurisdiction of the National Mediation Board.

Time is of the essence. What can the unions do next? May they proceed to court, or is this a representation matter within the exclusive province of the NMB? Decide. [*Local 2702 v. Western Airlines*, 125 LRRM 2153 (9th Cir.)]

11. The Pacific & Arctic Railway halted operations between Skagway, Alaska, and the Yukon Territory. The union filed grievances,

and a three-member arbitration panel, consisting of a union member, a carrier member, and a neutral member, met to hear the grievances. On the evening of the first hearing day, the railroad's attorney encountered the union member and the neutral member going out to dinner; the union member paid for the dinner. When the hearing resumed, the railroad's attorney questioned the *ex parte* contacts. A heated discussion ensued, with the neutral member characterizing the objection as "trivial." An exchange between the neutral member and the attorney followed:

THE ARBITRATOR: Sir, I don't care what your plans are. Now, will you stop interrupting the board? If you say you're through, you're through.

MR. ROBINSON: I'm making a record. Are you preventing me from making a record?

THE ARBITRATOR: No, you can make no further record.

MR. ROBINSON: I can make no further record?

THE ARBITRATOR: As far as I'm concerned, you've said everything you can say.

The railroad withdrew from the hearing, and the neutral member continued the hearing with only the union present. Ultimately, the neutral member totally disregarded the carrier's arguments and decided the grievance in favor of the union. A second hearing was held in Skagway on another grievance. The railroad again refused to participate. After a short hearing, the neutral member and union member stayed in the area for several days and went on fishing trips together and took their meals together. The neutral member again ruled in favor of the union.

The carrier contended that the arbitration awards should be set aside because the conduct of the neutral member amounted to the functional equivalent of fraud.

The union contends that court decisions make clear that Congress specifically intended to keep railroad labor disputes out of the courts. It argues that arbitration is an informal process and that the hearing was conducted in a satisfactory manner. The union states that no evidence exists that the union member and neutral member ever discussed the matter they were arbitrating outside the hearing room.

On what grounds can a court set aside an arbitration award under the RLA? Why are the grounds for court review of arbitration awards so narrow? Decide. [*Pacific & Arctic Railway v. Transportation Union*, 952 F.2d 1144 (9th Cir.)]

CHAPTER 4

THE NATIONAL LABOR RELATIONS ACT

SECTION

SECTION 22: INTRODUCTION

Today's labor law is built on a framework of three federal statutes. Each of these statutes has an official title and a popular name. The National Labor Relations Act (NLRA), enacted in 1935, is frequently referred to as the Wagner Act. The Labor Management Relations Act (LMRA), enacted in 1947, is often called the Taft-Hartley Act. Title I of this Act continued a major portion of the Wagner Act but also contained drastic changes. Title I of the LMRA is often referred to as "the National Labor Relations Act, as amended." The Labor-Management Reporting and Disclosure Act (LMRDA), enacted in 1959, is also known as the Landrum-Griffin Act. A major purpose of this law is to protect union members from improper conduct by union officials. Title VII of this Act also amended certain sections of the NLRA, and these amendments are commonly referred to as "the Landrum-Griffin amendments to the NLRA." Chapter 9 of this book presents cases and text concerning the LMRDA as it relates to regulation of internal union conduct.

SECTION 23: HISTORICAL DEVELOPMENT

Building on the experience of the Railway Labor Act, Congress enacted the National Industrial Recovery Act (NIRA) in 1933. This law was the first in a series of President Franklin D. Roosevelt's New Deal enactments designed to lift the nation out of the Great Depression of the 1930s. The NIRA suspended the antitrust laws to permit employers within single industries to form trade associations that set production quotas and fixed prices under Codes of Fair Competition. To encourage participation by unions, Section 7(a) of the NIRA gave employees the right to organize without employer interference, stating that

> employees shall have the right to organize and bargain collectively through representatives of their own choosing, and shall be free from the interference, restraint, or coercion of employers of labor, or their agents, in the designation of such representatives or in self-organization or in other concerted activities for the purpose of collective bargaining or other mutual aid or protection; ...

This declaration had a profound impact. Unions used it as a basis for telling unorganized workers that President Roosevelt wanted them to join a union. And many employers refused to recognize newly formed unions, leading to many strikes for union recognition. As a result, President Roosevelt created the National Labor Board to bring compliance with Section 7(a) and to mediate controversies under the NIRA. The Board, however, lacked any meaningful power.

Faced with mounting labor disputes, in June 1934, Congress, passed a joint resolution authorizing the president to establish a new board as a part of the NIRA, called the National Labor Relations Board, and later known as the "Old NLRB." This board had the authority to investigate disputes arising under Section 7(a) and to conduct secret ballot representation elections. However, it lacked real power to enforce Section 7(a). In May 1935, when the NIRA was declared unconstitutional by the Supreme Court in *Schechter Poultry Corp. v. United States*,[1] the Old NLRB went out of existence.

---

[1] 295 U.S. 495 (1935).

THE WAGNER ACT

Undeterred by the adverse decision in *Schechter Poultry*, Congress enacted a comprehensive labor code on July 5, 1935, called the National Labor Relations Act (popularly called the Wagner Act after its chief legislative sponsor, Senator Robert F. Wagner of New York). In drafting this legislation, Congress drew heavily upon experience secured under the Railway Labor Act of 1926 and Section 7(a) of the NIRA, hoping that by so doing, it would avoid an adverse constitutional interpretation by the Supreme Court. The National Labor Relations Act was grounded in the federal government's power, granted in Article I, Section 8, of the Constitution, to regulate interstate commerce. The Act was designed so that the secret ballot election would take the place of the recognition strike.

The two most significant portions of the National Labor Relations Act were embodied in Sections 7 and 8. The substantive rights of employees were stated in Section 7 as follows:

> Employees shall have the right to ... form, join, or assist labor organizations, to bargain collectively through representatives of their own choosing, and to engage in other concerted activities for the purpose of collective bargaining or other mutual aid or protection....

The rights granted by Section 7 were protected against employer interference by Section 8, which listed the following five unfair labor practices:

1. Interference with efforts of employees to form, join, or assist labor organizations or to engage in concerted activities for mutual aid or protection;
2. Domination of a labor organization (which outlawed the company-formed or company-assisted labor union);
3. Discrimination in hiring or tenure to influence union affiliation or discourage union activities;
4. Discrimination for filing charges or giving testimony under the Act;
5. Refusal to bargain collectively with a duly designated representative of the employees.

Employers immediately undertook action to have the new law reviewed by the Supreme Court in an effort to have it declared unconstitutional for, among other things, being in excess of federal power to regulate interstate commerce. The classic case on this issue is *National Labor Relations Board v. Jones & Laughlin Steel Corp.*, which is presented in this section. The constitutionality of the law was upheld by a 5–4 decision.

The labor movement secured phenomenal growth and strength because of the broad protection of Sections 7 and 8.

THE TAFT-HARTLEY ACT

During the years that the original NLRA was in effect, it was subjected to continuous attack by employer groups. They argued that legislative sponsorship of labor unions under the Wagner Act had, instead of restoring equality in bargaining power, served to tip the balance measurably in favor of labor.

In the context of numerous strikes and the fear that union power would lead to serious inflation after World War II, the Labor Management Relations Act of 1947, sponsored by Senator Robert Taft and Congressman Fred Hartley, Jr., became law after a veto by President Truman was overridden. The Act created an independent NLRB General Counsel to be appointed by the president, with responsibility to act as prosecutor and to supervise board attorneys, while the five-person board would perform quasi-judicial functions under the law. New language was added to Section 7 providing that employees shall have the right to refrain from all of the activities listed in Section 7. It set forth six union unfair labor practices, declared the closed shop illegal, and prohibited secondary boycotts. Section 301 of the LMRA granted federal courts jurisdiction to resolve disputes arising out of collective bargaining agreements. Under Section 303, employers were granted the right to sue unions for damages arising out of secondary boycotts, with recovery allowed only from union assets.

THE LANDRUM-GRIFFIN ACT

Public hearings in 1957 and 1958 by the Senate Select Committee on Improper Activities in the Labor Management Field, known by the name of its chairman John McClellan as the McClellan Committee, convinced Congress that legislation was necessary to regulate the internal affairs of unions and eliminate corrupt practices. Accordingly, Congress passed the Labor-Management Reporting and Disclosure Act of 1959 (the Landrum-Griffin Act). The Act also amended the NLRA, including the tightening of the ban on secondary boycotts, and added a new union unfair labor practice, Section 8(b)(7), to outlaw extended picketing for recognitional purpose.

HEALTH CARE INSTITUTION AMENDMENTS

In 1974, the NLRA was amended to eliminate an exclusion in Section 2(2) of the Act of nonprofit hospitals and to create a new category of employer called "health care institution," which included "any hospital, convalescent hospital, health maintenance organization, health clinic, nursing home, extended care facility, or other institution devoted to the care of sick, infirm and aged persons."[2] A new Section 8(g) was added to the NLRA, setting forth a special notice requirement that must be met before a union can picket or strike a health care institution.

CASE 4.1 | NLRB v. JONES & LAUGHLIN STEEL CORP.
SUPREME COURT OF THE UNITED STATES, 301 U.S. 1 (1937).

[The National Labor Relations Board found that Jones & Laughlin Steel Corporation had discharged ten employees at its Aliquippa, Pennsylvania, plant because of their union activity and for the purpose of discouraging membership in the union. The Board ordered these employees reinstated with full back pay and ordered that the employer cease and desist from such conduct. When the employer failed to comply with the Board's

continued

---

[2] 29 U.S.C. § 152 (14).

order, the Board petitioned the court of appeals to enforce the order. The court of appeals denied the petition, holding that the Board's order lay beyond the range of federal power. The Supreme Court granted certiorari.]

HUGHES, C. J....

Effects of the unfair labor practice in respondent's enterprise.—Giving full weight to respondent's contention with respect to a break in the complete continuity of the "stream of commerce" by reason of respondents' manufacturing operations, the fact remains that the stoppage of those operations by industrial strife would have a most serious effect upon interstate commerce. In view of respondent's far-flung activities, it is idle to say that the effect would be indirect or remote. It is obvious that it would be immediate and might be catastrophic.... When industries organize themselves on a national scale, making their relation to interstate commerce the dominant factor in their activities, how can it be maintained that their industrial labor relations constitute a forbidden field into which Congress may not enter when it is necessary to protect interstate commerce from the paralyzing consequences of industrial war? We have often said that interstate commerce itself is a practical conception. It is equally true that interference with that commerce must be appraised by a judgment that does not ignore actual experience....

The Act does not compel agreements between employers and employees. It does not compel any agreement whatever. It does not prevent the employer "from refusing to make a collective contact and hiring individuals on whatever terms" the employer "may by unilateral action determine." The Act expressly provides in Section 9(a) that any individual employee or a group of employees shall have the right at any time to present grievances to their employer. The theory of the Act is that free opportunity for negotiation with accredited representatives of employees is likely to promote industrial peace and may bring about the adjustments and agreements which the Act in itself does not attempt to compel.... The Act does not interfere with the normal exercise of the right of the employer to select its employees or to discharge them. The employer may not, under cover of that right, intimidate or coerce its employees with respect to their self-organization and representation, and, on the other hand, the Board is not entitled to make its authority a pretext for interference with the right of discharge when that right is exercised for other reasons than such intimidation and coercion. The true purpose is the subject of investigation with full opportunity to show the facts. It would seem that when employers freely recognize the right of their employees to their own organizations and their unrestricted right of representation there will be much less occasion for controversy in respect to the free and appropriate exercise of the right of selection and discharge....

The order of the Board required the reinstatement of the employees who were found to have been discharged because of their "union activity" and for the purpose of "discouraging membership in the union." That requirement was authorized by the Act. Section 10(c), 29 U.S.C.A. Section 160(c). In *Texas & N.O.R. Co. v. Railway & S.S. Clerks, supra,* a similar order for restoration to service was made by the court in contempt proceedings for the violation of an injunction issued by the court to restrain an interference with the right of employees as guaranteed by the Railway Labor Act of 1926. The requirement of restoration to service of employees discharged in violation of the provisions of the Act was thus a sanction imposed in the enforcement of a judicial decree. We do not doubt that Congress could impose a like sanction for the enforcement of its valid regulation. The fact that in the one case it was a judicial sanction, and in the other a legislative one, is not an essential difference in determining its propriety.

Our conclusion is that the order of the Board was within its competency and that the Act is valid as here applied. The judgment of the Circuit Court of Appeals is reversed and the case is remanded for further proceedings in conformity with this opinion.

Reversed.

Case Questions

1. What action did the Board take after investigation of the above charges?
2. Did the court of appeals uphold the Board? On what ground?
3. Does the NLRA compel agreements between employers and employees?

SECTION 24: ADMINISTRATION

The National Labor Relations Board (NLRB) enforces the National Labor Relations Act. Its two principal functions are (1) conducting secret ballot elections to determine whether a majority of employees want to be represented by a union ("representation cases") and (2) preventing and remedying unfair labor practices that employers and unions commit. The Board carries out these functions through two independent offices: the Board and the Office of General Counsel.

The Board is a five-member body that is appointed by the president, with approval of the Senate, for five-year terms, the term of one member expiring each year.[3] While the Act is silent on the matter, a tradition has developed that the president's party will hold a 3:2 majority of appointments and the position of the chairman. The Board acts as a quasi-judicial body, deciding appeals from the decisions of administrative law judges (ALJs). The full Board renders decisions in cases involving significant policy-making matters, while the ordinary work of the Board is adjudicated through three-member panels.

The General Counsel of the Board is appointed for a four-year term by the president and approved by the Senate, with the following powers:

> The general counsel is to have general supervision and direction of all attorneys employed by the Board, excluding the trial examiners [administrative law judges] and the legal assistants to the individual members of the Board, and of all the officers and employees in the Board's regional offices, and is to have the final authority to act in the name of, but independently of any direction, control, or review by, the Board in respect of the investigation of charges (under Section 10) and the issuance of complaints of unfair labor practices, and in respect of the prosecution of such complaints before the board.[4]

---

[3] The Congresses that enacted the Wagner Act and Taft-Hartley Act expected that the Labor Board members would be nonpartisan, neutral adjudicators of the disputes brought before them for resolution. *See* James J. Brudney, *The National Labor Relations Board In Comparative Context—Isolated and Politicized: The NLRB's Uncertain Future*, 26 COMP. LAB. L. & POL'Y J. 221, 243 (2005). Presidents Roosevelt and Truman filled appointments to the Board with nonpartisan appointees. Starting with President Eisenhower, appointment practices changed, and since 1970, a majority of appointments to the Board have come from management and union law practices rather than nonpartisan and neutral backgrounds. In the second Reagan administration and into the George H. W. Bush administration, greater Senatorial control over the appointment process occurred. Board appointments in both the George H. W. Bush and Clinton administrations tended to come in "packaged deals," whereby Senate power brokers, in consultation with industry and labor interest groups, insisted that the president acquiesce to some of its specific choices as the price of the Senate confirming his Board nominee(s). Moreover, in both of these administrations and continuing in the George W. Bush (Bush II) administration, recess appointments have been utilized while the Senate and White House bargained over packaged deals. The Clinton Board was perceived by employer groups as providing greater protections for workers than intended by the NLRA, and the Bush II Board was perceived by union leaders and many academicians as regularly denying or impairing the statutory rights it was charged with protecting. With the adjournment of Congress in January 2008, the Bush II Board consisted of just two members. Wilma B. Liebman, a Democrat whose term expires August 27, 2011, and Chairman Peter C. Schaumber, a Republican whose term expires August 27, 2010. Due to Senatorial tactics, no appointments were made to the Board during 2008, giving the new president, Barack Obama, three appointments to make upon taking office.

[4] House Report No. 510, 80th Congress, at p. 37, Section 3(d) of the NLRA.

Under the Taft-Hartley Act, Congress placed the functions of investigation and prosecution with the Office of the General Counsel and placed the quasi-judicial functions of deciding the merits of a controversy with the National Labor Relations Board. Under the Wagner Act, the NLRB had acted in the concurrent roles of investigator, prosecutor, and judge. The Taft-Hartley Act allowed independence of judgment on the part of the General Counsel; the General Counsel was responsible to the president and the Senate and not to the National Labor Relations Board, as it had been formerly.

There are 32 regional offices, 3 subregional offices, and 17 resident offices of the NLRB located throughout the United States and its territories. (See Figure 4.1, page 58.) A **regional director** is in charge of every region, assisted by a staff of attorneys, field examiners, and clerical personnel. All matters subject to the NLRA, except in unusual circumstances, must be initially filed with the regional director for the region in which the situation arose. In representation cases involving the Board's function of conducting secret ballot elections, the process is started by the filing of a "petition" with the regional director; in unfair labor practice cases the process is initiated by filing a "charge" with the regional director. The Board has delegated its authority over representation matters to the regional directors. The General Counsel has delegated authority to issue complaints in unfair labor practice cases to the regional directors. Thus, the Board has appellate jurisdiction over election decisions emanating from the regional offices, and the General Counsel has appellate authority over regional directors' rulings on charges of unfair labor practices.

The formal hearing on an unfair labor practice complaint issued under the authority of the General Counsel is conducted by an administrative law judge (ALJ).[5] In unfair labor practice hearings, the administrative law judge functions very much like a trial court judge: hearing witnesses, ruling on admissibility of evidence, making findings of fact, and drawing conclusions of law. The administrative law judge's decision may be appealed to the Board in Washington, D.C., by any party involved in the case. Administrative law judges are free from supervision by the Board. The Board appoints them based on merit from a civil service roster.

SECTION 25: PROCEDURES

An employee who believes that an employer or a union is engaged in one or more unfair labor practices may file charges with the appropriate regional office of the National Labor Relations Board. A union or an employer may also file charges. Section 10(b) of the Act provides that the Board may not issue a complaint based on conduct that occurred more than six months before the filing and service of the charge. This six-month time limit for filing may be suspended, however, where the charging party did not have actual or constructive knowledge of the unfair labor practice when it occurred but filed within six months of obtaining knowledge of the conduct. After the charges are filed, the case is processed as follows. (See also Figure 4.2 on page 59.)

---

[5] Until 1972, the title was "trial examiner."

FIGURE 4.1 | NATIONAL LABOR RELATIONS BOARD MAP SHOWING BOUNDARIES OF REGIONAL, SUBREGIONAL, AND RESIDENT OFFICES

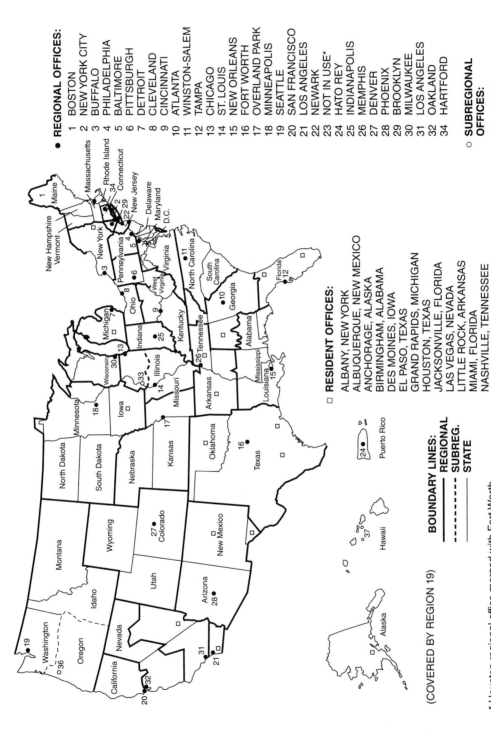

● **REGIONAL OFFICES:**

1 BOSTON
2 NEW YORK CITY
3 BUFFALO
4 PHILADELPHIA
5 BALTIMORE
6 PITTSBURGH
7 DETROIT
8 CLEVELAND
9 CINCINNATI
10 ATLANTA
11 WINSTON-SALEM
12 TAMPA
13 CHICAGO
14 ST. LOUIS
15 NEW ORLEANS
16 FORT WORTH
17 OVERLAND PARK
18 MINNEAPOLIS
19 SEATTLE
20 SAN FRANCISCO
21 LOS ANGELES
22 NEWARK
23 NOT IN USE*
24 HATO REY
25 INDIANAPOLIS
26 MEMPHIS
27 DENVER
28 PHOENIX
29 BROOKLYN
30 MILWAUKEE
31 LOS ANGELES
32 OAKLAND
34 HARTFORD

○ **SUBREGIONAL OFFICES:**

33 PEORIA
36 PORTLAND
37 HONOLULU

□ **RESIDENT OFFICES:**

ALBANY, NEW YORK
ALBUQUERQUE, NEW MEXICO
ANCHORAGE, ALASKA
BIRMINGHAM, ALABAMA
DES MOINES, IOWA
EL PASO, TEXAS
GRAND RAPIDS, MICHIGAN
HOUSTON, TEXAS
JACKSONVILLE, FLORIDA
LAS VEGAS, NEVADA
LITTLE ROCK, ARKANSAS
MIAMI, FLORIDA
NASHVILLE, TENNESSEE
SAN ANTONIO, TEXAS
SAN DIEGO, CALIFORNIA
TULSA, OKLAHOMA
WASHINGTON, DISTRICT OF COLUMBIA

BOUNDARY LINES:
——— REGIONAL
– – – SUBREG.
——— STATE

(COVERED BY REGION 19)

* Houston regional office merged with Fort Worth. Houston became a resident office.
* Peoria regional office merged with St. Louis and is now a subregional office of Region 14.

FIGURE 4.2 | BASIC PROCEDURES IN CASES INVOLVING CHARGES OF UNFAIR LABOR PRACTICES

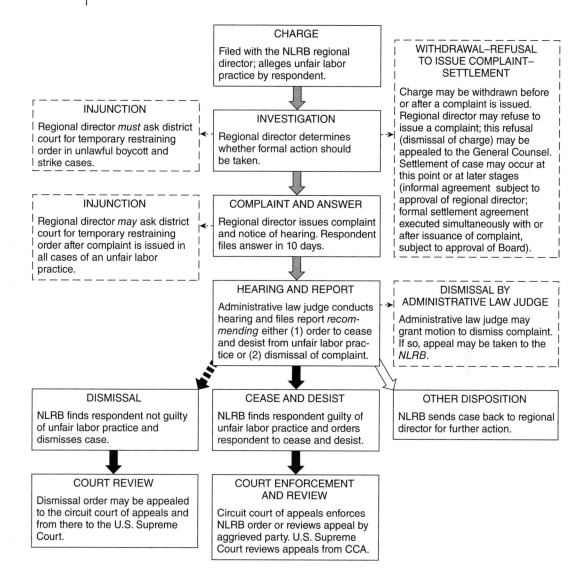

1. The charges are investigated by a professional staff member. During this investigation, charges may be adjusted, withdrawn, dismissed, or otherwise closed without formal action.
2. A formal complaint is issued by the regional director if the charges are found to be well grounded and the case is not settled by adjustment.
3. A public hearing on the complaint is held before an administrative law judge. The case is prosecuted by an attorney from the regional staff, acting on behalf of the General Counsel.

4. The administrative law judge's findings and recommendations are served on the parties and sent to the Board in Washington. At this point, the case is transferred to the Board in Washington. Unless either of the parties files a statement of exceptions to the judge's finding within 28 days, the judge's recommended order takes the full effect of an order by the Board. Parties who disagree with the judge's findings may file a brief to support their exceptions and request an oral argument before the Board. Exceptions are, in effect, an appeal from the administrative law judge's decisions.

5. The Board reviews the case and issues a decision and an order. It is the Board's policy not to overrule an ALJ's credibility determinations unless the incorrectness is shown by a "clear preponderance of all the relevant evidence."[6]

6. In case a union or an employer fails to comply with a Board order, the Board may ask the appropriate U.S. Court of Appeals for a judgment enforcing its order. Also, any party to the case who is aggrieved by the Board's order may appeal to an appropriate U.S. Court of Appeals.

7. The Board or an aggrieved party may petition the Supreme Court of the United States to review the decision of the court of appeals. Failure to obey a final court judgment is punishable as civil or criminal contempt of court or both.

If the regional director refuses to issue a complaint, the charging party may appeal to the General Counsel's Office of Appeals in Washington, D.C., where recommendations are made to the General Counsel, who has final authority over the issuance of complaints. If the General Counsel approves the decision not to issue the complaint, there is no further appeal. On the other hand, the General Counsel may reverse the regional director's decision and order that a complaint be issued.

The General Counsel's authority over the issuance of complaints provides a legal basis from time to time for an activist role in presenting new and novel legal theories to the Board for adjudication.

COURT REVIEW OF BOARD DETERMINATIONS ON FACTS

Section 10(e) of the Taft-Hartley amendments of 1947 stipulates that "the findings of the Board with respect to questions of fact if supported by substantial evidence of record considered as a whole shall be conclusive." Interpreting this language, the Supreme Court in *Universal Camera Corp. v. NLRB* said that a reviewing court may only set aside the Board's findings on two fairly conflicting views on questions of fact "when it cannot conscientiously find that the evidence supporting that decision is substantial when viewed in the light that the record in its entirety furnishes, including the body of evidence opposed to the Board's view."[7]

---

[6] IUE Local 745 (McGraw Edison), 268 NLRB 308 (1983); but see Marshall Engineered Products Co., 351 NLRB No. 47, p. 4 (Sept. 29, 2007).

[7] 340 U.S. 474 (1951).

COURT REVIEW OF BOARD DETERMINATIONS ON LAW AND POLICY

In *Chevron, U.S.A., Inc., v. Natural Resources Defense Council, Inc.*,[8] the Supreme Court set forth a rule of deference to administrative agencies in matters of statutory interpretation when U.S. Courts of Appeals are reviewing final orders of administrative agencies. If Congress has directly addressed the question at issue, the agency must give effect to this congressional intent. However, if the statute is silent or ambiguous on the question at issue, the agency's formulation of policy and rules in filling statutory gaps will be upheld by the court as long as they are rational and consistent with the Act.

In determining whether the Labor Board's decisions are entitled to the deference annunciated in *Chevron*, courts nevertheless exercise some subjective leeway in their analysis to consider factors such as the quality of the Board's reasoning, the relevancy of the Board's experience, and the impartiality of the Board majority.

SECTION 26: JURISDICTION: EMPLOYERS UNDER THE ACT

On the same day that the Supreme Court rendered the *Jones & Laughlin* decision, upholding the Act of 1935 on all contested constitutional grounds and placing interstate manufacturing operations within the scope of the federal commerce power, four companion cases were simultaneously handed down, all of which upheld the constitutionality and coverage of the Act.[9] Thus, in one fell swoop, manufacturing, textiles, transport, and newspapers were included in the employer coverage. Jurisdiction of the Board, however, is still based on Sections 2(6) and (7) of the Act. The term **commerce** is defined in Section 2(6) and the term **affecting commerce** in Section 2(7). The broadness of the latter is herein indicated: "The term 'affecting commerce' means in commerce, or burdening or obstructing commerce or the free flow of commerce, or having led or tending to lead to a labor dispute burdening or obstructing commerce or the free flow of commerce." Purely local activities are not under the jurisdiction of the National Labor Relations Board.

The term **employer** is defined by Section 2(2). This section excludes from the Act's coverage the following employers:

1. Federal, state, or municipal corporations;
2. Federal Reserve banks;
3. Railroad companies under the Railway Labor Act, airlines, and related companies;
4. Labor organizations in their representation capacity but not in the capacity of hiring their own employees.

Although the interpretation of the jurisdictional provisions of the statute has given the Board broad authority, the Board has for reasons of administrative convenience and policy exercised its authority only in situations falling within certain standards. First adopted and published in 1950, the standards have been revised from time to time.

---

[8] 467 U.S. 837 (1984).

[9] *Associated Press v. NLRB*, 301 U.S. 103; *NLRB v. Friedman-Marks Clothing Co.*, 301 U.S. 58; *NLRB v. Fruehauf Trailer Co.*, 301 U.S. 49; and *Washington V & M Coach Co. v. NLRB*, 301 U.S. 142 (1937).

In every Board proceeding, the first question investigated is the question of the Board's jurisdiction. Once the existence of general authority over the subject matter is established, the Board then determines whether to proceed by ascertaining if the employer's operations satisfy the following standards. In applying these standards, the Board considers the total operations of the employer, even though the particular labor dispute involves only a portion of those operations. The Board's jurisdictional standards are as follows:

1. *Nonretail businesses*: Sales of goods to consumers in other states directly or indirectly through others (called outflow) of at least $50,000 a year or purchases of goods from suppliers in other states directly or indirectly through others (called inflow) of at least $50,000 a year.
2. *Office buildings*: Total annual income of at least $100,000 of which $25,000 or more is paid by other organizations that meet any of the standards except standard 1 (nonretail).
3. *Retail enterprises*: At least $500,000 total annual volume of business.
4. *Public utilities*: At least $250,000 total annual volume of business.
5. *Newspapers*: At least $200,000 total annual volume of business.
6. *Radio, telegraph, television, and telephone business*: At least $100,000 total annual volume of business.
7. *Hotels and motels*: At least $500,000 total annual volume of business. (In 1967, the Board extended this yardstick to include jurisdiction over permanent or residential apartment houses with annual revenues meeting this standard.)
8. *Taxicab companies*: At least $500,000 total annual volume of business.
9. *Transit systems*: At least $250,000 total annual volume of business.
10. *Transportation enterprises, links, and channels of interstate commerce*: At least $50,000 total annual income from furnishing interstate transportation services or $50,000 or more from performing services for enterprises that meet any of the standards except the indirect outflow and indirect inflow standards established for nonretail businesses.
11. *Associations*: Regarded as single employers in that the annual business of all members is totaled to determine whether any of the standards apply.
12. *Privately operated health care institutions*: At least $250,000 total annual volume of business for hospitals; at least $100,000 for nursing homes, visiting nurses' associations, and related facilities; and at least $250,000 for all other types of private health care institutions defined in the 1974 amendments to the Act. The statutory definition includes "any hospital, convalescent hospital, health maintenance organization, health clinic, nursing home, extended care facility, or other institution devoted to the care of the sick, infirm, or aged person." Public hospitals are excluded from NLRB jurisdiction by Section 2(2) of the Act.
    Church-operated hospitals, including a hospital operated by the Seventh Day Adventist Church, are subject to the jurisdiction of the NLRB; exercising this jurisdiction is not in violation of the First Amendment or the Religious Freedom Restoration Act.[10]

---

[10] 332 NLRB No. 59 (2000).

13. *Baseball*: In 1969, the Board asserted jurisdiction over organized baseball. The case is reported in this section.
14. *Nonprofit, private education institutions*: In 1970, the Board asserted jurisdiction over private universities and colleges having annual operating expenses of at least $1 million. Professors classified as managerial employees are excluded from the protection of the Act.
15. *U.S. Postal Service*: The Board was empowered to assert jurisdiction over Postal Service employees under the Postal Reorganization Act (PRA) of 1970. Postal employees do not have the right to strike, however. Binding arbitration is provided for in Section 1207 of the PRA in the event of collective bargaining impasses.

In addition, the Board exercises jurisdiction over all enterprises that affect commerce when their operations have a substantial impact on national defense. Also, all businesses in the District of Columbia come under the jurisdiction of the Board.

Ordinarily, if an enterprise does the total annual volume of business listed in the standard, it will necessarily be engaged in activities that "affect" commerce.

The Board has established the policy that when an employer whose operations affect commerce refuses to supply the Board with information concerning total annual business, the Board may dispense with this requirement and exercise jurisdiction.

Under its jurisdictional standards, the Board has applied the Act to such employers as law firms,[11] accounting firms,[12] the American Arbitration Association,[13] and gambling casinos.[14] The Board has exercised jurisdiction over Indian-owned casinos.[15] The Board has declined jurisdiction in the horse-racing industry.[16] However, the Board's exercise of jurisdiction over jai alai players at the Volusia Jai Alai Palace in Daytona Beach was upheld by the court of appeals.[17] In the racetrack cases, the Board declined jurisdiction because the rapid turnover of employees and the irregular nature of employment prevented effective regulation. However, jai alai players constituted a stable workforce with sufficient continuity to enable the Board to conduct meaningful elections. The Board also found that the jai alai players had a special need for union representation because their individual player contracts were printed in English, whereas almost all of the players were Spanish-speaking natives of Mexico or Spain who understood little or no English.

The Board has asserted jurisdiction over state banks owned by foreign governments doing business in the United States, rejecting the argument that these banks are immune under the Foreign Sovereign Immunities Act.[18]

---

[11] Foley, Hoag & Eliot, 229 NLRB 456 (1977), and Kleinberg, Kaplan et al., 253 NLRB 450 (1980).

[12] Ernst and Ernst National Warehouse, 228 NLRB 590 (1977).

[13] American Arbitration Association, Inc., 225 NLRB 291 (1976).

[14] El Dorado Club, 220 NLRB 291 (1975).

[15] San Manuel Indian and Bingo Casino, 345 NLRB No. 79 (2005), *enforced* 475 F.3d 1306 (D.C. Cir. 2007).

[16] Walter A. Kelley, 139 NLRB 744 (1962), and Centennial Turf Club, 192 NLRB 698 (1971).

[17] *Florida Board of Business Regulation, Division of Pari-Mutuel Wagering v. NLRB*, 686 F.2d 1362 (11th Cir. 1982).

[18] *State Bank of India v. NLRB*, 808 F.2d 526 (7th Cir. 1986).

The Board asserted jurisdiction over professional baseball in *American League and Association of Umpires*, presented next, rejecting arguments that the sport has an insubstantial effect on interstate commerce and that umpires should be considered supervisors within the meaning of the Act.

The Board has not taken jurisdiction over the real estate brokerage business, holding it to be essentially local in nature.[19] The Board was denied jurisdiction over lay teachers in "church-operated" schools by the Supreme Court in *NLRB v. Catholic Bishop of Chicago*, presented in this section. The Board has extended the *Catholic Bishop* decision to religious schools operated by lay boards of directors and administrators[20] and church-operated colleges[21] on a case-by-case basis, refusing to exercise jurisdiction over an employer if it would create a "significant risk of infringement" of First Amendment rights.[22]

CASE 4.2	AMERICAN LEAGUE AND ASSOCIATION OF UMPIRES
	180 NLRB No. 30 (1969).

The Petitioner [Association of National Baseball League Umpires] seeks an election in a unit of umpires employed by the American League of Professional Baseball Clubs (hereinafter called the Employer or the League). The Employer, while conceding the Board's constitutional and statutory power to exercise jurisdiction herein, nevertheless urges the Board, as a matter of policy, not to assert jurisdiction pursuant to Section 14(c) of the Act.

The Employer is a nonprofit membership association consisting of 12 member clubs located in 10 states and the District of Columbia. Operating pursuant to a constitution adopted and executed by the 12 member clubs, the Employer is engaged in the business of staging baseball exhibitions and, with its counterpart the National League of Professional Baseball Clubs, constitutes what is commonly known as "major league baseball." The Employer currently employs, among other persons, the 24 umpires requested herein, and one umpire-in-chief....

We have carefully considered the positions of the parties, and the amicus briefs, and we find that it will best effectuate the mandates of the Act, as well as national labor policy, to assert jurisdiction over this Employer....

We can find, neither in the statute nor in its legislative history, any expression of a Congressional intent that disputes between employers and employees in this industry should be removed from the scheme of the National Labor Relations Act. In 1935, 1947, and again in 1959, Congress examined the nation's labor policy as reflected in the National Labor Relations Act; and Congress has consistently affirmed

continued

---

[19] Seattle Real Estate Board, 130 NLRB 608 (1961).

[20] Jewish Day School and AFT Local 3648, 283 NLRB 757 (1987).

[21] Trustees of St. Joseph's College, 282 NLRB 65 (1986).

[22] In *Carroll College Inc.*, 345 NLRB No. 17 (2005), the employer, a private liberal arts college located in Wisconsin and affiliated with the Presbyterian Church, did not contest the Board's assertion of jurisdiction. Thus, the Board did not apply its *Catholic Bishop* test to determine whether the exercise of jurisdiction over the employer involves a significant risk of infringement of religious rights that would exempt the entity from the NLRA. Rather, the college contended that it was exempt from coverage under the Religious Freedom Restoration Act (RFRA), 42 U.S.C. § 2000 bb-1 (2005). The Board rejected the college's contentions under the RFRA because it did not meet the burden of proof of showing that the application of the act substantially burdened its ability to freely exercise its sincere religious beliefs in any way. Hypothetical or mere potential transgressions are not enough. *But see, Ukiah Valley Medical Center*, 332 NLRB 602 (2000) where Seventh Day Adventist religious practices prohibit workers from belonging to or supporting labor unions.

the Act's basic policy, as expressed in Section 1, of encouraging collective bargaining by "protecting the exercise by workers of full freedom of association, self-organization, and designation of representatives of their own choosing." Nowhere in Congress' deliberations is there any indication that these basic rights are not to be extended to employees employed in professional baseball or any other professional sport. We do not agree that Congress, by refusing to pass legislation subjecting the sport to the antitrust laws when it considered the regulation of baseball and other sports under the antitrust statutes, sanctioned a government-wide policy of "non-involvement" in all matters pertaining to baseball. Indeed, to the extent that Congressional deliberation on the antitrust question has reference to the issue before us, it indicates agreement that players' rights to bargain collectively and engage in concerted activities are to be protected rather than limited.

There is persuasive reason to believe that future labor disputes—should they arise in this industry—will be national in scope, radiating their impact far beyond individual state boundaries. As stated above, the Employer and its members are located and conduct business in 10 states and the District of Columbia. The stipulated commerce data establishes that millions of dollars of interstate commerce are involved in its normal business operations. The nature of the industry is such that great reliance is placed upon interstate travel. Necessarily, then, we are not here confronted with the sort of small, primarily intrastate employer over which the Board declines jurisdiction because of failure to meet its prevailing monetary standards. Moreover, it is apparent that the Employer, whose operations are so clearly national in scope, ought not have its labor relations problems subject to diverse state labor laws.

The Employer's final contention, that Board processes are unsuited to regulate effectively baseball's international aspects, clearly lacks merit, as many if not most of the industries subject to the Act have similar international features.

Accordingly, we find that the effect on interstate commerce of a labor dispute involving professional baseball is not so insubstantial as to require withholding assertion of the Board's jurisdiction, under Section 14(c) of the Act, over Employers in that industry, as a class. As the annual gross revenues of this Employer are in excess of all our prevailing monetary standards, we find that the Employer is engaged in an industry affecting commerce, and that it will effectuate the policies of the Act to assert jurisdiction herein.

1. The Employer at the hearing denied that the petitioner was a labor organization within the meaning of Section 2(5) of the Act. The record shows, however, that the Petitioner is an organization in which employees participate, and which exists for the purpose of dealing with employers concerning wages and other conditions of employment. Accordingly, we find that the Petitioner is a labor organization within the meaning of Section 2(5) of the Act.

2. A question affecting commerce exists concerning the representation of certain employees of the Employer within the meaning of Section 9(c)(1) and Sections 2(6) and (7) of the Act.

3. The Employer contends that the petition should be dismissed on the ground that the umpires who sought to be represented are supervisors as defined in Section 2(11) of the Act. It is not contended that umpires have authority to hire, fire, transfer, discharge, recall, promote, assign, or reward. We think it equally apparent that umpires do not "discipline" or "direct" the workforce according to the common meaning of those terms as used in the Act.

The record indicates that an umpire's basic responsibility is to ensure that each baseball game is played in conformance with the predetermined rules of the game. Thus, the umpire does not discipline except to the extent he may remove a participant from the game for violation of these rules. Testimony shows that after such a removal the umpire merely reports the incident to his superiors, and does not himself fine, suspend, or even recommend such action. As the final arbiter on the field, the umpire necessarily makes decisions which may favor one team over another, and which may determine to some extent the movements of various players, managers, and other personnel on the ball field. The umpire does not, however, direct the workforce in the same manner and for the same reasons as a foreman in an industrial setting. As every fan is aware, the umpire does not—through the use of independent judgment—tell a player how to bat, how to field, to work harder or exert more effort, nor can he tell a manager which players to play or where to play them. Thus, the umpire merely sees to it that the game is played in compliance with the rules.

continued

It is the manager and not the umpire who directs the employees in their pursuit of victory.

Accordingly, we find that the umpires are not supervisors, and thus the Employer's motion to dismiss on this ground is hereby denied. We further find that the following employees of the Employer constitute a unit appropriate for the purposes of collective bargaining within the meaning of Section 9(b) of the Act:

All persons employed as umpires in the American League of Professional Baseball Clubs, but excluding all other employees, office clerical employees, guards, professional employees and supervisors as defined in the Act.

An election by secret ballot shall be conducted among the employees in the unit found appropriate, as early as possible, but not later than 30 days from the date below....

Case Questions

1. Are employers in the baseball industry subject to the jurisdiction of the Board under Section 14(c)?
2. Is the association of umpires a labor organization within the meaning of Section 2(5)?
3. Are umpires supervisors as defined by Section 2(11) of the Act?

| CASE 4.3 | NLRB v. Catholic Bishop of Chicago
Supreme Court of the United States, 440 U.S. 490 (1979). |

[The National Labor Relations Board exercised jurisdiction over the lay faculty members at two Catholic high schools in the Chicago Diocese and exercised jurisdiction over five Catholic high schools in the Fort Wayne–South Bend Diocese. All of the high schools in question seek to provide a traditional secondary education, but oriented to the tenets of the Roman Catholic faith. Religious training is mandatory at all of the schools in question. And the schools are certified by the states of Illinois and Indiana, respectively. The Board supervised elections for both groups of schools, and the unions prevailed. The Board certified the unions as the representatives of the lay teachers, but the schools declined to recognize or to bargain with the unions. Section 8(a)(5) unfair labor practice charges were brought by the unions and upheld by the Board. The Court of Appeals for the Seventh Circuit denied enforcement of the Board's order. The Supreme Court granted certiorari.]

BURGER, C. J....

In recent decisions involving aid to parochial schools we have recognized the critical and unique role of the teacher in fulfilling the mission of a church-operated school. What was said of the schools in *Lemon v. Kurtzman*, 403 U.S. 602, 617(1971), is true of the schools in this case: "Religious authority necessarily pervades the school system." The key role played by teachers in such a school system has been the predicate for our conclusions that governmental aid channeled through teachers creates an impermissible risk of excessive governmental entanglement in the affairs of the church-operated schools....

... Inevitably the Board's inquiry will implicate sensitive issues that open the door to conflicts between clergy-administrators and the Board, or conflicts with negotiators for unions. What we said in *Lemon* applies as well here: "... parochial schools involve substantial religious activity and purpose."

"The substantial religious character of these church-related schools gives rise to entangling church-state relationships of the kind the Religion Clauses sought to avoid." Mr. Justice Douglas emphasized this in his concurring opinion in Lemon, noting "the admitted and obvious fact that the *raison d'être* of parochial schools is the propagation of religious faith."

The church-teacher relationship in a church-operated school differs from the employment relationship in a public or other non-religious school. We see no escape from conflicts flowing from the Board's exercise of jurisdiction over teachers in church-operated schools and the consequent serious First Amendment questions that would follow. We therefore turn to an examination of the National Labor Relations Act to decide whether it must be read to confer jurisdiction that would in turn require a decision on the constitutional claims raised by respondents.

There is no clear expression of an affirmative intention of Congress that teachers in church-operated schools should be covered by the Act. Admittedly, Congress defined the Board's jurisdiction in very broad terms; we must therefore examine the legislative history of the Act to determine whether Congress contemplated that the grant of jurisdiction would include teachers in such schools.

continued

In enacting the National Labor Relations Act in 1935, Congress sought to protect the right of American workers to bargain collectively. The concern that was repeated throughout the debates was the need to assure workers the right to organize to counterbalance the collective activities of employers which had been authorized by the National Industrial Recovery Act. But congressional attention focused on employment in private industry and on industrial recovery.

Our examination of the statute and its legislative history indicates that Congress simply gave no consideration to church-operated schools....

Affirmed.

BRENNAN, J. (joined by WHITE, MARSHALL, and BLACKMUN, J. J.), Dissenting ...

The Court today holds that coverage of the National Labor Relations Act does not extend to lay teachers employed by church-operated schools. That construction is plainly wrong in light of the Act's language, its legislative history, and this Court's precedents. It is justified solely on the basis of a canon of statutory construction seemingly invented by the Court for the purpose of deciding this case. I dissent....

Case Questions

1. Is religious training mandatory at all of the schools in question?
2. Does the Court see inevitable church-state entanglements if the Board were allowed to exercise jurisdiction over teachers in church-operated schools?
3. Did Congress express the clear intent to bring teachers in church-operated schools within the jurisdiction of the NLRA?

SECTION 27: JURISDICTION: AGENTS, "CONTINGENT" WORKERS

This section considers the criteria employed by the courts in distinguishing between the three legal relations of principal, agent, and independent contractor in reviewing NLRB orders. An employer who acts in his or her own capacity and right does so as a **principal** and entails the full legal responsibility of a principal. When an employer acts through others who are given express or implied authority to act for the employer, the employer remains responsible as a principal because an **agency** relation has been created. This rule of imputed liability applies as long as the agent acts within the scope of express or implied authority. Acts of an agent beyond this authority are not imputable to the employer unless they are subsequently ratified by the employer.

The legal relation of **independent contractor** is that of a principal. An independent contractor contracts and performs independent acts. A contractor is liable for those acts as long as the contractor's performance is free from the control or intervention of another person or agency.

The National Labor Relations Act introduces these concepts in three sections:

1. Section 2(2) provides: "The term 'employer' includes any person acting as an agent of an employer, directly or indirectly."
2. Section 2(13) states: "In determining whether any person is acting as an 'agent' of another person so as to make such other person responsible for his acts, the question of whether the specific acts performed were actually authorized or subsequently ratified shall not be controlling."
3. Section 2(3) excludes independent contractors from the term employee.

A supervisor generally acts for and commits the employer. An employer can generally be relieved of liability if the unfair labor practices committed were those of an independent contractor rather than an agent or a joint employer. An employer remains jointly liable, however, if the employer procures the commission of an unfair labor practice by third persons over whom the employer retains express or covert power of control.

In deciding whether a group of individuals are employees within the meaning of Section 2(3) of the Act rather than independent contractors and thus entitled to the rights and protections of the NLRA, including the right to petition for Board elections for the purposes of collective bargaining, a multifactor test developed under the common law of agency is used. These factors include (1) the extent of control exercised over the details of the work by the employer, (2) whether the individual employed is in a distinct occupation or business, (3) whether the individual has an opportunity to make an entrepreneurial profit, (4) what skill is required of the worker, (5) whether the employer or worker supplies the tools and the place of work, (6) how long the person is employed, and (7) whether the work is a part of the regular business of the employer. In the Board's *Roadway Package System, Inc.*, decision, presented in this section, the Board determined that the drivers were "employees" covered under the NLRA.

FedEx Corp. of Memphis, Tennessee, acquired Roadway Package System, Inc., in 1998. FedEx Ground is the parent of FedEx Home Delivery, and it continued the business model of "owner-operators" as independent contractors utilized by Roadway. NLRB Regional Director Rosemary Pye found that the drivers in Wilmington, Massachusetts, were employees under the Act, not independent contractors, because the company "exercises substantial control" over how drivers perform their jobs, the vehicles must display a company logo, drivers must wear a company uniform, and the company "unilaterally establishes the rates of compensation." Misclassification of employees as independent contractors subjects owners to fines by the IRS; payment of back state worker's compensation and unemployment compensation premiums; and in some states, payment for work-related expenses.[23]

In *Dial-a-Mattress Operating Corp.*,[24] a Board majority held that the status of 39 owner-operators in the Long Island–New York area weighed more heavily toward independent contractor status than employee status. The owner-operators hired their own employees and helpers, owned and had complete control over their own vehicles, had the opportunity to make an entrepreneurial profit, and could decline work without penalty.

There is growing awareness that contingent workers—including independent contractors, on-call workers, temporary help–agency workers, and contract–company employees—make up an ever-increasing portion of the nation's labor force.[25] There is some evidence that contracting or leasing of employees is being used to

---

[23] For articles on FedEx liabilities, see DLR No. 247, A-3 (Dec. 27, 2007) and DLR No. 60, AA-1 (Mar. 28, 2008).

[24] Dial-a-Mattress and IBT Local 363, 326 NLRB 884 (1998).

[25] See http://www.bls.gov/cps/USDL05-1433.

evade the letter and spirit of labor laws.[26] The Presidential Commission on the Future of Worker-Management Relations, chaired by former Labor Secretary John Dunlop and popularly known as the Dunlop Commission, devoted several days of hearings to this subject. In a May 1994 fact-finding report, the Dunlop Commission stated in part:

> The growing number of "contingent" and other non-standard workers poses the problem of how to balance employers' needs for flexibility with workers' needs for adequate income protections, job security, and the application of public laws that these arrangements often preclude, including labor protection and labor-relations statutes.

CASE 4.4	ROADWAY PACKAGE SYSTEM, INC., AND TEAMSTERS LOCAL 63 326 NLRB 842 (1998).

[Drivers at Roadway Package System, Inc. (RPS or Roadway), terminals at Ontario and Pomona, California, filed separate election petitions seeking a unit of all pickup and delivery drivers at each respective terminal. The two cases were consolidated for handling before the Board. Roadway operates a nationwide package pickup and delivery service with over 5,000 drivers. Some 22 drivers work out of both Ontario and Pomona terminals. The drivers at Ontario and Pomona own or lease vans to perform their work for Roadway. The vehicles must meet precise specifications set by Roadway, which are "custom designed for RPS" and are leased from Bush Leasing or purchased from former RPS drivers. Each driver must wear a Roadway-approved uniform, displaying the RPS emblem that is consistent with RPS standards as promulgated from time to time by RPS. Roadway contends that the drivers are independent contractors because they control their own work schedules, they are not subject to discipline, and their compensation is based on performance-related components. Moreover, Roadway asserts the drivers are entrepreneurs, receive no benefits, and are responsible for their own income tax withholding. The Teamsters contend that Roadway controls customer rates and business volume, which are the main determinants of each driver's compensation, and that the drivers have no genuine opportunity to realize financial gains through entrepreneurial initiative.]

continued

---

[26] See Yvonne Abraham, "Building Industry Wages Probed: Immigrant Labor Scheme Alleged," *The Boston Sunday Globe*, pp. 1, B5 (Nov. 27, 2005). This article reports a scheme set up to lower employer costs and increase profits while giving employers "plausible deniability." Phase I, a construction company, accepts a building project and employs subcontractors to complete the construction. All income and expenditures of this company are reported for taxes to the IRS. Phase II, the subcontracting company, receives payment from the construction company and pays certain lead employees as "independent contractors." The subcontractor reports to the IRS all income and expenditures including payments to lead workers deemed independent contractors. Phase III, each lead worker, misclassified as an independent contractor, receives payments from the subcontractor and keeps his wages and passes the rest on to men working under him, who are often undocumented workers and are not reported as employees of any of the principal companies. At Phase III, no income is reported to the IRS, no workers' compensation insurance is provided, nor are overtime wages paid. The article reveals that some 30 percent of construction workers in the state are misclassified according to the Center for Labor Market Studies at Northeastern University.

A study by the Fiscal Policy Institute indicated that in New York City, 50,000 of the city's 200,000 construction workers were employed "off the books" or misclassified as independent contractors in 2005, avoiding employment laws and resulting in the loss of $272 million in unpaid payroll taxes as well as the loss of workers' compensation, unemployment, and disability insurance premiums and $70 million in lost personal income taxes. DLR No. 236, A-9 (Dec. 10, 2007).

From the Opinion of the Board

Legal Principles

Section 2(3) of the Act, as amended by the 1947 Labor Management Relations Act (the Taft-Hartley Act), provides that the term "employee" shall not include "any individual having the status of independent contractor." The meaning and ramifications of this 1947 amendment were first considered by the Supreme Court in *NLRB v. United-Insurance Co. of America*, 390 U.S. 254 (1968). In that case, the Court declared that

> [t]he obvious purpose of this amendment was to have the Board and the courts apply general agency principles in distinguishing between employees and independent contractors under the Act.... And both petitioners and respondents agree that the proper standard here is the law of agency. Thus there is no doubt that we should apply the common-law agency test here in distinguishing an employee from an independent contractor. [390 U.S. at 256.]

The parties and amici in the instant case rely on the Restatement, but they debate whether any of the factors listed in Section 220 are more or less indicative of employee status. Citing the language contained

---

*This section provides, in pertinent part:

1. A servant is a person employed to perform services in the affairs of another and who with respect to the physical conduct in the performance of the services is subject to the other's control or right of control.
2. In determining whether one acting for another is a servant or an independent contractor, the following matters of fact, among others, are considered:
   (a) The extent of control which, by the agreement, the master may exercise over the details of the work.
   (b) Whether or not the one employed is engaged in a distinct occupation or business.
   (c) The kind of occupation, with reference to whether, in the locality, the work is usually done under the direction of the employer or by a specialist without supervision.
   (d) The skill required in the particular occupation.
   (e) Whether the employer or the workman supplies the instrumentalities, tools, and the place of work for the person doing the work.
   (f) The length of time for which the person is employed.
   (g) The method of payment, whether by the time or by the job.
   (h) Whether or not the work is part of the regular business of the employer.
   (i) Whether or not the parties believe they are creating the relation of master and servant.
   (j) Whether the principal is or is not in the business.

in Subsections (1) and 2(a), Roadway and several amici argue that the "most important" or "predominant" factor to be considered is whether an employer has a "right to control" the manner and means of the work. In contrast, the Petitioner and the AFL-CIO assert that all the factors should be weighed in the equation, as evidenced by the opening paragraph of Subsection 2 of Section 220.*

The Supreme Court has clearly stated that "all of the incidents of the relationship must be assessed and weighed with no one factor being decisive." See *United Insurance*, 390 U.S. at 258; ....

To summarize, in determining the distinction between employee and an independent contractor under Section 2(3) of the Act, we shall apply the common-law agency test and consider all the incidents of the individual's relationship to the employing entity.

Application of the Common-Law Agency Test

Guided by the legal principles set forth above ... we now apply the common-law agency test to the present situation involving the Ontario and Pomona drivers. We find that the dealings and arrangements between these drivers and Roadway, including those reflective of the changes made by the 1994 Agreement, have many of the same characteristics of the employee-employer relationship presented in *United Insurance*.

A. Analysis of Factors

As in *United Insurance*, the drivers here do not operate independent businesses, but perform functions that are an essential part of one company's normal operations; they need not have any prior training or experience, but receive training from the company; they do business in the company's name with assistance and guidance from it; they do not ordinarily engage in outside business; they constitute an integral part of the company's business under its substantial control; they have no substantial proprietary interest beyond their investment in their trucks; and they have no significant entrepreneurial opportunity for gain or loss. All these factors weigh heavily in favor of employee status, and are fully supported by the following facts....

... While a few operate as incorporated businesses, all the Ontario and Pomona drivers do business in the name of Roadway. Wearing an "RPS-approved uniform," the drivers operate uniformly marked vehicles. In fact, the vehicles are custom designed by Roadway and produced to its specifications by Navistar. The

continued

vehicles are identical as to make, model, internal shelving, and rear door, differing only as to chassis and payload (three choices depending on the size of the driver's primary service area). All the vehicles clearly display Roadway's name, logo, and colors. Thus, the drivers' connection to and integration in Roadway's operations are highly visible and well publicized.

The drivers have a contractual right to use this customized truck in business activity outside their relationship with Roadway, though none of the Ontario and Pomona drivers (and only 3 out of Roadway's 5000 drivers nationwide) have used their vehicles for other commercial purposes. This lack of pursuit of outside business activity appears to be less a reflection of entrepreneurial choice by the Ontario and Pomona drivers and more a matter of the obstacles created by their relationship with Roadway.

Roadway's drivers are prohibited under the 1994 Agreement from conducting outside business for other companies throughout the day. The drivers' commitment to Roadway continues through the evening hours when they must return their vehicles to the terminal to interface with Roadway's evening line-haul operations. Typically, most drivers then take their vehicles out of circulation. They leave their vehicles overnight at the terminal to take advantage of loading of the next day's assignments by Roadway's package handlers. As a consequence, their vehicles remain out of service during these off-work hours. Even if the drivers want to use their vehicles for other purposes during their off-work hours, there are several obvious built-in hindrances. First, the vehicles are not readily available. Second, before the driver can use his vehicle for other purposes, he must mask any marking reflecting Roadway's name or business. Every vehicle utilized by the driver has been dictated in detail—color, size, internal configuration including the internal shelving and door—by Roadway's operations. The vehicles are also not easily flexible or susceptible to modifications or adaptations to other types of use. Thus, these constraints on the drivers' use of their vehicles during their off-work hours "provide minimal play for entrepreneurial initiative and minimize the extent to which ownership of a truck gives its driver entrepreneurial independence." Roadway has simply shifted certain capital costs to the drivers without providing them with the independence to engage in entrepreneurial opportunities.

Truck ownership can suggest independent contractor status where, for example, an entrepreneur with a truck puts it to use in serving his or another business' customers. But, the form of truck ownership, here, does not eliminate the Ontario and Pomona drivers' dependence on Roadway in acquiring their vehicles. Roadway's indirect control is further seen in that it requires the drivers to acquire and maintain their own specialty vans, and Roadway eases the drivers' burden through its arrangement and promotion of Navistar vans sold or leased through Bush Leasing....

Other support for employee status can be found in Roadway's compensation package for the drivers. Here, Roadway establishes, regulates, and controls the rate of compensation and financial assistance to the drivers as well as the rates charged to customers. Generally speaking, there is little room for the drivers to influence their income through their own efforts or ingenuity. Whatever potential for entrepreneurial profit does exist, Roadway suppresses through a system of minimum and maximum number of packages and customer stops assigned to the drivers. For example, when a driver becomes busier and the number of packages or customer stops grows, his territory may be unilaterally reconfigured, and the extra packages or stops are reassigned if the driver has already attained the maximum level for his primary service area that has been already determined by Roadway. "[I]t is clear that, unlike the genuinely independent businessman, the drivers' earnings do not depend largely on their ability to exercise good business judgment, to follow sound management practices, and to be able to take financial risks in order to increase their profits." *Standard Oil Co.*, supra, 230 NLRB at 972....

Roadway stresses that two items in the 1994 Agreement—the driver's proprietary interest in his service area and his right to sell all or part of his area to the "highest bidder"—allow the drivers to influence their profits like entrepreneurs. We disagree because Roadway has imposed substantial limitations and conditions on both new features of the driver's relationship such that neither one retains any significant entrepreneurial characteristics....

The testimonial evidence shows that the sales by drivers Gonzales, Irions, Hawkins and Steenburgen took place at Roadway's behest, if not direction to the drivers, to sell or risk having their entire contract terminated. No gain was shown. In a system of over 5000 drivers assigned to over 300 terminals, we find that these few forced sales, given their circumstances, are insufficient to support a finding of independent contractor status....

continued

Conclusion

Weighing all the incidents of their relationship with Roadway, we conclude that the Ontario and Pomona drivers are employees and not independent contractors ... we find that the following employees of Roadway constitute an appropriate unit for the purposes of collective bargaining within the meaning of Section 9(b) of the Act:

Included: All pickup and delivery drivers employed by the Employer at its facility located at 1235 Grand Avenue, Pomona, California 91766.

Excluded: All other employees, including Temporary B drivers, office clerical employees, guards, and supervisors as defined in the Act.

We remand both cases to the Regional Director for further processing consistent with our decision.

Case Questions

1. What did Roadway contend?
2. What "test" did the Board follow in determining whether the drivers were "employees" or "independent contractors" under the NLRA?
3. How did the Board decide this case?

SECTION 28: JURISDICTION: EMPLOYEES UNDER THE ACT

Because one of the major policy objectives of the National Labor Relations Act is the protection of those employee organizational rights guaranteed by Section 7, the definition of the term **employee**, embodied in Section 2(3), becomes a matter of prime importance.

Section 2(3), the definitions section of the NLRA, states:

The term "employee" shall include any employee, and shall not be limited to the employees of a particular employer, unless this subchapter explicitly states otherwise, and shall include any individual whose work has ceased as a consequence of, or in connection with, any current labor dispute or because of any unfair labor practice, and who has not obtained any other regular and substantially equivalent employment, but shall not include any individual employed as an agricultural laborer, or in the domestic service of any family or person at his home, or any individual employed by his parent or spouse, or any individual having the status of an independent contractor, or any individual employed by an employer subject to the Railway Labor Act, as amended from time to time, or by any other person who is not an employer as herein defined.

In *NLRB v. Town and Country Electric, Inc.*,[27] presented in this section, the Supreme Court held that the Board's broad literal reading of the statutory definition of "employee" set forth in Section 2(3) of the NLRA was entitled to considerable deference, holding that paid union organizers can qualify as employees of a company and be entitled to the protections of the NLRA. Town & Country Electric Co. had terminated a newly hired individual when it found out that he was also being paid by a union in order to help the union organize the company. In *Lechmere, Inc., v. NLRB*,[28] the Supreme Court held that employers who enforce

---

[27] 516 U.S. 85 (1995). In *Starcom, Inc., v. NLRB*, 161 LRRM 2233 (7th Cir. 1999), the Seventh Circuit enforced the NLRB's cease-and-desist order against a contractor's refusal to hire qualified union "salts" but refused to enforce the Board's remedial order because the Board had not demonstrated how many salters would have been hired but for the employer's hostility toward unionization.

[28] 502 U.S. 527 (1992).

their no-solicitation rules cannot be compelled to allow nonemployee union organizers on their private property to distribute organizational literature. Because of the reduced access of outsider organizers to company property under the *Lechmere* rule, many unions are utilizing a strategy based on the *Town & Country* decision of "salting" the workforces of companies that unions have targeted for organizational campaigns as outside organizers take employment with the targeted companies.

In the Labor Board's *FES, a Division of Thermo Power*[29] decision, it established a framework for analyzing refusal-to-consider and/or hire cases by making clear the elements of the violation, the burdens of the parties, and the stage at which issues are to be litigated. To establish a discriminatory refusal-to-hire violation, the General Counsel must, at the hearing on the merits, show (1) that the respondent was hiring, or had concrete plans to hire, at the time of the alleged unlawful conduct; (2) that the applicants had experience or training relevant to the announced or generally known requirements of the positions for hire, or in the alternative, that the employer has not adhered uniformly to such requirements or that the requirements were themselves pretextual or were applied as a pretext for discrimination; and (3) that antiunion animus contributed to the decision not to hire the applicants. If established, the respondent-employer must show that it would not have hired the applicants even in the absence of their union activity or affiliation. In *FES*, the ALJ found that nine union pipefitter-applicants would have been hired as welders by FES but for the company's antiunion animus and ordered back pay and instatement for each applicant; this order was adopted by the Board. The Third Circuit Court of Appeals enforced the Board's order.[30]

In the September 29, 2007, *Toering Electric Co.* decision involving an overt salting case from 1996, where a union organizer submitted a batch of 18 résumés in response to a blind help-wanted ad for electricians and the employer made no response, the Labor Board, with a 3-2 majority, materially altered its *FES* framework, imposing on the General Counsel, who is responsible for investigating charges and prosecuting complaints before the Board, the ultimate burden of proving in hiring discrimination cases that the alleged discriminatee had a genuine interest in seeking to establish an employment relationship with the employer. If this burden is met, the existing *FES* framework will apply.

The dissent pointed out that under this rule, if the General Counsel cannot prove that an applicant would have accepted a job offer from the employer, the applicant is not a statutory employee and there can be no violation of the Act and no remedy even if the employer's refusal to hire or consider the applicant was motivated solely by antiunion animus. The dissent stated that the Board majority, without the benefit of briefs from interested parties, without oral argument, and without a request for it to reconsider the long-established precedent enduring over 170 hiring discrimination cases tried before the Board's administrative law

---

[29] 331 NLRB 9, 34 (2000).

[30] *NLRB v. FES (A Division of Thermo Power)*, 301 F.3d 83 (3d Cir. 2002). In *Fluor Daniel, Inc., v. NLRB*, 332 F.3d 961 (6th Cir. 2003), *cert. den.* 125 S.Ct. 964 (2005), the Sixth Circuit Court of Appeals approved the Board's *FES* test for refusal-to-consider and/or hire cases.

judges since the issuance of *FES*, legalized hiring discrimination involving salts in some cases.

As set forth in Section 2(3), the following workers are not protected by the Act:

1. Workers under the Railway Labor Act;
2. Employees of employers not covered by the Act;
3. Independent contractors;
4. Domestic servants in the home;
5. Persons employed by parents or spouses;
6. Agricultural workers;
7. Supervisors.

The exclusion of workers under the Railway Labor Act follows the jurisdictional aspects of that Act as defined in Chapter 2 of this text. Of course, the employees of employers not covered by the law are similarly not covered. As set forth in the previous section, independent contractors are not covered by the Act. Domestic servants in the home are not covered by this federal legislation because of their lack of impact on interstate commerce.[31] A condominium association's argument that employees who performed various maintenance and cleaning services in individual units of owners were domestic employees excluded from coverage under Section 2(3) of the Act was rejected by the Eleventh Circuit Court of Appeals. The court held that the employees' relationship was no different from an employee performing similar work for apartment house or office building employers and therefore the Teamsters should be certified as the bargaining unit's representative.[32] In the interest of family harmony, persons employed by parents or spouses are not covered by the Act.[33] A discussion of matters relating to agricultural workers and supervisory, managerial, and professional employees follows.

AGRICULTURAL WORKERS

Union-organizing activity among farmworkers has been accompanied by considerable strife, in part because there is no uniform statutory framework for the conduct of collective bargaining in the farm sector. Section 2(3) specifically excludes agricultural laborers from federal labor relations law. Thus, the regulation of labor relations in the farm sector is left to the individual states. Most states do not provide comparable protection and rights for agricultural workers. Agricultural workers are specifically excluded from the coverage of many state labor relations acts. However, Hawaii's and Wisconsin's state labor relations acts are broad enough to include farmworkers within the coverage of the acts. Also, the California

---

[31] Ankh Services, Inc., 243 NLRB 478 (1979).

[32] *Shore Club Condominium Association v. NLRB*, 400 F.3d 1336 (11th Cir. 2005).

[33] See Winco Petroleum Co., 241 NLRB 1118 (1979), where the Board looked beyond the corporate form of business organization in deciding that an employee-wife, whose husband was an officer and a majority stockholder in the employer corporation, was excluded from protection under the Act by Section 2(3), even though her employer was, technically speaking, the corporation.

Agricultural Labor Relations Act extends organization, representation, and collective bargaining rights to agricultural workers. The Massachusetts labor relations law provides coverage only where the employer has a permanent workforce of more than four agricultural workers, and the law expressly provides that it will not apply if a contract with migrant workers has been approved by the federal government. The Arizona Agriculture Employment Relations Act has among its controversial features a ban on certain boycott activities, a restriction on use of consumer boycotts, and a restriction on harvest-time strikes by authorizing issuance of a 10-day injunction against a strike, with the condition, however, that the dispute be submitted to binding arbitration.

Although agricultural laborers are clearly excluded from the Section 2(3) definition of employee, the Act does not define the term **agricultural laborer**. The Board and courts had significant difficulty interpreting the meaning of this exclusion until 1947, when Congress applied the Fair Labor Standards Act (FLSA) definition of **agriculture** to Board proceedings.

SUPERVISORY, MANAGERIAL, AND PROFESSIONAL EMPLOYEES

While the NLRA excludes *supervisors* from the protections of the Act and *managerial employees* are excluded as a matter of Board policy, *professional employees* are an expressly covered category. Judgment and discretion are common functions to the status of each of these classifications, and expanded or adjusted definitions of statutory terms can have the effect of removing classes of workers from the rights and protections of the Act.[34]

SUPERVISORS. Section 2(3) of the NLRA excludes supervisory employees from the definition of employees protected by the Act. Section 2(11) of the Act defines "supervisor" as:

> any individual having the authority, in the interest of the employer, to hire, transfer, suspend, lay off, recall, promote, discharge, assign, reward, or discipline other employees, or responsibility to direct them, or to adjust their grievances, or effectively to recommend such action, if in connection with the foregoing the exercise of such authority is not of a merely routine or clerical nature, but requires the use of independent judgment.

The text of Section 2(11) contains a three-part test for determining supervisory status. Employees fall within this statutory exclusion from coverage and rights under the Act if (1) they hold the authority to engage in or effectively recommend any one of the 12 listed supervisory functions (that is, hire, transfer, suspend, lay off, recall, promote, discharge, assign, reward, discipline other employees, responsibly direct them, or adjust their grievances); (2) their exercise of such authority is

---

[34] The outcome of Board-conducted elections can be affected by the composition of the voting unit. Employers and unions aggressively pursue their legal options to obtain a voting unit that will most likely yield a favorable outcome from their respective points of view. A unit clarification hearing preceding a union election held before an NLRB hearing officer may resolve issues on who will be allowed to vote in the Board election. Whether certain individuals are excluded as supervisors or managerial, or are protected as professionals may be pivotal to the outcome of the election and the rights of individual employees.

not merely routine or clerical in nature, but requires the use of independent judgment; and (3) their authority is held in the interest of the employer.[35] The burden of proving supervisory status is on the party asserting that such status exists.[36]

In *Oakwood Healthcare, Inc.,*[37] the Board examined whether 12 permanent acute care charge nurses at the Oakwood Heritage Hospital were statutory supervisors based on their role in assigning nursing personnel to patients and directing the nursing staff in the performance of their duties. The Board majority found that the 12 nurses were Section 2(11) supervisors because they had the authority to "assign" and exercised independent judgment in making these assignments in the interest of their employer. The Board majority adopted definitions for the terms **assign, responsibility to direct,** and *independent judgment* as those terms are used in Section 2(11) of the Act. It defined the term **assign** in sum as "designation of overall duties to an employee, not the ad hoc instruction that the employee perform a discrete task." In addition to the term assign, the function of "responsibility to direct" is one of the 12 listed functions of supervisory status. While the Board found that the hospital did not meet its burden of proof that the charge nurses "responsibly directed"[38] employees within the meaning of Section 2(11), nevertheless, the nurses were still excluded as supervisors, because an employee needs only perform one of the 12 enumerated supervisory functions to fall within the supervisory exclusion. In explaining the definition of **independent judgment** in relation to the authority to "assign," the Board stated that "[t]he authority to effect an assignment must be independent [free of the control of others], it must involve a judgment [forming an opinion or evaluation by discerning and comparing data], and the judgment must involve a degree of discretion that rises above the 'routine or clerical.'"[39]

The *Oakwood Healthcare* dissent stated that the majority's decision threatens to create a new class of workers under federal labor law—workers who have neither the genuine prerogatives of management nor the statutory rights of ordinary employees. It states that most professionals, who have some supervisory responsibilities in the sense of directing another's work, fall into that category.

MANAGERIAL EMPLOYEES. **Managerial employees** are employees whose responsibilities to their employers are not such that they fit within the Section 2(11) definition of supervisory employees. Managerial employees are excluded from the coverage of the Act—not by explicit statutory language, but as a matter of Board policy. This policy received unanimous approval in the Supreme Court's *NLRB v. Bell Aerospace Co.*

---

[35] *Public Service Company of Colorado v. NLRB,* 405 F.3d 1071, 1076 (10th Cir. 2005) (citing Kentucky River, 532 U.S. at 711–12).

[36] Dean & Deluca New York, Inc., 338 NLRB 1046, 1047 (2003).

[37] Oakwood Healthcare, Inc., 348 NLRB No. 37 (Sept. 29, 2006).

[38] In defining the term "responsibly to direct" with accountability, the Board stated "... it must be shown that the employer delegated to the putative supervisor the authority to direct the work and the authority to take corrective action, if necessary. It also must be shown that there is a prospect of adverse consequences for that putative supervisor if he/she does not take these steps." *Id.* slip op. at 7.

[39] *Id.* slip op. at 8.

decision.[40] The Court defined **managerial employees** as "those who formulate, determine, and effectuate an employer's policies."[41]

PROFESSIONAL EMPLOYEES. **Professional employees** are within the protection of the Act. Section 2(12) of the Act sets forth a definition of **professional employee:**

> ... any employee engaged in work (i) predominantly intellectual and varied in character as opposed to routine mental, manual, mechanical, or physical work; (ii) involving the consistent exercise of discretion and judgment in its performance; (iii) of such a character that the output produced or the result accomplished cannot be standardized in relation to a given period of time; (iv) requiring knowledge of an advanced type in a field of science or learning customarily acquired by a prolonged course of specialized intellectual instruction and study in an institution of higher learning or a hospital, as distinguished from a general academic education from an apprenticeship or from training in the performance of routine mental, manual, or physical processes....

Examples of professional employees are engineers, physicians, nurses, reporters, and symphony orchestra musicians.

The issue of whether full-time faculty members are "professional employees" covered by the Act or "managerial employees" excluded from the rights and protection of the Act was considered by the Supreme Court in *NLRB v. Yeshiva University*, presented in this section. In a 5–4 decision, the Court ruled that the faculty members were managerial employees. The NLRB makes its determination on the managerial status of faculty members on a case-by-case basis.[42] The Board does not consider part-time faculty at private universities to be managerial employees and has determined that part-time faculty may constitute an appropriate unit for collective bargaining.[43]

At the same time Congress acted to exclude supervisors from the NLRA's protection, it explicitly extended those same protections to professionals. The inclusion of professionals and the exclusion of supervisors give rise to some tension in the statutory text of the Act. However, in *NLRB v. Kentucky River Community Care, Inc.*,[44] a 5–4 Supreme Court majority ruled that the test for supervisory status set forth in Section 2(11) of the Act applies no differently to professionals than to other employees. It rejected the Board's determination that nurses were not supervisors within the meaning of the NLRA, despite their direction of patient care by nurse's aides, based on a statutory interpretation that the nurses do not use "independent judgment" as referenced in Section 2(11) when they exercise "ordinary professional or technical judgment in directing less skilled employees to deliver

---

[40] 416 U.S. 267 (1974).

[41] 444 U.S. 672, 103 LRRM 2526 (1980).

[42] See *Loretto Heights College v. NLRB*, 742 F.2d 1245 (10th Cir. 1984) (faculty, not managerial); *Trustees of Boston University*, 281 NLRB 110 (1986) (faculty found to be managerial); LeMoyne-Owen College 345 NLRB No. 93 (2008) (faculty found to be managerial employees and excluded from coverage under the Act).

[43] University of San Francisco, 265 NLRB 571 (1982).

[44] 352 U.S. 706 (2001).

services in accordance with employer-specified standards." As a result, the Board's order to the Kentucky mental health care facility to include six registered nurses in a bargaining unit was not enforced.

CASE 4.5	NLRB v. TOWN & COUNTRY ELECTRIC, INC.
	SUPREME COURT OF THE UNITED STATES, 516 U.S. 85 (1995).

[Town & Country Electric, Inc., a nonunion electrical contractor, wanted to hire licensed Minnesota electricians for construction work at a paper mill in International Falls, Minnesota. Town & Country, through an employment agency, advertised for job applicants, but it refused to interview 10 of 11 union applicants who responded to the advertisements. Its employment agency hired one union applicant whom Town & Country interviewed, but he was dismissed after three days on the job.

The 11 members of the union, the International Brotherhood of Electrical Workers, filed charges with the National Labor Relations Board claiming that Town & Country and the employment agency had refused to interview or retain them because of their union membership. The National Labor Relations Board, in the course of its decision, determined that all 11 job applicants, including 2 union officials and the 1 member briefly hired, were "employees" as the Act defines that word. The Board recognized that under well-established law, it made no difference that the 10 members who were simply applicants were never hired. Moreover, the Board concluded with respect to the meaning of the word *employee* that it did not matter that the union members intended to try to organize the company if they secured the advertised jobs, nor that the union would pay them while they went about their organizing.

The U.S. Court of Appeals for the Eighth Circuit reversed the Board, holding that the Board had incorrectly interpreted the statutory word *employee*. In the court's view, the term *employee* does not cover those who work for a company while a union simultaneously pays them to organize that company. Since this determination was in conflict with decisions by the District of Columbia Circuit and the Second Circuit, the Supreme Court granted certiorari to resolve the conflict.]

BREYER, J....

The National Labor Relations Act seeks to improve labor relations ("eliminate the causes of certain substantial obstructions to the free flow of commerce," 29 U.S.C. § 151 (1988 ed.)) in large part by granting specific sets of rights to employers and to employees. This case grows out of a controversy about rights that the Act grants to "*employees*," namely, rights "to self-organization, to form, join, or assist labor organizations, to bargain collectively ... and to engage in other concerted activities for the purpose of collective bargaining or other mutual aid or protection." § 157. We granted certiorari to decide only that part of the controversy that focuses upon the meaning of the word "employee," a key term in the statute, since these rights belong only to those workers who qualify as "employees" as that term is defined in the Act. See, *e.g.*, § 158(a)(1) ("unfair labor practice" to "interfere with ... *employees* in the exercise of the rights guaranteed in Section 157 of this title") (emphasis added)....

Several strong general arguments favor the Board's position. For one thing, the Board's decision is consistent with the broad language of the Act itself—language that is broad enough to include those company workers whom a union also pays for organizing. The ordinary dictionary definition of "employee" includes any "person who works for another in return for financial or other compensation." American Heritage Dictionary 604 (3d ed. 1992). See also Black's Law Dictionary 525 (6th ed. 1990) (an employee is a "person in the service of another under any contract of hire, express or implied, oral or written, where the employer has the power or right to control and direct the employee in the material details of how the work is to be performed"). The phrasing of the Act seems to reiterate the breadth of the ordinary dictionary definition, for it says "[t]he term 'employee' shall include *any* employee." 29 U.S. C. § 152(3) (1988 ed.) (emphasis added). Of course, the Act's definition also contains a list of exceptions, for example, for independent contractors, agricultural laborers, domestic workers, and employees subject to the

continued

Railway Labor Act, 45 U.S.C. § 151 *et seq*; but no exception applies here.

For another thing, the Board's broad, literal interpretation of the word "employee" is consistent with several of the Act's purposes, such as protecting "the right of employees to organize for mutual aid without employer interference," ...

Further, a broad, literal reading of the statute is consistent with cases in this Court such as, say, ... *Phelps Dodge Corp. v. NLRB*, 313 U.S., at 185–186, ... (job applicants are "employees")....

Finally, at least one other provision of the 1947 Labor Management Relations Act seems specifically to contemplate the possibility that a company's employee might also work for a union. This provision forbids an employer (say, the company) from making payments to a person employed by a union, but simultaneously exempts from that ban wages paid by the company to "any ... employee of a labor organization, who is *also* an employee" of the company. 29 U.S.C. § 186(c)(1) (1988 ed., Supp. V) (emphasis added). If Town & Country is right, there would not seem to be many (or any) human beings to which this last phrase could apply....

... The company refers to a Union resolution permitting members to work for nonunion firms, which,

the company says, reflects a union effort to "salt" nonunion companies with union members seeking to organize them. Supported by *amici curiae*, it argues that "salts" might try to harm the company....

... [T]he law offers alternative remedies for Town & Country's concerns, short of excluding paid or unpaid union organizers from all protection under the Act.... A Company faced with unlawful (or possibly unlawful) activity can discipline or dismiss the worker, file a complaint with the Board, or notify law enforcement authorities....

For these reasons the judgment of the Court of Appeals is vacated, and the case is remanded for further proceedings consistent with this opinion.

It is so ordered.

Case Questions

1. What factors did the Board rely on in making its decision?
2. Did the Supreme Court approve the NLRB's rationale?
3. Did the Supreme Court offer direction to employers on how to deal with problems that could arise when dealing with paid union organizers as employees?

CASE 4.6   NLRB v. YESHIVA UNIVERSITY
SUPREME COURT OF THE UNITED STATES, 444 U.S. 672 (1980).

[Yeshiva University is a private university that conducts a broad range of arts and sciences programs at its five undergraduate and eight graduate schools in New York City. On October 30, 1974, the Yeshiva University Faculty Association (Union) filed a representation petition with the National Labor Relations Board (Board). The Union sought certification as bargaining agent for the full-time faculty members at 10 of the 13 schools. The University opposed the petition on the grounds that all of its faculty members are managerial or supervisory personnel and hence not employees within the meaning of the National Labor Relations Act (the Act). A Board-appointed hearing officer held hearings over a period of five months, generating a voluminous record.

The University administrative structure is similar to that of many private universities, with ultimate authority being vested in a Board of Trustees. Faculty power at Yeshiva's schools extends beyond strictly academic concerns. The faculty at each school make recommendations to the dean or director in every case of faculty hiring, tenure, sabbaticals, termination, and promotion. Although the final decision is reached by the central administration on the advice of the dean or director, the overwhelming majority of faculty recommendations are implemented. In addition, some faculties make final decisions regarding the admission, expulsion, and graduation of individual students. Others have decided questions involving teaching loads, student absence policies, tuition and enrollment levels, and in one case the location of a school.

continued

A three-member panel of the Board granted the Union's petition and directed an election in a bargaining unit consisting of all full-time faculty members at the affected schools. The Board concluded that the faculty are professional employees entitled to the protection of the Act because "faculty participation in collegial decision making is on a collective rather than individual basis, it is exercised in the faculty's own interest rather than in the interest of the employer, and final authority rests with the Board of Trustees." The Union won the election and was certified by the Board. The University refused to bargain, reasserting its view that the faculty are managerial. The Board ordered the University to bargain. However, the court of appeals denied the enforcement petition. The Supreme Court granted certiorari.]

POWELL, J....

Managerial employees are defined as those who "formulate and effectuate management policies by expressing and making operative the decisions of their employer." These employees are "much higher in the managerial structure" than those explicitly mentioned by Congress, which "regarded [them] as so clearly outside the Act that no specific exclusionary provision was thought necessary." Managerial employees must exercise discretion within or even independently of established employer policy and must be aligned with management. Although the Board has established no firm criteria for determining when an employee is so aligned, normally an employee may be excluded as managerial only if he represents management interests by taking or recommending discretionary actions that effectively control or implement employer policy.

The Board does not contend that the Yeshiva faculty's decision making is too insignificant to be deemed managerial. Nor does it suggest that the role of the faculty is merely advisory and thus not managerial. Instead, it contends that the managerial exclusion cannot be applied in a straightforward fashion to professional employees because those employees often appear to be exercising managerial authority when they are merely performing routine job duties....

The controlling consideration in this case is that the faculty of Yeshiva University exercise authority which in any other context unquestionably would be managerial. Their authority in academic matters is absolute. They decide what courses will be offered, when they will be scheduled, and to whom they will be taught. They debate and determine teaching methods, grading policies, and matriculation standards. They effectively decide which students will be admitted, retained, and graduated. On occasion their views have determined the size of the student body, the tuition to be charged, and the location of a school. When one considers the function of a university, it is difficult to imagine decisions more managerial than these. To the extent the industrial analogy applies, the faculty determines within each school the product to be produced, the terms upon which it will be offered, and the customers who will be served.

The Board nevertheless insists that these decisions are not managerial because they require the exercise of independent professional judgment. We are not persuaded by this argument. There may be some tension between the Act's exclusion of managerial employees and its inclusion of professionals, since most professionals in managerial positions continue to draw on their special skills and training. But we have been directed to no authority suggesting that tension can be resolved by reference to the "independent professional judgment" criterion proposed in this case....

Moreover, the Board's approach would undermine the goal it purports to serve: To ensure that employees who exercise discretionary authority on behalf of the employer will not divide their loyalty between employer and union. In arguing that a faculty member exercising independent judgment acts primarily in his own interest and therefore does not represent the interest of his employer, the Board assumes that the professional interests of the faculty and the interests of the institution are distinct, separable entities with which a faculty member could not simultaneously be aligned. The Court of Appeals found no justification for this distinction, and we perceive none. In fact, the faculty's professional interests—as applied to governance at a university like Yeshiva—cannot be separated from those of the institution....

We certainly are not suggesting an application of the managerial exclusion that would sweep all professionals outside the Act in derogation of Congress' expressed intent to protect them. The Board has recognized that employees whose decision making is limited to the routine discharge of professional duties in projects to which they have been assigned cannot be excluded from coverage even if union membership

continued

arguably may involve some divided loyalty. Only if an employee's activities fall outside the scope of the duties routinely performed by similarly situated professionals will he be found aligned with management. We think these decisions accurately capture the intent of Congress, and that they provide an appropriate starting point for analysis in cases involving professionals alleged to be managerial.*

Affirmed.

BRENNAN, J. (joined by WHITE, MARSHALL, and BLACKMUN, J. J.), dissenting ...

[In their dissent, the justices argue that the touchstone of managerial status is an alliance with management and the pivotal inquiry is whether the employee in performing duties represents the employee's own interests or those of the employer. They criticize the majority, saying that the Court fails to understand that whatever influence the faculty wields in university decision making is attributable solely to their collective expertise as professional educators, and not to any managerial or supervisory prerogatives. They go on to state:]

...Finally, the Court's perception of the Yeshiva faculty's status is distorted by the rose-colored lens through which it views the governance structure of the modern-day university. The Court's conclusion that the faculty's professional interests are indistinguishable from those of the administration is bottomed on an idealized model of collegial decision making that is a vestige of the great medieval university. But the university of today bears little resemblance to the "community of scholars of yesteryear." Education has become "big business," and the task of operating the university enterprise has been transferred from the faculty to an autonomous administration, which faces the same pressure to cut costs and increase efficiencies that confront any large industrial organization. The past decade of budgetary cutbacks, declining enrollments, reductions in faculty appointments, curtailment of academic programs, and increasing calls for accountability to alumni and other special interest groups has only added to the erosion of the faculty's role in the institution's decision making process.

These economic exigencies have also exacerbated the tensions in university labor relations as the faculty and administration more and more frequently find themselves advocating conflicting positions not only on issues of compensation, job security, and working conditions but even on subjects formerly thought to be the faculty's prerogative. In response to this friction, and in an attempt to avoid the strikes and work stoppages that have disrupted several major universities in recent years, many faculties have entered into collective bargaining relationships with their administrations and governing boards. An even greater number of schools—Yeshiva among them—have endeavored to negotiate and compromise their differences informally by establishing avenues for faculty input into university decisions on matters of professional concern.

Today's decision, however, threatens to eliminate much of the administration's incentive to resolve its disputes with the faculty through open discussion and mutual agreement....

[The dissent believes that the notion of a faculty member's professional competence depending on undivided loyalty to management is antithetical to the whole concept of academic freedom.]

---

*We recognize that this is a starting point only, and that other factors not present here may enter into the analysis in other contexts. It is plain, for example, that professors may not be excluded merely because they determine the content of their own courses, evaluate their own students, and supervise their own research. There thus may be institutions of higher learning unlike Yeshiva where the faculty are entirely or predominantly nonmanagerial. There also may be faculty members at Yeshiva and like universities who properly could be included in a bargaining unit. It may be that a rational line could be drawn between tenured and untenured faculty members, depending upon how a faculty is structured and operates. But we express no opinion on these questions, for it is clear that the unit approved by the Board was far too broad.

Case Questions

1. State the issue before the Supreme Court.
2. What was the Court's decision on the issue?
3. Identify the faculty powers and functions that the Court majority deemed "managerial decisions."
4. What was the dissent's view of the Court's perception of the status of the Yeshiva faculty?

SECTION 29: JURISDICTION: PREEMPTION

The creation of federal labor legislation in the form of the NLRA raises the jurisdictional issue of whether employers and employees covered by the Act must look exclusively to the NLRB and the federal court system for redress or if they may seek an alternative state-created remedy in a state court. This issue is deceptively complicated and must be dealt with by reference to a legal concept that is derived from the "supremacy clause" of the U.S. Constitution and is referred to as the **preemption doctrine.**

The supremacy clause is found in Article VI, Section 2, of the Constitution, which states, "This Constitution and The Laws of the United States which shall be made in Pursuance thereof ... shall be the supreme Law of the Land; and the judges in every State shall be bound thereby, anything in the Constitution or Laws of any State to the Contrary notwithstanding." The preemption doctrine is a natural extension of the supremacy clause and mandates that a state law cannot stand either where it is in direct conflict with a federal law or where there is evidence that Congress intended to foreclose state action in the particular area in question. Congressional preemptive intent can be established by express language in a statute or implied from either the pervasiveness of the federal law or the need for uniformity of regulation in the field.

With respect to the NLRA, the Supreme Court has held that the Act does not preempt all state laws and remedies in the area of labor relations. The Court stated in *Garner v. Teamsters Local 776*[45] that the Act "leaves much to the states, though Congress has refrained from telling us how much. We must spell out from conflicting indications of Congressional will the area in which state action is permissible."

In spelling out this congressional will, the Supreme Court has established a general rule for determining when preemption is appropriate and from this rule has carved out several key exceptions.

GENERAL RULE

The general rule of preemption in the labor relations field was established in the landmark Supreme Court decision in *San Diego Building Trades Council v. Garmon*, presented next. In *Garmon*, the Court held that in the absence of an overriding state interest, such as that involved in controlling violence, state courts must defer to the exclusive competence of the NLRB in cases in which the activity that is the basis of the litigation is "arguably subject" to the protections of Section 7 or the prohibitions of Section 8 of the NLRA. The basic premise of this rule is that there is a clear need for uniformity of regulation in the field of labor relations. Allowing alternative state laws and remedies where the activity in question is "arguably subject" to Section 7 or 8 of the NLRA would unduly interfere with national labor policy.

In *Sears Roebuck and Co. v. San Diego County District Council of Carpenters,*[46] an important case in which the Supreme Court upheld the application of California's

---

[45] 346 U.S. 485 (1953).

[46] 436 U.S. 180 (1978).

trespass laws to picketing that was either arguably protected or arguably prohibited by Sections 7 and 8 of the NLRA, the *Garmon* rule was refined. The Court stated that the preemption inquiry cannot end with a determination that an activity is arguably subject to Section 7 or 8 of the Act for state action to be preempted. It must further be concluded that the legal theory or issue presented to the state court is very similar to that which could have been presented to the NLRB, thus creating an unacceptable risk of interference with the NLRB's jurisdiction. It must also be found that the party who could have presented the issue to the NLRB had not done so and the other party had no acceptable means of doing so.

ALLOWABLE STATE ACTION

Where the activity that is being litigated is a matter of overriding state interest, the courts have, in many instances, declined to apply the *Garmon* "arguably subject" rule of preemption and have allowed state action. Three areas in which state action has been consistently allowed are violence, libel, and fair representation. In *Machinists, Lodge 76 v. Wisconsin Employment Relations Commission*,[47] the Supreme Court held that the states retain the power "to regulate conduct physically injuring or threatening injury to persons or property." The Supreme Court sustained the jurisdiction of a state court to award damages in a civil action for libel instituted under state law by an employer subject to the NLRA in *Linn v. United Plant Guard Workers, Local 114.*[48] The Court recognized "an overriding state interest" in protecting its residents from malicious libel. In *Vaca v. Sipes*[49] the Supreme Court carved out a further exception to the *Garmon* preemption doctrine for cases involving a breach of a union's duty of fair representation. In *Vaca*, the Court held that a state court did have jurisdiction in an action alleging breach of a collective bargaining agreement and seeking damages for a breach of a union's duty of fair representation, even though the conduct complained of was arguably protected or prohibited by the NLRA.

There are specific instances where Congress has expressly stated that state laws are not to be preempted because of federal labor legislation. The two most important examples are found in Section 301 of the LMRA and Section 14(b) of the NLRA. Under Section 301, federal and state courts have concurrent jurisdiction over suits for violations of collective bargaining agreements, even though the conduct involved may be "arguably subject" to Section 7 or 8 of the NLRA. Section 14(b) of the NLRA specifically grants states the power to pass right-to-work laws. In *Retail Clerks v. Schermerhorn*,[50] the Supreme Court upheld the right of a state to enforce such a law. The Court said, "Since it is plain that Congress left the States free to legislate in that field, we can only assume that it intended to leave unaffected the power to enforce those laws."

---

[47] 427 U.S. 132 (1976).

[48] 383 U.S. 53 (1996).

[49] 386 U.S. 171 (1967).

[50] 375 U.S. 96 (1963).

IMPERMISSIBLE STATE AND MUNICIPAL ACTIONS

A second preemption doctrine (in addition to the *Garmon* rule) exists based on the Supreme Court's *Machinists, Lodge 76 v. Wisconsin Employment Relations Commission* decision. The so-called *Machinists* preemption rule precludes state and municipal regulation concerning conduct that Congress intended to be unregulated. In *Golden State Transit Corp. v. Los Angeles*, presented in this section, the city of Los Angeles was found to have violated the *Machinists'* rule. It interfered in a labor dispute between the Teamsters and a major taxi operator by conditioning the renewal of the operator's franchise on the settlement of the labor dispute, thus interfering with the normal bargaining and self-help process contemplated by Congress under the NLRA.[51]

After the Supreme Court's 1986 *Golden State* decision, the matter was returned to the district court on the issue of whether the transit company could bring a "civil rights" damages suit under Section 1983 against the city. Both the trial court and the court of appeals concluded that the private employer had no right to compensatory damages. However, the Supreme Court reversed, holding that where a state (or city) attempts to abridge a personal liberty created by the National Labor Relations Act—the right to withstand a strike—a suit against the state under Section 1983 is viable.[52]

In *Chamber of Commerce v. Brown*, the Supreme Court found that a California statute prohibiting employers that receive state grants or funds of more than $10,000 per year from using any portion of these funds "to assist, promote or deter union organizing" is preempted by the NLRA under the *Machinist* preemption rule. Citing *Golden State Transit*, the Court stated, "[w]hat Congress left unregulated is as important as the regulations that it imposed." The Court pointed out that noncoercive speech is protected by Sections 8(a) and 8(b) as well as Section 7 and Section 8(c) of the NLRA. The *Chamber of Commerce* case is presented in this section.

CASE 4.7	SAN DIEGO BUILDING TRADES COUNCIL V. GARMON SUPREME COURT OF THE UNITED STATES, 359 U.S. 236 (1959).

[A union picketed an employer seeking an agreement by which the employer would retain only those workers who were union members or who applied for union membership within 30 days. The employer sought an injunction and damages in state court, both of which were granted. Concurrently, proceedings had been instituted before the NLRB. The Board, however, declined jurisdiction because the amount of interstate commerce involved did not meet its monetary standards. On appeal, the state supreme court held that since the NLRB declined jurisdiction, the state courts had power over the dispute. The case reached the U.S. Supreme Court, which

continued

---

[51] The NLRA does not preempt a municipality when it acts as a "market participant" in the furtherance of its propriety interests as opposed to its regulatory interests, as determined in *Building & Trades Council v. Associated Builders*, 507 U.S. 218 (1993).

[52] *Golden State Transit Corporation v. City of Los Angeles*, 493 U.S. 103 (1989).

remanded it. On remand, the state supreme court set aside the injunction but sustained the award of damages. Once again the case was appealed to the U.S. Supreme Court.]

FRANKFURTER, J....

In determining the extent to which state regulation must yield to subordinating federal authority, we have been concerned with delimiting areas of potential conflict; potential conflict of rules of law, of remedy, and of administration. The nature of the judicial process precludes an *ad hoc* inquiry into the special problems of labor-management relations involved in a particular set of occurrences in order to ascertain the precise nature and degree of federal-state conflict there involved, and more particularly what exact mischief such a conflict would cause. Nor is it our business to attempt this. Such determinations inevitably depend upon judgments on the impact of these particular conflicts on the entire scheme of federal labor policy and administration. Our task is confined to dealing with classes of situations. To the National Labor Relations Board and to Congress must be left those precise and closely limited demarcations that can be adequately fashioned only by legislation and administration. We have necessarily been concerned with the potential conflict of two law-enforcing authorities, with the disharmonies inherent in two systems, one federal, the other state, of inconsistent standards of substantive law and differing remedial schemes. But the unifying consideration of our decisions has been in regard to the fact that Congress has entrusted administration of the labor policy for the Nation to a centralized administrative agency, armed with its own procedures, and equipped with its specialized knowledge and cumulative experience.

> Congress did not merely lay down a substantive rule of law to be enforced by any tribunal competent to apply law generally to the parties. It went on to confide primary interpretation and application of its rules to a specific and specially constituted tribunal and prescribed a particular procedure for investigation, complaint and notice, and hearing and decision, including judicial relief pending a final administrative order. Congress evidently considered that centralized administration of specially designed procedures was necessary to obtain uniform application of its substantive rules and to avoid these diversities and conflicts likely to result from a variety of local procedures and attitudes towards labor

controversies.... A multiplicity of tribunals and diversity of procedures are quite as apt to produce incompatible or conflicting adjudications as are different rules of substantive law....

When it is clear or may fairly be assumed that the activities which a State purports to regulate are protected by Section 7 of the National Labor Relations Act, or constitute an unfair labor practice under Section 8, due regard for the federal enactment requires that state jurisdiction must yield. To leave the states free to regulate conduct so plainly within the central aim of federal regulation involves too great a danger of conflict between power asserted by Congress and requirements imposed by state law. Nor has it mattered whether the states have acted through laws of broad general application rather than laws specifically directed towards the governance of industrial relations. Regardless of the mode adopted, to allow the states to control conduct which is the subject of national regulation would create potential frustration of national purposes.

At times it has not been clear whether the particular activity regulated by the states was governed by Section 7 or Section 8 or was, perhaps, outside both these sections. But courts are not primary tribunals to adjudicate such issues. It is essential to the administration of the Act that these determinations be left in the first instance to the National Labor Relations Board. What is outside the scope of this Court's authority cannot remain within a state's power and state jurisdiction too must yield to the exclusive primary competence of the Board....

The case before us is such a case. The adjudication in California has throughout been based on the assumption that the behavior of the petitioning unions constituted an unfair labor practice. This conclusion was derived by the California courts from the facts as well as from their view of the Act. It is not for us to decide whether the National Labor Relations Board would have, or should have decided these questions in the same manner. When an activity is arguably subject to Section 7 or Section 8 of the Act, the states as well as the federal courts must defer to the exclusive competence of the National Labor Relations Board if the danger of state interference with national policy is to be averted.

To require the states to yield to the primary jurisdiction of the National Board does not ensure Board adjudication of the status of a disputed activity. If the Board decides, subject to appropriate federal

continued

judicial review, that conduct is protected by Section 7, or prohibited by Section 8, then the matter is at an end, and the States are ousted of all jurisdiction. Or, the Board may decide that an activity is neither protected nor prohibited, and thereby raise the question whether such activity may be regulated by the States. However, the Board may also fail to determine the status of the disputed conduct by declining to assert jurisdiction, or by refusal of the general counsel to file a charge, or by adopting some other disposition which does not define the nature of the activity with unclouded legal significance. This was the basic problem underlying our decision in *Guss v. Utah Labor Relations Board*, 353 U.S. 1. In that case we held that the failure of the National Labor Relations Board to assume jurisdiction did not leave the states free to regulate activities they would otherwise be precluded from regulating. It follows that the failure of the Board to define the legal significance under the Act of a particular activity does not give the states the power to act. In the absence of the Board's clear determination that an activity is neither protected nor prohibited or of compelling precedent applied to essentially undisputed facts, it is not for this Court to decide whether such activities are subject to state jurisdiction. The withdrawal of this narrow area from possible state activity follows from our decision in *Weber* and *Guss*. The governing consideration is that to allow the states to control activities that are potentially subject to federal regulation involves too great a danger of conflict with national labor policy.

Reversed.

Case Questions

1. Why did the NLRB decline jurisdiction?
2. According to the Court, to which body did Congress entrust the administration of national labor policy?
3. What is the basic premise behind the Court's holding that the state courts must yield to federal law?
4. Does the failure of the Board to define the legal significance under the NLRA of a particular activity give the states the power to act?

CASE 4.8   GOLDEN STATE TRANSIT CORP. V. LOS ANGELES
SUPREME COURT OF THE UNITED STATES, 475 U.S. 608 (1986).

[While Golden State's application to renew its franchise to operate 400 Yellow Cab taxis in the city of Los Angeles was pending before the City Council, the taxi drivers represented by the Teamsters went on strike. At the Council meeting that evening and at later meetings, Teamster representatives argued against renewal because of the labor dispute. Thereafter the Council conditioned renewal of the franchise on settlement of the labor dispute by March 31. When the dispute was not settled by this date, the franchise expired. Golden State filed suit against the city, contending that the city's action of conditioning the franchise renewal on settlement of the labor dispute was preempted by the NLRA, a position rejected by the district court and affirmed by the court of appeals.]

BLACKMUN, J....

There is no question that the Teamsters and Golden State employed permissible economic tactics. The drivers were entitled to strike—and to time the strike to coincide with the council's decision—in an attempt to apply pressure on Golden State.... And Golden State was entirely justified in using its economic power to withstand the strike in an attempt to obtain bargaining concessions from the union....

The parties' resort to economic pressure was a legitimate part of their collective bargaining process.... But the bargaining process was thwarted when the city in effect imposed a positive durational limit on the exercise of economic self-help. The District Court found that the council had conditioned the franchise on a settlement of the labor dispute by March 31. We agree with the Court of Appeals that this finding is amply supported by the record. The city's insistence on a settlement is pre-empted if the city "[entered] into the substantive aspects of the bargaining process to an extent Congress has not countenanced."

That such a condition—by a city or the Labor Board—contravenes congressional intent is demonstrated by the language of the NLRA and its

continued

legislative history. The NLRA requires an employer and a union to bargain in good faith, but it does not require them to reach agreement. Section 8(d) as amended... (duty to bargain in good faith "does not compel either party to agree to a proposal or require the making of a concession")...("The theory of the Act is that free opportunity for negotiation...may bring about the adjustments and agreements which the Act in itself does not attempt to compel").

The Act leaves the bargaining process largely to the parties.... It does not purport to set any time limits on negotiations or economic struggle. Instead, the Act provides a framework for the negotiations; it "is concerned primarily with establishing an equitable process for determining terms and conditions of employment."... See also § 1, as amended, of the NLRA ... (Act achieves national policy "by encouraging the practice and procedure of collective bargaining")....

... "[F]ederal law intended to leave the employer and the union free to use their economic weapons against one another." *Belknap, Inc. v. Hale*, 463 U.S. at 500. We hold, therefore, that the city was preempted from conditioning Golden State's franchise renewal on the settlement of the labor dispute....

The summary judgment entered for the city is reversed and the case is remanded for further proceedings consistent with this opinion.

It is so ordered.

Case Questions

1. Summarize the essential facts of the case.
2. Did the city's action add restrictions where Congress intended that none should exist?

CASE 4.9 | CHAMBER OF COMMERCE OF THE UNITED STATES V. BROWN
UNITED STATES SUPREME COURT, 128 U.S. 2408 (2008).

[Organizations whose members do business with the State of California, including the U.S. Chamber of Commerce, sued the State to enjoin enforcement of "Assembly Bill 1889" (AB 1889), which, among other things, prohibits employers that receive state grants of more than $10,000 in state program funds per year from using the funds "to assist, promote, or deter union organizing." The District Court granted the plaintiffs partial summary judgment, holding that the National Labor Relations Act (NLRA) preempts AB 1889 because it regulates employer speech about union organizing under circumstances in which Congress intended free debate. The Ninth Circuit reversed, concluding that Congress did not intend to preclude States from imposing such restrictions on the use of their own funds. The U.S. Supreme Court agreed to hear the case.]

STEVENS, J....

Congress' express protection of free debate forcefully buttresses the pre-emption analysis in this case. Under

Machinists, congressional intent to shield a zone of activity from regulation is usually found only "implicit[ly] in the structure of the Act," *Livadas v. Bradshaw*, 512 U.S. 107, 117, n. 11 (1994), drawing on the notion that "'[w]hat Congress left unregulated is as important as the regulations that it imposed,'" *Golden State Transit Corp. v. Los Angeles*, 493 U.S. 103, 110 (1989) (*Golden State II*). In the case of noncoercive speech, however, the protection is both implicit and explicit. Sections 8(a) and 8(b) demonstrate that when Congress has sought to put limits on advocacy for or against union organization, it has expressly set forth the mechanisms for doing so. Moreover, the amendment to § 7 calls attention to the right of employees to refuse to join unions, which implies an underlying right to receive information opposing unionization. Finally, the addition of § 8(c) expressly precludes regulation of speech about unionization "so long as the communications do not contain a 'threat of reprisal or force or promise of benefit.'" *Gissel Packing*, 395 U.S., at 618....

continued

In NLRA pre-emption cases, "'judicial concern has necessarily focused on the nature of the activities which the States have sought to regulate rather than on the method of regulation adopted.'"... ("Pre-emption analysis ... turns on the acutal content of [the State's] policy and its real effect on federal rights".).

... As the statute's preamble candidly acknowledges, the legislative purpose is not the efficient procurement of goods and services, but the furtherance of a labor policy. See 2000 Cal. Stats. ch. 872, § 1. Although a State has a legitimate proprietary interest in ensuring that state funds are spent in accordance with the purposes for which they are appropriated, this is not the objective of AB 1889. In contrast to a neutral affirmative requirement that funds be spent solely for the purposes of the relevant grant or program, AB 1889 imposes a targeted negative restriction on employer speech about unionization. Furthermore, the statute does not even apply this constraint uniformly. Instead of forbidding the use of state funds for all employer advocacy regarding unionization, AB 1889 permits use of state funds for *select* employer advocacy activities that promote unions. Specifically, the statute exempts expenses incurred in connection with, *inter alia*, giving unions access to the workplace, and voluntarily recognizing unions without a secret ballot election. §§ 16647(b), (d)...

The statute also imposes deterrent litigation risks. Significantly, AB 1889 authorizes not only the California Attorney General but also any private taxpayer—including, of course, a union in a dispute with an employer—to bring a civil action against suspected violators for "injunctive relief, damages, civil penalties, and other appropriate equitable relief."

§ 16645.8. Violators are liable to the State for three times the amount of state funds deemed spent on union organizing §§ 16645.2(d), 16645.7(d), 16645.8(a). Prevailing plaintiffs, and certain prevailing taxpayer intervenors, are entitled to recover attorney's fees and costs, § 16645.8(d), which may well dwarf the treble damages award. Consequently, a trivial violation of the statute could give rise to substantial liability....

... AB 1889's enforcement mechanisms put considerable pressure on an employer either to forgo his "free speech right to communicate his views to his employees," *Gissel Packing*, 395 U.S., at 617, or else to refuse the receipt of any state funds. In so doing, the statute impermissibly "predicat[es] benefits on refraining from conduct protected by federal labor law," *Livadas*, 512 U.S., at 116, and chills one side of "the robust debate which has been protected under the NLRA," *Letter Carriers*, 418 U.S., at 275....

[*Reversed and remanded.*]

Case Questions

1. What is the meaning of the term "noncoercive speech" widely referenced in the Court's opinion?

2. Preemption under the *Machinists* rule forbids both the NLRB and the states from regulating conduct that Congress intended "be unregulated and left to be controlled by the free play of economic forces." How does the *Machinist* rule apply to the present case?

3. Does AB 1889 impose an equal restriction on employer and union speech about unionization?

SECTION 30: MAJORITY BARGAINING RIGHTS

Section 7 of the National Labor Relations Act guarantees employees the right to form, join, or assist labor organizations; to bargain collectively through representatives of their own choosing; and to engage in other concerted activity for the purpose of collective bargaining or other mutual aid or protection. Section 7 also guarantees employees the right to refrain from all of these activities, except to the extent that such right may be affected by a union security agreement as authorized by Section 8(a)(3) of the Act. The right of a group of employees to select or reject a bargaining representative through the secret ballot procedures set forth in Section 9 of the Act is the very heart of the NLRA.

The Board has delegated most of its authority over representation cases to the regional directors, retaining a limited right to review their decisions. Regional directors have the authority to:

1. Decide whether a question concerning representation exits;
2. Determine appropriate bargaining units;
3. Direct and conduct elections;
4. Certify the results of elections;
5. Rule on challenged ballots and objections to the election.

In carrying out their responsibilities under the Act, regional directors, and the Board, when called upon to review regional directors' decisions, must resolve many difficult questions concerning freedom of speech and electioneering activity, management conduct, and union activities. Individual employees and factions are protected against discriminatory treatment. After determination of the majority's choice of a bargaining representative, all employees in the bargaining unit are subject to uniform conditions and terms agreed to by the employer and the union, as set forth in their collective bargaining agreement.

SECTION 31: THE APPROPRIATE BARGAINING UNIT

The NLRA authorizes the Board to select an appropriate unit so as to assure the fullest freedom of collective bargaining. The Act, however, includes many statutory mandates. Professional and nonprofessional workers may not be included in the same unit unless a majority of professionals first vote to be part of an overall unit. Separate craft units may not be found inappropriate by reason of prior certifications unless the craft majority so votes. Plant guards may not be included in a unit with other employees of the same employer.

The NLRB has broad discretion in determining an appropriate bargaining unit dispute. The common employment interests of workers, such as skill and training requirements, functional unity, and the history of bargaining and personnel policy, are a primary consideration.

Relevant to unit determinations are managerial and supervisory organizations and functions that, along with skill and similar functional considerations, may result in separating truck drivers or maintenance or custodial workers from a plantwide unit. On the basis of pertinent facts, technical employees with different group interests may be excluded from a unit of production and maintenance workers. Employees in a confidential capacity in the effecting of management-labor policies or those with supervisory responsibilities are excluded from any unit for collective bargaining.

The following guidelines have been applied to decide what employees will be grouped or whether, in the case of multiple-plant or store operations under unitary management, separate or combined employee units should be formed.

1. The physical location of production facilities is a factor. If the facilities are fairly close together, the Board has tended to favor a combined unit embracing workers in all plants.
2. A difference in the skill requirements of the work to be performed by employees usually leads to a separation. The routine worker and the skilled employee are

subjected to differing wage and working condition benefits and otherwise have little in common. At any rate, under the *Globe* doctrine, skilled employees must be given the right to vote on the question of a separate unit or a plantwide unit.[53]

3. The degree of ownership and managerial integration is also a factor in deciding whether employees should be grouped or separated for bargaining purposes. Are the facilities in question commonly owned? Would cessation of activity in one facility adversely affect performance in the others? Are managerial policies centrally formulated and uniformly applied to all facilities? Are conditions of employment essentially uniform among the several plants? Are employees frequently transferred and interchanged? If the answers are in the affirmative, the Board has favored a homogeneous unit.

4. The collective bargaining history of an employer has often led the Board to separate or combine bargaining units based on the employer's previous experience. If a particular employer has formerly enjoyed amicable relations with its employees under separate or combined units, such forms will generally be favored for present purposes.

5. The extent of organization is the final consideration entering into the Board's resolve to separate or combine for negotiation and representation purposes. The extent of organization is the degree to which employees in individual plants of multiple-plant companies have presently organized. Under the Wagner Act, the Board could decide that employees in Plant A were entitled to representation as a single unit even though the employees in Plants B and C had not, as yet, been sufficiently organized to call for an election. Some limitation is placed upon the Board's discretion in this regard by the 1947 NLRA. Section 9(c)(5) provides that "in determining whether a unit is appropriate ... the extent to which the employees have organized shall not be controlling." Thus, by legislative mandate, if other factors favor a multiple-plant unit, the Board may not base a plant unit decision upon a finding that the present extent of organization militates against a multiple-plant unit. This proviso does not outlaw consideration by the Board of organizational extent; it merely limits the *weight* the Board can accord it in deciding whether to separate or combine for appropriate unit purposes.

The Board engaged in rulemaking to resolve issues relating to appropriate bargaining units in the health care industry, establishing eight bargaining units that will be found appropriate at acute care hospitals. They are (1) all registered nurses, (2) all physicians, (3) all other professionals, (4) all technical employees, (5) all skilled maintenance employees, (6) all business office clerical employees, (7) all guards, and (8) all other nonprofessional employees. The *American Hospital Association v. NLRB*[54] decision affirmed the Board's authority to establish the units through its rulemaking authority.

The following two cases, *American District Telegraph* and *NLRB v. Hendricks County Rural Electric Membership Corp.*, illustrate situations where it might be appropriate to separate employees for bargaining purposes.

---

[53] Globe Machine and Stamping Co., 3 NLRB 294 (1937).

[54] 499 U.S. 606 (1991).

CASE 4.10	AMERICAN DISTRICT TELEGRAPH
	160 NLRB No. 82 (1966).

Employer, who is engaged in furnishing protective services by means of electric devices which it installs and maintains, employs several classifications of servicemen. Employer also operates a one-man division responsible for selling, installing, and repairing background music systems.

The union seeks to represent all of the above employees, as well as all porters. Employer contends that all of the servicemen are guards, that the background music director is a supervisor, and that these employees should consequently be excluded from any bargaining unit.

Of employer's several classifications of servicemen, only the S-2 group was specifically charged with duties related to enforcing rules to protect property or the safety of persons on customers' premises. This group was armed, wore uniforms, worked irregular hours, and was primarily responsible for detaining intruders apprehended in response to alarms....

The remaining classifications, S-1 and S-3, comprised servicemen whose duties principally involved installing and repairing the electric devices or monitoring signals therefrom.

Although the music director worked in a separate administrative office building and was on a separate payroll, he remained under the supervision of the District Manager who was responsible for the servicemen.

Although the union asserts that the S-2's are primarily mechanics and have only incidental duties with respect to apprehension of intruders, the stipulation of the parties states the reverse. In view of this, as well as the fact that they are uniformed and armed, the S-2's are guards within the meaning of the Act....

In contrast to the situation in *ADT Company*, 112 NLRB 80, there is no evidence that the regular S-1's have any responsibility other than prompt restoration of service through repairs. The instant situation being more akin to *American District Telegraph Co.*, 128 NLRB 345, the S-1's, accordingly, are not guards within the meaning of the Act.

Although the S-3's may well be an integral part of ADT's protection operation, there is nothing in the Act which requires that they be deemed guards on that basis alone. Since they have none of the characteristics of the servicemen previously determined to be guards, but merely monitor signals, they are includable in the non-guard unit.

The music director appears to have none of the statutory indicia of supervisory status, but does seem to have a community of interests with the regular S-1's and S-3's. Consequently, he shall also be included in the non-guard unit.

Case Questions

1. Whom did the Union seek to represent in one bargaining unit?
2. Discuss the differences between the various classifications of service persons.

CASE 4.11	NLRB v. HENDRICKS COUNTY RURAL ELECTRIC MEMBERSHIP CORP.
	SUPREME COURT OF THE UNITED STATES, 454 U.S. 170 (1981).

[Mary Weatherman was the personal secretary to the general manager and chief executive of Hendricks County Rural Electric Membership Corporation (Hendricks). She had been employed by the cooperative for nine years. In May 1977, she signed a petition seeking reinstatement of a close friend and fellow employee who had lost his arm in the course of employment with Hendricks and had been dismissed.

Several days later she was discharged. Weatherman filed an unfair labor practice charge with the NLRB, alleging that the discharge violated Section 8(a)(1) of the Act. Hendricks's defense was that Weatherman was denied the Act's protection because as a "confidential" secretary, she was implicitly excluded from the Act's definition of "employee" in Section 2(3). The administrative law judge (ALJ) rejected this argument. He noted that

continued

the Board's decisions had excluded from bargaining units only those "confidential employees ... who assist and act in a confidential capacity to persons who formulate, determine, and effectuate management policies in the field of labor relations." Applying this "labor-nexus" text, the ALJ found that Weatherman was not such a "confidential employee." He also determined that Hendricks had discharged Weatherman for activity—signing the petition—protected by Section 7 of the Act. The ALJ thus sustained Weatherman's unfair labor practice charge. The Board affirmed and ordered that Weatherman be reinstated with back pay. The U.S. Court of Appeals for the Second Circuit denied enforcement of the Board's order. The Supreme Court granted certiorari.]

BRENNAN, J....

Section 2(3) of the NLRA provides that the "term 'employee' shall include *any* employee..." (emphasis added), with certain stated exceptions such as "agricultural laborers," "supervisors" as defined in § 2 (11), and "independent contractors." Under a literal reading of the phrase "any employee," then, the workers in question are "employees." But for over 40 years, the NLRB, while rejecting any claim that the definition of "employee" in § 2(3) excludes confidential employees, has excluded from the collective bargaining units determined under the Act those confidential employees satisfying the Board's labor-nexus test. Respondents argue that contrary to the Board's practice, all employees who may have access to confidential business information are impliedly excluded from the definition of employee in § 2(3)....

In 1935 the Wagner Act became law. The Act's broad objectives were to "encourag[e] the practice and procedure of collective bargaining and ... protec [t] the exercise by workers of full freedom of association, self-organization, and designation of representatives of their own choosing, for the purpose of negotiating the terms and conditions of their employment or other mutual aid or protection." The employees covered by the Act were defined in § 2(3): "The term 'employee' shall include any employee ... but shall not include any individual employed as an agricultural laborer, or in the domestic service of any family or person at his home, or any individual employed by his parent or spouse." Although the Act's express exclusions did not embrace confidential employees, the Board was soon faced with the

argument that all individuals who had access to confidential information of their employers should be excluded, as a policy matter, from the definition of "employee." The Board rejected such an implied exclusion, finding it to have "no warrant under the Act." But in fulfilling its statutory obligation to determine appropriate bargaining units under § 9 of the Act, for which broad discretion has been vested in the Board, the Board adopted special treatment for the narrow group of employees with access to confidential, labor-relations information of the employer. The Board excluded these individuals from bargaining units composed of rank-and-file workers. The Board's rationale was that "management should not be required to handle labor relations matters through employees who are represented by the union with which the [c]ompany is required to deal and who in the normal performance of their duties may obtain advance information of the [c]ompany's position with regard to contract negotiations, the disposition of grievances, and other labor relations matters." *Hoover Co.*, 55 NLRB 1321, 1323 (1944)....

In 1946, in *Ford Motor Co.*, 66 NLRB 1317, 1322, the Board refined slightly the labor-nexus test because in its view the "definition [was] too inclusive and needlessly preclude[d] many employees from bargaining collectively together with other workers having common interests." Henceforth, the Board announced, it intended "to limit the term 'confidential' so as to embrace only those employees who assist and act in a confidential capacity to persons who exercise 'managerial' functions in the field of labor relations." This was the state of the law in 1947 when Congress amended the NLRA through the enactment of the Taft-Hartley Act....

The Court of Appeals, and the respondents here, rely on dictum [, a statement within an opinion which lacks the force of law,] in a footnote to *NLRB v. Bell Aerospace*, 416 U.S. 267 (1974), to suggest that the Eightieth Congress believed that all employees with access to confidential business information of their employers had been excluded from the Wagner Act by prior NLRB decisions and that Congress intended to freeze that interpretation of the Wagner Act into law. The *Bell Aerospace* dictum is:

> In 1946 in Ford Motor Co., 66 NLRB 1317, 1322, the Board had narrowed its definition of "confidential employees" to embrace only

continued

those who exercised "'managerial' functions in the field of labor relations." The discussion of "confidential employees" in both the House and Conference Committee Reports, however, unmistakably refers to that term as defined in the House bill, which was not limited just to those in "labor relations." Thus, although Congress may have misconstrued recent Board practice, it clearly thought that the Act did not cover "confidential employees" even under a broad definition of that term.

Obviously this statement was unnecessary to the determination whether *managerial* employees are excluded from the Act, which was the question decided in *Bell Aerospace*. In any event, the statement that Congress "clearly thought that the Act did not cover 'confidential employees,' even under a broad definition of that term," is error. The error is clear in light of our analysis ... of the legislative history of the Taft-Hartley Act pertinent to the question....

The Court's ultimate task here is, of course, to determine whether the Board's "labor-nexus" limitation on the class of confidential employees who, although within the definition of "employee" under § 2(3), may be denied the inclusion in bargaining units has "a reasonable basis in law." Clearly the NLRB's longstanding practice of excluding from bargaining units only those confidential employees satisfying the Board's labor-nexus test, rooted firmly in the Board's understanding of the nature of the collective bargaining process, and Congress' acceptance of that practice, fairly demonstrates that the Board's treatment of confidential employees does indeed have "a reasonable basis in law." ...

... In this court respondent Hendricks does not argue that Weatherman came within the labor-nexus test as formulated by the Board, but rather concedes that Weatherman did not have "confidential duties 'with respect to labor policies.'" Because there is therefore no dispute in this respect, and in any event no suggestion that the Board's finding regarding labor nexus was not supported by substantial evidence, we conclude that the Court of Appeals erred in holding that the record did not support the Board's determination that Weatherman was not

a confidential employee with a labor nexus.* We therefore reverse the judgment of the Court of Appeals in *Hendricks* insofar as enforcement of the Board's order was denied, and remand with direction to enter an order enforcing the Board's order.

It is so ordered.

POWELL, J. (joined by BURGER, C. J., and REHNQUIST and O'CONNOR, J. J.), dissenting ...

After today's decision, labor must accept into its rank confidential secretaries who are properly allied to management. And these confidential employees, who are privy to the daily affairs of management, who have access to confidential information, and who are essential to management's operation may be subjected to conflicts of loyalty when the essence of their working relationship requires undivided loyalty. The basic philosophy of the labor relations laws, the expressed intent of Congress, and the joint desire of labor and management for undivided loyalty all counsel against such a result.

Case Questions

1. Did Hendricks argue before the Supreme Court that all employees who may have access to confidential business information are impliedly excluded from the definition of "employee" in Section 2(3)?
2. What is the Board's labor-nexus test?
3. What is the Board's rationale for excluding from bargaining units certain confidential employees under its labor-nexus test?
4. Was Congress under the impression that the NLRA did not cover confidential employees when it passed the Taft-Hartley Act in 1947?

---

*We do not suggest that personal secretaries to the chief executive officers of corporations will ordinarily not constitute confidential employees. *Hendricks* is an unusual case, inasmuch as Weatherman's tasks were "deliberately restricted so as to preclude her from" gaining access to confidential information concerning labor relations. 236 NLRB 1616, 1619 (1978). Whether Hendricks imposed such constraints on Weatherman out of specific distrust or merely a sense of caution, it is unlikely that Weatherman's position mirrored that of executive secretaries in general.

SECTION 32: MULTIEMPLOYER BARGAINING UNITS

Multiemployer bargaining units exist in many industries and are strictly consensual arrangements between a union and a group of employers. Multiemployer bargaining presents an opportunity to both the employer group and the union to achieve informed and efficient bargaining and contract administration. Also, since all the employer members of the group will be obligated under their collective bargaining contract to pay the same wages and benefits to their employees and will be subject to the same contractual work rules, major competitive factors are removed between the employer members of the group. This is seen as an advantage by employers. Consistent wages, benefits, and work rules for employees working for different employers in the same industry and geographical area are sought-after union objectives.

All employer members of the group must stipulate that they intend to be bound by group rather than individual action. The union having representative status must also assent. The Board will not sanction the creation of a multiemployer unit over the objection of any party. Once the unit is formed, the multiemployer group has substantially the same bargaining responsibilities as any single employer under the Act.

The *Bonanno Linen Service v. NLRB* decision presented next deals with an employer's unilateral withdrawal from a multiemployer unit because of a bargaining impasse. Once consent has been given and negotiations have begun, neither an employer nor the union may withdraw without mutual consent absent "unusual circumstances."[55] The "unusual circumstances" exception has been limited to extreme situations, such as where the employer is subject to extreme financial pressures or the unit has dissipated so as no longer to be viable. In *NLRB v. D.A. Nolt, Inc.*, the Court of Appeals found that secret negotiations between the union and the multiemployer unit deprived Nolt of its right to withdraw prior to the commencement of negotiations.[56] In *Bonanno*, the Supreme Court upheld the Board's determination that a bargaining impasse is not an unusual circumstance justifying unilateral withdrawal from the unit.

CASE 4.12	BONANNO LINEN SERVICE V. NLRB SUPREME COURT OF THE UNITED STATES, 454 U.S. 404 (1982).

[Charles D. Bonanno Linen Service, Inc., was a member of the New England Linen Supply Association, a group of 10 employers formed to negotiate with Teamsters Local Union No. 25 as a multiemployer unit. On February 19, 1975, Bonanno authorized the Association's negotiating committee to represent it in the anticipated negotiations for a new contract. The Union and the Association held 10 bargaining sessions during March and April. On April 30, the negotiators agreed upon a proposed contract, but four days later the Union members rejected it. By May 15, the Union and the Association had reached an impasse over the method of compensation: the Union demanded that the drivers be paid on commission, while the

continued

---

[55] *Hass Electric, Inc., v. NLRB*, 299 F.3d 23 (1st Cir. 2002).

[56] 406 F.3d 200 (3d Cir. 2005).

Association insisted on continuing payment at an hourly rate. Several meetings failed to break the impasse, and on June 23, the union initiated a selective strike against Bonanno. In response, most of the Association members locked out their drivers. Despite sporadic meetings, the stalemate continued throughout the summer.

Bonanno hired permanent replacements for all of its striking drivers. On November 21, it notified the Association and the Union that it was "withdrawing" from the Association with respect to negotiations because of the ongoing impasse with Teamsters Local 25. Shortly thereafter the Association ended the lockout and continued multiemployer negotiations. Several negotiating sessions took place between December and April, without Bonanno participating. In the middle of April, the Union abandoned its demand for payment on commission and accepted the Association's offer of a revised hourly wage rate. With this development, the parties agreed on a new contract dated April 23, 1976, that was given retroactive effect to April 18, 1975. In a letter dated April 29, the Union informed Bonanno that because the Union had never consented to the withdrawal, it considered Bonanno to be bound by the settlement just reached.

The NLRB held that a bargaining impasse did not justify Bonanno's unilateral withdrawal from the multiemployer unit and that such an attempt was a violation of Sections 8(a)(5) and 8(a)(1) of the NLRA by refusing to execute the collective bargaining agreement later executed by the Union and the Association. The court of appeals enforced the Board's order, and the Supreme Court granted certiorari.]

WHITE, J....

I.

The standard for judicial review of the Board's decision in this case was established by *Labor Board v. Truck Drivers Union*, 353 U.S. 87, (1957) (*Buffalo Linen*). There the Union struck a single employer during negotiations with a multiemployer bargaining association. The other employers responded with a lockout. Negotiations continued, and an agreement was reached. The Union, claiming that the lockout violated its rights under §§ 7 and 8 of the Act, then filed charges with the Board. The Board rejected the claim, but the Court of Appeals held that the lockout was an unfair practice.

This Court in turn reversed. That the Act did not expressly authorize or deal with multiemployer units or with lockouts in that context was recognized. Nonetheless, multiemployer bargaining had "long antedated the Wagner Act" and had become more common as employers, in the course of complying with their duty to bargain under the Act, "sought through group bargaining to match increased union strength." Furthermore, at the time of the debates on the Taft-Hartley amendments, Congress had rejected a proposal to limit or outlaw multiemployer bargaining. The debates and their results offered "cogent evidence that in many industries multiemployer bargaining was a vital factor in the effectuation of the national policy of promoting labor peace through strengthened collective bargaining." Congress' refusal to intervene indicated that it intended to leave to the Board's specialized judgment the resolution of conflicts between union and employer rights that were bound to arise in multiemployer bargaining....

Thus, the Court of Appeals' rejection of the Board's justification of the lockout as an acceptable effort to maintain the integrity of the multiemployer unit and its refusal to accept the lockout as a legitimate response to the whipsaw strike had too narrowly confined the exercise of the Board's discretion.

Multiemployer bargaining has continued to be the preferred bargaining mechanism in many industries,[*] and as *Buffalo Linen* predicted, it has raised a variety of problems requiring resolution. One critical question concerns the rights of the union and the employers to terminate the multiemployer bargaining arrangement. Until 1958, the Board permitted both employers and the Union to abandon the unit even in the midst of bargaining. But in *Retail Associates, Inc.*, 120 NLRB 388, 41 LRRM 1502 (1958), the Board announced guidelines for withdrawal from multiemployer units. These rules, which reflect an increasing emphasis on the stability of multiemployer units, permit any party to withdraw prior to the date set for negotiation of a new contract or the date on which negotiations actually

---

[*]A recent survey of major collective bargaining agreements (those covering 1,000 or more employees) found that of 1,536 major agreements, 648 (42 percent) were multiemployer agreements and that 3,238,400 employees were covered by these agreements. U.S. Bureau of Labor Statistics, Dept. of Labor, Bull. No. 2065, Characteristics of Major Collective Bargaining Agreements—January 1, 1978, at 12, table 1.8 (1980).

continued

begin, provided that adequate notice is given. Once negotiations for a new contract have commenced, however, withdrawal is permitted only if there is "mutual consent" or "unusual circumstances" exist.

The Board's approach in *Retail Associates* has been accepted in the courts, as have its decisions that unusual circumstances will be found where an employer is subject to extreme financial pressures or where a bargaining unit has become substantially fragmented. But as yet there is no consensus as to whether an impasse in bargaining in a multiemployer unit is an unusual circumstance justifying unilateral withdrawal by the Union or by an employer. After equivocating for a time, the Board squarely held that an impasse is not such an unusual circumstance.

II.

We agree with the Board and with the Court of Appeals. The Board has recognized the voluntary nature of multiemployer bargaining. It neither forces employers into multiemployer units nor erects barriers to withdrawal prior to bargaining. At the same time, it has sought to further the utility of multiemployer bargaining as an instrument of labor peace by limiting the circumstances under which any party may unilaterally withdraw during negotiations. Thus, it has reiterated the view expressed in *Hi-Way Billboards* that an impasse is not sufficiently destructive of group bargaining to justify unilateral withdrawal. As a recurring feature in the bargaining process, impasse is only a temporary deadlock or hiatus in negotiations "which in almost all cases is eventually broken either through a change of mind or the application of economic

force." *Charles D. Bonanno Linen Service*, 243 NLRB 1093 (1979). Furthermore, an impasse may be "brought about intentionally by one or both parties as a device to further, rather than destroy, the bargaining process." Hence, "there is little warrant for regarding an impasse as a rupture of the bargaining relation which leaves the parties free to go their own ways." As the Board sees it, permitting withdrawal at impasse would as a practical matter undermine the utility of multiemployer bargaining.**

[Affirmed.]

Case Questions

1. State the Board's guidelines for withdrawal from multiemployer units as set forth in *Retail Associates*.

2. Is an impasse in bargaining in a multiemployer unit an unusual circumstance justifying unilateral withdrawal?

3. What is an impasse in bargaining?

**The Board explains that if withdrawal were permitted at impasse, the parties would bargain under the threat of withdrawal by any party who was not completely satisfied with the results of the negotiations. That is, parties could precipitate an impasse in order to escape any agreement less favorable than the one expected. In addition, it is precisely at and during impasse, when bargaining is temporarily replaced by economic warfare, that the need for a stable, predictable bargaining unit becomes acute so that the parties can weigh the costs and possible benefits of their conduct.

SECTION 33: CRAFT SEVERANCE

At the heart of labor-management relations is the bargaining unit. It is all-important that the bargaining unit be truly appropriate and not contain a mix of antagonistic interests or submerge the legitimate interests of a small group of employees in the interest of a larger group. The Board has the responsibility of determining which group of employees should be considered appropriate. In the *Mallinckrodt Chemical Works*[57] decision, the Board spelled out the policy guidelines that it would use in determining whether the severance of a bargaining

---

[57] 162 NLRB 387 (1966).

unit composed of the craft workers in a larger unit would be appropriate. The guidelines are summarized as follows:

1. The makeup of the proposed unit—whether it consists of a distinct and homogeneous group of skilled craft workers;
2. The history of collective bargaining of the employees involved;
3. The extent to which the employees in the proposed unit have established and maintained their separate identity during the period of inclusion in a broader unit;
4. The history and pattern of collective bargaining in the industry involved;
5. The degree of integration of the employer's production processes;
6. The qualifications of the union seeking to "carve out" a separate unit.

These Board guidelines are applicable not only to craft severance situations in organized plants but also to the initial formation of units in unorganized plants.[58]

SECTION 34: DETERMINING EMPLOYEES' CHOICE

Section 9(a) of the NLRA provides for union recognition and bargaining rights when questions regarding the majority representation status for an appropriate bargaining unit are resolved in favor of a union. The fundamental mandate of the NRLA is found in Section 9(a) stating:

> Representatives designated or selected for the purposes of collective bargaining by the majority of the employees in a unit appropriate for such purposes, shall be the exclusive representatives of all the employees in such unit for the purposes of collective bargaining in respect to rates of pay, wages, hours of employment or other conditions of employment.

The NLRB's function under Section 9 of the Act is to ascertain through its election procedures whether a majority of employees want a particular union to be their exclusive bargaining representative. The Board also conducts decertification proceedings that determine whether a certified or recognized union continues to represent a majority of the employees in a bargaining unit.[59]

RECOGNITION WITHOUT A BOARD ELECTION

An employer may voluntarily recognize a union without a Board election when the employer has no reasonable doubt as to its employees' preference for the union in question. The employer must act with due care in ascertaining the majority status of the union, however.[60] A **card check** majority is a legitimate means for establishing an employer's duty to bargain. In recent years, unions have sought to avoid Board-supervised election procedures for several reasons, including (1) delays that may occur between the filing of a representation petition and the actual Board

---

[58] E. I. duPont, 162 NLRB 413 (1966).

[59] Section 9(c).

[60] An employer commits an unfair labor practice in violation of Section 8(a)(2) of the Act should it recognize a minority union; Section 8(b)(1)(A) makes it an unfair labor practice for a union to coerce employees in the solicitation of employee card support.

election; (2) the employer's advantage of regular communication with employees while they are at work compared to the union's lack of access to employees; and (3) employer intimidation that may occur with a lack of effective Board remedies, such as a usual Board remedy for employer election misconduct being a rerun election with the posting of notices not to violate the Act in the future—after going through a year of litigation. Unions now seek to negotiate **card check agreements** along with **neutrality agreements** with employers to bypass NLRB elections. The language of a typical authorization card may state in relevant part:

> Desiring to become a member of the above Union of the International Brotherhood of Teamsters, Chauffeurs, Warehousemen and Helpers of America, I hereby make application for admission to membership. I hereby authorize you or your agents or representatives to act for me as collective bargaining agent on all matters pertaining to rates of pay, hours or any other condition of employment.[61]

A typical card check agreement may provide for recognition of a union after a designated neutral third party confirms that the union has obtained authorization cards from an agreed-upon percentage of the bargaining unit, such as a majority of eligible employees, or a set majority percentage ranging from 51 percent up to 65 percent. Most neutrality agreements are obtained by strong unions in highly unionized industries, such as the UAW in the auto industry, or by unions that deal with employers who deal directly with the public and are susceptible to union pressure from the likes of hotel and restaurant employee unions. Card check and/or neutrality agreements may be negotiated with compaines that have an existing bargaining relationship with a union, with the agreement to apply to new facilities that are opened or acquired in the future. A UAW neutrality agreement with ALCOA stated in part:

> The company agrees to a position of neutrality in the event that the Union seeks to represent any nonrepresented employees of the Aluminum Company of America. Neutrality means that the Company shall not comment negatively concerning the integrity or character of the Union or its officials. The Company's commitment to remain neutral shall cease if the Union, its agents, or its supporters comment negatively on the integrity or character of the Aluminum Company of America or its representatives.

RECOGNITION BAR DOCTRINE

In *Keller Plastics Eastern, Inc.*,[62] an employer's voluntary recognition of a union based on a showing of majority status—as opposed to certification after a Board election—barred a decertification petition or a rival union's petition for "a reasonable period of time." The *Keller Plastics* Board reasoned that when an employer voluntarily recognizes a union in good faith based on a showing of majority support, the parties are permitted a reasonable period to bargain for a first contract without challenge to the union's majority status. In *Dana Corp.*,[63] the Board

---

[61] This authorization card was used by the Teamsters in the landmark *NLRB v. Gissel Packing Co.* case, presented subsequently in this chapter.

[62] 157 NLRB 583 (1966).

[63] 351 NLRB No. 28 (Sept. 29, 2007).

majority modified this "recognition bar doctrine" and held that an employer's voluntary recognition of a union does not bar a decertification petition or rival union petition that is filed within 45 days of the notice of recognition. The Board majority expressed preference for the exercise of employee free choice in Board elections as opposed to reliance on authorization cards that are inferior to the election process.

The Board majority raised three points in this regard:

1. Unlike votes cast in privacy by Board secret election ballots, card signings are public actions and susceptible to group pressure exerted at the moment of choice. The election is held under the watchful eye of a neutral Board agent and observers from the parties. A card signing has none of these protections. There is good reason to question whether card signings in such circumstances accurately reflect employees' true choices concerning union representation....
2. Union card solicitation campaigns have been accompanied by misinformation or a lack of information about employees' representational options....
3. Like a political election, a Board election presents a clear picture of employee voter preference at a single moment....

Under the Board's new policy, an employee or a rival union has the right to file a petition during a 45-day period following the posting of an official NLRB notice that a union has been voluntarily recognized. The petition will be processed if it is supported by 30 percent of the bargaining unit.

The dissent states that nothing in the majority's decision justifies the radical departure of the well-settled, judicially approved *Keller Plastics* precedent, and it relegates voluntarily recognition to disfavored status. The dissent states in part:

> An employer has the right to refuse to voluntarily recognize a union and demand an election .... One important reason employers choose voluntary recognition is to avoid the time, expense, and disruption of an election. That rationale, however, is critically undermined by the majority's modifications. An employer has little incentive to recognize a union voluntarily if it knows that its decision is subject to second-guessing through a decertification petition. Furthermore, even if an employer does choose to recognize a union voluntarily, the majority's new window period leaves the parties' bargaining relationship open to attack by a minority of employees at the very outset of the relationship, when it is at its most vulnerable [point]....[64]

CERTIFICATION PROCEDURES

The Board's election procedures are initiated by the filing of a **representation petition** with the appropriate regional office of the NLRB. This petition may be filed by any individual or labor organization acting on behalf of a substantial number of employees. This petition must be supported by a showing that at least 30 percent of the employees involved want the union to be their bargaining representative or want to have an NLRB election to make such a determination.[65] This so-called showing of interest to the Board may be demonstrated by signed

---

[64] *Id.* slip op. p. 10.

[65] Section 9(c)(1)(B).

authorization cards or a signed petition. Unions commonly obtain authorization cards far in excess of the 30 percent figure because the chances of winning a representation election are slim when a union has been able to obtain authorization cards from only 30 percent of the employees.

Employees in a bargaining unit are limited to one valid election in a 12-month period.[66] A petition to seek an election when a valid election has been held within the previous 12 months is untimely.

Although most representation petitions are filed by unions, an employer may also file a petition when the employer is confronted with a demand that a union be recognized as the exclusive bargaining representative of the employees.[67] Thus, where a union asks for a meeting to negotiate an agreement or sets up a picket line demanding recognition, the employer may file a petition for an election.

The language of the Act does not provide any standards or procedures whereby a union may intervene in a representation case started by a rival union or an employer. If the intervening union submits some timely showing of interest "of any percentage" among the employees involved, the Board will allow that union to appear on the ballot in order to ensure full expression of employee choice and to prevent objection and delay by an excluded union.

After the representation petition is filed by a union at the regional office of the Board, the regional staff determines (1) whether the Board's jurisdictional standards (set forth in Section 26 of this book) have been met, (2) whether the required 30 percent showing of interest by employees has been met, and (3) whether the bargaining unit involved is appropriate. The regional staff then seeks to obtain an agreement of the parties to a "consent election." Two options exist. A **consent election agreement** provides for an election conducted by the regional office with final authority over any disputes vested in the regional director. A **stipulation for certification** also provides for a consent election to be conducted by the regional office, but final determination of any disputes is vested in the Board itself after the regional director has made interim recommendations. The election date is usually within 42 days of the filing of the petition. Employees are eligible to vote if they had employee status on the date of the election and were also employed in the appropriate bargaining unit at the end of the payroll period immediately preceding the date on which an election was directed by the Board or consented to by the parties. Economic strikers are allowed to vote in an election conducted within 12 months of the start of a strike.[68]

DECERTIFICATION PROCEDURES

Decertification proceedings challenge whether a certified or recognized union continues to represent a majority of the employees in the bargaining unit.

EMPLOYEE OPTIONS.   Section 9(c)(1)(A) provides that a decertification petition may be filed by employees. This petition, like a representation petition, must be

---

[66] Section 9(c)(3).

[67] Section 9(c)(1)(B).

[68] Section 9(c)(3).

supported by a 30 percent showing of the employees involved, signifying that they do not want the certified or recognized union to be their bargaining representative or want to have a Board election make such a determination. This showing is commonly accomplished by signatures on a petition.

A decertification petition may not be initiated by an employer, a supervisor, or another agent of the employer. Thus, if the regional staff's investigation of the petition shows that the employer or a supervisor initiated, circulated, or sponsored the employees who filed a decertification petition, the petition will be dismissed.[69] Once the decertification petition has been properly filed with the Board, the regular NLRB election rules apply and management may actively participate in the campaign to decertify the union.

The *Caterair International v. NLRB* decision, presented in this section, sets forth the extensive fact pattern evidencing that management exercised a pervasive influence in procuring employee signatures for a union decertification election. This conduct tainted the decertification petition and destroyed the company's basis for withholding recognition of the union and refusing to bargain with the union. The company had to recall, with partial back pay, the unfair-labor-practice strikers and terminate its replacement workers, wasting the company's economic and managerial resources and incurring significant legal costs. The company ultimately settled the dispute for $5 million.

During the year following certification, after a Board secret ballot election, a union has an irrebuttable presumption of a continuing majority status in the unit and no petition challenging the majority status of the union will be considered by the Board.[70] It is called a **certification year bar.**

EMPLOYER OPTIONS.   In dealing with an incumbent union requesting renewal of its collective bargaining contract, an employer who questions the union's continuing majority status may request a formal Board-supervised election, called an RM (Representation Management) election by the Board, based on the legislative history of Section 9(c)(1)(B) of the Act. However, to obtain such an RM election the employer must demonstrate that it had "objective reasonable doubt" about the majority status of the union.[71]

In the Board's *Levitz Furniture Company of the Pacific, Inc.,*[72] decision, a Board majority held that an employer may unilaterally (without a Board supervised election) withdraw recognition from an incumbent union only when it can prove that the union has actually lost the support of a majority of employees in the

---

[69] Maywood Plant of Grede Plastics, 235 NLRB 363 (1978), as modified in *NLRB v. Maywood Plant of Grede Plastics*, 628 F.2d 1 (D.C. Cir. 1980). But see *Connecticut Distributors, Inc., v. NLRB*, 681 F.2d 127 (2d Cir. 1982).

[70] *Ray Brooks v. NLRB*, 348 U.S. 96 (1954).

[71] In general see *Allentown Mack Sales and Service, Inc., v. NLRB*, 522 U.S. 359 (1988), where a 5–4 majority of the U.S. Supreme Court upheld the Board's "good faith reasonable doubt" test. A different 5–4 majority of the Court, however, determined that the Board failed to recognize several objective indicators that supported the employer's decision to conduct an independent poll of its workforce.

[72] See *Levitz Furniture Co. of the Pacific*, 333 NLRB 717 (2001). See also *MacDonald Partners, Inc.*, 342 NLRB No. 63 (2004).

bargaining unit. The Board's prior "good faith reasonable doubt" test was overruled as a basis for refusing to bargain. The Board majority reasoned that withdrawal of recognition in the absence of proof of actual majority loss undermined important policies by destroying bargaining relationships and depriving employees of their chosen representative.[73]

In *Parkwood Development Center, Inc., v. NLRB*, the Board determined that the employer violated Section 8(a)(5) of the NLRA by withdrawing recognition from the union without proving "actual loss" of majority support as required by *Levitz*.

CASE 4.13	CATERAIR INTERNATIONAL V. NLRB
	UNITED STATES COURT OF APPEALS, 22 F.3D 114 (D.C. CIR. 1994).

[Caterair is a company that furnishes meals to the airline industry. On March 11, 1991, Teamster Local 572 filed charges with the NLRB alleging that management solicitation of signatures for a decertification petition and management coercion of signatures were in violation of Sections 8(a)(1) and (3) of the NLRA. The Board issued a multicount complaint alleging that management solicitation had impermissibly tainted the decertification petition, thus invalidating Caterair's reliance, and that the resulting strike was motivated by Caterair's unfair labor practices.

Twenty-eight employees testified on behalf of the union before the ALJ, the majority of them relating either that managers had solicited their signatures or that they had witnessed managers talking to groups of employees and asking them to sign papers. None of the testifying employees had actually signed the petition. Four managers testified, denying that they had solicited employee signatures for the petition. At least one manager testified that he often carried around a clipboard and asked employees to sign work-related documents. The ALJ credited the employee-witnesses' testimony and discredited the conflicting managers' testimony, concluding that the managers had engaged in "widespread and conspicuous" solicitation of employees' signatures in violation of Section 8(a)(1) of the National Labor Relations Act. The ALJ determined that Caterair had violated Section 8(a)(5) of the Act by relying upon the tainted decertification petition as the basis for

withdrawing recognition of, and refusing to bargain with, the Union. The ALJ also concluded that the strike was motivated by Caterair's unfair labor practices, a conclusion Caterair does not now challenge. The ALJ ordered Caterair to cease and desist from interfering with its employees' rights under Section 7 of the National Labor Relations Act to form, join, or assist labor organizations of their own choosing. The ALJ also ordered Caterair to reinstate strikers to their former jobs and to provide back pay from the date of the Union's unconditional offer to return to work, October 3, 1991. Finally, the ALJ ordered Caterair to recognize and bargain with the Union upon its request as the collective bargaining representatives of employees in the unit. The Board adopted these findings and Caterair appealed.]

WALD, C. J....

In February 1991, Caterair employed roughly 750 unit employees and fifty-seven managers at the three facilities. Approximately 450 of those employees and thirty-nine managers worked at the largest of those three facilities ("Facility A"). Caterair employed about 275 unit employees and fourteen managers at the second facility ("Facility B"). The smallest facility employed only twenty-five unit employees and four managers ("Facility C"). As of February 1991, 403 unionized employees, or 54% of the unit, had authorized Caterair to deduct union dues and fees from their paychecks.

continued

---

[73] A third option exists for employers of conducting an internal poll of employees regarding continued support for a union. The employer, however, must demonstrate that it had a good faith reasonable doubt about the majority status of the union, and the polling must not be coercive in violation of Section 8(a)(1). The *Levitz Furniture* Board did not address polling in its decision. The restrictions applicable to polling under Section 8(a)(1) case law make polling an undesirable method of resolving questions about the majority status of a union.

In December 1990 and January 1991, three employees asked Caterair's human resources director how to decertify the Union. The company prepared fliers responsive to their inquiries describing the process by which employees could request their fellow employees to sign a decertification petition expressing disaffection with the Union and requesting that the Board hold an election. These fliers stated that the petition had to be filed with the Board between sixty and ninety days prior to the expiration of the contract, a period that would run between March 2 and March 31, 1991. They also indicated that the petition had to be signed by at least 30% of the unit employees. One document explained that if more than 50% of employees signed the petition, Caterair could lawfully refuse to negotiate with the Union. The human resources director provided these informational sheets to the three inquiring employees and made them available to others upon request.

On or around February 22, 1991, employee Xiomara Menendez and others prepared a decertification petition stating that signers "d[id] not want the Union" to represent them any longer. During a one-week period beginning February 22, Menendez and about eight other employees solicited signatures at Facility A. Employee Bonnie Metcalf and three other employees simultaneously sought signatures at Facility B.

The evidence, as credited by the ALJ, suggests that on or around February 22, several managers at both facilities began actively to solicit employees' signatures. Caterair's transportation manager at Facility A, Jose Castillo, called employee Luz Davalos at her desk to inquire whether she had "signed the paper to get rid of the Union." ... When Davalos replied that she did not know what Castillo was referring to, Castillo said he would "send somebody else later to talk to" her. Thirty minutes later, employee Dolores Vasquez visited Davalos at her desk and asked her to "sign the paper to get rid of the Union" and told her "not to be a dummy." Davalos refused to sign. Manager Castillo approached Davalos in the cafeteria two hours later, asking her whether someone had come by to talk to her already. She responded affirmatively and reiterated that she would not sign anything. Davalos told three other employees about her encounter with Manager Castillo....

During the same week, the production manager at Facility A, Alberto Pacheco, approached employee Rosa Rayas at her work area and inquired whether she had signed the petition "to get the Union out." ... When she said no, Manager Pacheco told her that if she did not sign, the Union would charge her "more than $200" in back dues.... He stated that the "Union was no good" because "the Union actually was a Mafia." ... Pacheco also told her that her signature was necessary because "they only needed a few more signatures to finish the amount of signatures that the Government requires to get the Union out." ... Rayas refused to sign.

On February 21 or 22, employee Carlos Sosa saw the sanitation manager at Facility A, Saul Monroy, talking to employees while holding a sheet of paper. Shortly thereafter, Monroy approached Sosa and asked him to sign a petition containing about nine signatures so that employees could "obtain better salaries, cheaper health program, and more days' vacation." ... Sosa was not able to get a good look at the petition, because Monroy had obscured the top of the page. Sosa refused to sign.

Manager Monroy solicited employee Jose Vasquez sometime between February 22 and 24 at the entrance to the dishwashing department. Monroy carried a clipboard and asked Vasquez to "sign the list." ... After Vasquez asked what the list was for, Monroy responded "that he was taking the signatures so that the Union will stay *in*." ... Vasquez testified that everyone at the company knew he was pro-Union. He stated that he had been forewarned by fellow employees that this was merely a maneuver on Monroy's part to get him to sign the decertification petition to *oust* the Union. Vasquez did not sign.

On or around February 26, Manager Monroy brought a clipboard to employee Alfred Mercado at his work area in the dishwashing department and asked him to sign a piece of paper. Monroy refused to tell Mercado what the piece of paper was for, although Mercado assumed it was the decertification petition that he had heard talk of around the workplace.... Mercado refused to sign.

Manager Monroy approached employee Victor Saldana in late February in the dishroom. He showed Saldana a clipboard on which he was collecting signatures, but obscured the actual petition under a white sheet of paper. Monroy asked Saldana if he would "sign to be able to get the Union out." ... Monroy told Saldana that signing would be "good" for him, and asked him "Why do you have to pay $15 per month and when they fire you, you're not going to get any help?" ... Saldana refused to sign and testified that he later told six or seven employees about the exchange.

continued

On February 26, the assistant manager at Facility B, Oscar Peralta, spoke with employee Israel Lopez in the cafeteria in the presence of employee Teresa Reveco and six or seven others. Peralta handed Lopez "a petition to get the Union out" and asked him to sign it. Tr. of February 4, 1992 Hearing (Testimony of Israel Lopez), at 108. Lopez observed a paper that was approximately three-fourths full of signatures. Explaining to Peralta that he was a Union Shop Steward, Lopez refused to sign. Lopez later witnessed Peralta soliciting the signature of employee Hector Hernandez. *See id.* at 112. Lopez heard Hernandez refuse to sign. Lopez told as many as twenty employees about his exchange with Manager Peralta.

Although Caterair vigorously disputes the conclusions of the ALJ drawn from such evidence, contending that the evidence does not sustain the ALJ's inference that managers solicited any actual signatures on the petition, the ALJ also credited the testimony of several employees that they saw managers talking to groups of employees and handing them sheets of paper to sign during this period....

By March 4, 1991, the decertification petition contained 428 employee signatures, representing 57% of the bargaining unit. Several employees filed the petition with the Board on that day so as to begin the process of official decertification. In a March 15 letter, the Union asked Caterair to bargain for a new contract. Caterair responded by letter of March 20 that it had a "good faith doubt" about the Union's majority status, citing the decertification petition supported by a majority of employees. Caterair refused to begin negotiations with the Union on a new contract.

After several employees discussed the possibility of striking over Caterair's refusal to bargain, the general manager of Facility A, Jose Ramirez, called employee Daniel Godoy into his office in early April. Ramirez told Godoy that he knew Godoy had been "agitating" among the employees in an effort to initiate a strike. Ramirez told Godoy that his actions were illegal and that he could be fired.... On May 22, the Union held an employee meeting at which the employees voted by written ballot to go on strike in response to Caterair's refusal to negotiate. The margin in favor of a strike was 318 to 6, that is, 42% of the total unit voted in favor of striking.

According to further testimony credited by the ALJ, management attempts to dissuade strikers continued. In late May, human resources director

Millie Bisono told employee Jerry Hayes that he would be fired if he joined the strike.... On May 31, labor relations director Roberto Velazquez had a conversation with employee Fulgencio Plascencia in which Velazquez stated that Caterair "did not want the Union" and that all striking employees would be "automatically fired." ... Velazquez told employee Castulo Flores the same thing the next day....

The strike began on June 3, 1991, and involved 289 striking employees, or 39% of the unit. Sixty-one of the striking employees had previously signed the decertification petition. Caterair began hiring permanent replacements for the strikers almost immediately. Caterair unilaterally granted a wage increase of 4–6% to employees on August 31, 1991, during the pendency of the strike.

The Union ended the strike in early October and made an unconditional offer by letter of October 3, 1991, to have the strikers return to work. The letter called the strike an unfair labor practice strike and asked the company to dismiss replacement employees and reinstate the striking workforce. Caterair refused to reinstate any of the strikers and denied that the strike had been motivated by Caterair's unfair labor practices.

[The Court of Appeals held that the evidence warranted a finding that the employer's management exercised a pervasive influence in procuring employee signatures for the "union decertification petition." The court enforced the Board's order, in part, to the extent that it required Caterair to cease and desist from committing unfair labor practices. Under the cease-and-desist order Caterair is required to bargain with the Union. Company employees remain free under the cease-and-desist order to petition for decertification.]

Case Questions

1. Was it proper for the director of human resources to prepare fliers responsive to employee inquiries as to how to decertify the union?

2. Evaluate the effects of the adverse decisions of the NLRB and the court of appeals on Caterair.

3. Advise the human resources director what she should have done after preparing the flier on how to decertify the union.

CASE 4.14	PARKWOOD DEVELOPMENT CENTER, INC., V. NLRB
	UNITED STATES COURT OF APPEALS 521 F.3D 404 (D.C. CIR. 2008).

[The employer, Parkwood, runs a home for the developmentally disabled in Valdosta, Georgia. Until 2003, the employees who worked at the home were represented by the United Food and Commerical Workers Union. Parkwood and the union were parties to a collective bargaining agreement ("CBA") that was scheduled to expire March 8, 2003.

On December 2, 2002, Parkwood was presented with a petition, signed by a majority of its employees at the home, announcing that they no longer wanted to be represented by the union. Believing that the union no longer enjoyed majority support, Parkwood told the union of the petition that same day and declared it would cease dealing with the union upon expiration of the CBA. From that moment onward, Parkwood refused to negotiate with the union for a successor agreement.

On March 7, 2003, the day before expiration of the CBA, the union presented to Parkwood a counterpetition, also signed by a majority of the employees at the home, declaring a renewed desire for union representation and "revoke[ing], rescind[ing] and cancel[ling]" the earlier petition. Parkwood was unmoved by this eleventh-hour show of support for the union. When the CBA expired the next day, Parkwood refused to recognize the union or bargain with it for a new agreement.

The union filed charges with the Board alleging, among other things, that Parkwood violated § 8(a)(5) of the NLRA by unlawfully withdrawing recognition from the union. The Board found that the employer violated Section 8(a)(5) of the Act and imposed an affirmative bargaining order, and Parkwood appealed.]

GRIFFITH, C.J....

Parkwood contends that the Board should have measured majority support on December 2, 2002, the date the company announced its intent to withdraw recognition in response to the employees' petition, rather than on March 8, 2003....

A.

Prior to *Levitz*, an employer could withdraw recognition from a union on the basis of good-faith doubt as to the union's continued support among a majority of employees in the bargaining unit. See *Levitz*, 333 N.L.R.B. at 717 (citing *Celanese Corp.*, N.L.R.B 664 (1951)). In applying this rule, the Board measured

good-faith doubt at the time the employer announced it.... Noting that the Board cannot ignore its own precedent, *see Manhattan Ctr, Studios, Inc. v. NLRB*, 452 F.3d 813, 816 (D.C. Cir. 2006), Parkwood argues that the Board was bound by pre-*Levitz* precedent to measure actual loss of majority support in the same way it once measured good-faith doubt, namely, on the day evidence of actual loss first came to light.

This argument fails to account for *Levitz*, which explicitly overruled *Celanese* and removed good-faith doubt as a sufficient basis for withdrawing recognition from a union. 333 N.L.R.B. at 717. *Levitz* changed *what* the Board measures in scrutinizing a withdrawal of recognition, shifting from good-faith doubt to actual loss of majority support. Implicit in this decision is a corresponding change in *how* the Board will take its measurements. The Board's pre-*Levitz* decisions never addressed the issue presented by the facts in this case, so there was no binding precedent on this point from which it could depart. That the Board was not bound by its precedent to choose the earlier measuring point is apparent from our recent decision in *Highlands Hospital Corp. v. NLRB*, 508 F.3d 28 (D.C. Cir. 2007). In *Highlands*, we approved the Board's decision to consider post-petition employee conduct in determining whether there was an actual loss of majority support. *Id.* at 31–32. We could not have so held if the Board's precedent required it to measure actual loss in the same way it had once measured good-faith doubt...

B.

In *Abbey Medical*, the Board described the employer's power to effect " 'an anticipatory withdrawal of recognition' in relation to a future contract," which allows an employer to honor an existing CBA but question the union's right to bargin for a new agreement upon its expiration. 264 N.L.R.B. at 969. To withdraw anticipatorily, an employer must "demonstrate that, on the date of withdrawal ... the union in fact had lost its majority status, or [that the] withdrawal was predicated on a reasonable doubt based on objective considerations of the union's majority status." *Id.* To avoid semantic confusion, anticipatory withdrawal must be distinguished from withdrawl of recognition. Anticipatory withdrawal occurs prior to expiration of a CBA and does not obviate the employer's obligations under the existing agreement.

continued

Withdrawal of recognition occurs after expiration of a CBA, at which time the employer is free of contractual obligation.

Parkwood took full advantage of *Abbey Medical*. During the period that began with the employees' petition and ended with their counter-petition, Parkwood lawfully declined to bargain with the Union for a new CBA. But nothing in *Abbey Medical* permitted Parkwood to ignore subsequent indicators of majority support in deciding whether to withdraw recognition....

We deny Parkwood's petition for review and grant the Board's cross-application to enforce its order.

So ordered.

Case Questions

1. Is "good faith doubt" a sufficient basis for an employer to withdraw recognition from a union?

2. What action should Parkwood have taken in view of the conflicting petitions, the first one expressing the position that a majority of employees did not want to be represented by the union and a subsequent petition expressing a majority support for the union?

SECTION 35: REPRESENTATION ELECTIONS

Under the NLRA, the regional staff conducts representation elections by consent of the parties or by order of the Board. Such concerns as time and place, standards and rules of conduct, eligibility to vote, use of observers, electioneering, and handling of challenges are settled by agreement or by ruling of the Board agent if no agreement seems possible. The time, standards of conduct, electioneering rules, and other details are designed to ensure the voters the opportunity to determine the wishes of the majority by a free and unimpeded expression of individual choice.

The first question is the bargaining unit or the arrangements to allow craft workers or professionals to help decide the unit by their votes. The next issue, eligibility to vote, depends upon the status of each employee on the payroll at some date prior to and also on the election date. An employee must be on the active payroll during the eligibility period and must also be working for the employer at the time of the election. Employees who are on leave, temporarily laid off, or on vacation may vote if they are present at the polling place.

An economic striker who has been replaced is eligible to vote in any election held within 12 months of the commencement of the strike, under Section 9(c)(3) of the Act. Replacements of economic strikers are considered eligible to vote as permanent employees, provided that they were employed on both the eligibility date and the election date. Unfair-labor-practice strikers are entitled to vote regardless of the 12-month statutory restriction; replacements for these strikers are not. In order to be certified as bargaining agent, a labor union or an individual candidate must receive a majority of the valid votes cast in the appropriate unit.

In representation elections involving two or more unions, the requirement of majority choice for certification may cause the necessity of a runoff election when a majority of those voting reject the "no union" option, while no one union received a majority vote. Section 9(c) of the amended NLRA states: "In any election where none of the choices on the ballot receives a majority, a runoff shall be conducted, the ballot providing for a selection between the two choices receiving the largest and second largest number of valid votes cast in the election."

An employer may challenge the result of an election by filing objections to the conduct of the balloting or to violations of the rules. If sustained, the objections may cause the invalidation of the election, the remedying of irregularities, and a new vote with the notice of invalidation sometimes stating why the first election was held void.

SECTION 36: ELECTION CONDUCT AND FREE SPEECH

The Board has promulgated preelection rules (sometimes referred to as "Board rules") restricting the parties in their electioneering activities so that the election proceedings can best determine the true desires of employees. Section 8(a)(1) of the National Labor Relations Act prohibits employer interference or coercion, and Section 8(c) of the Act prohibits employer statements that contain threats of reprisal or promises of benefits. A distinction is made between conduct that violates Board rules and conduct that violates the Act. The importance of the distinction is based primarily on the remedies available to the Board. A violation of a Board rule may result in the limited remedy of setting aside the election and rerunning it. A violation amounting to an unfair labor practice may also result in the posting of notice that an unfair labor practice has been committed and that the employer will no longer engage in such conduct and in the setting aside of the election and the ordering of a new election. However, in extreme cases involving unfair labor practices, where the employer's conduct was so pervasive as to render a fair rerun election unlikely and the union previously had an authorization card majority, the employer may be required to bargain without a rerun election. An example of a violation of Board rules that is not an unfair labor practice would be the failure of an employer to provide a timely list of names and addresses of employees eligible to vote. Examples of election conduct that are unfair labor practices in violation of Section 8(a)(1) are threats to close the plant or discharge union sympathizers or threats to discontinue benefits such as coffee breaks, wash-up time, or employee discounts.

PREELECTION RULES

The Board has developed a body of rules that impose restrictions on the preelection activities of the parties. The Board prohibits all electioneering activities at polling places.[74] The Board, in its *Peerless Plywood* decision,[75] formulated its "24-hour rule," which prohibits both unions and employers from delivering speeches to captive audiences within 24 hours of an election. The obvious rationale for such a rule is to preserve free elections and prevent any party from obtaining undue advantage. In its *Excelsior Underwear*[76] decision, the Board promulgated a rule requiring an employer to provide a list of names and addresses of all employees eligible to vote in a representation election. The

---

[74] Alliance Ware, Inc., 92 NLRB 55 (1950), and Michelm, Inc., 170 NLRB 46 (1968).

[75] Peerless Plywood Co., 107 NLRB 427 (1953).

[76] Excelsior Underwear, Inc., 156 NLRB 1236 (1966). The rule was accepted by the Supreme Court in *NLRB v. Wyman-Gordan Co.*, 394 U.S. 759 (1969).

so-called *Excelsior List* must be filed with the regional director within seven days after an election has been directed or agreed upon. This list is then made available to the union or unions seeking to represent the employees. In *Woodman's Food Markets, Inc.*,[77] the Board held that in determining whether an employer has substantially complied with its obligation under the *Excelsior* rule, it will continue to consider the percentage of omissions from the voter eligibility list; it will consider other factors as well, including whether the number of omissions is determinative and whether it equals or exceeds the number of additional votes needed by the union to prevail in the election. It will also consider the employer's explanation for the omissions. The Board noted that its *Excelsior* policy was designed to enhance the availability of information and arguments both for and against union representation to employees so that they might render a more informed judgment at the ballot box. In the Board's *Merchant's Transfer Co.*[78] decision, where the Union lost an election by two votes and the *Excelsior* list provided by the employer contained 13 incorrect addresses out of 58 employees, the hearing officer found that the employer acted in a "grossly negligent manner" in assembling the list. The election was set aside, and a rerun election ordered.

Violation of the previous rules and other rules promulgated by the Board is grounds for setting aside an election even if the conduct does not amount to an unfair labor practice. Conduct that is an unfair labor practice under the Act is also viewed as a violation of the Board's election rules.[79]

EMPLOYER FREE SPEECH AND SECTION 8(C)

Section 8(c) states that "the expressing of any views, argument, or opinion ... shall not constitute or be evidence of an unfair labor practice ... if such expression contains no threat of reprisal or force or promise of benefit."

The Supreme Court, in the *NLRB v. Gissel Packing Co., Inc.*, case, reported in this section, considered the question of whether certain specific statements made by an employer to its employees constituted an election-voiding threat of reprisal and thus fell outside the protection of the First Amendment and Section 8(c) of the Act. In *Gissel*, the Court established guidelines for employer preelection statements and predictions concerning the effect of unionization on a company. An employer is free to state only what the employer reasonably believes will be the likely economic consequences of unionization that are outside the employer's control.

However, as set forth in *Chamber of Commerce of the United States v. Brown*, the U.S. Supreme Court referenced the statement in *Gissel* by the Court that Section 8(c) "... merely implements the First Amendment," but the *Chamber of Commerce* Court pointed out that the enactment of Section 8(c) also manifested a

---

[77] 332 NLRB No. 48 (2000).

[78] 330 NLRB 1165 (2000).

[79] Dal-Tex Optical Co., 137 NLRB 1782 (1962).

congressional intent to encourage free debate on issues dividing labor and management[80]. In the *Chamber of Commerce v. Brown* decision, the Court found that a California statute prohibiting employers that receive state grants or funds of more than $10,000 per year from using any portion of these funds "to assist, promote, or deter union organizing" was preempted by the NLRA under the *Machinists v. Wisconsin Employment Relations Commission* rule. Section 7 and Section 8(a), Section 8(b), and Section 8(c) protect **noncoercive speech** by employers, employees, and unions.

Just as the free speech proviso of Section 8(c) of the Act will not protect an employer whose statements are found to be a threat of reprisal and a violation of Section 8(a)(1), so also a promise of benefit by an employer who times the promise to influence a representation election also violates Section 8(a)(1). This is known as the *Exchange Parts* rule.[81] In *Hineline's Meat Plant, Inc.*,[82] the Board set aside an election where the employer announced a new profit-sharing plan to employees 11 days before the election. Relying on the *Exchange Parts* rule, the Board found that since the announcement could have been delayed until after the election, it was possible that the company had timed the announcement to influence the employees' vote. Consequently, the Board found a violation of Section 8(a)(1) and set aside the election.

No-Solicitation Rules

While Section 7 of the Act gives employees the statutory right to self-organization, employers have the undisputed prerogative to make rules to maintain discipline in their establishments. *Republic Aviation Corp. v. NLRB*,[83] is the seminal case balancing those interests with respect to oral solicitation in the workplace. The employer in *Republic Aviation* maintained a rule prohibiting solicitation anywhere on company property and discharged an employee for soliciting for the union during nonworking time. The Board adopted a presumption that restricting oral solicitation on nonworking time was unlawful, absent special circumstances. The Supreme Court affirmed the Board's finding that the employer's rule and its enforcement violated Section 8(a)(1). Although the solicitation occurred on the employer's property, the Court found insufficient justification to allow the employer to prohibit it. Generally speaking, employers may prohibit union solicitation by employees during work periods. During nonworking time, however, employers may prohibit activity and communication only if legitimate efficiency and safety reasons exist and if the prohibitions are not manifestly intended to impede employees' exercise of their rights under Section 7. In the *Armstrong Tire* case, the Board stated that "[t]he

---

[80] The *Chamber of Commerce v. Brown* decision is presented in Section 29 of this chapter. Note that the underpinnings of the *Chamber of Commerce* decision is built on the *Gissel* precedent, yet the tone of *Chamber of Commerce* is more expansive, "favoring uninhibited, robust and wide-open debate in labor disputes."

[81] *NLRB v. Exchange Parts Co.*, 375 U.S. 405 (1964).

[82] Hineline's Meat Plant, Inc., 193 NLRB 135 (1971).

[83] 324 U.S. 793 (1945).

burden rests upon an employer to establish that safety conditions actually require an invasion of the normal exercise by his employees of self-organization rights during nonworking time."[84]

DISTRIBUTION OF LITERATURE. In *Eastex v. NLRB*,[85] the Supreme Court held that employees have a right under the "mutual aid or protection" language of Section 7 of the NLRA to distribute a newsletter in nonworking areas of the plant during nonworking time. The newsletter in *Eastex* set forth the union's views on right-to-work laws and on a presidential veto of a minimum wage bill. The Court found that the employees were already rightfully on the employer's property, so it was up to the company to show that its management interests would be prejudiced by distribution of the newsletter to which it objected. The Court found that the company had made no such showing. The Court stated that any incremental intrusion on the company's property rights from the distribution would be minimal.

E-MAIL AND SECTION 7. The Labor Board's *Register-Guard*[86] decision involves a case of first impression before the agency. Both the majority and the dissenting opinions are discussed since appellate review may well ultimately establish the applicable precedent. The Eugene Newspaper Guild represents some 150 employees of the *Register-Guard*, a newspaper in Eugene, Oregon. The employer had a written policy that prohibited use of company-owned communication systems, including e-mail, for "non-job-related solicitations." The union alleged that the policy and its enforcement against the union president for sending three union-related e-mails was a violation of the NLRA. In a 3-2 decision, the Board majority found that absent discrimination against the union, employees have no statutory right to use company-owned e-mail for Section 7 communications regarding union business. The ALJ determined that since the employer had permitted personal use of e-mails for a wide variety of nonbusiness purposes, it could not validly prohibit e-mails dealing with Section 7 subjects. The Board majority, however, fashioned a new policy on what constitutes discriminatory enforcement by adopting the Seventh Circuit Court of Appeals' analysis that unlawful discrimination consists of disparate treatment of communications of a similar character.[87] Thus, although the employer permitted personal e-mail solicitations, the employer had not permitted e-mails soliciting support for any outside organization. The Board viewed the union as an outside organization and determined that the employer lawfully enforced its policy regarding two of three e-mails sent by the union president that solicited support for the union.

The dissent asserted that ownership does not give the employer the absolute right to exclude Section 7 e-mails—"that where an employer has given employees access to

---

[84] Armstrong Tire and Rubber Co., 119 NLRB 382 (1958).

[85] 437 U.S. 556 (1978).

[86] The Guard Publishing Co. dba The Register-Guard 351 NLRB No. 70 (2007).

[87] See *Fleming Companies v. NLRB* 349 F.3d 968 (7th Cir. 2003); *Guardian Industries Corp. v. NLRB*, 49 F.3d 317 (7th Cir. 1999).

e-mail for regular, routine use in their work, banning all nonwork-related 'solicitations' is presumptively unlawful absent special circumstances." The dissent objects to the Board majority's overruling bedrock Board precedent about the meaning of discrimination as applied to Section 7 rights, asserting that the NLRA does not merely give employees the right to be free from discrimination based on union activity, but also gives them the affirmative right to engage in concerted group action for mutual benefit and protection.

NECESSITY OF NONDISCRIMINATORY ENFORCEMENT OF RULES. Employers have every right to establish work rules to properly conduct their businesses. In *St. Margaret Mercy Healthcare Centers v. NLRB*,[88] a hospital rule forbids solicitation in patient care areas. Under this rule, a nurse received a disciplinary sanction for engaging in union solicitation at a nurses' station. The Board found that "employee solicitation at the nurses' station was a common practice, and included a wide variety of solicitations, including solicitations for Girl Scout cookies, March of Dimes, United Way, Secretary's Day and Boss' Day, and 'going away' parties, and other social occasions, and the hawking of 'beach balm' a product 'created by a registered nurse to control bikini line irritation.'" Moreover, management was aware of these solicitations and even participated in some of them. The Court of Appeals for the Seventh Circuit considered that with the exception of the balm, the solicitations were charitable or social rather than commercial. The court rhetorically asked, "But what difference can that make? The hospital's rule forbids solicitations in patient care areas, period, yet the only solicitations in patient care areas, period, yet the only solicitations that have ever drawn a rebuke from management are ... those in support of union activities." The court found that substantial evidence of record supported the finding that the hospital discriminated against the nurse in violation of Section 8(a)(3) for engaging in union solicitation at the nurses' station.

CASE 4.15	NLRB v. GISSEL PACKING CO., INC. SUPREME COURT OF THE UNITED STATES, 395 U.S. 575 (1969).

[Partial statement of facts relating to the Sinclair Company, one of the four cases considered by the Court in its *Gissel* opinion.

After the president of the company learned of the union's organizational drive, he made speeches, issued pamphlets and leaflets, and sent letters conveying the message that the union was strike-happy and that a vote for the union could result in the plant's being shut down. Moreover, he informed the employees

that because of their age, they could have difficulty finding other employment. The union lost the election, and the union filed charges before the Board. The Board found that under the "totality of the circumstances," the company's activities amounted to a violation of Section 8(a)(1). Because the company's activities tended to foreclose the possibility of holding a fair new election, it ordered the company to bargain as requested with the union. The Court of Appeals for

continued

---

[88] 519 F.3d 373 (2208).

the First Circuit enforced the Board's order, and the company appealed to the Supreme Court, arguing that the statements made by the employer were protected by the First Amendment and that a bargaining order was inappropriate.]

WARREN, C. J....

...We consider finally petitioner Sinclair's First Amendment challenge to the holding of the Board and the Court of Appeals for the First Circuit. At the outset we note that the question raised here most often arises in the context of a nascent union organizational drive, where employers must be careful in waging their antiunion campaign. As to conduct generally, the ... gradations of unfair labor practices, with their varying consequences, create certain hazards for employers when they seek to estimate or resist unionization efforts. But so long as the differences involve conduct easily avoided, such as discharge, surveillance, and coercive interrogation, we do not think that employers can complain that the distinctions are unreasonably difficult to follow. Where an employer's antiunion efforts consist of speech alone, however, the difficulties raised are not so easily resolved. The Board has eliminated some of the problem areas by no longer requiring an employer to show affirmative reasons for insisting on an election and by permitting him to make reasonable inquiries. We do not decide, of course, whether these allowances are mandatory. But we do note that an employer's free speech right to communicate his views to his employees is firmly established and cannot be infringed by a union, or the Board. Thus, Section 8(c) merely implements the First Amendment by requiring that the expression of "any views, argument or opinion" shall not be "evidence of an unfair labor practice," so long as such expression contains "no threat of reprisal or force or promise of benefit" in violation of Section 8(a)(1). Section 8(a)(1), in turn, prohibits interference, restraint or coercion of employees in the exercise of their right to self-organization.

Any assessment of the precise scope of employer expression, of course, must be made in the context of its labor relations setting. Thus, an employer's rights cannot outweigh the equal rights of the employees to associate freely, as those rights are embodied in Section 7 and protected by Section 8 (a)(1) and the proviso to Section 8(c). And any balancing of those rights must take into account the economic dependence of the employees on their employers, and the necessary tendency of the former, because of that relationship, to pick up intended implications of the latter that might be more readily dismissed by a more disinterested ear. Stating these obvious principles is but another way of recognizing that what is basically at stake is the establishment of a non-permanent, limited relationship between the employer, his economically dependent employee and his union agent, not the election of legislators or the enactment of legislation whereby that relationship is ultimately defined and where the independent voter may be freer to listen more objectively and employers as a class freer to talk. Compare *New York Times Co. v. Sullivan*, 376 U.S. 254 (1964).

Within this framework, we must reject the Company's challenge to the decision below and the findings of the Board on which it was based. The standards used below for evaluating the impact of an employer's statements are not seriously questioned by petitioner and we see no need to tamper with them here. Thus, an employer is free to communicate to his employees any of his general views about unionism or any of his specific views about a particular union, so long as the communications do not contain a "threat of reprisal or force or promise of benefit." He may even make a prediction as to the precise effects he believes unionization will have on his company. In such a case, however, the prediction must be carefully phrased on the basis of objective fact to convey an employer's belief as to demonstrably probable consequences beyond his control or to convey a management decision already arrived at to close the plant in case of unionization. See *Textile Workers v. Darlington Mfg. Co.*, 380 U.S. 263, 274, n. 20 (1965). If there is any implication that an employer may or may not take action solely on his own initiative for reasons unrelated to economic necessities and known only to him, the statement is no longer a reasonable prediction based on available facts but a threat of retaliation based on misrepresentation and coercion, and as such without the protection of the First Amendment. We therefore agree with the court below that "conveyance of the employer's belief, even though sincere, that unionization will or may result in the closing of the plant is not a statement of fact unless, which is most improbable, the eventuality of closing is capable of proof." 397 F.2d, at 160. As stated elsewhere, an

continued

employer is free only to tell "what he reasonably believes will be the likely economic consequences of unionization that are outside his control," and not "threats of economic reprisal to be taken solely on his own volition." *NLRB v. River Togs, Inc.*, 382 F.2d 198, 202 (C.A. 2d Cir. 1967).

Equally valid was the finding by the court and the Board that petitioner's statements and communications were not cast as a prediction of "demonstrable economic consequences," 397 F.2d 157, 160, but rather as a threat of retaliatory action. The Board found that petitioner's speeches, pamphlets, leaflets, and letters conveyed the following message: That the company was in a precarious financial condition; that the "strike-happy" union would in all likelihood have to obtain its potentially unreasonable demands by striking, the probable result of which would be a plant shutdown, as the past history of labor relations in the area indicated; and that the employees in such a case would have great difficulty finding employment elsewhere. In carrying out its duty to focus on the question "What did the speaker intend and the listener understand," Cox, Law and the National Labor Policy 44 (1960), the Board could reasonably conclude that the intended and understood import of that message was not to predict that unionization would inevitably cause the plant to close but to threaten to throw employees out of work regardless of the economic realities. In this connection, we need go no further than to point out (1) that petitioner had no support for its basic assumption that the union, which had not yet even presented any demands, would have to strike to be heard, and that it admitted at the hearing that it had no basis for attributing other plant closings in the area to unionism; and (2) that the Board has often found that employees, who are particularly sensitive to rumors of plant closings, take such hints as coercive threats rather than honest forecasts.

Petitioner argues that the line between so-called permitted predictions and proscribed threats is too vague to stand up under traditional First Amendment analysis and that the Board's discretion to curtail free speech rights is correspondingly too uncontrolled. It is true that a reviewing court must recognize the Board's competence in the first instance to judge the impact of utterances made in the context of the employer-employee relationship, see *NLRB v. Virginia Electric & Power Co.*, 314 U.S. 469, 479 (1941). But an employer, who has control over that relationship and therefore knows it best, cannot be heard to complain that he is without an adequate guide for his behavior. He can easily make his views known without engaging in "brinkmanship" when it becomes all too easy to "overstep and tumble over the brink," *Wausau Steel Corp. v. NLRB*, 377 F.2d 369, 372 (C.A. 7th Cir. 1967). At the least he can avoid coercive speech simply by avoiding conscious overstatements he has reason to believe will mislead his employees.

[Affirmed.]

Case Questions

1. State the basis of Sinclair's challenge to the Board's decision.
2. Discuss the free speech differences between a union representation election and the election of a legislator or the enactment of legislation.
3. What standards did the Supreme Court set forth for evaluating employer statements to employees during an organizational campaign?

SECTION 37: ELECTION PROPAGANDA AND MISREPRESENTATIONS

During a representation election campaign, it is inevitable that statements will be made that are factually inaccurate. It is up to the parties to correct the misstatements, half-truths, allegations, or inaccuracies of their opponent. Ultimately, it is up to the employees to evaluate the statements made by employer representatives and union advocates in making their decision to vote for or against union representation. Under certain circumstances where one party does not have an opportunity to reply, a campaign misrepresentation could very well affect the outcome of an election. The Board has been called upon by the losing parties to set aside such elections and to order rerun elections on the basis of violation of its electioneering rules, even though the conduct did not amount to an unfair labor practice. The Board's changing position on this matter is discussed later on.

In *Bausch & Lomb, Inc., v. NLRB*,[89] the Second Circuit Court affirmed the NLRB's invalidation of a representation election in which an employer mailed a letter to employees two days before the election, informing them that the union local at another company plant had recently agreed to a contract without a Christmas bonus provision. The letter failed to mention that the union had obtained a wage increase and extended sick pay in exchange for dropping its Christmas bonus demand. The union lost the election. In rejecting the company's allegation that the Board had abused its discretion in invalidating the election, the court noted that the test set forth in the Board's *Hollywood Ceramics*[90] case had been satisfied. First, the misstatement was of a material fact; the employees would obviously be concerned with such a valuable right. Second, the union did not have time to reply; the letter was received just two days prior to the election. Third, the company was in a position to have "special knowledge" of the facts. Finally, the employees lacked independent knowledge with which to evaluate the statement.

In 1977, after 15 years' experience under *Hollywood Ceramics*, a majority of the Board decided in *Shopping Kart Food Market, Inc.*,[91] over a vigorous dissent, to overrule *Hollywood Ceramics*. The Board stated in *Shopping Kart* that it would "no longer probe into the truth or falsity of the parties' campaign statements" but would instead recognize and rely on employees "as mature individuals who are capable of recognizing campaign propaganda for what it is and discounting it." The majority also held that the Board would intervene "in instances where a party has engaged in such deceptive campaign practices as improperly involving the Board and its processes, or the use of forged documents which render the voters unable to recognize the propaganda for what it is." Twenty months after its *Shopping Kart* decision, a Board majority reversed *Shopping Kart* and reinstated its *Hollywood Ceramics* rule.[92] Reversing itself again four years later, a Board majority reverted to the *Shopping Kart* policy in its *Midland National Life Insurance* decision.[93] As presently applied, the *Shopping Kart–Midland National Life* rule applies to misrepresentations by either side. And, as is evident from the *North American Directory* decision, presented in this section, the rule is now court-approved.

---

[89] 451 F.2d 873 (2d Cir. 1971).

[90] 140 NLRB 221 (1962).

[91] 228 NLRB 1311 (1977).

[92] General Knit of California, Inc., 239 NLRB 619 (1978).

[93] 263 NLRB 387 (1982).

CASE 4.16	NORTH AMERICAN DIRECTORY CORP. V. NLRB
	U.S. COURT OF APPEALS, THIRD CIRCUIT, 939 F.2D 74 (1991).

[North American Directory Corporation prints telephone directories at its plant in Hazleton, Pennsylvania. In 1989, the Graphic Communications Union, Local 735-S, sought to organize the Hazleton plant's 64 production and maintenance employees and filed its petition with the Board on June 14, 1989. North American and Local 735-S executed a standard stipulated election agreement calling for an election on July 20, 1989, and each side began distributing campaign literature. North American printed flyers on company memorandum letterhead that bore the company's distinctive printing press logo. They were mailed in company envelopes and concluded with the exhortation "Vote Union No on July 20th." On the day before the election, North American workers received a plain envelope containing a memo on what appeared to be paper copied from a company memorandum letterhead. The memo contrasted an alleged attempt to reduce the salary of second-shift workers by 25 cents with the amount of North American Vice President David Pilcher's weekly salary, a fact not generally known to the workers. It concluded with the amended exhortation "Vote Union—on July 20th." The existence of this mailing was not made known to North American until the afternoon of July 19, 1989. Since the election was scheduled to begin at the first- and third-shift change at 6:30 the following morning, less than 24 hours later, North American did not attempt to speak to its employees about the matter (because of the *Peerless Plywood* rule). The election resulted in a vote of 38 for and 26 against the union.

North American filed an objection to the election results, alleging that the forged letter confused voters as to whether there had been a last-minute change in North American's policy. The Board's regional director conducted an investigation. The regional director recommended that North American's objection to the certification of the union be overruled and that the local be certified as the bargaining representative. The Board issued its decision certifying Local 735-S. Following certification, Local 735-S demanded recognition by North American, but the company refused to bargain with the local because of the forged pre-election mailing. Local 735-S filed an unfair labor practice charge, upon which the Board's General Counsel filed a complaint and motion for summary judgment. The Board granted the motion for summary

judgment and issued a cease-and-desist order on June 25, 1990. North American petitioned for review of the cease-and-desist order, and the Board applied for enforcement.]

SMITH, B., D. J....

The Board [in *Midland National Life Insurance*] reviewed its regulation of campaign propaganda from the adoption of the National Labor Relations Act through *Gummed Products Company*, 112 NLRB 1092 (1955), in which the Board set aside an election for misrepresentation of facts, the announcement of the "laboratory conditions" test of *Hollywood Ceramics Company, Inc.*, 140 NLRB 221, 224 (1962), that test's overruling in *Shopping Kart Food Market, Inc.*, 228 NLRB 1311 (1977), and its revival by *General Knit of California*, 239 NLRB 619 (1978). Concluding that the cost of attempting to police the content of pre-election propaganda exceeded any benefit realized in the dissemination of more accurate information to voting workers, the Board announced its current policy:

> In sum, we rule today that we will no longer probe into the truth or falsity of the parties' campaign statements, and that we will not set elections aside on the basis of misleading campaign statements. We will, however, intervene in cases where a party has used forged documents which render the voters unable to recognize propaganda for what it is. Thus, we will set an election aside not because of the substance of the representation, but because of the deceptive manner in which it was made, a manner which renders employees unable to evaluate the forgery for what it is.

Later in the same year, the Board announced that it would treat misrepresentations of Board actions or positions the same as other propaganda. Affiliated Midwest Hospital, Inc., d/b/a Riveredge Hospital, 264 NLRB 1094, 1095 (1982). In the following year, the Board held that it would apply *Midland Life Insurance* to objections alleging misrepresentations of law. Metropolitan Life Insurance Co., 266 NLRB 507 (1983).

The regional director found that the forged memorandum was readily identifiable as having been prepared by someone other than North American and as

continued

containing pro-union propaganda, and concluded that an employee could not reasonably believe that North American had changed its opinion at the last minute and was now asking them to vote for Local 735-S. The Board subsequently adopted his findings and conclusions. This Court must uphold the Board's findings if supported by substantial evidence. *Molded Acoustical Products v. NLRB*, 815 F.2d 934, 937 (3d Cir.), cert. denied, 484 U.S. 925, 108 S.Ct. 286, 98 L. Ed.2d 247 (1987). The test applied by the Board and endorsed by this Circuit to evaluate claims of improper preelection influence is an objective one, and requires reference in this matter only to the allegedly misleading information.

North American's campaign literature bore a distinctive letterhead with "North American Directory Corporation" and a printing press logo across the top. The company memorandum form was headed by boldface lines stating "Memo To:"; "From:"; "Subject:"; and "Date:"; the page ended with an outline boldface postscript "VOTE UNION NO ON JULY 20TH." The forged memorandum bore the same letterhead, but the "From" line is omitted and the text of the memo is in a different type-face which appears to be the product of someone's home computer printer. The postscript is altered, apparently by applying correction fluid to the "NO" in "VOTE UNION NO ON JULY 20TH" and drawing a dash where "NO" had appeared on the original. The forgery is, in short, an amateur production which appears as such even to the observer unfamiliar with North American's election propaganda. Additionally, the regional director quite properly observed that there was no reason for the employees to believe that North American, after campaigning vigorously against the Union, had reversed its stance on the eve of the election. The Board's conclusion that it was recognizable as partisan propaganda is supported by substantial evidence....

The Order is enforced.

Case Questions

1. What is the rationale for the *Shopping Kart–Midland National Life Insurance* decision?
2. Under the Board's *Shopping Kart–Midland* decision, will the Board intervene in all cases involving forged documents?
3. Were the voters in the *North American* case unable to recognize the forged memorandum as propaganda?

SECTION 38: BARGAINING RIGHTS BASED ON AUTHORIZATION CARDS

In *NLRB v. Gissel Packing Co.*, portions of which are reported in this section, the Supreme Court set forth the law regarding Board bargaining orders based on authorization cards. The bargaining order remedy is utilized by the Board in the following type of situation. A union conducts an organizational campaign and obtains authorization cards from a majority of the employees in an appropriate bargaining unit.[94] On the basis of these cards, the union demands recognition, which is refused on the grounds that the cards are inherently unreliable indicators of employee desires. The employer then conducts an antiunion campaign, during which the employer commits unfair labor practices. Following the union loss and the filing of charges with the Board, the Board will set aside the election if it finds that the unfair labor practices had the effect of undermining the union's majority. The Board will then either order a rerun election or, if the employer's conduct was so pervasive as to render a fair rerun election unlikely, certify the union on the basis of its authorization card majority and order the employer to bargain with it.

---

[94] The *Gissel* decision included four separate cases that were heard before the Supreme Court at the same time. The cards used in all four campaigns unambiguously authorized the union to represent the signing employee for collective bargaining purposes; there was no reference to elections.

Certain employer violations are consistently regarded by the Board and the courts as highly coercive of employees' Section 7 rights. These violations, sometimes referred to as *hallmark violations*, will support the issuance of a *Gissel* bargaining order unless some significant mitigating circumstance exists.[95] Hallmark violations include plant closures or threats of plant closures, unlawful discharge of union adherents, threats of job loss, or granting of significant benefits to employees.[96]

In its *Mercedes Benz of Orland Park*[97] decision, the Board restated the basis for evaluating the appropriateness of a *Gissel* bargaining order, stating:

> In *Gissel*, the Supreme Court "identified two types of employer misconduct that may warrant the imposition of a bargaining order; outrageous and pervasive unfair labor practices (category I) and less extraordinary cases marked by less pervasive practices which nonetheless still have the tendency to undermine majority strength and impede the election processes (category II)." The Court found that, in determining a remedy in category II cases, the Board can take into consideration the extensiveness of an employer's unfair labor practices in determining whether the "possibility of erasing the effects of past practices and ensuring a fair election ... by the use of traditional remedies, though present, is slight and employee sentiments once expressed by authorization cards would, on balance, be better protected by a bargaining order."

In *Gissel*, the Supreme Court left undetermined the issue of whether it would be appropriate to find a Section 8(a)(5) violation and grant a bargaining order in cases where the employer has knowledge, on the basis of cards or other circumstantial evidence, that the union has a valid majority and the employer refuses to recognize the union but refrains from committing independent unfair labor practices. In *Summer & Co. (Linden Lumber) v. NLRB*,[98] the Supreme Court addressed this issue, holding that absent independent unfair labor practices, a bargaining order will not be issued unless the employer and the union have agreed on an alternate means of resolving the issue of majority status. Where such an agreement has not been undertaken, the Court ruled that the burden of invoking the Board's election procedures is on the union seeking to represent the employer's workers. The policy to be served by the *Linden* rule is that of encouraging voluntarism while ensuring that the preferred route of a secret election is available to those who do not find any alternate route more acceptable.

CASE 4.17	**NLRB v. Gissel Packing Co., Inc.** Supreme Court of the United States, 395 U.S. 575 (1969).

[The portion of this case dealing with Sinclair's First Amendment challenges to the holding of the Board and the Court of Appeals for the First Circuit (Case No. 585) is reported in Section 36 of this chapter.]

WARREN, C. J....
These cases involve the extent of an employer's duty under the National Labor Relations Act to recognize a union that bases its claim to representative status

continued

---

[95] Michael's Painting, Inc., 377 NLRB No. 140 (2002); *NLRB v. Center Construction Co.* 482 F.3d 425 (6th Cir. 2007).

[96] See General Counsel Memorandum 99-8, November 10, 1999.

[97] 333 NLRB No. 127 slip op. at 1 (2001).

[98] 419 U.S. 301 (1974).

solely on the possession of union authorization cards, and the steps an employer may take, particularly with regard to the scope and content of statements he may make, in legitimately resisting such card-based recognition. The specific questions facing us here are whether the duty to bargain can arise without a Board election under the Act; whether union authorization cards, if obtained from a majority of employees without misrepresentation or coercion, are reliable enough generally to provide a valid, alternate route to majority status; whether a bargaining order is an appropriate and authorized remedy where an employer rejects a card majority while at the same time committing unfair labor practices that tend to undermine the union's majority and make a fair election an unlikely possibility; and whether certain specific statements made by an employer to his employees constituted such an election-voiding unfair labor practice and thus fell outside the protection of the First Amendment and Section 8(c) of the Act. For reasons given below, we answer each of these questions in the affirmative....

In each of the cases from the Fourth Circuit, the course of action followed by the Union and the employer and the Board's response were similar. In each case, the Union waged an organizational campaign, obtained authorization cards from a majority of employees in the appropriate bargaining unit, and then, on the basis of the cards, demanded recognition by the employer. All three employers refused to bargain on the ground that authorization cards were inherently unreliable indicators of employee desires; and they either embarked on, or continued, vigorous antiunion campaigns that gave rise to numerous unfair labor practice charges. In *Gissel*, where the employer's campaign began almost at the outset of the Union's organizational drive, the Union (petitioner in No. 691) did not seek an election, but instead filed three unfair labor practice charges against the employer, for refusing to bargain in violation of Section 8(a)(5), for coercion and intimidation of employees in violation of Section 8(a)(1), and for discharge of Union adherents in violation of Section 8(a)(3).* In *Heck's*, an election sought by the Union was never held because of nearly identical unfair labor practice charges later filed by the Union as a result of the employer's antiunion campaign, initiated after the Union's recognition demand. And in *General Steel*, an election petitioned for by the Union and won by the employer was set aside by the Board because of the unfair labor practices committed by the employer in the preelection period.

In each case, the Board's primary response was an order to bargain directed at the employers, despite the absence of an election in *Gissel* and *Heck's* and the employer's victory in *General Steel*. More specifically, the Board found in each case that (1) the Union had obtained valid authorization cards from a majority of the employees in the bargaining unit and was thus entitled to represent the employees for collective bargaining purposes; and (2) that the employer's refusal to bargain with the Union in violation of Section 8(a)(5) was motivated not by a "good faith" doubt of the Union's majority status, but by a desire to gain time to dissipate that status. The Board based its conclusion as to the lack of good faith doubt on the fact that the employers had committed substantial unfair labor practices during their antiunion campaign efforts to resist recognition. Thus, the Board found that all three employers had engaged in restraint and coercion of employees in violation of Section 8(a)(1)— in *Gissel*, for coercively interrogating employees about Union activities, threatening them with discharge and promising them benefits; in *Heck's*, for coercively interrogating employees, threatening reprisals, creating the appearance of surveillance, and offering benefits for opposing the Union; and in *General Steel*, for coercive interrogation and threats of reprisals, including discharge. In addition, the Board found that the employers in *Gissel* and *Heck's* had wrongfully discharged employees for engaging in Union activities in violation of Section 8(a)(3). And, because the employers had rejected the card-based bargaining demand in bad faith, the Board found that all three

---

*At the outset of the Union campaign, the Company vice president informed two employees, later discharged, that if they were caught talking to Union men, "you ... things will go." Subsequently, the union presented oral and written demands for recognition, claiming possession of authorized cards from 31 of the 47 employees in the appropriate unit. Rejecting the bargaining demand, the Company began to interrogate employees as to their Union activities; to promise them better benefits than the Union could offer; and to warn them that if the "union got in, [the vice president] would just take his money and let the union run the place," that the Union was not going to get in, and that it would have to "fight" the Company first. Further, when the Company learned of an impending Union meeting, it arranged, so the Board later found, to have an agent present to report the identity of the Union's adherents. On the first day following the meeting, the vice president told the two employees referred to above that he knew they had gone to the meeting and that their work hours were henceforth reduced to half a day. Three hours later, the two employees were discharged.

continued

had refused to recognize the Unions in violation of Section 8(a)(5).

Only in *General Steel* was there any objection by an employer to the validity of the cards and the manner in which they had been solicited, and the doubt raised by the evidence was resolved in the following manner. The customary approach of the Board in dealing with allegations of misrepresentation by the Union and misunderstanding by the employees of the purpose for which the cards were being solicited has been set out in *Cumberland Shoe Corp.*, 144 NLRB 1268 (1963), and reaffirmed in *Levi Strauss & Co.*, 172 NLRB No. 57 ... (1968). Under the *Cumberland Shoe* doctrine, if the card itself is unambiguous (i.e., states on its face that the signer authorizes the Union to represent the employee for collective bargaining purposes and not to seek an election), it will be counted unless it is proved that the employee was told that the card was to be used *solely* for the purpose of obtaining an election. ...

The first issue facing us is whether a union can establish a bargaining obligation by means other than a Board election and whether the validity of alternate routes to majority status, such as cards, was affected by the 1947 Taft-Hartley amendments. The most commonly traveled route for a union to obtain recognition as the exclusive bargaining representative of an unorganized group of employees is through the Board's election and certification procedures under Section 9(c) of the Act; it is also, from the Board's point of view, the preferred route. A union is not limited to a Board election, however, ...

In short, we hold that the 1947 amendments did not restrict an employer's duty to bargain under Section 8(a)(5) solely to those unions whose representative status is certified after a Board election.

We next consider the question whether authorization cards are such inherently unreliable indicators of employee desires that whatever the validity of other alternate routes to representative status, the cards themselves may never be used to determine a union's majority and to support an order to bargain. ...

That the cards, though admittedly inferior to the election process, can adequately reflect employee sentiment when that process has been impeded, needs no extended discussion, for the employers' contentions cannot withstand close examination. The employers argue that their employees cannot make an informed choice because the card drive will be over before the employer has had a chance to present his side of the unionization issues. Normally, however, the union will inform the employer of its organization drive early in order to subject the employer to the unfair labor practice provisions of the Act; the union must be able to show the employer's awareness of the drive in order to prove that his contemporaneous conduct constituted unfair labor practices on which a bargaining order can be based if the drive is ultimately successful. ...

The employers' second complaint, that the cards are too often obtained through misrepresentation and coercion, must be rejected also in view of the Board's present rules for controlling card solicitation, which we view as adequate to the task where the cards involved state their purpose clearly and unambiguously on their face. We would be closing our eyes to obvious difficulties, of course, if we did not recognize that there have been abuses, primarily arising out of misrepresentations by union organizers as to whether the effect of signing a card was to designate the union to represent the employee for collective bargaining purposes or merely to authorize it to seek an election to determine that issue. And we would be equally blind if we did not recognize that various courts of appeals and commentators have differed significantly as to the Board's *Cumberland Shoe* doctrine to cure such abuses.

In resolving the conflict among the circuits in favor of approving the Board's *Cumberland* rule, we think it sufficient to point out that employees should be bound by the clear language of what they sign unless that language is deliberately and clearly canceled by a union adherent with words calculated to direct the signer to disregard and forget the language above his signature. There is nothing inconsistent in handing an employee a card that says the signer authorizes the union to represent him and then telling him that the card will probably be used first to get an election. Elections have been, after all, and will continue to be, held in the vast majority of cases; the union will still have to have the signatures of 30 percent of the employees when an employer rejects a bargaining demand and insists that the union seek an election. We cannot agree with the employers here that employees as a rule are too unsophisticated to be bound by what they sign unless expressly told that their act of signing represents something else. In addition to approving the use of cards, of course, Congress has expressly authorized reliance on employee signatures alone in other areas of labor

continued

relations, even where criminal sanctions hang in the balance, and we should not act hastily in disregarding congressional judgments that employees can be counted on to take responsibility for their acts.…

Remaining before us is the propriety of a bargaining order as a remedy for a Section 8(a)(5) refusal to bargain where an employer has committed independent unfair labor practices which have made the holding of a fair election unlikely or which have in fact undermined a union's majority and caused an election to be set aside. We have long held that the Board is not limited to a cease and desist order in such cases, but has the authority to issue a bargaining order without first requiring the union to show that it has been able to maintain its majority status.… And we have held that the Board has the same authority even where it is clear that the union, which once had possession of cards from a majority of the employees, represents only a minority when the bargaining order is entered. *Franks Bros. Co. v. NLRB*, 321 U.S. 702 (1944). We see no reason now to withdraw this authority from the Board. If the Board could enter only a cease and desist order and direct an election or a rerun, it would in effect be rewarding the employer and allowing him "to profit from [his] own wrongful refusal to bargain." *Frank Bros. supra*, at 704, while at the same time severely curtailing the employees' right freely to determine whether they desire a representative. The employer could continue to delay or disrupt the election process and put off indefinitely his obligation to bargain,** and any election held under these circumstances would not be likely to demonstrate the employees' true, undistorted desires.…***

… If the Board finds that the possibility of erasing the effects of past practices and of ensuring a fair election (or a fair rerun) by the use of traditional remedies, though present, is slight and that employee sentiment once expressed through cards would, on balance, be better protected by a bargaining order, then such an order should issue.…

We emphasize that under the Board's remedial power there is still a third category of minor or less extensive unfair labor practices, which, because of their minimal impact on the election machinery, will not sustain a bargaining order. There is, the Board says, no *per se* rule that the commission of any unfair practice will automatically result in a Section 8(a)(5) violation and the issuance of an order to bargain.…

It is so ordered.

Case Questions

1. Summarize the *Cumberland Shoe* doctrine.
2. What did the Supreme Court say about the Board's *Cumberland* doctrine?
3. Did the Supreme Court hold that the Taft-Hartley amendments limited an employer's duty to bargain under Section 8(a)(5) solely to those unions whose representative status was certified after a Board election?
4. Under *Gissel*, when may the Board issue a bargaining remedy?

**The Board indicates here that its records show that in the period between January and June 1968, the median time between the filing of an unfair labor practice charge and a Board decision in a contested case was 388 days. But the employer can do more than just put off his bargaining obligation by seeking to slow down the Board's administrative processes. He can also affect the outcome of a rerun election by delaying tactics, for figures show that the longer the time between a tainted election and a rerun, the lesser are the union's chances of reversing the outcome of the first election.

***A study of 20,153 elections held between 1960 and 1962 shows that in over two-thirds of the cases, the party who caused the election to be set aside won in the rerun election. See Pollitt, NLRB Rerun Elections: A Study, 41 N.C.L. Rev. 209, 212 (1963).

SECTION 39: REMEDIAL POWERS

A complete treatment of all remedy possibilities is beyond the scope of this section. Orders against employer and union unfair labor practices are tailored to rectify the varied and sometimes unique misconduct in individual cases. The number of possibilities is great. Under Section 9 of the NLRA, the Board has authority to issue appropriate orders to remedy a broad range of violations concerning representation matters. For example, in the previous section, the *Gissel* bargaining order remedy was established.

TEMPORARY REMEDIES

Under Section 10(j) of the Act, the Board has the discretionary authority to seek injunctive relief in a federal district court in unfair labor practice cases. Section 10(j) remedies are ordinarily used against alleged employer unfair labor practices to preserve the status quo while the parties are awaiting the resolution of their basic dispute by the Board.[99] Section 10(l) *requires* the Board to seek temporary injunctive relief against unions in matters such as secondary boycotts, hot cargo agreements, recognitional picketing, and jurisdictional disputes. Section 10(k) frees federal district courts from the restriction of the Norris-LaGuardia Act in the preceding situations. It is important to remember that Section 10(j) and (l) injunctions are temporary and can be utilized only while charges are being processed by the Board.

In *Silverman v. Major League Baseball PRC, Inc.*,[100] the Regional Director for Region 2 of the NLRB, Daniel Silverman, sought and obtained a Section 10(j) temporary injunction against major league baseball club owners, ordering the clubs to abide by the terms of the expired collective bargaining agreement until a new agreement was reached or an impasse occurred. The injunction cleared the way for the end of the baseball players' 234-day strike in 1995–96. The court of appeals decision, upholding the issuance of the injunction, is presented in this section.

FINAL REMEDIES

Under Section 10(a), the Board is given the broad responsibility "to prevent any person from engaging in any unfair labor practice." The Board has the authority under 10(b) to investigate charges, issue complaints, and order hearings. Under Section 10(c), if the Board determines on the preponderance of the testimony taken at a Board hearing that a person has engaged, or is engaging, in an unfair labor practice, the Board will state its findings of fact and issue an order requiring such a person to "cease and desist from such unfair labor practice, and take such affirmative action, including reinstatement of employees with or without back pay, as will effectuate the policies of this Act." If a person should choose not to comply with the Board's order, the Board may petition an appropriate U.S. Court of Appeals for enforcement of its order under Section 10(e). Similarly, any person aggrieved by an order of the Board may file a petition for review of the order with the U.S. Court of Appeals without waiting for the Board to seek enforcement.

SELECTED BOARD ORDERS

In the *Phelps Dodge* case, the U.S. Supreme Court held that the Board has the power under Section 10(c) of the NLRA to order an employer to make whole any employees who have suffered loss of earnings because of the employer's discrimination in violation of Section 8(a)(3) of the Act.[101] The usual order in union activity discrimination cases includes reinstatement of the wronged employees with back

---

[99] See *McLeod v. General Electric Co.*, 366 F.2d 847 (1966).

[100] 67 F.2d 1054 (2d Cir. 1995).

[101] *Phelps Dodge Corp. v. NLRB*, 313 U.S. 177 (1941).

pay and a further requirement that the employer post a notice that it will not engage in further discriminatory activity and will take the affirmative action ordered by the Board. A wronged employee does have an obligation to mitigate damages by seeking other suitable employment. In *Reserve Supply Corp. and NLRB*,[102] the U.S. Court of Appeals sustained a Board order requiring an employer to pay 6 percent interest on the back pay amount owed an employee. In *Florida Steel Corp. and United Steelworkers of America*,[103] the Board dropped its 15-year application of a 6 percent back pay interest rate and adopted the adjusted prime rate used by the Internal Revenue Service to set interest on the underpayment or overpayment of federal taxes.

The usual remedy for Section 8(a)(5) refusal-to-bargain violations is a cease-and-desist order from failing to bargain and an affirmative order to bargain collectively about wages, hours, and working conditions at the request of the appropriate union. The Board may not order a party to agree to specific contractual items, however. In the *H. K. Porter* decision, presented in this section, the Supreme Court denied enforcement of an order that would have compelled the employer to agree to a checkoff of union dues.

Usually the remedy for Section 8(b)(1)(A) and (B) cases of union restraint or coercion is a cease-and-desist order and the posting of a notice of compliance by the union.

In the *Radio Officers*[104] case, the Supreme Court held that the Board may issue a back-pay order against a union for causing an employer to discriminate against an employee in violation of Section 8(b)(2). When both a union and an employer are charged, the usual remedy is an order holding both liable, reinstatement with back pay, and a posting of suitable notices.

Violations of Section 8(b)(4), which prohibits unions from engaging in strikes or boycotts to accomplish certain purposes, are temporarily remedied by Section 10(l) mandatory injunctions as previously mentioned. Final determinations by the Board may include cease-and-desist orders and posting of appropriate notices.

REMEDIES AVAILABLE TO UNDOCUMENTED ALIENS

The Supreme Court held that illegal aliens are employees within the meaning of Section 2(3) of the Act in *Sure-Tan, Inc., v. NLRB*.[105] The Court also held that the employer's retaliatory notification to the Immigration and Naturalization Service after illegal alien employees voted for a union constituted a constructive

---

[102] 317 F.2d 785 (1963).

[103] 231 NLRB 651 (1977).

[104] *Radio Officers Union, AFL v. NLRB*, 347 U.S. 17 (1954).

[105] 467 U.S. 883 (1984). In *Agri Processor Co., Inc., v. NLRB*, 2008 U.S. App. LEXIS 7648, where the UFCW union won a representation election and the employer subsequently ran the Social Security numbers given by all voting employees and discovered many of the voters were undocumeted workers, the D.C. Circuit enforced a Board bargaining order that the employer had an obligation to bargain with the union. Continuing the tension between the NLRA and IRCA, the Board rejected the employer's contention that undocumented aliens are not "employees" protected by the NLRA, finding that such a position ignores the Act's plain language and the Supreme Court's *Sure-Tan, Inc., v. NLRB* decision.

discharge. Moreover, the Court determined that the employees were entitled to reinstatement when they legally reentered the country (conditional reinstatement) and that back pay must be tolled during the aliens' illegal presence in the United States.

Subsequent to the *Sure-Tan* decision, the Immigration Reform and Control Act (IRCA)[106] became law in November 1986. Under this Act, civil penalties are imposed on employers who knowingly hire illegal aliens. This law was designed to discourage illegal immigration by the elimination of job opportunities through employer sanctions. In the *APRA Fuel Oil Buyers Group, Inc.*,[107] decision, the NLRB considered the effect the IRCA should have on NLRA remedies and determined that conditional reinstatement and limited back pay was available to undocumented workers who have been subjected to unfair labor practices.

In *Hoffman Plastic Compounds, Inc., v. NLRB*, presented in this section, the U.S. Supreme Court reviewed the Board's back-pay policy for undocumented workers, deciding in a 5–4 decision that the federal immigration policy, as expressed by Congress in the Immigration Reform and Control Act of 1986, foreclosed the NLRB from awarding back pay to an undocumented alien who was never legally authorized to work in the United States. *Hoffman* thus abrogated the Board's *APRA Fuel Oil Buyers Group, Inc.*, decision as to back pay.

The *Hoffman* decision does not preclude the Board from imposing a conditional reinstatement order against an employer who flouts the NLRA and IRCA by hiring and firing known undocumented workers. Because the employee must comply with IRCA prior to reinstatement, a conditional order satisfies the Court's concern that the Act not conflict with IRCA's extensive employment verification system. However, where an employer, as in *Hoffman*, establishes that it would not have hired or retained the discriminatee had it known of his or her undocumented status during the period of employment, such a remedy is inappropriate.[108]

| CASE 4.18 | H. K. PORTER CO., INC., v. NLRB
SUPREME COURT OF THE UNITED STATES, 397 U.S. 99 (1970). |

BLACK, J....

After an election respondent United Steelworkers Union was, on October 5, 1961, certified by the National Labor Relations Board as the bargaining agent for the employees at the Danville, Virginia, plant of the petitioner, H. K. Porter Co. Thereafter negotiations commenced for a collective bargaining agreement. Since that time the controversy has seesawed between the Board, the Court of Appeals for the District of Columbia Circuit, and this Court. This delay of over eight years is not because the case is exceedingly complex, but appears to have occurred chiefly because of the skill of the company's negotiators in taking advantage of every opportunity for delay in an Act more noticeable for its generality than for its precise prescriptions. The entire lengthy dispute mainly revolves around the union's desire to have the company agree to "check off" the dues owed to the union by its members, that

continued

---

[106] Pub. L. 99-603, also known as the Simpson-Rodino Act.

[107] 320 NLRB 408 (1995).

[108] Office of the General Counsel, Memorandum GC 02-06 (July 19, 2002).

is, to deduct those dues periodically from the company's wage payments to the employees. The record shows, as the Board found, that the company's objection to a checkoff was not due to any general principle or policy against making deductions from employees' wages. The company does deduct charges for things like insurance, taxes, and contributions to charities, and at some other plants it has a checkoff arrangement for union dues. The evidence shows, and the Court below found, that the company's objection was not because of inconvenience, but solely on the ground that the company was "not going to aid and comfort the union." Efforts by the union to obtain some kind of compromise on a checkoff request were all met with the same staccato response to the effect that the collection of union dues was the "union's business" and the company was not going to provide any assistance. Based on this and other evidence the Board found, and the Court of Appeals approved the finding, that the refusal of the company to bargain about the checkoff was not made in good faith, but was done solely to frustrate the making of any collective bargaining agreement....

We granted certiorari to consider whether the Board in these circumstances had the power to remedy the unfair labor practice by requiring the company to agree to check off the dues of the workers. 396 U.S. 817. For reasons to be stated we hold that while the Board does have power under the National Labor Relations Act, 61 Stat. 136, as amended, to require employers and employees to negotiate, it is without power to compel a company or a union to agree to any substantive contractual provision of a collective bargaining agreement.

Since 1935 the story of labor relations in this country has largely been a history of governmental regulation of the process of collective bargaining. In that year Congress decided that disturbances in the area of labor relations led to undesirable burdens on and obstructions of interstate commerce, and passed the National Labor Relations Act, 49 Stat. 449....

The object of this Act was not to allow governmental regulation of the terms and conditions of employment, but rather to ensure that employers and their employees could work together to establish mutually satisfactory conditions. The basic theme of the Act was that through collective bargaining the passions, arguments, and struggles of prior years would be channeled into constructive, open discussions leading, it was hoped, to mutual agreement. But it was recognized from the beginning that agreement might in some cases be impossible, and it was never intended that the Government would in such cases step in, become a party to the negotiations and impose its own views of a desirable settlement. This fundamental limitation was made abundantly clear in the legislative reports accompanying the 1935 Act....

In 1947 Congress reviewed the experience under the Act and concluded that certain amendments were in order.

Accordingly Congress amended the provisions defining unfair labor practices and said in Section 8(d) that:

> For the purposes of this section, to bargain collectively is the performance of the mutual obligation of the employer and the representative of the employees to meet at reasonable times and confer in good faith with respect to wages, hours, and other terms and conditions of employment or the negotiation of an agreement, or any question arising thereunder, and the execution of a written contract incorporating any agreement reached if requested by either party, but such obligation does not compel either party to agree to a proposal or require the making of a concession.

In discussing the effect of that amendment, this Court said it is "clear that the Board may not, either directly or indirectly, compel concessions or otherwise sit in judgment upon the substantive terms of collective bargaining agreements." *NLRB v. American Ins. Co.*, 343 U.S. 395, 404 (1952). Later this court affirmed that view stating that "it remains clear that Section 8(d) was an attempt by Congress to prevent the Board from controlling the settling of the terms of collective bargaining agreements." *NLRB v. Insurance Agents*, 361 U.S. 477, 487 (1960). The parties to the instant case are agreed that this is the first time in the 35-year history of the Act that the Board has ordered either an employer or a union to agree to a substantive term of a collective bargaining agreement....

... The Board's remedial powers under Section 10 of the Act are broad, but they are limited to carrying out the policies of the Act itself. One of these fundamental policies is freedom of contract. While the parties' freedom of contract is not absolute under the Act, allowing the Board to compel agreement when the parties themselves are unable to agree would violate the fundamental premise on which

continued

the Act is based—private bargaining under governmental supervision of the procedure alone, without any official compulsion over the actual terms of the contract.

In reaching its decision the Court of Appeals relied extensively on the equally important policy of the Act that workers' rights to collective bargaining are to be secured. In this case the Court apparently felt that the employer was trying effectively to destroy the union by refusing to agree to what the union may have considered its most important demand. Perhaps the court, fearing that the parties might resort to economic combat, was also trying to maintain the industrial peace that the Act is designed to further. But the Act as presently drawn does not contemplate that unions will always be secure and able to achieve agreement even when their economic position is weak, that strikes and lockouts will never result from a bargaining impasse. It cannot be said that the Act forbids an employer or a union to rely ultimately on its economic strength to try

to secure what it cannot obtain through bargaining. It may well be true, as the Court of Appeals felt, that the present remedial powers of the Board are insufficiently broad to cope with important labor problems. But it is the job of Congress, not the Board or the courts, to decide when and if it is necessary to allow governmental review of proposals for collective bargaining agreements and compulsory submission to one side's demands. The present Act does not envision such a process.

Reversed and remanded.

Case Questions

1. Summarize the facts of the case.
2. What is a checkoff? How important is it to a union?
3. What is the issue before the Supreme Court?
4. What was the Supreme Court's decision on this issue?

CASE 4.19	HOFFMAN PLASTIC COMPOUNDS, INC., V. NLRB
	SUPREME COURT OF THE UNITED STATES, 122 S. CT. 1275 (2002).

[Petitioner Hoffman Plastic Compounds, Inc., custom-formulates chemical compounds for businesses that manufacture pharmaceutical, construction, and household products. In May 1988, it hired Jose Castro to operate various blending machines that "mix and cook" the particular formulas per customer order. Before being hired for this position, Castro presented documents that appeared to verify his authorization to work in the United States. In December 1988, the United Rubber, Cork, Linoleum, and Plastic Workers of America, AFL-CIO, began a union-organizing campaign at petitioner's production plant. Castro and several other employees supported the organizing campaign and distributed authorization cards to coworkers. In January 1989, Hoffman laid off Castro and other employees engaged in these organizing activities. Three years later, January 1992, the Board found that Hoffman unlawfully selected four employees, including Castro, for layoff "in order to rid itself of known union supporters" in violation of Section 8(a)(3) of the NLRA. To remedy this violation, the Board ordered that Hoffman (1) cease and desist from further violations of the NLRA, (2) post a detailed notice to its

employees regarding the remedial order, and (3) offer reinstatement and back pay to the four affected employees. Hoffman entered into a stipulation with the Board's General Counsel and agreed to abide by the Board's order.

In June 1993, the parties proceeded to a compliance hearing before an administrative law judge to determine the amount of back pay owed to each discriminatee. On the final day of the hearing, Castro testified that he was born in Mexico and that he had never been legally admitted to, or authorized to work in, the United States. He admitted gaining employment with Hoffman only after tendering a birth certificate belonging to a friend who was born in Texas. He also admitted that he used this birth certificate to fraudulently obtain a California driver's license and a Social Security card, and to fraudulently obtain employment following his layoff by Hoffman. Based on this testimony, the ALJ found the Board precluded from awarding Castro back pay or reinstatement, as such relief would be contrary to *Sure-Tan, Inc., v. NLRB*, and in conflict with IRCA, which makes it unlawful for employers knowingly to hire undocumented

continued

workers or for employees to use fraudulent documents to establish employment eligibility.

In September 1998, four years after the ALJ's decision, and seven years after Castro was fired, the Board reversed with respect to back pay. Citing its earlier decision in *APRA Fuel Oil Buyers Group, Inc.*, the Board determined that "the most effective way to accommodate and further the immigration policies embodied in [IRCA] is to provide the protections and remedies of the [NLRA] to undocumented workers in the same manner as to other employees." The Board thus found that Castro was entitled to $66,951 of back pay, plus interest. It calculated this back pay award from the date of Castro's termination to the date Hoffman first learned of Castro's undocumented status, a period of 3½ years. A dissenting Board member would have affirmed the ALJ and denied Castro all back pay.

Hoffman filed a petition for review of the Board's order in the court of appeals. A panel of the court of appeals denied the petition for review. 208 F.3d 639 (2001). The Supreme Court granted certiorari.]

REHNQUIST, C. J....

This case exemplifies the principle that the Board's discretion to select and fashion remedies for violations of the NLRA, though generally broad, ... is not unlimited, see, *eg.*, *NLRB v. Fansteel Metallurgical Corp.*, 306 U.S. 240, 257–258 (1939); *Southern S.S. Co. v. NLRB*, 316 U.S. 31, 46–47 (1942).... Since the Board's inception, we have consistently set aside awards of reinstatement or backpay to employees found guilty of serious illegal conduct in connection with their employment. In *Fansteel*, the Board awarded reinstatement with backpay to employees who engaged in a "sit down strike" that led to confrontation with local law enforcement officials. We set aside the award, saying:

> We are unable to conclude that Congress intended to compel employers to retain persons in their employ regardless of their unlawful conduct, —to invest those who go on strike with an immunity from discharge for acts of trespass or violence against the employer's property, which they would not have enjoyed had they remained at work. 306 U.S., at 255, 59 S.Ct. 490....

Our decision in *Sure-Tan* followed this line of cases and set aside an award closely analogous to the award challenged here. There we confronted for the first time a potential conflict between the NLRA and federal immigration policy, as then expressed in the Immigration and Nationality Act (INA), 66 Stat. 163, as amended, 8 U.S.C. § 1101 *et seq.* Two companies had unlawfully reported alien-employees to the INS in retaliation for union activity. Rather than face INS sanction, the employees voluntarily departed to Mexico. The Board investigated and found the companies acted in violation of § § 8(a)(1) and (3) of the NLRA. The Board's ensuing order directed the companies to reinstate the affected workers and pay them six months' backpay.

We affirmed the Board's determination that the NLRA applied to undocumented workers, reasoning that the immigration laws "as presently written" expressed only a "peripheral concern" with the employment of illegal aliens. 467 U.S., at 892, ... "For whatever reason," Congress had not "made it a separate criminal offense" for employers to hire an illegal alien, or for an illegal alien "to accept employment after entering this country illegally." *Sure-Tan, supra,* at 892–893, ... Therefore, we found "no reason to conclude that application of the NLRA to employment practices affecting such aliens would necessarily conflict with the terms of the INA." 467 U.S., at 893, 104 S.Ct. 2803.

With respect to the Board's selection of remedies, however, we found its authority limited by federal immigration policy. See *id.*, at 903, 104 S.Ct. 2803 ("In devising remedies for unfair labor practices, the Board is obliged to take into account another 'equally important Congressional objective.' ") ... Thus, to avoid "a potential conflict with the INA," the Board's reinstatement order had to be conditioned upon proof of "the employees' legal reentry." "Similarly," with respect to backpay, we stated: "[T] he employees must be deemed 'unavailable' for work (and the accrual of backpay therefore tolled) during any period when they were not lawfully entitled to be present and employed in the United States." "In light of the practical workings of the immigration laws," such remedial limitations were appropriate even if they led to "[t]he probable unavailability of the [NLRA's] more effective remedies." *Id.*, at 904....

The *Southern S.S. Co.* line of cases established that where the Board's chosen remedy trenches upon a federal statute or policy outside the Board's competence to administer, the Board's remedy may be required to yield. Whether or not this was the situation at the time of *Sure-Tan*, it is precisely the situation today. In 1986, two years after *Sure-Tan*, Congress enacted

continued

IRCA, a comprehensive scheme prohibiting the employment of illegal aliens in the United States. § 101(a)(1), 100 Stat. 3360, 8 U.S.C. § 1324a. As we have previously noted, IRCA "forcefully" made combating the employment of illegal aliens central to "[t]he policy of immigration law." ... It did so by establishing an extensive "employment verification system," § 1324a(a)(1), designed to deny employment to aliens who (a) are not lawfully present in the United States, or (b) are not lawfully authorized to work in the United States, § 1324a(h)(3). This verification system is critical to the IRCA regime. To enforce it, IRCA mandates that employers verify the identity and eligibility of all new hires by examining specified documents before they begin work. § 1324a(b). If an alien applicant is unable to present the required documentation, the unauthorized alien cannot be hired § 1324a(a)(1)....

Similarly, if an employer unknowingly hires an unauthorized alien, or if the alien becomes unauthorized while employed, the employer is compelled to discharge the worker upon discovery of the worker's undocumented status. § 1324a(a)(2). Employers who violate IRCA are punished by civil fines, § 1324a(e)(4)(A), and may be subject to criminal prosecution, § 1324a(f)(1). IRCA also makes it a crime for an unauthorized alien to subvert the employer verification system by tendering fraudulent documents. § 1324c(a). It thus prohibits aliens from using or attempting to use "any forged, counterfeit, altered, or falsely made document" or "any document lawfully issued to or with respect to a person other than the possessor" for purposes of obtaining employment in the United States. § § 1324c(a)(1)–(3). Aliens who use or attempt to use such documents are subject to fines and criminal prosecution. 18 U.S.C. § 1546(b). There is no dispute that Castro's use of false documents to obtain employment with Hoffman violated these provisions.

Under the IRCA regime, it is impossible for an undocumented alien to obtain employment in the United States without some party directly contravening explicit congressional policies. Either the undocumented alien tenders fraudulent identification, which subverts the cornerstone of IRCA's enforcement mechanism, or the employer knowingly hires the undocumented alien in direct contradiction of its IRCA obligations. The Board asks that we overlook this fact and allow it to award backpay to an illegal alien for years of work not performed, for wages that could not lawfully have been earned, and for a job obtained in the first instance by a criminal fraud. We find, however, that awarding backpay to illegal aliens runs counter to policies underlying IRCA, policies the Board has no authority to enforce or administer. Therefore, as we have consistently held in like circumstances, the award lies beyond the bounds of the Board's remedial discretion....

[A]warding backpay in a case like this not only trivializes the immigration laws, it also condones and encourages future violations. The Board admits that had the INS detained Castro, or had Castro obeyed the law and departed to Mexico, Castro would have lost his right to backpay.... Castro thus qualifies for the Board's award only by remaining inside the United States illegally.... Similarly, Castro cannot mitigate damages, a duty our cases require, ... without triggering new IRCA violations, either by tendering false documents to employers or by finding employers willing to ignore IRCA and hire illegal workers. The Board here has failed to even consider this tension. See 326 N.L.R.B., at 1063, n. 10 (finding that Castro adequately mitigated damages through interim work with no mention of ALJ findings that Castro secured interim work with false documents)....

We therefore conclude that allowing the Board to award backpay to illegal aliens would unduly trench upon explicit statutory prohibitions critical to federal immigration policy, as expressed in IRCA. It would encourage the successful evasion of apprehension by immigration authorities, condone prior violations of the immigration laws, and encourage future violations. However broad the Board's discretion to fashion remedies when dealing only with the NLRA, it is not so unbounded as to authorize this sort of an award.

Lack of authority to award backpay does not mean that the employer gets off scot-free. The Board here has already imposed other significant sanctions against Hoffman—sanctions Hoffman does not challenge.... These include orders that Hoffman cease and desist its violations of the NLRA, and that it conspicuously post a notice to employees setting forth their rights under the NLRA and detailing its prior unfair practices.... Hoffman will be subject to contempt proceedings should it fail to comply with these orders.... (Congress gave the Board civil contempt power to enforce compliance with the Board's orders). We have deemed such "traditional remedies" sufficient to effectuate national labor policy regardless of whether the "spur and catalyst" of backpay accompanies them. *Sure-Tan*, 467 U.S., at 904, 104 S.Ct. 2803. See also *id.*, at 904, n. 13, 104 S.Ct. 2803 ("This threat of contempt sanctions ... provides a significant deterrent

continued

against future violations of the [NLRA]"). As we concluded in *Sure-Tan*, "in light of the practical workings of the immigration laws," any "perceived deficienc[y] in the NLRA's existing remedial arsenal," must be "addressed by congressional action," not the courts. *Id.*, at 904, 104 S.Ct. 2803. In light of IRCA, this statement is even truer today....

The judgment of the Court of Appeals is reversed.

It is so ordered.

JUSTICE BREYER, with whom JUSTICE STEVENS, JUSTICE SOUTER, and JUSTICE GINSBURG join, dissenting ...

I cannot agree that the backpay award before us "runs counter to," or "trenches upon," national immigration policy. *Ante*, at 1282, 1283 (citing the Immigration Reform and Control Act of 1986 (IRCA)). As *all* the relevant agencies (including the Department of Justice) have told us, the National Labor Relations Board's limited backpay order will *not* interfere with the implementation of immigration policy. Rather, it reasonably helps to deter unlawful activity that *both* labor laws *and* immigration laws seek to prevent. Consequently, the order is lawful....

The Court does not deny that the employer in this case dismissed an employee for trying to organize a union—a crude and obvious violation of the labor laws.... And it cannot deny that the Board has especially broad discretion in choosing an appropriate remedy for addressing such violations.... Nor can it deny that in such circumstances backpay awards serve critically important remedial purposes.... Those purposes involve more than victim compensation; they also include deterrence, *i.e.*, discouraging employers from violating the Nation's labor laws....

Without the possibility of the deterrence that backpay provides, the Board can impose only future-oriented obligations upon law-violating employers—for it has no other weapons in its remedial arsenal.... And in the absence of the backpay weapon, employers could conclude that they can violate the labor laws at least once with impunity. See *A.P.R.A. Fuel Oil Buyers Group, Inc.*, 320 N.L.R.B. 408, 415, N. 38 (1995) (without potential backpay order employer might simply discharge employees who show interest in a union "secure in the knowledge" that only penalties were requirements "to cease and desist and post a notice"); ... Hence the backpay remedy is necessary; it helps make labor law enforcement credible; it makes clear that violating the labor laws will not pay....

Case Questions

1. Does federal immigration policy, as expressed in the IRCA, preclude the Board from awarding back pay to an undocumented alien who has never been legally authorized to work in the United States?
2. Does the employer get off scot-free for its violation of the NLRA because back pay is not allowed?
3. Does the dissent believe that the back pay remedy best serves as a deterrent against unlawful activity that both the NLRA and the IRCA seek to prevent?

CHAPTER QUESTIONS AND PROBLEMS

1. Review the *Town & Country* decision and the text materials in Section 28, setting forth the Board's *FES* framework for analyzing refusal-to-consider and/or hire cases and the *Toering Electric Co.* modification of the framework. Employers have been very reluctant to comply with the Supreme Court's *Town & Country* decision, as evidenced by the many cases involving "salts" considered by the NLRB and the courts. Since the Supreme Court's 1996 *Town & Country* decision, five anti-salting bills have been considered and have failed to pass in Congress, including the Truth in Employment Act of 2007 (H.R. 2670 and S.1520, 110th Cong. 2007). Does an administrative agency, the NLRB, have the power to change the law regarding the employee status of "salts" under the NLRA where Congress has considered but failed to make changes to the statute? Is the NLRB's *Toering Electric Co.* decision an appropriate interpretation of the NLRA under the *Chevron* framework set forth in Section 14 of Chapter 2?

2. Wurtland Nursing, a rehabilitation center, withdrew recognition of the SEIU Local 1199 after it received an "RD" petition signed by a majority of employees in the unit that stated the following:

We the Employee's [sic] of Wurtland nursing and rehab wish for a vote to remove the union S.E.I.U. 1199.

Under the *Levitz Furniture* standard, "an employer may unilaterally withdraw recognition from an incumbent union only where the union has actually lost the support of the majority of the bargaining unit employees … and the employer bears the burden of showing, through objective evidence, an actual loss of the union's majority status at the time of the withdrawal of recognition." Did the employer violate Section 8(a)(5) in this case, or was this petition proof that the union had actually lost support of a majority of employees, allowing the employer to unilaterally withdraw recognition from the union? [Wurtland Nursing & Rehabilitation Center, 351 NLRB No. 50 (Sept. 29, 2007).

3. In July 1999, the Seattle Mariners baseball team moved from the King County-owned-and-operated Kingdome to newly constructed Safeco Field and hired 450 employees, some of whom were previously employed by King County at the Kingdome. The employer and union entered into a written neutrality/card check agreement prior to the move, pursuant to which the employer agreed to remain neutral during the organizing campaign and the parties designated an arbitrator to perform the card check. In September, the union submitted authorization cards to the arbitrator, and by letter dated September 24, the arbitrator certified that the union possessed majority status. On September 22, a group of "no-union" employees sent a petition to the arbitrator, signed by more than 30 percent of the employees, indicating that they did not want union representation. By letter dated September 28, the arbitrator notified the

group that he had already completed his duties under the neutrality/card check agreement. Following this card check certification by the arbitrator, the employer and union began negotiations for a first collective bargaining agreement. Based on the facts, the regional director concluded that the employer's voluntary recognition of the union based on the union's majority status did not create a "recognition bar" to the decertification petition filed by the no-union group. What did the regional director mean by determining that the voluntary recognition by the employer did not create a "recognition bar"? How would you decide this case under the Board's *Dana Corp.* decision? [*Baseball Club of Seattle, LP*, 335 NLRB 563]

4. The Resort Hotel Association represents several member hotels in their dealings with the various unions that represent workers at the hotels. Every hotel hires professional musicians to play for extended periods of time in hotel lounges, dining rooms, and ballrooms. Over the years, the association has bargained with the American Federation of Musicians and reached agreements governing the employment of union-based members and bandleaders in hotels. One year, after evaluating the situation, the association refused to bargain with the musicians union. The association claimed that the band members were not "employees" of the hotels within the meaning of the Act. Furthermore, the association contended that the bandleaders were not "supervisors" representing the hotel, but rather independent contractors free to conduct their business without hotel interference, including the hiring and firing of musicians.

The federation filed Section 8(a)(1) and (5) unfair labor practice charges against the association with the NLRB for refusing to bargain with the union. The union contended that the working conditions of musicians on extended engagements, such as method of payment and privileges, were identical to those of other hotel employees. Furthermore, because the hotel controlled the times the bands played, the type of music played, and the locations in which the bands played, the musicians were in effect "employees" of the hotel under Section 2(3). Because the band leaders helped the hotels effect their control, the union also claimed that bandleaders were hotel "supervisors" under Section 2(11).

What factors must be considered by the NLRB when deciding whether individuals are employees, independent contractors, or supervisors under the Act? How should the musicians and bandleaders be classified in this case? Decide. [*Hilton International Co. v. NLRB*, 111 LRRM 2669 (2d Cir.)]

5. The Health Care Institution (HCI) maintained a no-solicitation rule, which, on its face, prohibits solicitation for any purpose during working time and in immediate patient care areas. Before and after the union's organizing campaign began, HCI was inconsistent with its enforcement of this policy. For example, the employer warned and/or disciplined employees engaged in union solicitation activity. But it allowed institutional commercial solicitations (sales of Avon, Mary Kay cosmetics, Tupperware, and Pampered Chef products), individual commercial solicitations (sales of homemade foods, jewelry, and holiday crafts), school fund-raising solicitations (sales of candy, candles, and wrapping paper items), and personal solicitations (collection of money for various families). HCI believes that under the *Register Guard* rule, since it did not permit communications of similar character to union organizing, it lawfully enforced its rule against employees engaged in union solicitation activity. The union disagreed. Decide. [Office of General Counsel, *Register Guard* cases, Case No. 2 DLR No. 97, E-6 (May 20, 2008)]

6. One Monday, a labor organization affiliated with the International Ladies Garment Workers Union began an organization drive among the employees of Whittal & Shon, Inc., On the following Monday, six of the employees who were participating in the union drive were discharged. Immediately after the firings, the head of the company gave a speech to the remaining workers in which he made a variety of antiunion statements and threats. The union filed a complaint with the NLRB, alleging that the six employees were fired because they were engaging in organizational activity and that they were thus discharged in violation of the NLRA.

Assuming that the NLRA was violated, it could take two to three years before the NLRB obtains a final binding order compelling the employer to reinstate the six employees. Under the NLRA must the employees wait this long to get their jobs back? What action may be taken by the Board in this case? [*Silverman v. Whittal & Shon, Inc.*, 125 LRRM 2150 (S.D.N.Y.)]

7. The facts before the Board when it made its decision are: The Firestone Tire and Rubber Company employs 15,000 production and maintenance employees in 11 plants across the nation. All production and maintenance employees have been represented by the United Rubber Workers of America since 1948. Two thousand of the employees represented by the URW are skilled tradespeople. These skilled workers are members of nearly 50 different crafts and include machinists, carpenters, crane operators, and refrigeration mechanics. The rubber manufacturing production process is highly integrated, and these skilled workers spend up to 90 percent of their working time in production areas repairing production machinery.

A union called the International Society of Skilled Trades seeks to sever all skilled trades from the URW and to represent the various skilled workers in one unit. This would be the first such dual representation of production and maintenance workers in the rubber industry.

What factors must the Board consider before it allows craft severance? Based on the facts of this case, should the skilled trades be severed into their own unit? Explain. [*Firestone Tire and Rubber Co.*, 223 NLRB 955, 91 LRRM 156]

8. The Saint Joseph News-Press publishes a morning newspaper in Saint Joseph, Missouri. Haulers pick up the bundled papers at the plant and bring them to common drop points, where carriers pick them up. Carriers deliver papers to the customers. They also place papers in newspaper racks, deliver to dealers, and drop newspapers at the post office to be mailed to subscribers. When hired, carriers do not complete applications. They sign a contract with the newspaper expressly describing them as independent contractors. The contract grants the carrier the nonexclusive right to purchase, sell, and deliver the newspaper in a designated area and to control the method and means of making deliveries. Carriers sign the contracts as individuals; none are incorporated. Thirty days' notice is required for either party to terminate the contract without cause. The newspaper can terminate the contract for cause without notice. The contract prohibits carriers from displaying the newspaper's insignia while delivering newspapers and requires carriers to provide their own vehicles and auto insurance. The General Counsel asserts that the carriers did not operate as independent businesses and performed functions integral to the newspaper's business and had little opportunity for entrepreneurial gain or loss and little or no bargaining power. The newspaper contends that the carriers are independent contractors excluded from the protection of the act. Decide. [*St. Joseph News-Press and Teamsters Union Local 460*, 345 NLRB No. 31.]

9. Hasbro Industries maintains a printing division at its main plant in Pawtucket, Rhode Island. The Graphic Arts International Union notified Hasbro and the Board that it had obtained authorization cards from 11 of the 18 employees in the printing division. An election date was accordingly set. Prior to the election, Hasbro sent a letter signed by the management to the employees. The letter stated that employees and their families faced "real risks" if they made "the wrong decision." The letter concluded that the employees faced the loss of benefits and "the tragedy of permanent replacement" in the event a strike occurred. Another letter listed 28 benefits the employees risked losing if the union won the election. Mr. Feldman, a Hasbro manager, told one printing department employee that Hasbro would "never let another union in here." He also stated that Hasbro would subcontract out the printing division's work rather than deal with a union. The union subsequently lost the election. After the election, Feldman told an employee that the printing division would have been closed if the union had won. In addition, Hasbro granted higher-than-normal pay raises to the printing division immediately after the election. At this time, Hasbro knew that the union had filed objections to the election and had asked the NLRB to set aside the election and order Hasbro to bargain on the basis of the union's authorization card majority.

Is the company's conduct within the company's rights under the NLRA? Explain. Should the NLRB issue the bargaining order requested by the union? Explain. [*NLRB v. Hasbro Industries*, 109 LRRM 2911 (1st Cir.)]

10. The Communication Workers Union sought to represent certain service employees of Electro Protective Corporation as part of a communications craft bargaining unit. The company sells, installs, monitors, and services alarm systems. The employees in question respond to alarms at customers' premises, protecting the premises until the police or customers arrive. The employees also reset the alarm systems and provide any maintenance that the systems require. These employees drive radio-dispatched vans, wear uniforms, and are provided with nightsticks. They face the possibility of personal confrontation with intruders. The union insisted that these workers were maintenance

personnel who could be represented by their unit. The company contended that these employees were guards under Section 9(b)(3) and therefore must be excluded from the unit in question.

Are these employees guards under the Act? What difference would the absence of uniforms and nightsticks make? [*Electro Protective Corporation*, 251 NLRB 154, 105 LRRM 1254]

11. The unionized employees of Duo-Fast Corporation were scheduled to vote in a decertification election on June 15 to determine whether Teamsters Local 210 would continue to be their bargaining representative. At a June 7 meeting with the represented employees, a Duo-Fast manager distributed a leaflet signed by him that compared the health benefits of the unionized employees with the benefits provided to Duo-Fast's nonunion employees. The benefits received by the nonunion employees were generally better. The leaflet stated, "I'm not promising you better medical benefits if you vote 'No' on June 15, but you should know our nonunion employees' medical benefits." The leaflet concluded: "[G]ive me and Duo-Fast a chance to show you that you don't need Local 210. Vote 'No' on June 15." When he distributed the leaflet, the manager stated that if the union was voted out, the employees would receive "basically this type of coverage." The manager answered employees' questions at other meetings held on June 9, 13, and 14. When he was asked when the medical coverage would go into effect, the manager responded "immediately" or "most likely right away." At some of the meetings, however, the manager stated that he was not promising anything.

On June 15, Local 210 lost the decertification election. The union filed a complaint with the NLRB charging the employer with interfering with the election by promising the employees better health benefits if they voted the union out. Local 210 asked for a new election.

Should another election be held? Decide. [*Duo-Fast Corp.*, 122 LRRM 1136 (NLRB)]

12. Michael's Painting Co., Inc., of Van Nuys, California, became aware of an organizing campaign by the Painters Union in late March 1998. On March 27, the company employed 12 painters, with some 22 other painters being on layoff status. The union had obtained 18 signed authorization cards from a majority of the employees in the 34-person unit by March 27. On that afternoon, employees picketed at the offices of Michael's with signs protesting the alleged failure to pay prevailing wages. The signs stated "We need a Union," "Michael's Painting is unfair," "It is alright to be Union." Union business agent Alexander Lopez spoke to owner Laurie Abikasis. Lopez told her that he had signed union authorization cards. Later in the day Mrs. Abikasis told employees that the company did not want the union and did not need the union. She also said that she and her co-owner husband, Michael, would close the company rather than become a union shop. She also said she could not afford to be union—that she would go broke if she became a union shop and that the union agents were parasites. On Monday, March 30, Lopez asked Michael Abikasis to recognize the union based on the authorization cards. He stated that he would look into the matter and discuss it with Lopez at a later date. Thereafter, employees Lainez, Duenas, Romero, Martin Vega, and Carlos Vega were turned away from work by Mr. Abikasis and never again allowed to return to work. That afternoon Mrs. Abikasis told each of the employees that their paychecks could not be released unless the employees first provided a green card, Social Security number, or driver's license; the culture in the company had been lax in this regard previously. The employees were paid later that day. The two owners transferred all of the assets and work of that company to a newly formed company "Painting LA, Inc." During a job interview

on April 20, 1998, one of the fired workers was interrogated by the employer about his and other employees' union activities.

Identify the unfair labor practices evident in the preceding fact pattern. Is "Painting LA, Inc." an "alter ego" of Michael's Painting, Inc.? If so, should the NLRB impose a *Gissel* bargaining order or should it conduct an election to determine employee choice on the question of representation? [*Michael's Painting, Inc.*, 337 NLRB No. 140]

13. Union organizers Dooley and King applied for driver positions at Casino Ready Mix, Inc., a nonunion operation in Las Vegas, Nevada, in response to Casino's advertisement for drivers. Both wore shirts identifying themselves as organizers for the union as well as baseball caps with union logos when they applied in person on April 8. Each stated his organizer status on his application. The company received their applications and told them they were not hiring. In fact, the company hired four other drivers between April 8 and 21. And evidence existed that the company president had stated that he would never allow a union to represent his employees. Both Dooley and King were qualified drivers. The employer believed that "disabling conflicts" existed in this case and, if hired, the two union organizers would engage in activities inimical to the employer's operations. Dooley and King believe that they were not hired in violation of Section 8(a)(3) of the act. Decide. [*Casino Ready Mix, Inc., v. NLRB*, 321 F. 3d 1190 (D.C. Cir.)]

EMPLOYER UNFAIR LABOR PRACTICES

CHAPTER 5

SECTION

SECTION 40: PROTECTION OF EMPLOYEE RIGHTS

Employees have rights to form, join or exist labor organizations and they also have right to refrain from such activities.

THE RIGHT TO FORM, JOIN, OR ASSIST LABOR ORGANIZATIONS

Section 1 of the NLRA set forth the policy of the 1935 Act in part as follows:

> ...to encourag[e] the practice and procedures of collective bargaining ... and protect the exercise by workers of full freedom of association, self organization and designation of

135

representatives of their own choosing, for the purposes of negotiating the terms and conditions of their employment or other mutual aid or protection.

The design of Section 7 of the 1935 Act was to implement the policy stated in Section 1 of the NLRA. With the heading "Rights of Employees," it stated as follows:

> Section 7. Employees shall have the right to self-organization, to form, join or assist labor organizations, to bargain collectively through representatives of their own choosing, and to engage in other concerted activities for the purpose of collective bargaining or other mutual aid or protection.

Section 7 of the 1935 statute provided that employees shall have "the right to self organization and the right to form, join or assist labor organizations" and the right "to engage in other concerted activities for the purpose of collective bargaining or other mutual aid or protection." And Section 8 of the Act made it an unfair labor practice for an employer "to interfere with, restrain, or coerce employees" in the exercise of their rights "guaranteed in Section 7."

THE RIGHT OF EMPLOYEES TO REFRAIN FROM SUCH ACTIVITIES

Employees' rights were expanded by the Taft-Hartley Amendments to the NLRA in 1947, which added to the language of Section 7 the guarantee that employees also had the right "to refrain from any and all such activities." The policy behind this amendment was stated in Section 1(b) of the 1947 statute, reading "... to protect the rights of individual employees in their relations with labor organizations...." The 1947 amendments contained union unfair labor practices, Sections 8(b)(1) and 8(b)(2), to protect employees in their relations with labor organizations.

CONCERTED ACTIVITIES

Section 7 provides protection for employees engaged in concerted activities in forming unions and their involvement in the collective bargaining process, as well as refraining from such activities. It also protects employees engaged in "other concerted activities" concerning "other mutual aid or protection." To be protected as a "concerted activity" under the Act, it is not necessary that an employee have an official union title or designation that he or she is authorized to represent fellow employee interests. The test is whether the individual acted with the purpose of furtherance of the goals of a group of employees. For example, an employee's complaint about his employer's favoritism among crew members did not lose the protection of the Act, as the employee was expressing concern that other employees had raised and it was raised at a meeting, an appropriate place to raise such a concern.[1]

The *Meyers Industries* rule established that activities of a single employee are "concerted" under the Act when undertaken with or on the authority of other employees and not solely by or on behalf of the individual.[2] Thus, the Labor

---

[1] Media General Operations, Inc., 341 NLRB No. 18 (2004).

[2] 268 NLRB 493 (1984), *rev'd sub nom. Prill v. NLRB*, 755 F.2d 941 (D.C. Cir), *cert. denied sub nom. Meyers Indus. v. Prill*, 474 U.S. 971 (1985), *decision on remand*, 281 NLRB 882, (1986), *aff'd sub. nom. Prill v. NLRB*, 835 F.2d 1481 (D.C. Cir. 1987), *cert. denied sub nom. Meyers Indus. v. NLRB*, 487 U.S. 1205 (1988).

Board found that a longshoreman's threat to stop working if drinking water did not arrive by a certain time constituted protected concerted activity as it was a logical outgrowth of his and other employees' concerns about having drinking water available at the worksite.[3] In *Hollings Press, Inc.*, however, a female employee was terminated for purportedly attempting to coerce coworkers to testify on her behalf at a hearing on a sexual harassment complaint against her supervisor. The Board found that while the employee's request for help from others was "concerted activity," it was not for "mutual aid or protection" under Section 7, but rather was aimed only at aiding or protecting her own interests.[4]

SECTION 41: FREEDOM FROM INTERFERENCE

Under the broad and all-inclusive wording of Section 8(a)(1), employers may not interfere with, restrain, or coerce employees in any of their Section 7 rights. Whatever unfair labor practice an employer commits, it automatically means a violation of this subsection also. Moreover, aside from such indirect derivative applications of this catch-all clause, independent violations of Section 8(a)(1) occur where an employer commits such acts as these:[5]

THREATENING WORKERS; PROMISING BENEFITS

Implying the loss of jobs, promising or granting benefits, or suggesting the loss of benefits related to voting for or joining a union or for unionizing an operation has been held to be illegal. In its *Aluminum Casting and Engineering Co.* decision,[6] the Board found a Section 8(a)(1) violation where the employer withheld its annual pay increase during a union-organizing campaign because the employer sought to influence its employees' decision. In a June 27 leaflet distributed to all employees, the employer unambiguously attributed to the union the responsibility for the absence of the wage increase, stating that the union "stuck its nose in." Neither granting nor withholding a wage increase during an organizational campaign is illegal per se. It is the benefit manipulation that is the basis of the Section (8)(a)(1) violation. A promise "to take care" of those voting against the union, a promise to "get a raise next week" for an employee taking the employer's side, or a warning that a company would close and move to another location or go out of business entirely before it would deal with a union may be the basis of a finding of interference.

---

[3] Golden Stevedoring Co., 335 NLRB 410 (2001).

[4] 343 NLRB No. 45 (2004).

[5] A single case involving charges filed against an employer under Section 8(a) of the Act may include allegations of more than one subsection of the Act. The Board considers a violation of Sections 8(a)(2) through 8(a)(5) also to be a derivative violation of Section 8(a)(1). Some 16,887 charges were filed against employers in the fiscal year ended September 30, 2006, as reported in the Board's recent *Annual Report*, with 2,560 charges involving an independent Section 8(a)(1) charge, 391 involving Section 8(a)(2), 7,158 involving Section 8(a)(3), 662 involving Section 8(a)(4), and 8,467 involving Section 8(a)(5). *Seventy-First Annual Report of the NLRB*, issued September, 2007.

[6] 328 NLRB No. 2 (April 9, 1999).

In its *Hughes Drywall*[7] decision, the Board found that the employer's threat to call police on a union conducting "area standards" picketing and the false accusation that a picketer had urinated on a company truck and its insistence that the picketer be arrested was a Section 8(a)(1) violation. The Board decided that the employer's conduct attempting to interfere with area-standards picketing by threatening and causing an arrest was an attempt to interfere with the union's protected activity under Section 7. The Board ordered the contractor to reimburse the union for litigation costs and to arrange for the expungement of all records of the illegal arrest. In *ELC Electric, Inc.,*[8] the employer's vice president of operations responded to a question on health insurance during a mandatory meeting of employees where employees were urged not to vote for representation by a union. The vice president stated that "he was looking into insurance for the employees." The Board found that this statement interfered with the election and violated Section 8(a)(1) by impliedly promising to improve health insurance benefits.

Inquiring on Union Interest

An employer's interrogation of employees as to union allegiance or activity may be coercive in itself and unlawful. Questioning job applicants or employees on union sentiment, inquiring as to fellow workers' interests in a union, or using systematic interrogation regardless of threats or promises have all been held unlawful in themselves. Creative indirect methods of inquiring about employee sentiments may also prove unlawful, such as an employer's distribution of "Vote No" coffee mugs that compelled employees to either take the mug or reveal their pro-union beliefs.[9] An employer may lawfully poll employees concerning representation attitudes. However, such policy will be an unfair labor practice under the rule of the *Struknes Construction Co.*[10] case unless the following safeguards are observed:

    a. The purpose of the poll must be to determine the truth of a union's claim of majority.
    b. This purpose must be communicated to the employees.
    c. Assurances against reprisal must be given.
    d. The employees must be polled by secret ballot.
    e. The employer must not have engaged in unfair labor practices or otherwise created a coercive atmosphere.

Prohibiting Union Activity

An employer may have a rule against union activity on company working time if fairly applied and if not for discriminating purposes between unions. Such a rule during nonworking time is illegal unless it can be shown that the rule is necessary tomaintain order and discipline or to ensure safe work conditions and production. In its *Meijer, Inc.,*[11]

---

[7] Roger Hughes Drywall, 334 NLRB No. 49 (2005).

[8] 344 NLRB No. 144 (2005).

[9] Circuit City Stores, Inc., 324 NLRB 147 (1997).

[10] 165 NLRB 1062 (1967).

[11] 344 NLRB No. 115 (2005).

decision, the Board found that a supermarket chain's no-solicitation policy was too broad in prohibiting employees from distributing union literature in its retail stores' parking areas during nonworking time, because the employer failed to demonstrate a business justification for the policy.

Once an employer permits use of the bulletin board for union purposes, the employer generally may not remove notices or discriminate against employees who post notices that the employer finds distasteful, absent a showing by the employer of "special circumstances." To be "special," the circumstances must justify the restriction of the employees' Section 7 rights. Examples include the need to maintain discipline of employees and to avert violence.[12]

Employees have the right to wear union insignia, such as union stickers or buttons, while at work and to place these insignia on company-owned hard hats, absent special circumstances inherent in the business.[13] Employees have no right, however, to place stickers on an employer's walls or machines.[14]

The peculiar needs of retail operations are recognized by the Board in allowing store rules to prohibit union discussion or solicitation on the selling floors at any time. Such a rule may not legally apply to the entire store premises at all times, nor may management have a rule restricting employees if, at the same time, it engages in antiunion communications with employees.

The right to talk with fellow workers on nonworking time regarding grievances may not be restricted by management. The Board has found that such rules would obstruct the self-organization and representation rights of employees. Also, the Board has found that an employer violated Section 8(a)(1) by maintaining a discipline rule prohibiting "negative conversations" about associates or managers. The Board determined that such a rule would bar employees from discussing coworker complaints about managers, causing them to refrain from engaging in protected activities.[15]

ESPIONAGE AND SURVEILLANCE

An employer violates Section 8(a)(1) if management or its agent attempts surveillance over employee union activities, spies on union conversation or conduct, or even creates the impression of watching such activity. In the *Montgomery Ward*[16] decision, using detectives for this purpose was found unlawful.

In the Board's *Tenent Health System Hospitals, Inc.,*[17] decision, it applied the rule that absent proper justification, the photographing of employees engaged in concerted activities violates Section 8(a)(1) of the Act because it has the tendency to intimidate. Approximately 120 informational picketers traversed about 300 feet of the public sidewalk fronting the Garfield Medical Center. Picketers carried signs with such legends as "Garfield Unfair to Nurses," "Honk if You Support Nurses,"

---

[12] Southwestern Bell Tel. Co., 276 NLRB No. 110, 120 LRRM 1145 (1985), and *Republic Aviation Corp. v. NLRB*, 324 U.S. 793 (1945).

[13] Malta Construction Co., 276 NLRB 1494, 120 LRRM 1209 (1985).

[14] *NLRB v. Payless Cashway Lumber, Inc.*, 505 F.2d 24, 26 (8th Cir. 1974).

[15] KSL Claremont Resort, Inc., 344 NLRB No. 105 (2005).

[16] 269 NLRB 904 (1984).

[17] 2002 WL 31402769.

"Say NO to Corporate Greed," and "We Deserve a Contract." Picketers chanted, "We want a contract now." Under the hospital's direction, employee Ariel Shen photographed the picketing activity. In all, she took more than 50 photographs for the stated purpose of memorializing the written content of the picket signs, showing whether picketers blocked the driveway, and showing whether they entered the hospital's property. On the facts before the Board, no basis existed for the hospital to reasonably have anticipated misconduct by the informational picketers. A mere suspicion that something might happen to justify the recordation is insufficient when balanced against the tendency of interference with protected rights.

In the Board's *Saia Motor Freight Line, Inc.*,[18] decision, where some 30 to 40 handbillers did in fact interfere with the flow of traffic into and out of a struck company's terminal and the company did not photograph the handbillers until the police were unable to minimize traffic congestion, the Board found that the company had a legitimate safety concern because of the potential for accidents. Accordingly, the Board concluded that the employer did not engage in surveillance or create the impression of surveillance in violation of Section 8(a)(1) of the Act.

FILING A MERITLESS LAWSUIT

The Board has authority to find a violation of Section 8(a)(1) of the Act and order appropriate relief where an employer files an objectively baseless lawsuit against a union or employees in retaliation for a lawful strike, picketing, or other concerted activity protected under Section 7 of the NLRA. If an employer's lawsuit, although ultimately nonmeritorious, is reasonably based, the Board may not find a Section 8(a)(1) violation involving a retaliatory motive even if the employer involved acted with antiunion animus or ill will toward the employees and union involved. In BE&K Construction *Co. v. NLRB*,[19] the Supreme Court explained that a nonmeritorious lawsuit may be reasonably based even though it is ultimately unsuccessful. Even though the suit may attack activity that is ultimately determined to be protected, the suit nevertheless enjoys First Amendment protection if the plaintiff employer reasonably believes the conduct is unprotected and illegal. Similarly, the Court reasoned that inferring a retaliatory motive from evidence of animus would condemn genuine petitioning in circumstances where the plaintiff's "purpose is to stop conduct he reasonably believes is illegal." For the Court, then, a retaliatory-motive standard incorrectly "broadly covers a substantial amount of genuine petitioning."[20]

---

[18] 333 NLRB No. 87 (2001).

[19] 122 S. Ct. 2390 (2002).

[20] See BE & K Construction Co., 351 NLRB No. 29 (2007) where, on remand from the Supreme Court, a 3–2 Board majority found that all "reasonably based" lawsuits, both ongoing and completed, and ultimately unsuccessful, are immune from liability under the NLRA in order to protect the First Amendment right to petition, without regard for the existence of a retaliatory motive on the part of the employer for filing the lawsuit. The dissent would have remanded the case to evaluate whether the unsuccessful suit was brought with a retaliative motive such as to impose litigation costs on the union, balancing the protection of Section 7 rights of employees with the employer's constitutional right of accesss to the courts.

The General Counsel's guidance, memorandum GC-08-02 (Dec. 27, 2007), directs that the Region first investigate whether the suit is "reasonably based"; if so, the Region should dismiss the charge. And if the Region determines that the suit is baseless, it should fully investigate the evidence that the suit was brought with a retaliatory motive and process the matter against the employer through the Division of Advice.

COWORKER PRESENCE AT INVESTIGATORY INTERVIEWS

In 1973, the National Labor Relations Board issued its *Weingarten* decision, which held that an employer violated Section 8(a)(1) of the National Labor Relations Act when it denied an employee's request for the presence of a union representative at an investigatory interview that the employee reasonably believed might result in disciplinary action.[21] The Board's decision was upheld by the Supreme Court in *NLRB v. Weingarten, Inc.*, in 1975,[22] and is presented in this section. The *Weingarten* right of an employee to request the presence of a coworker at an investigatory interview was extended to nonunion workplaces by the Board's 1982 *Material Research Corp.* decision.[23] Three years later, in 1985, the Board reversed itself in *Sears, Roebuck Co.*, holding that *Weingarten* principles do not apply in nonunion settings.[24] In the Board's year 2000 *Epilepsy Foundation of Northeast Ohio* decision, it reimposed its *Materials Research* holding, concluding that unrepresented employees have a right to have a coworker present during investigatory interviews.[25] The Court of Appeals for the District of Columbia Circuit upheld the Board's renewed meaning of the statutory language in question, stating in part:

> ... It is a fact of life in NLRB lore that [the meaning of] certain substantive provisions of the NLRA invariably fluctuate with the changing compositions of the Board. Because the Board's new interpretation is reasonable under the Act, it is entitled to deference.[26]

And three years later, with the changing composition of the Board, on June 9, 2004, in a 3–2 decision, the Board reversed itself again in its *IBM Corp.* decision, presented in this section, and ruled that nonunion employees do not have the right to have a coworker present during an investigatory interview.

CASE 5.1	NLRB v. J. WEINGARTEN, INC. SUPREME COURT OF THE UNITED STATES, 420 U.S. 251 (1975).

[During an investigatory interview at which an employee of Weingarten was being interrogated about reported thefts at a Weingarten store, the employee requested, but was denied, the presence at the interview of her union representative. The union filed an unfair labor practice charge with the NLRB, which held that the employer had committed an unfair labor practice. The NLRB issued a cease-and-desist order; however, the court of appeals reversed, holding that an employee has no need for union assistance at such an interview. The decision was appealed to the Supreme Court.]

BRENNAN, J....

The Board's construction that Section 7 creates a statutory right in an employee to refuse to submit without union representation to an interview which he reasonably fears may result in his discipline was announced in its decision and order of January 28,

continued

---

[21] 202 NLRB 446 (1973).

[22] 420 U.S. 251, 260 (1978).

[23] 262 NLRB 1010 (1982).

[24] 274 NLRB 230 (1985). See also *Slaughter v. NLRB*, 794 F.2d 128 (3d Cir. 1986).

[25] 331 NLRB 676 (2000).

[26] 268 F.3d 1095 (D.C. Cir. 2001).

1972, in *Quality Mfg. Co.*, 195 N.L.R.B. 197.... In its opinions in that case and in *Mobil Oil Corp.*, 196 N.L.R.B. 1052, decided May 12, 1972, three months later, the Board shaped the contours and limits of the statutory right.

First, the right inheres in Section 7's guarantee of the right of employees to act in concert for mutual aid and protection. In *Mobil Oil*, the Board stated:

> An employee's right to union representation upon request is based on Section 7 of the Act which guarantees the right of employees to act in concert for "mutual aid and protection." The denial of this right has a reasonable tendency to interfere with, restrain, and coerce employees in violation of Section 8(a)(1) of the Act. Thus, it is a serious violation of the employee's individual right to engage in concerted activity by seeking the assistance of his statutory representative if the employer denies the employee's request and compels the employee to appear unassisted at an interview which may put his job security in jeopardy. Such a dilution of the employee's right to act collectively to protect his job interests is, in our view, unwarranted interference with his right to insist on concerted protection, rather than individual self-protection, against possible adverse employer action.

Second, the right arises only in situations where the employee requests representation. In other words, the employee may forgo his guaranteed right and, if he prefers, participate in an interview unaccompanied by his union representative.

Third, the employee's right to request representation as a condition of participation in an interview is limited to situations where the employee reasonably believes the investigation will result in disciplinary action. Thus the Board stated in *Quality*:

> We would not apply the rule to such run-of-the-mill shop-floor conversations as, for example, the giving of instructions or training or needed corrections of work techniques. In such cases there cannot normally be any reasonable basis for an employee to fear that any adverse impact may result from the interview, and thus we would then see no reasonable basis for him to seek the assistance of his representative.

Fourth, exercise of the right may not interfere with legitimate employer prerogatives. The employer has no obligation to justify his refusal to allow union representation, and despite refusal, the employer is free to carry on his inquiry without interviewing the employee, and thus leave to the employee the choice between having an interview unaccompanied by his representative, or having no interview and forgoing any benefits that might be derived from one....

Fifth, the employer has no duty to bargain with any union representative who may be permitted to attend the investigatory interview. The Board said in *Mobil*, "We are not giving the Union any particular rights with respect to pre-disciplinary discussions which it otherwise was not able to secure during collective bargaining negotiations."... The Board thus adhered to its decisions distinguishing between disciplinary and investigatory interviews, imposing a mandatory affirmative obligation to meet with the union representative only in the case of the disciplinary interview. *Texaco, Inc., Houston Producing Division*, 168 NLRB 361 (1967)....

The Board's holding is a permissible construction of "concerted activities for ... mutual aid or protection" by the agency charged by Congress with enforcement of the Act, and should have been sustained.

The action of an employee in seeking to have the assistance of his union representative at a confrontation with his employer clearly falls within the literal wording of Section 7 that "[e]mployees shall have the right to engage in ... concerted activities for the purpose of ... mutual aid or protection." *Mobil Oil Corp. v. NLRB*, 482 F.2d 842, 847 (7th Cir. 1973). This is true even though the employee alone may have an immediate stake in the outcome; he seeks "aid or protection" against a perceived threat to his employment security. The union representative whose participation he seeks is, however, safeguarding not only the particular employee's interest, but also the interests of the entire bargaining unit by exercising vigilance to make certain that the employer does not initiate or continue a practice of imposing punishment unjustly. The representative's presence is an assurance to other employees in the bargaining unit that they, too, can obtain his aid and protection if called upon to attend a like interview....

The Board's construction plainly effectuates the most fundamental purposes of the Act. In Section 1, 29 U.S.C. Section 151, the Act declares that it is a goal of national labor policy to protect "the

continued

exercise by workers of full freedom of association, self-organization, and designation of representatives of their own choosing, for the purpose of ... mutual aid or protection." To that end the Act is designed to eliminate the "inequality of bargaining power between employees ... and employers." Requiring a lone employee to attend an investigatory interview which he reasonably believes may result in the imposition of discipline perpetuates the inequality the Act was designed to eliminate, and bars recourse to the safeguards the Act provided to redress the perceived imbalance of economic power between labor and management. *American Ship Building Co. v. NLRB*, 380 U.S. 300, 316.... Viewed in this light, the Board's recognition that Section 7 guarantees an employee's right to the presence of a union representative at an investigatory interview in which the risk of discipline reasonably inheres is within the protective ambit of the section "read in the light of the mischief to be corrected and the end to be attained." *NLRB v. Hearst Publications, Inc.*, 322 U.S. 111, 124 (1944).

The Board's construction also gives recognition to the right when it is most useful to both employee and employer. A single employee confronted by an employer investigating whether certain conduct deserves discipline may be too fearful or inarticulate to relate accurately the incident being investigated, or too ignorant to raise extenuating factors. A knowledgeable union representative could assist the employer by eliciting favorable facts, and save the employer production time by getting to the bottom of the incident occasioning the interview. Certainly his presence need not transform the interview into an adversary context. Respondent suggests nonetheless that union representation at this stage is unnecessary because a decision as to employee culpability or disciplinary action can be corrected after the decision to impose discipline has become final. In other words, respondent would defer representation until the filing of a formal grievance challenging the employer's determination of guilt after the employee has been discharged or otherwise disciplined. At that point, however, it becomes increasingly difficult for the employee to vindicate himself, and the value of representation is correspondingly diminished. The employer may then be more concerned with justifying his actions than re-examining them....

The responsibility to adapt the Act to changing patterns of industrial life is entrusted to the Board. The Court of Appeals impermissibly encroached upon the Board's function in determining for itself that an employee has no "need" for union assistance at an investigatory interview. "While a basic purpose of Section 7 is to allow employees to engage in concerted activities for their mutual aid and protection, such a need does not arise at an investigatory interview." 485 F.2d, at 1138. It is the province of the Board, not the courts, to determine whether or not the "need" exists in light of changing industrial practices and the Board's cumulative experience in dealing with labor-management relations. For the Board has the "special function of applying the general provisions of the Act to the complexities of industrial life," *NLRB v. Erie Resistor Corp.*, 373 U.S. 221, 236, ... and its special competence in this field is the justification for the deference accorded its determination. *American Ship Building Co. v. NLRB*, 380 U.S., at 316.... Reviewing courts are of course not "to stand aside and rubber stamp" Board determinations that run contrary to the language or tenor of the Act, *NLRB v. Brown*, 380 U.S. 278, 291.... But the Board's construction here, while it may not be required by the Act, is at least permissible under it, and insofar as the Board's application of that meaning engages in the "difficult and delicate responsibility" of reconciling conflicting interests of labor and management, the balance struck by the Board is "subject to limited judicial review." *NLRB v. Truck Drivers*, 353 U.S. 87, 96.... In sum, the Board has reached a fair and reasoned balance upon a question within its special competence, its newly arrived at construction of Section 7 does not exceed the reach of that section, and the Board has adequately explicated the basis of its interpretation.

The statutory right confirmed today is in full harmony with actual industrial practice. Many important collective bargaining agreements have provisions that accord employees rights of union representation at investigatory interviews. Even where such a right is not explicitly provided in the agreement a "well-established current of arbitral authority" sustains the right of union representation at investigatory interviews which the employee reasonably believes may result in disciplinary action against him. *Chevron Chemical Co.*, 60 Lab. Arb. 1066, 1071 (1973)....

continued

Judgment of Court of Appeals reversed and case remanded with direction to enter a judgment enforcing the Board's order.

Case Questions

1. What Section 7 guarantee does the Court stress in its opinion?

2. Does the Court's opinion give an unlimited right to an employee to have a union representative present when the employee is being questioned?

3. What is the Court's primary reason for leaving unfair labor practice determinations to the NLRB rather than the courts?

<table>
<tr><td>**CASE 5.2**</td><td>IBM CORP.
174 LRRM 1537 (BNA 2004).</td></tr>
</table>

[IBM Corporation's facility at Research Triangle Park, North Carolina, is a nonunion facility. In response to allegations of harassment contained in a letter from a former employee, an IBM manager interviewed three employees individually in October 2001, after denying each employee's request to have a counselor present during the interview. All three were discharged approximately a month after the interviews. An administrative law judge, applying the *Epilepsy Foundation* precedent, found that IBM violated Section 8(a)(1) of the Act by denying each employee's request for the presence of a coworker. A Board majority reversed the *Epilepsy* precedent in IBM.]

From the Opinion of the Board

... Our reexamination of *Epilepsy Foundation* leads us to conclude that the policy considerations supporting that decision do not warrant, particularly at this time, adherence to the holding in *Epilepsy Foundation*. In recent years, there have been many changes in the workplace environment, including ever-increasing requirements to conduct workplace investigations, as well as new security concerns raised by incidents of national and workplace violence.

Our consideration of these features of the contemporary workplace leads us to conclude that an employer must be allowed to conduct its required investigations in a thorough, sensitive, and confidential manner. This can best be accomplished by permitting an employer in a nonunion setting to investigate an employee without the presence of a coworker.... We find the Charging Parties were not entitled to a coworker during the interviews.... Accordingly, we dismiss the complaint.

[Member Schaumber joined the majority opinion's finding that policy considerations support the denial of the *Weingarten* right to the nonunionized workplace. He believes that the *Weingarten* right is unique to employees represented by a Section 9(a) bargaining representative.]

[Members Liebman and Walsh, Dissenting]

... What is at stake is the Act's guarantees for workers who are not represented by a union, today the great majority of American workers.[*] The Act applies to these workers, whether they know it or not, and whether or not the Board is prepared to give full recognition to that fact.... [M]odest as the *Weingarten* right is, it brings a measure of due process to workplace discipline, particularly in nonunion workplaces, where employees and their representatives typically are at-will employees, who may be discharged or disciplined for any reason not specifically prohibited by law. "[T]he presence of a co-worker gives an employee a potential witness, advisor, and advocate in an adversarial situation, and, ideally, militates against the imposition of unjust discipline by the employer." *Epilepsy Foundation*, 268 F.3d at 1100.... They have overruled a sound decision not because they must, and not because they should, but because they can.... We dissent.

---

[*]According to the Bureau of Labor Statistics, in 2003, only 8.2 percent of private-sector employees were unionized. U.S. Department of Labor, Bureau of Labor Statistics.

continued

Case Questions

1. Section 7 of the NLRA states in part, "[e]mployees shall have the right ... to engage in concerted activities for the purposes of ... mutual aid or protection." The Board's construction of this language in *Weingarten* was that it created a statutory right in an employee to refuse to submit to an interview that the employee reasonably feared may result in discipline without union representation. Does this same language provide the same rights to unrepresented employees?

2. Did the [Dissent] concede that the Board [Majority] could legally overrule the *Epilepsy Foundation* precedent?

3. List some advantages and disadvantages to having a coworker present at an investigatory interview.

SECTION 42: DOMINATION OF LABOR ORGANIZATIONS

Section 2(5) of the NLRA broadly defines a **labor organization** as follows:

> The term "labor organization" means any organization of any kind, or any agency or employee representation committee or plan, in which employees participate and which exists for the purpose, in whole or in part, of dealing with employers concerning grievances, labor disputes, wages, rates of pay, hours of employment, or conditions of work.

Section 8(a)(2) of the Act provides that it shall be an unfair labor practice for an employer:

> to dominate or interfere with the formation or administration of any labor organization or contribute financial or other support to it: Provided, that subject to rules and regulations made and published by the Board pursuant to section 6, an employer shall not be prohibited from permitting employees to confer with him during working hours without loss of time or pay.

These provisions outlawing company-dominated labor organizations were a critical part of the Wagner Act, as revealed by the Act's legislative history. Senator Wagner stated in part:

> Genuine collective bargaining is the only way to attain equality of bargaining power.... The greatest obstacles to collective bargaining are employer-dominated unions, which have multiplied with amazing rapidity since the enactment of [the National Industrial Recovery Act]. Such a union makes a sham of equal bargaining power.... (O)nly representatives who are not subservient to the employer with whom they deal can act freely in the interest of employees. For these reasons the very first step toward genuine collective bargaining is the abolition of the employer-dominated union as the agency for dealing with grievances, labor disputes, wages, rates, or hours of employment.[27]

Congress thus brought within the coverage of the Act a broad range of employee groups, and it sought to ensure that such groups were free to act independently of their employer in representing employee interests.

---

[27] *Legislative History of the NLRA of 1935* (GPO, 1949), 15–16.

Employer-formed and employer-dominated unions are outlawed by the NLRA in Section 8(a)(2). The Board can draw inferences as to domination in those cases where a company contributes aid financially or otherwise to the union, is instrumental in a union's formation, or has its agents or supervisory staff solicit membership. The Board makes its decision on domination under the "totality of conduct" doctrine; namely, many little acts when summed up may place the conduct in the unfair labor practice category, even when the acts are unimportant taken individually. It is common for companies today to utilize employee involvement (EI) techniques such as joint employee-management committees that meet and look into safety issues and product quality issues. Such committees have proved to be very successful in helping employers make workplaces safer and have increased product quality, employee morale, and productivity. In unionized companies, these committees are often sanctioned by the unions, with union officers participating on the committees. However, where an employer is seeking to avoid bargaining with a union, the company cannot use a "safety and progress committee" to discuss and resolve an unlimited range of employee problems.[28] Nor may an employer support and use EI committees as a means to supplant or substitute for a union as the exclusive bargaining representative on wages, hours, working conditions, and grievances.

In *Electromation, Inc.*, presented in this section, the NLRB decided that certain **action committees** set up by the employer amounted to an illegal labor organization in violation of Section 8(a)(2) of the Act. The decision was a narrow one, however, and was not intended to suggest that employee committees formed under other circumstances for other purposes would necessarily be deemed a labor organization.

Quality circles are EI groups whose purpose is to utilize employee expertise in examining operational problems such as work quality, labor efficiency, and material waste. Other committees are sometimes called **quality of work-life programs**, whereby management draws on the creativity of its employees by including them in decisions that affect their work life. As long as these employee-management cooperative programs or committees do not usurp the traditional role of a union concerning collective bargaining about wages, hours, working conditions, and grievances, they may be utilized by employers because they are outside the Section 2(5) definition of **labor organization**.

Employers have a range of options to communicate with, learn from, and inform employees. For example, an employer may schedule a brainstorming session on safety with both employees and management participation. In such a situation, there is no "dealing with" employees because the session is not designed as a bilateral mechanism to make and respond to specific proposals.[29]

In the Board's *Syracuse University*[30] 2–1 decision, it considered whether the University's Staff Complaint Process (SCP), established by the employer to handle complaints by nonbargaining unit employees about disciplinary actions against

---

[28] *Szabo v. U.S. Marine Corp.*, 819 F.2d 714 (7th Cir. 1987).

[29] E.I. DuPont Co., 311 NLRB 893, 894 (1993).

[30] 350 NLRB No. 63 (Aug. 15, 2007).

them, was a labor organization within the meaning of Section 2(5) of the Act and, if so, whether the university was in violation of Section 8(a)(2) for establishing the SCP. The SCP consists of three-person panels made up of two employees and one management official with the adjudicative function of resolving the appropriateness of disciplinary actions against employees. The Board majority found that the SCP was not a labor organization within the meaning of Section 2(5) because its purpose was not to "deal with" the employer on terms and conditions of employment—it did not make proposals to management, nor did it represent the employees. Rather, it served a mere adjudicative function. And while a management official served on each three-member panel, there was no evidence that the official "dealt with" the two employees as if they were on opposing sides. Applying *Electromation Inc.* criteria, the dissent would find that the SCP was a labor organization and that the university violated Section 8(a)(2) of the Act by establishing it.

An employer has unilateral mechanisms to elicit the views of its workforce as a whole, including suggestion boxes for employees to present proposals to management or surveys and general employee polls. What it cannot do is create a committee of employees acting as a representative body along with employer representatives for dealing with each other, meeting on company property during working hours to address and agree on work rules, wages, and benefit issues.[31]

CASE 5.3	ELECTROMATION, INC.
	309 NLRB 990 (1992).

[The respondent, Electromation, manufactures electrical components and employs some 200 employees. These employees were not represented by a labor organization during the relevant time period involved in this case. In late 1988, the company cut expenses by altering the existing employee attendance bonus policy and, in lieu of a wage increase for 1989, it distributed year-end lump-sum payments based on length of service. Shortly after these changes, the company received a petition signed by 68 employees expressing displeasure with the new attendance policy. Thereafter, on January 11, company president John Howard met with a selected group of eight employees and discussed with them a number of issues, including wages, bonuses, incentive pay, attendance programs, and leave policy. Howard testified that it was decided after the January 11 meeting that "it was very unlikely that further unilateral management action to resolve these problems was going to come anywhere near making everybody happy ...

and we thought that the best course of action would be to involve the employees in coming up with solutions to these issues." Howard testified further that management came up with the idea of "action committees" as a method to involve employees.

On January 19, the company posted a memorandum to all employees announcing the formation of five action committees and posted sign-up sheets for each action committee. The memorandum explained that each action committee would consist of six employees and one or two members of management as well as the employee benefits manager, Loretta Dickey, who would coordinate all the action committees. The sign-up sheets explained the responsibilities and goals of each committee. No employees were involved in the drafting of the policy goals expressed in the sign-up sheets. The company determined the number of employees permitted to sign up for the action committees, and it informed two employees who had signed up for more than one committee that

continued

---

[31] See *Webcor Packaging, Inc., v. NLRB*, 118 F.3d 1115 (6th Cir. 1997), *cert. denied*, 522 U.S. 1108 (1998).

each would be limited to participation on one committee. After the action committees were organized, the Company posted a notice to all employees announcing the members of each committee and the dates of the initial committee meetings. The action committees were designated as (1) Absenteeism Infractions, (2) No Smoking Policy, (3) Communication Network, (4) Pay Progression for Premium Positions, and (5) Attendance Bonus Program.

Dickey testified that management expected that employee members on the committees would "kind of talk back and forth" with the other employees in the plant and get their ideas, and that, indeed, the purpose of the postings was to ensure that "anyone [who] wanted to know what was going on, they could go to these people" on the action committees. The company paid employees for time spent on committee work and supplied necessary materials. The Teamsters Union made a demand for recognition on February 13. On March 15, Howard informed employees that "due to the Union's campaign, the Company would be unable to participate in the committee meetings and could not continue to work with the committees until after the election," which was to be held on March 31.]

From the Opinion of the Board

... This case presents the issue of whether "Action Committees" composed, in part, of the Respondent's employees constitute a labor organization within the meaning of Section 2(5) of the Act and whether the Respondent's conduct vis-à-vis the "Action Committees" violated Section 8(a)(2) and (1) of the Act. In the notice of hearing of May 14, 1991, the Board framed the pertinent issues as follows:

1. At what point does an employee committee lose its protection as a communication device and become a labor organization?
2. What conduct of an employer constitutes domination or interference with the employee committee?....

...Congress viewed the abolition of employer-dominated organizations as essential to the Act's purpose. After Congress passed the Act in 1935, a first order of business for the Board, backed by the Supreme Court, was to weed out employer-dominated organizations. Indeed, the very first unfair labor practice case decided by the Board raised the issues of whether an organization was a labor organization under Section 2(5) and whether the employer

had dominated that organization in violation of Section 8(a)(2) and (1). *Pennsylvania Greyhound Lines*, 1 NLRB 1 (1935), *enfd. denied* in part 91 F.2d 178 (3d Cir. 1937), *revd.* 303 U.S. 261 (1938). In that case, the Board, as affirmed by the Supreme Court, found that the organization at issue was an employee representation plan under Section 2(5), that the organization was entirely the creation of management, which planned it, sponsored it, and foisted it on employees who had never requested it, and that the organization's functions were described and given to it by management. 1 NLRB at 13–14.

The Greyhound plan was entirely typical of the "employee representation plans or committees" perceived as so pernicious by Senator Wagner and ultimately by Congress. Greyhound management founded the association in 1933. The manager charged with establishing the association wrote that

> it is to our interest to pick out employees to serve on the committee who will work for the interest of the company and will not be radical. This plan of representation should work out very well providing the proper men are selected, and considerable thought should be given to the men placed on this responsible Committee.

Thus, Greyhound usurped from the employees their protected right to a bargaining representative of their own choosing when it set up and accorded recognition to a "committee" that was in no way an agent of the employees or loyal to their interests—although Greyhound management certainly intended that the committee appear to possess both those attributes.

In considering the interplay between Section 2(5) and Section 8(a)(2), we are guided by the Supreme Court's opinion in *NLRB v. Cabot Carbon Co.*, 360 U.S. 203 (1959). In *Cabot Carbon* the Court held that the term "dealing with" in Section 2(5) is broader than the term "collective bargaining" and applies to situations that do not contemplate the negotiation of a collective bargaining agreement....

... [O]ur inquiry is two-fold. First, we inquire whether the entity that is the object of the employer's allegedly unlawful conduct satisfies the definitional elements of Section 2(5) as to (1) employee participation, (2) a purpose to deal with employers, (3) concerning itself with conditions of employment or other statutory subjects, and (4) if an "employee

continued

representation committee or plan" is involved, evidence that the committee is in some way representing the employees. Second, if the organization satisfies those criteria, we consider whether the employer has engaged in any of the three forms of conduct proscribed by Section 8(a)(2)....

Applying these principles to the facts of this case, we find, in agreement with the judge, that the Action Committees constitute a labor organization within the meaning of Section 2(5) of the Act; and that the Respondent dominated it, and assisted it, i.e., contributed support, within the meaning of Section 8(a)(2).

First, there is no dispute that employees participated in the Action Committees. Second, we find that the activities of the committees constituted dealing with an employer. Third, we find that the subject matter of that dealing—which included the treatment of employee absenteeism and employee remuneration in the form of bonuses and other monetary incentives —concerned conditions of employment. Fourth, we find that the employees acted in a representational capacity within the meaning of Section 2(5). Taken as a whole, the evidence underlying these findings shows that the Action Committees were created for, and actually served, the purpose of dealing with the Respondent about conditions of employment....

There can also be no doubt that the Respondents' conduct vis-à-vis the Action Committees constituted "domination" in their formation and administration. It was the Respondent's idea to create the Action Committees. When it presented the idea to employees on January 18, the reaction, as the Respondent's President Howard admitted, was "not positive." Howard then informed employees that management would not "just unilaterally make changes" to satisfy employees' complaints. As a result, employees essentially were presented with the Hobson's choice of accepting the status quo, which they disliked, or undertaking a bilateral "exchange of ideas" within the framework of the Action Committees, as presented by the Respondent. The Respondent drafted the written purposes and goals of the Action Committees which defined and limited the subject matter to be covered by each Committee, determined how many members would compose a committee and that an employee could serve on only one committee, and appointed management representatives to the Committees to facilitate discussions. Finally, much of the evidence supporting the domination finding also

supports a finding of unlawful contribution of support. In particular, the Respondent permitted the employees to carry out the committee activities on paid time within a structure that the Respondent itself created....

In sum, this case presents a situation in which an employer alters conditions of employment and, as a result, is confronted with a workforce that is discontented with its new employment environment. The employer responds to that discontent by devising and imposing on the employees an organized Committee mechanism composed of managers and employees instructed to "represent" fellow employees. The purpose of the Action Committees was, as the record demonstrates, not to enable management and employees to cooperate to improve "quality" or "efficiency," but to create in employees the impression that their disagreements with management had been resolved *bilaterally*. By creating the Action Committees the Respondent imposed on employees its own *unilateral* form of bargaining or dealing and thereby violated Section 8(a)(2) and (1) as alleged.

[The NLRB ordered the company to immediately disestablish and cease giving assistance or any other support to the Action Committees.]

[*Concurring opinions were filed by three of the four Board members participating in the decision.*]

[Note: The Teamsters Union lost the initial representation election at Electromation, Inc.,: however, a rerun election was ordered, and the union won this election and was certified. Eventually, a collective bargaining contract was negotiated. In October 1993, a decertification petition was filed, but the employees again voted for the union. The parties thereafter reached an agreement on a three-year contract.]

Case Questions

1. Assess the fairness of the following statement in light of the *Pennsylvania Greyhound Lines* precedent case: "An employer-dominated organization robs employees of the freedom to choose their own representative."

2. Read Section 8(a)(2) of the Act and identify the three forms of employer conduct prohibited by this section of the Act.

3. Did the employer's conduct in this case constitute "domination" in the foundation and administration of the Action Committees?

SECTION 43: DISCRIMINATION AS TO HIRE AND TENURE

In the *Jones & Laughlin Steel* decision in Chapter 4, the Supreme Court discussed how Section 8 of the NLRA forbids all forms of employer discrimination tending to encourage as well as discourage membership in a labor union. This rule is subject to the proviso that an employer may lawfully terminate an individual in instances where the labor organization is functioning under authority of a union shop or maintenance-of-membership agreement and the union seeks the discharge of an employee because of failure to pay dues or initiation fees. (See Section 47 of this chapter.)

The NLRB has found evidence of discrimination against active union supporters where the employer:

1. Gives inconsistent reasons for discharge;
2. Discharges on the strength of past misdeeds that were condoned;
3. Neglects to give customary warning prior to discharge;
4. Discharges for a rule generally unenforced;
5. Applies disproportionately severe punishment to union supporters;
6. Effects layoffs in violation of seniority status with disproportionate impact on union supporters.

The NLRA preserves the right of the employer to maintain control over the workforce in the interest of discipline, efficiency, and pleasant and safe customer relations. Employees, on the other hand, have the right to be free from coercive discrimination resulting from union activity. Job applicants, as in the *Phelps Dodge* case referenced in Chapter 4, also receive the same protection from illegal discrimination.

At times, these two rights may collide. For example, an employee may be discharged for apparently two reasons: (1) violation of a valid company rule and (2) union activity. The former is given by the employer as the reason for termination; the latter remains unstated on the employer's part, causing the labor organization to file a Section 8(a)(3) charge against the employer. These are known as **dual-motive** cases.

The *Wright Line*[32] decision set forth a new standard to be applied to all Section 8(a)(3) cases and cases turning on employer motivation, including dual-motive situations. Under the Board's *Wright Line* test, the General Counsel must make on behalf of the dismissed employee a prima facie showing sufficient to support the inference that protected conduct such as union activity was a "motivating factor" in the employer's decision. After this showing, the burden shifts to the employer, who must demonstrate that the employee would have been dismissed for legitimate business reasons even absent the protected conduct.

The Board restated the *Wright Line* test in a 1996 decision as follows:

> The General Counsel has the burden to persuade that antiunion sentiment was a substantial or motivating factor in the challenged employer decision. The

---

[32] 251 NLRB 1083 (1980).

burden of persuasion then shifts to the employer to prove its affirmative defense that it would have taken the same action even if the employees had not engaged in protected activity.[33]

This two-step standard reconciles the rights of the employee and the employer. The first step, a prima facie showing that protected conduct was a motivating factor in the dismissal, allows the administrative law judge and the Board to consider whether the evidence shows that it is likely that the employee's rights have been violated by the employer. The second step, where the burden of persuasion shifts to the employer to prove that the employee would have been dismissed for legitimate business reasons even absent the protected conduct, allows the administrative law judge and the Board to consider the evidence and interests of the employer in dismissing the employee.

The General Counsel's case on behalf of an employee may be insufficient to show that union activity was a motivating factor in the dismissal. On the other hand, where a prima facie case is made for an employee, the ALJ and the Board may determine that the reasons offered by the employer for the discharge were a "pretext."[34] Reasons for termination not accepted by the Board have been noted at the start of this section. Examples of legitimate reasons for termination may be dishonesty, assault on a supervisor or fellow employee, aggravated sexual harassment, gross insubordination, unlawful strike activity, use of intoxicants or drugs on company premises, or discharge in accordance with progressive discipline for absences and tardiness.

The *Transportation Management Corp.* decision of the Supreme Court, which unanimously confirmed the *Wright Line* test, is presented in this section. In *Emerson Electric Company v. NLRB*,[35] the Court of Appeals for the Eighth Circuit held that the employee's support of a union plus the supervisor's knowledge of the employee's union activities were not sufficient to support an inference that the employee's discharge was motivated by antiunion considerations.

---

[33] The *Wright Line* test was approved in 1983 by the U.S. Supreme Court in the *NLRB v. Transportation Management* decision, reported in this section. In the U.S. Supreme Court's *Office of Workers Compensation Programs, Department of Labor v. Greenwich Collieries* decision, 512 U.S. 267 (1994), the Court made clear that the ultimate burden of persuasion remains with the General Counsel, regardless of the language used in the 1983 *Transportation Management* case. The Court added that once the General Counsel establishes that antiunion animus was a motivating factor, the employer bears the burden of establishing any affirmative defense. Accordingly, the Board restated the *Wright Line* test in terms of burden to persuade in its *Manno Electric* decision, 321 NLRB 278 at footnote 12 (1996).

[34] In modern-day labor relations, an employer will rarely, if ever, baldly assert that it has disciplined an employee because it detests unions or will not tolerate employees engaging in union or other protected activities. Instead, it will generally advance what it asserts to be a legitimate business reason for its action. Examination of the evidence may reveal, however, that the asserted justification is a sham in that the purported rule or circumstance advanced by the employer did not exist or was not, in fact, relied upon. When this occurs, the reason advanced by the employer may be termed *pretextual*. Because no legitimate business justification for the discipline exists, there is, by strict definition, no dual motive. Nevertheless, the *Wright Line* steps are applicable to all such Section 8(a)(3) cases.

[35] 573 F.2d 543 (8th Cir. 1978).

CASE 5.4	NLRB v. Transportation Management Corp.
	Supreme Court of the United States, 462 U.S. 393 (1983).

[Prior to his discharge, Sam Santillo was a bus driver for respondent Transportation Management Corp. On March 19, 1979, Santillo talked to officials of the Teamsters Union about organizing the drivers who worked with him. Over the next four days, Santillo discussed with his fellow drivers the possibility of joining the Teamsters and distributed authorization cards. On the night of March 23, George Patterson, who supervised Santillo and the other drivers, told one of the drivers that he had heard of Santillo's activities. Patterson referred to Santillo as two-faced and promised to get even with him. Later that evening Patterson talked to Ed West, who was also a bus driver for respondent. Patterson asked, "What's with Sam and the union?" Patterson said that he took Santillo's actions personally, recounted several favors he had done for Santillo, and added that he would remember Santillo's activities when Santillo again asked for a favor. On Monday, March 26, Santillo was discharged. Patterson told Santillo that he was being fired for leaving his keys in the bus and taking unauthorized breaks. Santillo filed charges with the Board, and the General Counsel issued a complaint contending that Santillo was discharged because of his union activities in distributing authorization cards to fellow employees. The administrative law judge (ALJ) determined that Patterson's disapproval of Santillo's practice of leaving his keys in the bus was clearly a pretext and that the practice of leaving keys in buses was commonplace among company employees. The company identified two types of unauthorized breaks: coffee breaks and stops at home. With respect to both coffee breaks and stopping at home, the ALJ found that Santillo was never cautioned or admonished about such behavior and that the employer had not followed its customary practice of issuing three written warnings before discharging a driver. The ALJ also found that the taking of coffee breaks during work hours was normal practice and that the company tolerated the practice unless the breaks interfered with the driver's performance of his duties. The ALJ found that the company had never taken any adverse personnel action against an employee because of such behavior. The Board adopted the ALJ's findings and expressly applied its *Wright Line* decision. The First Circuit Court of Appeals refused to enforce the Board's order. The Supreme Court granted certiorari.]

WHITE, J....

The Court of Appeals for the First Circuit refused enforcement of the *Wright Line* decision because in its view it was error to place the burden on the employer to prove that the discharge would have occurred had the forbidden motive not been present. The General Counsel, the Court of Appeals held, had the burden of showing not only that a forbidden motivation contributed to the discharge but also that the discharge would not have taken place independently of the protected conduct of the employee. The Court of Appeals was quite correct, and the Board does not disagree, that throughout the proceedings, the General Counsel carries the burden of proving the elements of an unfair labor practice. Section 10(c) of the Act, 29 U.S.C. § 160(c), expressly directs that violations may be adjudicated only "upon the preponderance of the testimony" taken by the Board. The Board's rules also state "the Board's attorney has the burden of pro[ving] violations of Section 8." 29 CFR § 101.10(b). We are quite sure, however, that the Court of Appeals erred in holding that § 10(c) forbids placing the burden on the employer to prove that absent the improper motivation he would have acted in the same manner for wholly legitimate reasons....

We assume that the Board could reasonably have construed the Act in the manner insisted on by the Court of Appeals.... The Board has instead chosen to recognize, as it insists it has done for many years, what it designates as an affirmative defense that the employer has the burden of sustaining. We are unprepared to hold that this is an impermissible construction of the Act.... "[T]he Board's construction here, while it may not be required by the Act, is at least permissible under it...," and in these circumstances its position is entitled to deference....

The Board's allocation of the burden of proof is clearly reasonable in this context, for the reason stated in *NLRB v. Remington Rand*, 94 F.2d 862 (1938), a case on which the Board relied when it began taking the position that the burden of persuasion could be shifted. The employer is a wrongdoer; he has acted out of a motive that is declared illegitimate by the statute. It is fair that he bear the risk that the influence of legal and illegal motives cannot be separated, because he knowingly created the risk and

continued

because the risk was created not by innocent activity but by his own wrongdoing....

The Board was justified in this case in concluding that Santillo would not have been discharged had the employer not considered his efforts to establish a union. At least two of the transgressions that purportedly would have in any event prompted Santillo's discharge were commonplace, and yet no transgressor had ever before received any kind of discipline. Moreover, the employer departed from its usual practice in dealing with rules infractions; indeed, not only did the employer not warn Santillo that his actions would result in being subjected to discipline, it never even expressed its disapproval of his conduct. In addition, Patterson, the person who made the initial decision to discharge Santillo, was obviously upset with Santillo for engaging in such protected activity. It is thus clear that the Board's finding that Santillo would not have been fired if the employer had not had an anti-union animus was "supported by sub-

stantial evidence on the record considered as a whole," 29 U.S.C. § 160(f).

Accordingly the judgment is
Reversed.

Case Questions

1. According to the General Counsel's position, why was Santillo fired by his employer?
2. Why was Santillo fired according to the company?
3. Did the Supreme Court find that the Board was justified in concluding that Santillo would not have been discharged had the employer not considered his efforts to establish a union?
4. Did the Supreme Court agree with the court of appeals that Section 10(c) of the Act forbids placing the burden on the employer to prove that, absent the improper motivation, the employer would have acted in the same manner for wholly legitimate reasons?

SECTION 44: DISCRIMINATORY LOCKOUTS

The legality of a layoff or lockout of employees during bargaining raises issues concerning the motive of the employer and the effect on the employee's rights. If a defensive act is undertaken to protect the employer's business in the face of a threatened strike or to improve the employer's bargaining position rather than to interfere with bargaining rights or union activity, no violation of the Act occurs. The NLRB had been inclined to conclude that anything is illegal except a strictly defensive shutdown. The courts, however, have been willing to allow the employer more freedom temporarily to use a lockout, as in the *Brown* case presented next, reversing the NLRB ruling of illegality.

In the so-called *Buffalo Linen* decision, *Truck Drivers Local 449 v. NLRB*,[36] the Board determined that a lockout for defending a multiemployer bargaining unit was legal. The Supreme Court agreed. In *Buffalo Linen*, one employer member was struck as a whipsaw tactic by the union to pressure the others, and the others legally locked out their employees to defend their position. However, a lockout to force a union to accept multiemployer bargaining rather than to protect the existing unit is an illegal offensive lockout according to the Board.[37]

In *American Shipbuilding Co. v. NLRB*,[38] the "defensive lockout" theory of *Brown* was extended. The Supreme Court reversed the Board's ruling of discrimination. The Supreme Court found no antiunion or antibargaining motives in an employer's shutdown designed to improve the employer's economic position in

---

[36] 353 U.S. 87 (1956).

[37] Great Atlantic and Pacific Tea Co., 145 NLRB 361 (1963).

[38] 380 U.S. 300 (1965).

negotiating. The Court held that "there is nothing in the Act which gives employees the right to insist on their contract demands, free from the sort of economic disadvantage which frequently attends bargaining disputes. Therefore, we conclude that where the intention proven is merely to bring about a settlement of a labor dispute on favorable terms, no violation of Section 8(a)(3) is shown."

CASE 5.5	NATIONAL LABOR RELATIONS BOARD V. BROWN, D.B.A. BROWN FOOD STORES

SUPREME COURT OF THE UNITED STATES, 380 U.S. 278 (1965).

BRENNAN, J....

The respondents, who are members of a multiemployer bargaining group, locked out their employees in response to a whipsaw strike against another member of the group [Food Jet, Inc.]. They and the struck employer continued operations with temporary replacements. The National Labor Relations Board found that the struck employer's use of temporary replacements was lawful under *Labor Board v. Mackay Radio & Telegraph Co.*, 304 U.S. 333, but that the respondents had violated Sections 8(a)(1) and (3) of the National Labor Relations Act by locking out their regular employees and using temporary replacements to carry on business. 137 NLRB 73. The Court of Appeals for the Tenth Circuit disagreed and refused to enforce the Board's order. 319 F.2d 7. We granted certiorari, 375 U.S. 962. We affirm the Court of Appeals....

The Board's decision does not rest upon independent evidence that the respondents acted either out of hostility toward the Local or in reprisal for the whipsaw strike. It rests upon the Board's appraisal that the respondent's conduct carried its own indicia of unlawful intent, thereby establishing, without more, that the conduct constituted an unfair labor practice. It was disagreement with this appraisal, which we share, that led the Court of Appeals to refuse to enforce the Board's order.

It is true that the Board need not inquire into employer motivation to support a finding of an unfair practice where the employer conduct is demonstrably destructive of employee rights and is not justified by the service of significant or important business ends. See, e.g., *Labor Board v. Erie Resistor Corp.*, 373 U.S. 221. We agree with the Court of Appeals that, in the setting of this whipsaw strike and Food Jet's

continued operations, the respondents' lockout and their continued operations with the use of temporary replacements, viewed separately or as a single act, do not constitute such conduct.

We begin with the proposition that the Act does not constitute the Board as an "arbiter of the sort of economic weapons the parties can use in seeking to gain acceptance of their bargaining demands." In the absence of proof of unlawful motivation, there are many economic weapons which an employer may use that either interfere in some measure with concerted employee activities, or which are in some degree discriminatory and discourage union membership, and yet the use of such economic weapons does not constitute conduct that is within the prohibition of either Section 8(a)(1) or Section 8(a)(3). Even the Board concedes that an employer may legitimately blunt the effectiveness of an anticipated strike by stockpiling inventories, readjusting contract schedules, or transferring work from one plant to another, even if he thereby makes himself "virtually strikeproof." As a general matter he may completely liquidate his business without violating either Section 8(a)(1) or Section 8(a)(3), whatever the impact of his action on concerted employee activities. *Textile Workers v. Darlington Mfg. Co.*, Nos. 37 and 41, decided today. Specifically, he may in various circumstances use the lockout as a legitimate economic weapon. And in *American Ship Building Co. v. Labor Board*, No. 255, decided today, we hold that lockout is not an unfair labor practice simply because used by an employer to bring pressure to bear in support of his bargaining position after an impasse in bargaining negotiations has been reached.

In the circumstances of this case, we do not see how the continued operations of respondents and their use of temporary replacements any more imply

continued

hostile motivation, nor how they are inherently more destructive of employee rights, than is the lockout itself. Rather, the compelling inference is that this was all part and parcel of respondents' defensive measure to preserve the multiemployer group in the face of the whipsaw strike....

... In determining here that the respondents' conduct carried its own badge of improper motive, the Board's decision, for the reasons stated, misapplied the criteria for governing the application of Section 8(a)(1) and (3). Since the order therefore rested on

an "erroneous legal foundation," the Court of Appeals properly refused to enforce it.

Affirmed.

Case Questions

1. What factual difference existed between the *Buffalo Linen* case referred to in the text and the *Brown* case?
2. Why did the Court reverse the Board's decision?
3. What is an illegal lockout?
4. What is meant by a **whipsaw strike?**

SECTION 45: PERMANENT SHUTDOWNS

As distinct from a temporary shutdown or layoff, the permanent shutdown of a unionized company raises some other difficult questions. In the liquidation of an operation, a violation of Section 8(a)(3) may be found by the NLRB if union membership or avoidance of collective bargaining is found to be the controlling motivation. A Section 8(a)(3) violation does not exist where legitimate economic considerations rather than antiunion reasons were the controlling factors.

In the *Darlington Manufacturing Co.* case, presented in this section, a recently unionized company owned by a multiplant parent corporation was liquidated. Some economic factors, as well as unionization, contributed to its shutting down. The employer's claim of an absolute right to go out of business was denied by the NLRB. The court of appeals refused to enforce the Board's order, and the matter was remanded to the Board by the Supreme Court for further evidence as to any coercive impact of the shutdown on employees at other plants of the parent corporation. The Court held that the mill closing was an unfair labor practice under Section 8(a)(3) "if motivated by a purpose to chill unionism in any of the remaining plants ... much the same as that found to exist in runaway shop and temporary closing cases." On remand to the Board, the employer's closing and liquidation of the plant was found to be in violation of Section 8(a)(3). As a remedy, the employer was ordered to offer terminated employees jobs at other plants where work was available, with travel and moving expenses to be paid by the employer for those who accepted such work. The employer was ordered to pay back wages to the employees less their interim earnings until such time as they obtained comparable employment or were offered comparable jobs at the employer's other plants.[39] The litigation continued thereafter before the Board and the courts until December 1980 when the parent corporation agreed to pay $5 million in back pay. Prior to this agreement, no employee terminated as a result of the closing of the textile mill in 1956 had received any compensation for the unlawful shutdown. The settlement agreement marked the end of the most protracted labor dispute in American history.

---

[39] 165 NLRB 1074 (1967), *enforced* 397 F.2d 760 (4th Cir. 1968).

| TEXTILE WORKERS OF AMERICA V. DARLINGTON MANUFACTURING CO.
SUPREME COURT OF THE UNITED STATES, 380 U.S. 263 (1965).

HARLAN, J....

We here review a judgment of the Court of Appeals refusing to enforce an order of the National Labor Relations Board which found respondent Darlington guilty of an unfair labor practice by reason of having permanently closed its plant following petitioner union's election as the bargaining representative of Darlington's employees.

Darlington Manufacturing Company was a South Carolina corporation operating one textile mill. A majority of Darlington's stock was held by Deering Milliken, a New York "selling house" marketing textiles produced by others. Deering Milliken in turn was controlled by Roger Milliken, president of Darlington, and by other members of the Milliken family. The National Labor Relations Board found that the Milliken family, through Deering Milliken, operated 17 textile manufacturers, including Darlington, whose products, manufactured in 27 different mills, were marketed through Deering Milliken.

In March 1956 petitioner Textile Workers Union initiated an organizational campaign at Darlington which the company resisted vigorously in various ways, including threats to close the mill if the union won a representation election. On September 6, 1956, the union won an election by a narrow margin. When Roger Milliken was advised of the union victory, he decided to call a meeting of the Darlington board of directors to consider closing the mill. Mr. Milliken testified before the Labor Board:

> I felt that as a result of the campaign that
> had been conducted and the promises and
> statements made in these letters that had
> been distributed [favoring unionization], that
> if before we had had some hope, possible hope
> of achieving competitive [costs] ... by taking
> advantage of new machinery that was being
> put in, that this hope had diminished as a
> result of the election because a majority
> of the employees had voted in favor of the
> union... (R. 457).

The board of directors met on September 12 and voted to liquidate the corporation, action which was approved by the stockholders on October 17. The plant ceased operations entirely in November, and all plant machinery and equipment was sold piecemeal at auction in December.

The Union filed charges with the Labor Board claiming that Darlington had violated Section 8(a)(1) and (a)(3) of the National Labor Relations Act by closing its plant, and Section 8(a)(5) by refusing to bargain with the union after the election. The Board, by a divided vote, found that Darlington had been closed because of the antiunion animus of Roger Milliken, and held that to be a violation of Section 8(a)(3). The Board also found Darlington to be part of a single integrated employer group controlled by the Milliken family through Deering Milliken; therefore Deering Milliken could be held liable for the unfair labor practices of Darlington. Alternatively, since Darlington was a part of the Deering Milliken enterprise, Deering Milliken had violated the Act by closing part of its business for a discriminatory purpose. The Board ordered back pay for all Darlington employees until they obtained substantially equivalent work or were put on preferential hiring lists at the other Deering Milliken mills. Respondent Deering Milliken was ordered to bargain with the union in regard to details of compliance with the Board order. 139 NLRB 241.

On review, the Court of Appeals ... denied enforcement by a divided vote. 325 F.2d 682. The Court of Appeals held that even accepting *arguendo* the Board's determination that Deering Milliken had the status of a single employer, a company has the absolute right to close out a part or all of its business regardless of antiunion motives. The court therefore did not review the Board's finding that Deering Milliken was a single integrated employer. We granted certiorari, 377 U.S. 903, to consider the important questions involved. We hold that so far as the Labor Relations Act is concerned, an employer has the absolute right to terminate his entire business for any reason he pleases, but disagree with the Court of Appeals that such right includes the ability to close part of a business no matter what the reason. We conclude that the case must be remanded to the Board for further proceedings....

[The Court hereinafter considers whether the closing, if discriminatorily motivated, is in violation of Section 8(a)(3) of the NLRA.]

We consider first the argument, advanced by the petitioner union but not by the Board, and rejected by the Court of Appeals, that an employer may not go completely out of business without running afoul of the Labor Relations Act if such action is prompted by

continued

a desire to avoid unionization. Given the Board's finding on the issue of motive, acceptance of this contention would carry the day for the Board's conclusion that the closing of this plant was an unfair labor practice, even on the assumption that Darlington is to be regarded as an independent unrelated employer. A proposition that a single businessman cannot choose to go out of business if he wants to would represent such a startling innovation that it should not be entertained without the clearest manifestation of legislative intent or unequivocal judicial precedent so construing the Labor Relations Act. We find neither.

So far as legislative manifestation is concerned, it is sufficient to say that there is not the slightest indication in the history of the Wagner Act or of the Taft-Hartley Act that Congress envisaged any such result under either statute....

We are not presented here with the case of a "runaway shop," whereby Darlington would transfer its work to another plant or open a new plant in another locality to replace its closed plant. Nor are we concerned with a shutdown where the employees, by renouncing the union, could cause the plant to reopen. Such cases would involve discriminatory employer action for the purpose of obtaining some benefit from the employees in the future. We hold here only that when an employer closes his entire business, even if the liquidation is motivated by vindictiveness toward the union, such action is not an unfair labor practice....

The closing of an entire business, even though discriminatory, ends the employer-employee relationship; the force of such a closing is entirely spent as to that business when termination of the enterprise takes place. On the other hand, a discriminatory partial closing may have repercussions on what remains of the business, affording employer leverage for discouraging the free exercise of Section 7 rights among remaining employees of much the same kind as that found to exist in the "runaway shop" and "temporary closing" cases. Moreover, a possible remedy open to the Board in such a case like the remedies available in the "runaway shop" and "temporary closing" cases, is to order reinstatement of the discharged employees in the other parts of the business. No such remedy is available when an entire business has been terminated. By analogy to those cases involving a continuing enterprise we are constrained to hold, in disagreement with the Court of Appeals, that a partial closing is an unfair labor practice under Section 8(a)(3) if motivated by a purpose to chill

unionism in any of the remaining plants of the single employer and if the employer may reasonably have foreseen that such closing would likely have that effect.

While we have spoken in terms of a "partial closing" in the context of the Board's finding that Darlington was part of a larger single enterprise controlled by the Milliken family, we do not mean to suggest that an organizational integration of plants or corporations is a necessary prerequisite to the establishment of such a violation of Section 8(a)(3). If the persons exercising control over a plant that is being closed for antiunion reasons (1) have an interest in another business, whether or not affiliated with or engaged in the same line of commercial activity as the closed plant, of sufficient substantiality to give promise of their reaping a benefit from the discouragement of unionization in that business; (2) act to close their plant with the purpose of producing such a result; and (3) occupy a relationship to the other business which makes it realistically foreseeable that its employees will fear that such business will also be closed down if they persist in organization activities, we think that an unfair labor practice has been made out.

Although the Board's single employer finding necessarily embraced findings as to Roger Milliken and the Milliken family which, if sustained by the Court of Appeals, would satisfy the elements of "interest" and "relationship" with respect to other parts of the Deering Milliken enterprise, that and the other Board findings fall short of establishing the factors of "purpose" and "effect" which are vital requisites of the general principles that govern a case of this kind.

Thus, the Board's findings as to the purpose and foreseeable effect of the Darlington closing pertained *only* to its impact on the Darlington employees. No findings were made as to the purpose and effect of the closing with respect to the employees in the other plants comprising the Deering-Milliken group. It does not suffice to establish the unfair labor practice charged here to argue that the Darlington closing necessarily had an adverse impact upon unionization in such other plants. We have heretofore observed that employer action which has a foreseeable consequence of discouraging concerted activities generally does not amount to a violation of Section 8(a)(3) in the absence of a showing of motivation which is aimed at achieving the prohibited effect. See *Teamsters Local v. Labor Board*, 365 U.S. 667, and the concurring opinion therein, at 677. In an area which trenches

continued

so closely upon otherwise legitimate employer prerogatives, we consider the absence of Board findings on this score a fatal defect in its decision....

In these circumstances, we think the proper disposition of this case is to require that it be remanded to the Board so as to afford the Board the opportunity to make further findings on the issue of purpose and effect.

It is so ordered.

Case Questions

1. State the facts of the case.
2. May an employer close down its business for any reason it pleases?
3. What remedy did the Board order?
4. Summarize the rule promulgated by the Supreme Court.

SECTION 46: DISCRIMINATION FOR CONCERTED ACTIVITIES

Different types of strikes and pressure tactics will be discussed in Chapter 7 with explanations of the extent of legal protection for the participants. During an economic strike, an employer may legally replace such strikers permanently. However, **economic strikers** who unconditionally apply for reinstatement and make known their continued availability are entitled to reinstatement by the employer as long as a vacancy exists for which they are qualified. If the strikers have been permanently replaced, they are entitled to reinstatement when permanent replacements leave their jobs. Strikers violating the unfair labor practices of Section 8(b) or a no-strike contract provision or engaging in other serious misconduct may be lawfully discharged on a nondiscriminatory basis. Employer **unfair labor practice strikers** receive full reinstatement protection regardless of the replacements, with back pay ordered from the date of a refusal to reemploy upon request up to the date of reemployment in the vast majority of cases.

When strikers' job rights exist, it is illegal for the employer to deprive strikers of seniority rights by giving superior seniority or superseniority to replacements or to those strikers returning to work first. In *NLRB v. Erie Resistor Corp.*,[40] a strike was called when bargaining on a new contract reached an impasse. The company, under intense competitive pressures, decided to continue production operations, and after a period of weeks, it notified the union that it would begin hiring replacements. Several weeks later the company informed the union that it had decided to award 20 years additional seniority—for credit against future layoffs—to replacements and strikers who returned by a certain date. The union charged that this granting of superseniority during a strike was an unfair labor practice. The Supreme Court held that such action unavoidably discouraged protected collective activities and must have been so intended. A weighing process was used to consider the conflict between the employer's interest in operating its business in a particular way and the employees' interest in concerted economic action. Answering the problem, the Court said the employer's asserted business purpose did not balance the violation of the strikers' rights in the light of the federal law's deference to the strike weapon.

The *Great Dane Trailer* case presented next deals with another type of employer action affecting economic strikers. In this case, the employer paid accrued vacation benefits to nonstrikers and announced the extinction of these benefits to strikers. The Supreme Court considered the factor of employer motivation in the context of a Section 8(a)(3) violation and set forth the controlling principles.

---

[40] 373 U.S. 221 (1963).

CASE 5.7	NLRB v. GREAT DANE TRAILER, INC.
	SUPREME COURT OF THE UNITED STATES, 388 U.S. 26 (1967).

WARREN, C. J....

The issue here is whether, in the absence of proof of an antiunion motivation, an employer may be held to have violated Sections 8(a)(3) and (1) of the National Labor Relations Act when it refused to pay striking employees vacation benefits accrued under a terminated collective bargaining agreement while it announced an intention to pay such benefits to striker replacements, returning strikers, and nonstrikers who had been at work on a certain date during the strike.

The respondent company and the union entered into a collective bargaining agreement which was effective by its terms until March 31, 1963.... In essence, the company agreed to pay specified vacation benefits to employees who, during the preceding year, had worked at least 1,525 hours. It was also provided that, in the case of a "lay-off, termination or quitting," employees who had served more than 60 days during the year would be entitled to pro rata shares of their vacation benefits. Benefits were to be paid on the Friday nearest July 1 of each year.

The agreement was temporarily extended beyond its termination date, but on April 30, 1963, the union gave the required 15 days' notice of intention to strike over issues which remained unsettled at the bargaining table. Accordingly, on May 16, 1963, approximately 350 of the company's 400 employees commenced a strike which lasted until December 26, 1963. The company continued to operate during the strike, using nonstrikers, persons hired as replacements for strikers, and some original strikers who had later abandoned the strike and returned to work. On July 12, 1963, a number of the strikers demanded their accrued vacation pay from the company. The company rejected this demand, basing its response on the assertion that all contractual obligations had been terminated by the strike and, therefore, none of the company's employees had a right to vacation pay. Shortly thereafter, however, the company announced that it would grant vacation pay—in the amounts and subject to the conditions set out in the expired agreement—to all employees who had reported for work on July 1, 1963. The company denied that these payments were founded on the agreement and stated that they merely reflected a new "policy" which had been unilaterally adopted.

The refusal to pay vacation benefits to strikers, coupled with the payments to nonstrikers, formed the basis of an unfair labor practice complaint filed with the Board while the strike was still in progress.... [The Board held that the company had violated Sections 8(a)(3) and 8(a)(1) of the NLRA, and the Fifth Circuit Court of Appeals denied enforcement of the Board's order.]

But inquiry under Section 8(a)(3) does not usually stop at this point. The statutory language "discrimination ... to ... discourage" means that the finding of a violation normally turns on whether the discriminatory conduct was motivated by an antiunion purpose. *American Ship Building Co. v. Labor Board*, 380 U.S. 300 (1965). It was upon the motivation element that the Court of Appeals based its decision not to grant enforcement, and it is to that element which we now turn. In three recent opinions we considered employer motivation in the context of asserted Section 8(a)(3) violations. *American Ship Building Co. v. Labor Board, supra*; *Labor Board v. Brown*, 380 U.S. 278 (1965); and *Labor Board v. Erie Resistor Corp., supra*....

From this review of our recent decisions, several principles of controlling importance here can be distilled. First, if it can reasonably be concluded that the employer's discriminatory conduct was "inherently destructive" of important employee rights, no proof of an antiunion motivation is needed and the Board can find an unfair labor practice even if the employer introduces evidence that the conduct was motivated by business considerations. Second, if the adverse effect of the discriminatory conduct on employee rights is "comparatively slight," an antiunion motivation must be proved to sustain the charge *if* the employer has come forward with evidence of legitimate and substantial business justifications for the conduct. Thus, in either situation, once it has been proved that the employer engaged in discriminatory conduct which could have adversely affected employee rights to *some* extent, the burden is upon the employer to establish that he was motivated by legitimate objectives since proof of motivation is most accessible to him.

Applying the principles to this case then, it is not necessary for us to decide the degree to which the challenged conduct might have affected employee rights. As the Court of Appeals correctly noted, the

continued

company came forward with no evidence of legitimate motives for its discriminatory conduct. 363 F.2d at 134. The company simply did not meet the burden of proof, and the Court of Appeals misconstrued the function of judicial review when it proceeded nonetheless to speculate upon what *might have* motivated the company. Since discriminatory conduct carrying a potential for adverse effect upon employee rights was proved and no evidence of a proper motivation appeared in the record, the Board's conclusions were supported by substantial evidence, *Universal Camera Corp. v. Labor Board*, 340 U.S. 474 (1951), and should have been sustained.

The judgment of the Court of Appeals is reversed and the case is remanded with directions to enforce the Board's order.

It is so ordered.

Case Questions

1. What is the issue that the Supreme Court is called upon to resolve?
2. What are the controlling principles set forth by the Supreme Court concerning the significance of employer motivation in the context of an alleged Section 8(a)(3) violation?
3. What was the holding of the case?

SECTION 47: UNION SECURITY AND "RIGHT-TO-WORK" LAWS

Union security clauses contained in collective bargaining contracts have been a source of tension between those who object to joining and supporting unions and the union adherents, who assert that it is a fundamental necessity that the unions be able to generate the economic resources through periodic dues to provide appropriate representation. Right-to-work laws prohibit certain union security agreements in certain states.

Union Security Clauses and the Rights of Objectors

Sections 8(a)(3) and 8(b)(2) authorize the parties to collective bargaining agreements to enter into agreements by which employees working under such agreements, as a condition of continued employment, are required to maintain membership in a union. This is a so-called union shop clause or agreement. Under the NLRA, employees subject to a union shop agreement must be allowed a minimum of 30 days to join a union. Section 8(f) provides an exception to the 30-day requirement, permitting the enforcement of a seven-day union shop agreement in the construction industry because of the occasional nature of work in that industry.

The union shop agreement permitted by Section 8(a)(3) does not require full union membership, but only dues-paying membership. Thus, a union can compel an employer to terminate an employee for failure to be a member of the union only when the employee is unwilling to meet the initiation fee and union dues required of all employees working under the collective bargaining agreement. The rationale for the dues-paying requirement of the Act is that all employees who receive the benefits of a union's representation of the employees in contract negotiations and contract administration, including the costs of arbitration of grievances, should share in the costs of such services.[41] Nonmembers should not be allowed to "free ride" on the dues paid by union members.

---

[41] See *William F. Buckley v. Television & Radio Artists*, 496 F.2d 305 (2d Cir. 1974).

Much less commonly used than the union shop form of union security agreement is the agency shop agreement, which requires all unit employees, both union and nonunion, to pay a representation or agency fee, or union dues, as a condition of employment.

A problem exists, however, with union or agency shop agreements under which all employees must pay the union representation fees, in that unions expend some funds for activities that are not related to collective bargaining. In *Communication Workers of America v. Beck*,[42] the Supreme Court determined that collective bargaining agreements negotiated in the private sector are unlawful to the extent that nonunion employees must pay fees for union representation, which include the financing of activities other than the negotiation and administration of the collective bargaining agreement, and the nonunion employees object to the financing of such activities. In *NLRB v. Studio Transportation Drivers Local 399*, presented in this section, the Teamsters Union was found to have committed a Section 8(b)(1)(a) unfair labor practice in its method of calclating *Beck* objector's dues.

In its *California Saw and Knife Works*[43] decision, the Board ruled in a series of consolidated cases that (1) unions must timely inform newly hired nonmembers of their *Beck* rights, and such notice may be provided in a union newspaper if reasonable perusal would alert nonmembers of their *Beck* policy; (2) unions may not insist that nonmember objections be sent to the union by registered mail; (3) unions need not calculate agency fee reductions on a unit-by-unit basis and may include as a fee for union representation litigation expenses, including expenses external to a unit that may ultimately inure to the benefit of unit employees; and (4) unions may consolidate arbitration hearings regarding challenges to dues reduction calculations and may require challengers to bear the cost of their travel expenses for such hearings.

In *UFCW Locals 951, 7, and 1036 v. NLRB*,[44] certain individuals employed by Meijer, Inc., a food retailer, asserted their *Beck* rights and objected to paying for the organizing costs expended by the union in attempting to organize other food retailers. Citing *California Saw*, the Board majority found that organizing expenditures were properly charged to objectors because there is a direct, positive relationship between wage levels of union-represented employees and the level of organization of employees of employers in the same competitive market. The decision was enforced by the Ninth Circuit Court of Appeals.[45]

In *PWU, Local 707 v. NLRB*, the court held that a union is in violation of its duty of fair representation if it seeks the discharge of employees for nonpayment of

---

[42] 487 U.S. 735 (1988).

[43] 320 NLRB 224 (1995).

[44] 307 F.3d 760 (9th Cir. 2002).

[45] In *Pirlott v. NLRB*, 522 F.3d 423 (D.C. Cir. 2008), the D.C. Court of Appeals granted the Board's application for enforcement of Board findings that the Teamsters Local 75 failed to show that its organizing activities were permissible expenditures under *Beck* for objecting nonmembers David and Sherry Pirlott, employees of Schreiber Foods in Green Bay, Wisconsin. The Board found that the testimony before the ALJ amounted to a literature review that supported the general proposition that organizing will allow unions to raise wages more than they otherwise would, but such was not sufficient evidence to meet its burden of proof under *Meijer*.

dues without first informing the employees of their *Beck* and *California Saw* rights that they have the right to remain nonmembers of the union and that as nonmembers, they have "the right (1) to object to paying for union activities not germane to the union's duties as bargaining agent and to obtain a reduction in fees for such activities; (2) to be given sufficient information to enable the employee to intelligently decide whether to object; and (3) to be apprised of any internal union procedures for filing objections."[46]

RIGHT-TO-WORK LAWS

Section 14(b) of the NLRA permits states that have passed so-called right-to-work laws to prohibit union shop and agency shop agreements. Some 22 states, primarily in the South and West, have enacted such laws.[47]

Unions are philosophically opposed to right-to-work laws because they allow all employees (both union and nonunion) to receive the benefits derived from the continuing negotiations of collective bargaining contracts and their administration, including the right to representation by a union in the processing of grievances, which nonunion employees do not pay for through union dues or an agency fee. They are free riders according to the unions' viewpoint.

Unions have attacked the validity of right-to-work laws on various fronts. The *Retail Clerks Local 1625 v. Schermerhorn* case disposed of the union's preemption claim raised on reargument.[48] The Supreme Court held that although most labor disputes are within the exclusive jurisdictional province of federal agencies and courts, Congress, in granting the states the power to prohibit certain union security devices, also extended to them the authority to enforce that prohibition. The Supreme Court has also rejected various claims based on the constitutional guarantees of free speech, due process, and freedom to contract. Right-to-work legislation is an area of obvious and continuing importance in the labor field.

In *Lord v. Local 2088 IBEW*,[49] the Eleventh Circuit Court of Appeals held that a union shop provision in a collective bargaining agreement applicable to employees working at federal enclaves in Florida was legal under the NLRA. It was thus enforceable against employees, even though the provision was prohibited under Florida's right-to-work law.

---

[46] *PWU, Local 707 v. NLRB*, 161 F.3d 1047 (7th Cir. 1998).

[47] The following states have passed right-to-work laws: Alabama, Arizona, Arkansas, Florida, Georgia, Idaho, Iowa, Kansas, Louisiana, Mississippi, Nebraska, Nevada, North Carolina, North Dakota, Oklahoma, South Carolina, South Dakota, Tennessee, Texas, Utah, Virginia, and Wyoming. On September 25, 2001, Oklahoma became the 22nd state with a right-to-work law, which was approved by voters on that date. The state's governor touted it as an economic development tool, stating, "As of today, Oklahoma is open for business. Passage of Right-to-Work is just the latest in a series of reforms and changes designed to make Oklahoma the most attractive business destination in America."

[48] 375 U.S. 96 (1963).

[49] 646 F.2d 1057 (11th Cir. 1981).

CASE 5.8	NLRB v. Studio Transportation Drivers, Local 399
	United States Court of Appeals for the Ninth Circuit 525 F.3d 898 (2008).

[Hyo Choi Lim is employed by a subsidiary of Universal Studios. Local 399's collective bargaining agreement includes a union security clause. Union security clauses require all employees to become members of the union within a certain period of time after being hired. Lim notified the union that he was asserting his rights as a *Beck* objector. Under that decision, employees who work under collective bargaining agreements with union security clauses can refuse to join the union as long as they agree to pay their fair share of representational expenses. The union conceded Lim's right to refuse to join the union under *Beck*, but informed him that his fair share of representational expenses would be 99.6 percent of dues owed by union members. Lim challenged the union's decision to use "liquidated damages" obtained in the sum of $26,705 from arbitration awards payable to the union to fund nonrepresentational expenses such as political and charitable donations. From the Board's determination that the union had violated the NLRA, it appealed to the Court of Appeals to enforce its order.]

PREGERSON, C. J. ...

In *Communications Workers of America v. Beck*, the Supreme Court held that "§ 8(a)(3) permits an employer and a union to enter into an agreement requiring all employees to become union members as a condition of continued employment, but the 'membership' that may be so required has been 'whittled down to its financial core.'"... *Beck* held that § 8(a)(3) "authorizes the exaction of only those fees and dues necessary to 'performing the duties of an exclusive representative of the employees in dealing with the employer on labor-management issues.'"... The fees and dues exacted for performing representational duties are sometimes called "fair share" fees, because they represent the fair and reasonable cost of providing representational services to

each employee represented by the union, whether such employee is a *Beck* objector or full-fledged union member. *Beck* objectors are thus not required to pay for expenses that are not germane to representation, such as political or charitable donations....

... The "liquidated damages" in this case were derived from arbitration that had been funded partially by *Beck* objectors like Lim. Therefore, the Board held that the union could not offset these "liquidated damages" from its nonrepresentational expenses.

The Board's interpretation is rational and consistent with the Act. Whenever a union's representational expenses generate secondary income—be it interest and dividend income in *Chevron Chemical Co.* or "liquidated damages" in this case—the union could use those funds for representational expenses, which would in turn lower the dues required of full union members and *Beck* objectors alike. Therefore, in choosing to spend the secondary income on political and charitable contributions rather than on representational expenses, the union is essentially increasing the dues required of *Beck* objectors in order to pay for these contributions. That is exactly what the Supreme Court prohibited in *Beck*.

[Order enforced. Granted.]

Case Questions

1. State the union membership requirement under Section 8(a)(3) of the NLRA as interpreted by the Supreme Court's *Beck* decision.
2. What did the Court find wrong with the union spending funds, which it had lawfully been awarded in arbitration proceedings, on political candidates supportive of union ideals and on charitable contributions for the good of the community?

SECTION 48: DISCRIMINATION FOR NLRB ACTION

Under Section 8(a)(4), an employer may not "discharge or otherwise discriminate against an employee because he has filed charges or given testimony under this act." This provision protects employees from discharge, layoff, or other working-conditions discrimination for testifying or making out a charge or an affidavit in any NLRB proceedings. It applies to laid-off employees and applicants for open jobs if they are refused employment due to appearing at an NLRB hearing.

Discharging an employee or discriminating against an employee or applicant for testifying, filing a charge, or refusing to withdraw charges has been found to be a Section 8(a)(4) violation.[50]

In *Alamo Rent-a-Car*, the employer questioned an employee about whether he had any knowledge about allegations in an NLRB complaint. The employee stated that he knew nothing about it and signed a statement to that effect. Later, he testified at the unfair labor practice hearing in detail regarding the complaint, and thereafter, he was discharged for lying to the employer. The Board found that he was discharged for his testimony before the ALJ, not for lying, and that the discharge was in violation of Section 8(a)(4).[51]

SECTION 49: DUTY OF EMPLOYER TO BARGAIN

The extent of this duty of an employer to bargain is set forth in the NLRA. The employer must bargain over so-called mandatory subjects of bargaining and need not bargain over so-called permissive subjects of bargaining. A wide range of questions on employers' obligations to bargain have been considered by the Supreme Court and are developed as follows.

PERTINENT PROVISIONS OF THE ACT

Section 1 of the NLRA declares the policy of the United States to protect commerce "by encouraging the practice and procedure of collective bargaining and by protecting the exercise by workers of full freedom of association, self-organization, and designation of representatives of their own choosing, for the purpose of negotiating the terms and conditions of their employment." To effect this policy, Section 8(a)(5) provides that it is an unfair labor practice for an employer "to refuse to bargain collectively with the representatives of his employees subject to the provisions of Section 9(a)." Section 8(d) defines "to bargain collectively" as "the performance of the mutual obligation of the employer and the representative of the employees to meet at reasonable times and confer in good faith with respect to wages, hours, and other terms and conditions of employment." Section 9(a) declares: "Representatives designated or selected for the purposes of collective bargaining by the majority of the employees in a unit appropriate for such purposes, shall be the exclusive representatives of all the employees in such unit for the purpose of collective bargaining in respect to rates of pay, wages, hours of employment, or other conditions of employment."

Together these provisions establish the obligation of the employer to bargain collectively "with respect to wages, hours, and other terms and conditions of employment" with "the representatives of his employees" designated or selected by the majority "in a unit appropriate for such purposes."

The procedural requirements are partly defined by Section 8(d), including the following duties: (1) to meet at reasonable times and confer in good faith; (2) to

---

[50] See *NLRB v. Scrivener*, 405 U.S. 117 (1972); Caterpillar, Inc., 322 NLRB 674 (1996).

[51] 336 NLRB 1155 (2001).

execute a written contract if agreement is reached but without legal compulsion on either party to agree or to make any concessions; (3) for termination or modification of an existing contract, to give a 60-day notice to the other party with an offer to confer for negotiating proposals and a 30-day notice to federal and state mediation services of a pending dispute over the new agreement; and (4) to have no strikes or lockouts during the 60-day notice period, subject to loss of employee status for so striking.

Mandatory Subjects of Bargaining

In *NLRB v. Wooster Division of the Borg-Warner Corp.*,[52] the Supreme Court approved a distinction between mandatory and permissive subjects of bargaining. The duty to bargain imposed by Sections 8(a)(5) and 8(b)(3), the Court held, is limited to the subjects delineated in Section 9(a): "rates of pay, wages, hours of employment, or other conditions of employment." As to these items, classified as mandatory unless a party has waived its rights by previous agreement, the parties must bargain. The decision on what subjects are mandatory within the classification of Section 9(a) is made by the Board and the courts.

Some obvious examples of the meaning of the term **wages** are basic hourly rates of pay, piece rates, shift differentials, incentive plans, severance pay, and paid holidays and vacations. Bonuses are considered mandatory subjects when they are compensation for services rendered but not when they are given as a gift. Profit-sharing plans and stock purchase plans are also considered mandatory subjects. In the *Southern Nuclear Operating Co. v. NLRB* decision, presented in this section, future retirement benefits of current employees were determined to be mandatory subjects of bargaining as part of current employees' overall compensation packages.

The case law over "hours" has crystallized to the point that controversy in this area is almost nonexistent. Almost every issue related to hours of employment is now considered a mandatory subject of bargaining.

Several items under the phrase "terms and conditions of employment" have consistently been considered mandatory subjects of bargaining. These include seniority provisions, promotions, layoff and recall provisions, no-strike-no-lockout clauses, grievance procedures, and work rules. In *Brewers and Malters, Local No. 6, IBT v. NLRB*,[53] the D.C. Circuit Court of Appeals affirmed a Board decision that installing hidden surveillance cameras in work and break areas without first bargaining with the union is a violation of Section 8(a)(5). While such is a "term and condition of employment" and a mandatory subject of bargaining, the decision does not prevent an employer from using hidden surveillance cameras after bargaining over the issue. That is, after the employer bargains over the proposal and the reasons for it, it need not apprise the union of the exact location or the time they will be used.

---

[52] 356 U.S. 342 (1958).

[53] 414 F.3d 36 (D.C. Cir. 2005).

Subcontracting, business closings, and relocating bargaining unit work are three areas of controversy. In the *Fibreboard* decision, presented in this section, the Supreme Court ruled that a decision to subcontract work was a mandatory subject of bargaining. The Court limited its holding to the type of subcontracting in that case, which involved the replacement of employees in an existing bargaining unit with those of an independent contractor.[54] Thus, a ready-mix concrete company violated Section 8(a)(5) by selling its trucks to owner-operators and utilizing these independent contractors to perform the delivery work formerly performed by its employees, where it failed to bargain to impasse on the matter.[55]

In the Supreme Court's *First National Maintenance Corp.* decision, presented in this section, the Court announced a balancing test regarding an employer's duty to bargain over an economically motivated decision to close down part of its business. While the Court held that the union did not have a right to participate in the decision-making process on the question of whether to shut down part of the business, the Court held that the union did have a right to bargain over the *effects* of the decision.

In the NLRB's *Dubuque Packing Co.*[56] decision, the Board announced its test for determining whether an employer has a mandatory obligation to bargain over the relocation of bargaining unit work. The test requires the following:

1. The burden is initially on the General Counsel to establish that the employer's decision involved a relocation of work unaccompanied by a basic change in the nature of the employer's operation.
2. If so established, a *prima facie* case is made that the relocation decision is a mandatory subject of bargaining.
3. The burden shifts to the employer at this point, and the employer has two alternative defenses:
   a. The employer may produce evidence rebutting the *prima facie* case by establishing that the work performed at the new location varies significantly from the work performed at the former plant, (1) establishing that the work performed at the former plant is to be discontinued entirely and not moved to the new location or (2) establishing that the employer's decision involves a change in the scope and direction of the enterprise.
   b. Alternatively, the employer may proffer a defense to show by a preponderance of the evidence that (1) labor costs (direct and/or indirect) were not a factor in the decision or (2) even if labor costs were a factor in the decision, the union could not have offered labor cost concessions that could have changed the employer's decision to relocate.

---

[54] See *NLRB v. Wehr Constructors, Inc.*, 159 F.3d 946 (6th Cir. 1998), in which the Sixth Circuit refused to follow the *Fibreboard* precedent because the work subcontracted after union certification had not previously been performed by the existing union employees and no evidence was presented that the employer's continuation of its previously lawful subcontracting caused the employer to replace any existing employees.

[55] *Naperville Ready Mix, Inc., v. NLRB*, 242 F.3d 744 (7th Cir. 2001).

[56] 303 NLRB No. 66 (1991).

PERMISSIVE SUBJECTS OF BARGAINING

Those subjects that the Board and the courts have held not mandatory are classified as "permissive." If a subject is permissive, refusal to bargain over it does not violate Sections 8(a)(5) or (b)(3). When a permissive subject is included in a collective bargaining agreement, it is not transformed into a mandatory subject. Therefore, a party has no obligation to bargain over a permissive subject, despite the fact that past contracts contained a provision dealing with that subject.

Thus, where the Board has defined a bargaining unit, the unit may be altered by agreements of the parties, but a party may not seek the modification or exclusion of certain employees to the point of impasse.[57] The parties may agree upon an interest arbitration clause, but neither party may insist on its inclusion to the point of impasse.[58] Also, where an employer demands that charges against it before the NLRB be withdrawn as a precondition to contract negotiations, such is a Section 8(a)(5) unfair labor practice because the employer has caused an impasse over a permissive subject of bargaining.[59] Internal union affairs, required use of union labels, indemnification clauses, performance bonds, and union recognition clauses are considered permissive subjects of bargaining. In *Allied Chemical Workers Local 1 v. Pittsburgh Plate Glass Co.*,[60] the Supreme Court held that benefits of already retired employees were not mandatory subjects of bargaining and that an employer's unilateral modification of a contract term did not breach its duty to bargain where that modification related to a permissive rather than a mandatory subject of bargaining. In an interesting sidelight to an antitrust suit in *Robertson v. The National Basketball Association*,[61] the district court held that the player draft, the reserve clause, and merger or noncompetition agreements are permissive, rather than mandatory, subjects of bargaining. It is important to note, however, that in the private sector, the Board and the courts are more inclined to find a subject mandatory and tend to classify subjects as permissive only where they are clearly beyond the scope of Section 9(a). Moreover, astute employers and unions tend to bargain for benefits that help hire, retain, and advance qualified workers regardless of the subject matter. For example, where an immigrant workforce is utilized, parties have negotiated that the employer would begin to offer English language classes, forklift instruction, and other educational opportunities to help workers in their job advancement.

COURT DECISIONS ON SCOPE OF BARGAINING OBLIGATION

The question of good faith bargaining arises in many ways, one aspect being employer unilateral action on mandatory bargaining subjects without good faith negotiations with employee representatives. It also may involve an employer communicating directly with employees as to its bargaining position. The Board held in

---

[57] Canterbury Gardens, 238 NLRB 864 (1978).

[58] Columbus Pressmen, 219 NLRB 268 (1975).

[59] Stackpole Components Co., 232 NLRB 723 (1977).

[60] 404 U.S. 157 (1971).

[61] 389 F. Supp. 867 (S.D.N.Y. 1975).

the *General Electric*[62] case that presenting to union negotiators an insurance proposal and other proposals as rigid "fair-and-firm" offers or on a "take-it-or-leave-it" basis is illegal. Also illegal is attempting to bypass national negotiators by directly dealing with local unions. General Electric's collective bargaining policy, called **Boulwarism** for the company vice president who formulated the bargaining concept of a fair-and-firm offer that would be subject to change only if new information showed the company wrong, was thus held to be an unfair labor practice. The Board found this technique "calculated to disparage the union and to impose, without substantial alteration, respondent's fair and firm proposal, rather than to satisfy the true standards and good faith collective bargaining required by the statute."

As a general rule, bypassing a union and dealing directly with employees so as to undermine a certified bargaining agent is unlawful. In the *C & C Plywood*[63] decision, the Supreme Court upheld a Board determination that an employer's inauguration of a premium pay plan during the term of a collective bargaining agreement, without prior consultation with the union, violated Section 8(a)(5).

A further significant requirement imposed by collective bargaining arises from rulings that any relevant information for intelligent consideration of the employer's position under a union's representation responsibility must be provided to the union upon request.[64] Included have been such matters as job description information; job classification wage data (within the unit or outside if comparable); time study data and the right to make independent check studies; financial data as to employer inability to meet union demands; and competitive wage data to support claimed noncompetitive rates. An unwillingness to cooperate in these areas may result in a finding of employer refusal to bargain and a cease-and-desist order.

Surface bargaining—appearing to negotiate while intending to avoid reaching a contract—violates Section 8(a)(5) of the Act. In *NLRB v. Hardesty Co.,*[65] the Eighth Circuit Court of Appeals upheld the Board's decision that Hardesty Co., a ready-mix concrete distributor, engaged in surface bargaining as part of a plan to seek a decertification election as soon as the protected one-year certification period ended. While Section 8(d) specifically provides that the obligation to bargain in good faith does not compel either party to agree to a proposal or require the making of a concession, a party cannot negotiate with the intent to avoid reaching a contract. When the behavior of the company was examined at the bargaining table as well as away from the table, the Section 8(a)(5) violation became evident. The Court stated:

> The record shows that the parties easily reached agreement on a number of issues and that the negotiations proceeded smoothly for several months until Hardesty withdrew some of its initial proposals and thereafter introduced regressive proposals, proposing the elimination of overtime (which averaged ten hours per week, per employee in the unit), bonuses, and the 401(k) plan. Of itself, such hard-bargaining might not amount to a Section 8(a)(5) violation. However, in this case, the Board found that the explanation for Hardesty's bargaining positions were not to be found in the Company's

---

[62] General Electric Co., 150 NLRB 192 (1965), *enforced* 418 F.2d (1969).

[63] *NLRB v. C & C Plywood*, 385 U.S. 421 (1967).

[64] See *NLRB v. Truit Mfg. Co.*, 351 U.S. 149 (1956).

[65] 308 F.3d 859 (8th Cir. 2002).

somewhat perfunctory statements. Rather, the explanation for the Company's course of conduct was provided by the Company's away-from-the-table behavior, consisting mostly of statements by supervisors concerning the Company's preferred method of dealing with the Union. Given the evidence of record, we cannot say that the Board erred in concluding that Hardesty had no intention of reaching an agreement, that its plan was to wait until a decertification vote might be had in order to get rid of the Union.[66]

CASE 5.9	FIBREBOARD PAPER PRODUCTS CORP. V. NLRB
	SUPREME COURT OF THE UNITED STATES, 379 U.S. 203 (1964).

[After receiving union proposals for contract revisions for the benefit of the maintenance workers at the company's Emeryville, California, plant, the company advised the union that negotiations for a new contract would be pointless because it had definitely decided to contract out the work performed by the employees covered by the agreement upon the expiration of the agreement. The company planned to replace these employees with an independent contractor's employees and expected that substantial savings would be effected by this contracting out of the work. The Board ordered the company to reinstate the maintenance operation with the union employees, reinstate the employees with back pay, and fulfill its statutory bargaining obligation. The court of appeals granted the Board's enforcement petition, and the Supreme Court agreed to hear the case.]

WARREN, C. J....

I. Section 8(a)(5) of the National Labor Relations Act provides that it shall be an unfair labor practice for an employer "to refuse to bargain collectively with the representatives of his employees." Collective bargaining is defined in Section 8(d) as

the performance of the mutual obligation of the employer and the representative of the employees to meet at reasonable times and confer in good faith with respect to wages, hours, and other terms and conditions of employment.

"Read together, these provisions establish the obligation of the employer and the representative of its employees to bargain with each other in good faith with respect to 'wages, hours, and other terms and conditions of employment....' The duty is limited to

those subjects, and within that area neither is legally obligated to yield. *Labor Board v. American Ins. Co.,* 343 U.S. 395. As to other matters, however, each party is free to bargain or not to bargain...." *Labor Board v. Wooster Div. of Borg-Warner Corp.,* 356 U.S. 342, 349. Because of the limited grant of certiorari, we are concerned here only with whether the subject upon which the employer allegedly refused to bargain—contracting out of plant maintenance work previously performed by employees in the bargaining unit, which the employees were capable of continuing to perform—is covered by the phrase "terms and conditions of employment" within the meaning of Section 8(d).

The subject matter of the present dispute is well within the literal meaning of the phrase "terms and conditions of employment."...

... As the Court of Appeals pointed out,

it is not necessary that it be likely or probable that the union will yield or supply a feasible solution but rather that the union be afforded an opportunity to meet management's legitimate complaints that its maintenance was unduly costly.

We are thus not expanding the scope of mandatory bargaining to hold, as we do now, that the type of "contracting out" involved in this case—the replacement of employees in the existing bargaining unit with those of an independent contractor to do the same work under similar conditions of employment—is a statutory subject of collective bargaining under Section 8(d). Our decision need not and does not encompass other forms of "contracting out" or "subcontracting" which arise daily in our complex economy....

continued

[66] *Id.* at 866.

The judgment of the Court of Appeals is affirmed.

Case Questions

1. What company action caused this complaint?
2. What remedy did the Board order?
3. With this decision, did the Supreme Court expand the scope of mandatory bargaining to include all subcontracting situations?

CASE 5.10	FIRST NATIONAL MAINTENANCE CORP. V. NLRB
	SUPREME COURT OF THE UNITED STATES, 452 U.S. 666 (1981).

[Petitioner, First National Maintenance Corporation (FNM), supplies its customers a contracted-for labor force and supervision in return for reimbursement of its labor costs plus a management fee. FNM terminated a part of its business, that of performing maintenance work at the Greenpark Care Center, a nursing home in Brooklyn, New York, solely for economic reasons, and the 35 FNM employees working there were discharged. The NLRB held that FNM had a duty to bargain under Sections 8(a)(5) and 8(d) with the certified representative of its employees over the decision to close a part of its business, the maintenance operation at the Greenpark Care Center, and the court of appeals enforced the Board's order.]

BLACKMUN, J....

The Court of Appeals' decision in this case appears to be at odds with decisions of other Courts of Appeals, some of which decline to require bargaining over any management decision involving "a major commitment of capital investment" or a "basic operational change" in the scope or direction of an enterprise, and some of which indicate that bargaining is not mandated unless a violation of § 8(a)(3) (a partial closing motivated by antiunion animus) is involved....

Because of the importance of the issue and the continuing disagreement between and among the Board and the Courts of Appeals, we granted certiorari.

... The present case concerns a ... type of management decision, one that had a direct impact on employment, since jobs were inexorably eliminated by the termination, but had as its focus only the economic profitability of the contract with Greenpark, a concern under these facts wholly apart from the employment relationship. This decision, involving a change in the scope and direction of the enterprise, is akin to the decision whether to be in business at all, "not in [itself] primarily about conditions of employment though the effect of the decision may be necessarily to terminate employment." Cf. *Textile Workers v. Darlington Co.*, 380 U.S. 263 (1965) ("an employer has the absolute right to terminate his entire business for any reason he pleases"). At the same time, this decision touches on a matter of central and pressing concern to the union and its member employees: the possibility of continued employment and the retention of the employees' very jobs.

Petitioner contends it had no duty to bargain about its decision to terminate its operations at Greenpark. This contention requires that we determine whether the decision itself should be considered part of petitioner's retained freedom to manage its affairs unrelated to employment.*... Management must be free from the constraints of the bargaining process to the extent essential for the running of a profitable business. It also must have some degree of certainty beforehand as to when it may proceed to reach decisions without fear of later evaluations labeling its conduct an unfair labor practice. Congress did not explicitly state what issues of mutual concern to union and management it intended to exclude from mandatory bargaining. Nonetheless, in view of an employer's need for unencumbered decision making, bargaining over management decisions that have a substantial impact on the continued availability of employment should be required only if the benefit, for labor-management relations and the collective bargaining process, outweighs the burden placed on the conduct of the business....

---

*There is no doubt that petitioner was under a duty to bargain about the results or effects of its decision to stop the work at Greenpark, or that it violated that duty. Petitioner consented to enforcement of the Board's order concerning bargaining over the effects of the closing and has reached agreement with the union on severance pay.

continued

Both union and management regard control of the decision to shut down an operation with the utmost seriousness. As has been noted, however, the Act is not intended to serve either party's individual interest, but to foster in a neutral manner a system in which the conflict between these interests may be resolved. It seems particularly important, therefore, to consider whether requiring bargaining over this sort of decision will advance the neutral purposes of the Act.

A union's interest in participating in the decision to close a particular facility or part of an employer's operations springs from its legitimate concern over job security. The Court has observed: "The words of [§ 8(d)] ... plainly cover termination of employment which ... necessarily results" from closing an operation. The union's practical purpose in participating, however, will be largely uniform; it will seek to delay or halt the closing. No doubt it will be impelled, in seeking these ends, to offer concessions, information, and alternatives that might be helpful to management or forestall or prevent the termination of jobs. It is unlikely, however, that requiring bargaining over the decision itself, as well as its effects, will augment this flow of information and suggestions. There is no dispute that the union must be given a significant opportunity to bargain about these matters of job security as part of the "effects" bargaining mandated by § 8(a)(5). And, under § 8(a)(5), bargaining over the effects of a decision must be conducted in a meaningful manner and at a meaningful time, and the Board may impose sanctions to ensure its adequacy. A union, by pursuing such bargaining rights, may achieve valuable concessions from an employer engaged in a partial closing. It also may secure in contract negotiations provisions implementing rights to notice, information, and fair bargaining.

Moreover, the union's legitimate interest in fair dealing is protected by § 8(a)(3), which prohibits partial closings motivated by antiunion animus, when done to gain an unfair advantage. *Textile Workers v. Darlington Co.*, 380 U.S. 263, 58 LRRM 2657 (1965). Under § 8(a)(3) the Board may inquire into the motivations behind a partial closing. An employer may not simply shut down part of its business and mask its desire to weaken and circumvent the union by labeling its decision "purely economic."

Thus, although the union has a natural concern that a partial closing decision not be hastily or unnecessarily entered into, it has some control over the effects of the decision and indirectly may ensure that the decision itself is deliberately considered. It also

has direct protection against a partial closing decision that is motivated by an intent to harm a union.

Management's interest in whether it should discuss a decision of this kind is much more complex and varies with the particular circumstances. If labor costs are an important factor in a failing operation and the decision to close, management will have an incentive to confer voluntarily with the union to seek concessions that may make continuing the business profitable. At other times, management may have great need for speed, flexibility, and secrecy in meeting business opportunities and exigencies. It may face significant tax or securities consequences that hinge on confidentiality, the timing of a plant closing, or a reorganization of the corporate structure. The publicity incident to the normal process of bargaining may injure the possibility of a successful transition or increase the economic damage to the business. The employer also may have no feasible alternative to the closing, and even good faith bargaining over it may be both futile and cause the employer additional loss.

There is an important difference, also, between permitted bargaining and mandated bargaining. Labeling this type of decision mandatory could afford a union a powerful tool for achieving delay, a power that might be used to thwart management's intentions in a manner unrelated to any feasible solution the union might propose....

We conclude that the harm likely to be done to an employer's need to operate freely in deciding whether to shut down part of its business purely for economic reasons outweighs the incremental benefit that might be gained through the union's participation in making the decision, and we hold that the decision itself is *not* part of § 8(d)'s "terms and conditions," over which Congress has mandated bargaining.

The judgment of the Court of Appeals, accordingly, is reversed and the case is remanded to that court for further proceedings consistent with this opinion.

It is so ordered.

JUSTICE BRENNAN, with whom JUSTICE MARSHALL joins, Dissenting ...

The Court bases its decision on a balancing test. It states that "bargaining over management decisions that have a substantial impact on the continued availability of employment should be required only if the benefit, for labor-management relations and the collective bargaining process, outweighs the burden placed on the conduct of the business." I cannot agree with this test, because it takes into account only the

continued

interests of *management*; it fails to consider the legitimate employment interests of the workers and their Union. This one-sided approach hardly serves "to foster in a neutral manner" a system for resolution of these serious, two-sided controversies.

Apparently, the Court concludes that the benefit to labor-managment relations and the collective bargaining process from negotiation over partial closings is minimal, but it provides no evidence to that effect. The Court acknowledges that the Union might be able to offer concessions, information, and alternatives that might obviate or forestall the closing, but it then asserts that "[i]t is unlikely, however, that requiring bargaining over the decision ... will augment this flow of information and suggestions." Recent experience, however, suggests the contrary. Most conspicuous, perhaps, were the negotiations between Chrysler Corporation and the United Auto Workers, which led to significant adjustments in compensation and benefits, contributing to Chrysler's ability to remain afloat. Even where labor costs are not the direct cause of a company's financial difficulties, employee concessions can often enable the company to continue in operation—if the employees have the opportunity to offer such concessions....

Case Questions

1. Why did the Supreme Court decide to hear the case?
2. State the test the Court applied in determining whether the partial closing was a mandatory subject of bargaining.
3. Did the Court conclude that the partial closing was a mandatory subject of bargaining?
4. Under the *FNM* decision, may an employer shut down part of its business in order to weaken a union's position at the employer's other operations by labeling the decision as "purely economic"?
5. Did FNM have a mandatory obligation to bargain about the "effects" of its decision to stop work at Greenpark?

CASE 5.11	SOUTHERN NUCLEAR OPERATING CO. v. NLRB
	UNITED STATES COURT OF APPEALS, D.C. CIRCUIT, 524 F.3D 1350 (2008).

[In 2000, four subsidiaries of the Southern Company made modifications to the health care and life-insurance benefits of their future retirees without negotiating with their employees' unions. The unions filed unfair labor practice charges against these subsidiaries, and the National Labor Relations Board determined that the subsidiaries violated Sections 8(a)(1) and 8(a)(5) of the National Labor Relations Act by making the changes without bargaining collectively. The subsidiaries petitioned for review, and the Board cross-applied for enforcement of its order.]

GRIFFITH, C. J. ....

The Companies ask us to set aside the Board's conclusion that they were required to bargain collectively before making the 2000 changes. We first consider the Companies' argument that the NLRA left them free to make the changes unilaterally.

Section 8(a)(5) of the NLRA makes it an unfair labor practice for an employer to "refuse to bargain collectively with the representatives of his employees." 29 U.S.C. § 158(a)(5). Section 8(d) requires employers to bargain collectively before introducing changes "with respect to wages hours, and other terms and conditions of employment." *Id.* § 158(d). An employer violates Section 8(a)(5) by making any unilateral changes to the mandatory bargaining subjects covered by Section 8(d), *NLRB v. Katz*, 369 U.S. 736, 743(1962). The Companies argue that their unilateral changes to the OPRBs [Other Post-Retirement Benefits] were permissible because the future retirement benefits of current employees are not mandatory bargaining subjects under Section 8(d). We are not persuaded.

The governing principle is found in *Allied Chemical & Alkali Workers of America, Local Union No. 1 v. Pittsburgh Plate Glass Co.*, 404 U.S. 157 (1971). In that case, the Supreme Court held that retirement benefits for workers who have already retired are not mandatory bargaining subjects because retirees are not "employees" under the NLRA and are therefore not protected by the Act. *See id.* at 168 ("The ordinary meaning of 'employee' does not include retired workers; retired employees have ceased to work for another for hire.") But the Court also made clear that retirement benefits for current employees *are* mandatory bargaining subjects: "To be

continued

sure, the future retirement benefits of active workers are part and parcel of their overall compensation and hence a well-established statutory subject of bargaining." *Id.* at 180. Because the 2000 modifications affected future retirement benefits of current employees, the Companies were required to bargain over them with the unions.

The Companies argue that the statement in *Pittsburgh Plate Glass* about future retirement benefits is a *dictum* and should not supply a rule of decision in this case. We have more faith than do the Companies in Supreme Court declarations that begin with "To be sure...." *See United States v. Oakar*, 111 F.3d 146, 153 (D.C. Cir. 1997) (stating that "carefully considered language of the Supreme Court, even if technically *dictum*, generally must be treated as authoritative") (quotation marks omitted). But even if the question were an open one, the Companies' argument fails because "classifications of bargaining subjects as 'terms [and] conditions' of employment is a matter concerning which the Board has special expertise." *Local Union No. 189, Amalgamated Meat Cutters & Butcher Workmen of N. Am. v. Jewel Tea Co.*, 381 U.S. 676, 685–86 (1965); *see also Ford Motor Co. v. NLRB*, 441 U.S. 488, 497

(1979) ("Construing and applying the duty to bargain ... [lies] at the heart of the Board's function."). The Board has decided that future retirement benefits fit in Section 8(d)'s basket of mandatory bargaining subjects. This decision, particularly in light of the Board's expertise, is rational and therefore lawful. *See id.* at 495 (noting that the Board's "judgment as to what is a mandatory bargaining subject is entitled to considerable deference"). No one could doubt that current employees are rightly concerned about the retirement benefits that they will receive in the future. Giving them the right to bargain collectively over those benefits is certainly sensible....

[*The Board's order is enforced in relevant parts.*]

Case Questions

1. Does an employer violate the NLRA by making a unilateral change in a "mandatory" subject of bargaining?
2. Did the employer's modification to the health care and life insurance benefits of future retirees without input from the unions constitute unilateral changes in mandatory subjects of bargaining?
3. Find an example of a "permissive" subject of bargaining in the Court's opinion.

SECTION 50: SUCCESSOR EMPLOYERS' OBLIGATIONS UNDER THE NLRA

It is common under our economic system for businesses to merge or be acquired by other businesses. The manner in which the changes in business ownership take place is varied and often indirect and complex. There may be an outright sale of a business operation, with the new employer continuing to employ the same employees at the same plant. The new employer may hire many new employees while continuing to employ some of the predecessor's employees. The new employer may acquire the assets of the plant or business but change the operation of the business. The union representing the predecessor's employees may believe that the new owner is a "successor" employer with an obligation to bargain with the union. The new owner may believe that it is not a successor and that it has no legal obligations to the predecessor's union and employees.

In *NLRB v. Burns International Security Services, Inc.*,[67] the Supreme Court stated that a mere change of employers or ownership in the employing industry does not affect the Board's certification of a bargaining unit. The successor's obligation to bargain is based on the language of Sections 8(a)(5) and 9(a) of the NLRA—an employer must bargain with the "representatives designated or selected for the purposes of collectively bargaining by the majority of the employees in a

---

[67]406 U.S. 272, 279 (1972).

unit appropriate for such purposes." In *Burns*, the Supreme Court approved the rule that a mere change in ownership does not destroy the presumption of continuing employee support for a certified union.[68]

UNION RECOGNITION

In determining whether a new employer must recognize a union that has represented the predecessor's employees, the NLRB looks to the totality of the circumstances to determine whether there have been changes that have significantly altered the employees' working conditions, expectations, and needs for representation. Factors considered by the Board in determining whether a new employer is obligated to recognize a union are the following:

1. *Continuity of the workforce*: A majority of the employees must have worked for the predecessor employer for the union to succeed. If the new owner purposefully avoids hiring union members to escape designation as a *Burns* successor, the majority requirement is waived, and the employer will ordinarily be subject to a bargaining order.[69]
2. *Continuity of operations*: The Board looks to the continuity of the functions performed by the employees, the continuation of the business at the same location with the same or similar equipment, and the continuity of customers.
3. *Continuity of the appropriateness of the unit*: The bargaining unit of the new employer must continue to be appropriate for a successorship finding.
4. *Hiatus*: A hiatus between the cessation of production of the old employer and the commencement of the new employer's operations will be considered by the Board. However, it does not preclude a successorship finding where the hiatus period is viewed as the normal concomitant of a new management and a new approach to a failing business.
5. *Employer defenses*: The new employer may avoid the successorship obligations to recognize and bargain with a union where the continuity and hiatus factors do not support a finding of successorship. The new employer may also avoid these obligations if it has not committed unfair labor practices and demonstrates a bona fide doubt as to the union's lack of majority support.[70]

OBLIGATIONS OF SUCCESSOR EMPLOYERS

The obligation of a new employer to negotiate the initial terms and conditions of employment depends on whether the new employer is an ordinary successor or a "perfectly clear successor." A new employer is generally free to set the initial terms

---

[68] *Id.* at 277–79. See also Aircraft Magnesium, 265 NLRB 1344, 1345 (1982).

[69] Hudson River Aggregates, Inc., 246 NLRB 192 (1979), and Potter's Drug Enterprises, 233 NLRB 15 (1977).

[70] In its *MV Transportation* decision, 337 NLRB No. 129 (July 17, 2002), the Board decided that an incumbent union in a successorship situation is entitled to a rebuttable presumption of continuing majority status, which will not serve as a bar to an otherwise valid decertification, rival union, or employer petition or other valid challenge to the union's majority status.

of employment for the employees of a predecessor, without bargaining with the incumbent union.[71] However, where it is "perfectly clear" that the new employer intends to retain the unionized employees of its predecessor as a majority of its own workforce under essentially the same terms as their former employment, then the new employer becomes a "perfectly clear successor" and must bargain with the union about the initial terms of employment.

In *Dupont Dow Elastomers, LLC v. NLRB,*[72] the Sixth Circuit Court of Appeals ruled that a joint venture between E.I. du Pont de Nemours & Co. and Dow Chemical Co. was a "perfectly clear successor" of the parent companies and was therefore required to bargain with the union involved before setting initial terms and conditions of employment. The successor joint venture wanted to retain the trained workers who manufactured synthetic rubber products, and its communications with the predecessor employees were crafted to ensure that it would not lose these experienced workers to other employers. The joint venture offered employment to these workers, 97 percent of whom accepted. It then, without bargaining with the union, changed classifications, overtime policy, and the severance program. This action was found to be a Section 8(a)(5) refusal-to-bargain unfair labor practice.

Situations exist where a new employer may be ordered to abide by the terms of the predecessor's collective bargaining agreement. A new employer is under no obligation to hire a predecessor's employees. However, where it is determined that a successor employer discriminates against hiring predecessor employees because of their union membership, seeking to avoid dealing with a union, the employer loses its right to set initial terms and conditions of employment, and it may be ordered to rescind any changes in those terms and compensate employees for losses in order to put them in a position they would have been in but for the successors' unlawful conduct.[73]

A successor employer is distinguished from an "alter ego" employer. An entity is an alter ego of another discontinued entity where it is "merely a disguised continuance of the old employer." In alter ego cases, the Board determines whether there is a continuation of ownership and control of the new enterprise by the former owner, stating it will find alter ego status "where the two enterprises have substantially identical management, business purpose, operations, equipment, customers, and supervision, as well as ownership."[74] The alter ego employer is bound by the terms of the predecessor's collective bargaining agreement.

DETERMINING WHEN THE BARGAINING OBLIGATION ATTACHES

The bargaining obligation can normally be determined at the time of the transaction or when operations of the new employer begin. However, in circumstances where a new employer is reopening a shutdown plant or is operating at a substantially

---

[71] *NLRB v. Burns International Security Service, Inc.*, 406 U.S. 272, 298–99 (1972).

[72] 296 F.3d 495 (6th Cir. 2002).

[73] *U.S. Marine Corporation v. NLRB*, 944 F.2d 1305 (7th Cir. 1991).

[74] Crawford Door Sales Co., 226 NLRB 1144, 94 LRRM 1393 (1976).

reduced capacity, a delay in making the determination may be appropriate until, as the Supreme Court stated in *Burns*, "the successor employer has hired his full complement of employees."[75] This "full-complement" principle, however, has not been interpreted to require that the bargaining obligation determination be postponed until the business is operating at its maximum capacity or until the employer has completed hiring all of its bargaining unit employees. The Board has applied, and the courts have agreed, that in cases in which the successorship obligation cannot be determined at the very outset of the transaction, fixing the appropriate date at which the bargaining obligation arises "involves balancing the objective of ensuring maximum employee participation in the selection of a bargaining agent against the goal of permitting employees to be represented as quickly as possible."[76] Accordingly, a "substantial and representative complement" standard is applied in such situations, as set forth in the *Fall River Dyeing & Finishing Corp. v. NLRB* decision, portions of which follow.

CASE 5.12 | FALL RIVER DYEING & FINISHING CORP. V. NLRB
SUPREME COURT OF THE UNITED STATES, 482 U.S. 27 (1987).

[For more than 30 years, Sterlingwale, which was owned by the Ansin family, operated a textile dyeing and finishing plant at Fall River, Massachusetts. In early 1982, Sterlingwale ran out of cash and, as a result, began to liquidate the company. It laid off employees and sold part of its inventory. In July 1982, the firm's remaining assets were sold by a professional liquidator, and Arthur Friedman, the president of Fall River Dyeing, acquired Sterlingwale's equipment and real property through another Friedman company. On September 20, 1982, Fall River began hiring employees at the former Sterlingwale premises. On October 19, 1982, the union demanded recognition from the new employer. At that time, 18 of the 21 individuals employed by Fall River Dyeing were former Sterlingwale employees. By January 15, 1983, the first shift at Fall River was in full operation, with 36 of the 55 employees hired being former Sterlingwale employees. By April 15, 1983, the workforce had expanded to 107 employees, with 52 being former Sterlingwale employees. The Board held that as of January 15, 1983, the company employed a substantial and representative complement of employees and that Fall River

was a successor employer to Sterlingwale. It held that Fall River had violated Sections 8(a)(5) and (1) of the NLRA by refusing to recognize and bargain with the union once its successoral obligation arose. The Court of Appeals for the First Circuit enforced the Board's order, and the Supreme Court granted certiorari.]

BLACKMUN, J....

Fifteen years ago in *NLRB v. Burns International Security Services, Inc.*, 406 U.S. 272 (1972), this Court first dealt with the issue of a successor employer's obligation to bargain with a union that had represented the employees of its predecessor. In *Burns*, about four months before the employer transition, the security guard employees of Wackenhut Corp. had chosen a particular union as their bargaining representative and that union had negotiated a collective bargaining agreement with Wackenhut. Wackenhut, however, lost its service contract on certain airport property to Burns. Burns proceeded to hire 27 of the Wackenhut guards for its 42-guard operation at the airport. Burns told its guards that, as a condition of their employment, they must join

continued

---

[75] *NLRB v. Burns*, 406 U.S. at 295.
[76] *NLRB v. Pre-Engineered Bldg. Products*, 603 F.2d 134, 136 (10th Cir. 1979). See also *Premium Foods, Inc. v. NLRB*, 709 F.2d 623 (9th Cir. 1983).

the union with which Burns already had collective bargaining agreements at other locations. When the union that had represented the Wackenhut employees brought unfair labor practice charges against Burns, this Court agreed with the Board's determination that Burns had an obligation to bargain with this union....

... We cited with approval, Board and Court of Appeals decisions where it "ha[d] been consistently held that a mere change of employers or of ownership in the employing industry is not such an 'unusual circumstance' as to affect the force of the Board's certification within the normal operative period if a majority of employees after the change of ownership or management were employed by the preceding employer." *Id.*, at 279....

In addition to recognizing the traditional presumptions of union majority status, however, the Court in *Burns* was careful to safeguard "'the rightful prerogative of owners independently to rearrange their business.'" *Golden State Bottling Co. v. NLRB*, 414 U.S. 168, 182 (1973), quoting *John Wiley & Sons, Inc., v. Livingston*, 376 U.S. 543, 549 (1964). We observed in *Burns* that, although the successor has an obligation to bargain with the union, it "is ordinarily free to set initial terms on which it will hire the employees of a predecessor," 406 U.S., at 294, and it is not bound by the substantive provisions of the predecessor's collective bargaining agreement. *Id.*, at 284. We further explained that the successor is under no obligation to hire the employees of its predecessor, subject, of course, to the restriction that it not discriminate against union employees in its hiring. *Id.*, at 280, and n. 5; see also *Howard Johnson Co. v. Hotel Employees*, 417 U.S. 249, 262, and n. 8 (1974). Thus, to a substantial extent the applicability of *Burns* rests in the hands of the successor. If the new employer makes a conscious decision to maintain generally the same business and to hire a majority of its employees from the predecessor, then the bargaining obligation of § 8(a)(5) is activated. This makes sense when one considers that the employer *intends* to take advantage of the trained workforce of its predecessor.

Accordingly, in *Burns* we acknowledged the interest of the successor in its freedom to structure its business and the interest of the employees in continued representation by the union. We now hold that a successor's obligation to bargain is not limited to a situation where the union in question has been recently certified. Where, as here, the union has a rebuttable

presumption of majority status, this status continues despite the change in employers. And the new employer has an obligation to bargain with that union so long as the new employer is in fact a successor of the old employer and the majority of its employees were employed by its predecessor....

A.

In *Burns* we approved the approach taken by the Board and accepted by courts with respect to determining whether a new company was indeed the successor to the old. 406 U.S., at 280–281, and n. 4. This approach, which is primarily factual in nature and is based upon the totality of the circumstances of a given situation, requires that the Board focus on whether the new company has "acquired substantial assets of its predecessor and continued, without interruption or substantial change, the predecessor's business operations." *Golden State Bottling Co. v. NLRB*, 414 U.S., at 184. Hence, the focus is on whether there is "substantial continuity" between the enterprises. Under this approach, the Board examines a number of factors: whether the business of both employers is essentially the same; whether the employees of the new company are doing the same jobs in the same working conditions under the same supervisors; and whether the new entity has the same production process, produces the same products, and basically has the same body of customers....

Although petitioner does not challenge the Board's "substantial continuity" approach, it does contest the application of the rule to the facts of this case. Essentially for the reasons given by the Court of Appeals, 775 F.2d, at 430, however, we find that the Board's determination that there was "substantial continuity" between Sterlingwale and petitioner and that petitioner was Sterlingwale's successor is supported by substantial evidence in the record. Petitioner acquired most of Sterlingwale's real property, its machinery and equipment, and much of its inventory and materials. It introduced no new product line. Of particular significance is the fact that, from the perspective of the employees, their jobs did not change. Although petitioner abandoned converting dyeing in exclusive favor of commission dyeing, this change did not alter the essential nature of the employees' jobs, because both types of dyeing involved the same production process. The job classifications of petitioner were the same as those of Sterlingwale; petitioner's employees worked

continued

on the same machines under the direction of supervisors, most of whom were former supervisors of Sterlingwale. The record, in fact, is clear the petitioner acquired Sterlingwale's assets with the express purpose of taking advantage of its predecessor's workforce.

We do not find determinative of the successorship question the fact that there was a 7-month hiatus between Sterlingwale's demise and petitioner's start-up. Petitioner argues that this hiatus, coupled with the fact that its employees were hired through newspaper advertisements—not through Sterlingwale employment records, which were not transferred to it—resolves in its favor the "substantial continuity" question. Yet such a hiatus is only one factor in the "substantial continuity" calculus and thus is relevant only when there are other indicia of discontinuity. Conversely, if other factors indicate a continuity between the enterprises, and the hiatus is a normal start-up period, the "totality of the circumstances" will suggest that these circumstances present a successorship situation.

For the reasons given above, this is a case where the other factors suggested "substantial continuity" between the companies despite the 7-month hiatus. Here, moreover, the extent of the hiatus between the demise of Sterlingwale and the start-up of petitioner is somewhat less than certain. After the February layoff, Sterlingwale retained a skeleton crew of supervisors and employees that continued to ship goods to customers and to maintain the plant. In addition, until the assignment for the benefit of the creditors late in the summer, Ansin was seeking to resurrect the business or to find a buyer for Sterlingwale. The Union was aware of these efforts. Viewed from the employees' perspective, therefore, the hiatus may have been much less than seven months. Although petitioner hired the employees through advertisements, it often relied on recommendations from supervisors, themselves formerly employed by Sterlingwale, and intended the advertisements to reach the former Sterlingwale workforce.

Accordingly, we hold that, under settled law, petitioner was a successor to Sterlingwale. We thus must consider if and when petitioner's duty to bargain arose.

B.

In *Burns*, the Court determined that the successor had an obligation to bargain with the union because a majority of its employees had been employed by Wackenhut. The "triggering" fact for the bargaining obligation was this composition of the successor's workforce. The Court, however, did not have to consider the question *when* the successor's obligation to bargain arose: Wackenhut's contract expired on June 30 and Burns began its services with a majority of former Wackenhut guards on July 1. In other situations, as in the present case, there is a start-up period by the new employer while it gradually builds its operations and hires employees. In these situations, the Board, with the approval of the Courts of Appeals, has adopted the "substantial and representative complement" rule for fixing the moment when the determination as to the composition of the successor's workforce is to be made. If, at this particular moment, a majority of the successor's employees had been employed by its predecessor, then the successor has an obligation to bargain with the union that represented these employees.

This rule represents an effort to balance "'the objective of ensuring maximum employee participation in the selection of a bargaining agent against the goal of permitting employees to be represented as quickly as possible.'" 775 F.2d, at 430–431, quoting *NLRB v. Pre-Engineered Building Products, Inc.*, 603 F.2d 134, 136 (CA10 1979). In deciding when a "substantial and representative complement" exists in a particular employer transition, the Board examines a number of factors. It studies "whether the job classifications designated for the operation were filled or substantially filled and whether the operation was in normal or substantially normal production." See *Premium Foods, Inc., v. NLRB*, 709 F.2d 623, 628 (CA9 1983). In addition, it takes into consideration "the size of the complement on that date and the time expected to elapse before a substantially larger complement would be at work ... as well as the relative certainty of the employer's expected expansion." *Ibid.*

Petitioner contends that the Board's representative complement rule is unreasonable, given that it injures the representation rights of many of the successor's employees and that it places significant burdens upon the successor, which is unsure whether and when the bargaining obligation will arise. According to petitioner, if majority status is determined at the "full complement" stage, all the employees will have a voice in the selection of their bargaining representative, and this will reveal if the union truly has the support of most of the successor's employees. This approach, however, focuses only on the interest in

continued

having a bargaining representative selected by the majority of the employees. It fails to take into account the significant interest of employees in being represented as soon as possible. The latter interest is especially heightened in a situation where many of the successor's employees, who were formerly represented by a union, find themselves after the employer transition in essentially the same enterprise, but without their bargaining representative. Having the new employer refuse to bargain with the chosen representative of these employees "disrupts the employees' morale, deters their organizational activities, and discourages their membership in unions." *Franks Bros. Co. v. NLRB*, 321 U.S. 702, 704 (1944). Accordingly, petitioner's "full complement" proposal must fail....

We conclude, however, that in this situation the successor is in the best position to follow a rule the criteria of which are straightforward. The employer generally will know with tolerable certainty when all its job classifications have been filled or substantially filled, when it has hired a majority of the employees it intends to hire, and when it has begun normal production. Moreover, the "full complement" standard advocated by petitioner is not *necessarily* easier for a successor to apply than is the "substantial and representative complement." In fact, given the expansionist dreams of many new entrepreneurs, it might well be more difficult for a successor to identify the moment when the "full complement" has been attained, which is when the business will reach the limits of the new employer's initial hopes, than it would be for this same employer to acknowledge the time when its business has begun normal production —the moment identified by the "substantial and representative complement" rule.

We therefore hold that the Board's "substantial and representative complement" rule is reasonable in the successorship context....

C.

We also hold that the Board's "continuing demand" rule is reasonable in the successorship situation. The successor's duty to bargain at the "substantial and representative complement" date is triggered only when the union has made a bargaining demand. Under the "continuing demand" rule, when a union has made a premature demand that has been rejected by the employer, this demand remains in force until

the moment when the employer attains the "substantial and representative complement." See, *e.g., Aircraft Magnesium*, 265 N.L.R.B., at 1345, n. 9; *Spruce Up Corp.*, 209 N.L.R.B., at 197....

The judgment of the Court of Appeals is affirmed. *It is so ordered.*

POWELL, J., joined by C. J. BURGER and J. O'CONNOR, Dissenting ...

... The Court acknowledges that when petitioner completed the employment of its anticipated workforce in April 1983, less than 50 percent of its employees formerly had worked for Sterlingwale. It nevertheless finds that the new company violated its duty to bargain, because at an earlier date chosen by the Board, a majority of the workforce formerly had worked for Sterlingwale. The NLRB concluded that even though petitioner was still in the process of hiring employees, by the middle of January it had hired a "substantial and representative complement," when its first shift was adequately staffed and most job categories had been filled....

... [U]nless the delay or uncertainty of future expansion would frustrate the employees' legitimate interest in early representation—a situation not shown to exist here—there is every reason to wait until the full anticipated workforce has been employed....

... The decision today "balances" these interests by over-protecting the latter and ignoring the former. In an effort to ensure that some employees will not be deprived of representation for even a short time, the Court requires petitioner to recognize a union that has never been elected or accepted by a majority of its workers....

Case Questions

1. Is a successor under an obligation to hire the employees of its predecessor?
2. Did the fact that there was a seven-month hiatus between the shutdown of Sterlingwale and the start-up of Fall River demonstrate that Fall River was not a successor?
3. At what point in time does the Board determine whether a new employer's workforce is made up of a majority of employees of the predecessor?
4. When did the dissenting justices believe the majority status should have been determined?

SECTION 51: REJECTION OF LABOR CONTRACTS UNDER CHAPTER 11 OF THE BANKRUPTCY CODE

The Bankruptcy Code provides a statutory procedure whereby a financially troubled business debtor may petition the bankruptcy court for "reorganization."[77] Under Chapter 11 of the Bankruptcy Code, a rehabilitation plan is filed with the courts. Creditors' acceptance of the plan is then sought, and ultimately a plan is approved or confirmed by the court. The business debtor usually remains in possession of the business and its assets after filing a Chapter 11 petition and is referred to as a *debtor in possession*. The purpose of a Chapter 11 petition is to financially rehabilitate the business.

The Supreme Court's *NLRB v. Bildisco and Bildisco, Debtor in Possession,*[78] decision dealt with the issues that arise after a business files for reorganization under Chapter 11 of the Bankruptcy Code. May a business—the debtor in possession—be permitted to reject a collective bargaining agreement without demonstrating that its reorganization will fail unless rejection of the labor contract is permitted? The Supreme Court did not approve such a strict standard for rejection of a labor contract by a bankruptcy court. Instead, the Court held that a collective bargaining agreement may be rejected if "the debtor can show that the collective bargaining agreement burdens the estate, and [if] after careful scrutiny the equities balance in favor of rejecting the labor contract." May a debtor in possession unilaterally modify or terminate its labor contracts when a Chapter 11 petition is filed, or must it wait until the bankruptcy court approves its motion to reject the labor contract? The *Bildisco* Court held that the debtor in possession could unilaterally terminate or reject a labor contract after filing a petition in bankruptcy before formal rejection is approved by the bankruptcy court. This action was found not to be in violation of Sections 8(a)(5) and (d) of the NLRA. However, the Court set forth bargaining requirements before the debtor could petition the court for rejection and also noted the debtor's obligation to bargain over the terms and conditions of a possible new contract.

The Bankruptcy Amendments and Federal Judges Act of 1984 overturned that part of the *Bildisco* decision that allowed for the unilateral rejection of a collective bargaining contract before approval by a bankruptcy court. The 1984 Act added certain other requirements for rejection of labor contracts. It requires bankruptcy court approval of "necessary" contract modifications before the debtor in possession (employer in bankruptcy) can reject the contract. Three provisions of the Act are of particular importance:

1. Section 1113(b)(1) provides that prior to filing an application for rejection of a contract, the debtor must make a proposal to the union "which provides for

---

[77] The foundation of the current law of bankruptcy is the Bankruptcy Reform Act of 1978, 11 U.S.C. §§ 101 *et seq.* (2005), and is commonly referred to as the "Bankruptcy Code." The Bankruptcy Abuse Prevention and Consumer Protection Act of 2005 (BAPCPA) Pub. L. No 109-8, 119 Stat.23, modifies the provisions of the code governing individual bankruptcies, impacts financially distressed small businesses, and establishes a comprehensive procedural framework to manage transnational insolvencies. The law relating to rejection of labor contracts was not modified, however, by BAPCPA and is set forth in the text of this section.

[78] 465 U.S. 513 (1984).

those necessary modifications in the employees' benefits and protections that are necessary to permit the reorganization of the debtor and assures that all creditors, the debtor and all of the affected parties are treated fairly and equitably." The language "assures that all creditors, the debtor and all of the affected parties are treated fairly and equitably" was added to the Act because Congressman Morrison of Connecticut pointed to a Chapter 11 proceeding where the Wilson Food Co. unilaterally rejected its labor contract. Bargaining unit employees absorbed a 25 percent pay cut, while all creditors received 100 cents on the dollar. Congressman Morrison expressed the belief that employees should not be asked to make greater financial sacrifices than other creditors, and after debate, the language was added to the Act.

2. The court can approve the application for rejection only after bargaining on the proposal required by Section 1113(b)(1) and, under Section 1113(c)(2), only after it is demonstrated at a court hearing that the union refuses to accept such a proposal "without good cause."

3. Where the requirements of Sections 1113(b)(1) and (c)(2) are met, the court will then apply "the balance of the equities" standard applied in *Bildisco*, with the additional requirement that the balance of the equities "clearly" favors rejection of the labor contract. If so found by the court, the court will approve the application for rejection or modification of the labor contract.

The terrorist attacks on September 11, 2001, have had a severe impact on the airline industry. Most major U.S. airlines have restructured their costs through the bankruptcy process in conformity with Sections 1113(b) and 1113(c), with the parties themselves ultimately reaching agreements on labor cost reductions, allowing the carrier involved to be cost-competitive with low-cost and previously restructured airlines.[79]

In *Wheeling-Pittsburgh Steel Corp., Debtor in Possession v. Steelworkers*,[80] the Third Circuit Court of Appeals set forth the meaning of the term *necessary* as used in Section 1113(b)(1) of the Bankruptcy Code. Because the 1984 legislation contained no definition of the word *necessary*, the Third Circuit relied on the legislative history to give meaning to the term. The study of the legislative history showed that the language of Section 1113(b)(1) was based on Senator Packwood's amendment. Senator Packwood noted concerning the amendment that

> only modifications which are necessary to a successful reorganization may be proposed. Therefore, the debtor will not be available to exploit the bankruptcy procedure to rid itself of unwanted features of the labor agreement that have no relation to its financial condition and its reorganization and which earlier were agreed to by the debtor. The word "necessary" inserted twice into this provision clearly emphasizes this required aspect of the proposal which the debtor must offer and guarantees the sincerity of the debtor's good faith in seeking contract changes.[81]

---

[79] See "Airlines" DLR No. 220 (Nov. 16, 2005), but see "Airlines" DLR No. 237 (Dec. 12, 2005).
[80] 791 F.2d 1074 (3d Cir. 1986).
[81] 130 Cong. Rec. § 8898 (daily ed. June 29, 1984).

The court in *Wheeling-Pittsburgh* held that the reasons given by the bankruptcy court in concluding that the debtor's proposal was "necessary" and "fair and equitable" were not persuasive. The bankruptcy court "failed to give any persuasive rationale for the disproportionate treatment of the employees who were being asked to take a five-year agreement under a worse-case scenario without any possibility for restoration or share in the event of a better than anticipated recovery."

In *Truck Driver's Local 807 v. Carey*,[82] the Second Circuit Court of Appeals utilized a different standard than the "minimum modifications" language of Senator Packwood's amendment, stating:

> In sum, we conclude that the necessity requirement places on the debtor the burden of proving that its proposal is made in good faith, and that it contains necessary, but not absolutely minimal, changes that will enable the debtor to complete the reorganization process successfully.

The Second Circuit's "necessary" requirement focuses on the long-term goal of the debtor's successful reorganization as opposed to the short-term horizon of the Third Circuit's reading of the "necessary" requirement with its minimum modifications that would permit reorganization.[83]

CHAPTER QUESTIONS AND PROBLEMS

1. The UAW (union) filed a representation petition on May 15, 2000, to represent some 650 production workers at Stanadyne Automobile Corporation's plant in Windsor, Connecticut, and the Board scheduled the election for June 29, 2000. Before the election, the employer had no rule prohibiting employees from talking about any topic they chose during working hours. After the petition was filed, supervisors informed employees that the employees were not allowed to discuss the union or solicit union support during working hours and that violations could result in being disciplined or fired.

   On June 6, CEO William Gurley delivered a prepared speech to groups of employees in which he stated in part:

   "It has come to my attention that some union supporters, not all, but some are harassing fellow employees.... Harassment of any type is not tolerated by this company and will be dealt with."

   The union lost the election and filed unfair labor practice charges against the employer. The employer admits that the supervisors should not have told employees that they were not allowed to discuss the union or solicit support during working hours, and it does not challenge a finding that this activity was a violation of rights protected by Section 7 of the NLRA. The employer insists, however, that CEO Gurley had a right to promulgate the no-harassment rule on June 6 and this rule could not be construed to prohibit protected activity. The union disagrees. Decide. [*UAW v. NLRB*, 520 F.3d. 102 (2d Cir. 2008)].

2. The management of Bill Johnson's Restaurants, doing business as The Big Apple Restaurant, informed the employees of new

---

[82] 816 F.2d 82, 90 (2d Cir. 1987).

[83] See *in re American Provision Co.*, 44 B.R. 907, 909 (1984), and *in re Horizon Natural Res. Co.*, 316 B.R. 268 (2004), for prerequisites for determining whether a collective bargaining agreement should be rejected.

restrictions regarding the employees' use of the company phone, the procedure for calling in sick, and the chewing of gum at work. During a later discussion in front of a supervisor, one of the employees, Mrs. Helton, suggested that the servers needed a union. The following day, Mrs. Helton, a senior employee, was fired because a company vice president "didn't like her attitude." In response to the firing, several employees petitioned the NLRB to institute an unfair labor practice action against the restaurant. Several employees also picketed in front of the restaurant without obstructing the parking lot or entrances. The picketers urged the public to boycott the business, and they also distributed leaflets to that effect. Sherry Sturgeon, a manager, told the picketers that they were not funny and she would "have the last laugh." The management then filed a civil action in state court for business interference, trespass, and libel. The complaint sought $500,000 in damages and an injunction.

When the NLRB decided the Helton discharge case, it also ordered the restaurant to withdraw its state court action. The NLRB ruled that the suit was an intrusion upon the Board's jurisdiction and constituted a unfair labor practice. The restaurant refused to comply with the Board's order and appealed.

What factors must be considered when deciding whether the state lawsuit may be pursued? What was the result in this case? Decide. [*Bill Johnson's Restaurants v. NLRB*, 108 LRRM 3044 (9th Cir.); 461 U.S. 731. But see *BE & K Construction Co. v. NLRB*, 536 U.S. 516 (2002), on *remand* 351 NLRB No. 29, (2007)].

3. The United Transportation Workers went on strike after their contract expired with Safeway Trails Bus Company. The company submitted to the union a new proposal for ratification. John Lantz, the union's chief negotiator, decided that this latest proposal was very similar to the contract recently rejected by the membership and therefore did not submit it for approval by the membership. Lantz informed the company of this decision. The company thereafter mailed copies of its proposal to all employees asking each to act "in the interest of his own personal welfare." The company repeatedly sent employees letters outlining its final offer and questioning the qualifications of representative Lantz. At one point, the company president offered to meet with any three employees other than Lantz to settle on a contract. The president told some striking employees they were "following the wrong man."

The union claimed that Safeway had not bargained in good faith in violation of Section 8(a)(5) by attempting to undermine union authority. The company denied these charges and claimed that its communication with the employees was protected by Section 8(c).

Is Safeway's conduct protected or prohibited under the NLRA? Decide. [*Safeway Trails, Inc., v. NLRB*, 102 LRRM 2328 (D.C. Cir.)]

4. Jenny Allen, a General Motors employee, was observed by a GM security guard at a bowling alley near the plant during working hours. Allen's supervisor and the plant labor relations manager then questioned Allen on three separate occasions. During the first two interrogations, Allen, a union committeeperson, never requested that a union representative accompany her, and she denied being at the bowling alley. When questioned a third time on the plant floor, Allen requested union representation. The supervisor ignored Allen's request. Allen continued to answer questions and finally admitted that she had been at the bowling alley during working hours. Allen was discharged the next day.

Allen and her union claimed that General Motors engaged in a Section 8(a)(1) unfair labor practice when it denied Allen's request for union representation. General Motors cited Allen's failure to request a union representative at two previous interrogations and her willingness to answer questions without union representation as evidence against this charge.

Has a Section 8(a)(1) unfair labor practice occurred? Decide. [*General Motors Corp. v. NLRB*, 109 LRRM 3345 (6th Cir.)]

5. During his tenure at Tera Advanced Services Corporation, Dan Malloy had received many warnings concerning below-average attitude and productivity, including a "final warning" and company probation in January. After this warning, however, Malloy's attitude and production improved so greatly that his supervisor told the operations manager that the warnings had been successful and no further disciplinary action was needed. On February 4, Malloy attended a company lunch where employees were allowed to ask questions of Tera's project manager, James Long. In front of other employees, Malloy asked Long how he would feel about the formation of a union for the employees. Malloy proceeded to cite the advantages of a union. Long was visibly angered by the question and exclaimed after the lunch "who the hell does he think he is, asking to form a union at Tera." Long then demanded to see Malloy's personnel file, and he determined that his record was "terrible." He decided to discharge Malloy. Long ordered a memorandum compiled outlining Malloy's employment record. The following day Dan Malloy was discharged. Malloy claimed before the NLRB that he was discharged because of his question at the lunch. He claimed that asking that question was a protected activity. He believed that Tera had committed Section 8(a)(3) and (1) unfair labor practices. Tera Corporation contended Malloy would have been discharged even if he had not attended the company lunch and supported its position with the memorandum Long had ordered compiled.

What factors must the Board consider in deciding this case? Is there sufficient evidence of Section 8(a)(3) and (1) violations? Decide.

[*Tera Advanced Services Corp.*, 259 NLRB No. 125, 109 LRRM 1053]

6. David Stark submitted an application to the maintenance department at Wyman-Gordon Company. Stark was a journeyman mill-wright with nine years' experience at a neighboring company at the time of his application to Wyman-Gordon. Stark was vice president of the local industrial workers' union. In his preliminary interview with the company, Ms. Peevler asked if Stark was involved in union activity, and Stark detailed his involvement to her. She informed Stark that Wyman-Gordon was a nonunion shop and asked how he felt about this. Ms. Peevler's notes from the interview characterize Stark's response to this question as "seems to lean toward third-party intervention." Company officials testified that Stark's qualifications were "exactly what we were looking for." Stark was not employed by the company. Stark claimed that he was discriminated against. Wyman-Gordon denied that any discrimination had occurred.

Is a job applicant (as opposed to an employee) entitled to protection from anti-union discrimination? On the facts of this case, has any discrimination taken place? Decide. [*Wyman-Gordon Co. v. NLRB*, 108 LRRM 2085 (1st Cir.)]

7. Hospitality Motor Inns began to bargain with the Hotel Employees Union after the NLRB certified the results of a representation election. A few days prior to this election, Hospitality had promoted the leading activist of the union among the employees to a supervisory position. Hospitality refused to entertain union proposals on dues check-offs or union security, and the company insisted upon a broad management rights clause that would permit unilateral acts by the company regarding wages and other terms of employment. Hospitality cited "philosophical reasons" to justify its rejection of union proposals, including "no discrimination" and "no individual contracts" clauses in the agreement. After

six months of bargaining sessions, the company's position did not change and no agreement was reached.

The union petitioned the Board, alleging that Hospitality Inns was bargaining in bad faith contrary to Section 8(a)(5) and (1). The company claimed that good faith bargaining does not require it to make "concessions" to the union. Decide. [*NLRB v. Hospitality Motor Inns*, 109 LRRM 2945 (6th Cir.)]

8. Since 1978, the International Association of Machinists, Lodge 1899, has been the certified bargaining representative of certain food service employees of Marriott In-Flite Services. In 1980, without bargaining with the union, Marriott unilaterally bestowed an 11 percent wage increase and an additional holiday on these employees. Marriott contended that it had honestly doubted that the Machinists represented a majority of these employees since the fall of 1979, and therefore it did not bargain with the Machinists. The Machinists alleged that the granting of wage and benefit increases without bargaining was a violation of Section 8(a)(5) and (1) of the NLRA. Decide. [Marriott Corp., 259 NLRB 157, 108 LRRM 1317]

9. Four days after a three-week strike, during which strike a number of employees continued to work, the union posted Jack London's "Definition of a Scab" on the union bulletin boards on company premises. It read as follows:

Definition of a Scab

After God had finished the rattlesnake, the toad, and the vampire, he had some awful substance left with which he made a SCAB. A SCAB is a two-legged animal with a corkscrew soul, a water-logged brain, and a combination backbone made of jelly and glue. Where others have hearts, he carries a tumor of rotten principles.

When a SCAB comes down the street men turn their backs and angels weep in Heaven, and the devil shuts the gates of Hell to keep him out. No man has the right to SCAB, so long as there is a pool of water deep enough to drown his body in, or a rope long enough to hang his carcass

with. Judas Iscariot was a gentleman ... compared with a SCAB; for betraying his master, he had the character to hang himself—a SCAB hasn't.

Essau sold his birthright for a mess of porrage. Judas Iscariot sold his Saviour for thirty pieces of silver. Benedict Arnold sold his country for a promise of a commission in the British Army. The modern strikebreaker sells his birthright, his country, his wife, his children and his fellow men for an unfulfilled promise from his employer, trust or corporation.

Essau was a traitor to himself. Judas Iscariot was a traitor to his God. Benedict Arnold was a traitor to his country.

A strikebreaker is a traitor to himself, a traitor to his God, and a traitor to his country, a traitor to his family and a traitor to his class.

There is Nothing Lower than a Scab.

The company ordered the postings removed from the bulletin boards under threat of disciplinary action. The company stated that it acted because the postings would create animosity among employees.

The union contended that the company violated the employees' Section 7 rights and Section 8(a)(1) of the Act. The union contended that it had legitimate interest in strengthening employee support and cohesion for future economic strikes. The company contended that the postings were beyond the protection of Sections 7 and 8(a)(1).

Which party has the burden of proof in this case? Has the Act been violated? Decide. [Southwestern Bell Tel. Co., 276 NLRB 1053, 120 LRRM 1145]

10. Local 35 of the United Food and Commercial Workers Union was certified by the NLRB as bargaining representative of the employees of Fountainhead Development Corporation in July. Fountainhead operated the Blu-Fountain Manor Nursing Home. Immediately after certification, the union began collective bargaining negotiations with Fountainhead. The negotiations were not fruitful, and in October, the employees began an economic strike against Fountainhead.

The union filed unfair labor practice charges against Fountainhead in February relating to access to Fountainhead's financial records. Fountainhead hired strike replacements.

On May 1, Jarm Enterprises purchased the Blu-Fountain Manor Nursing Home. Jarm immediately retracted the employee benefits package extended by Fountainhead and rehired, under new terms, all Fountainhead employees who had been working at the time of the transfer of ownership, including the striker replacements. In addition, Jarm did the following: instituted new personnel policies, eliminated certain supervisory positions and job classifications, introduced a new computerized billing system, and initiated $60,000 worth of repairs to the nursing home.

On May 8, the union contacted Jarm with an unconditional offer to return to work and a request to commence collective bargaining. Jarm refused both offers, claiming that it was a new employer that was not subject to labor relationships established with Fountainhead. Furthermore, Jarm asserted that the union did not represent its current employees. Jarm could have rehired the striking union members because in the months following May 8, the company hired a number of employees that exceeded the number of striking employees.

The union filed an unfair labor practice charge against Jarm, claiming the company was obligated to bargain. Jarm contended that it was a radically different enterprise and was in no way bound to deal with the union and its strikers.

Should the union's charge be upheld? Decide. [*NLRB v. Jarm Enterprises, Inc.*, 121 LRRM 3105 (7th Cir.)]

11. Kathy Denaple worked in a nonsupervisory capacity at a missile component plant operated by Rockwell International. The Communications Workers of America began a successful organizing campaign among Rockwell's employees. Denaple supported the campaign by attending meetings and distributing authorization cards. In September, Denaple's supervisor, Bernice Cash, asked her if she was involved with the union. When Denaple responded that it was none of Cash's business, Cash stated that union involvement would hurt Denaple's work record.

One morning the following January, supervisors Cash and Cheek held a meeting at which Cheek told the employees in Denaple's department that they spent too much time in the washrooms and that the music from their radio headsets was too loud. Denaple contradicted Cheek at the meeting by stating that the music was not loud and, in fact, was softer than the sound of the wire-cutting machine in their area. Denaple also reminded the supervisors of Rockwell's unfulfilled promise to remove the noisy machines. After this meeting, the supervisors discussed issuing Denaple a written warning for speaking out. Later that same day an employee complained that Denaple was laughing loudly and excessively at her workstation. The supervisors issued Denaple a written warning for "allowing excessive laughing to disturb a work group."

In February, six employees were discharged by Rockwell after urinalysis revealed that they had used drugs. After the tests, but before the discharges, one of the tested employees had asked Denaple to find out if the union could help him if he was fired. She agreed. During the morning on which the employees were fired, Denaple was discussing the firings with a coworker when a supervisor cautioned Denaple that she was already in enough trouble and that she should return to her workstation. Denaple complained to the supervisor that the firings were unfair and asked if all employees would be tested. Later that day Denaple asked Cash for time off to attend to personal business. Cash refused permission although she noted that Denaple's attendance had improved of late. Denaple told Cash that she had to leave. The supervisor told Denaple that she would not be fired if she left, but she explicitly refused to grant Denaple's request. Nevertheless, Denaple left the premises.

Cash shared this latest incident with the other supervisors, and they consulted Rockwell's manager of employee relations, Wanda Saed, by phone. Saed ordered Denaple terminated. The next day Denaple was terminated for "work-related behavior and attendance."

The union asserted that Denaple was fired because she engaged in protected activity. The employer claimed that Denaple was fired because she was an insubordinate employee with an attendance problem.

Have any unfair labor practices occurred? Could the General Counsel bring a case on behalf of Denaple challenging her dismissal? Decide. [*Rockwell International v. NLRB*, 125 LRRM 2132 (11th Cir.)]

12. The Chrysler Corporation sold its marine engine division to the U.S. Marine Corporation (USM) on January 13, 1984. USM estimated, based on data provided by its marketing and manufacturing departments, that it would need a full complement of 396 workers on the job by June 1984. USM wanted to reopen the plant as quickly as possible and needed a skilled workforce to do so. It reopened the plant under changed terms and conditions of employment, with all 219 workers being former Chrysler employees. On January 30, 1984, it hired its last Chrysler employee, with its employee totals that day being 261 employees, 227 of whom had worked for Chrysler. Thirty-four Chrysler employees were not hired, although USM's total workforce ranged up to 323 workers through August 31, 1984. On January 25, when 222 of their 231 workers were former Chrysler employees, the union requested recognition. The request filtered up the organization, and figures on the number of former Chrysler workers hired in the rather disorganized hiring process that took place in January were compiled and indicated

to top management that as of January 30, 1984, 223 Chrysler workers had been hired. On January 31, 1984, Mr. Hoag, the general manager of the USM operation, changed the full complement projection from 396 to 460 workers, increasing the production schedules for engines by some 130 engines, with no justification.

In February, the union filed charges with the Board, claiming that USM had unlawfully refused to bargain and had discriminated against the 34 Chrysler employees it refused to hire. USM responded that it had no obligation to recognize the union because less than half of the 460 expected employees were former Chrysler employees.

Did USM have the right to change the terms and conditions of employment when it reopened the plant? Did it have an obligation to recognize and bargain with the union in late January? Was the failure to hire the 34 remaining Chrysler workers after January 31 a Section 8(a)(3) violation? Decide. [*U.S. Marine Corp. v. NLRB*, 944 F.2d 1305 (7th Cir.)]

13. Polaroid Corporation announced the formation of an Employee-Owners Influence Council (EOIC) in January 1993 and invited all 8,000 employees to apply to serve on the committee. Some 150 employees applied, and the company interviewed and selected 30 employees. The company provided the facilities for the EOIC and paid all expenses to serve three-, four-, or five-year terms. A Polaroid organizational specialist conducted each meeting where management made proposals to the group on such topics as family and medical leave, a termination policy, medical benefits, and an employee stock ownership plan (ESOP). Polaroid consistently polled or otherwise questioned the group to determine the majority view of the group on the topic discussed, and this view then effectively constituted the proposal of the EOIC, to which Polaroid thereafter responded by word or deed. For example, Polaroid's Chief

Executive Officer Booth stated to the EOIC at the October 20 meeting that he would come back and discuss solutions with employees, and in fact he did come back to the EOIC with a decision. In internal publications to its workforce, Polaroid repeatedly emphasized the significant input of the EOIC on the decisions made by management. Polaroid encouraged EOIC members to communicate with other employees about issues and to report back to the EOIC the views of these employees. Mr. Booth encouraged EOIC members to tell him what other employees were expressing.

Did the employer violate Section 8(a)(2) by creating a labor organization under Section 2(5) in setting up and implementing EOIC? Or was the employer entitled to exercise its First Amendment and basic managerial rights to conduct brainstorming sessions with its employees? Decide. [Polaroid Corp., 329 NLRB 424]

14. Tasty Baking Company (TBC) operates a plant in Philadelphia, Pennsylvania, where approximately 700 workers produce baked goods on daytime and overnight shifts. In 1994, Teamsters Union Local 115 began an organizing drive among TBC employees. The union lost a representation election in April 1995, but upon the union's objection, the board set aside the results and ordered a new election in March 1996. In mid-June, Production Operations Director Thomas Kenney demoted Edwina Flannery, the wife of well-known union activist and "oven man" Michael Flannery, from the supervisory position she had held for nearly five years. This demotion took place despite management's recent assurances that her position was safe and that she was the company's "newest rising star." On August 10, 1995, after Edwina Flannery's demotion, Superintendent Charles Britsch told her that the fact that her husband was outside the plant distributing union literature "was not helping [her] chances of staying on day work," and that if he continued, she "could

very seriously end up on night work." She responded that he was "a grown man" and that she could not tell him what to do. Michael Flannery continued leafleting, and a month later the company transferred his wife to night shift. On January 16, 1996, Michael Flannery received a disciplinary warning from his supervisor, alleging that Flannery had twice failed to remove crumbs from the crumbs depositor. Flannery filed a written grievance, protesting that it was not his responsibility to remove the crumbs. When Flannery met with Britsch to discuss the grievance on January 18, Britsch said that the warning stemmed from the company's new "get tough" policy. Britsch also said that he and Flannery were "enemies" and that while Flannery might think that he was doing the right thing for the employees, Britsch believed that he (Britsch) was "doing the right thing for Tasty Bake and will do whatever I have to do to keep the union out."

On January 26, 1996, Operations Director Kenney met with an employee, William Martin, to discuss Martin's suggestion that metal detectors be installed at the entrance to the workplace. Kenney told Martin that the suggestion was "stupid" and speculated that Michael Flannery was behind it. Martin denied this, and then told Kenney that Michael Flannery should not have received the "crumbs" warning because it was Martin's, not Flannery's, responsibility to remove the crumbs from the depositor. Kenney responded that he did not care whose job it was, and "that he had told Mike that if Mike f**ked him, he would f**k Mike back." Kenney then told Martin that, "if you f**k me, I'll f**k you back," and concluded: "[N]ow I'm getting Mike. I told him I was going to do it. Now I'm doing it."

On January 31, 1996, sanitation employee Robert Nolan, another vocal union supporter, received a three-day suspension and was subsequently issued a written warning for "insubordination" resulting from an incident with Linda Casey, a substitute floor monitor. According to Nolan, he had been making a telephone call during his usual break time when Casey began "yelling and screaming" at him to get off the phone. Nolan told Casey that he was talking to his wife and asked to see his regular floor monitor. Casey refused to let Nolan explain or see his monitor and instructed him to get off the phone and return to work, which Nolan did. Nolan testified that thereafter, his regular monitor told him not to worry about the incident. Nonetheless, Nolan received a written warning and a three-day suspension for insubordination.

On April 11, 1996, Kenney approached Michael Flannery during his shift and said, "[I] don't believe you. After what happened to your wife, you're still pushing the union and calling OSHA [the Occupational Safety & Health Administration]. Are you going to make me fire you?" Two months later, on June 6, 1996, Flannery received a warning for reporting wrong "oven times" to other employees. Flannery received the warning notwithstanding that he had disputed the allegation and had been told that he would merely receive a memo to his file.

TBC contends that Britsch's references to people "screwing up" and to the new "get tough" policy had nothing to do with union activity and contends that Kenney had never made any reference to Flannery calling OSHA. Moreover, among other points, TBC states that it demoted Edwina Flannery as part of a reorganization because she couldn't get the job done. She received a positive performance evaluation in 1994. TBC points out that supervisors are not protected under the Act. And it states that because of her demotion, she lost seniority and was thus eligible only for night shift work. TBC contends that the Board has no authority to order Edwina reinstated as a supervisor, especially one that is on the union's side.

From the General Counsel's point of view, what section(s) of the NLRA would you contend were violated in this case? The company has presented its contentions regarding legitimate business reasons for its actions. Apply the *Wright Line* test and decide the unfair labor practices complaints. Discuss what protection, if any, Edwina Flannery is entitled to under the Act. If the Act was violated, what should be the remedy? [*Tasty Baking Co. v. NLRB*, 254 F.3d 114 (D.C. Cir. 2001)]

15. Richard Wehrli was the sole or part owner of Naperville Ready Mix, Inc., T&W Trucking, and Wehrli Equipment Co., which respectively provided ready-mix concrete, hauling services, and truck repair services for the ready-mix concrete business. During contract negotiations with Teamster Local 673, Wehrli announced that he was going to sell the delivery trucks to owner-operators. He supplied the financing for buying the trucks, required buyers to give first priority to Naperville's hauling needs, restricted purchasers from working for competitors, sold subsidized fuel, provided truck repair services, and allowed free truck storage on site. The trucks continued to haul concrete exclusively for the employer, drivers continued to receive their orders from the same dispatcher, and the owner stipulated that the purpose of the change was to lower labor costs.

Wehrli contends that the business decided, for entrepreneurial reasons, to sell substantial assets and close part of its business and that under *First National Maintenance*, his companies had no duty to bargain over this entrepreneurial decision. The companies recognize the obligation to bargain over the effects of the decision. And he contends the basic decision to close part of the business is unaffected by any decision to later engage in subcontracting, regardless of labor costs being a factor in the decision. The General Counsel contends that *Fibreboard* is controlling in this case. What arguments can you make in support of the General Counsel's position? If you were an administrative Law Judge, what would be your recommended decision?

[*Naperville Ready Mix, Inc., v. NLRB*, 242 F.3d 744 (7th Cir. 2001)]

16. Cindy Adams worked as a salesperson at the nonunion Wal-Mart store in Wasilla, Alaska. On March 10, 2001, while walking to the employees' break room for lunch, she met Ken Stanhope in the hallway, who asked about her father, a Wal-Mart employee out on worker's compensation. She responded, and they continued to speak about her father. Stanhope then changed the subject, asking what she thought about the union, and she replied she did not want a union. Stanhope replied that her father was pro-union and urged her to check out a pro-union Internet site. According to a statement written by Cindy Adams, she asserted that Stanhope said management were "all f—ken pricks and they would f—ken lie to your face without even batting an eye. And so we needed a union to stop management and make it safe for associates." Adams said that as Stanhope talked, he moved closer to her, and she became uncomfortable and twice moved back from him and ended the conversation, saying she was missing out on her lunch. While the ALJ did not believe Cindy Adams' testimony to be reliable or truthful, management acted upon her written version of events, and an investigation was conducted by comanagers Bruce Manderson and Marlene Munsell. On March 16, the two comanagers conducted a meeting with Stanhope, investigating the allegations of Cindy Adams against him. Stanhope immediately requested the presence of his own witness, which was denied, and he was ordered to sit and continue with the interview, and he was sent home while the managers continued the investigation. On March 17, after Stanhope reported for work, accompanied by an assistant manager and with, at the manager's request, a police officer standing nearby, Manderson approached Stanhope at the food court and asked him to follow him to his office. Stanhope replied that he would not go anywhere unless he had a witness. The request was denied, and thereafter, he was terminated for creating a hostile work environment and using foul language. Manderson testified that Stanhope's refusal to cooperate in the investigation without a witness present was a factor in the decision to discharge him. Does the "*Weingarten* right" apply in this case? Did Wal-Mart commit a Section 8(a)(1) unfair labor practice by denying Stanhope's request for a witness on March 16, 2001, and continuing the interview without the presence of his requested witness? Did it violate Section 8(a)(1) by terminating Stanhope on March 17 after he refused to attend a subsequent investigatory interview without the presence of a witness? Decide. [See the ALJ's decision to the Board's Wal-Mart Stores, Inc., and UFCWIU, Local 343 decision, 343 NLRB No. 127.]

REGULATION OF UNION ACTIVITIES

SECTION

SECTION 52: UNION UNFAIR LABOR PRACTICES

In the favorable environment provided by the Norris-LaGuardia Act and the Wagner Act, unions flourished in the period from 1935 to 1947. Union membership expanded from 3 million members to 15 million members during this period. Organized labor was perceived as a powerful political force during the years of World War II, with union leaders being appointed to important governmental positions. With the increasing strength of labor unions, the public became more aware of the abuses of certain unions. During World War II, the United Mine Workers conducted two crippling coal strikes. These strikes were looked upon with disdain by many citizens who believed the strikes hurt the war effort. The fairness of the closed shop, as well as the use of boycotts, was questioned. The laxity and corruption in the administration of union dues, as well as certain pay for no work or featherbedding practices, were called into question by the media, academicians, and political office holders and candidates. During 1946, after the end of World War II, strikes occurred in many major industries, including the steel and auto industries. In this climate, the Taft-Hartley legislation was vigorously debated. The Taft-Hartley amendments to the NLRA were enacted on June 23, 1947, when Congress overrode President Truman's veto. The amendments contained new restrictions on unions, including Section 8(b), which prohibited six union unfair labor practices.

The first two union unfair labor practices involving (1) the prohibition of union coercion of employees in the exercise of the right to refrain from union activities, as set forth in Section 8(b)(1) of the Act, and (2) the prohibition against unions causing employers to discriminate against employees in order to discourage or encourage union membership, as set forth in Section 8(b)(2) of the Act, currently generate over 80 percent of union unfair labor practices charges filed with the NLRB.[1] Union refusal to engage in good faith bargaining, a violation of Section 8(b)(3), is not common. Employers continue to file charges for unions' failure to engage in concessionary bargaining, but most of the time, it is in the unions' best interest to engage in bargaining with employers. Section 8(b)(4), dealing with prohibited strikes and boycotts, is a complex subject matter that has led to clarifying legislation and much litigation. A major portion of this and the subsequent chapter will deal with these and related topics. Restrictions on excessive dues and initiation fees, as set forth in Section 8(b)(5), and the prohibition against featherbedding practices found in Section 8(b)(6) are not currently common issues before the Labor Board. Section 8(b)(7) was added to the NLRA in 1959 as part of the Landrum-Griffin Act, making it an unfair labor practice for unions to engage in extended picketing for recognitional purposes.

COERCION BY LABOR UNIONS

The first union unfair labor practice is predicated upon the Section 7 right of employees to refrain from union activities as well as to participate in them. Section 8(b)(1) provides as follows:

> It shall be an unfair labor practice for a labor organization or its agents to restrain or coerce (A) employees in the exercise of the rights guaranteed in Section 7; provided that this paragraph shall not impair the right of a labor organization to prescribe its own rules with respect to the acquisition or retention of membership therein; or, (B) an employer in the selection of his representatives for the purposes of collective bargaining or the adjustment of grievances.

---

[1] Some 6,140 cases were filed against labor organizations in the fiscal year ending September 30, 2006, as reported in the Board's recent *Annual Report*, with 4,658 charges involving Section 8(b)(1), 40 involving Section 8(b)(2), 319 involving Section 8(b)(3), 451 involving Section 8(b)(4), 3 involving Section 8(b)(6), and 67 involving Section 8(b)(7). *Seventy-First Annual Report of the NLRB*, issued September 2007.

Congressional reasoning including Section 8(b)(1) can clearly be determined from an extract of Senate Report 105, 80th Congress:

> The committee heard many instances of union coercion of employees such as that brought about by threats of reprisal against employees and their families in the course of organizing campaigns; also, direct interference by mass picketing and other violence. Some of these acts are made illegal by state law, but we see no reason why they should not also constitute unfair labor practices to be investigated by the National Labor Relations Board, and at least deprive the violators of any protection furnished by the Wagner Act. We believe that the freedom of the individual workman should be protected from duress by the union as well as from duress by the employer.

The legislative history of this provision indicates that Congress had no intention to prohibit the normal exercise by unions of the right to appeal to employees or members by persuasive speech or conduct that carried no threat of force or reprisal.

The prohibition of union restraint on employees' rights contains the proviso that allows unions to prescribe their own membership rules; and such will be dealt with in detail in the chapter on regulating internal union affairs. Section 8(b)(1)(A), however, has been applied to prevent union coercion to force upon employees membership or representation by a union. Threatening harm by pickets or strikers in the presence of union officials who do not repudiate them to nonstriking employees constitutes a violation of Section 8(b)(1)(A).

Under Section 8(b)(1)(B), union coercion of an employer's rights to select its bargaining representatives is forbidden. This restriction applies to a union strike threat for insistence on bargaining with the company owners or executives rather than with an attorney engaged to negotiate for the management. It has been applied to unions striking to compel members of an employer association to sign individual agreements in conflict with an established multiemployer single unit.

CAUSING EMPLOYER TO DISCRIMINATE

Section 8(b)(2) makes it an unfair labor practice for a union "to cause or attempt to cause an employer to discriminate against an employee in violation of Section 8(a)(3) or to discriminate against an employee with respect to whom membership in such organization has been denied or terminated on some ground other than the employee's failure to tender the periodic dues and the initiation fees uniformly required as a condition of acquiring or retaining membership." Under the NLRA as amended in 1947, an employer is obligated to discharge an employee upon notice by the union if the following circumstances prevail:

1. A valid **union shop, maintenance-of-membership,** or **agency shop** agreement is in force.[2]

---

[2] See definitions in Glossary. Note that in all three forms of union security arrangements, the statutory mandates of Section 8(a)(3) and Section 8(b)(2) apply, relating only to "dues paying" or financial support requirements, and do not compel full union membership. An agency shop may be regulated or prohibited by the states under Section 14(b) in so-called right-to-work law states.

2. The employee has been denied membership in the labor association for failure to pay a reasonable initiation fee or is expelled from membership because the employee has failed to pay dues that are reasonable under Section 8(b)(5).
3. The contractual requirement of union membership is not effective before the 30th day after the date of employment or after the start of the contract period, whichever comes later. However, under Section 8(f) of the 1959 amendments to the Act, it is not an unfair labor practice for an employer in the construction industry to make an agreement with a labor organization representing employees in that industry requiring membership after the seventh day of employment on the job.

Examples of union actions in violation of Section 8(b)(2) include forcing agreements on employers requiring that only those "satisfactory" to the union be hired and union-caused discharges because the employee was a "troublemaker" or a "bad actor," tried to organize a rival union, or was otherwise disliked by the union members. Although the right of a union to determine its own rules for membership is protected explicitly by Section 8(b), employees' jobs or the job conditions fall outside lawful union discrimination. The Board also has found violations of Section 8(b)(1) and (2) in union discrimination for racial reasons.

REFUSAL BY UNION TO BARGAIN

The original National Labor Relations Act imposed no explicit duty upon a labor organization to engage in good faith bargaining, presumably under the theory that such a provision would be superfluous since the basic purpose of a labor association is to represent employees for purposes of collective bargaining. The amended Act, in Section 8(b)(3), imposes an affirmative duty upon unions. This union requirement, like that for employers, includes the duties stated in Section 8(d) of the law to give 60-day notice of proposed changes in agreements, with the status quo to be maintained during the notice period.

The union duty to bargain in good faith also includes the same procedural requirements that the employer must meet, including a willingness to consider in good faith the position of the other party. Insisting on clauses that fall outside the scope of mandatory bargaining subjects constitutes a union violation of Section 8(b)(3), as the reciprocal of Section 8(a)(5).

EXCESSIVE INITIATION FEES AND DUES

Labor organizations that operate under permitted forms of union security may not, by virtue of Section 8(b)(5), charge excessive or discriminatory dues or initiation fees. The General Counsel of the NLRB has issued a statement that shows a disposition to handle each charge on this issue as it arises, with the determination of unfair labor practice resting on a study of custom in the trade, the earnings made by the constituents, and the extent of protection offered to them. Thus, what might be considered excessive in one case may be entirely reasonable in another. In *Television and Radio Artists (WBEN, Inc.),*[3] a Section 8(b)(5) violation was found

---

[3] 208 NLRB 377 (1974). But see *George Banter Co. v. NLRB,* 626 F.2d 354 (4th Cir. 1980).

when the initiation fee was raised from $100 to $250 by the union in order to impede the employer from hiring parttime employees.

FEATHERBED PRACTICES: EMPLOYER PAYMENTS TO UNION REPRESENTATIVES

Featherbedding is the receiving of compensation for work that is not required by the employer or that is not tendered or performed by the employee recipients of the compensation. The work or services in question may not, in the employer's opinion, be at all necessary but, through industry usage, may have become customary. Section 8(b)(6) of the NLRA makes unlawful those attempts to cause an employer to "pay ... for services which are not performed or not to be performed." Its phrasing permits certain make-work forms of featherbedding, which would include those situations where two employees do the work that, conceivably or reasonably, one worker could do. Section 8(b)(6) is inapplicable, then, where unnecessary work is performed. The test is **performance** and not **necessity of performance**, as stated by the Supreme Court in its *American Newspaper Publishers Ass'n. v. NLRB* decision.[4]

Section 8(b)(6) must also be read along with Section 302 of the LMRA. Although Section 302(a) of the LMRA prohibits an employer from paying "any money or any other thing of value" to a union official, Section 302(c)(1) makes an exception for payments to union officials who are also employees of the employer "as compensation for, or by reason of, his service as an employee of such an employer." In *IAM, Local 964 v. BF Goodrich*,[5] the chief shop steward James Cifu was entitled under the parties' collective bargaining agreement to draw his salary and benefits while working primarily on "the investigation and prosecution of union grievances." Goodrich sought a declaratory judgment voiding the provision providing pay and benefits to Cifu, arguing that such payment was in violation of Section 302(a) as money paid to a union official while conducting union business. The Ninth Circuit Court of Appeals determined that Cifu, even in his capacity as a union representative, served the company's interests since services "rendered by union stewards benefit unions and corporations alike." Moreover, the court supported its decision based on the fact that Cifu worked from an office on the shop floor under immediate supervision of the employer, not a union hall free from corporate control. Also, he carried out his work on the shop floor, where his conduct was observable and subject to the policies and norms of the employer. Accordingly, the court held that payments made to Cifu fall within the Section 302(c)(1) exception covering compensation for "services as an employee of such an employer."

SECTION 53: PICKETING: TYPES AND CONSTITUTIONAL PARAMETERS

In addition to strike activity, which will be discussed in the succeeding chapter, two other forms of economic pressure may be applied against employers in labor disputes. They are picketing and boycott activities. The use of picketing and the

---

[4] 345 U.S. 100 (1953).

[5] 387 F.3d 1046 (9th Cir. 2004).

boycott and the protection of property may cause a conflict of rights. The Constitution and the labor laws do not establish any absolute right to picket or boycott regardless of purpose or effect, according to the views of the courts. The intent, the circumstances, and the result usually receive consideration.

Picketing of an establishment may take a number of forms, may be engaged in for a variety of reasons or purposes, and may or may not coexist with a strike. Two major forms of picketing exist—*primary* and *secondary picketing*. The **primary picket** results when workers in a given establishment patrol around it with placards, usually to inform workers and the public that the employer is unfair to union labor. A strike may or may not have been called. The gist of the primary picket is a dispute with the employer whose establishment is being patrolled. The **secondary picket**, which is a species of secondary boycott, involves the stationing of pickets around the place of business of a customer or supplier of the primary employer with whom the union has a dispute in order to cause others to refrain from dealing with the primary employer. Other forms of picketing will be discussed in subsequent sections along with the legal parameters for each category.

The *Thornhill* case presented in this section involves the constitutionality of a state statute that prohibited *all* picketing as a misdemeanor. *Thornhill* is a landmark case in labor law because it held that the dissemination of information about the facts of a labor dispute must be regarded as within that area of free discussion that is guaranteed by the First and Fourteenth Amendments of the U.S. Constitution. Also presented in this section is the *Meadowmoor Dairies, Inc.*, case. Violent picketing is unlawful in all jurisdictions, and the *Meadowmoor* court reconciles its decision with that of *Thornhill v. Alabama*.

While Section 8(b)(1) of the NLRA prohibits union coercion, including violence, states have a basic constitutional right to regulate and enjoin violence occurring in the context of a labor dispute.

CASE 6.1	THORNHILL V. ALABAMA
	SUPREME COURT OF THE UNITED STATES, 310 U.S. 88 (1940).

MURPHY, J....

Petitioner, Byron Thornhill, was convicted in the Circuit Court of Tuscaloosa County, Alabama, of the violation of Section 3448 of the State Code of 1923. The Code Section reads as follows: "Section 3448. Loitering or picketing forbidden. Any person or persons, who, without a just cause or legal excuse therefor, go near to or loiter about the premises or place of business of any other person, firm, corporation or association of people, engaged in a lawful business, for the purpose, or with intent of influencing, or inducing other persons not to trade with, buy from, sell to, have business dealings with, or be employed by such persons, firm, corporation, or association of persons, for the purpose of hindering, delaying, or interfering with or injuring any lawful business or enterprise of another, shall be guilty of a misdemeanor; but nothing herein shall prevent any person from soliciting trade or business for a competitive business."

At the close of the case for the State, petitioner moved to exclude all the testimony taken at the trial on the ground that Section 3448 was violative of the Constitution of the United States. The Circuit Court overruled the motion, found petitioner "guilty of Loitering and Picketing as charged in the complaint," and entered judgment accordingly. The judgment was affirmed by the Court of Appeals, which considered the constitutional question and sustained the section on the authority of two previous decisions in the Alabama courts.

The proofs consist of the testimony of two witnesses for the prosecution. It appears that petitioner on the morning of his arrest was seen "in company

continued

with six or eight other men" "on the picket line" at the plant of the Brown Wood Preserving Company. Some weeks previously a strike order had been issued by a Union, apparently affiliated with the American Federation of Labor, which had as members all but four of the approximately 100 employees of the plant. Since that time a picket line with two picket posts of six to eight men each had been maintained around the plant 24 hours a day. The picket posts appear to have been on Company property, "on a private entrance for employees, and not on any public road." One witness explained that practically all of the employees live on Company property. No demand was ever made upon the men not to come on the property. There is no testimony indicating the nature of the dispute between the Union and the Preserving Company, or the course of events which led to the issuance of the strike order, or the nature of the efforts for conciliation.

The Company scheduled a day for the plant to resume operations. One of the witnesses, Clarence Simpson, who was not a member of the union, reporting to the plant on the day indicated, was approached by petitioner who told him that "they were on strike and did not want anybody to go up there to work." None of the other employees said anything to Simpson, who testified: "Neither Mr. Thornhill nor any other employee threatened me on the occasion testified to. Mr. Thornhill approached me in a peaceful manner and did not put me in fear; he did not appear to be mad." "I then turned and went back to the house, and did not go to work." The other witness, J. M. Walden, testified: "At the time Mr. Thornhill and Clarence Simpson were talking to each other, there was no one else present, and I heard no harsh words and saw nothing threatening in the manner of either man." For engaging in some or all of these activities, petitioner was arrested, charged, and convicted as described.

The freedom of speech and of the press, which are secured by the First Amendment against abridgment by the United States, are among the fundamental personal rights and liberties which are secured to all persons by the Fourteenth Amendment against abridgment by a state.

The safeguarding of these rights to the ends that men may speak as they think on matters vital to them and that falsehoods may be exposed through the processes of education and discussion is essential to free government. Those who won our independence had confidence in the power of free and fearless reasoning and communication of ideas to discover and spread political and economic truth. Noxious doctrines in those fields may be refuted and their evil averted by the courageous exercise of the right of free discussion. Abridgment of freedom of speech and of the press, however, impairs those opportunities for public education that are essential to effective exercise of the power of correcting error through the processes of popular government.

Section 3448 has been applied by the State courts so as to prohibit a single individual from walking slowly and peacefully back and forth on the public sidewalk in front of the premises of an employer, without speaking to anyone, carrying a sign or placard on a staff above his head stating only the fact that the employer did not employ union men affiliated with the American Federation of Labor; the purpose of the described activity was concededly to advise customers and prospective customers of the relationship existing between the employer and its employees and thereby to induce such customers not to patronize the employer. *O'Rourke v. City of Birmingham*, 27 Ala. App. 133, 168 So. 206, certiorari denied 232 Ala. 355, 168 So. 209. The statute as thus authoritatively construed and applied leaves room for no exceptions based upon either the number of persons engaged in the proscribed activity, the peaceful character of their demeanor, the nature of their dispute with an employer, or the restrained character and the accurateness of the terminology used in notifying the public of the facts of the dispute....

We think that Section 3448 is invalid on its face.

The freedom of speech and of the press guaranteed by the Constitution embraces at least the liberty to discuss publicly and truthfully all matters of public concern without previous restraint or fear of subsequent punishment....

The range of activities proscribed by Section 3448, whether characterized as picketing or loitering or otherwise, embraces nearly every practicable, effective means whereby those interested—including the employees directly affected—may enlighten the public on the nature and causes of a labor dispute. The safeguarding of these means is essential to the securing of an informed and educated public opinion with respect to a matter which is of public concern.

The State urges that the purpose of the challenged statute is the protection of the community from the violence and breaches of the peace, which, it asserts, are the concomitants of picketing. The power and the duty of the State to take adequate steps to preserve the peace and to protect the privacy, the lives, and the

continued

property of its residents cannot be doubted. But no clear and present danger of destruction of life or property, or invasion of the right of privacy, or breach of the peace can be thought to be inherent in the activities of every person who approaches the premises of an employer and publicizes the facts of a labor dispute involving the latter. We are not now concerned with picketing en masse or otherwise conducted which might occasion such imminent and aggravated dangers to these interests as to justify a statute narrowly drawn to cover the precise situation giving rise to the danger. Compare *American Steel Foundries v. Tri-City Council*, 257 U.S. 184, 205.... Section 3448 in question here does not aim specifically at serious encroachments on these interests and does not evidence any such care in balancing these interests against the interest of the community and that of the individual in freedom of discussion on matters of public concern.

It is not enough to say that Section 3448 is limited or restricted in its application to such activity as takes place at the scene of the labor dispute. "The streets are natural and proper places for the dissemination of information and opinion; and one is not to have the exercise of his liberty of expression in appropriate places abridged on the plea that it may be exercised in some other place." *Schneider v. State*, 308 U.S. 147, 161.... *Hague v. C.I.O.*, 307 U.S. 496, 515, 516.... The danger of breach of the peace or serious invasion of rights of property or privacy at the scene of a labor dispute is not sufficiently imminent in all cases to warrant the legislature in determining that such place is not appropriate for the range of activities outlawed by Section 3448.

Reversed.

Case Questions

1. State the gist of Section 3448 of the Alabama Code.
2. What facts gave rise to the *Thornhill* indictment?
3. Did the Supreme Court hold Section 3448 invalid on its face?
4. What defense of the statute was made by the state? How was the defense disposed of?

CASE 6.2	MEADOWMOOR DAIRIES, INC.
	SUPREME COURT OF THE UNITED STATES, 312 U.S. 287 (1941).

FRANKFURTER, J....

The Supreme Court of Illinois sustained an injunction against the Milk Wagon Drivers' Union over the latter's claim that it involved an infringement of the freedom of speech guaranteed by the Fourteenth Amendment. Since this ruling raised a question intrinsically important, as well as affecting the scope of *Thornhill v. Alabama*, 310 U.S. 88, and *Carlson v. California*, 310 U.S. 106, we brought the case here.

The "vendor system" for distributing milk in Chicago gave rise to the dispute. Under that system, which was fully analyzed in *Milk Wagon Drivers' Union v. Lake Valley Farm Products*, 311 U.S. 91, milk is sold by the dairy companies to vendors operating their own trucks who resell to retailers. These vendors departed from the working standards theretofore achieved by the Union for its members as dairy employees. The Union, in order to compel observance of the established standards, took action against dairies using the vendor system. The present respondent, Meadowmoor Dairies, Inc., brought suit against the Union and its officials to stop interference with the distribution of its products. A preliminary injunction restraining all union conduct, violent and peaceful, was promptly issued, and the case was referred to a master for report. Besides peaceful picketing of the stores handling Meadowmoor's products, the master found that there had been violence on a considerable scale. Witnesses testified to more than fifty instances of window-smashing; explosive bombs caused substantial injury to the plants of Meadowmoor and another dairy using the vendor system and to five stores; stench bombs were dropped in five stores; three trucks of vendors were wrecked, seriously injuring one driver, and another was driven into a river; a store was set on fire and in large measure ruined; two [vendors'] trucks were burned; a storekeeper and a truck driver were severely beaten; workers at a dairy which, like Meadowmoor, used the vendor system, were held up with guns and severely beaten about the head while being told "to join the union"; carloads of men followed vendors' trucks, threatened the drivers, and in one instance shot at the truck and driver. In more than a dozen of these occurrences,

continued

involving window-smashing, bombings, burnings, the wrecking of trucks, shootings, and beatings, there was testimony to identify the wrongdoers as union men. In the light of his findings, the master recommended that all picketing, and not merely violent acts, should be enjoined. The trial court, however, accepted the recommendations only as to acts of violence and permitted peaceful picketing. The reversal of this ruling by the [Illinois] Supreme Court, 371 Ill. 377, 21 N.E. 2d 308, directing a permanent injunction as recommended by the master, is now before us.

The question which thus emerges is whether a state can choose to authorize its courts to enjoin acts of picketing in themselves peaceful when they are enmeshed with contemporaneously violent conduct which is concededly outlawed. The Constitution is invoked to deny Illinois the power to authorize its courts to prevent the continuance and recurrence of flagrant violence, found after an extended litigation to have occurred under specific circumstances, by the terms of a decree familiar in such cases....

The starting point is *Thornhill's* case. That case invoked the constitutional protection of free speech on behalf of a relatively modern means for "publicizing, without annoyance or threat of any kind, the facts of a labor dispute." 310 U.S. 100. The whole series of cases defining the scope of free speech under the Fourteenth Amendment are facets of the same principle in that they all safeguard modes appropriate for assuring the right to utterance in different situations. Peaceful picketing is the workingman's means of communication.

It must never be forgotten, however, that the Bill of Rights was the child of the Enlightenment. Back of the guarantee of free speech lay faith in power of an appeal to reason by all the peaceful means for gaining access to the mind. It was in order to avert force and explosions due to restrictions upon rational modes of communication that the guarantee of free speech was given a generous scope. But utterance in a context of violence can lose its significance as an appeal to reason and become part of an instrument of force. Such utterance was not meant to be sheltered by the Constitution....

To maintain the balance of our federal system, insofar as it is committed to our care, demands at once zealous regard for the guarantees of the Bill of Rights and due recognition of the powers belonging to the state. Such an adjustment requires austere judgment, and a precise summary of the result may help to avoid misconstruction.

We do not qualify the *Thornhill* and *Carlson* decisions. We reaffirm them. They involved statutes baldly forbidding all picketing near an employer's place of business. Entanglement with violence was expressly out of those cases. The statues had to be dealt with on their face, and therefore we struck them down. Such an unlimited ban on free communication declared as the law of a state by a state court enjoys no greater protection here....

The exercise of the state's power which we are sustaining is the very antithesis of a ban on all discussion in Chicago of a matter of public importance. Of course we would not sustain such a ban. The injunction is confined to conduct near stores dealing in respondent's milk, and it deals with this narrow area precisely because the coercive conduct affected it. An injunction so adjusted to a particular situation is in accord with the settled practice of equity, sanctioned by such guardians of civil liberty as Mr. Justice Cardozo. Compare *Nann v. Raimist*, 255 N.Y. 307, 174 N.E. 690. Such an injunction must be read in the context of its circumstances. Nor ought state action be held unconstitutional by interpreting the law of the state as though, to use a phrase of Mr. Justice Holmes, one were fired with a zeal to pervert. If an appropriate injunction were put to abnormal uses in its enforcement, so that encroachments were made on free discussion outside the limits of violence, as for instance discussion through newspaper or on the radio, the doors of this Court are always open.

The injunction which we sustain is "permanent" only for the temporary period for which it may last. It is justified only by the violence that induced it and only so long as it counteracts a continuing intimidation. Familiar equity procedure assures opportunity for modifying or vacating an injunction when its continuance is no longer warranted....

Affirmed.

Case Questions

1. Describe the "vendor system" of milk distribution.
2. Had the union previously resorted to violence?
3. What question does the U.S. Supreme Court say is before it?
4. Did the Court qualify the *Thornhill* decision?
5. Is the scope of the injunction confined to a particular physical area?
6. State the rule of law developed by the case.

SECTION 54: MASS PICKETING

Another form of peaceful picketing that may be illegal is that in which the pickets are so massed as to contain elements of implicit coercion growing out of the force of numbers. Some courts have been disposed to limit substantially the number of pickets on station or patrol and the manner of their position. Others have been more liberal as long as the picketing retained its essentially peaceful character.

The modern judicial view on this question continues to be found in the *Carnegie-Illinois* decision, presented in this section, which sets forth an example of unlawful mass picketing, properly enjoined by a state court.

Care must be exercised in drafting statutes that restrict individuals' right to picket. There must be a compelling state interest shown, and the regulation must be content-neutral, must be narrowly drawn, and must allow alternative means of expression. In the *Nash* case, presented in this section, the state of Texas mass picketing statute was struck down for being unconstitutionally overbroad.

CASE 6.3	CARNEGIE-ILLINOIS STEEL CORP. v. UNITED STEELWORKERS OF AMERICA
	SUPREME COURT OF PENNSYLVANIA, 353 PA 420 (1946).

MAXEY, C. J....

On January 25, 1946, a large group of pickets, estimated to be from 100 to 200 in number, standing three deep, extended across the gate and blocked the entrance to plaintiff's Homestead plant and thus denied access to the plant to individuals below the rank of superintendent....

There were ... injunction affidavits filed all purporting to show that supervisory officials were denied access to plaintiff's plant and that the defendant labor union and its officials and agents had arrogated to itself and themselves the authority to determine what employees of the plaintiff corporation should and should not, respectively, enter the corporation's plant, and that the Union enforced its assumed authority by massing approximately 200 pickets at the gate leading into the plant.

The court below in response to the above bill of complaint, supported by the above injunction affidavits and others, granted the injunction prayed for....

... When this case reached this court and the record was before us, it then became our duty to decide whether or not the facts showed that what the defendants were doing constituted a "holding" or "seizure" of the plant or any part of it. The holding or seizure of even one gateway to the plant entitled the plaintiff to the protection of a court of equity just as fully as

would the seizure of an entire plant. When a "picket line" becomes a picket *fence* it is time for government to act. Collective coercion is not a legitimate child of collective bargaining. The forcible seizure of an employer's property is the very essence of communism.

Injunctions are not issued against picketing when the latter's only purposes are to advertise the fact that there is a strike in a certain plant and to persuade workers to join in the strike and to urge the public not to patronize the employer. For these purposes, a limited number of pickets is all that is necessary. But when hundreds of pickets are massed, as at least 200 were here at a single gate, it is obvious that this force was not mustered for a peaceful purpose....

We dismiss this appeal....

Case Questions

1. What workers did the pickets exclude from the plant?
2. Suppose regular production workers were the only ones excluded. Would this have made a difference in the decision of the court?
3. How many pickets were at the main entrance?
4. How did the court characterize the picket line in its analogy?
5. State the rule of law of this case.

CASE 6.4	NASH V. TEXAS
	U.S. DISTRICT COURT, 632 F. SUPP. 951 (E.D. TEX. 1986).

[The plaintiff John Nash, the president of Rubber Workers Local 746, and some 90 other individuals were arrested by Tyler, Texas, police officers for unlawful picketing at the Schoellkopf Products Co. plant in Tyler, Texas, under Texas mass picketing statute. The arrests forced the collapse of a strike against the company. Some three weeks after the arrests began, the plaintiffs received a preliminary injunction against the police in federal court and now seek declaratory relief that the mass picketing statute unconstitutionally infringed their First Amendment rights.]

JUSTICE, C. J....

I.

On September 18, 1978, the National Labor Relations Board certified Local 746 of the United Rubber Workers ("the union") as the collective bargaining representative of an appropriate unit of employees at the Schoellkopf Products plant in Tyler....

During the period from September 1978, to February 8, 1979, the union bargained with Schoellkopf Products, without any disruption of work at the company's Tyler plant. On February 8, 1979, the union began engaging in protected concerted activity, in the form of a strike, against the company. Picket lines were thereafter established at the entrance to the company's plant in Tyler....

On March 14, 1979, the company filed a suit in a state court against the union, John Nash, and another union member, seeking a temporary restraining order, a temporary injunction, and a permanent injunction against the union's picketing activities. A temporary restraining order was granted, *ex parte*, ... on March 14, 1979, restraining picketing and other alleged activities of the union and Local 746.

On March 15, 1979, the company's president Hugo Schoellkopf, arranged for a meeting to be held in the office of the City Manager of Tyler, Texas, at 11:00 A.M. Schoellkopf, executive vice president Delbert Chandler, plant manager Jeff Keasler, and company attorney Erich Klein represented the company. Also present were City Manager Ed Wagoner, Assistant City Manager Terry Childress, Chief of Police Willie Hardy, and the executive director of the Tyler Chamber of Commerce, Freeman Carney. Neither the City Attorney, State District Attorney,

nor any union representative was invited to attend this meeting. According to Schoellkopf, the purpose of the meeting was to ensure that the City of Tyler and its Police Chief would enforce the mass picketing statute at the company's Tyler plant. At the gathering, copies of the statute were made available to the city officials by the company representatives....

From March 15, 1979, to March 28, 1979, approximately 90 arrests were made for "unlawful picketing." In arresting the picketers, the police cited three alleged violations of the mass picketing statute, Article 5154d, as follows:

1. Under the "numbers-distance" provision, § 1, paragraph 1, anyone who approached the two picketers within fifty-foot markers laid out by police and union members was arrested, even a person intending to relieve a picketer on duty;
2. A picketer who caused a vehicle driven on the access and exit roads to the plant to stop, even momentarily, was arrested, allegedly pursuant to § 1, paragraph 2; and
3. Any striker or sympathizer who shouted "scab" or who was accused of uttering a profanity was arrested, supposedly in accordance with § 2 [an intimidating language provision] of the statute.

No arrests were made for alleged acts or threats of violence, destruction of property, or resisting arrest.

The arrests of the union's attorneys were particularly notable. Ken Miller, Esquire, and Joe Beam, Esquire, counsel for Local 746, approached the picket line on March 15, 1979, at about 4:30 in the afternoon. Each identified himself to the police as an attorney for the picketing union members. Without regard to these facts, the Tyler police officers on the scene arrested each attorney for unlawful picketing, handcuffed both, and placed them, first, in the police paddy wagon and, later, in a patrol car. The two attorneys were afterwards taken to jail, booked, and processed. They were ultimately released on bail near midnight on March 15, 1979....

II.

Section 1, paragraph 1, the Numbers-Distance Provision.

The numbers-distance section of the mass picketing statute makes it illegal for "more than two (2) pickets

continued

at any time" to be "within either fifty (50) feet of any entrance to the premises being picketed, or within fifty (50) feet of any other picket or pickets." Tex.Rec.Civ.Stat.Ann. art. 5154d § 1, paragraph 1 (Vernon 1971). This provision, therefore, regulates the time, place, and manner of speech, for the enforcement of this section is not, facially, affected by the content of speech.

The Supreme Court has held that a state may regulate the time, place, and manner of speech, if there is a compelling state interest justifying the restriction. *Heffron v. International Society for Krishna Consciousness*, 452 U.S. 640, 649 (1981). If a compelling interest is shown, nonetheless, the regulation must be content-neutral, narrowly drawn so as to least restrict protected speech, allow alternative means of expression, and, as well, be rationally related to the state interest it is designed to further. Consequently, in preparation for determining whether the questioned statute was drawn with sufficient precision, its potential for misuse must be pragmatically confronted....

It is unquestioned that a state may legitimately regulate violence at a picket line, because the First Amendment protects only "peaceful" picketing. *See, e.g., Thornhill,* 310 U.S. 88, 102 (1940) ("the dissemination of information concerning the facts of a labor dispute must be regarded as within the area of free discussion that is guaranteed by the constitution"). A state, therefore, has a "substantial" interest in arresting violent picketers. But the statute under consideration is not aimed at violence *per se.* The state characterizes Article 5154d as a preventive measure, and, in fact, the statute "prohibit[s] *conduct* which often *le[ads] to ... violence." Sherman v. State,* 626 S.W. 2d 520, 524 (Tex.Cr.App. 1981) (emphasis added). Furthermore, the state admits that the goal of preventing violence "is achieved at considerable expense to an individual's or group of individuals' right to effectively communicate." Intervenor's Supplemental Pre-Trial Brief at 9. The Supreme Court has stressed that, while a state has a compelling interest in restricting violent behavior at a picket line, it has no substantial interest in regulating acts that might lead to violence.

In *Thornhill,* the Supreme Court declared unconstitutionally overbroad an anti-picketing statute similar in many respects to the Texas mass picketing statute. There, the Court determined that the declared state interest, the "protection of the community from the violence and breaches of the peace," did not sufficiently justify the statute that was adopted. *Thornhill,*

310 U.S. at 105. The court emphasized in *Thornhill* that, because there was no picketing *"en masse,"* claims of a state interest in protecting the community were not credible, and that free speech could be abridged only where the clear danger of a substantive evil arises.

As in *Thornhill,* the numbers-distance formula here in issue is not limited to *"en masse"* picketing, for it prohibits more than two persons from standing near an entrance of a business. The presence of two picketers, both standing 50 feet from a company entrance and from one another, cannot forebode such violence that there is a "significant and legitimate state interest" in arresting those picketers and thereby curtailing their speech. Moreover, the Texas statute is even more restrictive than the statute challenged in *Thornhill.* The *Thornhill* statute applied only to the picketing of businesses. The Texas statute, on the other hand, applies to picketing at "any premises." Additionally, the *Thornhill* statute applied only to labor picketing, whereas the Texas statute reaches more broadly, and realistically could be employed to proscribe picketing activities in many other contexts.

The state has not suggested any other compelling state interest that would justify the anti-picketing statute. For example, the Texas statute is not specifically directed at the state interest in protecting public order at critical locations. Anti-picketing statutes in issue before the Supreme Court have: assured peaceful ingress to and egress from public buildings, *Cameron v. Johnson,* 390 U.S. 611 (1968); regulated picketing near a school, *Grayned v. City of Rockford,* 408 U.S. 104 (1972); and restricted picketing at or near a courthouse, *Cox v. Louisiana,* 379 U.S. 559 (1965). The reach of the Texas statute, to the contrary, is far more extensive than the regulations that have been upheld, and closely resembles enactments that have been declared unconstitutionally overbroad.

... The numbers-distance provision facially does not allow adequate "breathing space"; its overbreadth—its unnecessary stifling of First Amendment rights—renders it unconstitutional.

III.

Section 2, The Intimidating Language Provision.

Section 2 states:

> It shall be unlawful for any person, singly or in concert with others, by use of insulting, threatening or obscene language, to interfere with, hinder, obstruct, or intimidate, or seek to interfere with,

continued

hinder, obstruct, or intimidate, another in the exercise of his lawful right to work, or to enter upon the performance of any lawful vocation, or from freely entering or leaving any premises.

Section 2 expressly regulates speech and is thus a content-based statute; as such, it is necessary that it be rigorously tested....

In this case, the statute proscribes such broad categories of speech that the meaning of the words, "insult," "threaten," "obscene," "interfere with," "hinder," "obstruct," and "intimidate," becomes unclear.

By way of illustration, it would seem obvious that a protester should not be prosecuted for calling another person a "nerd," but, if a police officer conceived that the intimidating language provision was violated by its use, the statute would allow the prosecution. Because of that, a picketer must speculate as to which words are punishable. But due process requires that persons be given fair notice of what actions are illegal, and that the discretion allowed law enforcement officers be limited by explicit statutory standards. *Kolender v. Lawson*, 455 U.S. 999 (1983). As presently drawn, the statute manifestly could have a chilling effect on those who are unclear regarding what is unlawful, and these individuals, on that account, well might restrict "their conduct to that which is unquestionably safe," *Baggett v. Bullitt*, 377 U.S. 360, 372 (1964).

The circumstance of this case indicate that union members who called non-strikers "scabs" had no intention of violating § 2. Nevertheless, the police so interpreted the statute as to arrest the union members for simply using that word. The situation here was not one...in which any word was said with the requisite degree of force, by a sufficient number of persons, to create a "fighting words" reaction; and

there was no evidence of threatened violence in connection with use of the term. The workers who were leaving the plant were in vehicles, and there were few face-to-face confrontations. If this statute were allowed to stand, local law enforcement officers conceivably could find such pejorative words as "strikebreaker" or "fink" to be in violation of § 2. Cf. *Cohen v. California*, 403 U.S. at 16 (refusing to forbid public display of single four-letter expletive when the prohibition would also create a substantial risk of suppressing ideas). Certainly, those contemplating picketing will have no assurance that this will not be the case. Therefore, "persons of common intelligence" cannot determine what words to avoid to remain within the laws; moreover, the discretion of law enforcement officers has not been sufficiently limited.

Conclusion

Picketing claims a historic place in the history of America, providing an opportunity for diverse groups to express their ideas publicly. Article 5154d is not drafted with the precision necessary to save it from the challenges made to its constitutionality. Both § 2 and § 1, paragraph 1, of Article 5154 are in disregard of the First Amendment, since both are unconstitutionally overbroad. Additionally, § 2 is unconstitutionally vague.

Case Questions

1. Summarize the facts of the case.
2. Assess the fairness of the *ex parte* temporary restraining order granted on March 14.
3. Was the 50-foot provision justified by the state's interest in preventing violence?
4. What purpose does picketing serve?

SECTION 55: UNION ACCESS TO PRIVATE PROPERTY

The NLRB and the courts have had difficulty resolving questions regarding the extent of employee and nonemployee union organizers' rights to have access to an employer's property. The Supreme Court's *Lechmere, Inc., v. NLRB* decision, presented in this section, sharply narrowed the circumstances under which nonemployees may have access to an employer's property.

THE CONFLICTING RIGHTS

Section 7 of the NLRA guarantees employees the right to self-organization. Section 8(a)(1) of the NLRA prohibits employers from interfering with, restraining, or coercing employees in the exercise of their Section 7 rights. For Section 7 rights to be meaningful, their effectiveness depends in some measure on the ability of employees to learn the advantages and disadvantages of unionization from others. "Others" who are interested in discussing the advantages of unionization are non-employee union organizers. Although Section 7 rights are the workers' rights, unions and their agents derivatively have been given the protection of Section 7.[6]

Union organizers and other union adherents, seeking to initiate an organizational campaign at a nonunion company, based on their derivative Section 7 rights, have often engaged in activities inconsistent with traditional notions of private property rights. It is up to the NLRB and the courts to seek a proper accommodation between organizational rights and property rights. The Supreme Court first set forth guiding principles for resolving conflicts between Section 7 rights and property rights in its *NLRB v. Babcock & Wilcox Co.*[7] decision in the following language:

> Organization rights are granted to workers by the same authority, the National Government, that preserves property rights. Accommodation between the two must be obtained with as little destruction of one as is consistent with the maintenance of the other. The employer may not affirmatively interfere with organization; the union may not always insist that the employer aid organization. But when the inaccessibility of employees makes ineffective the reasonable attempts by nonemployees to communicate with them through the usual channels, the right to exclude from property has been required to yield to the extent needed to permit communication of information on the right to organize.[8]

In *Babcock,* a case involving an industrial plant employer's refusal to allow non-employee union organizers access to its private parking lot to distribute organizational literature to employees, the Court held that the nonemployee organizers were not entitled access to company property because the employees lived in nearby communities and could be reached by "the usual methods of imparting information" (i.e., by literature sent through the mail, home visits, and telephone calls). Under *Babcock,* an employer may prohibit the distribution of union literature by nonemployee organizers if (1) "reasonable efforts by the union through other available channels of communication will enable it to reach the employees with its message ..."[9] and (2) the employer does not discriminate against the union by allowing other distributions.

THE SHORT-LIVED FIRST AMENDMENT THEORY

Some 12 years after its *Babcock & Wilcox* decision, the Supreme Court considered the case of *Amalgamated Food Employees Local 590 v. Logan Valley Plaza, Inc.*[10] This case involved organizational picketing of a supermarket located in a shopping mall by nonemployee union organizers. Rather than treat this case under the principles set forth in *Babcock,* the Supreme Court held that shopping center picketing

---

[6] See *Sears, Roebuck & Co. v. San Diego Dist. Council of Carpenters,* 436 U.S. 180, 206 n. 42 (1978); *Central Hardware Co. v. NLRB,* 407 U.S. 539, 542 (1972).

[7] 351 U.S. 105 (1956).

[8] *Id.* at 112.

[9] *Id.* at 112.

[10] 391 U.S. 308 (1968).

was protected under the First Amendment, notwithstanding the fact that the picketing took place on private property. The Court's rationale was that the shopping center was open to the public and was the functional equivalent of a city "business block" and for the purpose of the First Amendment must be treated in substantially the same manner.

In *Central Hardware v. NLRB*,[11] decided four years after *Logan Valley*, the Supreme Court limited the applicability of *Logan Valley*. Union organizers had engaged employees in Central's single store parking lot in violation of the store's no-solicitation policy. The Court did not believe that a parking lot serving a single store was the functional equivalent of a "business block." The Court ruled that *Babcock* and not *Logan Valley* was the controlling precedent.

In *Hudgens v. NLRB*,[12] decided in 1976, the Supreme Court effectively overruled *Logan Valley*, holding that there is no First Amendment right to picket on the premises of a privately owned shopping center. The *Hudgens* case dealt with a shopping mall's interference with the picketing of a shoe store at the mall by the shoe company's unionized warehouse workers in furtherance of their economic strike against that employer. The Court, returning to its *Babcock* precedent, remanded the case to the Board, instructing it to seek a proper accommodation between the Section 7 rights of employees and private property rights, "with as little destruction of one as is consistent with the maintenance of the other." On remand, the Board decided that the proper accommodation between Section 7 rights and private property rights required that the warehouse workers be allowed to picket.[13]

The NLRB's Formulation of a Standard under Babcock

In a number of decisions, the Board grappled with the basic question of how to accommodate the exercise of rights guaranteed under Section 7 with a property owner's right to protect its property from union trespassers. Ultimately, in its *Jean Country*[14] decision, the Board devised a test that involved assessment and weighing of the interrelated facts concerning (1) the strength of the union's Section 7 rights, (2) the strength of the employer's property rights, and (3) the availability of reasonable and effective alternative means of communication.

The Lechmere, Inc., v. NLRB Challenge to Jean Country

Local 919 of the United Food and Commercial Workers sought to organize the 200 workers at a newly opened Lechmere store located in a strip mall in Newington, Connecticut. On June 18, union organizers began leafletting cars at this so-called Lechmere mall, but the organizers were ordered by store officials to leave the parking lot, and the leaflets were removed by security guards. The union placed five advertisements in the *Hartford Courant* in an attempt to organize Lechmere's workforce, with little evidence that affected employees actually saw the

---

[11] 407 U.S. 539 (1972).

[12] 424 U.S. 507 (1976).

[13] 230 NLRB 414 (1977).

[14] 129 LRRM 1201 (1988).

ads. The union also took down the license plate numbers of cars parked where employees had been told to park, and the union obtained certain names and addresses from the Registry of Motor Vehicles. Ultimately it obtained 41 names and addresses from all their efforts, but half of the individuals had unlisted telephone numbers. The union filed unfair labor practice charges against Lechmere because of its refusal to allow representatives of Local 919 to engage in organizational activity in the parking lot. The Board decided that Lechmere had committed an unfair labor practice by barring union representatives from handbilling in the parking lot, and Lechmere petitioned for review of the Board's order.

Lechmere, Inc., believed that it had the absolute right to ban the nonemployee union organizers from its property under the *Babcock* decision. It posted on each set of doors to its premises 6″ × 8″ signs stating:

> TO THE PUBLIC. No Solicitation, Canvassing,
> Distributing of Literature or Trespassing
> by Non-Employees in or on Premises.

And Lechmere strictly enforced this no-solicitation rule in its store and parking lots. Lechmere also believed that the union did have reasonable alternative means of communicating with Lechmere's employees through the "usual channels" as stated in *Babcock*.

After the NLRB's decision in favor of the union, the Court of Appeals for the First Circuit approved and applied the *Jean Country* test in upholding the Board's order.[15] The court found that the union's Section 7 interest in disseminating organizational information to employees was "robust." The strength of Lechmere's property right was not quite as strong, according to the court, even though Lechmere was a co-owner and followed a strict no-solicitation rule, because of the public nature of the parking lot, and the union activity did not disrupt business, constitute harassment, or impede traffic flow. The third *Jean Country* test—whether the union had open to it other reasonable and effective means of reaching the workforce—also weighed in favor of the union according to the court. The court reasoned that although the union had expended considerable time and effort, it was able to compile merely a skeletal employee roster. The mail, which is not an effective alternative to personal contact, was impractical because of the incomplete list of names and addresses. Newspaper advertising was futile. Television advertising of the organizational message would be expensive, and in the context of reaching 200 workers in a market of 900,000 people would be extravagantly wasteful. Much the same can be said for radio and newspaper advertising. The court concluded that the Board had a rational basis for its conclusions in this case, and it supported the Board's holding that Lechmere violated Section 8(a)(1) of the NLRA by barring union representatives from organizational activity in the mall's parking lots.

The Supreme Court rejected the *Jean Country* balancing test as it applied to nonemployee union organizers as contrary to its handling in *Babcock*. The Court explained that under *Babcock*, an employer may not be compelled to allow distribution of union literature by nonemployee organizers on its property except under

---

[15] 914 F.2d 313 (1ˢᵗ Cir. 1990).

the very narrow circumstances where the location of the property and the living quarters of the employees place the employees beyond the reach of reasonable union efforts to communicate with the employees. Examples of such isolated locations are logging camps, mining camps, and mountain resort hotels. The Supreme Court majority found that the union organizers had reasonable access to employees outside the employer's property.

LECHMERE'S IMPACT

As a result of *Lechmere, Inc.*, employers who have and enforce a no-solicitation policy on their private property as a general rule cannot be compelled to allow nonemployee union organizers on their property to distribute organizational literature.[16] However, where employers do not exclude other organizations, such as political or charitable groups, from soliciting on their property, they may find themselves subject to disparate treatment claims by unions under *Babcock & Wilcox,* which allows no-solicitation rules against unions so long as the employer does not discriminate against unions by allowing other distributions.[17] Contrary precedents exist in the Sixth Circuit. In *Albertsons, Inc., v. NLRB,*[18] the Sixth Circuit Court of Appeals refused to enforce a Board ruling that five Albertsons supermarkets in Oregon and Washington[19] had discriminated against the United Food and Commercial Workers Union (UFCW) when it banned the union from distributing union materials in organizing drives at their stores, which activities Albertsons stated were in violation of its no-solicitation policy. In fact, Albertsons had allowed charitable, civic, and educational groups to solicit its customers near the entrances to their stores, including the Salvation Army, and various youth, school, and veterans groups. The Board believes the employer's tolerance of nonemployee charitable solicitations is probative evidence of discrimination against nonemployee organizing activity. However, the Sixth Circuit believes that for discrimination to exist, it

---

[16] Broader free speech rights under California law lead to a different outcome in that state. It was state property law that created the interest entitling employers such as Lechmere to exclude outside union organizers from company-owned store parking lots. California's state constitution provides broader free speech rights than the First Amendment to the U.S. Constitution. California law permits reasonably exercised free speech at privately owned shopping centers and adjacent walkways and parking lots. In the *NLRB v. Calkins* decision, 187 F.3d 1080 (9th Cir. 1999), the Ninth Circuit Court of Appeals upheld the Board's determination that a California grocery store committed a Section 8(a)(1) unfair labor practice by having outside union organizers arrested for handbilling and picketing in the store's private parking lot. In *Glendale Associates Ltd. v. NLRB*, 347 F.3d 1145 (9th Cir. 2003), a shopping mall's restriction of union handbilling literature that named a mall tenant, the Disney Store, Inc., was a violation of the free speech provision of the California Constitution. The Ninth Circuit enforced the Board's order for the mall to cease prohibiting the handbilling, which was protected by Section 7 of the NLRA.

[17] Riesbeck Food Markets, Inc., 315 NLRB 940 (Dec. 16, 1994). But see *Register-Guard*, 351 NLRB No. 70 (2007).

[18] 301 F.3d 441 (6th Cir. 2002).

[19] While the dispute arose at stores in Oregon and Washington, which are part of the Ninth Circuit Court of Appeals, Albertsons, Inc., also has stores in Michigan and Tennessee, which are located in the Sixth Circuit. Knowing favorable precedents existed in the Sixth Circuit, Albertsons brought its appeal of the Board's decision to this circuit.

must be among comparable groups or activities and the activities themselves under consideration must be comparable; and it points out that Albertsons did not allow nonunion organizers of another union to disseminate union information that it banned the UFCW for disseminating. Employees continue to have their Section 7 organizational rights on company property. The rights of employee economic strikers on private property continue to be under the guidance of the *Hudgens* principle under which the Board, on a case-by-case basis, seeks a proper accommodation between Section 7 rights and private property rights, "with as little destruction of one as is consistent with the maintenance of the other."

In its *Leslie Homes, Inc.*, decision,[20] a Labor Board majority held that the *Lechmere* decision leaves the NLRB little choice but to bar almost all activity on an employer's private property, including area-standards picketing.

CASE 6.5	LECHMERE, INC., V. NLRB
	SUPREME COURT OF THE UNITED STATES, 502 U.S. 527 (1992).

[Petitioner Lechmere, Inc., owns and operates a retail store located in a shopping plaza in Newington, a suburb of Hartford, Connecticut. Lechmere is also part owner of the plaza's parking lot, which is separated from a public highway by a 46-foot-wide grassy strip, almost all of which is public property. In a campaign to organize Lechmere employees, nonemployee union organizers from Local 919 of the UFCW union placed handbills on the windshields of cars parked in the employees' part of the parking lot. After Lechmere denied the organizers access to the lot, they picketed from the grassy strip. In addition, they were able to contact directly some 20 percent of the employees. The union filed an unfair labor practice charge with the Board, alleging that Lechmere had violated the NLRA by barring the organizers from its property. An administrative law judge ruled in the union's favor. The Board affirmed, and the court of appeals enforced the Board's order.]

THOMAS, J....

A.

Section 7 of the NLRA provides in relevant part that "[e]mployees shall have the right to self-organization, to form, join, or assist labor organizations." 29

U.S.C. § 157. Section 8(a)(1) of the Act, in turn, makes it an unfair labor practice for an employer "to interfere with, restrain, or coerce employees in the exercise of rights guaranteed in [§ 7]." 29 U.S.C. § 158(a)(1). By its plain terms, thus, the NLRA confers rights only on *employees*, not on unions or their nonemployee organizers. In *NLRB v. Babcock & Wilcox Co.*, 351 U.S. 105 (1956), however, we recognized that insofar as the employees' "right of self-organization depends in some measure on [their] ability ... to learn the advantages of self-organization from others," *id.*, at 113, § 7 of the NLRA may, in certain limited circumstances, restrict an employer's right to exclude nonemployee union organizers from his property. It is the nature of those circumstances that we explore today....

[In *Babcock*, the Board ordered the company to allow the nonemployee organizers to distribute literature on its parking lot and walkways; the court of appeals refused to enforce the order; and the Supreme Court decided to hear the case.] While recognizing that "the Board has the responsibility of 'applying the Act's general prohibitory language in the light of the infinite combinations of events which might be charged as violative of its terms,'" 351 U.S., at 111–112 (quoting *NLRB v. Stowe Spinning*

continued

---

[20] 316 NLRB 29 (1995).

Co., 336 U.S. 226, 231 (1949)), we [the Supreme Court] explained that the Board had erred by failing to make the critical distinction between the organizing activities of employees (to whom § 7 guarantees the right of self-organization) and nonemployees (to whom § 7 applies only derivatively). Thus, while "[n]o restriction may be placed on the employees' right to discuss self-organization *among themselves,* unless the employer can demonstrate that a restriction is necessary to maintain production or discipline," 351 U.S., at 113 (emphasis added) (citing *Republic Aviation Corp. v. NLRB,* 324 U.S. 793, 803 (1945)), "no such obligation is owed non-employee organizers," 351 U.S., at 113. As a rule, then, an employer cannot be compelled to allow distribution of union literature by nonemployee organizers on his property. As with many other rules, however, we recognized an exception. Where "the location of a plant and the living quarters of the employees place the employees beyond the reach of reasonable union efforts to communicate with them," *ibid.,* employers' property rights may be "required to yield to the extent needed to permit communication of information on the right to organize," *id.,* at 112....

B.

Jean Country, as noted above, represents the Board's latest attempt to implement the rights guaranteed by § 7....

... *Babcock's* teaching is straightforward: § 7 simply does not protect nonemployee union organizers *except* in the rare case where "the inaccessibility of employees makes ineffective the reasonable attempts by nonemployees to communicate with them through the usual channels," 351 U.S., at 112. Our reference to "reasonable" attempts was nothing more than a common sense recognition that unions need not engage in extraordinary feats to communicate with inaccessible employees—*not* an endorsement of the view (which we expressly rejected) that the Act protects "reasonable" trespasses. Where reasonable alternative means of access exist, § 7's guarantees do not authorize trespasses by nonemployee organizers, *even* (as we noted in *Babcock, id.,* at 112) "under ... reasonable regulations" established by the Board.

Jean Country, which applies broadly to "all access cases," 291 N.L.R.B., at 14, misapprehends this critical point. Its principal inspiration derives not from *Babcock,* but from the following sentence in *Hudgens:* "[T]he locus of th[e] accommodation [between § 7 rights and private property rights] may fall at differing points along the spectrum depending on the nature and strength of the respective § 7 rights and private property rights asserted in any given context." 424 U.S., at 522. From this sentence the Board concluded that it was appropriate to approach every case by balancing § 7 rights against property rights, with alternative means of access thrown in as nothing more than an "especially significant" consideration. As explained above, however, *Hudgens* did not purport to modify *Babcock,* much less to alter it fundamentally in the way *Jean Country* suggests. To say that our cases require accommodation between employees' and employers' rights is a true but incomplete statement, for the cases also go far in establishing the *locus* of that accommodation where nonemployee organizing is at issue. So long as nonemployee union organizers have reasonable access to employees outside an employer's property, the requisite accommodation has taken place. It is *only* where such access is infeasible that it becomes necessary and proper to take the accommodation inquiry to a second level, balancing the employees' and employers' rights as described in the *Hudgens* dictum.... At least as applied to nonemployees, *Jean Country* impermissibly conflates these two stages of the inquiry—thereby significantly eroding *Babcock's* general rule that "an employer may validly post his property against nonemployee distribution of union literature," 351 U.S., at 112. We reaffirm that general rule today, and reject the Board's attempt to recast it as a multifactor balancing test.

C.

The threshold inquiry in this case, then, is whether the facts here justify application of *Babcock's* inaccessibility exception. The ALJ below observed that "the facts herein convince me that reasonable alternative means [of communicating with Lechmere's employees] *were* available to the Union," 295 N.L.R.B. No. 15, ALJ slip op., at 9 (emphasis added). Reviewing the ALJ's decision under *Jean Country,* however, the Board reached a different conclusion on this point, asserting that "there was no reasonable, effective alternative means available for the Union to communicate its message to [Lechmere's] employees." 295 N.L.R.B. No. 15, Board slip op., at 4–5.

continued

We cannot accept the Board's conclusion, because it "rest[s] on erroneous legal foundations." As we have explained, the exception to *Babcock's* rule is a narrow one. It does not apply wherever nontrespassory access to employees may be cumbersome or less-than-ideally effective, but only where "the *location of a plant* and the *living quarters* of the employees place the employees *beyond the reach* of reasonable union efforts to communicate with them," 351 U.S., at 113 (emphasis added). Classic examples include logging camps, … mining camps, … and mountain resort hotels, …. *Babcock's* exception was crafted precisely to protect the § 7 rights of those employees who, by virtue of their employment, are isolated from the ordinary flow of information that characterizes our society. The union's burden of establishing such isolation is, as we have explained, "a heavy one," and one not satisfied by mere conjecture or the expression of doubts concerning the effectiveness of nontrespassory means of communication.

The Board's conclusion in this case that the union had no reasonable means short of trespass to make Lechmere's employees aware of its organizational efforts is based on a misunderstanding of the limited scope of this exception. Because the employees do not reside on Lechmere's property, they are presumptively not "beyond the reach," *Babcock, supra,* at 113, of the union's message. Although the employees live in a large metropolitan area (Greater Hartford), that fact does not in itself render them "inaccessible" in the sense contemplated by *Babcock.* Their accessibility is suggested by the union's success in contacting a substantial percentage of them directly, via mailings, phone calls, and home visits. Such direct contact, of course, is not a necessary element of "reasonably effective" communication; signs or advertising also may suffice. In this case, the union tried advertising in local newspapers; the Board said that this was not reasonably effective because it was expensive and might not reach the employees. 295 N.L.R.B. No. 15, Board slip op., at 4–5. Whatever the merits of that conclusion, other alternative means of communication were readily available. Thus, signs (displayed, for example, from the public grassy strip adjoining Lechmere's parking lot) would have informed the employees about the union's organizational efforts. (Indeed, union organizers picketed the shopping center's main entrance for months as employees came and went every day.) *Access* to employees, not *success* in winning them over, is the critical issue—although success, or lack

thereof, may be relevant in determining whether reasonable access exists. Because the union in this case failed to establish the existence of any "unique obstacles," that frustrated access to Lechmere's employees, the Board erred in concluding that Lechmere committed an unfair labor practice by barring the nonemployee organizers from its property.

* * *

The judgment of the First Circuit is therefore reversed, and enforcement of the Board's order denied.

It is so ordered.

JUSTICE WHITE, with whom JUSTICE BLACKMUN joins, Dissenting….

In the case before us, the Court holds that *Babcock* itself stated the correct accommodation between property and organizational rights; it interprets that case as construing §§7 and 8(a)(1) of the National Labor Relations Act to contain a general rule forbidding third-party access, subject only to a limited exception where the union demonstrates that the location of the employer's place of business and the living quarters of the employees place the employees beyond the reach of reasonable efforts to communicate with them. The Court refuses to enforce the Board's order in this case, which rested on its prior decision in *Jean Country*, 291 N.L.R.B. 11 (1988), because, in the Court's view, *Jean Country* revealed that the Board misunderstood the basic holding in *Babcock*, as well as the narrowness of the exception to the general rule announced in that case.

For several reasons, the Court errs in this case….

… [T]he Court in *Babcock* recognized that actual communication with nonemployee organizers, not mere notice that an organizing campaign exists, is necessary to vindicate § 7 rights, 351 U.S., at 113. If employees are entitled to learn from others the advantages of self-organization, *ibid.*, it is singularly unpersuasive to suggest that the union has sufficient access for this purpose by being able to hold up signs from a public grassy strip adjacent to the highway leading to the parking lot.

Second, the Court's reading of *Babcock* is not the reading of that case reflected in later opinions of the Court. We have consistently declined to define the principle of *Babcock* as a general rule subject to narrow exceptions, and have instead repeatedly reaffirmed that the standard is a neutral and flexible rule of accommodation.

continued

Third, and more fundamentally, *Babcock* is at odds with modern concepts of deference to an administrative agency charged with administering a statute....

Case Questions

1. State the *Babcock* rule as set forth in the majority opinion. Is the exception to the rule a broad one?

2. State the two-stage test set forth in *Lechmere* to determine if an accommodation between employees' and employer's rights have taken place.

3. Did the nonemployee union organizers have reasonable access to Lechmere employees outside the employer's property?

4. Did the dissent agree that there was sufficient access given the union organizers as they were able to hold up signs from a grassy strip adjacent to the highway?

SECTION 56: ORGANIZATIONAL AND RECOGNITIONAL PICKETING: INFORMATIONAL PICKETING

The Labor-Management Reporting and Disclosure Act of 1959 comprehensively addressed the issues regarding organizational and recognitional picketing by amending the NLRA with an additional union unfair labor practice in Section 8(b)(7). In enacting this unfair labor practice, Congress sought to provide statutory protection to employers who, though innocent of misconduct or illegality, might be subjected to long, extended, and harassing picketing. The effect of such picketing, in some cases, would force employers to illegally grant recognition to an uncertified union that did not, in fact, command sufficient employee support to win an election under the provisions of Section 9 of the NLRA. Informational or, as it is often called, "area-standards" picketing is not subject to Section 8(b)(7).

The summary language of Section 8(b)(7) reads as follows:

(b) It shall be an unfair labor practice for a labor organization or its agents—

(7) to picket or cause to be picketed, or threaten to picket ... any employer where an object thereof is forcing or requiring an employer to recognize or bargain with a labor organization ... unless such labor organization is currently certified as the representative of such employees:

(A) where the employer has lawfully recognized ... any other labor organization and a question concerning representation may not appropriately be raised under section 9(c) of this Act,

(B) where within the preceding twelve months a valid election under section 9(c) of this Act has been conducted, or

(C) where such picketing has been conducted without a petition under section 9(c) being filed [to secure NLRB resolution of representation right] within a reasonable period of time *not to exceed thirty days* from the commencement of such picketing.[21]

To illustrate the manner in which the above three provisions operate, let us take an assumed set of facts and proceed with the action, with initial focus upon Subsections (A) and (B) above. An uncertified union is peacefully picketing an

---

[21] Brackets and italics added.

employer for recognition even though the employer is already legally bargaining under the circumstances detailed in (A) and (B) above. The employer may then file an unfair labor practice charge under Section 8(b)(7) with the NLRB. If the Board finds that the employer's statement truly represents the facts of the case, it will find the union responsible for the commission of an unfair labor practice and take appropriate steps for the cessation of the practice.

Let us now examine Subsection (C) above, altering the facts in one particular. Assume that there is, at present, no union representative and the uncertified union peacefully pickets to secure recognition by the employer. If, after 30 days of picketing, no party files a petition for an election under Section 9(c), the picketing becomes violative of Section 8(b)(7) and subject to injunctive relief.

Suppose, however, that one of the parties involved in the organizational picketing does file such petition within the prescribed 30 days. Under the language of Section 8(b)(7)(C), "The Board shall *forthwith,*[22] without regard to the provisions of Section 9(c)(1) or the absence of a showing of substantial interest on the part of the labor organization, direct an election ... and shall certify the results thereof."

The *NVE Constructors, Inc., v. NLRB* decision, presented in this section, contains a discussion of how Section 8(b)(7)(C) was designed to work and allowed the construction union in this case the limited right to engage in recognitional picketing.

So-called area-standards or informational picketing is permissible picketing not subject to Section 8(b)(7)(C) because this picketing does not have an organizational or recognitional objective. This type of picketing is common to the construction and retailing industries and is a form of protest against a nonunion business whose wage scales or terms of employment are below those of other area firms. The Board will, however, look beyond a union's assertion of area-standards picketing for evidence of recognitional or organizational objectives. Thus, picketing with demands broader than necessary to achieve area standards, coupled with an offer to the employer to negotiate, has supported a finding that the union had a recognitional objective.[23]

CASE 6.6	NVE Constructors, Inc., v. NLRB
	U. S. Court of Appeals, 934 F.2d 1084 (9TH Cir. 1991).

[From January 5 to January 14, 1988, Laborers' International Union of North America, Local No. 1184 (the union) picketed the construction site where NVE Constructors, Inc., (NVE) was a general contractor on a state prison project. At the gate reserved for NVE employees, the union displayed picket signs that stated: "NVE, No Contracts. Laborers' Local 1184, AFL-CIO." As a result of the picketing, NVE did not receive deliveries of concrete scheduled for January 5–7, 1988. At the time of the picketing, NVE was not a party to a collective bargaining agreement with the union. There were 20 NVE employees at the jobsite, but those employees had not designated the union as their bargaining representative. According to the union's business agent, the purpose of the picketing was "to obtain a contract either by authorization from the people

continued

---

[22] Italics added. This means that an election is held on an expedited schedule.

[23] *NLRB v. Electrical Workers Local 265,* 602 F.2d 1091 (8th Cir. 1979).

through authorization cards or the contractor or contractors signing a prehire agreement voluntarily." The picketing stopped on January 13, 1988, after NVE filed an unfair labor practice charge alleging a violation of Section 8(b)(7)(C) of the Act. The Board dismissed the complaint, concluding that "at least with respect to any employer, which has employees, we do not believe that recognitional and organizational picketing by a minority union in the construction industry is prohibited by Section 8(b)(7)(C) of the Act if the picketing meets the time limitations set forth in that section." NVE petitioned for review.]

BEEZER, C. J....

Section 8(b)(7) of the Act makes it an unfair labor practice for a union to picket to force an employer to recognize or bargain with it if the employer has already recognized another union or if there has been a representation election within the preceding 12 months. If neither of these situations exist, such picketing may be conducted for "a reasonable period not to exceed 30 days from the commencement of such picketing to gain recognition." The union may not picket beyond this time without filing a petition for a representation election. *Id.*

The purpose of section 8(b)(7) is "to ensure that employees [are] free to make an uncoerced choice of bargaining agent." This was accomplished in section 8(b)(7)(C) by encouraging "prompt resort to the Board's election machinery, rather than protracted picketing, as the method for resolving questions concerning representation."

Section 8(f) of the Act provides that it is not an unfair practice for unions and employers in the construction industry to enter into collective bargaining agreements even though the employees of that employer have not designated the union as their lawful bargaining representative. These agreements are known as "prehire agreements." ...

... [A]t the same time it enacted section 8(f), Congress included a provision protecting employers from being pressured to enter into agreements with minority unions. If the picketed employer doubts that the union enjoys the support of a majority of its employees, the employer may file an election petition. *See* NLRA § 8(b)(7)(C). When an election petition is filed in a situation in which a noncertified union is picketing, the Board must direct an expedited representation election, without first investigating the petition to determine whether a question of representation exists. *See id.* §§ 8(b)(7)(C), 9(c). If the election demonstrates that a majority of the employees do not support the union, section 8(b)(7)(B) bars the union from picketing for twelve months.

NVE argues that the effect of the Board's decision is to legalize the "very top-down organizing weapon Congress condemned in enacting" section 8(b)(7)(C)....

... In the case of section 8(f), Congress acted to limit the potential top-down effects of allowing prehire agreements by allowing employees to invalidate a prehire agreement by petitioning for a representation or decertification election at any time during the period covered by the agreement. 29 U.S.C. § 158(f) (1988).

The Board's interpretation of sections 8(b)(7)(C) and 8(f) is "rational and consistent with the Act." ...

Section 8(b)(7)(C) is intended "to encourage prompt resort to the Board's election machinery, rather than protracted picketing, as the method for resolving questions concerning representation." ...

More serious interference with work has not persuaded the Board to shorten the [30-day] period. In *Walters Foundation,* 203 NLRB 397, for example, the Board did not find unreasonable a 22-day period of picketing, and in *Colson & Stevens Constr. Co.,* 137 NLRB 1650, the Board found the period of picketing not to be unreasonable where suppliers refused to cross the picket lines for 29 days. Furthermore, nothing in the present case prevented NVE from filing for an expedited election and resolving quickly the issue of the union's majority support. The Board's determination that the picketing did not exceed a reasonable period of time is thus reasonable and supported by the record.

The petition for review of the Board's order is DENIED.

Case Questions

1. How are employers protected under the Act from being pressured to enter prehire agreements with minority unions?
2. How are employees protected from the effects of a prehire agreement in which a minority union is allowed to reach an agreement with the employer?

SECTION 57: JURISDICTIONAL DISPUTES

In Section 8(b)(4)(D), some additional economic pressures by unions are prohibited. Where the purpose of a strike or boycott is to compel work assignment to members of a trade, craft, class, or organization in the absence of a Board certification or ruling concerning that particular work, a violation occurs.

This particular violation receives a different, accelerated treatment since the Act gives the parties 10 days after notice of charges filed for attempting to adjust the dispute. If satisfactory evidence of adjustment or of an agreed-upon method for adjustment is submitted within 10 days, the proceeding ends. Otherwise, under Section 10(k), the dispute may be heard and determined by the Board.[24] A complaint may issue if the violation continues. In addition to the usual cease-and-desist orders, the Board may also obtain from a court a temporary restraining order against jurisdictional or work assignment unfair activity prior to issuing its complaint. Thus, a neutral employer and the public should receive prompt relief from a jurisdictional struggle between unions.

Such strife may continue over long periods, however, where two unions are contesting each other's right. For example, in one case, the respondent union contended that the case was a moot one since the work had been completed before any restraining order was issued. The court found grounds, however, to believe that the dispute would be renewed on future jobs. Although the parties had agreed on voluntary methods of adjustment, the court of appeals upheld the Board's authority to resolve the matter by a cease-and-desist order.[25]

Interesting questions arise as to the purpose of union activity where both unlawful and also protected objectives are said to be present. The picketing respondent union may claim its sole aim to be consumer or public information, while the Board may believe work reassignment to be the objective. If any basis exists for the latter conclusion, even though multiple objectives are present, the Board will proceed under the Section 8(b)(4)(D) provision, and the courts agree to this.

In making work assignment determinations, the criteria used include past practice and customs, existing contracts, efficiency and economy of operations, previous certification of bargaining units, or other significant considerations. Usually several significant considerations may be in conflict, the problem then being to decide which will have the controlling weight. The courts do not upset the NLRB judgments in such matters.

After a charge is filed under Section 8(b)(4)(D), Section 10(k) then requires the Board to hold a hearing to resolve the jurisdictional dispute unless "the parties to such dispute" adjust or agree upon a method for the voluntary adjustment of the dispute. Ever since Section 10(k) was enacted, the Board has consistently interpreted the phrase "parties to such dispute" to include the employer as well as the disputing unions. The Board has refused to dismiss the Section 10(k) proceedings when the unions, but not the employer, have agreed to settle. In the *NLRB v. Plasterers'*

---

[24] Laborers International Union, Local 113, and Super Excavators, Inc., 327 NLRB 113 (1998).

[25] *Douds v. Local Union No. 46, Wood, Wire, and Metal Lathers Int'l. Ass'n.*, 245 F.2d 223 (3d Cir. 1957).

Local 79[26] decision, presented next, the Supreme Court upheld the Board's interpretation and reversed the District of Columbia Circuit's decision that an employer had no right to insist upon participation in a Section 10(k) proceeding.

In *NLRB v. Local 825, Operating Engineers (Burns and Roe)*,[27] the Supreme Court determined that a strike against neutral employers, with the object of forcing a change in a work assignment by the primary employer, amounted to coercion to "cease doing business" with the primary employer in violation of Section 8(b)(4)(B). Strikes to force assignment of work thus can violate both Section 8(b)(4)(D) and Section 8(b)(4)(B).

SECTION 58: SECONDARY ACTIVITY: "ALLY" AND "COMMON SITUS" DOCTRINES

The thrust of Section 8(b)(4)(ii)(B), the principal secondary boycott section of the Act, is to protect neutral employers from the effects of labor disputes between other employers and their employees. This protection has been limited by rulings that have recognized the right of striking employees, under certain circumstances, to picket "allies" of their employer, to picket common situs locations where neutral as well as primary employer activity is present, and (again under certain circumstances) to conduct secondary consumer boycotts.

THE "ALLY" DOCTRINE

In *NLRB v. Denver Building & Construction Trades Council*,[28] the Supreme Court stated that Section 8(b)(4) reflects "the dual congressional objectives of preserving the right of labor organizations to bring pressure to bear on offending employers in primary labor disputes and of shielding unoffending employers and others from pressures and controversies not their own." This policy then protects unoffending or innocent third parties from labor disputes that are not their affair. Under the so-called ally doctrine, an employer who performs the "struck work" of a primary employer is no such innocent party and is not protected under Section 8(b)(4).[29] The ally doctrine is also applied to those employers who, because of common ownership, control, and integration of operations, become so identified with the primary employer that the businesses are considered as a single enterprise.

COMMON SITUS PICKETING AND RESERVED GATES

The line between legitimate primary and unlawful secondary activity is relatively easy to draw where the primary and secondary employers have separate work sites. A more difficult problem is presented in the common situs cases where both the struck or primary employer and the secondary or neutral employer are carrying on

---

[26] 404 U.S. 116 (1971).

[27] 400 U.S. 297 (1971).

[28] 341 U.S. 675 (1951).

[29] *Douds v. Metropolitan Federation*, 75 F. Supp 672 (S.D.N.Y. 1948).

business activities at the same location. In the *Moore Dry Dock Co.* case,[30] where a union that had a dispute with a shipowner was refused permission to enter a shipyard to picket alongside the ship and thus set up a picket line at the entrance to the secondary employer's shipyard, the Board set forth standards outlining the types of picketing permissible in common situs situations. The Board ruled that picketing is primary and beyond the scope of Section 8(b)(4) when the following take place:

1. The picketing is strictly limited to times when the common situs of the dispute is located on the secondary employer's premises.
2. At the time of picketing, the primary employer is engaged in its normal business at the situs.
3. The picketing is limited to places reasonably close to the location of the situs.
4. The picketing discloses clearly that the dispute is with the primary employer.

A company may reserve a certain plant gate or entrance to its premises for the exclusive use of an outside contractor. If a union has a labor dispute with the company and pickets the company's premises, including the gate so reserved for the employees of the outside contractor, the union may be held to have violated Section 8(b)(4)(B). The U.S. Supreme Court has stated the circumstances under which such a violation may be found as follows:

> There must be a separate gate, marked and set apart from other gates; the work done by the employees who use the gate must be unrelated to the normal operations of the employer, and the work must be of a kind that would not, if done when the plant were engaged in its regular operations, necessitate curtailing those operations.[31]

However, if the reserved gate is used by employees of both the company and the contractor, the picketing would be considered primary and not a violation of Section 8(b)(4)(B).

The *Wilhelm Construction Co., Inc.,* case, presented in this section, involves a violation of Section 8(b)(4) of the NLRA in a "reserve gate" context.

CASE 6.7	F. A. WILHELM CONSTRUCTION CO., INC., V. CARPENTERS
	U.S. COURT OF APPEALS, 293 F. 3D 935 (6TH CIR. 2002).

[The Carpenters Union, representing union carpenters in the Louisville, Kentucky, area, unsuccessfully sought to have Dant Clayton Co. and Dailey Seating Co. enter into collective bargaining contracts with the carpenters union. Dailey had a subcontract to install the seating for the construction of the University of Louisville's new stadium. F. A. Wilhelm Construction Co., Inc., had the contract for the construction of a portion of the stadium's concrete superstructure and employed union

carpenters on this project and was subject to a collective bargaining contract with the union that contained a no-strike clause. Dailey Seating Co. employed a nonunion workforce. On December 4, 1997, the union told Dailey that there would be a picket line established against it the following morning. Union representatives walked around the project that day advising all union members, including Wilhelm workers, that picketing would begin against Dailey the following day, and they

continued

---

[30] Sailors Union of the Pacific (Moore Dry Dock Co.), 92 NLRB 547 (1950). See also OCAW Local 1-591 and BN Railroad, 325 NLRB 45 (1998).

[31] *United Steelworkers v. NLRB & Carrier Corp.*, 376 U.S. 492 (1964). See also Local 7, SMWIA, 345 NLRB No. 119 (2004).

requested volunteers to staff the picket line. A union wallet card was distributed stating on one side "GOOD UNION BUILDING TRADESMEN do not work behind banners even with 4 gates." The other side read:

> Which side are you on? Picketing has been described by the Supreme Court as the "working man's means of communication." A picket is a message to you that some of your fellow workers are engaged in a labor dispute and need your help. It is your constitutional right as an American citizen to decide how you will respond to that picket. Under the law your union cannot help you make that decision. You can seek guidance only from your conscience then decide, "Which side am I on?"

In response to the union's activities, the project manager set up a "reserve gate system." When Dailey Seating Company's name appeared on the reserved gate, other jobsite workers from the construction trades went to work for their respective contractors or subcontractors utilizing the other entrances to the project while the carpenters union picketed Gate 1, the reserved gate for Dailey's workers. When the leader of the National Carpenters Union wrote a letter to the local union advising that the strike was improperly affecting Wilhelm Construction Co., a union contractor with a no-strike clause, the union ceased picketing at the jobsite and the carpenters went back to work for Wilhelm. Wilhelm Construction Co. sued the carpenters union under Section 303 of the NLRA for damages resulting from an illegal secondary boycott arising from a violation of Section 8(b)(4) of the NLRA. From a judgment for Wilhelm the parties cross-appealed.]

MERRITT, C. J....

The establishment of a reserved gate system is common in the construction industry, particularly where numerous employers work at a site but only one employer is experiencing labor unrest. Under a reserve gate system, one gate, or entrance, called the "primary" gate, is reserved for the exclusive use of the "primary" contractor that is the target of the picket line, as well as its subcontractors, vendors and guests; other gates or entrances are reserved for use by contractors and others not involved in the dispute. Generally, once a reserved gate system is in place, the union must confine its picketing to the primary gate. The system is designed to keep neutral parties out of the dispute and avoid the need for them to

cross picket lines. Reserve gate systems are usually effective because unions confine their picketing to the gate reserved for the targeted contractor and the project is not shut down....

Under the Act, when a union has a problem with the "primary" employer, it must focus its activities on that employer only. It may not exert pressure, whether direct or indirect, on other neutral or unrelated "secondary" employers. Encouraging employees to engage in a concerted activity against their employer in order to have that employer refuse to deal with the primary employer is illegal. The question is a factual one as to the union's intent. Accordingly, in determining whether a union has violated Section 8(b)(4), the court must decide if the union's actions were directed at the secondary employer or merely had ancillary consequences for that employer. It is not necessary that the sole object of the strike be focused on the secondary employer if one of the union's objectives was to influence the secondary employer to bring pressure to bear on the primary employer. Whether the union was motivated by a secondary objective is a question of fact and is to be determined by the totality of the union's conduct under the circumstances.

The question for the district court, therefore, was one of intent. The district court concluded, and we agree, that representatives of the union violated Section 8(b)(4) when they explicitly enlisted advance help from Wilhelm employees to form a picket line against Dailey. The direct solicitation by defendant of Wilhelm's union employees before any picket line had been established demonstrates that defendant's likely objective was to keep Wilhelm employees off the job. A reasonable inference from the evidence demonstrates that defendant intended to embroil Wilhelm in its labor dispute against Dailey by recruiting Wilhelm workers to staff the picket lines in advance of the creation of the picket....

Section 303 of the National Labor Relations Act, provides a private cause of action for damages arising from a violation of Section 8(b)(4). The district court awarded Wilhelm $44,547.76 in damages....

Once liability is established, Wilhelm is entitled to recover all damages, "directly and proximately" caused from the violations from the Act by the union...

[*The matter was remanded to the district court for calculation of damages according to the direction of the Court of Appeals.*]

continued

Case Questions

1. Did the reserve gate system work as intended in this case?

2. Does the plaintiff in a Section 303 lawsuit for damages arising from a violation of Section 8 (b)(4) of the NLRA have to prove that the union's actions were directed at the secondary employer?

3. What evidence exists that the carpenters union intended to exert pressure on the neutral or secondary employer in this case, Wilhelm Construction Co.?

SECTION 59: SECONDARY ACTIVITY: CONSUMER PICKETING, HANDBILLING, AND BANNERING

The terms **picketing, handbilling,** and **bannering** are often associated with secondary boycott litigation. The *Tree Fruits, Safeco Title Insurance*, and *DeBartolo II* Supreme Court precedents provide developing guidance for the murky statutory language of Section 8(b)(4) of the NLRA.

SECONDARY PICKETING AND THE PUBLICITY PROVISO

The "publicity proviso" to Secion 8(b)(4) states that:

> nothing contained in such paragraph shall be construed to prohibit publicity, other than picketing, for the purpose of truthfully advising the public, including consumers and members of a labor organization, that a product or products are produced by an employer with whom the labor organization has a primary dispute and are distributed by another employer, as long as such publicity does not have an effect of inducing any individual employed by any person other than the primary employer in the course of his employment to refuse to pick up, deliver, or transport any goods, or not to perform any services, at the establishment of the employer engaged in such distribution....

A union thus has the right to publicize a dispute with a primary employer at retail establishments that sell the goods of the primary employer. Truthful handbills, billboards, newspaper advertisements, and radio and television messages are all clearly protected. Despite the "other than picketing" language of the publicity proviso, the Supreme Court held in *Tree Fruits* that consumer picketing limited to asking customers not to purchase the struck product at the neutral employer's store is legal. When the purpose of the picketing is to cut off all trade with the neutral employer, it is a Section 8(b)(4)(ii)(B) violation. The *Tree Fruits* decision is presented in this section.

In the *Safeco Title Insurance* decision, also presented in this section, a union's secondary picketing against the central product sold by neutral employers—title insurance—was held to be a violation of the language and purpose of Section 8(b)(4)(ii)(B) because it was reasonably calculated to induce customers not to patronize the neutral employers at all.

HANDBILLING AS PROTECTED FREE SPEECH

In *DeBartolo II*, presented in this section, where a union distributed handbills at all entrances to a Tampa, Florida, shopping mall urging a total consumer boycott of all 85 stores in the mall and where the union had a labor dispute with only one building contractor hired to build a single store at the mall, the Supreme Court found that peaceful handbilling unaccompanied by picketing that urged a consumer boycott of the neutral employers was not a violation of Section 8(b)(4) of the NLRA. The Court pointed out in *DeBartolo II* that picketing is "a mixture of conduct and communication and the conduct often provides the most persuasive deterrent to third persons about to enter a business establishment," whereas hand-bills "depend entirely on the persuasive force of the idea." The Court thus avoided the serious First Amendment free speech issue in that handbilling lacked the characteristics of picketing that often proves to be threatening or coercive conduct within the meaning of §8(b)4(ii)(B).

In *NLRB v. Servette, Inc.*,[32] union representatives contacted managers of supermarkets, advised them that they were engaged in a strike against Servette, and requested that they discontinue handling merchandise supplied by Servette. The union representatives also warned that handbills asking the public not to buy Servette products would be passed out in front of those stores that refused to cooperate. The court found that warnings that threatened distribution of handbills were not "threats" within the meaning of Section 8(b)(4)(ii), reasoning that the statutory protection for the distribution of handbills would be undermined if a threat to engage in protected conduct were not itself protected.

Bannering

In *Overstreet v. Carpenters Local 1506*, the Ninth Circuit refused to enjoin the union's use of large 4′ × 15′ banners near the neutral employers' premises that proclaimed "SHAME ON [Name of neutral retailer]" and "Labor Dispute" in smaller letters in the corners of the banners.[33] The banners were placed a good distance away from the jobsite, and none of the entrances to the retailers were blocked. The Court rejected the General Counsel's argument that the banners constituted coercion under Section 8(b)(4)(ii)(B) because it was tantamount to "signal" picketing. Rather, applying *DeBartolo II*, the Court concluded that the banners were speech protected by the First Amendment, similar to handbills, and were truthful statements of the union's issue with the secondary employers.

The legality of union's use of mock funerals or oversized rat balloons or bannering activities often turns on whether the means by which the union delivers its message is coercive, threatening, restraining, or intimidating. In *Sheet Metal Workers Local 15 (Brandon Medical Center) v. NLRB*, the D.C. Circuit Court of Appeals concluded that the union did not violate Section 8(b)(4)(ii)(B) by staging a "mock funeral" near a neutral hospital and that it was not the functional equivalent of picketing "because it had none of the coercive character of picketing."[34] In *Kentou v. Sheet Metal Workers Local 15*, the Eleventh Circuit affirmed the issuance of a Section 10(l) injunction, also involving a mock funeral near a neutral hospital,

---

[32] 377 U.S. 46 (1964).

[33] 409 F.3d.1199 (9th Cir. 2005).

[34] 491 F.3d 429 (D.C. Cir. 2007).

where the union's conduct was found to be in violation of Section 8(b)(4)(ii)(B) because the activity involved patrolling and a "mixture of conduct and communication intended to provide the most persuasive deterrent to third persons about to enter" the hospital.[35]

CASE 6.8

NLRB V. FRUIT AND VEGETABLE PACKERS AND WAREHOUSEMEN, LOCAL 760 (TREE FRUITS, INC.)
SUPREME COURT OF THE UNITED STATES, 377 U.S. 58 (1964).

BRENNAN, J....

Under Section 8(b)(4)(ii)(B) of the National Labor Relations Act, as amended, it is an unfair labor practice for a union "to threaten, coerce, or restrain any person," with the object of "forcing or requiring any person to cease using, selling, handling, transporting, or otherwise dealing in the products of any other producer ... or to cease doing business with any other person...." A proviso excepts, however,

> publicity, other than picketing, for the purpose of truthfully advising the public ... that a product or products are produced by any employer with whom the labor organization has a primary dispute and are distributed by another employer, as long as such publicity does not have an effect of inducing any individual employed by any person other than the primary employer in the course of his employment to refuse to pick up, deliver, or transport any goods, or not to perform any services, at the establishment of the employer engaged in such distribution.

The question in this case is whether the respondent unions violated this section when they limited their secondary picketing of retail stores to an appeal to the customers of the stores not to buy the products of certain firms against which one of the respondents was on strike.

Respondent Local 760 called a strike against fruit packers and warehousemen doing business in Yakima, Washington. The struck firms sold Washington State apples to the Safeway chain of retail stores in and about Seattle, Washington. Local 760, aided by respondent Joint Council, instituted a customer boycott against the apples in support of the strike. They placed pickets who walked back and forth before the customers' entrances of 46 Safeway stores in Seattle. The

pickets—two at each of 45 stores and three at the 46th store—wore placards and distributed handbills which appealed to Safeway customers, and to the public generally, to refrain from buying Washington State apples, which were only one of numerous food products sold in the stores. Before the pickets appeared at any store, a letter was delivered to the store manager informing him that the picketing was only an appeal to his customers not to buy Washington State apples, and that the pickets were being expressly instructed "to patrol peacefully in front of the customer entrances of the store, to stay away from delivery entrances and not to interfere with the work of your employees, or with deliveries to or pickups from your store." A copy of written instructions to the pickets—which included the explicit statement that "you are also forbidden to request that the customers not patronize the store"—was enclosed with the letter. Since it was desired to assure Safeway employees that they were not to cease work, and to avoid any interference with pickups or deliveries, the pickets appeared after the stores opened for business and departed before the stores closed. At all times during the picketing, the store employees continued to work, and no deliveries or pickups were obstructed. Washington State apples were handled in normal course by both Safeway employees and the employees of other employers involved. Ingress and egress by customers was not interfered with in any manner.

A complaint issued on charges that this conduct violated Section 8(b)(4) as amended. The case was submitted directly to the National Labor Relations Board on a stipulation of facts and the waiver of a hearing and proceedings before a Trial Examiner. The Board held, following its construction of the statute in *Upholsterers Frame & Bedding Workers Twin*

continued

---

[35] 18 F.3d 1259, 1265–1266 (11th Cir. 2005).

City Local No. 61, 132 NLRB 40, that "by literal wording of the proviso [to Section 8(b)(4)] as well as through the interpretative gloss placed thereon by its drafters, consumer picketing in front of a secondary establishment is prohibited." 132 NLRB 1172, 1176. Upon respondents' petition for review and the Board's cross-petition for enforcement, the Court of Appeals for the District of Columbia Circuit set aside the Board's order.... We granted certiorari, 374 U.S. 804....

We have examined the legislative history of the amendments to Section 8(b)(4)....

No Conference Report was before the Senate when it passed the compromise bill, and it had the benefit only of Senator [John] Kennedy's statement of the purpose of the proviso. He said the proviso preserved

> the right to appeal to consumers by methods other than picketing asking them to refrain from buying goods made by nonunion labor and to refrain from trading with a retailer who sells such goods.... We were not able to persuade the House conferees to permit picketing in front of that secondary shop, but were able to persuade them to agree that the union shall be free to conduct informational activity short of picketing. In other words, the union can hand out handbills at the shop ... and can carry on all publicity short of having ambulatory picketing....

This explanation does not compel the conclusion that the Conference Agreement contemplated prohibiting any consumer picketing at a secondary site beyond that which urges the public, in Senator Kennedy's words, to "refrain from trading with a retailer who sells such goods." To read into the Conference Agreement, on the basis of a single statement, an intention to prohibit all consumer picketing at a secondary site would depart from our practice of respecting the congressional policy not to prohibit peaceful picketing except to curb "isolated evils" spelled out by the Congress itself.

Peaceful consumer picketing to shut off all trade with the secondary employer unless he aids the union in its dispute with the primary employer, is poles apart from such picketing which only persuades his customers not to buy the struck product. The proviso indicates that no more than the Senate conferees' constitutional doubts led Congress to authorize publicity other than picketing which persuades the customers of a secondary employer to stop all trading with him, but not such publicity which has the

effect of cutting off his deliveries or inducing his employees to cease work. On the other hand, picketing which persuades the customers of a secondary employer to stop all trading with him was also to be barred.

In sum, the legislative history does not support the Board's finding that Congress meant to prohibit all consumer picketing at a secondary site, having determined that such picketing necessarily threatened, coerced, or restrained the secondary employer. Rather, the history shows that Congress was following its usual practice of legislating against peaceful picketing only to curb "isolated evils."

This distinction is opposed as "unrealistic" because, it is urged, all picketing automatically provokes the public to stay away from the picketed establishment. The public will, it is said, neither read the signs and handbills, nor note the explicit injunctions that "This is not a strike against any store or market." Be that as it may, our holding today simply takes note of the fact that a broad condemnation of peaceful picketing, such as that urged upon us by petitioners, has never been adopted by Congress, and an intention to do so is not revealed with that "clearest indication in the legislative history," which we require.

We come then to the question whether the picketing in this case, confined as it was to persuading customers to cease buying the product of the primary employer, falls within the area of secondary consumer picketing which Congress did clearly indicate its intention to prohibit under Section 8(b)(4)(ii). We hold that it did not fall within that area, and therefore did not "threaten, coerce, or restrain" Safeway. While any diminution in Safeway's purchases of apples due to a drop in consumer demand might be said to be a result which causes respondents' picketing to fall literally within the letter of the statute and yet not within the statute, because not within its spirit, nor within the intentions of its makers. When consumer picketing is employed only to persuade customers not to buy the struck product, the union's appeal is closely confined to the primary dispute. The site of the appeal is expanded to include the premises of the secondary employer, but if the appeal succeeds, the secondary employer's purchases from the struck firm are decreased only because the public had diminished its purchases of the struck product. On the other hand, when consumer picketing is employed to persuade customers not to trade at all with the secondary employer, the

continued

latter stops buying the struck product, not because of a falling demand, but in response to pressure designed to inflict injury on his business generally. In such case, the union does more than merely follow the struck product; it creates a separate dispute with the secondary employer.

We disagree therefore with the Court of Appeals that the test of "to threaten, coerce, or restrain" for the purposes of this case is whether Safeway suffered or was likely to suffer economic loss. A violation of Section 8(b)(4)(ii)(B) would not be established merely because respondents' picketing was effective to reduce Safeway's sales of Washington State apples, even if this led or might lead Safeway to drop the item as a poor seller.

The judgment of the Court of Appeals is vacated and the case is remanded with direction to enter judgment setting aside the Board's order.

It is so ordered.

Case Questions

1. What was the union conduct complained of by Safeway stores?
2. On what grounds did the NLRB prohibit the picketing?
3. How does the Supreme Court view the legality of this boycott?
4. Is peaceful secondary activity against one product of a multiproduct retailer prohibited by the NLRA according to the *Tree Fruits* decision?

NLRB v. Retail Clerks, Local 1001 (Safeco Title Insurance Co.)
SUPREME COURT OF THE UNITED STATES, 447 U.S. 607 (1980).

[Safeco Title Insurance Co. underwrites real estate title insurance in the state of Washington. It maintains close business relationships with five local title companies. These local title companies search land titles, perform escrow service, and sell title insurance; and over 90 percent of their gross income derives from the sale of Safeco insurance. Local 1001 of the Retail Store Employees Union became the certified bargaining representative for certain Safeco employees in 1974. When contract negotiations between Safeco and the union reached an impasse, the employees went on strike. The union picketed Safeco's office in Seattle, and it also picketed each of the five local title companies. The pickets carried signs declaring that Safeco had no contract with the union. A typical sign read:

> Safeco Nonunion Does not Employ
> Members of or Have Contract with Retail Store
> Employees Local 1001

Union members also distributed handbills advising the public of the strike and asking consumers to support the strike by canceling their Safeco policies. Safeco and one of the title companies filed complaints with the NLRB charging that the union had engaged in an unfair labor practice by picketing in order to promote a secondary boycott against the title companies. No issue was raised concerning the distribution of handbills.

The Board concluded that the union's picketing violated Section 8(b)(4)(ii)(B) of the NLRA. The U.S. Court of Appeals for the District of Columbia Circuit set aside the Board's order, holding that *Tree Fruits* leaves neutrals susceptible to whatever consequences may flow from secondary picketing against the consumption of products of an employer involved in a labor dispute. The Supreme Court granted a writ of certiorari.]

POWELL, J....

The question is whether § 8(b)(4)(ii)(B) of the National Labor Relations Act forbids secondary picketing against a struck product when such picketing predictably encourages consumers to boycott a neutral party's business....

Section 8(b)(4)(ii)(B) of the National Labor Relations Act makes it "an unfair labor practice for a labor organization ... to threaten, coerce, or restrain" a person not party to a labor dispute "where ... an object thereof is ... forcing or requiring [him] to cease using, selling, handling, transporting, or otherwise dealing in the products of any other producer ... or to cease doing business with any other person...."

... The product picketed in *Tree Fruits* was but one item among the many that made up the retailer's trade. If the appeal against such a product succeeds, the Court

continued

observed, it simply induces the neutral retailer to reduce his orders for the product or "to drop the item as a poor seller." The decline in sales attributable to consumer rejection of the struck product puts pressure upon the primary employer, and the marginal injury to the neutral retailer is purely incidental to the product boycott. The neutral therefore has little reason to become involved in the labor dispute. In this case, on the other hand, the title companies sell only the primary employer's product and perform the services associated with it. Secondary picketing against consumption of the primary product leaves responsive consumers no realistic option other than to boycott the title companies altogether. If the appeal succeeds, each company "stops buying the struck product, not because of a falling demand, but in response to pressure designed to inflict injury on [its] business generally." Thus, "the union does more than merely follow the struck product; it creates a separate dispute with the secondary employer." Such an expansion of labor discord was one of the evils that Congress intended § 8(b)(4)(ii)(B) to prevent.

As long as secondary picketing only discourages consumption of a struck product, incidental injury to the neutral is a natural consequence of an effective primary boycott. But the Union's secondary appeal against the central product sold by the title companies in this case is "reasonably calculated to induce customers not to patronize the neutrals at all." The resulting injury to their business is distinctly different from the injury that the Court considered in *Tree Fruits.* Product picketing that reasonably can be expected to threaten neutral parties with ruin or substantial loss simply does not square with the language or the purpose of § 8(b)(4)(ii)(B). Since successful secondary

picketing would put the title companies to a choice between their survival and the severance of their ties with Safeco, the picketing plainly violates the statutory ban on the coercion of neutrals with the object of "forcing or requiring [them] to cease ... dealing in the [primary] produc[t] ... or to cease doing business with" the primary employer. § 8(b)(4)(ii)(B).

The Court of Appeals suggested that application of § 8(b)(4)(ii)(B) to the picketing in this case might violate the First Amendment. We think not. Although the Court recognized in *Tree Fruits* that the Constitution might not permit "a broad ban against peaceful picketing," the Court left no doubt that Congress may prohibit secondary picketing calculated "to persuade the customers of the secondary employer to cease trading with him in order to force him to cease dealing with, or to put pressure upon, the primary employer." Such picketing spreads labor discord by coercing a neutral party to join the fray....

The judgment of the Court of Appeals is reversed and the case is remanded with directions to enforce the National Labor Relations Board's order.

So ordered.

Case Questions

1. Was the union's distribution of handbills a violation of Section 8(b)(4)(ii)(B) of the NLRA?
2. State the rule of the case.
3. Compare the impact on neutral employers of responsive consumer action in the *Tree Fruits* case with that in the *Safeco* case.
4. Does the *Safeco* decision modify the *Tree Fruits* decision?

CASE 6.10

DEBARTOLO CORP. (DEBARTOLO II) V. FLORIDA GULF COAST BUILDING AND CONSTRUCTION TRADES COUNCIL
SUPREME COURT OF THE UNITED STATES, 485 U.S. 568 (1988).

[The Supreme Court in *DeBartolo I* remanded the case to the Board. On remand, the Board held that the handbilling violated Section 8(b)(4)(ii)(B), which forbids a union to "threaten, coerce, or restrain" any person where an object is to force the person to cease doing business with another person. Because it had serious doubts about Section 8(b)(4)'s constitutionality under the Board's interpretation, the court of appeals applied *NLRB v. Catholic Bishop of Chicago,* 440 U.S. 490,

and ruled that neither the statute's language nor its legislative history revealed a clear congressional intent to proscribe such handbilling. The court thus denied enforcement of the Board's order. The Supreme Court granted certiorari.]

WHITE, J....
This case centers around the respondent union's peaceful handbilling of the businesses operating in a

continued

shopping mall in Tampa, Florida, owned by petitioner, the Edward J. DeBartolo Corporation (DeBartolo). The union's primary labor dispute was with H. J. High Construction Company (High) over alleged substandard wages and fringe benefits. High was retained by the Wilson Company (Wilson) to construct a department store in the mall, and neither DeBartolo nor any of the other 85 or so mall tenants had any contractual right to influence the selection of contractors.

The union, however, sought to obtain their influence upon Wilson and High by distributing handbills asking mall customers not to shop at any of the stores in the mall "until the Mall's owner publicly promises that all construction at the Mall will be done using contractors who pay their employees fair wages and fringe benefits."* The handbills' message was that "[t]he payment of substandard wages not only diminishes the working person's ability to purchase

---

*The Handbill read:

"PLEASE *DON'T SHOP AT EAST LAKE SQUARE MALL* PLEASE

"The FLA. GULF COAST BUILDING TRADES COUNCIL, AFL-CIO, is requesting that you do not shop at the stores in the East Lake Square Mall because of The Mall ownership's contribution to substandard wages.

"The Wilson's Department Store under construction on these premises is being built by contractors who pay substandard wages and fringe benefits. In the past, the Mall's owner, The Edward J. DeBartolo Corporation, has supported labor and our local economy by ensuring that the Mall and its stores be built by contractors who pay fair wages and fringe benefits. Now, however, and for no apparent reason, the Mall owners have taken a giant step backwards by permitting our standards to be torn down. The payment of substandard wages not only diminishes the working person's ability to purchase with earned, rather than borrowed, dollars, but it also undercuts the wage standard of the entire community. Since low construction wages at this time of inflation means decreased purchasing power, do the owners of East Lake Mall intend to compensate for the decreased purchasing power of workers of the community by encouraging the stores in East Lake Mall to cut their prices and lower their profits?

"CUT-RATE WAGES ARE NOT FAIR UNLESS MERCHANDISE PRICES ARE ALSO CUT-RATE.

"We ask for your support in our protest against substandard wages. Please do not patronize the stores in the East Lake Square Mall until the Mall's owner publicly promises that all construction at the Mall will be done using contractors who pay their employees fair wages and fringe benefits.

"IF YOU MUST ENTER THE MALL TO DO BUSINESS, please express to the store managers your concern over substandard wages and your support of our efforts.

"We are appealing only to the public—the consumer. We are not seeking to induce any person to cease work or to refuse to make deliveries."

---

with earned, rather than borrowed, dollars, but it also undercuts the wage standard of the entire community." The handbills made clear that the union was seeking only a consumer boycott against the other mall tenants, not a secondary strike by their employees. At all four entrances to the mall for about three weeks in December 1979, the union peacefully distributed the handbills without any accompanying picketing or patrolling....

... [W]here an otherwise acceptable construction of a statute would raise serious constitutional problems, the Court will construe the statute to avoid such problems unless such construction is plainly contrary to the intent of Congress. *Catholic Bishop,* supra. at 499–501, 504....

[We] conclude, as did the Court of Appeals, that [§ 8(b)(4)] is open to a construction that obviates deciding whether a congressional prohibition of handbilling on the facts of this case would violate the First Amendment.

The case turns on whether handbilling such as involved here must be held to "threaten, coerce, or restrain any person" to cease doing business with another, within the meaning of § 8(b)(4)(ii)(B)....

The Board ... found that the handbilling "coerced" mall tenants and explained in a footnote that "[a]ppealing to the public not to patronize secondary employers is an attempt to inflict economic harm on the secondary employers by causing them to lose business. As the case law makes clear, such appeals constitute 'economic retaliation' and are therefore a form of coercion." 273 N.L.R.B., at 1432, n. 6. Our decision in *Tree Fruits,* however, makes untenable the notion that *any* kind of handbilling, picketing, or other appeals to a secondary employer to cease doing business with the employer involved in the labor dispute is "coercion" within the meaning of § 8(b)(4)(ii) (B) if it has some economic impact on the neutral....

NLRB v. Retail Store Employees, 447 U.S. 607 (1980) (*Safeco*), in turn, held that consumer picketing urging a general boycott of a secondary employer aimed at causing him to sever relations with the union's real antagonist was coercive and forbidden by § 8(b)(4). It is urged that *Safeco* rules this case because the union sought a general boycott of all tenants in the mall. But "picketing is qualitatively 'different from other modes of communication.'" *Babbitt v. Farm Workers,* 442 U.S. 289, 311, n. 17 (1979), (quoting *Hughes v. Superior Court,* 339 U.S. 460, 465 (1950)), and *Safeco* noted that the picketing there actually threatened the neutral with ruin or

continued

substantial loss. As Justice Stevens pointed out in his concurrence in *Safeco, supra*, at 619, picketing is "a mixture of conduct and communication" and the conduct element "often provides the most persuasive deterrent to third persons about to enter a business establishment." Handbills containing the same message, he observed, are "much less effective than labor picketing" because they "depend entirely on the persuasive force of the idea." *Ibid.* Similarly, the Court stated in *Hughes v. Superior Court, supra*, at 465:

> Publication in a newspaper, or by distribution of circulars, may convey the same information or make the same charge as do those patrolling a picket line. But the very purpose of a picket line is to exert influences, and it produces consequences, different from other modes of communication.

In *Tree Fruits*, we could not discern with the "requisite clarity" that Congress intended to proscribe all peaceful consumer picketing at secondary sites. There is even less reason to find in the language of § 8(b)(4)(ii), standing alone, any clear indication that handbilling, without picketing, "coerces" secondary employers. The loss of customers because they read a handbill urging them not to patronize a business, and not because they are intimidated by a line of picketers, is the result of mere persuasion, and the neutral who reacts is doing no more than what its customers honestly want it to do....

The Board's reading of § 8(b)(4) would make an unfair labor practice out of any kind of publicity or communication to the public urging a consumer boycott of employers other than those the proviso specifically deals with. On the facts of this case, newspaper, radio, and television appeals not to patronize the mall would be prohibited; and it would be an unfair labor practice for unions in their own meetings to urge their members not to shop in the mall. Nor could a union's handbills simply urge not shopping at a department store because it is using a nonunion contractor, although the union could safely ask the store's customers not to buy there because it is selling mattresses not carrying the union label. It is difficult, to say the least, to fathom why Congress would consider appeals urging a boycott of a distributor of a non-union product to be more deserving of protection than nonpicketing persuasion of customers of other neutral employers such as that involved in this case....

In our view, interpreting § 8(b)(4) as not reaching the handbilling involved in this case is not foreclosed either by the language of the section or its legislative history. That construction makes unnecessary passing on the serious constructional questions that would be raised by the Board's understanding of the statute. Accordingly, the judgment of the Court of Appeals is *Affirmed.*

Case Questions

1. Why didn't the Supreme Court give its usual deference to the Board's interpretation of the statute in this case?
2. Is picketing qualitatively different from handbilling?
3. Did the Court conclude that the handbilling in this case had a coercive effect on the secondary employers?
4. Assume that the Bakery Workers' Union is on strike against a bakery whose products are sold at a local supermarket. Compare the action the union may take against the local supermarket under *Tree Fruits* and *DeBartolo II*.

SECTION 60: HOT CARGO AGREEMENTS

After Section 8(b)(4) was enacted to make illegal secondary economic activity for the purpose of compelling one employer to cease doing any business with another person, the problem of contracts providing for such results remained. In 1959, Section 8(e), the so-called **hot cargo** section of the Act, was added. This section prohibits collective bargaining agreements whereby members of the contracting bargaining unit need not handle nonunion or struck goods of other employers; it also prohibits contracts whereby the employer ceases to do business with any person. The Newspaper Deliverers Union and the *New York Post*'s collective bargaining contract, which provides that the *Post* "shall not distribute its newspaper ... through any wholesaler unless such wholesaler is under written collective agreement with the Union," was held to be an unenforceable "hot cargo" provision by the Labor Board. The Board pointed out that the union's attempt to obtain the distribution work on Long Island for the employees of a union signatory employer rather than nonunion wholesalers was contrary to Section 8(e) and also a violation of Section 8(b)4.[36]

Explicit exceptions to the prohibitions of Section 8(e) were made for two industries, garment manufacturing and building construction, where subcontracting commonly is practiced under the contractual requirements that only unionized shops will be used.

The *United Rentals* case, presented in this section, is an example of a collective bargaining agreement clause protected by the Section 8(e) exception for workers at construction sites, which forbids the signatory contractors from subcontracting work at their construction site to any firm that has not signed a collective bargaining agreement with the Laborers Union.

The construction industry proviso to Section 8(e) has been interpreted to allow unions in this industry to use economic pressures to secure hot cargo subcontracting clauses limited to work to be done at the site of the construction. The Board and the courts, however, have held that it is not legal for unions to use any economic pressure to enforce such clauses.[37] The union's recourse is to bring a Section 301 lawsuit.

A union may, under certain circumstances, use economic pressure to enforce a **work preservation clause**. In the *National Woodwork* decision, reported in this section, the Court held that it is not a Section 8(b)(4)(B) violation for a union to picket its immediate employer for the purpose of preserving work traditionally performed by union members that the employer is in a position to award, even if it might cause the employer to terminate contractual relations with another employer. In *NLRB v. Pipefitters Local 638*,[38] however, the Supreme Court held that it was a Section 8(b)(4)(B) violation for a union to undertake economic activity against its immediate employer, a plumbing and pipe fitting contractor, when that employer was not in a position to award the work. In *Pipefitters*, the subcontractor's employees refused to install climate control units where the internal piping of the units was performed at the factory according to the general contractor's job specifications. This work traditionally had been performed by union members at various construction sites. Although the labor agreement between the subcontractor and the union contained a valid work preservation clause, the Court found the activity in question secondary in nature because the subcontractor lacked the "right of control" over the choice of materials to be used. The Court reasoned that the union activity was a secondary boycott because it had the effect of unlawfully pressuring the subcontractor to "cease doing business" with the general contractor. In the circumstances of *National Woodwork*, the "cease doing business" consequences were incidental to the primary activity, whereas in *Pipefitters*, the union, if it was to obtain the work, must have intended to exert pressure on another employer.

---

[36] Newspaper and Mail Deliverers' Union of N.Y., 337 NLRB No. 91 (2002).

[37] See *NLRB v. IBEW, Local 769*, 405 F.2d 159 (9th Cir. 1968).

[38] 429 U.S. 507 (1977).

Garment industry unions were treated more favorably by Congress than construction industry unions and may use economic pressure to obtain and enforce hot cargo clauses in their collective bargaining agreements.

| CASE 6.11 | UNITED RENTALS HIGHWAY TECHNOLOGIES, INC., V. INDIANA CONSTRUCTORS, INC. |

UNITED STATES COURT OF APPEALS, SEVENTH CIRCUIT, 518 F.3D 526 (2008).

[United Rentals is in the "traffic control" segment of the highway construction market. The firms in this market help to protect highway construction workers from being hit by vehicles using the stretch of the highway that the workers are building, repairing, or rebuilding. When construction activity is about to begin, employees of the traffic control firm place cones, barrels, concrete blocks, or other barricades in position to block or alter traffic lanes. The workers also paint stripes on the road to indicate the new lanes, install warning signs to guide drivers using the highway, and place guardrails to keep vehicles from veering off onto what may be a nonexistent shoulder. The traffic control firm owns and stores the barricades, signs, guardrails, and other safety devices and brings them to the construction site as needed. The firm installs its devices before construction begins and removes them when it is finished. If flaggers are required, they may be supplied by the traffic control firm or by the general contractor.

Road work in Indiana is done almost entirely by contractors who belong to a trade association called Indiana Constructors, which has for many years negotiated collective bargaining agreements for its members with the Laborers International Union. In 2004, the collective bargaining agreement in force was modified to forbid the association's members to subcontract work at a construction site to a firm that had not signed a collective bargaining agreement with the Laborers Union. This was a blow to United Rentals because it had a collective bargaining agreement with another union. Also, it did not want to bargain with the Laborers Union when that agreement expired. It filed a charge with the NLRB that Indiana Constructors and the Laborers Union were violating the NLRB's "hot cargo" provision. Section 8(e) of the provision forbids a union and an employer to agree that the employer will refuse to deal with another employer, as Indiana Constructors had agreed with the Laborers Union to do with respect to United Rentals. The Board's General Counsel declined to file a complaint, and United Rentals brought suit against the union

in federal court under Section 303 of the Taft Hartley Act, which forbids a union to enter an agreement prohibited by the hot cargo provision. The federal district court granted summary judgement in favor of the union, and United Rentals appealed.]

POSNER, C. J....

Before Congress enacted the hot cargo provision, along with its exception for the construction industry, in 1959, hot cargo clauses had been pervasive in the industry, had been upheld repeatedly as lawful, and had not caused the problems associated with closed shops—though one reason, inapplicable to this case, was that most construction workers are hired from hiring halls; the halls are operated by unions but the unions are required to refer all comers, and not just workers represented by a union, to contractors and subcontractors, *Woelke & Romero Framing, Inc., v. NLRB*, 456 U.S. 645, 664-65 (1982); *Lucas v. NLRB*, 333 F.3d 927, 932 (9th Cir. 2003).

So one reason for the construction-industry exception was just a desire to ratify an acceptable status quo.... But another was to prevent friction at construction jobsites.... More than just work stoppages were at stake. Much construction work is dangerous, including road construction in the presence of highway traffic; and there was concern that the frictions engendered by union workers working side by side at a construction job site with nonunion workers or workers belonging to another union would reduce safety as well as efficiency. *Woelke & Romero Framing, Inc., v. NLRB*, supra, 456 U.S. at 662.

Before there was a separate market in traffic control there was no impediment to the general contractor's requiring whatever subcontractor performed traffic control for the contractor to bargain collectively with the general contractor's union. For a time after traffic control broke off and became a separate business, general contractors and construction workers' unions did not insist that the employees of traffic control subcontractors be represented by the

continued

general contractor's union, though even in that transitional period the collective bargaining agreement between the Indiana Constructors and the Laborers Union said that the union "encourages its members to utilize subcontractors who are signatory to collective bargaining agreements with the Laborers Union. Such subcontractors help to promote peace and harmony of the jobsite and to avoid labor dispute interruption of work." The modification in the collective bargaining agreement of which United Rentals complains restores fully the practice that prevailed before traffic control became a separate market....

United Rentals points out that its employees are not engaged in construction, but rather in a preparatory or ancillary activity. But the statutory exception is not for construction workers as such; it is for workers at a construction site; and traffic control workers work at highway construction sites.... Placing traffic

control workers within the exception...creates a clear rule. March down the road of attempting to distinguish "real" construction workers from other workers at the construction site and you will quickly find yourself in a trackless wilderness....

[The court determined that the hot cargo provision in this case did not raise any "traditional antitrust concerns" and was not in violation of the Sherman Act.]

Affirmed.

Case Questions

1. What rationale exists for the construction industry proviso allowing unions in the construction industry to negotiate hot cargo provisions in their collective bargaining agreements?
2. Since United Rentals employees are not engaged in construction, are they exempt from the construction industry proviso?

CASE 6.12	NATIONAL WOODWORK MANUFACTURERS ASSOCIATION V. NLRB
	SUPREME COURT OF THE UNITED STATES, 386 U.S. 612 (1967).

BRENNAN, J....

Under The Landrum-Griffin Act amendments enacted in 1959, Section 8(b)(4)(A) of the National Labor Relations Act became Section 8(b)(4)(B) and Section 8(e) was added. The questions here are whether, in the circumstances of this case, the Metropolitan District Council of Philadelphia and Vicinity of the United Brotherhood of Carpenters and Joiners of America, AFL-CIO (hereafter the Union), committed the unfair labor practices prohibited by Section 8(e) and 8(b)(4)(B).

Frouge Corporation, a Bridgeport, Connecticut, concern, was the general contractor on a housing project in Philadelphia. Frouge had a collective bargaining agreement with the Carpenters' International Union under which Frouge agreed to be bound by the rules and regulations agreed upon by local unions with contractors in areas in which Frouge had jobs. Frouge was therefore subject to the provisions of a collective bargaining agreement between the Union and an organization of Philadelphia contractors, the General Building Contractors Association, Inc. A sentence in a provision of that agreement entitled Rule 17 provides that "... No member of this District Council will handle...any

doors ... which have been fitted prior to being furnished on the job ..." Frouge's Philadelphia project called for 3,600 doors. Customarily, before the doors could be hung on such projects, "blank" or "blind" doors would be mortised for the knob, routed for the hinges, and beveled to make them fit between jambs. These are tasks traditionally performed in the Philadelphia area by the carpenters employed on the jobsite. However, precut and prefitted doors ready to hang may be purchased from door manufacturers. Although Frouge's contract and job specifications did not call for premachined doors, and "blank" or "blind" doors could have been ordered, Frouge contracted for the purchase of premachined doors from a Pennsylvania door manufacturer which is a member of the National Woodwork Manufacturers Association, petitioner in No. 110 and respondent in No. 111. The Union ordered its carpenter members not to hang the doors when they arrived at the jobsite. Frouge thereupon withdrew the prefabricated doors and substituted "blank" doors which were fitted and cut by its carpenters on the jobsite.

The National Woodwork Manufacturers Association filed charges with the National Labor Relations Board against the Union alleging that by including

continued

the "will not handle" sentence of Rule 17 in the collective bargaining agreement the Union committed the unfair labor practice under Section 8(e) of entering into an "agreement … whereby the employer … agrees to cease or refrain from handling … any of the products of any other employer …," and alleging further that in enforcing the sentence against Frouge, the Union committed the unfair labor practice under Section 8(b)(4)(B) of "forcing or requiring any person to cease using … the products of any other … manufacturer…."

The Court of Appeals for the Seventh Circuit held that the "will not handle" agreement violated Section 8(e) without regard to any "primary" or "secondary" objective, and remanded to the Board with instructions to enter an order accordingly.

The Landrum-Griffin Act amendments of 1959 were adopted only to close various loopholes in the application of Section 8(b)(4)(A) which had been exposed in Board and court decisions….

This loophole closing measure … did not expand the type of conduct which Section 8(b)(4)(A) condemned. Although the language of Section 8(e) is sweeping, it closely tracks that of Section 8(b)(4)(A), and just as the latter and its successor Section 8(b)(4)(B) did not reach employees' activity to pressure their employer to preserve for themselves work traditionally done by them, Section 8(e) does not prohibit agreements made and maintained for that purpose….

However, provisos were added to Section 8(e) to preserve the *status quo* in the construction industry, and exempt the garment industry from the prohibitions of Sections 8(e) and 8(b)(4)(B). This action of the Congress is strong confirmation that Congress meant that both Sections 8(e) and 8(b)(4)(B) reach only secondary pressures. If the body of Section 8(e) applies only to secondary activity, the garment industry proviso is a justifiable exception which allows what the legislative history shows it was designed to allow, secondary pressures to counteract the effects of sweatshop conditions in an industry with a highly integrated process of production between jobbers, manufacturers, contractors and subcontractors. First, this motivation for the proviso sheds light on the central theme of the body of Section 8(e), from which the proviso is an exception. Second, if the body of that provision and Section 8(b)(4)(B) were construed to prohibit primary agreements and their maintenance, such as those concerning work preser-

vation, the proviso would have the highly unlikely effect, unjustified in any of the statute's history, of permitting garment workers, but garment workers only, to preserve their jobs against subcontracting or prefabrication by such agreements and by strikes and boycotts to enforce them. Similarly, the construction industry proviso, which permits "hot cargo" agreements only for jobsite work, would have the curious and unsupported result of allowing the construction worker to make agreements preserving his traditional tasks against jobsite prefabrication and subcontracting, but not against non-jobsite prefabrication and subcontracting. On the other hand, if the heart of Section 8(e) is construed to be directed only to secondary activities, the construction proviso becomes, as it was intended to be, a measure designed to allow agreements pertaining to certain secondary activities on the construction site because of the close community of interests there, but to ban secondary-objective agreements concerning non-jobsite work, in which respect the construction industry is no different from any other. The provisos are therefore substantial probative support that primary work preservation agreements were not to be within the ban of Section 8(e)….

The Woodwork Manufacturers Association and *amici* who support its position advance several reasons, grounded in economic and technological factors, why "will not handle" clauses should be invalid in all circumstances. Those arguments are addressed to the wrong branch of government. It may be that the time has come for a reevaluation of the basic content of collective bargaining as contemplated by the federal legislation. But that is for Congress….

The determination whether the "will not handle" sentence of Rule 17 and its enforcement violated Section 8(e) and 8(b)(4)(B) cannot be made without an inquiry into whether, under all the surrounding circumstances, the Union's objective was preservation of work for Frouge's employees, or whether the agreements and boycott were tactically calculated to satisfy union objectives elsewhere. Were the latter the case, Frouge, the boycotting employer, would be a neutral bystander, and the agreement or boycott would, within the intent of Congress, become secondary. There need not be an actual dispute with the boycotted employer, here the door manufacturer, for the activity to fall within this category, so long as the tactical object of the agreement and its maintenance is

continued

that employer, or benefits to other than the boycotting employees or other employees of the primary employer thus making the agreement or boycott secondary in its aim. The touchstone is whether the agreement or its maintenance is addressed to the labor relations of the contracting employer *vis-à-vis* his own employees. This will not always be a simple test to apply. But "[h]owever difficult the task of drawing of lines more nice than obvious, the statute compels the task."

That the "will not handle" provision was not an unfair labor practice in this case is clear. The finding of the Trial Examiner, adopted by the Board, was that the objective of the sentence was preservation of work traditionally performed by the jobsite carpenters. This finding is supported by substantial evidence, and therefore the Union's making of the "will not handle" agreement was not a violation of Section 8(e).

Similarly, the Union's maintenance of the provision was not a violation of Section 8(b)(4)(B). The Union refused to hang prefabricated doors whether

or not they bore a union label, and even refused to install prefabricated doors manufactured off the jobsite by members of the Union. This and other substantial evidence supported the finding that the conduct of the Union on the Frouge jobsite related solely to preservation of the traditional tasks of the jobsite carpenters.

The judgment is affirmed in No. 110, and reversed in No. 111.

It is so ordered.

Case Questions

1. Define the term "hot cargo clause".
2. Why was Section 8(e) of the Landrum-Griffin Act made law?
3. What test did the Supreme Court set out for determining whether the "will not handle" clause and its enforcement was in violation of Section 8(e) and Section 8(b)(4)(B)?
4. State the findings of the Supreme Court concerning the objective of the union's "will not handle" clause.

SECTION 61: DAMAGES FROM BOYCOTTS AND PICKETING

In addition to unfair labor practice and injunction procedures providing redress against illegal boycotts and for picketing activities, the Labor Management Relations Act of 1947 provides for damage suits in the federal courts. Section 303 makes it unlawful for any labor organization to engage in conduct prohibited by Section 8(b)(4) of the National Labor Relations Act, which includes all the boycott and picketing activities previously discussed in this chapter.

Suits for damages, with judgments and costs enforceable against the union's assets but not against individual members, are specifically permitted by Section 303.

In the *Wilhelm* case presented in Section 58 of this chapter, a construction company successfully brought a Section 303 private action against the carpenters union for damages arising from violation of Section 8(b)(4).[39]

CHAPTER QUESTIONS AND PROBLEMS

1. Distinguish between the strike and the boycott and between the boycott and the picketing weapons in labor disputes.
2. Can secondary activity be found at a single building construction site? On a primary employer's own property?
3. To what extent may consumer picketing be carried out legally?
4. What are the dual objectives of Section 8(b)(4) of the NLRA?

---

[39] *F. A. Wilhelm Construction Co., Inc., v. Carpenters,* 293 F.3d 935 (6th Cir. 2002).

5. What was the purpose of including unfair labor practices for labor organizations in the NLRA in 1947?

6. Does Section 8(b)(3) regarding a labor organization's duty to bargain collectively impose any more duties than Section 8(a)(5) regarding an employer's duty to bargain collectively? Explain.

7. The Wine and Liquor Store Employees Union had a union security clause in its collective bargaining agreement with Oz Liquor Company. The agreement provided that when an employment vacancy occurs, the company must give the union 24 hours to produce a member for the job. After 24 hours, the company could hire a person "provided such person makes application to, and is accepted by the union." Oz further agreed to employ only "employees in good standing with the union," with the union being the "sole judge of the good standing of its members." The company also agreed to discharge any employee upon receipt of notice that the employee was "no longer a member in good standing in the union." The company refused to discharge certain employees who the union claimed were not members in good standing. The union sought arbitration to enforce the terms of the collective bargaining contract. Oz Liquor, however, petitioned the NLRB to rule the union security clause unlawful under Sections 8(b)(1) and (2).

    How should the Board decide this case? [*Distillery Workers*, 261 NLRB 1070, 110 LRRM 1184]

8. J. R. Stevenson Corporation was engaged in a large construction project for which it needed intrasite and intersite truck drivers belonging to the Teamsters Union. Part of the collective bargaining agreement with the Teamsters required that Stevenson provide a heated trailer with a telephone at the site and hire a shop steward for the site. Stevenson paid Arpod Korchma $20,000 per year to serve as shop steward. As shop steward, however, Korchma remained inside the heated trailer during working hours, emerging only to check the union cards of drivers as they entered the site gate. Stevenson eventually objected to the presence of Korchma, claiming that it had no use for him and that he performed no work or traditional Teamster duties. Stevenson charged the Teamsters with featherbedding in violation of Section 8(b)(6). The union denied that it was engaging in this practice.

    What factors must the Board consider in deciding a featherbedding case? What was the result in this case? [Teamster Local 456, 212 NLRB 968, 87 LRRM 1101]

9. Jimmy Hunter, business agent for Pipefitters Local 101, arranged a meeting with Ben Jenkins, the president of Interstate Plumbing and Heating Corporation. He told Jenkins that he had in his possession authorization cards signed by a "clear majority" of Interstate's shop employees, appointing Local 101 as their exclusive bargaining agent. Hunter asked Jenkins to recognize the union immediately because it would "save [Jenkins] a lot of grief" and they could "get down to business." Jenkins said that he would bargain with Hunter only if a fair election were held with secret ballot voting. Hunter left Jenkins's office and supervised the immediate formation of a picket line in front of Interstate's shop. After some five weeks, no election had been requested, but the picketing continued. Jenkins petitioned the NLRB to stop the picketing. The union claimed that the pickets were not violent and merely informed the public that Interstate refused to negotiate with the union.

    Is this picketing lawful under the NLRA? Decide. [Sheet Metal Workers, 260 NLRB 1332, 110 LRRM 1010]

10. The members of Teamsters Local 391 established a picket line immediately upon commencement of a lawful strike against their employer, Seaboard Foods, Inc., of Rocky Mount, North Carolina. After patrolling in front of the plant, the union members were arrested for violating a Rocky Mount

ordinance prohibiting picketing on a public way without a permit. The ordinance required a 72-hour advance notice for the permit. The permit could be denied by the city manager or police chief if the picketing would "create hazardous traffic conditions" or "disturb the convenience of the public." The ordinance also placed specific limitations on picketing, allowed only ten picketers, required single-file processions only on the sidewalk, and allowed picket signs no larger than two feet. After failing in their attempt to secure a permit, the members of Local 391 were arrested again when they resumed picketing.

The union challenged the Rocky Mount ordinance as unconstitutional. The city defended its ordinance as necessary to protect the safety and welfare of the citizens. Decide. [*Teamsters Local 391 v. Rocky Mount*, 109 LRRM 3114 (4th Cir.)]

11. Local 182, International Union of Electrical Workers, went on strike at the General Electric (GE) plant in Hickory, North Carolina, on October 24. The union immediately established a picket line in front of the plant and bordering a major intersection. One of the roads served as the principal approach route for a neighboring local hospital. The presence of the picketers snarled traffic and delayed medical personnel bound for the hospital. Employees at GE who chose to work had their cars damaged and were subjected to thrown rocks and verbal insults as they passed through the group of 79 strikers. On November 3, GE obtained a preliminary injunction in state court enjoining Local 182 from assaulting GE employees, damaging property, and obstructing public roads and plant gates. The injunction also prohibited mass picketing by limiting the number of pickets at any one time to six.

The union claimed the state court had no power to grant this injunction because labor activity is under the exclusive jurisdiction of the NLRB. GE disagreed and wanted the injunction continued permanently in the event of any future labor strike.

May the state court grant this injunction? If so, may GE extend the injunction to cover future disputes? [*General Electric v. Local 182*, 106 LRRM 2191 (N.C. Ct. App.)]

12. Arlie Heald, business agent for Local 265 (IBEW), had been told by Roger Trautwein, president of RP&M Electric Company, that RP&M might be interested in signing a collective bargaining agreement with the union for its employees. After several attempts by Heald to begin negotiations with RP&M, Trautwein told him that the company was no longer interested. The union did not file a Section 9(c) recognition petition on behalf of the RP&M employees, but Heald did send a letter to Trautwein citing the "substandard wages, hours, and working conditions" of the RP&M employees. The union stated in the letter that it recognized the right of RP&M to be nonunion. However, the union asked Trautwein to pay his employees "union scale wages" and offer working conditions similar to those secured by the union. If RP&M did not comply with this request, Heald promised to inform the public through picketing of the substandard employment conditions at RP&M. For two months, pickets from Local 265 patrolled RP&M jobsites with signs stating, "RP&M Electric does not pay Union scale wages," which caused some disruption of work.

RP&M filed unfair labor practice charges with the NLRB and claimed that the union violated Section 8(b)(7) by picketing for recognition. The union defended its action as informational picketing sanctioned under Section 8(b)(7) of the NLRA.

What factors should the NLRB weigh when deciding this case? Is Local 265's picketing lawful? Decide. [*NLRB v. Electrical Workers Local 265*, 102 LRRM 1694 (8th Cir.)]

13. Ashton Company was the general contractor on a construction project for American Smelting and Refining Company. Ashton had received objections from members of Local 741 of the Plumbers Union when it

designated that the installation of all process piping, including air and water pipes, was to be performed by members of the Laborers International Union. After the plumbers began to picket the construction site, the dispute was taken before the NLRB pursuant to Section 10(k) of the Act. The Board found that the work should be performed by the Laborers International Union and ruled that the decision of the Impartial Jurisdictional Dispute Board, which had ruled in favor of the Plumbers Union, was not binding on the contractor. After the Board's ruling, the plumbers resumed picketing at the jobsite, causing delays in deliveries and forcing some members of craft unions not to report to work. The pickets demanded that Ashton recognize the ruling of the Impartial Board and award the pipe work to the Plumbers Union.

Ashton Company charged Local 741 with engaging in an unfair labor practice. The union maintained that it had the right to inform other workers and the public about Ashton's refusal to give pipe work to plumbers.

May the union lawfully inform others in this manner? Decide. [*United Ass'n. of Journeyman & Appren. of the Plumbing and Pipefitting Industry*, 259 NLRB No. 123, 109 LRRM 1062]

14. R. H. Drukker & Company, a nonunion general contractor, was engaged to construct a restaurant and adjacent office building on a large site in New Jersey. Drukker completed preliminary work on the Red Lobster Restaurant and had moved some of its excavating equipment to the office building site 500 feet away when pickets arrived from Local 825 of the Operating Engineers. The union established a picket line that covered entrances to both of Drukker's projects. The union's signs claimed that Drukker's employees received less than union wages and endured substandard working conditions but also stated that Local 825 had "no dispute with any other employer at this site."

Although Drukker removed its employees and equipment from the Red Lobster job, the union continued to picket that area. Employees of neutral employers chose not to cross the picket line, halting progress on the Red Lobster job for two weeks. The job superintendent of the Red Lobster site informed Local 825 that Drukker was no longer at that site, and the union withdrew to concentrate its efforts on the office project. Before leaving, however, the union business agent warned that as soon as Drukker returned, so would the pickets. Work by other contractors immediately resumed on the restaurant.

The NLRB ruled that the union had engaged in unlawful activity by picketing the Red Lobster site. Local 825 appealed this ruling to the circuit court. What factors must the circuit court weigh to determine the legality of the union's conduct? Decide. [*NLRB v. Operating Engineers, Local 825*, 108 LRRM 2480 (3d Cir.)]

15. The United Paperworkers International Union engaged in a lawful strike against Duro Paper Bag Company. In furtherance of its dispute with Duro, the union established pickets at two local Kroger Supermarkets. The pickets' signs and handbills announced a "consumer boycott of Duro Paper Bag Co." and urged customers to ask Kroger for boxes or bring their own bags to transport their purchases from the market. On the first day of picketing, 4,300 customers passed through the two stores, but Kroger was only able to furnish 115 customers with boxes before it exhausted its supply. Kroger claimed that it could furnish boxes to only 2.5 percent of its customers. On at least one occasion, a woman abandoned her purchased items at the cash register when her request for a box instead of a Duro bag could not be satisfied. The woman refused to pay and use what she termed "scab bags."

Kroger claimed before the NLRB that the union was engaged in a secondary boycott in violation of Section 8(b)(4)(ii)(B). The union insisted that its picketing activity was legal under the *Tree Fruits* and *Safeco* decisions. Decide. [*Kroger Co. v. NLRB*, 105 LRRM 2897 (6th Cir. 1980). Paperworkers, Local 832, 258 NLRB 67, 108 LRRM 1073]

16. Texaco, Inc., operates a refinery in Anacortes, Washington, and contracts with independent contractors to process a refinery by-product into a commercially usable product at a separate on-site coking unit. Alpha Omega Construction, Inc., was the coking contractor from 1990 through 1995. Texaco awarded the contract to Western Plant Services, Inc., (WPS) on June 1, 1995. To protest the failure of WPS to hire former Omega workers represented by the Oil, Chemical and Atomic Workers (OCAW) union, the union began picketing gates 6 and 7 at the Texaco refinery, gates reserved for WPS's workers and suppliers. Burlington Northern Railroad (BN) had been assigned a separate reserved gate at the BN's spur track. BN was under contract with Texaco to transport the products produced by WPS at the coking facility. Neither BN nor Texaco had a labor dispute with OCAW. However, on June 3 and June 5, an OCAW union member picketed the BN reserved gate area and the main line, respectively, disrupting BN's service under its contract with Texaco to transport products from the coking facility operated by independent contractor WPS. The General Counsel contended that the picketing of the BN reserved gate was secondary picketing in violation of Section 8(b)(4)(B). Because employers other than WPS were working at the facility, the General Counsel contended that *Moore Dry Dock* standards should apply to the common situs picketing. OCAW contended that it was lawful primary situs picketing under the *Steelworkers v. NLRB & Carrier Corp.* decision. Decide. [*OCAW v. Burlington Northern Railroad*, 325 NLRB 45]

LEGALITY OF STRIKES

SECTION 62: TYPES OF STOPPAGES

The strike is perhaps the most potent weapon possessed by labor to force its demands upon an employer. Its usual concomitant is the establishment of a picket line. Sometimes the boycott is simultaneously employed against an especially resistant employer.

The **strike** may generally be defined as a temporary and concerted withdrawal of workers from an employer's service to enforce their demands, the workers retaining a contingent interest in their jobs. The degree to which workers retain a vested or contingent interest in the positions they leave will depend largely upon the purpose of the strike, the means employed to effect the strike, and the success of the employer in securing effective replacements. Interpretations under the National Labor Relations Act have clarified the status of workers engaging in the various forms of strikes. The determination of a striker's status becomes important with respect to deciding questions of reinstatement of workers, awarding of back pay, and deciding questions on the rights of individuals to participate in representation elections.

While the general definition has been given, it is important to distinguish the several forms of strike activity. The **primary strike** involves a withdrawal of a single employer's workers who seek a direct and immediate benefit to themselves. The **secondary strike** involves a withdrawal of another employer's workers who thereby exert pressure on their own employer in the expectation that the employer will, in turn, bring pressure upon an employer with whom the union has a dispute. Thus, the unionized workers of X Company withdraw to force X to bring pressure upon the Y Company with whom the union has an unsettled dispute. The secondary strike has sympathetic elements but is distinguishable from a sympathetic strike in that to fall in the secondary rather than the sympathetic category, the strike in question must be conducted for the direct benefit of the union involved. If the strike is for the direct benefit of some other union and if the strikers secure only an incidental benefit from the strike, then we have a **sympathetic** or **sympathy strike**.

The **general strike** involves work cessation by most, if not all, workers in a particular industry, such as coal or steel, or most, if not all, workers in a particular city. In its widest and most serious application, the workers of an entire nation are involved. European countries have seen more national general strikes, which may be traced to the broad economic and political character of this strike form. Strongly unified labor employs the general strike for the assertion of strength to protest against adverse industrywide conditions of employment or antilabor legislation. The general strike was restricted by the inclusion in the amended National Labor Relations Act of 1947 of Sections 206–210 on national emergency strikes. Usage of the general strike weapon is not subject to executive action and injunction.

The **sit-down strike** covers a cessation of work by employees without withdrawal from the plant. In a sit-down strike, employees remain at their workstations but machines and tools remain idle. The **slowdown** is a variant of the sit-down. In a slowdown, there is no withdrawal from the workstation and the cessation of work is only partial. In a **partial strike**, only some of the workers leave their workstations. This technique has been employed successfully in large-scale firms when a union selects a vulnerable department or departments and strikes only in those areas. No merchandise can enter or leave, especially if outside unions give sympathetic aid by respecting picket lines established at the receiving and shipping docks. The bulk of union members continue working and draw their pay, as long as the employer does not lock them out.

The **wildcat strike** is one for which the parent union disclaims responsibility. Presumably, or in fact, it is unauthorized and generally is in breach of a collective agreement.

A **jurisdictional strike** involves a dispute between two or more unions. In order to compel the employer to take sides, one or both unions instigate a strike. New materials and new production methods, especially in the building trades, often precipitate controversy between two or more unions, where each seeks to obtain work assignments for its own members.

A **whipsaw strike** is a strike against one strategically situated employer in order to weaken the opposition of other employers or force them to capitulate, one company being played off against other companies. The *Brown Food Stores* case, in Chapter 5, is an example.

The National Labor Relations Board lumps all of the above strike variants into three broad groupings. The first may be termed the economic strike; the second, the employer unfair labor practice strike; and the third, the union unfair labor practice strike. The **economic strike** is concerned with demands regarding hours of work, wages, and working conditions. The **employer unfair labor practice strike** involves a strike by employees that is called in retaliation against unfair employer practice. (See Chapter 5.) These unfair practices include the denial to workers of the right to bargain collectively, discrimination against union members and other proscribed interferences with legitimate collective activity. The third type of strike under the National Labor Relations Act is designated a **union unfair labor practice strike** or an **unprotected activity strike**. Activities made unfair by the amendments of 1947 and 1959, activities in violation of no-strike agreements, and other strikes that remove the strikers from the protection of the law will be discussed in the following sections to show how the rights of strikers differ in each type of situation.

SECTION 63: EMPLOYER UNFAIR LABOR PRACTICE STRIKES

In a strike by lawful, nonviolent methods to protest an unfair labor practice committed by the struck employer, strikers are protected from discharge or from the loss of employment by replacements. Replacements may be hired to fill the strikers' jobs, but only for the period until the strikers seek to return to work.

The *Mastro Plastics* case, reported next, established the right of employees striking against employer violations of the NLRA to reinstatement with limited back pay rights. Under *Mastro Plastics*, back pay was to be paid for the period of time after the striking employees made an unconditional offer to return to work, which was ignored by the employer. This remedy was sustained notwithstanding an agreement prohibiting strikes and also the failure of the employees to observe obligations that would otherwise have been in effect except for the employer's unfair labor practices.

In *John Cuneo, Inc., v. NLRB*,[1] the court of appeals endorsed the Board's holding that even though a strike began as an economic strike for recognition of the union, it was converted to an unfair labor practice strike when the company engaged in widespread unfair labor practices following the union's bid for recognition based on authorization cards. The precedent decision was the Board's *Drug Package Co.*[2] ruling, which held that striking employees are entitled to reinstatement as unfair labor practice strikers when an employer engages in unfair practices that undermine the process for choosing union representatives.

---

[1] 681 F.2d 11 (D.C. Cir. 1982).
[2] 228 NLRB 108 (1977).

| CASE 7.1 | MASTRO PLASTICS CORP. V. NLRB |
| | SUPREME COURT OF THE UNITED STATES, 350 U.S. 270 (1956). |

[Mastro Plastics Corporation and its sister corporation F. A. Reeds Company (Mastro or petitioners) manufactured plastic parts for musical instruments at a plant in New York City. Their employees were represented by Carpenters Local 3127. In August 1950, Local 65 of the Warehouse Workers Union began a campaign to represent Mastro/F. A. Reeds employees. Mastro bitterly opposed the movement, believing Local 65 to be communist-controlled. Believing that the Carpenters were too weak to cope successfully with Local 65, Mastro asked the Carpenters to transfer their bargaining rights to Local 318, International Brotherhood of Paper Mill Workers, AFL. When the Carpenters declined to do so, Mastro selected a committee of employees to visit Local 318, obtain membership cards, and seek members for that union. The cards were distributed during working hours, and Mastro paid the employees for time spent in the campaign, including attendance at a meeting of Local 318. Mastro's officers and supervisors instructed employees to sign these cards and indicated that those refusing to do so would be "out."

On September 28, Local 65 filed with the NLRB its petition for certification as bargaining representative. On October 24, Local 318 intervened in the representation proceedings and asked that it be certified. However, many employees revoked their applications for membership in Local 318 and reaffirmed their adherence to the Carpenters. This was followed on October 31 by the Carpenters' refusal to consent to an election on the ground that petitioners had unlawfully assisted Local 318 in the campaign.

On November 10, 1950, Mastro's president discharged Frank Ciccone because of his activity in support of the Carpenters and his opposition to Local 318. The discharge precipitated a strike. There was no disorder, but the plant was shut down until December 11; and it was March 9, 1951, before the Carpenters, on behalf of Mastro employees, made an unconditional request to return to work. Mastro ignored that request, and neither Ciccone nor any of the other 76 striking employees were reinstated.]

BURTON, J...

This case presents two principal questions: (1) whether in the collective bargaining contract before us, the union's undertaking "to refrain from engaging in any strike or work stoppage during the term of this agreement" waives not only the employees' rights to strike for economic benefits but also their right to strike solely against unfair labor practices of their employers, and (2) whether Par. 8(d) of the National Labor Relations Act, as amended, deprives individuals of their status as employees if, within the waiting period prescribed by Par. 8(d)(4), they engage in a strike solely against unfair labor practices of their employers. For the reason hereafter stated, we answer each in the negative.

Petitioners admitted that they had discharged the employees in question and had not rehired them. They denied, however, that in so doing they had committed any unfair labor practices. Their first affirmative defense was that the waiver of the right to strike, expressed by their employees in their collective bargaining contract, applied to strikes not only for economic benefits but to any and all strikes by such employees, including strikes directed solely against unfair labor practices of the employer.

Petitioners' other principal defense was that the existing strike began during the statutory waiting period initiated by the employees' request for modifications of the contract and that, by virtue of Section 8(d) of the Act, the strikers had lost their status as employees. That defense turned upon petitioners' interpretation of Section 8(d), applying it not only to strikes for economic benefits but to any and all strikes occurring during the waiting period, including strikes solely against unfair labor practices of the employer.

The trial examiner made findings of fact sustaining the complaint and recommended that petitioners be ordered to cease and desist from the interference complained of and be required to offer Ciccone and the 76 other discharged employees full reinstatement, together with back pay for Ciccone from November 10, 1950, and for the other employees from March 9, 1951. With minor modifications, the Board adopted the examiner's findings and conclusions and issued the recommended order.

Because of the importance of the issues in industrial relations and in the interpretation of the National Labor Relations Act, as amended, we granted certiorari. 348 U.S. 910.

continued

Apart from the issues raised by petitioners' affirmative defenses, the proceedings reflect a flagrant example of interference by the employers with the expressly protected right of their employees to select their own bargaining representative. The findings disclose vigorous efforts by the employers to influence and even to coerce their employees to abandon the Carpenters as their bargaining representatives and to substitute Local 318. Accordingly, unless petitioners sustain at least one of their affirmative defenses, they must suffer the consequences of their unfair labor practices violating Section 8(a)(1), (2) and (3) of the Act, as amended.

In the absence of some contractual or statutory provision to the contrary, petitioners' unfair labor practices provide adequate ground for the orderly strike that occurred here. Under those circumstances, the striking employees do not lose their status and are entitled to reinstatement with back pay, even if replacements for them have been made. Failure of the Board to enjoin petitioners' illegal conduct or failure of the Board to sustain the right to strike against that conduct would seriously undermine the primary objectives of the Labor Act. While we assume that the employees, by explicit contractual provision, could have waived their right to strike against such unfair labor practices and that Congress, by explicit statutory provision, could have deprived strikers, under the circumstances of this case, of their status as employees, the questions before us are whether or not such a waiver was made by the Carpenters in their 1949–1950 contract and whether or not such a deprivation of status was enacted by Congress in Section 8(d) of the Act, as amended in 1947....

As neither the collective bargaining contract nor Section 8(d) of the National Labor Relations Act, as amended, stands in the way, the judgment of the Court of Appeals is

Affirmed.

Case Questions

1. What unfair labor practices did the employer commit?
2. Was the agreement a strike deterrent? Why or why not?
3. What did the Court find as to the legality of the union conduct?

SECTION 64: PERMANENT REPLACEMENT OF STRIKERS

Since the 1938 Supreme Court decision in *NLRB v. Mackay Radio & Telegraph Co.*,[3] an employer has been allowed to hire permanent replacements for economic strikers. In dicta in Justice Roberts's majority opinion in *Mackay*, he stated that it was not "an unfair labor practice to replace the striking employees with others in an effort to carry on the business."[4] Additionally, he stated that it was not an unfair labor practice "to reinstate only so many of the strikers as there were vacant places to be filled."[5] Under *Mackay*, then, an employer can refuse to reinstate strikers at the conclusion of an economic strike if it has replaced them with permanent employees.

LIMITATIONS ON THE EMPLOYER

Restrictions, limitations, and special rules are applied to the general *Mackay* rule allowing permanent replacements.

---

[3] 304 U.S. 333 (1938).

[4] *Id.* at 345.

[5] *Id.* at 346.

REINSTATEMENT RIGHTS FOR ECONOMIC STRIKERS.   Section 2(3) of the NLRA provides that an individual whose work has ceased as a consequence of a labor dispute continues to be an employee if the individual has not obtained regular and substantially similar employment. If at the conclusion of a strike an employer refuses to reinstate striking employees to vacant positions, the effect is to discourage employees from exercising their rights to organize and strike guaranteed by Sections 7 and 13 of the NLRA. In *NLRB v. Fleetwood Trailer Company, Inc.,*[6] the Supreme Court dealt with the question of an employer's obligation to rehire economic strikers who unconditionally applied for reinstatement at the end of a strike if no work existed for them at that time. The employer contended in *Fleetwood* that the right of strikers to jobs must be judged as of the date they apply for reinstatement, which was August 20; because no jobs were available on that date, the employer argued, their requests were properly rejected. On October 8 and 16, the employer hired six new employees for jobs that six strikers were qualified to fill. The six strikers were ultimately reinstated by December 14. The Supreme Court ruled that the six strikers should have been rehired as soon as jobs became available and that therefore the employer had violated Sections 8(a)(1) and (3) of the NLRA by hiring six new employees rather than reinstating the strikers in October. On the basis of the Supreme Court's decision in *Fleetwood*, the NLRB set forth a comprehensive rule on the reinstatement rights of economic strikers in its *Laidlaw Corporation* decision.[7] The *Laidlaw* rule states that

> economic strikers who unconditionally apply for reinstatement at a time when their positions are filled by permanent replacements: (1) remain employees; (2) are entitled to full reinstatement upon departure of replacements unless they have in the meantime acquired regular and substantially equivalent employment, or the employer can sustain his burden of proof that the failure to offer full reinstatement was for legitimate and substantial business reasons....[8]

In *NLRB v. Oregon Steel Mills, Inc.,*[9] the employer placed the names of former strikers on a preferential reinstatement list after the union made an unconditional offer to end a strike at the steel mills. The employer reinstated a number of employees from this list. However, it then utilized the services of a temporary employment agency to provide temporary workers to do other work formerly done by strikers instead of returning available qualified former strikers from the preferential hiring list. The Board and the U.S. Court of Appeals for the Ninth Circuit placed the burden of proof on the employer to demonstrate a legitimate and substantial business reason for refusal to reinstate the strikers to available positions, and they determined the burden had not been met. The Board held, and the court of appeals affirmed, that it was a violation of Section 8(a)(3) and inherently destructive of employee rights for the employer to utilize a temporary service agency to supply workers when qualified former strikers were available on the preferential reinstatement list.

---

[6] 389 U.S. 375 (1967).

[7] 171 NLRB 1336 (1968).

[8] *Id.* at 1369–70.

[9] 47 F.3d 1536 (9th Cir. 1995).

As set forth previously, under the *Mackay* rule, employers may refuse to reinstate strikers at the conclusion of an economic strike if it has replaced them with permanent employees. But under the *Laidlaw* rule, economic strikers have certain reinstatement rights. In representation election situations, employers may have occasion to address employees about the employer's right to hire replacements under *Mackay*. However, election results against union representation will be set aside if the employer's agent tells employees in a campaign speech before an election, without other explanation, that "union strikers can lose their jobs" and that "you could end up losing your job by being displaced with a permanent worker." Such statements have a coercive effect in violation of Section 8(a)(1).[10] In such a context, the employer must also reference the *Laidlaw* right to return to the job.

Special Rule for "Unfair Labor Practice Strikers." Unfair labor practice strikers are individuals who go on strike to protest an unfair labor practice of an employer, as opposed to going on strike for better wages, hours, and working conditions and being classified as "economic strikers." If an employer fires a union leader because of the leader's union activity—a Section 8(a)(1) and (3) unfair labor practice—and the discharge precipitates a strike, the employer may hire replacement workers, but only for the period until the strikers return to work. When the strikers protesting the unfair labor practice make an unconditional request to return to work, the employer may not continue to employ the replacement workers in preference to the strikers. Should the employer do so, it would be liable to pay the unfair labor practice strikers back wages for the period of time after its failure to reinstate them.[11]

In *Poly-America, Inc., v. NLRB*,[12] 19 employees walked off the job at the company's plastic products manufacturing plant in Grand Prairie, Texas, on November 14 over a pay issue relating to a meeting with the company's owner on November 6. Since the walkout was over an economic issue, the strike thus began as an economic strike. The evidence showed that the company discharged the 19 economic strikers on the night of November 14, not allowing them to return to work after their walkout, before any replacement hires were made. The discharge constituted an unfair labor practice under Section 8(a)(1) and 8(a)(3) of the Act and had the effect of converting the strike from an economic strike to an unfair labor practice strike for which reinstatement with back pay is an appropriate remedy.

Rejection of Preference for Trainees over Returning Strikers. In *Eastern Air Lines, Inc., v. Airline Pilots Association International*,[13] the U.S. Court of Appeals for the Eleventh Circuit dealt with the question of whether Eastern was obligated to reinstate striking pilots prior to awarding pilot positions to new-hire pilots

---

[10] Baddour, Inc., 303 NLRB 275 (1991).

[11] *Mastro Plastics Corp. v. NLRB*, 350 U.S. 270 (1956).

[12] 206 F.3d 465 (5th Cir. 2001).

[13] 920 F.2d 722 (11th Cir. 1990).

who had not completed all requirements to fly revenue flights. The striking pilots had made unconditional offers to return to work by the end of the strike on November 22, 1989. As of that date, at least 227 new-hire replacement pilots remained in training, not having obtained certificates from the FAA permitting them to fly regular revenue flights. Eastern contended that the new-hire pilots, who were still in training, were permanent employees and as such should not be displaced by returning strikers. The court of appeals ruled that the trainees were not permanent replacements. The court was reluctant to support Eastern's position because giving preference to trainees over returning strikers discouraged employees from exercising their rights to organize and to strike and undermined the preservation of the employer-employee relationship both during and after the strike. Accordingly, the court rejected Eastern's preference for trainees over returning strikers and remanded the case to the district court for further proceedings.

EMPLOYER CONTRACTUAL OBLIGATIONS TO REPLACEMENT WORKERS. In *Belnap, Inc., v. Hale*,[14] the employer hired "permanent" replacements for striking employees. Later, as part of a strike settlement agreement with the union, the employer agreed to reinstate the strikers, and the replaced employees were laid off. These employees sued Belnap, Inc., in a state court to recover damages for misrepresentation and breach of contract. The Supreme Court held that the causes of action in state court of the replacement workers who were laid off at the end of the strike were not preempted by the NLRA. However, in the majority opinion, the Court suggested an approach for employers that would allow the employer to call the replacements "permanent" and yet allow the employer to make a strike settlement with the union, if expedient, that would reinstate strikers and lead to the layoff of the replacement workers. The Supreme Court formulation suggests that employers hiring "permanent" replacements could condition their offering of permanent employment, subject only to settlement with the union in question and/or a Board unfair labor practice order directing reinstatement of strikers. The Court said such a conditional offer would not render the replacements temporary employees. And should the employer totally prevail in the strike, the employer may keep the replacements if it chooses to do so. Thus, the potential for "permanency" exists. The Court stated in regard to the conditional offers:

> We perceive no substantial impact on the availability of settlement of economic or unfair labor practice strikes if the employer is careful to protect itself against suits like this in the course of contracting with strike replacements. Its risk of liability if it discharges replacements pursuant to a settlement or to a Board order would then be minimal....[15]

In the Board's *Jones Plastic & Engineering Co. (Camden Division) and United Steelworkers*[16] decision, the employer hired replacement workers during a strike. Subsequently, the union made an unconditional offer to return to work on behalf

---

[14] 463 U.S. 491 (1983).

[15] *Id.* at 505, 506.

[16] 351 NLRB No. 11 (2007).

of all striking employees. The employer responded that it had a full complement of permanent replacement employees and that returning strikers would be placed on a preferential recall list. The status of the replacement workers determined the outcome of this case before the Board. The replacements were required to sign a statement stating that they were "permanent replacement[s]," but that they could be "terminated ... at any time, with or without cause." The statement then stated, "I further understand that my employment may be terminated as a result of a strike settlement agreement .... or by order [of] the National Labor Relations Board." The three-member Board majority believed that the at-will disclaimer in the first part of the signed statement did not detract from the otherwise valid showing of permanent replacement status. The majority concluded that the employer did not violate the act by refusing to reinstate the striking employees immediately. The two dissenting Board members believed that although the employer used the terms **permanent replacement,** it undercut that term by failing to give the replacements assurances that they had any rights vis-á-vis the strikers and that the evidence failed to support a finding that the employer and the replacements shared an understanding that the replacements were permanent.

OTHER DECISIONS RESTRICTING CERTAIN EMPLOYER TACTICS. The Supreme Court dealt with creative incentives extended by employers to induce striking employees to return to work in two other major cases. In *NLRB v. Erie Resistor Corp.,*[17] the Supreme Court upheld the Board's decision prohibiting employers from granting super seniority to strike replacements and strike crossovers (striking employees who later crossed over the picket line to return to work before the termination of the strike) because of the damage super seniority would do to the right to strike and the future bargaining relationship of the parties.

In *NLRB v. Great Dane Trailers, Inc.,*[18] the Supreme Court upheld the Board's decision that an employer's payment of vacation benefits to replacements, crossovers, and nonstrikers but not to strikers violated the Act because of its destructive effect on the right to strike. The Court stated that paying accrued benefits to one group while announcing the extinction of the same benefits to another group surely would have the effect of discouraging present or future concerted activities.

REINSTATEMENT RIGHTS OF FULL-TERM STRIKERS VERSUS JUNIOR NONSTRIKERS

In *TWA v. Independent Federation of Flight Attendants* [IFFA], presented in this section, the Supreme Court dealt with the issue of whether senior flight attendants who unconditionally offered to return to work at the end of a strike may displace junior flight attendants who crossed picket lines to work during the strike. TWA argued that it would be anomalous to require crossovers to be displaced when

---

[17] 373 U.S. 221 (1963).

[18] 388 U.S. 26 (1967).

newly hired, permanent employees cannot be displaced under the *Mackay* decision. The Court accepted this view of the *Mackay* decision, holding that crossovers need not be displaced in order to reinstate more senior full-term strikers. The *TWA* decision adds a new device for employers to use to break a strike. The legal rights of employers to promise employees who refrain from participating in a strike or who return to work during a strike that they will not be displaced from desirable jobs at the end of the strike by more senior striking workers gives employers a potent new weapon that can be threatened at the bargaining table or utilized in economic conflict should a strike ensue. With the risk of losing their positions to permanent replacements or to junior crossover employees, senior employees may be very reluctant to support a strike.

Loss of Recognition as a Result of Hiring Permanent Replacements

In *NLRB v. Curtin Matheson Scientific, Inc.,*[19] the Supreme Court dealt with the question of whether the NLRB, in evaluating an employer's claim that the employer had a reasonable basis for doubting a union's majority support, must presume that the permanent employees hired to replace the strikers oppose the union. On May 25, when the bargaining unit consisted of 27 employees, the union began an economic strike. Five employees immediately crossed the picket line. On June 25, the employer hired 29 replacement workers for the 22 strikers. The union ended its strike on July 20. On that date, the employer notified the union that it doubted that the union was supported by a majority of the employees in the unit, and it withdrew recognition from the union. As of July 20, the bargaining unit consisted of 29 strikers (not currently working), 25 replacement workers, and 5 crossover employees. The Board reversed the ALJ's determination that the employer had a reasonably based good faith doubt of the union's majority status, holding that it would not use any presumptions with respect to replacement workers' union sentiments, but would instead take a case-by-case approach and require additional evidence of lack of union support. The Supreme Court upheld the Board's approach because the employer's antiunion presumption could allow an employer to eliminate a union in its entirety merely by hiring a sufficient number of replacements and thereby avoid good faith bargaining over a strike settlement.[20]

While the *Curtin Matheson* decision went against the employer's mandatory, antiunion presumption, nevertheless an employer can rebut the presumption of majority support of a union after the certification year is over, either by showing that the union in fact lacks majority support or by demonstrating a sufficient objective basis for doubting the union's majority status.[21] The hiring of a significant number of permanent replacements under the *Mackay* rule may still ultimately undermine a union's majority status.

---

[19] 494 U.S. 775 (1990).

[20] *Id.* at 1553.

[21] *Id.* at 1549–1550.

| CASE 7.2 | TWA v. IFFA
SUPREME COURT OF THE UNITED STATES, 489 U.S. 426 (1989). |

[At the conclusion of a strike between TWA and the flight attendants' union, IFFA, TWA refused to displace permanent replacements or junior nonstriking attendants (crossover employees) with senior full-term strikers, many of whom were therefore left without an opportunity to return to work. The IFFA filed the instant action contending that, assuming the strike was economic, the full-term strikers were entitled to displace the newly hired replacements and the less senior crossover attendants under the terms of the pre-strike collective bargaining agreement. The district court denied relief for the most part, but the court of appeals, relying on judicial interpretation of the National Labor Relations Act (NLRA), reversed the lower court's ruling that the more senior full-term strikers could not displace junior crossovers. The question considered before the Supreme Court was whether an employer is required to lay off junior crossover employees in order to reinstate more senior full-term strikers at the conclusion of a strike.]

O'CONNOR, J....

I.

We have observed in the past that carefully drawn analogies from the federal common labor law developed under the NLRA may be helpful in deciding cases under the RLA. Thus, as in this case, those lower courts that have examined the reinstatement rights of strikers under the RLA have turned to NLRA precedents for guidance.

We first considered the reinstatement rights of strikers under the NLRA in *NLRB v. Mackay Radio & Telegraph Co.*, 304 U.S. 333 (1938). In *Mackay Radio*, radio and telegraph operators working in the San Francisco offices of a national telecommunications firm went on strike. In order to continue operations, the employer brought employees from its other offices to fill the strikers' places. At the conclusion of the strike, the striking operators sought to displace their replacements in order to return to work. We held that it was not an unfair labor practice under § 8 of the NLRA for the employer to have replaced the striking employees with others "in an effort to carry on the business," or to have refused to discharge the replacements in order to make room for the strikers at the conclusion of the strike. *Id.* at 345–346. As we

then observed, "[t]he assurance by [the employer] to those who accepted employment during the strike that if they so desired their places might be permanent was not an unfair labor practice nor was it such to reinstate only so many of the strikers as there were vacant places to be filled." *Id.*, at 346. On various occasions we have reaffirmed the holding of *Mackay Radio*....

... Both the RLA and the NLRA protect an employee's right to choose not to strike. 45 U.S.C. § 152 Fourth; 29 U.S.C. § 157, and, thereby, protect employees' rights to "the benefit of their individual decisions not to strike...." Accordingly, in virtually every strike situation there will be some employees who disagree with their union's decision to strike and who cannot be required to abide by that decision. It is the inevitable effect of an employer's use of the economic weapons available during a period of self-help that these differences will be exacerbated and that poststrike resentments may be created. Thus, for example, the employer's right to hire permanent replacements in order to continue operations will inevitably also have the effect of dividing striking employees between those who, fearful of permanently losing their jobs, return to work and those who remain stalwart in the strike. In such a situation, apart from the "pressure on the strikers *as a group* to abandon the strike," to which the dissent refers, a "competition" may arise *among* the striking employees to return to work in order to avoid being displaced by a permanent replacement. Similarly, employee awareness that an employer may decide to transfer working employees to necessary positions previously occupied by more senior striking employees will isolate employees fearful of losing those positions and employees coveting those positions from employees more committed to the strike. Conversely, a policy such as TWA employed here, in creating the incentive for individual strikers to return to work, also "puts pressure on the strikers *as a group* to abandon the strike," *ibid.*, in the same manner that the hiring of permanent replacements does.

To distinguish crossovers from new hires in the manner IFFA proposes would have the effect of penalizing those who decided not to strike in order to benefit those who did. Because permanent replacements need not be discharged at the conclusion of a strike in which the union has been unsuccessful,

continued

a certain number of prestrike employees will find themselves without work. We see no reason why those employees who chose not to gamble on the success of the strike should suffer the consequences when the gamble proves unsuccessful. Requiring junior crossovers, who cannot themselves displace the newly hired permanent replacements, "who rank lowest in seniority," to be displaced by more senior full-term strikers is precisely to visit the consequences of the lost gamble on those who refused to take the risk. While the employer and union in many circumstances may reach a back-to-work agreement that would displace crossovers and new hires or an employer may unilaterally decide to permit such displacement, nothing in the NLRA or the federal common law we have developed under that statute requires such a result. That such agreements are typically one mark of a successful strike is yet another indication that crossovers opted not to gamble; if the strike was successful the advantage gained by declining to strike disappears....

Reversed.

JUSTICE BRENNAN, with whom JUSTICE MARSHALL joins, Dissenting ...

The issue in this case is whether under the ... RLA an employer, in allocating available jobs among members of a bargaining unit at the conclusion of a strike, may discriminate against full-term strikers by giving preference to employees who crossed the picket line to return to work before the strike was over. Because I conclude that such discrimination on the basis of union activity is "inherently destructive" of the right to strike, as guaranteed by both the RLA and the National Labor Relations Act (NLRA), I dissent.

Case Questions

1. The labor law governing labor disputes in the airline industry is the Railway Labor Act. May the Supreme Court look to cases decided under the NLRA when deciding a case under the RLA?
2. May an employer and union reach an agreement in conjunction with the end of a strike that would displace crossovers and permanent replacements?
3. Did the Court recognize in its decision that individual employees have a right to choose not to strike?
4. Did the Supreme Court see TWA's guarantees to crossovers that they would not be displaced by senior full-term strikers as an unlawful employer tactic destructive to the right to strike?

SECTION 65: UNPROTECTED STRIKE ACTIVITY

A strike may be declared unlawful if it has an unlawful purpose or object or if unlawful means are employed to accomplish a lawful purpose. In either situation, participants are not protected against discharge by their employer.

In most instances, the NLRA defines which strike objectives will be deemed unlawful. Section 8(b)(4) prohibits labor organizations from utilizing certain types of strikes, picketing, and boycotts if they fall into the "secondary" or "jurisdictional" category. Moreover, as amended, Sections 8(b)(7) and 8(e) prohibit any primary or secondary strike, picketing, or boycott where the object is as follows:

1. To force an employer to join an employer organization;
2. To force a self-employed person to join a labor union;
3. To force one employer to cease dealing with another person;
4. To require recognition after another union has obtained bargaining rights by certification under the Act where redetermination of such rights is barred.

Common examples of unlawful means are the sit-down strike, the partial strike, the wildcat strike, and the use of violence during strike activities. With respect to violence, a distinction is drawn between aggravated violence, which deprives employees of the Act's protection, and less aggravated acts of misconduct, which do not deprive employees of protection.[22] This distinction is illustrated in the *Ohio Power* decision, which follows.

In the *Winston-Salem Journal* decision, the Board determined that a union officer's cursing and disruptive behavior did not cause loss of protected status because he was speaking out about unfair treatment at work in a meeting with his employer.[23] However, the U.S. Court of Appeals denied enforcement of the Board's order, holding that the speech in question using language such as "b____d," "a redneck son of a b____h," and other words of a similar nature are devoid of substantive content and of meaningful value that could convey a message of grievance or concern.[24]

CASE 7.3	OHIO POWER CO. v. NLRB
	U.S. COURT OF APPEALS, 539 F.2D 575 (6TH CIR. 1976).

ENGEL, C. J....

In the early morning hours of October 21, 1973, a truck collided with a power pole adjacent to a two-lane asphalt highway outside the corporate limits of Bellaire, Ohio. The collision severed the pole in half, severely damaged the truck, and shut off electrical power in the vicinity. Alvin E. Mayer, a working foreman, and Kenneth Dawson, an area foreman, were reached at their home and together they traveled in one of the company's 35 ft. elbow trucks to the scene to restore electric service and to remove the pole butt which was then blocking the road. Dawson and Mayer arrived upon the scene at approximately 1:30 AM and brought their truck to a halt in the eastbound lane of the road just west of the accident scene. Meanwhile word of the power failure had reached a striking employee, Joseph Campbell, who lived nearby. Campbell and two other striking employees, Larry Campbell and Gabriel Gasbarre, drove to the scene, arriving there in advance of the company truck bringing Mayer and Dawson. Shortly before, Joseph Campbell had an unsatisfactory telephone conversation with the dispatcher on duty in the company offices in an effort to find out what had happened and what was being done to correct the power shutoff. The three strikers brought picket signs with them, but upon arrival, decided to leave them in the car....

According to Mayer, following a conversation between himself and Joseph Campbell in the middle of the road, Mayer turned toward the accident scene only to have Campbell grab him from behind and throw him to the ground, Mayer falling on his left side but sustaining only a scraped elbow and [a scraped] small finger.

In contrast, Joseph Campbell claimed that the two men were talking when Campbell slipped down off the truck and collided "chest-to-chest" with Mayer, causing him to slip and fall on gravel which had accumulated on the pavement.

Mayer and Dawson reported the incident to the company that night, and thereafter a letter was sent to Joseph Campbell notifying him that he was discharged for an "act of unprovoked aggression against a supervisor."

The company contends that Campbell's conduct was sufficiently serious to warrant discharge. The company notes that it is undisputed that at the time when the repair truck arrived on the scene, Campbell left the group of onlookers and began talking to Mayer about how thin his patience was growing, and that the exchange between the two men was heated. Further ... it is undisputed that Campbell came down from the fender of the repair truck where he was sitting and collided with Mayer, knocking Mayer backwards and onto the ground. Further,

continued

---

[22] Cook Family Foods, Inc., 323 NLRB 413 (1997).

[23] 341 NLRB No. 18 (2004).

[24] 394 F.3d 207 (4th Cir. 2005).

Campbell thereafter attempted to interfere with efforts to remove the broken utility pole and reopen the blocked highway to traffic, until directed to refrain by a police officer at the scene.

We begin our analysis by noting our standard of review ... on this point:

> [N]ot every impropriety committed during [Section 7] activity places the employee beyond the protective shield of the act. The employee's right to engage in concerted activity may permit some leeway for impulsive behavior, which must be balanced against the employer's right to maintain order and respect....

We have recognized in many cases that an employer is not required to countenance all misconduct by an employee, and we have carefully examined the acts of the employee to determine whether they are beyond the pale of protected activity under Section 7....

We conclude that Campbell's misconduct was sufficiently serious to justify his dismissal.... The supervisors were engaged in emergency repair work at approximately 1:30 AM. When the truck arrived, Campbell left the area where the other strikers and the onlookers were gathered and jumped up on the fender of the company's truck. The record indicates that at this point the two supervisors had just begun to survey the area where the accident had occurred, and did not as yet know whether there were any downed power lines or live wires.

According to Campbell's own testimony, he began a discussion with Mayer stating how his patience was getting thin. Apparently, Campbell's statements angered Mayer because at this point Mayer came at Campbell and as Campbell arose from the truck, the two men bumped "chest-to-chest." The force of the collision knocked Mayer back and he slipped onto the ground. He sustained slight injuries from the fall. Although there was no evidence that either man had to be restrained subsequent to the bumping incident,

onlookers apparently considered the situation quite serious. Police Officer Warnock testified that immediately after Mayer fell, he came over to Campbell and told him to back away, so there would not be any trouble.... [The Court found that as a result, the Company was within its rights to discharge Campbell.]

The facts leading to Larry Greene's discharge are in most respects undisputed. On August 10, 1973, Greene and two other strikers were walking to picket the site of a repair job being performed by the company in Steubenville. As Greene and the others reached the southeast corner of the intersection of North and 4th Streets, a company truck which had just left the worksite stopped for a red light at the intersection. In it were line foreman Ross Lee Cunningham and working foreman Walt Williams. Cunningham was driving. Greene yelled "Don't you know we're on strike?" and made some comments that the two non-union men were not observing safety rules. Greene then ran out into the intersection, grabbed Cunningham's cigar from his mouth and threw it to the ground. Based solely upon this incident, Greene was discharged.

The conduct complained of was an isolated expression which did not upon the circumstances create a safety hazard jeopardizing either company equipment or personnel. At the time of his discharge Greene was the Recording Secretary for the Union and the evidence suggests that the incident was exaggerated and that Greene's discharge for the alleged misconduct was pretextual.... [The Court held that] Greene's admitted misconduct was not so serious as to justify his discharge....

Case Questions

1. What balancing test does the court employ in determining whether an employee's act of violence justifies the employee's dismissal?

2. Why does the court find that Greene's dismissal was not justified?

SECTION 66: EFFECTS OF STRIKES IN VIOLATION OF NLRA NOTICE REQUIREMENTS

Section 8(d) of the NLRA imposes a mandatory duty upon the parties to negotiate in good faith to reach an agreement concerning wages, hours, and other terms and conditions of employment. The Labor Management Relations Act of 1947 established the Federal Mediation and Conciliation Service (FMCS) to assist the parties in resolving any impasse concerning the achievement of initial agreements or the renegotiation of existing agreements. Section 8(d)(1) requires the party desiring to modify an existing agreement to serve written notice on the other party within 60 days of the expiration of a collective bargaining contract, and Section 8(d)(3) requires notice to the FMCS and any comparable state agency within 30 days after the Section 8(d)(1) notice of the existence of a dispute is given. Section 8(d)(4) provides for a 60-day cooling-off period after notice is given to the FMCS during which neither strikes nor lockouts may occur.

Section 8(d) provides a severe penalty for engaging in a strike without the requisite written notice being given, that is, the individuals forfeit their status as employees under the Act and become unprotected activity strikers. In *Boghosian Raisin Packing Co.*,[25] Teamsters Local 616 drafted a written notice to FMCS on February 19, 1999, of a pending dispute with the employer raisin packing company as mandated under Section 8(d)(3), but inadvertently failed to mail the notice. After negotiations broke down in late September, the union notified the company that it had complied with Section 8(d)'s notice requirements to the FMCS and would strike on October 1. The company's attorney contacted the FMCS and found out that the union had not filed the required notice. The union struck on October 1. On the afternoon of October 1, 1999, when the union learned from the company's attorney that the FMCS notice had not been given, it offered to return to work and resume negotiations. The strike continued to October 5, 1999, when the company terminated 42 of the 45 strikers. A Board majority determined that the strikers lost their protected status as employees by going on strike without giving the Section 8(d)(3) notice to the FMCS. Replacement workers were subsequently hired, and thereafter the company legally withdrew recognition of the union.

In 1974, the NLRA was amended to cover employees working in private hospitals. Expanded notice periods were incorporated into Section 8(d) to facilitate the peaceful settlement of the health care disputes. Section 8(g) of the NLRA requires that a 10-day notice be given to a health care institution and the FMCS of a labor organization's intent to strike or picket. The notice is intended to provide the health care institution with advance warning of strike and picket activity so that it can make arrangements for the continued care of patients.

Any employee who engages in a strike during any of the notice periods set forth in Section 8(d) or 8(g) would lose the protections of the NLRA, becoming an unprotected activity striker, as discussed in the previous section.

In *Minnesota Licensed Practical Nurses Assn. v. NLRB*, presented in this section, the Eighth Circuit Court of Appeals upheld a 3–2 Board decision that 22 LPNs who began a strike four hours after the time designated in their Section 8(g) notice lost their protected employees' status under the Section 8(d) so-called "loss of status" provision.

---

[25] 342 NLRB No. 32 (2004).

CASE 7.4	MINNESOTA LPN ASSOCIATION V. NLRB
	UNITED STATES COURT OF APPEALS, 406 F.3D 1020 (8TH CIR. 2005).

[The Union is the certified collective bargaining representative of LPNs employed by the Alexandria Clinic. In August 1999, after months of unsuccessful bargaining, the Clinic announced that it would implement its final offer. In response, the nurses voted to strike. The Union gave the 10 days' written notice required by § 8(g), advising the Clinic that the strike would commence at 8 AM on September 10, 1999. However, the Union secretly advised the nurses that they could delay the commencement of the strike up to 72 hours.* The strike leaders decided that the bargaining unit nurses should report for duty on September 10 and walk off the job at noon. They did not notify the Clinic of this plan. On the morning of September 10, temporary replacement nurses hired by the Clinic reported before 8:00. Fourteen bargaining unit nurses also reported for duty without warning. The Clinic responded by having the replacements wait in a lounge area so as not to disturb the patients. The bargaining unit nurses left just before noon, again without warning the Clinic or their supervising physicians. Eight other nurses not on duty that morning later joined the strike. Patient care was not affected, as the replacement nurses were present to take over at noon on September 10. Citing the strike delay without notice, the Clinic fired the striking nurses for engaging in unlawful activity. After a hearing, the administrative law judge held that the Union did not violate § 8(g) and therefore the Clinic committed an unfair labor practice by discharging the nurses. A divided Board reversed. The Union petitioned the Court of Appeals to review the Board's decision.]

LOKEN, C. J....

The Board [stated]:

As made clear in Section 8(g), the "appropriate period" is the waiting period after a notice that gives the date and time for a strike. Obviously, if there is no notice, there can be no lawful strike. Concededly, in the instant case, there was a notice and the employees did not strike within the period set by the notice. However, the employees did strike thereafter, *and there was no notice with respect to that strike*. ... In sum, the strike was without notice, and it was therefore unlawful.

*   *   *   *   *

... [T]his conclusion results in the nurses losing their protected employee status under Section 8(d) for engaging in an unlawful strike, and subjects them to lawful discharge.

... The Union delayed the strike a disruptive one-half day with no notice of the delay. Prior to this case, the Board had never upheld this tactic.

The nurses engaged in a strike in violation of § 8(g), thereby lost their protected status by reason of § 8(d), and were lawfully discharged by their employer. The individual nurses may have acted in good faith in relying upon unsound advice from the Union and its legal counsel. But that does not justify rewarding their unlawful activity by imposing a back pay and reinstatement remedy on their employer, whose conduct was entirely lawful. The petition for review is denied.

[Denied.]

---

*An e-mail from the Union advisor to the nurses explained: "We can go at 8:00 [on Friday, September 10]; or just have everyone go to lunch and not come back; or work as usual on Friday, but not show up for Urgent Care Saturday—and have them wondering about Monday (when no one will come to work)!"

Case Questions

1. Assess the "delayed start" tactic used by the union in this case.
2. What were the consequences of the unsound advice from the union in this case?

SECTION 67: NO-STRIKE AGREEMENTS

Because the purpose of collective bargaining is to promote industrial stability, it is common for the parties to negotiate a no-strike clause into their collective bargaining contracts. In the *Standard Concrete Products* case, reported in this section, the court points out that the right to strike may be relinquished by appropriate provisions in the collective bargaining agreements, provided the relinquishment is expressed in clear and unmistakable language. In *Standard Concrete*, however, the court found that there was not an explicit contractual waiver of the employees' right to engage in a sympathy strike.

In *John Morrell Co. v. UFCW, Local 304A*,[26] where workers at Morrell's Sioux Falls plant engaged in a six-month sympathy strike in 1987 in support of striking Sioux City, Iowa, workers, Morrell sued the union, seeking damages for earnings lost because of the sympathy strike. A jury returned a verdict in favor of the company for $24.6 million in damages. The U.S. Court of Appeals for the Eighth Circuit ruled that the workers had engaged in an illegal sympathy strike and that the union was liable to the company for damages. The ruling was based on the no-strike clause in the contract, along with another provision of the contract that allowed Sioux Falls workers to refuse to perform work transferred from other meat packing companies facing strikes but required workers to perform work transferred from other Morrell plants that were on strike. If employees could engage in sympathy strikes, the court said, such a provision would be meaningless.

| **CASE 7.5** | STANDARD CONCRETE PRODUCTS, INC., V. TEAMSTERS LOCAL 952
 UNITED STATES COURT OF APPEALS, 353 F.3D 668 (9TH CIR. 2003). |

[Teamsters Local 952 represented the employees at the Standard Concrete Products, Inc., plant in Corona, California. It also represented employees at three sites in Orange County, California, in a separate bargaining unit with a separate collective bargaining agreement. Failing to make progress in negotiating a new collective bargaining agreement, Local 952's Corona bargaining unit went on strike on January 5, 2000, and extended picket lines to the three facilities in Orange County. The Orange County bargaining unit participated in a sympathy strike and refused to cross the Corona bargaining unit's picket line. The employer sued Local 952 in the U.S District Court for damages for breach of the no-strike clause in the Orange County CBA. From a judgment for Standard Concrete for $802,237, the Union appealed.]

PREGERSON, C. J....

Section 7 of the National Labor Relations Act guarantees workers and unions the right to engage in a sympathy strike, i.e., to refuse to cross the picket line of another bargaining unit that is on strike

against its employer. *Oil, Chem. and Atomic Workers Int'l Union, Local 1-547 v. NLRB*, 842 F.2d 1141, 1143 (hereinafter *Local 1-547*) (9th Cir. 1988). The right to strike and sympathy strike may be waived in a CBA. To do so, the union must make a "clear and unmistakable" waiver in the CBA. *Children's Hosp.*, 283 F.3d at 1192; *Local 1-547*, 842 F.2d at 1143. We require a specific "clear and unmistakable" waiver of a Union's right to sympathy strike because:

> [I]f a Union is negotiating away employees' rights that are fundamental to the collective bargaining process, any proposed contract must unambiguously put those employees on notice of the waiver.
>
> Children's Hosp., 283 F.3d at 1192

In *Children's Hospital* we made clear that "[a] general no-strike clause that does not specify whether sympathy strikes are included or excluded does not, simply by virtue of its incorporation in a collective bargaining agreement, constitute such a clear and unmistakable waiver [of sympathy strikes]." *Children's*

continued

[26] 949 F.2d 266 (8th Cir. 1990). But see Englehard Corp. 342 NLRB No. 5 (2004).

Hosp., 283 F.3d at 1192. We must "examine the relevant extrinsic evidence to determine if the parties intended that general [no-strike] language to include sympathy strikes." *Id.* at 1194. The burden is on the "employer to show by clear and unmistakable evidence that a general waiver of the right to strike includes sympathy strikes." *Id.* at 1195....

We find that *Children's Hospital* is controlling. There is evidence in the *express text* of the Orange County CBA that the parties did not intend to bar sympathy strikes when they agreed to a general no strike clause. Article IX, Section 1 of the Orange County CBA provides: "No employee shall be discharged or discriminated against because of his/her membership in the Union or Union activities, including his/her refusal to cross a picket line approved by the Union." If Standard Concrete intended the no

strike clause to encompass a ban on sympathy strikes, it would not have agreed to safeguard the jobs of Local 952 members that refuse to cross a picket line.

We conclude that Local 952 did not make a clear and unmistakable waiver of its members' right to refuse to cross the picket line of another union or bargaining unit of the same union.

Reversed.

Case Questions

1. What is a "sympathy strike?"
2. Does a general no-strike clause that does not reference "sympathy strikes" constitute a waiver of the right to participate in a sympathy strike?

SECTION 68: NORRIS-LAGUARDIA AND NO-STRIKE INJUNCTIONS

Section 4 of the Norris-LaGuardia Act prohibits federal court injunctions in labor disputes. Section 301 of the Labor Management Relations Act provides that employers and unions may sue each other whenever a breach of a collective bargaining contract takes place. Section 301, however, does not include any statutory provision insulating cases brought under Section 301 from the prohibition against injunctions in the Norris-LaGuardia Act. Are federal courts then allowed to use the injunction as a remedy in breach of collective bargaining agreement (Section 301) cases? We must analyze the Supreme Court decisions that have construed these statutes for our answer.

In *Textile Workers Union v. Lincoln Mills*,[27] the U.S. Supreme Court allowed the use of an injunction to compel an employer to fulfill its obligation to arbitrate under an existing collective bargaining agreement. However, in *Sinclair Refining Co. v. Atkinson*,[28] the Court refused to enjoin a strike by a union, even though the collective bargaining agreement in effect at the time of the strike contained a no-strike clause and an arbitration clause. In *Sinclair*, Mr. Justice Black wrote for the majority that Section 301 did not modify the Norris-LaGuardia Act insofar as the statute prohibited injunctions in labor disputes and that federal district courts were without jurisdiction to order injunctive relief. In *Avco Corp. v. Aero Lodge*,[29] the Supreme Court in effect negated the employer's right to seek injunctive

---

[27] 353 U.S. 448 (1957).

[28] 370 U.S. 195 (1962).

[29] 390 U.S. 557 (1968).

relief to enforce a no-strike clause in a state court (remember, Norris-LaGuardia prohibitions against the use of injunctions apply only to federal courts) by allowing the union to remove the case from the state court to a federal court. The *Boys Markets* decision, reported in this section, overruled *Sinclair*. In *Boys Markets*, the Supreme Court held that there must be an accommodation between the seemingly absolute terms of the Norris-LaGuardia Act and the policy considerations underlying Section 301. The Court concluded that the federal courts do have limited injunctive powers in Section 301 cases. The Court does caution that this decision is "a narrow one," and only under certain limited circumstances may a court enjoin a strike in violation of a contractual no-strike clause.

In the *Buffalo Forge Co. v. Steelworkers*[30] decision, the Supreme Court held that a prerequisite for the issuance of *Boys Markets* injunctive relief is that the strike must be over an issue that the parties are obligated to arbitrate. In *Buffalo Forge*, two production and maintenance locals of the Steelworkers were parties to collective bargaining agreements containing broad no-strike clauses and grievance arbitration procedures. Two office and technical employee units were certified as Steelworkers locals. After several months of negotiations for a first contract with the employer, the office employees were on strike. Several days later, the production and maintenance employees went on strike. The company sought an injunction against this strike. The Court held that since the cause of the sympathy strike—the impasse in the office workers' negotiations—was not subject to arbitration between the production workers and the company, the relief sought was not granted. The Court ruled that the *Boys Markets* exception to the Norris-LaGuardia Act was limited to arbitrable disputes and that the Norris-LaGuardia Act, aside from the *Boys Markets* exception, does not permit the intrusion of the courts at the preliminary injunction stage to enjoin actual or threatened contract violations.

Following the *Buffalo Forge* precedent, the Supreme Court held in *Jacksonville Bulk Terminals v. International Longshoremen's Ass'n* [ILA] that an employer may not obtain injunctive relief pending arbitration where the dispute underlying the work stoppage is not arbitrable. In *Jacksonville Bulk Terminals*, the underlying dispute related to the then Soviet Union's intervention in Afghanistan, which led the ILA to refuse to handle goods arriving from or destined for the Soviet Union. This dispute, the Court majority held, was plainly not arbitrable under the collective bargaining agreement.[31]

---

[30] 428 U.S. 397 (1976).

[31] Please note that in a case arising out of the same ILA protest of the Soviet intervention in Afghanistan and involving an importer, Allied International and J. T. Clark Stevedoring Co., the union refusal to unload Russian goods on ships docking in Boston was found to be an unlawful secondary boycott in violation of Section 8(b)(4)(B) of the NLRA. The case, *International Longshoremen's Ass'n v. Allied International, Inc.*, 456 U.S. 212 (1982), was brought against the ILA under Section 303 of the LMRA for damages caused by the boycott. Following the Supreme Court's decision in *Jacksonville*, the U.S. district court entered a judgment of $8,055,490 plus interest in favor of Allied, which was upheld on appeal. See *Allied Plywood Corp. v. ILA*, 814 F.2d 32 (1st Cir. 1987).

CASE 7.6 | BOYS MARKETS, INC., V. RETAIL CLERKS UNION, LOCAL 778
SUPREME COURT OF THE UNITED STATES, 398 U.S. 235 (1970).

[Boys Markets, Inc. (petitioner), had a collective bargaining agreement with the Retail Clerks Union (respondent). A company supervisor and certain other company employees who were not part of the Retail Clerks bargaining unit rearranged merchandise in the frozen food cases of one of the company's supermarkets. A union representative insisted that the merchandise be restocked by union personnel, because the bargaining unit work had been wrongfully taken away from union personnel. When Boys Markets refused to do so, a strike was called, and the union began to picket the market. The company sought an injunction against the strike and an order compelling arbitration of the dispute, as the collective bargaining agreement contained a no-strike clause and a grievance-arbitration procedure to resolve disputes under the agreement. Upon removal from a state court, the U.S. district court ordered the parties to arbitrate the dispute and enjoined the strike. The court of appeals reversed, considering itself bound by the *Sinclair* decision. The Supreme Court granted certiorari.]

BRENNAN, J....

At the outset, we are met with respondent's contention that *Sinclair* ought not to be disturbed because the decision turned on a question of statutory construction which Congress can alter at any time. Since Congress has not modified our conclusions in *Sinclair*, even though it has been urged to do so, respondent argues that principles of **stare decisis** should govern the present case.

We do not agree that the doctrine of *stare decisis* bars a re-examination of *Sinclair* in the circumstances of this case. We fully recognize that important policy considerations militate in favor of continuity and predictability in the law. Nevertheless, as Mr. Justice Frankfurter wrote for the Court, "[S]tare decisis is a principle of policy and not a mechanical formula of adherence to the latest decision, however recent and questionable, when such adherence involves collision with a prior doctrine more embracing in its scope, intrinsically sounder, and verified by experience." It is precisely because *Sinclair* stands as a significant departure from our otherwise consistent emphasis upon the congressional policy to promote the peaceful settlement of labor disputes through arbitration

and our efforts to accommodate and harmonize this policy with those underlying the anti-injunction provisions of the Norris-LaGuardia Act that we believe *Sinclair* should be reconsidered. Furthermore, in light of developments subsequent to *Sinclair*, in particular our decision in *Avco Corp. v. Aero Lodge*, 735, 390 U.S. 557 (1968), it has become clear that the *Sinclair* decision does not further but rather frustrates realization of an important goal of our national policy.

Nor can we agree that conclusive weight should be accorded to the failure of Congress to respond to *Sinclair* on the theory that congressional silence should be interpreted as acceptance of the decision. The Court has cautioned that "[i]t is at best treacherous to find in congressional silence alone the adoption of a controlling rule of law." Therefore, in the absence of any persuasive circumstances evidencing a clear design that congressional inaction be taken as acceptance of *Sinclair*, the mere silence of Congress is not a sufficient reason for refusing to reconsider the decision.

We have also determined that the dissenting opinion in *Sinclair* states the correct principles concerning the accommodation necessary between the seemingly absolute terms of the Norris-LaGuardia Act and the policy considerations underlying Section 301(a). Although we need not repeat all that was there said, a few points should be emphasized at this time.

The literal terms of Section 4 of the Norris-LaGuardia Act must be accommodated to the subsequently enacted provisions of Section 301(a) of the Labor-Management Relations Act and the purposes of arbitration. Statutory interpretation requires more than concentration upon isolated words; rather, consideration must be given to the total corpus of the pertinent law and the policies which inspired ostensibly inconsistent provisions.

The Norris-LaGuardia Act was responsive to a situation totally different from that which exists today. In the early part of this century, the federal courts generally were regarded as allies of management in its attempt to prevent the organization and strengthening of labor unions; and in this industrial struggle the injunction became a potent weapon which was wielded against the activities of labor groups. The

continued

result was a large number of sweeping decrees, often issued *ex parte*, drawn on an *ad hoc* basis without regard to any systematic elaboration of national labor policy.

In 1932 Congress attempted to bring some order out of the industrial chaos that had developed and to correct the abuses which had resulted from the interjection of the federal judiciary into union-management disputes on the behalf of management. See Declaration of Public Policy, Norris-LaGuardia Act, Section 2, 47 Stat. 70 (1932). Congress, therefore, determined initially to limit severely the power of the federal courts to issue injunctions "in any case involving or growing out of any labor dispute...." 47 Stat. 70. Even as initially enacted, however, the prohibition against federal injunctions was by no means absolute. See Norris-LaGuardia Act, Sections 7, 8, 9, 47 Stat. 70 (1932). Shortly thereafter Congress passed the Wagner Act, designed to curb various management activities which tended to discourage employee participation in collective action.

As labor organizations grew in strength and developed toward maturity, congressional emphasis shifted from protection of the nascent labor movement to the encouragement of collective bargaining and administrative techniques for the peaceful resolution of industrial disputes. This shift in emphasis was accomplished, however, without extensive revision of many of the older enactments, including the anti-injunction section of the Norris-LaGuardia Act. Thus it became the task of the courts to accommodate, to reconcile the older statutes with the more recent ones.

The principles elaborated in *Trainmen v. Chicago River R.R.*, 353 U.S. 30 (1957), are equally applicable to the present case. To be sure, *Chicago River* involved arbitration procedures established by statute. However, we have frequently noted, in such cases as *Lincoln Mills*, the *Steelworkers Trilogy*, and *Lucas Flour*, the importance which Congress has attached generally to the voluntary settlement of labor disputes without resort to self-help and more particularly to arbitration as a means to this end. Indeed, it has been stated that *Lincoln Mills*, in its exposition of Section 301(a), "went a long way towards making arbitration the central institution in the administration of collective bargaining contracts."

The *Sinclair* decision, however, seriously undermined the effectiveness of the arbitration technique

as a method peacefully to resolve industrial disputes without resort to strikes, lockouts, and similar devices. Clearly, employers will be wary of assuming obligations to arbitrate specifically enforceable against them when no similarly efficacious remedy is available to enforce the concomitant undertaking of the union to refrain from striking. On the other hand, the central purpose of the Norris-LaGuardia Act to foster the growth and viability of labor organizations is hardly retarded—if anything, this goal is advanced— by a remedial device which merely enforces the obligation that the union freely undertook under a specifically enforceable agreement to submit disputes to arbitration. We conclude, therefore, that the unavailability of equitable relief in the arbitration context presents a serious impediment to the congressional policy favoring the voluntary establishment of a mechanism for the peaceful resolution of labor disputes, that the core purpose of the Norris-LaGuardia Act is not sacrificed by the limited use of equitable remedies to further this important policy, and consequently that the Norris-LaGuardia Act does not bar the granting of injunctive relief in the circumstances of the instant case.

Our holding in the present case is a narrow one. We do not undermine the vitality of the Norris-LaGuardia Act. We deal only with the situation in which a collective bargaining contract contains a mandatory grievance adjustment or arbitration procedure. Nor does it follow from what we have said that injunctive relief is appropriate as a matter of course in every case of a strike over an arbitrable grievance. The dissenting opinion in *Sinclair* suggested the following principles for the guidance of the district courts in determining whether to grant injunctive relief—principles which we now adopt:

> A District Court entertaining an action under Section 301 may not grant injunctive relief against concerted activity unless and until it decides that the case is one in which an injunction would be appropriate despite the Norris-LaGuardia Act. When a strike is sought to be enjoined because it is over a grievance which both parties are contractually bound to arbitrate, the District Court may issue no injunctive order until it first holds that the contract does have that effect; and the employer should be ordered to arbitrate, as a

continued

condition of his obtaining an injunction against the strike. Beyond this, the District Court must, of course, consider whether issuance of an injunction would be warranted under ordinary principles of equity—whether breaches are occurring and will continue, or have been threatened and will be committed; whether they have caused or will cause irreparable injury to the employer; and whether the employer will suffer more from the denial of an injunction than will the union from its issuance. 370 U.S., at 228.

In the present case there is no dispute that the grievance in question was subject to adjustment and arbitration under the collective bargaining agreement and that the petitioner was ready to proceed with arbitration at the time an injunction against the strike was sought and obtained. The District Court also concluded that, by reason of respondent's violations of its no-strike obligation, petitioner "has suffered irreparable injury and will continue to suffer irreparable injury." Since we now overrule *Sinclair*, the holding of the Court of Appeals in reliance on *Sinclair* must be reversed. Accordingly, we reverse the judgment of the Court of Appeals and remand the case with directions to enter a judgment affirming the order of the District Court.

It is so ordered.

BLACK J., Dissenting ...

Although Congress has been urged to overrule our holding in *Sinclair*, it has steadfastly refused to do so.

... When the law has been settled by an earlier case then any subsequent "reinterpretation" of the statute is gratuitous and neither more nor less than an amendment: it is no different in effect from a judicial alteration of language that Congress itself placed in the statute.

Altering the important provisions of a statute is a legislative function. And the Constitution states simply and unequivocally: "All legislative Powers herein granted shall be vested in a Congress of the United States...." U.S. Const., Art. I. It is the Congress, not this Court, that responds to the pressures of political groups, pressure entirely proper in a free society....

Case Questions

1. How did the labor dispute that led to this litigation arise?
2. What are the issues before the Supreme Court?
3. Does the majority believe that the doctrine of stare decisis bars a reexamination of the *Sinclair* decision handed down in 1962?
4. What guiding principles adopted by the Court are to be utilized by district courts in determining whether to grant injunctive relief?

SECTION 69: NATIONAL EMERGENCY STRIKES

Limitations are imposed on the use of the federal court injunction by the Federal Anti-Injunction Act of 1932. However, these restrictions do not apply to suits initiated by the government to protect the public interest from actual or threatened national emergency strikes.[32]

Several strikes in 1946, particularly in the bituminous coal industry, were stimulants for inclusion of Section 3 206–210, dealing with national emergencies, in the Labor Management Relations Act (Taft-Hartley Act or LMRA) of 1947. These are in purpose parallel to Section 10 of the Railway Labor Act.

Under these provisions of the Act, as in the emergency strike provisions of the Railway Labor Act, the president is authorized to appoint a board of investigation, which submits a report to the president concerning the issues in dispute. The Labor Management Relations Act of 1947 under Sections 206–210 enables the government to secure what amounts to an 80-day injunction forestalling strikes or lockouts affecting all or a substantial part of an industry in interstate commerce when such

---

[32] See *United States v. United Mine Workers*, 330 U.S. 258 (1947).

disputes imperil the national health or safety. During the interim, the government mediation service is to be invoked, but recommendations for settlement are not mandatory on the disputants. If an accord is not reached, the NLRB must poll the workers as to whether they want to accept the employer's last offer in settlement. If the last offer is not acceptable, the injunction is dissolved, and the president refers the case to Congress for such "appropriate action" as it deems advisable.

The Taft-Hartley provisions do not provide for a compulsory method of dispute settlement but leave ultimate disposition of an unresolved national emergency case in the hands of Congress upon referral by the president. The Act of 1947, Sections 206–210, expresses congressional intentions to leave open all legitimate methods of labor union self-help, subject to delaying action by presidential injunctive intervention. The Act provides facilities for mediation and conciliation in the hope that the parties will reach a settlement and avoid a crippling strike.

In *United Steelworkers of America v. United States*,[33] the Supreme Court upheld the authority of the government to secure an injunction under Sections 206–210. In this case, a steel strike impeded production of vital weapons needed for defense.

At the other end of the spectrum, however, the Supreme Court in *Youngstown Sheet and Tube v. Sawyer*[34] denied that the existence of emergency alone, in the absence of prior congressional authority, gave the president constitutional power to effect a seizure of major American steel mills. The president attempted to accomplish this seizure by executive order in a steel strike stalemate in 1951.

Presidential action was initiated in October 2002 to deal with a prolonged dispute between the Pacific Maritime Association (PMA) and the International Longshore and Warehouse Union (ILA) in order to interrupt a lockout by the PMA affecting 29 ports on the West Coast and some 10,500 longshore workers. The lockout began on September 27, 2002, and presidential action under the Taft-Hartley Act was invoked on October 7, 2002. The U.S. District Court's order approving a stipulated preliminary injunction is set forth in this section. The parties were able to resolve their dispute during the 80-day cooling-off period imposed under Taft-Hartley.

CASE 7.7	UNITED STATES V. PACIFIC MARITIME ASSOCIATION AND ILA
	U.S. DISTRICT COURT, 2002 WL 31324099 (N.D. CAL.).

ALSUP, J....

Introduction

In this action for injunctive relief under the emergency provisions of the Labor Management Relations Act of 1947, commonly known as the Taft-Hartley Act, this order APPROVES the stipulation of the parties imposing injunctive relief.

Statement

At the direction of President George W. Bush, the United States commenced this action for injunctive relief on October 8, 2002, under the emergency provisions of the Labor Management Relations Act of 1947, 29 U.S.C. 176-180. The President invoked the Act to interrupt a lockout by the Pacific Maritime

continued

---

[33] 361 U.S. 39 (1959).

[34] 343 U.S. 579 (1952).

Association and its members affecting 29 ports on the West Coast and 10,500 longshore workers represented by the International Longshore and Ware-house Union. The lockout began on September 27, following a breakdown in negotiations over a new collective-bargaining agreement, the old one having expired over the summer.

Prior to suit, on October 7, the President appointed a board of inquiry pursuant to Section 206 after finding that (1) the lockout affected a substantial part of the maritime industry and (2) the lockout, if permitted to continue, would imperil national health and safety. The board of inquiry issued its report on October 8. The board concluded that the PMA and the ILWU would not resolve the port shutdown within a reasonable time. After receiving the report, the President directed the Attorney General to initiate this action....

Analysis

Section 208 of the Taft-Hartley Act provides:

> Upon receiving a report from a board of inquiry the President may direct the Attorney General to petition any district court of the United States having jurisdiction of the parties to enjoin such strike or lockout or the continuing thereof, and if the court finds that such threatened or actual strike or lockout—
>
> (i) affects an entire industry or a substantial part thereof engaged in trade, commerce, transportation, transmission, or communication among the several States or with foreign nations, or engaged in the production of goods for commerce; and
>
> (ii) if permitted to occur or to continue, will imperil the national health or safety, it shall have jurisdiction to enjoin any such strike or lockout, or the continuing thereof, and to make such other orders as may be appropriate.
>
> 29 U.S.C. 178(a). For the reasons stated at the hearing on October 8 ... this order finds that both statutory factors have been met.

With respect to the first statutory factor, the lockout at 29 ports along the West Coast and resultant work stoppage have affected a substantial part of the nation's maritime industry, an industry intimately engaged in "trade, commerce, transportation, transmission, or communication among the several States or with foreign nations." Specifically, the 29 affected West Coast ports are crucial gateways to America's trade routes to Asia and the Pacific. Indeed, the affected ports annually handle over 50 percent of the nation's containerized imports and exports, with a total annual value of bulk cargo at $300 billion....

The second statutory factor is met as well. The lockout and resultant work stoppage "if permitted to occur or to continue, will imperil the national health or safety." 29 U.S.C. 178(a)(ii). This order reiterates the finding made in open court on October 8 that both national health *and* national safety will be imperiled by the lockout's continuation. A continuation of the closure of West Coast ports will endanger the national economy and labor force. Key industries directly and substantially affected, as stated, include the transportation and agricultural industries. Continuation of the closure would harm the national economy still recovering from recession.

At the October 8 hearing, the ILWU raised two points. It first argued that the invocation of the Taft-Hartley Act was the product of "collusion" between the United States and the PMA. This was rejected as speculation and, at all events, beside the point, since all persons, including both the PMA and the ILWU, have the right to petition the government for redress of grievance. The focus must be on whether the government has proven the statutory preconditions for emergency relief—not on the politics behind its decision to seek relief. The ILWU's second argument was that the lockout was on the verge of collapsing and, thus, there was no need for injunctive relief. This was rejected on the facts given the government's powerful showing of the massive logjam of imports and exports paralyzing the West Coast. Even if the lockout eventually might have collapsed of its own weight, estimating when a voluntary end to the shutdown might have come would have been guesswork. Again, the statutory findings are plainly indicated. That is the end of the inquiry at the district court. *United Steel Workers of America v. United States*, 361 U.S. 39, 41 (1959).

... [T]he Court has considered on its own whether a Taft-Hartley injunction provoked by a management lockout, as here, can be directed not only at the lockout but also at any future strike or other work slowdown by a union. This case is evidently the first to arise primarily from a lockout. This order concludes that in such circumstances the injunction may extend beyond enjoining a lockout and also may enjoin a strike, including a work slow down. The Act expressly refers to a "threatened ... strike" as a basis

continued

for an injunction. "The term 'strike' includes … any concerted slow-down or other concerted interruption of operations by employees." 29 U.S.C. 142(2). The findings of the board of inquiry demonstrate that the lockout was, at least in part, occasioned by work slow-downs in various ports. In this charged environment, it is clear that a "strike" is "threatened" within the meaning of the Act. Although the massive grid-lock at West Coast ports is primarily attributable to the PMA's lockout, and although the lockout will now be enjoined, concerted slow-downs by longshore workers would greatly exacerbate an existing national emergency. Therefore, there is a sufficient basis to extend the injunction to prohibit both lock-outs and strikes at this juncture.

Moreover, in the past Taft-Hartley decisions generated by strikes, the preliminary injunctions swept broadly to prohibit both strikes and lockouts, at least insofar as can be determined from the published decisions. At all events, under Section 208 of the Act, the Court has the authority "to make such other orders as may be appropriate." 29 U.S.C. 178(a)(ii)....

Conclusion

For the reasons stated, this order APPROVES the stipulated preliminary injunction.

It is so ordered.

Case Questions

1. Did the ILA prove that the invocation of the Taft-Hartley Act was the product of "collusion" between the United States and the PMA?
2. The 2002 case was the first case to arise primarily from a lockout by an employer. Did the court have the right to issue a Taft-Hartley injunction not only against the lockout but also against any future strike?

CHAPTER QUESTIONS AND PROBLEMS

1. Distinguish between economic, unprotected, and employer unfair labor practice strikes.
2. What are the reinstatement rights of economic strikers as opposed to unfair labor practice strikers?
3. Evaluate the effectiveness of the strike weapon for unions versus the employers' economic weapons.
4. The International Ladies Garment Workers' Union obtained 59 signed authorization cards from the 86 employees at the Robin-American Zipper factory in Hialeah, Florida. In late November, the union informed the president of the company, Benbast, that it wanted to be recognized as the representative for the employees. Benbast insisted upon an NLRB election, and one was scheduled for the following March. Between November and January, supervisors and managers interrogated a number of employees who had signed authorization cards and threatened some with dismissal if the union won the election. In December, the company also closed an entire department (where the employees had unanimously signed cards) without warning. In January, a union representative confronted Benbast over the layoff of two pro-union employees and charged that his actions were antiunion. In response to these developments, 50 employees went on strike in mid-February. The strikers offered to return before the election. However, they were told that they had been replaced and were no longer needed.

   Before the NLRB, the union insisted that the striking employees be reinstated immediately. The company maintained that the strikers were not entitled to reinstatement until a vacancy occurred among the replacements.

   Are the strikers entitled to the immediate reinstatement of their jobs? Decide. [*NLRB v. Robin-American Corp.*, 108 LRRM 2229 (5th Cir.)]
5. A collective bargaining agreement existing between the Elevator Manufacturers' Association of New York and Local 1 of the Elevator Workers Union contained a no-strike clause and a provision requiring

arbitration of all "differences and disputes regarding the application and construction" of the agreement. The agreement also contained a provision governing emergency callbacks for employees after hours. When elevator repair was needed during the evening, employees who were called to work from the "night call list" were entitled to time-and-a-half wages. Otis Elevator, a signator of the agreement, instituted a policy under which it would screen all after-hours calls for elevator service. Otis would determine whether service was required immediately or whether repair could be postponed until the following workday. The union objected to the Otis "screening" system and requested that the policy be changed. Otis contended that it had a right to screen out "emergency" calls and refused to change its policy. In response to the company's policy, the union directed its members not to perform *any* after-hours work for Otis.

The union rejected a suggestion by Otis that the issue should be determined through the contractual grievance machinery. Subsequently, Otis petitioned the U.S. district court for an injunction against the union's refusal to work overtime. The union argued that the court could not issue an injunction under the Norris-LaGuardia Act. May an injunction be issued by a court against a strike? If so, under what circumstances? Should an injunction be issued in this case? Decide. [*Elevator Manufacturers' Association v. Local 1*, 111 LRRM 2631 (2d Cir.)]

6. Harding Glass Industries was a member of a multiemployer bargaining association called the Topeka Area Glazing Contractors Association. The association's collective bargaining agreement with the Glass Workers' Union expired on July 31. Although the union and the association did bargain over a new contract, the union went on strike on August 1 when no agreement had been reached. Harding's adamant opposition to a shift rotation clause in the agreement brought

the negotiations to a standstill. At one bargaining session, Jack Zander, the union business agent, exclaimed in exasperation, "If it weren't for Harding, we could settle this damn thing." With negotiations at an impasse, Harding informed Zander that it was withdrawing from the association so that it could bargain separately with the union. Zander objected and demanded that Harding continue bargaining in the association. Harding did not take part in any further bargaining. Subsequently, on November 3, the union and the association agreed on a three-year contract. On the basis of this agreement, the striking Harding employees returned to their plant. The company barred their return, stating that it had no contract with the employees and that it had permanently replaced the strikers.

The union claimed that its Harding members were entitled to immediate reinstatement and back pay because Harding had engaged in unfair labor practices. Harding maintained that it had the right to replace workers who went on strike over an economic issue.

Are the strikers entitled to immediate reinstatement by Harding Industries? Decide. [*Harding Glass Industries v. NLRB*, 109 LRRM 3044 (10th Cir.)]

7. Vincent Venditto and Todd Needham were hired as machine operators for Waveline, Inc., of Fairfield, New Jersey. Venditto and Needham commenced their employment under the customary 60-day probationary period at Waveline. After the expiration of 60 days, Waveline would decide whether to retain new employees or let them go. After Needham and Venditto had worked only 26 days, the newly certified Clothing and Textile Workers Union called a strike pending negotiation of a collective bargaining agreement with Waveline. Venditto and Needham went along with the two-month strike and were eager to return to their jobs when a collective bargaining agreement was signed ending the strike. When Venditto and Needham

unconditionally offered to return to work with the other workers, they were told that they had been terminated. Although Waveline had always allowed probationary employees to complete the 60-day trial period, the company had terminated Venditto and Needham after only 26 days of work, thus depriving them of poststrike reinstatement.

The union charged that Waveline had violated the Act by, in effect, discharging two employees engaged in a lawful economic strike. Waveline defended its action as the mere execution of its probationary prerogative.

May Waveline lawfully terminate Venditto and Needham? Decide. [*Waveline, Inc.*, 258 NLRB No. 87, 108 LRRM 1139]

8. James Stockwell was among the members of Machinists Lodge 65 who commenced a lawful economic strike on May 5 against their employer, Overhead Door Corporation. Several of the strikers eventually offered to return to work when the company began to hire replacement workers in the fall. On October 9, Stockwell phoned Overhead Door and offered to return to work. The company notified Stockwell on October 10 that his former job had been filled. Nonetheless, Stockwell expressed his desire to accept any other position, and on October 14, the company offered him a position on the second shift. Stockwell told Overhead Door that he would let them know the following day if he accepted the job. The company did not hear from Stockwell again until December 15, by which time all positions had been taken by replacements.

Before the NLRB, the union contended that Overhead Door was obligated to recall Stockwell before hiring additional replacement workers after he offered to return on October 9. The company maintained that it was free to hire replacements when Stockwell failed to accept the job he was offered.

Has Overhead Door unlawfully failed to recall this economic striker under the NLRA? Decide. [*Overhead Door Corp.*, 261 NLRB 657, 110 LRRM 1113]

9. William Chapman, Edwin Russ, and Antoinette Rhoads were among the members of UAW who were on strike in support of union demands during collective bargaining with their employer, E-Systems, Inc., After two months of strike activity, agreement was reached, and the company placed all of the strikers except Chapman, Russ, and Rhoads on a preferential hiring list. These employees were cited for strike misconduct and were formally discharged. Chapman had admitted that on a windy, rainy day during the strike, his umbrella had accidentally blown into a truck that was crossing the picket line. The umbrella scratched the paint on the truck. Chapman had immediately contacted the owner and made restitution. Several persons saw Russ reach out and snap back the antenna of a car as it attempted to leave the E-Systems plant. Russ pleaded no contest to a charge of criminal mischief for this act. Antoinette Rhoads had repeatedly joined in a blocking of the main plant gate, obstructing the arrival and departure of nonstriking employees. Rhoads also struck a nonstriker on the shoulder, causing a bruise.

The union challenged the discharges before the Board as too severe for the type of behavior that had occurred. The company maintained that the three employees engaged in aggravated strike misconduct and should be discharged.

What factors should the Board consider in deciding this case? Should the discharges be upheld by the Board? Decide [*NLRB v. E-Systems, Inc.*, 107 LRRM 2094 (5th Cir.)]

10. The collective bargaining agreement covering Southern California Edison Company and its employees represented by the IBEW stated in Article I that the company recognized all employee rights under Section 7 of the NLRA. In Article II, the union promised, in exchange for a company no-lockout promise, not to strike until the "methods provided for the settlement of disputes in the agreement have been utilized." Article V required

unresolved grievances under the agreement to be submitted to arbitration. Two IBEW members were subjected to company discipline when they refused to cross picket lines. One employee refused to cross a line at Edison manned by striking Edison employees represented by the Utilities Workers. Gary Blum refused to cross a picket line established by strikers at the Freightliner Corporation when Edison sent him there on a service call. Blum was sent home and subsequently suspended for five days.

The union objected to this discipline, claiming that its members had a statutory right not to cross picket lines. By disciplining the employees, the IBEW charged that Edison had interfered with protected activity in violation of the collective bargaining agreement and Section 8(a)(1). Edison maintained that employees could not refuse to work under any circumstances because this privilege had been waived by the union through the no-strike clause.

Is the right to honor a picket line protected under the NLRA? If so, has the IBEW waived this right? Decide. [*NLRB v. Southern California Edison*, 107 LRRM 2667 (9th Cir.)]

11. Zartic, Inc., employed approximately 425 people, including a number of Mexican-Americans. In early July, two Zartic workers were severely burned on the job, and the employees began complaining about safety issues and working conditions. The employees also discussed the possibility of striking.

On July 18 and 19, James Wells, a Zartic employee who was also a member of the Ku Klux Klan, solicited fellow employees to sign a leaflet designating the American Workers Union (AWU) as their bargaining representative. The leaflet stated that the AWU would try to obtain dismissal of all green card and illegal aliens, a wage increase, improved insurance and retirement benefits, a new leave system, new work rules, and a reasonable overtime policy. Early on July 20, Wells and 25 other men dressed in KKK garb

picketed Zartic's plant, carrying signs that contained derisive comments about Mexican-Americans, as well as slogans calling for better working conditions and benefits. Many Zartic employees refused to report for work, and the AWU pamphlets were distributed to the striking employees.

Zartic immediately began hiring replacements and obtained from the district court a temporary restraining order that prohibited any picketing designed to force Zartic to terminate or refuse to employ persons of Mexican ancestry. The order specifically did not prohibit picketing or labor activity tied to a legitimate labor dispute.

By Tuesday, July 21, the picket signs were altered so that references to Mexican-Americans were eradicated. Although a company policy authorized termination of any employee with three unexcused absences, Zartic management decided not to fire the striking employees. Instead, the company informed the employees that day that they had been permanently replaced, but they were placed on a preference recall list. On Wednesday, July 22, the strikers abandoned the strike and offered unconditionally to return to work. When Zartic refused, picketing resumed until August 9. Between July 22 and August 9, Zartic hired 102 new employees. During the same period, Zartic did not recall any of the strikers.

The General Counsel alleged that Zartic engaged in an unfair labor practice by refusing to rehire striking employees. Zartic contended that the strike had an illegal objective, and thus the strikers had no reinstatement rights under the NLRA.

Were the Zartic strikers entitled to reinstatement? Decide. [*Zartic, Inc., v. NLRB*, 124 LRRM 2807 (11th Cir.)]

12. In May, the nurses' union at Waterbury Hospital went out on strike, and the hospital was shut down. In mid-June, the hospital began hiring replacements and gradually opened many units. In order to induce nurses to take employment during the strike and in

an attempt to induce some striking nurses to return to work, the hospital guaranteed replacement and crossover nurses their choice of positions and shifts. If a preferred position was in a unit that was not open at that time, the hospital guaranteed that the individual would be placed in that position at the end of the strike. The strike ended in October, and as the striking workers returned to work, the hospital began opening units that had been closed during the strike. It staffed many of these positions with nonstrikers. The nurses who had filled the positions prior to the strike and who were waiting to return to work believed that they should have been called to fill these positions rather than the junior replacements and crossover nurses who had held other positions during the strike. Decide this case based on the *Mackay Radio* and *TWA v. IFFA* decisions. [*The Waterbury Hospital v. NLRB*, 950 F.2d 849 (2d Cir.)]

13. Pirelli Cable Corporation and IBEW Local 2236 began talks over terms of a new collective bargaining agreement in March 1994 to replace their contract, which would expire on May 1, 1994. Pirelli sought economic concession from the union, and the union talked to the membership about the possibility of a strike. On April 20, 1994, a letter was sent to all Pirelli employees expressing Pirelli's concerns about a potential strike and encouraging the employees to continue good faith negotiations. The two-page body of the letter addressed the financial difficulties Pirelli had encountered, noting specifically that both the demand for, and price of, its products had declined. Attached to the letter was a two-page list of nine questions and answers designed to convey information about the consequences of a decision to strike. Among the questions and answers was the following:

Q   If I go on strike, can I lose my job?

A   Yes. The Company can continue operating the plant, and can hire strike replacements. If you strike in an attempt to force the Company to agree to the Union's economic demands or to force the Company to withdraw its economic demands, the Company may permanently replace you. When the strike ends you would not have a job if you had been permanently replaced.

Subsequent negotiations led to a final offer by the company, and it was rejected by the 200-person union membership. The union called a strike on May 5, 1994. The employer hired replacement workers, and the plant continued to operate. On June 20, the union made an unconditional offer to return to work. Pirelli told the union that replacement workers had been hired and that strikers would be put on a preferential hiring list.

In July 1994, some of Pirelli's employees circulated a petition and obtained 127 signatures of workers wanting the union decertified. The petition was presented to the management, which withdrew recognition of the union.

The union contends that the Q&A letter was threatening and coercive of employees' Section 7 rights in violation of Section 8(a)(1) of the Act. The union contends that because the employer violated Section 8(a)(1), the strikers were unfair labor practice strikers and should have been returned to work immediately upon their unconditional offer to return to work on June 20, 1994. The union contends that the decertification petition was tainted because of the employer's unfair labor practices.

The employer contends that the Q&A letter was explanatory of the problems and not threatening, and thus not an unfair labor practice. It asserts that there was no causal link between the single Q&A on replacements in the Q&A letter and the subsequent strike. Rather, it asserts that the strike was an economic strike. It also contends that the decertification petition was an exercise of employee rights, untainted by the employer. Decide. [*Pirelli Cable Corp. v. NLRB*, 141 F.3d 503 (4th Cir.)].

Dispute Settlement Law | CHAPTER **8**

SECTION 70: INTRODUCTION

The Railway Labor Act and the Labor Management Relations Act both seek to create the proper setting for formalized collective bargaining between the parties, with the parties themselves being responsible for reaching an agreement on matters in dispute. Private negotiation, then, is the foundation of the dispute settlement process in the United States. Government intervention is limited to enforcing the duties of the parties toward one another and facilitating, through mediation and fact-finding, the obligation to reach and maintain collective bargaining agreements. This chapter will, in part, discuss the procedures available for dispute settlement when a stalemate in bargaining occurs.

Labor-management disputes commonly occur over the meaning or application of the terms of an existing collective bargaining agreement. Very often the parties themselves are able to adjust such disputes through a contractually agreed upon grievance procedure. Where the parties are unable to adjust a dispute, most collective bargaining contracts require that the dispute be resolved through arbitration, and these contracts correspondingly prohibit resort to a strike or lockout as a means for resolving the dispute. This chapter will discuss the law relating to arbitration.

The law governing the resolution of national emergency disputes is also discussed in this chapter.

SECTION 71: DEFINITIONS AND TERMS

It is important to understand the terms that are applied to labor dispute settlement. Six commonly used terms are explained next

1. **Negotiation** is the act of settling the issues of a labor dispute directly between the immediate parties to the dispute, namely, between the representatives of each through the medium of collective bargaining. It is the first phase of dispute settlement. If it fails, it may be followed by the conciliatory devices of mediation and/or arbitration on the one hand or self-help in the form of strike or picket pressure on the other.

2. **Mediation** is the act of a third-party intermediary directed toward inducing the parties to a labor dispute to agree to a collective contract. It is synonymous with the term **conciliation**. It is directed to forestall resort to self-help pressure tactics or to stop their exercise if they have already begun. Pure mediation does not concern itself with the direct settlement of the issues at stake; the mediator makes no decision for the parties. The mediator usually acts in the role of a neutral expert to aid the parties to the dispute in resuming or continuing their bargaining efforts. In some cases, the mediator may be called upon to make findings of fact looking to a solution, but the mediator's recommendations do not bind the parties.

3. **Fact-finding** covers a nonbinding report of the issues, contentions, and findings of a neutral expert, with or without recommendations for settling differences.

4. **Voluntary arbitration** is the act of resolving a dispute between the parties through the medium of a neutral third party whom the parties empower to decide the issue(s) relating to the dispute.

   The most familiar type of voluntary arbitration is **grievance** or **rights arbitration** where the subject of the arbitration is a claimed violation of the terms of an existing collective bargaining contract. The term **rights** is used because the claim relates to an asserted right or entitlement under an existing contract. **Interest arbitration** involves disputes over the formation of a new collective bargaining agreement. Interest arbitration is not common in the private sector. An arbitrator's decision is binding on the parties and is enforceable in the courts.

5. **Compulsory arbitration** may be defined as arbitration that is compelled by a state or a federal statute rather than being obligatory by agreement of the parties.

6. **Alternative dispute resolution (ADR)** refers to any procedure agreed to by the parties to a dispute in which they call on the services of a neutral party to assist them in reaching agreement and thus avoid litigation. Types of ADR

include negotiation, mediation, fact-finding, and arbitration. "Minitrials" may also be utilized as a creative solution to complex disputes. For example, the parties may agree to exchange certain essential information and documents and then put on their case in a limited time frame before a neutral person selected by the parties. Decision makers from both sides are present at the hearing to assess the relative merit of the positions articulated by the attorneys of the parties. The neutral may be asked for his or her opinion about the likely outcome of the case should it be arbitrated or litigated. And settlement discussions are pursued at the conclusion of the "trial" stage.

With the exception of arbitration, the goal of ADR is to provide a forum for the parties themselves to work toward a voluntary, consensual agreement, as opposed to having a judge, an arbitrator, or another authority decide the case.

In addition to serving as a potential means of avoiding the expense, delay, and uncertainty associated with traditional litigation, ADR is intended as a means of improving communication between the parties. ADR thus provides a forum for creative solutions to disputes to better meet the needs of the parties.

In the *IUE and General Electric* arbitration case presented in this section, note that the company employs a professional union relations officer whose job is in part to determine whether discipline should be administered and, if so, to see that it is administered on a consistent and appropriate basis from the employer's perspective. Most non dismissal discipline penalties administered by companies are either accepted by the employees involved or not challenged by unions to the point of an arbitration. However, with a large workforce, disagreements between a company and a union over the propriety or the amount of discipline in certain cases result in the use of the arbitration process. The arbitrator in a discipline case is called upon to determine whether the discipline of the employee in question was for "just cause." The reference to just cause refers to the language in the collective bargaining contract. The source of the arbitrator's authority is the collective bargaining contract. The arbitrator has no authority to add to or modify this contract in any way but must interpret it as written. In addition to disciplinary arbitrations, arbitrators are commonly called upon to resolve disputes over the meaning of contract language concerning such matters as promotions, seniority, bumping and recall rights, overtime pay and distribution, vacation issues, holiday issues, work schedules, fringe benefits, subcontracting issues, and jurisdictional disputes.

| **CASE 8.1** | IUE AND GENERAL ELECTRIC CO.
74 LAB. ARB. 338 |

From the Opinion of the Arbitrator:
The evidence indicates that the Grievant [A___] was away from his own work area on his coffee break, standing with a can of hot water in one hand and a cup in the other when the Supervisor, B___, approached him for the clerical information in ques-

tion. It was 8:50 am, a period when an employee would reasonably be on a coffee break. Mr. B___ believed that he needed additional information in order to price a ticket for a hose clamp. However, the record indicates that there was sufficient information on the card for an informed person to find the price

continued

for the clamp. The Foreman pressed A___ for the information, and A___, refusing to give information on the ticket, told the Foreman not to jump all over him or he would tell him to stick the tickets.... The Foreman at that time did not take this individual off his coffee break, ... nor did he advise him to give him the information after his break, but pressed on for the information. The Grievant then advised the Foreman to see the Group Leader for the information. The Foreman again pressed for the information and was told to see the Group Leader and stick the tickets.... Mr. B___ again sought the information and asked him to come in to his office to discuss the matter in private; the Grievant said he would not do so because he was on his coffee break. At that point Mr. B___ offered to leave the tickets with A___ to give him information after his coffee break; and A___ refused the tickets saying "stick them...."

The Union contends that Mr. B___ provoked the incident by asking for ridiculous information at a time when A___ was on a coffee break. I find that Mr. B___ honestly believed that he needed the information to properly price the clamp. And, I find that Mr. B___ did not set out to provoke an incident with the Grievant.

The Union contends that the Grievant was not refusing a legitimate work order because he was in a non-working period on his coffee break. The Grievant, a shop steward, should have known very well that he could have challenged the Foreman's action in seeking information while an employee was on a coffee break by filing a grievance. The Foreman's directive was not in the category of those extenuating circumstances, such as a hazard to the employee's health or requiring an employee to do an illegal act, which would allow an employee to refuse an order. The Grievant had an obligation to respond to his foreman's directive and had the right to file a grievance concerning the propriety of the directive.

The Company's Union Relations Officer, the individual who made the determination that the Grievant was guilty of the charges and assessed the suspension, identified the factors he took into consideration in reaching his determination.... He did not consider the fact that A___ was on a coffee break to be an extenuating circumstance:

Q. Did you consider an extenuating circumstance that he was on his coffee break?

A. No, I didn't consider that at all.

Q. You thought that he had the same obligation?

A. As any other person.

Q. To work during his coffee break as he would at any other time?

A. At the direction of a supervisor, certainly.

Q. But this supervisor didn't take him off coffee break.

A. Well, when you get directions from a supervisor, it is understood that you are no longer on coffee break, you are now working.

Q. That is what you understand?

A. And I am sure that most employees do. (Tr. 109, 110)

I find that a fair and just appraisal of the incident required that the Company consider the fact that the Grievant was on his coffee break, on non-working time. The information sought was not of pressing importance. And... the Foreman's handling of the matter while not provocation was not without error in that he continuously pressed for the information while the Grievant stood with a coffee cup and a can of hot water in his hands and did not initially inform the Grievant that the matter could be handled after the coffee break, or advise the Grievant his coffee break should be delayed until the information was obtained.

The Grievant did, in fact, clearly violate the work rules in question. The "work now grieve later" principle should have been well-known to him as a shop steward. And, with recent previous discipline for insubordination, the gravity of the situation should have been very clear to him. To the contrary, the Grievant chose to openly challenge Mr. B___'s authority by his refusal to give information, either during or after his coffee break; and such is insubordination. And, the language used to his supervisor in refusing the directive was clearly abusive and intolerable.*

I find that the discipline of a four-week suspension should be reduced to a three-week suspension to reflect the extenuating circumstances discussed above. I find that there was just cause for a disciplinary suspension of three weeks....

---

*Author's note: The expletives used by A___ appear in the arbitrator's opinion but have been deleted here for the sake of decorum.

continued

Case Questions

1. What is the source of the arbitrator's authority?
2. What is the rationale for the "work now grieve later" principle?

3. Based on the facts, could the disciplined employee have brought a successful Section 8(a)(3) charge against the employer?

SECTION 72: ASSISTING NEGOTIATIONS

Mandatory bargaining laws date back to 1926. Both the Railway Labor Act and the National Labor Relations Act impose a mandatory duty on management and union representatives to negotiate in a bona fide effort to reach an agreement covering conditions of employment and other related matters affecting management or union authority or employee welfare. If grievances develop over the interpretation and application of the collective bargaining agreement, resolution is ordinarily mandated through the grievance-arbitration machinery contained in the collective bargaining agreement.

Negotiations may fail to resolve differences notwithstanding good faith efforts of the participants. Sometimes economic, political, or personality differences preclude a mutually acceptable adjustment between a union and management. A strike threat or an actual strike may add to the difficulties because the interests and the viewpoints of the union and management representatives may then become more inflexible.

Labor disputes differ from negotiations between commercial interests where disagreement can result in the termination of efforts at further dealing and where disputes over language of an existing agreement can be decided by a court. A buyer may simply look for another seller and a seller for a different buyer. In labor negotiations, however, no alternative exists because employers and unions are not free agents. In the absence of an accord, a stoppage of operations will usually occur when no acceptable substitute or supplement can be found; court action is not a possibility to settle nonlegal disputes. Neutral third-party intervention by mediation is the usual course of resolving these labor disputes.

The Labor Management Relations Act of 1947 established the Federal Mediation and Conciliation Service (FMCS) by Title II with the function of aiding the parties to labor difficulties "to settle such disputes through conciliation and mediation." The FMCS is an independent agency reporting directly to the Office of the President of the United States. Its duties may be summarized as follows, as given in Section 203 of the Labor Management Relations Act of 1947:

1. "The Service may proffer its services in any labor dispute... whenever in its judgment such dispute threatens to cause a substantial interruption of commerce."
2. "If the Director (of the Service) is not able to bring the parties to agreement by conciliation... he shall seek to induce the parties voluntarily to seek other means of settling the dispute without resort to strike, lockout, or other coercion."

3. "The Service is directed to make (itself) available in the settlement of grievance disputes only as a last resort and in exceptional cases."

4. Although parties to disputes are encouraged to use the service, "the failure or refusal of either party to agree to any procedure suggested by the Director shall not be deemed a violation on any duty or obligation imposed by the Act."

The Federal Mediation and Conciliation Service concerns itself primarily with disputes arising from new agreement negotiations and from conflict as to what shall be the changes in the renegotiation of an existing agreement.[1] Most of the states also have provided for the mediation of labor disputes by ad hoc or permanent mediators or boards of conciliation.

SECTION 73: NLRB DEFERRAL TO ARBITRATION

In arbitration of grievances, the arbitrator is appointed by the parties pursuant to an arbitration clause in a collective bargaining agreement. The powers and duties of an arbitrator are limited by the terms of the collective bargaining agreement. Arbitration is generally confined to the question of whether a particular action was valid under the collective bargaining agreement. The arbitrator is concerned, then, with private rights under a private agreement between private parties. In contrast, the NLRB has the statutory obligation to resolve unfair labor practice charges under the amended National Labor Relations Act. The Board's powers are statutory. It is concerned with public rather than private rights. What is the law when a particular action affects both a private contractual right and a public right guaranteed by statute? The answer to that question has been a changing one, tied to the changing political climate and the resulting changing membership of the Board.

DEFERRAL TO EXISTING ARBITRATION AWARDS

As a general rule, the NLRB has the statutory power to resolve unfair labor practice charges in matters relating to contract interpretation and is not ousted from jurisdiction by the existence of contract grievance arbitration machinery. However, under the Board's *Spielberg* standards, the Board will defer to an existing arbitration award when (1) the arbitration proceedings were fair and regular, (2) all parties had agreed to be bound by the award, and (3) the results were not "clearly repugnant to the purposes and policies of the Act."[2] Thus, if a party was not allowed to be present at an arbitration proceeding, to present or cross-examine witnesses, or to have a reasonable time to prepare its case, the Board would not defer to the award and would consider the unfair practice charge on its merits.

---

[1] FMCS mediators were actively involved in more than 5,300 collective bargaining contract negotiations in every major industry during FY 2007, enabling the parties to reach agreements in 3,818 of those cases. Some 173 work stoppages occurred during FY 2007, down from 268 in FY 2006. See http://www.fmcs.gov/assets/files/annual20reports/fy2007_Annual_Report.pdf.

[2] Spielberg Mfg. Co., 112 NLRB 1080 (1955).

The *Spielberg* requirement that the award not be "repugnant to the purposes and policies of the Act" has received significant Board focus over the years. The Board required a showing that the statutory unfair labor practice issue was in fact brought to the arbitrator's attention[3] and that the statutory unfair labor practice issue was actually discussed in the arbitrator's decision.[4] In *Suburban Motor Freight, Inc.*,[5] the Board held that it would not honor the results of an arbitration proceeding under *Spielberg* unless the unfair labor practice issue before the Board was both presented to and considered by the arbitrator. Under *Suburban Motor Freight*, an individual was allowed first to present the matter to an arbitrator as a contract violation and then, where the resolution was unsatisfactory and the matter not barred by the six-month time limit for filing charges with the Board set forth in Section 10(b) of the NLRA, to present the same matter to the Board as a statutory violation cast in statutory rather than the contractual terms.

In *Olin Corp.*,[6] the Board overruled *Suburban Motor Freight*. The Board in *Olin* restated its commitment to follow the basic *Spielberg* standards. The Board also added the following analysis that is to be applied to determine whether the arbitrator has adequately considered the unfair labor practice issue: (1) The contractual issue must be factually parallel to the unfair labor practice issue, and (2) the arbitrator must have been presented generally with the facts relevant to resolving the unfair labor practice issue. The *Olin* Board majority also changed existing law by requiring the General Counsel, in representing the charging party, to establish that the arbitral process was deficient such that the Board should not defer to the award.

The *NLRB v. Yellow Freight Lines, Inc.*, decision, presented in this section, upholds the Board's decision not to defer to an arbitrator's decision under *Spielberg-Olin* because the arbitrator was not presented generally with all of the facts relevant to resolving the unfair labor practice issue. The court held that the Board was not required to defer to specific facts found by the arbitrator.

Required Grievance Arbitration Machinery instead of Board Proceedings

Board policy changed in the last four decades on the matter of whether and in what type of cases grievants are required to use contractual grievance arbitration machinery instead of Board proceedings. The changes reflected the different Board majorities over this period of time.

In its 1971 *Collyer Insulated Wire* decision,[7] the Board announced that it would defer, at least contingently, to available contract arbitration procedures where alleged wrongful conduct may violate both the contract and the NLRA. Under *Collyer*, the Board held that it would dismiss charges where grievance

---

[3] Max Factor & Co., 239 NLRB 99 (1978).

[4] Clara Barton Terrace Convalescent Center, 225 NLRB 1028 (1976).

[5] 247 NLRB 2 (1980). See also *NLRB v. Designcraft Jewel Industries*, 109 LRRM 3341 (2d Cir. 1982).

[6] 268 NLRB 573 (1984).

[7] 192 NLRB 837 (1971).

arbitration machinery was available to the parties to resolve disputes even though an award had not been rendered or arbitration proceedings had not been instituted. Factors to be considered include whether (1) the dispute arose within the confines of an established collective bargaining agreement, (2) there was a claim of employer animosity toward employee rights, (3) the parties' contract provides for arbitration, and (4) the dispute is well suited to resolution by arbitration. The Board retained jurisdiction for the limited purpose of ensuring compliance with the *Spielberg* standards once the arbitration award was rendered.

Although *Collyer* involved an employer who had allegedly violated Section 8(a)(5) of the Act by making unilateral changes in certain wages and working conditions, it was soon extended to cover other violations. For example, in 1972 in *National Radio Co.*,[8] where an employer allegedly violated Section 8(a)(3) of the Act by discharging a union official for failing to notify his supervisor that he was going to another part of the plant on a grievance matter, the Board deferred under the *Collyer* rule. The impact of *Collyer*, however, was severely cut back by the Board in its 1977 *General American Transportation Corp. (GATC)* decision.

In its 1984 *United Technologies*[9] decision, a new Board majority overruled *GATC* and returned to the Board's deferral policy set forth in *Collyer* and *National Radio*.

In the Board's *Wonder Bread*[10] decision, it followed the *Collyer and United Technologies* precedents and deferred considering a Section 8(a)(5) refusal to bargain unfair labor practice charge relating to the company's unilateral requirement of its Route Sales Representatives to submit to physical examinations, including possible drug testing, pursuant to U.S. Department of Transportation regulations. The employer contended that it had a right to take this action under general language in the management's rights clause in the collective bargaining agreement. The union filed a grievance and also filed a Section 8(a)(5) refusal to bargain charge with the Board. Since the employer expressed a willingness to use the grievance-arbitration process and the union filed the grievance and the subject of the grievance was amenable to the grievance-arbitration process, the Board deferred to arbitration process, retaining jurisdiction to review the matter under its *Speilberg* standards after the issuance of the arbitrator's award.

In *United Cerebral Palsy of New York City*,[11] the Board refused to dismiss unfair labor practice charges against the employer and to defer the case to arbitration under *Collyer* because the underlying dispute was not well suited to resolution by arbitration. The Board found that deferral under *Collyer* was not appropriate where the employer made a number of changes to mandatory subjects of bargaining in a new employee handbook and required employees to sign an acknowledgment agreeing to the changes. The Board determined that this conduct amounted to a repudiation of collective bargaining principles in violation of Section 8(a)(5) of the Act.

---

[8] 198 NLRB 527 (1972).
[9] 268 NLRB 557 (1984).
[10] 343 NLRB No. 14 (2004).
[11] 347 NLRB No. 60 (2006).

COURT REVIEW OF DEFERRAL DECISION

As set forth previously, cases deferred under *United Technologies* pending arbitration are reviewed by the Board under its *Spielberg-Olin* standards after arbitration to ensure that individuals' statutory rights under the NLRA have been protected by the arbitral proceedings. Thereafter, a court of appeals may be called upon to review the Board's decision to defer to a decision of an arbitrator. Or a court of appeals may consider an individual's challenge to an NLRB order that requires the individual to exhaust the grievance procedure of the union contract prior to filing an unfair labor practice charge. In *Hammontree v. NLRB*,[12] the U.S. Court of Appeals for the D.C. Circuit approved the Board's *United Technologies* decision. Moreover, it identified some instances where deferment may be impermissible, such as where the interests of the union are adverse to that of the individual or deferment poses an undue financial burden upon one of the parties.

| CASE 8.2 | NLRB v. YELLOW FREIGHT SYSTEMS, INC. |
| | U.S. COURT OF APPEALS, 930 F.2D 316 (3D CIR. 1991). |

[The NLRB petitioned the court to enforce its order finding that Yellow Freight had violated Sections 8(a)(1) and 8(a)(3) of the NLRA. The company contended that the Board's order should not be enforced because it failed to defer to specific facts found by an arbitrator that Lonnie Bedell assaulted a supervisor.]

SLOVITER, C. J.

I.

Facts and Procedural History

Lonnie Bedell was hired in 1983 as a dock worker at Yellow Freight's Carlstadt, New Jersey, facilities. His testimony as to the relevant facts set forth below was credited by the ALJ following a hearing. In April 1986, Bedell observed JoAnne DeGrosa, the sales secretary, crying in the company parking lot after she had dropped her keys. DeGrosa told Bedell that she had been sexually harassed by branch manager Dan Hamlin and sales manager Kenny Dore. Bedell reported the incident to his shop steward the following evening and requested that the steward discuss the allegations with Dore. Dore approached Bedell a day later, and told him that DeGrosa was not a union member and that the matter was none of Bedell's business.

The sexual harassment continued, and DeGrosa was discharged three months later. Bedell accompanied DeGrosa to the New Jersey Division of Civil Rights, assisted her in filing a claim with the Equal Employment Opportunity Commission, and signed an affidavit on her behalf. Thereafter, Bedell posted on the union's bulletin board a newspaper advertisement for an upcoming television series on workplace sexual harassment. As he did so, Bedell commented to a supervisor that Dore and Hamlin "shouldn't have done that to JoAnne DeGrosa."

Shortly after these events occurred Bedell's supervisors began to give him more arduous and dangerous assignments, such as transporting heavier loads without mechanical assistance and working in the hazardous area of the dock where corrosive liquids are stored, even though he was the most senior dock worker at the Carlstadt facility. Bedell also was subjected to frequent workplace harassment. Although he apparently complained on several occasions to his supervisors and to the union officials, Bedell continued to be harassed. Bedell left the

continued

---

[12] 925 F.2d 1486 (D.C. Cir. 1991).

Carlstadt facility in 1987 and transferred to Yellow Freight's new terminal in Elizabeth, New Jersey. Dore was then appointed as the operations manager in Elizabeth. Bedell was again assigned harder and more demeaning work than he had been assigned before he assisted JoAnne DeGrosa, such as cleaning the coffee room and working without the use of the forklift truck and drag line.

Bedell filed his own charge with the Equal Employment Opportunity Commission on January 19, 1988, in which he asserted that he was being subjected to constant harassment in retaliation for the assistance he rendered to DeGrosa in opposing Dore's and Hamlin's sexual harassment practices. On February 3, 1988, Bedell was assigned to unload and move 40 cartons, each weighing 24 pounds. While he was in the process of placing them into three carts his supervisor Joseph Smidt ordered him to consolidate the cartons into two carts.

Bedell and Yellow Freight contest the events that followed this order. Bedell contends that he told Smidt that he would follow the order but added "and I am not a piece of shit," in protest of the continuous harassment. Yellow Freight claims that he refused to follow the order, exclaiming "because you're a big piece of shit.... [a]nd you're a scum bag, too." Smidt testified that Bedell came toward him waving his hands up and down and staring with a crazed look in his eyes. Smidt is 6 feet 2 inches tall, weighs 260 pounds, is 20 years younger than Bedell, and is a judo and karate champion. Bedell weighs 170 pounds. Smidt testified that he nevertheless feared bodily injury because he had heard rumors that Bedell carried a gun and had used it to threaten others. Smidt testified he turned and walked quickly to Dore's office. Bedell testified Smidt walked away and talked to the shift operation manager who was 30 or 40 feet away, and who told Bedell to go to Dore's office.

Bedell was thereafter discharged for disobeying a direct order and assaulting a supervisor. Bedell filed a second complaint with the Equal Employment Opportunity Commission, alleging that he was fired in retaliation for filing his first EEOC complaint.

Bedell also filed a grievance based on his discharge which was arbitrated at a two-day hearing. Bedell retained personal counsel to represent him who also represented the union, Local 641 of the International Brotherhood of Teamsters, Chauffers, Warehousemen

and Helpers of America, AFL-CIO. Bedell was permitted to call his own witnesses and to cross-examine Yellow Freight's witnesses.

The hearing was limited, without objection by Yellow Freight, to the issue of whether there was just cause for Bedell's termination under the collective bargaining agreement entered into between Yellow Freight and the union. Bedell's lawyer stated on the record that he did not intend to raise any of the issues pertaining to Bedell's EEOC charges. The arbitrator found that although Bedell did not disobey a direct order, he did assault his supervisor, and there was therefore just cause for his discharge. He noted in his opinion that, "[t]he grievant's credibility was substantially diminished by the fact that he did not previously grieve what he characterized as unfair treatment when he was ordered to push his carts and not to use the drag line." Bedell appealed the arbitrator's decision to the Superior Court of New Jersey, which affirmed without opinion.

Finally, Bedell filed charges with the National Labor Relations Board alleging that his discharge by Yellow Freight constituted an unfair labor practice. The administrative law judge conducted a hearing after the arbitrator's decision was made. The ALJ found that Yellow Freight committed unfair labor practices in violation of sections 8(a)(1) and 8(a)(3) of the NLRA because Bedell was harassed and discharged for supporting DeGrosa's sexual harassment claim. In so finding, the administrative law judge concluded that much of the testimony supporting Yellow Freight's allegations that Bedell committed an assault was not credible. The ALJ refused to defer to the arbitrator's finding that Bedell had assaulted his supervisor, noting, "[i]t would not be appropriate to do so as the conflicting accounts presented to me for resolution are necessarily enmeshed with the evidence bearing on the EEOC matters."

The Board affirmed the ALJ's rulings, findings, and conclusions. It adopted the recommended order which directed Yellow Freight to (1) cease and desist from discriminating against and coercing employees in the exercise of their rights guaranteed by the NLRA; and (2) reinstate Bedell with back pay and full seniority and remove from his files any reference to his unlawful discharge; ...

The Board itself, recognizing the value of arbitration under certain circumstances, has voluntarily and

continued

as a matter of its own discretion adopted a deferral policy under which it will defer to an arbitrator's award provided certain conditions are met: the proceedings appear to have been fair and regular, all parties have agreed to be bound, the decision of the arbitrator is not clearly repugnant to the purposes and policies of the Act, and the arbitrator has adequately considered the unfair labor practice issue. *See, e.g., Olin Corp.,* 268 N.L.R.B. 573, 573–574 (1984); *Spielberg Mfg. Co.,* 112 N.L.R.B. 1080 (1955); *NLRB v. Al Bryant, Inc.,* 711 F.2d 543, 549 (3d Cir. 1983), *cert. denied,* 464 U.S. 1039 (1984).

Although we have held that it is the court's responsibility to ensure that the Board follow its own policies, we review the Board's deferral decisions for abuse of discretion only....

The motivations and the credibility of the parties and their witnesses may take on an entirely new light once the additional facts related to the unfair labor practice charge are introduced. In the present case, for example, the administrative law judge had reason to question the credibility of Yellow Freight's witnesses' version of the facts in light of the evidence presented to him regarding Bedell's past employment relationship with his supervisors. On the other hand, the arbitrator never heard much of the evidence of Dore's harassment of Bedell in retaliation for Bedell's assistance of DeGrosa. Moreover, the arbitrator, who discounted Bedell's credibility on the ground that Bedell had not previously grieved his treatment, was apparently unaware that Bedell had

complained about harassment in the EEOC claim that he filed shortly before his discharge.

Because the evidence related to the unfair labor practice claim, here the history of discrimination and Bedell's earlier efforts to alleviate the conditions under which he was forced to work, was not presented to the arbitrator, the ALJ did not abuse his discretion in concluding that the conflicting accounts of Bedell's actions on the day he was discharged from Yellow Freight were "necessarily enmeshed with the evidence bearing on the EEOC matter," and that deference to the arbitrator's fact finding was therefore not warranted.

Conclusion

For the foregoing reasons, we will enforce in its entirety the decision of the National Labor Relations Board ordering Yellow Freight to reinstate Lonnie Bedell with back pay and to cease and desist from engaging in unfair labor practices.

Case Questions

1. Summarize the facts and procedural background of the case.
2. Under the *Spielberg-Olin* policy of deferral to existing arbitration awards, was the ALJ obligated to defer to the arbitrator's decision that Bedell had assaulted his supervisor and was discharged for just cause?
3. Can additional facts change the credibility determinations of witnesses?

SECTION 74: THE COURTS AND THE ARBITRATION PROCESS

In *Atkinson v. Sinclair Refining Co.,* the Supreme Court held that it is the responsibility of a court to determine whether a union and an employer have agreed to arbitration.[13] Additionally, the Court held in *Sinclair* that the scope of the arbitration clause remains a matter for judicial decision. Once a court finds that the parties are subject to an agreement to arbitrate and that agreement extends to "any difference" between them, then a claim that a particular grievance is barred by an equitable defense is itself an arbitrable issue under the agreement.[14] In

---

[13] 370 U.S. 238, 241 (1962).
[14] *Operating Engineers, Local 150 v. Flair Builders, Inc.,* 80 LRRM 2441 (1972).

John Wiley & Sons v. Livingston, where an employer refused to arbitrate on the ground that the union had failed to follow grievance procedures required by the collective bargaining agreement, the Supreme Court ordered arbitration, holding that "once it is determined... that the parties are obligated to submit the subject matter of a dispute to arbitration, 'procedural' questions which grow out of the dispute and bear on its final disposition should be left to the arbitrator."[15] In *Nolde Brothers v. Local 358 BCWU*,[16] the Supreme Court held that the obligation of parties to arbitrate under an arbitration clause of a collective bargaining agreement survives, despite the fact that the agreement has been terminated, when the dispute is over an obligation allegedly created by the expired agreement. However, in *Litton Financial Printing Division v. NLRB*,[17] the Supreme Court limited the scope of its ruling in *Nolde*, stating that for a grievance to be arbitrable, it must involve facts and occurrences that arose before expiration of the agreement. In *Litton*, the Court held that the company need not arbitrate a dispute over a layoff of six of the most senior workers at a plant, where the layoffs occurred almost one year after the collective bargaining agreement had expired.

In *Textile Workers v. Lincoln Mills*,[18] the Supreme Court held that under Section 301 of the LMRA, the courts could compel performance of an arbitration provision. In the *Steelworkers Trilogy*,[19] the Supreme Court further expanded the use of Section 301 suits not only to compel performance of grievance arbitration agreements but also to enforce arbitration awards. And in *Groves v. Ring Screw Works*,[20] a unanimous Supreme Court ruled that even where a collective bargaining contract does not provide for binding arbitration of a discipline dispute, nevertheless under Section 301 of the LMRA, two discharged employees were entitled to have the federal courts resolve the question of whether their termination was for "just cause" under the collective bargaining contract.

Litigation involving the courts and arbitration is commonly resolved by reference to doctrines found in the famous *Steelworkers Trilogy*, consisting of the *American Manufacturing*,[21] *Warrior & Gulf*,[22] and *Enterprise Wheel*[23] decisions. In *American Manufacturing*, the Court held that the function of the courts is limited to ascertaining whether the party seeking arbitration is making a claim

---

[15] 376 U.S. 543 (1964).

[16] 430 U.S. 243 (1977).

[17] 501 U.S. 190 (1991).

[18] 353 U.S. 448 (1957).

[19] *United Steelworkers v. American Mfg. Co.*, 363 U.S. 561 (1960); *United Steelworkers v. Warrior & Gulf Navigation Co.*, 363 U.S. 574 (1960); and *United Steelworkers v. Enterprise Wheel & Car Corp.*, 363 U.S. 593 (1960).

[20] 498 U.S. 168 (1990).

[21] *United Steelworkers v. American Mfg. Co.*, 363 U.S. 561 (1960).

[22] *United Steelworkers v. Warrior & Gulf Navigation Co.*, 363 U.S. 574 (1960).

[23] *United Steelworkers v. Enterprise Wheel & Car Corp.*, 363 U.S. 593 (1960).

that on its face is governed by the contract.[24] In *Enterprise Wheel*, the Court held that the courts have no authority to substitute their interpretations of contractual provisions for interpretations rendered by arbitrators where the authority to interpret has been granted to arbitrators. The Court stated:

> The question of interpretation of the collective bargaining agreement is a question for the arbitrator. It is the arbitrator's construction which was bargained for; and so far as the arbitrator's decision concerns construction of the contract, the courts have no business overruling him because their interpretation of the contract is different from his.[25]

In *Warrior & Gulf*, the Court announced a strong presumption of arbitrability as follows:

> To be consistent with the congressional policy in favor of settlement of disputes by the parties through the machinery of arbitration ... (a)n order to arbitrate the particular grievance should not be denied unless it may be said with positive assurance that the arbitration clause is not susceptible of an interpretation that covers the asserted dispute. Doubts should be resolved in favor of coverage.[26]

In *Wright v. Universal Maritime Services Corp.*,[27] the U.S. Supreme Court refused to apply the presumption of arbitrability to a case in which an employer contended that its collective bargaining agreement with the union required the union to arbitrate "all matters" regarding "terms and conditions of employment," including a dispute over whether the employer violated the Americans with Disabilities Act (ADA) when it refused to allow a longshoreman, Caesar Wright, to return to work after being released by his doctor for duty. The employer also contended that the arbitration clause barred the employee from seeking relief on his own under the ADA.

The Supreme Court resolved the dispute before it by refusing to apply the presumption of arbitrability to the *Wright* case, allowing Wright to pursue legal remedies under the ADA. It stated that the presumption of arbitrability does not extend beyond the reach of the underlying rationale that justifies it, which is that arbitrators are in a better position than the courts to interpret the terms of a collective bargaining agreement.[28] And the Court pointed out that the dispute ultimately concerned not the application or interpretation of a collective bargaining agreement but the meaning of a federal statute, the ADA.

---

[24] 363 U.S. at 563.

[25] 363 U.S. at 599.

[26] 363 U.S. at 582, 583.

[27] 525 U.S. 70 (1998).

[28] In *Warrior & Gulf* at page 581, the Supreme Court set forth, in part, the rationale for the presumption of arbitrability, stating:

> The labor arbitrator performs functions which are not normal to the courts; the considerations which help fashion judgments may indeed be foreign to the competence of the court.
>
> Arbitrators are experts in interpreting contractual disputes involving wages, hours, and working conditions. Unlike federal judges, their practices do not ordinarily deal with public laws and remedies.

SECTION 75: JUDICIAL REVIEW OF ARBITRATION DECISIONS

Arbitration offers employers and unions a relatively fast and inexpensive method of resolving disputes that may arise under their collective bargaining agreements. Because the parties themselves select the arbitrator, who is usually an expert on the issue in dispute, there is usually prompt compliance with the arbitrator's award. Were the parties able to challenge the award through the courts on a wide range of theories, the advantages of low cost and the finality of the arbitration process would be lost.[29] The courts have been keenly aware of this situation and allow challenges to arbitrators' decisions only on very narrow grounds. It is most unusual indeed for a losing party to succeed in a court challenge to an arbitration decision.[30]

PLAIN LANGUAGE OF THE CONTRACT

As set forth in the *Enterprise Wheel*[31] decision of the *Steelworkers Trilogy*, the courts have no business overruling an arbitrator because their interpretation of the contract is different from that of the arbitrator. However, the arbitrator may not ignore the plain language of the contract. Should an arbitrator do so, the award may be successfully challenged in court. Thus, should a union and an employer agree in their collective bargaining contract in clear and unambiguous language that possession of drugs on company property is grounds for immediate termination and an arbitrator later reinstates a person found to have possessed drugs on company property, the decision of the arbitrator may be vacated by the courts.[32] It should be pointed out that it is a most infrequent occurrence for an arbitrator to ignore the clear and unambiguous language of the contract. Usually there is some ambiguity in the contract. Where the arbitrator is even arguably construing the contract but the court is convinced the arbitrator has made a serious error, the court may not overturn the arbitrator's decision.

FRAUD AND DISHONESTY

Decisions procured by the parties through fraud or through an arbitrator's dishonesty need not be enforced by the courts. Such decisions are most infrequent occurrences.

PUBLIC POLICY

In recent years, suits have been filed in the courts to vacate arbitrators' awards on the theory that to reinstate certain discharged employees would be "contrary to public policy."

---

[29] It is common to find language in collective bargaining agreements setting forth the contractual authority of the arbitrator such as "The parties agree that the decision of the arbitrator shall be final and binding on the parties and that the arbitrator shall have no authority to add to, subtract from, or modify this agreement."

[30] See *Appalachian Regional Healthcare, Inc., v. Kentucky Nurses Assn.*, 237 DLR A-1 (6th Cir. 2007).

[31] *United Steelworkers v. Enterprise Wheel & Car Corp.*, 363 U.S. 593, 599 (1960).

[32] *S. D. Warren Co. (Warren II) v. UPIU*, 128 LRRM 2175 (1st Cir. 1988).

In *Paperworkers v. Misco, Inc.*,[33] the Supreme Court held that the lower courts were in error in vacating an arbitrator's award on asserted public policy grounds. The Supreme Court pointed out that the court of appeals made no attempt to review existing laws and legal precedents in order to demonstrate that they had established a "well defined and dominant" public policy. Only under the narrow circumstances of the existence of a well-defined public policy and a clear showing that the policy was violated may a court vacate an award. In *Misco*, the Supreme Court stated:

> In *W. R. Grace [v. Rubber Workers*, 461 U.S. 757, 766 (1983)] we recognized that "a court may not enforce a collective bargaining agreement that is contrary to public policy," and stated that "the question of public policy is ultimately one for resolution by the courts." 461 U.S., at 766. We cautioned, however, that a court's refusal to enforce an arbitrator's *interpretation* of such contracts is limited to situations where the contract as interpreted would violate "some explicit public policy" that is "well defined and dominant, and is to be ascertained 'by reference to the laws and legal precedents and not from general considerations of supposed public interests.'" *Ibid.* (quoting *Muschany v. United States*, 324 U.S. 49, 66 (1945)). In *W. R. Grace*, we identified two important public policies that were potentially jeopardized by the arbitrator's interpretation of the contract: obedience to judicial orders and voluntary compliance with Title VII. We went on to hold that enforcement of the arbitration award in that case did not compromise either of the two public policies allegedly threatened by the award. Two points follow from our decision in *W. R. Grace*. First, a court may refuse to enforce a collective bargaining agreement when the specific terms contained in that agreement violate public policy. Second, it is apparent that our decision in that case does not otherwise sanction a broad judicial power to set aside arbitration awards as against public policy. Although we discussed the effect of that award on two broad areas of public policy, our decision turned on our examination of whether the award created any explicit conflict with other "laws and legal precedents" rather than an assessment of "general considerations of supposed public interests." Id., at 766. At the very least, an alleged public policy must be properly framed under the approach set out in *W. R. Grace*, and the violation of such a policy must be clearly shown if an award is not to be enforced.[34]

As a hypothetical example, were an arbitrator to foolishly reinstate an individual to a truck driver position when the individual's license to drive had been suspended for a two-year period, an employer could successfully seek to vacate that award in court. There is a well-defined and dominant public policy set forth in the law that only those with valid licenses may drive trucks, and this policy would have been violated when the arbitrator reinstated the individual to the truck driver position.

A judge reviewing a decision of an arbitrator in the context of the breadth of cases before federal district courts or the U.S. courts of appeals may believe the arbitrator's award to be outrageous and may desire to correct the perceived error.[35] Under a loose and expansive view of *W. R. Grace v. Rubber Workers*,

---

[33] *UPIU v. Misco, Inc.*, 484 U.S. 29 (1987).

[34] *Id.* at 43.

[35] See *Northwest Airlines v. ALPA*, 808 F. 2d 76, at 83 (D.C. Cir. 1987), where the court recognized that there is something called "judicial chutzpah" and the court declined the employer's invitation to impose its own brand of justice in determining applicable public policy.

some judges had refused to enforce arbitrators' awards that varied from the judges' notions of public policy. The Supreme Court's *Misco, Inc.*, decision sought with just limited success to restrict such judicial intervention by reasserting the narrowness of the precedent cases and holding that refusal to enforce an award for contravention of public policy is justified only when such a policy is well defined, dominant, and ascertained by reference to laws and legal precedents rather than general considerations of supposed public interests. Judicial deference to arbitration awards—with narrow exceptions involving an arbitrator's ignoring the plain language of the contract, fraud, and the narrow application of the public policy exception—is of critical importance to the institution of arbitration. The parties need the relatively inexpensive, relatively speedy, final, and expert justice provided by arbitration. The erosion of the concept of finality and the expense of judicial appeals is contrary to the principles of the *Steelworkers Trilogy* and our national labor policy. Where employers want to restrict arbitrators' discretion in areas such as drug possession and use, or intentional safety violations, they have the right to narrow the arbitrators' authority by specific contract language in the collective bargaining agreement when negotiating new collective bargaining contracts. The *Eastern Coal* decision presented in this section validates the *Steelworkers Trilogy* upon which the law of labor arbitration has been structured over the past five decades and sets forth a blueprint for a narrow application of the public policy exception.

| CASE 8.3 | EASTERN ASSOCIATED COAL CORPORATION v. UMW, DISTRICT 17 |
| | SUPREME COURT OF THE UNITED STATES, 531 U.S. 57 (2000). |

[A labor arbitrator returned a heavy truck operator, James Smith, to service with specific stringent conditions after the operator had failed a second random drug test within a 15-month interval by testing positive for marijuana use. The employer sought to have the arbitrator's award vacated in federal court on the basis that the award contravened the public policy against the operation of dangerous machinery by workers who test positive for drugs. The federal district court, while recognizing a strong regulation-based public policy against drug use by workers who perform safety-sensitive functions, held that the employee's conditional reinstatement did not violate that policy and ordered the enforcement of the arbitration award. The court of appeals affirmed. The Supreme Court granted certiorari.]

BREYER, J....

Eastern claims that considerations of public policy make the arbitration award unenforceable. In considering this claim, we must assume that the collec-tive-bargaining agreement itself calls for Smith's reinstatement. That is because both employer and union have granted to the arbitrator the authority to interpret the meaning of their contract's language, including such words as "just cause." See *Steelworkers v. Enterprise Wheel & Car Corp.*, 363 U.S. 593, 599 (1960). They have "bargained for" the "arbitrator's construction" of their agreement. *Ibid.* And courts will set aside the arbitrator's interpretation of what their agreement means only in rare instances. *Id.*, at 596. Of course, an arbitrator's award "must draw its essence from the contract and cannot simply reflect the arbitrator's own notions of industrial justice." *Paperworks v. Misco, Inc.*, 484 U.S. 29, 38 (1987). "But as long as [an honest] arbitrator is even arguably construing or applying the contract and acting within the scope of his authority," the fact that "a court is convinced he committed serious error does not suffice to overturn his decision." *Ibid.*; see also *Enterprise Wheel, supra*, at 596, 80 S.Ct. 1358 (the "proper" judicial approach to a labor arbitration award is to

continued

"refus[e]... to review the merits"). Eastern does not claim here that the arbitrator acted outside the scope of his contractually delegated authority. Hence we must treat the arbitrator's award as if it represented an agreement between Eastern and the union as to the proper meaning of the contract's words "just cause." See St. Antoine, Judicial Review of Labor Arbitration Awards: A Second Look at *Enterprise Wheel* and Its Progeny, 75 Mich. L.Rev. 1137, 115 (1977). For present purposes, the award is not distinguishable from the contractual agreement.

We must then decide whether a contractual reinstatement requirement would fall within the legal exception that makes unenforceable "a collective-bargaining agreement that is contrary to public policy." *W. R. Grace & Co. v. Rubber Workers*, 461 U.S. 757, 766, 103 S.Ct. 2177, 76 L.Ed.2d 298 (1983). The Court has made clear that any such public policy must be "explicit," "well defined," and "dominant." *Ibid.* It must be "ascertained 'by reference to the laws and legal precedents and not from general considerations of supposed public interests.'" *Ibid.* And, of course, the question to be answered is not whether Smith's drug use itself violates public policy, but whether the agreement to reinstate him does so. To put the question more specifically, does a contractual agreement to reinstate Smith with specified conditions, run contrary to an explicit, well-defined, and dominant public policy, as ascertained by reference to positive law and not from general considerations of supposed public interests? See *Misco, supra*, at 43, 108 S.Ct. 364....

We agree, in principle, that courts' authority to invoke the public policy exception is not limited solely to instances where the arbitration award itself violates positive law. Nevertheless, the public policy exception is narrow and must satisfy the principles set forth in *W.R. Grace* and *Misco*. Moreover, in a case like the one before us, where two political branches have created a detailed regulatory regime in a specific field, courts should approach with particular caution pleas to divine further public policy in that area.

Eastern asserts that a public policy against reinstatement of workers who use drugs can be discerned from an examination of that regulatory regime, which consists of the Omnibus Transportation Employee Testing Act of 1991 and DOT's implementing regulations....

In Eastern's view, these provisions embody a strong public policy against drug use by transportation workers in safety-sensitive positions and in favor of random drug testing in order to detect that use. Eastern argues that reinstatement of a driver who has twice failed random drug tests would undermine that policy—to the point where a judge must set aside an employer-union agreement requiring reinstatement.

Eastern's argument, however, loses much of its force when one considers further provisions of the Act that make clear that the Act's remedial aims are complex. The Act says that "rehabilitation is a critical component of any testing program," § 2(7), 105 Stat. 953, that rehabilitation "should be made available to individuals, as appropriate," *ibid.*, and that DOT must promulgate regulations for "rehabilitation programs," 49 U.S.C. § 31306(e). The DOT regulations specifically state that a driver who has tested positive for drugs cannot return to a safety-sensitive position until (1) the driver had been evaluated by a "substance abuse professional" to determine if treatment is needed, 49 CFR § 382.605(b) (1999); (2) the substance-abuse professional has certified that the driver has followed any rehabilitation program prescribed, § 382.605(c)(2)(i); and (3) the driver has passed a return-to-duty drug test, § 382.605(c)(1). In addition, the driver must be subject to at least six random tests during the first year after returning to the job. Neither the Act nor the regulations forbid an employer to reinstate in a safety-sensitive position an employee who fails a random drug test once or twice. The congressional and regulatory directives require only that the above-stated prerequisites to reinstatement be met....

Regarding drug use by persons in safety-sensitive positions, then, Congress has enacted a detailed statute. And Congress has delegated to the Secretary of Transportation authority to issue further detailed regulations on that subject. Upon careful consideration, including public notice and comment, the Secretary has done so. Neither Congress nor the Secretary has seen fit to mandate the discharge of a worker who twice tests positive for drugs. We hesitate to infer a public policy in this area that goes beyond the careful and detailed scheme Congress and the Secretary have created.

We recognize that reasonable people can differ as to whether reinstatement or discharge is the more

continued

appropriate remedy here. But both employer and union have agreed to entrust this remedial decision to an arbitrator. We cannot find in the Act, the regulations, or any other law or legal precedent an "explicit," "well defined," "dominant" public policy to which the arbitrator's decision "runs contrary." *Misco*, 484 U.S., at 43; *W. R. Grace*, 461 U.S., at 766. We conclude that the lower courts correctly rejected Eastern's public policy claim. The judgment of the Court of Appeals is

   Affirmed.

[The concurring opinion of Justice Scalia, joined by Justice Thomas, criticizes the majority's statement that "[w]e agree, in principle, that courts' authority to invoke the public policy exception is not limited solely to instances where the arbitrator's award itself violates positive law." Justice Scalia complained that this dictum opens the door to "fluid public policy arguments of the sort presented by the petitioner, [Eastern Coal]." Justice Scalia believes that it is hard to imagine how an arbitration award could violate public policy as identified in *W. R. Grace*, *Misco*, and *Eastern Coal* without actually conflicting with positive law. In sum, he believes that dictum "is not worth the candle."]

Case Questions

1. What is the employer's view as to the origin of "explicit," "well-defined," and "dominant" public policy that makes the agreement to reinstate Smith contrary to public policy?
2. Did the Supreme Court accept the employer's position? Explain.

SECTION 76: SEIZURE OF VITAL INDUSTRY

Sections 206–210 of the LMRA set out procedures for the resolution of national emergency strikes. Provision is made for presidential Boards of Inquiry, the injunctive process to forestall such strikes for 80 days, interim mediation and conciliation to restore bargaining, strike ballots, and ultimate reporting by the president to Congress for legislative action, all other efforts having failed. The procedures are both complex and dilatory; it must be emphasized that the LMRA does not require compulsory arbitration because ultimately the right of the union to call a strike is preserved.

CHAPTER QUESTIONS AND PROBLEMS

1. Was conciliation and mediation affected by the 1947 Act? If so, how?
2. Is compulsory arbitration constitutional?
3. Is a voluntary arbitration decision enforceable? If so, how?
4. James Ray, a member of the Bakery Workers Union, was employed at Cotton Brothers Baking Company. Ray, who had a history of tardiness and absenteeism at Cotton Brothers, experienced automobile problems one morning; this delayed his arrival at work. When he subsequently arrived at work, Ray was told that he was fired. The union filed a grievance on behalf of Ray, objecting to the discharge. In accordance with the collective bargaining agreement, an arbitration hearing was held. The arbitrator, after weighing testimony and evidence, ordered Ray reinstated with back pay. The arbitrator found that Cotton Brothers had not properly and objectively investigated Ray's automobile breakdown; therefore, it did not have just cause to fire him. Cotton refused to reinstate Ray in compliance with the arbitrator's award. Ray and the union petitioned the U.S. district court to enforce the arbitrator's award. Cotton asked the court to overturn the arbitrator's decision, claiming that, based on the evidence, the dismissal was

unquestionably for just cause under the labor agreement.

Should the court grant Cotton Brothers' request and overrule the arbitrator? Decide. [*Local 370 v. Cotton Bros. Baking Co.,* 110 LRRM 2234 (5th Cir.)]

5. Thomas Huber, the shop steward for the Machinists Union at G&H Products, Inc., was discharged for encouraging employees to engage in insubordination. He had told employees not to fill out a new system of time cards until the company handed over sufficient information to the union explaining the reason for new time cards. Pursuant to the labor agreement, the union contested the discharge through arbitration. The arbitrator heard evidence and testimony on the subject, including the union's contention that the discharge of Huber was a Section 8(a)(3) unfair labor practice of antiunion discrimination by the company. The arbitrator concluded that Huber was disciplined for insubordination, not for exercising his rights as a union steward. He found no evidence of an unfair labor practice and upheld the discharge.

The union asked the NLRB to find that G&H had engaged in an unfair labor practice by discharging Huber. The company asked the Board to defer to the existing arbitration decision on the discharge.

What factors must the Board consider before it defers to an arbitrator's decision? Should the Board defer in this case? Decide. [*G&H Products, Inc.,* 261 NLRB 298, 110 LRRM 1036]

6. The labor agreement in effect between the Retail Clerks Union and Alpha Beta Company governing its grocery store employees contained a no-strike provision and a sympathy strike provision that allowed covered employees to refuse to cross a picket line sanctioned by the Central Labor Council of the San Francisco Bay area. The Teamsters struck several supermarkets, including Alpha Beta, and sporadically set up sanctioned picket lines at Alpha Beta stores. In support of the strike, 20 Alpha Beta employees refused to report for work, citing the sympathy strike provision of their labor agreement. Alpha Beta fired all 20 employees, claiming that they had breached the no-strike provision of the agreement because there were no picket lines at the stores where they were working. The union objected to the firings and invoked the grievance procedure of the labor agreement, which provided for an adjustment meeting and arbitration for "a dispute or difference of opinion arising out of the agreement." The adjustment meeting produced a "final and binding settlement agreement" that allowed the fired employees to return to work. Alpha Beta then informed the union that it wanted to have an arbitrator determine whether the sympathy strike provision of the agreement allowed these employees to strike in the absence of a picket line. The union refused to engage in arbitration, claiming that there was no longer any dispute, as the settlement agreement returned the employees to work. Alpha Beta petitioned the U.S. district court to compel arbitration.

May the courts compel parties to arbitrate under the facts of this case? Decide. [*Alpha Beta Co. v. Retail Clerks, Local 428,* 110 LRRM 2169 (9th Cir.)]

7. A U.S. district court issued a *Boys Markets* injunction enjoining a strike by the United Mine Workers against King Coal Company. The union was about to strike over whether a laboratory technician was included in the bargaining unit covered by the labor agreement. In addition to its injunction, the court ordered the parties to resolve their dispute through binding arbitration provided in the labor agreement. The arbitrator ruled in favor of the union and found that the laboratory employee was a member of the bargaining unit. Prior to the decision of the arbitrator, however, King Coal had filed a "unit clarification petition" with the NLRB

asking the Board to decide whether the laboratory employee was a member of the unit. The NLRB subsequently held that the laboratory employee should be excluded from the unit.

King Coal asked the court to declare the arbitrator's award unenforceable. The union asked the court either to enforce the arbitrator's award or dissolve the injunction that bars it from striking.

Should the court enforce the arbitrator's decision? Should the *Boys Markets* injunction be continued? Decide. [*King Coal v. UMW*, 110 LRRM 2786 (N.D. Ala.)]

8. One day in February, Ernest Swiger, a 10-year employee of Wheeling-Pittsburgh Steel Corporation, was operating an ore bridge crane. The crane is an elevated structure that moves north and south on four legs along tracks while the operator sits in a trolley that moves east and west along the moving bridge. The operator controls a 14-ton bucket that picks up ore and other materials. Around 11:30 AM, some fellow employees motioned for Swiger to come down from the crane. They told Swiger that the crane was swaying unusually and that the back legs were lifting off their mounts. Swiger then noticed that several critical bolts were missing from the structure and that others were so rusty they could be broken by hand.

When the shift supervisor noticed the crane was not operating, he approached Swiger and the other men. The men, including Brian Maguire, described to the supervisor the erratic movements they had seen. Swiger told the supervisor that he did not believe the crane was safe to operate. The collective bargaining agreement in effect at the Wheeling plant provided that when an employee believed working conditions were unsafe, consultations between union and plant officials at various levels would be held to resolve the matter. Maguire took the first step in the process by notifying the union safety representative. In the meantime, the

supervisor had the crane inspected as provided in the labor agreement and was told it was safe to operate. He ordered Swiger back to work. Swiger refused to operate the crane until it was repaired. Swiger was immediately suspended, then discharged at 2:45 PM.

The second-shift crane operator, Robert Coulter, also refused to work in the crane. At this point, the plant general supervisor and the union safety representative decided that the crane should be repaired. As a result, millwrights began replacing the bolts. Coulter began operating the crane at 9:00 PM. Coulter was not disciplined.

An arbitrator ruled that Swiger was discharged for just cause under the contract for refusing to operate the crane. When the matter was brought before an administrative law judge, the ALJ refused to defer to the arbitrator's decision because he believed that the arbitrator (a) mistakenly believed that repairs were made before Swiger was suspended, (b) never heard testimony from Coulter but was told by company witnesses simply that Coulter had agreed to operate the crane after Swiger had refused, and (c) did not hear testimony from the other employees about the crane's legs lifting off the tracks. The ALJ heard testimony from Coulter and the other employees as well as from the same witness that had appeared before the arbitrator and concluded that Wheeling's discharge of Swiger violated Section 8(a)(1) and (3) of the act. The ALJ concluded Swiger's refusal to operate the crane was protected concerted activity.

Wheeling-Pittsburgh contended that the ALJ abused his discretion in refusing to defer. The company asserted that deferral should not be avoided merely because the employee might present a better case the second time around.

What factors must be considered in examining whether deferral is appropriate? Should the Board uphold the ALJ's refusal to defer? Decide. [*Wheeling-Pittsburgh Steel Corp. v. NLRB*, 125 LRRM 2825 (6th Cir.)]

9. Carpenters, painters, plumbers, and maintenance workers of the Denver Hilton Hotel were members of the International Union of Operating Engineers (IUOE). The hotel's five electricians were represented by the International Brotherhood of Electrical Workers (IBEW).

On July 1, the IUOE began an economic strike against Hilton. Some of the other hotel employees, including IBEW member electricians Thomas Harberson and Bill Talley, honored the IUOE picket line. On July 6, Hilton began hiring replacements for its maintenance department. Two of the replacement maintenance workers, Mike Bozic and Tim Jude, performed some electrical work for the remainder of the strike.

On July 12, Hilton and the IUOE reached an agreement through which all of the striking IUOE members were reinstated immediately. When Harberson and Talley returned to the hotel, they were informed that they had been permanently replaced during the strike. Hilton placed the two IBEW men on a preferential rehire list.

The collective bargaining agreement between Hilton and IBEW provided that employees could not be "disciplined or discharged" for refusing to cross a legitimate picket line. Accordingly, Hilton had the right to replace, but not to discharge, the two men as long as they were replaced before the end of the strike.

The IBEW filed a grievance on behalf of Harberson and Talley, claiming that the hotel did not have the right to permanently replace these two sympathy strikers because it amounted to "discipline or discharge," forbidden under the contract. Before the arbitration board, Hilton contended that the men were not discharged or disciplined and asserted its right to replace striking employees. Hilton managers explained that Bozic and Jude had replaced the men and performed electrical work during the strike. The arbitrator ruled that the facts demonstrated that the two men had not been discharged

but were merely replaced. The arbitrator further ruled that Hilton had not violated Section 8(a)(3) by placing the two men on a recall list because the employer had the right to replace, but not to discharge, the strikers.

The IBEW also filed an unfair labor practice charge against Hilton, alleging that Hilton had violated Section 8(a)(3) by refusing to reinstate Harberson and Talley. An ALJ heard evidence that Bozic and Jude were hired not as electricians but as maintenance workers. Furthermore, the ALJ heard evidence that Bozic and Jude were given no expectation that their jobs were to be permanent when they were hired, although Hilton records had since been altered. None of this evidence had been presented to the arbitrator. Accordingly, the ALJ refused to defer to the arbitrator's decision and ruled that when Harberson and Talley returned to work, they had not yet been replaced. Accordingly, Hilton violated Section 8(a)(3) by refusing to reinstate the two employees.

Hilton asked the Board to overrule the ALJ and defer to the arbitrator's award. The employer asserted that the unfair labor practice issues and contractual issues were factually parallel and were fully aired before the arbitrator.

Must Hilton demonstrate the regularity of the arbitration process to prevail? Should the Board defer in this case? Decide. [*Harberson v. NLRB,* 125 LRRM 2667 (10th Cir.)]

10. Veronica Lewis was employed by Spann Building Maintenance at the Meramec Building in St. Louis. In January, Spann announced a reduction in force at the Meramec Building. Although Lewis was affected, under the collective bargaining agreement, her seniority level entitled her to reassignment to another location serviced by Spann. Lewis initially refused to transfer because of transportation problems but later tried to avail herself of the contractual provision. One day in February, Lewis confronted her supervisor in the Meramec Building about the transfer. Following a loud exchange, Lewis was first

suspended and then terminated for improper conduct and the use of abusive language toward the supervisor.

The union filed a grievance on behalf of Lewis. Under the labor agreement, there was a three-step grievance procedure culminating in arbitration at the option of the union. Lewis's grievance progressed through the first and second steps without settlement. The union then notified Spann of its desire to arbitrate the grievance and twice requested that an arbitrator be selected. Settlement negotiations continued, and Spann eventually offered reinstatement to Lewis without back pay or seniority. When the reinstatement offer was rejected, the union decided internally that the purpose of the grievance process had been satisfied and that the union would not pursue arbitration. This decision was not communicated to Spann, however, and the grievance, as well as the request for selection of an arbitrator, was not withdrawn. Dissatisfied with the union's decision, Lewis filed an unfair labor practice charge with the NLRB, alleging that Spann had violated Section 8(a)(1) by discharging her in retaliation for the exercise of her rights under the collective bargaining agreement.

What factors must the Board consider before hearing Lewis's complaint? Will Lewis's unfair labor practice charge be heard by the Board? Decide. [*Lewis v. NLRB*, 123 LRRM 2469 (8th Cir.)]

11. On November 6, the union filed a third-step grievance alleging that the employer, United Technologies Corporation, through its general foreman Peterson, intimidated, coerced, and harassed shop steward Wilson and employee Sherfield at a first-step grievance meeting by threatening disciplinary action against Sherfield if she appealed her grievance to the second step. The grievance that was the subject of the first-step meeting alleged that Sherfield had been "repeatedly harassed, intimidated, and discriminated against" by her foreman, Cote, and that Cote had engaged in an "act of aggression" against her. The act of aggression referred to an incident in which Cote had responded to Sherfield's request for certain parts by allegedly tossing a bag of parts weighing approximately one-third of an ounce at her workbench. At some point during the first-step meeting, Cote apologized to Sherfield, whereupon general foreman Peterson denied the grievance and urged everyone to return to work. Shop steward Wilson and Sherfield indicated that they would appeal the grievance to the second step. Peterson then told Sherfield that the company had been nice to her and that they had not disciplined her in the past because of her rejects. Wilson stated that Peterson's statement could be construed as a threat. Peterson denied that he was threatening Sherfield; rather, he said he was merely telling Sherfield what could and would happen. The employer requested that the matter be submitted to arbitration. The request was refused by the union, and it filed a charge with the NLRB, alleging that the employer violated Section 8(a)(1) by threatening employee Sherfield with discipline if she processed a grievance to the second step.

Should the NLRB defer to the parties' contract arbitration procedures in this case? What factors must be considered to make this determination? [*United Technologies Corp.*, 268 NLRB No. 83.]

Regulating Internal Union Conduct:

ERISA: RICO

SECTION 77: INTRODUCTION

We have seen how labor organizations are legally permitted to engage in conduct that is prohibited to other groups by such statutes as the antitrust laws. Under the 1947 amendments to the NLRA, union responsibilities toward employees and employers were added to the law. The employees' right to refrain from union activities received statutory protection, and union membership can no longer be demanded as a condition of hiring under closed-shop agreements. The 1947 amendments also prohibited unions from coercing employees or from forcing employers to discriminate. Other responsibilities were imposed by the provisions, making it unfair for a union to charge a discriminatory or excessive initiation fee or to have dues deducted by the employer unless individually authorized by each member of the bargaining unit.

Dissatisfaction with the conduct of some unions and companies toward employees and with the abuse of power of union officers resulted in investigation by Congress that brought about the Labor-Management Reporting and Disclosure Act (LMRDA) of 1959. The law imposed further duties and responsibilities on labor unions and their officials for the protection of the members and required certain employer disclosures as well. In this chapter, the duties imposed on unions in relation to workers and union members will be discussed and explained under existing law.

Although the union organization and its officials are generally not opponents of the employees who make up the membership, conflicts do arise between the union, on the one hand, and individuals or dissident groups, on the other, over rights or interests. Disputes arise also over the application of the fair representation principle underlying the collective bargaining statutes. As in the other political activities and institutions based on majority rule, the individual's freedom may be sacrificed to protect the benefits or the bargaining power of the group or to enhance the long-run bargaining position of the organization. A labor organization's constitution and bylaws usually provide internal procedures to remedy unfair or arbitrary action by union officials. Thereafter, administrative or judicial remedies may be pursued.

SECTION 78: UNION'S DUTY OF FAIR REPRESENTATION (DFR)

Union officials have a duty to provide fair and nondiscriminatory representation for all persons in a bargaining unit. Within the membership group or between the members and their union officials there exists the duty to fulfill obligations established in the collective bargaining agreement. Union members may bring a Section 301 lawsuit against both their employer and their union when they believe the union has violated its duty of fair representation (DFR) in connection with the rights due them under the collective bargaining agreement. However, as seen in the *Ramey v. District 141, IAM* case, presented in this section, a union cannot negotiate adverse seniority standing for a group of union members in retaliation for the group's support of a rival union.

CASE 9.1	RAMEY V. DISTRICT 141, IAM UNITED STATES COURT OF APPEALS, 378 F.3D 269 (2D CIR. 2004).

[Shuttle mechanics employed by Eastern Airlines "transitioned" in 1989 from Eastern to the successor carrier Trump Shuttle, which purchased the shuttle operation in bankruptcy proceedings. In 1990, these mechanics voted out the International Association of Machinists (IAM) union as their representative and chose a rival union, the Aircraft Mechanics Fraternal Association (AMFA). U.S. Airways acquired rights to the shuttle routes in 1992 with "single carrier status." The IAM, which represented U.S. Air mechanics, resumed its

continued

status as the representative of former Eastern mechanics. In March 1998, U.S. Air announced its intention to integrate the shuttle workforce with its regular workforce. The IAM negotiated seniority status for the former Eastern mechanics as of the date they started working at Trump Shuttle, asserting that they had resigned from Eastern prior to accepting employment at Trump. The former Eastern mechanics sued the IAM, contending that the union had breached its duty of fair representation by failing to bargain for full seniority rights for them based on their Eastern Airlines service. A jury found for the plaintiffs, and the union appealed.]

MESKILL, C. J....

"The statutory duty of fair representation was developed [decades] ago." *Vaca v. Sipes*, 386 U.S. 171, 177 (1967). "[A] union breaches this duty ... when its conduct toward a member of the bargaining unit is arbitrary, discriminatory, or in bad faith." *Marquez v. Screen Actors Guild*, 525 U.S. 33, 44 (1998). Put differently, a breach occurs when a union fails to "serve the interests of all members without hostility or discrimination toward any, exercise its discretion with complete good faith and honesty, [or] avoid arbitrary conduct." Vaca, 386 U.S. at 177. "[A] union may not, without a legitimate purpose, take action favoring some of its members at the expense of others." *Teamsters Local Union No. 42 v. NLRB*, 825 F.2d 608, 611 (1st Cir. 1987) (citing Laborers and Hod Carriers Local No. 341 v. NLRB, 564 F.2d 834, 840 (9th Cir. 1977). Additionally, "a union violates [its duty] when it causes an employer to discriminate against employees on arbitrary, hostile, or bad faith grounds." *Barton Brands*, 529 F.2d at 799.

Although our review of a union's collective bargaining "must be highly deferential [and must] recogniz[e] the wide latitude that [unions] need for the effective performance of their bargaining responsibilities," *Airline Pilots Association v. O'Neill*, 499 U.S. 65, 78 (1991), "a union may not juggle the seniority roster for no reason other than to advance one group of employees over another" or to punish a disfavored group, *Rakestraw v. United Airlines*, 981 F.2d 1524, 1535 (7th Cir. 1992) ("[W]hen a union attempts to prefer [one group of] workers based solely on [their loyalty to their guild]," it has breached its duty.).

Finally, a union is not permitted to ignore its own policies to punish a minority group within the union. *Nellis v. Air Line Pilots Association*, 815 F. Supp. 1522, 1533 (E.D. Va. 1993).

The jury found that IAM violated these principles. Rather than treating plaintiffs as having transitioned from Eastern—a policy IAM announced in the Eastern bankruptcy proceeding—IAM instead opted to treat them as having resigned in order to strip them of their seniority status for no reason other than animus....

In this case, there was ample evidence, when viewed in the aggregate, to support the verdict. IAM claimed at trial that its motivation for stripping plaintiffs of their Eastern seniority was their having resigned from Eastern. This claim was belied by the position it had taken during the Eastern bankruptcy proceeding that plaintiffs were to be considered as merely having transitioned from Eastern to Trump. Once plaintiffs showed that IAM's purported neutral motivation was pretextual, they only needed to convince the jury that the single other motivation suggested by either party—animus as a result of plaintiffs' association with AMFA—was the reason for IAM's adverse decision.

Plaintiffs met this burden by producing various pieces of evidence pointing to this rationale. For instance, at least one plaintiff testified to personal knowledge of the acrimony between IAM and AMFA. Further, at least one IAM official testified as to the hostility between the groups. In addition, with respect to plaintiffs themselves, the minutes of an IAM local lodge stated that plaintiffs "voted for AMFA. IAM will now go for their jobs." Similarly, various IAM union members petitioned IAM officials not to accord plaintiffs their Eastern seniority because they voted in favor of AMFA. Viewing this evidence in the aggregate and in light of Attorney Lee Seham's corroborating testimony that IAM officials were themselves hostile towards those associated with AMFA, the jury reasonably could have believed that IAM was swayed by the sentiments expressed by its members and officials.

Conclusion

For these reasons, we affirm.

continued

Case Questions

1. Does a union have the general democratic right to favor loyal members and disfavor disloyal members when negotiating collective bargaining agreements with an employer?

2. Was the IAM able to prove that it had an independent rational basis supporting its decision to deny the plaintiffs Eastern seniority, in that they had resigned from Eastern prior to being hired by Trump Shuttle?

UNION'S DUTY IN PROCESSING GRIEVANCES

In *Vaca v. Sipes*,[1] presented in this section, the Supreme Court set forth the requirements imposed upon a union in processing an employee's grievance under a collective bargaining contract. The Court held that the union has the discretion to make decisions "in good faith" and "in a non-arbitrary manner" as to the merits of any particular grievance. Citing the case of *Ford Motor Company v. Huffman*,[2] the majority opinion stated that while a union "may not arbitrarily ignore a meritorious grievance or process it in perfunctory fashion, we do not agree that the individual employee has an absolute right to have his grievance taken to arbitration regardless of the provisions of the applicable agreement." In the absence of evidence of personal hostility to the member or of any bad faith, the Court said that a union could not be found to have breached its duty of fair representation to the member when it decided not to arbitrate the grievance as not meritorious. In a dissent, Justice Black said that the majority imposed too much of a burden on the employee by requiring that the employee prove the union had acted in bad faith or arbitrarily.

In *Hines v. Anchor Motor Freight*,[3] the Supreme Court held that a union had breached its duty of fair representation to several of its members who were accused of dishonesty by permitting their discharge when a minimum of investigation would have resulted in their exoneration. As a result of the breach, the employees were relieved from any express or implied requirement that their dispute be settled through contractual procedures. The effect of the *Hines* decision is that while ordinarily an adverse arbitration award is final and binding on the grievant and a bar to a court suit for damages, proof of a breach of the duty of fair representation removes the bar of finality from the arbitral decision.

UNION'S DUTY IN CONTRACT NEGOTIATIONS

In *ALPA v. O'Neill*, presented in this section, the U.S. Supreme Court stated that the tripartite (three-part) standard announced in *Vaca v. Sipes* also applied to a union's duty of fair representation in contract negotiations with an employer.

---

[1] 386 U.S. 171 (1967).
[2] 345 U.S. 330 (1953).
[3] 424 U.S. 554 (1976).

A union thus breaches its duty of fair representation in contract negotiations if its actions are (1) arbitrary, (2) discriminatory, or (3) in bad faith. The Court set forth a standard dealing with when a union's conduct would be considered "arbitrary" within the *Vaca* rule; that being, when and only when, in light of the factual landscape at the time of the union's actions (as opposed to a retrospective view of the facts), the union's behavior is so far outside a wide range of reasonableness as to be irrational. The Court found that *ALPA's* strike settlement with Continental Airlines was well within the "wide range of reasonableness" that a union is allowed in its contract negotiations.

APPORTIONMENT OF DAMAGES IN DFR CASES

Although in *Vaca v. Sipes* the Supreme Court held that the union did not breach its duty of fair representation, nevertheless the Court, in an attempt to broadly settle the issues of the law of fair representation, considered what damages would be owed a wrongfully discharged employee if a union did breach its duty of fair representation. The *Vaca v. Sipes* precedent was an important focal point in the case of *Bowen v. United States Postal Service*.[4] In *Bowen*, the Supreme Court majority held that where a union is found to have breached its duty of fair representation in representing an employee wrongfully discharged by an employer, the union, in addition to the employer, may be held liable for the damages that it caused. Under *Bowen*, an employer who wrongfully discharges an employee protected by a collective bargaining agreement containing an arbitration clause is responsible for the back pay that accrues prior to the hypothetical date upon which an arbitrator would have issued an award, had the employee's union taken the matter to arbitration. And all back pay damages that accrue after this date are the sole responsibility of the union. Four dissenting justices maintained that the employer should be held primarily liable for all back pay because the employer could have stopped the accumulation of back pay by reinstating the employee. The dissenting justices also argued that the majority's ruling will cause unions to take unmeritorious grievances to arbitration lest they expose the union to the risk of back pay liability under the *Bowen* decision. In *IBEW v. Foust*,[5] the Supreme Court ruled that a union may not be held liable for punitive damages for breach of its duty of fair representation because the potentially substantial awards of punitive damages would impact adversely on the union's exercise of discretion in deciding what claims to pursue to arbitration.

The issue of what statute of limitations applies in an employee suit against an employer and a union alleging the employer's breach of the collective bargaining agreement and the union's breach of its duty of fair representation was considered by the Supreme Court in *Del Costello v. Teamsters*.[6] The Supreme Court adopted a six-month statute of limitations for nationwide application to such cases,

---

[4] 459 U.S. 212 (1983).

[5] 442 U.S. 42 (1979).

[6] 462 U.S. 151 (1983).

choosing by analogy the six-month statute of limitations for making charges of unfair labor practices under Section 10(b) of the NLRA rather than the short (or long) state law statutes of limitations. In *West v. Conrail*,[7] the Supreme Court held that a case is within the statute of limitations as long as the complaint is filed within the six-month limitation period.

CASE 9.2	VACA V. SIPES
	SUPREME COURT OF THE UNITED STATES, 386 U.S. 171 (1967).

[Benjamin Owens filed suit in a Missouri state court against his union for "arbitrarily, capriciously and without just or reasonable reason or cause" refusing to take his grievance with Swift Company to arbitration. Owens, an employee who suffered from high blood pressure, took an extended sick leave. He was later certified by his family physician as fit to resume work. The employer's doctor examined him and refused reinstatement. The employee received a second authorization from another outside doctor but ultimately was permanently discharged for poor health. The union processed a grievance on behalf of the employee through the prearbitration steps of the collective bargaining agreement, but based on a negative medical opinion that the union itself had required and paid for, the union refused to take the case to arbitration. The employee brought suit against the union, including Vaca, a union official, under Section 301 of the LMRA for damages for failure to represent him fairly in processing his grievance with the employer. The Missouri Supreme Court sustained a jury award of damages in favor of the employee. During the appeal, Owens died and the administrator of his estate, Niles Sipes, was substituted as a party. The Supreme Court of the United States, on appeal, held that the union has the discretion to make decisions "in good faith and in a nonarbitrary manner" as to the merits of any particular grievance.]

WHITE, J....

A.

... [T]he question which the Missouri Supreme Court thought dispositive of the issue of liability was whether the evidence supported Owens' assertion that he had been wrongfully discharged by Swift, regardless of the Union's good faith in reaching a contrary conclusion. This was also the major concern of the plaintiff at trial: the bulk of Owens' evidence was directed at whether he was medically fit at the time of discharge and whether he had performed heavy work after that discharge.

A breach of the statutory duty of fair representation occurs only when a union's conduct toward a member of the collective bargaining unit is arbitrary, discriminatory, or in bad faith.... Though we accept the proposition that a union may not arbitrarily ignore a meritorious grievance or process it in perfunctory fashion, we do not agree that the individual employee has an absolute right to have his grievance taken to arbitration regardless of the provisions of the applicable collective bargaining agreement. In L.M.R.A. § 203(d), Congress declared that "Final adjustment by a method agreed upon by the parties is ... the desirable method for settlement of grievance disputes arising over the application or interpretation of an existing collective bargaining agreement." In providing for a grievance and arbitration procedure which gives the union discretion to supervise the grievance machinery and to invoke arbitration, the employer and the union contemplate that each will endeavor in good faith to settle grievances short of arbitration. Through this settlement process, frivolous grievances are ended prior to the most costly and time-consuming step in the grievance procedures. Moreover, both sides are assured that similar complaints will be treated consistently, and major problem areas in the interpretation of the collective bargaining contract can be isolated and perhaps resolved. And finally, the settlement

continued

---

[7] 124 LRRM 3137 (1987).

process furthers the interest of the union as statutory agent and as coauthor of the bargaining agreement in representing the employees in the enforcement of that agreement....

If the individual employee could compel arbitration of his grievance regardless of its merit, the settlement machinery provided by the contract would be substantially undermined, thus destroying the employer's confidence in the union's authority and returning the individual grievant to the vagaries of independent and unsystematic negotiation. Moreover, under such a rule, a significantly greater number of grievances would proceed to arbitration. This would greatly increase the cost of the grievance machinery and could so overburden the arbitration process as to prevent it from functioning successfully. *See NLRB v. Acme Ind. Co.*, 385 U.S. 432, 438, 87 S.Ct. 565, 569, 17 L.Ed.2d 495; Ross, Distressed Grievance Procedures and Their Rehabilitation, in Labor Arbitration and Industrial Change, Proceedings of the 16th Annual Meeting, National Academy of Arbitrators 104 (1963). It can well be doubted whether the parties to collective bargaining agreements would long continue to provide for detailed grievance and arbitration procedures of the kind encouraged by L.M.R.A. § 203(d), *supra*, if their power to settle the majority of grievances short of the costlier and more time-consuming steps was limited by a rule permitting the grievant unilaterally to invoke arbitration. Nor do we see substantial danger to the interests of the individual employee if his statutory agent is given the contractual power honestly and in good faith to settle grievances short of arbitration. For these reasons, we conclude that a union does not breach its duty of fair representation, and thereby open up a suit by the employee for breach of contract, merely because it settled the grievance short of arbitration....

For these same reasons, the standard applied here by the Missouri Supreme Court cannot be sustained. For if a union's decision that a particular grievance lacks sufficient merit to justify arbitration would constitute a breach of the duty of fair representation because a judge or jury later found the grievance meritorious, the union's incentive to settle such grievances short of arbitration would be seriously reduced. The dampening effect on the entire grievance procedure of this reduction of the union's freedom to settle claims in good faith would surely be substantial. Since the union's statutory duty of fair representation protects the individual employee from arbitrary abuses of the settlement device by providing him with recourse against both employer (in a § 301 suit) and union, this severe limitation on the power to settle grievances is neither necessary nor desirable. Therefore, we conclude that the Supreme Court of Missouri erred in upholding the verdict in this case solely on the ground that the evidence supported Owens' claim that he had been wrongfully discharged.

B.

Applying the proper standard of union liability to the facts of this case, we cannot uphold the jury's award, for we conclude that as a matter of federal law the evidence does not support a verdict that the Union breached its duty of fair representation....

In administering the grievance and arbitration machinery as statutory agent of the employees, a union must, in good faith and in a nonarbitrary manner, make decisions as to the merits of particular grievances. See *Humphrey v. Moore*, 375 U.S. 335, 349–350; *Ford Motor Co. v. Huffman*, 345 U.S. 330, 337–339. In a case such as this, when Owens supplied the Union with medical evidence supporting his position, the Union might well have breached its duty had it ignored Owens' complaint or had it processed the grievance in a perfunctory manner.... But here the Union processed the grievance into the fourth step, attempted to gather sufficient evidence to prove Owens' case, attempted to secure for Owens less vigorous work at the plant and joined in the employer's efforts to have Owens rehabilitated. Only when these efforts all proved unsuccessful did the Union conclude both that arbitration would be fruitless and that the grievance should be dismissed. There was no evidence that any Union officer was personally hostile to Owens or that the Union acted at any time other than in good faith. Having concluded that the individual employee has no absolute right to have his grievance arbitrated under the collective bargaining agreement at issue, and that a breach of the duty of fair representation is not established merely by proof that the underlying grievance was meritorious, we must conclude that the duty was not breached here....

Reversed.

continued

Case Questions

1. May an individual employee compel his or her union to progress his or her grievance to arbitration when the employee is convinced that he or she has been wrongfully terminated?

2. What discretion, if any, does the union have in making decisions on the merits of grievances?

3. If a union arbitrarily refuses to progress a member's grievance to arbitration, what legal recourse is available to the member?

CASE 9.3	ALPA v. O'Neill
	SUPREME COURT OF THE UNITED STATES, 499 U.S. 65 (1991).

[After Continental Airlines, Inc., filed a petition for reorganization under Chapter of the Bankruptcy Code, it repudiated its collective bargaining agreement with petitioner Air Line Pilots Association, International (ALPA). An acrimonious strike ensued, during which Continental hired replacement pilots and reemployed several hundred crossover strikers. Two years into the strike, Continental announced in its Bid 1985-5 that it would fill a large number of anticipated vacancies using a system that allowed working pilots to bid for positions. Although ALPA authorized strikers to submit bids, Continental announced that all of the positions had been awarded to working pilots. ALPA and Continental then agreed to end the strike, dispose of some related litigation, and reallocate the positions covered by the 85-5 bid. Striking pilots were offered the option of settling all outstanding claims with Continental and participating in the 85-5 bid positions' allocations, electing not to return to work and receiving severance pay, or retaining their individual claims against Continental and becoming eligible to return to work only after all of the settling pilots had been reinstated. Thus, striking pilots received some of the positions previously awarded to the working pilots. After the settlement, some of the former striking pilots filed suit in the district court against ALPA, charging that the union had breached its duty of fair representation. The court granted ALPA's motion for summary judgment, but the court of appeals reversed.]

STEVENS, J....

We granted certiorari to clarify the standard that governs a claim that a union has breached its duty of fair representation in its negotiation of a back-to-work agreement terminating a strike. We hold that the rule announced in *Vaca v. Sipes*, 386 U.S. 171, 190

(1967)—that a union breaches its duty of fair representation if its actions are either "arbitrary, discriminatory, or in bad faith"—applies to all union activity, including contract negotiation. We further hold that a union's actions are arbitrary only if, in light of the factual and legal landscape at the time of the union's actions, the union's behavior is so far outside a "wide range of reasonableness," *Ford Motor Co. v. Huffman*, 345 U.S. 330, 338 (1953), as to be irrational....

The union maintains, not without some merit, that its view that courts are not authorized to review the rationality of good faith, nondiscriminatory union decisions is consonant with federal labor policy. The Government has generally regulated only "the *process* of collective bargaining," *H.K. Porter Co., v. NLRB*, 397 U.S. 99, 102 (1970) (emphasis added), but relied on private negotiation between the parties to establish "their own charter for the ordering of industrial relations." As we stated in *NLRB v. Insurance Agents*, 361 U.S. 477, 488 (1960), Congress "intended that the parties should have wide latitude in their negotiations, unrestricted by any governmental power to regulate the substantive solution of their differences."

There is, however, a critical difference between governmental modification of the terms of a private agreement and an examination of those terms in search for evidence that a union did not fairly and adequately represent its constituency. Our decisions have long recognized that the need for such an examination proceeds directly from the union's statutory role as exclusive bargaining agent. "[T]he exercise of a granted power to act in behalf of others involves the assumption toward them of a duty to exercise the power in their interest and behalf." *Steele v. Louisville & Nashville R. Co.*, 323 U.S. 192, 202 (1944).

continued

ALPA suggests that a union need owe no enforceable duty of adequate representation because employees are protected from inadequate representation by the union political process. ALPA argues, as has the Seventh Circuit, that employees "do not need ... protection against representation that is inept but not invidious" because if a "union does an incompetent job ... its members can vote in new officers who will do a better job or they can vote in another union." ...

... We have repeatedly noted that the *Vaca v. Sipes* standard applies to "challenges leveled not only at a union's contract administration and enforcement efforts but at its negotiation activities as well." *Communications Workers v. Beck*, 487 U.S. 735, 743 (1988) (internal citation omitted); ...

As we acknowledged above, Congress did not intend judicial review of a union's performance to permit the court to substitute its own view of the proper bargain for that reached by the union. Rather, Congress envisioned the relationship between the courts and labor unions as similar to that between the courts and the legislature. Any substantive examination of a union's performance, therefore, must be highly deferential, recognizing the wide latitude that negotiators need for the effective performance of their bargaining responsibilities.... For that reason, the final product of the bargaining process may constitute evidence of a breach of duty only if it can be fairly characterized as so far outside a "wide range of reasonableness," *Ford Motor Co. v. Huffman*, 345 U.S., at 338, that it is wholly "irrational" or "arbitrary."

... A settlement is not irrational simply because it turns out in *retrospect* to have been a bad settlement. Viewed in light of the legal landscape at the time of the settlement, ALPA's decision to settle rather than give up was certainly not illogical. At the time of the settlement, Continental had notified the union that all of the 85-5 bid positions had been awarded to working pilots and was maintaining that none of the strikers had any claim on any of those jobs....

Given the background of determined resistance by Continental at all stages of this strike, it would certainly have been rational for ALPA to recognize the possibility that an attempted voluntary return to work would merely precipitate litigation over the right to the 85-5 bid positions. Because such a return would not have disposed of any of the individual claims of the pilots who ultimately elected option one or option two of the settlement, there was certainly a realistic possibility that Continental would not abandon its bargaining position without a complete settlement.

At the very least, the settlement produced certain and prompt access to a share of the new jobs and avoided the costs and risks associated with major litigation. Moreover, since almost a third of the striking pilots chose the lump-sum severance payment rather than reinstatement, see n. 1, *supra*, the settlement was presumably more advantageous than a surrender to a significant number of striking pilots. In labor disputes, as in other kinds of litigation, even a bad settlement may be more advantageous in the long run than a good lawsuit. In all events, the resolution of the dispute over the 85-5 bid vacancies was well within the "wide range of reasonableness," 345 U.S., at 338, that a union is allowed in its bargaining....

The judgment of the Court of Appeals is reversed and the case is remanded for further proceedings consistent with this opinion.

It is so ordered.

Case Questions

1. What is the "tripartite" standard announced in *Vaca v. Sipes* that applies to a union's duty of fair representation in contract negotiations?
2. When is a union's conduct in relation to contract negotiations "arbitrary" within the *Vaca v. Sipes* rule?
3. Was ALPA's settlement with Continental irrational? Explain.

SECTION 79: MEMBERS' RIGHTS UNDER THE UNION'S CONSTITUTION

As we have seen, unions have a duty of fair representation (DFR) to their members in the bargaining unit in regard to the collective bargaining agreement, and members may enforce these rights in a DFR Section 301 lawsuit against both their employer and their union. Certain rights of members in relation to their union are established by the union constitution, and members may also pursue these rights in a Section 301 lawsuit. Statutory rights under the LMRDA, which protect members' rights to free speech and fair hearings in regard to union discipline, as well as rights concerning the election of union officers, are covered in a subsequent section.

In *Wooddell v. IBEW*,[8] the Supreme Court found that Section 301(a) of the LMRDA authorized the federal courts to consider a breach of contract claim by an individual member based on his international and local unions' constitutions. The Court recognized that union constitutions are an important form of contract between international unions and their local unions, with members being the beneficiaries of these contracts. The Court reasoned that since individual members can bring a Section 301 breach of contract suit to enforce terms of a collective bargaining agreement, individual members may also sue under Section 301 based on their union constitutions. The Supreme Court thus allowed Gus Wooddell to sue his union for damages and punitive relief where the union allegedly violated Wooddell's rights under the constitution because he had opposed a union dues increase. In this suit, the Court found unconvincing the union's argument that the federal courts would be inundated with trivial suits dealing with intraunion affairs. In *Shea v. McCarthy*,[9] the U.S. Court of Appeals for the Second Circuit allowed a former officer to sue the union's president for the alleged breach of the Teamsters' constitution when McCarthy fired Shea because he would not support McCarthy's candidate for union president. The Court stated that it did not foresee a plethora of trivial lawsuits by extending this right to sue individual union officers for equitable relief.

SECTION 80: UNION DISCIPLINE: SECTION 8(b)(1)(A)

Section 8(b)(1)(A) protects employees' rights in their relations with labor organizations. The main clause of the section makes it an unfair labor practice for a union to "restrain or coerce employees in the exercise of the rights guaranteed in Section 7." A proviso reduces the sweep of the section: "*Provided*, that this paragraph shall not impair the right of a labor organization to prescribe its own rules with respect to the acquisition or retention of membership therein." The problem inherent in Section 8(b)(1)(A), then, is the seeming conflict between the main clause, which offers employees protection of their Section 7 rights, and the proviso, which protects from Board action certain union disciplinary rules that may abridge those rights.

FINES AND RIGHT TO RESIGN

In *NLRB v. Allis-Chalmers Mfg. Co.*,[10] the Supreme Court sustained an NLRB decision finding that union discipline in the form of fines for crossing a picket line involved internal union matters that were not subject to the employees' right to refrain from concerted activities under Section 7.

---

[8] 502 U.S. 93 (1991).

[9] 953 F.2d 29 (2d Cir. 1992).

[10] 388 U.S. 175 (1967).

In *Scofield v. NLRB*,[11] the Supreme Court held that union fines imposed on members who exceeded a union piecework rule were lawful. In *Scofield*, the Supreme Court set forth the standards for lawful imposition of union fines: "Section 8(b)(1)(A) leaves a union free to enforce a properly adopted rule which reflects a legitimate union interest, impairs no policy Congress has imbedded in the labor laws, and is reasonably enforced against union members who are free to leave the union and escape the rule." The third *Scofield* standard, of reasonable enforcement against union members, has been modified by the Supreme Court in *NLRB v. Boeing Co.*[12] In *Boeing*, the Court held that when union disciplinary fines against members do not interfere with the employer-employee relationship or otherwise violate a policy of the NLRA, the Board does not have authority to determine the reasonableness of the fines in making a ruling on whether the fines are an unfair labor practice. If the Board investigated a fine's reasonableness, the Court held, it would be delving into internal union affairs in a manner that Congress did not intend. The Court recognizes that state courts will continue to have jurisdiction to determine reasonableness in a fine enforcement context. The dissenting opinions in *Boeing* argued that it is no answer to say that the reasonableness of a fine may be tested in a state court suit because individual employees are often indigent and such a suit is likely to be no contest. Under Board procedures, the General Counsel represents the employee without cost to the employee if the employee's charge has merit. Further, the dissenting justices argued that state judges have no expertise in labor-management relations and that national standards to be set by the Board are needed in the matter of union disciplinary fines.

In *NLRB v. Textile Workers (Granite State Joint Board)*,[13] the Supreme Court found that the union's imposition of court-collectible fines against former members, who had resigned during a lengthy strike that they had previously voted for, constituted illegal interference with employees' freedom to refrain from collective activities. Because nothing in the union's constitution or in any contract limited this right to resign or to work thereafter, the fines interfered with rights guaranteed in Section 7 in violation of Section 8(b)(1)(A).

In *Pattern Makers' League of North America v. NLRB*,[14] where a provision of the union's constitution prohibited union members from resigning during a strike, the Supreme Court held that such a provision violated the congressional policy of voluntary unionism implicit in Section 8(a)(3) of the Act and curtailed the vitality of Section 7 of the Act. The Court held that the union rule was contrary to the second *Scofield* standard ("impairs no policy Congress has imbedded in the labor law") and was a violation of Section 8(b)(1)(A). Thus, a union member may now

---

[11] 394 U.S. 423 (1969).

[12] 412 U.S. 67 (1973). But see Operating Engineers, Local 3 (Specialty Crushing), 331 NLRB No. 60 (2002), where the Board found that the union violated Section 8(b)(1)(A) by disciplining union members who worked nonunion where the union had no uniform rule or policy for disciplining members who worked nonunion.

[13] 409 U.S. 213 (1972).

[14] 473 U.S. 95 (1985).

avoid union fines by tendering a resignation before acting in a manner inconsistent with the union's rules.

Union Discipline of Supervisor Members

Union membership in skilled trades, such as the electrical, plumbing, or carpentry trades, is a valuable right that many union members are reluctant to give up in order to accept a higher-paying supervisory position that may last only until the completion of a specific construction job. Employers needing competent supervisors are more than willing to accept union members as their supervisors. Union discipline of these supervisor union members for violation of union rules has led to much litigation.

The U.S. Supreme Court, in *Florida Power and Light Co. v. IBEW*,[15] considered the issue of whether a union committed an unfair labor practice under Section 8(b)(1)(B) when it disciplined its supervisor members for crossing picket lines and performing rank-and-file struck work during a lawful economic strike against the employer. The Court held that the NLRB erred in finding that the union violated Section 8(b)(1)(B). The Court pointed out that a union's discipline of supervisor members can violate Section 8(b)(1)(B) when it adversely affects their conduct in performing their duties or when they are acting in the capacity of grievance adjusters or collective bargainers on behalf of an employer. The Court found that Congress addressed the problem of supervisors' loyalty to the employer not through Section 8(b)(1)(B), but instead through Sections 2(3), 2(11), and 14(a). These sections of the NLRA permit an employer to refuse to hire union members as supervisors because of their union activities or membership and to refuse to engage in collective bargaining with them. In *American Broadcasting Companies, Inc., v. Writers Guild*,[16] the Supreme Court refused to adopt the union's contention that *Florida Power* immunizes union discipline of supervisor members who work during a strike regardless of the work they perform. The Court found that ample leeway is already accorded to a union in permitting it to discipline any member, even a supervisor, for performing struck work but that to carry over to the case of purely supervisory work would be an inappropriate extension and interference with the employer's prerogative. Thus, the Court held that the union could not discipline supervisor members who cross a picket line during a strike and perform their normal supervisory duties, including the adjustment of grievances.

In *NLRB v. IBEW*, presented in this section, the Supreme Court held that a union does not violate Section 8(b)(1)(B) when it disciplines a supervisor member who does not participate as the employer's representative for collective bargaining or adjustment of grievances and whose employer has no collective bargaining agreement with the union.

---

[15] 417 U.S. 790 (1974).

[16] 437 U.S. 411 (1978).

CASE 9.4	NLRB v. IBEW
	SUPREME COURT OF THE UNITED STATES, 481 U.S. 573 (1987).

[Albert Schoux worked as a supervisor for Royal Electric Company, and Ted Choate worked as a supervisor for Nutter Electric Company. Both were members of the International Brotherhood of Electrical Workers (IBEW), and neither of their employers had collective bargaining agreements with the IBEW. The union found that both individuals had violated the union's constitution by working for employers who did not have contracts with the union and fined Schoux $8,200 and Choate $6,000. The employers filed Section 8(b)(1)(B) unfair labor charges. The Board entered an order against the union, but the court of appeals refused to enforce the order. The Supreme Court granted certiorari.]

BRENNAN, J....

I.

The question for decision is whether a union "restrain[s] or coerce[s] ... an employer in the selection of his representatives for the purposes of collective bargaining or the adjustment of grievances," 29 U.S.C. § 158(b)(1)(B), when it disciplines a supervisor union member who does not participate in collective bargaining or adjust contractual grievances, and whose employer has not entered into a collective bargaining agreement with the union.

II.

The structure of the NLRA reveals that in § 8(b)(1)(B) Congress addressed "a separate and far more limited problem than that of conflict of loyalties." Florida Power, 417 U.S., at 811, n. 21. One need only compare the scope of § 8(b)(1)(B) with that of other sections of the Act: § 8(b)(1)(B) covers only individuals selected as the employer's representatives "for the purposes of collective bargaining or the adjustment of grievances," while the total class of supervisors "is defined by § 2(11) to include individuals engaged in a substantially broader range of activities." 417 U.S., at 811, n. 21....

We conclude that the union discipline at issue was not an unfair labor practice. Although both Schoux and Choate were supervisors within the meaning of § 2(11), neither had grievance adjustment or collective bargaining responsibilities protected by § 8(b)(1)(B). The possibility that a § 2(11) supervisor might someday perform § 8(b)(1)(B) functions and that past discipline might then have an adverse effect on the performance of such duties is simply too speculative to support a finding that an employer has been "restrain[ed] or coerce[d]" "in the selection of his representatives for the purposes of collective bargaining or the adjustment of grievances."

III.

The Court of Appeals found, as a matter of law, that the Union did not have a collective bargaining relationship with Royal or Nutter, and that it did not seek to represent their employees in the future. It held that such a finding precluded union liability for violation of § 8(b)(1)(B). The NLRB argues, however, that even under these circumstances, the Union's enforcement of its no-contract-no-work rule against its supervisor-members would restrain or coerce Royal and Nutter by affecting the way in which the supervisor-members performed their § 8(b)(1)(B) tasks and by restricting the selection of § 8(b)(1)(B) representatives.... [W]e find that the absence of a collective bargaining relationship between the union and the employer, like the absence of § 8(b)(1)(B) responsibilities in a disciplined supervisor-member, makes the possibility that the Union's discipline of Schoux and Choate will coerce Royal and Nutter too attenuated to form the basis of an unfair labor practice charge....

Both the structure of the NLRA and recent developments in its interpretation suggest that employers are no longer restrained or coerced in their selection of representatives by union discipline of supervisor-members. The statute itself reveals that it is the employer, not the supervisor-member, who is protected from coercion by the statutory scheme. It is difficult to maintain that an *employer* is restrained or coerced because a *union member* must accept union expulsion or other discipline to continue in a supervisory position. The employer's problem—that the supervisor-member might decline to serve as a representative or align with the union during a strike and deprive the

continued

employer of services—is of its own making. A dissenting member of the Board has said:

> "Having been afforded the opportunity to refuse to hire union members as supervisors, the opportunity to discharge supervisors for involvement in union affairs, the opportunity to incorporate into a collective-bargaining agreement the permissible extent of a supervisor-member's functioning during a strike and, indeed, the opportunity to provide additional incentives making it worthwhile for all union members to forfeit union benefits upon taking supervisory positions, the employer, having forsaken such opportunities, cannot now be heard to argue that the union is affecting its selection of the very grievance adjustment or collective bargaining representative it permits to retain union membership." New York Typographical Union No. 6 (Triangle Publications), 216 N.L.R.B. 896, 901 (1975) (Member Fanning, dissenting)....

... Recently this Court decided in *Pattern Makers v. NLRB*, 473 U.S. 95 (1985), that union members have a right to resign from a union *at any time* and avoid imposition of union discipline. The employer may order its representatives to leave the union immediately and there is no barrier to a supervisor-member's obedience to that order. The very least that may be derived from *Pattern Makers* is that union rules or discipline that merely diminish an employer-representative's willingness to serve no longer restrain[s] or coerce[s] the *employer* in its selection of a § 8(b)(1)(B) representative.

IV.

Section 8(b)(1)(B) was enacted to protect the integrity of the process of grievance adjustment and collective bargaining—two private dispute resolution systems on which the national labor laws place a high premium. Although some union discipline might impermissibly affect the manner in which a supervisor-member carries out § 8(b)(1)(B) tasks or coerce the employer in its selection of a § 8(b)(1)(B) representative, union discipline directed at supervisor-members without § 8(b)(1)(B) duties, working for employers with whom the union neither has nor seeks a collective bargaining relationship, cannot and does not adversely affect the performance of § 8(b)(1)(B) duties. Consequently, such union action does not coerce the employer in its selection of § 8(b)(1)(B) representatives. The order of the Court of Appeals for the Ninth Circuit is therefore

Affirmed.

Case Questions

1. Why did the employers rather than Schoux and Choate file the Section 8(b)(1)(B) unfair labor practice charges?
2. When is discipline of a supervisor member prohibited under Section 8(b)(1)(B)?
3. Were Schoux and Choate Section 8(b)(1)(B) supervisors?
4. Why was Section 8(b)(1)(B) made a part of the NLRA?

SECTION 81: RIGHTS OF MEMBERS

A number of statutory rights are incorporated in the Reporting and Disclosure Act of 1959 in Title I, the "Bill of Rights" provisions. The basic rights of equal treatment with regard to nominations and voting, assembly, free expression, and appeal to the courts or to other government agencies are included. Thus, an elected business agent had the right to bring a Section 101(a)(2) LMRDA lawsuit against the union when a union trustee removed him from office for opposing the trustee's proposal to raise union dues.[17]

Legislative rights have precedence over inconsistent provisions of a union constitution or bylaws. The law further provides, however, that it is not to be applied

---

[17] *Sheet Metal Workers v. Lynn*, 487 U.S. 639 (1989).

as to impair "reasonable rules" concerning a member's responsibility to the organization and to the performance of its obligations.

Freedom of participation in all membership affairs, such as elections, referendums, meetings, and discussions, is specifically provided for with the qualifying condition that the matter is "properly before the meeting, subject to the organization's established and reasonable rules pertaining to the conduct of meetings." In *Hall v. Cole*,[18] the respondent John Cole, at a regular meeting of the membership of petitioner Seafarers Union, introduced a set of resolutions alleging various instances of undemocratic actions and shortsighted policies on the part of the union officers. The resolutions were defeated, and Cole was expelled from the union on the grounds that his presentation of the resolutions violated a union rule proscribing "deliberate and malicious vilification with regard to the execution of the duties of any office." After exhausting his intraunion remedies, respondent filed suit under Section 102 of the LMRDA, claiming that his expulsion violated his right of free speech as secured by Section 101(a)(2) of the Act. He regained his union membership and was awarded $5,500 in legal fees by the trial court. The Supreme Court, considering only the issue of the propriety of awarding the legal fees, held that a trial judge has the inherent equitable power to award legal fees whenever overriding considerations indicate the need for such recovery. The Court found such considerations, since Cole's vindication of free speech rights worked to the benefit of all members of the union.

In *Steelworkers v. Sadlowski*,[19] the Supreme Court upheld a union rule banning all nonmember campaign contributions for union office. The Court majority held that the union rule did not violate a union member's right to free speech and assembly under Section 101(a)(2) of the LMRDA. The Court found the rule to be a "reasonable restriction" that protects the union's interest in limiting outside influence on the union. The dissent disagreed that the union's absolute, unbending no-contribution rule was a reasonable restriction on a union member's right to speak, assemble, and run for office. The dissent pointed out that mounting an effective challenge to an incumbent union leader requires a substantial war chest if the campaign is to be effective and to have any reasonable chance of succeeding.

An increase of dues or assessments and changes in initiation fees can be made only by a majority of members voting in a secret ballot or in a convention. The Disclosure Act of 1959 specifies different requirements for national unions and for local unions.

Members may not be restricted in their right to initiate proceedings before an administrative agency or a court of law. However, a member may first be required to exhaust reasonable internal union hearing procedures before initiating an external action, and the internal union procedures may not take longer than four months to complete.

Collective bargaining agreements must be available for all employees affected, whether members or not and whether negotiated by the local or by a parent organization. They may bring civil actions to gain relief in a federal court. They have the right for just cause to examine union records and accounts and to have copies of all documents and information that the LMRDA requires the union to submit to the Secretary of Labor.

---

[18] 412 U.S. 1 (1973).
[19] 457 U.S. 102 (1982).

Title IV of the LMRDA establishes democratic standards for all elections, including the following:

1. Secret ballots in local union elections
2. Opportunity for members to nominate candidates
3. Advance notice of elections
4. Freedom of choice among all candidates
5. Observers at polling and at ballot-counting stations for all candidates
6. Publication of results and preservation of records for one year
7. Prohibition of any income from dues or assessments being used to support candidates for union office
8. Provision for the frequency of elections for officers and advance opportunity of each candidate to inspect the membership name and address lists along with other detailed procedural requirements for balloting

In *Masters, Mates & Pilots v. Brown*,[20] the Supreme Court decided that the union had violated Section 401(c) of the LMRDA when it denied a candidate for president of the union his request for the addresses of the 8,500 union members before the union's nominating convention. The candidate, Timothy Brown, wanted to mail campaign literature to the members. The union had denied Brown's request because it argued that it had a "reasonable" union rule barring all candidates from mailing literature before the convention. The Court found that Brown's request was reasonable, and the union did not advance any basis to show that the request was unreasonable.

In *Steelworkers v. Usery*, presented in this section, the Secretary of Labor brought an action to invalidate an election under Section 401(e) of the LMRDA because the election had been conducted subject to a "meeting attendance" rule that made 96.5 percent of the members of a local ineligible to hold office. The Supreme Court found the rule invalid. In *Dunlop v. Bachowski*,[21] the Secretary declined to bring suit on behalf of a union member who had claimed fraud when defeated in a union election. The Supreme Court held that the Secretary has a duty to provide an aggrieved union member with a statement of reasons for not bringing suit. However, the Secretary's decision, while subject to court review, is reversible only if shown to be "arbitrary and capricious."

| CASE 9.5 | UNITED STEELWORKERS OF AMERICA V. USERY
SUPREME COURT OF THE UNITED STATES, 429 U.S. 305 (1977). |

[A provision of the constitution of the United Steelworkers of America International Union limited eligibility to run for a local union office to members who have attended at least one-half of the local's regular meetings for three years previous to the election of officers. The Secretary of Labor brought an action

continued

---

[20] 498 U.S. 466 (1991).
[21] 421 U.S. 560 (1975).

to invalidate the 1970 election of officers of Local 3489, contending that the provision limiting eligibility violated Section 401(e) of the LMRDA. Section 401(e) provides that every union member in good standing shall be eligible to be a candidate and to hold office, subject to "reasonable qualifications." At the time of the challenged election, 96.5 percent of the members of Local 3489 were ineligible to hold office because of the eligibility rule. The district court dismissed the complaint, finding no violation. The court of appeals reversed, and the union appealed to the U.S. Supreme Court.]

BRENNAN, J....

The LMRDA does not render unions powerless to restrict candidacies for union office. The injunction in Section 401(e) that "every member in good standing shall be eligible to be a candidate and to hold office" is made expressly "subject to ... reasonable qualifications uniformly imposed." But "Congress plainly did not intend that the authorization ... of 'reasonable qualifications ...' should be given a broad reach. The contrary is implicit in the legislative history of the section and its wording...." *Wirtz v. Hotel Employees*, 391 U.S. 492, at 499. The basic objective of Title IV of LMRDA is to guarantee "free and democratic" union elections modeled on "political elections in this country" where "the assumption is that voters will exercise common sense and judgment in casting their ballots." Thus, Title IV is not designed merely to protect the right of a union member to run for a particular office in a particular election. "... Congress emphatically asserted a vital public interest in assuring free and democratic union elections that transcends the narrower interest of the complaining union member...." The goal was to "protect the rights of rank-and-file members to participate fully in the operation of their union through processes of democratic self-government, and, through the election process, to keep the union leadership responsive to the membership."

Whether a particular qualification is "reasonable" within the meaning of Section 401(e) must therefore "be measured in terms of its consistency with the Act's command to unions to conduct 'free and democratic' union elections." *Wirtz v. Hotel Employees, supra*, 391 U.S., at 499. Congress was not concerned only with corrupt union leadership. Congress chose the goal of "free and democratic" union elections as a preventive measure "to curb the possibility of abuse

by benevolent as well as malevolent entrenched leadership." *Hotel Employees* expressly held that the check was seriously impaired by candidacy qualifications which substantially deplete the ranks of those who might run in opposition to incumbents, and therefore held invalid the candidacy limitation there involved that restricted candidacies for certain positions to members who had previously held union office. "Plainly, given the objective of Title IV, a candidacy limitation which renders 93% of union members ineligible for office can hardly be a 'reasonable qualification.'" ...

Petitioners ... argue that the rule is reasonable within Section 401(e) because it encourages attendance at union meetings, and assures more qualified officers by limiting election to those who have demonstrated an interest in union affairs, and are familiar with union problems. But the rule has plainly not served these goals. It has obviously done little to encourage attendance at meetings, which continue to attract only a handful of members. Even as to the more limited goal of encouraging the attendance of potential dissident candidates, very few members, as we have said, are likely to see themselves as such sufficiently far in advance of the election to be spurred to attendance by the rule.

As for assuring the election of knowledgeable and dedicated leaders, the election provisions of LMRDA express a congressional determination that the best means to this end is to leave the choice of leaders to the membership in open democratic elections, unfettered by arbitrary exclusions. Pursuing this goal by excluding the bulk of the membership from eligibility for office, and thus limiting the possibility of dissident candidacies, runs directly counter to the basic premise of the statute. We therefore conclude that Congress in guaranteeing every union member the opportunity to hold office, subject only to "reasonable qualifications," disabled unions from establishing eligibility qualifications as sharply restrictive of the openness of the union political process as is petitioners' attendance rule.

Judgment affirmed.

Case Questions

1. What is the basic objective of Title IV of the LMRDA?
2. What does the Court focus on in finding the meeting attendance rule invalid?
3. How does the union defend the rule?

SECTION 82: UNION AND MANAGEMENT REPORTING REQUIREMENTS

The Labor Management Relations Act of 1947 contained provisions for reports and affidavits, but unions were not required to comply unless they wanted to obtain the services of the National Labor Relations Board. Some organizations preferred to forgo access to the Board rather than meet these filing conditions.

The Labor-Management Reporting and Disclosure Act (LMRDA) of 1957 rescinded this 1947 provision and replaced it with a mandatory reporting requirement. Every labor union *must* now file with the Secretary of Labor a complete report containing the following:

1. The name and title of each officer
2. The initiation fees and work permit fees required of members or others and regular dues or other fees required of members
3. The provisions as to membership qualifications or restrictions, assessments, benefit plan participation, authorization for fund disbursements, audits, the calling of meetings for the selection of officers or representatives and for their discipline or removal, the discipline of members, the authorization of bargaining demands and strikes, the ratification of contracts, and the issuance of work permits

Any changes in union constitutions, bylaws, or rules must be reported. Section 201(b) of the LMRDA requires the filing of an annual report containing the following information:

1. Assets and liabilities at the beginning and end of the fiscal year;
2. Receipts and their sources;
3. Salary and allowances and other disbursements to anyone receiving more than $10,000 total from the union and any affiliated organization;
4. Any loan aggregating over $250 with full details;
5. Any other disbursements.

In *AFL-CIO v. Chao*,[22] the U.S. Court of Appeals for the District of Columbia Circuit upheld the Secretary of Labor's changes to the financial reporting requirements under Section 201(b) of the LMRDA. The Secretary's new rule amends Form LM-2 and requires unions to itemize general receipts and disbursements. The rule requires in part that unions must identify the vendors and other entities that receive union receipts and disbursements of $5,000 or more during the fiscal year and must itemize all accounts receivable and payable of $5,000 or more at the end of the fiscal year. The rule was promulgated by the Secretary to fully inform union members about their union's financial condition and operations and to deter the misuse of funds.

All the information reported to the Secretary of Labor must be made available to the members under Section 201(c) of the LMRDA.

---

[22] 409 F.3d 377 (D.C. Cir. 2005).

SECTION 83: EMPLOYEE RETIREMENT INCOME SECURITY ACT (ERISA)

Section 302 of the Labor Management Relations Act prohibits any employer from paying, and any employee representative from receiving, "any money or other thing of value," with specified exceptions, under penalty of fine or imprisonment. The exceptions include such lawful transactions as paying checkoff dues deductions to the union where the employee has signed a written authorization for such wage deduction and assignments. Another exception allows the employer to make payments into a trust fund for the sole benefit of employees and their dependents. In 1958, a Welfare and Pension Plans Disclosure Act required that details of all such funds must be filed with the Secretary of Labor and made available to each beneficiary. This law was superseded by the Employee Retirement Income Security Act (ERISA) of 1974,[23] which sets forth fiduciary standards for administering such funds as well as vesting requirements and funding responsibilities for pension plans. Bargaining over the benefits contained in pension plans and health and welfare plans continues to be covered by the NLRA.

FIDUCIARY STANDARDS AND REPORTING REQUIREMENTS

ERISA requires that persons administering a pension fund must handle it so as to protect the interest of the employees. The fact that an employer contributed all or part of the money does not entitle the employer to use the fund as though it were still owned by the employer. Persons administering pension plans must make detailed reports to the Secretary of Labor.

Commonly a "benefits claims committee" is set up under the plan to make determinations about coverage issues, and courts will not disturb the findings of a benefits committee unless the determinations are "arbitrary and capricious." For example, Joe Gustafson, who provided chauffeur services for senior executives at NYNEX for a number of years, while classified as an independent contractor, sought benefits under ERISA because he asserted he was a common law employee of NYNEX. While the court determined he was in fact an employee entitled to overtime compensation under the Fair Labor Standards Act, the court was compelled to defer to the benefits committee's determination that Gustafson was not an employee under the NYNEX plan because he was not "on the payroll" as required by the plan guidelines. The court found that such a determination was not arbitrary or capricious.[24]

Regardless of their job title, persons involved in the exercise of discretion regarding the administration or management of a pension plan are fiduciaries, and their breach of fiduciary duties may be binding on their employers. In *Varity Corp. v. Howe*, reported in this section, the Supreme Court recognized a cause of action under ERISA Section 502(a)(3) for individual plaintiffs for relief because a

---

[23] Pub. L. 93-406, 88 Stat. 829, 29 U.S.C. §§ 1001–1381. A number of subsequent acts have also affected private pensions.

[24] *Gustafson v. Bell Atlantic Corp.*, 171 F. Supp. 2d 311 (S.D.N.Y. 2001).

fiduciary's misrepresentation caused the plaintiffs' injury. The Court applied common law "trust law" principles to decide whether there was a breach of fiduciary duty.

VESTING

Vesting refers to the right of an employee to pension benefits paid into a pension plan in the employee's name by the employer. Prior to ERISA, many pension plans did not vest accrued benefits until after 20 to 25 years of service by an employee. Thus, an employee who was forced to terminate service after 18 years would not receive any pension rights or benefits whatsoever. Under ERISA, employers implementing pension plans must select one of two minimum vesting schedules, either 100 percent vesting after five years of service with no vesting prior to five years or gradual vesting over seven years with 20 percent vesting per year after three, four, five, six, and seven years. Special rules apply to multiemployer benefit plans, and participants need not be fully vested until completion of 10 years of service.

An "anti-cutback" provision, ERISA Section 204(g), prohibits any amendment of a pension plan that would reduce a participant's "accrued benefits," including changes to a plan that result in the suspension of payments of early retirement benefits already accrued. In *Central Laborers' Pension Fund v. Heinz*,[25] Thomas Heinz took early retirement from his job as a construction worker. When he retired in 1996, the plan listed "disqualifying employment" to include a job as a construction worker but not as a supervisor. Heinz took employment as a supervisor and received benefits under the plan. In 1998, the plan was amended to disqualify "any" construction industry job. Heinz was successful in his suit to recover his suspended benefits since the change to the plan was a violation of the "anti-cutback" provision of ERISA.

In the past, it was common for pension plans to contain "break-in-service" clauses whereby employees who left their employment for a period longer than one year for any reason other than an on-the-job injury lost valuable pension eligibility rights. Under the Retirement Equity Act of 1984,[26] which was designed to provide greater pension equity for women, an individual can leave the workforce for up to five consecutive years and still retain eligibility for pension benefits. Also, under the Retirement Equity Act, the spouse of a plan participant must give consent to any election to waive the survivor annuity option required by the Act.

The vesting of health care benefits (as opposed to pension benefits) is a matter of contract. In *Sprague v. General Motors Corp.*, the employer told employees about to retire, in a summary plan description, that the terms of the current plan entitled them to health insurance at no cost throughout retirement and that the terms of the current plan were subject to change. Subsequently, GM changed health care coverage, implementing deductibles and copayments that could cost up to $1,500 a year, costs that would previously have been paid by GM. The full bench of the Sixth Circuit Court of Appeals determined that no summary language

---

[25] 541 U.S. 739 (2004).

[26] Pub. L. No. 98-397, 98 Stat. 1426.

or plan language stated that the benefits were vested. And because GM unambiguously reserved the right to change the health insurance benefits, the retirees' arguments were without merit.[27]

FUNDING

ERISA requires that contributions be made to pension funds on a basis that is actuarially determined so that the pension fund will be sufficiently large to make the payments that will be required of it. The Treasury Department is authorized to issue regulations, opinions, variances, and waivers pertaining to funding. ERISA established an insurance plan, called the Pension Benefit Guaranty Corporation (PBGC), to protect employees should the employer go out of business. Under the Retirement Protection Act of 1994, companies with pension plans that are less than 90 percent funded must provide their employees and retirees with an easy-to-understand notice of the plan's funding level and PBGC guarantees for plans that terminate so that individuals will know the extent to which their pension plans are funded and the extent of the federal guarantees.

In the case of defined benefit plans, the entire investment risk is on the employer that sponsors the plan. The employer must cover any underfunding that may result from the plan's poor performance. However, if the plan becomes overfunded, the employer may reduce or suspend its contributions.[28]

In *Beck v. PACE International Union*, the paperworkers' union represented employees covered by defined-benefit pension plans sponsored and administered by Crown Paper Company, which had filed for bankruptcy. ERISA allows employers to terminate their pension plans voluntarily, so long as the terminated plans have sufficient assets to cover benefit liabilities. When purchasing annuities to cover benefit liabilities, Crown discovered that it had overfunded some of its pension plans that would have allowed it to retain a projected $5 million reversion for the benefit of its creditors, after satisfying all obligations to plan participants. The union proposed that Crown terminate the plans in question by merging them with the union's own multiemployer plan. Under the union proposal, Crown would be required to convey *all* plan assets to the multiemployer plan. Crown declined this proposal, and the union brought suit. The Supreme Court held that Crown did not have a fiduciary duty under ERISA to consider a merger with the multiemployer plan as a method of terminating the Crown plans.[29]

TIME LIMITS

While ERISA does not set forth a statute of limitations for benefit plan participants to file suits contesting the denial of benefits by a plan provider, the courts have determined that the time limit begins to run when a plan administrator denies or

---

[27] 133 F.3d 388 (6th Cir. 1998), *cert. denied*, 524 U.S. 923 (1998).

[28] *Hughes Aircraft Co. v. Jacobson*, 523 U.S. 1093 (1998).

[29] 127 S.Ct. 2310 (2007).

repudiates a claim of benefits notwithstanding the existence of an earlier date in plan documents.[30] The length of this limitation period is determined by state law.

CASE 9.6	VARITY CORP. V. HOWE SUPREME COURT OF THE UNITED STATES, 516 U.S. 489 (1996).

[Charles Howe and the other respondents used to work for Massey-Ferguson, Inc., a farm equipment manufacturer, and a wholly owned subsidiary of the petitioner, Varity Corporation. (Because the lower courts found that Varity and Massey-Ferguson were "alter egos," the Supreme Court referred to them interchangeably.) These employees were all participants in, and beneficiaries of, Massey-Ferguson's self-funded employee welfare benefit plan—an ERISA-protected plan that Massey-Ferguson itself administered. In the mid-1980s, Varity became concerned that some of Massey-Ferguson's divisions were losing too much money and developed a business plan to deal with the problem.

The business plan—which Varity called "project Sunshine"—amounted to placing many of Varity's money-losing eggs in one financially rickety basket. It called for a transfer of Massey-Ferguson's money-losing divisions, along with various other debts, to a newly created, separately incorporated subsidiary called Massey Combines. The plan foresaw the possibility that Massey Combines would fail. But it viewed such a failure, from Varity's business perspective, as closer to a victory than to a defeat. That is because Massey Combines' failure would not only eliminate several of Varity's poorly performing divisions but would also eradicate various debts that Varity would transfer to Massey Combines and which, in the absence of reorganization, Varity's more profitable subsidiaries or divisions might have to pay.

Among the obligations that Varity hoped the reorganization would eliminate were those arising from the Massey-Ferguson benefit plan's promises to pay medical and other nonpension benefits to employees of Massey-Ferguson's money-losing divisions. Rather than terminate those benefits directly (as it had retained the right to do), Varity attempted to avoid the undesirable fallout that could have accompanied cancellation by inducing the failing divisions' employees to switch employers and thereby voluntarily release Massey-Ferguson from its obligation to provide them benefits.

To persuade the employees of the failing divisions to accept the change of employer and benefits, Varity called them together at a special meeting and talked to them about its likely financial viability and the security of their employee benefits. The thrust of Varity's remarks was that the employees' benefits would remain secure if they voluntarily transferred to Massey Combines. As Varity knew, however, the reality was very different. Indeed, the district court found that Massey Combines was insolvent from the day of its creation and that it hid $46 million negative net worth by overvaluing its assets and underestimating its liabilities.

After the presentation, about 1,500 Massey-Ferguson employees accepted Varity's assurances and voluntarily agreed to transfer. Unfortunately for these employees, Massey Combines ended its first year with a loss of $88 million and ended its second year in a receivership, under which its employees lost their nonpension benefits. Many of those employees (along with several retirees whose benefit obligations Varity had assigned to Massey Combines) brought this lawsuit, seeking the benefits they would have been owed under their old Massey-Ferguson plan had they not transferred to Massey Combines.

The U.S. district court ordered appropriate equitable relief to address the harm caused by the deception, including reinstatement to the old plan. The court of appeals affirmed. The Supreme Court granted certiorari.]

BREYER, J....

ERISA protects employee pensions and other benefits by providing insurance (for vested pension rights, see ERISA § 4001 *et seq.*), specifying certain plan characteristics in detail (such as when and how pensions vest, see §§ 201–211), and by setting forth

continued

---

[30] See *Sun Life Assurance Co. of Canada v. White*, 488 F.3d 240 (4th Cir. 2007).

certain general fiduciary duties applicable to the management of both pension and nonpension benefit plans. See § 404. In this case, we interpret and apply these general fiduciary duties and several related statutory provisions.

In doing so, we recognize that these fiduciary duties draw much of their content from the common law of trusts, the law that governed most benefit plans before ERISA's enactment....

We begin with the question of Varity's fiduciary status. In relevant part, the statute says that a "person is a fiduciary with respect to a plan," and therefore subject to ERISA fiduciary duties, "to the extent" that he or she "exercises any discretionary authority or discretionary control respecting management" of the plan, or "has any discretionary authority or discretionary responsibility in the administration" of the plan. ERISA § 3(21)(A).

Varity was *both* an employer *and* the benefit plan's administrator, as ERISA permits.... Varity argues that when it communicated with its Massey-Ferguson workers about transferring to Massey Combines, it was not administering or managing the plan; rather, it was acting only in its capacity as an *employer* and not as a plan *administrator*.

The District Court, however, held that when the misrepresentations regarding employee benefits were made, Varity was wearing its "fiduciary," as well as its "employer," hat....

... The ordinary trust law understanding of fiduciary "administration" of a trust is that to act as an administrator is to perform the duties imposed, or exercise the powers conferred, by the trust documents. See Restatement (Second) of Trusts § 164 (1957); 76 Am.Jur.2d, Trusts § 321 (1992). Cf. ERISA § 404(a). The law of trusts also understands a trust document to implicitly confer "such powers as are necessary or appropriate for the carrying out of the purposes" of the trust.... Conveying information about the likely future of plan benefits, thereby permitting beneficiaries to make an informed choice about continued participation, would seem to be an exercise of a power "appropriate" to carrying out an important plan purpose. After all, ERISA itself specifically requires administrators to give beneficiaries certain information about the plan....

... [R]easonable employees, in the circumstances found by the District Court, could have thought

that Varity was communicating with them *both* in its capacity as employer *and* in its capacity as plan administrator. Reasonable employees might not have distinguished consciously between the two roles. But they would have known that the employer was their plan's administrator and had expert knowledge about how their plan worked. The central conclusion ("your benefits are secure") could well have drawn strength from their awareness of that expertise, and one could reasonably believe that the employer, aware of the importance of the matter, so intended.

We conclude, therefore, that the factual context in which the statements were made, combined with the plan-related nature of the activity, engaged in by those who had plan-related authority to do so, together provide sufficient support for the District Court's legal conclusion that Varity was acting as a fiduciary....

... Varity says that when it made the statements that most worried the District Court—the statements about Massey Combines' "bright future"—it must have been speaking only as employer (and not as fiduciary), for statements about a new subsidiary's financial future have virtually nothing to do with administering benefit plans. But this argument parses the meeting's communications too finely. The ultimate message Varity intended to convey—"your benefits are secure"—depended in part upon its repeated assurances that benefits would remain "unchanged," in part upon the detailed comparison of benefits, and in part upon assurances about Massey Combines' "bright" financial future. Varity's workers would not necessarily have focused upon each underlying supporting statement separately, because what primarily interested them, and what primarily interested the District Court, was the truthfulness of the ultimate conclusion that transferring to Massey Combines would not adversely affect the security of their benefits. And, in the present context ..., Varity's statements about the security of benefits amounted to an act of plan administration. That Varity intentionally communicated its conclusion through a closely linked set of statements (some directly concerning plan benefits, others concerning the viability of the corporation) does not change this conclusion.

We do not hold, as the dissent suggests, ... that Varity acted as a fiduciary simply because it made statements about its expected financial condition or because "an ordinary business decision turn[ed] out

continued

to have an adverse impact on the plan." Instead, we accept the undisputed facts found, and factual inferences drawn, by the District Court, namely that Varity *intentionally* connected its statements about Massey Combines' financial health to statements it made about the future of benefits, so that its intended communication about the security of benefits was rendered materially misleading. See App. to Pet. for Cert. 64a-65a, ¶¶ 65, 68. And we hold that making intentional representations about the future of plan benefits in that context is an act of plan administration....

The second question—whether Varity's deception violated ERISA-imposed fiduciary obligations—calls for a brief, affirmative answer. ERISA requires a "fiduciary" to "discharge his duties with respect to a plan solely in the interest of the participants and beneficiaries." ERISA § 404(a). To participate knowingly and significantly in deceiving a plan's beneficiaries in order to save the employer money at the beneficiaries' expense, is not to act "solely in the interest of the participants and beneficiaries." As other courts have held, "[l]ying is inconsistent with the duty of loyalty owed by all fiduciaries and codified in section 404(a)(1) of ERISA,"....

The remaining question before us is whether or not the remedial provision of ERISA that the beneficiaries invoked, ERISA § 502(a)(3), authorizes this lawsuit for individual relief....

> "Sec. 502. (a) A civil action may be brought— ...
> "(3) by a participant, beneficiary, or fiduciary (A) to enjoin any act or practice which violates any provision of this title or the terms of the plan, or (B) to obtain other appropriate equitable relief (i) to redress such violations or (ii) to enforce any provisions of this title or the terms of the plan; ...

The District Court held that the third subsection, which we have italicized, authorized this suit and the relief awarded. Varity concedes that the plaintiffs satisfy most of this provision's requirements, namely that the plaintiffs are plan "participants" or "beneficiaries," and that they are suing for "equitable" relief to "redress" a violation of § 404(a), which is a "provision of this title." Varity does not agree, however, that this lawsuit seeks equitable relief that is *appropriate*." ...

... [W]e believe that granting a remedy is consistent with the literal language of the statute, the Act's purposes, and pre-existing trust law.

For these reasons, the judgment of the Court of Appeals is

Affirmed.

JUSTICE THOMAS, with whom JUSTICE O'CONNOR and JUSTICE SCALIA join, Dissenting ...

In *Massachusetts Mut. Life Ins. Co. v. Russell*, 473 U.S. 134, 105 S.Ct. 3085, 87 L.Ed.2d 96 (1985), we held that actions for fiduciary breach under §§ 409 and 502(a)(2), 29 U.S.C. §§ 1109, 1132(a)(2) (1988 ed.), the provisions of ERISA specifically designed for civil enforcement of fiduciary duties, must "be brought in a representative capacity on behalf of the plan as a whole." *Id.*, at 142, n. 9, 105 S.Ct., at 3090, n. 9. The Court today holds that § 502(a)(3), 29 U.S.C. § 1132(a)(3), the catchall remedial provision that directly follows § 502(a)(2), provides the individual relief for fiduciary breach that we found to be unavailable under § 502(a)(2). This holding cannot be squared with the text or structure of ERISA, and to reach it requires the repudiation of much of our reasoning in *Russell*. The Court also finds that Varity was subject to fiduciary obligations under ERISA because it engaged in activity of a "plan-related nature" that plan participants reasonably perceived to be conducted in the employer's capacity as plan fiduciary. *Ante*, at 1073. This holding, like the first, has no basis in statutory text. Because these holdings are fundamentally at odds with the statutory scheme enacted by Congress, I respectfully dissent....

Case Questions

1. Was Varity acting as a fiduciary at the special meeting held with workers, or was it acting as an employer giving an optimistic view of a new venture?

2. Did Varity's deception violate ERISA-imposed fiduciary duties?

3. Does ERISA § 502(a)(3) authorize lawsuits for individualized equitable relief for breach of fiduciary obligations?

PROTECTION FROM DISCRIMINATION AND ENFORCEMENT RIGHTS

Section 510 of the Act prohibits the discharge of, or any discrimination against, an employee for exercising any right under the Act, or in order to prevent the vesting of an employee's pension benefits. The Act grants individuals the right to sue for damages in federal courts. The *Ingersoll-Rand Co. v. McClendon* decision, presented in this section, determined that an employee may not sue his employer in state court on state contract and tort theories based on the claim that his employer had fired him to prevent him from receiving a pension.[31] The employee's only remedy is to bring a civil action in U.S. district court based on Section 510 of ERISA.

ERISA authorizes the Secretary of Labor and employees to bring court actions to compel the observance of the statutory requirements.

COBRA NOTIFICATION REQUIREMENTS ON HEALTH INSURANCE PLANS

ERISA applies to health insurance plans without the vesting and funding guarantees applicable to pension benefits under ERISA. The Consolidated Omnibus Budget Reconciliation Act (COBRA)[32] requires the sponsor of a group health plan to provide each qualified beneficiary who would lose coverage under a health insurance plan as a result of a qualifying event (such as termination from employment), other than by reason of gross misconduct, the option of continuation of coverage under the plan. Each employee must be given written notice of his or her right to continue coverage, for a period of time between 18 and 36 months, depending on the qualifying event. The employee is responsible for payment of premiums for the period. An individual may bring suit under ERISA for civil penalties and damages for failure to comply with the COBRA notification requirements.[33] Small businesses employing fewer than 20 persons are exempt from the notification requirements.

CONFLICT WITH STATE LAWS

The Supreme Court has been called upon to resolve questions as to the applicability of state laws to pension plans governed by ERISA. In *Alessi v. Raybestos-Manhattan*,[34] the Supreme Court held that a New Jersey law that prohibited private pension plans governed by ERISA from reducing a retiree's benefits by the amount of a workers' compensation award was preempted by ERISA. The Court held, moreover, that Congress had approved the type of provision in question, which permitted offsets of pension benefits based on workers' compensation awards. In *Mackey v. Lanier Collections Agency & Service, Inc.*,[35] the Supreme

---

[31] But see *Rush Prudential HMO, Inc., v. Moran*, 122 S. Ct. 451 (2002), which determined that ERISA does not preempt the Illinois HMO Act, thus allowing a patient who was a participant in an employee benefit plan to sue her HMO for reimbursement for microneurolysis surgery.

[32] 29 U.S.C., §§ 1161–68.

[33] *Martinez v. Dodge Printing Centers, Inc.*, 123 B.R. 77 (D. Col. 1991).

[34] 451 U.S. 504 (1981).

[35] 486 U.S. 825 (1988).

Court held that ERISA does not preempt state general garnishment laws that give creditors access to employee *welfare* benefit funds governed by ERISA, funds that provide vacation and holiday benefits to employees. Section 206(d)(1) of ERISA protects *pension* benefits, however, from garnishment under state laws.

CASE 9.7	INGERSOLL-RAND CO. v. McCLENDON
	SUPREME COURT OF THE UNITED STATES, 498 U.S. 133 (1990).

[After petitioner, Ingersoll-Rand Company, fired respondent, Perry McClendon, McClendon filed a wrongful discharge action under various state law tort and contract theories, alleging that a principal reason for his termination was the company's desire to avoid contributing to his pension fund. The Texas court granted the company summary judgment, and the state court of appeals affirmed, ruling that McClendon's employment was terminable at will. The Texas Supreme Court reversed and remanded for trial, holding that public policy required recognition of an exception to the employment-at-will doctrine. Therefore, recovery would be permitted in a wrongful discharge action if the plaintiff could prove that "the principal reason for his termination was the employer's desire to avoid contributing to or paying benefits under the employee's pension fund." In distinguishing federal cases holding similar claims preempted by the Employee Retirement Income Security Act of 1974 (ERISA), the court reasoned that McClendon was seeking future lost wages, recovery for mental anguish, and punitive damages rather than lost pension benefits. The U.S. Supreme Court granted certiorari.]

O'CONNOR, J....

... [T]he Texas cause of action would be pre-empted because it conflicts directly with an ERISA cause of action. McClendon's claim falls squarely within the ambit of ERISA § 510, which provides:

"It shall be unlawful for any person to discharge, fine, suspend, expel, discipline, or discriminate against a participant or beneficiary for exercising any right to which he is entitled under the provisions of an employee benefit plan ... *or for the purpose of interfering with the attainment of any*

right to which such participant may become entitled under the plan...." 29 U.S.C. § 1140 (emphasis added).

By its terms § 510 protects plan participants from termination motivated by an employer's desire to prevent a pension from vesting. Congress viewed this section as a crucial part of ERISA because, without it, employers would be able to circumvent the provision of promised benefits. We have no doubt that this claim is prototypical of the kind Congress intended to cover under § 510.

"[T]he mere existence of a federal regulatory or enforcement scheme," however, even a considerably detailed one, "does not by itself imply pre-emption of state remedies." *English v. General Electric Co.*, 496 U.S.___, ___ (1990) (slip op., at 14). Accordingly, "'we must look for special features warranting preemption.'"

Of particular relevance in this inquiry is § 502(a)—ERISA's civil enforcement mechanism. That section as set forth in 29 U.S.C. §§ 1132(a)(3), (e), provides, in pertinent part:

"A civil action may be brought—
"(3) by a participant ... (A) to enjoin any act or practice which violates any provision of this subchapter or the terms of the plan, or (B) to obtain other appropriate equitable relief (i) to redress such violations or (ii) to enforce any provisions of this subchapter or the terms of the plan;
"(e)(1) Except for actions under subsection (a)(1)(B) of this section, the district courts of the United States shall have *exclusive jurisdiction of civil actions under this subchapter brought by ... a participant.*" (Emphasis added.)

continued

REGULATING INTERNAL UNION CONDUCT **313**

In *Pilot Life* we examined this section at some length and explained that Congress intended § 502(a) to be the exclusive remedy for rights guaranteed under ERISA, including those provided by § 510: ...

It is clear to us that the exclusive remedy provided by § 502(a) is precisely the kind of "special featur[e]" that "warrant[s] preemption" in this case. As we explained in *Pilot Life*, ERISA's legislative history makes clear that "the preemptive force of § 502(a) was modeled on the exclusive remedy provided by § 301 of the Labor Management Relations Act, 1947 (LMRA)." ... "Congress was well aware that the powerful pre-emptive force of § 301 of the LMRA displaced" all state-law claims, "even when the state action purported to authorize a remedy unavailable under the federal provision." In *Metropolitan Life Ins. Co. v. Taylor*, 481 U.S. 58 (1987), we again drew upon the parallel between § 502(a) and § 301 of the LMRA to support our conclusion that the preemptive effect of § 502(a) was so complete that an ERISA preemption defense provides a sufficient basis for removal of a cause of action to the federal forum notwithstanding the traditional limitation imposed by the "well-pleaded complaint" rule. *Id.*, at 64–67.

We rely on this same evidence in concluding that the requirements of conflict preemption are satisfied in this case. Unquestionably, the Texas cause of action purports to provide a remedy for the violation of a right expressly guaranteed by § 510 and exclusively enforced by § 502(a). Accordingly we hold that

"'[w]hen it is clear or may fairly be assumed that the activities which a State purports to regulate are protected" by § 510 of ERISA, "due regard for the federal enactment requires that state jurisdiction must yield.'"

The preceding discussion also responds to the Texas court's attempt to distinguish this case as not one within ERISA's purview. Not only is § 502(a) the exclusive remedy for vindicating § 510-protected rights, there is no basis in § 502(a)'s language for limiting ERISA actions to only those which seek "pension benefits." It is clear that the relief requested here is well within the power of federal courts to provide. Consequently, it is no answer to a pre-emption argument that a particular plaintiff is not seeking recovery of pension benefits.

The judgment of the Texas Supreme Court is reversed.

It is so ordered.

Case Questions

1. Does ERISA prohibit an employer from discharging an employee when the employer is motivated by a desire to prevent a pension from vesting?

2. Because McClendon was not seeking lost pension benefits but rather future lost wages, recovery for mental anguish, and punitive damages, his claim was not governed by ERISA. Assess the validity of this position.

SECTION 84: POLITICAL CONTRIBUTIONS AND EXPENDITURES

The Labor Management Relations Act of 1947 contained a provision concerning union political expenditures. Its Section 304 presented the amended Section 313 of the Federal Corrupt Practices Act. As amended, the section included unions, as well as previously covered corporations, under the bans imposed on expending or contributing funds in federal election activities. This section was incorporated into the Federal Election Campaign Act of 1976 as Section 321.[36] This law prohibits unions from spending funds derived from dues in connection with federal political election campaigns. A union may, however, establish a separate fund to make political expenditures if such funds are financed by voluntary contributions from union members. Moreover, Section 321 excludes from the prohibitions expenditures for communications to union members and their families.

---

[36] Pub. L. No. 94-283, 29 U.S.C. § 441b(a).

In *Pipefitters Local 562 v. United States,*[37] the Supreme Court found that union political funds are legal if they are segregated from regular dues and assessments, they are earmarked for political activity purposes with the members so informed, and there is no actual or threatened reprisal by job or membership discrimination in connection with the collection of the members' contributions.

SECTION 85: ANTIRACKETEERING LAWS

The "AntiRacketeering," or Hobbs, Act[38] is intended to prevent anyone from obstructing or affecting commerce by robbery or extortion. Extortion under the Act refers to obtaining property from a consenting party by the wrongful use of actual or threatened force, violence, or fear or under color of official right. The Supreme Court held in *United States v. Enmons*[39] that union members could not be prosecuted under the Hobbs Act on a charge of conspiracy to extort higher wages from a company by the use of wrongful force, even though strikers fired rifles at three company transformers and blew up a substation. The Court ruled that "wrongful force" under the Hobbs Act means force with a wrongful objective, and in this case, the objective of higher wages through collective bargaining was legitimate. The Court pointed out that strike violence is properly prosecuted under state criminal laws.[40]

The Racketeer Influenced and Corrupt Organizations Act (RICO) was enacted by Congress in 1970. RICO authorizes criminal and civil actions against persons who use any income derived from racketeering activity to invest in an enterprise, control an enterprise through racketeering activity, and conduct an enterprise's affairs through a pattern of racketeering activity.[41] Under RICO, **racketeering activity** is defined as conduct that violates certain state laws and is punishable by imprisonment for more than one year and conduct that violates numerous federal criminal statutes, including federal laws that restrict loans and payments to labor organizations and punish embezzlement from union funds.[42] In criminal and civil actions under RICO, a **pattern of racketeering activity** must be established by proving that at least two acts of racketeering activity (so-called predicate acts) have been committed by the defendant within a period of 10 years.[43] Conviction under

---

[37] 407 U.S. 385 (1972). See *First National Bank v. Belloti*, 435 U.S. 765 (1978).

[38] 18 U.S.C. § 1951.

[39] 410 U.S. 396 (1973).

[40] In *United States v. Thordarson*, 107 LRRM 2505 (9th Cir. 1981), the court of appeals stated that using explosives and arson to destroy vehicles was not the sort of union picket line violence that the *Enmons* court feared would be transformed into federal crimes under the Hobbs Act. It held that union members who used such violence in support of their demands could be prosecuted under the Racketeer Influenced and Corrupt Organizations Act (RICO).

[41] 18 U.S.C. § 1962(a) to (d).

[42] 18 U.S.C. § 1961(1)(A) to (C).

[43] In *Sedima, SPRL v. Imrex Co.*, 473 U.S. 479 (1985), the Supreme Court noted that civil actions under RICO should not be maintained on the basis of two predicate acts if the acts are not part of a pattern but rather are isolated incidents of racketeering. *Id.* at 3285 n. 14.

RICO's criminal provisions may result in a $25,000 fine and up to 20 years' imprisonment as well as forfeiture of all property and financial interest acquired through racketeering activity.[44] A successful civil plaintiff may recover treble damages, costs, and attorney fees.[45]

RICO has various applications in the field of labor relations. Criminal prosecutions under RICO have been brought to address corrupt practices by union officials. Both the RICO Act and Hobbs Act were applied to the defendants in the *United States v. Stolfi* decision, presented in this section.[46] In addition, RICO's civil provisions have been invoked by unions and union members to support actions for damages against employers and union officials.[47]

An example of civil RICO's impact on union affairs is seen in *Hunt v. Weatherbee*.[48] In *Hunt*, a union member brought a civil action under RICO against several of her union's officials and her employers based on alleged acts of coercion and extortion that she alleged were part of a prolonged pattern of sexual harassment, discrimination, and violation of contractual rights. The court ruled that the predicate acts alleged by Hunt were not isolated acts but were sufficient to support a RICO claim because the incidents of sexual harassment and discrimination established a pattern of racketeering activity.

In *Trollinger v. Tyson Foods, Inc.*, the Sixth Circuit held that an employer's violations of immigration law may serve as predicate acts where legal workers have sufficiently direct injuries for RICO standing where it was alleged that the company, by hiring and harboring illegal immigrants, paid their legally authorized employees less than market rates.[49] The plaintiffs sought to recover damages in the amount of triple the difference between their artificially depressed wages and competitive market wages. On remand, the U.S. district court granted the employer's motion for summary judgment. While there was a basis for a jury to find that Tyson concealed unauthorized employees at one of its plants, the plaintiffs did not provide evidence that retention of unauthorized employees actually caused the depression of wages in this case.[50]

Employers and unions are increasingly concerned with the threat posed by civil RICO claims. Any number of actions may subject employers and union officials to treble damages as well as to the stigma resulting from being found to be a "racketeer."

---

[44] 18 U.S.C. § 1963.

[45] 18 U.S.C. § 1964.

[46] See, e.g., *United States v. Collack*, 124 LRRM 2334 (5th Cir. 1986) and *United States v. Pecora*, 122 LRRM 3196 (3d Cir. 1986).

[47] *Butchers Union Local No. 498 v. SDC Investments, Inc.*, 631 F. Supp. 1001 (E.D. Cal. 1986).

[48] 626 F. Supp. 1097 (D. Mass. 1986).

[49] 370 F.3d 602 (6th Cir. 2004).

[50] 543 F. Supp. 2d 842 (E.D. Tenn. 2008).

CASE 9.8   UNITED STATES V. STOLFI
U.S. COURT OF APPEALS, 889 F.2D 378 (2D CIR. 1989).

[Defendants Stolfi and Casalino, officers of Teamsters Local 875, were convicted of violating the RICO Act and the Hobbs Act. They appealed the convictions, contending that the RICO charges were improper and the Hobbs Act charge insufficient.]

WINTER, C. J....

This case involves the criminal activities of officers of the Teamsters Union in their dealings with the Wedtech Corporation. After Wedtech's management learned of discussions of unionization among Wedtech employees, the company became fearful that the employees would select a union that would engage in arm's-length bargaining. A principal shareholder and officer of Wedtech had previously dealt with Local 875 in his capacity as the owner of a machine shop in the Bronx and was confident that he could develop a collusive relationship with it. Soon thereafter, in April 1977, Wedtech recognized Local 875 and signed a collective agreement that, *inter alia*, required Wedtech to make contributions to the union's welfare benefit fund, the Louis Hirsch Memorial Welfare Fund ("Fund").

As officers of Local 875, Stolfi and Casalino were responsible for negotiating with Wedtech on behalf of the Wedtech employees and the Fund. Local 875 and the Fund also shared offices, and the evidence showed that appellants had influence over the operation of the Fund. Wedtech realized the value of a good relationship with Stolfi and Casalino and for a period of years made monthly cash payments of $5,000 to them. In return, Wedtech enjoyed relative freedom from labor disputes and was even able to use non-union labor on some projects, causing a reduction in contributions to the Fund. In 1983, Wedtech also paid the appellants $25,000 for negotiating what Wedtech officers considered a "viable" collective bargaining agreement after the unionized Wedtech employees exhibited dissatisfaction with their less-than-aggressive bargaining representative. Finally, Wedtech was threatened by Local 17 of the Brotherhood of Carpenters and Joiners ("carpenters' local") with work stoppages and violence as a result of the use of non-union labor. Stolfi and Casalino made their good offices available to aid Wedtech in its difficulties with the carpenters, and Wedtech gave

appellants $100,000 to pay off the carpenters' local, which thereafter ceased its threatening behavior. In addition, Stolfi embezzled money from the Fund through a false insurance claim and kickbacks from the purchase of real and fictitious dental equipment by a Fund dentist.

In 1988, Stolfi and Casalino were charged in an 11-count indictment. The charges pertinent to this appeal were a RICO violation and RICO conspiracy in conjunction with the Wedtech payoffs. The RICO charges against Stolfi also included embezzlement and receipt of kickbacks from the Fund as predicate crimes. Also pertinent to the appeal was a Hobbs Act count involving the extorted $100,000 payoff that resolved the dispute with the carpenters' local.

RICO Section 1962(c) makes it unlawful for "any person employed by or associated with any enterprise" to conduct or participate in the conduct of the enterprise's affairs through "a pattern of racketeering activity." The indictment in this case alleged that the RICO "enterprise" was composed of Local 875 and the Fund, and the jury specifically found that the RICO enterprise had been established as alleged.

Appellants' challenge to their RICO convictions is that they were entitled to an instruction advising the jury that it should consider their contention that Local 875 and the Fund constituted two separate enterprises rather than the single enterprise charged in the indictment. Judge Mukasey declined to offer that instruction....

A RICO enterprise is ... distinguishable from a criminal conspiracy in that it has cumulative aspects, whereas separate and distinct conspiratorial agreements must be charged and proven individually. Local 875 and the Fund may often have functioned as separate and distinct organizations and may have been capable of being separate enterprises for RICO purposes. That does not, however, preclude a finding that Local 875 and the Fund were jointly a RICO enterprise where appellants connected them by participating in them through a pattern of racketeering activity....

[The Court therefore held that Local 875 and the Fund were jointly a RICO "enterprise" and that defendants' participation became a crime when it involved a pattern of racketeering activities.]

continued

Appellants also argue that the government failed to prove that their receipt of payments from Wedtech to prevent disruption by the carpenters' local constituted aiding and abetting of a Hobbs Act violation. The argument is baseless. Extortion through threats of economic loss from violence or work stoppages falls within the Hobbs Act's prohibitions, *see United States v. Robilotto*, 828 F.2d 940, 944–945 (2d Cir. 1987), *cert. denied*, 484 U.S. 1011, 108 S.Ct. 711, 98 L.Ed.2d 662 (1988), and such extortion was shown in the instant case. Wedtech reasonably believed "first, that the [carpenters' local] had the power to harm [Wedtech], and second, that the [local] would exploit that power to [Wedtech's] detriment." *United States v. Capo*, 817 F.2d 947, 951 (2d Cir. 1987) (in banc); *see also United States v. Covino*, 837 F.2d 65, 68 (2d Cir. 1988). The instant case is, therefore, not like *Capo*, where the victims made payments, not to avoid a threatened loss, but only to improve their chances of obtaining a benefit. *Cf.* 817 F.2d at 950–954.

It is of course true that Wedtech feared the pertinent harm not from appellants but from the carpenters' local. However, to prove aiding and abetting, the government need show only that appellants "associated themselves" with the carpenters' criminal venture, participated in it as something that they wished to bring about, or sought by their action to make it succeed. *See United States v. Clemente*, 640 F.2d 1069, 1078–79 (2d. Cir.). The evidence was more than sufficient to make that showing. Appellants conducted the negotiations leading to the payoff and transmitted it for the express purpose of avoiding the threatened harm to Wedtech. This knowing participation as intermediaries is more purposeful than the participation of the "steerer" in *Clemente*, who merely advised the victim concerning a payoff. *See* 640 F.2d at 1073. Because Stolfi and Casalino unmistakably sought to make the extortionate scheme succeed, the fact that they did not share in the $100,000 is irrelevant. *See Clemente*, 640 F.2d at 1079–80.

Affirmed.

Case Questions

1. Comment on Wedtech's concern that the employees would select a union that would engage in arm's-length bargaining.
2. Under what circumstances may two separate enterprises become a singular RICO enterprise?
3. Assess the fairness of the Hobbs Act conviction where the defendants did not seek or receive a single dollar for their activities in resolving the carpenters' dispute.

CHAPTER QUESTIONS AND PROBLEMS

1. How are union members given protection by the law from unfair or arbitrary treatment by union officers or a union majority?
2. What reporting requirements are contained in the federal laws regulating unions?
3. What financial responsibility does a union have at law? Where does this liability rest?
4. Kay Rollinson had long been an outspoken critic of the leadership in Local 879 of the Hotel Employees Union. After a local election in which she was elected vice president, Rollinson filed charges with the international union, alleging certain violations of the union constitution and the LMRDA. The international union ordered a new election, and this time Rollinson chose to run for financial secretary/business agent. Shortly before the election, however, a local trial board found her guilty of using foul language toward union officers; accusing officers of illegal actions; holding unauthorized meetings in the ladies' room; disseminating information to members containing derogatory remarks about union officers; beating on the office door of the business agent; and creating an atmosphere of distrust, ill will, and disservice. The trial board suspended her from active membership for one year, fined her $850, and barred her from union meetings.

Without fully appealing the discipline through union procedures, Rollinson petitioned the U.S. district court to enjoin the union from disciplining her as her activity was protected under LMRDA's "Bill of Rights." She also requested the court to order her attorney fees to be paid by the union.

The union argued that Rollinson was not entitled to relief in court until she exhausted the appeals process within the union and that under no circumstances was she entitled to attorney fees.

Is Rollinson entitled to the relief she has requested from the court? Decide. [*Rollinson v. Hotel Employees, Local 879*, 110 LRRM 2489 (9ᵗʰ Cir.)]

5. Three members of the Dallas area local of the American Postal Workers Union asked the Secretary of Labor to set aside a union election pursuant to Section 401(e) and Section 402(b) of the LMRDA. The members challenged the validity of a provision of the union constitution that required candidates for any union office to have attended 12 regular union meetings within the 24 months prior to election in order to be eligible for nomination to any union office. This provision rendered 2,544 (97.85 percent) of the union's 2,600 members ineligible for nomination because they did not comply with the meeting attendance requirement. The union insisted that its requirement was a reasonable qualification for candidacy under Section 401(e) as it guaranteed an informed union leadership and encouraged attendance at meetings.

Should the election be set aside? Explain your decision. [*Donovan v. Postal Workers, Dallas Local*, 110 LRRM 2510 (N.D. Tex)]

6. The Executive Board of Theatrical Stage Employees Local 44 voted unanimously to expel local president James Myers from membership for allegedly accepting a $100 bribe from a prospective union member. The verdict was rendered after a hearing before a 17-person Internal Union Conduct Board at which Myers maintained his innocence of any wrongdoing. Myers had told the local secretary, Don Bennaducci, before the hearing that he had accepted the $100 to buy a truck camper cap as a favor for the

prospective member and not to illegally advance the individual's seniority as was alleged. However, Myers learned that before the board made its decision, Bennaducci, who served as union prosecutor at the hearing, told one individual, Joe Peck, an Executive Board member, that Myers had told him he accepted the money "for a favor" and "admitted the act alleged against him." Bennaducci then asked Peck to remove himself as nonvoting chairman at the hearing and function as a voting board member. Peck complied with this request and later joined in the vote to expel Myers.

Myers sued the union claiming that his right to a full and fair hearing under Section 101(a)(5) of the LMRDA was violated because Peck could not function as an impartial trier of fact after his conversation with Bennaducci. The union contended that the court must give great deference to union disciplinary hearings and claimed that Peck's vote did not make a great difference in the final decision of the unanimous 17-member board.

Has Myers been denied a full and fair hearing in violation of Section 101(a)(5)? Decide. [*Myers v. Theatrical Stage Employees*, 109 LRRM 2799 (9ᵗʰ Cir.)]

7. Bartenders Union Local 165 operated an exclusive hiring hall from which it referred all bartenders employed by hotels belonging to the Nevada Resort Association. William Dickson, a bartender who wanted to be referred to employment through the union hall, asked the union business manager to allow him to look at the union's hiring records because he suspected another bartender had been improperly referred to a job ahead of him. The business manager refused to show the hiring records to Dickson or any other member of the union. The manager claimed that the records were confidential.

At Dickson's request, the General Counsel issued a complaint against Local 165 for violating Section 8(b)(1)(A) of the NLRA. The General Counsel believed that the denial of access to the records was tantamount to union denial of fair representation. The union, relying on *Vaca v. Sipes*, maintained that it had not acted in bad faith or in an arbitrary manner by preserving the confidentiality of its records.

Has the union breached its duty of fair representation toward Dickson? Decide. [*Bartenders Local 165*, 261 NLRB No. 67, 110 LRRM 1063]

8. The Executive Board of Pressmen's Union Local 4 requested union members Gil Fouler and Mike Tenorio to appear before it during its investigation of a barroom fight they had been in with another union member. Fouler and Tenorio considered the barroom incident nonunion business and visited Executive Board member Paul Trimble at work to inform him that they would not be appearing. Fouler asked Trimble to "walk outside to talk." Trimble refused and later told his supervisors that he had a "threatening confrontation" with the two employees. Because of this report by Trimble, Fouler and Tenorio were discharged from their jobs at the S.F. Newspaper Printing Company. Upon hearing of the discharge, the union president filed a grievance. However, he also immediately prepared "travel cards" that would allow the two men to obtain union jobs in locations other than northern California. The union's investigation of the alleged confrontation focused on Trimble. The union did not ask Fouler and Tenorio for their version of the incident. A grievance committee ruled to uphold the discharges, and the union accepted this ruling, deciding not to pursue the grievance to arbitration.

Fouler and Tenorio alleged before the NLRB that the union breached its duty of fair representation in violation of Section 8(b)(1)(A) by making no effort to obtain their side of the story. The union claimed that it handled the grievance properly under the Act.

What factors must the Board consider in deciding this case? Has the union breached its duty of fair representation? Decide. [*Tenorio v. NLRB*, 110 LRRM 2939 (9th Cir.)]

9. Melvin Nance was chairman of the fair employment practices committee for the UAW Local 212 at a Chrysler Corporation plant. In his capacity as chairman, he filed a charge with the NLRB, alleging that the union had failed to fairly represent a union member in the pursuit of a grievance with Chrysler. When the union leadership learned of the charge Nance had filed against the union with the NLRB, they removed him from his position as chairman of the fair employment practices committee. Nance filed another charge with the Board, alleging that his removal from union office for filing a charge with the Board was a coercive unfair labor practice in violation of Section 8(b)(1)(A). The union maintained that the removal was a strictly internal union affair not prohibited by Section 8(b)(1)(A), as Nance's removal did not affect his employment status or cause him to suffer any loss of seniority, money, or union membership. The union stated that it had the right to fill its offices with whoever it believed would best serve the union and its membership.

Has the union violated NLRA by removing Nance from his union office? Decide. [*UAW Local 212*, 257 NLRB 637, 108 LRRM 1003]

10. Local 11 of the Hotel and Restaurant Employees International Union was the collective bargaining representative for hotel, catering, and food service employees in the Los Angeles area. Local 11 consisted of approximately 16,500 members, 48 percent of whom understood only Spanish. For this reason, Local 11 had its collective bargaining agreements, monthly newsletters, and various notices printed in Spanish and English. At ratification and nomination meetings that occurred every three years, contemporaneous English/Spanish translation was provided for discussions.

Local 11 had monthly meetings at which approximately 50 to 75 members debated union issues such as expenditures, salaries of officers, complaints, and other matters.

Translation of the monthly meetings only occurred when a Spanish-speaking member had a question or comment. The translation was performed by a bilingual union officer, not by an independent professional translator.

Angel Zamora and other Spanish-speaking members petitioned Local 11, through established procedures, to provide a qualified translator at all monthly meetings who would offer simultaneous translations of events. The union officers brought the issue before the members at the next monthly meeting. The union secretary announced that translation would be provided, but the members overrode the secretary's decision by majority vote. The issue was debated further at subsequent monthly meetings, but it was repeatedly voted down by a majority. When the union secretary tried once more to provide for translation at the monthly meetings, the membership voted to conduct monthly meetings solely in English.

Zamora commenced an action against Local 11 in federal district court, alleging that failure to provide simultaneous translation by a professional translator at the monthly meetings was a violation of his equal participation and freedom-of-speech rights under Section 101(a)(1) of the LMRDA.

What is the standard under which the court will review Zamora's allegation? How should the court decide this case? If Zamora does prevail, is he entitled to his attorneys' fees? Decide. [*Zamora v. Hotel Employees Local 11*, 125 LRRM 2538 (9ᵗʰ Cir.)]

11. Lynn Breininger filed suit under Section 301 against his union, the Sheet Metal Workers' Union, asserting that the union violated its duty of fair representation to him by discriminating against him in hiring hall referrals. He alleged that he was denied job referrals by union officials at the union's hiring hall in retaliation for his opposition to those officials at a recent union election. The hiring hall was established under a multiemployer collective bargaining agreement. He alleged that the union's conduct was arbitrary, discriminatory, and in bad faith. The union defended that Breininger failed to allege a fair representation claim, as the union was acting essentially as an employer in the hiring hall context, matching up job requests with available personnel. It stated that it did not "represent" the employees as bargaining agent in this function.

What standard applies to determine whether a union has violated its duty of fair representation? Do you believe that a union is relieved of its duty of fair representation when it is required to act essentially as an employer in the operation of a hiring hall, allocating jobs to competing applicants? Decide. [*Breininger v. Sheet Metal Workers, Local No. 6*, 493 U.S. 67]

PUBLIC EMPLOYMENT AND LABOR LAW

CHAPTER **10**

SECTION 86: INTRODUCTION

This chapter will review the legislation and other legal aspects of labor relations in the public service. The increasing unionization and use of collective bargaining by government workers requires an understanding of the differences of doctrine and of legal premises that distinguish government as an employer from the nongovernmental enterprise. The common law, the legislation, and the economic environment that have influenced labor relations in what is commonly known as the private sector are largely inapplicable in the government area. Insofar as labor relations are concerned, some significant differences also exist between national, state, and local levels of government in regard to labor legislation, administration, and collective bargaining practices.

As a starting point, the first section of the chapter focuses on the right of government employees to strike. This topic is a dominant public interest issue in the area of government employee collective bargaining; an overview of the philosophies of government employee bargaining may be gained from the cases in the section. The following sections contain materials on the legal framework for regulating and guiding collective negotiations and for handling disputes at each level of government. A final section discusses the topic of congressional power over the employment standards of state and local governments.

SECTION 87: STRIKES BY GOVERNMENT EMPLOYEES

In its definition of the term **employer,** the National Labor Relations Act expressly excludes the United States, wholly owned government corporations, states, and municipal corporations. Thus, public employees, with an exception for Postal Service employees to be explained later in this chapter, have no rights under the NLRA. This does not mean, however, that the collective bargaining process is not afforded recognition by governmental bodies. The Federal Service Labor-Management Relations Statute (FSLMRS), which is part of the Civil Service Reform Act of 1978, sets forth a statutory basis for federal employees to form, join, and assist labor organizations. Although not uniform as to scope and policy, state and municipal governments generally allow employees collective bargaining rights.

Section 7116(b)(7) of the Federal Service Labor-Management Relations Statute makes calling, participating in, or condoning a strike, work stoppage, or slowdown of an agency an unfair labor practice. If a union should intentionally violate Section 7116(b)(7), through either its actions or its failure to take action, the Federal Labor Relations Authority (FLRA) may revoke the union's certification or take other appropriate actions. The *PATCO v. FLRA* decision, reported in this section, upheld the FLRA's revocation of the air traffic controllers union certification for repeatedly violating the law against federal employees striking.

Concerning the air traffic controllers' strike, which began on August 3, 1981, President Reagan gave the striking controllers 48 hours to return to work or forfeit their jobs. More than 11,000 controllers were terminated after failing to comply with the president's order to return to work. A federal employee against whom an agency takes adverse action in the form of removal from service (termination) or suspension of more than 14 days has the option of appealing the agency's decision under the Civil Service Reform Act of 1978 to the Merit Systems Protection Board (MSPB) or through a negotiated grievance arbitration procedure.[1] Because of the decertification of the controllers union, PATCO, the claims for reinstatement of the terminated controllers were heard before the Merit Systems Protection Board. In the case of Robert Campbell and 53 other terminated strikers working in the Denver area, the Board held that the Federal Aviation Administration made out a prima facie case of strike participation by showing that an employee was absent from duty without authorization during the strike period. It denied the appeals.[2] In the cases of James Brennan and John Coleman, individuals who had worked in the New York Air Traffic Control Center, the Board ordered them reinstated because they were on authorized jury duty at the time they were charged with striking.[3]

---

[1] See 5 U.S.C. § 7513(d) and 5 U.S.C. § 712(e)(1).

[2] *Campbell v. D.O.T.,* Docket No. DEO 75281F0675 (1983).

[3] *Adams, Brennan and Coleman v. D.O.T.,* Docket No. NY075281F0424 (1983).

In June 1987, a new labor organization, the National Air Traffic Controllers Association, was certified to represent air traffic controllers in their collective bargaining with the Federal Aviation Administration.

In 1993, President Clinton lifted the ban on rehiring controllers who went on strike in 1981. By 2000, some 4,500 of the strikers had sought reemployment with the FAA, and 715 of the strikers were rehired.[4]

The right of public employees in state and municipal service to strike is prohibited by statute or court decision in most states.[5] However, despite these legal prohibitions, and in the face of severe penalties against unions, union officers, and individual union members, many public employee labor organizations have engaged in strikes in recent years. The *DeLury* case, presented in this section, reports on the famous New York City sanitation strike. *DeLury* demonstrates the use of the injunctive and punitive powers given the judiciary under the Taylor Act and gives the rationale for the state's policy in forbidding public employee strikes.

The California Supreme Court, in *County Sanitation District No. 2 of Los Angeles County v. Local 660*, SEIU, decided that public employee strikes are legal unless the strike poses an imminent threat to public health or safety. The *County Sanitation* case, presented in this section, is the first decision by a state supreme court specifically rejecting the common law principle that public employee strikes are illegal unless expressly authorized by legislation.

CASE 10.1	PROFESSIONAL AIR TRAFFIC CONTROLLERS ORGANIZATION V. FLRA U.S. COURT OF APPEALS, 110 LRRM 2676 (D.C. CIR. 1982).

EDWARDS, C. J....

Federal employees have long been forbidden from striking against their employer, the federal government, and thereby denying their services to the public at large. The United States Code presently prohibits a person who "participates in a strike ... against the Government of the United States" from accepting or holding a position in the federal government,

continued

---

[4] For current earnings of air traffic controllers, see www.bls.gov/oco/ocos108.htm. Some 172 rehired air traffic controllers sued the FAA, arguing that it had arbitrarily assigned the returnees GS-9 trainee-level pay on their return to service and did not take into account their prior air traffic controller experience. The D.C. Circuit Court of Appeals held that the lawsuit was in violation of the six-year statute of limitations, which started to run with the FAA's 1993 recruitment notice. See *Harris v. FAA*, 353 F.3d 1006 (D.C. Cir. 2004).

[5] Limited right of certain classifications of public employees to strike exists in Alaska, Hawaii, Idaho, Illinois, Minnesota, Montana, Ohio, Oregon, Pennsylvania, Vermont, and Wisconsin. Vermont allows public employees to strike if public health and safety are not endangered and if all impasse resolution machinery has been exhausted. Alaska law creates for strike-right purposes three categories, scaled to the degree to which an interruption in service can be tolerated: the right to strike is denied to protective services; the right is granted with limits to utility, sanitation, and school employees; and the right is granted without limit to all others. As will be seen in *County Sanitation District No. 2 of LA County v. Local 660*, by court decision, strikes by public employees in California are not unlawful at common law unless it is clearly demonstrated that the strikes create a substantial and imminent threat to the health and safety of the public. Following the California precedent, the Louisiana Supreme Court has also recognized that public employees, including teachers, possess a right to strike, except for strikes that clearly endanger public health and safety. *Davis v. Henry*, 555 So. 2d 457 (La. 1990).

5 U.S.C. § 311(2) (1976), and violation of this section is a criminal offense, 18 U.S.C. § 1918(3) (1976). Newly hired federal employees are required to execute an affidavit attesting that they have not struck and will not strike against the government, 5 U.S.C. § 3333(a) (1976). In addition, since the inception of formal collective bargaining between federal employee unions and the federal government, unions have been required to disavow the strike as an economic weapon. Since 1969, striking has been expressly designated a union unfair labor practice.

In 1978, Congress enacted the Civil Service Reform Act, Title VII of which provides the first statutory basis for collective bargaining between the federal government and employee unions. Title VII in no way reduced the existing legal proscriptions against strikes by federal employees and unions representing employees in the federal service. Rather, the Act added a new provision applicable to federal employee unions that strike against the government. Under section 7120(f) of Title VII, Congress provided that the Federal Labor Relations Authority ("FLRA" or "Authority") shall "revoke the exclusive recognition status" of a recognized union, or "take any other appropriate disciplinary action" against any labor organization, where it is found that the union has called, participated in or condoned a strike, work stoppage or slowdown against a federal agency in a labor management dispute. 5 U.S.C. § 7120(f) (Supp. IV 1980).

In this case we review the first application of section 7120(f) of the FLRA. After the Professional Air Traffic Controllers Organization ("PATCO") called a nationwide strike of air traffic controllers against the Federal Aviation Administration ("FAA") in the summer of 1981, the Authority revoked PATCO's status as exclusive bargaining representative for the controllers. For the reasons set forth below, we affirm the decision of the Authority.

I. Background

A. The PATCO Strike

The Professional Air Traffic Controllers Organization has been the recognized exclusive bargaining representative for air traffic controllers employed by the Federal Aviation Administration since the early 1970's. Faced with the expiration of an existing collective bargaining agreement, PATCO and the FAA began negotiations for a new contract in early 1981. A tentative agreement was reached in June, but was overwhelmingly rejected by the PATCO rank and file. Following this rejection, negotiations begin again in late July. PATCO announced a strike deadline of Monday, August 3, 1981.

Failing to reach a satisfactory accord, PATCO struck the FAA on the morning of August 3. Over 70 percent of the nation's federally employed air traffic controllers walked off the job, significantly reducing the number of private and commercial flights in the United States.*

In prompt response to the PATCO job actions, the government obtained restraining orders against the strike, and then civil and criminal contempt citations when the restraining orders were not heeded. The government also fired some 11,000 striking air traffic controllers who did not return to work by 11:00 AM on August 5, 1981.** In addition, on August 3, 1981, the FAA filed an unfair labor practice charge against PATCO with the Federal Labor Relations Authority. On the same day, an FLRA Regional Director issued a complaint on the unfair labor practice charge, alleging strike activity prohibited by 5 U.S.C. § 7116(b)(7) (Supp. IV 1980) and seeking revocation of PATCO's certification under the Civil Service Reform Act. The complaint noticed a hearing for one week later, August 10, 1981.

---

*Only 2,308 of the 9,034 controllers scheduled to work beginning with the 11:00 AM shift on August 3 reported. Attendance increased somewhat on succeeding days, so that by Saturday, August 8, 3,434 of the 9,286 scheduled controllers reported. During the first five days of the strike, the FAA was required to cancel some 26,000 flights and operate at 69 percent of normal capacity. Professional Air Traffic Controllers Org., No. 3-CO-105, slip op. at 3 (Aug. 14, 1981) (Fenton, A.L.J.).

**On the morning of the first day of the strike, President Reagan gave the striking controllers 48 hours to return to work or forfeit their jobs. Air Traffic Controllers Strike, 17 Weekly Comp. Pres. Doc. 845 (Aug. 3, 1981). Those who did not return to work on their first scheduled shift after 11:00 AM on August 5 were terminated. See *Professional Air Traffic Controllers Org. v. United States Dept. of Transp.*, 529 F. Supp. 614 (D. Minn. 1982).

continued

B. Federal Labor Relations Authority Proceedings

John H. Fenton, Chief Administrative Law Judge of the FLRA, conducted hearings on the unfair labor practice charge on the afternoon of August 10. The general counsel of the FLRA presented testimony establishing that on the morning of August 3 pickets assembled at entrances to Air Traffic Control Centers in Leesburg, Virginia, Chicago, Illinois, Ronkonkoma, New York, and Longmont, Colorado, and at the Airport Tower in Atlanta, Georgia. In each instance, the picketers carried signs that informed the public that they were air traffic controllers belonging to a particular PATCO Local and that PATCO was on strike. Attendance records presented by FAA witnesses indicated that only 2,308 of the 9,034 air traffic controllers scheduled to work nationwide on August 3 actually reported. FAA officials from the various facilities also identified striking air traffic controllers, including PATCO Local officers, in photographs of the picketing outside of the Air Traffic Control Centers. In several cases the persons identified, including the PATCO Local officers, were scheduled to work at the time the photographs were taken.

In addition to this evidence, an FAA official identified PATCO National President Robert E. Poli in two videotaped news conferences. In one videotape Mr. Poli was recorded as stating:

> If we have not received a settlement proposal which our negotiating team determines should be offered to the membership, I will order the count to begin. After the tallying has been completed and following verification of the necessary support, the strike will begin on the day shift on Monday, August the 3rd.

In the second videotape, apparently made after the strike had begun and after a temporary restraining order had been issued, Mr. Poli was recorded as saying: "The question is will the strike continue. The answer is yes."

In response, PATCO offered no evidence to suggest that a strike had not occurred, to substantiate its assertion that the FLRA's evidence only demonstrated a number of separate strikes by PATCO Locals, or to establish that PATCO had made any efforts to prevent or stop the strike....

II. PATCO's Violation of the Ban on Federal Employer Strikes

... We conclude that section 7120(f) entrusts the Federal Labor Relations Authority with extensive authority to remedy illegal strikes, work stoppages and slowdowns by federal employee unions. The section clearly permits the FLRA to employ the extreme measure of revoking a union's exclusive recognition status—a remedy unknown to private sector labor law—if the union commits or condones any of these unfair labor practices....

The FLRA's Exercise of Its Discretion

We have concluded that the FLRA has substantial discretion under section 7120(f) to decide whether or not to revoke the exclusive recognition status of a union found guilty by the FLRA of striking or condoning a strike against the government. A concomitant of this conclusion is that the courts have only a limited role in reviewing the FLRA's exercise of its remedial discretion....

... The FLRA's decision to revoke PATCO's exclusive recognition status was not an abuse of discretion. The union is a repeat offender that has willfully ignored statutory proscriptions and judicial injunctions. It has shown little or no likelihood of abiding by the legal requirements of labor-management relations in the federal sector. If the extreme remedy that Congress enacted cannot properly be applied to this case, we doubt that it could ever properly be invoked....

Affirmed.

Case Questions

1. Summarize the evidence supporting the finding by the FLRA that the air traffic controllers national union participated in a strike in violation of Section 7116(b)(7).
2. Was revocation of PATCO's certification required by Section 7120(f) of Title VII of the Civil Service Reform Act?
3. What effect does revocation of a union's "exclusive recognition status" have on the viability of a union?
4. Did the FLRA abuse its discretion in this case?

CASE 10.2	CITY OF NEW YORK v. DeLURY
	NEW YORK STATE COURT OF APPEALS, 23 N.Y. 2D 175 (1968).

FULD, C. J....

We recently decided, in *Rankin v. Shanker* (23 N.Y. 2d 111), that public employee and labor organizations representing them were not entitled to a trial by jury in a criminal contempt proceeding for the violation of Section 210, Subdivision 1, of the Taylor Law.* In so holding, we concluded that a legislative classification "which differentiates between strikes by public employees and employees in private industry" is reasonable and does not offend against the constitutional guarantee of equal protection of the law (23 N.Y. 2d, at p. 118). The case now before us calls upon the Court to determine, primarily, whether the Taylor Law's mandate that public employees shall not strike and that labor organizations representing them shall not cause or encourage a strike violates due process requirements of the state or federal Constitution.

---

*The Taylor Law was enacted in 1967 (L. 1967, Ch. 392: Civil Service Law, Art. 14, Sections 200–212) to supersede the Condon-Wadlin Act (L. 1947, Ch. 391, adding Civil Service Law, former Section 22-a renum. by L. 1958, Ch. 790; former Section 108 of Civil Service Law). Like its predecessor, the Taylor Law prohibits strikes by public employees (Section 210, Subd. 1), but unlike Condon-Wadlin, it does not mandate termination of employment for its violation. The Taylor Law grants to all public employees (which, broadly speaking, includes all employees in the service of the State or any subdivision thereof) rights that in the main they did not formerly possess, namely, the right to be represented by employee organizations of their own choosing and the right to negotiate collectively with public employers and, in addition, the right to require public employers to negotiate and to enter into collective agreement with them. It sets up a Public Employment Relations Board—known as PERB—to "resolve disputes concerning the representation status of employee organizations" and to assist in the "voluntary resolution of disputes between public employers and employee organizations." It also authorizes under the so-called "home rule" section (Civil Service Law, Section 212) the adoption by local governments of "provisions and procedures" that are "substantially equivalent" to those of the Taylor Law. The New York City equivalent to such law is Local Law no. 53 of 1967, but the parties did not utilize the machinery therein provided for resolving disputes between the city and municipal employee organizations. All public employees, whether or not covered by the "home rule" section (Section 212), are subject to the statutory mandate of Section 210, Subdivision 1, of the Civil Service Law prohibiting them from striking.

At about seven o'clock on the morning of February 2, 1968, virtually all of the sanitation men in the City of New York—employees of the Department of Sanitation—failed, without excuse, to report for work. Later in the day, at a demonstration in front of City Hall, members of the Uniformed Sanitationmen's Association (referred to herein as the "Union") were addressed by their president, the defendant DeLury, in these words:

> Your sentiments before was go-go-go. I'd accept a motion for go-go-go (cheers). All in favor signify by saying yes (cheers). All opposed (boos). I didn't come here to bargain, I took a firm position with the City, I gave the members a final offer of this union. Now I want to show discipline here this morning—or this afternoon—I don't want to show where there is confusion in the members—You got a job at the locations to see that this is effective 100% (cheers).

A nine-day strike, ending on the night of February 10, resulted. During that period, few, if any, of the sanitation men reported for work, in consequence of which garbage and refuse accumulated on the city streets at the rate of 10,000 tons a day. This constituted a serious health and fire threat; indeed, the Commissioner of Health characterized the "garbage situation" as "a serious one to the health of the city" and the Fire Commissioner declared that the Fire Department "experienced a marked increase in the number of outside rubbish fires."

On February 2, the very day the work stoppage began, the City instituted the present action to enjoin the defendants from "striking" and moved for a preliminary injunction. A temporary restraining order was granted which enjoined the carrying on of the strike and required the leaders of the Union to instruct the members to return to work. Three days later, on February 5, the Court at Special Term granted a preliminary injunction, which again contained a directive to DeLury that he shall "forthwith instruct all members [of the Union] not to engage or participate in any strike, concerted stoppage of work or concerted slowdown against the plaintiff." Although because of the

continued

health and fire hazards involved, immediate compliance with the orders was vital, the members of the Union, as previously noted, remained away from their jobs until February 10.

An application, brought on by order to show cause, to punish the Union and DeLury for criminal contempt for willfully disobeying the restraining order, came on for hearing before the court; the testimony adduced concerning the strike and its effects, as well as the conduct of DeLury, was substantially as outlined above....

At the conclusion of the hearings, the court, dismissing charges which had also been asserted against other officers, found DeLury and the Union guilty of criminal contempt for willfully disobeying its lawful mandate. It sentenced DeLury to 15 days in jail and fined him $250 and it fined the Union $80,000. In addition, the court ordered that the Union's right to dues checkoff be forfeited for a period of 18 months.* The Appellate Division affirmed Special Term's orders and granted the defendants leave to appeal to our court on a certified question.

We consider, first, the defendant's contention that the Taylor Law is unconstitutional on the ground that, in prohibiting strikes by public employees it deprives them of due process of law. Manifestly, neither the Fourteenth Amendment to the Federal Constitution nor the Bill of Rights of the State Constitution (Art. 1) grants to any individual an absolute right to strike....

... Substantial reasons are at hand for the almost universal condemnation of strikes by public employees. As Professor George W. Taylor, an outstanding authority in the field of labor relations and one of the architects of the Taylor Law, put it (*Public Employment: Strikes or Procedures?, 20 Industrial and Labor Relations Rev. 617*),

> One of the vital interests of the public which should be considered in the government-employee relationship is the ability of representative government to perform the functions of levying taxes and, through the budgeting of governmental resources, of establishing priorities among the government services desired by the body politic.

Quite obviously, the ability of the Legislature to establish priorities among government services would be destroyed if public employees could, with impunity, engage in strikes which deprive the public of essential services. The striking employees, by paralyzing a city through the exercise of naked power, could obtain gains wholly disproportionate to the services rendered by them and at the expense of the public and other public employees. The consequence would be the destruction of democratic legislative processes because budgeting and the establishment of priorities would no longer result from the free choice of the electorate's representatives but from the coercive effect of paralyzing strikes of public employees....

...There was here indisputable proof not only of deliberate disobedience of the explicit provisions of the Taylor Law but willful defiance of the court's lawful mandates as well. Such defiance, the more egregious when committed by employees in the public sector, is not to be tolerated.

The order appealed from should be affirmed, with costs, and the question certified answered in the affirmative.

Case Questions

1. What was defendant DeLury's role in the dispute?

2. What action did the lower court take against the defendant and the union for violating the preliminary injunction?

3. In Professor Taylor's view, does condemnation of strikes by public employees effect a valid policy for a state government?

---

*Author's note: On December 20, 21, and 22, 2005, Local 100 of the Transit Workers Union (TWU) engaged in an illegal strike against its public employer, the Metropolitan Transportation Authority (MTA), shutting down public transportation in New York City for 60 hours. The union is funded by a dues checkoff procedure whereby the MTA automatically deducts $21.94 from each member's paycheck every two weeks, for a total of $570.44 per year. With some 33,700 union members, the MTA deducts $19.8 million a year and remits it to the union. The New York State trial court delayed revoking TWU dues checkoff rights until June 2007 through November 2007 to allow the union to continue to receive dues while it paid $2.5 million in fines for engaging in the unlawful strike. Without the MTA's payroll deduction of union dues, the union's collection of dues from its members decreased by $1.1 million in the period from June through August. As a result, staff reductions occurred and the work of the union was curtailed.

| COUNTY SANITATION DISTRICT NO. 2 OF LOS ANGELES
COUNTY v. LOCAL 660, SEIU
SUPREME COURT OF CALIFORNIA, 38 CAL 3D 564 (1985).

[Since 1973, the district and Local 660 have bargained concerning wages, hours, and working conditions pursuant to the Meyers-Milias-Brown Act (MMBA). Each year these negotiations have resulted in a binding labor contract or memorandum of understanding (MOU). On July 5, 1976, approximately 75 percent of the district's employees went out on strike after negotiations between the district and the union for a new wage and benefit agreement reached an impasse and failed to produce a new MOU. The district promptly filed a complaint for injunctive relief and damages and was granted a temporary restraining order. The strike continued for approximately 11 days, during which time the district was able to maintain its facilities and operations through the efforts of management personnel and certain union members who chose not to strike. On July 16, the employees voted to accept a tentative agreement, the terms of which were identical to the district's offer prior to the strike. The district then proceeded with the instant action for tort damages. The trial court found the strike to be unlawful and in violation of the public policy of the state of California and thus awarded the district $246,904 in compensatory damages, prejudgment interest in the amount of $87,615.22, and costs of $874.65.]

BROUSSARD, J....

Common law decisions in other jurisdictions at one time held that no employee, whether public or private, had a right to strike in concert with fellow workers. In fact, such collective action was generally viewed as a conspiracy and held subject to both civil and criminal sanctions. Over the course of the 20th century, however, courts and legislatures gradually acted to change these laws as they applied to private-sector employees; today, the right to strike is generally accepted as indispensable to the system of collective bargaining and negotiation, which characterizes labor-management relations in the private sector.

By contrast, American law continues to regard public-sector strikes in a substantially different manner. A strike by employees of the United States government may still be treated as a crime, and strikes by state and local employees have been explicitly allowed by courts or statute in only ten states.

Contrary to the assertions of the plaintiff as well as various holdings of the Court of Appeal, this Court has repeatedly stated that the legality of strikes by public employees in California has remained an open question....

Before commencing our discussion, however, we must note that the legislature has also chosen to reserve judgment on the general legality of strikes in the public sector. As Justice Grodin observed in his concurring opinion in *El Rancho Unified School District v. National Education Assn.*, 33 Cal. 3d 946, 964, "the Legislature itself has steadfastly refrained from providing clearcut guidance." With the exception of firefighters, no statutory prohibition against strikes by public employees in this state exists. The MMBA, the statute under which the present controversy arose, does not directly address the question of strikes....

In sum, the MMBA establishes a system of rights and protections for public employees which closely mirrors those enjoyed by workers in the private sector. The legislature, however, intentionally avoided the inclusion of any provision which could be construed as either a blanket grant or prohibition of a right to strike, thus leaving the issue shrouded in ambiguity. In the absence of clear legislative directive on this crucial matter, it becomes the task of the judiciary to determine whether, under the law, strikes by public employees should be viewed as a prohibited tort.

... The Court of Appeal and various lower courts in this and other jurisdictions have repeatedly stated that, absent a specific statutory grant, all strikes by public employees are per se illegal. A variety of policy rationales and legal justifications have traditionally been advanced in support of this common law "rule," and numerous articles and scholarly treatises have been devoted to debating their respective merits. The various justifications for the common law prohibition can be summarized into four basic arguments. First—the traditional justification—that a strike by public employees is tantamount to a denial of governmental authority/sovereignty. Second, the terms of public employment are not subject to bilateral collective bargaining, as in the private sector, because they are set by the legislative body through unilateral law-making. Third, since legislative bodies are responsible

continued

for public employment decision making, granting public employees the right to strike would afford them excessive bargaining leverage, resulting in a distortion of the political process and an improper delegation of legislative authority. Finally, public employees provide essential public services which, if interrupted by strikes, would threaten the public welfare.

... The first of these justifications, the sovereignty argument, asserts that government is the embodiment of the people, and hence those entrusted to carry out its function may not impede it. This argument was particularly popular in the first half of the 20th century, when it received support from several American presidents.

The sovereignty concept, however, has often been criticized in recent years as a vague and outdated theory based on the assumption that "the King can do no wrong." As Judge Harry T. Edwards has cogently observed, "the application of the strict sovereignty notion—that governmental power can never be opposed by employee organizations—is clearly a vestige from another era, an era of unexpanded government.... With the rapid growth of the government, both in sheer size as well as in terms of assuming services not traditionally associated with the 'sovereign,' governmental employees understandably no longer feel constrained by a notion that 'The King can do no wrong.' The distraught cries by public unions of disparate treatment merely reflect the fact that, for all intents and purposes, public employees occupy essentially the same position vis a vis the employer as their private counterparts." (Edwards, *The Developing Labor Relations Law in the Public Sector* (1972) 10 Duq. L. Rev. 357, 359–360.)...

The second basic argument underlying the common law prohibition of public-employee strikes holds that since the terms of public employment are fixed by the legislature, public employers are virtually powerless to respond to strike pressure, or alternatively that allowing such strikes would result in "government by contract" instead of "government by law." This justification may have had some merit before the California legislature gave extensive bargaining rights to public employees. However, at present, most terms and conditions of public employment are arrived at through collective bargaining under such statutes as the MMBA....

The remaining two arguments have not served in this state as grounds for asserting a ban on public employee strikes but have been advanced by commentators and by courts of other states....

The first of these arguments draws upon the different roles of market forces in the private and public spheres. This rationale suggests that because government services are essential and demand is generally inelastic, public employees would wield excessive bargaining power if allowed to strike....

In sum, there is little, if any empirical evidence which demonstrates that governments generally capitulate to unreasonable demands by public employees in order to resolve strikes. The result of the strike in the instant case clearly suggests the opposite. During the 11-day strike, negotiations resumed, and the parties subsequently reached an agreement on a new MOU, the terms of which were *precisely the same* as the District's last offer prior to the commencement of the strike. Such results certainly do not illustrate a situation where public employees wielded excessive bargaining power and thereby caused a distortion of our political process.

The fourth and final justification for the common law prohibition is that interruption of government services is unacceptable because they are essential. As noted above, in our contemporary industrial society the presumption of essentiality of most government services is questionable at best. In addition, we tolerate strikes by private employees in many of the same areas in which government is engaged, such as transportation, health, education, and utilities; in many employment fields, public and private activity largely overlap....

We of course recognize that there are certain "essential" public services, the disruption of which would seriously threaten the public health or safety. In fact, defendant union itself concedes that the law should still act to render illegal any strikes in truly essential services which would constitute a genuine threat to the public welfare. Therefore, to the extent that the "excessive bargaining power" and "interruption of essential services" arguments still have merit, specific health and safety limitations on the right to strike should suffice to answer the concerns underlying those arguments....

It is universally recognized that in the private sector, the bilateral determination of wages and working conditions through a collective bargaining process, in which both sides possess relatively equal strength, facilitates understanding and more harmonious relations between employers and their employees. In the absence of some means of equalizing the parties' respective bargaining positions, such as a credible strike threat, both sides are less likely to bargain in good

continued

faith; this in turn leads to unsatisfactory and acrimonious labor relations and ironically to more and longer strikes. Equally as important, the possibility of a strike often provides the best impetus for parties to reach an agreement at the bargaining table, because *both* parties lose if a strike actually comes to pass. Thus by providing a clear incentive for resolving disputes, a credible strike threat may serve to avert, rather than to encourage, work stoppages....

Plaintiff's argument that only the legislature can reject the common law doctrine prohibiting public-employee strikes flies squarely in the face of both logic and past precedent. Legislative silence is not the equivalent of positive legislation and does not preclude judicial reevaluation of common law doctrine. If the courts have created a bad rule or an outmoded one, the courts can change it....

For the reasons stated above, we conclude that the common law prohibition against public-sector strikes should not be recognized in this state. Consequently, strikes by public-sector employees in this state as such are neither illegal nor tortious under California common law. We must immediately caution, however, that the right of public employees to strike is by no means unlimited. Prudence and concern for the general public welfare require certain restrictions....

After consideration of the various alternatives before us, we believe the following standard may properly guide courts in the resolution of future disputes in this area: strikes by public employees are not unlawful at common law unless or until it is clearly demonstrated that such a strike creates a substantial and imminent threat to the health or safety of the public. This standard allows exceptions in certain essential areas of public employment (e.g., the prohibition against firefighters and law enforcement personnel) and also requires the courts to determine on a case by case basis whether the public interest overrides the basic right to strike....

Thoughtful judges and commentators, however, have questioned the wisdom of upholding a per se prohibition of public employee strikes. They have persuasively argued that because the right to strike is so inextricably intertwined with the recognized fundamental right to organize and collectively bargain, some degree of constitutional protection should be extended to the act of striking in both the public and private sectors.

As Judge J. Skelly Wright declared in his concurrence in *United Federation of Postal Clerks v. Blount, supra,* "[i]f the inherent purpose of a labor organization is to bring the workers' interests to bear on management, the right to strike is, historically and practically, an important means of effectuating that purpose. A union that never strikes, or which can make no credible threat to strike, may wither away in ineffectiveness. That fact is not irrelevant to the constitutional calculations. Indeed, in several decisions, the Supreme Court has held that the First Amendment right of association is at least concerned with essential organizational activities which give the particular association life and promote its fundamental purposes.... [Citations.] I do not suggest that the right to strike is co-equal with the right to form labor organizations.... But I do believe that the right to strike is, at least, within constitutional concern and should not be discriminatorily abridged without substantial or 'compelling' justification." (325 F. Supp. 879, 885.) ...

We conclude that it is not unlawful for public employees to engage in a concerted work stoppage for the purpose of improving their wages or conditions of employment, unless it has been determined that the work stoppage poses an imminent threat to public health or safety. Since the trial court's judgment for damage in this case was predicated upon an erroneous determination that defendants' strike was unlawful, the judgment for damages cannot be sustained.

The judgment is reversed.

[Four of the seven justices adopted the rule of law legalizing strikes. Two others filed a concurring opinion, agreeing with the majority only insofar as it struck down the damage award, concluding that damages should not be awarded for a peaceful public-sector strike regardless of whether the strike is legal or illegal. They contended that the question of the legality of strikes could and should again be sidestepped. One judge, Justice Lucas, dissented, issuing a sharply worded opinion that public employees do not have, nor should they have, a right to strike. He also criticized the majority for attempting to fashion a rule of law outlawing some but not all strikes, preferring to let the California legislature resolve the problem.]

Case Questions

1. Do strikes by public employees result in public employers making extraordinary concessions?
2. Did the court believe that it was required to leave the question of the common law doctrine prohibiting the right to strike to the legislature?
3. State the rule of the case.

SECTION 88: FEDERAL EMPLOYMENT

The legal structure underlying collective activities of federal government employees has developed slowly compared with that regulating nongovernment unionization and bargaining.

In the early part of the 20th century, the executive power of the president was used to prevent lobbying activities by federal employee representatives. President Theodore Roosevelt issued executive orders to prevent lobbying efforts of federal employees. He prohibited federal officers, employees, and their associations from soliciting pay increases in Congress under the penalty of dismissal. In the next administration, President William Howard Taft repeated these restrictive executive orders. Congress moderated this restraint as to postal employees by enacting the Lloyd-LaFollette Act of 1912 to allow organizations unaffiliated with labor organizations to present their grievances to Congress without retaliation.

The National Labor Relations Act of 1935 explicitly excluded all government agencies and their employees from coverage.

Executive Order 10988

Soon after John F. Kennedy became president in 1961, a task force on employer-employee relations in the federal service was appointed to investigate labor relations in the federal government. The task force proposed that the government should respond affirmatively to organization by any considerable group of employees for "collective dealing." The recommendations resulted in the signing of Executive Order 10988 on January 17, 1962, by President Kennedy. The order provided that most civilian employees could organize and that organized employee groups in appropriate units would be recognized.

Each agency's management was itself responsible for determining appropriate bargaining units and also deciding whether a majority of the employees in such a unit had designated a labor organization as their representative. A panel of qualified arbitrators was made available for assisting in resolving disputes by investigating the facts and then rendering advisory opinions, subject to management's acceptance or rejection. Pursuant to Executive Order 10988, a Code of Fair Labor Practices was adopted in 1963.

Executive Order 11491

To improve the program, President Nixon in 1969 signed Executive Order 11491, clarifying the responsibilities of employees, their representatives, and government officials. Under this system final authority no longer rested with the department concerned, for a permanent Federal Labor Relations Council was created to interpret the executive order, to make major policy decisions, and to hear appeals on various matters. Under the executive order, arbitration of grievances was allowed, subject to certain exceptions that could be reviewed by the Federal Labor Relations Council. Also, the Federal Service Impasses Panel, an agency within the council, was authorized by the order "to take any action it considers necessary to settle an impasse."

POSTAL SERVICE EMPLOYEES

The Postal Reorganization Act of 1970[6] created the U.S. Postal Service as an independent agency within the executive branch of the federal government. The underlying policy of that Act is that performance, not politics, is to determine promotion and tenure of Postal Service employees.

Under the Postal Reorganization Act, the NLRB is authorized to determine appropriate bargaining units, supervise representation elections, and enforce the unfair labor practice provisions of the NLRA. Wages, hours, and working conditions are determined through collective bargaining between the appropriate postal unions and the Postal Service. Because postal employees do not have the right to strike, the Postal Reorganization Act provides for fact-finding procedures and then binding arbitration if a bargaining impasse exists after 180 days from the start of negotiations.

Supervisory and managerial employees of the Postal Service, like their counterparts in the private sector, do not have collective bargaining rights; however, they are assured pay differentials over those they supervise.

FEDERAL SERVICE LABOR-MANAGEMENT RELATIONS STATUTE

On January 11, 1979, the Federal Service Labor-Management Relations Statute (FSLMRS) of 1978 became effective.[7] This statute provides a permanent legislative basis for labor-management relations in the federal sector, as opposed to the impermanent structure that existed under the presidential executive orders.

The statute is clearly modeled on the NLRA, with the establishment of a three-member Federal Labor Relations Authority (FLRA) to administer the program and the creation of the Office of General Counsel with authority to investigate and prosecute unfair labor practice cases. The statute also provides for judicial review and enforcement of most cases.

COVERAGE.   The statute covers all executive agencies, the Library of Congress, and the U.S. Government Printing Office. Specifically excluded agencies include the General Accounting Office, the Federal Bureau of Investigation, the Central Intelligence Agency, the National Security Agency, and the Tennessee Valley Authority.[8] In addition, the statute empowers the president to issue an executive order excluding any agency or subdivision from coverage under the program if that agency or subdivision is primarily engaged in intelligence, counterintelligence, or investigative or national security work and if the provisions of the statute cannot be applied to it in a manner consistent with national security requirements and consideration.

ADMINISTRATION.   The principal agency charged with administering the statute is the Federal Labor Relations Authority. The FLRA is an independent agency consisting of three members appointed by the president for five-year terms. The FLRA has

---

[6] 39 U.S.C. §§ 1200 *et seq.*

[7] Pub. L. 95-454, 5 U.S.C. §§ 7101 *et seq.*, 92 Stat. 1191. This law was enacted as part of the Civil Service Reform Act of 1978. Pub. L. 95-454, 92 Stat. 1111.

[8] 5 U.S.C. § 7103(a)(d).

responsibility to determine the appropriateness of bargaining units, supervise and conduct elections to select an exclusive representative, resolve negotiability disputes, conduct hearings and resolve complaints of unfair labor practices, and resolve exceptions to arbitrators' awards.[9] Like the NLRB, the FLRA may delegate to regional directors the authority to determine whether a group of employees is an appropriate bargaining unit. Regional directors may also supervise and conduct elections. The FLRA may delegate to administrative law judges its authority to determine if any person is engaged in an unfair labor practice. Decisions by the regional directors and administrative law judges are appealable to the FLRA.

Final decisions of the FLRA are appealable to the U.S. court of appeals except for unit determination case decisions. The FLRA also has the power to petition any U.S. court of appeals for enforcement of its orders and for appropriate temporary relief or restraining orders.[10]

The statute establishes the Office of General Counsel of the FLRA. The General Counsel is appointed by the president for a five-year term, but may be removed at any time by the president. The General Counsel is empowered to investigate and prosecute unfair labor practice cases.[11]

The statute continues the Federal Service Impasses Panel essentially unchanged from Executive Order 11491. The panel's primary function is to assist parties in resolving bargaining impasses and to take necessary actions consistent with the law to resolve such impasses.[12]

EMPLOYEE RIGHTS. Under Section 7102 of the statute, federal employees have the right "to form, join, or assist a labor organization, or to refrain from such activity, freely and without fear of penalty or reprisal."

Under Section 7114 (a)(2) B of the FSLMRS, an employee reasonably believing an investigatory interview could result in discipline against him or her is entitled to active union representation at such an interview, whether the interview is conducted by a management official who is a party to the collective bargaining agreement or is conducted by an investigator of the Office of Inspector General.[13] This section of the FSLMRS gives federal-sector employees so-called *Weingarten* rights.[14] The *NASA v. FLRA* decision, presented in this section, sets forth the Supreme Court's decision on this matter.

COLLECTIVE BARGAINING. Agencies and exclusive representatives have an obligation under the statute to "meet at reasonable times and to consult and bargain in a good faith effort to reach agreement with respect to conditions of employment." The statute defines "conditions of employment" as "personnel policies, practices, and

---

[9] 5 U.S.C. § 7105. For examples of the FLRA's review of arbitrators' awards, see NTEU and DHS, Customs and Border Protection, 62 FLRA No. 72 (Apr. 4, 2008) and Metal Trades Council and Puget Sound Naval Shipyard, 62 FLRA No. 74 (May 6, 2008).

[10] 5 U.S.C. § 7123.

[11] 5 U.S.C. § 7104(f)(2).

[12] 5 U.S.C. § 7119(c).

[13] *NASA v. FLRA*, 527 U.S. 229 (1999).

[14] *NLRB v. J. Weingarten, Inc.*, 420 U.S. 251 (1975).

matters whether established by rule, regulation, or otherwise, affecting working conditions."[15] It should be noted that the parties do not ordinarily bargain over wages. Wages for blue-collar employees are set according to the Coordinated Federal Wage System, under which blue-collar workers are paid wages comparable to those paid in private industry for similar types of work. Thus, a federal employee working as an electrician would be paid a rate of pay comparable to that of an electrician working in the private sector.[16] The General Schedule (GS) is the basic pay schedule for so-called white-collar federal employees. Pay increases for employees covered by this schedule are ultimately up to the president, who reviews recommended pay increases in the context of "economic conditions affecting the general public."[17]

The *Fort Stewart Schools v. FLRA*[18] decision embodies an exception to the rule that agencies do not have to bargain about wages and benefits with unions that represent federal employees who have their wages and benefits fixed by law in accordance with the General Schedule of the Civil Service Act. The U.S. Supreme Court concluded in the *Fort Stewart Schools* case that wages and benefits were included in the words "conditions of employment" as used in Section 7103(a)(14) of the FSLMRS for those white-collar federal employees who earn wages that are exempt from the GS schedule. That is, those few federal agencies that have the power to set wages and benefits are required to bargain over them.

The duty to negotiate in good faith is set forth in Section 7114(b) of the statute. It includes the duty of approaching negotiations with a "sincere resolve" to reach agreement, having negotiators with necessary authority meeting at reasonable times and places, and executing a written document to reflect agreement. The statute also requires that the agency furnish the exclusive representative with available and necessary information normally maintained by the agency in order for the union to bargain intelligently. To have full discussions of issues subject to the collective bargaining process, unions may well desire a list of the home addresses of employees represented by each union, including the addresses of nonunion employees. However, the Supreme Court, in *U.S. Department of Defense v. FLRA*,[19] held that such information would be an unwarranted invasion of employees' privacy and thus not within an exemption from the Freedom of Information Act. The Court also determined that the FSLMRS did not entitle the union to the addresses. The statute contains a strong "management rights" clause as well.[20]

---

[15] 5 U.S.C. § 7103(a)(14).

[16] Blue-collar employees include most recognized trades, crafts, and skilled and unskilled manual labor employees outside the Postal Service. Union members do participate in Local Wage Survey Committees, which do the survey work in collaboration with the Bureau of Labor Statistics to establish the job comparability wage data of private-sector jobs to government jobs.

[17] The Federal Pay Comparability Act, 5 U.S.C. § 5305, covers 1.3 million white-collar workers under the General Schedule. The prime objective of the Act is to provide comparable pay with private industry. A Federal Employees Pay Council was created by the Act, but it has essentially an advisory role. Ultimately, it is the president who issues final executive orders adjusting pay for white-collar federal employees.

[18] 495 U.S. 641 (1990).

[19] 510 U.S. 487 (1994).

[20] 5 U.S.C. § 7106. See *U.S. Government Printing Office v. IBEW, Local 121*, 62 FLRA No. 80 (May 20, 2008).

Negotiations are prohibited on matters covered by a federal statute and on specified management rights, including the agency's mission, budget, and organization and the right to manage the agency's workforce.[21] When good faith negotiations fail to produce a collective bargaining agreement, the parties may submit their dispute to the Federal Service Impasse Panel (FSIP). The FSIP is an entity within the Federal Labor Relations Authority, composed of a chairman and six members appointed by the president, with the ultimate authority to make binding determinations on contract terms in dispute.[22]

Under the statute, all labor-management relations agreements must include a grievance procedure with binding arbitration as the final step.[23] In general, nearly all matters related to an employee's employment are encompassed within the expanded grievance procedure unless the parties agree to exclude them as a result of their negotiations.

Employees covered by collective bargaining agreements may grieve any discipline assessed against them under the negotiated grievance procedures.[24] Federal-sector employees eligible under the Civil Service Reform Act of 1978 (CSRA) have an alternative forum to challenging serious disciplinary actions such as termination, suspension for more than 14 days, and reduction in grade or pay and may do so before the federal Merit Systems Protection Board (MSPB).[25] However, an individual cannot appeal discipline to both forums.

In the *U.S. Postal Service v. Gregory* case, the U.S. Supreme Court was called upon to reconcile the authority of the MSPB to deal with disciplinary action tied to pending union grievances. While three disciplinary actions that the Postal Service took against Maria Gregory were pending in grievance proceedings pursuant to the Postal Service's collective bargaining agreement with the National Association of Letter Carriers union, the Postal Service terminated her employment after a fourth violation. Ms. Gregory elected to appeal her dismissal to the MSPB. An MSPB administrative law judge concluded that the Postal Service had shown that Gregory overestimated her overtime beyond permissible limits as charged and that her termination was reasonable in light of her three prior violations, which were still pending grievances being processed by her union but were analyzed independently by the ALJ. The matter was ultimately appealed to the U.S. Supreme Court, which decided that the MSPB, when determining the reasonableness of the penalty imposed upon an employee, may independently review prior disciplinary actions that are still the subject of pending grievances. Ms. Gregory's case was remanded for further

---

[21] 5 U.S.C. § 7106(a)(2)A–D. The Secretary of the Department of Homeland Security issued regulations for the department referred to as Human Resources Management Systems on February 1, 2005, 70 Fed. Reg. 5272. In *National Treasury Employees Union v. Chertoff*, 385 F.Supp.2d 1 (D. D.C. 2005), the U.S. District Court enjoined interpretation of sections of these regulations because the secretary retained numerous avenues under the regulations to unilaterally declare contract terms null and void, making collective bargaining negotiations illusory.

[22] 5 U.S.C. § 7119(c).

[23] 5 U.S.C. § 7121.

[24] 5 U.S.C. § 7121.

[25] 5 U.S.C. §§ 7512–7513.

proceeding because one of her disciplinary actions had been overturned in arbitration before the MSPB rendered its decision and the board had not been informed of the event.[26]

Employees with grievances against an agency who allege discrimination based on race, color, creed, national origin, sex, age, or physical handicap may choose to bring a complaint under the separate statutory equal employment opportunity procedure or the negotiated grievance arbitration procedure, but not both.[27] Either party has the right to file with the FLRA an exception to an arbitrator's award on grounds similar to those applied by federal courts to private-sector awards. If no exception is taken after 30 days, the award is final and binding on the parties.[28]

AGENCY UNFAIR LABOR PRACTICES.   Section 7116(a) of the statute sets forth eight management unfair labor practices. It parallels in part the unfair labor practice provisions of the NLRA. It is, for example, an unfair labor practice for agency management to interfere with the exercise of employee rights or to discipline or discriminate against an employee because the employee engaged in union activity or filed a complaint or petition under the statute. Also, it is an unfair labor practice to refuse to negotiate in good faith with a labor organization or to refuse to cooperate in impasse procedures. Further, it is an unfair labor practice for an agency to enforce a regulation that is in conflict with any prior collective bargaining agreement or to otherwise fail to comply with the statute.

UNION UNFAIR LABOR PRACTICES.   Section 7116(b) of the statute sets forth eight union unfair labor practices. As under the NLRA, labor organizations in the federal sector are prohibited from interfering with employee rights or attempting to cause an agency to discriminate against an employee because of the employee's exercise of rights under the statute. Federal-sector unions must negotiate in good faith and cooperate in impasse procedures and decisions.

It is an unfair labor practice under Section 7116(b)(4) for a federal-sector union to discriminate against an employee on the basis of race, color, creed, national origin, sex, age, preferential or nonpreferential civil service status, political affiliation, marital status, or handicap.

Finally, it is an unfair labor practice under Section 7116(b)(7) for a union to call or condone a strike or work slowdown. Picketing that interferes with an agency's operations is also prohibited under this section. However, informational picketing that does not interfere with operations is expressly allowed.

REMEDIES FOR UNFAIR LABOR PRACTICES.   When the FLRA determines that an unfair labor practice has occurred, an appropriate remedy could include an order (1) to cease and desist, (2) to require a renegotiation with retroactive effect, or (3) to reinstate an employee with back pay.[29] The statute also authorizes the award of

---

[26] 122 S. Ct. 431 (2001).

[27] 5 U.S.C. § 7121(d).

[28] 5 U.S.C. § 7122.

[29] 5 U.S.C. § 7118(a)(7).

attorney fees in certain unfair labor practice and grievance cases where an employee has suffered an unwarranted or unjustified personnel action resulting in the loss of all or part of the employee's pay.[30]

IMPACT OF THE LAW. In the private sector, bargaining over wage issues is considered by the parties to be the most important part of the negotiation process. Unions make demands and submit supporting data for wages and other economic benefits based on the union's economic analysis of the company's ability to pay the increased wages. Companies present information and arguments based on their competitive position and their ability to pay. In the negotiation process, wage proposals are made over a period of time—a period that may include a strike or lockout—until new wage rates are agreed upon. Reaching agreement on wage issues is commonly the most difficult part of negotiating a collective bargaining contract. The noneconomic issues concerning hours and working conditions, in the setting of intensive negotiation over the economic issues, have a way of being resolved quickly by the parties by tying a final offer or acceptance on the economic issues to acceptance or withdrawal of important noneconomic issues. In the federal sector, the agencies and exclusive representatives ordinarily do not bargain over wages and are limited to bargaining over conditions of employment, which consist of personnel policies, practices, and matters affecting working conditions. Personnel policies and practices are indeed most important to employees working in the federal sector. However, with wages not a component of bargaining in most agencies, the impact of the Federal Service Labor-Management Relations Statute is not comparable to the impact of the NLRA or state and local government bargaining laws.

While some 60 percent of civilian, nonpostal, federal service employees are represented by unions, the actual number of union members as opposed to represented employees is relatively small. For example, over one-half of the employees in National Treasury Employees Union units do not belong to the union, and a large percentage of federal employees represented by the American Federation of Government Employees (NAGE) do not pay union dues. Union security arrangements are prohibited under the FSLMRS.

CASE 10.4	NATIONAL AERONAUTICS AND SPACE ADMINISTRATION v. FLRA
	SUPREME COURT OF THE UNITED STATES, 527 U.S. 229 (1999).

[In January 1993, in response to information supplied by the Federal Bureau of Investigation (FBI), the National Aeronautics and Space Administration's (NASA's) Office of Inspector General (OIG) conducted an investigation of certain threatening activities of an employee of the George C. Marshall Space Flight center in Huntsville, Alabama, which is also a component of NASA. A NASA-OIG investigator contacted the employee to arrange for an interview and, in response to the employee's request, agreed that both the employee's lawyer and union representative could attend. The conduct of the interview gave rise to a complaint by the union representative that the investigator had improperly limited the union representative's participation. The union filed a charge with the Federal Labor Relations Authority (Authority), alleging that NASA

continued

---

[30] 5 U.S.C. § 5596(b)(1)(A)(i).

and its OIG had committed an unfair labor practice. The administrative law judge (ALG) ruled for the union with respect to its complaint against NASA-OIG. The ALJ concluded that the OIG investigator was a "representative" of NASA within the meaning of Section 7114(a)(2)(B) and that certain aspects of the investigator's behavior had violated the right to union representation under that section. On review, the Authority agreed that the NASA-OIG investigator prevented the union representative from actively participating in the examination. The Eleventh Circuit granted the Authority's application for enforcement of its order. The U.S. Supreme Court granted certiorari.]

STEVENS, J....

... The question presented by this case is whether an investigator employed in NASA's Office of Inspector General (NASA-OIG) can be considered a "representative" of NASA when examining a NASA employee, such that the right to union representation in the FSLMRS may be invoked....

On October 12, 1978, Congress enacted the Inspector General Act (IGA), 5 U.S.C. App. § 1 et seq., p. 1381, which created an Office of Inspector General (OIG) in each of several federal agencies, including the National Aeronautics and Space Administration (NASA). The following day, Congress enacted the Federal Service Labor-Management Relations Statute (FSLMRS), 5 U.S.C. § 7101 et seq., which provides certain protections, including union representation, to a variety of federal employees....

The FSLMRS provides, in relevant part,

"(2) An exclusive representative of an appropriate unit in an agency shall be given the opportunity to be represented at—

"(B) any examination of an employee in the unit by a representative of the agency in connection with an investigation if—

"(i) the employee reasonably believes that the examination may result in disciplinary action against the employee; and

"(ii) the employee requests representation."
5 U.S.C. § 7114(a)....

Employing ordinary tools of statutory construction, in combination with the Authority's position on the matter, we have no difficulty concluding that § 7114(a) (2) (B) is not limited to agency investigators representing an "entity" that collectively bargains with the employee's union....

... The right Congress created in § 7114 (a) (2) (B) vindicates obvious countervailing federal policies. It provides a procedural safeguard for employees who are under investigation by their agency, and the mere existence of the right can only strengthen the morale of the federal workforce. The interest in fair treatment for employees under investigation is equally strong whether they are being questioned by employees in NASA's OIG or by other representatives of the agency. And, as we indicated in *Weingarten*, representation is not the equivalent of obstruction. See 420 U.S., at 262–264. In many cases the participation of a union representative will facilitate the fact-finding process and a fair resolution of an agency investigation—or at least Congress must have thought so.

Whenever a procedural protection plays a meaningful role in an investigation, it may impose some burden on the investigators or agency managers in pursuing their mission. We must presume, however, that Congress took account of the policy concerns on both sides of the balance when it decided to enact the IGA and, on the heels of that statute, § 7114(a)(2)(B) of the FSLMRS.

[Affirmed.]

JUSTICE THOMAS, with whom THE CHIEF JUSTICE, JUSTICE O'CONNOR, and JUSTICE SCALIA join, Dissenting ...

In light of the independence guaranteed Inspectors General by the Inspector General Act of 1978, 5 U.S.C. App. § 1 et seq., p 1381, investigators employed in the Office of Inspector General (OIG) will not represent agency management in the typical case. There is no basis for concluding, as the Federal Labor Relations Authority did, that in this case the investigator from OIG for the National Aeronautics and Space Administration was a "representative of the agency" within the meaning of 5 U.S.C. § 7114(a) (2) (B). I respectfully dissent....

Case Questions

1. How did the Supreme Court rule in this case?
2. What policy argument exists for granting federal employees who are under investigation by their agency, the right to have active union representation not only when the investigator is acting directly for the management of the government agency, but also when the investigator is from the agency's Office of Inspector General?

SECTION 89: STATE AND LOCAL EMPLOYMENT

Before the issuance of Executive Order 10988 in 1962, labor associations at all levels of government had lobbied for improvements in benefits and conditions rather than participating in formal collective bargaining or direct negotiation. After 1962, with the encouragement of organizing at the national level, state and local government workers renewed their efforts to get collective bargaining agreements. These efforts were accepted by the electorate, by local government officials, and by management. State legislation was enacted to prescribe standards and procedures for state and local government employer-employee consultation or negotiation for agreements.

Legislation for collective negotiations also came out of studies by a task force that was established by the National Governors' Conference. A number of state studies were undertaken by legislative or tripartite committees or by a combination of legislative and bipartisan representatives in the industrialized and urbanized states where public-sector bargaining problems had developed, including New York, New Jersey, Michigan, Illinois, Pennsylvania, Rhode Island, Minnesota, and Connecticut. In a few states with restrictive employee relations legislation, the laws were revised. Some of the states undertook to draft and enact collective bargaining laws for the first time.

COVERAGE

Approximately two-thirds of the states have enacted legislation that permits public-sector collective bargaining, with some 30 states having comprehensive public-sector labor relations laws.[31] The legislative pattern that has emerged is far from consistent. The coverage of some state laws includes both state and municipal employees. In some states, only municipal employees are covered; in others, only state employees. Separate statutes governing the collective bargaining rights of teachers, police officers, and firefighters are found in many states, whereas some states classify all employees together. The varying nature of this legislation is the result of the different needs and different political climates of the states.

Most municipal labor relations come under the preemptive jurisdiction of state legislation, a pattern that originated with the enactment of the Wisconsin Municipal Employee Relations Act of 1959. However, some state collective bargaining laws allow municipalities to establish local labor relations agencies through local legislation. This form of legislation is important because the majority of all government employment is performed at the local level. One municipality that has taken advantage of local legislation is New York City. Faced with the problems inherent in dealing with over 100 local unions affiliated with over 50 parent unions, the city passed an ordinance establishing an Office of Collective Bargaining.

---

[31] Some states, while having no public bargaining laws, do allow voluntary bargaining based on court decisions structured on constitutional rights to free speech and assembly. The following states do not have public employee labor relations laws governing state, county, and municipal employees: Alabama, Arizona, Arkansas, Colorado, North Dakota, South Carolina, Virginia, and West Virginia.

BARGAINING UNITS IN THE PUBLIC SECTOR

The private-sector concept of exclusive recognition has been successfully extended into the public sector. Most of the statutes governing public-sector collective bargaining authorize the recognition of a single organization as the exclusive representative for the employees. In most instances, a union is certified through a Public Employment Relations Board (PERB), which is legislatively created and is similar in concept to the NLRB.

Exclusive recognition in the public sector has given rise to a unique problem because of "sunshine" laws in certain states. Sunshine laws require that formal action by state or local governmental bodies be deliberated and adopted only at *public* meetings. As a result, in some jurisdictions, the public is given an opportunity to indirectly involve itself in contract negotiations by commenting on proposals as they arise. In *City of Madison, Joint School District No. 8 v. Wisconsin Employment Relations Comm'n*,[32] the U.S. Supreme Court held that a school board had not committed an unfair labor practice by permitting a teacher to speak in opposition to a teachers union proposal at a public school board meeting. The Court reasoned that such statements are merely opinions and do not represent an attempt at negotiation on the part of either the individual teacher or the school board.

PUBLIC-SECTOR UNION SECURITY CLAUSES

A primary area of contention in both the private and the public sectors has been the issue of union security. A union security clause in a collective bargaining agreement, in the case of a **union shop**, requires employees, as a condition of employment, to maintain union membership, with dues being deducted or checked off by the employer as a payroll deduction. An **agency shop** union security arrangement requires that every employee represented by the union, even though not a union member, must pay to the union, as a condition of employment, a service charge usually equal in amount to union dues.

In the private sector, the NLRA does not permit a union, over the objections of dues-paying nonmember employees, to expend funds on activities unrelated to collective bargaining and contract administration.[33] In the public sector, it was thought the union security clauses might be unconstitutional, as a state or local government is an actual party to the agreement and thus directly participates in the restriction of the nonunion employees' freedom of association protected by the First and Fourteenth Amendments. In *Abood v. Detroit Board of Education*,[34] the Supreme Court decided the issue. It upheld the constitutionality of an agency shop clause in a collective bargaining agreement between a union and a school board, but with a serious qualification. Unions that have won security agreements in the public-sector must provide an internal remedy by which those opposing ideological expenditures unrelated to collective bargaining, such as political contributions, can be reimbursed the percentage of their dues that went to such expenditures. This can

---

[32] 429 U.S. 167 (1976).

[33] *Communication Workers of America v. Beck*, 487 U.S. 735 (1988).

[34] 431 U.S. 209 (1977).

be determined by an accounting of which of the union's expenditures were related to collective bargaining, contract administration, and grievance adjustment and were unrelated to those matters.

In the *Chicago Teachers Union v. Hudson* decision, presented in this section, the U.S. Supreme Court set forth three requirements for a union's collection of agency fees: (1) an adequate explanation of the basis for the fee, (2) a reasonably prompt opportunity to challenge the amount of the fee before an impartial administrator, and (3) an escrow for the amounts reasonably in dispute while such challenges are pending. The First Amendment is not violated when a state requires that its public-sector unions receive affirmative authorization from a nonmember before spending the nonmember's agency fee for election-related purposes.[35]

In *Lehnert v. Ferris Faculty Ass'n*,[36] the Supreme Court cataloged certain union expenses for inclusion in the amount to be paid by the objecting individuals. Under *Lehnert*, objectors must share in the cost of supporting affiliate and parent unions that can be a resource for the local union, as well as the expense for articles in the union newspaper concerning teaching and education and costs associated with preparation for a strike that could have been illegal under state law if it had occurred.

SCOPE OF BARGAINING

In the *Borg-Warner* case, discussed in Chapter 5, the Supreme Court classified the subjects of bargaining as either mandatory or permissive. Although this decision related to the NLRA and the private sector, the Court's approach has been adopted in the public sector. However, because of the vast network of laws, rules, and regulations governing public employers, it is first necessary to determine whether the public employer legally has the power to agree to a given subject. For example, where a state statute sets the minimum number of teacher evaluations at two a year, it is impermissible for a school board to agree to only one evaluation a year.[37] If a matter is an **impermissible subject** of collective bargaining, there is no obligation to bargain on the subject, and any agreement that purports to deal with the subject is unenforceable.

Once it is determined that the subject may be agreed to, the analysis shifts to determine whether it is a mandatory or permissive subject of bargaining. As you will recall from Chapter 5, Section 49, a **mandatory subject** of bargaining is one the parties are required to negotiate over and a **permissive subject** of bargaining is one the parties may negotiate over but upon which neither can insist to the point of impasse.

---

[35] *Davenport v. Washington Education Assn.*, 127 S.Ct. 2372 (2007).

[36] 500 U.S. 507 (1991). For a recent application of *Lehnert*, see *Otto v. Pennsylvania State Education Assn.*, 330 F.3d 125 (2003).

[37] See *Springfield Education Ass'n v. Springfield School District* No. 19, 549 P.2d 1141 (Or. App. 1976): where a state statute vests power to discipline teachers on a school board, one jurisdiction has determined that it is impermissible for the school board to agree to submit its decisions to arbitration, *Raines v. Independent School District No. 6 of Craig County*, 796 P.2d 303 (Colo. 1990). See also *Chicago School Reform Board of Trustees v. Chicago Teachers Union*, 721 N.E.2d 676 (Ill. App. 1999) and *Land v. Board of Education of City of Chicago*, 781 NE 2d 249 (Ill. 2002).

Mandatory subjects of collective bargaining in the state and local sectors have, in most instances, been legislatively defined in terms similar to those found in the NLRA, encompassing "wages, hours, and other terms and conditions of employment." The term **wages** has been held to include overtime pay, vacation pay, severance pay, pensions, and shift differentials. One wage item that has not been held to be a mandatory subject of bargaining but that unions have persisted in trying to include in a collective bargaining agreement is the wage parity provision. A wage parity provision provides that a particular group's wage schedule, such as the wage schedule of firefighters, will be adjusted upward to equal that obtained in a subsequent agreement by a different group, such as the police. The Connecticut Supreme Court in *Fire Fighters, Local 1219 v. Connecticut Labor Relations Board* held that all wage parity clauses that burden the later negotiation of a second union's contract are void and unenforceable.[38] However, courts in New York and California have upheld the right of public employees to secure wage parity clauses.[39]

The term **hours**, it is generally agreed, encompasses the length of time employees are required to work. There is, however, an area of disagreement over whether the term includes the scheduling of an employee's hours. Ohio has held that the scheduling of hours is a mandatory subject of bargaining,[40] whereas Oregon has held it to be merely permissive.[41]

The most difficulty has been in interpreting "other terms and conditions of employment." This is also the case in the private sector. Unlike the private sector, public-sector collective bargaining legislation often contains "management prerogative" language. The Pennsylvania statute, for example, provides that "public employers shall not be required to bargain over matters of inherent managerial policy ... and selection and direction of personnel."[42]

The special statutes for police, firefighters, and teachers contain broad managerial prerogative language. The statutory reservation of managerial prerogatives, therefore, creates an overlap problem with the mandatory subjects of bargaining contained in the phrase "other terms and conditions of employment." Some courts have resolved the problem by stating that despite such statutory language, if an item is "significantly" related to wages, hours, or other terms and conditions of employment, then the parties are required to negotiate. However, the majority of courts apply a balancing test, weighing the competing interests and deciding which is more compelling.[43]

Because of the statutory reservations of managerial prerogatives and the fiscal squeeze that has hit state and local governments, the courts and various public

---

[38] 370 A.2d 952 (Conn. 1976). See *Town of Madison v. IBPO*, 1999 WL42321 (Conn. Super.).

[39] *Banning Teachers Ass'n v. Public Employment Relations Bd.*, 750 P.2d 313 (Cal. 1988); *County of Sullivan v. Sullivan County Employees Association, Inc.*, 235 A.D.2d 748 (N.Y. 1997); *Baltimore v. Baltimore Firefighters*, 776 A.2d 219 (Md. App. 2001).

[40] *State Employment Relations Bd. v. City of Bedford Heights*, 534 N.E.2d 115 (Ohio 1987).

[41] *Marion County Law Enforcement Ass'n v. Marion County*, 883 P.2d 222 (Or. 1994).

[42] Purdon's Pa. Stat. Ann. Title 43 Section 1101.702 (2000).

[43] *Crawford County v. Pennsylvania Labor Relations Bd. and AFSCME*, 659 A.2d 1078 (1995).

employment relations boards have not been as inclined to hold items to be mandatory subjects of bargaining as the courts and the NLRB have in the private sector. This has necessarily weakened the union position in public sector collective bargaining because permissive subjects cannot be insisted upon to the point of impasse.

In *I.A.F. v. Town of Bellingham*,[44] the town contended that it was its management prerogative to make the decision to allow or disallow 24-hour shifts of firefighters and that the union's proposal for 24-hour shifts to an arbitration panel was beyond the scope of interest arbitration. However, the court held that "shift structure hours" were "hours of employment" and as such were mandatory subjects of bargaining. The court enforced the arbitration award in favor of the firefighters.

CONTRACTUAL IMPASSE SETTLEMENT PROCEDURES

When an impasse is reached in public sector contractual negotiations, the parties have several means of resolving their differences. As in the private sector, negotiation and mediation play an important role—a majority of all public sector disputes are settled through these devices. Three procedures that are generally not found in the private sector but that are receiving some acceptance in the public sector are fact-finding, interest arbitration,[45] and final offer selecting.

Fact-finding has come into use in the public sector from the "public interest" segments of the private sector, such as the transportation and utilities industries. In this procedure, a neutral person or panel conducts a hearing at which the opposing parties present their positions and supporting evidence on the issues. The fact finder thereafter issues settlement recommendations that are not binding but that, it is hoped, will bring the dispute to an end.

Interest arbitration is similar in form to fact-finding but has an important distinguishing feature. Unlike fact-finding, which results in recommendations, interest arbitration results in a final and binding decision setting the terms of the settlement with which the parties are legally required to comply. Interest arbitration may be either compulsory (when mandated by law) or voluntary (when the parties utilize the procedure of their own volition). Where not mandated by law, interest arbitration is a permissive subject of bargaining, and both parties must agree to its inclusion in their labor contract for it to be continued.[46]

The third mode of impasse settlement is final offer selection. Final offer selection is similar to interest arbitration; however, the arbitrator is restricted to selecting the last offer of one of the parties. This procedure may be varied to allow the arbitrator to make the selection on an issue-by-issue basis. The factors given weight by the arbitrator or arbitration panel vary from state to state, but may include the following:

1. The financial ability of the municipality to meet costs;
2. The interests and welfare of the public;

---

[44] 67 Mass. App. Ct. 502 (2006); 450 Mass. 1011 (2007).

[45] Interest arbitration involves the settlement of the terms of a contract, whereas, in the more familiar grievance arbitration, the subject is a claimed violation of the terms of an existing contract.

[46] *Pasco Police Officers Ass'n v. City of Pasco*, 938 P.2d 827 (Wash. 1997).

3. The hazards of employment; physical, educational, and mental qualifications; the job training required; and the skills involved;

4. A comparison of wages, hours, and conditions of employment of the employees involved in the arbitration proceedings with the wages, hours, and conditions of employment of other employees performing similar services and with other employees generally in public and private employment in comparable communities;

5. The decisions and recommendations of a fact-finder;

6. The average consumer prices for goods and services, commonly known as the cost of living;

7. The overall compensation presently received by the employees, including direct wages and fringe benefits;

8. Changes in any of the foregoing circumstances during the pendency of the arbitration proceedings.

CASE 10.5   CHICAGO TEACHERS UNION V. HUDSON
SUPREME COURT OF THE UNITED STATES, 475 U.S. 292 (1986).

[The Chicago Teachers Union has been the exclusive collective bargaining representative of the Chicago Board of Education's educational employees since 1967. Approximately 95 percent of the employees are members of the union. Until 1982, the members' dues financed the entire cost of the union's collective bargaining and contract administration, and nonmembers received the benefits of the union's representation without making any contributions to its cost. In an attempt to solve this "free rider" problem, the union and the board entered into an agreement requiring the board to deduct "proportionate share payments" from nonmembers' paychecks. The union determined that the "proportionate share" assessed on nonmembers was 95 percent of union dues. Union officials computed the 95 percent fee on the basis of the union's financial records for the fiscal year ending on June 30, 1982. They identified expenditures unrelated to collective bargaining and contract administration (which they estimated as $188,549.82). They divided this amount by the union's income for the year ($4,103,701.38) to produce a percentage of 4.6; the figure was then rounded off to 5 percent to provide a cushion to cover any inadvertent errors. The union also established a procedure for considering nonmembers' objections to the deductions. After the deduction was made, a nonmember could object by writing the union president. The objection would then meet a three-stage procedure: (1) the union's executive committee would consider the objection and within 30 days notify the objector of its decision; (2) if the objector disagreed with that decision and appealed within another

30 days, the union's executive board would consider the objection; and (3) if the objector continued to protest after the executive board's decision, the union's president would select an arbitrator. If an objection was sustained at any stage, the remedy would be a reduction in future deductions and a rebate for the objector. Annie Hudson and other objecting nonmembers of the union brought suit in federal district court, challenging the union procedure on the grounds that it violated their First Amendment rights to freedom of expression and association and their Fourteenth Amendment due process rights and also permitted the use of their proportionate share for impermissible purposes. The district court rejected challenges and upheld the procedure. The court of appeals reversed, holding that the procedure was constitutionally inadequate.]

STEVENS, J....
In *Abood v. Detroit Board of Education*, 431 U.S. 209 (1977), "we found no constitutional barrier to an agency shop agreement between a municipality and a teacher's union insofar as the agreement required every employee in the unit to pay a service fee to defray the costs of collective bargaining, contract administration, and grievance adjustment. The union, however, could not, consistently with the Constitution, collect from dissenting employees any sums for the support of ideological causes not germane to its duties as collective bargaining agent." *Ellis v. Railway Clerks*, 466 U.S. 435, 447 (1984). The *Ellis* case was primarily

continued

concerned with the need "to define the line between union expenditures that all employees must help defray and those that are not sufficiently related to collective bargaining to justify their being imposed on dissenters." *Ibid.* In contrast, this case concerns the constitutionality of the procedure adopted by the Chicago Teachers Union, with the approval of the Chicago Board of Education, to draw that necessary line and to respond to nonmembers' objections to the manner in which it was drawn....

I.

The procedure that was initially adopted by the Union and considered by the District Court contained three fundamental flaws. First, as in *Ellis*, a remedy which merely offers dissenters the possibility of a rebate does not avoid the risk that dissenters' funds may be used temporarily for an improper purpose. "[T]he Union should not be permitted to exact a service fee from nonmembers without first establishing a procedure which will avoid the risk that their funds will be used, even temporarily, to finance ideological activities unrelated to collective bargaining." *Abood*, 431 U.S., at 244 (concurring opinion). The amount at stake for each individual dissenter does not diminish this concern. For, whatever the amount, the quality of respondents' interest in not being compelled to subsidize the propagation of political or ideological views that they oppose is clear. In *Abood*, we emphasized this point by quoting the comments of Thomas Jefferson and James Madison about the tyrannical character of forcing an individual to contribute even "three pence" for the "propagation of opinions which he disbelieves." A forced exaction followed by a rebate equal to the amount improperly expended is thus not a permissible response to the nonunion employees' objections.

Second, the "advance reduction of dues" was inadequate because it provided nonmembers with inadequate information about the basis for the proportionate share. In *Abood*, we reiterated that the non-union employee has the burden of raising an objection, but that the union retains the burden of proof: "'Since the unions possess the facts and records from which the proportion of political to total union expenditures can reasonably be calculated, basic considerations of fairness compel that they, not the individual employees, bear the burden of proving such proportion.' "*Abood*, 431 U.S., at 239–240, n. 40, quoting *Railway Clerks v. Allen*, 373 U.S. 113,

122 (1963). Basic considerations of fairness, as well as concern for the First Amendment rights at stake, also dictate that the potential objectors be given sufficient information to gauge the propriety of the union's fee. Leaving the non-union employees in the dark about the source of the figure for the agency fee—and requiring them to object in order to receive information—does not adequately protect the careful distinctions drawn in *Abood*.

In this case, the original information given to the non-union employees was inadequate. Instead of identifying the expenditures for collective bargaining and contract administration that had been provided for the benefit of nonmembers as well as members— and for which nonmembers as well as members can fairly be charged a fee—the Union identified the amount that it admittedly had expended for purposes that did not benefit dissenting nonmembers. An acknowledgment that nonmembers would not be required to pay any part of 5 percent of the Union's total annual expenditures was not an adequate disclosure of the reasons why they were required to pay their share of 95 percent.

Finally, the original Union procedure was also defective because it did not provide for a reasonably prompt decision by an impartial decision maker. Although we have not so specified in the past, we now conclude that such a requirement is necessary. The non-union employee, whose First Amendment rights are affected by the agency shop itself and who bears the burden of objecting, is entitled to have his objections addressed in an expeditious, fair, and objective manner....

Thus, the original Union procedure was inadequate because it failed to minimize the risk that non-union employees' contributions might be used for impermissible purposes, because it failed to provide adequate justification for the advance reduction of dues, and because it failed to offer a reasonably prompt decision by an impartial decision maker.

II.

... We need not hold, however, that a 100 percent escrow is constitutionally required. Such a remedy has the serious defect of depriving the Union of access to some escrowed funds that it is unquestionably entitled to retain. If, for example, the original disclosure by the Union had included a certified public accountant's verified breakdown of expenditures, including some categories that no dissenter could reasonably

continued

challenge, there would be no reason to escrow the portion of the nonmember's fees that would be represented by those categories. On the record before us, there is no reason to believe that anything approaching a 100 percent "cushion" to cover the possibility of mathematical errors would be constitutionally required. Nor can we decide how the proper contribution that might be made by an independent audit, in advance, coupled with adequate notice, might reduce the size of any appropriate escrow.

Thus, the Union's 100 percent escrow does not cure all of the problems in the original procedure. Two of the three flaws remain, and the procedure therefore continues to provide less than the Constitution requires in this context.

III.

We hold today that the constitutional requirements for the Union's collection of agency fees include an adequate explanation of the basis for the fee, a reasonably prompt opportunity to challenge the amount of the fee before an impartial decision maker, and an escrow for the amounts reasonably in dispute while such challenges are pending.

The determination of the appropriate remedy in this case is a matter that should be addressed in the first instance by the District Court. The Court of Appeals correctly reversed the District Court's original judgment and remanded the case for further proceedings. That judgment of reversal is affirmed, and those further proceedings should be consistent with this opinion.

It is so ordered.

Case Questions

1. What was the "free rider" problem the union and Board of Education tried to resolve?
2. Would not a rebate equal to the amount improperly expended resolve the nonmember employees' objections?
3. What was constitutionally wrong with the original information given to the nonmember employees?
4. State the constitutional requirements for a union to collect agency fees.

SECTION 90: CONGRESSIONAL POWER OVER STATE EMPLOYMENT STANDARDS

The Fair Labor Standards Act (FLSA) did not apply to employees of state and local governments when enacted, but under the 1974 amendments to the FLSA, the Act covered virtually all state and local government employees. In *National League of Cities v. Usery*,[47] the Supreme Court held that FLSA and its minimum wage and overtime provisions were not applicable to states in areas of "traditional governmental functions." The divided Court held that the 1974 amendments were unconstitutional in that Congress had wielded its power in a way that deeply impaired the states' ability to function effectively within the federal system embodied in the Constitution. In *Garcia v. San Antonio Metropolitan Transit Authority*,[48] after experiencing a growing number of problems in applying the "traditional governmental functions" test, a sharply divided Supreme Court overruled *National League of Cities*. The Court held that the "traditional governmental functions" test was unsound and inconsistent with the principles of federalism and pointed out that states are protected by the political process from overreaching by the federal government. The four dissenting judges disagreed, asserting that the majority had failed to point out how the states' role in the political process guaranteed that the federal government would not infringe on state sovereignty.

---

[47] 426 U.S. 833 (1976).

[48] 469 U.S. 528 (1985).

Although the Supreme Court has not actually overturned *Garcia v. San Antonio Metropolitan Transit Authority*, the Court has recently adopted a very different approach toward federal-state government relations, based in part on the language of the Tenth Amendment, which states, "The powers not delegated to the United States ... are reserved to the States." A new majority of the Court has reasserted what it perceives as a "residual sovereignty" of the states from the era before the ratification of the U.S. Constitution in 1788. This judicial reassertion of states' rights is found in the *Alden v. Maine* and *Kimel v. Florida Board of Regents* cases, discussed next.

SOVEREIGN IMMUNITY OF STATES IN FLSA SUITS

In *Alden v. Maine*,[49] a group of probation officers filed suit against their employer, the state of Maine, in state court action, alleging the state had violated the overtime provisions of the Fair Labor Standards Act, and the group sought compensatory and liquidated damages. The state trial court dismissed the suit on the basis of sovereign immunity, and the state's appeals court affirmed. In a 5–4 decision, the U.S. Supreme Court ruled that the powers delegated to Congress under Article I of the U.S. Constitution do not include the power to subject nonconsenting states to private lawsuits in federal courts for overtime pay and liquidated damages under the FLSA. The majority maintained that the doctrine of state sovereign immunity supports its position.

The doctrine that a sovereign could not be sued without its consent was universal in the states when the Constitution was drafted and ratified; and the leading advocates for ratification of the Constitution gave explicit assurances during the ratification debates that the Constitution would not strip the states of sovereign immunity. The majority pointed out that a state does not have a right to disregard the Constitution or valid federal laws and that the state of Maine is now in full compliance with the FLSA. Maine exercised its sovereign immunity defense to the lawsuit for damages. The dissent disagreed with the majority's position, pointing out that state employees are left without a meaningful way to enforce their rights under the FLSA in states that do not waive their immunity and consent to such suits. The dissent believed that it is a fundamental principle that when there is a right, there must be a remedy.

STATE EMPLOYEE ACTIONS UNDER THE ADEA

In *Kimel v. Florida Board of Regents*,[50] three separate sets of plaintiffs filed suit under the Age Discrimination Employment Act (ADEA) against their state employers, Florida and Alabama, and the U.S. Supreme Court dealt with state sovereign immunity defenses and congressional power to enact the ADEA. The 1974 amendments to the FLSA, referred to in the first paragraph of this section, not only extended the FLSA to state and local government employees, but also extended application of the ADEA's substantive requirements to the states. The Supreme

---

[49] 527 U.S. 706 (1999).

[50] 528 U.S. 62 (2000).

Court has interpreted the Eleventh Amendment of the U.S. Constitution as not providing for federal jurisdiction over suits by private citizens against nonconsenting states.[51] However, in *Fitzpatrick v. Ditzer*,[52] the Supreme Court held that under Section 5 of the Fourteenth Amendment, Congress may abrogate states' sovereign immunity if there is a clear expression of intent to lift such immunity and if it acts under a valid grant of constitutional authority. In *Kimel v. Florida Board of Regents*, involving private citizen suits against states under the ADEA, Congress made it very clear that it intended to lift the sovereign immunity of the states when it applied the ADEA's substantive requirements to the states. However, the Supreme Court majority held that the ADEA was not appropriate legislation under Section 5 of the Fourteenth Amendment and therefore the abrogation of the states' sovereign immunity was invalid.[53] The Court applied a test found in *City of Boerne v. Flores* that for remedial legislation to be appropriate under Section 5 of the Fourteenth Amendment, "there must be congruence and proportionality between the injury to be prevented or remedied and the means adopted to that end."[54] The *Kimel* court majority pointed out that age is not a suspect classification under the Equal Protection Clause of the Fourteenth Amendment, and a review of the ADEA's legislative record reveals Congress had virtually no reason to believe state and local governments were unconstitutionally discriminating against their employees on the basis of age. The Court pointed out that although employees cannot bring ADEA suits against state employers, these employees are protected by state age discrimination statutes in almost every state of the Union.

SUITS AGAINST STATES UNDER TITLE I OF THE ADA

Title I of the Americans with Disabilities Act prohibits private employers from discriminating against individuals with disabilities who, with or without reasonable accommodations, are qualified to perform the essential functions of a job. In *Board of Trustees of the University of Alabama v. Garret*,[55] the Supreme Court held in a 5–4 decision that private suits to enforce Title I of the Americans with Disabilities Act against state governments are barred by the Eleventh Amendment. The Court determined that while Congress affirmatively authorized suits against the states when it passed the ADA, Title I of the ADA was not legislation implementing the provisions of the Fourteenth Amendment and thus could not subject a nonconsenting state to suit. The Court relied upon its *City of Cleburne v. Cleburne*

---

[51] *Seminole Tribe of Florida v. Florida*, 517 U.S. 44 (1996).

[52] 427 U.S. 445, 456 (1976).

[53] The Fourteenth Amendment provides, in relevant part:

> "Section 1 … No state shall make or enforce any law which shall abridge the privileges or immunities of citizens of the United States, nor shall any State deprive any person, of life, liberty, or property, without due process of law; nor deny to any person within its jurisdiction the equal protection of the laws."
>
> "Section 5. The Congress shall have the power to enforce, by appropriate legislation, the provisions of this article."

[54] 521 U.S. 507, 520 (1997).

[55] 351 U.S. 356 (2001).

Living Center, Inc.,[56] precedent that distinctions based upon disability are not constitutionally suspect and that "States are not required by the Fourteenth Amendment to make special accommodations for the disabled, so long as their actions towards such individuals are rational." The Court pointed out that in passing Title I of the ADA, Congress identified no historic pattern of unconstitutional behavior by state governments.

CHAPTER QUESTIONS AND PROBLEMS

1. How has the federal government provided for bargaining rights for federal employees?
2. Is the FSLMRS's impact on the federal sector comparable to the NLRA's impact on the private sector? Explain.
3. What remedies may the FLRA employ once it determines that an unfair labor practice has occurred?
4. Is the right of state and municipal employees to bargain impeded by having no legal right to strike? What substitutes do the laws provide?
5. Michael Murphy, a member of the Postal Workers union, was employed at the San Francisco Bulk Mail Center. Murphy arrived at the center for his 9 AM shift one morning and observed a group of his coworkers and union officers gathered in front of the center's main entrance with picket signs. Murphy was told that a picket line was being erected but that anyone who wanted to work could cross the line. Fearing threats and verbal abuse if he attempted to cross the line, Murphy phoned the center and stated that the picket line prevented his arrival at work. Murphy then joined the pickets in their patrol until he learned that the strike had not been sanctioned by the union. Murphy refused to cross the picket line for the next three days; however, he did not take part in any more picketing. Murphy was discharged by the Postal Service, which had informed him that strikes against the U.S. government were illegal. An arbitrator subsequently ru-

led that discharge was too severe a punishment for Murphy, given the extent of his strike activity, and ordered him to be reinstated without back pay.

The Postal Service refused to abide by the arbitrator's ruling, citing federal law, which required that a striking U.S. government employee be discharged. The union asked the federal district court to enforce the arbitrator's award.

Should the court order Murphy to be reinstated? Decide. [*Postal Workers v. Postal Service,* 110 LRRM 2764 (9th Cir.)]

6. Rule 54A of the Rules and Regulations of the Chicago Police Department prohibited "the joining or retaining membership in, or soliciting other members to join any labor organization whose membership is not exclusively limited to full-time law enforcement officers." Three Chicago police officers attempted to organize police for Local 1975, United Paperworkers International Union, AFL-CIO. Although the composition of Local 1975 was exclusively restricted to full-time sworn police officers, the international did not restrict its membership, and it comprised various occupations.

The union and the three officers challenged Rule 54A as an unconstitutional restriction of their First Amendment right of freedom of association. The city defended the rule as essential to secure the impartiality of police in labor disputes. Chicago contended that the neutrality of police would be

---

[56] 473 U.S. 432 (1985).

destroyed if they had loyalty to diverse fellow union members and confronted those members in the line of duty.

Should the court hold this rule unconstitutional? Decide. [*Mescall, Chicago Police Local 1975 v. Rochford*, 109 LRRM 2813 (7th Cir.)]

7. New Hampshire's Public Employee Labor Relations Act included a section, RSA 273-A:13, that stated: "Strikes and other forms of job action by public employees are hereby declared to be unlawful." Negotiations between the Manchester Firefighters' Association and the city of Manchester for a new collective bargaining contract deteriorated when the union concluded that the city was no longer bargaining in good faith as the state's labor relations act required. The disillusioned members of the association began a "sickout," a form of job action in which members reported an inability to work because of illness. The results of this sickout left Manchester fire stations manned by half crews. The city obtained a cease-and-desist order from the New Hampshire Public Employee Relations Board, which was subsequently enforced by a state court against the association. The court also fined the association and its officers for noncompliance with the cease-and-desist order.

The association appealed the orders and injunction, claiming that the city had also broken the law by failing to perform its statutory duty to bargain in good faith. The association claimed that the city "provoked" the strike and, therefore, was not entitled to seek fines and an injunction against the association. The city of Manchester disagreed and claimed the sickout endangered the public health and safety.

If Manchester has bargained in bad faith, should the city be allowed to seek a stoppage of the firefighters' sickout? Decide. [*City of Manchester Firefighters' Association*, 1979–81 PBC (CCH) ¶ 36,879, N.H. Sup. Ct.]

8. The City Council of Vernon, California, enacted a resolution that unilaterally prohibited city employees from maintaining personal property with city property. The resolution was specifically targeted against firefighters who, while off duty, would wash their personal cars at city facilities. This car-washing practice had been taking place for several years and was fairly widespread throughout the department.

The Vernon Fire Fighters Union charged the city with unilateral action that violated the California "meet and confer" act. This act required municipal officials to meet and confer with union officials before acting on any subject within the union's scope of representation or terms and conditions of employment. The city denied the existence of any obligation to bargain with the union over this subject. The city maintained that the decision to ban car washing was a managerial policy decision that did not need to be discussed with the union.

Must the city bargain with the union over its decision to ban car washing? Decide. [*Vernon Fire Fighters Local 2312 v. City of Vernon*, 1979–81 PBC (CCH) ¶ 37,066, California Court of Appeals]

9. William Lowary was a geography teacher in the Lexington, Ohio, local school system. The Lexington Teachers Association (LTA) was the exclusive bargaining representative for all teachers employed by the Lexington Board of Education. Lowary was not a member of the LTA or any teachers union organization.

Lowary's employment contract contained a provision that incorporated an agency shop section of the LTA collective bargaining agreement. The contract stated that money would be deducted from his paycheck and provided to the LTA as a fair-share fee. Lowary never specifically authorized any deductions from his salary, however, and he did not receive any information concerning the ultimate use of deducted funds or the procedure for obtaining a rebate.

When the school board began deducting $29.65 (an amount equal to the union dues paid by LTA members) from each of his paychecks, Lowary objected. He went to U.S. district court to seek an injunction against the deducting of further monies from his salary on the grounds that his constitutional rights had been violated.

May a public school system constitutionally deduct union dues from a nonunion teacher's salary? If so, has the LTA and the Lexington Board of Education acted properly in this case? Decide. [*Lowary v. Lexington Board of Education*, 124 LRRM 2516 (N.D. Ohio)]

Occupational Safety and Health Law

SECTION 91: PURPOSE AND SCOPE

Reflecting persistently severe safety and health statistics over previous years, more than 14,000 workers were killed and over 2,000,000 were injured in industrial accidents in 1970. It was estimated that there were 300,000 new cases of occupational disease being discovered annually. The net effect on workers and on the economy was staggering. In response, Congress passed the Occupational Safety and Health Act (OSH Act) of 1970.[1] The stated purpose of the Act is "to assure so far as possible every working man and woman in the Nation safe and healthful working conditions and to preserve our human resources."[2]

The OSH Act attempted to reach this goal through the following ways:

1. By encouraging employers and employees in their efforts to reduce the number of occupational safety and health hazards;
2. By providing for the development and promulgation of occupational safety and health standards;
3. By providing an effective enforcement program;
4. By providing that employers and employees have separate but dependent responsibilities and rights;
5. By providing for research in the field of occupational safety and health, including the psychological factors involved, and by developing innovative methods, techniques, and approaches for dealing with occupational safety and health problems;
6. By encouraging the states to assume the fullest responsibility for the administration and enforcement of their occupational safety and health laws.

Congress passed the OSH Act pursuant to its powers under the commerce clause of the Constitution.[3] By defining the OSH Act as reaching those businesses "affecting interstate commerce,"[4] Congress provided a broad jurisdictional base. With few exceptions, the coverage of the OSH Act extends to all employers and employees in the United States and its territories. However, it does not apply to federal or state governments as employers.[5] Other important exceptions are those who are self-employed and domestic servants.[6]

SECTION 92: ADMINISTRATION

To effect its purpose, the OSH Act created three new federal agencies: the Occupational Safety & Health Administration (OSHA), the National Institute of Occupational Safety and Health (NIOSH), and the Occupational Safety and Health Review Commission (OSHRC).

OSHA is the primary administrative agency created by the Act. It is within the Department of Labor. It has the authority, through the Secretary of Labor, to promulgate standards, conduct inspections, and seek enforcement action where there

---

[1] 29 U.S.C. §§ 651 et seq. The Bureau of Labor Statistics issues data on fatal occupational injuries by industries in the fall of each year for the preceding year on its web site at http://www.bls.gov/iif/oshwc/cfoi/cftb0205.pdf. The BLS Census of Fatal Occupational Injuries for 2006 listed 5,703 fatal work injuries nationwide. There were 1,329 deaths in highway accidents, with 832 of the deaths in the transportation and warehousing sector. Construction-sector workplace deaths were 1,226. There were 516 workplace homicides for the year.

[2] 29 U.S.C. § 651(b).

[3] U.S. Const., art. 1, § 8, cl. 3.

[4] 29 U.S.C. § 652.

[5] 29 U.S.C. § 653.

[6] 29 C.F.R., Section 1975.

has been noncompliance. In litigation concerning OSHA, the courts commonly make reference only to the Secretary of Labor as the administrative actor, as OSHA's authority to act is through the Secretary of Labor.

NIOSH is primarily an occupational health research center. It studies various safety and health problems, provides technical assistance to OSHA, and recommends standards for OSHA's adoption.

OSHRC is fully autonomous from OSHA. Its sole function is to adjudicate contested enforcement actions undertaken by OSHA through the Department of Labor. OSHA recommends penalties to OSHRC for violations, but it is only OSHRC that may actually assess penalties. A party can appeal an OSHRC decision to the appropriate federal circuit court of appeals. For example, after an accident at Staley Manufacturing Co.'s Decatur, Illinois, plant in which an employee was fatally asphyxiated, OSHA inspectors issued citations for multiple violations of the OSH Act. The employer challenged the citations before the OSHRC. Upon review by the U.S. court of appeals, the court affirmed OSHRC's decision, finding that the company's "plain indifference" to act on the hazards at the workplace and train employees how to handle the hazards was a willful violation of the Act, allowing for civil penalty of no more than $70,000 for each violation.[7] OSHRC consists of three members appointed by the president for staggered six-year terms.

Conflicts have occurred between the Secretary of Labor (OSHA) and the OSHRC over which of these two independent agencies has the right to "settle the law" as to the meaning of ambiguous regulations. This conflict was resolved in favor of the Secretary of Labor by the Supreme Court in the *Martin v. OSHRC* decision.[8] The Secretary of Labor has the power to promulgate regulations and interpret ambiguous regulations in addition to its enforcement powers. The OSHRC is limited to non-policy-making adjudicatory powers typically exercised by a court in the agency review context. It (1) makes authoritative findings of fact and (2) applies the Secretary's reasonable standards to those facts in making a decision. Should the Secretary's interpretation of a regulation be unreasonable, then the OSHRC is free not to enforce the Secretary's action.

SECTION 93: STANDARDS

The Secretary of Labor is given broad authority to promulgate standards for OSHA.[9] The Act provides for the issuance of three types of standards: interim, permanent, and emergency.

INTERIM STANDARDS

Interim standards were those which the Secretary was given the power to establish for two years following the effective date of the Act. These were generally taken from preexisting national consensus standards.

---

[7] *A. E. Staley Manufacturing Co. v. Chao*, 295 F.3d 1341 (D.C. Cir. 2002).

[8] *Martin v. OSHRC*, 499 U.S. 144 (1991).

[9] 29 U.S.C. § 655(b).

PERMANENT STANDARDS

Permanent standards are either newly created or revised from original interim standards. The Secretary is empowered to take suggestions concerning standards from such interested parties as unions, employers, and NIOSH. An advisory committee may also be appointed to assist in the promulgation of permanent standards.

Once OSHA has developed a proposed or amended standard, it must publish its proposal in the *Federal Register*. The public is given at least 30 days in which to respond.[10] Failure to publish its proposal will cause the standard to be vacated.[11] If an interested party requests a public hearing, OSHA must schedule one and publicize it. Within 60 days after the close of the public comment and hearing phase, OSHA is required to publish the new standard and the date it will become effective. The Secretary has the authority to delay its effective date. In *Industrial Union Dept., AFL-CIO v. Hodgson*,[12] a delay of four years for a standard on asbestos dust was deemed within the scope of the Secretary's power. OSHA issued a final rule on employer-paid personal protective equipment for general industry, shipyards, marine terminals, longshoring, and construction on November 15, 2007. The standard had been proposed in 1999, and a union lawsuit was pending to compel the issuance of the rule. It is anticipated that the rule providing employer-paid protective equipment, such as steel-toed boots and protective gloves, will decrease 21,000 occupational injuries each year.[13]

When the new standard is published, the Secretary must give reasons for its adoption. In *Dry Color Manufacturers' Ass'n v. Department of Labor*,[14] a case involving carcinogenic chemicals, the court vacated the newly promulgated standards because the Secretary inadequately explained the basis for their adoption.

An example of a standard would be the field sanitation standard issued by OSHA in April 1987 requiring agricultural employers with 11 or more employees to provide potable drinking water as well as toilet and hand-washing facilities. The standard is designed to protect workers against four main hazards: communicable intestinal diseases; heat-related illnesses, including heat stroke; urinary tract infections; and agrichemical exposures. The standard has reduced the number of cases of these illnesses by nearly two-thirds.

TEMPORARY EMERGENCY STANDARDS

The Secretary may bypass most of the above formalities and create temporary emergency standards when it is believed that workers are in grave danger from exposure to toxic substances or other newly discovered hazards.[15] In *Florida Peach*

---

[10] 29 U.S.C. § 655(b)(1).

[11] *Synthetic Organic Chemical Manufacturers' Ass'n v. Brennan*, 503 F.2d 1155 (3d Cir. 1974). See also *Fabi Construction Co. v. Secretary of Labor*, 508 F.3d 1077 (D.C. Cir. 2007).

[12] 499 F.2d 467 (D.C. Cir. 1974).

[13] See *Daily Lab. Rpt.* (BNA) No. 220 (Nov. 15, 2007) p. A-1.

[14] 486 F.2d 198 (3d Cir. 1973).

[15] 29 U.S.C. § 655(c).

Growers Ass'n, Inc., v. Department of Labor,[16] a case concerned with an emergency standard established for a specific type of pesticide, the court held that death or injury need not occur before a temporary emergency standard is promulgated, but there must be a genuinely serious emergency before it can be issued.

The temporary emergency standard becomes effective when published. The Secretary must give the reasons for its issuance and then institute the normal procedures for promulgating permanent standards, because the emergency standard is only effective for six months.[17]

STANDARDS FOR APPEAL

Any person who is adversely affected by an OSHA standard may file a petition challenging its validity in the appropriate U.S. court of appeals at any time prior to the 60th day after issuance. The filing of an appeal will not delay the enforcement of a standard unless the court of appeals orders that the enforcement be held in abeyance for the duration of the appeal.[18]

The Secretary's standard will be upheld by the courts if the standard is supported by substantial evidence. However, the Secretary must first demonstrate that the standard addresses a "significant risk" of material health impairment. This requirement of demonstrating a significant risk was developed in the *Industrial Union Department v. American Petroleum Institute*[19] decision of the U.S. Supreme Court.

DEMONSTRATION OF SIGNIFICANT RISK

The U.S. Supreme Court, in *Industrial Union Department v. American Petroleum Institute,* held that the Act requires the Secretary of Labor to initially find that a proposed standard is reasonably necessary or appropriate to protect employees against a significant risk of material health impairment before the Secretary is empowered to adopt a standard. The case involved standards for employee exposure to benzene, a toxic substance produced mostly by the petrochemical industry and used in manufacturing motor fuels, solvents, detergents, pesticides, and other organic chemicals. Industrial health experts were long aware that exposure to benzene could lead to various types of nonmalignant diseases. However, in the 1970s, a number of studies tied workers exposed to high concentrations of benzene to a significantly increased risk of leukemia. In March 1978, the Secretary of Labor decided to lower the permissible exposure limit for benzene in the air from its then current ten-parts-per-million standard to one part per million. The one-part-per-million standard was the lowest level technologically and economically feasible. The industrial producers and users of benzene challenged the validity of the new benzene standard. A Supreme Court plurality decided that the Secretary had failed to find that a significant risk existed for employees under the

---

[16] 489 F.2d 120 (5th Cir. 1974).

[17] 29 U.S.C. § 655(c)(3).

[18] 29 U.S.C. § 655(f).

[19] 448 U.S. 607 (1980).

ten-parts-per-million standard. The Court then pointed out that the evidence linking benzene exposure to cancer, on which the Secretary relied, did demonstrate a linkage but at exposure levels far above the current permissible level of ten parts per million. The Court stated that OSHA, by assuming that no safe exposure level existed, had evaded its burden of determining that a significant risk was posed by exposure under the ten-parts-per-million standard. The Court held that the burden of proof is on OSHA and the Secretary of Labor to demonstrate the need for a new standard.

Government estimates of the cost of compliance with the one-part-per-million standard were $500 million, and industry estimates placed the cost up to $5 billion. The Court delayed consideration of the question of whether the Act requires the Secretary to do a cost-benefit analysis of a proposed standard for toxic substances. This question was addressed in the *American Textile Manufacturers Institute v. Donovan* decision, presented in this section.

Cost-Benefit Analysis and the Substantial Evidence Test

In the *American Textile Manufacturers Institute v. Donovan* decision, the U.S. Supreme Court held that the Occupational Safety & Health Administration and the Secretary of Labor were not required under the Act to determine that the costs of the standard bear a reasonable relationship to its benefits, for Congress itself balanced costs and benefits under Section 6(b)(5) of the Act in its mandate to OSHA to adopt the most protective, "feasible" standard. The Court found, applying the substantial evidence test, that economic feasibility was supported by "substantial evidence in the record considered as a whole."

Variances—Exemption from Standards

Employers may seek an exemption from a standard they believe is inappropriate to their particular situation. This is known as a **variance** and is classified as either temporary or permanent.[20]

A temporary variance may be granted when an employer cannot comply with a standard by its effective date. However, the employer must establish that all possible measures are being taken to protect employees and that all steps necessary for compliance are also being instituted. The employees must be informed of the requested variance. Temporary variances can be granted for a period of one year and are renewable twice, each time for a period of six months.[21]

A permanent variance may be granted to an employer who can prove that its particular methods provide as safe a work site as would be forthcoming through compliance with the OSHA standard. OSHA generally inspects the premises before granting a permanent variance. The employees must be informed of the application for the variance and of their right to request a hearing on the matter. Within six months after a permanent variance has been granted, the employee may petition OSHA to modify or revoke the variance. OSHA can take similar steps on its own initiative.

---

[20] 29 U.S.C. § 655(f).
[21] 29 C.F.R., § 1905.

CASE 11.1	AMERICAN TEXTILE MANUFACTURERS INSTITUTE V. DONOVAN
	SUPREME COURT OF THE UNITED STATES, 452 U.S. 490 (1981).

[The Secretary of Labor, acting through the Occupational Safety & Health Administration, promulgated the so-called Cotton Dust Standard limiting occupational exposure to cotton dust, exposure to which induces byssinosis, a serious and potentially disabling respiratory disease known in its more severe manifestations as "brown lung" disease. Petitioners, representing the cotton industry, challenged the validity of the standard in the court of appeals, contending that the Act requires OSHA to demonstrate that the standard reflects a reasonable relationship between the costs and benefits associated with the standard, that OSHA's determination of the standard's "economic feasibility" was not supported by substantial evidence, and that the wage guarantee requirement contained in the standard was beyond OSHA's authority. The court of appeals upheld the standard in all major respects.]

BRENNAN, J....

I.

Byssinosis, known in its more severe manifestations as "brown lung" disease, is a serious and potentially disabling respiratory disease primarily caused by the inhalation of cotton dust.* Byssinosis is a "continuum ... disease," that has been categorized into four grades. In its least serious form byssinosis produces both subjective symptoms, such as chest tightness, shortness of breath, coughing, and wheezing, and objective indications of loss of pulmonary functions. In its most serious form, byssinosis is a chronic and irreversible obstructive pulmonary disease, clinically similar to

chronic bronchitis or emphysema, and can be severely disabling. At worst, as is true of other respiratory diseases including bronchitis, emphysema, and asthma, byssinosis can create an additional strain on cardiovascular functions and can contribute to death from heart failure. One authority has described the increasing seriousness of byssinosis as follows:

"In the first few years of exposure [to cotton dust], the symptoms occur on Monday, or other days after absence from the work environment; later, symptoms occur on other days of the week; and eventually, symptoms are continuous, even in the absence of dust exposure." A. Bouhuys, Byssinosis in the United States, Exhibit 6-16, Joint App. 15.

While there is some uncertainty over the manner in which the disease progresses from its least serious to its disabling grades, it is likely that prolonged exposure contributes to the progression. It also appears that a worker may suddenly contract a severe grade without experiencing milder grades of the disease.

Estimates indicate that at least 35,000 employed and retired cotton mill workers, or 1 in 12 such workers, suffers from the most disabling form of byssinosis. The Senate Report accompanying the Act cited estimates that 100,000 active and retired workers suffer from some grade of the disease. One study found that over 25 percent of a sample of active cotton preparation and yarn manufacturing workers suffer at least some form of the disease at a dust exposure level common prior to adoption to the current standard. Other studies confirm these general findings on the prevalence of byssinosis.

---

*Descriptions of the disease by individual mill workers, presented in hearings on the Cotton Dust Standard before an administrative law judge, are more vivid:

"When they started speeding the looms up the dust got finer and more and more people started leaving the mill with breathing problems. My mother had to leave the mill in the early fifties. Before she left, her breathing got so short she just couldn't hold out to work. My stepfather left the mill on account of breathing problems. He had coughing spells til [sic] he couldn't breathe, like a child's whooping cough. Both my sisters who work in the mill have breathing problems. My husband had to give up his job when he was only fifty-four years old because of the breathing problems." Ct. of App. J. A. 3791.

"I suppose I had a breathing problem since 1973. I just kept on getting sick and began losing time at the mill. Every time that I go into the mill I get deathly sick, choking and

vomiting losing my breath. It would blow down all that lint and cotton and I have clothes right here where I have wore and they have been washed several times and I would like for you all to see them. That will not come out in washing."

"I am only fifty-seven years old and I am retired and I can't even get to go to church because of my breathing. I get short of breath just walking around the house or dressing [or] sometimes just watching T.V. I cough all the time." Id., at 3793.

"... I had to quit because I couldn't lay down and rest without oxygen in the night and my doctor told me I would have to get out of there.... I couldn't [sic] even breathe, I had to get out of the door so I could breathe and he told me not to go back in [the mill] under any circumstances." Id., at 3804.

Byssinosis is not a newly discovered disease, having been described as early as in the 1820s in England, Joint App. 401–405, and observed in Belgium in a study of 2,000 cotton workers in 1845, Exhibit 6-16, Joint App. 15.

continued

Not until the early 1960s was byssinosis recognized in the United States as a distinct occupational hazard associated with cotton mills. In 1966, the American Conference of Governmental Industrial Hygienists (ACGIH), a private organization, recommended that exposure to total cotton dust be limited to a "threshold limit value" of 1,000 micrograms per cubic meter of air (1000 µg/m^3) averaged over an 8-hour workday. The United States government first regulated exposure to cotton dust in 1968, when the Secretary of Labor, pursuant to the Walsh-Healey Act, 41 U.S.C. § 35(e), promulgated airborne contaminant threshold limit values, applicable to public contractors, that included the 1000 µg/m^3 limit for total cotton dust. 34 Fed. Reg. 7953 (1969). Following passage of the Act, in 1970, the 1000 µg/m^3 standard was adopted as an "established federal standard" under § 6(a) of the Act, 29 U.S.C. § 655(a)....

[In 1974] the Director of the National Institute for Occupational Safety and Health (NIOSH), pursuant to the Act, 29 U.S.C. §§ 669(a)(3), 671(d)(2), submitted to the Secretary of Labor a recommendation for a cotton dust standard with a permissible exposure limit (PEL) that "should be set at the lowest level feasible, but in no case at an environmental concentration as high as 0.2 mg lint-free cotton dust/cu.m.," or 200 µg/m^3 of lint-free respirable dust....

The Cotton Dust Standard promulgated by OSHA establishes mandatory PELs over an 8-hour period of 200 µg/m^3 for yarn manufacturing, 750 µg/m^3 for slashing and weaving operations, and 500 µg/m^3 for all other processes in the cotton industry. These levels represent a relaxation of the proposed PEL of 200 µg/m^3 for all segments of the cotton industry.

OSHA chose an implementation strategy for the standard that depended primarily on a mix of engineering controls, such as installation of ventilation systems, and work practice controls, such as special floor sweeping procedures. Full compliance with the PELs is required within four years, except to the extent that employers can establish that the engineering and work practice controls are feasible. During this compliance period, and at certain other times, the Standard requires employers to provide respirators to employees. Other requirements include monitoring of cotton dust exposure, medical surveillance of all employees, annual medical examinations, employee education and training programs, and the posting of warning signs. A specific provision also under challenge in the instant case requires employers to transfer employees unable to wear respirators to another position, if available, having a dust level at or below the Standard's PELs, with "no loss of earnings or other employment rights or benefits as a result of the transfer."

II.

The principal question presented in this case is whether the Occupational Safety and Health Act requires the Secretary, in promulgating a standard pursuant to § 6(b)(5) of the Act, 29 U.S.C. § 655(b)(5), to determine that the costs of the standard bear a reasonable relationship to its benefits. Relying on §§ 6(b)(5) and 3(8) of the Act, 29 U.S.C. §§ 655(b)(5), 652(8), petitioners urge not only that OSHA must show that a standard addresses a significant risk of material health impairment, see *Industrial Union Department v. American Petroleum Institute, supra*, slip op., at 29 (plurality opinion),** but also that OSHA must demonstrate that the reduction in risk of material health impairment is significant in light of the costs of attaining that reduction. Respondents on the other hand contend that the Act requires OSHA to promulgate standards that eliminate or reduce such risks "to the extent such protection is technologically and economically feasible." To resolve this debate, we must turn to the language, structure, and legislative history of the Occupational Safety and Health Act.

A.

The starting point of our analysis is the language of the statute itself. Section 6(b)(5) of the Act, 29 U.S.C. § 655(b)(5) (emphasis added), provides:

> The secretary, in promulgating standards dealing with toxic materials or harmful physical agents under this subsection, shall set the standard

---

**In distinct contrast with its Cancer Policy, OSHA expressly found that "exposure to cotton dust presents a significant health hazard to employees," 43 Fed. Reg. 27350, col. 1, and that "cotton dust produced significant health effects at low levels of exposure," *id.*, at 27358, col. 2. In addition, the agency noted that "grade 1/2 byssinosis and associated pulmonary function decrements are significant health effects in themselves and should be prevented in so far as possible." *Id.*, at 27354, col. 2. In making its assessment of significant risk, OSHA relied on dose response curve data (the Merchant Study) showing that 25 percent of employees suffered at least Grade 1/2 byssinosis at a 500 µg/m^3 PEL and that 12.7 percent of all employees would suffer byssinosis at the 200 µg/m^3 PEL standard *Id.*, at 27358, col. 2 and 3. It is difficult to imagine what else the agency could do to comply with this Court's decision in *Industrial Union Department v. American Petroleum Institute.*

continued

which most adequately assures, *to the extent feasible,* on the basis of the best available evidence, that no employee will suffer material impairment of health or functional capacity even if such employee has regular exposure to the hazard dealt with by such standard for the period of his working life.

Although their interpretations differ, all parties agree that the phrase "to the extent feasible" contains the critical language in § 6(b)(5) for purposes of this case.

The plain meaning of the word "feasible" supports respondents' interpretation of the statute. According to Webster's Third New International Dictionary of the English Language, "feasible" means "capable of being done, executed, or effected." *Id.,* at 831 (1976). … Thus, § 6(b)(5) directs the Secretary to issue the standard that "most adequately assures … that no employee will suffer material impairment of health," limited only by the extent to which this is "capable of being done." In effect, then, as the Court of Appeals held, Congress itself defined the basic relationship between cost and benefits, by placing the "benefit" of worker health above all other considerations save those making attainment of this "benefit" unachievable. Any standard based on a balancing of costs and benefits by the Secretary that strikes a different balance than that struck by Congress would be inconsistent with the command set forth in § 6(b)(5). Thus, cost-benefit analysis by OSHA is not required by the statute because feasibility analysis is. See *Industrial Union Department v. American Petroleum Institute, supra,* slip op., at 32 (MARSHALL, J., dissenting).

B.

Even though the plain language of § 6(b)(5) supports this construction, we must still decide whether § 3(8), the general definition of an occupational safety and health standard, either alone or in tandem with § 6(b)(5), incorporates a cost-benefit requirement for standards dealing with toxic materials or harmful physical agents. Section 3(8) of the Act, 29 U.S.C. § 652(8) (emphasis added), provides:

> The term "occupational safety and health standard" means a standard which requires conditions, or the adoption or use of one or more practices, means, methods, operations, or processes, *reasonably necessary or appropriate* to provide safe or healthful employment and places of employment.

Taken alone, the phrase "reasonably necessary or appropriate" might be construed to contemplate some balancing of the costs and benefits of a standard. Petitioners urge that, so construed, § 3(8) engrafts a cost-benefit analysis requirement on the issuance of § 6(b)(5) standards, even if § 6(b)(5) itself does not authorize such analysis. We need not decide whether § 3(8), standing alone, would contemplate some form of cost-benefit analysis. For even if it does, Congress specifically chose in § 6(b)(5) to impose separate and additional requirements for issuance of a subcategory of occupational safety and health standards dealing with toxic materials and harmful physical agents: it required that those standards be issued to prevent material impairment of health *to the extent feasible.* Congress could reasonably have concluded that *health* standards should be subject to different criteria than *safety* standards because of the special problems presented in regulating them.

Agreement with petitioners' argument that § 3(8) imposes an additional and overriding requirement of cost-benefit analysis on the issuance of § 6(b)(5) standards would eviscerate the "to the extent feasible" requirement. Standards would inevitably be set at the level indicated by cost-benefit analysis, and not at the level specified by § 6(b)(5). For example, if cost-benefit analysis indicated a protective standard of 1000 µg/m^3 PEL, while feasibility analysis indicated a 500 µg/m^3 PEL, the agency would be forced by the cost-benefit requirement to choose the less stringent point. We cannot believe that Congress intended the general terms of § 3(8) to countermand the specific feasibility requirement of § 6(b)(5). Adoption of petitioners' interpretation would effectively write § 6(b)(5) out of the Act. We decline to render Congress' decision to include a feasibility requirement nugatory, thereby offending the well-settled rule that all parts of a statute, if possible, are to be given effect. Congress did not contemplate any further balancing by the agency for toxic material and harmful physical agents standards, and we should not "impute to Congress a purpose to paralyze with one hand what it sought to promote with the other."

C.

The legislative history of the Act, while concededly not crystal clear, provides general support for respondents' interpretation of the Act. The congressional reports and debates certainly confirm that Congress meant

continued

"feasible" and nothing else in using that term. Congress was concerned that the Act might be thought to require achievement of absolute safety, an impossible standard, and therefore insisted that health and safety goals be capable of economic and technological accomplishment. Perhaps most telling is the absence of any indication whatsoever that Congress intended OSHA to conduct its own cost-benefit analysis before promulgating a toxic material or harmful physical agent standard. The legislative history demonstrates conclusively that Congress was fully aware that the Act would impose real and substantial costs of compliance on industry, and believed that such costs were part of the cost of doing business.

III.

Section 6(f) of the Act provides that "[t]he determinations of the Secretary shall be conclusive if supported by substantial evidence in the record considered as a whole." 29 U.S.C. § 655(f). Petitioners contend that the Secretary's determination that the Cotton Dust Standard is "economically feasible" is not supported by substantial evidence in the record considered as a whole. In particular, they claim (1) that OSHA underestimated the financial costs necessary to meet the Standard's requirements; and (2) that OSHA incorrectly found that the Standard would not threaten the economic viability of the cotton industry....

OSHA derived its cost estimate for industry compliance with the Cotton Dust Standard after reviewing two financial analyses, one prepared by the Research Triangle Institute (RTI), an OSHA-contracted group, the other by industry representatives (Hocutt-Thomas). The agency carefully explored the assumptions and methodologies underlying the conclusions of each of these studies. From this exercise the agency was able to build upon conclusions from each which it found reliable and explain its process for choosing its cost estimate....

RTI evaluated the likely economic impact on the cotton industry and the United States economy of OSHA's original proposed standard, an across-the-board 200 µg/m^3 PEL. RTI had estimated a total compliance cost of $2.7 billion for a 200 µg/m^3 PEL, and used this estimate in assessing the economic impact of such a standard.... OSHA estimated total compliance costs of $656.5 million for the final Cotton Dust Standard, a Standard less stringent,

than the across-the-board 200 µg/m^3 PEL of the proposed standard. Therefore, the agency found that the economic impact of its Standard would be "much less severe" than that suggested by RTI for a 200 µg/m^3 PEL estimate of $2.7 billion....

Relying on its comprehensive economic evaluation of the cotton industry's ability to absorb the $2.7 billion compliance cost of a 200 µg/m^3 PEL standard, RTI concluded that "nothing in the RTI study indicates that the cotton textile industry as a whole will be seriously threatened." Therefore, it follows *a fortiori* that OSHA's estimated compliance cost of $656.6 million is "economically feasible." Even if OSHA's estimate were understated, we are fortified in observing that RTI found that a standard more than four times as costly that a standard more than four times as costly was nevertheless economically feasible.

The Court of Appeals found that the agency "explained the economic impact it projected for the textile industry," and that OSHA has "substantial support in the record for its ... findings of economic feasibility for the textile industry." 617 F.2d, at 662. On the basis of the whole record, we cannot conclude that the Court of Appeals "misapprehended or grossly misapplied" the substantial evidence test.

IV.

The final Cotton Dust Standard places heavy reliance on the use of respirators to protect employees from exposure to cotton dust, particularly during the 4-year interim period necessary to install and implement feasible engineering controls. One part of the respirator provision requires the employer to give employees unable to wear a respirator the opportunity to transfer to another position, if available, where the dust level meets the standard's PEL. When such a transfer occurs, the employer must guarantee that the employee suffers no loss of earnings or other employment rights or benefits. Petitioners do not object to the transfer provision, but challenge OSHA's authority under the Act to require employers to guarantee employees' wage and employment benefits following the transfer....

... Because the Act in no way authorizes OSHA to repair general unfairness to employees that is unrelated to achievement of health and safety goals, we conclude that OSHA acted beyond statutory authority when it issued the wage guarantee regulation.

Affirmed in part, reversed in part.

continued

Dissenting Opinions

[Justice Stewart in his dissent observed that all parties to the case agree that the statute requires that the standard must at least be economically feasible. "[E]verybody would also agree, I suppose, that in order to determine whether or not something is economically feasible, one must have a fairly clear idea of how much it is going to cost." Justice Stewart states, "Because I believe that OSHA failed to justify its estimate of the cost of the cotton dust standard on the basis of substantial evidence, I would reverse the judgment before us without reaching the question whether the Act requires that a standard, beyond being economically feasible, must meet the demands of a cost-benefit examination."

Justice Rehnquist, joined in dissent by Chief Justice Burger, states that the majority ruling leaves open the possibility that the Secretary of Labor may engage in a cost-benefit analysis, although not required by the Act to do so. He rejects the view of the majority opinion which forbids a weighing of costs versus benefits. Justice Rehnquist submits that the statutory phrase "to the extent feasible" provides no meaningful guidance to federal administrators and therefore represents an unconstitutional delegation of legislative authority to the executive branch of government.]

Case Questions

1. What is byssinosis?
2. Did OSHA demonstrate that the Cotton Dust Standard was reasonably necessary or appropriate to protect employees against a significant risk of health impairment as required by the *Industrial Union Department v. American Petroleum Institute* decision?
3. Does the Occupational Safety and Health Act require the Secretary of Labor, in promulgating a standard pursuant to Section 6(b)(5), to determine that the costs of the standard bear a reasonable relationship to its benefits?
4. Was the Secretary of Labor's determination on economic feasibility supported by substantial evidence?
5. Did the Secretary (OSHA) make the necessary determinations that the wage guarantee requirement was related to the achievement of a safe and healthful work environment?

SECTION 94: EMPLOYER DUTIES

Under the Occupational Safety and Health Act, employers have three major responsibilities. The first two relate directly to the maintenance of a hazard-free workplace; the third, to recordkeeping and reporting procedures to monitor occupational injuries and illnesses.

THE SPECIFIC AND GENERAL DUTY CLAUSES

The language of Section 5(a) of the Act creates both a specific and a general duty on the employer to maintain a safe work site:

Each employer
1. shall furnish to each of his employees employment and a place of employment which are free from recognized hazards that are causing or are likely to cause death or serious physical harm to his employees;
2. shall comply with occupational safety and health standards promulgated under the Chapter.[22]

The second clause relates specifically to standards already defined by OSHA, and the question of compliance is basically one of statutory fact.

It is the first clause, Section 5(a)(1) of the Act, known as the **general duty clause**, that has been the cause of much confusion and litigation. As more OSHA

---

[22] Section 5(a) of the Occupational Safety and Health Act, 29 U.S.C. § 654(a).

standards have been promulgated, it has lost some of its initial significance; however, the general duty clause remains a vital aspect of the Act.

If an OSHA standard was directly applicable to an alleged hazardous condition, OSHRC believed that a general duty citation was inappropriate and that the specific OSHA standard preempted the general duty clause.[23] However, in *UAW v. General Dynamics Land Systems Division*, reported in this section, the Third Circuit Court of Appeals rejected this position, holding that if an employer knows that a specific OSHA standard will not protect its workers against a particular hazard, its duty under Section 5(a)(1) will not be discharged no matter how faithfully the employer observes the specific standard.

In order to establish a violation of the general duty clause, the Secretary of Labor must prove that (1) the employer failed to render its workplace free of a hazard, (2) the hazard was recognized either by the cited employer or generally within the employer's industry, (3) the hazard was causing or was likely to cause death or serious physical harm, and (4) there was a feasible means by which the employer could have eliminated or materially reduced the hazard. In *OSHA v. K-Mart*,[24] the Review Commission found a general duty clause violation for failing to protect employees from hazards arising out of the operation of a cardboard box compactor. The hazard at issue was the possibility of a crushing injury due to movement of the ram during routine operation of the baler. The commission stated that a recognized hazard is a workplace condition or practice that is known to be hazardous by either the industry in general or the employer in particular. The commission pointed out that K-Mart's recognition of the hazard was evidenced by the instructions the store manager gave shortly after the baler was first installed prohibiting any employee from placing any part of the body within the baler at any time. The commission pointed to the evidence that at the time of the employee's injury, it had been over two years since K-Mart had held a training session on the safe operation of the machine, and it found that all four elements necessary to prove the Secretary of Labor's case had been met.

OSHA uses the general duty clause to address the major problems associated with back injuries in the workplace.[25]

MULTIEMPLOYER DUTY PROBLEMS

A problem concerned with employer duty has developed in the construction field because of subcontracting procedures. Subcontracting has resulted in multiple employers conducting business on the same work site. Responsibility for a violation under the Act is limited by the definition of employers set forth in Section 3(5) of the Act, which broadly applies to persons "engaged in a business affecting commerce who have employees." In *Brennan v. OSHA (Underhill Construction Corp.)*, the precedent was established that a general contractor who created or

---

[23] A. Prokasch & Sons Sheet Metal, 1980 CCH OSHD ¶ 24,840 (1980).

[24] 1982 CCH OSHD ¶ 26,333 (1982).

[25] See DeClercq and Lund, "Back Injuries, OSHA General Duty Clause Citations, and the NIOSH Lifting Guidelines," *Labor Law Journal* (Dec. 1991): 807–13.

controlled a hazard to which one or more employees of another employer were exposed could be cited for OSHA violations even though none of its own employees were exposed.[26] However, in *Secretary of Labor v. Summit Constructors, Inc.*, the commission overturned this long-standing precedent and held that general contractors cannot be held responsible for OSHA violations created by subcontractors to which only employees of the subcontractor are exposed.[27]

RECORDKEEPING AND REPORTING REQUIREMENTS

Before occupational safety and health problems can be corrected, there must be a method for ascertaining the dimensions of the problem. One procedure required by the Occupational Safety and Health Act is that employers of eight or more employees maintain records of occupational injuries and illnesses.[28]

An occupational injury is any injury that results from a work-related accident involving a single incident, such as a cut, fracture, or sprain. An occupational illness is any condition resulting from exposure to environmental factors at the work site. All occupational injuries and illnesses must be recorded if they result in death, loss of consciousness, transfer to another job, medical treatment (other than first aid), or one or more lost workdays.[29] The employer is required to use specific OSHA forms and must present the records if an OSHA compliance officer requests them. Once a year the records must be posted to provide employees with the information so compiled.

In *Kaspar Wire Works, Inc., v. Secretary of Labor*,[30] the U.S. Court of Appeals for the District of Columbia upheld "per instance" penalties totaling $224,050 assessed by the OSHRC against a manufacturer of custom wire products for willfully failing to comply with OSHA's recordkeeping requirements for occupational accidents. The company failed to record some 357 injuries on OSHA form No. 200, including injuries as serious as finger amputations, broken bones, and severe burns.

In addition to this recordkeeping required because of injuries and illness from specific known exposure to environmental factors at the work site, OSHA has issued a broad "records access rule," which requires employers to provide their employees, OSHA, and employee representatives access to records voluntarily created by the employers that contain information relating to the medical and exposure histories of employees exposed to toxic substances or harmful physical agents. The rule was challenged in *Louisiana Chemical Ass'n v. Bingham*[31] and found to be a proper exercise of OSHA's authority under the Act. The court determined that the rule will serve to establish a primary database regarding long-term exposure to toxic substances and harmful physical agents and that such a pool of information will be of great utility to medical/industrial research in the isolation and identification of latent occupational diseases and health hazards yet unknown.

---

[26] 513 F.2d 1032 (2d Cir. 1975).

[27] 2007 WL 2265137 (OSHRC 2007).

[28] 29 C.F.R., § 1904 (2000).

[29] 29 C.F.R., § 1904.12 (2000).

[30] 268 F.3d 1123 (D.C. Cir. 2001).

[31] 1983 CCH OSHD ¶ 26,351 (1983).

CASE 11.2	UAW v. GENERAL DYNAMICS LAND SYSTEMS DIVISION
	U.S. COURT OF APPEALS, 815 F.2D 1570 (D.C. CIR. 1987).

[General Dynamics (G.D.) manufactures M-1 tanks in a Department of Defense facility called the Detroit Arsenal Tank Plant. The tanks have internal hydraulic systems that sometimes leak during assembly. For several months prior to November 1983, G.D. employees had used a solvent called 1,1,2 trichloro 1,2,2 trifluoroethane (solvent or freon) to clean up the oil spills. The solvent evaporates quickly. While it is less toxic than other commercial solvents, in its gaseous state, it is heavier than air and may cause serious illness or death. It tends to accumulate in assembly line pits and tank hulls, displacing oxygen and creating a risk of asphyxiation. In high concentrations, it may also cause cardiac arrhythmia and eventual arrest. On November 29, 1983, OSHA cited G.D. for violations of Section 5(a)(1), the general duty clause of the Act and OSHA's specific standard for governing an employee's exposure to the solvent or freon. This citation followed several incidents in which employees became ill following exposure to the solvent's fumes. One incident occurred on September 21, 1983. It involved employee Charles Paling, who, after entering a tank and pouring approximately two gallons of solvent to clean a hydraulic leak, exited and used a portable device to ventilate the tank. This procedure was in apparent compliance with the ventilation requirement in a safety bulletin. Paling then reentered the tank. Another employee later discovered him inside the driver's compartment shaking and foaming from the mouth. Soon thereafter an employee at another G.D. plant died from exposure to the solvent fumes. After a hearing, the administrative law judge found that G.D. had been in compliance with the specific OSHA standard regulating employee exposure to freon (the freon standard). The ALJ then dismissed the charge, alleging a general duty clause violation, believing the specific standard preempted the general duty clause. The ALJ's decision became a final order of the OSHRC, and the UAW and the Secretary of Labor appealed.]

BUCKLEY, J....

I.

... The ALJ's opinion ... refers to the general principle of statutory construction that the specific takes precedence over the general as a basis for preemption. General Dynamics urges us to accept this reasoning,

noting that the principle is contained in the maxim *expressio unius est exclusio alterius*.... First, this maxim can apply only if we assume *a priori* that the specific standard is exclusive of the general duty of the Act. More important, however, we cannot defeat clear and unambiguous statutory language with a Latin maxim anymore than we can with legislative history.

We conclude that the Act does not empower the Secretary, and hence OSHA, to absolve employers who observe specific standards from duties otherwise imposed on them by the general duty clause. To the degree that the final order makes such a claim, it is in error.

II.

The final order also relies on an OSHA preemption regulation, 29 C.F.R. § 1910.5(c)(1), which General Dynamics here supplements with another, namely, 29 C.F.R. § 1910.5(f). Section 1910.5(c)(1) provides:

> if a particular standard is specifically applicable to a condition, practice, means, method, operation, or process, it shall prevail over any different general standard which might otherwise be applicable to the same condition, practice, means, method, operation, or process.

Section 1910.5(f) provides:

> an employer who is in compliance with any standard in this part shall be deemed to be in compliance with the requirement of section 5(a)(1) of the Act, but only to the extent of the condition, practice, means, method, operation, or process covered by the standard.

... Both presumption regulations were promulgated pursuant to OSHA's authority under section 6 of the Act, 29 U.S.C. § 655 (1982). Section 6 authorizes the Secretary to promulgate safety standards. It nowhere suggests that the Secretary may promulgate standards that displace the general duty imposed by section 5(a)(1). When we compare the lack of statutory support for the construction of sections 1910.5(c)(1) and (f) that the Commission and General Dynamics reach, and the clear and unambiguous language of the general duty clause, there is no contest. On the facts in this case, section 5(a)(1) can no more be denied legal effect on the basis of OSHA's preemption regulations than it can on the basis of its specific standard.

continued

III.

Any apparent conflict between section 5(a)(2) or the preemption regulations on the one hand, and the general duty clause on the other, is resolved when one focuses on the words "recognized hazard" in section 5(a)(1). As the Commission has pointed out in *Con Agra, Inc., McMillan Co. Division*, 1983–84 O.S.H. Dec. (CCH) ¶ 26,420, at 33,523 (1983):

> In order to establish a section 5(a)(1) violation, the Secretary must prove: (1) the employer failed to render its workplace free of a hazard, (2) the hazard was recognized either by the cited employer or generally within the employer's industry, (3) the hazard was causing or likely to cause death or serious physical harm, and (4) there was a feasible means by which the employer could have eliminated or materially reduced the hazard.

This analysis emphasizes the fact that the duty to protect employees is imposed on the employer, and the hazards against which he has the obligation to protect necessarily include those of which he has specific knowledge. Therefore if (as is alleged in this case) an employer knows a particular safety standard is inadequate to protect his workers against the specific hazard it is intended to address, or that the conditions in his place of employment are such that the safety standard will not adequately deal with the hazards to which his employees are exposed, he has a duty under section 5(a)(1) to take whatever measures may be required by the Act, over and above those mandated by the safety standard, to safeguard his workers. In sum, if an employer knows that a specific standard will not protect his workers against a particular hazard, his duty under section 5(a)(1) will not be discharged no matter how faithfully he observes that standard. Scienter is key.

By the same token, absent such knowledge, an employer may rely on his compliance with a safety standard to absolve him from liability for any injury actually suffered by employees as a consequence of a hazard the standard was intended to address, and he will be deemed to have met his obligations under the general duty clause with respect thereto. In other words, compliance with a safety standard will not relieve an employer of his duty under section 5(a)(1); rather, it satisfies that duty. It is in this sense that it may be said that an OSHA standard preempts obligations under the general duty clause....

IV.

We hold that the part of the Commission's final order vacating the statutory charge is not in accordance with law because it impermissibly construes regulations in a manner unauthorized by the clear and unambiguous language of the Act.... We therefore grant both petitions for review, vacate that part of the Commission's final order that vacates the section 5(a)(1) portion of the citation, and remand the cases to the Commission with instructions to address the merits of the section 5(a)(1) citation.

It is so ordered.

Case Questions

1. Summarize the facts of the case.
2. Can a standard issued by the Secretary of Labor displace the statutory general duty standard?
3. If an employer knows that a specific standard will not protect its workers against a particular hazard but can prove that it is in full compliance with the specific standard, can the employer be held to be in violation of the general duty clause?

SECTION 95: PROTECTION FROM RETALIATION

Section 11(c) of the OSH Act protects employees from retaliation for exercising rights granted by the Act. In the *Whirlpool Corp. v. Marshall* decision, presented in this section, the Supreme Court upheld a regulation of the Secretary of Labor under which an employee has a right to refuse to perform an assigned job if (1) the employee has a reasonable apprehension that death or serious injury may result due to a dangerous condition and (2) the employee is unable to apprise OSHA of the danger before the refusal. The Court held that the regulation was permissible based on the Act's language, structure, and legislative history and that the employer violated Section 11(c) by suspending two employees when they refused to walk on an elevated screen that the employees reasonably believed was unsafe. On remand to the district court, back pay was awarded to the employees.

In *Reich v. Cambridgeport Air Systems, Inc.*,[32] the U.S. Court of Appeals for the First Circuit held that a federal district court acted within its authority under Section 11(c) of the OSH Act in ordering double back pay damages in a retaliatory discharge action. Section 11(c) authorizes "all appropriate relief," and the court of appeals determined that this language gives district courts authority to award compensatory and even such traditional other relief as exemplary (punitive) damages, where such relief is, in fact, appropriate. The court determined that the double damages with their exemplary component were appropriate in the *Cambridgeport* case, where the employer intentionally retaliated against one employee who had reported workplace health violations to OSHA and fired another employee as an example to others. This case is a landmark decision in that it is the first in which a court awarded compensatory and exemplary damages in a retaliatory discharge action. Such damages are now being sought by the Department of Labor in all appropriate retaliatory discharge actions.

CASE 11.3 | WHIRLPOOL CORPORATION V. MARSHALL
SUPREME COURT OF THE UNITED STATES, 445 U.S. 1 (1980).

[Virgil Deemer and Thomas Cornwell, employees at the Whirlpool Corporation's plant in Marion, Ohio, refused to comply with a supervisor's order that they perform maintenance work on certain mesh screens located some 20 feet above the plant floor. Twelve days before this incident a fellow employee had fallen to his death from the screens. After the refusal, the men were ordered to punch out and leave the plant. They were not paid for the remaining six hours of their shift, and written reprimands for insubordination were placed in their employment files. Section 11(c)(1) of the Occupational Safety and Health Act provides that no employer shall discharge or in any manner discriminate against an employee because the employee filed a complaint with OSHA or testified in any OSHA proceeding or exercised any right afforded by the Act. A regulation issued by the Secretary of Labor under the Act provides that an employee with no reasonable alternative who refuses in good faith to be exposed to a dangerous condition will be protected against subsequent discrimination. The Secretary of Labor filed suit in U.S. district court against Whirlpool, contending that Whirlpool's actions against Deemer and Cornwell constituted "discrimination" under the Secretary's regulation and Section 11(c)(1) of the Act.

Whirlpool contended that the regulation encouraged workers to engage in "self-help" and unlawfully permitted a "strike with pay." The court held that the Secretary's regulation was inconsistent with the Act and denied relief. The U.S. court of appeals reversed this decision, and Whirlpool appealed.]

STEWART, J....

The petitioner company maintains a manufacturing plant in Marion, Ohio, for the production of household appliances. Overhead conveyors transport appliance components throughout the plant. To protect employees from objects that occasionally fall from these conveyors, the petitioner has installed a horizontal wire mesh guard screen approximately 20 feet above the plant floor. This mesh screen is welded to angle-iron frames suspended from the building's structural steel skeleton.

Maintenance employees of the petitioner spend several hours each week removing objects from the screen, replacing paper spread on the screen to catch grease drippings from the material on the conveyors, and performing occasional maintenance work on the conveyors themselves. To perform these duties, maintenance employees usually are able to stand on the

continued

---

[32] 26 F.3d 1187 (1st Cir. 1994).

iron frames, but sometimes find it necessary to step onto the steel mesh screen itself.

In 1973 the company began to install heavier wire in the screen because its safety had been drawn into question. Several employees had fallen partly through the old screen, and on one occasion an employee had fallen completely through to the plant floor below but had survived. A number of maintenance employees had reacted to these incidents by bringing the unsafe screen conditions to the attention of their foreman. The petitioner company's contemporaneous safety instructions admonished employees to step only on the angle-iron frames.

On June 28, 1974, a maintenance employee fell to his death through the guard screen in an area where the newer, stronger mesh had not yet been installed. Following this incident, the petitioner effectuated some repairs and issued an order strictly forbidding maintenance employees from stepping on either the screens or the angle-iron supporting structure. An alternative but somewhat more cumbersome and less satisfactory method was developed for removing objects from the screen. This procedure required employees to stand on power raised mobile platforms and use hooks to recover the material.

On July 7, 1974, two of the petitioner's maintenance employees, Virgil Deemer and Thomas Cornwell, met with the plant maintenance superintendent to voice their concern about the safety of the screen. The superintendent disagreed with their view, but permitted the two men to inspect the screen with their foreman and to point out dangerous areas needing repair. Unsatisfied with the petitioner's response to the results of this inspection, Deemer and Cornwell met on July 9 with the plant safety director. At that meeting, they requested the name, address, and telephone number of a representative of the local office at the Occupational Safety and Health Administration (OSHA). Although the safety director told the men that they "had better stop and think about what [they] were doing," he furnished the men with the information they requested. Later that same day, Deemer contacted an official of the regional OSHA office and discussed the guard screen.

The next day, Deemer and Cornwell reported for the night shift at 10:45 PM. Their foreman, after himself walking on some of the angle-iron frames, directed the two men to perform their usual maintenance duties on a section of the old screen. Claiming

that the screen was unsafe, they refused to carry out this directive. The foreman then sent them to the personnel office, where they were ordered to punch out without working or being paid for the remaining six hours of the shift. The two men subsequently received written reprimands, which were placed in their employment files....

... [C]ircumstances may sometimes exist in which the employee justifiably believes that the express statutory arrangement does not sufficiently protect him from death or serious injury. Such circumstances will probably not often occur, but such a situation may arise when (1) the employee is ordered by his employer to work under conditions that the employee reasonably believes pose an imminent risk of death or serious bodily injury, and (2) the employee has reason to believe that there is not sufficient time or opportunity either to seek effective redress from his employer or to apprise OSHA of the danger.

Nothing in the Act suggests that those few employees who have to face this dilemma must rely exclusively on the remedies expressly set forth in the Act at the risk of their own safety. But nothing in the Act explicitly provides otherwise. Against this background of legislative silence, the Secretary has exercised his rule making power under 29 U.S.C. § 657(g)(2) and has determined that, when an employee in good faith finds himself in such a predicament, he may refuse to expose himself to the dangerous condition, without being subjected to "subsequent discrimination" by the employer.

The regulation clearly conforms to the fundamental objective of the Act—to prevent occupational deaths and serious injuries. The Act, in its preamble, declares that its purpose and policy is "to assure so far as possible every working man and women in the Nation safe and healthful working conditions and to *preserve* our human resources." 29 U.S.C. § 651(b). (Emphasis added.)

To accomplish this basic purpose, the legislation's remedial orientation is prophylactic in nature. See *Atlas Roofing Co. v. Occupational Safety Comm'n*, 430 U.S. 422. The Act does not wait for an employee to die or become injured. It authorizes the promulgation of health and safety standards and the issuance of citations in the hope that these will act to prevent deaths or injuries from ever occurring. It would seem anomalous to construe an Act so directed and constructed as prohibiting an employee, with no other

continued

reasonable alternative, the freedom to withdraw from a workplace environment that he reasonably believes is highly dangerous.

Moreover, the Secretary's regulation can be viewed as an appropriate aid to the full effectuation of the Act's "general duty" clause. That clause provides that "[e]ach employer ... shall furnish to each of his employees employment and a place of employment which are free from recognized hazards that are causing or are likely to cause death or serious physical harm to his employees." 29 U.S.C. § 654(a)(1). As the legislative history of this provision reflects, it was intended itself to deter the occurrence of occupational deaths and serious injuries by placing on employers a mandatory obligation independent of the specific health and safety standards to be promulgated by the Secretary. Since OSHA inspectors cannot be present around the clock in every workplace, the Secretary's regulation ensures that employees will in all circumstances enjoy the rights afforded them by the "general duty" clause.

[The Court next considered and rejected Whirlpool's contention that the legislative history is contrary to the Secretary's regulation. The Court explained its view as follows:]

When it rejected the "strike with pay" concept, therefore, Congress very clearly meant to reject a law unconditionally imposing upon employers an obligation to continue to pay their employees their regular pay checks when they absented themselves from work for reasons of safety. But the regulation at issue here does not require employers to pay workers who refuse to perform their assigned tasks in the face of imminent danger. It simply provides that in such cases the employer may not "discriminate" against the employees involved. An employer "discriminates" against an employee only when he treats that employee less favorably than he treats others similarly situated.

[In a footnote to the decision, the Court applied the above principles to the situation of Mr. Deemer and Mr. Cornwell. The Court stated that the placing of reprimands in their personnel files clearly represents discrimination. The Court stated that whether the denial of work and pay for the six-hour period also represented discrimination was a question not before the Court.]

The judgment of the Court of Appeals is *Affirmed*.

Case Questions

1. Was the supervisor's order to perform maintenance duties on the old section of the screen contrary to the company's directive not to step on the screen or the angle iron supporting the structure?
2. Summarize the protection afforded employees by the Secretary's regulation.
3. Does the Secretary of Labor's regulation aid in giving full effect to the OSHA's general duty clause?
4. Does the Secretary's regulation require the employer to pay employees who refuse to perform work in the face of imminent danger?

SECTION 96: INSPECTION

In order to enforce its standards, OSHA is empowered to conduct work site inspections in every establishment covered by the Act. To make the best use of a limited staff, safety and health inspections are classified into priority categories. The highest priority is assigned to situations involving fatalities or serious injuries. Information on these occurrences comes to OSHA as a result of employer recordkeeping and reporting obligations. The second priority is given to valid employee complaints. Under the Act, employees are protected from discrimination for exercising their right to inform OSHA of possible violations.[33] The next priority is assigned to

---

[33] 29 U.S.C. § 660(c).

target programs aimed at typically high-hazard industries. The final priority is given to the general inspection, which is conducted randomly when time permits.

The employer is usually given no advance notice of an inspection, and any person giving such notice improperly can be fined or imprisoned.[34] An exception exists for instances of imminent danger where advance notice would enable the employer to abate the danger as quickly as possible.

When the compliance officer arrives, the officer must present the proper identification. Moreover, although the language of the OSH Act appears to eliminate the need for a warrant,[35] the Supreme Court, in the *Marshall v. Barlow's, Inc.*, decision, reported in this section, held that OSHA must secure a warrant before a compliance officer can conduct an inspection. Three exceptions exist to the *Barlow's* decision, however. No warrant is needed (1) if the employer consents to the inspection, (2) if the site is open to public view, or (3) if an emergency situation exists. It is common for OSHA compliance officers to ask employers for permission to inspect the premises prior to obtaining a warrant, and most employers grant such permission. A videotape taken by a compliance officer without a warrant from the roof of the Peabody Hotel in Orlando showing two employees working on structural steel more than 80 feet above ground without "fall protection devices" mandated by a specific OSHA regulation was not a Fourth Amendment violation on which to base the exclusion of the videotape. The court held there was no reasonable expectation of privacy because anyone on the side of the hotel could observe the activities on the construction site, and thus there was no reasonable expectation of privacy.[36] In order for the emergency exception to apply, imminent danger to employees would have to exist, making it impossible for inspectors to take the time to obtain a warrant.

Both the employer and the employees may designate a representative to accompany the compliance officer. In *Chicago Bridge v. OSHRC*,[37] the Seventh Circuit Court of Appeals ruled that the language of the OSH Act made such a right mandatory and not at the discretion of the compliance officer.

On the inspection tour, the compliance officer may observe conditions, take photos, make instrument readings, take samples, and inspect records. The officer is also authorized to question employers, their agents, and their employees in private.

At the conclusion of the inspection, the compliance officer goes over the findings with the employer in a "closing conference." At this time, the employer learns of possible violations. The officer reports to the area director, who then decides whether to issue a citation and propose a penalty. The area director has six months within which to take action.

Any trade secrets that are observed by the compliance officer must be kept confidential. Any officer who violates the confidentiality of an employer's trade secret may be subject to a fine and/or imprisonment.[38]

---

[34] 29 U.S.C. § 666(p).

[35] 29 U.S.C. § 657(a).

[36] *Secretary of Labor v. Wilson*, 1998 CCH OSHD ¶ 31,501 (4th Cir. 1998).

[37] 535 F.2d 371 (7th Cir. 1976).

[38] 29 U.S.C. § 664 (1970).

| CASE 11.4 | MARSHALL V. BARLOW'S, INC.
SUPREME COURT OF THE UNITED STATES, 436 U.S. 307 (1978). |

WHITE, J....

Section 8(a) of the Occupational Safety and Health Act of 1970 (OSHA) empowers agents of the Secretary of Labor (the Secretary) to search the work area of any employment facility within the Act's jurisdiction. The purpose of the search is to inspect for safety hazards and violations of OSHA regulations. No search warrant or other process is expressly required under the Act.

On the morning of September 11, 1975, an OSHA inspector entered the customer service area of Barlow's, Inc., an electrical and plumbing installation business located in Pocatello, Idaho. The president and general manager, Ferrol G. "Bill" Barlow, was on hand; and the OSHA inspector, after showing his credentials, informed Mr. Barlow that he wished to conduct a search of the working areas of the business. Mr. Barlow inquired whether any complaint had been received about his company. The inspector answered no, but that Barlow's, Inc., had simply turned up in the agency's selection process. The inspector again asked to enter the nonpublic area of the business; Mr. Barlow's response was to inquire whether the inspector had a search warrant. The inspector had none. Thereupon, Mr. Barlow refused the inspector admission to the employee area of his business. He said he was relying on his rights as guaranteed by the Fourth Amendment of the United States Constitution.

The Secretary urges that warrantless inspections to enforce OSHA are reasonable within the meaning of the Fourth Amendment. Among other things, he relies on Section 8(a) of the Act, 29 U.S.C. Section 657(a), which authorizes inspection of business premises without a warrant and which the Secretary urges represents a congressional construction of the Fourth Amendment that the courts should not reject. Regretfully, we are unable to agree....

This Court has already held that warrantless searches are generally unreasonable, and that this rule applies to commercial premises as well as homes. In *Camara v. Municipal Court*, 387 U.S. 523, 528–529 (1967), we held:

> [E]xcept in certain carefully defined classes of cases, a search of private property without proper consent is "unreasonable" unless it has been authorized by a valid search warrant.

On the same day, we also ruled:

> As we explained in Camara, a search of private houses is presumptively unreasonable if conducted without a warrant. The businessman, like the occupant of a residence, has a constitutional right to go about his business free from unreasonable official entries upon his private commercial property. The businessman, too, has that right placed in jeopardy if the decision to enter and inspect for violation of regulatory laws can be made and enforced by the inspector in the field without official authority evidenced by a warrant. See v. City of Seattle, 387 U.S. 541, 543 (1967).

The Secretary urges that an exception from the search warrant requirement has been recognized for "pervasively regulated business[es]," *United States v. Biswell*, 406 U.S. 311, 316 (1972), and for "closely regulated" industries "long subject to close supervision and inspection." *Colonnade Catering Corp. v. United States*, 397 U.S. 72, 74, 77 (1970). These cases are indeed exceptions, but they represent responses to relatively unique circumstances. Certain industries have such a history of government oversight that no reasonable expectation of privacy, see *Katz v. United States*, 389 U.S. 347, 351–352 (1967), could exist for a proprietor over the stock of such an enterprise. Liquor (*Colonnade*) and firearms (*Biswell*) are industries of this type; when an entrepreneur embarks upon such a business, he has voluntarily chosen to subject himself to a full arsenal of governmental regulation.

Industries such as these fall within the "certain carefully defined classes of cases," referenced in *Camara, supra*, at 528. The element that distinguishes these enterprises from ordinary businesses is a long tradition of close government supervision, of which a person who chooses to enter such a business must already be aware. "A central difference between those cases [*Colonnade and Biswell*] and this one is that businessmen engaged in such federally licensed and regulated enterprises accept the burdens as well as the benefits of their trade, whereas the petitioner here was not engaged in any regulated or licensed business. The businessman in a regulated industry in effect consents to the restrictions placed upon him." *Almeida-Sanchez v. United States*, 413 U.S. 266, 271 (1973)....

continued

The Secretary ... stoutly argues that the enforcement scheme of the Act requires warrantless searches, and that the restrictions on search discretion contained in the Act and its regulations already protect as much privacy as a warrant would. The Secretary thereby asserts the actual reasonableness of OSHA searches, whatever the general rule against warrantless searches might be. Because "reasonableness is still the ultimate standard," *Camara v. Municipal Court, supra,* at 539, the Secretary suggests that the Court decide whether a warrant is needed by arriving at a sensible balance between the administrative necessities of OSHA inspections and the incremental protection of privacy of business owners a warrant would afford. He suggests that only a decision exempting OSHA inspections from the Warrant Clause would give "full recognition to the competing public and private interests here at stake." *Camara v. Municipal Court, supra,* at 539.

The Secretary submits that warrantless inspections are essential to the proper enforcement of OSHA because they afford the opportunity to inspect without prior notice and hence to preserve the advantages of surprise. While the dangerous conditions outlawed by the Act include structural defects that cannot be quickly hidden or remedied, the Act also regulates a myriad of safety details that may be amenable to speedy alteration or disguise. The risk is that during the interval between an inspector's initial request to search a plant and his procuring a warrant following the owner's refusal of permission, violations of this latter type could be corrected and thus escape the inspector's notice. To the suggestion that warrants may be issued *ex parte* and executed without delay and without prior notice, thereby preserving the element of surprise, the Secretary expresses concern for the administrative strain that would be experienced by the inspection system, and by the courts, should *ex parte* warrants issued in advance become standard practice.

We are unconvinced, however, that requiring warrants to inspect will impose serious burdens on the inspection system or the courts, will prevent inspections necessary to enforce the statute, or will make them less effective. In the first place, the great majority of businessmen can be expected in normal course to consent to inspection without warrant; the Secretary has not brought to this Court's attention any widespread pattern of refusal. In those cases where an owner does insist on a warrant, the Secretary argues that inspection efficiency will be

impeded by the advance notice and delay. The Act's penalty provisions for giving advance notice of a search, 29 U.S.C. Section 666(f), and the Secretary's own regulations, 29 CFR Section 1903.6, indicate that surprise searches are indeed contemplated. However, the Secretary has also promulgated a regulation providing that upon refusal to permit an inspector to enter the property or to complete his inspection, the inspector shall attempt to ascertain the reasons for the refusal and report to his superior, who shall "promptly take appropriate action, including compulsory process, if necessary." 29 CFR Section 1903.4. The regulation represents a choice to proceed by process where entry is refused; and on the basis of evidence available from present practice, the Act's effectiveness has not been crippled by providing those owners who wish to refuse an initial requested entry with a time lapse while the inspector obtains the necessary process. Indeed, the kind of process sought in this case and apparently anticipated by the regulation provides notice to the business operator. If this safeguard endangers the efficient administration of OSHA, the Secretary should never have adopted it, particularly when the Act does not require it. Nor is it immediately apparent why the advantages of surprise would be lost if, after being refused entry, procedures were available for the Secretary to seek an *ex parte* warrant and to reappear at the premises without further notice to the establishment being inspected.

Whether the Secretary proceeds to secure a warrant or other process, with or without prior notice, his entitlement to inspect will not depend on his demonstrating probable cause to believe that conditions in violation of OSHA exist on the premises. Probable cause in the criminal law sense is not required. For purposes of an administrative search such as this, probable cause justifying the issuance of a warrant may be based not only on specific evidence of an existing violation* but also on a showing that "reasonable legislative or administrative standards for conducting an ... inspection are satisfied with respect

---

*Section 8(f)(1), 29 U.S.C. Section 657(f)(1), provides that employees or their representatives may give written notice to the Secretary of what they believe to be violations of safety or health standards and may request an inspection. If the Secretary then determines that "there are reasonable grounds to believe that such violation or danger exists, he shall make a special inspection in accordance with the provisions of this Section as soon as practicable." The statute thus purports to authorize a warrantless inspection in these circumstances.

continued

to a particular [establishment]." *Camara v. Municipal Court, supra*, at 538. A warrant showing that a specific business has been chosen for an OSHA search on the basis of a general administrative plan for the enforcement of the Act derived from neutral sources such as, for example, dispersion of employees in various types of industries across a given area, and the desired frequency of searches in any of the lesser divisions of the area, would protect an employer's Fourth Amendment rights. We doubt that the consumption of enforcement energies in the obtaining of such warrants will exceed manageable proportions....

We hold that Barlow was entitled to a declaratory judgment that the Act is unconstitutional insofar as it purports to authorize inspections without warrant or its equivalent and to an injunction enjoining the Act's enforcement to that extent.

Case Questions

1. What exception from the search warrant requirement does the Secretary of Labor urge upon the Court as justification for OSHA's warrantless searches?

2. How does the Secretary of Labor respond to the argument that warrants are essential to protect the businessperson's privacy interest?

3. In order to secure a warrant after this decision, must the Secretary demonstrate probable cause to believe that conditions in violation of OSHA exist on the premises?

SECTION 97: CITATIONS AND PENALTIES

Section 17 of the OSH Act sets forth the types and degree of violations of the Act. Civil sanctions are provided for any willful, repeated, serious, or nonserious violation of the Act or any standard, rule, or order promulgated pursuant to the Act.[39] The Act provides for civil sanctions for each day during which a violation has not been corrected. A willful violation may result in the imposition of criminal sanctions. Criminal sanctions also may be imposed for giving unauthorized advance notice of inspections or for making false statements, representations, or certifications in any application, record, report, plan, or other document filed or required to be maintained under the Act.[40]

In reviewing the compliance officer's investigative report, the area director has specific guidelines within which to issue a citation and to propose a civil penalty. The gravity of the violation is the primary factor in determining penalties, and then the size of the business, the good faith of the employer, and the history of previous violations are considered in reduction of the gravity-based penalty. The types and degrees of violations are as follows:

1. **Willful:** Violations determined to be willful that cause an employee's death may result in a criminal violation of the Act as well as prosecution under state law. Willfulness is established by a conscious, intentional, deliberate decision.[41] An employer's good faith belief that its alternative program meets the objectives of an OSHA regulation is irrelevant in determining whether a violation is willful.[42] It also may be characterized by a careless disregard of the requirements of the Act or an indifference to employee safety. Criminal prosecutions are undertaken by the U.S. Department of Justice. Civil penalties for willful violations

---

[39] 29 U.S.C. § 666(a), (b), and (c), as amended by Pub. L. No. 101–508, § 3101(1) (2000).

[40] 29 U.S.C. § 666(f) and (g) (2000).

[41] *Lakeland Enterprises v. Chao*, 402 F.3d 739 (7th Cir. 2005).

[42] See *Flour Daniel v. OSHRC*, 295 F.3d 1232 (11th Cir. 2002).

may range up to $70,000 for each violation, with the minimum civil penalty being $5,000. The *John Carlo, Inc., v. Secretary of Labor* case, presented in this section, deals with a willful violation.

2. **Repeated:** A prior violation of the same standard constitutes a prima facie case of a substantially similar present "repeated violation." Penalties for repeated violations may range up to $70,000. In assessing the appropriate penalty, factors such as commonality (or lack of such) of supervisory control as well as the similarity (or lack thereof) of geographic location and time may be considered.

3. **Serious:** A violation there is a substantial likelihood that serious physical harm or death could result. Penalties of up to $7,000 may be assessed. Again the area director can take such factors as an employer's good faith into account in adjusting the penalty.[43]

4. **Nonserious:** A violation that has an immediate relationship to job safety but will probably not cause serious physical harm or death. The 1981 Labor-HEW Appropriations Act prohibited the assessment of penalties for nonserious violations unless 10 or more nonserious violations were cited. The maximum penalty is $7,000. This policy continues to be followed by OSHA.

5. *De minimus:* A violation that has no immediate relationship to job safety. A notice is issued but citations and proposed penalties are not.

The citations and proposed penalties are sent to the employer by certified mail. The citation must state with particularity the nature of the violation.[44] In addition, it fixes a reasonable time for the abatement of the violation, generally not exceeding 30 days. When longer periods are required, the employer must submit progress reports. The employer must also post the citation to inform employees of the action undertaken by OSHA. Employees have the right to contest the abatement period if they believe it is unreasonable.[45]

APPEAL OF THE CITATION AND/OR PENALTY

If the employer wants to challenge the citation, the period of abatement, or the proposed penalty, the employer has 15 working days from the time of receipt of the citation to notify the area director in writing.[46] This is known as a "notice of

---

[43] See, for example, *Secretary of Labor v. Ohio State Home Services*, 15 BNA OSHC 1492 (1992), where following a cave-in at a building excavation site, the Secretary proposed a penalty of $24,800 for certain serious and nonserious violations of the Act. The Review Commission reduced the penalty to $10,000 because of the owner's immediate compliance with the excavation standard and the fact that imposition of the $24,800 penalty would affect the owner's ability to stay in business. But see *Wal-Mart Stores, Inc., v. Secretary of Labor*, 406 F.3d 731 (D.C. Cir. 2005), involving the assessment of a $5,000 penalty for a serious violation where a conveyor system and some stacked boxes obstructed access to an emergency exit. Wal-Mart maintained that actual conditions, including employee training, the sprinkler system, other exits, and a nearby fire department, indicate the violation was *de minimis*. The Court of Appeals found no cause to disturb the ALJ's conclusion that the violation was serious, where employees could panic and forget their training, and other factors could eventuate in serious harm.

[44] 29 U.S.C. § 658(a).

[45] 29 U.S.C. § 659(c).

[46] 29 U.S.C. § 659(b).

contest." The notice of contest must also be posted to inform employees of the employer's actions and of their right to participate in the OSHRC procedures.

If contested, the first stage of review is a hearing before an administrative law judge who makes findings of fact and conclusions of law affirming, modifying, or vacating the citation and proposed penalty. It should be noted that no right to a jury trial exists under the Act.[47] Within 30 days of the judge's decision, any commissioner or aggrieved party may petition for discretionary OSHRC review.[48] After the administrative remedies have been pursued, a party may obtain judicial review in the appropriate U.S. court of appeals.[49]

The findings of the Commission with respect to questions of fact are conclusive if supported by "substantial" evidence.[50] If the employer challenges only the penalty, the citation is not subject to review by any court or agency. The violation is deemed to have been admitted by the employer.[51]

In *Brennan v. OSHRC and Interstate Glass Co.*,[52] the court held that when a proposed penalty is challenged, the Commission has wide discretionary power to increase, modify, or vacate the penalty.

AFFIRMATIVE DEFENSES

Several affirmative defenses are available to employers contesting a violation. It has been held by the Commission that impossibility of compliance gives an employer an absolute defense to a citation. This defense breaks down into three categories:

1. It is impossible to comply with the standard and still accomplish the work.
2. It is impossible to comply with the standard without damaging the work already done.
3. It is impossible to comply with the standard due to the structural inadequacy of the building or the device itself.

These have been most successfully raised by employers in the construction industry. However, a showing that the standards are merely impractical or difficult to comply with will not excuse performance.[53]

In *Bratton Furniture Manufacturing Co.*,[54] a charge of failure to guard a table saw with an automatically adjusting hood was dismissed by the Commission on the grounds that such a guard would make the dado operation for which the table saw was used impossible to perform.

---

[47] *Atlas Roofing Co. v. OSHRC*, 430 U.S. 442 (1977).

[48] 29 C.F.R., § 2200.91.

[49] 29 U.S.C. § 660(a). See *Bianchi Trison Corp. v. Chao*, 409 F.3d 196 (3d Cir. 2005), where the contractor for the demolition of Three Rivers Stadium in Pittsburg petitioned the Third Circuit Court of Appeals to review an OSHRC order upholding 35 charged violations of the OSH Act.

[50] 29 U.S.C. § 660(a).

[51] *Brennan v. OSHRC and Bill Echols Trucking Co.*, 487 F.2d 230 (5th Cir. 1973).

[52] 487 F.2d 438 (8th Cir. 1973). See also *J. L. Foti Construction Co.*, 1980 CCH OSHD ¶ 24,421 (1980).

[53] *Hobart Corp.*, 5 OSHC 1718 (1977).

[54] 1982 CCH OSHD ¶ 25,907 (1982).

CASE 11.5	JOHN CARLO, INC. v. SECRETARY OF LABOR
	U.S. COURT OF APPEALS, ELEVENTH CIRCUIT, 2008 CCH OSHD ¶ 32,929.

[John Carlo, Inc. (JCI) participated in a road improvement project in Jacksonville, Florida, which required crew members to install a sewer line down the middle of an existing roadway. At one location, the new line would cross under an existing gas line that was perpendicular to the proposed sewer line. JCI attempted to have the gas company relocate the gas line, but the company would not cooperate. JCI's supervisors resolved to address the problem when they encountered it. On March 30, 2004, the JCI crew worked in two stacked trench boxes, laying pipe up to the location where the pipeline crossed the trench for the sewer line. On March 31, 2004, however, the crew removed the top trench box because both boxes would not fit under the perpendicular gas line. The crew pulled the bottom box under the perpendicular gas line and prepared the bottom of the trench to lay one joint of the sewer pipe. Two crew members entered the trench and worked inside the trench box for at least 20–30 minutes. The trench walls above the box (approximately 6 feet) were not sloped or otherwise protected. While the employees were in the trench, a large clay ball dislodged, fell into the trench, and struck one employee, who eventually died as a result. Subsequent to the cave-in, JCI was able to slope the trench walls according to OSHA standards and complete the laying of the pipe at the same location without moving or removing the gas line. The ALJ found that JCI willfully violated Section 5(a)(1) of the Act and assessed a $50,000 penalty. The ALJ's decision became a final order of the OSHRC. JCI seeks review, arguing that the Secretary failed to establish a violation before the ALJ.]

PER CURIAM: ...

John Carlo, Inc. ("JCI") seeks review of a final order of the Occupational Safety and Health Review Commission in favor of the Secretary of Labor. After a trench collapse fatally injured a JCI employee, the Administrative Law Judge ("ALJ") found that JCI willfully violated 29 C.F.R. § 1926.652(a)(1) and assessed a $50,000 penalty. The Commission adopted the decision of the ALJ, which became the final order of the Commission. JCI argues that the Secretary failed to establish a violation before the ALJ and asks us to reverse the Commission's final order. We

find that substantial evidence supports the ALJ's decision. Accordingly, we affirm....

OSHA regulations require employers to protect employees working in excavations from cave-ins with an adequate protection system. 29 C.F.R. § 1926.652(a)(1). There are various types of protection systems including sloping and shoring....

After hearing testimony from the project superintendent (Lester Cox), the foreman (James Jacobs), and the employee who survived the accident, the ALJ concluded that Cox instructed Jacobs to use only the bottom trench box where the trench crossed under the gas line. Jacobs testified that he reminded Cox that this would leave the top portion of the trench unprotected. Jacobs said Cox explained that he realized the problem, but because JCI had bid the project based on six-foot-wide trenches, they could not slope the trench. Jacobs was present and supervised the crew at the time of the accident.

The ALJ imputed Jacobs' actual knowledge of the violation to JCI. The ALJ determined that, in light of the employee's death and the nature of the hazard, the "violation was a serious violation in that there was a substantial probability that death or serious physical harm could result from the violative conditions." The ALJ also determined that the violation was willful and held that JCI, "through Cox and Jacobs, was actually aware, at the time of the violative act, that the act was unlawful." Both Cox and Jacobs "knowingly and deliberately" violated the standard because it "was more expedient to place employees in an unprotected trench for 15 minutes to lay one joint of pipe than to take the time to adequately shore or slope the trench to protect employees."...

"We review the Commission's findings of fact to determine whether they are supported by substantial evidence on the record as a whole; if so, they are deemed conclusive." *J.A.M. Builders, Inc., v. Herman*, 233 F.3d 1350, 1352 (11th Cir. 2000)....

Moreover, we must uphold the Commission's legal determinations unless they are arbitrary, capricious, an abuse of discretion, or otherwise not in accordance with the law. *Fluor Daniel*, 295 F.3d at 1236.

After carefully considering the briefs, reviewing the record on appeal, and having had the benefit of oral

continued

argument, we find that substantial record evidence supports the ALJ's findings and the decision is in accordance with the law. Thus, we deny JCI's petition for review and uphold the Commission's final order.

Affirmed.

Case Questions

1. Having bid the job based on 6-foot-wide trenches and the discovery that the gas line obstruction would not allow for use of the top trench box, was it a reasonable risk for the employer to utilize the two employees in the trench for just 15 minutes to lay one joint of pipe?

2. Did the Court find that substantial evidence of record supported the ALJ's findings and that the decision was in accordance with the law?

SECTION 98: OVERLAPPING JURISDICTION

Under Section 653(b)(1) of the Act, OSHA is to have no jurisdiction where another federal agency has exercised statutory authority to prescribe safety or health rules. Employers have frequently claimed that safety regulations by another agency result in the regulated industry's exemption from OSHA. OSHA's response (which has been sustained by the courts) is that the other agency regulates certain working conditions but that those OSHA regulates are of a different type and are therefore not preempted. This line of reasoning was echoed by the court in *Labor Secretary v. Tidewater Pacific, Inc.,*[55] a case in which OSHA standards on confined space entries and machine guarding on oceangoing tugboats operating within U.S. territorial waters were upheld over the company's argument that such regulations were preempted by the U.S. Coast Guard, because the Coast Guard had not exercised its authority in this area.

In *Chao v. Mallard Bay Drilling, Inc.,*[56] presented in this section, the U.S. Supreme Court dealt with the issue of whether Section 4(b)(1) of the OSH Act preempted OSHA jurisdiction because the Coast Guard had exclusive authority to prescribe and enforce standards concerning occupational safety and health on vessels in navigable waters. The Court determined that the Coast Guard had not preempted OSHA's jurisdiction.

SECTION 99: VIOLENCE IN THE WORKPLACE

Employers have a legal obligation to protect their employees from acts of violence. Workplace violence includes a broad spectrum of misconduct ranging from homicide[57] and various kinds of physical assaults to domestic violence, stalking, threats, harassment, bullying, emotional abuse, intimidation, and other misconduct that creates anxiety, fear, and a climate of distrust in the workplace. Workplace

---

[55] 1998 CCH OSHD ¶ 31, 703 (9th Cir. 1998).

[56] 122 S.Ct. 738 (2002).

[57] In 2006, some 516 individuals were homicide victims at their workplace, down from 567 in 2005. See http://www.bls.gov/opub/ted/2007/aug/wk2/art02.htm.

violence can occur at the workplace, on official travel, at field locations, and at clients' homes or workplaces. It may be classified in the following ways:

1. **Criminal:** When the perpetrator has no legitimate relationship to the business or its employees and is usually committing a crime in conjunction with the violence (e.g., robbery, shoplifting, or trespassing).
2. **Customer or Client:** When the perpetrator has a legitimate relationship with the business and becomes violent being served by the business (e.g., customers, clients, patients, students, inmates, or any other group for which the business provides a service).
3. **Coworker:** When the perpetrator is an employee, a past employee of the business, or a contractor who works as a temporary employee on-site and who attacks or threatens another employee.
4. **Domestic Violence:** When the perpetrator, who has no legitimate relationship to the business (but has a personal relationship with the intended victim), threatens or assaults the employee at the workplace (e.g., family member, boyfriend, or girlfriend).[58]

Characteristics of potentially hazardous work environments include (1) working in direct contact with the public, (2) exchanging money with customers, (3) delivering goods and services, (4) working with unstable or volatile people, (5) working in high-crime areas, (6) working in small numbers (fewer than five people), and (7) working in community-based settings.[59]

EMPLOYER DUTIES UNDER OSHA

Section 5(a)(1) of the OSH Act sets forth the general duty clause, which provides in part that "each employer shall furnish to each of his employees employment and a place of employment which are free from recognized hazards that are causing or are likely to cause death or serious physical harm to his employees."[60] Criminal acts of violence in the workplace have been recognized as one of the hazards the employer must protect against; and employers have an obligation to assess the specific hazards in their workplaces and to provide training and procedures for dealing with "feasibly preventable hazards." For example, in its *Charter Barclay Hospital* decision, OSHA used the general duty clause to cite a psychiatric health care facility for failure to protect its employees from the recognized hazards of dealing with violent patients.[61]

OSHA encourages employers to develop and implement a Workplace Violence Prevention Plan in furtherance of each employer's obligations under the general duty clause. Essentials of a plan may include (1) a policy statement on management commitment and employee involvement, (2) an assessment and analysis of the workplace for security hazards, (3) prevention and control of those hazards,

---

[58] See BLS-NIOSH, a survey document for Survey of Workplace Violence Prevention, 2005, at http://www.bls.gov/iif/home.htm.

[59] *Id.*

[60] 29 U.S.C. § 654(a).

[61] 23 OHSA 646 (1993).

(4) training on how to prevent the hazards from occurring, and (5) recordkeeping and evaluation of the plan.[62]

WORKPLACE VIOLENCE LITIGATION

Victims of workplace violence may attempt to hold the employer of the perpetrator civilly responsible for the harm caused by the violence. However, workers' compensation laws may shield employers from liability to its own employees for workplace injuries caused by coworkers or third parties. Employer workers' compensation immunity does not apply to injured independent contractors.

An intentional tort exception may exist for employees when their employer does not act to prevent or eliminate a known threat.[63] Common tort liability theories raised against employers by customer, client, or third-person victims of an employee's violent conduct include employer vicarious liability for the torts of employees and negligent hiring and retention of employees, which are covered in Chapter 16.

RETALIATION FOR REPORTING THREATS OF VIOLENCE

An at-will employee possesses a tort action for wrongful termination of employment based on the public policy exception to the employment-at-will doctrine where an employee is discharged for reporting an incident or threat of workplace violence. The public policy supporting this exception is the requirement that employers provide a safe and secure workplace and that employees report credible threats of violence in the workplace.[64]

SECTION 100: STATE PROGRAMS

The Act specifically encourages states to adopt their own plans for dealing with occupational safety and health issues as long as their programs are "at least as effective" as the federal program.[65] However, the only way a state may regulate occupational safety and health issues regulated by OSHA is pursuant to a state

---

[62] The Bureau of Labor Statistics conducted a special survey for the National Institute for Occupational Safety and Health regarding the policies and training on workplace violence prevention for private industry and state and local government for 2005, http://www.bls.gov/iif/home.htm. State government reported a higher percentage of all types of workplace violence than did local government or private industry. See also Occupational Safety & Health Admin., Dep't. of Labor, *Guidelines for Preventing Workplace Violence for Health Care & Social Service Workers*, pp. 4–6 (2004), available at http://www.osha.gov/Publications/OSHA3148.pdf (describing the extent of the workplace violence problem in the health care and social service industries). See Nat'l Inst. of Occupational Safety & Health, "Violence in the Workplace: Developing and Implementing a Workplace Violence Prevention Program and Policy" http://www.ede.gov/NIOSH/violdev.html.

[63] See *Medlen v. Estate of Myers*, 273 F.App'x 464 (6th Cir. 2008), where an employee shot by coworker Myers was allowed to have his intentional tort claim against DaimlerChrysler heard in state court, alleging that DaimlerChysler had knowledge that Myers would harm employees in the plant and failed to protect employees from this harm.

[64] *Franklin v. The Monadnock Co.*, 59 Cal. Rptr. 3d 692 (2007); *Daoust v. Abbott Laboratories*, 2007 U.S. Dist. LEXIS 2138 (2007).

[65] 29 U.S.C. § 667(a)(2).

plan approved by the Secretary of Labor that displaces the federal standards in that state. Employers and employees are subject to only one set of regulations, be it federal or state. In *Gade v. National Solid Wastes Management Ass'n*, the state regulation establishing occupational safety and health standards for training hazardous waste workers, which was not approved by the Secretary of Labor and for which there was a federal standard in effect, was found to be preempted by the OSH Act.[66]

SECTION 101: STATE "RIGHT-TO-KNOW" LEGISLATION

So-called right-to-know laws have been enacted by many states in recent years. These laws guarantee individual workers the right to know if there are hazardous substances in their workplaces. Also, these laws commonly require an employer to make known to an employee's physician the chemical composition of certain substances in the workplace in connection with the diagnosis and treatment of an employee by the physician. Further, local fire and public health officials, as well as local neighborhood residents, are granted the right to know if local employees are working with hazardous substances that could pose health or safety problems.

The information disclosed varies from state to state. Common features in right-to-know laws are as follows:

1. Employers have an obligation to post on bulletin boards in the work area that employees have a right to request information about toxic substances in the work area. These notices commonly require the employer to state that no reprisals will be taken against employees who exercise their right to request information.
2. Employers have an obligation in some states to inform prospective and current employees of reproductive hazards, including whether radioactive materials are used in the workplace.
3. Employers have an obligation in some states to label containers of toxic substances.
4. Employers in some states must conduct training programs for employees that inform employees of the properties of the toxic substances in the workplace, train employees concerning the safe handling of the substances, and instruct employees on emergency treatment for overexposure to the substances.

CHAPTER QUESTIONS AND PROBLEMS

1. What is the stated purpose of the Occupational Safety and Health Act of 1970?
2. Under what circumstances may the Secretary of Labor bypass the formalities of OSHA and create temporary emergency standards?
3. Distinguish between an occupational injury and an occupational illness under the OSH Act.
4. What activities can a compliance officer undertake on an inspection tour?

---

[66] 505 U.S. 88 (1992).

5. Carl Frost, a maintenance mechanic for the Firestone Tire Company, was told to install a temporary chute in the carbon black tower at his plant during the night shift. The chute, which was located 40 feet up the tower, funneled the black substance used in tire manufacturing to conveyor belts at ground level. Frost and two other employees climbed the tower's ladder at 1 AM. The temperature was below freezing, and a steady snow was falling. The rungs of the ladder were ice-covered from the mist of a nearby cooling tower. Frost and the others made the climb and worked with flashlights between their teeth due to poor lighting on the tower. Frost and the others worked on the tower until 3:30 AM, when they returned to the ground to obtain a part needed for completion. At that time, the supervisor, Dan Aphe, instructed Frost to remove the chute he had just installed and hoist a permanent replacement chute weighing 150 pounds up the tower and install it. Frost refused, stating it was "too bad" on the tower. Aphe told Frost to do the job or clock out. Frost clocked out and was subsequently suspended without pay for two weeks.

Frost's union brought an OSHA Section 11(c) complaint on his behalf, charging Firestone with discrimination because Frost reasonably believed he was in danger of death or serious injury and had no alternative but to refuse the job. Firestone maintained that it had an inherent management right to properly discipline employees.

Has Firestone discriminated against Frost? Decide. [*Marshall v. Firestone Tire and Rubber Co.*, 8 OSHC 1637]

6. The Philadelphia area office of the Occupational Safety & Health Administration obtained a warrant to conduct an inspection of the premises of Metal Banks of America, Inc. The OSHA area director had received numerous complaints regarding unhealthy and hazardous employee exposure to lead at the plant. The warrant entitled the OSHA inspectors to enter Metal Banks' premises and engage in an extensive inspection, including "the questioning privately of any owner, operator, agent, employer, or employee of the establishment" and the inspection of "any area in the establishment where there is an occupational exposure to lead and copper." When the OSHA inspectors arrived at the plant, they were not allowed to conduct private interviews with employees on the premises and were denied access to shower facilities, lunchrooms, and change rooms provided for employees exposed to lead.

The Secretary of Labor asked the U.S. district court to find Metal Banks in contempt of court for impeding the OSHA investigation. Metal Banks defended its denial of private interviews by citing Section 657(e) of the Act, which guarantees the right of employer representatives to accompany the OSHA team during its inspections. Metal Banks contended, therefore, that private interviews were in conflict with its right to accompany the OSHA inspector. Metal Banks also contended that OSHA need not inspect the lunchrooms, shower facilities, and change rooms as there was no danger of lead exposure in those areas.

Has Metal Banks unlawfully impeded the OSHA inspection? Decide. [*Establishment Inspection of Metal Banks of America, Inc.*, 9 OSHC 1972]

7. De Trae Enterprises was employed as a masonry subcontractor at the Smithhaven Mall construction site in Lake Grove, New York. OSHRC found De Trae guilty of three separate violations of OSHA standards when it was revealed that De Trae employees were allowed to work in areas near unguarded floor openings, open-sided floors, and stairways without proper handrails. The evidence showed that De Trae, as a masonry subcontractor, had no control over creating the safety violations and that responsibility was that of the general contractor; that is, De Trae employees merely did masonry work in the vicinity of someone else's safety violations.

May De Trae be penalized for the safety violations? Decide. [*De Trae Enterprises v. Secretary of Labor and OSHRC*, 9 OSHC 1425 (2d Cir.)]

8. In response to a complaint filed by an employee, OSHA dispatched a compliance officer to Genessee Valley Industrial Packaging. When the officer arrived at the shop, he was greeted by a truck driver. The driver told the inspector that he had been asked to watch over the shop until the supervisor returned and asked the inspector to delay his inspection until that time. Nevertheless, the inspector began his investigation without a warrant, including the photographing of alleged violations of "saw guarding" requirements. The inspection was halted when the company president arrived and objected to the presence of the OSHA officer. Based on this partial inspection, the Secretary of Labor issued two charges of "saw guarding" violations against the company.

The company requested that these charges be dropped due to a warrantless inspection conducted by OSHA without consent of the employer. The Secretary of Labor argued that the OSHA inspector obtained consent from the truck driver, who was functioning as an assistant supervisor.

Has OSHA conducted a lawful inspection? Decide. [Genessee Valley Industrial Packaging, OSHD ¶ 24,279 (CCH)]

9. While a compliance officer from OSHA was engaged in a postinspection closing conference at the Swidzinski Construction Company work site, he observed a violation of an OSHA standard that requires "every open-sided floor or platform six or more feet above ground to have guardrails all around." The five-story building under construction had platforms made of wooden planks that protruded 6 feet out from each floor. The platforms enabled a crane to deliver pallets of concrete blocks directly to each floor by way of the platforms. An employee operating a forklift on the platform would wheel the pallet of blocks from the edge of the platform into the building, where they would be used. The officer observed a Swidzinski employee stand at the end of such a platform without a guardrail on the fourth floor and signal to the crane operator 41 feet below.

Because in the absence of a guardrail or another protective device this employee was exposed to the hazard of falling, the Secretary of Labor charged Swidzinski with a serious violation of OSHA standards. Swidzinski appealed this citation, claiming it was impossible to comply with the guardrail standard as the rail would prevent the crane from delivering stock to the fourth-floor platform and would impede construction on the fourth floor.

What factors must OSHRC consider when faced with an employer's impossibility defense? Is it impossible for Swidzinski to comply in this case? Decide. [Frank Swidzinski Co., 9 OSHC 1230]

10. The Occupational Safety & Health Review Commission found the R. L. Sanders Roofing Company in violation of the Occupational Safety and Health Act for its failure to provide a perimeter guardrail on one of its flat-roof projects. The Commission held that the company was obligated to provide the guardrail under the general duty clause of the Act and was liable for the injuries received by an employee in a 13-foot fall from the roof.

The company appealed this decision, claiming the general duty clause was not sufficient notice to the company that it must provide a guardrail. In addition, the company cited a regulation promulgated by the Secretary of Labor that requires an employer to install a rail and catch platform below the working areas of roofs with a slope of greater than 4 inches. Because a flat roof has a slope of 0 inches, R. L. Sanders maintained that this regulation explicitly exempted it from the duty to provide a safety rail around flat roofs. The Secretary of Labor disagreed and claimed that the cited regulation applied only to sloped roofs and that this employer was obligated to provide a guardrail for a flat roof under the general duty clause of the Act.

Should the company be held liable under the general duty clause or be exempt due to the Secretary's regulation? Decide. [*R. L. Sanders Roofing Co. v. OSHRC and Marshall*, 8 OSHC 1559 (5th Cir.)]

11. Paul Sund, an employee of Astra Pharmaceutical Products, Inc., was severely injured and hospitalized when a vat used in the production of chloroacetyl xylidine, an anesthetic ingredient, overflowed, spraying toxic chemicals in the immediate area. Sund, an employee with 20 years' experience, was tending the vat at the time of the overflow. OSHA inspector Goyda, dispatched to investigate this incident, spoke with some employees who helped wash down Sund. A fellow employee who saw Sund after the accident told Goyda that Sund was "covered from head to toe with chemical, including his head and mouth." Sund's supervisor told Goyda that it was "company policy" that the vat operator wear a respirator, chemical goggles, and gloves. Although no one testified as to exactly what type of protective gear Sund was wearing, the OSHRC found Astra in violation of a specific regulation that compels an employer to make sure that an employee engaged in an operation like Sund's is wearing full-body protection, including boots, chemical retardant clothes, a full face shield, and a self-contained breathing apparatus.

Astra appealed this decision to the court of appeals, claiming that there was not enough evidence to support a citation for a violation of the chemical clothing requirements as no one testified as to exactly what Sund was wearing.

What factors must the court consider when deciding whether to enforce or vacate an OSHRC decision? Should the court set aside this OSHRC decision? Decide. [*Astra Pharmaceutical Products v. OSHRC and Donovan*, 10 OSHC 1697 (1st Cir.)]

12. Robin Medlack, an OSHA compliance officer, was driving down Highway 32 toward Cincinnati when he observed workers at an apartment complex under construction near the roadway walking around the site without protective helmets. He also observed scaffolding being used without guardrails at the work site. Medlack reported these violations of OSHA standards to his supervisor, who dispatched Medlack to the Ackermann Enterprises construction site for further investigation. Medlack was told by an office secretary at the site that he would have to await the return of the company president or job superintendent before he could obtain consent to conduct an OSHA inspection. Because the job superintendent was expected back soon, the secretary allowed Medlack to wait by his car in the parking lot. While he was waiting in the lot, Medlack observed three workers riding in the elevated front bucket of a backhoe as it made eight to ten trips between buildings at the work site. Although he could see this occurrence plainly from 300 feet away, Medlack also took photographs of the workers with a zoom lens camera.

On the basis of Medlack's photos and observations, the Secretary of Labor cited Ackermann for a violation of Section 5(a)(1) of OSHA. Ackermann appealed this citation, claiming that the evidence obtained by Medlack was obtained in violation of the U.S. Constitution because Medlack did not have a warrant and an inspection was never consented to by Ackermann.

Was the evidence obtained by Medlack obtained unlawfully without a warrant? Decide. [Ackermann Enterprises, Inc. (Review Comm. Decision), 10 OSHC 1709]

13. Taylor Diving and Salvage Company conducts commercial diving operations in deep-water ports in the United States from installations on the outer continental shelf and from Coast Guard-inspected vessels. The Coast Guard has traditionally monitored and regulated the commercial diving industry. Published Coast Guard regulations provide rules for the "design, construction, and use of

equipment, and inspection, operation, and safety and health standards for commercial diving operations." One Coast Guard regulation requires that diving companies create records whenever a diver is involved in an accident and that they retain those records for six months.

In 1980, OSHA promulgated a Final Standard Regulating Access to Employee Medical Records. Under this standard, employers are required to maintain employee medical records and records of employee exposure to potentially toxic materials or harmful physical agents for 30 years. The standard provides for employee access to the records and for OSHA access so that the "detection, treatment and prevention of occupational disease may be improved."

Taylor and other diving companies asked a federal district court to rule that the OSHA standard is inapplicable to the diving industry because the preexisting Coast Guard regulations mandate similar recordkeeping and the Coast Guard is solely responsible for regulating occupational safety and health in the diving industry. The industry contended that it should not be burdened by dual regulation.

Is there any basis for Taylor's argument? If so, should Taylor prevail? Decide. [*Taylor Diving and Salvage Co. v. Department of Labor*, 13 OSHC 1111 (D.D.C.)]

14. Lakeland Enterprises, a water and sewer contractor, was engaged in a project on a public street in Marshfield, Wisconsin, when Chad Greenwood, an OSHA compliance officer, was driving by the project and noticed the excavation in progress. Greenwood observed Lakeland supervisory employee Ron Krueger excavating a trench with a backhoe. Greenwood also observed another employee, Tony Noth, working at the bottom of the trench. The trench contained neither a ladder nor a trench box, a device used to prop up the walls to prevent collapse. Greenwood began videotaping the scene, at which point Jim Gust, the project superintendent, asked him to step back and informed him that the road was closed. Greenwood explained that he was an OSHA compliance officer and indicated the nature of the inspection. While Gust and Greenwood were speaking, Noth began climbing up one of the walls of the trench. Greenwood observed loose dirt falling back into the trench, apparently unsettled by Noth's feet as he scaled the slope. Krueger later admitted that he knew Noth was not supposed to be working in the trench and that he failed to remove him. Greenwood took some soil samples and measured the trench dimensions. Lakeland's motion to suppress the evidence from the inspection because Greenwood's warrantless search of the excavation site was a violation of the Fourth Amendment was denied by the ALJ. The company was assessed a $49,000 civil penalty for a willful violation of the Act. What defenses will the company raise on appeal? How would you decide this case? [*Lakeland Enterprises of Rhinelander, Inc., v. Chao*, 402 F.3d 739 (7th Cir.)]

DISCRIMINATION LAWS: PROTECTED CLASSES UNDER TITLE VII AND THE CONSTITUTION

CHAPTER **12**

SECTION

SECTION 102: INTRODUCTION

Numerous major federal laws regulate the equal employment rights of individuals. The Civil Rights Act of 1866, commonly referred to as a legal action under Section 1981, remedies discrimination based on race. Title VII of the Civil Rights Act of 1964, as amended by the Equal Employment Opportunities Act of 1972 and the Civil Rights Act of 1991, forbids employer and union discrimination based on race, color, religion, sex, or national origin. The Pregnancy Discrimination Act requires employers to treat pregnancy and related medical conditions as any other medical disability with respect to terms and conditions of employment, including health care benefits. The Equal Pay Act of 1963 requires equal pay for men and women doing equal work. The Age Discrimination in Employment Act of 1967, as amended, forbids discriminatory hiring practices against job applicants and employees over the age of 40. The Rehabilitation Act of 1973 and Title I of the Americans with Disabilities Act of 1990, as amended in 2008, prohibit discrimination against qualified individuals with disabilities in employment-related matters.

Additionally, Executive Order 11246, which has the force and effect of a statute enacted by Congress, regulates contractors and subcontractors doing business with the federal government. This order forbids discrimination against minorities and women and in certain situations requires affirmative action to be taken regarding employment opportunities for minorities and women.

This chapter and all subsequent chapters treat in detail or in part aspects of employment discrimination law. Coverage includes the preceding statutes and executive order, the U.S. Constitution, and the court decisions construing them.

SECTION 103: TITLE VII AS AMENDED

The general purpose of Title VII of the Civil Rights Act of 1964 is the elimination of employer and union practices that discriminate against employees and job applicants on the basis of race, color, religion, sex, or national origin.

LEGISLATIVE BACKGROUND

The Civil Rights Act of 1964 was passed in response to the civil rights movement in the early 1960s protesting racial segregation of black Americans. On June 19, 1963, President John Kennedy submitted a bill to Congress, which later became the Civil Rights Act of 1964. Title I was a voting rights proposal, which had already been submitted to Congress. Title II addressed the subject of public accommodation, dealing with the denial of full accommodation rights to all Americans at restaurants, hotels, and other public places. Title VII dealt with discrimination in employment, but the approach taken in the initial bill was quite modest in comparison to Title VII as ultimately enacted in 1964. In 1963, then Vice President Lyndon Johnson advised President Kennedy to go to the source of the opposition to the bill—the South—and present the bill as a question of simple morality. Johnson believed that the people in the South were good people who knew that what was happening to black Americans was just not right.

On November 22, 1963, President Kennedy was assassinated while the bill was being considered by the Congress. The president's death gave impetus to passage of the bill and was considered by many to be a legislative monument to him. Title VII had been amended by opponents of the legislation, who added the word *sex* to the forms of prohibited discrimination, hoping that such an amendment would kill the entire legislation. However, the legislation was an idea whose time had come for Congress and President Johnson, and the bill was signed into law on July 2, 1964.

As Title VII is studied, it will become evident that this law has been the driving force in shaping fair employment practices in our society and ridding society of unfair practices whereby otherwise qualified workers are impeded from competing on an equal basis with fellow citizens for employment and promotional opportunities.

PROHIBITED PRACTICES AND COVERAGE

Title VII forbids discrimination in hiring, terms or conditions of employment, union membership and representation, and the referral of applicants by employment services. Title VII specifically forbids any employer to fail to hire; to discharge; to classify employees; or to discriminate with respect to compensation, terms, conditions, or privileges of employment in any way that would deprive any individual of employment opportunity due to race, color, religion, sex, or national origin. Title VII also prohibits retaliation against persons who file charges with the Equal Employment Opportunity Commission (EEOC) or participate in EEOC investigations.[1]

Title VII covers private employers, state and local governments, and educational institutions that have 15 or more employees.[2] The federal government, private and public employment agencies, labor organizations, and joint labor-management committees for apprenticeship and training also must abide by the law.

The employees of the U.S. Senate, the U.S. House of Representatives, and the executive branch are covered by Title VII, the Age Discrimination in Employment Act, and the Americans with Disabilities Act. However, each branch has its own enforcement procedures and remedies, and considerations of party affiliations, domicile, and political compatibility in employment decisions are not to be considered unfair employment practices.[3]

---

[1] U.S. EEOC Charge Statistics
FY 2007

	Charges	Percentage
Race	30,510	23.8%
Sex	24,826	19.3
National Origin	9,396	7.3
Religion	2,880	2.3
Retaliation	23,371	18.2
Age	19,103	14.9
Disability	17,734	13.8
Equal Pay Act	818	.7

This reflects the percentage of total charges that each type of allegation comprises.
Source: EEOC National Database, April 13, 2008. http://www.eeoc.gov/stats/charges.html.

[2] In *Arbaugh v. Y & H Corp.* d/b/a *The Moonlight Café*, 126 S. Ct. 1235 (2006), Jenifer Arbaugh claimed she was forced to leave her waitress job because her employer sexually harassed and assaulted her. She brought suit in federal district court under Title VII of the Civil Rights Act of 1964. The jury returned a verdict in her favor in the amount of $40,000. Two weeks after the verdict was entered, the defendant employer moved to dismiss the case, claiming that it was not an "employer" as defined in Title VII because it had fewer than the required, 15 employees. The district court granted the motion, holding that Title VII's 15-employee threshold is a jurisdictional requirement that can be raised at any time. The appellate court confirmed the dismissal, and Arbaugh petitioned the Supreme Court for relief. The Supreme Court held that the 15-employee numerosity threshold in Title VII is not a provision that must be met for the federal courts to have subject matter jurisdiction in a case, because Congress did not explicitly make it so, and Ms. Arbaugh's $40,000 judgment was reinstated. The numerosity requirement goes to the merits of the case, and the employer must raise the question at the beginning of the case, or the defendant is deemed to have waived this defense to liability.

[3] See Government Employee Rights Act of 1991, Pub. L. 102-166, Nov. 21, 1991, 105 Stat. 1088, 2 U.S.C. 1201. The EEOC has authority to enforce nondiscrimination laws in the federal sector through appropriate remedies, including back pay and compensatory damages, as set forth in *West v. Gibson*, 119 S. Ct. 1906 (1999).

THE EQUAL EMPLOYMENT OPPORTUNITY COMMISSION

The Equal Employment Opportunity Commission (EEOC) was created by Title VII. It is a five-member commission appointed by the president and confirmed by the Senate. Members are appointed for five-year staggered terms. The five-member commission makes equal employment opportunity policy and approves all litigation. The members do not "decide" individual cases under an administrative law system that is similar to the adjudicative procedures of the National Labor Relations Act.

The Office of the General Counsel coordinates and supervises the EEOC's litigation program in conjunction with the agency's field legal units to identify, investigate, and litigate cases of systemic discrimination, selecting some 300-plus "merits" lawsuits in a given year.[4] The EEOC initiates this selective litigation across the entire spectrum of the statutes it administers to develop the legal issues to serve as precedents for courts and arbitration tribunals handling the thousands of statutory employment claims each year.

The EEOC administers Title VII of the Civil Rights Act, the Pregnancy Discrimination Act, the Equal Pay Act, the Age Discrimination in Employment Act, the Rehabilitation Act, and Titles I and V of the Americans with Disabilities Act.

EEOC PROCEDURES

Where a state or local agency has the power to act on allegations of discriminatory practices, the charging party must file a complaint with that agency. The charging party must wait 60 days or until the termination of the state proceedings, whichever occurs first, before filing a charge with the EEOC. The commission then conducts an investigation to determine whether reasonable cause exists to believe that the charge is true. If such cause is found to exist, the EEOC attempts to remedy the unlawful practice through conciliation.

The EEOC undertakes mediation, investigative, and conciliation responsibilities through its regional offices. Figure 12-1 outlines the process. Prior to investigation of the charge by the EEOC, the agency offers the parties a form of alternative dispute resolution (ADR) called **mediation**. Participation in mediation is strictly voluntary. The mediators are unbiased neutral professionals, with no authority to decide who is right or wrong or to impose a settlement. A mediator assists the parties to reach a negotiated resolution of the charge of discrimination. If mediation is successful, the charge is withdrawn. If it is unsuccessful, the charge is returned to an investigative unit for processing.

The EEOC classifies incoming charges by letter-designated priorities, designating *A* charges as worthy cases for immediate handling, *B* charges as those requiring further investigation, and *C* charges as those that have a low likelihood of success. Cases where a restraining order may be deemed appropriate or where the charging party may be dying are placed in the highest priority *A* category, as are cases that appear to be litigation-worthy, have a potential for **class action** status, or present a

---

[4] For litigation statistics, see http://www.eeoc.gov.

FIGURE 12.1 | EEOC CHARGE PROCESSING

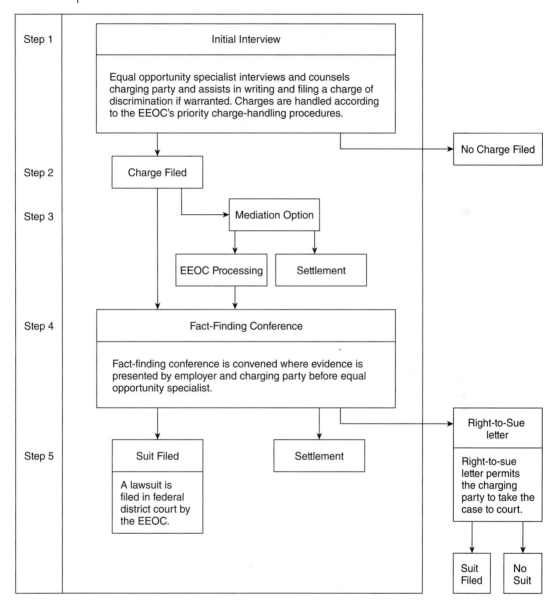

new or novel legal issue. Cases that appear to meet a high standard of proof are also classified in the *A* category. Cases where further investigation is required are classified as *B* cases. Examples of low-priority *C* cases are cases in which the charge is filed after the 300-day time limit for filing charges, cases in which the employer has too few employees to be subject to Title VII, and cases in which the offending party is not an employer.

After a charge is filed, the employer is notified and a fact-finding conference is convened. At this conference, both the charging party and the employer present evidence before the equal opportunity specialist, who tries to work out a settlement, if appropriate, satisfactory to both sides.

If the EEOC finds that there is reasonable cause to believe that discrimination has occurred but is unable to conciliate the charge, EEOC attorneys will consider the complaint for possible litigation. If the EEOC decides to litigate the case, a lawsuit will be filed in federal district court. If the EEOC decides not to litigate the case, a right-to-sue letter will be issued that permits the charging party to take the case to court. The fact that the EEOC does not choose to litigate a case does not mean that the case is without merit. The EEOC does not have funding to litigate all arguable cases. If successful, the charging party will recover attorney fees from the defendant.[5]

TIME LIMITS

At a minimum, a "charge" is a written statement filed with the EEOC that names the employer and generally describes the alleged discriminating act(s) and can be construed as a request by the employee for the agency to take action to vindicate his or her rights.[6]

The time limitation for filing charges with the EEOC is 180 days after the occurrence of the discriminatory act.[7] When the charging party is required to file first with a state or local agency, the time limit for filing charges is increased to 300 days after the occurrence of the discriminatory act or 30 days after receiving notice that the state has terminated its processing of the charge, whichever is earlier.[8] After the conclusion of proceedings before the EEOC, an individual claiming a violation of Title VII has 90 days after receipt of a right-to-sue letter from the EEOC to file a civil lawsuit in a federal district court.[9] If an aggrieved individual does not meet the time limit of Title VII, the individual may well lose the right to seek relief under the Act.[10] Limited exceptions exist where the time limits are

---

[5] The EEOC field legal units filed or intervened in 364 lawsuits in FY 2007, seeking relief for individuals it believes are victims of discrimination and do not have the resources to pursue legal remedies in federal courts under *right-to-sue* letters. The EEOC pursues systemic discrimination cases. For example, it recently successfully settled a suit against Walgreen Co., alleging discrimination against African-American retail management and pharmacy employees in promotion and assignment on behalf of a class of 10,000 members for $20 million. See 59 DLR A-9 (Mar. 27, 2008).

[6] *Federal Express Corp. v. Holowecki*, 128 S.Ct. 1147 (2008). The Court urged the EEOC to determine what revisions to its forms and processes are necessary to reduce the risk of future misunderstandings by those who seek its assistance.

[7] 42 U.S.C. §701(e).

[8] 42 U.S.C. § 706(e).

[9] 42 U.S.C. § 706(f)(l).

[10] Where an individual misses the relatively short time limits for filing a racial discrimination claim under Title VII, the individual may be able to bring a race discrimination case under 28 U.S.C. § 1981, the Civil Rights Act of 1866, which has a four-year statute of limitations applied under 28 U.S.C. § 1658. See *Jones v. R.R. Donnelley & Sons*, 541 U.S. 369 (2004).

considered "tolled" or suspended for equitable reasons. For example, in *Crown Cork & Seal Co. v. Parker*,[11] the Supreme Court decided that the 90-day limitation period for filing a court action after receiving a right-to-sue notice from the EEOC was tolled because of the filing of a class action suit by others where Parker was a member of the class.

In *National Railroad Passenger Corporation v. Morgan*,[12] Abner Morgan, a black male, alleged that he had been subjected to discriminatory acts in a racially hostile environment throughout his employment with Amtrak. Some of the alleged acts occurred within 300 days of the time Morgan filed his EEOC charge, but many took place prior to that time period. Hostile work environment claims are different in kind from discrete acts. Their very nature involves repeated conduct occurring over a series of days or perhaps years, and determining whether an actionable hostile environment claim exists requires an examination of all circumstances. Accordingly, a Supreme Court majority decided that a charge alleging a hostile work environment will not be time-barred if all acts constituting the claim are part of the same unlawful practice and at least one act falls within the 180- or 300-day filing periods.

The *Ledbetter v. Goodyear Tire & Rubber Co.*[13] decision established the rule that ongoing effects alone cannot breathe life into prior uncharged discrimination. Lilly Ledbetter introduced evidence that during the course of her nearly 20 years of employment with Goodyear Tire Co., several supervisors had given her poor evaluations because of her gender; that as a result, her pay was not increased as it should have been; and that these past decisions affected the amount of her pay throughout her employment. Ms. Ledbetter did not file a charge challenging any of the poor evaluations within 180 days "after the alleged unlawful practice occurred" as required by the Act. She argued that the paychecks issued during the 180-day period preceding the filing of her EEOC claim and a decision by Goodyear denying her a raise (which also occurred during the 180-day period) were unlawful because they carried forward intentionally discriminating disparities from prior years. The U.S. Supreme Court, in a 5-4 decision, held that a new violation does not occur and a new "charging period" does not commence upon the occurrence of subsequent nondiscriminatory acts that entail adverse results from past discrimination. Thus, her failure to challenge each of Goodyear's discrete acts of alleged intentionally discriminatory pay decisions within 180 days of each decision resulted in her loss of the legal right to pursue the claims.

---

[11] 462 U.S. 345 (1983). See also *Zipes v. TWA*, 455 U.S. 385 (1982), in which the Supreme Court held that the filing period is not a jurisdictional prerequisite and is subject to equitable waiver, estoppel, and tolling. In *Edelman v. Lynchburg College*, 122 S. Ct. 1145 (2002), the Supreme Court held that an EEOC regulation permitting an otherwise timely filer to verify a discrimination charge after the time for filing expired was a valid interpretation of Section 706 of Title VII.

[12] 122 S.Ct. 2061 (2002).

[13] 127 S.Ct. 2162 (2007). In January 2009, as this book goes to press, the Lilly Ledbetter Fair Pay Act (H.R.1.) was passed by the House, and would clarify that every paycheck resulting from an earlier discriminatory pay decision by an employer would constitute a violation of the Civil Rights Act provided the employee filed charges within 180 days of the discriminatory paycheck. The Senate passed the bill on January 22, 2009, and President Obama is expected to sign the bill into law.

COVERED EMPLOYEES

In *Robinson v. Shell Oil Co.*,[14] the oil company fired Charles Robinson. Shortly thereafter, Robinson filed a charge with the EEOC, alleging that he had been discharged because of his race. While that charge was pending, Robinson applied for a job with another company, and that company contacted Shell for an employment reference. Robinson claimed that Shell gave him a negative reference in retaliation for his having filed the EEOC charge; he then filed a retaliation charge with the EEOC based on this postemployment incident. Both the district court and the *en banc* Fourth Circuit agreed that the term "employees" in Section 704 (a) of Title VII referred only to current employees and that therefore Robinson did not have a claim cognizable under Title VII based on retaliation. A unanimous Supreme Court disagreed with the lower courts and held that a former employee is included within Section 704 (a)'s coverage. The Court stated that to cut former employees off from Title VII protection would undermine the effectiveness of the law.

THEORIES OF DISCRIMINATION

The Supreme Court has created and the Civil Rights Act of 1991 has codified two primary legal theories under which a plaintiff may prove a case of unlawful employment discrimination: disparate treatment and disparate impact (see Figure 12-2). A **disparate treatment** claim exists where an employer treats some individuals less favorably than others because of their race, color, religion, sex, or national origin. Proof of the employer's discriminatory motive is critical in a disparate treatment case.

A **disparate impact** claim exists where an employer's facially neutral employment practices, such as hiring or promotion examinations, though neutrally applied and making no adverse reference to race, color, religion, sex, or national origin, have a significantly adverse or disparate impact on a protected group *and* the employment practice in question is not shown to be job related and consistent with business necessity by the employer. Under the disparate impact theory, it is not a defense for an employer to demonstrate that the employer did not intend to discriminate. Technical rules exist concerning the burdens of proof and production of these two types of Title VII cases. Treatment of these rules is deferred to the next chapter so that the intervening text and materials may provide a foundation for better understanding the basis and application of these rules.

The EEOC itself in unusual situations may bring a **pattern-or-practice** case. A pattern-or-practice of discrimination lawsuit may be brought on behalf of a class of affected employees in disparate treatment cases. It is a two-phase process. The pattern-or-practice phase focuses on an employer's policy or practice, not on individual charges of discrimination and defenses against each of the individual charges. Once the pattern-or-practice of discrimination have been established, the process moves to the individual relief phase, where individual claims may be presented; the employer then has the opportunity to produce defenses to individual claims, and the individuals accordingly have the burden of proving that they were

---

[14] 33 DLR E-1 (Feb. 19, 1997).

FIGURE 12.2 | UNLAWFUL DISCRIMINATION UNDER TITLE VII OF THE CIVIL RIGHTS ACT OF 1964 AS AMENDED BY THE CIVIL RIGHTS ACT OF 1991

Discriminatory treatment in employment decisions on the basis of

Race
Color
Religion
Sex
National Origin

Disparate Treatment Theory	Disparate Impact Theory
Nonneutral practice or Nonneutral application	Facially neutral practice and Neutral application
Requires proof of discriminatory intent	Does not require proof of discriminatory intent Requires proof of adverse effect on protected group and Employer is unable to show that the challenged practice is job related for the position in question and is consistent with business necessity
Either party has the right to require a jury trial when seeking compensatory or punitive damages	No right to a jury trial
Remedy:	**Remedy:**
Reinstatement,hiring,or promotion Back pay less interim earnings Retroactive seniority Attorney and expert witness fees *plus* Compensatory* and punitive damages Damages capped for cases of sex and religious discrimination depending on size of employer. (The same cap applies to disability cases under the ADA.)	Reinstatement, hiring, or promotion Back pay less interim earnings Retroactive seniority Attorney and expert witness fees

Number of employees	Cap
100 or fewer	$ 50,000
101 to 200	100,000
201 to 500	200,000
Over 500	300,000

No cap on damages for race cases.

* Compensatory damages include future pecuniary losses and nonpecuniary losses such as emotional pain and suffering.

affected by the employer's discriminatory practices. If an individual claim is not challenged by the employer, a presumption of liability based on the pattern-or-practice finding turns into a finding of individual liability. In *EEOC v. Mitsubishi Motor Manufacturing of America, Inc.*,[15] the federal district court rejected the employer's argument that each individual who alleged sexual harassment against Mitsubishi must file a lawsuit rather than have the case proceed on behalf of all former and current female employees who may have been subjected to sexual harassment. The court then determined that it would follow the two-phase pattern-or-practice process set forth above. Within six months of this decision, the employer agreed to a $34 million settlement on behalf of 350 present and former female employees at the employer's Normal, Illinois, facility.[16]

DAMAGES AND JURY TRIALS

The broad scope of possible court-ordered remedies for violations of Title VII is covered in this and the subsequent chapter. Victims of discrimination are entitled to be made whole, including back pay and benefits less their interim earnings as well as front pay. Back pay is the amount of money an individual would have earned on the job but for the unlawful actions of the employer. Often there is a reduction from this figure for "outside earnings," which are the earnings of the plaintiff in other employment while he or she was wrongfully deprived of work or a promotion by the employer. "Front pay" is money awarded for lost compensation during the brief period of time between a court judgment and the actual reinstatement of the employee. A more common meaning of front pay is a monetary award in lieu of reinstatement when reinstatement is not viable because of continuing hostility between a plaintiff and the employer or its workers.[17] In the *Pollard* case, presented in this section, the U.S. Supreme Court determined that "front pay" is not subject to the statutory cap applicable to gender and religious discrimination. In addition to these remedies, which were available under the Civil Rights Act of 1964, the Civil Rights Act of 1991 provides further remedies for the victims of discrimination. Section 1981a(a)(1) of the 1991 Act provides for **compensatory**

---

[15] 990 F. Supp. 1059 (C.D. Ill. 1998).

[16] In *Davis v. Coca-Cola Bottling Co. Consolidated* (CCBCC), 516 F.3d 955, (11th Cir. 2008), the Court of Appeals dismissed a pattern or practice of race discrimination suit that a group of current and former Coca Cola Bottling employees brought against CCBCC because they failed to bring the claim as a "class action." The court reasoned that class status is necessary; otherwise, the named plaintiffs lack standing to pursue broad claims in which unnamed parties may have a stake. 27 DLR A-1 (Feb. 11, 2008).

[17] An example of front pay is an instance in which a manager testifies on behalf of an employee that the company indeed did discriminate against the employee and, as a result of testifying, that manager is subsequently removed from the position. Retaliation for testifying in a Title VII action is a violation of the law. The manager is entitled to back pay and benefits. The court may deem the manager's relationship with other managerial employees to be so poor that there is no longer a possibility that the manager can effectively function as such. The court would then order that the manager receive front pay—the pay he or she would have earned in the future had he or she been returned to work in a management position.

damages in cases of "intentional discrimination." (That is, compensatory damages may be recovered in "disparate treatment" cases only and may not be recovered in "disparate impact" cases.) Compensatory damages may include damages based on future pecuniary losses, emotional pain, suffering, inconvenience, loss of enjoyment of life, and other nonpecuniary losses.

Section 1981a(a)(1) also provides for **punitive damages** in cases of "intentional discrimination" (nondisparate impact cases). But Section 1981a(b)(1) adds a further qualifying factor for entitlement to punitive damages, that in addition to the employer's engaging in intentional discrimination, the employer has done so "with malice or with reckless indifference to the federally protected rights of an aggrieved individual." The meaning of this statutory language was considered *en banc* by the Court of Appeals for the District of Columbia in *Kolstad v. American Dental Ass'n*,[18] and the court majority concluded that the plaintiff had the obligation to demonstrate that the employer had engaged in some "egregious" misconduct in order to qualify for punitive damages. However, in its consideration of the *Kolstad* case, the U.S. Supreme Court disagreed and decided that the terms "malice" and "reckless indifference" used in Section 1981a(b)(1) focus on the actor's state of mind, not the showing of "egregious" misconduct.[19] The terms pertain to the employer's state of mind, not the extent of misconduct. However, evidence of egregious misconduct may be used to meet the plaintiff's burden of proof on the employer's state of mind. Ultimately, it must be shown that the employer discriminated in the face of a perceived risk that its actions were in violation of federal law in order for the employer to be liable for punitive damages.

The Supreme Court pointed out that there will be cases where intentional discrimination does not give rise to punitive damages under this standard because, for example, the employer reasonably, but erroneously, believed its discrimination satisfied a statutory exception to liability.[20]

The *Kolstad* analysis did not end on this point, but set forth an additional limitation on the awarding of punitive damages based on agency law. The Court recognized that an employer may have made every good faith effort to comply with Title VII, including having a written antidiscrimination policy and complaint procedure in effect, and yet a managerial agent nevertheless may violate Title VII. Full compensatory damages would be due the victim in such a case, but, the Court held, such an innocent employer may not be vicariously liable for punitive damages for the discriminatory employment decision of a managerial agent where the decision is contrary to the employer's good faith effort to comply with Title VII. Punitive damages may not be assessed against a governmental body.

The compensatory and punitive damages are capped according to the schedule set forth in Figure 12.2 for intentional discrimination based on sex, religion,

---

[18] 139 F.3d 958 (D.C. Cir. 1998).

[19] 119 S. Ct. 2118, 2125 (1999).

[20] *Id.* at 2125.

and nonracial national origin discrimination. There is no cap on intentional discrimination based on race or color.[21] It is common for a plaintiff to pursue more than one statutory claim for discrimination in a single lawsuit, such as a sexual harassment claim and a retaliation claim. Although the EEOC believes that the $300,000 cap allows $300,000 per claim in such a case, the courts in the Sixth, Seventh, and Tenth Circuits combine the separate damages awards into a single award capped at $300,000.[22]

In disparate treatment—intentional discrimination—cases, where compensatory and punitive damages are sought, either party may demand a jury trial. Successful plaintiffs are entitled to attorney fees and expert witness fees.

CONGRESSIONAL CHANGES OF SUPREME COURT DECISIONS

Between 1989 and 1991, the U.S. Supreme Court clearly reoriented Title VII jurisprudence to favor employers. The Civil Rights Act of 1991 modifies or reverses these decisions, augments the types of damages available to plaintiffs, and provides for jury trials in cases of intentional discrimination. The court decisions and the congressional corrections are presented at appropriate points throughout the chapters on fair employment practices.

EXTRATERRITORIAL EMPLOYMENT

In *EEOC v. Arabian American Oil Co.*,[23] Ali Boureslan, a naturalized U.S. citizen born in Lebanon and working in Saudi Arabia, was discharged by his employer, Arabian American Oil Company, a Delaware corporation. Boureslan claimed that he had been discriminated against because of his race, religion, and national origin. The U.S. Supreme Court held that Title VII does not apply extraterritorially to regulate employment practices of U.S. employers who employ U.S. citizens abroad.

The Civil Rights Act of 1991 contained the congressional response to this decision, amending both Title VII and the Americans with Disabilities Act to cover U.S. citizens employed in foreign countries by American-owned or controlled companies.[24] The 1991 Act contains an exemption if compliance with Title VII or the ADA would cause the company to violate the law of the foreign country in which it is located.

---

[21] Section 102(b)(4) of the Civil Rights Act of 1991. Technically, to obtain uncapped damages for discrimination based on race or color, one would file under 42 U.S.C. Section 1981. When the Civil Rights Act of 1866 was passed, which law is the basis for a Section 1981 lawsuit, the definition of *race* was broadly understood to prohibit discrimination based on ancestry or ethnic characteristics, protecting Arabs, Jews, Gypsies, Mexicans, Swedes, Germans, Greeks, Irish, etc. What might be deemed "national origin" discrimination today may be the subject matter of a Section 1981 "racial" lawsuit with uncapped damages.

[22] *Baty v. Wilamette Industries, Inc.*, 172 F.3d 1232 (10th Cir. 1999).

[23] 499 U.S. 244 (1991).

[24] Section 109 of the Civil Rights Act of 1991, Pub. L. 102-166, 105 Stat. 1071.

CASE 12.1	POLLARD V. E. I. DUPONT DE NEMOURS & CO.
	SUPREME COURT OF THE UNITED STATES, 532 U.S. 843 (2001).

[Sharon Pollard sued her former employer, E. I. du Pont de Nemours and Company (DuPont), alleging that she had been subjected to a hostile work environment based on her sex, in violation of Title VII. After a trial, the district court found that Pollard was subjected to coworker sexual harassment of which her supervisors were aware. The district court further found that the harassment resulted in a medical leave of absence from her job for psychological assistance and her eventual dismissal for refusing to return to the same hostile work environment. The court awarded Pollard $107,364 in back pay and benefits, $252,997 in attorney's fees, and $300,000 in compensatory damages—the maximum permitted under the statutory cap for such damages in 42 U.S.C. § 1981a(b)(3). The court observed that the award was insufficient to compensate Pollard, but that it was bound by an earlier Sixth Circuit holding that front pay—money awarded for lost compensation during the period between judgment and reinstatement or in lieu of reinstatement—was subject to the damages cap of §198la(b)(3). The Sixth Circuit affirmed.]

THOMAS, J....

Congress ... made clear through the plain language of the statute that the remedies newly authorized under § 1981a were *in addition to* the relief authorized by § 706(g). Section 1981a(a)(1) provides that, in intentional discrimination cases brought under Title VII, "the complaining party may recover compensatory and punitive damages as allowed in subsection (b) of [§ 1981a], *in addition to any relief authorized by section 706(g) of the Civil Rights Act of 1964*, from the respondent." (Emphasis added.) And § 1981a(b)(2) states that "[c]ompensatory damages awarded under [§ 1981a] shall not include backpay, interest on backpay, *or any other type of relief authorized under section 706(g) of the Civil Rights Act of 1964*." (Emphasis added.) According to these statutory provisions, if front pay was a type of relief authorized under § 706(g), it is excluded from the meaning of compensatory damages under § 1981a.

[T]he original language of §706(g) authorizing backpay awards was modeled after the same language in the NLRA. This provision in the NLRA had been construed to allow awards of backpay up to the date of reinstatement, even if reinstatement occurred after judgment. Accordingly, backpay awards made for the period between the date of judgment and the date of reinstatement, which today are called front pay awards under Title VII, were authorized under § 706(g).

As to front pay awards that are made in lieu of reinstatement, we construe §706(g) as authorizing these awards as well. We see no logical difference between front pay awards made when there eventually is reinstatement and those made when there is not. Moreover, to distinguish between the two cases would lead to the strange result that employees could receive front pay when reinstatement eventually is available but not when reinstatement is not an option—whether because of continuing hostility between the plaintiff and the employer or its workers, or because of psychological injuries that the discrimination has caused the plaintiff. Thus, the most egregious offenders could be subject to the least sanctions. Had Congress drawn such a line in the statute and foreclosed front pay awards in lieu of reinstatement, we certainly would honor that line. But, as written, the text of the statute does not lend itself to such a distinction, and we will not create one. The statute authorizes courts to "order such affirmative action as may be appropriate." 42 U.S.C. 2000e-5(g)(1). We conclude that front pay awards in lieu of reinstatement fit within this statutory term.

Because front pay is a remedy authorized under §706(g), Congress did not limit the availability of such awards in §1981a. Instead, Congress sought to expand the available remedies by permitting the recovery of compensatory and punitive damages in addition to previous available remedies, such as front pay.

* * *

The judgment of the Court of Appeals is reversed, and the case is remanded for further proceedings consistent with this opinion.

It is so ordered.

Case Questions

1. What are the traditional remedies available to victims of employment discrimination under § 706(g) of the Civil Rights Act of 1964?

continued

2. Did Congress in the Civil Rights Act of 1991 expand the remedies available to plaintiffs? Explain.

3. What are the two types of "front pay"? Is front pay an element of compensatory damages subject to the cap for sex and religious discrimination?

SECTION 104: RACE AND COLOR

The legislative history of Title VII of the Civil Rights Act demonstrates that a primary purpose of the Act is to provide fair employment opportunities for black Americans. The terms 'race' and 'color' as used in the Act clearly apply to blacks, and thus the protections of the Act are applied to blacks based on race or color. However, the word 'race' as used in the Act applies to all members of the four major racial groupings: white, black, Native American, and Asian-Pacific. Native Americans can file charges and receive the protection of the Act on the basis of national origin, race, or (in some instances) color. Individuals of Asian-Pacific origin may file discrimination charges based on race, color, or (in some instances) national origin. Although not a common situation, whites are also protected against discrimination because of race and color. For example, two white professors at a predominately black university were successful in discrimination suits against the university where it was held that the university discriminated against them based on race and color in tenure decisions.[25]

EMPLOYMENT ATMOSPHERE

The EEOC has determined that an employer is responsible for maintaining a working environment free of racial intimidation. Under this determination, for example, the employer must not tolerate racial or ethnic jokes by employees.

GROOMING POLICY

The courts have upheld evenhanded employer grooming policies, even where it has been argued that the employer's policy infringed on black employees' cultural identification.[26] However, a disparate impact case may be made for a black male employee who is unable to shave due to a severe dermatitis condition affecting only black males, where the employer is unable to demonstrate a business necessity for its grooming policy.[27]

---

[25] *Turgeon v. Howard University*, 32 FEP 927 (D.C. Cir. 1983). See also *Huckabay v. Moore*, 142 F.3d 233 (5th Cir. 1998).

[26] In *Brown v. D.C. Transit*, 523 F.2d 725, 10 FEP (D.C. Cir. 1975), the U.S. Court of Appeals for the District of Columbia held that a grooming policy barring muttonchops and long sideburns did not deprive black bus drivers of their racial identity so as to constitute a Title VII violation.

[27] In *Bradley v. Pizzaco of Nebraska, Inc.*, 939 F.2d 610 (8th Cir. 1991), the court held that the EEOC established a *prima facie* case of disparate impact on black males because of a no-beard policy, since 25 percent of all black males cannot shave because of pseudofolliculitis barbae (PFB); but the court held that the plaintiff had a mild case of PFB and could shave. The matter was remanded for handling of the business necessity stage of the disparate impact case.

ARREST AND CONVICTION INQUIRIES

In *Gregory v. Litton Systems Inc.*,[28] the Ninth Circuit Court of Appeals upheld a district court's order for damages and attorney fees awarded pursuant to Title VII of the Civil Rights Act. It was stipulated that Litton's decision not to hire Gregory as a sheet metal worker was predicated upon Gregory's statement in Litton's employment questionnaire that he had been arrested 14 times and not upon any consideration of convictions. The trial court held, and it was approved on appeal, that Litton's employment questionnaire, which required each applicant to reveal the applicant's arrest record, was discriminatory against black job seekers. It was held that Litton had not demonstrated that it had any reasonable business purpose for asking prospective employees about their arrest records.

The EEOC has taken the position that review of arrest records is irrelevant. The EEOC has also maintained that convictions cannot always be regarded as relevant to the ability of an individual to perform a job. The burden of proof is on the employer to justify inquiries into an applicant's arrest-conviction record.

In these circumstances, the employer's criminal record policy is unlawful absent a showing of "business necessity." However, employers generally will be able to justify their decision when the conduct that was the basis of the conviction is related to the position or the conduct was particularly egregious.[29] For example, business necessity would clearly allow an employer to reject an applicant for a security-sensitive position based on the applicant's criminal record of theft.[30]

In *El v. Southeastern Pennsylvania Transportation Authority (SEPTA)*, the Third Circuit Court of Appeals affirmed a jury's determination that SEPTA's hiring policy that disallowed hiring drivers with a violent criminal conviction for paratransit bus operator positions satisfied the "business necessity" defense.[31]

RESIDENCY REQUIREMENTS

In the *United States v. Villages of Elmwood Park and Melrose Park* case, presented in this section, the court struck down the villages' respective three- and five-year residency requirements for consideration of police and firefighting positions. These requirements were found to be artificial, arbitrary, and unnecessary barriers to employment that were unrelated to measuring job capabilities; thus, they were prohibited by Title VII.

---

[28] 472 F.2d 631 (9th Cir. 1972).

[29] EEOC Compliance Manual, § 15-VII(B)(2) (Apr. 19, 2006), available at http://www.eeoc.gov/policy/docs/race-color.html#VIB2conviction.

[30] But see a discussion on whether society should want ex-offenders to have a second chance at a legal lifestyle and what the alternatives are, as presented by C. N. O'Brien and J. J. Darrow, "Adverse Employment Consequence Triggered by Criminal Convictions," 42 *Wake Forest Law Review* 991 (Winter 2007).

[31] 479 F.3d 232 (3rd Cir. 2007).

SPECIFIC CASES

In the landmark *Griggs v. Duke Power* decision, which is presented in this section, an employer was found to have discriminated against blacks as to transfers and hiring by the use of tests and its educational requirement of a high school diploma, both of which were not job-related.

CASE 12.2	GRIGGS V. DUKE POWER CO.
	SUPREME COURT OF THE UNITED STATES, 401 U.S. 424 (1971).

BURGER, C. J....

We granted the writ in this case to resolve the question whether an employer is prohibited by the Civil Rights Act of 1964, Title VII, from requiring a high school education or passing of a standardized general intelligence test as a condition of employment in or transfer to jobs when (a) neither standard is shown to be significantly related to successful job performance, (b) both requirements operate to disqualify Negroes at a substantially higher rate than white applicants, and (c) the jobs in question formerly had been filled only by white employees as part of a long-standing practice of giving preference to whites.

Congress provided, in Title VII of the Civil Rights Act of 1964, for class actions for enforcement of provisions of the Act and this proceeding was brought by a group of incumbent Negro employees against Duke Power Company. All the petitioners are employed at the Company's Dan River Steam Station, a power generating facility located at Draper, North Carolina. At the time this action was instituted, the Company had 95 employees at the Dan River Station, 14 of whom were Negroes; 13 of these are petitioners here.

The District Court found that prior to July 2, 1965, the effective date of the Civil Rights Act of 1964, the Company openly discriminated on the basis of race in the hiring and assigning of employees at its Dan River plant. The plant was organized into five operating departments: (1) Labor, (2) Coal Handling, (3) Operations, (4) Maintenance, and (5) Laboratory and Test. Negroes were employed only in the Labor Department where the highest paying jobs paid less than the lowest paying jobs in the other four "operating" departments in which only whites were employed. Promotions were normally made within each department on the basis of job seniority.

Transferees into a department usually began in the lowest position.

In 1955 the Company instituted a policy of requiring a high school education for initial assignment to any department except Labor, and for transfer from the Coal Handling to any "inside" department (Operations, Maintenance, or Laboratory). When the Company abandoned its policy of restricting Negroes to the Labor Department in 1965, completion of high school also was made a prerequisite to transfer from Labor to any other department. From the time the high school requirement was instituted to the time of trial, however, white employees hired before the time of the high school requirement continued to perform satisfactorily and achieve promotions in the "operating" departments. Findings on this score are not challenged.

The Company added a further requirement for new employees on July 2, 1965, the date on which Title VII became effective. To qualify for placement in any but the Labor Department it became necessary to register satisfactory scores on two professionally prepared aptitude tests, as well as to have a high school education. Completion of high school alone continued to render employees eligible for transfer to the four desirable departments from which Negroes had been excluded if the incumbent had been employed prior to the time of the new requirement. In September 1965 the Company began to permit incumbent employees who lacked a high school education to qualify for transfer from Labor or Coal Handling to an "inside" job by passing two tests—the Wonderlic Personnel Test, which purports to measure general intelligence, and the Bennett Mechanical Comprehension Test. Neither was directed or intended to measure the ability to learn to perform a particular job or category of jobs. The requisite scores

continued

used for both initial hiring and transfer approximated the national median for high school graduates.*

The District Court had found that while the Company previously followed a policy of overt racial discrimination in a period prior to the Act, such conduct had ceased. The District Court also concluded that Title VII was intended to be prospective only and, consequently, the impact of prior inequities was beyond the reach of corrective action authorized by the Act.

The Court of Appeals was confronted with a question of first impression, as are we, concerning the meaning of Title VII. After careful analysis a majority of that court concluded that a subjective test of the employer's intent should govern, particularly in a close case, and that in this case there was no showing of a discriminatory purpose in the adoption of a diploma and test requirements. On this basis, the Court of Appeals concluded there was no violation of the Act.

The Court of Appeals reversed the District Court in part, rejecting the holding that residual discrimination arising from prior employment practices was insulated from remedial action. The Court of Appeals noted, however, that the District Court was correct in its conclusion that there was no finding of a racial purpose or invidious intent in the adoption of a high school diploma requirement or general intelligence test and that these standards had been applied fairly to whites and Negroes alike. It held that, in the absence of a discriminatory purpose, use of such requirements was permitted by the Act. In doing so, the Court of Appeals rejected the claim that because these two requirements operated to render ineligible a markedly disproportionate number of Negroes, they were unlawful under Title VII unless shown to be job-related. We granted the writ on these claims.

The objective of Congress in the enactment of Title VII is plain from the language of the statute. It was to achieve equality of employment opportunities and remove barriers that have operated in the past to favor an identifiable group of white employees over other employees. Under the Act, practices, procedures, or tests neutral on their face, and even neutral in terms of intent, cannot be maintained if they operate to "freeze" the status quo of prior discriminatory employment practices.

The Court of Appeals' opinion, and the partial dissent, agreed that, on the record in the present case,

"whites register far better on the Company's alternative requirements" than Negroes.** This consequence would appear to be directly traceable to race. Basic intelligence must have the means of articulation to manifest itself fairly in a testing process. Because they are Negroes, petitioners have long received inferior education in segregated schools and this Court expressly recognizes the differences in *Gaston County v. United States*, 395 U.S. 285 (1969). There, because of the inferior education received by Negroes in North Carolina, this Court barred the institution of a literacy test for voter registration on the ground that the test would abridge the right to vote indirectly on account of race. Congress did not intend by Title VII, however, to guarantee a job to every person regardless of qualifications. In short, the Act does not command that any person be hired simply because he was formerly the subject of discrimination, or because he is a member of a minority group. Discriminatory preference for any group, minority or majority, is precisely and only what Congress has proscribed. What is required by Congress is the removal of artificial, arbitrary, and unnecessary barriers to employment when the barriers operate invidiously to discriminate on the basis of racial or other impermissible classification.

Congress has now provided that tests or criteria for employment or promotion may not provide equality of opportunity merely in the sense of the fabled offer of milk to the stork and the fox. On the contrary, Congress has now required that the posture and condition of the jobseeker be taken into account. It has—to resort again to the fable—provided that the vessel in which the milk is proffered be one all seekers can use. The Act proscribes not only overt discrimination but also practices that are fair in form, but discriminatory in operation. The touch-stone is business necessity. If an employment practice which operates to exclude Negroes cannot be shown to be related to job performance, the practice is prohibited.

On the record before us, neither the high school completion requirement nor the general intelligence

---

* The test standards are thus more stringent than the high school requirement since they would screen out approximately half of all high school graduates.

** In North Carolina, 1960 census statistics show that while 34 percent of white males had completed high school, only 12 percent of Negro males had done so. U.S. Bureau of the Census of Population: 1960, Vol. 1, Characteristics of the Population, Part 35, Table 47.

Similarly, with respect to standardized tests, the EEOC in one case found that use of a battery of tests, including the Wonderlic and Bennett tests used by the Company in the instant case, resulted in 58 percent of whites passing the tests, as compared with only 6 percent of the blacks.

continued

test is shown to bear a demonstrable relationship to successful performance of the jobs for which it was used. Both were adopted, as the Court of Appeals noted, without meaningful study of their relationship to job-performance ability. Rather, a vice president of the Company testified, the requirements were instituted on the Company's judgment that they generally would improve the overall quality of the work force.

The evidence, however, shows that employees who have not completed high school or taken the tests have continued to perform satisfactorily and make progress in departments for which the high school and test criteria are now used. The promotion record of present employees who would not be able to meet the new criteria thus suggests the possibility that the requirements may not be needed even for the limited purpose of preserving the avowed policy of advancement within the Company. In the context of this case, it is unnecessary to reach the question whether testing requirements that take into account capability for the next succeeding position or related future promotion might be utilized upon a showing that such long-range requirements fulfill a genuine business need. In the present case the Company has made no such showing.

The Court of Appeals held that the Company had adopted the diploma and test requirements without any "intention to discriminate against Negro employees." We do not suggest that either the District Court or the Court of Appeals erred in examining the employer's intent; but good intent or absence of discriminatory intent does not redeem employment procedures or testing mechanisms that operate as "built-in headwinds" for minority groups and are unrelated to measuring job capability.

The Company's lack of discriminatory intent is suggested by special efforts to help the under-educated employees through Company financing of two-thirds the cost of tuition for high school training. But Congress directed the thrust of the Act to the *consequences* of employment practices, not simply the motivation. More than that, Congress has placed on the employer the burden of showing that any given requirement must have a manifest relationship to the employment in question.

The facts of this case demonstrate the inadequacy of broad and general testing devices as well as the infirmity of using diplomas or degrees as fixed measures of capability. History is filled with examples of men and women who rendered highly effective performance without the conventional badges of accomplishment in terms of certificates, diplomas, or degrees. Diplomas and tests are useful servants, but Congress has mandated the commonsense proposition that they are not to become masters of reality.

The Company contends that its general intelligence tests are specifically permitted by Section 703(h) of the Act. That section authorizes the use of "any professionally developed ability test" that is not "designed, intended *or used* to discriminate because of race...." (Emphasis added.)

The Equal Employment Opportunity Commission, having enforcement responsibility, has issued guidelines interpreting Section 703(h) to permit only the use of job-related tests. The administrative interpretation of the Act by the enforcing agency is entitled to great deference. See *e.g., United States v. City of Chicago*, 400 U.S. 8 (1970).... Since the Act and its legislative history support the Commission's construction, this affords good reason to treat the guidelines as expressing the will of Congress....

Nothing in the Act precludes the use of testing or measuring procedures, obviously they are useful. What Congress has forbidden is giving these devices and mechanisms controlling force unless they are demonstrably a reasonable measure of job performance. Congress has not commanded that the less qualified be preferred over the better qualified simply because of minority origins. Far from disparaging job qualifications as such, Congress has made such qualifications the controlling factor, so that race, religion, nationality, and sex become irrelevant. What Congress has commanded is that any tests used must measure the person for the job and not the person in the abstract.

The judgment of the Court of Appeals is, as to that portion of the judgment appealed from, reversed.

Case Questions

1. What is the question before the Supreme Court?
2. What was the objective of Congress in the enactment of Title VII?
3. Would the Court order the case against the employer to be dismissed if it found that the employer had adopted the diploma and test requirements without any intention to discriminate against minority employees?
4. As a result of the *Griggs* decision, may employers insist that both minority and white job applicants meet the applicable job qualifications by the use of testing or measuring procedures?

CASE 12.3	UNITED STATES V. VILLAGES OF ELMWOOD PARK AND MELROSE PARK
	U.S. DISTRICT COURT, ILLINOIS, 43 FEP 995 (1987).

[These actions were filed by the United States in December 1985, alleging a pattern or practice of unlawful discrimination in employment against black persons by the villages of Elmwood Park and Melrose Park in violation of Title VII of the Civil Rights Act of 1964. The United States moved for summary judgment on the issues of liability and prospective relief. The villages of Elmwood Park and Melrose Park are near the western boundary of the city of Chicago and are located within Cook County. According to the 1980 census, the labor force for Cook County is 20.7 percent black and for the Chicago standard metropolitan statistical area, it is 16.2 percent black. No blacks live in Elmwood Park, and 24 blacks live in Melrose Park. Both villages have a residency requirement of at least three years for police and firefighter applicants. The purposes of the requirement were said to be to "help its own" in granting employment opportunities and to maintain pride in the community through hiring individuals who live there. Most recruiting is done on a word-of-mouth basis.]

MARSHALL, D. J....

... In *Griggs v. Duke Power Co.*, 401 U.S. 424, 431 (1971) the Supreme Court ruled that Title VII of the Civil Rights Act of 1964, as amended, "proscribes not only overt discrimination, but also practices that are fair in form, but discriminatory in operation." Thus, employment practices that are shown to have a discriminatory impact on a group protected under Title VII, notwithstanding an absence of discriminatory intent, are prohibited unless shown to have a "manifest relationship to the employment in question." *Id.* at 432.

As the Court went on to say in *Griggs*, "Good intent or absence of discriminatory intent does not redeem employment practices ... which operate as 'built-in headwinds' for minority groups and are unrelated to measuring job capability." ...

In this case, the undisputed facts show that the practices of Elmwood Park and Melrose Park have had an overwhelmingly discriminatory impact. Elmwood Park has no black persons in its resident civilian labor force. Melrose Park has 24 out of 11,000 persons. Their durational residence requirements for police officer and firefighter applicants exclude all black persons residing in Cook County and the metropolitan statistical area from

employment in those categories in Elmwood Park and Melrose Park. The "philosophy" of the defendants to favor resident applicants over non-resident applicants for all other positions similarly disfavors all black persons in [the] labor market from employment. These practices are precisely the kind of "artificial, arbitrary and unnecessary barriers" which are "unrelated to measuring job capability" that Congress prohibited in enacting Title VII. *Griggs v. Duke Power Co.*, supra, at 431, 432. The effect of these durational residency requirements and the "philosophy" of favoring resident applicants over non-resident applicants reduces the proportion of blacks in the relevant labor force from approximately 13% and 18% (the percentages of black persons employed privately in the communities) to zero. Thus, all black persons are effectively barred from consideration for employment by the defendants. Unless these practices are necessary to the efficient operation of the defendants, they are unlawful. None of the reasons advanced by the defendants validate the requirements. Both defendants seek to help "our own." But helping "our own" only exacerbates the situation when all of "our own" are white. *Local 53 Asbestos Workers v. Vogler*, 407 F.2d 1047 (5th Cir. 1969).

"Pride in the community" is advanced as a reason. Perhaps there is a modicum of justification which requires residency for incumbent employees, i.e., after employment is effected, but we are at a loss to comprehend community pride as a valid condition precedent to employment. We note that there is no claim that a resident could perform the job more efficiently.

In addition to their use of durational residence requirements for police and firefighter applicants and their preferences for residence for all other village jobs, the defendants use "word-of-mouth" as the sole method of recruiting applicants for municipal vacancies. This is an additional barrier to black employment. It appears that there are no blacks living in Elmwood Park and only a handful in Melrose Park. In these circumstances, local networking will not convey information of job opportunities to non-whites. A word-of-mouth recruitment system limits information about job openings to the friends and relatives of incumbent employees and given the all-white nature of the defendants' work forces, disproportionately

continued

deprives qualified black applicants of the information they need to apply for village jobs.

In short, the employment requirements and techniques used by the defendant Villages have had the effect of excluding all blacks from consideration for employment and actual employment in the two communities. The justifications advanced by defendants for these patently discriminatory employment practices are no justification at all. Indeed, if anything, they call into question the good faith of the defendants. The United States of America is entitled to summary judgment under the disparate impact analysis on the issues of liability and prospective relief....

It is so ordered.

Case Questions

1. Because of the residency requirements, what percentage of blacks were effectively barred from consideration for employment by the villages?
2. Assess the fairness of the villages' recruiting procedures.
3. Did the court agree that the villages had presented valid justification for their residency requirements?

SECTION 105: RELIGION

Under Section 701(j), employers have a duty to accommodate their employees' or prospective employees' religious practices. Under Section 702, religious organizations are exempt from Title VII prohibitions against discrimination on the basis of religion.

EMPLOYER'S DUTY TO ACCOMMODATE

The 1972 amendments added to Title VII a definition of **religion** in Section 701(j), which provides:

> The term "religion" includes all aspects of religious observance and practice, as well as belief, unless an employer demonstrates that he is unable to reasonably accommodate to an employee's or prospective employee's religious observance or practice without undue hardship on the conduct of the employer's business.

RELIGIOUS OBSERVANCE DAYS.   Most cases involving allegations of religious discrimination revolve around the determination of whether an employer has made reasonable efforts to accommodate its employees' religious beliefs. The 1972 definition includes all aspects of religious observance, practice, and belief so as to require employers to make reasonable accommodations for employees whose religion may include observances, practices, and beliefs, such as Friday evening and Saturday religious observances, that differ from the employer's requirements regarding schedules or other business-related employment conditions. Failure to make accommodations is unlawful unless an employer can demonstrate that it cannot reasonably accommodate such beliefs, practices, or observances without undue hardship in the conduct of its business. The Supreme Court considered such an issue in *Trans World Airlines, Inc. v. Hardison*.[32] The Court of Appeals for the Eighth Circuit had ruled that TWA had not satisfied its duty to accommodate Hardison's religious views, which kept him from working Saturdays. Specifically, the court of appeals found that TWA could have permitted Hardison to work a four-day week despite the

---

[32] 432 U.S. 63 (1977).

fact that this would have caused shop functions to suffer unless TWA had breached its seniority system or incurred overtime expense by keeping someone on the job. The Supreme Court reversed, holding that TWA made reasonable efforts to accommodate Hardison, and to force it to comply with the court of appeals ruling would have created an undue hardship on TWA. Under *Hardison*, the employer and union need not violate a seniority provision of a valid collective bargaining agreement, the employer has no obligation to impose undesirable shifts on nonreligious employees, and the employer has no obligation to call in substitute workers if such accommodation would require more than *de minimis* cost.

Where an employer is called upon to make reasonable accommodations for the religious practice of an employee, both the employer and the employee may make proposals to achieve this accommodation. In *Ansonia Board of Education v. Philbrick*,[33] Ronald Philbrick, a teacher, sued his school board because the school board's accommodation to his need to take six days off each school year for the holy days of his religion was to allow him to take three paid religious observance days granted him under the teachers' collective bargaining contract and three unpaid leaves. He had proposed as the appropriate accommodation that he take the three paid religious leave days plus three paid personal business leave days or that he pay the cost of a substitute teacher for the three days at $30 per day, thus enabling him to receive his regular pay of $130 for each of these days. The Second Circuit agreed with Philbrick, holding that Title VII requires the employer to accept the employee's proposal unless it causes undue hardship to the employer's business. The Supreme Court held that the Second Circuit was in error and that the employer meets its obligation under Section 701(j) when it demonstrates that it has offered a reasonable accommodation to the employee, which removes the conflict between the employment requirement and the religious practices of the individual. The extent of the undue hardship to the employer's business is an issue only when the employer claims it is unable to offer a reasonable accommodation without hardship.[34]

RELIGIOUS BEHAVIOR AT WORK. The *Trans World Airlines, Inc. v. Hardison* and the *Philbrick* cases dealt with employees' refusal to work on certain days due to religious observance. In *Brown v. Polk County*, the U.S. Court of Appeals for the Eighth Circuit, sitting *en banc*, dealt with a public employee's religious behavior at work under Title VII and the First Amendment.[35] Isaiah Brown asserted that his First Amendment right to the free exercise of his religion was violated when the

---

[33] 42 FEP 359 (1986).

[34] In *Sturgill v. UPS Inc.*, 572 F.3d 1024 (8th Cir. 2008), a Seventh-day Adventist was successful in his Title VII lawsuit against UPS based on religious discrimination regarding his termination after he refused to complete his route on December 17, 2004, because working past sundown on a Friday violated his religious beliefs. In *EEOC v. Firestone Fibers and Textiles Co.*, 515 F.3d 307 (4th Cir. 2008), David Wise, a member of the Living Church of God, which prohibits working from sundown Friday to sundown Saturday, was unsuccessful in his lawsuit against his employer, alleging failure to accommodate his religious observance in violation of Title VII. While the employer provided various options to Wise, it could not reasonably accommodate all of the time needed to give him time off each week to avoid violation of the employer's attendance policy. Allowing excessive unpaid leave time would deprive other employees of their deserved shift preferences.

[35] 61 F.3d 650 (8th Cir. 1995).

county administrator ordered him to "cease any activities that could be considered to be religious proselytizing, witnessing, or counseling" while he was on the job. In a 6-5 decision returning Mr. Brown to work with back pay, the court majority stated:

> We may concede for the sake of argument that Polk County has a legal right to ensure that its workplace is free from religious activity that harasses or intimidates. But any interference with religious activity that the exercise of that right entails must be reasonably related to the exercise of that right and must be narrowly tailored to its achievement. See e.g., *Thomas v. Review Board*, 450 U.S. 707, 718, ... (1981). Here, there was not the least attempt to confine the prohibition to harassment or intimidating speech. Instead, Polk County baldly directed Mr. Brown to "cease any activities that *could be considered* to be religious proselytizing, witnessing, or counseling" (emphasis supplied). That order exhibited a hostility to religion that our constitution simply prohibits. It would seem to require no argument that to forbid speech "that could be considered" religious is not narrowly tailored to the aim of prohibiting harassment, although it is certainly capable of doing that. If Mr. Brown asked someone to attend his church, for instance, we suppose that "could be considered" proselytizing, but its prohibition runs afoul of the free exercise clause. Similarly, a statement to the effect that one's religion was important in one's life "could be considered" witnessing, yet for the government to forbid it would be unconstitutional.

The court held that an employer must accommodate employees' religious activities on the job to the extent the activities do not create undue hardship to the public employer by disrupting the work environment and forcing the employer to sustain real, nonhypothetical costs.

To establish a claim for religious discrimination, the plaintiff must establish a *prima facie* case by showing that he or she (1) has a bona fide religious belief that conflicts with an employment requirement, (2) informed the employer of such conflict, and (3) suffered an adverse employment action. If the plaintiff establishes those elements, the burden shifts to the employer to offer a legitimate, nondiscriminatory reason for the adverse employment action. Thereafter, the burden shifts back to the plaintiff to show that the reason offered by the employer is pretextual.[36]

BODY ART WORK RULES AND RELIGIOUS BELIEFS. In *Cloutier v. Costco*, the First Circuit Court of Appeals dealt with an employee's claim that her employer's ban on body art was a form of religious discrimination.[37] Kimberly Cloutier was a member of the Church of Body Modification. Costco grooming policy prohibited any "visible facial or tongue jewelry" in order to present a professional image to its customers. Ms. Cloutier wore an eyebrow ring as a religious practice. Costco offered to return her to work if she wore a Band-Aid or plastic retainer over the jewelry, but Ms. Cloutier said that such would violate her religious beliefs. EEOC's 1980 Guidelines broadly defines religion "to include moral or ethical beliefs as to what is right and wrong which are sincerely held with the strength of

---

[36] See *Turner v. Gonzales*, 424 F.3d 688, 694 (8th Cir. 2005).

[37] 390 F.3d 126 (1st Cir. 2004).

traditional religious views."[38] The Guidelines do not limit religion to theistic practices or to beliefs professed by organized religions.[39] Since Cloutier would not accept an accommodation short of exemption, the Court of Appeals determined that it was an undue hardship for the employer because an exemption would negatively impact the company's professionalism. However, in *EEOC v. Red Robin Gourmet Burgers, Inc.,*[40] the federal district court held that the employer failed to provide sufficient evidence of undue hardship in accommodating an exemption for an employee's religious tattoos surrounding his wrists that were in violation of the employer's grooming policy. The court looked for actual proof of the restaurant's assertion that the tattoos contravened the company's "family-oriented image," such as customer complaints or other evidence, as opposed to the mere assertion.

RELIGIOUS ORGANIZATION EXEMPTION

Section 702 of Title VII permits religious societies to grant hiring preferences in favor of members of their religion. The *Feldstein v. Christian Science Monitor* decision, presented in this section, is an example of the application of Section 702. Section 702 provides in pertinent part:

> This title shall not apply ... to a religious corporation, association, educational institution, or society with respect to the employment of individuals of a particular religion to perform work connected with the carrying on by such corporation, association, educational institution, or society of its activities.

In *Mormon Church v. Amos*, presented in this section, the Supreme Court upheld the constitutionality of the Section 702 exemption, holding that Section 702 was not in violation of the Establishment Clause of the First Amendment. Thus, the Mormon Church was allowed to terminate a building engineer who had worked at its nonprofit gymnasium for 16 years because he failed to maintain his qualifications for church membership. The decision to terminate was made on the basis of religion by the religious organization and was thus exempted from the Title VII prohibition against religious discrimination.

Section 703(e)(2) provides an exemption for educational institutions to hire employees of a particular religion if the institution is owned, controlled, or managed by a particular religious society. The exemption is a broad one and is not restricted to the religious activities of the institution.

---

[38] C.F.R. §§ 1605.1 (1980).

[39] The EEOC's definition of religion was derived from early Selective Service cases that moved beyond institutional religions and theistic belief structures in handling exemptions to the draft and military service. See *Welsh v. U.S.*, 398 U.S. 333, 343–44 (1970), which allows for expansion of belief systems to include nonreligious ethical or moral codes.

[40] 2005 U.S. Dist LEXIS 36219 (W.D. March 2005).

| CASE 12.4 | FELDSTEIN V. CHRISTIAN SCIENCE MONITOR
U.S. DISTRICT COURT, 30 FEP 1842 (E.D. MASS. 1983). |

[In January 1979, Mark Feldstein inquired at the *Christian Science Monitor* whether there would be job openings on its news reporting staff upon his graduation from college in June. At that time, Feldstein was a college student interested in pursuing a career in journalism. On making his inquiry, Feldstein was instructed to contact the personnel department of the church, where he was asked if he was a member of the Christian Science church. He indicated that he was not and was informed that he would stand little, if any, chance of becoming employed by the *Monitor* as a reporter, as only Christian Scientists were hired except in the rare circumstance that no qualified member of the church was available. Feldstein nevertheless requested and obtained an employment application for a reporter's position. The employment application, used for positions throughout the church, contained several questions relating to religious practice, including "Are you ... a member of the Mother Church? A branch Church member? Class taught?"; "Are you free from the use of liquor, tobacco, drugs, medicine?"; "Do you subscribe to the Christian Science periodicals?"; and "Are you a daily student of the lesson-sermon?" Inquiries were also directed to the applicant's present and past religious affiliation. References were sought from "two Christian Scientists who can comment on your character and your practice of Christian Science." The application closed with the following statement:

> The First Church of Christ, Scientist, may by law apply the test of religious qualifications to its employment policies. Those who meet this requirement and are otherwise qualified will be hired, promoted, and transferred without regard to their race, national origin, sex, color, or age.

Feldstein filed his application with the church in March 1979, together with a copy of his curriculum vitae, letters of recommendation, and a portfolio of newspaper articles that he had written. In April, he was notified by a church personnel representative that his application for employment as a reporter had been rejected. Feldstein alleged that his application for employment was not given a full consideration because he was not a Christian Scientist.]

MAZZONE, D. J....

Title VII of the Civil Rights Act of 1964 was originally passed as an expression of Congress' laudable intention to eliminate all forms of unjustified discrimination in employment, whether such discrimination be based on race, color, religion, sex, or national origin. This posed a sharp question under the Establishment Clause of the First Amendment to the United States Constitution as to whether Congress could properly regulate the employment practices, and specifically the preference of co-religionists, of religious organizations in matters related to their religious activities. As a result, the original Title VII contained an exemption from the operation of Title VII's proscriptions with respect to the employment of co-religionists to perform work related to the employer's religious activity. Church-affiliated educational institutions were also permitted to hire on the basis of religion.

In 1972, a number of amendments to Title VII were proposed in an effort to alter and expand the existing exemption for religious organizations....

... Title VII was amended to eliminate the qualification that only religious activities of religious organizations would be exempt from suit based on religious discrimination. Section 702 provides, as a result of the 1972 amendment:

> This subchapter shall not apply ... to a religious corporation, association, educational institution, or society with respect to the employment of individuals of a particular religion to perform work connected with the carrying on by such corporation, association, educational institution or society of its activities.

It is clear that the disposition of this matter turns on two key issues: first, whether the Monitor is a religious activity of a religious organization and therefore within the limited exemption provided by Congress in the Civil Rights Act of 1964; and second, if it is not a religious activity of a religious organization, whether the 1972 amendment to Title VII excluding from the scope of Title VII *all* activities of whatever nature of a religious organization is constitutional in light of the requirements of the Free Exercise and Establishment Clauses of the First Amendment.

It is self-evident, as well as uncontested, that the First Church of Christ, Scientist is a religious

continued

organization. The status of the Christian Science Publishing Society and of the Monitor is less clear. The plaintiff has argued that the Monitor is a highly regarded and impartial newspaper carrying news stories, articles, features, columns, and editorials that are secular in nature and content. The defendants take exception to this characterization of the Monitor and make reference to a number of facts in support of their position that the newspaper is a religious activity of a religious organization and therefore exempt from regulation under Title VII....

The deed of trust of the Publishing Society declares as its purpose "more effectually promoting and extending the religion of Christian Science."...

The plaintiff does not contest that the Christian Science Church is intimately involved with the management, the day-to-day operations, and the financial affairs of the Monitor. Paragraph 5 of his complaint states in part:

> Defendant First Church of Christ, Scientist is a nonincorporated religious association.... Control of the Church is vested in a Board of Directors who serve in accordance with terms set out in the Church Manual. Pursuant to the Church Manual, the Board has ultimate authority for and responsibility over the policy and operations of the Monitor....

... A religious activity of a religious organization does not lose that special status merely because it holds some interest for persons not members of the faith, or occupies a position of respect in the secular world at large. Though the "wall between church and state" is not absolute, I am nevertheless unwilling to involve the federal court in what is ultimately an internal administrative matter of a religious activity.

While fully crediting the plaintiff's statements that the Monitor holds itself out as an objective and unbiased reporter of world news and events, I cannot ignore the close and significant relationship existing between the Christian Science Church, the Publishing Society and the Monitor; or the declared purpose, both at the time of its founding and until the present, of the Monitor to promulgate and advance the tenets of Christian Science. I find the conclusion inescapable that the Monitor is itself a religious activity of a religious organization, albeit one with a recognized position and an established reputation in the secular community.

Having concluded that the Monitor is a religious activity of a religious organization, I find that the constitutionality of that part of Section 702 of Title VII, 42 U.S.C. § 2000e-1, that extends the exemption provided for religious organizations, to *all* their activities, secular and religious, is simply not here implicated.

Because I find that the Monitor is a religious activity of a religious organization, I find that it is permissible for the Monitor to apply a test of religious affiliation to candidates for employment. Therefore, I find as a matter of law that the defendants have not committed an unlawful employment practice under the Civil Rights Act of 1964. The defendants' motion for summary judgment is granted and the complaint is dismissed.

So ordered.

Case Questions

1. Does the *Christian Science Monitor* violate Title VII by giving preference to Christian Scientists when hiring reporters for the newspaper?
2. Does Section 702 of Title VII allow religious societies to hire coreligionists for secular activities as opposed to religious activities?

CASE 12.5 | MORMON CHURCH V. AMOS
SUPREME COURT OF THE UNITED STATES, 483 U.S. 327 (1987).

[Mayson worked for 16 years as a building engineer at the Mormon Church's Deseret Gymnasium in Salt Lake City. He was discharged from this job because he failed to qualify for a "temple recommend," which is issued only to individuals observing the church's standards, such as regular church attendance; tithing; and abstinence from coffee, alcohol, and tobacco. A class action suit was brought on behalf of Mayson, Amos, and others claiming that Section 702 was in violation of the Establishment Clause of the First Amendment when construed to allow religious employers to discriminate on religious grounds in hiring and granting tenure

continued

for nonreligious jobs. The district court held that Section 702 was unconstitutional as applied to secular activities, and it reinstated Mayson with back pay.]

WHITE, J....

This Court has long recognized that the government may (and sometimes must) accommodate religious practices and that it may do so without violating the Establishment Clause. It is well established, too, that "[t]he limits of permissible state accommodation to religion are by no means co-extensive with the noninterference mandated by the Free Exercise Clause." There is ample room under the Establishment Clause for "benevolent neutrality which will permit religious exercise to exist without sponsorship and without interference." At some point, accommodation may devolve into "an unlawful fostering of religion," but this is not such a case, in our view....

After a detailed examination of the legislative history of the 1972 amendment, the District Court concluded that Congress' purpose was to minimize governmental "interfer[ence] with the decision-making process in religions." We agree with the District Court that this purpose does not violate the Establishment Clause....

Appellees argue that § 702 offends equal protection principles by giving less protection to the employees of religious employers than to the employees of secular employers.... To dispose of appellees' Equal Protection argument, it suffices to hold—as we now do—that as applied to the nonprofit activities of religious employers, § 702 is rationally related to the legitimate purpose of alleviating significant governmental interference with the ability of religious organizations to define and carry out their religious missions.

It cannot be seriously contended that § 702 impermissibly entangles church and state; the statute effectuates a more complete separation of the two and avoids the kind of intrusive inquiry into religious belief that the District Court engaged in in this case....

The judgment of the District Court is reversed, and the case is remanded for further proceedings consistent with this opinion.

It is so ordered.

Case Questions

1. Why was Mayson fired from his job?
2. Does Section 702 allow a religious organization to refuse to hire or to continue in employment individuals who are not members of the religious organization where the positions involved are nonreligious jobs?
3. Why did Congress enact Section 702?

SECTION 106: SEX

The amendment adding the word "sex" to Section 703 of Title VII of the Civil Rights Act was adopted one day before the House passed the Act. It was added without legislative hearings and with little debate.[41] As a result, the courts do not have the benefit of a fully developed legislative history to be referred to in interpreting cases relating to sex discrimination. Courts therefore apply the plain and ordinary meaning of the word "sex," and under such application, employers who discriminate against female or male employees because of their sex are held to be in violation of Title VII.

HEIGHT, WEIGHT, AND PHYSICAL ABILITY REQUIREMENTS

Under the *Griggs v. Duke Power* decision reported in a previous section, an employer must be ready to demonstrate that criteria used to make an employment decision that has a disparate impact on women, such as minimum height and

---

[41] The amendment adding the word *sex* was offered by Congressman Howard Smith of Virginia, then chairman of the Rules Committee, who was an opponent of Title VII. The amendment was adopted by a majority, most of whom later voted against Title VII. Apparently it was thought that the amendment adding the word *sex* might kill the entire legislation.

weight requirements, are in fact job-related. All candidates for a position requiring physical strength must be given an opportunity to demonstrate their capability to perform the work. Women cannot be precluded from consideration just because they have not traditionally performed such work. In *Boyd v. Ozark Airlines*,[42] a woman contended that the airline's minimum height requirement for pilots discriminated against her on the basis of sex. The evidence established that the airline's 5-foot-7-inch minimum height requirement had a disparate impact on women. While the court agreed that minimum height requirements for the position of pilot are valid, it held that the airline's requirements were excessive and ordered the airline's height requirements lowered to 5 feet 5 inches.

PREGNANCY-RELATED BENEFITS AND JOB PROTECTION

Title VII arguments concerning the matters of disability due to pregnancy and loss of competitive seniority due to pregnancy have been considered by the U.S. Supreme Court. In the landmark case of *General Electric v. Gilbert*,[43] the Supreme Court held that a disability plan that did not cover pregnancy was not violative of Title VII absent any indication that the exclusion of pregnancy benefits was a pretext for discriminating against women. However, in *Nashville Gas v. Satty*,[44] the Court held that a company policy that deprived female workers of their competitive seniority upon their return from maternity leave was violative of Title VII. In distinguishing *General Electric v. Gilbert*, the Court stated: "Here, by comparison, the [employer] has not merely refused to extend to women a benefit that men cannot and do not receive, but has imposed on women a substantial burden that men need not suffer."

In 1978, Title VII was amended by the Pregnancy Discrimination Act (PDA), which added to Section 701 a new subsection (k) clarification that the prohibitions against sex discrimination in the Act include discrimination in employment based on pregnancy, childbirth, or related medical conditions. The intent of the amendment was to reverse the *Gilbert* decision, which held that disability plans that exclude pregnancy do not discriminate on the basis of sex in violation of the Act. The amendment prevents employers from treating pregnancy, childbirth, and related medical conditions in a manner different from the treatment of other disabilities. Thus, women disabled due to pregnancy, childbirth, or other related medical conditions must be provided with the same benefits as other disabled workers. This includes temporary and long-term disability insurance, sick leave, and other forms of employee benefit programs. An employer who does not provide disability benefits or paid sick leave to other employees is not required to provide them for pregnant workers. Under the 1978 law, benefits do not have to be provided for abortion except where it is necessary to preserve the life of the mother or where medical complications have arisen from an abortion.[45]

---

[42] 419 F. Supp. 1061 (E.D. Mo. 1976).

[43] 429 U.S. 125 (1976).

[44] 434 U.S. 136 (1977).

[45] The Pregnancy Discrimination Act of 1978, Pub. L. 95-555 (1978).

In *Newport News Shipbuilding and Dry Dock Co. v. EEOC*,[46] the employer amended its health insurance plan after passage of the Pregnancy Discrimination Act of 1978 to provide for benefits for pregnancy-related conditions for its female employees, with the plan providing for less extensive benefits for the wives of male employees. The Supreme Court held that such a plan discriminated against married male employees as their benefits package was less than that provided to married female employees, which was contrary to the Pregnancy Discrimination Act. The dissent argued that the Pregnancy Discrimination Act plainly speaks of female employees affected by pregnancy and says nothing about spouses of male employees.

In addition to protecting women's rights to medical benefits related to pregnancy as set forth above, the PDA also protects women from termination or other adverse employment actions because of pregnancy. Thus, a catering manager who informs her employer that she will take a 12-week leave after childbirth, which would be during the busiest time of the year for the employer, and is subsequently fired by the employer for "customer complaints" and other asserted reasons may bring suit against the employer under the PDA. After establishing a *prima facie* case, and thereafter the employer showing its reasons for the termination, the plaintiff may show the employer's reasons are a pretext, or "phony reasons," pointing out, for example, that when she asked for documentation of the customer complaints, her supervisor said that he "did not want to review that shit."[47] In *Pruett v. Krause Gentile Corp.*,[48] two pregnant clerks working at a "Kum & Go" convenience store–gas station, who had been fired by the company and brought a PDA lawsuit, were able to survive a motion for summary judgment by showing the employer's reason for the terminations was a pretext. However, a genuine issue of material fact as to whether the pregnancies were considered in the decision to terminate must still be considered by the court.

In *Hall v. Nalco Co.*, the Seventh Circuit Court of Appeals reversed the trial court and concluded that Cheryl Hall presented a cognizable claim for sex discrimination under Title VII. Hall was terminated not for the gender-neutral condition of infertility as perceived by the trial court judge, but rather for the gender-specific quality of childbearing capacity involving in vitro fertilization, at which the Pregnancy Discrimination Amendments to Title VII were aimed.[49]

PENSION-RELATED BENEFITS

In the case of pension plans, employers have sometimes required their female employees to pay more into pension plan funds because, as a class, women outlive men and therefore receive benefits for a longer period of time. This practice was held to be in violation of Title VII by the Supreme Court in *City of Los Angeles v. Manhart*.[50] The Court reasoned that although the generalization that women live

---

[46] 462 U.S. 669 (1983).

[47] See *Newman v. Deer Path Inn*, 1999 U.S. Dist. LEXIS 19040.

[48] *Pruett v. Krause Gentile Corp.*, 226 F. Supp. 2d 983 (2002).

[49] 534 F.3d 644 (7th Cir. 2008).

[50] 435 U.S. 702 (1978).

longer than men was true, it was an insufficient reason for burdening those women to whom the generalization did not apply. Because it could not be known to whom the generalization did apply while an employee was alive, it could not be used to justify requiring larger payments from any female employee.

In *Arizona Annuity Plans v. Norris*,[51] the Supreme Court followed its *Manhart* ruling in holding that the pension annuity plans administered for employees of the state of Arizona, which pay a woman lower monthly retirement benefits than a man who has made the same contributions, were in violation of Title VII, constituting discrimination on the basis of sex.

GLASS CEILING

Because women and minorities continue to be underrepresented in management and decision-making positions in business, Congress, as part of Title II of the Civil Rights Act of 1991, set up a commission to identify the artificial barriers to the advancement of women and minorities in the workplace and to make recommendations for overcoming such barriers.[52] The Glass Ceiling Commission recommended that business and government take certain actions to break the glass ceiling. It recommended that in business, (1) all CEOs demonstrate commitment to workplace diversity, (2) all strategic business plans specify efforts to achieve diversity both at the senior management level and throughout the workforce, (3) all qualified individuals have an opportunity to compete based on ability and merit, (4) the organizations expand access to core areas of each business and establish formal mentoring programs to prepare minorities and women for senior positions, (5) the organizations provide formal training on company time, and (6) the organizations adopt policies that accommodate the balance between work and family responsibilities that impact career paths of all employees. The commission urged the government to (1) lead by example, (2) make certain that enforcement agencies have adequate resources to enforce laws, (3) improve data collection by government agencies, and (4) increase public exposure to diversity data.

DEVELOPING LAW REGARDING SEXUAL ORIENTATION AND TRANSSEXUALS

The EEOC and the courts have determined that the word **sex** as used in Title VII means a person's gender and not a person's sexual orientation.[53] In a 1992

---

[51] 463 U.S. 1073 (1983).

[52] Section 202 of the Civil Rights Act of 1991. The term *glass ceiling* was initially used to describe the apparently invisible barrier that has kept women from obtaining top jobs in management and relates to the continuing current situation where just 1 percent of our nation's CEOs are women. The Department of Labor has concluded that *glass ceiling* is best defined today as those artificial barriers based on attitudinal or organizational bias that prevent qualified individuals from advancing upward in their organization into management-level positions.

[53] See *Ulane v. Eastern Airlines, Inc.*, 642 F.2d 1081 (7th Cir. 1984). See also *Oiler v. Winn Dixie Stores, Inc.*, E.D. La. No 00-3114, Sept. 16, 2002, where a federal district court judge said that courts have uniformly held that Title VII does not prohibit discrimination based on sexual orientation, transvestism, transsexualism, or gender identity issues.

decision, *Dillon v. Frank*,[54] the U.S. Court of Appeals for the Sixth Circuit determined that a former postal employee who was taunted, ostracized, and physically beaten by coworkers because they believed he was a homosexual had no remedy under Title VII. The court pointed out that both criminal and tort law may protect individuals such as the former postal worker against such harassment. The court further indicated that Title VII is not all-inclusive, stating in part:

> We interpret Title VII to proscribe only specified discriminatory actions. What Title VII proscribes, although vitally important, is easily exceeded by what it does not. Employers or co-workers can still make the workplace unpleasant based on political belief ("damned Republican"), see *Reichman v. Bureau of Affirmative Action*, 536 F. Supp. 1149, 1176 (M.D. Pa. 1982) ("comments concerning the Arab-Israeli conflict and Menachem Begin were political opinions rather than disparagements of Judaism"); a co-worker's discussing sexual topics at work, see *Fair*, 742 F. Supp. at 155 ("petty, inappropriate remarks made by someone conducting himself in an improper and unprofessional manner" not sexual harassment); family antagonism ("damned Rockefeller"); college attended ("I'm a Harvardian, you Yalie"); eating practices ("how can you eat something that used to be alive"); rooting for particular sports teams ("the Dodgers are bums")....

In *Oncale v. Sundowner Offshore Services, Inc.*, presented in the following section, the Supreme Court concluded that sex discrimination consisting of same-sex harassment is actionable under Title VII. In *Schmedding v. Tromec Co.*,[55] the U.S. Court of Appeals for the Eighth Circuit reinstated a claim for sexual harassment under Title VII by a male employee who charged that male and female coworkers harassed him on the job with taunts concerning his presumed homosexuality. In order to have an actionable claim under Title VII, the plaintiff had to amend his complaint and delete the assertion that the harassment was based on "perceived sexual preference" and assert solely that the harassment was based on "sex," thus bringing his case within the *Oncale v. Sundowner Offshore Services, Inc.*, precedent.

In *Nichols v. Azteca Restaurant Enterprises, Inc.*,[56] an effeminate male was harassed by male coworkers, including being mocked for being "like a woman." In a 2-1 decision by the Ninth Circuit Court of Appeals finding employer responsibility under Title VII, the majority relied on the *Oncale* decision and the Supreme Court's *Price Waterhouse v. Hopkins*[57] decision, where an accounting firm was found to have violated Title VII by the denial of a partnership to the plaintiff because she was a forceful and aggressive woman who did not match sex (gender) stereotypes. Both the *Oncale* precedent and the "gender stereotyping discrimination" theory were subsequently used in *Rene v. MGM Grand Hotel, Inc.*,[58] where a butler sued the hotel for sexual harassment. The court reported the nature and extent of the harassment as follows:

> Rene provided extensive evidence that, over the course of a two-year period, his supervisor and several of his fellow butlers subjected him to a hostile work environment

---

[54] 952 F.2d 403 (6th Cir. 1992).

[55] 187 F.3d 862 (8th Cir. 1999).

[56] 256 F.3d 864 (9th Cir. 2001).

[57] 490 U.S. 642 (1989).

[58] 305 F.3d 1061 (9th Cir. 2002).

on almost a daily basis. The harassers' conduct included whistling and blowing kisses at Rene, calling him "sweetheart" and "muñeca" (Spanish for "doll"), telling crude jokes and giving sexually oriented "joke" gifts, ... On "more time than [Rene said he] could possibly count," the harassment involved offensive physical conduct of a sexual nature. Rene gave deposition testimony that he was caressed and hugged and that his coworkers would "touch [his] body like they would to a woman." On numerous occasions, he said, they grabbed him in the crotch and poked their fingers in his anus through his clothing. When asked what he believed was the motivation behind this harassing behavior, Rene responded that the behavior occurred because he is gay.

Relying on the *Oncale* precedent, the majority of the judges in this *en banc* review of the case determined that Rene suffered discrimination in comparison to other men; the offensive conduct was sexual; and it was also discriminatory. "That is precisely what Title VII forbids: 'discrimination ... because of ... sex,'" the majority opinion stated.

A concurring opinion relied on the gender stereotyping discrimination theory as follows:

> The similarities between *Nichols* and the present case are striking. In both cases, a male gay employee was "teased" or "mocked" by his male co-workers because he walked "like a woman." And in both cases, a male gay employee was referred to by his male co-workers in female terms—"she," "her," and "female whore" in *Nichols*; "sweet-heart" and "muñeca" ("doll") in the present case—to "remind [] [him] that he did not conform to their gender-based stereotypes." For the same reasons that we concluded in *Nichols* that "[the] rule that bars discrimination on the basis of sex stereotypes" set in *Price Waterhouse* "squarely applie[d] to preclude the harassment" at issue there, *Nichols*, 256 F.3d at 874–75, I conclude that this rule also squarely applies to preclude the identical harassment at issue here. Accordingly, this is a case of actionable gender stereotyping harassment.

Four dissenting judges believed that Rene's lawsuit was brought solely on the basis of his sexual orientation, which is not actionable under Title VII. The dissent stated in part:

> The degrading and humiliating treatment Rene describes is appalling and deeply disturbing. I agree with the eloquent words of the First Circuit: We hold no brief for harassment because of sexual orientation; it is a noxious practice, deserving of censure and opprobrium. But we are called upon here to construe a statute as glossed by the Supreme Court, not to make a moral judgment—and we regard it as settled law that, as drafted and authoritatively construed, Title VII does not proscribe harassment simply because of sexual orientation. (*Higgins*, 194 F.3d at 259).

It is clear that Title VII does not cover sexual orientation discrimination. However Title VII does provide protection for employees from same-sex harassment and there is developing acceptance of a gender stereotyping theory of discrimination under Title VII. Astute attorneys may often be able to marshal the facts of sexual orientation discrimination to fit the same-sex harassment or gender stereotyping theories. Indeed, a fact pattern similar to the 1992 *Dillon v. Frank* case may very well be remedied today under Title VII on the basis of these developing sexual harassment theories. While this area of the law is still unsettled and developing at this time, prudent and fair-minded employers should have a policy in place protecting employees from discrimination based on sexual orientation. Also, state and local laws prohibit employment discrimination on the basis of sexual orientation.[59]

For many years, it was uniformly held that Title VII's ban on sex discrimination in employment practices does not encompass discrimination against transsexuals. The decision of the U.S. Court of Appeals for the Eighth Circuit in *Sommers v. Budget Marketing, Inc.*, presented in this section, is a representative decision applicable in that judicial circuit. The *Sommers* decision contains a discussion of the meaning and application of the word *sex* as used in Title VII.[60] Recently, however, the Sixth Circuit determined that a transsexual claim is actionable pursuant to Title VII. The court explained its view in *Smith v. City of Salem, Ohio*[61] that, by definition, transsexuals are individuals who fail to conform to stereotypes about how those assigned a particular sex at birth should act, dress, and self-identify and accordingly such raises a claim of sex stereotyping pursuant to Title VII under *Price Waterhouse*, where the victim suffered discrimination for gender nonconformity.

CASE 12.6	AUDRA SOMMERS, A/K/A TIMOTHY K. CORNISH V. BUDGET MARKETING, INC. U.S. COURT OF APPEALS, 667 F.2D 748 (8TH CIR. 1982).

PER CURIAM....

Sommers claims to be "female with the anatomical body of a male."* Inasmuch as Sommers refers to

---

*A medical affidavit submitted by Sommers stated that a psychological female with anatomical features of a male is one type of transsexual but that transsexualism is not voluntarily assumed and is not a matter of sexual preference. A transsexual has been described as an individual who is mentally one sex but physically of the other, Annot., 63 A.L.R.3d 1199, n. 1 (1975), or as one born with the anatomical genitalia of one sex but whose self-identity is of the other sex. Annot., 78 A.L.R.3d 19, 54 (1977).

herself in the feminine gender, this court will likewise do so. As Audra Sommers, appellant was hired by Budget on April 22, 1980, to perform clerical duties. On April 24, 1980, Sommers's employment was terminated. Budget alleged Sommers was dismissed because she misrepresented herself as an anatomical female when she applied for the job. It further alleged that the misrepresentation led to a disruption of the company's work routine in that a number of female employees indicated they would quit if Sommers were permitted to use the restroom facilities assigned to

continued

---

[59] Some 19 states and the District of Columbia and over 130 localities have laws and ordinances protecting individuals from workplace sexual-orientation discrimination, including cities such as San Francisco, Berkeley, Chicago (Cook County), and Louisville. In *Quinn v. Nassau County Police Department*, 53 F. Supp.2d 347 (E.D.N.Y. 1999), the federal court in New York considered a long line of cases, all of which held that Title VII does not provide a remedy for a hostile environment created by taunts aimed at a plaintiff's homosexuality, including a post-*Oncale* decision, *Simonton v. Runyon*, 50 F. Supp 2d 159 (E.D.N.Y. 1999). The court decided however that *Simonton* was not controlling because it was a Title VII case, limited by the language of Title VII prohibiting discrimination against "any individual ... because of such individual's ... sex." In *Quinn*, the court decided to allow a jury's award of $300,000 in compensatory and punitive damages to stand in a case where a homosexual government employee working as a police officer was singled out for abuse in the workplace because of his homosexuality. The court pointed out that the case before it was not a Title VII case but a case based on the equal protection clause of the Fourteenth Amendment of the U.S. Constitution.

[60] Twelve states and the District of Columbia, along with scores of cities and counties and over 300 major businesses, have laws and policies banning workplace discrimination based on "gender identity and expression." "Gender identity" includes transsexuals, cross-dressers, and all others who identify with the gender other than their biological sex. See 124 DLR A-1 (June 27, 2008).

[61] 378 F.3d 566 (6th Cir. 2004); see also *Barnes v. Cincinnati*, 401 F.3d 729 (6th Cir. 2005).

female personnel. After exhausting administrative remedies, Sommers brought action against Budget, alleging that she had been discharged on the basis of sex in violation of Title VII of the Civil Rights Act of 1964....

... Sommers's amended complaint claimed she had been discriminated against because of her status as a female, that is, a female with the anatomical body of a male, and further stated that sexual conversion surgery had not been performed. Sommers nonetheless argued that the court should not be bound by the plain meaning of the term "sex" under Title VII as connoting either male or female gender, but should instead expand the coverage of the Act to protect individuals such as herself who are psychologically female, albeit biologically male. In response, Budget argued that Title VII provided no relief for a person like Sommers.

... The court entered summary judgment in favor of Budget. Sommers contends on this appeal that the district court erred in concluding that Title VII coverage did not extend to those discriminated against because of their transsexuality and therefore erred in awarding summary judgment to Budget. We disagree.

... Although this circuit has not previously considered the issue raised on this appeal, we are in agreement with the district court that for the purposes of Title VII the plain meaning must be ascribed to the term "sex" in absence of clear congressional intent to do otherwise. Furthermore, the legislative history does not show any intention to include transsexualism in Title VII. The amendment adding the word "sex" to the Civil Rights Act was adopted one day before the House passed the Act without prior legislative hearing and little debate. It is, however, generally recognized that the major thrust of the "sex" amendment was towards providing equal opportunities for women.

Also, proposals to amend the Civil Rights Act to prohibit discrimination on the basis of "sexual preference" have been defeated. Three such bills were presented in the 94th Congress and seven were presented to the 95th Congress. Sommers's claim is not one dealing with discrimination on the basis of sexual preference. Nevertheless, the fact that the proposals were defeated indicates that the word "sex" in Title VII is to be given its traditional definition, rather than an expansive interpretation. Because Congress has not shown an intention to protect transsexuals, we hold that discrimination based on one's transsexualism does not fall within the protective purview of the Act.

We are not unmindful of the problem Sommers faces. On the other hand, Budget faces a problem in protecting the privacy interests of its female employees. According to affidavits submitted to the district court, even medical experts disagree as to whether Sommers is properly classified as male or female. The appropriate remedy is not immediately apparent to this court. Should Budget allow Sommers to use the female restroom, the male restroom, or one for Sommers's own use?

Perhaps some reasonable accommodation could be worked out between the parties. The issue before this court is not whether such an accommodation can be reached. Rather, the issue is whether Congress intended Title VII of the Civil Rights Act to protect transsexuals from discrimination. As explained above, we hold that such discrimination is not within the ambit of the Act.

The decision of the district court granting summary judgment in favor of the employer is affirmed.

Case Questions

1. What did Sommers claim?
2. Does the Title VII ban on sex discrimination encompass discrimination based on transsexualism?

SECTION 107: EMPLOYER LIABILITY FOR SEXUAL HARASSMENT

In the mid-1970s, the first sexual harassment cases appeared. The early cases generally held that actions taken by an employer against an employee were not based on the employee's sex but rather on whether the employee would acquiesce to sexual demands made by an employer and, as such, did not fall under the protection of Title VII.[62] Public awareness of the extensive problems relating to sexual harassment in the workplace became a major media issue in the late 1970s. The trend of the early court decisions was quickly reversed, and sexual harassment became generally recognized by the courts as a form of sex discrimination prohibited by Title VII.[63] On November 10, 1980, the EEOC issued *Sex Discrimination Guidelines* specifically dealing with the problem of sexual harassment. The guidelines define sexual harassment as follows:

> Unwelcome sexual advances, requests for sexual favors, and other verbal or physical conduct of a sexual nature constitute sexual harassment when (1) submission to such conduct is made either explicitly or implicitly a term or condition of an individual's employment, (2) submission to or rejection of such conduct by an individual is used as a basis for employment decisions affecting such individual, or (3) such conduct has the purpose or effect of unreasonably interfering with an individual's work performance or creating an intimidating, hostile, or offensive working environment.

The guidelines were immensely helpful in publicizing the problems relating to sexual harassment and in informing employers of their obligations. The guidelines are not administrative "regulations," and courts are not bound by the EEOC guidelines. However, the Supreme Court in *Griggs v. Duke Power Company*, presented earlier, declared that EEOC guidelines should be shown "great deference" by the courts.[64] The courts, then, and not the EEOC, have the final voice in settling the legal issues involving sexual harassment in the workplace.

DEVELOPING CASE LAW: EMPLOYER LIABILITY FOR HARASSMENT BY SUPERVISORS

The first successful sexual harassment litigation against an employer involved Paulette Barnes, who had her job terminated after she refused her supervisor's sexual advances. The Court of Appeals for the District of Columbia Circuit, in *Barnes v. Costle*,[65] heard the argument made by the employer that Barnes was pursuing an improper legal theory. The employer argued that the action based on sex discrimination was improper because Barnes's supervisor terminated her job

---

[62] In *Tompkins v. Public Serv. Elec. & Gas Co.*, 422 F. Supp. 553 (D. N.J. 1976), the court held that sexual harassment did not constitute sexual discrimination under Title VII. So, also, the same result was reached in *Corne v. Bausch and Lomb, Inc.*, 390 F. Supp. 161 (D. Ariz. 1975), when a male supervisor made sexual advances toward female employees.

[63] See, e.g., *Gerber v. Saxon Bus. Prod., Inc.*, 552 F.2d 1032 (4th Cir. 1977). See also *Barnes v. Costle*, 561 F.2d 983 (D.C. Cir. 1977).

[64] *Griggs v. Duke Power Co.*, 401 U.S. 424, 433–34 (1971), and *Bushey v. New York Civ. Serv. Comm'n*, 733 F.2d 220 at 225 (2d Cir. 1984). In *Miller v. Department of Corrections*, 30 Cal. Rptr. 3d 797 (2005), the California Supreme Court, applying the California Fair Employment and Housing Act and relying in part on EEOC policy guidance, determined that a California prison warden's consensual sexual affair with three subordinate female employees who received preferential treatment may create a hostile environment that demeans other employees.

[65] 561 F.2d 983 (D.C. Cir. 1977).

because she had refused sexual advances, not because she was a woman. The court responded:

> But for her womanhood ... [Barnes's] participation in sexual activity would never
> have been solicited. To say, then, that she was victimized in her employment
> simply because she declined the invitation is to ignore the asserted fact that she was
> invited only because she was a woman subordinate to the inviter in the hierarchy of
> agency personnel.[66]

The court concluded that sex discrimination within the meaning of Title VII is not confined to disparate treatment solely limited to gender. Also, the court held that the employer was chargeable with the Title VII violations of its supervisor under the facts before it. This type of sexual harassment was later called quid pro quo harassment. **Quid pro quo** is a phrase commonly used in contract negotiations whereby parties negotiate "something for something," and in this employment context, a supervisor seeks sexual favors for benefits.

A different fact pattern was developed in the case of *Bundy v. Jackson*. Unlike Paulette Barnes, Sandra Bundy was not terminated for refusing her supervisor's advances. Her claim in part stated that "conditions of employment" as set forth in Title VII include the psychological and emotional work environment. The sexually stereotyped insults and demeaning propositions to which she was subjected and which caused her anxiety illegally poisoned the work environment. The Court of Appeals for the District of Columbia Circuit set forth the following relevant fact pattern in its decision:

> The District Court's decision that sexual intimidation was a "normal condition of
> employment" in Bundy's agency finds ample support in the District Court's own
> chronology of Bundy's experiences there. Those experiences began in 1972 when
> Bundy, still a GS-5, received and rejected sexual propositions from Delbert Jackson,
> then a fellow employee at the agency but now its Director and the named defendant
> in this lawsuit in his official capacity. It was two years later, however, that the
> sexual intimidation Bundy suffered began to intertwine directly with her employ-
> ment, when she received propositions from two of her supervisors, Arthur Burton
> and James Gainey.
>
> Burton became Bundy's supervisor when Bundy became an Employment
> Development Specialist in 1974. Shortly thereafter Gainey became her first-line
> supervisor and Burton her second-line supervisor, although Burton retained control
> of Bundy's employment status. Burton began sexually harassing Bundy in June 1974,
> continually calling her into his office to request that she spend the workday after-
> noon with him at his apartment and to question her about sexual proclivities.
> Shortly after becoming her first-line supervisor, Gainey also began making sexual
> advances to Bundy, asking her to join him at a motel and on a trip to the Bahamas.
> Bundy complained about these advances to Lawrence Swain, who supervised both
> Burton and Gainey. Swain casually dismissed Bundy's complaints, telling her that
> "any man in his right mind would want to rape you," and then proceeding himself
> to request that she begin a sexual relationship with him in his apartment. Bundy re-
> jected his request.[67]

---

[66] *Id.* at 990.
[67] 641 F.2d 934 (D.C. Cir. 1981).

The court held that Bundy had proved that she was a victim of sexual harassment in the context of a discriminatory work environment permitted by her employer. This type of sexual harassment, called hostile work environment harassment, even if it did not result in a loss of tangible benefits, is illegal sex discrimination. The court stated that injunctive relief was required. The court ordered the agency's director to establish and publicize procedures whereby harassed employees could complain to the director immediately and confidentially. Moreover, the director was ordered to promptly take all necessary steps to investigate and correct any harassment, including warnings and appropriate discipline directed at the offending party, and develop other means of preventing harassment within the agency. The court awarded attorney fees to Bundy. No compensatory or punitive damages were available as a remedy at that time.

The U.S. Supreme Court dealt with the issue of sexual harassment for the first time in 1986 in the case of *Meritor Savings Bank v. Vinson*, reported in this section. The Court distinguished between **quid pro quo** claims and **hostile environment** claims.[68] The *Meritor* court also stated that traditional agency law principles, embodied in the Restatement (Second) of Agency, are relevant in determining whether an employer is liable for the hostile work environment perpetrated by a supervisor or an employee.[69] The Court stated that Title VII does not make employers "always automatically liable for sexual harassment by their supervisors."[70]

As a result of the *Meritor* decision, courts of appeals have held that if a plaintiff established a quid pro quo claim, the employer was subject to vicarious liability.[71] It was also clear under *Meritor* that an employer may raise an affirmative defense based on agency law principles in hostile work environment cases. Because employer liability was certain if a quid pro quo case could be established, plaintiffs commonly sought to state their claims in quid pro quo terms, placing ever-expansive pressure on the definition of quid pro quo.[72] The Supreme Court in two 1998 decisions with the same holdings, discussed below, decided to diminish the significance of the distinctions between quid pro quo and hostile environment cases. The Court stated that it is now more useful to distinguish between harassment that results in a **tangible employment action** and harassment that creates a **hostile work environment,** because the dichotomy determines whether the employer can raise the affirmative defense to vicarious liability.[73]

---

[68] 477 U.S. at 65.

[69] 477 U.S. at 70–72.

[70] *Id.*

[71] *Davis v. Sioux City*, 115 F.3d 1365, 1367 (8th Cir. 1997); *Nichols v. Frank*, 42 F.3d 503, 513–14 (9th Cir. 1994); *Bouton v. BMW of North America, Inc.*, 29 F.3d 103, 106–107 (3d Cir. 1994); *Sauers v. Salt Lake County*, 1 F.3d 1122, 1127 (10th Cir. 1993); *Kauffman v. Allied Signal, Inc.*, 970 F.2d 178, 185–86 (10th Cir. 1992).

[72] See *Burlington Industries v. Ellerth*, 524 U.S. 742 (1998).

[73] *Id.*

The Supreme Court's Current Application

In *Burlington Industries, Inc. v. Ellerth*[74] and *Faragher v. City of Boca Raton*,[75] the Supreme Court set forth new rules on employer "vicarious liability"[76] for sexual harassment committed by supervisors. Under the Court's *Ellerth/Faragher* holdings, quid pro quo tangible employment action sexual harassment involves situations where a supervisor has taken significant adverse tangible employment action such as a discharge, a demotion, or an undesirable reassignment against a subordinate employee for the employee's refusal to submit to the supervisor's demand for sexual favors.

Hostile work environment continues as the second classification of sexual harassment under these decisions. With this type of harassment, an employee's economic benefits have not been affected by a supervisor's conduct, but the supervisor's sexually harassing conduct has nevertheless caused anxiety and "poisoned" the work environment. Such conduct may include unwelcome sexual flirtation, propositions, or other abuses of a sexual nature, including the use of degrading words or the display of sexually explicit or suggestive pictures.

TANGIBLE EMPLOYMENT ACTION CASES.   The phrases "tangible employment action" and "hostile work environment" illustrate the respective distinction between cases involving a threat that is carried out and offensive conduct in general, including unfulfilled threats. Where a plaintiff proves that a tangible employment action resulted from a refusal to submit to a sexual demand, the supervisor is acting with the authority of the company to cause the economic injury by, for example, docking another's pay or demoting an individual.[77] The employer is always vicariously liable for this quid pro quo harassment by a supervisor under the so-called aided-in-the-agency-relation standard. That is, the supervisor is aided in accomplishing the wrongful objective by the existence of the agency relation. The supervisor has been empowered by the employer as a distinct class of agent to make economic decisions affecting other employees under his or her control. The employer can raise no affirmative defense based on the presence of an employer's antiharassment policy in such a case.

---

[74] 524 U.S. 742 (1998).

[75] 524 U.S. 775 (1998).

[76] If the employer knew of sexual harassment by a supervisor and took no effective action to stop it, the victim has the right to bring a negligence action directly against the employer. This fact situation is unusual, however, because most employers discharge their duties with reasonable care and simply do not tolerate the supervisory misconduct. In most situations, the employer finds out about the harassment committed by a managerial agent, contrary to the good faith efforts of the employer to comply with Title VII, after a sexual harassment claim has been filed. The employer is "innocent" of wrongdoing, but the victim seeks to hold the employer "vicariously liable" under agency law. It is under these circumstances that the Supreme Court's *Burlington Industries, Inc. v. Ellerth*, 524 U.S. 742 (1998) and *Faragher v. City of Boca Raton*, 524 U.S. 775 (1998) decisions on the vicarious liability of employers under agency principles for supervisory harassment apply. The vicarious liability standard sets forth a "more stringent standard" for the employer than the "minimum standard" of negligence. *Ellerth*, 524 U.S. at 758.

[77] See *Hunt v. City of Markham*, 219 F.3d 1053 (5th Cir. 2000).

HOSTILE WORK ENVIRONMENT. In all other cases of sexual harassment involving supervisors, the classification of hostile work environment applies and the plaintiff must prove severe or pervasive conduct on the part of the supervisor to meet his or her burden of proof. Where no tangible employment action is taken, the employer may raise an affirmative defense to liability for damages by proving (1) it exercised reasonable care to prevent and promptly correct any sexually harassing behavior at its workplace and (2) the plaintiff employee unreasonably failed to take advantage of corrective opportunities provided by the employer. The existence of an employer sexual harassment policy and notification procedures will aid the employer in proving the affirmative defense in hostile environment cases. In *Burlington Industries v. Ellerth*, presented in this section, Kim Ellerth alleged that she was subject to constant sexual harassment by her supervisor, Ted Slowik, at Burlington Industries. Slowik made comments about her breasts, told her to "loosen up," and warned, "You know, Kim, I could make your life very hard or very easy at Burlington." When she was being considered for a promotion, Slowik expressed reservations that she was not "loose enough" and then reached over and rubbed her knee. She received the promotion, however. After other such incidents, she quit and filed charges alleging she was constructively discharged because of quid pro quo sexual harassment. She did not use Burlington's sexual harassment internal complaint procedures. Because she was not the victim of any significant tangible employment action, because she received the promotion she sought, and because Slowik never carried out any of his implied threats, she could not successfully pursue a quid pro quo automatic vicarious liability theory against Burlington. Rather, she was able to prove severe and pervasive conduct on the part of a supervisor under a hostile environment theory. The employer could defeat liability, however, by proving that it exercised reasonable care to prevent and correct sexual harassing behavior by its internal company complaint policies and that Ellerth unreasonably failed to take advantage of company procedures.[78]

CONSTRUCTIVE DISCHARGE ATTRIBUTABLE TO SUPERVISORS

In its *Pennsylvania State Police v. Suders* decision, presented in this section, the U.S. Supreme Court set out to clarify the application of its *Ellerth/Faragher* principles to "constructive discharge" cases where an employee resigns because of unendurable working conditions resulting from a "hostile work environment" created by a supervisor. When a supervisor engaged in harassing conduct against a subordinate takes "tangible employment action" by means of an **official act of the enterprise,** such as a transfer, pay cut, or demotion, which is duly noted in official records of the employer, the supervisor is aided by the agency relation, and the employer is vicariously liable to the subordinate, and the employer may not raise an affirmative defense. However, if there is no "official act," then the employer may raise an affirmative defense under the Supreme Court's *Suders* decision, presented later in this section.

---

[78] See also *Clark County Sch. Dist. v. Breeden*, 532 U.S. 268 (2001).

Supervisor-harassment claims asserting constructive discharges are thus divided according to the presense or absence of an "official act." In *Reed v. MBNA Marketing Systems, Inc.,*[79] the plaintiff claimed constructive discharge based on her supervisor's repeated sexual comments and a sexual assault. The supervisor's behavior involved no "official action like a dangerous job assignment to retaliate for the spurned advances." Therefore, the employer was not precluded from raising the *Ellerth/Faragher* affirmative defense.

In *Robinson v. Sappington,*[80] the plaintiff claimed that she was sexually harassed by the judge for whom she worked. A supervising judge decided to resolve the matter by transferring the plaintiff to a judge who resisted placing her on his staff. The Seventh Circuit Court of Appeals held that the employer was precluded from asserting the *Ellerth/Faragher* affirmative defense to the constructive discharge claim because the plaintiff's decision to resign resulted in part from the supervising judge's "official action" of transferring her to the judge who did not want her on his staff.

STANDING TO FILE A CLAIM AND APPLICABLE STANDARD FOR SUFFICIENCY OF HARASSMENT

Women and men are protected by Title VII from sexual harassment in the workplace and may bring a claim against a member of the opposite sex for sexual harassment. Although men may be victims of sexual harassment, in most cases, the perpetrators are men and the victims are women.[81] Federal courts across the country were split on the issue of whether Title VII applied to sexual harassment by males on males and females on females—referred to as "same-sex harassment." The *Oncale v. Sundowner Offshore Services, Inc.,* decision of the U.S. Supreme Court, presented in this section, settled this issue. The Court determined that there is no justification in the statutory language or Supreme Court precedents to exclude same-sex sexual harassment from coverage of Title VII.

The Court in *Oncale* set forth the standard to apply in judging whether the conduct in question amounts to sexual harassment. It stated that the objective severity of the harassment should be judged from the perspective of a reasonable person in the plaintiff's position, considering all of the circumstances. The Court made clear that it was not transforming Title VII into a general civility code for the American workplace, and it stated that Title VII forbids only behavior so objectively offensive as to alter the conditions of the victim's employment. "Common sense" and "context" must apply before courts and juries in determining whether the conduct is severely hostile and abusive according to the Court.[82]

---

[79] 333 F.3d 27 (1st Cir. 2003).

[80] 351 F.3d 317 (7th Cir. 2003).

[81] *David Huebshen v. Department of Health and Social Services,* 716 F.2d 1167 (7th Cir. 1983).

[82] See *Indest v. Freeman Decorating, Inc.,* 164 F.3d 258 (5th Cir. 1999); see also *Patt v. Family Health Sys., Inc.,* 280 F.3d 749 (7th Cir. 2002).

Prima Facie Case of Sexual Harassment

To establish a claim for a quid pro quo tangible employment action case of sexual harassment, a plaintiff must demonstrate the following:

1. That she or he belongs to a protected class;
2. That she or he was subject to unwelcome sexual harassment;
3. That the harassment was based on sex;
4. That as a result of the plaintiff's refusal to submit to a supervisor's sexual; demand, an adverse tangible employment action—official act of the enterprise— was taken against the plaintiff.

No affirmative defense exists for tangible employment action cases.

Because both men and women are protected, the first element may be established by a stipulation that the victim is a man or woman. Critical to proving a tangible employment action case is establishing element 2: the harassing event occurred and it was "unwelcome." Indeed, most courts give the benefit of the doubt to the victims on the issue of unwelcomeness in regard to supervisors' conduct, absent clear evidence to the contrary. Thus, supervisors should be warned that dating employees with less authority than themselves is fraught with problems, where the supervisors must evaluate, assign, transfer, and give raises and other job benefits in the context of personal relationships that are subject to change. Elements 3 and 4 can be developed based on the misconduct proven in element 2 and the tangible employment action taken of record.

A *prima facie* case for a hostile work environment sexual harassment case is established by demonstrating the same first three elements as required in a tangible employment action case. In addition, the plaintiff must demonstrate a fourth element: that the harassment was so severe and pervasive that it affected a "term, condition, or privilege of employment."

Concerning the second element, some types of conduct are so universally offensive in the workplace as to be clearly unwelcome, including groping, pinching, or touching private parts of the body. Other less obvious types of harassment, such as sexual jokes, gossip regarding one's sex life, or comments on an individual's body or sexual prowess, would require that the complainant take some steps to let it be known that the sexual advance or conduct was not welcome. The milder the conduct, the more responsibility the complainant has to express objection.[83]

The "based on sex" element requires a showing that the harassment occurred because of the complainant's sex and did not occur to members of the opposite sex. Thus, if a supervisor is equally abusive and demeaning to both men and women, there is no violation of Title VII even though a hostile work environment has been created.[84]

The "affecting a term, condition, or privilege of employment" fourth element requires a showing that the harassment complained of was so severe and pervasive as to alter the conditions of employment and create an abusive work environment.

---

[83] See *King v. Board of Regents of University of Wisconsin System*, 858 F.2d 533, 537 (7th Cir. 1990).

[84] But see *Steiner v. Showboat Operating Co.*, 25 F.3d 1459 (9th Cir. 1994).

The *Oncale* test of a "reasonable person in the plaintiff's position, considering all of the circumstances" is utilized to judge the objective severity of the harrassment.

When sexual harassment by a supervisor creates an unlawful hostile environment but does not result in a tangible employment action (official act of the enterprise), the employer can raise an affirmative defense to liability for damages, which it must prove by a preponderance of the evidence. The defense consists of two necessary elements: (1) The employer exercised reasonable care to prevent and promptly correct any harassment, and (2) the employee unreasonably failed to take advantage of any preventive or corrective opportunities provided by the employer or to otherwise avoid harm.[85]

EMPLOYER PREVENTIVE STEPS

The affirmative defense to sexual harassment makes evident the necessity for preventive steps by employers. An effective complaint procedure encourages employees to report harassing conduct before it becomes severe or pervasive;[86] and if an employee promptly uses that procedure, the employer can usually stop the harassment before actionable harm occurs.[87] However, the employer is shielded from liability under the affirmative defense only if it proves that it exercised reasonable care to "prevent and correct" the misconduct and the employee unreasonably failed to take advantage of the employer's procedures.[88] If the employer and employee-victim both exercise reasonable care, the employer's affirmative defense will fail. However, the employer's reasonable care policy and procedures should reduce the harm and damages.

An outline of employer preventive action follows:

A. Develop and implement a sexual harassment policy and communicate it to all employees. Set forth specific examples of conduct that will not be tolerated, such as:

- Unwelcome sexual advances, whether they involve physical touching or not

---

[85] In his article entitled "Smoke, Mirrors, and the Disappearance of 'Vicarious' Liability: The Emergence of a Dubious Summary-Judgment Safe Harbor for Employers Whose Supervisory Personnel Commit Hostile Environment Workplace Harassment," 38 *Houston Law Review* 1404 (2002), John Marks believes that the *Ellerth/Faragher* defense as it is currently used provides no recourse for the harm inflicted on the employee before lodging her or his complaint. He states that entirely denying recovery to innocent plaintiffs for suddenly imposed abuse that the employer, after the fact, remedies upon notice, is equivalent to granting the employer a windfall that resembles the immunity that common law once granted dog owners. Dog owners were granted immunity for the first bite their dog inflicted and were liable only for subsequent bites.

[86] *Ellerth*, 524 U.S. at 765.

[87] See *Indest v. Freeman Decorating, Inc.*, 168 F.3d 795, 803 (5th Cir. 1999).

[88] Care must be exercised to make certain that the employer's policies and procedures provide a reasonable process by which a victim can complain to the company of perceived harassment. Thus, if some employees do not speak English, posted policies and an employee handbook written in English is not reasonable. Where employers employ teenagers as part-time workers, special care must be taken to design and implement a preventive action plan reflective of the understanding and experience of average teenagers. In *EEOC v. V & J Foods, Inc.*, 507 F.3d 575 (7th Cir. 2007), Judge Posner took the owners of a Burger King restaurant to task where the employer hired teens and put them under another's supervision, yet did not have a reasonable harassment mechanism to allow relatively inexperienced teenagers to complain about sexual harassment by a supervisor.

- Sexual epithets, jokes, written or oral references to sexual conduct, gossip regarding one's sex life; comments on an individual's body; comments about an individual's sexual activity, deficiencies, or prowess
- Displaying of sexually suggestive objects, pictures, or cartoons
- Unwelcome leering, whistling, brushing against the body, sexual gestures, or suggestive or insulting comments
- Inquiries into one's sexual experiences
- Discussion of one's sexual activities

B. Establish ongoing educational programs to demonstrate unacceptable behavior. Keep exact business records of all educational programs offered to employees and maintain employee signatures attesting to their attendance at such programs. Such evidence may enable the employer to prove an affirmative defense.

C. Designate a responsible senior official to whom complaints of sexual harassment can be made. Avoid any procedure that requires an employee to first complain to the employee's supervisor, as that individual may be the offending person. Make certain complainants know that there will be no retaliation for filing a complaint.

D. Investigate all complaints promptly and thoroughly.

E. Keep the complaint and investigation as confidential as possible and limit all information to only those who need to know.

F. If a complaint has merit, impose appropriate and consistent discipline.

APPLICATION BEYOND SEXUAL HARRASSMENT

The *Ellerth* and *Faragher* rules regarding vicarious liability apply to harassment by supervisors regarding not only sex but also regarding race, color, religion, national origin, retaliation, age, or disability, according to the EEOC and certain courts.[89]

CASE 12.7 | MERITOR SAVINGS BANK V. VINSON
SUPREME COURT OF THE UNITED STATES, 477 U.S. 57 (1986).

[Mechelle Vinson (respondent) brought this action against Sidney Taylor, a vice president and branch manager of Meritor Savings Bank, and the bank (petitioners), claiming that during her four years at the bank, she had been constantly subjected to sexual harassment by Taylor in violation of Title VII. She testified to over 40 instances of sexual favors successfully sought by Taylor from 1974 to 1977, when these activities ceased after she started going with a steady boyfriend. Taylor denied allegations of sexual activity. He contended instead that respondent made her accusations in response to a business-related dispute.

The bank also denied respondent's allegations and asserted that any sexual harassment by Taylor was unknown to the bank and engaged in without its consent or approval. The district court denied relief, finding in part:

> If (respondent) and Taylor did engage in an intimate or sexual relationship during the time of (respondent's) employment with [the bank], that relationship was a voluntary one having nothing to do with her continued employment at [the bank] or her advancement or promotions at that institution.

continued

---

[89] "EEOC Guidance on Vicarious Employer Liability for Unlawful Harassment by Supervisors," EEOC Notice No. 915.002 (June 18, 1999), Part II and cases therein.

The court of appeals reversed the district court. The Supreme Court granted certiorari.]

REHNQUIST, J....

...[I]n 1980 the EEOC issued guidelines specifying that "sexual harassment" as there defined, is a form of sex discrimination prohibited by Title VII....

Since the guidelines were issued, courts have uniformly held, and we agree, that a plaintiff may establish a violation of Title VII by proving that discrimination based on sex has created a hostile or abusive work environment....

...[T]he District Court's conclusion that no actionable harassment occurred might have rested on its earlier "finding" that "[i]f [respondent] and Taylor did engage in an intimate or sexual relationship... that relationship was a voluntary one." But the fact that sex-related conduct was "voluntary," in the sense that the complainant was not forced to participate against her will, is not a defense to a sexual harassment suit brought under Title VII. The gravamen of any sexual harassment claim is that the alleged sexual advances were "unwelcome." While the question whether particular conduct was indeed unwelcome presents difficult problems of proof and turns largely on credibility determinations committed to the trier of fact, the District Court in this case erroneously focused on the "voluntariness" of respondent's participation in the claimed sexual episodes. The correct inquiry is whether respondent by her conduct indicated that the alleged sexual advances were unwelcome, not whether her actual participation in sexual intercourse was voluntary.

Petitioner contends that even if this case must be remanded to the District Court, the Court of Appeals erred in one of the terms of its remand. Specifically, the Court of Appeals stated that testimony about respondent's "dress and personal fantasies," which the District Court apparently admitted into evidence, "had no place in this litigation." The apparent ground for this conclusion was that respondent's voluntariness *vel non* in submitting to Taylor's advances was immaterial to her sexual harassment claim. While "voluntariness" in the sense of consent is not a defense to such a claim, it does not follow that a complainant's sexually provocative speech or dress is irrelevant as a matter of law in determining whether he or she found particular sexual advances unwelcome. To the contrary, such

evidence is obviously relevant. The EEOC guidelines emphasize that the trier of fact must determine the existence of sexual harassment in light of "the record as a whole" and "the totality of circumstances, such as the nature of the sexual advances and the context in which the alleged incidents occurred." ...

Although the District Court concluded that respondent had not proved a violation of Title VII, it nevertheless went on to consider the question of the bank's liability. Finding that "the bank was without notice" of Taylor's alleged conduct, and that notice to Taylor was not the equivalent of notice to the bank, the court concluded that the bank therefore could not be held liable for Taylor's alleged actions. The Court of Appeals took the opposite view, holding that an employer is strictly liable for a hostile environment created by a supervisor's sexual advances, even though the employer neither knew nor reasonably could have known of the alleged misconduct. The court held that a supervisor, whether or not he possesses the authority to hire, fire, or promote, is necessarily an "agent" of his employer for all Title VII purposes, since "even the appearance" of such authority may enable him to impose himself on his subordinates....

We therefore decline the parties' invitation to issue a definitive rule on employer liability, but we do agree with the EEOC that Congress wanted courts to look to agency principles for guidance in this area. While such common-law principles may not be transferable in all their particulars to Title VII, Congress' decision to define "employer" to include any "agent" of an employer, 42 U.S.C. § 2000e(b), surely evinces an intent to place some limits on the acts of employees for which employers under Title VII are to be held responsible. For this reason, we hold that the Court of Appeals erred in concluding that employers are always automatically liable for sexual harassment by their supervisors. For the same reason, absence of notice to an employer does not necessarily insulate that employer from liability.

Finally, we reject petitioner's view that the mere existence of a grievance procedure and a policy against discrimination, coupled with respondent's failure to invoke that procedure, must insulate petitioner from liability. While those facts are plainly relevant, the situation before us demonstrates why they are not necessarily dispositive. Petitioner's general nondiscrimination policy did not address sexual harassment in particular, and thus did not alert

continued

employees to their employer's interest in correcting that form of discrimination. Moreover, the bank's grievance procedure apparently required an employee to complain first to her supervisor, in this case Taylor. Since Taylor was the alleged perpetrator, it is not altogether surprising that respondent failed to invoke the procedure and report her grievance to him. Petitioner's contention that respondent's failure should insulate it from liability might be substantially stronger if its procedures were better calculated to encourage victims of harassment to come forward....

Accordingly, the judgment of the Court of Appeals reversing the judgment of the District Court is affirmed, and the case is remanded for further proceedings consistent with this opinion.

It is so ordered.

Case Questions

1. Is the fact that the sex-related conduct by an employee and her supervisor was "voluntary" a defense to a sexual harassment charge?
2. Was it proper for a trial court to consider evidence of sexually provocative speech or dress on the part of the complainant in a sexual harassment suit?
3. Did Taylor in fact make unwelcome sexual advances to Vinson?
4. What was wrong with the bank's nondiscrimination policy and grievance procedure?

CASE 12.8 | ONCALE V. SUNDOWNER OFFSHORE SERVICES, INC.
SUPREME COURT OF THE UNITED STATES, 523 U.S. 75 (1998).

[Joseph Oncale worked for Sundowner Offshore Services, Inc., as a roustabout on an oil platform in the Gulf of Mexico. On several occasions, he was forcibly subjected to sex-related, humiliating actions by three male crew members, two of whom had supervisory authority over him. Oncale's complaints to supervisory personnel produced no remedial action. Oncale eventually quit because of the sexual harassment. He filed a complaint against his employer, claiming that sexual harassment directed against him by coworkers in their workplace constituted "discriminat[ion] ... because of ... "sex" prohibited by Title VII of the Civil Rights Act. Relying on Fifth Circuit precedent, the district court held that Oncale, a male, had no Title VII cause of action for harassment by male coworkers. The Fifth Circuit affirmed.]

SCALIA, J....

Title VII of the Civil Rights Act of 1964 provides, in relevant part, that "[i]t shall be an unlawful employment practice for an employer...to discriminate against any individual with respect to his compensation, terms, conditions, or privileges of employment, because of such individual's race, color, religion, sex, or national origin." 78 Stat. 255, as amended, 42 U.S.C. § 2000e-2(a)(1). We have held that this not only covers "terms" and "conditions" in the narrow

contractual sense, but "evinces a congressional intent to strike at the entire spectrum of disparate treatment of men and women in employment." *Meritor Savings Bank, FSB v. Vinson*, 477 U.S. 57, 64 (1986). "When the workplace is permeated with discriminatory intimidation, ridicule, and insult that is sufficiently severe or pervasive to alter the conditions of the victim's employment and create an abusive working environment, Title VII is violated." *Harris v. Forklift Systems, Inc.*, 510 U.S. 17, 21 (1993) (citations and internal quotation marks omitted).

Title VII's prohibition of discrimination "because of...sex" protects men as well as women, *Newport News Shipbuilding & Dry Dock Co. v. EEOC*, 462 U.S. 669, 682 (1983)....

...[I]n the context of a "hostile environment" sexual harassment claim, the state and federal courts have taken a bewildering variety of stances. Some, like the Fifth Circuit in this case, have held that same-sex sexual harassment claims are never cognizable under Title VII. See also, *e.g., Goluszek v. H.P. Smith*, 697 F. Supp. 1452 (ND Ill. 1988). Other decisions say that such claims are actionable only if the plaintiff can prove that the harasser is homosexual (and thus presumably motivated by sexual desire). Compare *McWilliams v. Fairfax County Board of Supervisors*, 72 F.3d 1191 (CA4 1996), with *Wrightson v. Pizza*

continued

Hut of America, 99 F.3d 138 (CA4 1996). Still others suggest that workplace harassment that is sexual in content is always actionable, regardless of the harasser's sex, sexual orientation, or motivations. See *Doe v. Belleville*, 119 F.3d 563 (CA7 1997).

We see no justification in the statutory language or our precedents for a categorical rule excluding same-sex harassment claims from the coverage of Title VII....

Our holding ... must extend to sexual harassment of any kind that meets the statutory requirements.

Respondents and their **amici** contend that recognizing liability for same-sex harassment will transform Title VII into a general civility code for the American workplace. But that risk is no greater for same-sex than for opposite sex harassment, and is adequately met by careful attention to the requirements of the statute. Title VII does not prohibit all verbal or physical harassment in the workplace; it is directed only at *"discriminat[ion] ... because of ... sex."* We have never held that workplace harassment, even harassment between men and women, is automatically discrimination because of sex merely because the words used have sexual content or connotations. "The critical issue, Title VII's text indicates, is whether members of one sex are exposed to disadvantageous terms or conditions of employment to which members of the other sex are not exposed." *Harris, supra*, at 25 (GINSBURG, J., concurring)....

And there is another requirement that prevents Title VII from expanding into a general civility code:...the statute does not reach genuine but innocuous differences in the ways men and women routinely interact with members of the same sex and of the opposite sex. The prohibition of harassment on the basis of sex requires neither asexuality nor androgyny in the workplace; it forbids only behavior so objectively offensive as to alter the "conditions" of the victim's employment. "Conduct that is not severe or pervasive enough to create an objectively hostile or abusive work environment—an environment that a reasonable person would find hostile or abusive—is beyond Title VII's purview." *Harris*, 510 U.S., at 21, citing *Meritor*, 477 U.S. at 67. We have always regarded that requirement as crucial, and as sufficient to ensure that courts and juries to not mistake ordinary socializing in the workplace—such as male-on-male horseplay or intersexual flirtation—for discriminatory "conditions of employment."

We have emphasized, moreover, that the objective severity of harassment should be judged from the perspective of a reasonable person in the plaintiff's position, considering "all the circumstances." *Harris, supra*, at 23. In same-sex (as in all) harassment cases, that inquiry requires careful consideration of the social context in which particular behavior occurs and is experienced by its target. A professional football player's working environment is not severely or pervasively abusive, for example, if the coach smacks him on the buttocks as he heads onto the field—even if the same behavior would reasonably be experienced as abusive by the coach's secretary (male or female) back at the office. The real social impact of workplace behavior often depends on a constellation of surrounding circumstances, expectations, and relationships which are not fully captured by a simple recitation of the words used or the physical acts performed. Common sense, and an appropriate sensitivity to social context, will enable courts and juries to distinguish between simple teasing or roughhousing among members of the same sex, and conduct which a reasonable person in the plaintiff's position would find severely hostile or abusive.

Because we conclude that sex discrimination consisting of same-sex harassment is actionable under Title VII, the judgment of the Court of Appeals for the Fifth Circuit is reversed, and the case is remanded for further proceedings consistent with this opinion.

It is so ordered.

JUSTICE THOMAS, concurring....

I concur because the Court stresses that in every sexual harassment case, the plaintiff must plead and ultimately prove Title VII's statutory requirement that there be discrimination "because of ... sex."

Case Questions

1. Does the *Oncale* decision transform Title VII into a general civility code for the American workplace?

2. What standard should apply in judging whether the conduct in question amounted to sexual harassment?

3. What justification exists in the statutory language or Supreme Court precedents for a categorical rule excluding same-sex harassment claims from coverage of Title VII?

CASE 12.9	BURLINGTON INDUSTRIES, INC. v. ELLERTH
	SUPREME COURT OF THE UNITED STATES, 524. U.S. 742 (1998).

[Kimberly Ellerth quit her job after 15 months as a salesperson in one of Burlington Industries' many divisions, allegedly because she had been subjected to constant sexual harassment by one of her supervisors, Ted Slowik. Slowik was a midlevel manager who had authority to hire and promote employees, subject to higher approval, but was not considered a policy-maker. Against a background of repeated boorish and offensive remarks and gestures allegedly made by Slowik, Ellerth placed particular emphasis on three incidents where Slowik's comments could be construed as threats to deny her tangible job benefits. Ellerth refused all of Slowik's advances yet suffered no tangible retaliation and was, in fact, promoted. Moreover, she never informed anyone in authority about Slowik's conduct, despite knowing Burlington had a policy against sexual harassment. In filing this lawsuit, Ellerth alleged that Burlington engaged in sexual harassment and forced her constructive discharge in violation of Title VII. The U.S. Supreme Court decided to hear the case.]

KENNEDY, J....

[1.]

At the outset, we assume an important proposition yet to be established before a trier of fact. It is a premise assumed as well, in explicit or implicit terms, in the various opinions by the judges of the Court of Appeals. The premise is: a trier of fact could find in Slowik's remarks numerous threats to retaliate against Ellerth if she denied some sexual liberties. The threats, however, were not carried out or fulfilled. Cases based on threats which are carried out are referred to often as *quid pro quo* cases, as distinct from bothersome attentions or sexual remarks that are sufficiently severe or pervasive to create a hostile work environment. The terms *quid pro quo* and hostile work environment are helpful, perhaps, in making a rough demarcation between cases in which threats are carried out and those where they are not or are absent altogether, but beyond this are of limited utility.

Section 703(a) of Title VII forbids

"an employer—
   "(1) to fail or refuse to hire or to discharge any individual, or otherwise to discriminate against any individual with respect to his compensation,

terms, conditions or privileges of employment, because of such individual's ... sex." 42 U. S. C. § 2000e-2(a)(1).

"*Quid pro quo*" and "hostile work environment" do not appear in the statutory text. The terms appeared first in the academic literature, see C. MacKinnon, Sexual Harassment of Working Women (1979); found their way into decisions of the Courts of Appeals, see, *e.g.*, *Henson v. Dundee*, 682 F.2d 897, 909 (CA11 1982); and were mentioned in this Court's decision in *Meritor Savings Bank, FSB v. Vinson*, 477 U.S. 57 (1986). See generally E. Scalia, The Strange Career of Quid Pro Quo Sexual Harassment, 21 Harv. J. L. & Pub. Policy 307 (1998)....

...As use of the terms grew in the wake of *Meritor*, they acquired their own significance. The standard of employer responsibility turned on which type of harassment occurred. If the plaintiff established a *quid pro quo* claim, the Courts of Appeals held, the employer was subject to vicarious liability. The rule encouraged Title VII plaintiffs to state their claim as *quid pro quo* claims, which in turn put expansive pressure on the definition. The equivalence of the *quid pro quo* label and vicarious liability is illustrated by this case. The question presented on certiorari is whether Ellerth can state a claim of *quid pro quo* harassment, but the issue of real concern to the parties is whether Burlington has vicarious liability for Slowik's alleged misconduct, rather than liability limited to its own negligence. The question presented for certiorari asks:

"Whether a claim of quid pro quo sexual harassment may be stated under Title VII .... where the plaintiff employee has neither submitted to the sexual advances of the alleged harasser nor suffered any tangible effects on the compensation, terms, conditions or privileges of employment as a consequence of a refusal to submit to those advances?" *Pet. for Cert. i.*

We do not suggest the terms *quid pro quo* and hostile work environment are irrelevant to Title VII litigation. To the extent they illustrate the distinction between cases involving a threat which is carried out and offensive conduct in general, the terms are relevant when there is a threshold question whether a plaintiff can prove discrimination in violation of Title VII. When a plaintiff proves that a tangible employment

continued

action resulted from a refusal to submit to a supervisor's sexual demands, he or she establishes that the employment decision itself constitutes a change in the terms and conditions of employment that is actionable under Title VII. For any sexual harassment preceding the employment decision to be actionable, however, the conduct must be severe or pervasive. Because Ellerth's claim involves only unfulfilled threats, it should be categorized as a hostile work environment claim which requires a showing of severe or pervasive conduct. See *Oncale v. Sundowner Offshore Services, Inc.*, 523 U.S. 75, 81 (1998); *Harris v. Forklift Systems, Inc.*, 510 U.S. 17, 21 (1993)....

[2.]

We must decide, then, whether an employer has vicarious liability when a supervisor creates a hostile work environment by making explicit threats to alter a subordinate's terms or conditions of employment, based on sex, but does not fulfill the threat....

As *Meritor* acknowledged, the Restatement (Second) of Agency (1957) (hereinafter Restatement), is a useful beginning point for a discussion of general agency principles, 477 U.S., at 72....

[The Court reviewed agency law principles such as a master is responsible for the torts of his employees committed within the scope of their employment. Because a supervisor's conduct relating to sexual harassment of subordinate employees generally never serves the interests of the employer, the conduct is thus not within the scope of employment and the employer is not liable for it. The Court pointed out that an employer is negligent and therefore subject to direct liability under Restatement (Second) Agency § 219(2)(b) if it knew or should have known about the sexual harassment and failed to stop it. But the *Ellerth* case was not appealed on such a basis.

Ultimately, the Court reached the conclusion on the appropriate standard to apply when a party seeks to impose vicarious liability based on an agent's misuse of delegated authority and concluded that the appropriate analysis is the "aided in the agency relation" rule.]

At the outset, we can identify a class of cases where, beyond question, more than the mere existence of the employment relation aids in commission of the harassment: when a supervisor takes a tangible employment action against the subordinate. Every Federal Court of Appeals to have considered the

question has found vicarious liability when a discriminatory act results in a tangible employment action.... ("'If the plaintiff can show that she suffered an economic injury from her supervisor's actions, the employer becomes strictly liable without any further showing ...'"). In *Meritor*, we acknowledged this consensus. ("[T]he courts have consistently held employers liable for the discriminatory discharges of employees by supervisory personnel, whether or not the employer knew, or should have known, or approved of the supervisor's actions"). Although few courts have elaborated how agency principles support this rule, we think it reflects a correct application of the aided in the agency relation standard.

In the context of this case, a tangible employment action would have taken the form of a denial of a raise or a promotion. The concept of a tangible employment action appears in numerous cases in the Courts of Appeals discussing claims involving race, age, and national origin discrimination, as well as sex discrimination. Without endorsing the specific results of those decisions, we think it prudent to import the concept of a tangible employment action for resolution of the vicarious liability issue we consider here. A tangible employment action constitutes a significant change in employment status, such as hiring, firing, failing to promote, reassignment with significantly different responsibilities, or a decision causing a significant change in benefits....

When a supervisor makes a tangible employment decision, there is assurance the injury could not have been inflicted absent the agency relation. A tangible employment action in most cases inflicts direct economic harm. As a general proposition, only a supervisor, or other person acting with the authority of the company, can cause this sort of injury. A co-worker can break a co-worker's arm as easily as a supervisor, and anyone who has regular contact with an employee can inflict psychological injuries by his or her offensive conduct. See *Gary*, 59 F.3d, at 1397; *Henson*, 682 F.2d, at 910; *Barnes v. Costle*, 561 F.2d 983, 996 (CADC 1977) (MacKinnon, J., concurring). But one co-worker (absent some elaborate scheme) cannot dock another's pay, nor can one co-worker demote another. Tangible employment actions fall within the special province of the supervisor. The supervisor has been empowered by the company as a distinct class of agent to make economic decisions affecting other employees under his or her control.

continued

Tangible employment actions are the means by which the supervisor brings the official power of the enterprise to bear on subordinates. A tangible employment decision requires an official act of the enterprise, a company act. The decision in most cases is documented in official company records, and may be subject to review by higher level supervisors....

For these reasons, a tangible employment action taken by the supervisor becomes for Title VII purposes the act of the employer. Whatever the exact contours of the aided in the agency relation standard, its requirements will always be met when a supervisor takes a tangible employment action against a subordinate. In that instance, it would be implausible to interpret agency principles to allow an employer to escape liability, as *Meritor* itself appeared to acknowledge.

Whether the agency relation aids in commission of supervisor harassment which does not culminate in a tangible employment action is less obvious....

In order to accommodate the agency principles of vicarious liability for harm caused by misuse of supervisory authority, as well as Title VII's equally basic policies of encouraging forethought by employers and saving action by objecting employees, we adopt the following holding in this case and in *Faragher v. Boca Raton, post,* also decided today. An employer is subject to vicarious liability to a victimized employee for an actionable hostile environment created by a supervisor with immediate (or successively higher) authority over the employee. When no tangible employment action is taken, a defending employer may raise an affirmative defense to liability for damages, subject to proof by a preponderance of the evidence. The defense comprises two necessary elements: (a) that the employer exercised reasonable care to prevent and correct promptly any sexually harassing behavior, and (b) that the plaintiff employee unreasonably failed to take advantage of any preventive or corrective opportunities provided by the employer or to avoid harm otherwise. While proof that an employer had promulgated an anti-harassment policy with complaint procedure is not necessary in every instance as a matter of law, the need for a stated policy suitable to the employment circumstances may appropriately be addressed in any case when litigating the first element of the defense. And while proof that an employee failed to fulfill the corresponding obligation of reasonable care to avoid harm is not limited to showing any unreasonable failure to use any complaint procedure provided by the employer, a demonstration of such failure will normally suffice to satisfy the employer's burden under the second element of the defense. No affirmative defense is available, however, when the supervisor's harassment culminates in a tangible employment action, such as discharge, demotion, or undesirable reassignment.

Relying on existing case law which held out the promise of vicarious liability for all *quid pro quo* claims, see *supra,* at 7, Ellerth focused all her attention in the Court of Appeals on proving her claim fit within that category. Given our explanation that the labels *quid pro quo* and hostile work environment are not controlling for purposes of establishing employer liability, see *supra,* at 8, Ellerth should have an adequate opportunity to prove she has a claim for which Burlington is liable.

Although Ellerth has not alleged she suffered a tangible employment action at the hands of Slowik, which would deprive Burlington of the availability of the affirmative defense, this is not dispositive. In light of our decision, Burlington is still subject to vicarious liability for Slowik's activity, but Burlington should have an opportunity to assert and prove the affirmative defense to liability.

[Judgment affirmed.]

JUSTICE THOMAS, with whom JUSTICE SCALIA joins, Dissenting...

The Court today manufactures a rule that employers are vicariously liable if supervisors create a sexually hostile work environment, subject to an affirmative defense that the Court barely attempts to define. This rule applies even if the employer has a policy against sexual harassment, the employee knows about that policy, and the employee never informs anyone in a position of authority about the supervisor's conduct. As a result, employer liability under Title VII is judged by different standards depending upon whether a sexually or racially hostile work environment is alleged. The standard of employer liability should be the same in both instances: An employer should be liable if, and only if, the plaintiff proves that the employer was negligent in permitting the supervisor's conduct to occur....

Case Questions

1. What is tangible employment action in the context of a sexual harassment lawsuit?
2. Explain how an employer can be found to have "aided in the agency relation" and thus be liable for damages when the employer had no idea that a supervisor had turned down an employee for a position because the employee had rejected a sexual proposal.
3. Under what circumstances may an employer raise an affirmative defense to liability for damages in a sexual harassment case?

CASE 12.10 | PENNSYLVANIA STATE POLICE V. SUDERS
SUPREME COURT OF THE UNITED STATES, 542 U.S. 129 (2004).

[In March 1998, the Pennsylvania State Police (PSP) hired Nancy Suders to work as a police communications operator for the McConnellsburg barracks, where her male supervisors subjected her to a continuous barrage of sexual harassment. In June 1998, Suders told the PSP's Equal Employment Opportunity Officer, Virginia Smith-Elliott, that she might need help, but neither woman followed up on the conversation. Two months later Suders contacted Smith-Elliott again, this time reporting that she was being harassed and was afraid. Smith-Elliott told Suders to file a complaint, but did not tell her how to obtain the necessary form. Two days later Suders' supervisors arrested her for theft of her own computer-skills exam papers. Suders had removed the papers after concluding that the supervisors had falsely reported that she had repeatedly failed, when in fact, the exams were never forwarded for grading. Suders then resigned from the force and sued the PSP, alleging, *inter alia*, that she had been subjected to sexual harassment and constructively discharged, in violation of Title VII of the Civil Rights Act of 1964.

The District Court granted the PSP's motion for summary judgment. Although recognizing that Suders' testimony would permit a fact trier to conclude that her supervisors had created a hostile work environment, the court nevertheless held that the PSP was not vicariously liable for the supervisors' conduct because she unreasonably failed to avail herself of the PSP's antiharassment procedures. The Third Circuit Court of Appeals reversed and remanded the case for trial, ruling that a constructive discharge, if proved, constituted a "tangible employment action" that renders the employer liable and precludes an affirmative defense. The Supreme Court granted certiorari.]

GINSBURG, J....

Suders' claim is of the same genre as the hostile work environment claims the Court analyzed in *Ellerth* and *Faragher*. Essentially, Suders presents a "worse case" harassment scenario, harassment ratcheted up to the breaking point. Like the harassment considered in our pathmarking decisions, harassment so intolerable as to cause a resignation may be effected through co-worker conduct, unofficial supervisory conduct, or official company acts. Unlike an actual termination, which is *always* effected through an official act of the company, a constructive discharge need not be. A constructive discharge involves both an employee's decision to leave and precipitating conduct: The former involves no official action; the latter, like a harassment claim without any constructive discharge assertion, may or may not involve official action.

To be sure, a constructive discharge is functionally the same as an actual termination in damages-enhancing respects. As the Third Circuit observed, both "en[d] the employer-employee relationship," and both "inflic[t]...direct economic harm." 325 F. 3d, at 460 (internal quotation marks omitted). But when an official act does not underlie the constructive discharge, the *Ellerth* and *Faragher* analysis, we here hold, calls for extension of the affirmative defense to the employer. As those leading decisions indicate, official directions and declarations are the acts most likely to be brought home to the employer, the measures over which the employer can exercise greatest control. See *Ellerth*, 524 U.S., at 762. Absent "an official act of the enterprise," *ibid.*, as the last straw, the employer ordinarily would have no particular reason to suspect that a resignation is not the typical kind daily occurring in the work force.

continued

And as *Ellerth* and *Faragher* further point out, an official act reflected in company records—a demotion or a reduction in compensation, for example—shows "beyond question" that the supervisor has used his managerial or controlling position to the employee's disadvantage. See *Ellerth*, 524 U.S., at 760. Absent such an official act, the extent to which the supervisor's misconduct has been aided by the agency relation..., is less certain. That uncertainty, our precedent establishes,..., justifies affording the employer the chance to establish, through the *Ellerth/Faragher* affirmative defense, that it should not be held vicariously liable....

We agree with the Third Circuit that the case, in its current posture, presents genuine issues of material fact concerning Suders' hostile work environment and constructive discharge claims. We hold, however, that the Court of Appeals erred in declaring the affirmative defense described in *Ellerth* and *Faragher* never available in constructive discharge cases. Accordingly, we vacate the Third Circuit's judgment and remand the case for further proceedings consistent with this opinion.

It is so ordered.

JUSTICE THOMAS, Dissenting.

[Justice Thomas dissented because Suders did not proffer sufficient evidence of an adverse employment act taken because of her sex, nor has she proffered any evidence that the employer knew or should have known of the alleged harassment.]

Case Questions

1. From the point of view of direct economic harm, is a constructive discharge functionally the same as an actual termination? If so, should not both situations be governed by the same rule of law?

2. What justification exists for affording an employer the chance to establish an affirmative defense and avoid liability where "no official act of the enterprise" is tied to the proven constructive discharge caused by a supervisor?

SECTION 108: EMPLOYER LIABILITY FOR COWORKER AND NONEMPLOYEE SEXUAL HARASSMENT

Sexual harassment of employees by their coworkers is an issue faced by employers in today's workforce, as is the matter of employers' liability for the sexual harassment of their employees by nonemployees.

EMPLOYER LIABILITY FOR COWORKERS' SEXUAL HARASSMENT

Most employers are aware of the problems of sexual harassment and now have procedures through which employees can rectify coworker sexual harassment. Under the rules of conduct of many employers, a coworker may be subject to discipline up to and including discharge for the sexual harassment of fellow workers in the form of sexual flirtations, propositions, or other sexually degrading conduct.[90]

---

[90] See, for example, AT&T's affirmative action policy statement, which contains a section prohibiting sexual harassment. Under this section, "sexually harassing conduct in the workplace, whether committed by supervisors or non-supervisory personnel, is also prohibited. This includes: repeated offensive sexual flirtations, advances, propositions, continual or repeated verbal commentaries about an individual's body; sexually degrading words used to describe an individual; and the display in the workplace of sexually suggestive objects or pictures." In the AT&T and IBEW arbitration decision AAA 327-3, Arbitrator Robins upheld a five-day suspension concerning an offensive action in violation of the company's sexual harassment policy that the perpetrator believed to be a joke that would be seen as amusing by the individual who was the object of the action. See also Greyhound Lines, Inc. and IAM, AAA 325, p. 1, upholding discipline for "boisterous, profane or vulgar language."

Where the coworker's conduct is objectively severe or pervasive to alter the conditions of employment of a fellow worker and thus creates a hostile work environment, the employer can be held liable for this unlawful conduct.[91] However, the employer is liable only if it knew or should have known of the misconduct and yet failed to take prompt and reasonable corrective action.[92] The *Ellison v. Brady*[93] case, presented as end-of-chapter problem 13, presents a fact pattern allowing full discussion of the applicable standard to apply in determining whether or not the conduct in question was so objectively severe and pervasive as to amount to sexual harassment. In *Kyriazi v. Western Electric Co.*,[94] where three male coworkers teased and tormented the complainant Kyriazi and made wagers concerning her virginity, the court found that Kyriazi's supervisors were aware of the harassment and made no attempt to discipline the coworkers involved. Not only did the court find the employer liable for violating Title VII for this and other employer-imputed conduct, the court, under state law claims made by Kyriazi, assessed $1,500 punitive damages against each of the coworkers and explicitly prevented the employer from indemnifying these employees for their punitive damages.

An employer may be held to have violated Title VII of the Civil Rights Act of 1964 if it permits its employees to be subjected to sexual harassment by nonemployees. In such a case, the burden of proof would be on the complainant to show that the harassment in question created a hostile or abusive work atmosphere and that the employer knew or should have known of the harassment and failed to take reasonable measures to prevent it.

Presently, cases of sexual harassment by nonemployees relate to employers requiring employees to wear sexually provocative uniforms where the employers should reasonably know that wearing the uniforms would subject the employees to sexual harassment by nonemployees. In *EEOC v. Sage Realty Corp.*,[95] where a female lobby attendant was required to wear a uniform that resulted in her being subjected to sexual propositions and lewd comments by passersbys, the court found that the employer, Sage, had violated Title VII of the Act. The court accepted the principle that an employer may impose "reasonable" dress requirements but held that the employer did not have the unfettered discretion to force employees to wear sexually provocative uniforms.

There is much discussion presently about sexual harassment issues relating to waitresses who accept jobs at "sex appeal" restaurants, where they know they are required to wear "provocative" uniforms. Have the waitresses assumed the risk of harassment or "welcomed" it by taking such jobs? Can the employer protect itself from liability by having a published policy and practice of immediately removing

---

[91] In *Ballard v. Union Pacific R.R. Co.*, 2008 U.S. Dist. LEXIS 36450 (D. Neb. May 5, 2008), the court granted summary judgment for the employer, determining that the coworker conduct was a single act of vulgar behavior not based on sexual desire, and the court pointed out that Title VII is not designed to purge the workplace of vulgarity.

[92] *Star v. West*, 237 F.3d 1036 (9th Cir. 2001).

[93] 924 F.2d 872 (9th Cir. 1991).

[94] 461 F. Supp. 894 (D.N.J. 1978), enforced by 465 F. Supp. 1141 (D.N.J. 1979), modifying and enforcing, 476 F. Supp. 355 (D.N.J. 1979).

[95] *EEOC v. Sage Realty Corp.*, 25 E.P.D. ¶ 31,529 (S.D.N.Y. 1981).

offensive patrons from the premises? In Section 111, the "BFOQ" defense will be discussed. Can an employer hire only waitresses with sex appeal for a sex appeal motif restaurant? End-of-chapter problem 12 deals with these issues.

SECTION 109: NATIONAL ORIGIN DISCRIMINATION AND "ENGLISH ONLY" RULES

National origin discrimination extends Title VII protection to members of all nationalities.[96] As examples, national origin discrimination claims under Title VII have been brought on behalf of Spanish-surnamed persons; a person of Cajun descent; and persons of Hungarian, German, and Polish ancestry.[97] A disparate treatment of and retaliation Title VII lawsuit against Arizona web domain registrar Go Daddy Inc. on behalf of Youseff Boumama, a Muslim of Moroccan national origin, resulted in a verdict of $390,000 in back pay, compensatory and punitive damages because of national origin, and religious discrimination and a retaliatory termination.[98]

The judicial principles that have emerged from cases involving other forms of employment discrimination are generally applicable to cases involving allegations of national origin discrimination. Thus, physical standards such as minimum height requirements, which tend to exclude persons of a particular national origin because of the physical stature of the group, have been deemed unlawful where these standards cannot be justified by business necessity.[99]

Adverse employment decisions based on an individual's lack of English language skills have been considered violative of Title VII in those situations where the language requirement bears no demonstrable relationship to the successful performance of the job to which it is applied. In *Fragante* v. *City and County of Honolulu*, presented in this section, the U.S. Court of Appeals for the Ninth Circuit cautioned that it is an easy refuge for an employer to unlawfully discriminate against an individual because of national origin by falsely claiming that the individual lacked the necessary communication skills demanded by the job in question. The court found no national origin discrimination, however, because it determined that an honest assessment of Fragante's communication skills was made and that he was passed over not because of his accent, but because of the deleterious effect of his accent on his ability to communicate orally.

In the ever-expanding diversity of the American workforce, a significant number of workers prefer to speak a language other than English on the job. However, it is a valid company rule for an employer to require employees dealing with the public to speak only English to customers because politeness, helpfulness, and approachability

---

[96] State law may also apply to national origin discrimination. For example, five workers from India were successful in their national origin discrimination suit against their employer ADVO, Inc., under the California Fair Employment and Housing Act; *Chopra v. ADVO, Inc.* (Cal. Ct. App. No. A103168 [2004]).

[97] *Roach v. Dresser Industries*, 494 F. Supp. 215, (W.D. La. 1980).

[98] *CCH Labor Law Reports*, No. 1496, Rpt. 803 (Jan. 3, 2007).

[99] *Davis v. County of Los Angeles*, 13 FEP 1217 (9th Cir. 1976), and *League of United Latin American Citizens v. City of Santa Ana*, 410 F. Supp. 873 (C.D. Calif. 1976).

are business necessities and not a matter of abstract customer preference.[100] Moreover, EEOC guidelines provide that English-only rules are justified when customers speak only English, where efficiency requires cooperation among those who need to speak the same language, when supervisory personnel who speak only English need to monitor employees and their communications with customers, and when common language is necessary to promote workplace safety.[101]

In *Garcia v. Glour*,[102] the employer forbid bilingual sales employees to speak anything but English in the sales area while on the job. An expert witness testified that the Spanish language is the most important aspect of ethnic identification for Mexican–Americans. However, the court held that Garcia was discharged not because he was the victim of discrimination based on national origin, but rather because he had the ability to comply with the employer's "English-only" rule but did not do so.

Title VII does not prohibit discrimination on the basis of citizenship where an employer has a rule against employment of aliens and the application of the rule is not a pretext for excluding persons of a particular national origin.[103]

CASE 12.11	## FRAGANTE V. CITY AND COUNTY OF HONOLULU U.S. COURT OF APPEALS, 888 F.2D 591 (9ᵀᴴ CIR. 1989).

[Manuel Fragante applied for a clerk's job with the city and county of Honolulu. Although he placed high enough on a civil service eligibility list to be chosen for the position, he was not selected because of a perceived deficiency in relevant oral communication skills caused by his "heavy Filipino accent." Fragante brought suit, alleging that the defendants discriminated against him on the basis of his national origin, in violation of Title VII of the Civil Rights Act. At the conclusion of the trial, the district court found that the oral ability to communicate effectively and clearly was a legitimate occupational qualification for the job in question. And finding no proof of a discriminatory intent or motive by the defendant, the court dismissed Fragante's complaint. Fragante appealed.]

continued

---

[100] See *EEOC v. Sephora*, 419 F. Supp. 2d 408, 417 (S.D.N.Y. 2005). But see *EEOC v. Premier Operator Service, Inc.*, 113 F. Supp. 2d 1066 (N.D. Tex. 2000) where the court found the employer's English-only rule discriminatory, having an adverse impact on its employees' national origin in violation of Title VII.

[101] The Federal Motor Carrier Safety Administration requires anyone with a commercial driver's license to speak English well enough to talk with the police in order to communicate about the vehicle, its operations, and its loads. More than 17 percent of the nation's 7.4 million truck drivers are Hispanic, according to the Bureau of Labor Statistics. It is unknown how many speak both Spanish and English. Manual Castillo, a permanent resident of the United States (a green card holder), took his California commercial driver's license test in Spanish because it was the language he was most comfortable speaking. In July 2007, he was stopped in Alabama hauling a truckload of onions and issued a $500 ticket for being a "non-English speaking driver." He was not speeding or operating improperly and had no violations of record. In an interview in Spanish, he said he speaks English at the third-grade level. Police issued some 25,230 tickets in 2007 for failure to speak English well enough to communicate with police. Jay Reeves, "Federal Government Looks to Tighten English Law For Truckers," *Boston Globe*, July 18, 2008, p. A16.

[102] 618 F.2d 264, 22 FEP 1403 (5ᵗʰ Cir. 1980). See also *Garcia v. Spun Steak Co.*, 988 F.2d 1480 (9ᵗʰ Cir. 1993).

[103] *Espinoza v. Farah Manufacturing Co.*, 414 U.S. 86, 6 FEP 933 (1973).

TROTT, C. J....

I.

The Statute and Its Purpose

Preliminarily, we do well to remember that this country was founded and has been built in large measure by people from other lands, many of whom came here—especially after our early beginnings—with a limited knowledge of English. This flow of immigrants has continued and has been encouraged over the years. From its inception, the United States of America has been a dream to many around the world. We hold out promises of freedom, equality, and economic opportunity to many who only know these words as concepts. It would be more than ironic if we followed up our invitation to people such as Manuel Fragante with a closed economic door based on national origin discrimination. It is no surprise that Title VII speaks to this issue and clearly articulates the policy of our nation: unlawful discrimination based on national origin shall not be permitted to exist in the workplace. But, it is also true that there is another important aspect of Title VII: the "preservation of an employer's remaining freedom of choice." ...

Accent and national origin are obviously inextricably intertwined in many cases. It would therefore be an easy refuge in this context for an employer unlawfully discriminating against someone based on national origin to state falsely that it was not the person's national origin that caused the employment or promotion problem, but the candidate's inability to measure up to the communications skills demanded by the job. We encourage a very searching look by the district courts at such a claim.

An adverse employment decision may be predicated upon an individual's accent when—but only when—it interferes materially with job performance. There is nothing improper about an employer making an *honest* assessment of the oral communications skills of a candidate for a job when such skills are reasonably related to job performance. EEOC Compliance Manual (CCH) ¶ 4035 at 3877-78 (1986); see also *Mejia v. New York Sheraton Hotel*, 459 F. Supp. 375, 377 (S.D.N.Y. 1978) (Dominican chambermaid properly denied promotion to front desk because of her "inability to articulate clearly or coherently and to make herself adequately understood in ... English"); *Carino v. University of Oklahoma Board of Regents*, 750 F.2d 815, 819 (10th Cir. 1984) (plaintiff with a "noticeable" Filipino accent was improperly denied a position as supervisor of a dental laboratory where his accent did not interfere with his ability to perform supervisory tasks); *Berke*, 628 F.2d at 981 (employee with "pronounced" Polish accent whose command of English was "well above that of the average adult American" was improperly denied two positions because of her accent)....

...In a letter, dated June 28, 1982, the reasons why he was not selected were articulated as follows:

> As to the reason for your non-selection we felt the two selected applicants were both superior in their verbal communication ability. As we indicated in your interview, our clerks are constantly dealing with the public and the ability to speak clearly is one of the most important skills required for the position. Therefore, while we were impressed with your educational and employment history, we felt the applicants selected would be better able to work in our office because of their communication skills.

The interviewers' record discloses Fragante's third place ranking was based on his "pronounced accent which is difficult to understand." Indeed, Fragante can point to no facts which indicate that his ranking was based on factors other than his inability to communicate effectively with the public. This view was shared by the district court....

Fragante argues the district court erred in considering "listener prejudice" as a legitimate, nondiscriminatory reason for failure to hire. We find, however, that the district court did not determine defendants refused to hire Fragante on the basis that some listeners would "turn off" a Filipino accent. The district court after trial noted that: "Fragante, in fact, has a difficult manner of pronunciation and the Court further finds as a fact from his general testimony that he would often not respond directly to the questions as propounded...."

In sum, the record conclusively shows that Fragante was passed over because of the deleterious *effect* of his Filipino accent on his ability to communicate orally, not merely because he had such an accent.

The district court is
Affirmed.

Case Questions

1. Why do courts take a very careful look at non-selection decisions based on foreign accents?

2. Why was Fragante not selected for the clerk's position when he had higher tests scores than the two successful candidates?

SECTION 110: PROTECTION AGAINST RETALIATION

Section 704(a) sets forth Title VII's anti-retaliation provision in the following terms:

> "It shall be an unlawful employment practice for an employer to discriminate against any of his employees or applicants for employment ... because he has opposed any practice made an unlawful employment practice by this subchapter, or because he has made a charge, testified, assisted, or participated in any manner in an investigation, proceeding, or hearing under this subchapter."

Some U.S. courts of appeals had held that the retaliation provisions set forth in Section 704(a) of Title VII apply only to retaliation that takes the form of "ultimate employment actions" such as demotions, suspensions, and terminations and did not apply to ministerial matters such as reprimands and poor evaluations. The EEOC believed that the statute prohibits any adverse treatment that is based on a retaliatory motive and is reasonably likely to deter the charging party or others from engaging in protected activity. In *Burlington Northern & Santa Fe Railway Co. (BNSF) v. White*, presented in this section, the U.S. Supreme Court held that a plaintiff may pursue a retaliation claim under Title VII if the "employer's challenged action would have been material to a reasonable employee" and likely would have "dissuaded a reasonable worker from making or supporting a charge of discrimination." The Supreme Court specifically rejected more restrictive standards of proof that had been used by several U.S. courts of appeals. The Court stated that by focusing on the materiality of the challenged action and the perspective of a reasonable person, it believes that this standard will screen out trivial conduct while capturing those acts that are likely to dissuade employees from complaining or assisting in complaints about discrimination. BNSF believed that it was not retaliatory to assign the plaintiff, Ms. White, to do the work she was hired to do, that of a track laborer; and her suspension of 37 days was corrected, and she was made whole for her loss. The Supreme Court, applying the "materially adverse to a reasonable person" standard, disagreed with BNSF.

The *Burlington Northern* decision is significant regarding its findings as the "reach" of the Section 704 anti-retaliation provision. The Court stated that Title VII's anti-retaliation provision "does not confine the actions and harms it forbids to those that are related to employment or occur at the workplace." The Court reasoned that "[a]n employer can effectively retaliate against an employee by taking actions not directly related to his employment or by causing him harm outside the workplace." For example, in *Berry v. Stevinson Chevrolet*, the Tenth Circuit found an actionable retaliation claim where an employer filed false criminal charges against a former employee who complained about discrimination.[104]

EMPLOYER PREVENTIVE STEPS

Employers must be aware that the *Burlington Northern* decision extends the reach of Section 704 protections beyond the workplace and employment-related retaliatory acts and harms, widening the range of employer conduct subject to the Act.

---

[104] *Berry v. Stevinson Chevrolet*, 74 F.3d 980, 984, 986 (10th Cir. 1996).

The standard, involving questions of "materiality" of the employer action and ways the action would influence a "reasonable worker," will result in an increase in litigation involving issues of fact for juries to resolve as opposed to the resolution through the summary judgment process as was appropriate in some retaliation cases. The time-consuming pretrial procedures for building cases for jury trials and the trials themselves may add significant costs to employers and employees, with the employers responsible for their own attorneys' fees, damages, and attorneys' fees for the employees should the employees be successful in their litigation. Accordingly, employers must develop and implement effective anti-retaliation policies and procedures for their supervisors and employees. With the wide notoriety of the *Burlington Northern* decision, employers should expect to have to deal with an increased number of claims of alleged retaliation. (Retaliation claims under Title VII increased from 19,560 in FY 2006 to 23,371 in FY 2007.)

Employers should develop and implement an anti-retaliation preventive action plan. Each employer should:

- Post as part of its anti-discrimination and harassment policies a broad anti-retaliation policy that will be strictly enforced.
- Establish ongoing educational programs for all levels of supervision to ensure that managers understand actions that may be construed as retaliation and the possible consequences to the employer of retaliatory litigation. The plan should set forth the disciplinary consequences to company officials found responsible for retaliatory actions.
- Make certain that complainants of race, color, religion, sex, national origin, age, and disability know that there will be no retaliation for filing a complaint and that each individual who is interviewed or who testifies regarding such a complaint also will be informed of the company's no-retaliation policy.
- Human Resources (HR) specialists should be assigned to scrutinize any employer action against an employee who has previously complained about discrimination. Supervisors proposing disciplinary or "other" actions against a complainant must be able to demonstrate to the HR specialist that legitimate nondiscriminatory reasons exist for the proposed employer actions. As examples from the *Burlington Northern* case, when the roadmaster (company supervisor) concluded that Ms. White's foreman was in violation of the company's sexual harassment policy and should be disciplined and be required to attend a sexual harassment training session, the concurrent timing of his reassigning the victim to less desirable duties would have signaled a clear anti-retaliation violation to a Human Resources specialist, which would have resulted in the proposed action having been overruled by the specialist and litigation would have been avoided. So also when the track foreman and the roadmaster agreed to suspend Ms. White for insubordination without pay, believing that she had refused a direct order to ride with another foreman, mandatory consultation with a Human Resources specialist could have initially resulted in an immediate suspension "with pay" and an expedited investigation by the employer to ascertain the true facts of the incident, rather than a 37-day period without a paycheck, which was a materially adverse action, even though the employer ultimately determined that the discipline was not

warranted and she eventually received full back pay and benefits and the discipline was removed from her record.

APPLICATION BEYOND TITLE VII

In *CBOCS West Inc. v. Humphries*,[105] the U.S. Supreme Court, by a 7-2 vote, held that lawsuits brought under 42 U.S.C. § 1981 encompass claims of retaliation. Thus, Hedrick Humphries, a black former assistant manager of a Cracker Barrel Restaurant, will be able to pursue a retaliation claim under the Civil Rights Act of 1866 (42 U.S.C. § 1981). As set forth in Chapter 13, Section 120 of this book, Section 1981 allows a four-year statute of limitation period for intentional discrimination claims based on race and uncapped damages. Moreover, plaintiffs do not have to file an EEOC charge.

CASE 12.12	**BURLINGTON NORTHERN SANTA FE RAILWAY CO. v. WHITE** SUPREME COURT OF THE UNITED STATES, 126 S.CT. 2405 (2006).

[Shelia White was hired by the BNSF Railway as a track laborer at the Carrier's Tennessee Yard. She was the only woman in the track department. When hired, she was given the job of forklift operator, as opposed to the ordinary track laborer tasks. Three months after being hired, she complained to the roadmaster that her foreman treated her differently than he treated male employees and twice made inappropriate remarks. The foreman was suspended without pay for 10 days and ordered to attend sexual harassment training. Also at that time, the roadmaster reassigned the forklift duties to the former operator, who was "senior" to White, and assigned White to track labor duties. Six months into her employment, White refused to ride in a truck as directed by a different foreman, and she was suspended for insubordination. Some 37 days later, she was reinstated with full back pay, and the discipline was removed from her record. She filed a complaint with the EEOC, claiming the reassignment to track laborer duties was unlawful gender discrimination and retaliation for her complaint about her treatment by the foreman. The 37-day suspension led to a second retaliation charge. A jury rejected her gender discrimination claim and awarded her compensatory damages for her retaliation claims. BNSF appealed, contending that Ms. White was hired as a track laborer and it was not retaliatory to assign her to do the work she was hired to do. And it asserts that the suspension of 37 days was corrected, and she was made whole for her loss.]

BREYER, J....

To be sure, reassignment of job duties is not automatically actionable. Whether a particular reassignment is materially adverse depends upon the circumstances of the particular case, and "should be judged from the perspective of a reasonable person in the plaintiff's position, considering 'all the circumstances.'" *Oncale*, 523 U.S., at 81, 118 S.Ct. 998. But here, the jury had before it considerable evidence that the track labor duties were "by all accounts more arduous and dirtier"; that the "forklift operator position required more qualifications, which is an indication of prestige"; and that "the forklift operator position was objectively considered a better job and the male employees resented White for occupying it." 364 F. 3d, at 803 (internal quotation marks omitted). Based on this record, a jury could reasonably conclude that the reassignment of responsibilities would have been materially adverse to a reasonable employee.

Second, Burlington argues that the 37-day suspension without pay lacked statutory significance because Burlington ultimately reinstated White with backpay. Burlington says that "it defies reason to believe that Congress would have considered a rescinded investigatory suspension with full back pay" to be unlawful....

...White did receive backpay. But White and her family had to live for 37 days without income. They did not know during that time whether or when White could return to work. Many reasonable

continued

---

[105] 128 S.Ct. 1951 (2008).

employees would find a month without a paycheck to be a serious hardship. And White described to the jury the physical and emotional hardship that 37 days of having "no income, no money" in fact caused. 1 Tr. 154 ("That was the worst Christmas I had out of my life. No income, no money, and that made all of us feel bad.... I got very depressed"). Indeed, she obtained medical treatment for her emotional distress. A reasonable employee facing the choice between retaining her job (and paycheck) and filing a discrimination complaint might well choose the former. That is to say, an indefinite suspension without pay could well act as a deterrent, even if the suspended employee eventually received backpay. Cf. *Mitchell*, 361 U.S., at 292, 80 S.Ct, 332 ("[I]t needs no argument to show that fear of economic retaliation might often operate to induce aggrieved employees quietly to accept substandard conditions").

Thus, the jury's conclusion that the 37-day suspension without pay was materially adverse was a reasonable one.

[Affirmed]
It is so ordered.

Case Questions

1. Was the reassignment of Sheila White from forklift operator duties to track laborer duties unlawful gender discrimination and retaliation for her complaint about her treatment by the first foreman?

2. Can a rescinded disciplinary suspension with full back pay be considered a materially adverse employer action in violation of Title VII's prohibition against retaliation?

SECTION 111: TITLE VII: SECTION 703 EXCEPTIONS

Section 703 of the Act defines what employment activities are unlawful. This same section, however, also exempts several key practices from the scope of Title VII enforcement. The most important are the bona fide occupational qualification exception, the testing and educational requirement exception, and the seniority system exception.

Bona Fide Occupational Qualification Exception

Section 703(e) stipulates that it shall not be unlawful employment practice for an employer to hire employees on the basis of the religion, sex, or national origin in those certain instances where religion, sex, or national origin is a bona fide occupational qualification (BFOQ) reasonably necessary to the normal operation of a particular enterprise. The so-called BFOQ clause is construed narrowly by the courts, and the burden of proving the business necessity for any such restrictive occupational qualifications is on the employer.

In *Dothard v. Rawlinson*,[106] the Supreme Court, while recognizing that the BFOQ exception was meant to be an extremely narrow one, upheld as a BFOQ a male-only requirement for correctional counselor (guards) positions in male maximum security correctional institutions in Alabama. The Court referred to the substantial amount of testimony that the use of women as guards in "contact" positions under the existing conditions in Alabama maximum security male penitentiaries (which included 20 percent of the male prisoners being sex offenders housed throughout the facilities) would pose a substantial security problem directly linked to the sex of the prison guards.

---

[106] 433 U.S. 321, 15 FEP 10 (1977).

In *UAW v. Johnson Controls, Inc.*, presented in this section, the Supreme Court dealt with the difficult issues relating to employer fetal protection policies under Title VII. The Court found that the employer's fetal protection policy that barred all fertile women from jobs involving lead exposure exceeding OSHA standards was discriminatory, as only women employees were affected by the policy. And the Court rejected the employer's BFOQ defense. Moreover, it determined that the Pregnancy Discrimination Act contained its own BFOQ standard, which requires employers to treat potentially pregnant employees the same as other employees if their ability to do the work is the same. The Court held that Title VII mandates that decisions about the welfare of future children be left to the parents who conceive, bear, support, and raise them rather than to employers who hire those parents or to the courts.

CASE 12.13	## UAW v. JOHNSON CONTROLS SUPREME COURT OF THE UNITED STATES, 499 U.S. 187 (1991).

[Johnson Controls, Inc. (JCI) manufactures batteries. A primary ingredient in the battery manufacturing process is lead. Occupational exposure to lead entails health risks, including the risk of harm to any fetus carried by a female employee. After eight of its employees became pregnant while maintaining blood lead levels exceeding levels set by the Centers for Disease Control (CDC) as critical for a worker planning to have a family, respondent announced a policy barring all women, except those whose infertility was medically documented, from jobs involving actual or potential lead exposure exceeding the OSHA standard. Petitioners filed a class action in the district court, claiming that the policy constituted sex discrimination violative of Title VII of the Civil Rights Act of 1964, as amended. Among the individual plaintiffs were Mary Craig, who had chosen to be sterilized in order to avoid losing her job; Elsie Nason, a 50-year-old divorcee who had suffered a loss in compensation when she was transferred out of a job where she was exposed to lead; and Donald Penney, who had been denied a request for a leave of absence for the purpose of lowering his lead level because he intended to become a father. The court granted summary judgment for respondent, and the court of appeals affirmed. The Supreme Court granted certiorari.]

BLACKMUN, J....

I.

The bias in Johnson Controls' policy is obvious. Fertile men, but not fertile women, are given a choice as to whether they wish to risk their reproductive health for a particular job. Section 703(a) of the Civil Rights Act of 1964, 78 Stat. 255, as amended, 42 U.S.C. § 2000e-2(a), prohibits sex-biased classifications in terms and conditions of employment, in hiring and discharging decisions, and in other employment decisions that adversely affect an employee's status. Respondent's fetal-protection policy explicitly discriminates against women on the basis of their sex. The policy excludes women with childbearing capacity from lead-exposed jobs and so creates a facial classification based on gender....

First, Johnson Controls' policy classifies on the basis of gender and childbearing capacity, rather than fertility alone. Respondent does not seek to protect the unconceived children of all its employees. Despite evidence in the record about the debilitating effect of lead exposure on the male reproductive system, Johnson Controls is concerned only with the harms that may befall the unborn offspring of its female employees....

"The Pregnancy Discrimination Act has now made clear that, for all Title VII purposes, discrimination based on a woman's pregnancy is, on its face, discrimination because of her sex." *Newport News Shipbuilding & Dry Dock Co. v. EEOC*, 462 U.S. 669, 684 (1983). In its use of the words "capable of bearing children" in the 1982 policy statement as the criterion for exclusion, Johnson Controls explicitly classifies on the basis of potential for pregnancy. Under the PDA, such a classification must be regarded, for Title VII purposes, in the same light as explicit sex

continued

discrimination. Respondent has chosen to treat all its female employees as potentially pregnant; that choice evinces discrimination on the basis of sex.

We concluded above that Johnson Controls' policy is not neutral because it does not apply to the reproductive capacity of the company's male employees in the same way as it applies to that of the females. Moreover, the absence of a malevolent motive does not convert a facially discriminatory policy into a neutral policy with a discriminatory effect....

... We hold that Johnson Controls' fetal-protection policy is sex discrimination forbidden under Title VII unless respondent can establish that sex is a "bona fide occupational qualification."

II.

Under § 703(e)(1) of Title VII, an employer may discriminate on the basis of "religion, sex, or national origin in those certain instances where religion, sex, or national origin is a bona fide occupational qualification reasonably necessary to the normal operation of that particular business or enterprise." We therefore turn to the question whether Johnson Controls' fetal-protection policy is one of those "certain instances" that come within the BFOQ exception.

The BFOQ defense is written narrowly, and this Court has read it narrowly. We have read the BFOQ language of § 4(f) of the Age Discrimination in Employment Act of 1967 (ADEA), 81 Stat. 603, as amended, 29 U.S.C. § 623(f)(1), which tracks the BFOQ provision in Title VII, just as narrowly. Our emphasis on the restrictive scope of the BFOQ defense is grounded on both the language and the legislative history of § 703.

The wording of the BFOQ defense contains several terms of restriction that indicate that the exception reaches only special situations. The statute thus limits the situations in which discrimination is permissible to "certain instances" where sex discrimination is "reasonably necessary" to the "normal operation" of the "particular" business. Each one of these terms—certain, normal, particular—prevents the use of general subjective standards and favors an objective, verifiable requirement. But the most telling term is "occupational"; this indicates that these objective, verifiable requirements must concern job-related skills and aptitudes.

Johnson Controls argues that its fetal-protection policy falls within the so-called safety exception to the BFOQ. Our cases have stressed that discrimination on the basis of sex because of safety concerns is

allowed only in narrow circumstances. In *Dothard v. Rawlinson*, this Court indicated that danger to a woman herself does not justify discrimination. 433 U.S., at 335, 97 S. Ct. at 2729–2730. We there allowed the employer to hire only male guards in contact areas of maximum-security male penitentiaries only because more was at stake than the "individual woman's decision to weigh and accept the risks of employment." *Ibid*. We found sex to be a BFOQ inasmuch as the employment of a female guard would create real risks of safety to others if violence broke out because the guard was a woman. Sex discrimination was tolerated because sex related to the guard's ability to do the job—maintaining prison security. We also required in *Dothard* a high correlation between sex and ability to perform job functions and refused to allow employers to use sex as a proxy for strength although it might be a fairly accurate one....

Our case law, therefore, makes clear that the safety exception is limited to instances in which sex or pregnancy actually interferes with the employee's ability to perform the job. This approach is consistent with the language of the BFOQ provision itself, for it suggests that permissible distinctions based on sex must relate to ability to perform the duties of the job. Johnson Controls suggests, however, that we expand the exception to allow fetal-protection policies that mandate particular standards for pregnant or fertile women. We decline to do so. Such an expansion contradicts not only the language of the BFOQ and the narrowness of its exception but the plain language and history of the Pregnancy Discrimination Act.

The PDA's amendment to Title VII contains a BFOQ standard of its own: unless pregnant employees differ from others "in their ability or inability to work," they must be "treated the same" as other employees "for all employment-related purposes." 42 U.S.C. § 2000e(k). This language clearly sets forth Congress' remedy for discrimination on the basis of pregnancy and potential pregnancy. Women who are either pregnant or potentially pregnant, must be treated like others "similar in their ability ... to work." *Ibid*. In other words, women as capable of doing their jobs as their male counterparts may not be forced to choose between having a child and having a job....

The legislative history confirms what the language of the Pregnancy Discrimination Act compels. Both the House and the Senate Reports accompanying the legislation indicate that this statutory standard was chosen to protect female workers from being treated

continued

differently from other employees simply because of their capacity to bear children....

We conclude that the language of both the BFOQ provision and the PDA which amended it, as well as the legislative history and the case law, prohibit an employer from discriminating against a woman because of her capacity to become pregnant unless her reproductive potential prevents her from performing the duties of her job. We reiterate our holdings ... that an employer must direct its concerns about a woman's ability to perform her job safely and efficiently to those aspects of the woman's job-related activities that fall within the "essence" of the particular business.

III.

We have no difficulty concluding that Johnson Controls cannot establish a BFOQ. Fertile women, as far as appears in the record, participate in the manufacture of batteries as efficiently as anyone else. Johnson Controls' professed moral and ethical concerns about the welfare of the next generation do not suffice to establish a BFOQ of female sterility. Decisions about the welfare of future children must be left to the parents who conceive, bear, support, and raise them rather than to the employers who hire those parents. Congress has mandated this choice through Title VII, as amended by the Pregnancy Discrimination Act. Johnson Controls has attempted to exclude women because of their reproductive capacity. Title VII and the PDA simply do not allow a woman's dismissal because of her failure to submit to sterilization.

Nor can concerns about the welfare of the next generation be considered a part of the "essence" of Johnson Controls' business. Judge Easterbrook in this case pertinently observed: "It is word play to say that 'the job' at Johnson [Controls] is to make batteries without risk to fetuses in the same way 'the job' at Western Air Lines is to fly planes without crashing." 886 F.2d, at 913.

Johnson Controls argues that it must exclude all fertile women because it is impossible to tell which women will become pregnant while working with lead.... Johnson Controls' fear of prenatal injury, no matter how sincere, does not begin to show that substantially all of its fertile women employees are incapable of doing their jobs.

IV.

A word about tort liability and the increased cost of fertile women in the workplace is perhaps necessary. One of the dissenting judges in this case expressed concern about an employer's tort liability and concluded that liability for a potential injury to a fetus is a social cost that Title VII does not require a company to ignore. 886 F.2d, at 904–905. It is correct to say that Title VII does not prevent the employer from having a conscience. The statute, however, does prevent sex-specific fetal-protection policies. These two aspects of the Title VII do not conflict.

More than 40 States currently recognize a right to recover for a prenatal injury based either on negligence or on wrongful death. According to Johnson Controls, however, the company complies with the lead standard developed by OSHA and warns its female employees about the damaging effects of lead. It is worth noting that OSHA gave the problem of lead lengthy consideration and concluded that "there is no basis whatsoever for the claim that women of childbearing age should be excluded from the workplace in order to protect the fetus or the course of pregnancy." Instead, OSHA established a series of mandatory protections which, taken together, "should effectively minimize any risk to the fetus and newborn child." *Id.*, at 52966. Without negligence, it would be difficult for a court to find liability on the part of the employer. If, under general tort principles, Title VII bans sex-specific fetal-protection policies, the employer fully informs the woman of the risk, and the employer has not acted negligently, the basis for holding an employer liable seems remote at best....

V.

Our holding today that Title VII, as so amended, forbids sex-specific fetal-protection policies is neither remarkable nor unprecedented. Concern for a woman's existing or potential offspring historically has been the excuse for denying women equal employment opportunities. See, *e.g.*, *Muller v. Oregon*, 208 U.S. 412, 28 S. Ct. 324, 52 L.Ed. 551 (1908). Congress in the PDA prohibited discrimination on the basis of a woman's ability to become pregnant. We do no more than hold that the Pregnancy Discrimination Act means what it says.

It is no more appropriate for the courts than it is for individual employers to decide whether a woman's reproductive role is more important to herself and her family than her economic role. Congress has left this choice to the woman as hers to make.

The judgment of the Court of Appeals is reversed and the case is remanded for further proceedings consistent with this opinion.

It is so ordered.

continued

JUSTICE WHITE, with whom THE CHIEF JUSTICE and JUSTICE KENNEDY join, concurring in part and concurring in the judgment ... The Court properly holds that Johnson Controls' fetal-protection policy overtly discriminates against women, and thus is prohibited by Title VII unless it falls within the bona fide occupational qualification (BFOQ) exception, set forth at 42 U.S.C. § 2000e-2(e). The Court erroneously holds, however, that the BFOQ defense is so narrow that it could never justify a sex-specific fetal-protection policy. I nevertheless concur in the judgment of reversal because on the record before us summary judgment in favor of Johnson Controls was improperly entered by the District Court and affirmed by the Court of Appeals....

[Justice Scalia concurred in the judgment of the Court.]

Case Questions

1. Did Johnson Controls' "fetal-protection policy" discriminate against women?

2. JCI's fetal-protection policy was implemented only after eight employees became pregnant while maintaining blood lead levels exceeding the level set by the CDC as critical. Considering JCI's moral and ethical obligations to the unborn fetuses and its possible extensive lability in future lawsuits, should not the BFOQ defense be available to it?

3. Was JCI's policy within the so-called safety exception to the BFOQ?

4. Does the PDA contain a BFOQ standard of its own?

TESTING AND EDUCATIONAL REQUIREMENTS

Section 703(h) of the Act authorizes the use of "any professionally developed ability test [that is not] designed, intended, or used to discriminate." The Supreme Court held in *Griggs v. Duke Power Co.* that employment testing and educational requirements must be "job related;" that is, the employers must prove that the tests and educational requirements bear a demonstrable relationship to job performance. The Court ruled that the employer's lack of intention to discriminate against blacks was irrelevant when the effect was to discriminate. As stated by the Supreme Court in *Griggs*, "What Congress has commanded is that any tests used must measure the person for the job and not the person in the abstract."

The EEOC has issued *Uniform Guidelines of Employee Selection Procedures* to assist employers in their compliance with EEOC laws. The *Uniform Guidelines* establish a "four-fifths" rule of thumb for determining when an adverse impact exists in employee selection. If the selection rate for a protected class of employees is less than four-fifths of the selection rate for the rest of the workforce or the qualified applicant pool, the test or requirement has an adverse impact. Although some courts use the four-fifths rule as a guideline, it has not been universally adopted.[107]

The *Albermarle Paper Co. v. Moody* decision, presented in the next chapter, demonstrates the requirement that where tests used by an employer have an adverse impact on a protected class under the Act, the validation studies of these tests must be able to withstand strict scrutiny that they are job-related. Validation

---

[107] For an application of the "four-fifths" rule, see *Stout v. Potter*, 276 F.3d 1118, 1123 (9th Cir. 2002).

studies demonstrate the job relatedness or lack thereof in the selection procedure in question.[108]

The two most common methods of test validation are *content validation* and *criterion-related validation.*

Content validation is the measure of how well a test correlates to the specific job tasks that make up the job. In order for the test to withstand the strict scrutiny that it may be subject to in court, a detailed **job analysis** must be conducted by the employer, thoroughly analyzing the component functions of the job in question and identifying the tasks that make up the important elements of the job. Tests must then be designed to measure performance in these important functions. An example of a selection procedure based on content validity is the administration of typing and shorthand tests for a candidate for a secretarial position. An example of a content-validated job-related physical agility test for male and female state trooper candidates, agreed to in a consent decree between the state of Maine and the U.S. Justice Department, requires the following. Each applicant must be able to:

1. Push a standard-size vehicle a distance of 12 feet on a level surface.
2. Rescue an injured child from a school bus.
3. Carry one end of a stretcher with a 175-pound mannequin a distance of 200 feet.
4. Climb a flatbed truck.
5. Run 1.5 miles in a designated time period.[109]

Criterion-related validation is established by demonstrating that there is a significant positive correlation between success on the test (predictor) in question and comparative success on some measures of job performance (criteria). A **predictive** criterion validation study involves a test during the hiring process administered to a sample group with members of the sample group being selected without reference to their test scores. Later, the actual job performance of the sample group is evaluated and compared with the test scores to see if the test accurately predicted performance. The **concurrent** criterion validation study involves the administration of a test to current employees, with their actual job performance being compared with their test scores to see if the test has validity. An example of a criterion-related validation study would be either a predictive or a concurrent study to determine whether salespersons scoring higher on an intelligence test also tended to be among the better sales performers and whether this relationship was statistically significant.

Because of the fear of court rejection of employment tests in hiring practices and because of the expense involved in conducting job analyses, designing tests, and conducting validation studies, many employers abandoned the use of written tests. This is unfortunate because a properly designed test can be one of the least discriminatory ways of selecting employees.

---

[108] The *Uniform Guidelines of Employee Selection Procedures* represents a summary statement of legal and validation standards for determining the proper use of tests and other selection procedures in order to assist employers and others to comply with federal law prohibiting discriminatory employment practices. 29 C.F.R. § 1607.

[109] *United States v. Maine*, CA-83-0195P, May 26, 1983. See *Lamming v. SEPTA*, 308 F.3d 286 (3d Cir. 2002).

Courts will accept prior court-approved validation studies developed for a different employer in a different state or region so long as it is demonstrated that the job for which the test was initially validated is essentially the same job function for which the test is currently being used. Thus, a firefighters test that had been validated in a study in California was accepted as valid when later used in Richmond, Virginia. Such application is called **validity generalization**. Based on the use of validity generalization, employers seeking to use employment tests may be able to rely on validation studies for like job classifications prepared by other employers in the same industry or by professional test developers.

The Civil Rights Act of 1991 makes it an unlawful employment practice for an employer to adjust scores or use different cut-off scores or otherwise alter the results of employment tests on the basis of race, color, religion, sex, or national origin. This provision addresses the so-called race norming issue, whereby the results of hiring and promotion tests are adjusted to assure that a minimum number of minorities are included in application pools. The federal government's method of grading its General Aptitude Test Battery (GATB) based on percentiles within racial grouping was made unlawful by the 1991 law.

SENIORITY SYSTEM

Of the three major exceptions to Section 703, the one most important to workers is the seniority system exception found in Section 703(h). It provides that differences in employment conditions that result from a bona fide seniority system are sanctioned as long as the differences do not stem from an intention to discriminate. The term **seniority system** is generally understood to mean a set of rules that ensures that workers with longer years of continuous service for an employer will have a priority claim to a job over others with fewer years of service. Because such rules provide workers with considerable job security, organized labor has continually and successfully fought to secure seniority provisions in collective bargaining agreements.

In the *Teamsters v. United States*[110] decision, the court held that by virtue of Section 703(h), a bona fide seniority system does not become unlawful simply because it may perpetuate pre-Title VII discrimination. In *American Tobacco Co. v. Patterson*,[111] the Supreme Court held that Section 703(h) is applicable as well to bona fide seniority systems created after the passage of Title VII. As a result of the *American Tobacco* decision, even though a seniority system has disparate or adverse impact on a protected class of persons under the Act, such alone is insufficient to invalidate the seniority system. To invalidate a seniority system, it has to be shown that the system is not bona fide because the *actual motive* of the parties in adopting the seniority system was to discriminate. In *Pullman-Standard v. Swint*,[112] the Supreme Court recognized that adverse impact on minorities is part

---

[110] 431 U.S. 324 (1977).

[111] 456 U.S. 63 (1982).

[112] 456 U.S. 273 (1982).

of the evidence to be considered by the trial court in reaching a finding of fact on whether there was a discriminatory intent.

In *Firefighters Local 1784 v. Stotts*,[113] the city of Memphis planned to lay off employees due to budget cuts and had agreed with the city's unions that "seniority … shall govern layoffs and recalls." Minority firefighters sought a court injunction preventing the layoffs based on seniority in order to protect the employment gains of minority firefighters under court-approved consent decrees in 1974 and 1980. The district court approved and the court of appeals upheld a modified layoff plan that resulted in nonminority employees with more seniority than minority employees being laid off or reduced in rank. The Supreme Court reversed the lower courts, citing *Teamsters* as a precedent for its position that Section 703(h) permits, as in this case, the routine application of a seniority system absent proof of an intention to discriminate. The Supreme Court pointed out that there was no finding that any black protected from the layoffs had been an actual victim of discrimination and had received an award of competitive seniority.

In 1979, the International Brotherhood of Electrical Workers (IBEW) and AT&T Technologies executed a new collective bargaining agreement making seniority in "tester" jobs dependent upon the time spent in a tester position rather than the previous rule of plantwide seniority. Three years later, when a group of women were bumped from tester positions under the 1979 seniority language, they challenged the seniority provision in court, contending that the purpose of the 1979 change was to protect incumbent testers, who were mostly men, from female employees, who had greater plantwide seniority. In *Lorance v. AT&T Technologies, Inc.*,[114] the Supreme Court ruled that the lawsuit must be dismissed as time-barred as the women did not file their claim with the EEOC within the 180-day or 300-day requirements of Title VII. The Civil Rights Act of 1991 overturned the *Lorance* decision with respect to a seniority system that has been adopted for "intentionally discriminatory purposes." And the 1991 Act provides that a seniority system that *intentionally* discriminates, regardless of whether such discrimination is apparent, may be challenged when the system is adopted, when an individual becomes subject to it, or when a person is actually injured by it.[115]

SECTION 112: SELECTED CONSTITUTIONAL THEORIES ON DISCRIMINATION

Many employment discrimination problems have been approached on constitutional rather than statutory grounds, especially when public employees are involved. When statutory solutions, such as those provided by Title VII, are inapplicable, inadequate,

---

[113] 467 U.S. 561 (1984).

[114] 490 U.S. 900 (1989).

[115] Section 112, Civil Rights Act of 1991.

or too time-consuming, the constitutional guarantees of equal protection[116] and due process found in the Fifth and Fourteenth Amendments have been argued in an attempt to remedy the allegedly discriminatory employment practices.

RACE DISCRIMINATION

Since the passage of Title VII, cases involving alleged racially discriminatory employment practices have generally been argued in the courts on statutory, rather than constitutional, grounds. This was not the case, however, in *Washington v. Davis*.[117] Here, the Supreme Court was faced with the question of whether a written personnel test used by the District of Columbia's police department to measure verbal skill, and failed by a higher percentage of blacks than whites, was violative of the equal protection component of the due process clause of the Fifth Amendment. The district court ruled that the test was a reliable indication of job performance and was not designed to, and did not, discriminate against otherwise qualified blacks. The court of appeals reversed, basing its decision on the standards enunciated in *Griggs v. Duke Power Co.* The court of appeals held that the lack of discriminatory intent was irrelevant, that four times as many blacks as whites failed the test, and that such disproportionate impact sufficed to establish a constitutional violation. The Supreme Court reversed the court of appeals' decision and reinstated the order of the district court upholding the use of the test. The Supreme Court held that although disproportionate impact is not irrelevant, where a law or official conduct such as the administering of a personnel test is not designed to discriminate and serves legitimate governmental interests, it will not be struck down simply because it burdens blacks more than whites.

SEX DISCRIMINATION

The *Cleveland Board of Education v. LaFleur*[118] decision was initially successful in the court of appeals utilizing equal protection clause arguments against mandatory maternity leave rules for pregnant teachers. However, the Supreme Court sustained the court of appeals on the basis of the due process clause, finding the challenged maternity leave rules to be violative of due process because they created a conclusive presumption that every teacher who is four or five months pregnant is physically incapable of continuing her duties, whereas any such teacher's inability to continue past a fixed pregnancy period is an individual matter.

Freedom of the press contentions relating to employment opportunities advertising were considered by the U.S. Supreme Court. In *Pittsburgh Press Co. v. Pittsburgh Comm'n on Human Relations*,[119] the Supreme Court upheld an order of the

---

[116] In *Engquist v. Oregon Department of Agriculture*, 128 S.Ct. 2146 (2008), the U.S. Supreme Court held that "class of one" equal protection under the Fourteenth Amendment does not protect state government workers against termination for arbitrary reasons. The Court declined, in an employment context, to displace managerial discretion by judicial supervision.

[117] 426 U.S. 229 (1976).

[118] 414 U.S. 632 (1974).

[119] 413 U.S. 376 (1973).

Pittsburgh Commission on Human Relations that forbade placing help wanted advertisements under the heading "Jobs—Male Interest" and "Jobs—Female Interest." The majority of the Court took the position that the order came under the "commercial speech" exception to the First Amendment, whereas the four dissenters viewed it as a prior restraint on the press. The commission had ordered the *Pittsburgh Press* to stop using the headings in its help wanted columns after the National Organization for Women, Inc., complained.

Speaking for the Supreme Court, Mr. Justice Powell held that the case came under the commercial speech doctrine of *Valentine v. Chrestensen*,[120] which sustained a city ordinance that banned the distribution of a handbill soliciting customers for a tour of a submarine. The Court distinguished the commercial speech cases from the holding of *New York Times v. Sullivan*,[121] a libel suit in which the Court held that paid political advertising was entitled to First Amendment protection. The help-wanted advertisements in the *Pittsburgh Press*, the Court held, do not express a position on "whether as a matter of social policy, certain positions ought to be filled by members of one or the other sex.... Each is no more than a proposal of possible employment. The advertisements are thus classic examples of commercial speech." The Court added that nothing in its holding prevented the *Pittsburgh Press* from publishing advertisements commenting on the ordinance and the commission, or its enforcement practices, or the propriety of sex preferences in employment.

In his dissent, Chief Justice Burger called the decision "a disturbing enlargement of the 'commercial speech' doctrine." Mr. Justice Douglas argued that the newspaper could print whatever it pleased without censorship or restraint by government. The want ads express the preference of the employer for the kind of help the employer wants, Justice Douglas said, and the commission might issue an order against the employer if discrimination in employment was shown. Mr. Justice Stewart, whose dissent Justice Douglas joined, declared that the issue was whether government "can tell a newspaper in advance what it can print and what it cannot." Mr. Justice Blackmun also dissented, substantially for the reasons stated by Mr. Justice Stewart.

In *University of Pennsylvania v. EEOC*,[122] Rosalie Tung filed a charge with the EEOC, alleging discrimination on the basis of race, sex, and national origin, after she was denied tenure at the Wharton School. The university resisted an EEOC subpoena that sought Tung's tenure review file on the basis that it contained "confidential peer review information." The university argued that disclosure of peer evaluations would be a significant infringement on the university's First Amendment right of academic freedom, because the disclosure would have a "chilling effect" on candid evaluations by peers of tenure candidates. The Supreme Court rejected the university's position. It pointed out that Congress expressly extended Title VII's coverage to educational institutions without restriction on the right of access to evidence. The Court also stated that the claimed injury to academic freedom is

---

[120] 316 U.S. 52 (1942).

[121] 376 U.S. 254 (1964).

[122] 493 U.S. 182 (1990).

speculative, as confidentiality is not the norm in all peer review systems; and the Court could not assume that most peer evaluators would become less candid if the possibility of disclosure increased.

CHAPTER QUESTIONS AND PROBLEMS

1. Doyle Ollis, Jr., worked as a sales associate for HearthStone, a company in the business of building and selling homes. Ollis is a member of the Assemblies of God Church, which is a Protestant Christian church. John Smith is the owner and president of HearthStone. Smith believes in reincarnation and that a person's traumas in past lives can explain his or her behavior in the present life. During Ollis's tenure at HearthStone, on certain occasions, HearthStone used Mind Body Energy (MBE) sessions to "cleanse the negative energy" from its employees to enhance their work performance. HearthStone encouraged and paid for its employees to attend an MBE course that required participants to read *The Tibetan Book of Life*, which discussed Buddhist and Hindu teachings. HearthStone's core values include spirituality and the need to leave behind all experiences from past lives, as well as the beliefs that everything in the universe is connected (including animals and past lives) and that uncorrected problems from past lives must be corrected in the present life.

Ollis told his supervisor, Rachel Langford, that the MBE sessions made him uncomfortable, MBE was cultlike and conflicted with his religious beliefs, and he did not want to participate in MBE activities. Langford did not report Ollis's religious concerns to her boss, Smith, because Lanford feared losing her job if she did make the report. Langford advised Ollis to make a standing appointment with the least offensive MBE coach, but to cancel those appointments later to give management the impression that "he bought into MBE concepts." Ollis followed Langford's instructions and canceled 5 of his 12 appointments. Ollis further

testified that he also told Smith about his discomfort with MBE. Ollis expressed his disagreement with MBE at company sales meetings, and Ollis conveyed to Smith that MBE was fundamentally against his religious beliefs.

According to Smith, an employee's negative energy could be discovered through a machine that tests a person's electromagnetic energy field or through a manual process called "muscle testing." An example of muscle testing is to place two fingers together and to answer yes or no questions. If the fingers remain together, the answer is yes; whereas, if the fingers separate, the answer is no. Smith used muscle testing to make business decisions. Smith equates muscle testing "to someone who may pray before they make decisions."

In late September 2003, HearthStone hired Sarah Audas to work as a sales associate under Ollis's supervision. Approximately two weeks after Audas commenced work, she reported that she was uncomfortable with certain sexual comments Ollis made to her. Management investigated and terminated Ollis for "poor leadership and lack of judgment." Ollis filed a religious discrimination charge against HearthStone. HearthStone defended that Ollis was fired for sexual harassment. Ollis claimed at trial that Audas initiated the sex talk and that the sexual harassment charge was a setup and pretext. There was testimony indicating that HearthStone later terminated Audas after she reportedly "removed her clothing at a golf outing and was doing cart-wheels naked on a golf course." Applying the elements of a claim for religious discrimination, how would you decide this case? [*Ollis v. HearthStone Homes, Inc.*, 495 F.3d 570 (8th Cir 2007).]

2. Young, an African-American woman, sued the United Methodist Church under Title VII of the Civil Rights Act, claiming the church discriminated against her based on race and color in refusing to promote her from the status of probationary minister to that of "elder" in the church. Will a court be allowed to determine if Young was qualified for this promotion but was turned down because of her race and color? Decide. [*Young v. Northern Illinois Conference of United Methodist Church*, 21 F.3d 184 (7th Cir.)]

3. Mercy Prado worked for L. Luria & Son Inc., a Florida-based general merchandise retail chain. She worked as the customer service manager at Luria's Coral Gables store. The store had a policy for workers of not speaking Spanish on the job unless a customer spoke it first. Her boss prohibited all employees from speaking Spanish before the store opened and even on breaks. Ms. Prado contends that she was so humiliated by her boss's chants of "English, English, English" that she quit. Luria's defends that the store manager in question did not speak any Spanish. And the store contends that Prado quit because she did not like the long hours and the pressure. Ms. Prado does not deny that job-related stress existed. She stated that her boss stood outside the bathroom listening for Spanish and warned her to switch to English when she came out. Before quitting, she told her coworkers, "This is a nightmare!" Did the enforcement of the employer's English-only rule effect a constructive discharge of Ms. Prado? Decide. [See A. Davis, "English-Only Rules Spur Workers to Speak Legalese," *Wall Street Journal*, January 23, 1997, p. B-1]

4. Continental Photo, Inc., is a portrait photography company. Alex Riley, a black man, applied for a position as a photographer with Continental. Riley submitted an application and was interviewed. In response to a question on a written application, Riley indicated that he had been convicted for forgery, a felony, six years prior to the interview and had received a suspended sentence. He also noted that he would discuss the matter with his interviewer if necessary. The subject of the forgery conviction was subsequently not mentioned by Continental's personnel director in his interview with Riley. Riley's application for employment was eventually rejected. Riley inquired as to the reason for his rejection by Continental. The personnel director, Geuther, explained to him that the prior felony conviction disclosed on his application and an unsatisfactory test score were the reasons for his rejection.

Riley contended that the refusal to hire him because of his conviction record was actually discrimination against him because of his race in violation of Title VII. Riley believe that his successful completion of a five-year probation without incident and his steady work over the years qualified him for the job.

Continental maintained that because its photographers handle approximately $10,000 in cash per year, its policy of not hiring applicants whose honesty was questionable was justified. Continental's policy excluded all applicants with felony convictions.

What factors must be weighed in this case? Has Continental violated Title VII? Decide. Would the result be different if Riley had been a convicted murderer? Explain. [*Continental Photo, Inc.*, 26 FEP 1799 (EEOC)]

5. Sambo's Restaurants maintained a uniform grooming policy concerning each of its over one thousand establishments nationwide. The policy forbade restaurant managers and other restaurant personnel to wear facial hair, with an exception for a neatly trimmed mustache. Sambo's has consistently enforced this grooming policy since the restaurant chain's inception in 1957. Grooming standards similar to Sambo's were common in the restaurant industry. Sambo's believe that the grooming policy reflected the restaurant's public image as a family-oriented business

where food was served under sanitary conditions.

Mohen S. Tucker was a member of the Sikh religion. The practice of Sikhism forbade the cutting or shaving of facial hair and also required the wearing of a turban that covered the head. In accordance with the dictates of his religion, Tucker wore a long beard. Tucker applied for a position as a Sambo's restaurant manager. While filling out the application, he was informed of Sambo's grooming policy, which would require that he shave his beard or be denied the position. Tucker informed Sambo's that it was against his religion to shave his beard. Sambo's responded that no exceptions were allowed under the grooming policy for religious reasons and denied his application.

Tucker brought a court action through the EEOC, claiming that Sambo's had violated Title VII by refusing to accommodate his religious practice. Sambo's denied any religious discrimination.

What standard of review should be employed to decide this case? What factors will be relevant? Decide the case. [*EEOC v. Sambo's of Georgia, Inc.*, 27 FEP 1210 (N.D. Ga.)]

6. Mercy Health Center in Oklahoma City, Oklahoma, was a hospital that provided extensive medical services including obstetrical and gynecological care. The labor and delivery area of the hospital hosted an average of 148 deliveries a month. Between 40 and 50 percent of those births were life-threatening to the mother or infant and were therefore classified as high risk. Staff nurses in the labor and delivery area were involved in extensive contact with the expectant mother. Their duties included assessment and examination of the mother, which consisted of frequent contact with the mother's body. To minimize the tension, fear, and stress that accompanies the labor and delivery experience, Mercy did not hire males for the position of staff nurse in the labor and delivery area. The hospital cited its paramount concern for the privacy and comfort of the mother as a basis for its policy. Mercy also conducted a survey of parents involved in prenatal classes and found that 60 to 70 percent of the mothers and a larger percentage of the fathers objected to the use of male nurses in the labor and delivery area.

Andre Fontain applied for a job as a staff nurse in the labor and delivery area at Mercy. Because of the policy, he was denied employment.

Through the EEOC, Fontain alleged that Mercy discriminated against him on the basis of sex in violation of Title VII. The hospital denied the charge of discrimination.

Has Mercy violated Title VII? If so, what defense, if any, is available to the hospital? Decide the case. [*EEOC v. Mercy Health Center*, 29 FEP 159 (W.D. Okla.)]

7. DiMillo's Floating Restaurant on Long Wharf, Portland, Maine, ran a help wanted ad in the *Portland Press Herald*, which read in part:

Bartenders/Cocktail Service, Experienced Only. Applicants must be able to wear uniforms sizes 8 to 12.

Complaints were made to the Maine Human Rights Commission. Antonio DiMillo defended the ad in a newspaper interview, expressing the view that all over the country the restaurant industry routinely hires waitresses based on their size. DiMillo was quoted as saying: "Do you go out to eat and drink? Do you like to see a fat, big broad coming at you?"

Against whom, if anyone, does the ad discriminate? What responsibility, if any, does the newspaper have in publishing employment advertisements that are found to discriminate? [See page 13 of the *Portland Press Herald*, Vol. 121, No. 127, Thursday, Nov. 18, 1982.]

8. Sylvia Hayes worked as a staff technician in the radiology department of Shelby Memorial Hospital, a county hospital located in Birmingham, Alabama. In early October,

Hayes was told by her physician that she was pregnant. When Hayes informed the doctor of her occupation as an X-ray technician, the doctor advised Hayes that she could continue working until the end of April as long as she followed standard safety precautions. On October 8, Hayes told Gail Nell, the director of radiology at Shelby, that she had discovered she was two months pregnant. On October 14, Hayes was discharged by the hospital. The hospital's reason for terminating Hayes was its concern for the safety of her fetus given the X-ray exposure that occurs during employment as an X-ray technician.

Hayes brought an action under Title VII, claiming that her discharge was unlawfully based on her condition of pregnancy. She cited scientific evidence and the practice of other hospitals where pregnant women were allowed to remain in their jobs as X-ray technicians.

The hospital claimed that Hayes's discharge was based on business necessity. Specifically, the hospital claimed that the potential for future liability existed if an employee's fetus was damaged by radiation encountered at the workplace.

Has the hospital violated Title VII by discharging Hayes? What remedy, if any, is appropriate in this case? Decide the case. [*Hayes v. Shelby Memorial Hospital*, 29 FEP 1173 (N.D. Ala.)]

9. Glenwood H. MacDougal, chairman of the Office Occupations Department at Northern Maine Vocational Technical Institute in Presque Isle, claimed that between September 1985 and September 1986, he received in the mail sexually suggestive items. Poems, letters, and cards were all signed "Love, Charlene." MacDougal's attorney stated that MacDougal became emotionally upset because of this, was forced to seek psychological counseling, and had been out of work for over six weeks due to these emotional problems. MacDougal brought suit against three female teachers at the institute, charging them with sexual

harassment. MacDougal sought $1.6 million in damages.

The three teachers contended that there had been a history of good-humored practical jokes played by the faculty members at the school, that MacDougal himself participated, and that all they were doing was playing a practical joke on MacDougal. They claimed that they had no intention of harassing him.

Does the EEOC guidelines definition of sexual harassment apply to men? Assuming for the sake of discussion that men are protected from sexual harassment under the guidelines, was there a violation of the guidelines? What is the measure of damages in a case such as this? [*MacDougal v. Gregg, Boston Herald*, Feb. 26, 1987, p. 23]

10. A teenage female high school student named Salazar was employed part-time at Church's Fried Chicken restaurant. Salazar was hired and supervised by Simon Garza, the assistant manager of the restaurant. Garza had complete supervisory powers when the restaurant's manager, Garza's roommate, was absent. Salazar alleged that while she worked at the restaurant, Garza would refer to her and all other females by a Spanish term that she found objectionable. According to Salazar, Garza once purportedly made a lecherous comment about Salazar's body and repeatedly asked her about her personal life. On another occasion, Garza allegedly physically removed eyeshadow from Salazar's face because he thought that it looked ugly. Salazar also claimed that one night she was restrained in a back room of the restaurant while Garza and another employee fondled her. Later that night, when Salazar told a customer about what had happened, she was fired. Salazar believed she was fired because she disclosed this incident.

Salazar filed an action under Title VII against Garza and Church's Fried Chicken, Inc., alleging sexual harassment. The defendants moved for summary judgment. Garza, who has since stopped working at Church's, contended that even if Salazar's allegations were true, she had not established sexual harassment under Title VII. Church's, the corporate defendant, maintained that it should not be held liable under Title VII for Garza's harassment. Church's grounded its argument on the existence of a published "fair treatment policy" and a grievance procedure that was not invoked by Salazar.

If Salazar's allegations are true, has she stated an actionable case under Title VII? May Church's be held liable for Garza's actions? If the case proceeds to trial, what remedies may Salazar seek? [*Salazar v. Church's Fried Chicken, Inc.*, 44 FEP 472 (S.D. Tex.)]

11. Sandra Shope had worked as chief of county housing services in Loudoun County, Virginia, for some six years when Timothy Krawczel was made her boss. Shope testified that Krawczel pounded his fists on her desk and called her a "stupid woman" in front of coworkers and berated her as "weak like a woman." Krawczel told Shope "I'm the boss at home, and I will be the boss here." Shope testified that Krawczel never touched her or sought sexual favors. Krawczel was not abusive to men in the office, but the evidence suggested that other women in the office were subjected to "insults." The county defended that Krawczel was strict with Shope because she was not doing her job well. Shope responded that she worked more than 50 hours per week and was a respected housing official. Shope sought relief from the all-male County Board of Supervisors, but her complaints were ignored. She became physically ill as a result of the treatment by Krawczel and ultimately resigned.

Shope contends that the county and Krawczel constructively discharged her in violation of Title VII. She seeks back pay, compensatory damages for the pain and suffering involved, and punitive damages from Krawczel.

Can the county and Krawczel be guilty of sexual harassment where no sexual favors are sought and no sexual conduct is involved? Is the fact that Krawczel was not abusive to any male employees of any legal significance? Could the county be required to pay punitive damages? Decide. [*Shope v. Loudoun County, Washington Post*, col. 3, p. 1, June 20, 1992]

12. Hooters Inc. is an Atlanta-based restaurant chain with over 170 locations. The company hires only female waitresses. Hooters states that "a lot of places serve good burgers. The Hooters Girls, with their charm and all-American sex appeal, are what customers come for." The waitresses wear bright orange hot pants and tight white T-shirts or tank tops. Several waitresses brought suit against the restaurant for sexual harassment, alleging that it established a work environment in which its customers felt free to make sexual comments and advances to waitresses. Some argue that the provocative uniforms and the name of the restaurant itself should lead to liability for Hooters Inc. Others argue that waitresses should not be able to recover for conduct they clearly should have anticipated at the time they chose to work for Hooters. What effect should the *Vinson* decision's pronouncement on speech and dress have on such a case? What effect should management policy to immediately remove offensive patrons have on a court case? Decide.

Four Chicago men sued Hooters for its policy of hiring only female waitresses. They contend that such a policy is sex discrimination. In the sex appeal restaurant business, does Hooters Inc. have a BFOQ defense? Hooters Inc. has taken out full-page newspaper advertisements featuring a burly man with a blond wig wearing a Hooters uniform, holding a plate of chicken wings in protest against an EEOC recommendation that the restaurant hire male waiters. See *Wilson v. Southwest Airlines Co.*, 517 F. Supp 292 (N.D. Tex. 1981), where the BFOQ defense was narrowly applied against the airline's female-only flight attendants policy under a marketing scheme based on sex appeal.

Southwest is in the business of transporting passengers. What if a primary aspect of Hooters Inc. is not just to serve food and drink but also to provide sex appeal? Should the BFOQ defense succeed? Decide the case involving the four male applicants for the wait staff positions.

13. Kerry Ellison worked as a revenue agent for the Internal Revenue Service (IRS) in San Mateo, California. Sterling Gray's desk was 20 feet from Ellison's desk, two rows behind and one row over. Revenue agents in the San Mateo office often went to lunch in groups. In June, when no one else was in the office, Gray asked Ellison to lunch. She accepted. Ellison alleges that after the June lunch, Gray started to pester her with unnecessary questions and to hang around her desk. On October 9, Gray asked Ellison out for a drink after work. She declined but suggested that they have lunch the following week. She did not want to have lunch alone with him, and she tried to stay away from the office during lunchtime. One day during the following week, Gray uncharacteristically dressed in a three-piece suit and asked Ellison out for lunch again. Again, she did not accept.

On October 22, Gray handed Ellison a note he wrote on a telephone message slip, which read:

I cried over you last night and I'm totally drained today. I have never been in such a constant term oil (sic). Thank you for talking with me. I could not stand to feel your hatred for another day.

When Ellison realized that Gray wrote the note, she became shocked and frightened and left the room. Gray followed her into the hallway and demanded that she talk to him, but she left the building. Ellison later showed the note to Bonnie Miller, who supervised both Ellison and Gray. Miller said, "This is sexual harassment." Ellison asked Miller not to do anything about it. She wanted to try to handle it herself. Ellison asked a male co-worker to talk to Gray, to tell him that she was

not interested in him, and to leave her alone. The next day, Thursday, Gray called in sick.

Ellison did not work on Friday, and on the following Monday, she started four weeks of training in St. Louis, Missouri. Gray mailed her a card and a typed, single-spaced three-page letter. She describes this letter as "twenty times, a hundred times weirder" than the prior note. Gray wrote, in part:

I know that you are worth knowing with or without sex.... Leaving aside the hassles and disasters of recent weeks, I have enjoyed you so much over these past few months. Watching you. Experiencing you from O so far away. Admiring your style and elan.... Don't you think it odd that two people who have never even talked together, alone, are striking off such intense sparks.... I will [write] another letter in the near future.

Explaining her reaction, Ellison stated: "I just thought he was crazy. I thought he was nuts. I didn't know what he would do next. I was frightened."

She immediately telephoned Miller. Ellison told her supervisor that she was frightened and really upset. She requested that Miller transfer either her or Gray because she would not be comfortable working in the same office with him. Miller asked Ellison to send a copy of the card and letter to San Mateo. Miller then telephoned her supervisor, Joe Benton, and discussed the problem. That same day she had a counseling session with Gray. She informed him that he was entitled to union representation. During this meeting, she told Gray to leave Ellison alone. At Benson's request, Miller apprised the labor relations department of the situation. She also reminded Gray many times over the next few weeks that he must not contact Ellison in any way. Gray subsequently transferred to the San Francisco office on November 24. Ellison returned from St. Louis in late November and did not discuss the matter further with Miller.

After three weeks in San Francisco, Gray filed union grievances requesting a return to the San Mateo office. The IRS and the union settled the grievances in Gray's favor, agreeing to allow him to transfer back to the San Mateo office provided he spend four months in San Francisco and promise not to bother Ellison. On January 28, Ellison first learned of Gray's request in a letter from Miller explaining that Gray would return to the San Mateo office. The letter indicated that management decided to resolve Ellison's problem with a six-month separation and that it would take additional action if the problem recurred. After receiving the letter, Ellison was "frantic." On January 30, she filed with the IRS a formal complaint alleging sexual harassment. She also obtained permission to transfer to San Francisco temporarily when Gray returned.

Ellison filed a complaint in federal district court, and the court granted the government's motion for summary judgment on the grounds that Ellison had failed to state a *prima facie* case of sexual harassment due to a hostile work environment. Ellison appealed. From Gray's perspective, he could be portrayed by his attorney as a modern-day Cyrano de Bergerac wishing to woo Ellison by his words. There is no evidence that he harbored ill will toward her, and his representative would argue that Gray's conduct was isolated and trivial.

From Ellison's perspective, Gray's first note shocked her and the three-page letter truly frightened her. Her attorney would portray Gray's actions as poisoning Ellison's work environment and, in a most severe manner, adversely affecting her personal life. What standard should apply in judging the severity of the conduct to determine if it amounts to sexual harassment? Should it be a reasonable woman standard? How would such a standard differ from the *Oncale* standard of objective severity from the perspective of a reasonable person in the plaintiff's position, considering all the circumstances? Do men and women have different views on what constitutes sexual harassment? Did the

employer take proper corrective action if the victim ended up being transferred as a result of the harassment? Decide. [*Ellison v. Brady*, 924 F.2d 872 (9th Cir.)]

14. Patricia Baty was hired by Willamette Industries, a Kansas City corrugated box plant, in October 1993, and coworkers immediately began making sexual comments to her. She reported these incidents to her supervisor. Thereafter, the supervisor's brother, who was also a supervisor, put his arm around Baty's waist, grabbed her breast, and invited her to have drinks at a local bar. When she complained to her supervisor, he said his brother "got a little overzealous." Over the next several months, Baty reported ongoing sexual comments to various supervisors to no avail. In June and July, graffiti relating to her sexual prowess began appearing in the men's room. In July, the regional personnel manager, Jim Mertes, investigated anonymous complaints of sexual harassment and concluded that no sexual harassment occurred. He also conducted a 45-minute sexual harassment training seminar for managers and another for employees. Baty was terminated in November 1994 as a result of cost-cutting measures from a worldwide paper shortage. However, a budget approved three days before her termination projected an increase in production, and no other employees were terminated because of the paper shortage. Baty brought suit for sexual harassment and also claimed that she had been terminated in retaliation for her complaints about sexual harassment. The jury awarded her $40,000 in back pay, $146,000 in front pay, $145,000 in compensatory damages, and $1,000,000 in punitive damages. The district court judge reduced the damages to $38,063 in back pay, and $22,420 in front pay, and capped the consequential and punitive damages on both claims at $300,000.

Baty appealed, contending that her sexual harassment claim should be capped at $300,000 and her retaliation claim should be capped at $300,000 for a total of $600,000, according to the EEOC's interpretation of the statute. The employer disagreed.

Under the standards set forth in *Kolstad v. American Dental Ass'n*, should punitive damages have been assessed against the employer? Was it proper for the court to cap the consequential and punitive damages at $300,000? Decide. [*Baty v. Willamette Industries, Inc.*, 122 F.2d 1232 (10ᵗʰ Cir.)]

15. Beth Faragher worked part-time and summers as an ocean lifeguard for the Marine Safety Section of the city of Boca Raton, Florida. Bill Terry and David Silverman were her supervisors over the five-year period of her employment. During this period, Terry repeatedly touched the bodies of female employees without invitation and would put his arm around Faragher, with his hand on her buttocks. He made crudely demeaning references to women generally. Silverman once told Faragher, "Date me or clean the toilets for a year." She was not so assigned, however. The city adopted a sexual harassment policy addressed to all employees. The policy was not disseminated to the Marine Safety Section at the beach, however. Faragher resigned and later brought action against the city, claiming a violation of Title VII and seeking nominal damages, costs, and attorney fees. The city defended that Terry and Silverman were not acting within the scope of their employment when they engaged in harassing conduct and that the city should not be held liable for their actions. Are part-time employees covered by Title VII? Was Silverman's threat, "Date me or clean toilets for a year," a basis for quid pro quo vicarious liability against the city? Decide this case. [*Faragher v. City of Boca Raton*, 118 S. Ct. 2751]

PROCEDURES AND REMEDIES | CHAPTER 13

SECTION 113: BURDEN OF PROOF

As stated previously, there are two legal theories for a plaintiff to use in proving a case of unlawful discrimination: disparate treatment and disparate impact.

Disparate treatment is intentional employment discrimination where, for example, women are treated less favorably than men or blacks are treated less favorably than whites. The burden of proof for disparate treatment cases is developed in this section.

Disparate impact is a theory of employment discrimination that focuses on the consequences of an employer's selection procedures for hiring and promotions. The theory was developed in the *Griggs v. Duke Power Co.* decision. The practice occurs where an employer's facially neutral employment practices have a significant adverse or disparate impact on a protected group and the employer is unable to show that the practice is job-related. Proof of a discriminatory motive is not required. The burden of proof for disparate impact cases is also developed in this section.

PROOF IN DISPARATE TREATMENT CASES

In *McDonnell Douglas Corp. v. Green,*[1] the Supreme Court discussed how a *prima facie* showing of discrimination in the context of a disparate treatment (intentional discrimination) case may be established. The plaintiff must show (1) that he or she belongs to a group protected from discrimination under Title VII on the basis of characteristics such as race, color, national origin, sex, or religion; (2) that he or she applied and was qualified for a job for which the employer was seeking applicants; (3) that despite being qualified, he or she was rejected; and (4) that after he or she was rejected, the position remained open and the employer continued to seek applicants whose qualifications were similar to those of the plaintiff. Once such a *prima facie* case is established, the burden shifts to the employer to articulate some legitimate, nondiscriminatory reason for its action. If such a reason is forthcoming, then the plaintiff is afforded an opportunity to demonstrate by a preponderance of the evidence that the supposedly valid reasons for the employer's actions were in fact a cover-up or "pretext" for a discriminatory decision.

Confusion existed in the federal trial courts and appeals courts as to the precise nature of the shifts of burdens of proof and persuasion after the plaintiff made out a *prima facie* case under the **McDonnell Douglas** model. The *Texas Department of Community Affairs v. Burdine*[2] decision confirms that the employer rebuts a *prima facie* case by producing admissible evidence of a legitimate reason for its decision to reject the plaintiff. Legitimate, nondiscriminatory reasons offered by an employer could be lesser comparative qualifications, inability to work in harmony with others, or violations of employer rules. Once a *prima facie* case is rebutted by the employer, the plaintiff can prevail by showing that the employer was motivated by a discriminatory reason or that the employer's reason is not believable. Under *Burdine,* then, the employer has an intermediate burden of production, but the ultimate burden of proving that the defendant-employer intentionally discriminated against the plaintiff remains with the plaintiff at all times.

The Supreme Court made an additional attempt to clarify its numerous decisions on proof in disparate treatment (intentional discrimination) cases in *Postal Service v. Aikens,*[3] focusing in detail on its *McDonnell Douglas* and *Burdine* precedents. Under the *McDonnell Douglas/Burdine* model, as applied in *Aikens,* a three-stage process is followed. Stage 1 focuses on the plaintiff's burden to present sufficient evidence of discrimination to establish a *prima facie* case according to the elements set forth in *McDonnell Douglas.* At the end of the plaintiff's presentation of evidence, the district court may sustain the defendant-employer's motion to dismiss the case for lack of a *prima facie* case, and the case is terminated. Stage 2 is reached if the court determines that the plaintiff has made out a *prima facie* case. At this stage, the defendant must respond with evidence of a nondiscriminatory reason for the plaintiff's rejection. Stage 3 is sometimes referred to as the "pretext" stage in reference to *Burdine.* As set forth in *Burdine,* the

---

[1] 411 U.S. 792 (1972).

[2] 450 U.S. 248 (1981).

[3] 460 U.S. 711 (1983).

plaintiff has the right to offer additional evidence rebutting the employer's asserted reason for the rejection. Alternatively, the plaintiff may simply rely on the evidence of a discriminatory motive introduced as part of its *prima facie* case. The Civil Rights Act of 1991 allows either party to obtain a jury trial in these disparate treatment cases where compensatory or punitive damages are sought. It is at this third stage that the jury must reach the ultimate question of fact by deciding which party's explanation of the employer's motivation in rejecting the plaintiff for employment is to be believed. The jury will weigh all the evidence of record in reaching its decision, with the ultimate burden of proof on the plaintiff.

Some managers lack an understanding of the importance of preparing accurate written records regarding employee performance evaluations and don't really understand the need for accurate written statements in termination letters. A manager may verbally give an accurate negative performance appraisal to an employee, but write a marginally satisfactory written evaluation for the same period, not wanting to initiate a diminished salary increment for morale or cost of living reasons and in the expectation that the tough verbal warning will have a corrective effect. Months later, when the employee's poor performance continues, the employee will be terminated because of the poor performance. The termination letter may so state the cause as poor performance, or the manager may attempt to reduce the impact on the individual's future employment prospects by giving a termination letter citing adverse economic reasons affecting the company as the reason for termination. The discharged employee may later file a discrimination case. After the employee presents a *prima facie* case at Stage 1, the employer at Stage 2 will present its nondiscriminatory reason for the termination—poor performance—through the testimony of its manager. At Stage 3, the pretext stage, the employee will present the written "satisfactory" evaluation and/or the termination letter referring to economic reasons, contradicting the employer's position. The writings introduced at the pretext stage may well overwhelm the manager's testimony and result in the employee prevailing in the lawsuit. The consequences of an adverse outcome in court in a discrimination case based on race, color, religion, national origin, sex, age, or disability are severe in reputational and economic terms for any employer. Accuracy, therefore, in all employment correspondence is of critical importance.

In *St. Mary's Honor Center v. Hicks*,[4] decided after passage of the Civil Rights Act of 1991, the Supreme Court reaffirmed the *McDonnell Douglas/Burdine* model. The *Hicks* Court concluded:

We reaffirm today what we said in *Aikens*:

[The] question facing triers of fact in discrimination cases is both sensitive and difficult. The prohibitions against discrimination contained in the Civil Rights Act of 1964

---

[4] 509 U.S. 502 (1993). In *Hicks*, Melvin Hicks alleged that he was demoted and discharged because he is black, in violation of Title VII. A federal appeals court ruled that once Hicks proved that all of his employer's reasons for demoting and discharging him were not believable, he was entitled to judgment as a matter of law. In a 5-4 split, the Supreme Court reversed and held that once a plaintiff in a Title VII case shows that an employer's actual reasons for taking adverse job actions were not believable, a ruling in favor of the plaintiff is not required, but a jury can draw an inference that the employer intentionally discriminated against the plaintiff and no additional proof of discrimination is required by the plaintiff.

reflect an important national policy. There will seldom be 'eyewitness' testimony as to the employer's mental processes. But none of this means that trial courts or reviewing courts should treat discrimination differently from other ultimate questions of fact. Nor should they make their inquiry even more difficult by applying legal rules which were devised to govern the 'basic allocation of burdens and order of presentation of proof,' in deciding this ultimate question.[5]

As will be seen in later chapters, the *McDonnell Douglas* model is also applied to age and disability discrimination cases.

MIXED-MOTIVE CASES

In *Price Waterhouse v. Hopkins*,[6] the Supreme Court held that even after a plaintiff proved that gender discrimination was a motivating factor in an employment decision, an employer could avoid liability for intentional discrimination in so-called **mixed-motive cases** if the employer could demonstrate by a preponderance of the evidence that the same adverse employment decision would have been taken based on other business considerations containing no discriminatory motives. Ann Hopkins was not made a partner at the Price Waterhouse accounting firm. Some evidence indicated that she was abrasive with staff members, a legitimate reason not to promote a person to partner. Other evidence indicated that the selection process was influenced by gender stereotyping, including one partner who advised her to improve her chances for partnership by stating, "Walk more femininely, talk more femininely, dress more femininely, wear makeup, have your hair styled, and wear jewelry."[7] On remand from the Supreme Court, Hopkins was awarded the partnership, back pay, and attorney fees.

The Civil Rights Act of 1991 overturned the *Price Waterhouse v. Hopkins* decision in certain respects. The 1991 Act provides that if the plaintiff shows that a statutorily prohibited factor such as race, sex, or religion motivated an employment action, an unlawful employment practice is established at that point, even if other lawful factors also motivated the action. An employer can avail itself of a limited affirmative defense that restricts the remedies available to the plaintiff, however, if it demonstrates (meets the burdens of production and persuasion) that it would have taken the same adverse employment action such as a suspension or discharge of the plaintiff absent the impermissible motivating factor. If the employer is able to demonstrate that it would have taken the same action absent the unlawful motive, a court is limited to awarding attorney's fees, costs, and declaratory relief. However, the court may not award the plaintiff damages such as back pay; compensatory or punitive damages; or admission, reinstatement, hiring, or promotion. Of course, if the employer is not able to meet this shifting burden of proof, as was the case in the *Desert Palace Inc. v. Costa* decision, presented in this section, the plaintiff is entitled to full remedies. The *Desert Palace* case held that direct evidence

---

[5] *Id.* at 2756. See also *Kobrin v. University of Minn.*, 34 F.3d 698 (8th Cir. 1994) (plaintiff retains burden of persuading trier of fact of discrimination).

[6] 490 U.S. 228 (1989).

[7] *Id.* at 234.

of discrimination is not required in mixed motive cases and circumstantial evidence is probative of intentional discrimination.

DISPARATE IMPACT CASES: *WARDS COVE* AND THE 1991 ACT

In *Wards Cove Packing Co. v. Atonio*,[8] the Supreme Court changed the burden of proof in Title VII disparate impact (facially neutral practice with an adverse impact on a protected group) cases. Under *Wards Cove*, a plaintiff was required to (1) prove a relevant statistical disparity in the workplace and (2) demonstrate that a specific or particular employment practice created the disparate impact under attack. The burden then shifted to the employer to produce evidence that the identified practice was justified. This "business justification" test lessened the burden on the employer that had existed since *Griggs v. Duke Power*, which placed a "business necessity" affirmative defense on the employer. Moreover, under *Wards Cove*, the employer's burden was not to persuade but only to produce evidence in support of its position. The ultimate burden of proving the lack of business justification for the practice remains with the plaintiff. The Supreme Court recognized in *Wards Cove* that a plaintiff may establish unlawful disparate impact if it is shown that a less discriminatory "alternative practice" is available but the employer refuses to adopt it. However, consideration of cost and the burdens on the employer are relevant considerations.

The Civil Rights Act of 1991 (CRA 91) specifically responded to the *Wards Cove* decision. Section 2(2) of the 1991 Act set forth the finding that:

> (2) the decision of the Supreme Court in *Wards Cove Packing Co. v. Atonio*, 490 U.S. 642 (1989) has weakened the scope and effectiveness of Federal civil rights protections....

And Section 3(2) of the 1991 Act set forth as one of its purposes:

> (2) to codify the concepts of "business necessity" and "job-related" enunciated by the Supreme Court in *Griggs v. Duke Power Co.*, 401 U.S. 424 (1971), and in the other Supreme Court decisions prior to *Wards Cove Packing Co. v. Atonio*....

The 1991 law reaffirmed segments of *Wards Cove*, however. The case's discussion of the statistical comparisons needed to form a proper basis for initial inquiry still applies. Plaintiffs must still demonstrate that each particular challenged employment practice causes a disparate impact. An exception exists to this causation requirement where the plaintiff can demonstrate that the elements of the employer's decision-making process are not capable of separation for such a causation analysis. In such a situation, the process may be analyzed as one employment practice. The 1991 Act allows a plaintiff to prove a case of disparate impact by demonstrating that less discriminatory alternative employment practices could be utilized but the employer refuses to adopt such practices. The extent of the proof requirements and considerations of costs and employer needs were purposely left unresolved by Congress, to be settled according to the law "as it existed" on the day before the *Wards Cove* decision.

---

[8] 490 U.S. 642 (1989).

Disparate impact analysis is not limited to "objective" employment practices, such as testing or educational requirements. It is also applicable to subjective employment practices, such as personal interviews and performance appraisals.[9] However, the complaining party must nevertheless identify the particular element or practice within the process that causes the adverse impact. Thus, in *Stout v. Potter*,[10] where female postal inspectors brought a Title VII disparate impact action against the postmaster general alleging denial of promotion on the basis of sex, it was claimed that the employer's facially neutral screening process excludes female applicants due to gender. Since there was no evidence that the criteria in the employer's screening process operated as "built in headwinds" for female applicants, a motion for summary judgment for the employer was properly granted.

Disparate impact is not properly measured in terms of bottom-line results of a hiring process but rather at any point in the selection process where individuals are disproportionately excluded from equal employment opportunities.[11]

PROOF IN DISPARATE IMPACT CASES

Section 105 of the 1991 Act specifically overruled the *Wards Cove* burden of proof analysis; the Act codified the concepts of "business necessity" and "job-related" enunciated in *Griggs*. The new shifting burdens of proof scheme that resulted is as follows:

1. The plaintiff must "demonstrate" through relevant statistical comparisons that a particular facially neutral employment practice used in selecting or promoting employees "causes" a "disparate impact." A more complete discussion on statistical cases is presented in Section 114.
2. The defending employer may then proceed to "demonstrate" that a specific employment practice does not cause the disparate impact, *or*
3. The defending employer must demonstrate (with the burden of persuasion, not just production of evidence) that the challenged practice is "job-related" for the position in question and consistent with "business necessity."

An example of the application of the shifting burden test is found in *EEOC v. Dial Corp.*[12] In that case, the employer implemented a "work tolerance test" that all new employees were required to pass to obtain employment in its Armour Star brand sausage-making department. Ninety-seven percent of male applicants passed the test, with 38 percent of females passing the test. The EEOC "demonstrated" that the facially neutral work tolerance test "caused" a disparate impact on women. The defending employer did not deny that the employment practice in question caused the disparate impact. Rather, the employer responded that the test was "job-related" and "necessary" to reduce job-related injuries at the plant, and the employer submitted evidence that the number of job injuries was reduced after

---

[9] *Watson v. Fort Worth Bank and Trust Co.*, 487 U.S. 1232 (1988).

[10] 276 F.3d 1118 (9th Cir. 2002).

[11] *Connecticut v. Teal*, 457 U.S. 440 (1982).

[12] 2005 WL 2839977 (S.D. Iowa, 2005).

the testing program was implemented. However, the employer did not meet its burden of persuasion, because the company had initiated numerous other safety initiatives during the time period that likely led to the reduction in injuries at the plant. The employer was ordered to pay $3.4 million in damages to the 52 women denied a job after they failed the test.

In *Lanning v. SEPTA*,[13] the Southeastern Pennsylvania Transportation Authority was able to demonstrate that the challenged practice of requiring that all applicants for the job of a SEPTA transit police officer be able to run 1.5 miles in 12 minutes was "job-related" for the position of patrol officer and consistent with "business necessity" even though the pass rate for women was 12 percent compared to 60 percent for men. The court majority pointed out that nearly all women who trained for the run were able to pass the test.

CASE 13.1	DESERT PALACE INC. V. COSTA
	SUPREME COURT OF THE UNITED STATES, 539 U.S. 90 (2003).

[Petitioner Desert Palace, Inc., dba Caesar's Palace Hotel & Casino of Las Vegas, Nevada, employed respondent Catharina Costa as a warehouse worker and heavy equipment operator. She was the only woman in this job and in her local Teamsters' bargaining unit. Costa experienced a number of problems with management and her coworkers that led to an escalating series of disciplinary sanctions, including informal rebukes, a denial of privileges, and suspension. The employer finally terminated her after she was involved in a physical altercation in a warehouse elevator with fellow Teamsters' member Herbert Gerber. The employer disciplined both employees because the facts surrounding the incident were in dispute, but Gerber, who had a clean disciplinary record, was assessed a five-day suspension while Costa was fired. Ms. Costa subsequently filed this lawsuit against her employer in the United States District Court for sex discrimination. At trial, she presented evidence that (1) she was singled out for "intense stalking" by one of her supervisors, (2) she received harsher discipline than men for the same conduct, (3) she was treated less favorably than men in the assignment of overtime, and (4) supervisors repeatedly "stacked" her disciplinary record and "frequently used or tolerated" sex-based slurs against her. The District Court instructed the jury that "[t]he plaintiff has the burden of proving ... by a preponderance of the evidence" that she "suffered adverse work condi-

tions" and that her sex "was a motivating factor in any such work conditions imposed upon her." The District Court gave the jury the following mixed-motive instruction:

> You have heard evidence that the defendant's treatment of the plaintiff was motivated by the plaintiff's sex and also by other lawful reasons. If you find that the plaintiff's sex was a motivating factor in the defendant's treatment of the plaintiff, the plaintiff is entitled to your verdict, even if you find that the defendant's conduct was also motivated by a lawful reason.
>
> However, if you find that the defendant's treatment of the plaintiff was motivated by both gender and lawful reasons, you must decide whether the plaintiff is entitled to damages. The plaintiff is entitled to damages unless the defendant proves by a preponderance of the evidence that the defendant would have treated plaintiff similarly even if the plaintiff's gender had played no role in the employment decision.

The employer unsuccessfully objected to this instruction, claiming that Costa had failed to adduce "direct evidence" that sex was a motivating factor in her dismissal. The jury rendered a verdict for Costa, awarding back pay, compensatory damages, and punitive damages.

The Court of Appeals, *en banc*, concluded that a "plaintiff ... may establish a violation through a

continued

---

[13] 308 F.3d 286 (3d Cir. 2002).

preponderance of evidence (whether direct or circumstantial) that a protected characteristic played "a motivating factor." Based on that standard, the court of appeals held that respondent's evidence was sufficient to warrant a mixed-motive instruction and that a reasonable jury could have found that respondent's sex was a "motivating factor in her treatment." The Supreme Court granted certiorari.]

THOMAS, J....

... This case provides us with the first opportunity to consider the effects of the 1991 Act on jury instructions in mixed-motive cases. Specifically, we must decide whether a plaintiff must present direct evidence of discrimination in order to obtain a mixed-motive instruction under 42 U.S.C. § 2000e-2(m)....

Our precedents make clear that the starting point for our analysis is the statutory text. And where, as here, the words of the statute are unambiguous, the "'judicial inquiry is complete.'" Section 2000e-2(m) unambiguously states that a plaintiff need only "demonstrat[e]" that an employer used a forbidden consideration with respect to "any employment practice." On its face, the statute does not mention, much less require, that a plaintiff make a heightened showing through direct evidence....

Moreover, Congress explicitly defined the term "demonstrates" in the 1991 Act, leaving little doubt that no special evidentiary showing is required. Title VII defines the term "'demonstrates'" as to "mee[t] the burdens of production and persuasion." § 2000e(m)....

In addition, Title VII's silence with respect to the type of evidence required in mixed-motive cases also suggests that we should not depart from the "[c]onventional rul[e] of civil litigation [that] generally appl[ies] in Title VII cases." That rule requires a plaintiff to prove his case "by a preponderance of the

evidence," using "direct or circumstantial evidence," *Postal Service Bd. of Governors v. Aikens*, 460 U.S. 711, 714, n. 3 (1983). We have often acknowledged the utility of circumstantial evidence in discrimination cases. For instance, in *Reeves v. Sanderson Plumbing Products, Inc.*, 530 U.S. 133, 120 S.Ct. 2097, 147 L.Ed.2d 105 (2000), we recognized that evidence that a defendant's explanation for an employment practice is "unworthy of credence" is "one form of *circumstantial evidence* that is probative of intentional discrimination." *Id.*, at 147 (emphasis added). The reason for treating circumstantial and direct evidence alike is both clear and deep rooted: "Circumstantial evidence is not only sufficient, but may also be more certain, satisfying and persuasive than direct evidence." *Rogers v. Missouri Pacific R. Co.*, 352 U.S. 500, 508, n. 17....

In order to obtain an instruction under § 2000e-2(m), a plaintiff need only present sufficient evidence for a reasonable jury to conclude, by a preponderance of the evidence, that "race, color, religion, sex, and national origin was a motivating factor for any employment practice." Because direct evidence of discrimination is not required in mixed-motive cases, the Court of Appeals correctly concluded that the District Court did not abuse its discretion in giving a mixed-motive instruction to the jury. Accordingly, the judgment of the Court of Appeals is affirmed.

Case Questions

1. What is a mixed-motive case? Give an example from the text.
2. What remedy options exist in a mixed-motive case where the jury determines that the employer demonstrated that it would have taken the same employment action of termination in the absence of the impermissible motivating factor?

SECTION 114: STATISTICAL CASES

In *Hazelwood School District v. United States*,[14] the Supreme Court dealt with the matter of statistical proof in Title VII cases. The Hazelwood School District was formed by 13 rural school districts outside of St. Louis, Missouri. Of the more than 19,000 teachers employed in the St. Louis area, 15.4 percent were black.

---

[14] 433 U.S. 299, 15 FEP 1 (1977).

This figure included the St. Louis City School District, which had a policy of attempting to maintain a 50 percent black teaching staff. Apart from the city district, 5.7 percent of the teachers in the county were black according to the 1970 census. In the 1972–73 school year, Hazelwood employed 16 black teachers on its staff of 1,107 (1.4 percent), and by the 1973–74 school year, 22 of 1,231 (1.8 percent) of the teachers were black. The attorney general of the United States brought a "pattern or practice" of discrimination suit against the school district. This suit was unsuccessful in the U.S. District Court but successful in the U.S. Court of Appeals. The Supreme Court granted certiorari. In its decision, the Court set forth certain principles for statistical cases and remanded the case for further proceedings.

QUALIFIED LABOR MARKET

A "population-workforce" comparison makes a statistical comparison of the percentage of blacks, Hispanics, or women in the population of a specific geographic area to the number of blacks, Hispanics, or women employed by a defendant employer. In *Hazelwood*, the Supreme Court cautioned that the statistical data for such comparisons should be based on the "qualified" labor market. The Court stated:

> When special qualifications are required to fill particular jobs, comparisons to the general population (rather than to the smaller group of individuals who possess the necessary qualifications) may have little probative value.[15]

RELEVANT GEOGRAPHIC AREA

The *Hazelwood* decision emphasized the importance of determining the relevant geographic area for statistical comparison purposes. The objective is to define the area from which applicants are likely to come, absent discrimination. Thus, commuting patterns, availability of public transportation, and the geographic scope of the employer's recruiting practices are all relevant considerations. For example, if the employer recruits for executives on a nationwide basis, the relevant geographic area would be the entire country, and nationwide statistics would be applicable.

RELEVANT TIME FRAME

Hazelwood recognized the concept of "relevant time frame" statistics, which focuses on the employment decisions made during the relevant time period of the litigation rather than looking at "static" statistics. The relevant time period is after the effective date of Title VII. However, under the Supreme Court's *United Air Lines v. Evans*[16] decision, the Court considers discriminatory acts occurring before the charge-filing period to be the legal equivalent of acts occurring before the effective date of Title VII. Thus, the relevant time frame for a Title VII case is the period starting 300 days prior to the filing of a charge with the EEOC. For example, if an employer had few blacks in its workforce but in the two years prior to the filing of

---

[15] 433 U.S. 229, 308 n. 13 (1977); see also, *Stout v. Potter*, 276 F.3d 1118, 1123 (9th Cir. 2002).
[16] 431 U.S. 553, 14 FEP 1510 (1977).

a charge had hired blacks at a rate equal to or above the percentage of blacks in the workforce of the area, the relevant time frame analysis would lead to a finding that Title VII was not violated even though a "static analysis"—which is simply the actual percentage of blacks employed in the employer's total workforce on a given date regardless of hiring dates—would show a gross disparity. The *Evans* Court would consider the statistical significance of the static analysis, which would indicate the existence of past discrimination as "merely an unfortunate event in history which has no present legal consequences."

SUFFICIENCY OF STATISTICAL DISPARITY

Ultimately in a statistical case, a court is called upon to make determinations based on the statistical evidence before it. The Court in *Hazelwood* made it clear that the statistical disparity must be a "gross" disparity in order for there to be a finding of discrimination based on the statistical evidence. The *Hazelwood* Court set forth a "standard deviations" analysis that has been followed by numerous lower courts. The Supreme Court did not resolve the discrimination issue before it in *Hazelwood* and remanded the case to the district court for further proceedings on the geographic scope of the relevant labor market utilizing the statistical methodology explained in *Castaneda v. Partida.*[17] Footnote 17 of the *Hazelwood* decision states:

> Indeed, under the statistical methodology explained in *Castaneda* ... involving the calculation of the standard deviation as a measure of predicted fluctuations, the difference between using 15.4% and 5.7% as the areawide figure would be significant. If the 15.4% figure is taken as the basis for comparison, the expected number of Negro teachers, hired by Hazelwood in 1972–1973 would be 43 (rather than the actual figure of 10) of a total of 282, a difference of more than five standard deviations; the expected number in 1973–1974 would be 19 (rather than the actual figure 5) of a total of 123, a difference of more than three standard deviations. For the two years combined, the difference between the observed number of 15 Negro teachers hired (of a total of 405) would vary from the expected number of 62 by more than six standard deviations. Because a fluctuation of more than two or three standard deviations would undercut the hypothesis that decisions were being made randomly with respect to race, each of these statistical comparisons would reinforce rather than rebut the Government's other proof. If, however, the 5.7% areawide figure is used, the expected number of Negro teachers hired in 1972–1973 would be roughly 16, less than two standard deviations from the observed number of 10; for 1973–1974, the expected value would be roughly seven, less than one standard deviation from the observed value of 5; and for the two years combined, the expected value of 23 would be less than two standard deviations from the observed total of 15....
>
> These observations are not intended to suggest that precise calculations of statistical significance are necessary in employing statistical proof, but merely to highlight the importance of the choice of the relevant labor market area.

Please note in footnote 17 that the Supreme Court has adopted a rule of thumb for the number of standard deviations that would undercut the hypothesis that the decisions were being made randomly with respect to race and the like and that it is a greater than "two or three standard deviations" rule.

---

[17] 430 U.S. 482 (1977).

The binomial test used by the Supreme Court in *Castaneda* may be summarized in terms of a set of equations using the following symbols to represent the variables. Thus,

n = number of binomial trials in a particular experiment

p = probability of a success on each trial

e = expected number of successes

o = observed number of successes

SD = standard deviation

Z = Z statistic or Z score, which is the number of standard deviations by which the number of successes actually observed differs from the number expected

1. In *Castaneda*, the statistical analysis sought to assess whether the shortage in the number of Mexican-Americans called to serve on grand juries in Hidalgo County, Texas, could have occurred by chance. The total number of persons selected for grand jury was 870; thus, n = 870. Mexican-Americans made up 79.1 percent of the population from which grand jurors were drawn; thus, p = .791. The actual number of Mexican-Americans selected for grand jury duty was 339; thus, o = 339. To find the expected number of successes, multiply n times p (e = n × p): e = 870 × .791 = 688.

2. To calculate the standard deviation (SD), take the square root of the product of the number of trials, the probability of a success, and the probability of a failure:

$$(SD = \sqrt{n \times p \times (1 - p)} : SD = \sqrt{870 \times .791 \times .209} = \sqrt{143.83} = 11.99$$

3. To calculate the Z statistics or score, which is the number of standard deviations by which the number of successes actually observed differs from the number of successes expected, the numerator consists of the expected number minus the observed number:

$$Z = \frac{e - o}{SD} : Z = \frac{688 - 399}{11.99} = 29.1$$

A fluctuation of more than two or three standard deviations—that is, a Z score of greater than 2 or 3—would undercut the hypothesis that the selection process was being made randomly with respect to national origin. In *Castaneda*, the fluctuation was so great that the Court concluded that the statistical disparities established a *prima facie* case of discrimination against Mexican-Americans in the selection process.

An employee may also use statistics to show that an employer's justification for a discriminatory act is a pretext.[18] Moreover, gross statistical disparities may be probative of discriminatory intent, motive, or purpose.[19] In *Delcorte v. Jordan*,[20] the statistics supplied by plaintiffs, former employees of the Orleans Parish (New Orleans), Louisiana District Attorney's office, showed that on the date Eddie Jordan took office

---

[18] *Plemer v. Parsons-Gilbane*, 713 F.2d 1127 (5ᵗʰ Cir. 1983).

[19] *Walther v. Lone Star Gas Co.*, 977 F.2d 161. 162 (5ᵗʰ Cir. 1992).

[20] 497 F.3d 433 (5ᵗʰ Cir. 2007).

as district attorney, the racial composition of the non-attorney staff was 77 whites, 56 blacks, 2 Hispanics, and 1 Asian, but 72 days later, the composition had changed to 27 whites and 130 blacks. Of the 56 non-attorney employees Jordan terminated, 53 were white, 1 was Hispanic, and 2 were black. The plaintiffs' statistician testified that the probability that 53 out of the 56 terminated employees would be white if the terminations was race-neutral was less than 1 in 10,000; and the probability of the racial composition changing as it did in 72 days, if the decisions had been made randomly as asserted by the black district attorney, was less than one in a million. The Fifth Circuit Court of Appeals affirmed the jury's award of compensatory damages to the plaintiffs.

SECTION 115: TITLE VII COURT-ORDERED REMEDIES

The remedial powers of federal courts deciding Title VII actions include injunctions against unlawful practices; affirmative orders requiring the reinstatement or the hiring of employees; and the awarding of back pay, front pay, and seniority rights. Back pay orders are limited to a period of two years prior to the filing of the charge.[21] The Civil Rights Act of 1991 provides for increased damages, including compensatory and punitive damages, as summarized in Figure 12.2, page 395.

MAKE-WHOLE REMEDIES FOR VICTIMS

In the *Albemarle Paper Co.* decision, reported in this section, the Supreme Court held that back pay should be denied only in limited situations and for reasons that would not frustrate the purposes of Title VII. The *Bowman* decision reported in this section is an example of a remedy fashioned from legislative intent. There the Supreme Court held that the awarding of seniority rights was necessary to eradicate the effects of post–Title VII discrimination against black employees.

COURT-ORDERED AFFIRMATIVE ACTION FOR NONVICTIMS

In *Sheet Metal Workers' Local 28 v. EEOC*,[22] the Supreme Court held that district courts were not limited to awarding preferential relief only to the actual victims of unlawful discrimination. The courts may order preferential relief, such as requiring the employer to meet goals and timetables for the hiring of minorities, where an employer or labor union has engaged in persistent and egregious discrimination or where it is necessary to dissipate the lingering effects of pervasive discrimination. The Court stated, however, that in the majority of Title VII cases where Title VII has been found to have been violated, the district court will need only to order the employer or union to cease the unlawful practices and award make-whole relief to the individuals victimized by those practices.

AWARD OF ATTORNEY FEES

Section 706(k) of Title VII provides that the court in its discretion may allow the prevailing party, other than the EEOC and the United States, a reasonable attorney fee.

---

[21] 42 U.S.C. § 706(g).
[22] 478 U.S. 421 (1986).

In *New York Gaslight Club, Inc. v. Carey*,[23] the Supreme Court held that a federal court may allow the prevailing party attorney fees before a state administrative proceeding that Title VII requires federal claimants to invoke. The 1991 Act provides that the court may also award as part of the attorney fees a fee for expert witnesses.

The Supreme Court in *Christiansburg Garment Co. v. EEOC*[24] set forth a standard that allows district courts the discretion to award attorney fees to a prevailing defendant where the plaintiff's case is "frivolous, unreasonable, or without foundation." In *Arnold v. Burger King Corporation*,[25] the Fourth Circuit Court of Appeals affirmed an award of $10,744 in attorney fees against an unsuccessful plaintiff in a race discrimination case. The plaintiff, Arnold, a black male, was employed as a manager of a Burger King when several female employees formally complained to management that Arnold had sexually harassed them. The complaints accused Arnold of various incidents of misconduct, including propositions and acts of deliberate and suggestive physical conduct. Following the complaints, Arnold was discharged. He then filed a race discrimination charge with the EEOC. After the EEOC issued a right-to-sue letter, Arnold took his former employer to court, where his only evidence was testimony from several coworkers and friends attesting to his good character. Burger King cited evidence that the workforce was half white and half black, that the number of blacks in management had risen, and that a white employee involved in a less severe sexual harassment incident was fired before Arnold. The district court ruled that Arnold's case was frivolous and groundless from the outset and dismissed the case. The district court also awarded the $10,744 in attorney fees to be paid by Arnold, fees that were upheld by the court of appeals.

CASE 13.2	ALBEMARLE PAPER CO. V. MOODY
	SUPREME COURT OF THE UNITED STATES, 422 U.S. 405 (1975).

[Respondents, a certified class of present and former Negro employees, brought this action against petitioners, their employer, Albemarle Paper Company, and the employees union, seeking injunctive relief against "any policy, practice, custom or usage" at the plant violative of Title VII of the Civil Rights Act of

continued

---

[23] 477 U.S. 54, 22 FEP 1642 (1980).

[24] 434 U.S. 412 (1978).

[25] 32 FEP 1769 (4th Cir. 1983). See also *Weeks v. Samsung Heavy Industries Co.*, 1996 U.S. LEXIS 17832. But see *Weisberg v. Riverside Township Board of Education*, 272 Fed. Appx. 170 (3d Cir. 2008). Charles Weisberg received a head injury at work, and he sought quiet surroundings and other accommodations from his school board employer. At a deposition prior to his Americans with Disabilities Act lawsuit against the Board of Education, he was asked a number of questions about his actions the previous Monday night. He stated that he watched the Giants game at home, that because of his disability, he could not have attended the game. On the night in question, a private investigator for the school board videotaped Weisberg meeting a group of fans, tailgating, attending the entire game, and returning home at 2 A.M. A federal trial court granted summary judgment for the school board. The school board appealed the denial of its request for attorney fees. The appeals court determined that the trial court did not abuse its discretion on the matter of attorney fees. Although a disability was not established, "especially in light of Weisberg's credibility," the record indicated that he had "some sort of medical condition affecting his concentration, vision, mood and energy and his claim was not wholly without foundation."

1964, as amended by the Equal Employment Opportunity Act of 1972, and after several years of discovery, moved to add a class back pay demand. At this trial, the major issues were the plant's seniority system, its program of employment testing, and back pay. The district court found that following a reorganization under a new collective bargaining agreement, the Negro employees had been "locked" in the lower-paying job classification and ordered petitioners to implement a system of plantwide seniority. The court refused, however, to order back pay for losses sustained by the plaintiff class under the discriminatory system on the grounds that (1) Albemarle's breach of Title VII was found not to have been in "bad faith" and (2) respondents had initially disclaimed interest in back pay and delayed making their back pay claim until five years after the complaint was filed, thereby prejudicing petitioners. The court also refused to enjoin or limit Albemarle's testing program, which respondents had contended had a disproportionate adverse impact on blacks and was not shown to be related to job performance. The court concluded that "personnel tests administered at the plant have undergone validation studies and have been proven to be job-related." Respondents appealed on the back pay and preemployment test issues. The court of appeals reversed the district court's judgment.]

STEWART, J....

The District Court's decision must therefore be measured against the purposes which inform Title VII. As the Court observed in *Griggs v. Duke Power Co.*, the primary objective was a prophylactic one:

> It was to achieve equality of employment opportunities and remove barriers that have operated in the past to favor an identifiable group of white employees over other employees.

Back pay has an obvious connection with this purpose. If employers faced only the prospect of an injunctive order, they would have little incentive to shun practices of dubious legality. It is the reasonably certain prospect of a back pay award that "provide[s] the spur or catalyst which causes employers and unions to self-examine and to self-evaluate their employment practices and to endeavor to eliminate, so far as possible, the last vestiges of an unfortunate and ignominious page in this country's history."

It is also the purpose of Title VII to make persons whole for injuries suffered on account of unlawful employment discrimination. This is shown by the very fact that Congress took care to arm the courts with full equitable powers....

It follows that, given a finding of unlawful discrimination, back pay should be denied only for reasons which, if applied generally, would not frustrate the central statutory purposes of eradicating discrimination throughout the economy and making persons whole for injuries suffered through past discrimination. The courts of appeals must maintain a consistent and principled application of the back pay provision, consonant with the twin statutory objectives, while at the same time recognizing that the trial court will often have the keener appreciation of those facts and circumstances peculiar to particular cases.

The District Court's stated grounds for denying back pay in this case must be tested against these standards. The first ground was that Albemarle's breach of Title VII had not been in "bad faith." This is not a sufficient reason for denying back pay. Where an employer *has* shown bad faith—by maintaining a practice which he knew to be illegal or of highly questionable legality—he can make no claims whatsoever on the Chancellor's conscience. But, under Title VII, the mere absence of bad faith simply opens the door to equity; it does not depress the scales in the employer's favor. If back pay were awardable only upon a showing of bad faith, the remedy would become a punishment for moral turpitude, rather than a compensation for workers' injuries. This would read the "make whole" purpose right out of Title VII, for a worker's injury is no less real simply because his employer did not inflict it in "bad faith." Title VII is not concerned with the employer's "good intent or absence of discriminatory intent" for "Congress directed the thrust of the Act to the *consequences* of employment practices, not simply the motivation." To condition the awarding of back pay on a showing of "bad faith" would be to open an enormous chasm between injunctive and back pay relief under Title VII. There is nothing on the face of the statute or in its legislative history that justifies that creation of drastic and categorical distinctions between those two remedies....

[A synopsis of the remainder of the Court's opinion is as follows:

As is clear from *Griggs, supra,* and the Equal Employment Opportunity Commission's guidelines for employers seeking to determine through professional validation studies whether employment tests are job-related, such tests are impermissible unless shown, by professionally acceptable methods, to be "predictive

continued

of or significantly correlated with important elements of work behavior which comprise or are relevant to the job or jobs for which candidates are being evaluated." Measured against the standard, Albemarle's validation study is materially defective in that (1) it would not, because of the odd patchwork of results from its application, have "validated" the two general ability tests used by Albemarle for all the skilled lines of progression for which the two tests are, apparently, now required; (2) it compared test scores with subjective supervisorial rankings, affording no means of knowing what job performance criteria the supervisors were considering; (3) it focused mostly on job groups near the top of

various lines of progression, but the fact that the best of those employees working near the top of the lines of progression score well on a test does not necessarily mean that the test permissibly measures the qualifications of new workers entering lower level jobs; and (4) it dealt only with job-experienced white workers, but the tests themselves are given to new job applicants who are younger, largely inexperienced, and in many instances nonwhite.]

Accordingly, the judgment is vacated and remanded to the district court for proceedings consistent with this opinion.

It is so ordered.

CASE 13.3 | ## FRANKS V. BOWMAN TRANSPORTATION CO., INC.
SUPREME COURT OF THE UNITED STATES, 424 U.S. 747 (1976).

[A trucking company had discriminated against blacks after the passage of Title VII by denying them employment as over-the-road drivers. In holding that a remedy which included seniority rights was necessary, the Supreme Court reviewed the legislative intent behind Section 706(g) of the Act.]

BRENNAN, J....

Last term's *Albemarle Paper Company v. Moody*, 422 U.S. 405, 418 (1975), consistent with the congressional plan, held that one of the central purposes of Title VII is "to make persons whole for injuries suffered on account of unlawful employment discrimination." To effectuate this make-whole objective, Congress in Section 706(g) vested broad equitable discretion in the federal courts to order such affirmative action as may be appropriate, which may include, but is not limited to, reinstatement or hiring of employees, with or without back pay..., or any other equitable relief as the court deems appropriate. The legislative history supporting the 1972 Amendments of Section 706(g) of Title VII affirms the breadth of this discretion. The provisions of [Section 706(g)] are intended to give the courts wide discretion exercising their equitable powers to fashion the most complete relief possible.... [T]he Act is intended to make the victims of unlawful employment discrimination whole, and ... the attainment of this objective ... requires that persons aggrieved by the consequences and effects of the unlawful employment practice be so far as possible, restored

to a position where they would have been were it not for the unlawful discrimination. Section-by-Section Analysis of H.R. 1746, accompanying the Equal Employment Opportunity Act of 1972—Conference Report, 118 Cong. Rec. 7166, 7168 (1972). This is emphatic confirmation that federal courts are empowered to fashion such relief as the particular circumstances of a case may require to effect restitution, making whole insofar as possible the victims of racial discrimination in hiring. Adequate relief may well be denied in the absence of a seniority remedy slotting the victim in that position in the seniority system that would have been his had he been hired at the time of his application. It can hardly be questioned that ordinarily such relief will be necessary to achieve the make-whole purposes of the Act....

Case Questions

1. In *Albemarle*, did a showing that the employer had not acted in bad faith relieve the employer from a back pay obligation?

2. Why did the district court in *Albemarle* refuse to order a back pay remedy?

3. Does the Supreme Court agree with the district court's ruling in *Albemarle* that it has unfettered discretion in fashioning a remedy?

4. According to the House Report quoted in the *Bowman* decision, what is the primary intention of Title VII?

SECTION 116: CONSENT DECREES AND VOLUNTARY AFFIRMATIVE ACTION PLANS

Employers have an interest in affirmative action because it is fundamentally fair to have a diverse and representative workforce. Moreover, affirmative action is an effective means of avoiding litigation costs associated with discrimination cases while at the same time preserving management prerogatives and preserving rights to government contracts. Employers, under affirmative action plans (AAPs), may undertake special recruiting and other efforts to hire and train minorities and women and help them advance within the company. However, the plan may also provide job preferences for minorities and women. Such aspects of affirmative action plans have resulted in numerous lawsuits contending that Title VII of the Civil Rights Act of 1964, the Fourteenth Amendment, or collective bargaining contracts have been violated. The Supreme Court has not been able to settle the many difficult issues before it with a clear and consistent majority. The Court has decided cases narrowly, with individual justices often feeling compelled to speak in concurring or dissenting opinions.

PRIVATE SECTOR AAPs

The Supreme Court, in the landmark *Griggs v. Duke Power Co.* decision, made a statement on discriminatory preferences and Title VII:

> The Act does not command that any person be hired simply because he was formerly the subject of discrimination, or because he is a member of a minority group. Discriminatory preference for any group, minority or majority, is precisely and only what Congress has proscribed. What is required by Congress is the removal of artificial, arbitrary, and unnecessary barriers to employment when the barriers operate invidiously to discriminate on the basis of racial or other impermissible classification.

In *McDonald v. Santa Fe Trail Transportation Co.,*[26] the Supreme Court held that discrimination against whites was prohibited by Title VII. In *Regents of the University of California v. Bakke,*[27] the Supreme Court held that Allan Bakke, a white applicant for admission to the University of California Medical School at Davis, was denied admission to the school solely on racial grounds and that the Constitution forbids such.

It was in the above context that the Supreme Court considered the question of whether Title VII allows an employer and union in the private sector to implement an affirmative action plan that granted a racial preference to blacks where there was no finding of proven discrimination by a court but where there was a conspicuous racial imbalance in the employer's skilled craft workforce. The Court decided this question in *Steelworkers v. Weber*, presented in this section. The Court held that the employer could implement such a plan under Title VII. It thus rejected the contentions of the white male plaintiff that the selection of junior black employees over more senior white male employees discriminated against the white males because of their color and was "reverse discrimination" contrary to Title VII. The Court majority chose not to define in detail a line of demarcation between

---

[26] 427 U.S. 273, 12 FEP 1577 (1976).

[27] 438 U.S. 265, 17 FEP 1000 (1978).

permissible and impermissible affirmative action plans, but certain principles may be extracted from the majority opinion as to what is permissible:

1. The affirmative action must be in connection with a "plan."
2. There must be a showing that affirmative action is justified as a remedial measure. The plan then must be remedial to open opportunities in occupations closed to protected classes under Title VII or designed to break down old patterns of racial segregation and hierarchy. In order to make a determination that affirmative action is justified, the parties must make a self-analysis to determine if and where conspicious racial imbalances exist.
3. The plan must be voluntary.
4. The plan must not unnecessarily trammel the interests of whites.
5. The plan must be temporary.

The *Weber* decision was the cornerstone on which many subsequent Supreme Court decisions on affirmative action issues were structured.[28]

---

[28] For a retrospective analysis of the *Weber* decision, see University of Minnesota law professor Philip P. Frickey's Wisdom Lecture entitled "*Wisdom on Weber*" given on February 7, 2000, at the Tulane Law School and published 24 *Tul. L. Rev.* 1169 (2000). Professor Frickey stated in part at p. 1200:

> The story of Brian Weber may seem quite ironic. He helped propose the apprenticeship program that, in part because of pressure from federal contracting authorities, ended up with a racial quota attached to it that resulted in the denial of his application and his resulting lawsuit; as union steward, he had to assist in the administration of the program while the suit was pending; he obtained a first-class attorney by sheer fortuity; after losing the case, he obtained a college education in painful dribs and drabs at night and then was unable to find a position fitting his credentials and interests for four years; and then he traded in his blue collar for a white collar, switched from union to management, and became a highly successful manager intimately involved in the human resources of a company that, as a federal contractor, applied for and won an award from the federal government celebrating achievements in equal employment opportunity and diversity. The story is less ironic than it appears. Weber was never anything remotely like a racist. He was, and is, an ambitious person seeking to advance himself: indeed, at the moment, at the age of fifty-three, he is working on a Masters in Business Administration, which he hopes to receive this summer. By all accounts, he is also a fine fellow.... In 1993, the *Times-Picayune* ran a series on race relations and the economy. One feature involved an interview with Weber, who by that time was working for Wackenhut in New Orleans. Here is what he is quoted as saying, which, Weber has confirmed to me, remains accurate of his views today:
>
> Initially, I was active within the union, and I knew this was coming about when the union and the company began working out a plan where race would be the criteria for the training program instead of seniority. It was 50-50, one black and one white, even if the black had less seniority. You have to understand that in the union, everything works by seniority. When they did this, I was opposed to it. I thought it was not only illegal, but unfair. I voiced my opposition to this by filing a grievance with the union. But the union then dropped the grievance after a couple of steps, so I filed a complaint with the EEOC (Equal Employment Opportunity Commission). It took six months for them to investigate it. They gave me a right-to-sue letter, and I got an attorney. I went to federal court in New Orleans and talked to a clerk, who took me to the judge. The judge just happened to have someone in his office who had been active in civil rights and assigned him the case. But I must admit that over the years I was exposed to things that kind of altered my feelings somewhat. What I learned from it all is there's this class of people—females and minorities—who haven't been given the same opportunity. Theoretically, I would like to see it where no one would be given preferences. But they didn't start from the same level playing field. And understanding that, I've become more supportive of affirmative action programs. A lot of it had to do with being alert and aware of how people were feeling. What do you do with a society that put people on the side, and they haven't been given the opportunity? Even now, there's a lot of discrimination. I guess I've become more liberal because of what I've been exposed to through the lawsuit. ("Speaking Race," *Times-Picayune* (New Orleans), Nov. 16, 1993, at A7.)

PUBLIC SECTOR AAPS

In *Wygant v. Jackson Board of Education*,[29] where five judges wrote opinions on the issues before the Court, a sufficient number of justices supported various aspects of the concept of a public sector employer's right to implement a race-conscious affirmative action plan. However, the Court struck down a layoff preference for blacks as violative of the Fourteenth Amendment. Under *Wygant*, a majority of the Supreme Court justices recognized affirmative action in the public sector as permissible where (1) there is convincing evidence of prior discrimination by the governmental unit involved (the affirmative action is justified as a remedial measure) and (2) the means chosen to accomplish the remedial purpose is "sufficiently narrowly tailored" to achieve its remedial purpose. A majority of justices concluded, however, that the layoffs were not sufficiently narrowly tailored to survive the Fourteenth Amendment challenge.

The plurality opinion rejected the theory that providing minority role models for minority students to alleviate societal discrimination justified the layoff preference provision for black teachers, saying that such is insufficient to justify racial classifications.

Most of the justices agreed that the public employer does not have to wait for a court finding that it has been guilty of past discrimination before it takes action. However, compelling evidence of past discrimination must be shown before affirmative action preferences may be implemented.

In *Johnson v. Santa Clara County Transportation*,[30] involving public sector affirmative action, the Supreme Court applied the *Weber* principles and upheld the public employer's decision under a voluntary AAP to promote a qualified woman over a more qualified man. The AAP authorized the consideration of the successful candidate's female gender as one factor in the decision-making process. With close but lesser "other" qualifications as compared to the male candidate, the sex of the female candidate tilted the weight of the totality of factors in her favor.

The Supreme Court has dealt with three types of specific issues involving public sector AAPs and has reached narrow determinations on these issues as follows:

1. *Consideration of sex in AAPs*: In the *Johnson v. Santa Clara County Transportation* decision, referred to above, the Supreme Court decided that the public employer did not violate Title VII by promoting a female employee to the position of dispatcher over a more qualified male employee under the terms of its voluntary affirmative action plan.
2. *Promotion quotas*: In *United States v. Paradise*,[31] a sharply divided Court approved a promotion quota for the Alabama State Police, requiring that one black state trooper be promoted for each white state trooper. The plurality opinion found the quota "narrowly tailored" to serve its purpose. Justice Stevens, who cast the deciding vote, believed the relief to be proper because of the state agency's egregious past violations of the equal protection clause.

---

[29] 476 U.S. 267 (1986).

[30] 480 U.S. 616 (1987).

[31] 480 U.S. 149 (1987).

3. *Layoff preferences*: In *Wygant v. Jackson Board of Education*,[32] the Supreme Court struck down a layoff provision in a collective bargaining agreement that gave preferences to blacks. This provision was held to violate the equal protection clause of the Fourteenth Amendment. The plurality opinion stated in part:

> While hiring goals impose a diffuse burden, often foreclosing only one of several opportunities, layoffs impose the entire burden of achieving racial equality on particular individuals, often resulting in serious disruption of their lives. That burden is too intrusive. We therefore hold that, as a means of accomplishing purposes that otherwise may be legitimate, the Board's layoff plan is not sufficiently narrowly tailored. Other, less intrusive means of accomplishing similar purposes—such as the adoption of hiring goals—are available.[33]
>
> In reading Justice O'Connor's concurring opinion in Wygant in conjunction with the plurality decision, it is apparent that racially based layoff procedures are of dubious legality.

CONSENT DECREES

Citing *Steelworkers v. Weber*, the Supreme Court stated in *Firefighters Local 93 v. City of Cleveland*[34] that voluntary action available to employers and unions seeking to eradicate racial discrimination may include reasonable race-conscious relief that benefits individuals who are not actual victims of discrimination. In *Weber*, the voluntary action was the private contractual agreement between the employer and the union. In *Firefighters Local 93*, a federal district court approved a consent decree between the city of Cleveland and an organization of black and Hispanic firefighters who brought suit against the city, charging racial discrimination in promotions and assignments. The terms of a consent decree are arrived at through agreement of the parties to a lawsuit; the court reviews and approves it, and the decree is enforceable by the court. In the *Firefighters Local 93* case, while not a party to the lawsuit, Local 93 was recognized as an intervenor. Local 93 did not approve of the consent decree, which set forth a quota system for the promotion of minorities over a four-year period. Local 93 had contended before the district court that "promotions based upon a criterion other than competence, such as a racial quota system, would deny those most capable from their promotions and deny ... the City ... the best possible firefighting force."[35]

The Supreme Court rejected the union's argument that Section 706(g) of Title VII precludes the courts from approving consent decrees benefiting individuals who were not the actual victims of discrimination.

The importance of the *Local 93* decision is that while Section 706(g) restricts the district court's powers to order relief, such as hiring or promotion orders for individuals who have not actually suffered discrimination, a consent decree is not an "order of the court," according to the Supreme Court majority. Thus, it may

---

[32] 476 U.S. 267 (1986).

[33] *Id.* at 283.

[34] 478 U.S. 501 (1986).

[35] *Id.* at 507.

go beyond what a court could have ordered if the case had been litigated to its conclusion.

UNION OR INDIVIDUAL CHALLENGES TO CONSENT DECREES

In *Martin v. Wilks*,[36] black individuals brought suit against the city of Birmingham, Alabama, alleging that the city had engaged in racially discriminatory hiring and promotion practices in violation of Title VII. Consent decrees were eventually entered that included goals for hiring and promoting blacks as firefighters. Thereafter, white firefighters who had not intervened in the earlier litigation, which resulted in the consent decrees, challenged the employment decisions taken pursuant to the decrees. The Supreme Court allowed this challenge to the consent decrees.

The Civil Rights Act of 1991 altered the *Martin v. Wilks* decision. The 1991 law bars challenges to consent decrees by persons who had actual notice of the proposed order and a reasonable opportunity to present objections and those whose interests were adequately represented by another person who challenged the decree on the same legal grounds and similar facts, unless there has been an intervening change in the law or facts.[37]

CASE 13.4	STEELWORKERS V. WEBER SUPREME COURT OF THE UNITED STATES, 443 U.S. 193 (1979).

[In 1974, petitioners United Steelworkers of America (USWA) and Kaiser Aluminum & Chemical Corporation (Kaiser) entered into a master collective bargaining agreement covering terms and conditions of employment at 15 Kaiser plants. The agreement included an affirmative action plan designed to eliminate racial imbalances in Kaiser's craft workforces by reserving for black employees 50 percent of the openings in in-plant craft training programs until the percentage of black craft workers in a plant was commensurate with the percentage of blacks in the local labor force. This litigation arose from the operation of the affirmative action plan at Kaiser's Gramercy, Louisiana, plant where, prior to 1974, 1.83 percent of the skilled craft workers were black and the local workforce was approximately 39 percent black. Pursuant to the national agreement, Kaiser, rather than continuing its practice of hiring trained outsiders, established a

training program to train its production workers to fill craft openings. Kaiser selected trainees on the basis of seniority and race so that at least 50 percent of the trainees were black until the percentage of black skilled craft workers in the plant approximated the percentage of blacks in the local labor force. During the plan's first year of operation, seven black and six white craft trainees were selected from the plant's production workforce, with the most senior black trainee having less seniority than several white production workers whose bids for admission to the training program were rejected. Thereafter, respondent Brian Weber, one of those white production workers, instituted a class action in federal district court, alleging that because the affirmative action program had resulted in junior black employees receiving training in preference to senior white employees, respondent and other similarly situated white employees had been

continued

---

[36] 490 U.S. 755 (1989).

[37] Section 108 of the Civil Rights Act of 1991.

discriminated against in violation of the provisions of Section 703(a) and (d) of Title VII, which makes it unlawful to "discriminate.... because of.... race" in hiring and in the selection of apprentices for training programs. The district court held that the affirmative action plan violated Title VII, entered judgment in favor of the plaintiff class, and granted injunctive relief. The court of appeals affirmed, holding that all employment preferences based upon race, including those preferences incidental to bona fide affirmative action plans, violated Title VII's prohibition against racial discrimination in employment. The Supreme Court granted certiorari.]

BRENNAN, J....

We emphasize at the outset the narrowness of our inquiry. Since the Kaiser-USWA plan does not involve state action, this case does not present an alleged violation of the Equal Protection Clause of the Fourteenth Amendment. Further, since the Kaiser-USWA plan was adopted voluntarily, we are not concerned with what Title VII requires or with what a court might order to remedy a past proved violation of the Act. The only question before us is the narrow statutory issue of whether Title VII forbids private employers and unions from voluntarily agreeing upon bona fide affirmative action plans that accord racial preferences in the manner and for the purpose provided in the Kaiser-USWA plan. That question was expressly left open in *McDonald v. Santa Fe Trail Transp. Co.*, 427 U.S. 273 (1976), which held, in a case not involving affirmative action, that Title VII protects whites as well as blacks from certain forms of racial discrimination.

Respondent argues that Congress intended in Title VII to prohibit all race-conscious affirmative action plans. Respondent's argument rests upon a literal interpretation of §§ 703(a) and (d) of the Act. Those sections make it unlawful to "discriminate ... because of ... race" in hiring and in the selection of apprentices for training programs. Since, the argument runs, *McDonald v. Santa Fe Trail Transp. Co., supra*, settled that Title VII *forbids* discrimination against whites as well as blacks, and since the Kaiser-USWA affirmative action plan operates to discriminate against white employees solely because they are white, it follows that the Kaiser-USWA plan violates Title VII.

Respondent's argument is not without force. But it overlooks the significance of the fact that the Kaiser-USWA plan is an affirmative action plan voluntarily adopted by private parties to eliminate traditional patterns of racial segregation. In this context respondent's reliance upon a literal construction of §§ 703(a) and (d) and upon *McDonald* is misplaced. It is a "familiar rule, that a thing may be within the letter of the statute and yet not within the statute, because not within its spirit, nor within the intention of its makers." The prohibition against racial discrimination in §§ 703(a) and (d) of Title VII must therefore be read against the background of the legislative history of Title VII and the historical context from which the Act arose. Examination of those sources makes clear that an interpretation of the sections that forbade all race-conscious affirmative action would "bring about an end completely at variance with the purpose of the statute" and must be rejected.

Congress' primary concern in enacting the prohibition against racial discrimination in the Title VII of the Civil Rights Act of 1964 was with "the plight of the Negro in our economy." As Senator Clark told the Senate:

> The rate of Negro unemployment has gone up consistently as compared with white unemployment for the past 15 years. This is a social malaise and a social situation which we should not tolerate. That is one of the principal reasons why the bill should pass.

... Accordingly, it was clear to Congress that "[t]he crux of the problem [was] to open employment opportunities for Negroes in occupations which have been traditionally closed to them," and it was to this problem that Title VII's prohibition against racial discrimination in employment was primarily addressed....

Given this legislative history, we cannot agree with respondent that Congress intended to prohibit the private sector from taking effective steps to accomplish the goal that Congress designed Title VII to achieve. The very statutory words intended as a spur or catalyst to cause "employers and unions to self-examine and to self-evaluate their employment practices and to endeavor to eliminate, so far as possible, the last vestiges of an unfortunate and ignominious page in this country's history," *Albemarle Paper Co. v. Moody*, 422 U.S. 405 (1975), cannot be interpreted as an absolute prohibition against all private, voluntary, race-conscious affirmative action efforts to hasten the elimination of such vestiges....

Our conclusion is further reinforced by examination of the language and legislative history of § 703(j) of Title VII....

continued

... The section provides that nothing contained in Title VII "shall be interpreted to *require* any employer ... to grant preferential treatment ... to any group because of the race ... of such ... group on account of" a de facto racial imbalance in the employer's work force. The section does *not* state that "nothing in Title VII shall be interpreted to *permit*" voluntary affirmative efforts to correct racial imbalances. The natural inference is that Congress chose not to forbid all voluntary race-conscious affirmative action....

... In view of [the] legislative history and in view of Congress' desire to avoid undue federal regulation of private businesses, use of the word "require" rather than the phrase "require or permit" in § 703(j) fortifies the conclusion that Congress did not intend to limit traditional business freedom to such a degree as to prohibit all voluntary race-conscious affirmative action.

We therefore hold that Title VII's prohibition in §§ 703(a) and (d) against racial discrimination does not condemn all private, voluntary, race-conscious affirmative action plans.

We need not today define in detail the line of demarcation between permissible and impermissible affirmative action plans. It suffices to hold that the challenged Kaiser-USWA affirmative action plan falls on the permissible side of the line. The purposes of the plan mirror those of the statute. Both were designed to break down old patterns of racial segregation and hierarchy. Both were structured to "open employment opportunities for Negroes in occupations which have been traditionally closed to them."

At the same time, the plan does not unnecessarily trammel the interests of the white employees. The plan does not require the discharge of white workers and their replacement with new black hirees. Nor does the plan create an absolute bar to the advancement of white employees; half of those trained in the program will be white. Moreover the plan is a temporary measure....

We conclude, therefore, that the adoption of the Kaiser-USWA plan for the Gramercy plant falls within the area of discretion left by Title VII to the private sector voluntarily to adopt affirmative action plans designed to eliminate conspicuous racial imbalance in traditionally segregated job categories. Accordingly, the judgment of the Court of Appeals for the Fifth Circuit is reversed.

So ordered.

[BRENNAN, J., delivered the opinion of the Court, in which STEWART, WHITE, MARSHALL, and BLACKMUN joined. BLACKMUN, J., filed a concurring opinion. BURGER, C. J., filed a dissenting opinion. REHNQUIST, J., filed a dissenting opinion, in which BURGER, C. J., joined. POWELL and STEVENS, J. J., took no part in the consideration or decision of the cases.]

BURGER, C. J., Dissenting...

The court reaches a result I would be inclined to vote for were I a Member of Congress considering a proposed amendment of Title VII. I cannot join the Court's judgment, however, because it is contrary to the explicit language of the statute and arrived at by means wholly incompatible with long-established principles of separation of powers. Under the guise of statutory "construction," the Court effectively rewrites Title VII to achieve what it regards as a desirable result. It "amends" the statute to do precisely what both its sponsors and its opponents agreed the statute was not intended to do.

When Congress enacted Title VII after long study and searching debate, it produced a statute of extraordinary clarity, which speaks directly to the issue we consider in this case. In § 703(d) Congress provided:

> It shall be an unlawful employment practice for any employer, labor organization, or joint labor-management committee controlling apprenticeship or other training or retraining, including on-the-job training programs to discriminate against any individual because of his race, color, religion, sex, or national origin in admission to, or employment in, any program established to provide apprenticeship or other training.

Often we have difficulty interpreting statutes either because of imprecise drafting or because legislative compromises have produced genuine ambiguities. But here there is no lack of clarity, no ambiguity. The quota embodied in the collective-bargaining agreement between Kaiser and the Steelworkers unquestionably discriminates on the basis of race against individual employees seeking admission to on-the-job training programs. And, under the plain language of § 703(d), that is "an unlawful employment practice." ...

REHNQUIST, J., Dissenting...

Contrary to the Court's analysis, the language of § 703(j) is precisely tailored to the objection voiced time and

continued

again by Title VII's opponents. Not once during the 83 days of debate in the Senate did a speaker, proponent, or opponent, suggest that the bill would allow employers *voluntarily* to prefer racial minorities over white persons. In light of Title VII's flat prohibition on discrimination "against any individual ... because of such individual's race," § 703(a), 42 U.S.C. § 2000e–2(a) [42 U.S.C.S. § 2000e–2(a)], such a contention would have been, in any event, too preposterous to warrant response....

In light of the background and purpose of § 703(j), the irony of invoking the section to justify the result in this case is obvious. The Court's frequent references to the "voluntary" nature of Kaiser's racially discriminatory admission quota bear no relationship to the facts of this case. Kaiser and the Steelworkers acted under pressure from an agency of the Federal Government, the Office of Federal Contract Compliance, which found that minorities were being "underutilized" at Kaiser's plants. That is, Kaiser's workforce was racially imbalanced.

Bowing to that pressure, Kaiser instituted an admissions quota preferring blacks over whites, thus confirming that the fears of Title VII's opponents were well founded. Today, § 703(j), adopted to allay those fears, is invoked by the Court to uphold imposition of a racial quota under the very circumstances that the section was intended to prevent....

Case Questions

1. State the facts that led Kaiser to contract with the union concerning the affirmative action training program.
2. What did the Court state was the question before it?
3. Do you believe that the Supreme Court applied Section 703(d) as written by Congress in this case?
4. Does the Court set guidelines for what are permissible and impermissible affirmative action plans?

SECTION 117: REVERSE DISCRIMINATION AND AFFIRMATIVE ACTION PLANS

When an employer's affirmative action plan is not shown to be justified or when it "unnecessarily trammels" the interests of nonminority employees in regard to promotions, training, or other employment expectations, it is said that the employer's action is unlawful "reverse discrimination." In the so-called **reverse discrimination cases,** the courts apply the *Weber* principles to test the validity of the employer action in question.

In *Jurgens v. Thomas,*[38] a reverse discrimination suit brought by white male employees of the Equal Employment Opportunity Commission, the court held that the EEOC itself had acted contrary to the *Weber* decision in its promotion and hiring procedures. The court determined that clear evidence of preferences for minorities and women was found in the EEOC's affirmative action plans, its Special Hiring Plan for Hispanics, and its District Directors Selection Program. After extensive discussion and an analysis of statistics on the affirmative action plans, the court held that the evidence showed that through the process of reorganization, white male district directors were reduced from ten to two. Also, the Special Hiring Plan for Hispanics was discussed by the court in the lengthy decision. Hispanics constituted 6.8 percent of the national population but 12.9 percent of the EEOC workforce, and the plan called for a 10 percent hiring goal even in field

---

[38] 29 FEP 1561 (1982).

offices where the local population was less than 10 percent Hispanic. The preferences of this plan were not temporary, according to the court, because of the follow-up procedure built into the plan whereby those offices that did not meet initial hiring goals "committed" one or more positions to future recruitment of Hispanics. The court held that the affirmative action plans were not remedial because the jobs were not traditionally closed to women and minorities; nor were they temporary, for the preferences appeared in slightly different form in each of the seven plans at issue. The court held that *Weber's* language should not be read to permit an employer with statistical parity in its own plant to use "status" as a basis for decisions as a means of compensating for unremedied societal discrimination elsewhere. The court held that the EEOC's affirmative action plans unnecessarily trammeled the interests of the plaintiffs and violated Title VII.

In the *San Francisco Police Officers' Ass'n v. San Francisco* decision, presented in this section, the U.S. Court of Appeals applied the *Weber* standards and found that the city's decision to rescore promotional tests in order to achieve specific and identified racial and gender percentages for promotion purposes "unnecessarily trammeled" the interests of white male police officers.

In *Hopp v. Pittsburgh*,[39] the Third Circuit Court of Appeals upheld a decision in favor of nine white police officers who claimed that the city of Pittsburgh had discriminated against them on the basis of race. Because of an early retirement incentive for its police officers, nearly 50 percent of the city's police officers retired. In replacing the retiring police officers in part with certified police officers from other communities, the city was concerned that ranking these applicants according to their performance on a written examination as required by a court order might work against minority applicants, so the mayor and the city council adopted a new hiring procedure designed to give the city "greater flexibility in creating a police force that reflects our overall population." Under the new procedure, in addition to the written exam, the applicants were required to take an oral exam. Any applicant could be eliminated from consideration, regardless of his or her performance on the written exam, if the panel administering the oral exam determined that the applicant "failed" the oral exam. The examination panels did not ask a predetermined series of questions or even follow a routine set of procedures in administering the exam. Thus, each panel had complete and unreviewable discretion to decide who, among the otherwise qualified applicants, would become eligible to receive offers of employment. The nine white officers who performed satisfactorily on the written exam but were deemed unemployable after failing the oral exam were successful in their reverse discrimination lawsuit against the city and received back pay, front pay, and other relief.

AFFIRMATIVE ACTION AFTER *ADARAND CONSTRUCTORS, INC. V. PENA*

In its 1995 landmark *Adarand Constructors, Inc. v. Pena*[40] decision, the Supreme Court placed significant limits on the federal government's authority to implement

---

[39] 194 F.3d 434 (3d Cir. 1999). See also *Delcorte v. Jordan*, 497 F.3d 433 (5th Cir. 2007).
[40] 515 U.S. 200 (1995).

programs favoring businesses owned by racial minorities over white-owned businesses. The decision reinstated a reverse discrimination challenge to a federal program designed to provide highway construction contracts to "disadvantaged" subcontractors where race-based presumptions were used to identify such individuals. The Court found the program to be violative of the equal protection component of the Fifth Amendment's due process clause and announced a strict scrutiny standard for evaluating the racial classifications used in the federal government's Disadvantaged Business Enterprise program. This standard can be satisfied only by narrowly tailored measures that further compel governmental interest. The Court stated that programs based on disadvantage rather than race are subject only to the most relaxed judicial scrutiny. Six additional years of litigation ensued before the case involving Adarand Constructors, Inc., was finally concluded on procedural and jurisdictional grounds. *Adarand I*, as it is now called, is indeed the landmark Supreme Court decision setting forth the legal principles for evaluating affirmative action programs involving race and remedies.

Upon remand from the Supreme Court, the U.S. District Court for the District of Colorado held that the Disadvantaged Business Enterprise (DBE) program implemented by the Federal Highway Administration failed the strict scrutiny standard of review announced by the Supreme Court in *Adarand I* because it was not narrowly tailored.[41] On appeal, the Tenth Circuit Court of Appeals dismissed the case as moot because Adarand had been recently certified as a DBE.[42] The Supreme Court reversed the Court of Appeals' determination that the case was moot.[43] On remand, the Tenth Circuit decided that the DBE program and the subcontractor compensation clause (SCC) program that provided financial incentives to contractors to select DBE subcontractors did not meet *Adarand I's* strict scrutiny standard.[44] The Secretary of Transportation did not challenge these rulings and has since discontinued any and all use of SCC programs. The Supreme Court once again agreed to review the decision of the court of appeals, strictly limited to reviewing the new regulatory framework that the Tenth Circuit determined was in compliance with *Adarand I*, but the Supreme Court later dismissed the writ as improvidently granted.[45]

Following the Court's *Adarand I* decision, the EEOC issued a statement on affirmative action, stating in part:

> … Affirmative action is lawful only when it is designed to respond to a demonstrated and serious imbalance in the work force, is flexible, time-limited, applies only to qualified workers, and respects the rights of non-minorities and men.[46]

---

[41] *Adarand Constructors, Inc. v. Pena*, 965 F. Supp. (1997).

[42] *Adarand Constructors, Inc. v. Slater*, 169 F.3d 1292 (10ᵗʰ Cir. 1999).

[43] *Adarand Constructors, Inc. v. Slater*, 528 U.S. 216 (2000).

[44] *Adarand Constructors, Inc. v. Slater*, 228 F.3d 1147, 1187 (10ᵗʰ Cir. 2000).

[45] *Adarand Constructors, Inc. v. Mineta*, 534 U.S. 103 (2001).

[46] BNA *Daily Labor Report* No. 147, S-47, Aug. 1, 1995.

<table>
<tr><td>CASE 13.5</td><td>SAN FRANCISCO POLICE OFFICERS' ASS'N v. CITY AND COUNTY
OF SAN FRANCISCO
U.S. COURT OF APPEALS, 812 F.2D 1125 (9TH CIR. 1987).</td></tr>
</table>

[The city and county of San Francisco (City) and the Civil Service Commission (Commission) entered into a consent decree that required the City to employ good faith efforts to achieve particular goals for employment of women and minorities. The Police Officers' Association (POA) intervened in those actions and agreed to the consent decree. The consent decree specifically prohibited the City from unlawfully discriminating in any manner on the basis of sex, race, or national origin. In 1983, the City administered selection procedures for the positions of assistant inspector and sergeant. The promotional examinations had three parts: a multiple-choice test, a written examination, and an oral examination. Partway through the examination, the Commission set the weights for all three components. When the examinations were scored, the results showed an adverse impact on minorities in both ranks and a slight adverse impact on women for the assistant inspector examination. This adverse impact led the Commission to revise the scoring procedures for the examinations. The Commission regarded the multiple-choice and written examination components on a pass-fail basis and used the oral examination as the sole criterion for ranking candidates who passed the multiple-choice and written examinations. The police union brought suit, objecting to the new grading procedures. The district court ruled in favor of the City, and the union appealed.]

WIGGINS, C. J....

The critical issue in this case is whether the Commission acted lawfully in reweighing the examination components. The district court viewed this question in terms of fairness and held a fairness hearing in order to determine if the Commission's decision to reweigh was a valid affirmative action plan under *United Steelworkers of America v. Weber*, 443 U.S. 193 (1979).

In *Weber*, the Supreme Court identified four criteria that make an affirmative action plan valid under Title VII: (1) it is designed to break down old patterns of racial segregation and hierarchy; (2) it does not create an absolute bar to the advancement of nonminority employees; (3) it is a temporary measure, "not intended to maintain racial balance, but simply to eliminate a manifest racial imbalance"; and (4) it does not unnecessarily trammel the interests of

non-minority employees. *Weber*, 443 U.S. at 208. *Weber* did not hold that these criteria were absolute requirements, but did hold that these aspects of the plan in *Weber* placed it on the permissible side of the line between permissible and impermissible plans. Here, the district court found that reweighing fit all four *Weber* criteria and was therefore permissible. We reverse the district court because reweighing unnecessarily trammeled the interests of the non-minority police officers.

In analyzing whether the interests of nonminorities were unnecessarily trammeled, the district court focused on what rights the candidates possessed and how those rights were affected by reweighing. It determined that the City did not overtly take into account race or sex in the decision to reweigh....

We find that the district court clearly erred when it determined that the decision to reweigh was not a race and gender conscious act....

Reweighing unlawfully displaced candidates on the basis of their race and gender. The information about the candidates' performance on the individual components led the Commission to choose the oral component as the sole ranking device. If the results of the examinations had been different, the written component or the multiple-choice component might have been the new ranking device. Without readministering the test, the Commission examined the results from each component based on race and gender criteria and rescored the test to achieve specific and identified racial and gender percentages. This type of result-oriented scoring is offensive.

Candidates who participate in promotional examinations expect to have an equal opportunity to score well and to achieve promotion. This neutrality cannot exist if the City can rescore the examinations to achieve a particular race and gender balance after it analyzes the results. Permitting an employer to rescore examinations with knowledge of the ultimate results undermines the integrity of the examination process.

Moreover, candidates for promotion should be on notice of how their performance will be evaluated in order to prepare themselves effectively for an examination....

... Here ... the Commission's decision to reweigh unlawfully restricted the promotional opportunities

continued

of non-minority candidates because the tests were scored to achieve a particular racial result. It trammeled the interests of non-minorities, in that the candidates were led to believe that the promotions would be based on merit alone. This harm to non-minorities was unnecessary because a less burdensome alternative, such as administering a new selection procedure, would have better achieved the goals of the consent decree without violating Title VII.

The City was obligated under the consent decree to administer an examination that would not have an adverse effect on minorities and women. When it failed in its first attempt to achieve that goal, the City inappropriately attempted to take short-cuts to meet its obligations. It did so in order to save time. Although we are sympathetic to the City's time dilemma, using an unlawful procedure is not acceptable. The City was required either to validate its initial examination or, if it could not, to devise and administer an alternative selection procedure that did not have an adverse impact.

The City was additionally obligated under the consent decree not to practice racial or sexual discrimination—no more against white males than against others. The POA was a party to the consent decree. The POA has a right to insist that this unequivocal renunciation of all discrimination means what it says. The reweighing as practiced here violated the consent decree.

The judgment is reversed and remanded.

Case Questions

1. Did the district court determine that the decision to rescore the components of the exam was not a race- and gender-conscious act?

2. How did the Commission's decision to rescore the components of the exam unnecessarily trammel the interests of non-minorities?

3. Was the City's obligation under the consent decree not to practice racial or sexual discrimination applicable to white male police officers?

SECTION 118: THE ARBITRATION OPTION

With the exception of transportation employees, employers can craft arbitration agreements that require employees to arbitrate any employment dispute, including all federal statutory discrimination claims, and these mandatory arbitration clauses can be enforced in federal courts under the Federal Arbitration Act.[47] Courts do, however, require that the arbitration clauses be "fair." Moreover, a party agreeing to arbitration does not forgo substantive rights afforded by Title VII or alter federal antidiscrimination statutes. A fair arbitration clause requires adequate discovery, mandates that the arbitrator have authority to apply the same types of relief available from a court, and should not preclude an employee from vindicating statutory rights because of arbitration costs.

THE *GILMER/CIRCUIT CITY* PRECEDENTS

An individual may not have a judicial remedy where the individual is bound by a broad arbitration clause to arbitrate the dispute with an employer. In *Gilmer v. Interstate/Johnson Lane*, presented in this section, the U.S. Supreme Court held that Robert Gilmer's age discrimination lawsuit against his former employer could be stayed under Section 3 of the Federal Arbitration Act (FAA) and that he could be compelled to arbitrate his claim under Section 4 of the FAA. Gilmer's registration

---

[47] Federal Arbitration Act, 9 U.S.C. 82.

form with the New York Stock Exchange had a broad arbitration clause requiring arbitration of "any controversy" between registered representatives and member organizations. The *Gilmer* Court left for another day the question of whether the language in Section 1 of the FAA—"nothing herein contained shall apply to contracts of employment of seamen, railroad employees, or any other class of worker engaged in foreign or interstate commerce"—excludes all contracts of employment from enforcement under the FAA. This question was later addressed by the Supreme Court in *Circuit City Stores, Inc. v. Adams*,[48] a 5-4 decision that held that the FAA was intended to broadly apply to all employment contracts except transportation workers, who were explicitly excluded under Section 1 of the FAA.

CONTRACT DEFENSES PRECLUDE ARBITRATION

With the *Circuit City* decision broadly applying to all employment contracts except transportation workers covered under Section 1 of the FAA, from an employer's perspective, a major obstacle to the mandatory arbitration of statutory employment discrimination claims had been eliminated. The *Circuit City* Court did emphasize, relying on the *Gilmer* decision, that by agreeing to arbitration of statutory claims, an employee does not forgo substantive rights afforded by statute; the employee only submits to their resolution in an arbitral rather than a judicial forum. However, most mandatory arbitration clauses are unilaterally developed and promulgated by employers, and they are presented to employees on a take-it-or-leave-it basis for continuing or new employment. Employers commonly exercise some flexibility in negotiating salaries and certain benefits, but they generally are adamant that any future employment disputes be resolved through arbitration and not in the courts. However, employers are not free to impose unconscionable arbitration agreements on employees. The *Gilmer/Circuit City* guarantees that securing employees' statutory rights require procedural and remedial protection so that claimants can effectively pursue their statutory rights.

On remand from the U.S. Supreme Court, the Ninth Circuit Court of Appeals in *Circuit City II*[49] set out to examine the validity of the underlying arbitration agreement, applying "ordinary state law principles that govern the formation of contracts." The court pointed out that general contract defenses such as fraud, duress, or unconscionability, grounded in state contract law, may operate to invalidate arbitration agreements. Applying California contract law, the court determined that the Circuit City Dispute Resolution Agreement (DRA) was procedurally unconscionable because it was a contract of adhesion—a standard-form contract drafted by the party with superior bargaining power, which relegates the other party to take the contract or leave it. The court also found that the DRA was substantively unconscionable. Under the DRA, employees must arbitrate "any and all employment related claims ..." while Circuit City is not obligated to arbitrate their claims against employees, thus depriving the DRA of any modicum of being

---

[48] 122 S.Ct. 1302 (2001).
[49] 279 F.3d 889 (9th Cir. 2002).

bilateral.[50] Moreover, the remedies are limited under the DRA, including a one-year back pay limit and a two-year front pay limit, with a cap on punitive damages of an amount up to the greater of the amount of back pay and front pay awarded or $5,000. By contrast, in a civil lawsuit a plaintiff is entitled to all forms of relief. A further reason for finding it substantively unconscionable was the DRA's requirement that the employee split the cost of the arbitrator's fees with the employer.

The court of appeals in *Circuit City II* also analyzed the DRA from the perspective of the *Gilmer* guarantee that the arbitral forum allow the employee to effectively pursue statutory rights. Under this *Gilmer* analysis, the court concluded that the DRA (1) failed to provide all of the types of relief that would otherwise be available in court and (2) failed to ensure that the employee did not have to pay unreasonable arbitration costs or fees or expenses as a condition of access to the arbitration forum. While the court recognized that under state law it had discretion to sever the unconscionable provisions and order arbitration, it rejected this option because the unconscionable provisions pervaded the entire contract. Accordingly, the court of appeals reversed the district court's order compelling arbitration.[51]

In *Circuit City Stores v. Ahmed*,[52] the Ninth Circuit enforced the very same dispute resolution agreement (DRA) because Ahmed had been given an opportunity to opt out of the arbitration program. Thus, as to Ahmed, it was not a nonnegotiable contract of adhesion and thus not unconscionable. In *Ingle v. Circuit City Stores*, the Ninth Circuit held that the arbitration agreement that sales associate Catherine Ingle signed was procedurally and substantively unconscionable under California contract law.[53]

THE "FAIRNESS" REQUIREMENT

An arbitration agreement that is fundamentally unfair will be subject to challenge by attorneys seeking to avoid arbitration. In cases where the employer has "devised an arbitration agreement that functions as a thumb on [an employer's] side of the scale" in an employment dispute with an employee,[54] or where the arbitration agreement and employer actions "indicate a systematic effort to impose arbitration on an employee ... as an inferior forum that works to the employer's advantage,"[55] the employer may well find that it will be unable to enforce the agreement to arbitrate under the FAA in court. Contrary to the perception that business may be

---

[50] In *Zimmer v. CooperNeff Advisors, Inc.* 523 F.3d 224 (3d Cir. 2008), the U.S. Court of Appeals for the Third Court, relying on Pennsylvania law, held that a party challenging an arbitration agreement has the burden to show that it is unconscionable. Moreover, under state law, a presumption of unconscionability based on one party's reservation of judicial remedies was expressly rejected.

[51] In *Zuver v. Airtouch Communications, Inc.*, 153 Wash. 2d 293 (2004), the Washington Supreme Court decided that substantively objectionable provisions of an employment arbitration agreement dealing with limitation of remedies and confidentiality could be severed, but the remainder of the agreement to arbitrate enforced.

[52] 283 F.3d 1198 (9th Cir. 2002).

[53] 328 F. 3d 1165 (9th Cir. 2003); 408 F.3d 592 (2005).

[54] *Circuit City II*, 279 F.3d 889, 892 (9th Cir. 2002).

[55] *Armandariz v. Foundation Healthcare Services, Inc.*, 24 Cal. 4th 83, 124 (2001).

attempting to "stack the deck" against claimant-employees, in reality, most corporate boards and company executives devote significant human and economic resources to making sure that their companies are in full compliance with federal and state employment laws. The advantages to arbitration for both the employer and employees are that the matters at issue are resolved in an expeditious, timely, and just manner, before an expert on employment law, with lower overall costs and in a shorter period of time than litigation. The decision is final and binding on the parties, with a very limited review of the decision under Section 10 of the FAA. Should the employee be successful and the actions of the employer's agents be found to be contrary to employment law, the employer is informed of the decision much sooner than in litigation, and the employer can take appropriate corrective action in a more expeditious fashion. The remedies for the employee are the same as provided in a court, and the process is a private one, not a source of adverse publicity with loss of good will. Should the employee be unsuccessful in her or his claims, the controversy is resolved in a shorter period of time than litigation and the individual can move forward with her or his life, short of the years that are sometimes consumed in prolonged litigation.

A "fair" arbitration agreement may address the following elements:

1. The claimant-employee must be involved in the selection of the arbitrator.
2. The arbitrator must be knowledgeable in employment law and neutral, with no personal or financial interests in the result of the process.
3. The parties must have adequate discovery consistent with efficiency, economy, and justice, as determined by the arbitrator.
4. The parties shall present their cases in the ordinary course of such proceedings, with rulings reserved to the arbitrator, and such rulings shall be in accordance with the *Gilmer* directives that the parties not forgo their substantive rights.
5. The arbitrator must have the authority to provide the same statutory law and the same types of relief that would be available from a court, including attorney fees and costs if such relief is afforded under the applicable statute.
6. The decision of the arbitrator shall be final and binding on the parties, with judicial review as limited in Section 10 of the FAA. The employer must make certain that claimant-employee shall not be precluded from effectively vindicating statutory rights in an arbitral forum because of prohibitive arbitration costs. The *Green Tree* decision procedures will apply.[56]

---

[56] The U.S. Supreme Court's decision in *Green Tree Financial Corp.-Alabama v. Randolph*, 531 U.S. 74 (2000), dealt with a dispute involving alleged violations of federal lending statutes and an arbitration. It stated that the existence of large arbitration costs could preclude a litigant from effectively vindicating federal statutory rights in an arbitral forum and it provided a formula for resolving whether the plaintiff was faced with prohibitive arbitration expenses. In the labor arbitration context of *Blair v. Specialty Gases, Inc.*, 283 F.3d 595 (3d Cir. 2002), the Third Circuit applied the *Green Tree* formula to the issue of arbitrator's fees, with the claimant having the initial burden to come forward with some evidence to show that projected fees would be prohibitively expensive and with an eventual burden shift to the party seeking arbitration to come forward with contrary evidence. The court of appeals explained that Blair has limited discovery rights into the rates charged and cost of arbitration, such that the cost would deny her a forum to vindicate her statutory rights, with the burden shifting to the company to prove arbitration will not be prohibitively expensive; or the company may offer to pay all of the arbitrator's fees.

SCOPE OF COURT REVIEW OF ARBITRATION AWARDS UNDER THE FAA

When one is seeking judicial review of an arbitration award under the Federal Arbitration Act, the grounds specified in Sections 11 and 12 of the Act are the exclusive grounds for vacating or correcting the award. The *Hall Street Associates, LLC v. Mattel, Inc.* decision of the Supreme Court, presented in this section, sets forth the Court's ruling applicable to all arbitration awards, including labor and employment casses. Section 10 of the FAA lists the grounds for vacating an award, including (1) corruption, fraud, or undue means; (2) misconduct of the arbitrators; or (3) the arbitrators exceeding their power. The grounds for modifying or correcting an award under Section 11 of the FAA include (1) evident material miscalculation, (2) evident material mistake, and (3) imperfections on a matter of form not affecting the merits.

THE *WAFFLE HOUSE* EXCEPTION FOR THE EEOC

The Supreme Court's *Equal Employment Opportunity Commission v. Waffle House, Inc.* decision, presented in this section, resolved a major issue regarding arbitration of statutory employment claims, allowing the EEOC to pursue a full range of remedies in court for individuals who failed to pursue arbitration of their employment disputes under valid, enforceable arbitration agreements with their employers. This decision properly enhances the role of the EEOC in seeing to it that the federal employment laws under its enforcement authority are meaningfully carried out. Moreover, it affirms the EEOC's unencumbered right to initiate litigation to resolve developing legal issues to serve as precedents for the arbitration of statutory employment claims.

CASE 13.6	GILMER V. INTERSTATE/JOHNSON LANE SUPREME COURT OF THE UNITED STATES, 500 U.S. 20 (1991).

[Petitioner Robert Gilmer was required by his employer to register as a securities representative with the New York Stock Exchange (NYSE). His registration application contained an agreement to arbitrate any controversy arising out of a registered representative's employment or termination of employment. The employer terminated Gilmer at age 62. Thereafter, he filed a charge with the Equal Employment Opportunity Commission (EEOC) and brought suit in the district court, alleging that he had been discharged in violation of the Age Discrimination in Employment Act of 1967 (ADEA). The employer moved to compel arbitration. The court denied the motion based on *Alexander v. Gardner-Denver Co.* The court of appeals reversed, and the Supreme Court granted certiorari.]

WHITE, J....

We ... are unpersuaded by the argument that arbitration will undermine the role of the EEOC in enforcing the ADEA. An individual ADEA claimant subject to

an arbitration agreement will still be free to file a charge with the EEOC, even though the claimant is not able to institute a private judicial action. Indeed, Gilmer filed a charge with the EEOC in this case. In any event, the EEOC's role in combating age discrimination is not dependent on the filing of a charge; the agency may receive information concerning alleged violations of the ADEA "from any source," and it has independent authority to investigate age discrimination. See 29 CFR §§ 1626.4, 1626.13 (1990). Moreover, nothing in the ADEA indicates that Congress intended that the EEOC be involved in all employment disputes....

Gilmer also argues that compulsory arbitration is improper because it deprives claimants of the judicial forum provided for by the ADEA. Congress, however, did not explicitly preclude arbitration or other nonjudicial resolution of claims, even in its recent amendments to the ADEA. "[I]f Congress intended the substantive protection afforded [by the ADEA]

continued

to include protection against waiver of the right to a judicial forum, that intention will be deducible from text or legislative history." Mitsubishi, 473 U.S., at 628, 105 S.Ct. at 3354....

I.

In addition to the arguments discussed above, Gilmer vigorously asserts that our decision in *Alexander v. Gardner-Denver Co.*, 415 U.S. 36, ... precludes arbitration of employment discrimination claims. Gilmer's reliance on the case, however, is misplaced....

There are several important distinctions between the *Gardner-Denver* line of cases and the case before us. First, those cases did not involve the issue of the enforceability of an agreement to arbitrate statutory claims. Rather, they involved the quite different issue whether arbitration of contract-based claims precluded subsequent judicial resolution of statutory claims. Since the employees there had not agreed to arbitrate their statutory claims, and the labor arbitrators were not authorized to resolve such claims, the arbitration in those cases understandably was held not to preclude subsequent statutory actions. Second, because the arbitration in those cases occurred in the context of a collective bargaining agreement, the claimants there were represented by their unions in the arbitration proceedings. An important concern therefore was the tension between collective representation and individual statutory rights, a concern not applicable to the present case. Finally, those cases were not decided under the FAA, which, as discussed above, reflects a "liberal federal policy favoring arbitration agreements." *Mitsubishi*, 473 U.S., at 625. Therefore, those cases provide no basis for refusing to enforce Gilmer's agreement to arbitrate his ADEA claim.

II.

We conclude that Gilmer has not met his burden of showing that Congress, in enacting the ADEA, intended to preclude arbitration of claims under the Act. Accordingly, the judgment of the Court of Appeals is
   Affirmed.

JUSTICE STEVENS, with whom JUSTICE MARSHALL joins, Dissenting...

Section 1 of the Federal Arbitration Act (FAA) states:

> "[N]othing herein contained shall apply to contracts of employment of seamen, railroad employees, or any other class of workers engaged in foreign or interstate commerce."
> 9 U.S.C. § 1.

The Court today, in holding that the FAA compels enforcement of arbitration clauses even when claims of age discrimination are at issue, skirts the antecedent question of whether the coverage of the Act even extends to arbitration clauses contained in employment contracts, regardless of the subject matter of the claim at issue. In my opinion, arbitration clauses contained in employment agreements are specifically exempt from coverage of the FAA, and for that reason respondent Interstate/Johnson Lane Corporation cannot, pursuant to the FAA, compel petitioner to submit his claims arising under the Age Discrimination in Employment Act of 1967 (ADEA), 29 U.S.C. § 621 *et seq.*, to binding arbitration....

Case Questions

1. Is the EEOC's role in combating age discrimination dependent on filing an age discrimination charge?
2. Did Congress intend to preserve an individual's right to a judicial forum in an ADEA case from waiver?
3. Did the Court hold that the *Alexander v. Gardner-Denver* decision precluded arbitration of employment discrimination claims?

CASE 13.7 | HALL STREET ASSOCIATES, LLC v. MATTEL, INC.
| SUPREME COURT OF THE UNITED STATES, 128 S.CT. 1396 (2008).

[The dispute involves property owner Hall Street Associates, LLC, and tenant Mattel, Inc., over liability for the cost of environmental cleanup of the property. The parties agreed to arbitrate the matter and entered into a contractual agreement to expand the scope of the judicial review of the arbitrator's award beyond the grounds for vacating or correcting an award set forth in Sections 10 and 11 of the Federal Arbitration Act (FAA). The Court's decision in this case applies the grounds for vacating or correcting arbitration awards under the FAA and is of significance to labor and employment arbitration.]

continued

SOUTER, J....

The Act ... supplies mechanisms for enforcing arbitration awards: a judicial decree confirming an award, an order vacating it, or an order modifying or correcting it. §§ 9–11. An application for any of these orders will get streamlined treatment as a motion, obviating the separate contract action that would usually be necessary to enforce or tinker with an arbitral award in court. § 6. Under the terms of § 9, a court "must" confirm an arbitration award "unless" it is vacated, modified, or corrected "as prescribed" in §§ 10 and 11. Section 10 lists grounds for vacating an award, while § 11 names those for modifying or correcting one.

The Courts of Appeals have split over the exclusiveness of these statutory grounds when parties take the FAA shortcut to confirm, vacate, or modify an award, with some saying the recitations are exclusive, and others regarding them as mere threshold provisions open to expansion by agreement.... We now hold that §§ 10 and 11 respectively provide the FAA's exclusive grounds for expedited vacatur and modification...

Instead of fighting the text, it makes more sense to see the three provisions, §§ 9–11, as substantiating a national policy favoring arbitration with just the limited review needed to maintain arbitration's essential virtue of resolving disputes straightaway. Any other reading opens the door to the full-bore legal and evidentiary appeals that can "rende[r] informal arbitration merely a prelude to a more cumbersome and time-consuming judicial review process," *Kyocera*, 341 F.3d, at 998; cf.

Ethyl Corp. v. United Steelworkers of America, 768 F.2d 180, 184 (CA7 1985), and bring arbitration theory to grief in post-arbitration process....

In holding that §§ 10 and 11 provide exclusive regimes for the review provided by the statute, we do not purport to say that they exclude more searching review based on authority outside the statute as well. The FAA is not the only way into court for parties wanting review of arbitration awards: they may contemplate enforcement under state statutory or common law, for example, where judicial review of different scope is arguable. But here we speak only to the scope of the expeditious judicial review under §§ 9, 10, and 11, deciding nothing about other possible avenues for judicial enforcement of arbitration awards....

[*Remanded.*]

[*JUSTICES STEVENS, KENNEDY, and BRYER dissented.*]

Case Questions

1. Can the parties mutually agree to have a court vacate, modify, or correct an award under the FAA when the arbitrator's conclusions of law are erroneous?

2. What did the Court mean when it stated that "it makes more sense to see the three provisions, §§ 9–11, as substantiating a national policy favoring arbitration with just the limited review needed to maintain arbitration's essential virtue of resolving disputes straightaway"?

CASE 13.8 | EEOC v. WAFFLE HOUSE, INC.
SUPREME COURT OF THE UNITED STATES, 122 S.CT. 754 (2002).

[Like all prospective employees of Waffle House, Inc., Eric Baker signed an employment application that stated, "the parties agree that any dispute or claim" concerning his employment would be "settled by binding arbitration." Baker was hired as grill cook on August 10, 1994. Some 16 days later he suffered a seizure at work, and soon thereafter he was discharged by the employer. Baker filed a timely charge of discrimination with the EEOC, alleging that his discharge was a violation of the Americans with Disabilities Act (ADA). Baker did not initiate arbitration proceedings. After investigating and attempting without success to conciliate the charge of discrimination, the EEOC filed an enforcement action in a U.S. District Court, asserting that the

employer discharged Baker "because of his disability" in violation of his federal rights, and it sought specific relief designed to make Baker whole, including reinstatement, back pay, compensatory damages, and punitive damages. The employer filed a petition with the district court to compel arbitration under the Federal Arbitration Act, which was denied by the court. On appeal, the Fourth Circuit ruled that the arbitration agreement signed by Eric Baker barred the EEOC from seeking victim-specific relief for Mr. Baker. The Fourth Circuit determined that the EEOC's remedy options were limited to injunctive relief in a situation where an employee has signed a mandatory arbitration agreement. The matter was appealed to the Supreme Court.]

continued

STEVENS, J....

I.

... The FAA was enacted in 1925, 43 Stat. 883, and then reenacted and codified in 1947 as Title 9 of the United States Code. It has not been amended since the enactment of Title VII in 1964. As we have explained, its "purpose was to reverse the longstanding judicial hostility to arbitration agreements that had existed at English common law and had been adopted by American courts, and to place arbitration agreements upon the same footing as other contracts." *Gilmer v. Interstate/Johnson Lane Corp.*, 500 U.S. 20, 24 (1991). The FAA broadly provides that a written provision in "a contract evidencing a transaction involving commerce to settle by arbitration a controversy thereafter arising out of such contract ... shall be valid, irrevocable, and enforceable, save upon such grounds as exist at law or in equity for the revocation of any contract." 9 U.S.C. § 2. Employment contracts, except for those covering workers engaged in transportation, are covered by the FAA. *Circuit City Stores, Inc. v. Adams*, 532 U.S. 105 (2001).

The FAA provides for stays of proceedings in federal district courts when an issue in the proceeding is referable to arbitration, and for orders compelling arbitration when one party has failed or refused to comply with an arbitration agreement. See 9 U.S.C. §§ 3 and 4. We have read these provisions to "manifest a 'liberal federal policy favoring arbitration agreements.'" ... Absent some ambiguity in the agreement, however, it is the language of the contract that defines the scope of disputes subject to arbitration.... For nothing in the statute authorizes a court to compel arbitration of any issues, or by any parties, that are not already covered in the agreement. The FAA does not mention enforcement by public agencies; it ensures the enforceability of private agreements to arbitrate, but otherwise does not purport to place any restriction on a nonparty's choice of a judicial forum.

II.

The Court of Appeals based its decision on its evaluation of the "competing policies" implemented by the ADA and the FAA, rather than on any language in the text of either the statutes or the arbitration agreement between Baker and respondent. 193 F.3d, at 812. It recognized that the EEOC never agreed to arbitrate its statutory claim, *id.*, at 811 ("We must also recognize that in this case the EEOC is not a party to any arbitration agreement"),

and that the EEOC has "independent statutory authority" to vindicate the public interest, but opined that permitting the EEOC to prosecute Baker's claim in court "would significantly trample" the strong federal policy favoring arbitration because Baker had agreed to submit his claim to arbitration. *Id.*, at 812. To effectuate this policy, the court distinguished between injunctive and victim-specific relief, and held that the EEOC is barred from obtaining the latter because any public interest served when the EEOC pursues "make whole" relief is outweighed by the policy goals favoring arbitration. Only when the EEOC seeks broad injunctive relief, in the Court of Appeals' view, does the public interest overcome the goals underpinning the FAA....

If it were true that the EEOC could prosecute its claim only with Baker's consent, or if its prayer for relief could be dictated by Baker, the court's analysis might be persuasive. But once a charge is filed, the exact opposite is true under the statute—the EEOC is in command of the process. The EEOC has exclusive jurisdiction over the claim for 180 days. During that time, the employee must obtain a right-to-sue letter from the agency before prosecuting the claim. If, however, the EEOC files suit on its own, the employee has no independent cause of action, although the employee may intervene in the EEOC's suit. 42 U.S.C. § 2000e-5(f)(1) (1994 ed.). In fact, the EEOC takes the position that it may pursue a claim on the employee's behalf even after the employee has disavowed any desire to seek relief. Brief for Petitioner 20. The statute clearly makes the EEOC the master of its own case and confers on the agency the authority to evaluate the strength of the public interest at stake. Absent textual support for a contrary view, it is the public agency's province—not that of the court—to determine whether public resources should be committed to the recovery of victim-specific relief. And if the agency makes that determination, the statutory text unambiguously authorizes it to proceed in a judicial forum....

... Rather than attempt to split the difference, we are persuaded that, pursuant to Title VII and the ADA, whenever the EEOC chooses from among the many charges filed each year to bring an enforcement action in a particular case, the agency may be seeking to vindicate a public interest, not simply provide make-whole relief for the employee, even when it pursues entirely victim-specific relief. To hold otherwise would undermine the detailed enforcement scheme

continued

created by Congress simply to give greater effect to an agreement between private parties that does not even contemplate the EEOC's statutory function....

The judgment of the Court of Appeals is reversed, and the case is remanded for further proceedings consistent with this opinion.

It is so ordered.

JUSTICE THOMAS, with whom THE CHIEF JUSTICE and JUSTICE SCALIA join, Dissenting...

The Court holds today that the Equal Employment Opportunity Commission (EEOC or Commission) may obtain victim-specific remedies in court on behalf of an employee who had agreed to arbitrate discrimination claims against his employer. This decision conflicts with both the Federal Arbitration Act (FAA), 9 U.S.C. § 1 *et seq.*, and the basic principle that the EEOC must take a victim of discrimination as it finds

him. Absent explicit statutory authorization to the contrary, I cannot agree that the EEOC may do on behalf of an employee that which an employee has agreed not to do for himself. Accordingly, I would affirm the judgment of the Court of Appeals....

Case Questions

1. How did the Supreme Court majority respond to the court of appeals' determination that the EEOC's remedy options were limited to injunctive relief in a situation where an employee signed a mandatory arbitration agreement?
2. Is it possible for the EEOC to pursue entirely victim-specific relief and yet be seeking to vindicate a public interest? Explain.
3. Comment on the dissent's view that "Baker waived his right to seek relief for himself in a judicial forum by signing an arbitration agreement."

SECTION 119: EXECUTIVE ORDER 11246: AFFIRMATIVE ACTION PROGRAMS

The Civil Rights Act, federal funding laws, and federal licensing laws have provided statutory authority for requiring certain employers to take affirmative action to improve the job opportunities for women and minorities.[57] The Rehabilitation Act of 1973 requires affirmative action by federal departments and government contractors to improve job opportunities for the handicapped. The Vietnam Veterans Readjustment Act of 1974 requires certain federal contractors to develop written affirmative action plans to hire veterans of the Vietnam War. The major source of affirmative action requirements, however, is presidential Executive Order 11246.

THE OFFICE OF FEDERAL CONTRACT COMPLIANCE PROGRAMS

Under Executive Order 11246, the Secretary of Labor is charged with supervising and coordinating the compliance activities of the federal contracting agencies. The Secretary of Labor has established the Office of Federal Contract Compliance Programs (OFCCP) to administer the order. The OFCCP, having the responsibility

---

[57] Civil Rights Act of 1964, Title VII, as amended. Federal funding laws: Title VI of the 1964 Civil Rights Act prohibits employment discrimination in any program or activity receiving federal financial assistance when the primary objective of the program is employment; sex discrimination is prohibited in HEW's aid-to-education programs by the terms of the Education Amendments of 1972. Federal licensing laws: The Federal Communications Commission has taken the position that it has authority to require licensees to take affirmative action to improve job opportunities for women and minorities; the Securities and Exchange Commission has authority to require corporations registering securities to report on significant developments in their equal employment practices.

to implement equal opportunity in the federal procurement area, has set forth regulations that apply to service and supply contractors and subcontractors as well as construction contractors and subcontractors. The OFCCP has full responsibility for conducting service, supply, and construction compliance review for the Department of Defense, the General Services Administration, Housing and Urban Development, the Department of Transportation, the Department of Interior, the Environmental Protection Agency, the Treasury Department, the Department of Commerce, and the Small Business Administration.

Each contract that the federal government awards amounting to $50,000 or more must contain an equal employment clause that is binding on the contractor or subcontractor for the duration of the contract. The clause contains the following commitments by the contractor:

1. To not discriminate against any employee or job applicant because of race, color, sex, religion, or national origin;
2. To state in all employment advertisements that applicants will be considered on the basis of their qualifications;
3. To advise all unions of the employer's commitments;
4. To include the same type of equal employment opportunity agreement in every subcontract or purchase order.

Whenever the director of the OFCCP has reason to believe that a contractor has violated the equal employment opportunity clause in the contract, the director may initiate administrative proceedings to seek correction of the violation. Administrative procedures include a hearing before an administrative law judge and review of the findings and recommendations of the ALJ by the Department of Labor's Administrative Law Board. The OFCCP has the power to cancel or suspend contracts for failure to comply with a nondiscrimination clause. The OFCCP may also require contracting agencies to refrain from entering into new contracts with "debarred" or ineligible contractors.

The Beverly Enterprises, Inc. v. Herman decision, reported in this section, outlines the procedures followed by OFCCP in selecting companies for an affirmative action compliance review through its corporate management review (CMR) procedures.

Service and Supply Contracts

Service and supply contractors and subcontractors having 50 or more employees and a contract exceeding $50,000 must develop written affirmative action plans for the increased utilization of women and minorities. In assessing whether a contract exceeds $50,000, the OFCCP counts the total value of the various orders anticipated in certain blanket purchase agreements (BPAs) rather than counting each order as a single contract.

Some requirements for an acceptable affirmative action program are as follows:

1. An analysis of all major job categories at a facility must be conducted with explanations if minority group members are being underutilized in job categories.
2. Goals, timetables, and affirmative action commitments must be designed to correct any identifiable deficiencies. When deficiencies exist, the regulations require

the contractor to create specific goals and a timetable as part of its written affirmative action program.[58]

3. Support data for the program and analysis should be compiled and maintained as part of the contractor's affirmative action program.

CONSTRUCTION CONTRACTS

The primary difference between affirmative action approaches for construction contractors and service and supply contractors is that minority goals and timetables for construction contractors are set periodically for "covered geographic areas" by the director of the OFCCP using Standard Metropolitan Statistical Area (SMSA) data. The service and supply contractors generate their own goals and timetables on an individual basis. The director has used the SMSA data and will use census data to set the goals for minority utilization equal to the percentage of minorities in the civilian labor force in the relevant area. The director has set a 6.9 percent nationwide goal for the utilization of women by contractors working on federally assisted construction contracts of $100,000 or more. The goal is not on a trade-by-trade basis but applies in the aggregate.

EVALUATION GUIDELINES

The revised Labor Department regulations outlining the affirmative action obligations of federal contractors under Executive Order 11246 continue to include an 80 percent, or four-fifths, rule for determining underutilization of minorities and women. Under this rule, an adverse impact is presumed if the selection rate for minorities and women from the relevant applicant pool is less than four-fifths, or 80 percent, of the selection rate for whites or males. The 80 percent rule has been sharply criticized for failing to account for differences in sampling size and test results in the applicant population and has had mixed acceptance by the courts. This rule is subject to modification at any time. It is considered by the EEOC and the OFCCP as a practical device for reviewing company employee profiles to see if serious discrepancies exist in the hiring and promotion policies of a company.[59]

Under federal affirmative action regulations, all covered federal contractors are required to perform an annual evaluation of compensation practices to ensure that minorities and woman are treated fairly. On June 16, 2006, OFCCP issued Self-Evaluation Guidelines along with its final Guidelines on Systemic Compensation Discrimination.[60]

---

[58] The "goals and timetables" approach to affirmative action programs, required of federal contractors by the OFCCP, has been approved by several circuit courts. See *Contractors Ass'n of Eastern Pennsylvania v. Shultz*, 442 F.2d 159 (3d Cir. 1971); *Southern Illinois Builders Ass'n v. Ogilvie*, 471 F.2d 680 (7th Cir. 1972); and *Associated General Contractors of Massachusetts, Inc. v. Altshuler*, 490 F.2d 9 (1st Cir. 1973). These cases predate the so-called reverse discrimination cases of *Regents of the University of California v. Bakke*, 438 U.S. 265 (1978); *Steelworkers v. Weber*, 443 U.S. 193 (1979); *Fullilove v. Klutznick*, 448 U.S. 448 (1980); and *Adarand Constructors, Inc. v. Pena*, 515 U.S. 200 (1995).

[59] See *Lawrence Aviation Indus. v. Reich*, 1999 WL 494870 (2d Cir.).

[60] http://www.dol.gov/esa/regs/fedreg/notices/2006005458.htm.

SANCTIONS FOR NONCOMPLIANCE

Where it has been determined that a contracting firm has not made adequate good faith efforts to hire minority workers or women for federal or federally assisted projects, the OFCCP, after notice and a hearing, is authorized to debar the firm from participating in such projects.

Construction firms may apply to the OFCCP for reinstatement; however, they must show that they have made good faith efforts to increase minority hiring and must agree to additional terms set by the OFCCP. For example, a construction firm that had been debarred because of its failure to make good faith efforts to hire minorities on a federally assisted hospital project in New Haven, Connecticut, applied for reinstatement with the OFCCP. After an investigation established that the firm had made renewed efforts to comply with Executive Order 11246, it was reinstated with certain conditions.

Under the terms of the reinstatement order by the OFCCP, the firm was required to pay back wages of $13,606 to three workers who were found to have been victims of past discrimination. In addition, the company agreed to submit to the Labor Department copies of its monthly payroll records for at least two years and to employ minority apprentices and trainees at the completion of their training if employment opportunities were available.

Other terms of the agreement specified that the company was bound by any OFCCP-approved affirmative action requirements and that it must take certain specific affirmative actions. These included:

1. Maintaining a working environment free of harassment, intimidation, and coercion;
2. Developing on-the-job apprentice and trainee opportunities for minorities;
3. Conducting an inventory and evaluation of all minority personnel for promotional opportunities;
4. Establishing and maintaining a current list of minority recruitment sources and minority job applicants toward which it would direct recruitment efforts;
5. Encouraging minority employees to recruit other minority persons, including students, for summer or part-time work.

In *OFCCP v. Bruce Church, Inc.,*[61] the Secretary of Labor ordered the immediate debarment of a lettuce supplier to military bases for failure to submit its written affirmative action plan for inspection by the Labor Department. The supplier's contention that since each order was less than $50,000 it was not covered by Executive Order 11246 was rejected. The OFCCP counts the total value of the orders anticipated in assessing whether the $50,000 threshold of the executive order has been reached where blanket purchase orders are used by the government. In this case, the contractor had done $3,500,000 in business with the federal government over a six-year period. The contractor will remain ineligible under the debarment until it submits an affirmative action plan and satisfies the Labor Department that it is in compliance with the plan.

Short of debarment, the OFCCP may negotiate a consent decree with an employer to make victims whole and correct an identified problem. The OFCCP

---

[61] Case No. 87–OFC–7, June 30, 1987.

and the EEOC have an agreement under which they share information on pay discrimination cases. In an OFCCP glass ceiling review of the data regarding upward-mobility opportunities for women and minorities at U.S. Airways, a pay discrepancy between female employees in professional and executive-level salary grades was discovered, where female employees were being paid less than their male counterparts. On November 20, 1998, OFCCP and U.S. Airways negotiated a consent decree paying 30 women some $395,000 to rectify the discrepancies.

| CASE 13.9 | BEVERLY ENTERPRISES, INC. V. HERMAN
U.S. DISTRICT COURT, 130 F. SUPP. 2D 1 (D.D.C. 2000). |

[The plaintiff, Beverly Enterprises, Inc., operates nursing homes that provide care for veterans under contracts with the Veterans Administration. It challenged OFCCP's administrative search of the company's affirmative action files and other review of the company as a violation of its Fourth Amendment rights. From an adverse ruling by the Department of Labor's Administrative Law Board, the plaintiff appealed to the U. S. district court.]

URBINA, D. J....

The plaintiff is an Arkansas corporation that operates nursing homes that provide skilled nursing care for veterans. In various contracts with the Veterans Administration, the plaintiff has agreed to be bound by the affirmative-action provisions contained in Executive Order 11,246. Executive Order 11,246 requires that whenever the federal government purchases goods or services the government must insert a provision into the contract that prohibits the contractor from discriminating on the basis of race, sex, color, religion or national origin. The executive order also requires that contractors establish and update a written affirmative action program and allows the Secretary of Labor to set guidelines for verifying compliance. If a contractor fails to comply with these guidelines, the Secretary of Labor is empowered to terminate all contracts with that contractor and order that the government not deal with that contractor until it complies with the executive order.

One method by which the Department of Labor secures compliance with affirmative action programs is through a corporate management review ("CMR"), an administrative search that normally includes a review of the company's affirmative action files, an on-site review of the company's headquarters and an off-site analysis. The process for selecting companies for review begins when federal contractors, such as

the plaintiff, file an Equal Employment Opportunity Employer Information Report with the Equal Employment Opportunity Commission. The plaintiff's report lists the location of the plaintiff's headquarters, the number of employees, the number of facilities and the plaintiff's industry. This information is entered into a computer and given to the Office of Federal Contract Compliance Programs in the Department of Labor ("OFCCP").

The OFCCP organizes the list of company headquarters into separate geographical lists corresponding to the jurisdictional territory of each OFCCP local office. The national office then sends each local office a list of the companies, placed in random order, which have headquarters in its jurisdiction ("CMR candidate list"). Defendant OFCCP claims the only criteria that affect the order and composition of the CMR candidate list are: (1) the geographical location of the company's headquarters, (2) the number of facilities the company owns, (3) the status of the company as a federal contractor and (4) the number of people the company employs....

The OFCCP local offices then are assigned to conduct a certain number of CMRs each year by their regional office. The area director for each local office starts at the top of the CMR candidate list and decides whether the office can review the candidate. A company may be rejected for review if it is out of business, its contract is completed, its contract is worth less than $50,000, it has fewer than 50 employees, there is no evidence of its contract with the government, it was reviewed within the past two years, it was reporting to the OFCCP under a Conciliation Agreement or it is a signatory to a consent decree....

In 1998, the Little Rock, Arkansas office of the OFCCP was assigned to choose one company in its jurisdiction for a CMR. According to the defendants, the plaintiff's name was placed third on a list of three

continued

candidates that was given to area director Joel Maltbia by the national office. Mr. Maltbia claimed he rejected the first name on the list because the Federal Procurement Data System, the OFCCP's computer listing of federal contractors, did not list the company as having a current contract with the federal government. Mr. Maltbia eliminated the second name from the list because he believed that the company was already reporting to the OFCCP under a consent decree. By contrast, Mr. Maltbia found that the plaintiff did not meet any of the criteria for being rejected for review. Accordingly, Mr. Maltbia filled out rejection forms for the first two candidates on the list and recommended that the plaintiff be selected for review.

The plaintiff was informed of its selection in October 1998. Mr. Reilly, the plaintiff's deputy general counsel and vice-president, met with OFCCP officials later that month to discuss the criteria by which the plaintiff was selected for a CMR review. Mr. Reilly expressed concerns that the plaintiff was being targeted for review because its other 699 facilities had been selected for other types of review on many occasions in the past few years. During this time, the plaintiff's companies were found to be compliant 100% of the time. Mr. Reilly believed the meetings with OFCCP officials failed to address his concerns and he refused to let the defendant OFCCP conduct its review.

On May 17, 1999, defendant OFCCP filed an Administrative Complaint with the Department of Labor's Office of Administrative Law alleging that the plaintiff's refusal to submit to a CMR violated its obligations under Executive Order 11,246.... The plaintiff claimed it was not selected according to a neutral administrative plan, as required by the Fourth Amendment....

On July 22, 1999, the A.L.J. issued a recommended decision and order ("decision") to the Board finding that the plaintiff's selection for a Corporate Management Review was valid. Based on this finding, the A.L.J. recommended that the Administrative Law Board cancel the plaintiff's contracts with the government and bar the plaintiff and its subsidiaries from future government contracts until it complied with the requirements of Executive Order 11,246. On September 1, 1999, the Board issued an order in which it accepted the factual findings and recommendations of the A.L.J. with the exception of the A.L.J.'s recommendation to

immediately cancel the government's contracts with the plaintiff and its subsidiaries. Instead, the Board gave the plaintiff 30 days to comply with Executive Order 11,246 before any sanction would be imposed.

The plaintiff appealed the Board's decision to this court as contrary to the plaintiff's constitutional and procedural rights and also sought to limit the scope of the remedy....

An administrative search violates the Fourth Amendment unless the agency shows the company's selection for the search is based on: (1) specific evidence of an existing violation, (2) reasonable legislative or administrative standards that have been met with respect to that particular contractor or (3) an administrative plan containing specific neutral criteria. In this case, the defendants seek to prove that the plaintiff's selection for the search was made pursuant to an administrative plan containing specific neutral criteria. Deciding whether the defendant OFCCP used neutral criteria is a factual determination. Thus, the court will overturn the agency's decision only if it is not supported by substantial evidence.... The court holds that the proposed administrative search does not violate the Fourth Amendment because substantial evidence supports the agency's finding that the search was initiated pursuant to a neutral administrative plan....

The plaintiff requests that this court give it 30 days after the sanctions take effect so that it will have a chance to comply with the order. This request is consistent with the sanction's goal of compelling compliance. See *First Alabama Bank of Montgomery v. Donovan*, 692 F.2d 714, 722 (11th Cir. 1982) (purpose of sanctions under E.O. 11,246 is to encourage compliance, not to punish). Therefore, the court holds that the defendants may not debar the plaintiff unless the plaintiff fails to comply with the Board's final order within 30 days from the date that the Board issues its final judgment.

For the foregoing reasons, the court will grant the defendants' motion and deny the plaintiff's motion for summary judgment on the plaintiff's Fourth Amendment claims. The court further holds that it lacks sufficient information to determine whether the plaintiff's subsidiaries may be punished for its failure to meet its obligations under Executive Order 11,246. Thus, the court will remand this case to the Administrative Law Board of the Department of Labor for proceedings consistent with this opinion. The court also modifies the remedy to allow the plaintiff 30 days after the

continued

Administrative Review Board's final decision to comply with its responsibilities under Executive Order 11,246 before it may be sanctioned.

Case Questions

1. Did the OFCCP violate the Fourth Amendment rights of the plaintiff, a government contractor, against an unreasonable administrative search by the federal government?

2. Are sanctions issued against government contractors calculated to punish them for failure to live up to their affirmative action responsibilities under their contracts?

SECTION 120: OTHER REMEDY OPTIONS

Because of an EEOC case backlog or the desire to avoid EEOC procedures, grievants have sometimes chosen to circumvent Title VII procedures. There are three principal avenues other than the Title VII approach to remedy discriminatory employment practices: (1) district court action under the Civil Rights Act of 1866, (2) private grievance and arbitration proceedings, and (3) NLRA unfair labor practice proceedings.

THE CIVIL RIGHTS ACT OF 1866

Following the Civil War, Congress enacted the Civil Rights Act of 1866 pursuant to the congressional power to eradicate slavery provided by the Thirteenth Amendment, which had been ratified in 1865. To remove any doubt as to its constitutionality, the statute was reenacted in 1870 following ratification of the Fourteenth Amendment in 1868 and was codified as 42 U.S.C. Sections 1981 and 1982. Lawsuits under the Civil Rights Act of 1866 are commonly referred to as Section 1981 and Section 1982 lawsuits.

In *Johnson v. Railway Agency*,[62] the Supreme Court held that Section 1 of the Civil Rights Act of 1866, and therefore its derivative 42 U.S.C. Section 1981, provides an independent remedy for discrimination in employment. The Court noted that filing a Section 1981 claim does not foreclose the use of EEOC procedures.

In *General Building Contractors Ass'n v. Pennsylvania*,[63] the Supreme Court considered whether discrimination under Section 1981 could be proved by establishing that the defendant's policies had a disparate impact without proving intentional discrimination. The Court decided that Section 1981 can be violated only by purposeful discrimination.

In *Patterson v. McLean Credit Union*,[64] the Supreme Court read the language of Section 1981—"all persons ... shall have the same right ... to make and enforce contracts ... as enjoyed by white citizens"—as prohibiting racial discrimination in the making and enforcement of private contracts, that is, in hiring decisions or the right to enforce contracts. The Court held that Section 1981 did not provide a remedy for racial harassment on the job. This decision limiting the application of Section 1981

---

[62] 421 U.S. 454 (1975).

[63] 458 U.S. 375, 29 FEP 139 (1982).

[64] 491 U.S. 164 (1989).

was overturned by Congress in the Civil Rights Act of 1991, which specifies that Section 1981 covers all forms of racial discrimination in employment.[65]

In Chapter 11 of this text, the time limitation for filing charges concerning alleged violations of Title VII is set forth. Where an individual misses the relatively short filing deadlines under Title VII, the individual may be able to bring a race discrimination case under the longer time limits allowed in Section 1981. In *Jones v. R.R. Donnelley & Sons*[66] the Supreme Court held that the four-year statute of limitations period set forth in 28 U.S.C. § 1658 applies to all claims under the Civil Rights Act of 1866, codified in 28 U.S.C. § 1981.

Section 1981 covers only claims of intentional discrimination based on race. Jury trials, with uncapped punitive and compensatory damages, may be obtained.

In *Saint Francis College v. Al-Khazraji*, presented in this section, the plaintiff's Title VII claims had been dismissed as untimely, but the Supreme Court upheld his right to sue under Section 1981 alleging racial discrimination based on his Arabian ancestry. In a related case, *Shaare Tefila Congregation v. Cobb*, also presented in this section, the Supreme Court determined that Jews can, under Section 1982 of the Civil Rights Act of 1866, sue those who allegedly desecrated a synagogue, as Jews were among the peoples considered to be distinct races at the time the 1866 Act was passed.

The Civil Rights Act of 1871, codified as 42 U.S.C. Section 1983, may be the basis of an action against state or local governments in an employment context when citizens are deprived of rights, privileges, and immunities secured by the U.S. Constitution or federal statutes.[67]

In *Quinn v. Nassau County Police Department*,[68] a homosexual government employee working as a police officer was singled out for abuse in the workplace because of his sexual orientation. Since Title VII of the Civil Rights Act of 1964 does not prohibit discrimination against individuals because of their sexual orientation, Quinn brought a Section 1983 employment discrimination claim against the police department based on the Fourteenth Amendment of the U.S. Constitution's equal protection clause. He was awarded $380,000 in compensatory and punitive damages.

| CASE 13.10 | SAINT FRANCIS COLLEGE V. AL-KHAZRAJI
SUPREME COURT OF THE UNITED STATES, 481 U.S. 604 (1987). |

[Respondent, a U.S. citizen born in Iraq, was an associate professor of behavioral science at St. Francis College in Pennsylvania. He filed suit in federal district court against the college and its tenure committee, alleging that by denying him tenure nearly three years before, they had discriminated against him on the basis of his

continued

---

[65] Section 101 of the Civil Rights Act of 1991.

[66] 541 U.S. 369 (2004).

[67] In *Brown v. Polk County, Iowa*, 61 F.3d 650 (8th Cir. 1995), Isaiah Brown, a black man who identifies himself as a born-again Christian, was successful in part in a Section 1983 action against a county employer that required him to remove from his office all items with a religious connotation.

[68] 53 F. Supp. 2d 347 (E.D.N.Y. 1999).

Arabian race in violation of 42 U.S.C. Section 1981. His Title VII claims of discrimination based on national origin, religion, and race were dismissed as untimely. The district court granted a summary judgment for the college, finding that Section 1981 does not cover claims based on Arabian ancestry. The court of appeals reversed, holding that the respondent had properly alleged racial discrimination in that although Arabs are Caucasians under current racial classifications, Congress, when it passed what is now Section 1981, did not limit its protections to those who today would be considered members of a race different from the defendant's. The Supreme Court granted certiorari.]

WHITE, J....

Section 1981 provides:

> All persons within the jurisdiction of the United States shall have the same right in every State and Territory to make and enforce contracts, to sue, be parties, give evidence, and to the full and equal benefit of all laws and proceedings for the security for persons and property as is enjoyed by white citizens, and shall be subject to like punishment, pains, penalties, taxes, licenses, and exactions of every kind, and to no other.

Although § 1981 does not itself use the word "race," the Court has construed the section to forbid all "racial" discrimination in the making of private as well as public contracts. *Runyon v. McCrary*, 427 U.S. 160, 168, 174–175 (1976). The petitioner college, although a private institution, was therefore subject to this statutory command. There is no disagreement among the parties on these propositions. The issue is whether respondent has alleged *racial* discrimination within the meaning of § 1981.

Petitioners contend that respondent is a Caucasian and cannot allege the kind of discrimination § 1981 forbids. Concededly, *McDonald v. Santa Fe Trail Transportation Co.*, 427 U.S. 273 (1976), held that white persons could maintain a § 1981 suit; but that suit involved alleged discrimination against a white person in favor of a black, and petitioner submits that the section does not encompass claims of discrimination by one Caucasian against another. We are quite sure that the Court of Appeals properly rejected this position.

Petitioner's submission rests on the assumption that all those who might be deemed Caucasians today were thought to be of the same race when § 1981

became law in the 19th century; and it may be that a variety of ethnic groups, including Arabs, are now considered to be within the Caucasian race. The understanding of "race" in the 19th century, however, was different. Plainly, all those who might be deemed Caucasian today were not thought to be of the same race at the time § 1981 became law....

Encyclopedias of the 19th century ... described race in terms of ethnic groups, which is a narrower concept of race than petitioners urged. Encyclopedia Americana in 1858, for example, referred in 1854 to various races such as Finns, Gypsies, Basques, and Hebrews. The 1863 version of the New American Cyclopaedia divided the Arabs into a number of subsidiary races, represented the Hebrews as of the Semitic race, and identified numerous other groups as constituting races, including Swedes, Norwegians, Germans, Greeks, Finns, Italians, Spanish, Mongolians, Russians, and the like. The Ninth edition of the Encyclopedia Britannica also referred to Arabs, Jews, and other ethnic groups such as Germans, Hungarians, and Greeks, as separate races.

These dictionary and encyclopedic sources are somewhat diverse, but it is clear that they do not support the claim that for the purposes of § 1981, Arabs, Englishmen, Germans and certain other ethnic groups are to be considered a single race. We would expect the legislative history of § 1981, which the Court held in *Runyon v. McCrary* had its source in the Civil Rights Act of 1866, as well as the Voting Rights Act of 1870, to reflect this common understanding, which it surely does. The debates are replete with references to the Scandinavian races, Cong. Globe, 39th Cong., 1st Sess, 499 (1866) (remarks of Sen. Cowan), as well as the Chinese (remarks of Sen. Davis), Latin (remarks of Rep. Kasson during debate of home rule for the District of Columbia), Spanish (remarks of Sen. Davis during debate of District of Columbia suffrage) and Anglo-Saxon races (remarks of Rep. Dawson). Jews, Mexicans (remarks of Rep. Dawson), blacks, and Mongolians (remarks of Sen. Cowan), were similarly categorized. Gypsies were referred to as a race (remarks of Sen. Cowan)....

Based on the history of § 1981, we have little trouble in concluding that Congress intended to protect from discrimination identifiable classes of persons who are subjected to intentional discrimination solely because of their ancestry or ethnic characteristics. Such discrimination is racial discrimination that Congress intended § 1981 to forbid, whether or not

continued

it would be classified as racial in terms of modern scientific theory. The Court of Appeals was thus quite right in holding that § 1981, "at a minimum," reaches discrimination against an individual "because he or she is genetically part of an ethnically and physiognomically distinctive subgrouping of *homo sapiens.*" It is clear from our holding, however, that a distinctive physiognomy is not essential to qualify for § 1981 protection. If respondent on remand can prove that he was subjected to intentional discrimination based on the fact that he was born an Arab, rather than solely on the place or nation of his origin, or his religion, he will have made out a case under § 1981.

The judgment of the Court of Appeals is accordingly
Affirmed.

Case Questions

1. Why did the plaintiff bring a Section 1981 claim rather than rely on a Title VII claim?
2. Can a Section 1981 claim encompass a charge of discrimination by one Caucasian against another?
3. Did the plaintiff prove that St. Francis College had discriminated against him because of his Arabian ancestry?

| CASE 13.11 | SHAARE TEFILA CONGREGATION V. COBB |
| | SUPREME COURT OF THE UNITED STATES, 481 U.S. 615 (1987). |

[After their synagogue was painted with anti-Semitic slogans, phrases, and symbols, petitioners brought suit in federal district court alleging that the desecration by respondents violated 42 U.S.C. Section 1982. The district court dismissed petitioners' claims, and the court of appeals affirmed, holding that discrimination against Jews was not racial discrimination under Section 1982. The Supreme Court granted certiorari.]

WHITE, J....

We agree with the Court of Appeals that a charge of racial discrimination within the meaning of § 1982 cannot be made out by alleging only that the defendants were motivated by racial animus; it is necessary as well to allege that defendants' animus was directed towards the kind of group that Congress intended to protect when it passed the statute. To hold otherwise would unacceptably extend the reach of the statute.

We agree with petitioners, however, that the Court of Appeals erred in holding that Jews cannot state a § 1982 claim against other white defendants. That view rested on the notion that because Jews today are not thought to be members of a separate race, they cannot make out a claim of racial discrimination within the meaning of § 1982. That construction of the section we have today rejected in *Saint Francis College v. Al-Khazraji.* Our opinion in that case

observed that definitions of race when § 1982 was passed were not the same as they are today and concluded that the section was "intended to protect from discrimination identifiable classes of persons who are subject to intentional discrimination solely because of their ancestry or ethnic characteristics." As *St. Francis* makes clear, the question before us is not whether Jews are considered to be a separate race by today's standards, but whether, at the time § 1982 was adopted, Jews constituted a group of people that Congress intended to protect. It is evident from the legislative history of the section reviewed in *Saint Francis College,* a review that we need not repeat here, that Jews and Arabs were among the peoples then considered to be distinct races and hence within the protection of the statute. Jews are not foreclosed from stating a cause of action against other members of what today is considered to be part of the Caucasian race.

The judgment of the Court of Appeals is therefore reversed and the case is remanded for further proceedings consistent with this opinion.

Case Questions

1. Why did the district court dismiss the congregation's Section 1982 claim?
2. Can Jews state a Section 1982 claim against other white defendants?

GRIEVANCE-ARBITRATION AND TITLE VII

An employee may seek a remedy against discriminatory employment practices through the grievance and arbitration procedures in an existing collective bargaining agreement. The advantage to the grievance and arbitration process is that it can be implemented with far less delay than the Title VII procedures, a suit under the Civil Rights Act of 1866, or NLRB proceedings. A difficulty with arbitration in employment discrimination cases is that the individual grievant may be left without adequate representation in the arbitration proceedings. The Supreme Court recognized in *Vaca v. Sipes* that because the remedies of grievance arbitration are devised and controlled by the union and the employer, "they may very well prove unsatisfactory or unworkable for the individual grievant."[69]

In *Alexander v. Gardner-Denver Co.*,[70] the U.S. Supreme Court considered the question of whether an individual grievant's election to invoke grievance and arbitration machinery that resulted in an adverse arbitration award precludes the individual from filing a subsequent Title VII claim. The Court found that it did not. The Court held that Title VII was designed by Congress to supplement existing laws and institutions relating to employment discrimination and that the doctrine of election of remedies was inapplicable in the present context, which involved statutory rights distinctly separate from the employee's contractual rights, regardless of the fact that violation of both rights may have resulted from the same factual occurrence. The Court held, however, that the arbitral decision may be admitted as evidence at the Title VII trial in a federal court and set forth in its much-discussed footnote 24 the weight to be accorded the arbitral decision. Footnote 24 states:

> We adopt no standards as to the weight to be accorded an arbitral decision, since this must be determined in the court's discretion with regard to the facts and circumstances of each case. Relevant factors include the existence of provisions in the collective-bargaining agreement that conform substantially with Title VII, the degree of procedural fairness in the arbitral forum, adequacy of the record with respect to the issue of discrimination, and the special competence of particular arbitrators. Where an arbitral determination gives full consideration to an employee's Title VII rights, a court may properly accord it great weight. This is especially true where the issue is solely one of fact, specifically addressed by the parties and decided by the arbitrator on the basis of an adequate record. But courts should ever be mindful that Congress, in enacting Title VII, thought it necessary to provide a judicial forum for the ultimate resolution of discriminatory employment claims. It is the duty of courts to assure the full availability of this forum.

Employers favor arbitration because they have an equal voice with the union in the selection of the arbitrator, the decisions of arbitrators are final and binding on the parties, and remedies available in arbitration may be less than the statutory remedies for discrimination cases. Section 118 of the Civil Rights Act of 1991 encourages the use of arbitration "where appropriate." Employees, however, tend to believe that arbitration diminishes their rights. Employers who go to court seeking

---

[69] 386 U.S. 171, 185 (1967).

[70] 415 U.S. 147 (1974).

to compel individuals to arbitrate Title VII, Age Discrimination in Employment Act (ADEA), or Americans with Disabilities Act (ADA) claims under language found in the collective bargaining agreement will run into the Supreme Court's language set forth in *Wright v. Universal Maritime Services Corp.*[71] that:

> *Gardner-Denver* at least stands for the proposition that the right to a federal judicial forum is of sufficient importance to be protected against less-than-explicit union waiver in a collective bargaining agreement [CBA]. The CBA in this case does not meet that standard.

Under the *Wright* decision, where an employer sought to compel a longshoreman to arbitrate his ADA claim against the employer under an arbitration provision in the Longshoremen's Union contract containing language compelling arbitration of "all matters" regarding "terms and conditions of employment," such language was held not to be a "clear and unmistakable" waiver of an individual's right to a federal judicial forum in a federal statutory discrimination claim.[72]

In *Pyett v. Pennsylvania Building Co.*,[73] Steven Pyett, Thomas O'Connell, and Michael Phillips alleged that they had been transferred from their positions as night watchmen and replaced by younger security guards in violation of the Age Discrimination Employment Act. As union members, they were covered by a collective bargaining agreement that included a mandatory arbitration clause for discrimination claims, stating in part as follows: "All such claims shall be subject to the grievance and arbitration procedure as the sole and exclusive remedy for violations. Arbitrators should apply appropriate law in rendering decisions based upon claims of discrimination." The employer sought to compel arbitration. The U.S. District Court recognized the distinction between arbitration clauses in individual contracts governed by the *Gilmer* line of Supreme Court precedents and arbitration clauses in CBAs that are governed by the *Gardner-Denver* line of Supreme Court precedents and held that union-negotiated waivers of statutory rights in CBAs were unenforceable. The Second Circuit Court of Appeals affirmed the order of the District Court.

NLRA REMEDIES

An employer's racial discrimination is an unfair labor practice in violation of Section 8(a)(1) of the NLRA if it is found that this discrimination interferes with the affected employees' Section 7 rights to act concertedly for their own protection. In *Jubilee Manufacturing Co.*,[74] the Board pointed out that it was "by no means inevitable" that an employer's racial or sex discrimination would set one group of employees against the other. The Board stated that a finding of a violation of the NLRA would depend upon a showing of "the necessary direct relationship" between the alleged race or sex discrimination and interference with employee rights under Section 7.

---

[71] 525 U.S. 70 (1998).

[72] *Id.* at 82.

[73] 498 F.3d 88 (2d Cir. 2007).

[74] 202 NLRB 2 (1973).

In *King Soopers, Inc.*,[75] the Board found an employer to be in violation of Section 8(a)(1) of the NLRA for suspending a Spanish American employee for filing charges with the EEOC alleging promotional discrimination. The Board also found the union to be in violation of Section 8(b)(1)(A) for refusing to represent and process the grievances of the charging party. The Board's order held the company and the union jointly and severally liable for back pay damages. It should be pointed out that the NLRA does not protect picketing, handbilling, or other concerted activity by a group of minority employees seeking to bargain directly with an employer concerning alleged racial discrimination by the employer when the minority employees circumvented their elected bargaining representative and refused to participate in the contract grievance procedure.

In *Frank Briscoe v. NLRB*,[76] 12 ironworkers were laid off because of winter weather. Four of the laid-off ironworkers were black, and they filed Title VII charges of discrimination based on race. When the weather improved, the company began rehiring but refused to hire any of the 12 laid-off workers. The company stated that to rehire those who did not file charges would be evidence of discrimination. Some of the ironworkers obtained other work, and eight of the workers laid off in February, including three of the black workers who filed Title VII charges, brought unfair labor charges before the NLRB. The U.S. court of appeals held that the filing of a complaint with the Equal Employment Opportunity Commission by the black employees under Title VII could constitute "concerted activity" protected by Section 7 of the NLRA. The court determined that retaliation by the employer against those employees and the others affected thereby was an unfair practice giving rise to the remedial measures of the NLRA. The court held that the availability of a remedy from the EEOC under Title VII does not preclude a plaintiff from seeking and obtaining relief under the NLRA. Indeed, a remedy under the NLRA may provide a faster resolution to a problem than one under Title VII procedures.

Employers are also protected from racial and religious prejudice in relation to Board election activities. In *M & M Supermarkets, Inc. v. NLRB*,[77] the Eleventh Circuit Court of Appeals let it be clearly known that appeals to racial and religious prejudice have no place in our system of justice or in an NLRB-conducted election. During the course of an election campaign, the company's personnel director Patrick made a presentation to a small group of employees at which a union supporter began to berate the company's owners as follows:

> The damn Jews who run this Company are all alike. They pay us pennies out here
> in the warehouse, and take all their money to the bank. The Jews ought to remember
> their roots. Norton Malaver ought to remember his roots. Us blacks were out in the
> cotton field while they, the damned Jews, took their money from the poor hardworking
> people.

---

[75] 222 NLRB 80 (1976).

[76] 637 F.2d 946, 106 LRRM 2155 (3d Cir. 1981).

[77] 125 LRRM 2918 (11th Cir. 1987).

As Patrick attempted to defend the reputation of Norton Malaver and his family as liberal and community-minded people, Charles Wade angrily interrupted her and continued loudly....[78]

The union, which did not condone the remarks, won the election, and the Board issued a bargaining order. The court of appeals refused to enforce the order, stating that the remarks were "so inflammatory and derogatory that they inflamed racial and religious tensions against the ... owners of the company and destroyed the laboratory conditions necessary for a free and open election."[79]

CHAPTER QUESTIONS AND PROBLEMS

1. What remedies are available to individuals charging discriminatory employment practices?

2. What guidelines did the *Weber* Court set forth for permissible affirmative action plans?

3. On what authority do federal agencies require bidders on government contracts to formulate and carry out affirmative action plans?

4. If the program referred to in *Adarand Constructors, Inc. v. Pena* reserved a percentage of highway work for "disadvantaged subcontractors" and instead of using "race-based" presumptions to identify who were disadvantaged subcontractors used an economic standard to identify the disadvantaged subcontractors eligible for the program, would the Court's decision have been the same?

5. Manual Lerma, a Mexican-American, responded to an advertisement announcing the availability of a custodial position at the Harlingen, Texas, post office. The applications were independently rated. Lerma placed third on the hiring list with a score of 95 points out of 110. Immediately behind Lerma was a white male named Ricky Schwab with a rating of 94. Schwab had worked at the Harlingen post office on a temporary basis in the past. After interviewing the four top candidates, the postmaster appointed Schwab to the vacant custodial position. As a persuasive factor in his decision to choose Schwab over the other candidates, the postmaster cited the favorable recommendation of a supervisor who had observed Schwab during his temporary work at the post office.

Lerma brought a Title VII action against the Postal Service, alleging that the failure to hire him was discrimination based on his race and national origin.

The Postal Service contended that no discrimination took place, that Lerma failed to establish a *prima facie* case under Title VII, and that legitimate reasons existed for selecting Schwab over Lerma.

On the basis of the facts given, did Lerma establish a *prima facie* case under Title VII? If so, what must the defendant do to avoid liability? Decide. [*Lerma v. Balger*, 29 FEP 1829 (5th Cir.)]

6. The New Bedford Police Department required all police officers, both male and female, to satisfy a 5-foot-6-inch minimum height requirement. Maria Costa wanted to become a police officer. She had passed the city's physical examination and had scored 93 percent on the state civil service examination. Costa's successful completion of these requirements gained her a ranking as the number one candidate on the eligibility list

---

[78] *Id.* at 2919.

[79] *Id.* at 2922.

for female officers. When two vacancies for a female police officer occurred, Costa was interviewed for the position but was rejected due to her failure to satisfy the minimum height requirement. The second-ranked female applicant was also rejected under the height requirement. The city hired the third- and fourth-ranked women, who did meet the minimum height.

Costa brought an action under Title VII, producing undisputed evidence that less than 20 percent of women attain the height of 5 feet 6 inches. Therefore, Costa claimed that the police department's minimum height policy had a disparate impact on women in violation of Title VII.

The city denied this allegation by claiming that its policy did not result in a disparate impact on women as it hired women for the vacancies.

Does the city policy violate Title VII? Decide the case. [*Costa v. Markey*, 706 F.2d 1 (1st Cir.)]

7. In 1985, a U.S. district court approved an affirmative action plan for the Washington, D.C. (D.C.), fire department that required that 60 percent of new hires be black. D.C. itself was predominantly black, with 65 percent of the workforce and up to 75 percent of the applicants from D.C. being black. Twenty-nine percent of the entire metropolitan Washington, D.C., area, from which D.C. recruited firefighters, was black. In 1983, 80 percent of the new hires were black. In 1982, 67.5 percent of the new hires were black. Over a four-year period an average of 75 percent of those hired were black. Between 1980 and 1984, virtually every candidate who showed up to take the test for firefighter passed it because the cutoff score was set so low that even random answering of questions would lead to a passing mark. D.C.'s goal in its affirmative action plan was to achieve racial parity in its firefighting force.

The plaintiffs contended that the evidence was clear that the fire department was not engaging in hiring practices that discrim-

inated against blacks and that no dismantling of the structures of past discrimination remained for the courts. They contended that the plan and its goal were illegal.

D.C. stated that the fire department was just 38 percent black, while the working-age population of D.C. was 70 percent black. D.C. contended that "plantation politics" were practiced in D.C. for over a century. It stated that the plaintiffs urged D.C. to forget the bad old days of discrimination and concentrate on the purity of current practices; however, it argued that racial parity would be lost without the 60 percent hiring goal.

What standard must a court apply in reviewing whether a city's race-conscious affirmative action quotas are permissible? On the limited evidence before you, were D.C.'s hiring practices discriminatory considering the qualified and relevant labor market? Is D.C.'s goal of achieving racial parity constitutionally valid? Decide. [*Hammond v. Barry*, 42 EPD ¶ 36,804 (D.C. Cir.)]

8. The First Alabama Bank of Montgomery was a party to various contracts with the United States in which it agreed to be bound by the terms of Executive Order 11246. The bank formulated an affirmative action plan. The Office of Federal Contract Compliance Programs notified First Alabama that it wanted to review the compliance with Executive Order 11246, Section 503, of the Rehabilitation Act of 1973 and Section 402 of the Vietnam Veterans Readjustment Assistance Act of 1974. Accordingly, the OFCCP asked the bank to submit a copy of its affirmative action plan and other supporting documentation.

The bank refused to supply the requested information or to allow an OFCCP compliance officer to conduct an on-site review. The bank stated that it had undergone three compliance reviews under Executive Order 11246 in the last 10 years and had been found to be in compliance each time. Furthermore, the bank stated that it had been a defendant in a 10-year race discrimination action under Title VII during which it had filed quarterly reports with the court. The litigation had ended with a finding by the court that the bank did not discriminate against blacks in its hiring practices.

Given the bank's refusal to comply, the Department of Labor issued a complaint against the bank, asking that First Alabama be debarred from receiving government contracts until it convinced the Secretary of Labor that it was in compliance with the affirmative action obligations of Executive Order 11246. After notice and hearing, the Secretary's complaint was sustained and First Alabama was debarred.

Citing its compliance history and the favorable decision in the Title VII case, First Alabama sought judicial review of the debarment in district court.

Should the debarment decision be upheld as proper? If so, what must First Alabama do to renew its eligibility as a government contractor? [*First Alabama Bank of Montgomery, N.A. v. Donovan*, 30 FEP 4448 (11th Cir.)]

9. Clara Watson, who is black, was hired by the Fort Worth Bank and Trust Company in August 1973 and was promoted to teller in 1976. Between 1980 and 1981, Watson applied for four supervisory jobs, but white employees were selected for these positions. The bank, which had some 80 employees, had not developed formal criteria for evaluating candidates, but relied on the subjective judgment of supervisors who were acquainted with the candidates and the nature of the jobs to be filled.

In a Title VII lawsuit against the bank, the trial court, following a disparate treatment model, concluded that Watson had established a *prima facie* case; the bank had rebutted it by presenting legitimate, nondiscriminatory reasons for each challenged promotion decision; and Watson had failed to show that the reasons were pretexts. Watson presented evidence that showed that the bank had only one black supervisor from 1975 to 1983, and a statistician testified on her behalf that a white applicant had a four times better chance of being hired than a black applicant. Watson claimed that a disparate impact model analysis of the employer's subjective promotion policy standards indicated that she was discriminated against in violation of Title VII. The court refused to apply a disparate impact analysis to subjective promotion procedures such as job interviews and performance evaluations, saying that disparate impact analysis was meant to evaluate such objective criteria as testing or diploma requirements.

Watson contended that if an employer's undisciplined system of subjective decision making had precisely the same effect as a system pervaded by impermissible intentional discrimination, it was difficult to see why Title VII was not violated. She contended, moreover, that the *Griggs* decision would be nullified if disparate impact analysis were applied only to objective selection practices.

The bank contended that employers would have to abandon subjective methods of evaluating candidates for promotion, such as interviews or performance evaluations, if it were forced to defend disparate impact cases, and its only alternative would be to adopt a quota system to ensure that no plaintiff could establish a *prima facie* case. It stated that quota systems were clearly contrary to Title VII. Further, the bank stated that Watson had full opportunity to prove that the bank did not promote her because of her race, and she failed to prove her case.

Did the trial court err in failing to apply disparate impact analysis to Watson's claims of discrimination in promotion? Decide. [*Watson v. Fort Worth Bank and Trust Co.*, 47 FEP 102 (U.S. S.Ct.)]

10. Connie Cunico, a white woman, was employed by the Pueblo, Colorado, School District as a social worker. She and other social workers were laid off in seniority order as a result of the district's poor financial

situation. However, the school board there-after decided to retain Wayne Hunter, a black social worker with less seniority than Cunico, because he was the only black on the administrative staff. No racial imbalance existed in the relevant workforce; and black persons constituted 2 percent of the work-force. Cunico, who was rehired over two years later, claimed that she was the victim of reverse discrimination. She stated that she lost $110,361 in back wages, plus $76,000 in attorney fees and costs. The school district responded that it was correct in protecting with special consideration the only black administrator in the district under the general principles it set forth in its AAP.

Refer to the text discussion of *Wygant v. Jackson Board of Education*. Did the school board grant a layoff preference based on race in this case?

Using standards developed in *Weber* and *Johnson*, did the employer show that its affirmative action in retaining Hunter was justified as a remedial measure? Decide.

[*Cunico v. Pueblo School District No. 6*, 917 F.2d 431 (10th Cir.)]

11. Joe's Stone Crab Restaurant of South Miami Beach, Florida, had a reputation for hiring only male waiters. Women did not apply for waitstaff positions there because of this rep-utation for discrimination. In the five years before the EEOC brought suit against it, Joe's hired 108 male waiters and 0 females. After the suit was filed, female applicants com-posed 22 percent of the applicant pool and received 21 percent of the waitstaff jobs. In deciding the case dealing with the five-year period preceding the lawsuit, the district court looked at the workforce statistics and the radical workforce imbalance between the number of males hired (108) and the number of females hired (0) along with the statistical availability of qualified women in the labor market. Was Joe's Restaurant guilty of dis-parate impact discrimination based on the statistical disparities? How would you decide this case? [*EEOC v. Joe's Stone Crab, Inc.*, 220 F.3d 1263 (11th Cir)].

PAY EQUITY; AGE DISCRIMINATION

SECTION

SECTION 121: EQUAL PAY FOR EQUAL WORK

The principle of equal pay for equal work regardless of sex is set forth in the Equal Pay Act of 1963, which was enacted as Section 6(d) of the Fair Labor Standards Act (FLSA). The Equal Pay Act prohibits employers from discriminating against employees covered by the minimum wage provisions of the FLSA by paying lower wages to employees of one sex than to employees of the opposite sex for equal work in the same establishment on jobs that require equal skill, effort, and responsibility and are performed under similar working conditions.[1] The Equal Pay Act was intended as a broad charter of women's rights in the business world. The Act seeks to eliminate the depressing effects on living standards caused by reduced wages for female workers. The Act does not prohibit any variation in wage rates paid men and women, but only those variations based solely on sex. The Act sets forth four exceptions, allowing variances in wages to be based on (1) a seniority system, (2) a merit system, (3) a system that measures earnings by quantity or

---

[1] 29 U.S.C. § 206(d)(1).

515

quality of production, or (4) a differential based on any factor other than sex. For example, in *Brinkley v. Harbour Recreation Club*,[2] Ms. Brinkley was hired as general manager of the Harbour Recreation Club, a golf club in New Bern, North Carolina, at $50,000 per year. At the end of the first year of operation, the club lost $166,000. At that point, the club offered Ms. Brinkley a lower-rated job as restaurant manager, which she declined. Soon thereafter, the club terminated her for gross negligence. She was replaced by a male successor at $75,400 a year. Brinkley filed an Equal Pay Act claim based on the fact that the employer agreed to pay a male $25,400 more than it had paid her to do the same job she had done. The court found, however, that the male successor was paid a higher salary based on "factors other than sex," including his salary history and the fact that his 11 years of industry experience was superior to Brinkley's experience.[3]

The 1974 amendments to the FLSA make the Act applicable to employees of the federal government and state and local governments and their agencies.[4] Enforcement of the Act is the responsibility of the Equal Employment Opportunity Commission (EEOC).

Congress, in prescribing equal pay for equal work, did not require that the jobs in question be identical, but only that the jobs be "substantially equal."[5] In applying this "substantially equal" test, the courts have had no difficulty finding that it is the job content, not the job description, that is controlling.[6]

The courts have uniformly found that the enforcing federal agency bears the initial burden of proving that the employer pays employees of one sex less than employees of the other sex for performing equal work. Once the enforcing agency sustains its initial burden of proof, the burden shifts to the employer to show that the differential is justified by one of the four allowable exceptions.

In *Shultz v. Wheaton Glass Co.*,[7] the Third Circuit Court of Appeals found that a manufacturing plant's 10 percent pay differential for male selector-packers over the pay for female selector-packers, where the male selector-packers spent a relatively small portion of their time doing the additional tasks of "snap-up boys," a lower-paying classification requiring lifting and other unskilled tasks, was a violation of the Equal Pay Act. The court did not require the skill, effort, and responsibility of the female selector-packers' work to be precisely equal to the male selector-packers' work, but rather that the work be substantially equal.

---

[2] 180 F.3d 598 (4th Cir. 1999). In *Weber v. Infinity Broadcasting Corp.*, 2006 WL 891138 (E.D. Mich. 2006), country music radio disc jockey Erin Weber successfully sued her employer based on a number of theories, including a violation of the Equal Pay Act, where her starting salary was $64,000, while two new male DJs each were paid more than $100,000.

[3] In *Warren v. Solo Cup Co.* 516 F.3d 627 (7th Cir. 2008), the court found that paying a male tool crib attendant more than what a female tool crib attendant was paid because of his greater skill in using computers was based on "factors other than sex." It relied on a precedent that said "employers are permitted to compensate employees differently based on skills that are not specifically required in a given job description so long as the employer considers those skills when making the compensation decision."

[4] See Section 3(d) of the FLSA as amended in 1974, Pub. L. 93-259.

[5] *Shultz v. Wheaton Glass Co.*, 421 F.2d 259 (3d Cir. 1970).

[6] *Brennan v. Victoria Bank & Trust Co.*, 493 F.2d 896 (5th Cir. 1974).

[7] 421 F.2d 259 (3d Cir. 1970).

The *Corning Glass Works* decision, presented in this section, discusses several important aspects of the Equal Pay Act. This case was brought at a time when enforcement of the Act was the responsibility of the Department of Labor's Employment Standards Administration and court actions were brought in the name of the Secretary of Labor. The Equal Pay Act is now administered by the EEOC.

CASE 14.1	CORNING GLASS WORKS V. BRENNAN SUPREME COURT OF THE UNITED STATES, 415 U.S. 972 (1974).

MARSHALL, J....

These cases arise under the Equal Pay Act of 1963, 29 U.S.C. Section 206(d)(1), which added to the Fair Labor Standards Act the principle of equal pay for equal work regardless of sex. The principal question posed is whether Corning Glass Works violated the Act by paying a higher base wage to male night shift inspectors than it paid to female inspectors performing the same tasks on the day shift, where the higher wage was paid in addition to a separate night shift differential paid to all employees for night work. In No. 73-29, the Court of Appeals for the Second Circuit, in a case involving several Corning plants in Corning, New York, held that this practice violated the Act. 474 F.2d 226 (1973). In No. 73-695, the Court of Appeals for the Third Circuit, in a case involving a Corning plant in Wellsboro, Pennsylvania, reached the opposite conclusion. 480 F.2d 1254 (1973). We granted certiorari and consolidated the cases to resolve this unusually direct conflict between two circuits. Finding ourselves in substantial agreement with the analysis of the Second Circuit, we affirm in No. 73-29 and reverse in No. 73-695.

I.

Prior to 1925, Corning operated its plants in Wellsboro and Corning only during the day, and all inspection work was performed by women. Between 1925 and 1930, the company began to introduce automatic production equipment which made it desirable to institute a night shift. During this period, however, both New York and Pennsylvania law prohibited women from working at night. As a result, in order to fill inspector positions on the new night shift, the company had to recruit male employees from among its male day workers. The male employees so transferred demanded and received wages substantially higher than those paid to women inspectors engaged

on the two day shifts. During this same period, however, no plantwide shift differential existed and male employees working at night, other than inspectors, received the same wages as their day shift counterparts. Thus a situation developed where the night inspectors were all male, the day inspectors all female, and the male inspectors received significantly higher wages.

In 1944, Corning plants at both locations were organized by a labor union and a collective bargaining agreement was negotiated for all production and maintenance employees. This agreement for the first time established a plantwide shift differential, but this change did not eliminate the higher base wage paid to male night inspectors. Rather, the shift differential was superimposed on the existing differences in base wages between male night inspectors and female day inspectors.

Prior to the June 11, 1964, effective date of the Equal Pay Act, the law in both Pennsylvania and New York was amended to permit women to work at night. It was not until some time after the effective date of the Act, however, that Corning initiated efforts to eliminate the differential rates for male and female inspectors. Beginning in June 1966, Corning started to open up jobs on the night shift to women. Previously separate male and female seniority lists were consolidated and women became eligible to exercise their seniority, on the same basis as men, to bid for the higher paid night inspection jobs as vacancies occurred.

On January 20, 1969, a new collective bargaining agreement went into effect, establishing a new "job evaluation" system for setting wage rates. The new agreement abolished for the future the separate base wages for day and night shift inspectors and imposed a uniform base wage for inspectors exceeding the wage rate for the night shift previously in effect. All inspectors hired after January 20, 1969, were to

continued

receive the same base wage, whatever their sex or shift. The collective bargaining agreement further provided, however, for a higher "red circle" rate for employees hired prior to January 20, 1969, when working as inspectors on the night shift. This "red circle" rate served essentially to perpetuate the differential in base wages between day and night inspectors.

The Secretary of Labor brought these cases to enjoin Corning from violating the Equal Pay Act and to collect back wages allegedly due female employees because of past violations. Three distinct questions are presented: (1) Did Corning ever violate the Equal Pay Act by paying male night shift inspectors more than female day shift inspectors? (2) If so, did Corning cure its violation of the Act in 1966 by permitting women to work as night shift inspectors? (3) Finally, if the violation was not remedied in 1966, did Corning cure its violation in 1969 by equalizing day and night inspector wage rates but establishing higher "red circle" rates for existing employees working on the night shift?

II.

Congress' purpose in enacting the Equal Pay Act was to remedy what was perceived to be a serious and endemic problem of employment discrimination in private industry—the fact that the wage structure of "many segments of American industry has been based on an ancient but outmoded belief that a man, because of his role in society, should be paid more than a woman, even though his duties are the same." S. Rept. No. 176, 88th Cong., 1st Sess. (1963), at 1. The solution adopted was quite simple in principle: to require that "equal work be rewarded by equal wages." *Ibid.*

The Act's basic structure and operation are similarly straightforward. In order to make out a case under the Act, the Secretary must show that an employer pays different wages to employees of opposite sexes "for equal work on jobs the performance of which requires equal skill, effort, and responsibility, and which are performed under similar working conditions." Although the Act is silent on this point, its legislative history makes plain that the Secretary has the burden of proof on this issue, as both of the courts below recognized.

The Act also establishes four exceptions—three specific and one a general catchall provision—where different payment to employees of opposite sexes "is made pursuant to (i) a seniority system; (ii) a merit system; (iii) a system which measures earnings by

quantity or quality of production; or (iv) a differential based on any other factor other than sex." Again, while the Act is silent on this question, its structure and history also suggest that once the Secretary has carried his burden of showing that the employer pays workers of one sex more than workers of the opposite sex for equal work, the burden shifts to the employer to show that the differential is justified under one of the Act's four exceptions. All of the many lower courts that have considered this question have so held, and this view is consistent with the general rule that the application of an exemption under the Fair Labor Standards Act is a matter of affirmative defense on which the employer has the burden of proof.

The contentions of the parties in this case reflect the Act's underlying framework. Corning argues that the Secretary has failed to prove that Corning ever violated the Act because day shift work is not "performed under similar working conditions" as night shift work. The Secretary maintains that day shift and night shift work are performed under "similar working conditions" within the meaning of the Act....

Congress' intent, as manifested in [the Act's] history, was to use these terms to incorporate into the new federal act the well-defined and well-accepted principles of job evaluation so as to ensure that wage differentials based upon bona fide job evaluation plans would be outside the purview of the Act....

While a layman might well assume that time of day worked reflects one aspect of a job's "working conditions," the term has a different and much more specific meaning in the language of industrial relations. As Corning's own representative testified at the hearings, the element of working conditions encompasses two subfactors: "surroundings" and "hazards." "Surroundings" measure the elements, such as toxic chemicals or fumes, regularly encountered by a worker, their intensity, and their frequency. "Hazards" take into account the physical hazards regularly encountered, their frequency, and the severity of injury they can cause. This definition of "working conditions" is not only manifested in Corning's own job evaluation plans but is also well accepted across a wide range of American industry.

Nowhere in any of these definitions is time of day worked mentioned as a relevant criterion. The fact of the matter is that the concept of "working conditions," as used in the specialized language of job evaluation systems, simply does not encompass

continued

shift differentials. Indeed, while Corning now argues that night inspection work is not equal to day inspection work, all of its own job evaluation plans, including the one now in effect, have consistently treated them as equal in all respects, including working conditions. And Corning's Manager of Job Evaluation testified in No. 73-29 that time of day worked was not considered to be a "working condition.".…

The question remains, however, whether Corning carried its burden of proving that the higher rate paid for night inspection work, until 1966 performed solely by men, was in fact intended to serve as compensation for night work, or rather constituted an added payment based upon sex. We agree that the record amply supported the District Court's conclusion that Corning had not sustained its burden of proof. As its history revealed, "the higher night rate was in large part the product of the generally higher wage level of male workers and the need to compensate them for performing what were regarded as demeaning tasks." 474 F.2d, at 233. The differential in base wages originated at a time when no other night employees received higher pay than corresponding day workers and it was maintained long after the company instituted a separate plantwide differential which was thought to compensate adequately for the additional burdens of night work. The differential arose simply because men would not work at the low rates paid women inspectors, and it reflected a job market in which Corning could pay women less than men for the same work. That the company took advantage of such a situation may be understandable as a matter of economics, but its differential nevertheless became illegal once Congress enacted into law the principle of equal pay for equal work.…

The judgment in No. 73-29 is affirmed. The judgment in No. 73-695 is reversed and the case remanded to the Court of Appeals for further proceedings consistent with this opinion.

It is so ordered.

Case Questions

1. Summarize the facts of the case.
2. Who brought the two court actions against Corning Glass Works?
3. Does the statutory term "working conditions" encompass the time of day worked?

SECTION 122: THE *GUNTHER* DECISION AND COMPARABLE WORTH

In spite of the passage of the Equal Pay Act of 1963 and Title VII of the Civil Rights Act of 1964, a substantial earnings gap exists between the average earnings of women working full-time and the average earnings of men working full-time.[8]

The Equal Pay Act has been very successful in remedying pay disparity between men and women performing the same work for their employer. Thus, female full-time college professors earn about the same as male full-time college professors with similar qualifications; female autoworkers earn the same as male autoworkers doing the same work.

Advocates of the concept of **comparable worth** believe that female employees whose jobs are separate and distinct from jobs performed by male employees but are of comparable worth or value to the employer are entitled to wages comparable to those of male employees. Advocates of comparable worth believe that if comparable

---

[8] The disparity closed from 60 percent in 1965 to 72 percent in 1990, but has added only 5.3 percentage points over the subsequent 16 years, with the figure being 76.9 percent in 2006 (the latest data available). The weekly earnings were 80.2 percent for full-time workers in 2007, down from 80.8 percent in 2006. See Institute for Women's Policy Research, Fact Sheet, updated February 2008, http://www.iwpr.org/pdf/R260.pdf.

The reasons for the disparity are complicated and may include both women's own choices and discrimination. See D. Leonhardt, "Gender Pay Gap, Once Narrowing, Is Stuck in Place," *The New York Times*, http://www.nytimes.com/2006/12/24/business/24gap.html.

wages are not paid, female employees should be entitled to relief under Title VII of the Civil Rights Act of 1964. This theory has not been accepted in the courts.

SEX-BASED DISCRIMINATION IN JOB COMPENSATION

In *County of Washington v. Gunther*, presented in this section, the Supreme Court considered the claims of four women employed as matrons at the Washington County, Oregon, jail. These women claimed that the pay differential between them and male corrections officers was attributable to intentional sex discrimination even though the matron's job was not substantially the same job as that of the corrections officers. The Supreme Court set forth the narrow holding that the plaintiffs' claim of low pay because of discrimination based on sex was not barred by Section 703(h) of Title VII, the Bennett Amendment, merely because the plaintiffs did not perform work "equal" to that of the male corrections officers. The significance of the decision is that women may now bring a sex discrimination suit on the basis of low compensation even if they cannot prove that male coworkers are being paid higher wages for substantially the same job. The Court majority emphasized that its narrow holding did not require it to take a position on the issue of comparable worth.

COMPARABLE WORTH

The *Gunther* decision was widely acclaimed by advocates of comparable worth as a first step in the direction of court acceptance of that doctrine. In *AFSCME v. State of Washington (AFSCME I)*,[9] a U.S. district court judge held that the state violated Title VII by its failure to pay men and women the same wages for work of comparable, but not equal, worth. The judge found that the state's practice of taking prevailing market rates into account in setting employee wages had an adverse impact on women, who have historically received lower wages than men in the labor market. The judge ordered implementation of a salary schedule based on comparable worth and ordered back pay of up to $800 million.

In *AFSCME v. State of Washington (AFSCME II)*,[10] the Ninth Circuit Court of Appeals reversed the trial court's decision. The court of appeals rejected the doctrine of comparable worth, holding that reliance on market forces to set wages did not violate Title VII. The appeals court stated that the value of a job depends on factors other than just the actions performed on the job, factors such as the availability of workers and the effectiveness of unions in negotiating wages. Moreover, the court stated that the legislative history of Title VII did not indicate that Congress intended "to abrogate fundamental economic principles such as the laws of supply and demand."[11]

AFSCME and the state of Washington reached a pay equity agreement in resolution of the comparable worth dispute. This agreement called for the state to spend some $482.4 million over six years to raise salaries of certain underpaid workers.

---

[9] 578 F. Supp. 846 (W.D. Wash. 1983).

[10] 770 F.2d 1401 (9th Cir. 1985).

[11] *Id.* at 1407.

In *American Nurses Ass'n v. State of Illinois*,[12] a sex discrimination case brought by nurses against the state of Illinois, the Seventh Circuit Court of Appeals stated in part:

> An employer (private or public) that simply pays the going wage in each of the different types of jobs in its establishment, and makes no effort to discourage women from applying for particular jobs, would justifiably be surprised to discover that it may be violating federal law because each wage rate and therefore the ratio between them have been found to be determined by cultural or psychological factors attributable to the history of male domination of society; that it has to hire a consultant to find out how it must, regardless of market conditions, change the wages it pays, in order to achieve equity between traditionally male and traditionally female jobs; and that it must pay back pay to boot.[13]

In cases dealing with comparable worth issues, employers have a valid defense if they relied on market forces to set wages. The *Gunther* decision may be shown to be consistent with cases such as *AFSCME II* in that the compensation system in *Gunther* tied wages to market rates, but the violation of Title VII occurred when it did not pay the same percentage of the market rate to women as it did to men. The decision not to pay the women the full rate was attributable to intentional sex discrimination.

CASE 14.2	COUNTY OF WASHINGTON V. GUNTHER
	SUPREME COURT OF THE UNITED STATES, 452 U.S. 161 (1981).

[The plaintiffs were four women employed as matrons at the Washington County, Oregon, jail. The county also employed male corrections officers and deputy sheriffs. The matrons under Oregon law guarded female inmates, while the corrections officers and deputy sheriffs guarded male inmates. Effective February 1, 1973, the matrons were paid monthly salaries of between $525 and $668, while the salaries for the male guards ranged from $701 to $904. The plaintiffs filed suit under Title VII, alleging that they were paid unequal wages for work substantially equal to that performed by their male counterparts and, in the alternative, that part of the pay differential was attributable to intentional sex discrimination. The district court found that the male corrections officers supervised up to 10 times as many prisoners per guard as did the matrons and that the females devoted much of their time to less valuable clerical duties, such as processing fingerprint cards and mug shots, filing reports, keeping medical records, recording deputy sheriffs' activities, and censoring mail. The district court held that the plaintiffs' jobs were not substantially equal to those of the male guards, and the plaintiffs were thus not entitled to equal pay. The district court also dismissed the claim based on intentional sex discrimination, holding as a matter of law that sex-based wage discrimination cannot be brought under Title VII unless it would satisfy the "equal work" standard of the Equal Pay Act. The court of appeals reversed the district court on this point, and the Supreme Court granted certiorari.]

BRENNAN, J....

The question presented is whether § 703(h) of Title VII of the Civil Rights Act of 1964, restricts Title VII's prohibition of sex-based wage discrimination to claims of equal pay for equal work.

continued

---

[12] 783 F.2d 716 (7th Cir. 1986).

[13] *Id.* at 720.

I.

We emphasize at the outset the narrowness of the question before us in this case. Respondents' claim is not based on the controversial concept of "comparable worth," under which plaintiffs might claim increased compensation on the basis of a comparison of the intrinsic worth or difficulty of their job with that of other jobs in the same organization or community. Rather, respondents seek to prove, by direct evidence, that their wages were depressed because of intentional sex discrimination, consisting of setting the wage scale for female guards, but not for male guards, at a level lower than its own survey of outside markets and the worth of the jobs warranted. The narrow question in this case is whether such a claim is precluded by the last sentence of § 703(h) of Title VII, called the "Bennett Amendment."

II.

Title VII makes it an unlawful employment practice for an employer "to discriminate against any individual with respect to his compensation, terms, conditions, or privileges of employment, because of such individual's ... sex...." The Bennett Amendment to Title VII, however, provides:

> "It shall not be an unlawful employment practice under this subchapter for any employer to differentiate upon the basis of sex in determining the amount of the wages or compensation paid or to be paid to employees of such employer if such differentiation is authorized by the provisions in Section 206(d) of Title 29." Section 703(h).

To discover what practices are exempted from Title VII's prohibitions by the Bennett Amendment, we must turn to § 206(d) of Title 29—the Equal Pay Act—which provides the relevant part:

> "No employer having employees subject to any provisions of this section shall discriminate, within any establishment in which such employees are employed, between employees on the basis of sex by paying wages to employees in such establishment at a rate less than the rate at which he pays wages to employees of the opposite sex in such establishment for equal work on jobs the performance of which requires equal skill, effort, and responsibility, and which are performed under similar working conditions, except where such payment is made pursuant to (i) a seniority system; (ii) a merit system; (iii) a system which measures earnings by quantity or quality of

production; or (iv) a differential based on any other factor other than sex." 29 U.S.C. § 206(d)(1).

On its face, the Equal Pay Act contains three restrictions pertinent to this case. First, its coverage is limited to those employers subject to the Fair Labor Standards Act. Thus, the Act does not apply, for example, to certain businesses engaged in retail sales, fishing, agriculture, and newspaper publishing. Second, the Act is restricted to cases involving "equal work on jobs the performance of which requires equal skill, effort, and responsibility, and which are performed under similar working conditions." Third, the Act's four affirmative defenses exempt any wage differentials attributable to seniority, merit, quantity or quality of production, or "any other factor other than sex."

Petitioner argues that the purpose of the Bennett Amendment was to restrict Title VII sex-based wage discrimination claims to those that could also be brought under the Equal Pay Act, and thus that claims not arising from "equal work" are precluded. Respondents, in contrast, argue that the Bennett Amendment was designed merely to incorporate the four affirmative defenses of the Equal Pay Act into Title VII for sex-based wage discrimination claims. Respondents thus contend that claims for sex-based wage discrimination can be brought under Title VII even though no member of the opposite sex holds an equal but higher-paying job, provided that the challenged wage rate is not based on seniority, merit, quantity or quality of production, or "any other factor other than sex." The Court of Appeals found respondents' interpretation the "more persuasive." 623 F.2d at 1311, 20 FEP Cases, at 797. While recognizing that the language and legislative history of the provision are not unambiguous, we conclude that the Court of Appeals was correct....

The legislative background of the Bennett Amendment is fully consistent with this interpretation....

> "Mr. BENNETT. Mr. President, after many years of yearning by members of the fair sex in this country, and after very careful study by the appropriate committees of Congress, last year Congress passed the so-called Equal Pay Act, which became effective only yesterday.
> "By this time, programs have been established for the effective administration of this act. Now, when the civil rights bill is under consideration, in which the word 'sex' has been inserted in many places, I do not believe sufficient attention

continued

may have been paid to possible conflicts between the wholesale insertion of the word 'sex' in the bill and in the Equal Pay Act.

"The purpose of my amendment is to provide that in the event of conflicts, the provisions of the Equal Pay Act shall not be nullified.

"I understand that the leadership in charge of the bill have agreed to the amendment as a proper technical correction of the bill. If they will confirm that understand [sic], I shall ask that the amendment be voted on without asking for yeas and nays.

"Mr. HUMPHREY. The amendment of the Senator from Utah is helpful. I believe it is needed. I thank him for his thoughtfulness. The amendment is fully acceptable.

"Mr. DIRKSEN. Mr. President, I yield myself 1 minute.

"We were aware of the conflict that might develop, because the Equal Pay Act was an amendment to the Fair Labor Standards Act. The Fair Labor Standards Act carries out certain exceptions.

"All that the pending amendment does is recognize those exceptions, that are carried in the basic act.

"Therefore, this amendment is necessary, in the interest of clarification." 110 Cong. Rec. 13647 (1964).

As this discussion shows, Senator Bennett proposed the Amendment because of a general concern that insufficient attention had been paid to the relation between the Equal Pay Act and Title VII, rather than because of a *specific* potential conflict between the statutes. His explanation that the Amendment assured that the provisions of the Equal Pay Act "shall not be nullified" in the event of conflict with Title VII may be read as referring to the affirmative defenses of the Act. Indeed, his emphasis on the "technical" nature of the Amendment and his concern for not disrupting the "effective administration" of the Equal Pay Act are more compatible with an interpretation of the Amendment as incorporating the Act's affirmative defenses, as administratively interpreted, than as engrafting all the restrictive features of the Equal Pay Act onto Title VII....

Thus, although the few references by Members of Congress to the Bennett Amendment do not explicitly confirm that its purpose was to incorporate into Title VII the four affirmative defenses of the Equal Pay Act in sex-based wage discrimination cases, they are broadly consistent with such a reading, and do not support an alternative reading.

Our interpretation of the Bennett Amendment draws additional support from the remedial purposes of Title VII and the Equal Pay Act....

Under petitioner's reading of the Bennett Amendment, only those sex-based wage discrimination claims that satisfy the "equal work" standard of the Equal Pay Act could be brought under Title VII. In practical terms, this means that a woman who is discriminatorily underpaid could obtain no relief—no matter how egregious the discrimination might be—unless her employer also employed a man in an equal job in the same establishment, at a higher rate of pay. Thus, if an employer hired a woman for a unique position in the company and then admitted that her salary would have been higher had she been male, the woman would be unable to obtain legal redress under petitioner's interpretation. Similarly, if an employer used a transparently sex-biased system for wage determination, women holding jobs not equal to those held by men would be denied the right to prove that the system is a pretext for discrimination.

III.

Petitioner argues strenuously that the approach of the Court of Appeals places "the pay structure of virtually every employer and the entire economy ... at risk and subject to scrutiny by the federal courts." It raises the spectre that "Title VII plaintiffs could draw any type of comparison imaginable concerning job duties and pay between any job predominantly performed by women and any job predominantly performed by men." But whatever the merit of petitioner's arguments in other contexts, they are inapplicable here, for claims based on the type of job comparisons petitioner describes are manifestly different from respondents' claim. Respondents contend that the County of Washington evaluated the worth of their jobs; that the county determined that they should be paid approximately 95 percent as much as the male correctional officers; that it paid them only about 70 percent as much, while paying the male officers the full evaluated worth of their jobs; and that the failure of the county to pay respondents the full evaluated worth of their jobs can be proven to be attributable to intentional sex discrimination. Thus, respondents' suit does not require a court to make its own subjective assessment of the value of the male and female guard jobs, or to attempt by statistical technique or other method to quantify the effect of sex discrimination on the wage rates.

continued

We do not decide in this case the precise contours of lawsuits challenging sex discrimination in compensation under Title VII. It is sufficient to note that respondents' claims of discriminatory undercompensation are not barred by § 703(h) of Title VII merely because respondents do not perform work equal to that of male jail guards. The judgment of the Court of Appeals is therefore

Affirmed.

REHNQUIST, J., joined by BURGER, C. J., and STEWART and POWELL, J. J., Dissenting...

The Court today holds a plaintiff may state a claim of sex-based wage discrimination under Title VII without even establishing that she has performed "equal or substantially equal work" to that of males as defined in the Equal Pay Act. Because I believe that the legislative history of both the Equal Pay Act and Title VII clearly establish that there can be no Title VII claim of sex-based wage discrimination without proof of "equal work," I dissent....

Case Questions

1. What does the Bennett Amendment provide?
2. What did the employer argue was the purpose of the Bennett Amendment?
3. State the Supreme Court's decision.
4. If the equal work standard were to apply, could situations exist where a discriminatorily underpaid woman would be unable to obtain a remedy?

SECTION 123: AGE DISCRIMINATION

The Age Discrimination in Employment Act of 1967 (ADEA) as amended forbids discrimination against men and women over 40 years of age by employers, unions, employment agencies, and the federal government.[14] The U.S. Supreme Court has held that state and local government workers do not have the right to sue their employers for monetary damages under the ADEA.[15] However, state law prohibits age discrimination in nearly every state of the union.

Enforcement of the ADEA is the responsibility of the EEOC. Procedures and time limitations for filing and processing ADEA charges are the same as those under Title VII. After receiving a right-to-sue letter from the EEOC, the aggrieved person has 90 days to initiate a lawsuit in a federal court.

The *EEOC v. Liggett & Myers, Inc.*[16] decision involving a fact pattern the trial court referred to as a "sad saga beginning in 1971" resulted in back wages plus liquidated damages for over 100 terminated employees due to the employer's intentional violations of the ADEA. After more than four decades of experience under the ADEA, it is now fair to say that the law has curtailed widespread arbitrary age-biased terminations of older employees, as was evident in the *Liggett & Myers* case, and age is no longer used as a valid selection criterion in properly run workplaces. However, mature workers continue to experience great difficulties in the hiring process. In addition, a sizeable number of individual ADEA cases are pursued before the EEOC and the courts each year regarding assertions of unlawful or

---

[14] 29 U.S.C. § 623. Employees of the U.S. Senate, the U.S. House of Representatives, and the Executive Branch are also protected from age discrimination under special procedures set forth in the Government Employees Right Act of 1991. Pub. L. 102-166, November 21, 1991.

[15] *Kimel v. Florida Board of Regents*, 528 U.S. 62 (2000).

[16] 29 FEP 1611 (E.D.N.C. 1982).

pretextual reasons for terminations or failures to promote, and plaintiffs have very significant challenges in meeting their burdens of proof, as indicated in the *Zippittelli v. J.C. Penney Company* case presented in this section.[17] Employers presently must scrutinize criteria used in making reductions in forces because employers have the burden of production and persuasion when they raise "reasonable factors other than age" affirmative defenses in disparate impact ADEA claims, as required by a 2008 Supreme Court decision, *Meacham v. Knolls Atomic Power Laboratory.*[18]

DISPARATE TREATMENT

Most ADEA suits are brought on a disparate treatment theory of intentional discrimination because of age. Procedures are similar in many respects to those previously set forth in the text on Title VII. The burden-of-proof framework of the *McDonnell Douglas prima facie* case is commonly applied to ADEA disparate treatment cases. However, the *prima facie* showing of age discrimination does not require that the plaintiff's replacement (if any) be a person younger than the protected age group—that is, younger than 40 years old. In *O'Connor v. Consolidated Coin Caterers Corp.*,[19] the Supreme Court held that replacement by someone under 40 was not a necessary element of an ADEA *prima facie* case. The *McDonnell Douglas* model is not the exclusive method of assessing an ADEA disparate treatment case. For example, where there is direct evidence of discrimination, a determination may be made on that basis alone.

In the *Zippittelli v. J.C. Penney Company, Inc.* decision, presented in this section, the plaintiff, Joanne Zippittelli, had a conversation with her supervisor Ms. Benko where she told her supervisor that she suspected that she would not get the promotion she applied for because of her age. The supervisor asked her how old she was, and when Ms. Benko found out that Ms. Zippittelli was 63, the supervisor said that she would "probably not" get the position. This remark coupled with the fact that the plaintiff had better performance evaluations than the younger women awarded the promotion led the plaintiff to expend emotional and financial resources pursuing this ADEA claim in federal court. From the plaintiff's view, this was age discrimination. However, when analyzed by the court under a "direct evidence of discrimination" theory and under the *McDonnell Douglas* model, she had no case.

HOSTILE WORKING ENVIRONMENT

In the *Crawford v. Medina General Hospital* case, the U.S. Court of Appeals for the Sixth Circuit determined that a hostile working environment claim can be

---

[17] 2007 LEXIS 14243 (M.D. Pa. 2007). See K. M. Clermont and S. J. Schwab, "How Employment Discrimination Plaintiffs Fare in Federal Court," 1 *Journal of Empirical Legal Studies*, 429, 456 (2004) for the classic study by two Cornell University law professors who concluded, "Employment discrimination plaintiffs must swim against the tide—at pretrial, trial and appeal."

[18] 128 S.Ct. 2395 (2008).

[19] 517 U.S. 308 (1996).

brought under the ADEA.[20] However, the court held that the plaintiff did not meet her burden of proof in making out a *prima facie* case.

DISPARATE IMPACT

In *Smith v. City of Jackson, Mississippi*, presented in this section, the U.S. Supreme Court determined that disparate impact claims of age discrimination are permitted under the ADEA. The Court relied upon its Title VII *Griggs v. Duke Power Co.* precedent, which interpreted identical text to the ADEA, with the substitution of the word "age" for the words "race, color, religion, sex or national origin"; the narrowing of the coverage of the ADEA that permits employers to take actions that would otherwise be prohibited based on "reasonable factors other than age" (called the RFOA provision); and the EEOC regulations permitting disparate impact claims. The dissenting justices assert that in the nearly four decades since the law was enacted, the Court had never read it to impose liability on an employer without proof of discriminatory intent. The *Smith v. City of Jackson* court decided the disparate impact case before it against the petitioning police officers, finding that the city's larger pay raises to younger employees were based on a RFOA that responded to the city's legitimate goal of retaining its new police officers.

In *Meacham v. Knolls Atomic Power Laboratory*,[21] the Supreme Court held that the employer, defending a disparate impact claim under the Age Discrimination in Employment Act, has both the burden of production and the burden of persuasion when it raises the "reasonable factors other than age" (RFOA) affirmative defense. Knolls was required to reduce its workforce by some 31 jobs due to lack of work. Managers were instructed to score subordinates on three scales: "performance," "flexibility," and "critical skills." The scores were summed, along with points for years of service. Of the 31 employees laid off, 30 were at least 40 years old. Twenty-eight of these individuals sued Knolls on **disparate impact** (discriminatory results) claims under the ADEA, claiming that the workforce reduction process had a discriminatory impact on ADEA-protected employees. At trial, a statistical expert testified that the results so skewed according to age could rarely occur by chance and that scores for "flexibility" and "criticality," over which managers had the most discretionary judgment, had the firmest statistical ties to the outcomes. The jury found for Meacham and the other 27 plaintiffs. On appeal in August 2006, the Second Circuit's 2-1 decision overturned a $5 million jury verdict for the plaintiffs, with Knolls prevailing on its RFOA defense. However, the Court of Appeals expressed its conclusion in terms of the plaintiff's "failure to meet its burden of persuasion." The U.S. Supreme Court, as stated above, determined that the employer, Knolls, had both the burden of production and the burden of persuasion when it raised the RFOA defense. The Supreme Court vacated the Court of Appeals' 2006 decision and remanded the case to that court for further proceedings consistent with the proper legal rule.

---

[20] 69 EPD ¶ 44, 276 (6th Cir. 1996).

[21] *Meacham v. Knolls Atomic Power Laboratory*, 128 S.Ct. 2395 (2008).

AFTER-ACQUIRED EVIDENCE

In *McKennon v. Nashville Banner Publishing Co.*,[22] the Supreme Court held that an employee who is discharged in violation of the ADEA is not completely barred from relief when the employer subsequently discovers evidence of the employee's misconduct that would have been just cause for terminating the employee. Christine McKennon was terminated from her job as a confidential secretary by the Nashville Banner Publishing Company, publisher of the *Nashville Banner* newspaper, after 39 years of service due to "a reduction in force." She was then 62 years old. However, two days prior to her termination, the Banner hired a 26-year-old secretary. McKennon sued the *Banner* for age discrimination. In a deposition taken by the *Banner* in preparation for the ADEA lawsuit, the employer discovered that McKennon had copied certain confidential documents at work and had shown them to her husband. The *Banner* then sent her notification that such a breach of her responsibilities was a dismissal offense. The district court granted the *Banner's* motion for a summary judgment, determining that such a breach of confidentiality was a just cause for dismissal. Under the Supreme Court's decision, the plaintiff would receive back pay for an ADEA violation from the time of her discharge in violation of the Act until the employer discovered the after-acquired evidence that would justify her termination. The remedies of additional back pay, reinstatement, and front pay will generally be precluded when the after-acquired evidence justifies termination. The *McKennon* rule also should apply in Title VII, EPA, and ADA cases according to the EEOC.[23]

CASE 14.3	ZIPPITTELLI V. J.C. PENNEY COMPANY, INC.
	UNITED STATES DISTRICT COURT, 2007 LEXIS 14243 (M.D. PA. 2007).

[The promotion decision about which plaintiff Joanne Zippittelli complains came in 2004. In the summer of that year, plaintiff applied for the shift operations manager job after Personnel Manager James Johnson informed her it had become available. At the time, she was working as a general lead clerk in the Call Service Center. She was one of four women—all of whom had the same job title at the time—who applied for that job. Johnson interviewed the candidates, determining that three of the candidates, including the plaintiff, were qualified for the position. Johnson then ranked the three candidates, making plaintiff his third choice. Patti Cruikshank was Johnson's first choice, and after he consulted with his supervisor, J.C. Penney hired Cruikshank as shift operations manager.

Plaintiff blamed her age for her lack of success in seeking the promotion and told her supervisor, Anita Benko, of this suspicion. This supervisor asked her how old she was. When Benko found out she was 63, Benko said she would "probably not" get the position. Plaintiff made no formal complaint of age discrimination immediately after hearing this comment.

continued

---

[22] 513 U.S. 352 (1995).

[23] "EEOC Guidance on After-Acquired Evidence" No. 195, 002 (Dec. 14, 1995).

She did file a complaint of age discrimination with the Equal Employment Opportunity Commission in 2004, however. She received a right-to-sue letter from the EEOC in 2005. And the matter was tried in U.S. District Court.]

MUNLEY, J....

The Age Discrimination in Employment Act prohibits discrimination against an individual over age 40 with respect to "compensation, terms, conditions, or privileges of employment, because of an individual's age." ... To recover under the act, "a plaintiff must prove by a preponderance of the evidence that age was the determinative factor in the employer's decision at issue."...

Plaintiff here apparently contends that she has direct evidence of discrimination in the comment made by Anita Benko that she would "probably not" get a job after plaintiff revealed to Benko her age. We apply the same "direct evidence" test to claims of age discrimination that we do to claims of sex discrimination.... She points to only one remark about age from a person not involved in the decision about whether to promote her. Plaintiff could not convince a reasonable juror that this evidence proves that age was a substantial factor in the decision made by Johnson not to promote the plaintiff. Accordingly, we find that no direct evidence exists to prove that defendants discriminated on the basis of age.

Lacking direct evidence of discrimination, a plaintiff seeking recovery under the ADEA must first make out a prima facie case by showing (1) he is within the protected age class, i.e. over forty; (2) that he was qualified for the position at issue; (3) he was dismissed despite being qualified; and (4) he was replaced by a person sufficiently younger to permit an inference of age discrimination.... Once the plaintiff establishes this prima facie case, "the defendant has the burden of producing evidence that it had 'a legitimate, nondiscriminatory reason for the discharge.'" ... If the defendant produces such evidence, the burden shifts back to the plaintiff, who provide "evidence 'from which a factfinder could reasonably either (1) disbelieve the employer's articulated legitimate reasons[;] or (2) believe that an invidious discriminatory reason was more likely than not a motivating or determinative cause of the employer's action.'" ... Here, plaintiff was sixty-three years old at the time she applied for the promotion, and thus within the protected class. She has shown that she was qualified for the

position, regardless of age. She did not get the promotion applied for, and the job went to a woman younger than forty. Defendants agree that plaintiff has made out the prima facie case required by federal law.

Defendants argue, however, that it had legitimate, non-discriminatory reasons for its promotion decision and that plaintiff has no evidence with which to rebut that case.... [The defendants claim that their employment decision was based on a careful assessment of which employee best fit the demands of the position and that they found the plaintiff less qualified than the successful candidate in the area of ability to make independent decisions. The employer also found the candidate who was hired to be highly qualified based on her motivation to do the job and her ability to work with and inspire other employees.] We find that the defendants have met their burden, advancing legitimate non-discriminatory reasons to explain why they passed plaintiff over for a promotion. The burden now lies with plaintiff to demonstrate that defendants' reasons serve as pretext to avoid liability for their actual motivations.

In order to meet her burden of demonstrating that defendants' stated reasons for their promotion decision were pretext to mask a discriminatory motive, plaintiff must "[produce] sufficient evidence to raise a genuine issue of fact as to whether the employer's proffered reasons were not its true reasons for the challenged employment action." ... A plaintiff must do more, however, than simply demonstrate that the employer did not make the correct hiring decision: "to discredit the employer's proffered reason, the plaintiff cannot simply show that the employer's decision was wrong or mistaken, since the factual dispute at issue is whether a discriminatory animus motivated the employer, not whether the employer is wise, shrewd, prudent, or competent.'"

Plaintiff contends that she had better performance evaluations and that the younger worker actually promoted to the job had an inferior record in areas supposedly determinative of eligibility for promotion, like attendance. A jury could not use this evidence to find that defendants' stated reasons for its employment decision were mere pretext. That evidence could only be used to convince a jury that defendants were wrong in the employment decision they made, not that their mistake was motivated by an animus towards plaintiff because of her age. Federal courts do not sit to pass judgment on the wisdom of an employer's hiring

continued

decisions, but only on whether those decisions were made in a way that violated anti-discrimination law....

The only evidence plaintiff supplies of a discriminatory intent in relation to plaintiff's age comes in Benko's remark that plaintiff "probably" would not get the job when plaintiff revealed her age. We do not find this evidence sufficient for a jury to find that defendants' stated reasons served as a pretext to hide a discriminatory practice. Plaintiff has introduced no evidence that Benko was involved in the decision to award the promotion, nor that she was privy to the considerations of the managers who did make that decision. Benko made her remark in informal conversation, and it was not intended as any statement of company policy, formal or informal. Indeed, the comment seems to represent a pessimistic and sympathetic statement from a coworker who assumed that younger people had more advantages in the workplace. The remark was too temporally and situationally distant from the actual hiring decision to be seen as strong evidence of the employer's practice or attitude. This case is therefore like Brewer Quaker State Oil Refining Corp., 72 F.3d 326 (3d Cir. 1995). In that age discrimination lawsuit, the plaintiff pointed to a statement by the company's chief executive in a newsletter that two executives in their 40s represented the age group the company sought to hire and promote. The comment, made two years before the company decided to fire the plaintiff, seemed to the court simply a "stray remark" "made by a non-decisionmaker and temporally remote from the decision" in question. The comment was thus not worthy of "commanding weight."

The remark here is not relevant to the defendants' hiring decision. There is no evidence that the supervisor who made the remark had anything to do with the decision to promote Cruikshank instead of the plaintiff. Unlike the statement made by the Quaker State chief executive in a company publication, the statement here was made in an off-hand, informal way by a supervisor who had no role in the hiring decision. We cannot find that a jury could conclude that the statement was one that demonstrates that age was a motivating factor in the hiring decision that Johnson and J.C. Penney executives in Dallas made.

[Defendants' motion for summary judgment is GRANTED.]

Case Questions

1. If a conversation that an employee had with her supervisor about applying for a promotion results in a question about age and a response by the supervisor when she found out that the applicant was 63 that the applicant would "probably not" get the position, coupled with the fact that the applicant had better performance evaluations than the younger woman who was awarded the position, would not a reasonable layperson in the position of the applicant think that she had been discriminated against because of age?

2. Was the fact that the plaintiff had better performance evaluations than the younger worker promoted to the job evidence of discriminatory intent because of age?

3. Was Benko's remark that the plaintiff would "probably not get the job" when the plaintiff revealed her age sufficient evidence for a jury to find that the defendant's stated reasons served as a pretext to hide a discriminatory practice?

CASE 14.4	SMITH V. CITY OF JACKSON, MISSISSIPPI
	SUPREME COURT OF THE UNITED STATES, 544 U.S. 228 (2005).

[The City of Jackson, Mississippi, adopted a pay plan giving raises to all police officers and police dispatchers. In an effort to bring starting salaries up to regional averages, officers with less than five years' service received proportionately greater raises than those with more seniority, and most officers over 40 had more than five years of service. Petitioners, a group of older officers, filed suit under the ADEA, claiming that they were adversely affected by the plan because of their age.

The District Court granted the City summary judgment. On appeal, the Fifth Circuit ruled that disparate-impact claims are categorically unavailable under the ADEA. The U.S. Supreme Court granted certiorari.]

STEVENS, J....

During the deliberations that preceded the enactment of the Civil Rights Act of 1964, Congress considered

continued

and rejected proposed amendments that would have included older workers among the classes protected from employment discrimination. Congress did, however, request the Secretary of Labor to "make a full and complete study of the factors which might tend to result in discrimination in employment because of age and of the consequences of such discrimination on the economy and individuals affected." The Secretary's report, submitted in response to Congress' request, noted that there was little discrimination arising from dislike or intolerance of older people, but that "arbitrary" discrimination did result from certain age limits (hereinafter Wirtz Report).

In response to that report Congress directed the Secretary to propose remedial legislation, and then acted favorably on his proposal. As enacted in 1967, § 4(a)(2) of the ADEA, now codified as 29 U.S.C. § 623(a)(2), provided that it shall be unlawful for an employer "to limit, segregate, or classify his employees in any way which would deprive or tend to deprive any individual of employment opportunities or otherwise adversely affect his status as an employee, because of such individual's age...." 81 Stat. 603. Except for substitution of the word "age" for the words "race, color, religion, sex, or national origin," the language of that provision in the ADEA is identical to that found in § 703(a)(2) of the Civil Rights Act of 1964 (Title VII). Other provisions of the ADEA also parallel the earlier statute. Unlike Title VII, however, § 4(f)(1) of the ADEA, 81 Stat. 603, contains language that significantly narrows its coverage by permitting any "otherwise prohibited" action "where the differentiation is based on reasonable factors other than age" (hereinafter RFOA provision).

In determining whether the ADEA authorizes disparate-impact claims, we begin with the premise that when Congress uses the same language in two statutes having similar purposes, particularly when one is enacted shortly after the other, it is appropriate to presume that Congress intended that text to have the same meaning in both statutes. We have consistently applied that presumption to language in the ADEA that was "derived *in haec verba* from Title VII."

Our unanimous interpretation of § 703(a)(2) of the Title VII in *Griggs* is therefore a precedent of compelling importance.

Griggs, which interpreted the identical text at issue here, thus strongly suggests that a disparate-impact theory should be cognizable under the ADEA....

... It is, ... , in cases involving disparate-impact claims that the RFOA provision plays its principal role by precluding liability if the adverse impact was attributable to a nonage factor that was "reasonable." Rather than support an argument that disparate impact is unavailable under the ADEA, the RFOA provision actually supports the contrary conclusion....

The text of the statute, as interpreted in *Griggs*, the RFOA provision, and the EEOC regulations all support petitioners' view. We therefore conclude that it was error for the Court of Appeals to hold that the disparate-impact theory of liability is categorically unavailable under the ADEA....

Turning to the case before us, we initially note that petitioners have done little more than point out that the pay plan at issue is relatively less generous to older workers than to younger workers. They have not identified any specific test, requirement, or practice within the pay plan that has an adverse impact on older workers. As we held in *Wards Cove*, it is not enough to simply allege that there is a disparate impact on workers, or point to a generalized policy that leads to such an impact. Rather, the employee is "'responsible for isolating and identifying the *specific* employment practices that are allegedly responsible for any observed statistical disparities.'" 490 U.S., at 656 (emphasis added) (quoting *Watson*, 487 U.S., at 994). Petitioners have failed to do so. Their failure to identify the specific practice being challenged is the sort of omission that could "result in employers being potentially liable for 'the myriad of innocent causes that may lead to statistical imbalances....'" 490 U.S., at 657. In this case not only did petitioners thus err by failing to identify the relevant practice, but it is also clear from the record that the City's plan was based on reasonable factors other than age....

... In sum, we hold that the City's decision to grant a larger raise to lower echelon employees for the purpose of bringing salaries in line with that of surrounding police forces was a decision based on a "reasonable factor other than age" that responded to the City's legitimate goal of retaining police officers. Cf. *MacPherson v. University of Montevallo*, 922 F. 2d 766, 772 (CA11 1991)....

Accordingly, while we do not agree with the Court of Appeals' holding that the disparate-impact theory of recovery is never available under the ADEA, we affirm its judgment.

It is so ordered.

continued

Case Questions

1. Did the Court's decision make it easier for older workers to sue for age discrimination on the job?
2. Disparate impact claims exist where an employer's facially neutral employment practices such as the pay scale, benefits adjustments, or layoffs, though making no adverse references to age have a significantly adverse or disparate impact on older employees, and the specially identified practices in question are not shown to be based on reasonable factors other than age. What does the Court's ruling allowing disparate impact claims mean for employers when setting policies that may affect their older workers?
3. How did the Court decide the underlying controversy between the City and the older workers?

SECTION 124: PROHIBITED PRACTICES AND DAMAGES

Section 4(a) of the ADEA sets forth the employment practices that are unlawful under the Act, including the failure to hire because of age and the discharge of employees because of age. Labor organizations are prohibited from discriminating because of age or attempting to cause employees to violate the ADEA under Section 4(b) of the Act.

Examples of what not to do are set forth in excerpts from the *EEOC v. Liggett & Meyers, Inc.* decision, presented in this section. In this case, the employer was ordered to pay back wages and benefits plus liquidated damages to more than 100 terminated employees. The *Rhodes v. Guiberson Oil Tools* case, reported in this section, demonstrates the continuing problem of age discrimination in the workplace.

Liability under the ADEA depends on whether the protected trait—age—actually motivated the employer's decision. In *Hazen Paper Co. v. Biggins,*[24] the Supreme Court held that an employer did not violate the ADEA just by interfering with an older employee's pension benefits that would have vested by virtue of the employee's years of service. The employer's decision to fire an older employee solely because he had nine plus years of service and was close to having his pension vested upon completion of ten years of service was not discrimination based on "age." It was, however, a violation of Section 510 of ERISA to fire the employee in order to prevent the individual's pension from vesting. (See Section 83 of this text.) But it was not, without more evidence proving age as a motivating factor, a violation of the ADEA.

DAMAGES

It should be noted that Section 7(b) of the ADEA allows for the doubling of damages in cases of "willful violations" of the Act. Consequently, an employer who willfully violates the ADEA is liable not only for back wages and benefits but also for "an additional amount as liquidated damages." Thus, individuals such as the employee terminated in the *Hazen Paper Co.* case, referred to above, had an economic incentive to bring an ADEA lawsuit in an attempt to qualify for double damages under Section 7(b) of the ADEA.

---

[24] 507 U.S. 604 (1993).

In *Trans World Airlines, Inc. v. Thurston*,[25] the Supreme Court held that where an employer's officers acted nonrecklessly and in good faith in attempting to determine whether their prohibition against pilots exercising bumping rights to flight engineer positions upon mandatory retirement as pilots at age 60 would violate the ADEA, their conduct was not "willful." Although determined to be violative of the ADEA, the plaintiffs were not entitled to double damages. The plaintiffs were, however, entitled to back wages and benefits.

In the *Hazen Paper Co.* decision, the Supreme Court clarified the definition of "willful" as meaning that the employer knew or showed reckless disregard for the matter of whether the conduct was prohibited by the ADEA. Once a "willful" violation has been shown, the employee need not demonstrate that the employer's conduct was outrageous in order to qualify for liquidated damages.

In *IRS Commissioner v. Schleier*,[26] the Supreme Court ruled that back pay and liquidated damages recovered under the ADEA are not excludable from gross income under the Internal Revenue Code. Schleier had received $72,800 in back pay and an equal amount in liquidated damages under a class action settlement against United Airlines resulting from its policy of forcing pilots to retire at age 60. The Court ruled that the damages were not based upon tort or tort-type rights, which would have qualified for exclusion from gross income.

CASE 14.5	EEOC v. LIGGETT & MEYERS, INC.
	U.S. DISTRICT COURT, 29 FEP 1611 (E.D.N.C. 1982).

MERHIGE, D. J....

Plaintiff's case rests upon its contention that pursuant to a plan or pattern, a large number of defendant's employees were discriminated against by the defendant company by reason of each being 40 years of age or older.

Defendant, on the other hand, denies any such plan or pattern and indeed that any employee has been discriminated against, by reason of age or any other reason, in either being terminated from his or her respective position or not being offered another position....

The sad saga seems to have begun in February 1971 when the Company appointed J. C. Gfeller, then 35 years of age, as its director of sales. Shortly thereafter, he also became vice president in charge of the Sales Department. At the time, the Company's sales had declined from a high 68.9 billion in 1952 to 33.5 billion in 1970. Cigarette sales continued to decline, as did the Company's percentage share of the market.

The sales quota for 1971 was established at 39 billion cigarettes, but it was reduced to 35 billion in September, and 32 billion was the actual amount sold in 1971.

The Hiring of New Top Management

The Company hired Ken McAllister as president of the cigarette and tobacco division, and Jack Southard as vice president of marketing. Both had consumer package goods backgrounds.

In February 1971 the Company hired John Gfeller as vice president of sales. His business background was consumer package goods. Gfeller's charge was to help turn around the decline in the Company's cigarette sales. He was expected to show a dramatic improvement in sales within 18 months.

As senior sales officer it was Gfeller's responsibility to achieve and maintain the distribution of the product line—to make sure the right amount of the product line was in the right place at the right time, properly priced

continued

---

[25] 469 U.S. 111 (1985).

[26] 67 FEP 1745 (Sup. Ct. 1996).

and displayed. The sales responsibility ended at the retail shelf. Inducing the consumer to take the product off the shelf once the sales department got it there was the responsibility of marketing....

Manpower Planning and Analysis—Age and Minority Reports

In late February 1971, Gfeller requested an analysis of field sales personnel showing ages and minority representation. He requested for each management level an age breakout in five-year groups and the average age for each level. For minority groups he asked for a breakout showing the numbers of each level and the percentage they represented.

In April 1971, Gfeller hired Tom McMorrow as Director of Sales Planning. His job was to maximize promotion effectiveness and coordinate all promotion activities. Also he reviewed all communications between field and headquarters and put a new Headquarters Communication Program into effect.

Gfeller requested and received two updates of the age report—one dated July 31, 1971, and another dated September 30, 1971. This information showed the average age of sales representatives to be 33 and that of first-line managers to be 42....

McMorrow was appointed National Field Sales Manager on June 21, 1971, and was instructed by Gfeller to find out what the problems were in the field that were causing the continuing sales decline. McMorrow went into the field and worked with all levels of the sales force and called on customers....

... Based on his visits and investigation, McMorrow concluded that field sales had an inferior management team compared to those of companies he had formerly worked for.

Personnel Changes—Sales Department

Thus, the Company set out on an intensive program of personnel changes. Gfeller and McMorrow instructed top management personnel to move against certain older managers working under their supervision. If the top manager delayed or sought to justify keeping the older manager, he was informed that he was "not getting the message." The key phrase used was that certain individuals were "not able to adapt" to the new procedures to be used by the Company. Throughout this period, Gfeller and McMorrow emphasized that they wanted young and aggressive people, that older individuals were not able to

conform or adapt to the new procedures. In specific reference to R. E. Moran, the defendant's top division manager for the year 1971, they made statements such as "he is over the hill" and "he is too old to learn." They also had a frequent saying when it was suggested that an employee had numerous years of experience: that it was not twenty years' experience, but rather one year's experience twenty times. Gfeller also commented in specific reference to L. D'Erasmo, who was 27 years of age in 1971, and who replaced R. E. Moran as area sales manager on September 1, 1972, that he was just the type of young man needed.

The terminations under Gfeller's plan to reorganize the sales force began with the region managers. They were all replaced with younger people. The first one terminated was W. F. Barrow, then 41 years of age, who had been employed in September 1954 and had been promoted to Central Region Manager in July 1970. He was terminated on September 10, 1971, when Gfeller and McMorrow told him he was no longer needed. The only reason they gave him was that he had a "human relations problem." He had no notice from defendant of any deficiency in his duties prior to his termination date. In fact, less than two months earlier Gfeller had notified him by letter dated July 15, 1971, in pertinent part, as follows:

> My heartiest congratulations on your outstanding performance during the month of June in achieving and exceeding your assigned quota.
>
> This month was particularly important to all of us in that it was the first month of our recently assigned new specific sales objectives, the first month of your new incentive compensation program and the first month, as I view it, that you were given specific directions, specific tools and you dramatically demonstrated your individual and personal ability to rise to the occasion.

Barrow, so the Court finds, had a history of outstanding performance....

C. Schmidt was the second region manager to be terminated. He was then 46 years of age, had been employed for 21 years, and had in 1969 been promoted to Western Region Manager. Without prior notice, McMorrow came to his office on October 28, 1971, and read a letter to him from Gfeller stating that for the best interest of the Company he should be terminated. McMorrow told him that he (McMorrow) felt nervous about having Schmidt as his representative. The Court finds that McMorrow

continued

told Schmidt he felt him inadequate. Schmidt did not receive a copy of the Gfeller letter. At that time his region ranked first for the year to date of the four regions, having met 97.56% of the assigned quota. The only document in his personnel file relating to his dismissal is a termination form indicating his resignation was requested for inability to perform duties. The Court finds that shortly after Schmidt's discharge, McMorrow stated he "needed younger men," and further that Schmidt "was not competent." Age obviously was a factor. Effective November 1, 1971, Hal Grant was appointed Western Region Manager.

Shortly thereafter, Grant began terminations in California. On February 7, 1972, Grant went to the office of E. W. Gardiner (age 46), the San Francisco Department Manager, and terminated him as of that date. Gardiner had no prior knowledge that he was to be terminated. Grant told him he was too old for the job and indicated that Gardiner did not fit the new youthful image the Company wanted to project. At the time, Gardiner's department had a 9% share of the market, which was substantially higher than the defendant's share of the national market. Grant never notified him of any charged deficiencies in his performance. Gardiner (age 46) was replaced by T. Jennings (age 32). Thereafter, on August 7, 1972, the date he received his final salary check, Gardiner wrote a letter to the president of Liggett & Meyers in which, among other things, he specified how Grant had informed him "I was too old for the job." He received no response to the letter....

T. Jennings immediately began to complete the reorganization of the San Francisco Department. He terminated R. J. Asche (age 41) on March 7, 1972. Asche had been an employee for 17 years. There was no BDR [an evaluation of the employee, called a business development review, or BDR] or evaluation prepared on Asche. The records in his personnel file reflect that he was a highly qualified employee. Jennings told him that he was to be replaced by a younger person. Jennings stated to him that many were to be replaced by younger, more qualified persons. Asche heard Jennings place an order with an employment agency for individuals under 35. Asche offered to take any other job, including sales representative, but Jennings told him that he would not fit in, he would not be happy, and they had no room for him....

[Here the court sets forth the details of numerous terminations in the sales department.]

A similar pattern occurred in the terminations of older sales representatives. J. T. Owens (age 42) and V. H. Hall (age 42) were terminated as sales representatives in the Nashville division on September 15, 1972, by H. M. Clunan (age 26), who was hired as a supervisor in Nashville on July 3, 1972. Clunan and D. O. Johnson (age 25), who was hired as the assistant department manager for the Memphis district on May 29, 1972, had visited Nashville after Clunan's appointment. At the first meeting in Nashville, Johnson commented to Clunan in the presence of Owens that some of the gentlemen were too old to be in the business. Later, Johnson asked Owens what a man his age was doing in this business. At this time, the Nashville division had five sales representatives: M. D. Garner (age 37), E. V. Holt (age 34), H. Vance Owens (age 33), and Hall. Clunan kept the youngest, H. Vance, and terminated the remaining four. Clunan replaced them with K. Ingram (age 23), hired September 1, 1972, B. Marshall (age 25), hired September 1, 1972, R. Puettman (age 23), employed September 1, 1972 (transferred from Alabama), and S. Roberts (age 23), hired October 9, 1972. Clunan also hired L. Winn (age 26) on September 18, 1972.

Clunan gave Owens no reason for termination. On the termination report, Clunan gave the reason that he felt Owens "could not adapt to new configuration." On the payroll notification form, the reason given was that Owens was "not adapted to our type of work." ...

[The facts set forth above demonstrate that the company was in violation of the Age Discrimination in Employment Act. The court held that the company's disavowal of any discriminatory attitude on age was overcome by overwhelming evidence. It finds that although there may have been factors other than age considered, in each instance, age was one of the determining factors and that this is impermissible under the law. The court determined that the violations of the company were willful, thereby triggering liquidated damages in addition to the lost wages and benefits.]

So ordered.

Case Questions

1. What options did the employer have at its disposal to improve the performance of the sales

continued

department other than the massive terminations of its older employees?

2. Speculate as to why Gfeller and McMorrow favored younger employees over older employees.

3. If a person, wrongfully forced to take early retirement, signs a release not to sue the company for violation of the ADEA, is that release a defense in a subsequent ADEA lawsuit?

CASE 14.6 | RHODES V. GUIBERSON OIL TOOLS
U.S. COURT OF APPEALS, 75 F.3D 989 (5TH CIR. 1996).

[Calvin Rhodes began his employment with Dresser Industries in 1955 as a salesman to the oil industry. In the throes of a severe economic downturn, Rhodes took a job selling oil field equipment at another Dresser company that became Guiberson Oil. After seven months, he was discharged, being told that it was a reduction in force and that he would be eligible for rehiring. At that time, he was 56 years of age. Within two months, Guiberson Oil hired a 42-year-old salesperson to do the same job. Rhodes sued Guiberson Oil for violating the ADEA. A jury found for the plaintiff, but a divided panel of the court of appeals rendered judgment for the employer. The matter was reheard *en banc* before the court of appeals.]

DAVIS, C. J....

Lee Snyder terminated Rhodes on October 31, 1986. Mr. Snyder told Rhodes he was part of a reduction in force (RIF) because of adverse economic conditions that persisted in the oilfield. Snyder told Rhodes, however that Guiberson would consider him for reemployment. Rhodes' personnel file reflected this same reason for the discharge. It was uncontradicted that Rhodes' position remained unfilled for only 6 weeks and that Guiberson knew at the time of termination or soon after that Rhodes would be replaced....

Lee Snyder, Rhodes' supervisor, testified via deposition that more than one salesman was clearly needed for the territory. Jack Givens, who had been Snyder's supervisor, testified that he told Snyder to replace Rhodes. Givens also testified that the business required more than one salesman, and that Rick Attaway had been hired to replace Rhodes. James Sewell, Snyder's other supervisor, testified that Rhodes was told that his position was being eliminated and that this statement was not true. The evidence supports a finding that Guiberson did not tell Rhodes the truth about why it was discharging him.

Guiberson Oil's defense at trial was not that Rhodes was RIF'd, but that he was discharged because of his poor work performance. Here too, Rhodes presented evidence to counter Guiberson's assertion....

Guiberson officials' testimony ... provided support for Rhodes' contention that Guiberson's "productivity" justification of his termination was a pretext for age discrimination. Lee Snyder testified that the memo placed in Rhodes' file explaining that Rhodes lacked technical expertise in downhole operations was substantially true but noted that it was also a "CYA ... (cover your _ss)" letter. Snyder testified that Rhodes was a good salesman with strong customer contacts and noted that Jack Givens—Snyder's boss who instructed Snyder to fire Rhodes—once said that he could hire two young salesmen for what some of the older salesmen were costing. Snyder quickly backed away from this statement and said that Givens had said he could hire two *new* salesmen for what some of the *others* were costing him. Givens said he was not aware of telling Snyder this. He also admitted that he had never talked to any of Rhodes' customers about Rhodes' performance as a salesman.

James Sewell, Snyder's other supervisor, testified that he had been very impressed with Rhodes' sales plans and that technical ability was not necessary to sell the product. He also testified that Rhodes had a poor customer base, but admitted that he did not know who Rhodes' customers were, had not talked to any of Rhodes' customers, and had no documentation to support his testimony about Rhodes' poor performance.

Lloyd Allen, the other salesman in the New Orleans office with whom Rhodes was compared, at first testified that his sales were much higher than Rhodes' but clarified on cross-examination that Rhodes' sales during the period in question nearly matched his own. Allen also admitted that the records supporting his testimony may have been incomplete,

continued

that Rhodes may have made another sale for which Allen had not credited him, and that another salesman may have been responsible for one of the sales Allen credited to himself....

Based on this evidence, the jury was entitled to find that the reasons given for Rhodes' discharge were pretexts for age discrimination. The jury was entitled to find that Guiberson's state[d] reason for discharging Rhodes—RIF—was false. Additionally, the reason for discharge that Guiberson Oil proffered in court to meet Rhodes' prima facie case was countered with evidence from which the jury could have found that Rhodes was an excellent salesman who met Guiberson Oil's legitimate productivity expectations. Viewing this evidence in the light most favorable to Rhodes, a reasonable jury could have found that Guiberson Oil discriminated against Rhodes on the basis of his age.

Conclusion

After considering all of the evidence in the record under the standard set forth in *Boeing Co. v. Shipman*, we are convinced that the district court properly accepted the jury's verdict on liability and willfulness. Guiberson Oil's motion for JNOV was properly denied....

[Judgment affirmed.]

Case Questions

1. Why did the employer tell Rhodes that he was being terminated because of a RIF, and why did supervisor Snyder place a memo in Rhodes's file about lacking expertise in downhole operations?

2. Evaluate the statement attributed to Jack Givens, the person who directed that Rhodes be fired, that "I could hire two young salesmen for what some of the older salesmen are costing."

3. Was the jury entitled to find that the reasons given by the employer for Rhodes's discharge were pretexts for age discrimination?

SECTION 125: THE OLDER WORKERS BENEFIT PROTECTION ACT; ADEA EXEMPTIONS AND DEFENSES

The Older Workers Benefit Protection Act (OWBPA) of 1990 amended the ADEA by prohibiting age discrimination in employee benefits and establishing minimum standards for determining the validity of waivers of age claims.[27] The OWBPA establishes that the ADEA prohibition of discrimination in "compensation, terms, conditions, or privileges of employment" encompasses all employee benefits, including those provided under a bona fide employee benefit plan. The 1990 Act amends the ADEA by adopting an "equal benefit or equal cost" standard, which provides that older workers must be given benefits that are at least equal to those provided to younger workers unless the employer can prove that the cost of providing an equal benefit would be more for an older worker than for a younger one.[28]

Early retirement incentive plans are exempted from the "equal benefit or equal cost" standard so long as the plans are bona fide. Employers may make Social

---

[27] Pub. L. 101–422, Oct. 16, 1990. This law reverses the Supreme Court's 1989 ruling in *Public Employees Retirement System of Ohio v. Betts*, which had the effect of exempting employee benefit programs from the ADEA.

[28] In *AARP v. EEOC*, 489 F.3d 558 (3d Cir. 2007), the Third Circuit Court of Appeals found that the EEOC had the authority under Section 9 of the ADEA to promulgate a rule that permits employer-sponsored benefit plans to "coordinate" retiree health benefits with a retiree's eligibility for Medicare or a state-sponsored health benefit program. The exemption effectively allowed employers to reduce or eliminate plan benefits for retirees 65 or older. AARP had argued that the rule was in violation of the OWBPA.

Security "bridge" payments to early retirees until the affected individuals reach eligibility age.

EXEMPTIONS AND DEFENSES

Section 4(f) of the ADEA sets forth certain exemptions from the strictures of the Act for employers. Thus, where an individual is terminated because of a bona fide seniority plan, the employer is not responsible for an ADEA violation. Also, if the employer discharges or disciplines an employee for "good cause," the employer is not in violation of the Act. Thus if a 60-year-old employee is discovered stealing from an employer, the employer may terminate that individual without being in violation of the Act.

State and local governments may make age-based hiring and retirement decisions for firefighters and law enforcement officers if the particular age limitation was in effect on March 3, 1983, and the action taken is pursuant to a bona fide hiring or retirement plan that is not a subterfuge to evade the purposes of the Act.[29] The ADEA permits the compulsory retirement of certain bona fide executives or high policymaking personnel at age 65.[30]

Section 4(f) provides employer defenses for "reasonable factors other than age" (RFOA) and "bona fide occupational qualifications reasonably necessary to the normal operation of a particular business" (BFOQ).

Generally, the BFOQ defense is raised by employers in cases involving public safety. This was the defense in *Hodgson v. Greyhound Lines Inc.*[31] There the company had a policy of limiting new driver applicants to persons under the age of 35. The district court judge held that Greyhound failed to meet its "burden of demonstrating that its policy of age limitation is reasonably necessary to the normal and safe operation of its business." However, the judge's ruling was overturned by a three-member panel of the U.S. court of appeals, holding that Greyhound did not violate the Act because its hiring age limitation had a rational basis in fact to believe that elimination of the policy would increase the likelihood or risk of harm to its passengers and others. The courts generally require the employer to prove that the BFOQ are reasonably necessary to the essence of its business and that the employer has a factual basis for believing that all or substantially all persons within the affected class would be unable to perform the duties involved safely and efficiently.

From time to time, large-scale reductions in forces (RIFs) have taken place in many industries and in public sector occupations such as schoolteachers, police, and fire personnel. Where the RIFs take place according to a bona fide seniority plan, no violation of the Act occurs. Where no collective bargaining agreement restricts an employer as to the manner of a RIF, the employer has the right to use reasonable factors other than age (RFOA) in implementing the reduction in force. For example, the employer may consider the relative performances of employees in each classification in deciding which employee to terminate. However, the risks are high that an employer may be found to be in violation of the ADEA because

---

[29] See Age Discrimination Employment Amendments of 1996, Pub. L. 104–208.

[30] § 12(c)(1).

[31] 499 F.2d 859, 7 FEP 817 (7th Cir. 1974).

statistical and other evidence of discrimination may be developed, as cost-cutting workforce reduction decisions tend to encourage the termination of highly paid, experienced employees, who tend to be older employees.

WAIVERS

Faced with the need to reduce labor costs, the risks of ADEA lawsuits, and the desire to treat older workers "right," many employers have opted to provide early retirement incentive programs. Employers commonly require that employees electing to take early retirement waive all claims against the employer, including their rights or claims under the ADEA. Congress recognized the utility of these programs in the Older Workers Benefit Protection Act of 1990, but wanted to make sure that employees fully understood that they were making knowing and voluntary waivers of ADEA claims. Congress established specific statutory requirements that must be met before an employee can waive the right to litigate ADEA claims as set forth in the *Oubre v. Entergy Operations, Inc.*, decision of the Supreme Court, presented in this section. The burden of proof for establishing such a waiver rests with the employer, who must establish that all of the requirements have been met. The requirements include the following:

1. The waiver is part of a written agreement.
2. It makes specific reference to rights or claims under the ADEA and may refer to Title VII and all other claims.
3. It does not apply to rights or claims that may occur after the agreement had been signed.
4. It is exchanged for value that is in addition to what the employee would otherwise be entitled to receive.
5. The employee is given written advice from the employer to consult with an attorney.
6. The employee is given a 21-day waiting period to consider the agreement and a 7-day period to revoke the agreement. For an agreement in connection with an early retirement program offered to a group of employees, the waiting period is 45 days rather than 21 and the employer must disclose all eligibility factors and the terms and inclusions of the program.

The courts have determined that an effective release must comply with each OWBPA prerequisite and that substantial compliance with the act's requirements is not adequate.[32]

| CASE 14.7 | OUBRE V. ENTERGY OPERATIONS, INC.
SUPREME COURT OF THE UNITED STATES, 522 U.S. 422 (1998). |

[Dolores Oubre worked as a scheduler at a power plant in Killona, Louisiana, run by her employer, Entergy Operations, Inc. In 1994, she received a poor performance rating. Oubre's supervisor met with her on January 17, 1995, and gave her the option of either improving her performance during the coming year or

continued

---

[32] *Peterson v. Seagate US, LLC*, 2008 U.S. Dist. LEXIS 42179 (D. Minn. May 28, 2008).

accepting a voluntary arrangement for her severance. She received a packet of information about the severance agreement and had 14 days to consider her options, during which she consulted with attorneys. On January 31, Oubre decided to accept. She signed a release in which she "agree[d] to waive, settle, release and discharge any and all claims, demands, damages, actions, or causes of action … that I may have against Entergy." In exchange, she received six installment payments over the next four months, totaling $6,258. In procuring the release, Entergy failed to comply in at least three respects with the requirements for a release under the Age Discrimination in Employment Act (ADEA), as set forth in the Older Workers Benefit Protection Act (OWBPA): It did not (1) give Oubre enough time to consider her options, (2) give her seven days to change her mind, and (3) make specific reference to ADEA claims. After receiving her last severance payment, Oubre sued Entergy, alleging constructive discharge on the basis of her age in violation of the ADEA and state law. Entergy moved for summary judgment, claiming Oubre had ratified the defective release by failing to return or offer to return the monies she had received. The district court agreed and entered summary judgment for Entergy. The Fifth Circuit affirmed.]

KENNEDY, J....

In 1990, Congress amended the ADEA by passing the OWBPA. The OWBPA provides: "An individual may not waive any right or claim under [the ADEA] unless the waiver is knowing and voluntary.... [A] waiver may not be considered knowing and voluntary unless at a minimum" it satisfies certain enumerated requirements, including the three listed above. 29 U.S.C. § 626(f)(1).

The statutory command is clear: An employee "may not waive" an ADEA claim unless the waiver or release satisfies the OWBPA's requirements. The policy of the Older Workers Benefit Protection Act is likewise clear from its title: It is designed to protect the rights and benefits of older workers. The OWBPA implements Congress' policy via a strict, unqualified statutory stricture on waivers, and we are bound to take Congress at its word. Congress imposed specific duties on employers who seek releases of certain claims created by statute. Congress delineated these duties with precision and without qualification: An

employee "may not waive" an ADEA claim unless the employer complies with the statute. Courts cannot with ease presume ratification of that which Congress forbids.

The OWBPA sets up its own regime for assessing the effect of ADEA waivers, separate and apart from contract law. The statute creates a series of prerequisites for knowing and voluntary waivers and imposes affirmative duties of disclosure and waiting periods. The OWBPA governs the effect under federal law of waivers or releases on ADEA claims and incorporates no exceptions or qualifications. The text of the OWBPA forecloses the employer's defense, notwithstanding how general contract principles would apply to non-ADEA claims.

The rule proposed by the employer would frustrate the statute's practical operation as well as its formal command. In many instances a discharged employee likely will have spent the monies received and will lack the means to tender their return. These realities might tempt employers to risk noncompliance with the OWBPA's waiver provisions, knowing it will be difficult to repay the monies and relying on ratification. We ought not to open the door to an evasion of the statute by this device.

Oubre's cause of action arises under the ADEA, and the release can have no effect on her ADEA claim unless it complies with the OWBPA. In this case, both sides concede the release the employee signed did not comply with the requirements of the OWBPA. Since Oubre's release did not comply with the OWBPA's stringent safeguards, it is unenforceable against her insofar as it purports to waive or release her ADEA claim. As a statutory matter, the release cannot bar her ADEA suit, irrespective of the validity of the contract as to other claims.

In further proceedings in this or other cases, courts may need to inquire whether the employer has claims for restitution, recoupment, or setoff against the employee, and these questions may be complex where a release is effective as to some claims but not as to ADEA claims. We need not decide those issues here, however. It suffices to hold that the release cannot bar the ADEA claim because it does not conform to the statue. Nor did the employee's mere retention of monies amount to a ratification equivalent to a valid release of her ADEA claims, since the retention did not comply with the OWBPA any more than the

continued

original release did. The statute governs the effect of the release on ADEA claims, and the employer cannot invoke the employee's failure to tender back as a way of excusing its own failure to comply.

We reverse the judgment of the Court of Appeals and remand for further proceedings consistent with this opinion.

It is so ordered.

[Justice Thomas and Chief Justice Rehnquist dissent.]

Case Questions

1. How did the release violate the ADEA?
2. Did the Court find that the retention of the money given by the employer in compliance with the severance agreement served as ratification equivalent to a valid release of ADEA claims?
3. Does the employer have a right to a setoff against this employee for the money paid to her by the employer?

CHAPTER QUESTIONS AND PROBLEMS

1. In reviewing a claim under the Equal Pay Act, do the courts require that the jobs in question be identical?
2. As a result of the passage of the Equal Pay Act of 1963 and Title VII of the Civil Rights Act of 1964, have the overall earnings for women become roughly comparable to that of men?
3. Can an employer terminate older employees as a reduction in the employer's workforce without violating the ADEA?
4. Della Janich was employed as a matron at the Yellowstone County Jail in Montana. The duties of the position of matron resemble those of a parallel male position—jailer. Both employees have the responsibility for booking prisoners, showering and dressing them, and placing them in the appropriate section of the jail depending on the sex of the offender. Because 95 percent of the prisoners at the jail were men and 5 percent were women, the matron was assigned more bookkeeping duties than the jailer. At all times during Della's employment at the jail, her male counterparts received $125 more per month as jailers.

   Della brought an action under the Equal Pay Act alleging discrimination against her in her wages because of her sex. The county sheriff denied the charge.

   What factors must be considered by the court when deciding this case under the Equal

Pay Act? Decide the case. [*Janich v. Sheriff*, 29 FEP 1195 (D. Mont.)]

5. The Federal Aviation Administration (FAA) has promulgated a federal regulation that prohibits airlines from employing pilots or copilots past age 60. The FAA's rule is recognized by the courts as a bona fide occupational qualification under the ADEA due to the administration's recognition that the possible onset of disease or debilitating condition would pose a flight safety risk.

   Western Airlines maintained a policy that all flight deck personnel must retire at age 60. Flight deck personnel include the pilot, copilot, and second officer (sometimes referred to as a flight engineer). The duties of a flight engineer are performed at a separate instrument panel, where various systems necessary for the operation of the aircraft, such as the electrical and hydraulic systems, are monitored and adjusted. The engineer does not manipulate the flight controls, and in the event of an emergency, all pilots and copilots having previously served as flight engineers are qualified to perform the necessary duties.

   Ron worked as a flight engineer for Western Airlines for over 30 years. As his 60th birthday approached, he informed Western management that he wanted to continue working past age 60. The airline told Ron that as members of the flight deck, second officers were required to retire at 60 for the same reasons as pilots and copilots.

Ron, Criswell, and others brought an action against Western under the Age Discrimination in Employment Act, claiming that Western's mandatory retirement policy was a form of age discrimination against flight engineers. Western denied the claim.

What defenses, if any, are available to Western Airlines to support its retirement policy? Has Western engaged in age discrimination? Decide the case. [*Western Air Lines, Inc. v. Criswell et al*, 472 U.S. 400]

6. Carlyle Cline, age 42, was employed for 10 years by Roadway Express Company, most recently as a loading dock supervisor at a Roadway terminal in North Carolina. Cline had received periodic merit pay raises, and his personnel file contained an even amount of both complimentary and critical evaluations by supervisors. When R. W. Hass became vice president for Roadway's southern division, he decided that the division needed to "upgrade" the quality of its personnel. Hass directed terminal managers to "look at" employees who had been with the company for five years without being promoted and decide whether they should be replaced with higher-quality employees, preferably college graduates. Thus, the ultimate decision regarding "promotability" was left to the terminal managers. They were not told that they were not to consider age when determining promotability. After the announcement of the new policy, Cline was discharged and classified "unpromotable." The terminal manager compiled a list of negative comments from Cline's file as evidence that Cline was discharged for "poor work performance." Roadway immediately replaced Cline with a man in his early 30s.

Cline brought an action against Roadway under the Age Discrimination in Employment Act, claiming he was discharged "because of his age in violation of the Act." Roadway maintained that Cline was discharged because of poor work performance.

Has Roadway violated the ADEA? Decide the case. [*Cline v. Roadway Express*, 29 FEP 1365 (4th Cir.)]

7. Harris-Stowe State College devised a reduction-in-force plan that selected both tenured and nontenured faculty members for termination. Leftwich, a 47-year-old tenured biology professor, sued the college for age discrimination under the ADEA. The college articulated its rationale for the termination plan based on tenure, stating that younger, nontenured faculty would have new ideas and that since tenured faculty were generally paid more than untenured faculty, a greater cost savings per person would be achieved by eliminating some tenured positions. The college states that its RIF plan never referred to age and thus it clearly did not violate the ADEA. Leftwich disagrees. Decide. [*Leftwich v. Harris-Stowe State College*, 702 F.2d 686 (8th Cir.)]

8. Local 350 represents pipe fitters and plumbers in northern Nevada and parts of California. Together with industry employers, Local 350 operates a hiring hall. The hiring dispatcher keeps four "out-of-work lists" with different qualifications and priorities from which members are hired. The dispatcher sends members out to jobs in the order in which they signed up. Donald Pilot, a member of Local 350, retired in 1983. After retirement, he paid retired members' dues. In 1984, he decided to return to work and signed onto the out-of-work list. Local 350 removed his name from the list, stating he was not eligible. In a letter dated April 20, 1984, Local 350 informed Pilot that "as a retiree, having applied for and been granted pension, you are not presently eligible for dispatch through the UA Local 350 Hiring Hall." The EEOC claims that Local 350's policy violates 29 U.S.C. § 623(c)(2) because it discriminates against older workers.

Section 623(c)(2) provides:

It shall be unlawful for a labor organization....
(2) to limit, segregate, or classify its membership,

or fail or refuse to refer for employment any individual, in any way which would deprive or tend to deprive any individual of employment opportunities or otherwise adversely affect his status as an employee or as an applicant for employment, because of such individual's age.

Local 350 defends that its policy is not discriminatory because the "but for" cause of discrimination is not the retiree's age, but his voluntary decision to retire. Decide. [*EEOC v. Local 350, Plumbers and Pipefitters*, 982 F.2d 1305 (9th Cir.)]

9. Mary Ann Crawford filed suit against her employer, Medina General Hospital, as well as her supervisor, Darla Kermendy, alleging that the defendants discriminated against her in violation of the Age Discrimination in Employment Act of 1967 by creating a hostile working environment. Crawford was once passing the door of a room where a group of people were having a pizza party. One of the five looked out and saw her pass and said, "It's just my luck in an office with an old dumb side to have to sit on that side." Crawford claims that Kermendy was in the room at the time and "laughed and pointed and looked at [the woman making the comment]" and said, "Oh, that's good." That comment apparently referred to the fact that a number of the older women sat on one side of the office. Crawford claims that the side was referred to as "the old side, the dumb side, worthless side." Crawford asserts that the office is "totally divided" on the basis of age. She contends that in addition to verbal insults, the older women are "not included in anything," such as parties, as well as not provided information about minor changes in office procedures. She further contends that Kermendy "calls the young people in[to Kermendy's office] and questions them about what the older people are doing, what they are saying, and then she encourages them to go out and confront those people." She claims that Kermendy "called attention" to Crawford's "extremely sensitive hearing" in a staff meeting once and that Kermendy said that all another older worker who had false teeth "wanted for Christmas was her front teeth." It is Crawford's belief that these comments are age-related. Crawford herself referred to one coworker as "the widow" because "she always wears black." Crawford nicknamed one supervisor "Pat" because "at times [Crawford feel[s] [the supervisor is] pathetic." Another coworker is nicknamed "Sluggo" because "she reminds [Crawford] of that cartoon character." Another is "Freak" because "she wears outlandish clothes and hairdos and that type of thing." Crawford calls two coworkers "Miss Piggy" and another "fasto." ... Can a hostile working environment claim be brought under the ADEA? If so, how would you decide this case? [*Crawford v. Medina General Hospital*, 69 EPD ¶ 44, 276 (6th Cir.)]

Disability Discrimination Laws—Workers' Compensation, SSDI and the ADA—Medical and Military Leaves

CHAPTER **15**

SECTION

- 126 Discrimination against Disabled Workers
- 127 The Rehabilitation Act of 1973
- 128 The Amended Americans with Disabilities Act
- 129 Workers' Compensation: Relationship to the ADA
- 130 Accommodation between SSDI and the ADA
- 131 Family and Medical Leaves of Absence
- 132 Military Leaves and Reemployment Rights

SECTION 126: DISCRIMINATION AGAINST DISABLED WORKERS

Some 53 million Americans have one or more physical or mental disabilities. Some impairments are obvious, such as paraplegia or blindness. Others may not be readily noticeable, such as heart disease, high blood pressure, and diabetes. In some cases, persons have recovered from their disabilities but have encountered job discrimination because of their past medical records. Cancer and mental or emotional disorders are examples of past medical conditions that may be associated with job discrimination.

543

The right of "handicapped persons" to enjoy equal employment opportunities was established on the federal level with the enactment of the Rehabilitation Act of 1973.[1] Although not designed specifically as an employment discrimination measure but rather as a comprehensive plan to meet many of the needs of the handicapped, the Rehabilitation Act does contain three sections that provide guarantees against discrimination in employment. As set forth below in detail, Section 501 of the Act is applicable to the federal government itself, Section 503 applies to federal contractors, and Section 504 applies to the recipients of federal funds.

Title I of the Americans with Disabilities Act of 1990 (ADA)[2] extends employment protection for disabled persons beyond the federal level to state and local governmental agencies and to all private employers with 15 or more employees. The ADA refers to *qualified individuals with disabilities* as opposed to the term *handicapped persons* used in the Rehabilitation Act. In drafting the ADA, Congress relied heavily on the language of the Rehabilitation Act and its regulations. It was anticipated that the body of case law developed under the Rehabilitation Act would provide guidance in the interpretation and application of the ADA. However, protections for individuals were eroded by U.S. Supreme Court decisions in 1999 and 2002. With the cooperation and agreement of both the employer and disability communities the ADA Amendments Act of 2008 became law, effective January 1, 2009, effectively overturning the Supreme Court decisions and restoring the original Congressional intent to provide broad coverage to protect individuals who face discrimination on the basis of disability.

The EEOC is responsible for enforcing the employment provisions of the ADA under the same procedures as Title VII of the Civil Rights Act of 1964.[3]

Moreover, in cases of *intentional* disability discrimination, the Civil Rights Act of 1991 allows for reinstatement, hiring or promotion with back pay, and attorney fees plus compensatory and punitive damages, subject to the same cap on damages as applied to sex and religious discrimination cases. Congress specified that the capped compensatory and punitive damages are only available in "intentional" cases.

In cases involving bias on the basis of an asserted lack of reasonable accommodation for a disability, damages may not be awarded against a covered entity that makes a good faith effort to reasonably accommodate a person with a disability that would provide that individual with an equally effective opportunity.

Under the Rehabilitation Act, disabled individuals did not have the same private rights of action and remedies as are afforded disabled persons under the Civil Rights Act of 1991.

Workers' compensation laws are also considered in this chapter. The Occupational Safety and Health Act (OSHA) of 1970 has had a significant impact on the improvement of workplace safety and health. Workers' compensation laws and the resulting insurance costs assessed to employers based on the quantity and monetary amounts of claims also provide a significant incentive for employers to

---

[1] 29 U.S.C. §§ 701–794.

[2] Pub. L. 101-336, 42 U.S.C. §§ 12101–12117. ADA Amendments Act of 2008, P.L. 110-325 (Sept. 25, 2008).

[3] ADA §§ 107.

provide a safe work environment. Inevitably there will be occupational injuries, and some conflicts may arise as to employers' obligations to employees with occupational injuries covered under state workers' compensation laws and their obligations to disabled employees protected under the ADA who are not occupationally injured. However, with the existence of these federal and state laws and the general acceptance by the business and governmental communities of the fundamental fairness of providing the basic dignity of a work life for disabled Americans, there have been expanded opportunities in our society for disabled persons. The *Quaker Oats Co. v. Ciha* case, presented later in this chapter, not only sets forth some basic principles of workers' compensation law but also provides insight into the extensive accommodations made by an employer for a severely disabled employee.

The Family and Medical Leave Act (FMLA) entitles eligible employees to a medical leave for "a serious health condition that makes the employee unable to perform the functions of the employee's position."[4] An on-the-job injury may be medically certified as a serious health condition entitling the employee to notice that his or her workers' compensation absences will count as an FMLA leave. The FMLA, which also deals with employee leaves involving birth or adoption of a child and leave to care for a family member, is covered in this chapter.

SECTION 127: THE REHABILITATION ACT OF 1973

SECTION 501

Section 501 of the Rehabilitation Act requires the federal government as an employer to develop and implement affirmative action plans on behalf of handicapped employees. Congress enacted Section 501 with the expectation that governmental policy regarding the employment of handicapped individuals would serve as a model for other employers. In *Mantolete v. Bolger*,[5] a person with epilepsy sued the U.S. Postal Service under Section 501 because she was denied a position as a letter-sorting machine operator because of her handicap. The court of appeals overturned the trial court's decision in favor of the Postal Service. The case was remanded for further consideration based on the requirement that the Postal Service demonstrate that the individual's handicap would result in a reasonable probability of substantial harm to Mantolete and/or her coworkers if she were to work the machine. The court made clear that employment decisions cannot be based on unsubstantiated generalizations and stereotypes, but must instead be made on the basis of individual qualifications, taking into account the employee's handicap.

SECTION 503

Section 503 requires all contractors having federal contracts in excess of $2,500 to take affirmative action to employ the handicapped. Enforcement of Section 503 is carried out by the Department of Labor's Office of Federal Contract Compliance

---

[4] 29 U.S.C. §§ 2601-2654 (1993) at §§ 2612(a)(1).
[5] 767 F.2d 1416, 38 FEP 1081 (9th Cir. 1985).

Programs (OFCCP). There is no private right of action under Section 503.[6] A handicapped individual must file a complaint with the OFCCP within 180 days of the occurrence of the alleged discriminating act in violation of Section 503. The complaint will then be investigated, and thereafter the matter may be heard at an administrative hearing. If a finding of discrimination is made and the employer disagrees with the finding, the OFCCP will initiate legal proceedings. The vast majority of Section 503 cases are resolved at or prior to the hearing before the administrative law judge.

SECTION 504

Section 504 of the Rehabilitation Act deals with discrimination in broader terms than the affirmative action requirements of Section 503. Section 504 prohibits federally funded programs and government agencies from excluding from employment an "otherwise qualified handicapped individual ... solely by reason of [his or her] handicap." Enforcement of Section 504 rests with each federal agency providing financial assistance. The Attorney General of the United States has responsibility for the coordination of the enforcement efforts of the agencies. A private right of action for compensatory damages in cases of intentional discrimination exists under Section 504 so long as all administrative remedies have been exhausted.[7]

Under the Rehabilitation Act, as amended in 1974, a **handicapped person** is defined as one who (1) has a physical or mental impairment which substantially limits one or more of the person's major life activities, (2) has a record of such impairment, or (3) is regarded as having such an impairment. The term **major life activity** includes such functions as caring for oneself, seeing, speaking, or walking.

To be entitled to the protection of the Rehabilitation Act with respect to employment, the individual must meet the requirements set forth in the definition of a handicapped person and must be an "otherwise qualified ... individual" as set forth in Section 504. An **otherwise qualified individual** is one who can perform "the essential functions" of the job in question.

The *Cook v. State of Rhode Island Department of MHRH* decision, presented in this section, is an application of the Rehabilitation Act to the state's rejection of an extremely overweight individual for employment.

CONTAGIOUS DISEASES

In *School Board of Nassau County, Florida v. Arline,* presented in this section, the Supreme Court determined that a person afflicted with tuberculosis may be a handicapped person as defined in Section 504. The fact that such a person is also contagious does not remove that person from Section 504's coverage. Under *Arline,* a district court must determine whether the handicapped person is "otherwise qualified" under Section 504. The district court must conduct an individualized inquiry and make appropriate findings of fact based on reasonable medical judgments, given the state of medical knowledge, about (1) the nature of the risk (e.g., how

---

[6] See *Auffant v. Searle & Co.,* 25 FEP 1254 (D.P.R. 1981), and *Davis v. UAL, Inc.,* 622 F.2d 120, 26 FEP 1527 (2d Cir. 1981).

[7] See *Conrail v. Darrone,* 465 U.S. 624 (1984).

the disease is transmitted), (2) the duration of the risk (how long the carrier is infectious), (3) the severity of the risk (what the potential harm is to third parties), and (4) the probabilities that the disease will be transmitted and cause varying degrees of harm. In making these findings, courts normally should defer to the reasonable medical judgments of public health officials. Courts must then determine, in light of these findings, whether any "reasonable accommodation" can be made by the employer. Because the district court did not make the appropriate findings in *Arline*, the case was remanded.

In *Chalk v. U.S. District Court,*[8] the U.S. Court of Appeals for the Ninth Circuit relied on the *School Board of Nassau County v. Arline* decision in concluding that discrimination on the basis of AIDS violates the Rehabilitation Act. In the *Chalk* case, the court of appeals ruled that the Orange County Department of Education violated the Rehabilitation Act when it reassigned Vincent Chalk from his position as a teacher of hearing-impaired students to an administrative position after Chalk was diagnosed as having AIDS. The court ruled that Chalk, who was "handicapped" as a result of the disease, was "otherwise qualified" for classroom duty because the medical evidence indicated that the disease could not be transmitted through normal classroom contact.[9]

CASE 15.1	COOK V. RHODE ISLAND DEPARTMENT OF MHRH U.S. COURT OF APPEALS, 10 F.3D 17 (1ST CIR. 1993).

[Bonnie Cook applied for the position of institutional attendant at the Ladd Center, a state residential facility for retarded persons. She was 5'2" tall and weighed over 320 pounds. During a prehire physical examination administered by a nurse, no limitation was found that infringed on her ability to do the job. The Department of Mental Health, Retardation, and Hospitals (MHRH) refused to hire her because her obesity was a health risk to herself and she might put retarded residents at risk in emergency situations because of her limited mobility. The agency was also concerned over possible absenteeism and costs of workers' compensation injuries that could occur because of her obesity. Ms. Cook sued RI–MHRH under the Rehabilitation Act.]

SELYA, C. J....

At the times material hereto, defendant-appellant Department of Mental Health, Retardation, and Hospitals (MHRH), a subdivision of the Rhode Island state government, operated the Ladd Center as

a residential facility for retarded persons. Plaintiff-appellee Bonnie Cook worked at Ladd as an institutional attendant for the mentally retarded from 1978 to 1980, and again from 1981 to 1986. Both times she departed voluntarily, leaving behind a spotless work record. The defendant concedes that Cook's past performance met its legitimate expectations.

In 1988, when plaintiff reapplied for the identical position, she stood 5'2" tall and weighed over 320 pounds. During the routine pre-hire physical, a nurse employed by MHRH concluded that plaintiff was morbidly obese but found no limitations that impinged upon her ability to do the job. Notwithstanding that plaintiff passed the physical examination, MHRH balked. It claimed that Cook's morbid obesity compromised her ability to evacuate patients in case of an emergency and put her at greater risk of developing serious ailments (a "fact" that MHRH's hierarchs speculated would promote absenteeism and increase the likelihood of workers' compensation claims).

continued

---

[8] 46 FEP 279 (9th Cir. 1988).

[9] Also, HIV, the AIDS virus, is not considered under the ADA a pathogen transmitted by food contamination by infected persons who handle food.

Consequently, MHRH refused to hire plaintiff for a vacant IA-MR position.

Cook did not go quietly into this dark night. Invoking section 504, she sued MHRH in federal district court....

In due season, the parties tried the case to a jury. At the close of the evidence, appellant moved for judgment as a matter of law. The court reserved decision, *see* Fed.R.Civ.P. 50(a), and submitted the case on special interrogatories (to which appellant interposed no objections). The jury answered the interrogatories favorably to plaintiff and, by means of the accompanying general verdict, awarded her $100,000 in compensatory damages. The district court denied appellant's motions for judgment as a matter of law and for a new trial, entered judgment on the verdict, and granted equitable relief to the plaintiff. MHRH lost little time in filing a notice of appeal.

In handicap discrimination cases brought pursuant to federal law, the claimant bears the burden of proving each element of her [claim]. The elements derive from section 504 of the Rehabilitation Act, which provides in relevant part: "[n]o otherwise qualified individual ... shall, solely by reason of her or his disability, ... be subjected to discrimination under any program or activity receiving Federal financial assistance." ... To invoke the statute in a failure-to-hire case, a claimant must prove four things: (1) that she applied for a post in a federally funded program or activity, (2) that, at the time, she suffered from a cognizable disability, (3) but was, nonetheless, qualified for the position, and (4) that she was not hired due solely to her disability. Here, MHRH concedes that it received substantial federal funding for the operation of the Ladd Center....

Appellant counterattacks on two fronts. Neither foray succeeds.

1. *Mutability.* MHRH baldly asserts that "mutable" conditions are not the sort of impairments that can find safe harbor in the lee of section 504. It exacuates this assertion by claiming that morbid obesity is a mutable condition and that, therefore, one who suffers from it is not handicapped within the meaning of the federal law because she can simply lose weight and rid herself of any concomitant disability. This suggestion is as insubstantial as a pitchman's promise....

In deciding this issue, the jury had before it credible evidence that metabolic dysfunction, which leads to weight gain in the morbidly obese, lingers even after weight loss. Given this evidence, the jury

reasonably could have found that, though people afflicted with morbid obesity can treat the manifestations of metabolic dysfunction by fasting or perennial undereating, the physical impairment itself—a dysfunctional metabolism—is permanent. *Cf. Gilbert v. Frank,* 949 F.2d 637, 641 (2d Cir. 1991) (finding that kidney disease controllable by weekly dialysis constitutes a handicap under § 504 of the Rehabilitation Act); *Reynolds v. Brock,* 815 F.2d 571, 573 (9th Cir. 1987) (holding that epilepsy controllable by medication qualifies as a handicap under § 504). Hence, the jury's resolution of the mutability question rested on a sufficiently sturdy evidentiary platform....

... MHRH asseverates that, because morbid obesity is caused, or at least exacerbated, by voluntary conduct, it cannot constitute an impairment falling within the ambit of section 504. But, this asseveration rests on a legally faulty premise. The Rehabilitation Act contains no language suggesting that its protection is linked to how an individual became impaired, or whether an individual contributed to his or her impairment. On the contrary, the Act indisputably applies to numerous conditions that may be caused or exacerbated by voluntary conduct, such as alcoholism, AIDS, diabetes, cancer resulting from cigarette smoking, heart disease resulting from excesses of various types, and the like.... Consequently, voluntariness, like mutability, is relevant only in determining whether a condition has a substantially limiting effect.

Appellant's premise fares no better as a matter of fact. The instructions (to which appellant did not object) specifically restricted disabilities to those conditions "that the person affected is powerless to control." Given the plethoric evidence introduced concerning the physiological roots of morbid obesity, the jury certainly could have concluded that the metabolic dysfunction and failed appetite-suppressing neural signals were beyond plaintiff's control and rendered her effectively powerless to manage her weight.

The regulations implementing section 504 define "major life activities" to include walking, breathing, working, and other manual tasks. *See id.* § 84.3(j)(2)(ii). In this case, Dr. O'Brien testified that he refused to hire plaintiff because he believed that her morbid obesity interfered with her ability to undertake physical activities, including walking, lifting, bending, stooping, and kneeling, to such an extent that she would be incapable of working as an

continued

IA-MR. On this basis alone, the jury plausibly could have found that MHRH viewed plaintiff's suspected impairment as interfering with major life activities.

Proceeding to the merits, we think that the degree of limitation fell squarely to the jury and that the evidence warrants its finding that appellant regarded plaintiff as substantially impaired. By his own admission, Dr. O'Brien believed plaintiff's limitations foreclosed a broad range of employment options in the health care industry, including positions such as community living aide, nursing home aide, hospital aide, and home health care aide. Detached jurors reasonably could have found that this pessimistic assessment of plaintiff's capabilities demonstrated that appellant regarded Cook's condition as substantially limiting a major life activity—being able to work....

Here, the jury rationally could have concluded that MHRH's perception of what it thought to be plaintiff's impairment, as exhibited in its refusal to hire her for the IA-MR position, foreclosed a sufficiently wide range of jobs to serve as proof of a substantial limitation. Accordingly, the district court appropriately refused to direct a verdict for the employer.

The next stop on our odyssey requires us to consider whether there was sufficient evidence for the jury to conclude that plaintiff was "otherwise qualified" to work as an IA-MR. Once again, an affirmative answer emerges.

"An otherwise qualified person is one who is able to meet all of a program's requirements in spite of h[er] handicap." Although an employer is not required to be unfailingly correct in assessing a person's qualifications for a job, an employer cannot act solely on the basis of subjective beliefs. An unfounded assumption that an applicant is unqualified for a particular job, even if arrived at in good faith, is not sufficient to forestall liability under section 504....

Appellant's position, insofar as we can understand it, is that plaintiff's morbid obesity presented such a risk to herself and the Ladd Center's residents that she was not otherwise qualified, or, in the alternative, that it was reasonable for appellant to believe that she was not otherwise qualified. This protestation is undone by ... independent considerations....

We will not paint the lily. Several pieces of evidence loom large on this issue. Plaintiff received a satisfactory report following the physical examination conducted by appellant's own nurse; the IA-MR position for which she applied did not demand any elevated level of mobility, lifting ability, size, or stature; plaintiff had satisfactorily performed all her duties and responsibilities as an IA-MR during her previous five years of employment; and MHRH acknowledged that those duties and responsibilities have not changed. From this, and other, evidence, we believe that the jury lawfully could have found plaintiff, apart from any impairment, "otherwise qualified" to work as an IA-MR.

Our last port of call requires that we determine whether the evidence justified a finding that MHRH turned down plaintiff's request for employment due solely to her morbid obesity. This final piece of the puzzle is straightforward.

MHRH has not offered a hint of any non-weight-related reason for rejecting plaintiff's application. Rather, it has consistently conceded that it gave plaintiff the cold shoulder because Dr. O'Brien denied her medical clearance. The record is pellucid that Dr. O'Brien's refusal had three foci, each of which related directly to plaintiff's obesity. On this record, there was considerable room for a jury to find that appellant declined to hire Cook "due solely to" her perceived handicap.

Conclusion

We need go no further. In a society that all too often confuses "slim" with "beautiful" or "good," morbid obesity can present formidable barriers to employment. Where, as here, the barriers transgress federal law, those who erect and seek to preserve them must suffer the consequences. In this case, the evidence adduced at trial amply supports the jury's determination that MHRH violated section 504 of the Rehabilitation Act. And because MHRH refused to hire plaintiff due solely to her morbid obesity, there is no cause to disturb either the damage award or the equitable relief granted by the district court.

Affirmed.

Case Questions

1. Are extremely overweight individuals protected under the Rehabilitation Act from discrimination based on their morbid obesity?
2. Can a person be considered as having a disability and thus be eligible for the protections of the Act when that individual can rid herself of the "disability" by simply losing weight?
3. Assess the judge's remarks in the first three sentences of the conclusion of the decision.

CASE 15.2	SCHOOL BOARD OF NASSAU COUNTY, FLORIDA V. ARLINE
	SUPREME COURT OF THE UNITED STATES, 480 U.S. 273 (1987).

[Respondent Gene Arline was hospitalized for tuberculosis in 1957. The disease went into remission for the next 20 years, during which time she began teaching elementary school in Florida. In 1977, March 1978, and November 1978, she had relapses. After the latter two relapses, she was suspended with pay for the rest of the school year. At the end of the 1978–1979 school year, the school board discharged her after a hearing because of the continued recurrence of tuberculosis. After she was denied relief in state administrative proceedings, she brought suit in federal district court, alleging a violation of Section 504 of the Rehabilitation Act. The district court held that although Arline suffered a handicap, she was not a handicapped person under the statute as it was difficult "to conceive that Congress intended contagious diseases to be included within the definition of a handicapped person." The court of appeals reversed, and the Supreme Court granted certiorari.]

BRENNAN, J....

I.

In enacting and amending the Act, Congress enlisted all programs receiving federal funds in an effort "to share with handicapped Americans the opportunities for an education, transportation, housing, health care, and jobs that other Americans take for granted." 123 Cong. Rec. 13515 (1977) (statement of Sen. Humphrey). To that end, Congress not only increased federal support for vocational rehabilitation, but also addressed the broader problem of discrimination against the handicapped by including § 504, an antidiscrimination provision patterned after Title VII of the Civil Rights Act of 1964. Section 504 of the Rehabilitation Act reads in pertinent part:

> "No otherwise qualified handicapped individual in the United States, as defined in section 706(7) of this title, shall, solely by reason of his handicap, be excluded from participation in, be denied the benefits of, or be subjected to discrimination under any program or activity receiving Federal financial assistance...." 29 U.S.C. § 794.

In 1974 Congress expanded the definition of "handicapped individual" for use in § 504 to read as follows:

> "[A]ny person who (i) has a physical or mental impairment which substantially limits one or

more of such person's major life activities,
(ii) has a record of such an impairment, or
(iii) is regarded as having such an impairment." 29 U.S.C. § 706(7)(B).

The amended definition reflected Congress' concern with protecting the handicapped against discrimination stemming not only from simple prejudice, but from "archaic attitudes and laws" and from "the fact that the American people are simply unfamiliar with and insensitive to the difficulties confront[ing] individuals with handicaps." To combat the effects of erroneous but nevertheless prevalent perceptions about the handicapped, Congress expanded the definition of "handicapped individual" so as to preclude discrimination against "[a] person who has a record of, or is regarded as having, an impairment [but who] may at present have no actual incapacity at all." *Southeastern Community College v. Davis,* 442 U.S. 397, 405–406, n. 6 (1979).

In determining whether a particular individual is handicapped as defined by the Act, the regulations promulgated by the Department of Health and Human Services are of significant assistance.... The regulations are particularly significant here because they define two critical terms used in the statutory definition of handicapped individual. "Physical impairment" is defined as follows:

> "[A]ny physiological disorder or condition, cosmetic disfigurement, or anatomical loss affecting one or more of the following body systems: neurological; musculo-skeletal; special sense organs; respiratory, including speech organs; cardiovascular; reproductive, digestive, genitourinary; hemic and lymphatic; skin; and endocrine." 45 CFR § 84.3(j)(2)(i) (1985).

In addition, the regulations define "major life activities" as:

> "functions such as caring for one's self, performing manual tasks, walking, seeing, hearing, speaking, breathing, learning, and working." § 84.3j(2)(ii).

II.

Within this statutory and regulatory framework, then, we must consider whether Arline can be considered a handicapped individual. According to the testimony of Dr. McEuen, Arline suffered tuberculosis

continued

"in an acute form in such a degree that it affected her respiratory system," and was hospitalized for this condition. Arline thus had a physical impairment as that term is defined by the regulations, since she had a "physiological disorder or condition ... affecting [her] ... respiratory [system]." This impairment was serious enough to require hospitalization, a fact more than sufficient to establish that one or more of her major life activities were substantially limited by her impairment. Thus, Arline's hospitalization for tuberculosis in 1957 suffices to establish that she has a "record of ... impairment" within the meaning of 29 U.S.C. § 706(7)(b)(ii), and is therefore a handicapped individual.

Petitioners concede that a contagious disease may constitute a handicapping condition to the extent that it leaves a person with "diminished physical or mental capabilities," and concede that Arline's hospitalization for tuberculosis in 1957 demonstrates that she has a record of a physical impairment. Petitioners maintain, however, Arline's record of impairment is irrelevant in this case, since the School Board dismissed Arline not because of her diminished physical capabilities, but because of the threat that her relapses of tuberculosis posed to the health of others.

We do not agree with petitioners that, in defining a handicapped individual under § 504, the contagious effects of a disease can be meaningfully distinguished from the disease's physical effects on a claimant in a case such as this. Arline's contagiousness and her physical impairment each resulted from the same underlying condition, tuberculosis. It would be unfair to allow an employer to seize upon the distinction between the effects of a disease on others and the effects of a disease on a patient and use that distinction to justify discriminatory treatment.

Nothing in the legislative history of § 504 suggests that Congress intended such a result....

... Few aspects of a handicap give rise to the same level of public fear and misapprehension as contagiousness. Even those who suffer or have recovered from such noninfectious diseases as epilepsy or cancer have faced discrimination based on the irrational fear that they might be contagious. The Act is carefully structured to replace such reflexive reactions to actual or perceived handicaps with actions based on reasoned and medically sound judgments: the definition of "handicapped individual" is broad, but only those individuals who are both handicapped *and* otherwise qualified are eligible for relief. The fact that *some*

persons who have contagious diseases may pose a serious health threat to others under certain circumstances does not justify excluding from the coverage of the Act *all* persons with actual or perceived contagious diseases. Such exclusion would mean that those accused of being contagious would never have the opportunity to have their condition evaluated in light of medical evidence and a determination made as to whether they were "otherwise qualified." Rather, they would be vulnerable to discrimination on the basis of mythology—precisely the type of injury Congress sought to prevent. We conclude that the fact that a person with a record of a physical impairment is also contagious does not suffice to remove that person from coverage under § 504.

III.

The remaining question is whether Arline is otherwise qualified for the job of elementary school teacher. To answer this question in most cases, the District Court will need to conduct an individualized inquiry and make appropriate findings of fact. Such an inquiry is essential if § 504 is to achieve its goal of protecting handicapped individuals from deprivations based on prejudice, stereotypes, or unfounded fear, while giving appropriate weight to such legitimate concerns of grantees as avoiding exposing others to significant health and safety risks. The basic factors to be considered in conducting this inquiry are well established. In the context of the employment of a person handicapped with a contagious disease, we agree with *amicus* American Medical Association that this inquiry should include:

> "[findings of] facts, based on reasonable medical judgments given the state of medical knowledge, about (a) the nature of the risk (how the disease is transmitted), (b) the duration of the risk (how long the carrier is infectious), (c) the severity of the risk (what the potential harm is to third parties) and (d) the probabilities the disease will be transmitted and will cause varying degrees of harm." Brief for American Medical Association as *Amicus Curiae* 19.

In making these findings, courts normally should defer to the reasonable medical judgments of public health officials. The next step in the "otherwise-qualified" inquiry is for the court to evaluate, in light of these medical findings, whether the employer could reasonably accommodate the employee under the established standards for that inquiry.

continued

Because of the paucity of factual findings by the District Court, we, like the Court of Appeals, are unable at this stage of the proceedings to resolve whether Arline is "otherwise qualified" for her job. The District Court made no findings as to the duration and severity of Arline's condition, nor as to the probability that she would transmit the disease. Nor did the court determine whether Arline was contagious at the time she was discharged, or whether the School Board could have reasonably accommodated her. Accordingly, the resolution of whether Arline was otherwise qualified requires further findings of fact.

IV.

We hold that a person suffering from the contagious disease of tuberculosis can be a handicapped person within the meaning of the § 504 of the Rehabilitation Act of 1973, and that respondent Arline is such a person. We remand the case to the District Court to determine whether Arline is otherwise qualified for her position. The judgment of the Court of Appeals is *Affirmed.*

Case Questions

1. Why did the school board terminate Arline?
2. When a person with a record of physical impairment is also contagious, is that person removed from coverage under Section 504?
3. Did Congress seek to prevent discrimination against handicapped individuals based on the fear and mythology of contagiousness when it enacted Section 504?
4. Did the Court find that Arline was otherwise qualified?

SECTION 128: THE AMENDED AMERICANS WITH DISABILITIES ACT

The Americans with Disabilities Act of 1990 was amended by the ADA Amendments Act of 2008 (ADAAA), effective January 1, 2009. The amended act requires courts to apply a less demanding standard for coverage under the Act; and employer obligations to provide "reasonable accommodations" will be more common.

BACKGROUND

In the 1999 U.S. Supreme Court decision *Sutton v. United Airlines Inc.*[10] the Court held that "mitigating measures" must be considered in deciding whether an ADA plaintiff has a "disability" as defined in the act. Thus, if an individual was able to manage the symptoms of an impairment so as not to be substantially limited in a major life activity by using medication, prosthetics or other mitigating means, the individual was not "disabled" under the ADA. In lower court cases, a wide variety of impairments such as hearing impairments, diabetes, depression, and epilepsy were found not to be disabilities when evaluated in the corrected state by using medication or other mitigating means.

In the 2002 *Toyota Motor Manufacturing, Kentucky, Inc. v. Williams*[11] decision a unanimous Supreme Court applied a demanding standard for establishing the existence of a disability under the ADA, stating that the phrase "substantially limited in a major life activity" means "prevented or severely restricted in an activity that is of central importance to most people's daily lives." While the plaintiff, Ms. Williams, could not do certain types of assembly line jobs involving repetitive work with hands and arms extended at or above her shoulders for extended periods of time due to her carpal tunnel syndrome, she could perform household chores,

---

[10] 527 U.S. 471 (1999).

[11] 534 U.S. 184 (2002).

bathe, tend her flower garden, do laundry, fix breakfast and pick up around the house—which are manual tasks of central importance to people's daily lives. When considering what she could do as part of the evidence, the Court unanimously determined that Ms. Williams was not disabled under the ADA. Following the *Toyota* decision, numerous claims of ADA plaintiffs were extinguished at the threshold stage of proving the plaintiff had a disability, with judicial focus seemingly on what plaintiffs could do as opposed to what they could not do. For example, in *Squibb v. Memorial Medical Center*[12] a nurse's ADA claim based on three back injuries, where she presented evidence of difficulties in performing everyday activities, was unsuccessful. The court emphasized the tasks the plaintiff could perform in deciding that she was not "substantially limited in the major life activity of caring for herself."

Thus, under *Sutton* and *Toyota* an individualized analysis had applied in the courts, considering mitigating measures and/or the activities of the individual both on and off the job to determine whether there was a "substantial impairment in a major life activity." These Supreme Court precedents resulted in a dramatic reduction in the number of workers with disabilities protected under the Act. It is in this context that the ADA Amendments Act of 2008 became law. The ADAAA specifically overturned the *Sutton* and *Toyota* decisions, rejecting the strict interpretation of the definition of "disability," and making absolutely clear that the ADA is intended to protect all individuals facing discrimination in the workplace on the basis of disability.

PROVING A CASE

The Americans with Disabilities Act (ADA) as amended in 2008[13] prohibits employers from discriminating "against a qualified individual on the basis of a disability."[14] A qualified individual with a disability is one "who, with or without reasonable accommodation, can perform the essential functions of the employment position." Therefore, to establish a viable claim under the ADA, a plaintiff must prove by a preponderance of the evidence that (1) he or she has a disability; (2) he or she is qualified for the position; and (3) an employer discriminated against him or her because of a disability.

Following the language of the Rehabilitation Act Amendments, and the ADA of 1990, Section 3 of the ADAAA also defines the term "disability" in a three pronged definition as follows:

(1) DISABILITY: The term "disability" means, with respect to an individual —

(A) a physical or mental impairment that substantially limits one or more major life activities of such individual;

(B) a record of such an impairment; or

(C) being regarded as having such an impairment.[15]

1. *Subsection (A) of the Definition.* The Supreme Court in *Bragdon v. Abbott* stated that "consideration of subsection (A) of the definition proceeds in three

---

[12] 497 F.3d 775 (7th Cir. 2007).

[13] 42 U.S.C. §§ 12101-12117; P.L. 110-325, S. 3406 (Sept. 25, 2008).

[14] ADRAA Section 5(1).

[15] ADAAA Section 3(1).

steps. First, the court must determine whether the plaintiff has an impairment. Second, the court must identify the life activity upon which the plaintiff relies and determine whether it constitutes a major life activity under the ADA. Third, "tying the two statutory phrases together, [the court] ask[s] whether the impairment substantially limited the major life activity."[16] The definition of impairment has been adopted from the Rehabilitation Act.[17] The amended ADAAA sets forth in clear and unmistakable language that the definition of disability "shall be construed in favor of broad coverage of individuals under this Act, to the maximum extent permitted by the terms of this Act;" and mandates that the term "substantially limits" be construed accordingly. Moreover, the determination of whether an impairment substantially limits a major life activity must be made without regard to the ameliorative effects of mitigating measures (except the ameliorative effects of ordinary eyeglasses or contact lenses shall be considered in determination whether an impairment substantially limits a major life activity).[18]

The ADAAA includes a new expansive compilation of major life activities to confirm the Congressional purpose of providing a broad scope of protection to individuals under the ADA.[19]

2. *Subsection (B) of the Definition.* Under subsection (B) of the definition of disability, persons with a "record of impairment" may, through the use of medical and hospital records, establish the existence of an impairment that substantially limits an individual's major life activity. Also necessary to proving a case under subsection B is evidence that the employer had knowledge of the plaintiff's record of impairment. A person with a history of cancer that is currently in remission or a person with a history of mental illness are two examples of a record of impairment.

3. *Subsection (C) of the Definition.* Subsection (C) of the definition of disability, "being regarded as having such an impairment," is a third basis for ADA protection of a plaintiff. This part of the definition protects individuals from

---

[16] 524 U.S. 624 (1998).

[17] The Department of Health and Human Services issued regulations defining impairment under the ADA, adopting the Rehabilitation Act regulations without change as follows:

(1) Any physiological disorder, or condition, cosmetic disfigurement, or anatomical loss affecting one or more of the following body systems: neurological, musculoskeletal, special sense organs, respiratory (including speech organs), cardiovascular, reproductive, digestive, genito-urinary, hemic and lymphatic, skin, and endocrine; or

(2) Any mental or physical disorder, such as mental retardation, organic brain syndrome, emotional or mental illness, and specific learning disabilities. 29 C.F.R. § 1630. 2(h).

[18] Section 3 (4)(E)(ii).

[19] Section 3(2) of the Act provides:
MAJOR LIFE ACTIVITIES —

(A) IN GENERAL.—For purposes of paragraph (1), major life activities include, but are not limited to, caring for oneself, performing manual tasks, seeing, hearing, eating, sleeping, walking, standing, lifting, bending, speaking, breathing, learning, reading, concentrating, thinking, communicating, and working.

(B) MAJOR BODILY FUNCTIONS.—For purposes of paragraph (1), a major life activity also includes the operation of a major bodily function, including but not limited to, functions of the immune system, normal cell growth, digestive, bowel, bladder, neurological, brain, respiratory, circulatory, endocrine, and reproductive functions.

discrimination who are regarded and treated as though they have an impairment that substantially limits an individual's major life activity, even though they may not have such an impairment. While protected from discrimination under this "regarded as" prong, nevertheless these individuals are not entitled to "reasonable accommodation" under the Act.[20] In order to be entitled to receive reasonable accommodation an individual must establish protection under the first or second prong of the definition and actually have an impairment that substantially limits a major life activity or have a record of impairment. Minor or transitory conditions lasting six months or less are excluded from "regarded as" claims.[21]

Reasonable Accommodations Issues under the ADA

The ADA states that reasonable accommodations may include the following:

> [J]ob restructuring, part-time or modified work schedules, reassignment to a vacant position, acquisition or modification of equipment or devices, appropriate adjustment or modifications of examinations, training materials or policies, the provision of qualified readers or interpreters, and other similar accommodations for individuals with disabilities.[22]

An employer is not obligated under the ADA to make accommodations that would be an "undue hardship" on the employer. For example, before passage of the ADA, a supermarket meat cutter unable to carry meat from a refrigerator to a processing area might have been refused clearance to return to work after a back injury until he was able to perform all job functions. Today under the ADA, the employer would be obligated to provide that worker with a cart to help him perform the job, even if the cart cost $500. However, if the meat cutter was employed by a small business with limited financial resources, an "accommodation" costing $500 might be an undue hardship that the employer could lawfully refuse to make.

Seniority. Seniority systems provide for a fair and uniform method of treating employees, whereas employees with more years of service have priority over employees with less service when it comes to layoffs, job selection, and other benefits such as days off and vacation periods. Seniority rules not only apply under collective bargaining agreements but also apply to many nonunion job classifications and nonunion settings. An employer's showing that a required accommodation conflicts with seniority rules is ordinarily sufficient to show that the requested "accommodation" is not "reasonable." For example, in *U.S. Airways, Inc. v. Barnett*, presented in this section, Robert Barnett, a cargo handler for U.S. Airways, sought a less physically demanding job in the mailroom due to a back injury. Because a senior employee bid the job, U.S. Airways refused Barnett's request to accommodate his disability by allowing him to work the mailroom position. In a 5-4 decision, the U.S. Supreme Court determined that ordinarily such a requested

---

[20] ADAAA Section 6(h).

[21] ADAAA Section 4(3)(B).

[22] 42 U.S.C. § 12111 (9)(B).

accommodation is not "reasonable." Barnett was given the opportunity on remand to show that the company allowed exceptions to the seniority rules and that he fit within such exceptions.[23]

The "Reassignment" Accommodation.   Under the ADEA, a reasonable accommodation may include "reassignment to a vacant position."[24] The EEOC states in its enforcement guidance that where other accommodations have failed and reassignment to a vacant equivalent position is not an undue burden, an employer is obligated to reassign a qualified disabled employee to the position and the employee does not have to compete with other employees or applicants for the vacant position. Moreover, the EEOC states that the employee does not need to be the best-qualified individual for the position in order to obtain it as reassignment.[25]

The *Huber v. Wal-Mart Stores, Inc.* case dealt with the question of whether an employer has an obligation to reassign a qualified disabled employee to a vacant equivalent position where an employer has an established policy of hiring or promoting the most qualified applicant for the position; or does the employer satisfy its obligations under the Act by having the employee compete with all other applicants for the vacant position? The district court granted Huber's motions for summary judgment, and the Eighth Circuit Court of Appeals reversed the lower court's decision and remanded for entry of judgment in favor of Wal-Mart. The appeals court noted that automatic reassignment is not required and that the ADA is not an affirmative action statute.

In *Smith v. Midland Brake, Inc.*, the Tenth Circuit determined that if reassignment does not create an undue hardship for the employer, then the employee automatically gets the position, even though he or she is not the most qualified applicant.[26]

The U.S. Supreme Court agreed to hear the *Huber* case in order to resolve the conflict between circuits. However, the parties settled that lawsuit and the case was dismissed. The *Huber* decision, including reference to the *Midland Brake* decision, is presented in this section.

While the Supreme Court must resolve the underlying question in the future, it is well settled that employers do not have to assign a disabled employee to a position in which he or she is not otherwise qualified;[27] nor is the employer required to create a vacancy by "bumping" another employee.[28]

Reasonable Accommodation.   In *Vande Zande v. Wisconsin Department of Administration*,[29] the U.S. Court of Appeals for the Seventh Circuit rejected a claim

---

[23] *U.S. Airways v. Barnett*, 122 S.Ct. 1516 (2002).

[24] 42 U.S.C. § 12111 (9)(B).

[25] "EEOC Enforcement Guidance, Reasonable Accommodation and Undue Hardship under the ADA" at 17-18 (Oct. 17, 2002) at http://www.eeoc.gov/policy/docs/accommodation.html.

[26] 180 F.3d 1154, 1164-65 (10th Cir. 1999) (en banc).

[27] *Aka v. Washington Hospital Center*, 156 F.3d 184, 1305 (D.C. 1998).

[28] *Emrick v. Libby-Owens-Ford Co.*, 875 F.Supp 393, 397 (E.D. Tex. 1995).

[29] 3 ADA Cases 1636 (7th Cir. 1994).

of a state secretarial worker who was paralyzed from the waist down as a result of a spinal tumor that her employer did not fully accommodate her "reasonable accommodation" request. To accommodate her disability, the state modified the bathroom, built a ramp for her wheelchair, provided special adjustable furniture, paid half the cost of a cot, and modified her schedule to accommodate her medical appointments. Her supervisor refused her request for full-time work at home while recovering during an eight-week bout with pressure ulcers and refused to install a desktop computer at her home. The supervisor advised her that he would have a maximum of 20 hours a week for her to work at home and advised her to use her laptop computer at home. In finding for the employer, the court determined that the employer had done more than was required to accommodate the employee's disability under the ADA.

Failure to Take Appropriate Action.   The potential for employer liability for failure to take appropriate action regarding reasonable accommodation is made evident in the *Brady v. Wal-Mart Stores, Inc.* case.[30] The Second Circuit Court of Appeals affirmed a federal district court judgment for Patrick Brady under the ADA for $900,000, including $300,000 in punitive damages, for transferring 19-year-old Brady, who has cerebral palsy, from a job as a Wal-Mart pharmacy aide after a "few days" with no training to the job of collecting shopping carts and garbage in the parking lot. His supervisor, Ms. Chin, regarded Brady as "too slow" and "she knew there was something wrong with him." While Brady did not request reasonable accommodations, because his disability was obvious and known to the employer, Wal-Mart was obligated to engage in an "interactive process" regarding accommodating his disability.[31]

In *Gagliardo v. Connaught Laboratories, Inc.,*[32] Jane Gagliardo was successful in her ADA suit against her former employer. Gagliardo had been diagnosed with multiple sclerosis in the early 1990s. By 1995, her symptoms began affecting her work. The most severe symptom was fatigue, which affected her ability to think, focus, and remember. All of her symptoms were subject to being exacerbated by stress. She sought a "reasonable accommodation" under the ADA of having one major client removed from her job responsibility. The employer took no action on this request. And while Ms. Gagliardo continued to seek the accommodation to no avail, the employer began disciplining her for poor job performance and ultimately fired her in May 1996. An award of $300,000 as capped punitive damages under the ADA was upheld by the Third Circuit Court of Appeals along with $2 million in compensatory damages under the Pennsylvania Human Relations Act.

---

[30] *Brady v. Wal-Mart Stores, Inc.*, 531 F.3d 127 (2d Cir. 2008).

[31] Accommodations need not be perfect. For example, an employer granted an employee's request for a perfume-free workplace because of her extra sensitivity to perfume. When the employee sued the employer because some coworkers were violating the ban, the court of appeals determined that it was unreasonable for the plaintiff to expect perfect enforcement. *Kaufmann v. GMAC Mortgage Corp*, 229 Fed. Appx. 164 (3d Cir. 2007).

[32] 311 F.3d 565 (3d Cir. 2002).

EXCLUSIONS FROM COVERAGE

The Act excludes from its coverage employees or applicants who are "currently engaging in the illegal use of drugs." The exclusion does not include an individual who has been successfully rehabilitated from such use or is participating in or has completed supervised drug rehabilitation and is no longer engaging in the illegal use of drugs.[33]

In *Wallace v. Veterans Administration*,[34] Dorothy Wallace, a registered nurse, was a former drug abuser who had successfully undergone treatment for this condition and remained drug-free during the period prior to applying for a position as an intensive care nurse at a VA hospital. She was refused employment because her own physician recommended that she not administer narcotics to patients. The hospital considered this restriction a basis to reject her application because she could not fully perform the functions of a registered nurse. Wallace challenged the decision in court. Utilizing a fact-based analysis, the court found that less than 2 percent of a nurse's time in the intensive care unit of the VA hospital was spent handling narcotics. Further, the court found that through the less burdensome process of job restructuring, Wallace could be accommodated by having another nurse, if necessary, dispense narcotics to her patients. In addition, another option was also available as an accommodation. She could be assigned primarily to heart and liver patients who received no narcotics.

Alcoholics are not excluded from the coverage of the ADA. The ADA thus may protect an individual from discrimination based on his or her status as an alcoholic. However, alcoholics are not protected from the consequences of their conduct. In *Larson v. Koch Refining Co.*,[35] Lloyd Larson, a supervisor at the refinery, was terminated after he was arrested for drunk driving and assault. Larson argued that his employer violated the ADA when it failed to provide him alcohol counseling and other reasonable accommodations. The court held that the employer did not know of Larson's disability prior to his discharge. And a pattern of absenteeism coupled with the drunk driving and assault arrest gave the employer a valid basis to terminate this supervisor. The court relied on the "alcoholics are not protected from the consequences of their conduct" principle.

Title V of the Act states that homosexuality and bisexuality and behaviors such as transvestism, transsexualism, pedophilia, exhibitionism, compulsive gambling, kleptomania, pyromania, or psychoactive substance use disorders resulting from current illegal use of drugs are not—in and of themselves—considered disabilities.

PREEMPLOYMENT INQUIRIES

An employer may make preemployment inquiries into the ability of a job applicant to perform job-related functions. Under new user-friendly EEOC guidelines on preemployment inquiries under the ADA, an employer may ask applicants whether

---

[33] § 124.

[34] 683 F. Supp 758 (D. Kan. 1988). See also *Chairi v. City of League City*, 920 F.2d 311 (5th Cir. 1991).

[35] 920 F. Supp. 1000 (D. Minn. 1995).

they will need reasonable accommodations in the hiring process. If the answer is yes, the employer may ask for reasonable documentation of the disability.[36]

In general, the employer may not ask questions about whether an applicant will need reasonable accommodations to do the job. However, the employer may make preemployment inquiries regarding the ability of a job applicant to perform job-related functions.

After making a job offer contingent on passing a medical examination, an offer may be rescinded where the position in question poses a direct threat to the worker's own health or safety. For example, Mario Echazabal was initially offered a job at Chevron's El Segundo, California, oil refinery, but the offer was rescinded when company doctors determined that exposure to chemicals on the job would further damage his already reduced liver functions due to his hepatitis C and would potentially kill him. An affirmative defense then exists for employers not only where hiring an individual poses a direct threat to the health or safety of other employees in the workplace but also where there is a direct threat-to-self. However, the employer must make an individualized medical risk assessment of the employee's condition.[37]

CASE 15.3	U.S. AIRWAYS, INC. V. BARNETT
	SUPREME COURT OF THE UNITED STATES, 122 S.CT. 1516 (2002).

[After respondent Robert Barnett injured his back while he was a cargo handler for petitioner U.S. Airways, Inc., he transferred to a less physically demanding mailroom position. His new position later became open to seniority-based employee bidding under U.S. Airways' seniority system, and employees senior to him planned to bid on the job. U.S. Airways refused his request to accommodate his disability by allowing him to remain in the mailroom, and he lost his job. He then filed suit under the ADA, which prohibits an employer from discriminating against "an individual with a disability" who, with "reasonable accommodation," can perform a job's essential functions, unless the employer "can demonstrate that the accommodation would impose an undue hardship on the operation of [its] business." Finding that altering a seniority system would result in an "undue hardship" to both U.S. Airways and its nondisabled employees, the district court granted the company summary judgment. The Ninth Circuit reversed, holding that the seniority system was merely a factor in the undue hardship analysis and that a case-by-case, fact-intensive analysis is required to determine whether any particular assignment would constitute an undue hardship. The Supreme Court agreed to hear the case.]

BREYER, J....

I.

In answering the question presented, we must consider the following statutory provisions. First, the ADA says that an employer may not "discriminate against a qualified individual with a disability." Second, the ADA says that a "qualified" individual includes "an individual with a disability who, *with* or without *reasonable accommodation*, can perform the essential functions of" the relevant "employment position." § 12111(8) (emphasis added). Third, the ADA says that "discrimination" includes an employer's *"not making reasonable accommodations* to the known physical or mental limitations of an otherwise qualified ... employee, *unless* [the employer] can demonstrate that the accommodation would impose an *undue hardship* on the operation of [its] business." § 12112(b)(5)(A) (emphasis added).

continued

---

[36] *EEOC Guidance on Pre-employment Inquiries Under the ADA*, Oct. 10, 1995.
[37] *Chevron v. Echazabal*, 122 S.Ct. 2045 (2002).

Fourth, the ADA says that the term "'reasonable accommodation' may include ... reassignment to a vacant position." § 12111(9)(B)....

II.

The question in the present case focuses on the relationship between seniority systems and the plaintiff's need to show that an "accommodation" seems reasonable on its face, *i.e.*, ordinarily or in the run of cases. We must assume that the plaintiff, an employee, is an "individual with a disability." He has requested assignment to a mailroom position as a "reasonable accommodation." We also assume that normally such a request would be reasonable within the meaning of the statute, were it not for one circumstance, namely, that the assignment would violate the rules of a seniority system. See § 12111(9) ("reasonable accommodation" may include "reassignment to a vacant position"). Does that circumstance mean that the proposed accommodation is not a "reasonable" one?

In our view, the answer to this question ordinarily is "yes." The statute does not require proof on a case-by-case basis that a seniority system should prevail. That is because it would not be reasonable in the run of cases that the assignment in question trump the rules of a seniority system. To the contrary, it will ordinarily be unreasonable for the assignment to prevail.

A

Several factors support our conclusion that a proposed accommodation will not be reasonable in the run of cases. Analogous case law supports this conclusion, for it has recognized the importance of seniority to employee-management relations....

Most important for present purposes, to require the typical employer to show more than the existence of a seniority system might well undermine the employees' expectations of consistent, uniform treatment—expectations upon which the seniority system's benefits depend. That is because such a rule would substitute a complex case-specific "accommodation" decision made by management for the more uniform, impersonal operation of seniority rules. Such management decisionmaking, with its inevitable discretionary elements, would involve a matter of the greatest importance to employees, namely, layoffs; it would take place outside, as well as inside, the confines of a court case; and it might well take place fairly often. Cf. ADA, 42 U.S.C. § 12101(a)(1), (estimating that some 43 million Americans suffer from physical or mental disabilities). We can find nothing in the statute that suggests Congress intended to undermine seniority systems in this way. And we consequently conclude that the employer's showing of violation of the rules of a seniority system is by itself ordinarily sufficient.

B

The plaintiff (here the employee) nonetheless remains free to show that special circumstances warrant a finding that, despite the presence of a seniority system (which the ADA may not trump in the run of cases), the requested "accommodation" is "reasonable" on the particular facts. That is because special circumstances might alter the important expectations described above.... The plaintiff might show, for example, that the employer, having retained the right to change the seniority system unilaterally, exercises that right fairly frequently, reducing employee expectations that the system will be followed—to the point where one more departure, needed to accommodate an individual with a disability, will not likely make a difference. The plaintiff might show that the system already contains exceptions such that, in the circumstances, one further exception is unlikely to matter. We do not mean these examples to exhaust the kinds of showings that a plaintiff might make. But we do mean to say that the plaintiff must bear the burden of showing special circumstances that make an exception from the seniority system reasonable in the particular case. And to do so, the plaintiff must explain why, in the particular case, an exception to the employer's seniority policy can constitute a "reasonable accommodation" even though in the ordinary case it cannot.

III.

In its question presented, U.S. Airways asked us whether the ADA requires an employer to assign a disabled employee to a particular position even though another employee is entitled to that position under the employer's "established seniority system." We answer that *ordinarily* the ADA does not require that assignment. Hence, a showing that the assignment would violate the rules of a seniority system warrants summary judgment for the employer—unless there is more. The plaintiff must present evidence of that "more," namely, special circumstances surrounding the particular case that demonstrate the assignment is nonetheless reasonable....

[W]e vacate the Court of Appeals' judgment and remand the case for further proceedings consistent with this opinion.

continued

It is so ordered.

Case Questions

1. How does the Court answer the question "Does the ADA require an employer to assign a disabled employee to a particular position even though another employee is entitled to that position under the employer's established seniority system?"

2. Explain the special circumstances exception. Who has the burden of proof to show special circumstances?

CASE 15.4	HUBER V. WAL-MART STORES, INC.
	UNITED STATES COURT OF APPEALS, 486 F.3D 480 (CIR. 2007).

[Pam Huber worked for Wal-Mart as a dry grocery order filler earning $13.00 per hour, including a $0.50 shift differential. While working for Wal-Mart, Huber sustained a permanent injury to her right arm and hand. As a result, she could no longer perform the essential functions of the order filler job. The parties stipulated that Huber's injury is a disability under the ADA. Because of her disability, Huber sought, as a reasonable accommodation, reassignment to a router position, which the parties stipulated was a vacant and equivalent position under the ADA. Wal-Mart, however, did not agree to reassign Huber automatically to the router position. Instead, pursuant to its policy of hiring the most qualified applicant for the position, Wal-Mart required Huber to apply and compete with other applicants for the router position. Ultimately, Wal-Mart filled the job with a non-disabled applicant and denied Huber the router position. Wal-Mart indicated that although Huber was qualified with or without an accommodation to perform the duties of the router position, she was not the most qualified candidate. The parties stipulated that the individual hired for the router position was the most qualified candidate. Wal-Mart later placed Huber at another facility in a maintenance associate position (janitorial position), which paid $6.20 per hour. Huber continues to work in that position and now earns $7.97 per hour.

Huber filed suit under the ADA, arguing she should have been reassigned to the router position as a reasonable accommodation for her disability. Wal-Mart filed a motion for summary judgment, contending that it had a legitimate non-discriminatory policy of hiring the most qualified applicant for all job vacancies and was not required to reassign Huber to the router position. Huber filed a cross motion for summary judgment, and the district court granted Huber's motion. Wal-Mart appealed.]

RILEY, C. J....

To make a prima facie case in a reasonable accommodation claim under the ADA, the plaintiff must show she (1) has a disability within the meaning of the ADA, (2) is a qualified individual, and (3) suffered an adverse employment action as a result of the disability. To be a qualified individual within the meaning of the ADA, an employee must (1) possess the requisite skill, education, experience, and training for her position; and (2) be able to perform the essential job functions, with or without a reasonable accommodation.

Here, the parties do not dispute Huber (1) has a disability under the ADA, (2) suffered an adverse employment action, or (3) possessed the requisite skills for the router position. The parties' only dispute is whether the ADA requires an employer, as a reasonable accommodation, to give a current disabled employee preference in filling a vacant position when the employee is able to perform the job duties, but is not the most qualified candidate.

The ADA states the scope of reasonable accommodation may include:

> [J]ob restructuring, part-time or modified work schedules, *reassignment to a vacant position*, acquisition or modification of equipment or devices, appropriate adjustment or modifications of examinations, training materials or policies, the provision of qualified readers or interpreters, and other similar accommodations for individuals with disabilities.

42 U.S.C. § 12111(9)(B) (emphasis added).

continued

Huber contends Wal-Mart, as a reasonable accommodation, should have automatically reassigned her to the vacant router position without requiring her to compete with other applicants for that position. Wal-Mart disagrees, citing its non-discriminatory policy to hire the most qualified applicant. Wal-Mart argues that, under the ADA, Huber was not entitled to be reassigned automatically to the router position without first competing with other applicants. This is a question of first impression in our circuit. As the district court noted, other circuits differ with respect to the meaning of the reassignment language under the ADA.

The Tenth Circuit in *Smith v. Midland Brake, Inc.*, 180 F.3d 1154, 1164-65 (10th Cir. 1999) (en banc), stated:

> [I]f the reassignment language merely requires employers to consider on an equal basis with all other applicants an otherwise qualified existing employee with a disability for reassignment to a vacant position, that language would add nothing to the obligation not to discriminate, and would thereby be redundant....
>
> Thus, the reassignment obligation must mean something more than merely allowing a disabled person to compete equally with the rest of the world for a vacant position.

In the Tenth Circuit, reassignment under the ADA results in automatically awarding a position to a qualified disabled employee regardless whether other better qualified applicants are available, and despite an employer's policy to hire the best applicant.

On the other hand, the Seventh Circuit in *EEOC v. Humiston-Keeling, Inc.*, 227 F.3d 1024, 1027-28 (7th Cir. 2000), explained:

> The reassignment provision makes clear that the employer must also consider the feasibility of assigning the worker to a different job in which his disability will not be an impediment to full performance, and if the reassignment is feasible and does not require the employer to turn away a superior applicant, the reassignment is mandatory.

In the Seventh Circuit, ADA reassignment does not require an employer to reassign a qualified disabled employee to a job for which there is a more qualified applicant, if the employer has a policy to hire the most qualified applicant. Wal-Mart urges this court to adopt the Seventh Circuit's approach and to conclude (1) Huber was not entitled, as a reasonable accommodation, to be reassigned automatically to the router position, and (2) the ADA only requires Wal-Mart to allow Huber to compete for the job,

but does not require Wal-Mart to turn away a superior applicant. We find this approach persuasive and in accordance with the purposes of the ADA. As the Seventh Circuit noted in *Humiston-Keeling:*

> The contrary rule would convert a nondiscrimination statute into a mandatory preference statute, a result which would be both inconsistent with the nondiscriminatory aims of the ADA and an unreasonable imposition on the employers and coworkers of disabled employees. A policy of giving the job to the best applicant is legitimate and nondiscriminatory. Decisions on the merits are not discriminatory.

Id. at 1028. "[T]he [ADA] is not a mandatory preference act." Id.

We agree and conclude the ADA is not an affirmative action statute and does not require an employer to reassign a qualified disabled employee to a vacant position when such a reassignment would violate a legitimate nondiscriminatory policy of the employer to hire the most qualified candidate. This conclusion is bolstered by the Supreme Court's decision in *U.S. Airways, Inc. v. Barnett*, 535 U.S. 391, 406, (2002), holding that an employer ordinarily is not required to give a disabled employee a higher seniority status to enable the disabled employee to retain his or her job when another qualified employee invokes an entitlement to that position conferred by the employer's seniority system. We previously have stated in *dicta* that "an employer is not required to make accommodations that would subvert other, more qualified applicants for the job." *Kellogg v. Union Pac. R.R. Co.*, 233 F.3d 1083, 1089 (8th Cir. 2000) (per curiam).

Thus, the ADA does not require Wal-Mart to turn away a superior applicant for the router position in order to give the position to Huber. To conclude otherwise is "affirmative action with a vengeance. That is giving a job to someone solely on the basis of his status as a member of a statutorily protected group." *Humiston-Keeling*, 227 F.3d at 1029.

Here, Wal-Mart did not violate its duty, under the ADA, to provide a reasonable accommodation to Huber. Wal-Mart reasonably accommodated Huber's disability by placing Huber in a maintenance associate position. The maintenance position may not have been a perfect substitute job, or the employee's most preferred alternative job, but an employer is not required to provide a disabled employee with an accommodation that is ideal from the employee's perspective, only an accommodation that is reasonable.

continued

See *Cravens v. Blue Cross & Blue Shield* of Kan. City, 214 F.3d 1011, 1019 (8th Cir. 2000). In assigning the vacant router position to the most qualified applicant, Wal-Mart did not discriminate against Huber. On the contrary, Huber was treated exactly as all other candidates were treated for the Wal-Mart job opening, no worse and no better.

Conclusion

We reverse the judgment of the district court, and we remand for entry of judgment in favor of Wal-Mart consistent with this opinion.

Case Questions

1. Pam Huber sustained a permanent injury while working for Wal-Mart and could no longer perform her order filler job. The parties agreed that she was qualified for the vacant router position, possessing the required skill, education, experience, and training. The ADA requires reasonable accommodation, including "reassignment to a vacant position." Do you believe the quoted reassignment language means something more than allowing her to compete equally with all other candidates for this vacant position? Explain.

2. Comment on the court's statement "Wal-Mart reasonably accommodated Huber's disability by placing Huber in a maintenance associate position."

3. Read the introductory text for the EEOC's position. What is your view of this position?

SECTION 129: WORKERS' COMPENSATION: RELATIONSHIP TO THE ADA

At common law, the employer is not liable to an injured employee if the employee is harmed by a fellow employee. Nor is the employer liable if the employee is harmed by an ordinary hazard of the work, because the employee assumed such risks. If the injured employee is contributorily negligent, regardless of the employer's negligence, the employer is not liable at common law. The rising incidence of industrial accidents due to the use of more powerful machinery and the growth of the industrialized labor force led to the statutory modification of common law rules relating to liability of employers for industrial accidents. Workers' compensation statutes have been adopted in every state.[38] These laws entitle workers or their dependents to compensation for work-related injuries, occupational diseases, or work-related deaths, without regard to fault or negligence as to the cause of the injuries, diseases, or deaths.

In exchange for compensation under workers' compensation statutes, workers lose their right to sue their employers in court except for intentional torts. Thus, even if an injury is caused by an employer's clear negligence, the employee's sole remedy is limited to that provided in the workers' compensation statute. Recoveries under these statutes are much less than what could be recovered in comparable common law lawsuits. The *Halliman v. Los Angeles School District* case, presented in this section, is an example of the application of the exclusive remedy

---

[38] Workers' compensation statutes do not cover railroad workers, longshore workers, and federal employees. Railroad workers are covered by the Federal Employers' Liability Act (FELA), 45 U.S.C. §§ 51–59; longshore and harbor workers are covered by the Longshoremen's and Harbor Workers' Compensation Act (LHWCA), 33 U.S.C. §§ 901–950; and federal employees are covered by the Federal Employees' Compensation Act (FECA), 5 U.S.C. §§ 8101 *et seq*. One example of the developing common law applicable to FELA suits is found in *Consolidated Rail Corp. v. Gottshall*, 512 U.S. 532 (1994), when the Supreme Court held that a claim for negligent infliction of emotional distress is a valid legal theory under FELA, with a "zone of danger test" to be used for determining who may recover under the theory.

rule. However, the exclusive remedy provisions in workers' compensation laws do not bar employees from pursuing ADA claims.[39]

BENEFITS

For most injuries and occupational diseases "arising out of and in the course of employment," the workers' compensation statutes usually provide (1) immediate medical benefits; (2) prompt periodic wage replacement, very often computed as a percentage of weekly wages (ranging from 50 percent to 80 percent of the injured employee's wage) for a specified number of weeks; (3) if applicable, a death benefit of a limited amount; (4) payment for loss of function or disfigurement (for example, loss of function and disfigurement payment due to a loss of an arm may be set at $31,000 by statute); and (5) vocational retraining services if the employee is unable to return to the former employment as a result of an injury.

A body of law continues to be developed concerning whether an employee received an injury "arising out of and in the course of employment." In *BeVan v. Liberty Northwest Insurance Corp.*,[40] a customer sales worker took her 15 minute mid-morning break at 11:45 a.m. and drove to her nearby house to care for her dog. On her return, she was injured in a car accident. Her injuries were found to have arisen "in the course of her employment" and thus were covered by workers' compensation under a four-factor test: (1) She was under pay during her break, (2) she was entitled to the break, (3) no restrictions limited where she could go on her break, and (4) the activity did not constitute a substantial personal deviation because she left work regularly during her breaks and would have returned on time but for the accident and could not have gone home during her usual lunch period because of an employer meeting. Injuries suffered off the premises during unpaid lunch breaks are not covered by workers' compensation, however, since the employee is free from the control and obligations of employment during this period of time. Injuries occurring off premises while going and coming to work are generally not compensable. However, as will be seen in the *Quaker Oats Co. v. Ciha* case, presented in this section, an exception exists that provides for coverage of employees who are injured while on a "special errand" for the employer.

PROCEEDINGS

Workers' compensation proceedings are brought before a special administrative agency called a workers' compensation or industrial accident board. Workers' compensation laws, being remedial in purpose, are broadly and liberally construed and embrace all activities that can reasonably be included within their coverage. The *Gacioch v. Stroh Brewery Co.* case, presented in this section, is an illustration of the liberal application of a workers' compensation statute.

---

[39] There is no cause of action for workers' compensation claims in the federal district courts. Workers' compensation claims for work-related injuries are handled before state administrative agencies such as industrial accident boards. Should an employer fail to make reasonable accommodations for the same disability, the employer may pursue ADA claims by filing a charge with the EEOC. See *Ridgway v. Metropolitan Museum of Art*, 2007 U.S. Dist. LEXIS 2007 (S.D.N.Y. Apr. 10, 2007).

[40] 174 P.3d 518 (Mont. 2008).

ADA Impact on Workers' Compensation

Under the Americans with Disabilities Act, employers may no longer inquire about job applicants' physical and mental conditions and workers' compensation histories. Prior to the ADA, it was common for employers to ask job applicants about their medical history and whether the applicants had received compensation for injuries. In some states, if an applicant intentionally misrepresented a preexisting disability in his or her employment application, the employer was allowed to raise this misrepresentation as a complete defense to a later workers' compensation claim by the individual. Because employers may no longer ask such questions, it appears that such misrepresentation defenses are no longer viable.

Many workers' compensation claimants fall within the definition of a "qualified individual with a disability" under the ADA. In a workers' compensation case, once an injured worker recovers and want to return to work, the employer may require that individual to take a medical examination to see if the individual can safely perform the essential functions of the job, with or without reasonable accommodation. Such a medical evaluation must be job-related and consistent with business necessity. That is, instead of administering general strength tests, only functional capacities relating to the job in question can be tested. If the recovered worker can perform the essential job functions, the worker must be returned to work under the ADA.

Prior to the ADA, many employers had the policy of requiring that employees be capable of performing the "full duties of a position, 100 percent" in order to be returned to work. Under the ADA, employers must make reasonable accommodation for those workers who can otherwise perform the essential functions of the job.[41] However, employers are not required to provide accommodation that represents undue hardship. Thus, as discussed previously on page 559, a supermarket meat cutter, who was out on workers' compensation for a back injury and is released to return to work by his or her physician, may be found to be able to perform all of the functions of a job, except for being unable to carry meat from the loading dock to the processing area. The supermarket can no longer flatly refuse to return this individual to work without being in violation of the ADA. It would have to make available a cart or device to enable this worker to perform the unloading function. This "accommodation" may cost the employer $500 for the cart or device. Such an accommodation on its face would be reasonable for a large supermarket chain. However, if the employer of the meat cutter was a small store and the owner had very limited financial resources, such an accommodation might be an undue hardship that the employer could lawfully refuse to make.

An employer may recognize a special obligation to create a light duty position for an employee who suffered an occupational injury while performing service for the employer and as a consequence is unable to do his or her regular duties. The employer is not legally obligated to create a light duty position for a nonoccupationally injured employee with a disability as a reasonable accommodation. The

---

[41] EEOC, *Technical Assistance Manual on the Employment Provisions of the ADA*, at IX-4 (January 1992).

ADA does not require employers to create positions as a form of reasonable accommodation.[42]

The ADA, through the "accommodation" process, may return many injured workers to their prior jobs, which in the past would not be open to them. This may well reduce the overall amount of time workers are out on disabilities and may result in substantial reductions in the overall cost of workers' compensation.

CASE 15.5	HALLIMAN V. LOS ANGELES UNIFIED SCHOOL DISTRICT
	CALIFORNIA COURT OF APPEALS, 163 CAL. APP. 3D 46, 209 CAL. RPTR. 175 (1984).

[Robert Halliman was employed as a teacher by the Los Angeles Unified School District at Milliken Junior High School. On November 4, 1982, a minor student, Louis "R," intentionally threw a rock at him, hitting him on the head and seriously injuring him. The same student had committed previous assaults on the school grounds, including an assault earlier that very day. Halliman and his wife brought suit against the Los Angeles Unified School District and the student's parents, seeking damages. Halliman contended that the defendants had the power and ability to prevent the student's conduct by appropriate disciplinary action but did not do so, ignoring their duty to protect students and teachers. The school district filed a motion for a summary judgment on the grounds that the Workers' Compensation Act provided the exclusive remedy for Halliman's injury. From a summary judgment in favor of the school district, Halliman appealed.]

ARGVELLES, A. J....

In this appeal from a judgment favoring a school district, we are called upon to determine whether workers' compensation is the exclusive remedy for a teacher's injuries caused by a student's unprovoked assault while the teacher is acting within the scope of his employment....

We find ... that plaintiffs have failed to state facts negating application of the exclusive remedy provision of the workers' compensation laws in their complaint....

We disagree with plaintiffs' contention that *Meyer v. Graphic Arts International Union* (1979) 88 Cal. App. 3d 176, 151 Cal. Rptr. 597, is dispositive of the issue in their favor. *Meyer* involved injury by a coemployee of

plaintiff, and there had been reported prior acts of aggression by that person against the complaining employee followed by the employer's ratification or acquiescence in failing to discipline, censure, criticize, suspend or discharge the offending coemployee. Here, as defendant correctly points out, the assailant was not a coemployee but a student for whom the plaintiff teacher, among other employees at the school, was responsible. The record before us discloses no reports of prior assaults upon plaintiff teacher by the same student. Additionally, the student's school records indicated that he had, indeed, been previously suspended and otherwise disciplined for prior assaults.

In *Adler v. Los Angeles Unified School Dist.* (1979) 98 Cal. App. 3d 280, 288, 159 Cal. Rptr. 528, though the case was decided on other grounds, the court presumed that where a teacher was injured in a classroom attack by a student, the available workers' compensation remedy barred a civil lawsuit for damages against the employer by virtue of Labor Code section 3601. Under the facts of this case, we so hold.

Plaintiffs argue that a student in this context is akin to an employer's agent or a coemployee who is "under the control" of the employer; and, therefore, the school district "employer" comes within the statutory exception to the exclusive remedy provisions of the workers' compensation laws for intentional acts of agents and coemployees. But, teacher and student are not equals, standing shoulder to shoulder in the classroom or on the playground, with the same status, rights, duties, responsibilities, maturity, judgment, knowledge and skill. If an analogy is to be drawn, a more appropriate one would liken the student to raw

continued

---

[42] See *EEOC Enforcement Guidance: Workers' Compensation and the ADA* issued by the EEOC on Sept. 3, 1996, Questions and Answers 23, 24, 26, and 27.

material which must be wrought by the employee into a finished product.

Thus, we find it helpful in addressing plaintiff's contentions to refer to those cases where the alleged intentional misconduct of the employer does not go beyond failure to assure a safe working environment. The California Supreme Court in *Johns-Manville Products Corp. v. Superior Court* (1980) 27 Cal. 3d 465, 165 Cal. Rptr. 858, 612 P.2d 948, reviewed cases where the employer concealed inherent dangers in the material its employees were required to handle, or made false representations in that regard, or allowed an employee to use a machine without proper instruction. Workers' compensation was held to be the exclusive remedy for any injuries thus suffered. The Supreme Court concluded that the workers' compensation laws provided "the sole remedy for additional compensation against an employer whose employee is injured in the first instance as the result

of a deliberate failure to assure that the physical environment of the workplace is safe."

The facts of the present case do not justify a departure from such precedent.

[Judgment affirmed.]

Case Questions

1. State the issue before the court.
2. Why did the Hallimans bring an action for damages in a court of law when Halliman was clearly entitled to benefits under the workers' compensation law?
3. When an employee is injured as a result of an employer's deliberate failure to provide a safe workplace, may the employee sue the employer for damages in a court of law?
4. Is there an exception to the exclusive remedy provisions of the workers' compensation laws for intentional acts of agents or "coemployees"?

CASE 15.6	QUAKER OATS V. CIHA
	SUPREME COURT OF IOWA, 552 N.W. 2D 143 (1996).

[Bradley Ciha was assigned as the on-call maintenance supervisor for the Memorial Day weekend. After completing call-in service at the employer's plant, he returned home by a scenic, less direct route, and was seriously injured in a motorcycle accident. Quaker Oats, the employer, believed it was not responsible for the injuries of an employee going or coming to work; but if an exception existed for a special errand, the employer believed Ciha deviated from this errand by taking the indirect route home. Quaker Oats did not believe that "reasonable appliances" under the workers' compensation law included modifications costing $20,788 to Ciha's home and a van conversion costing $24,509, nor did it believe Ciha's wife should be paid for nursing care expenses. Finally, the employer did not believe that Ciha was 80 percent "permanent partial" disabled, as the employer modified the workplace and continued to provide full-time employment for Ciha. The matter was appealed from the industrial commissioners' office to the district court to the state supreme court.]

McGIVERIN, C. J....

Ciha first returned to work at Quaker Oats in January 1992 in a new position as materials supervisor. In this position, he works at a computer (with

the aid of an adaptive device and telephone headset) in the company's purchasing department. With the aid of a modified computer, Ciha analyzes inventory and makes purchases on behalf of Quaker Oats. Quaker Oats greatly aided in Ciha's return to work by adapting the workplace and position in order for Ciha to be able to perform the job.* It is apparent Ciha has progressed well in the new position.

In his position as materials supervisor, he receives the same base salary, not including raises, as that of an area maintenance supervisor. Ciha no longer has the same opportunity, however, to earn overtime as he had as an area maintenance supervisor....

In order to return to work, Ciha relied on the county's disabled persons transportation service to and from Quaker Oats. Based on the hours of the transportation service, however, Ciha was not able to return to work full-time.

---

*Upon Ciha's return to work, Quaker Oats installed an automatic door specifically for his use. Also, a group of five Quaker Oats employees were responsible for assisting Ciha with transportation throughout the plant, changing his catheter bags, and knowing of his whereabouts at all times.

continued

Ciha was readmitted to Craig for one week in March 1992 for a comprehensive evaluation. At the time of his readmittance, Ciha did not own a van and did not drive. While at Craig, Ciha had his driving potential assessed. A driving specialist from the hospital concluded Ciha would need to purchase a specially modified van in order to be able to drive independently. At some time thereafter, Ciha purchased the recommended van.

After considering all arguments raised by the parties, we believe substantial evidence supports the commissioner's conclusion that Ciha was on a special errand at the time of his injury....

...The fact that Ciha was contacted on Sunday while he was on 204 duty was truly "special:" it was unusual, sudden, and unexpected....

...Notwithstanding our conclusion that the special errand exception to the going and coming rule applies in the present case, Quaker Oats contends Ciha had "deviated" from his trip home from the plant to such an extent that he abandoned his employment at the time of the accident. The commissioner and district court rejected this argument, and we do the same....

...In concluding Ciha did not deviate from his special errand, the commissioner stated:

> [Ciha] testified that he often took [the Ellis road] route home because it was more scenic, it had less traffic, it had fewer stop lights, and the actual difference in miles between this route and the more direct route was minimal. [Ciha's] call to his wife from the plant to start the grill for their meal shows that his purpose was to return home, and that he had no other destination other than to return to his residence. The record does not show a deviation from the course of the employment.

...Of the expenses awarded by the commissioner under Iowa Code section 85.27, Quaker Oats only challenges the award of costs for home modifications, van conversion, and home nursing services. The commissioner and district court found the home modification and van conversion expenses to be reasonable "appliances" under section 85.27. In addition, the commissioner found the claimed expenses for home nursing services and the claimed value of those services to be reasonable.

Iowa Code section 85.27 provides in pertinent part:

> The employer, for all injuries compensable under this chapter or chapter 85A, shall furnish reasonable surgical, medical, dental, osteopathic, chiropractic, podiatric, physical rehabilitation, nursing, ambulance and hospital services and supplies therefor and shall allow reasonably necessary transportation expenses incurred for such services. The employer shall also furnish reasonable and necessary crutches, artificial members and appliances....

...Quaker Oats does not dispute that the cost of Ciha's wheelchair is compensable under section 85.27; therefore, the question becomes whether the home modifications and van conversion completed to accommodate an admittedly covered appliance (a wheelchair) are compensable under the same statute.

> An "appliance" is defined as hearing aids, corrective lenses, orthodontic devices, dentures, orthopedic braces, or any other artificial device used to provide function or for therapeutic purposes.
>
> Appliances which are for the correction of a condition resulting from an injury ... are compensable under Iowa Code section 85.27....
>
> We begin with the unusually strong medical evidence of necessity and of the record that [the claimant's] family status and past lifestyle reveal no other use for the van. That evidence refutes any contention that the van is a frill or luxury and reveals what can be described as an appliance, not greatly different from crutches or a wheelchair. The point is that a van is necessary in order to make [the claimant's] wheelchair fully useful....

Under the unique facts of the present case, we conclude substantial evidence supports the commissioner's ruling that the home modifications and van conversion were reasonable appliances under Iowa Code section 85.27.

In addition to the claimed home modification and van conversion expenses, Ciha also sought $58,447 in home nursing services performed by his wife after his return home from the hospital in Colorado. At the arbitration hearing, Quaker Oats unsuccessfully contended the claimed home nursing services were not reasonable expenses under section 85.27, and also that the claimed amount of the services set forth in an affidavit prepared by Kim Ciha was unreasonable.

On appeal, Quaker Oats does not dispute that it had a duty under Iowa Code section 85.27 to provide reasonable nursing services to Ciha if his injury was compensable (which we have concluded it is). In addition, Quaker Oats agrees the services performed

continued

by Kim were "nursing" services as contemplated by section 85.27. Quaker Oats contends, however, that $58,447 in home nursing expenses claimed by Ciha is unreasonable. The commissioner and district court disagreed and we must affirm this decision if supported by substantial evidence.

In ordering Quaker Oats to pay Ciha's home nursing services, the commissioner stated the following:

> The record shows that [Ciha's] wife received special training to perform the functions of a nurse for her husband, including digital manipulation to stimulate a bowel movement.
>
> ....
>
> In the instant case, [Ciha's] spouse, although not a nurse or LPN, did have to receive special training to perform the services. The services themselves are clearly medical nursing services and not general care services such as dressing, bathing, feeding, etc. [Ciha's] spouse's nursing services are held to be compensable under Iowa Code section 85.27....

...We believe the affidavit and Kim's testimony establish the reasonableness of the claimed home nursing care expenses by a preponderance of the evidence. We conclude substantial evidence supports the commissioner's finding on this issue.

As a final issue, Quaker Oats contends the commissioner erred in ruling that Ciha had sustained an eighty percent permanent partial industrial disability. Quaker Oats argues Ciha's disability is only fifty to sixty percent because it, Ciha's employer, went to great lengths to accommodate claimant and also that claimant has suffered no loss of earnings.

As we have stated on many occasions, "[i]ndustrial disability measures an injured worker's lost earning capacity." ... Factors that should be considered include the employee's functional disability, age, education, qualifications, experience, and the ability of the employee to engage in employment for which the employee is fitted....

As a result of the accident and resulting quadriplegia, Ciha is wheelchair-bound, cannot control his bowel functions, and his lifestyle has been severely limited from that prior to the injury. He requires extensive, daily care and attention by his wife, relatives, and co-workers as he no longer has the ability to perform many basic daily living functions. Also, as a thirty-eight year old man, it cannot be reasonably disputed that Ciha's employability outside of the Quaker

Oats workforce has been significantly and negatively affected by his injury. Although we applaud the efforts of Quaker Oats in modifying the workplace to accommodate Ciha's disability, such efforts are not determinative of Ciha's industrial disability rating. *See Thilges v. Snap-On Tools Corp.,* 528 N.W.2d 614, 617 (Iowa 1995) ("[W]e are satisfied that the commissioner was correct in viewing loss of earning capacity in terms of the injured worker's present ability to earn in the competitive job market without regard to the accommodation furnished by one's present employer.").

In finding eighty percent industrial disability, the commissioner concluded the following:

> [D]efendant [Quaker Oats] has gone to great effort to accommodate claimant's [Ciha's] devastating disability. Defendant has set up a team of five co-employees to assist claimant, installed a special elevator, etc. These efforts are very appropriate, and defendant is to be commended for putting claimant back to work under difficult circumstances. However, defendant also obtains an advantage by doing so in that claimant's disability is reduced from what it otherwise would be. Although claimant's position is not a "make work" job and involves a significant contribution to his employer, nevertheless if claimant were to be suddenly thrust into the job market, his ability to compete with other workers for positions would be limited in the most extreme sense. Clearly, without the accommodation, claimant's disability would be permanent and total. Claimant's industrial disability is found to be [eighty] percent.

We conclude there is substantial evidence to support the commissioner's decision on this issue.

Affirmed.

Case Questions

1. Assess the extent of the accommodations the employer made to allow Ciha to be able to return to work.

2. Because Bradley Ciha suffered no loss of earnings, how can he be considered 80 percent permanent partial disabled?

3. Under Section 85.27, "The employer shall also furnish reasonable and necessary crutches, artificial members, and appliances...." Did the legislature authorize a home modification ($20,788) and a van conversion ($24,509) under the term *appliances*?

CASE 15.7 | GACIOCH V. STROH BREWERY CO.
MICHIGAN COURT OF APPEALS, 466 N.W. 2D 303 (1991).

[Gacioch sought workers' compensation benefits for chronic alcoholism, asserting that the condition arose out of his employment with the brewery and resulted in his disability. The Workers' Compensation Appeal Board (WCAB) awarded benefits, and the employer appealed.]

NEFF, J....

Defendants appeal from a decision of the Workers' Compensation Appeal Board, which essentially found that the decedent's alcoholism and the resulting disability were compensable under the Workers' Disability Compensation Act.

Reduced to its essence, the lengthy opinion of the appeal board reached the following conclusions:

1. The decedent clearly had the disease of alcoholism and whether this disease was an occupational disease or an ordinary disease of life is irrelevant if the disease was aggravated, accelerated, or contributed to by the employment, thereby resulting in disability. Aggravation or acceleration of or contribution to the decedent's underlying condition would constitute a personal injury under the Workers' Disability Compensation Act.

2. Alcoholism, like cardiovascular disease, is an ordinary disease of life, and the allegation is that the course of the disease was contributed to by the employment. Therefore, *Kostamo v. Marquette Iron Mining Co.,* 405 Mich. 105, 274 N.W.2d 411 (1979), and *Miklik v. Michigan Special Machine Co.,* 415 Mich. 364, 329 N.W.2d 713 (1982), apply to the case at bar.

3. While the decedent was predisposed to alcoholism before he was hired by defendant, he was not an alcoholic when he was hired. The unique circumstances of the employment shaped the course of the decedent's disease, aggravating and accelerating the underlying predisposition to alcoholism to the point of uncontrolled addiction, thus constituting a personal injury under the act.

4. The aggravation or acceleration of the decedent's alcoholic propensities occurred as a circumstance of the employment relationship.

5. Whether a personal injury analysis or an occupational disease analysis is employed in this case, the decedent's condition is compensable. An ordinary disease of life can be compensable as an occupational disease if exposure to the disease is increased by inherent characteristics of the employment, as existed in this case. *Mills v. Detroit Tuberculosis Sanitarium,* 323 Mich. 200, 35 N.W.2d 239 (1948).

After review of the record, the parties' briefs, and oral argument, we conclude that the WCAB correctly decided this case, and, accordingly, we affirm and adopt the board's opinion and order.

Affirmed.

Case Questions

1. Can ordinary diseases of life be compensable as an occupational injury or disease under a workers' compensation act?

2. Based on a "common-sense viewpoint of the average person in society" test, do you believe that Gacioch's disability should be a compensable industrial accident or an occupational disease? Explain.

SECTION 130: ACCOMMODATION BETWEEN SSDI AND THE ADA

Social Security taxes provide employees with three types of insurance protections: (1) retirement benefits under Old-Age and Survivors Insurance; (2) disability benefits under Social Security Disability Insurance (SSDI); and (3) hospitalization benefits under Medicaid.[43] Disabled individuals who do not have sufficient work history to qualify for SSDI may be entitled to Supplemental Security Income payments (SSI) based strictly on need.

---

[43] 42 U.S.C. § 4236(2)(A).

SSDI benefits are available to individuals with disabilities who cannot perform their previous work or substantial other gainful work. In *Cleveland v. Policy Management Systems Corp.*,[44] the U.S. Supreme Court dealt with the question of whether an individual's statement in her SSDI application for disability benefits that she was "disabled" and "unable to work" precluded her from later pursuing an ADA claim that she could "perform the essential functions" of her job with "reasonable accommodation." Carolyn Cleveland, after suffering a stroke and losing her job, obtained SSDI benefits, claiming she was unable to work due to her disability. The week before her SSDI award, Cleveland brought an ADA lawsuit against her former employer, contending that it had terminated her employment without reasonably accommodating her disability. The U.S. district court, affirmed by the Fifth Circuit Court of Appeals, granted summary judgment against her because by applying for and receiving SSDI benefits, she had conceded that she was totally disabled and she was therefore estopped from pursuing the essential elements of the ADA claim that she could perform the essential functions of her job with reasonable accommodation. The Fifth Circuit determined that Cleveland did not overcome a rebuttable presumption of judicial estoppel.

The Supreme Court disagreed, stating:

> The Social Security Disability Insurance (SSDI) program provides benefits to a person with a disability so severe that she is 'unable to do [her] previous work' and 'cannot ... engage in any other kind of substantial gainful work which exists in the national economy.' §223(a) of the Social Security Act. This case asks whether the law erects a special presumption that would significantly inhibit an SSDI recipient from simultaneously pursuing an action for disability discrimination under the Americans with Disabilities Act of 1990 (ADA), claiming that 'with ... reasonable accommodation' she could 'perform the essential functions' of her job.

We believe that, in context, these two seemingly divergent statutory contentions are often consistent, each with the other. Thus, pursuit and receipt of SSDI benefits does not automatically estop the recipient from pursuing an ADA claim. Nor does the law erect a strong presumption against the recipient's success under the ADA. Nonetheless, an ADA plaintiff cannot simply ignore her SSDI contention that she was too disabled to work. To survive a defendant's motion for summary judgment, she must explain why the SSDI contention is consistent with her ADA claim that she could "perform the essential functions" of her previous job, at least with "reasonable accommodation."[45]

---

[44] 526 U.S. 795 (1998).

[45] Cleveland had not been given an opportunity to explain to the trial court how her SSDI contention was consistent with her ADA claim that she could do her job with reasonable accommodation. She had submitted an affidavit from her treating physician that the accommodations she sought, training and additional time to complete her work, could allow her to perform the essential functions of her job.

SECTION 131: FAMILY AND MEDICAL LEAVES OF ABSENCE

The federal Family and Medical Leave Act of 1993 (FMLA)[46] entitles an eligible employee, whether male or female, to a total of 12 workweeks of unpaid leave during any 12-month period (1) due to the birth or adoption of the employee's son or daughter; (2) in order to care for the employee's spouse, son, daughter, or parent with a serious health condition; or (3) because of a "serious health condition" that makes the employee unable to perform the functions of the employee's position. In the case of an employee's serious health condition or that of a covered family member, the employer may require verification of the condition and may require that the employee use any accrued paid vacation, personal, medical, or sick leave toward any part of the 12-week leave provided by the Act. When an employee requests leave due to the birth or adoption of a child, the employer may require that the employee use all available paid personal, vacation, and family leave, but not sick leave, toward any FMLA leave.

The Secretary of Labor has issued regulations necessary to carry out the FMLA. Under FMLA and Labor Department regulations, an employer cannot penalize an employee for time missed due to FMLA leave.[47] An employer cannot count FMLA leave in an adverse manner regarding hiring, promotion, or discipline. Moreover, an employer may not take FMLA leave into consideration regarding bonuses for perfect attendance or safety. In *Dierlam v. Wesley Jessen Corp.*,[48] a federal court in Illinois determined that Valerie Dierlam was entitled to the full amount of a "stay bonus" promised by the new owner of the company under which employees as of November 1, 2000, were eligible for a lump sum payment of 50 percent of their annual base salary if they remained employed and actively working for the company as of September 30, 2001. The full amount of the bonus was $30,027.50. In May 2001, Dierlam was granted a 12-week FMLA leave for the adoption of a child. The employer prorated and reduced her stay bonus by $8,407 to reflect her 12-week FMLA leave. The court found that the stay bonus was clearly analogous to a perfect attendance bonus and concluded that Dierlam may not be disqualified, either partially or wholly, for the taking of the FMLA leave.

The FMLA requires that an employee taking covered leave "be restored by the employer to the position of employment held by the employee when the leave commenced; or...to an equivalent position with equivalent benefits [and] pay...."[49] However, the Labor Department regulations provide that an employer does not have to reinstate an employee who would have been terminated if he or she did not take FMLA leave.[50] With employers relying on the Labor Department regulation and employees relying on the language of the Act, litigation is common. In *Brenlla v. LaSorsa Buick*, when Magda Brenlla returned to her position at

---

[46] 29 U.S.C. § 2601 *et seq.*

[47] See 29 U.S.C § 2645. See also 239 C.F.R. § 825.215 (C)(2).

[48] 222 F. Supp.2d 1052 (2002).

[49] 29 U.S.C. § 2614 (a)(1).

[50] 29 C.F.R. § 825.216 (a)(1).

LaSorsa Buick in the Bronx, New York, after quadruple bypass surgery, she was terminated by the owner, who told her he decided to consolidate the positions of office manager and controller, even though he had no business plan for restructuring and soon thereafter had to hire additional help in the office. The judge upheld a jury verdict of $320,000, finding that the jury had ample evidence to conclude that the real reason for her termination was her FMLA leave.[51]

ELIGIBILITY

To be eligible for an FMLA leave, an employee must have been employed by a covered employer for at least 12 months and worked at least 1,250 hours during the 12-month period preceding the leave.[52] "Covered" employers are those that employ 50 or more employees at the time the leave is requested.[53] Upon return from an FMLA leave, the employee is entitled to be restored to the same or an equivalent position, with equivalent pay and benefits.

NOTICE

The Act requires an employee to give 30 days' notice for parental leave, if practicable. The FMLA does not set forth a notice period for the employee to notify an employer of the need for an FMLA leave for the other reasons set forth in the Act. The Department of Labor has instituted a regulation on this matter, requiring an employee to give the employer 30 days' notice if the leave is foreseeable and "as soon as practicable" when it is not foreseeable. The leave may be taken intermittently or on a reduced schedule basis, and notice need be given only one time.

In *McCarron v. British Telecom*,[54] a federal court in Pennsylvania determined that an absent employee's voicemail request to a human resources manager for "family leave to deal with a family situation"—without further explanation as sought by the employer, who left the employee a voicemail message stating the company "needed proper paper work to support the request"—was insufficient to initiate the protection of the FMLA and to set aside the employee's dismissal for absenteeism. The court stated, "Although there is no precise definition as to what constitutes 'sufficient notice,' an employee is required to provide his employer with enough information for the employer to determine that the leave qualifies under the Act."[55]

---

[51] *Brenlla v. LaSorsa Buick*, 2002 WL 1059117 (S.D.N.Y. 2002).

[52] In *Grace v. USCAR*, 521 F.3d 655 (6th Cir. 2008), the Sixth Circuit held that an employment agency, Bartech, and a partnership of U.S. automobile manufacturers doing research for the industry called USCAR were joint employers of Rosalyn Grace that were obligated to honor her FMLA-qualifying leave.

[53] In *Bellum v. PCE Constructors, Inc.*, 407 F.3d 734 (5th Cir. 2005), the Court of Appeals upheld a DOL regulation filling in a gap in the law providing an exception to the definition of "eligible employee," excluding employees of employers who have less than 50 employees within a 75-mile radius of the worksite, 29 U.S.C. § 2612(a)(1)(D). The court approved a DOL regulation that measured the 75 miles in road miles as opposed to "as the crow flies" and held that a construction employee who took medical leave for heart surgery was not covered by the FMLA.

[54] 2002 WL 1832843 (E.D. Pa.).

[55] *Id.* at 4.

To comply with the Secretary of Labor's regulations, the employer should give notice to an employee that the leave he or she is taking will count against FMLA entitlement. The Labor Department had a regulation stating that the employer shall be denied any credit for leave granted before the notice is given to the employee.[56] In *Ragsdale v. Wolverine Worldwide, Inc.*,[57] the employer granted 30 weeks of unpaid sick leave to an employee without notifying her that 12 weeks of the leave counted as FMLA leave. The employee sought an additional 12 weeks under the department's notice penalty regulation. The Supreme Court determined in a 5-4 decision that the Department of Labor lacked authority to grant more than 12 weeks of FMLA leave in one year and thus struck down the penalty provision in the regulation. However, a proposed DOL regulation provides remedial relief for losses caused by the employer's "violation of FMLA regulations."[58]

A Department of Labor regulation prohibits waiver or release of an employee's FMLA rights unless the waiver or settlement of a FMLA claim has the prior approval of the DOL or a court.[59]

DAMAGES

The FMLA provides specific statutory relief for violations of the provisions of the Act, including pay to the employee for damages equal to lost wages and benefits or any actual monetary losses, plus interest, plus an equal amount in liquidated damages,[60] and appropriate equitable relief such as reinstatement, employment, or promotion. As determined in the *Drew v. Waffle House, Inc.* decision, presented in this section, front pay is payment in lieu of reinstatement and is a form of equitable relief and thus is not calculated in determining the liquidated damage figure.

Should a covered employer refuse to allow an employee to take a FMLA qualifying leave or retaliate against an employee for taking such a leave, that individual may file a complaint with the local office of the Wage and Hour Division of the Department of Labor.[61] Or the individual may seek a private remedy by filing an action in federal court. In *Duckworth v. Pratt & Whitney, Inc.*,[62] the First Circuit Court of Appeals decided that a former employee could pursue a private right of action against his former employer under the FMLA based on the allegation that

---

[56] 29 C.F.R § 825.200(a).

[57] *Ragsdale v. Wolverine Worldwide, Inc.*, 122 S.Ct. 1155 (2002).

[58] See 73 Fed. Reg. 7875 (Feb. 11, 2008).

[59] 29 C.F.R. § 825.220(d). See also *Taylor v. Progress Energy, Inc.*, 415 F.3d 364 (4th Cir. 2005).

[60] See *Arban v. West Publishing Co.*, 345 F.3d 390 (6th Cir. 2003), where the U.S. Court of Appeals required the doubling of a jury verdict of $130,000 under the FMLA provision providing for liquidated damages, unless the employer is able to prove it acted "in good faith ..." and had reasonable grounds to believe it was not in violation of the FMLA. 29 U.S.C. § 2617(a)(iii).

[61] DOL will not seek enforcement if the employee did not have a serious health condition to justify the leave and did not give proper notice or if the employee tried to use the FMLA as an excuse for a poor attendance record.

[62] 152 F.3d 1 (1st Cir. 1998).

the employer refused to rehire him because of his previous use of the FMLA's protected right to take medical leave.

A two-year statute of limitations applies to all claims under the FMLA, except in the case of "willful violations," to which a three-year statute of limitations applies. In *Bass v. Potter* (USPS),[63] the Tenth Circuit Court of Appeals adopted the U.S. Supreme Court's *McLaughlin v. Richland Shoe Co.* interpretaion of "willful" under the Fair Labor Standards Act—"whether the employer either knew or showed reckless disregard for whether its conduct was prohibited by the statue."[64] Tony Boss's claim against the U.S. Postal Service did not produce evidence of a willful violation of the FMLA, and his claim filed after the two-year limitation period was thus time-barred.

CASE 15.8	DREW v. WAFFLE HOUSE, INC.
	SUPREME COURT OF SOUTH CAROLINA, 571 S.E.2D 89 (2002).

[Norma Drew was employed by Waffle House, Inc., as a restaurant manager in Hardeeville, South Carolina. In March 1993, she injured herself on the job while trying to secure a wind-blown sign in the restaurant parking lot. As a result, she had shoulder surgery for which she was authorized to take 12 weeks of leave from work. Although her supervisor authorized an extension of her leave, she was fired for absenteeism when she reported back to work. She subsequently sued her employer, which ultimately resulted in a jury verdict in her favor on her cause of action alleging a violation of the FMLA. By agreement of the parties, damages were submitted to the trial judge for determination. Pursuant to the FMLA, the judge awarded $103,273 in back pay for her pretrial loss of wages, plus prejudgment interest of $32,756.90. He further awarded $304,845.69 in "front pay." Finally, he calculated the amount of liquidated damages by adding the amount of back pay, prejudgment interest, and front pay, for a total of $440,875.59 in liquidated damages. On appeal, Waffle House contested the award of front pay, claiming it was highly speculative because it was based on the assumption that Drew would have worked for Waffle House for another 19 years until her retirement at age 65. The South Carolina Court of Appeals agreed and

modified the front pay award from $304,845.69 to $84,251.80, based on four years of front pay rather than 19. Waffle House further argued to the court of appeals that the front pay award should not have been included in the calculation of liquidated damages. The court of appeals agreed and reduced the liquidated damages award from $440,875.59 to $136,029.90. The Supreme Court of South Carolina agreed to review the court of appeals decision.]

MOORE, J....

Issues

1. Was front pay properly included in the calculation of liquidated damages?
2. Was the amount of front pay proper?

Discussion

1. Liquidated damages

The FMLA provides specific statutory relief for a violation of its provisions. Under 29 U.S.C. § 2617 (a)(1), an employer who violates the Act is liable to the employee:

    (A) for *damages* equal to—
    (i) the amount of—

continued

---

[63] 522 F.3d 1098 (10th Cir. 2008).

[64] *McLaughlin v. Richard Shoe Co.*, 486 U.S. 128 (1988).

(I) any wages, salary, employment benefits, or other compensation denied or lost to such employee by reason of the violation; or

(II) in a case in which wages, salary, employment benefits, or other compensation have not been denied or lost to the employee, any actual monetary losses ...;

(ii) the *interest on the amount described in clause* (i) calculated at the prevailing rate; and

(iii) an additional amount as liquidated damages equal to the sum of the amount described in clause (i) and the interest described in clause (ii)....; and

(B) for such *equitable relief* as may be appropriate, including employment, reinstatement, and promotion. (emphasis added).

Under this statute, the liquidated damages award is affected by whether front pay is classified as "damages" under clause (a)(l)(A)(i) or "equitable relief under clause (a)(l)(B) because relief classified as equitable is not included in the calculation of liquidated damages. Citing federal case law, the Court of Appeals ruled front pay was equitable relief and therefore should not be included in the calculation of liquidated damages.

The classification of front pay as legal or equitable relief impacts a substantial right of the plaintiff and therefore federal case law controls....

Applying federal precedent, we hold front pay is equitable relief under clause (a)(l)(B). Because liquidated damages do not include equitable relief, the Court of Appeals properly excluded front pay from the calculation of liquidated damages.

2. Amount of front pay award

The Court of Appeals held the front pay award for nineteen years was "highly speculative and unsupported by the record." It then held, without explanation, that under its view of the preponderance of the evidence, four years' front pay was "a more appropriate award." Petitioner [Drew] contends the evidence supports the award because petitioner testified she would have worked at Waffle House until she retired at age sixty-five....

Front pay is awarded as a complement or as an alternative to reinstatement. *Duke*, 928 F.2d at 1424. If reinstatement is shown to be infeasible, for instance because of a hostile atmosphere, front pay may be awarded in lieu thereof or to reimburse the employee until the time of reinstatement. *See generally Pollard*, 532 U.S. at 853–54, 121 S.Ct. 1946.

Under the FMLA, an employee is entitled to reinstatement upon return from leave. 29 U.S.C. § 2614 (a)(l)(A). Once an employee proves she was denied reinstatement, the employer must prove the employee would have been laid off in any event for some other reason in order to defeat a claim for reinstatement. *Smith v. Diffee Ford-Lincoln-Mercury, Inc.*, 298 F.3d 955 (10th Cir. 2002); *see also* 29 C.F.R. § 825.216(a) ("An employer must be able to show that an employee would not otherwise have been employed at the time reinstatement is requested in order to deny restoration to employment."). Similarly, the employer must bear the burden of proving the employee is not entitled to front pay, which is awarded in lieu of reinstatement, if the employee seeks front pay rather than reinstatement.

It is uncontested petitioner was denied reinstatement upon her return from FMLA leave. She claimed front pay based on her entitlement to reinstatement. It was Waffle House's burden to show petitioner would have been terminated for an unrelated reason while on FMLA leave, or that her continued employment would have been limited, in order to defeat or reduce the claim for front pay; in the alternative, Waffle House could have asserted the feasibility of reinstatement in lieu of a front pay award. Waffle House failed to carry its burden on this issue. We defer to the trial judge's judgment and affirm the award of front pay. The Court of Appeals's decision vacating the award is reversed.

[Affirmed in part; reversed in part.]

Case Questions

1. What significance is applied to classifying front pay as appropriate "equitable relief" rather than as "damages" in the calculation of liquidated damages?

2. Calculate the proper amount of damages owed Ms. Drew.

3. Assess the quality of the employer's decision to pay front pay to Ms. Drew rather than reinstate her to her manager's position.

SECTION 132: MILITARY LEAVES AND REEMPLOYMENT RIGHTS

The Uniformed Services Employment and Reemployment Rights Act (USERRA) was enacted in 1994 to encourage noncareer service in the armed services, minimize the disruption experienced in the civilian careers of reservists, and promote prompt reemployment of reservists upon return from military leave.[65] In the context of over 500,000 reservists being mobilized between September 11, 2001, and the spring of 2008, the USERRA has and will have a broad impact on American employers as it provides reemployment and benefit protection rights for returning military personnel and prohibits discrimination against individuals because of their application for or performance of military service.[66]

PROTECTIONS

Section 4312 of the USERRA generally requires returning reservists to be "promptly reemployed" and returned to the same or comparable positions of like seniority, status, and pay they would have had if they had not been activated. Moreover, Section 4316(c) of the Act provides that persons reemployed under the Act shall not be discharged from employment within a year of their reemployment if their period of service was over 180 days. For service more than 30 days, the protective period is 180 days. However, the employer may terminate an individual for cause regardless of the duration of service.

Section 4312(a)(3) and (4) provides protection for those disabled while in the service and requires employers to make reasonable efforts to accommodate each employee's disability so that he or she may return to the same or comparable positions or, if no longer qualified for that position, allow for the transfer to a position the disabled serviceperson can perform closest to the prior position in terms of seniority, status, and pay.

Section 4323 of the Act provides a full range of remedies, including back pay for loss of wages and benefits as well as liquidated damages in an amount equal to the actual damages when the employer's failure to comply with the Act was willful. The Department of Labor has issued USERRA regulations.[67] Enforcement of the Act is performed by the U.S. Justice Department's Division of Civil Rights. Employers are required to post notices of USERRA rights in prominent places at the worksite, as published by the Department of Labor.

---

[65] 38 U.S.C. § 4301 (2005).

[66] 38 U.S.C. § 4312, 4316, and 4317 (2005).

[67] Federal Register Vol. 70 No. 242 (Dec. 19, 2005).

DEFENSES

In addition to an employer's right to terminate a reemployed serviceperson for cause,[68] employers may be excused from reemploying or continuing employment of persons under § 4312(d)(1) of the Act where the employer's circumstances have so changed as to make reemployment impossible, unreasonable, or an undue hardship. The burden of proof on the matter is on the employer.

In *Duarte v. Agilent Technologies, Inc.,*[69] the U.S. District Court determined that the employer violated the USERRA, which provides that returning military are entitled to be returned to the same or equivalent position with their employer and cannot be discharged within one year of reemployment except for cause. Duarte was called to active duty in the Marine Corps Reserve from November 2002 to July 2003. On his return, Duarte was given his same pay but his status was diminished by being assigned a temporary assignment rather than acting as a primary consultant to one of the employer's business groups. Faced with financial hardship necessitating a reduction in its payroll, the employer eliminated Duarte's temporary assignment and terminated him in November 2003 for what it believed was economic "cause." The court disagreed. Duarte was within the one-year protective period of the Act. He was returned to work in the diminished status of a temporary assignment that was a direct result of his military service. The employer did not succeed on its defenses of cause or economic hardship. Duarte was awarded back pay of $114,500, front pay of $324,000, less $55,000 in severance benefits already paid him, for a total of $384,000 in damages. Liquidated damages equal to $384,000 were declined because the employer's actions were not deemed willful.

DISCRIMINATION AND RETALIATION PROTECTION

As opposed to the protections contained in Section 4312, Section 4311 of the Act provides separate and distinct statutory protection against discrimination of employees on the basis of military service and retaliation against individuals, whether military or not, who give testimony or statements on behalf of a USERRA claimant. An example of discrimination on the basis of military service is found in *Mills v. Earthgrains Baking Co.*[70] An affidavit by the company's former HR director stated that if the company had known Mills was in the Guard, they would not have hired him. The court allowed the case to go to trial because there was enough evidence to show that Mills's status as a reservist was a substantial or motivating factor in his termination.

---

[68] The burden of proof in "for-cause" terminations was addressed by the First Circuit. In *Velazquez-Garcia v. Horizon Lines of PR, Inc.,* 473 F.3d 11 (1st Cir. 2007), the First Circuit Court of Appeals reinstated a U.S. Marine Corps Reservist's USERRA claim against his employer that he had been discharged from his job due to his military service. The court did so because the trial court had incorrectly allocated the burden of proof. Rather than apply the three-pronged *McDonell Douglas* framework regarding burdens of proof, the trial court should have applied the NLRA-*Wright Line* two-pronged, burden-shifting approach. The plaintiff made out his prima facie case, and the burden then shifted to the employer to demonstrate, by a preponderance of the evidence, that it would have fired him regardless of his military status. The case was remanded for trial.

[69] 366 F. Supp. 2d 1039 (D. Colo. 2005).

[70] 2004 WL 1749500 (E.D. Tenn. 2004).

CHAPTER QUESTIONS AND PROBLEMS

1. Are individuals who are perceived as having handicaps, but in fact either have recovered from the disability or are not handicapped, covered by the Rehabilitation Act of the ADA?

2. Are all workers with occupational injuries protected by the ADA?

3. Mazir Coleman drove a school bus for the Casey County, Kentucky, Board of Education for four years. In 1978, Coleman's left leg was amputated. Coleman was fitted with an artificial leg and underwent extensive rehabilitation to relearn driving skills. When his driving skills had been sufficiently relearned over the course of four years, Coleman applied to the county board of education for a job as a school bus driver. The county refused to accept Coleman's application. The county board said that they had no alternative but to deny Coleman a bus-driving job because a Kentucky administrative regulation required it. That regulation states in part that "No person shall drive a school bus who does not possess both of these natural bodily parts: feet, legs, hands, arms, eyes, and ears. The driver shall have normal use of the above named body parts."

    Coleman brought an action under the Rehabilitation Act claiming discrimination based on his physical handicap. The county board of education denied this charge, claiming that the reason they rejected Coleman was because of the requirement of the state regulation.

    May Coleman maintain an action of employment discrimination in light of the state regulation on natural body parts? What factors must be proved to establish his case? Decide the case. [*Coleman v. Casey County Board of Education*, 26 FEP 357 (N.D. Ky.)]

4. The New York City Police Department was a recipient of federal funds subject to the Rehabilitation Act of 1973. When Officer Heron, a three-year veteran of the department, began having attendance problems, a police psychologist suggested that Heron turn in his gun and be placed on nonpatrol duty. Despite these actions, Heron's attendance problems continued, and it was eventually discovered that Heron was addicted to heroin.

    The department immediately initiated disciplinary proceedings against Heron and sought to dismiss him. After a hearing, Heron was dismissed and denied eligibility for continuing health or pension benefits.

    Heron alleged that his condition was due to job-related stress and exposure to dangerous and violent incidents. He challenged his dismissal in federal court because the department had a policy of not dismissing alcoholic officers. He alleged that the initiation of disciplinary action against him was prohibited by Section 504 of the Rehabilitation Act of 1973 because he was an otherwise qualified person disciplined solely because of his handicap.

    What factors must the court consider in evaluating Heron's claim? What result should the court reach in this case? Decide. [*Heron v. McGuire*, 42 FEP 31 (2d Cir.)]

5. The collective bargaining contract between the National Machinists Union (NMU) and Life Bread Company set forth a "no fault" attendance program that assessed points for absences and tardiness regardless of fault. Article XIII states in part:

ATTENDANCE POLICY AND GUIDE
PURPOSE
In order for the company to meet its customer requirements and maintain a competitive position in the market, it is essential that an employee be at work on time.

The purpose of this guide is to outline and define the company's objectives concerning attendance and the methods to be used in order to attain these objectives.

PROCEDURE

1. Effective November 1, 2008, all employees will have a clean record.
2. Records of absences and lateness will be maintained on all employees.
3. Each occurrence will have a point value:
   A. DOCUMENTED ABSENCE . . . . 5 POINTS
   B. LATENESS . . . . 5 POINTS
   C. *LEAVE EARLY . . . . 5 POINTS
   D. EXCESSIVE LATENESS
      (Employees who punch in more than three hours after the start of their scheduled shift) . . . 10 POINTS
   E. UNEXCUSED ABSENCE . . . . . 15 POINTS
   F. UNEXCUSED ABSENCE WITHOUT NOTIFICATION . . . 25 POINTS
   G. PERFECT ATTENDANCE—FOR EACH MONTH OF PERFECT ATTENDANCE AN EMPLOYEE WILL RECEIVE . . . 5 POINTS CREDIT
4. ...
   C. When an employee reaches seventy-five (75) Points, final counseling session will be conducted between the employee, his/her supervisor, and the manufacturing manager and the company general manager. A written record will be made with a copy sent to the union. A union representative may be present.
   D. When an employee reaches one hundred (100) Points, the employee will be terminated.
5. INDUSTRIAL ACCIDENT
   When an employee is hurt and is absent as a result of an industrial accident, he/she will not be charged with an absence.

The contract provides a bonus for perfect attendance; and after a year, each assessment of points is removed from an employee's record.

John O'Reilly joined the company after graduation from high school and had nine years of service as of December 2008. He played softball and bowled for company teams and often stayed out late having a "few beers" after these events. John was late for his 6 AM shift more than most employees. John also lost a lot of time due to a documented asthma condition he had had all of his life. In the past, John had come close to being assessed 100 points, which would have allowed his discharge.

In December 2008, John seriously injured his back while working on a bread-molding machine. The injury resulted in two back operations and extensive physical therapy. John was assigned to light duty during this period, and no points were assessed for any loss of time or lateness due to this injury. However, as a result of some car problems, some oversleeping, and some asthma attacks, his attendance record was assessed 115 points in July 2009, and he was terminated under Article XIII(4)(D) of the collective bargaining contract.

What is a "no-fault" attendance program?

Was the termination of O'Reilly justified under the contract? Is the contract in compliance with the ADA? Explain.

6. Excellent Lumber Milling Corporation has created light duty assignments for three disabled workers seriously injured on the job when they could no longer perform their regular duties as a result of their job-related injuries. A fourth employee, Clare Patrick, can no longer perform the heavy labor duties of a lumber stacker at the mill because of a disability caused by a serious off-the-job auto accident. As a disabled individual, she requests the employer to create a light duty position for her as a reasonable accommodation under the ADA. The company president denied Patrick's request, pointing out that she had not been injured on the job. Did the company violate the ADA by treating individuals with job-related disabilities differently from an individual with a disability caused by an off-the-job accident? Decide. [See "EEOC Enforcement Guidance: Workers' Compensation and the ADA, Question and Answer 27."]

7. Beverly C. was fired from her position as a clerk-typist for county government in Maryland because of outbursts and rude behavior directed at her supervisors. She had a manic-depressive disorder and believed that she should not have been fired. Rather, because of her handicap, she believed the employer should have made reasonable accommodations, including restructuring her job duties, changing her work schedule to alleviate stressful periods, relocating her from her current supervisor, and exempting her from normal performance reviews. The county had made efforts to accommodate C's problems through extensive training opportunities, job counseling, a medical leave, and offers to work with a psychiatrist. Did the employer violate the ADA by refusing to make the changes sought by the disabled individual and by terminating her for her outbursts and rude behavior to her supervisors? Decide. [DLR No.9, Jan. 13, 1995.]

8. Robert Maddox served as an assistant football coach at the University of Tennessee. The university did not know that he was an alcoholic with three arrests, two of which involved alcohol, prior to his employment by the university. On May 26, Maddox, while intoxicated, backed his car across a major public highway at a high rate of speed and was arrested and charged with driving under the influence and public intoxication. This incident received considerable attention from the regional press. Thereafter, the university investigated the charges and then sent him a written notice of termination, stating three reasons for the university's action: (1) his criminal acts, (2) the bad publicity, and (3) the university's determination that Maddox no longer possessed the qualifications necessary to serve as an assistant football coach.

   Maddox brought an action against the university, alleging that his termination was discriminatory because of his alcoholism and thus violated his rights under both the Rehabilitation Act and the ADA. In support of his action, Maddox alleged that the drunk driving incident constituted a causally connected manifestation of his alcoholism. In response, the university filed a motion for summary judgment, alleging that it had terminated Maddox for his misconduct rather than his disability. Can a person have a disability because of alcoholism and thus be within the protection of the Rehabilitation Act and the ADA? Under a different scenario, suppose the athletic director (AD) indirectly found out that an assistant football coach was an alcoholic through admissions made by the coach at an Alcoholics Anonymous meeting and when confronted by the AD, admitted to having a history of excessive use of alcohol. Could the AD terminate the at-will assistant coach based on the individual's own admissions? How would you decide the *Maddox* case under the two disabilities acts? [*Maddox v. University of Tennessee*, 62 F.3d 843 (6th Cir.)]

9. Bryant is the administrator of the estate of the deceased and the guardian of the deceased's minor child. Bryant sued Wal-Mart for damages following the death of the deceased based on the theory of unlawful false imprisonment. While working on the night restocking crew, the deceased suffered a stroke. Medical personnel arrived six minutes later but could not enter the store because management had locked all doors of the store and no manager was present to open the door. By the time the medical crew entered the store to assist her, they were unable to revive her, and she died 15 minutes later. Bryant contended that false imprisonment occurred from the time the deceased became ill until the time the medical team was able to enter the store. Wal-Mart claimed that Bryant's exclusive remedy was under the Workers' Compensation Act. Was Wal-Mart incorrect? Decide. [*Bryant v. Wal-Mart Stores, Inc.*, 417 S.E.2d 688 (Ga. Ct. App.)]

10. Overton suffered from depression and was made sleepy at work by medication taken for this condition. Also, because of his medical condition, Overton needed a work area away from public access and needed substantial

supervision to complete his tasks. The employer terminated him because of his routinely sleeping on the job, his inability to maintain contact with the public, and his need for supervision. Overton defended that he is a disabled person under the ADA and the Rehabilitation Act, fully qualified to perform the essential functions of the job, and that the employer had an obligation to make reasonable accommodations, such as allowing him catnaps as needed and providing extra supervision. Decide. [*Overton v. Reilly*, 977 F.2d 1190 (7th Cir.)]

11. While on an FMLA leave related to the birth of her son, Catherine Marzano was notified in writing that her position was being eliminated as a result of a reduction in force (RIF) caused by financial difficulties. Shortly thereafter, in October 1993, she went to see her boss, and he told her "how his wife had collected unemployment so that she could stay at home with their kids, and how [Marzano] might be better off if she could stay at home with her son and collect unemployment." On November 1, 1993, her boss circulated a memo advertising three positions. Marzano was never advised of or considered for these positions. Marzano asserted that pregnancy is the kiss of death with the employer, with many employees being terminated after taking maternity leave. The employer asserted that it acted out of legitimate business and economic considerations when it eliminated 9 out of some 50 positions in the unit, including Marzano's. Marzano responded that it was a reshuffling of employees, not a legitimate RIF. Did the employer violate the FMLA by terminating Marzano during her leave? Decide. [*Marzano v. Computer Science Corp., Inc.,* 91 F.3d 497 (3d Cir.)]

12. Donald Dilley worked as a truck driver for SuperValu, Inc., for approximately 18 years. He was the fifth most senior driver out of the 42 drivers on the company's seniority roster. During the course of his employment, he developed back problems and eventually became subject to a 60-pound lifting restriction imposed by his physician. SuperValu contends that in light of this restriction, Dilley was unable to perform the essential functions of his truck-driving position. Dilley asked the company for a "reasonable accommodation" by assigning him to a route or routes that did not require heavy lifting. SuperValu contended that Dilley's requested accommodation—returning to a truck driver position—" was unreasonable as a matter of law because it would have required SuperValu to violate the terms of its collective bargaining agreement with the union representing its warehouse employees." Because the driving positions are subject to a seniority system, SuperValu contended that Dilley could have been "bumped" from any of the driving positions for which he might have been qualified and that keeping him in the position if he were "bumped" would have violated the collective bargaining agreement. Dilley insisted that his seniority made such displacement unlikely. With no job to occupy, Dilley was terminated by the company. Dilley sued SuperValu, claiming a violation of the ADA for failure to make a reasonable accommodation. Decide. [*Dilley v. SuperValu, Inc.,* 296 F.3d 958]

13. Jeffrey Haight's reserve unit was called up for duty on August 23, 2004, but he was released on August 28, 2004, due to an injury. He sought his job back as a bar manager at Luckie's Lounge on September 6, 2004, but the owner stated she only had a cook's job available and wanted to check out her legal obligations with her attorney. She refused to put him on the schedule as bar manager. Bitter at the way he was treated, Haight altered Luckie's Lounge's web site on September 7, 2004, dismantling links to the menu, specials, and events. He brought suit under Section 4312 of the USERRA, which states the reservist "shall be promptly reemployed." Decide. [*Haight v. Katch, LLC, dba Luckie's Lounge & Grill* 2005 WL 246443 (D. Neb.)]

CHAPTER 16

EMPLOYMENT RELATIONSHIPS: CONTRACTUAL AND TORT THEORIES

SECTION

SECTION 133: EMPLOYMENT AT WILL, EXCEPTIONS, AND DISCRIMINATION CLAIMS

The relationship of employer and employee exists when, pursuant to an express or implied agreement of parties, one person, the employee, undertakes to perform services or to do work under the direction and control of another, the employer, for compensation. In most instances of individual employment contracts, the employment contract does not state any time or duration. It is an employment-at-will contract.[1] In contrast, the employment contract may state that it shall last for a specified period of time; an example would be a contract to coach a university basketball team for five years. An employer cannot terminate a contract for a definite period of time at an earlier date without justification as contemplated by the parties to that agreement. Under the classic at-will rule, both the employer and employee are free to terminate the relationship with or without cause.

The employment-at-will rule set forth in *Payne v. Western & Atlantic R.R. Co.* states:

> [M]en must be left, without interference to buy and sell where they please, and to discharge or retain employees at will for good cause or for no cause, or even for bad cause without thereby being guilty of an unlawful act per se. It is a right which an employee may exercise in the same way, to the same extent, for the same cause or want of cause as the employer.[2]

This rule, which gives an employer the right to terminate an employee for any reason—good cause, no cause, or bad cause—has been uniformly recognized throughout the country. However, judicial and, in some instances, legislative intervention has had an impact on the application of the rule in some 45 states. In *Texas Farm Bureau Mutual Insurance Companies v. Sears*, the Texas Supreme Court expressed its view of the employment-at-will doctrine and refused to recognize the existence of a tort action for failure to investigate an at-will employee's alleged misconduct with ordinary care prior to termination.

The court stated in part:

> By definition, the employment-at-will doctrine does not require an employer to be reasonable, or even careful, in making its termination decisions. If the at-will doctrine allows an employer to discharge an employee for bad reasons without liability, surely an employer should not incur liability when its reasons for discharge are carelessly formed. Engrafting a negligence exception on our at-will employment jurisprudence would inevitably swallow the rule....[3]

The court decisions that have carved out exceptions to the employment-at-will doctrine may be classified as follows:

1. The tort theory that a discharge violates established public policy (the so-called whistleblowing cases also are structured on public policy);
2. The tort theory of abusive discharge;

---

[1] An interesting discussion on the distinction between a legally enforceable employment contract for a definite period of time as opposed to a contract terminable at will is found in *Rooney v. Tyson*, 91 N.Y.2d 685, 697 N.E.2d 571 (1998). The case involved a lawsuit against boxer Mike Tyson by his former trainer Kevin Rooney for breach of an oral contract. New York's highest court held that if an employer made a promise, either express or implied, not only that the employer would pay for the service but also that the employment should continue for a period of time that is definite or capable of being determined, that employment is not terminable at will after the employee has begun the service or given the consideration. With the substantive law being settled by the state court, the Second Circuit Court of Appeals reinstated a $4,415,615 verdict for Rooney.

[2] 82 Tenn. 507, 518–19 (1884).

[3] 84 S.W.3d 604 (Tex. 2002).

3. The contract theory of express or implied guarantee of continued employment except for just-cause terminations;
4. The theory of an implied covenant of good faith and fair dealing in employment contracts.

Common to the court decisions on these developing exceptions to the employment-at-will doctrine are of judicial warnings on the narrowness of each decision. The employment-at-will doctrine continues to be a viable doctrine, subject to the developing exceptions. In a few jurisdictions, courts have stated that changes in the employment-at-will doctrine must await legislative action.

Most collective bargaining agreements contain a provision whereby the employer agrees that no employee subject to the agreement will be discharged without just cause. These agreements provide for arbitration on whether the employer had just cause for a discharge, with the burden of proof being on the employer. Over half of the approximately 15 million workers employed in the public sector by the federal government and state and local governments are protected by tenure processes or civil service against termination of employment without good cause. Also, a small number of managerial and professional employees have been successful in negotiating individual employment contracts in which the employer and the individual agree that the employer cannot terminate the employment during the duration of the contract unless there is good and sufficient cause. In the private sector, workers covered by union collective bargaining contracts that protect against termination without just cause constitute some 7.8 percent of the nation's workforce.[4] Protected employees in the public sector and employees with employment contracts constitute less than 10 percent of the workforce. Thus, more than 80 percent of the nation's workforce is employed at will or for indefinite durations and does not have the "good-cause" or "just-cause" protection against terminations negotiated by unions, granted by governmental bodies, or negotiated by individuals.

The National Conference of Commissioners on Uniform State Laws adopted the Model Employment Termination Act, which individual states may enact to protect the millions of at-will workers employed in the United States from being discharged without good cause.

Individuals are protected against discriminatory discharges principally by Title VII of the Civil Rights Act, the Age Discrimination in Employment Act, and the Americans with Disabilities Act. An at-will employee who is terminated may believe that there was a discriminatory motive to the discharge. Also, that employee may believe that one or more of the exceptions to the employment-at-will doctrine are applicable to that employee's discharge. The result is that a terminated individual may join claims based on exceptions to the employment-at-will doctrine and a claim based on discrimination. In *Murphy v. American Home Products Corp.*,[5] the New York Court of Appeals rejected four of the plaintiff's theories of wrongful discharge based on tort and contract law and reinstated the plaintiff's fifth theory, that of age

---

[4] For the latest information on union membership, see http://www.bls.gov/news.release/union2.toc.htm.
[5] 461 N.Y.2d 232 (1983).

discrimination. In *Marzano v. Computer Science Corp., Inc.*,[6] the plaintiff brought a lawsuit against her former employer, alleging gender discrimination based on pregnancy, breach of an implied-in-fact employment contract, and violation of a state Family and Medical Leave Act (FMLA). The court upheld her right to pursue the discrimination and FMLA claims.

A discussion of the four exceptions to the employment-at-will doctrine and the new model act follows.

PUBLIC POLICY

The courts in a number of jurisdictions have carved out an exception to the employment-at-will doctrine when the discharge is contrary to established public policy. In *Palmateer v. International Harvester*,[7] a so-called whistleblowing case, the court awarded damages for the wrongful discharge of an employee who was discharged in retaliation for his reporting to the police that a coemployee was engaged in criminal activities. The court held that the discharge violated an important public policy. In *Sheets v. Teddy's Frosted Foods*,[8] the court held that a cause of action in tort existed for wrongful discharge from employment where a quality control director alleged that he had been dismissed in retaliation for his insistence that the employer comply with the Food, Drug, and Cosmetic Act.

In some states, whistleblower laws have been enacted to protect employees who disclose employer practices that endanger public health and safety.

In *Phipps v. Clark Oil & Refining Corp.*,[9] the court found that an at-will employee could sue for wrongful termination after he was discharged for refusing his supervisor's directive in violation of the Clean Air Act to pump leaded gasoline into an automobile equipped to receive only unleaded gasoline.

The most frequent application of the public policy exception is in response to employees who are discharged in retaliation for filing workers' compensation claims.[10] The courts' concern in these cases is that the statute would not be effective if employees feared that the consequence of filing a compensation claim would be their discharge from employment.

In most states, the public policy exception to the employment-at-will doctrine is a narrow one and is applied only if the plaintiff can satisfy a two-part test: (1) The discharge must violate some well-established public policy expressed in a constitution, statutes, or regulations promulgated pursuant to the statutes; (2) There must be no other remedy available to protect the interest of the aggrieved individual or society.

In *McGarrity v. Berlin Metals, Inc.*,[11] taking the facts in the light most favorable to the plaintiff, the court's source of the public policy allegedly violated by

---

[6] 91 F.3d 497 (3d Cir. 1996).

[7] 85 Ill.2d 124, 421 N.E.2d 876 (1981).

[8] 179 Conn. 471, 424 A.2d 385 (1980). See also *Lynch v. Blanke Baer, Inc.*, 901 S.W.2d 147 (Mo. App. 1995).

[9] 396 N.W.2d 588 (Minn. App. 1986).

[10] *Wallace v. Milliken & Co.*, 406 S.E.2d 358 (S.C. 1991); *Blier v. Wellington Sears Co.*, 2000 Ala.LEXIS 16.

[11] 774 N.E.2d 71 (2002).

the employer was the termination of the company's chief financial officer (CFO) for his refusal to incur personal liability for felony fraud, refusal to file a false tax return, and refusal to abdicate his corporate responsibilities as CFO.

The *Adams v. Uno Restaurants, Inc.* case, presented in this section, is an example of the application of a state whistleblower law.

ABUSIVE DISCHARGE

The leading case for the abusive discharge tort theory exception to the employment-at-will doctrine is *Monge v. Beebe Rubber Co.*[12] In this case, a female employee was discharged for declining to date her supervisor. A similar situation today would be handled under the post-*Monge* Title VII theory of sexual harassment, with a remedy including reinstatement with back pay and capped compensatory and punitive damages.

The elements of the tort of intentional or reckless infliction of emotional distress in a constructive discharge context is set forth in *Travis v. Alcorn Laboratories, Inc.*[13] The plaintiff must prove extreme and outrageous conduct by the employer, motivated to inflict emotional distress, whose conduct was so intolerable that a reasonable person would be compelled to quit.

EXPRESS OR IMPLIED GUARANTEE OF CONTINUED EMPLOYMENT

Some courts construe statements by employers concerning continued employment, which previously had been viewed as having no binding effect, as a contractual basis for requiring good cause for the discharge of an employee. Also, written personnel policies used as guidelines for the employer's supervisors have been interpreted as being rules restricting the employer's right to discharge at will without proof of good or just cause.

In *Duldulao v. St. Mary Nazareth Hospital Center*,[14] an 11-year employee, Nora Duldulao, was fired without notice for unsatisfactory performance. The hospital's *Employee Handbook* provided that an employee could be terminated for enumerated causes following "proper notice and investigation." Duldulao contended before the Supreme Court of Illinois that such a provision had a limiting effect on her at-will employment status and created an enforceable contract that barred the hospital from terminating her without following the safeguards of notice and an investigation. The court agreed, holding that an employee handbook or other policy statement created enforceable contractual rights if the traditional requirements for contract formation were present. The court set forth the requirements as follows: (1) The language must contain a promise clear enough that an employee would reasonably believe that an offer has been made, (2) the statement must be disseminated to the employee in such a manner that the employee is aware of its contents and reasonably believes it to be an offer, and (3) the employee must accept the offer by continuing to work after learning of the policy statement. According to the court, the employee's continued work constitutes consideration for the promise.

---

[12] 114 N.H. 130, 316 A.2d 549 (1974).

[13] 504 S.E.2d 419 (W.Va.1998).

[14] 115 Ill.2d 482, 505 N.E.2d 314 (1987).

GOOD FAITH AND FAIR DEALING

Another development in the law governing the employment relationship is the recognition of a covenant of good faith and fair dealing in the employment relationship. For example, in *Fortune v. National Cash Register Co.*,[15] the court for the first time in Massachusetts recognized a common law contract action of "wrongful" or "bad faith" termination for an at-will employee. This case involved an employer's termination of a commission salesperson in order to deprive him of benefits and bonuses to which he was entitled. The court was offended by the overreaching and malicious acts of the company at the expense of the employee for the sole benefit of the employer. The court held that there existed an implied covenant of good faith and fair dealing in certain employment relationships.

In *Foley v. Interactive Data Corp.*,[16] the Supreme Court of California held that an employee who claims to be fired in violation of a covenant of good faith and fair dealing is limited to a contract claim and remedies such as reinstatement and lost wages. The court held that the covenant of good faith and fair dealing applies to employment contracts and that breach of covenant may give rise to contract but not tort damages. Thus, Foley could obtain reinstatement and back pay under a contract theory but was not eligible for the much greater damages that could be recovered under a tort theory, including recovery for emotional distress and punitive damages.

RETALIATION

Section 1985(2) of the Civil Rights Act of 1871 protects employees from intimidation and retaliation—or injury to [their] person or property—because of their cooperation with the government in federal court proceedings. In *Haddle v. Garrison*, reported in this section, the U.S. Supreme Court allowed a claim for damages under Section 1985(2). The Court rejected lower court holdings that an at-will employee discharged pursuant to a conspiracy to retaliate against the employee because of his grand jury cooperation in a Medicare fraud inquiry had suffered no constitutionally protected "property interest" injury because of the termination, because employment at will is not "property" for purposes of the due process clause. The Court pointed out that the gist of the wrong at which Section 1985(2) is directed is not deprivation of property but intimidation or retaliation against witnesses in federal court proceedings; it concluded that injury to "property" in Section 1985(2) refers to existing principles of tort law that provide a remedy for wrongful interference with at-will employment relationships.[17]

---

[15] 373 Mass. 96, 364 N.E.2d 1251 (1977). See also *Cleary v. American Airlines, Inc.*, 111 Cal. App. 3d 443, 168 Cal. Rptr. 722 (1980), and *Khanna v. Microdata Corp.*, 170 Cal. App. 3d 250, 215 Cal. Rptr. 860 (1985).

[16] 47 Cal. App. 3d 654 (1988).

[17] A statutory right exists for at-will employees who are terminated in retaliation for cooperating with a federal criminal prosecution or are terminated in violation of the public policy to provide truthful testimony. See *Fitzgerald v. Salsbury Chemical, Inc*, 613 N.W.2d 275 (Iowa 2000).

PUBLIC EMPLOYEE WHISTLEBLOWERS

In *Garcetti v. Ceballos*,[18] the U.S. Supreme Court held that any statement made within the organization by a public employee that can be considered part of his or her official duties is made in his or her capacity as an employee and not a citizen and carries no First Amendment protection against employer discipline. Deputy District Attorney Ceballos determined that an affidavit used to obtain a critical search warrant contained serious misrepresentations. After writing a memo to his supervisors expressing his concerns, he claimed he was subjected to a series of retaliatory actions. Ceballos sued in federal court, contending that his memo was protected under the First Amendment. The district court granted summary judgment against him. In upholding the district court, the Supreme Court stated that the controlling factor in the case was that Ceballos' "expressions were made pursuant to his duties as a calendar deputy."[19]

The fact that a citizen works for the government does not remove all speech protections for that citizen. Employer restrictions on speech are properly placed "only [on] the expressions an employee makes pursuant to his or her official responsibilities, not to statements or complaints ... that are made outside the duties of employment."[20]

Complaints by government employee whistleblowers are analyzed by evaluating the nature of the complaint as it relates to their job duties and their reporting responsibilities in their chain of command. In *Charles v. Grief*,[21] a systems analyst employed by the Texas Lottery Commission complained to state legislators of race discrimination and retaliation. The Fifth Circuit Court of Appeals held that he was protected by the First Amendment because his complaints were not related to his official job responsibilities, although he became aware of them while at work, and he complained to officials outside his chain of command.

THE MODEL ACT

The Model Employment Termination Act would extend relief to terminated workers who could make claims for wrongful termination under a "good-cause" standard. The model act defines an "employee" as an individual who works for the employer for at least one year and includes within its protection supervisors, managers, and confidential employees. Employers continue to have the right to terminate employees for serious misconduct and to lay off employees for economic reasons and to otherwise exercise "honest business judgment."

---

[18] 126 S.Ct. 1951 (2006).

[19] *Id.* at 1956, 1959–1960.

[20] *Id.* at 1961.

[21] 2008 U.S. App. LEXIS 6275 (5th Cir. Mar. 26, 2008).

In exchange for good-cause protection, the act extinguishes all common law rights against the employer, including "violation of public policy" tort claims and related claims such as defamation actions and claims for intentional infliction of emotional distress. Civil Rights Act theories and actions under collective bargaining agreements are not affected by the model act.

Under the model act, a terminated employee may file for arbitration up to 180 days after the effective date of the termination. The ordinary remedy for termination without good cause is reinstatement with back pay. Thus, the act eliminates jury trials and compensatory and punitive damages.

The Model Employment Termination Act has not been adopted by any state at this writing. Were it to apply in all states, it is estimated that annually some 150,000 to 200,000 terminated workers could make claims under the act. It would provide American workers protection against wrongful termination that is presently afforded workers in the European Union as well as in Japan and Canada.

EMPLOYER REACTIONS

As a result of cases similar to *Duldulao*, some nonunion employers have inserted conspicuous statements in employment applications that applicants must sign, indicating that they understand that the employment offered is "at will." Employers have revised their personnel manuals and employee handbooks and have issued directives to all employees that no assurance of continued employment exists and that the employers are not obligated to have good cause to terminate employees, just as employees are free to leave their positions with the employers. While simultaneously reserving their at-will termination powers, many employers also may design specific, apparently fair termination procedure and promulgate antiharassment policies and procedures, as seen in the *Semple v. FedEx* decision, presented in this section. Of course, where employers' actions are in fact arbitrary or capricious, impetus is provided for the organization of the employees by unions.

Most employers have no interest in terminating employees without good and sufficient cause. They have taken steps to assure that terminations are in fact for good cause and that a solid case exists for each termination should the employee in question sue on an unjust dismissal theory. Employers have standardized their termination methods. Employers often require that every disciplined employee be advised in writing of the infraction, the expected corrective action, and the fact that further misconduct could lead to additional discipline up to and including discharge. When a termination appears to be warranted, most employers require that at least two supervisors be involved and that they take care to ensure that the reasons for the termination are accurate and consistent with the documentation concerning the employee's deficiencies. Moreover, employers should inform the employee of the basis of the proposed termination and give the employee an opportunity to be heard before the dismissal notice is issued.

CASE 16.1	ADAMS V. UNO RESTAURANTS, INC.
	SUPREME COURT OF RHODE ISLAND, 18 IER CASES 998 (2002).

[After a jury returned a verdict in favor of the plaintiff, Gerald K. Adams, finding that his employer, the Warwick, Rhode Island, Pizzeria Uno, had wrongfully terminated Adams in violation of the state's Whistleblowers Act,* the trial court set aside the jury's award of $7,500 in damages, and Adams appealed to the state's Supreme Court.]

PER CURIAM...

On May 20, 1996, the plaintiff, who had been employed by the defendant for several years, arrived for his nighttime line cooking shift at the defendant's Warwick restaurant. Shortly after his shift began, the plaintiff noticed that the kitchen floor was saturated with a foul-smelling liquid coming from drains and backing up water onto the floor. He complained of illness and went home, at which time he contacted the Department of Health about the drainage problem in the restaurant's kitchen. A Department of Health representative visited the restaurant that evening and noticed that the floor drains were backed up and that the floor was wet and slippery. She ordered the kitchen staff to dispose of all the food they had touched with their bare hands and closed the restaurant for the night, leaving instructions to sanitize the kitchen area and clear all the drains. She also inquired about which employee went home sick. The restaurant reopened the next day after sanitizing the kitchen.

On May 22, 1996, two days after the incident, the plaintiff, who was not scheduled to work that day, returned to the restaurant curious to determine whether there was any hostility toward him resulting from his having called the Department of Health. The plaintiff testified that he was summarily ordered by David Badot, the restaurant's manager, to come into his office and that Badot proceeded to shout at him while inquiring whether he had contacted the Department of Health. The plaintiff testified that he

shouted back at Badot and acknowledged that he had indeed called the Department of Health. Badot then accused the plaintiff of stealing one of the defendant's softball team shirts and of taking a work schedule home. Badot then left his office, and the plaintiff followed him out into the general cooking area, where other employees were present. The shouting match between Badot and the plaintiff continued and in the course thereof, the plaintiff told Badot that he "was going to follow him back to Massachusetts on this, and [he] was going to blow the intelligence out of his head." The plaintiff then left the restaurant. Badot claimed to have perceived the plaintiff's words as threatening and instructed an employee to call the police. When the plaintiff later heard that the police were looking for him, he voluntarily went to the Warwick police station, whereupon he was then charged with disorderly conduct, arraigned, and pled not guilty. No trial on the charge ensued. The charge was later filed. One year later his record of arrest and charge automatically was expunged pursuant to the case filing statute.

Shortly thereafter, the plaintiff commenced this civil action against the defendant alleging therein that he had been unlawfully terminated only because he had notified the Department of Health regarding the unsanitary kitchen conditions existing at the defendant's Warwick Pizzeria Uno Restaurant & Bar....

After examining the evidence in the light most favorable to the plaintiff, the trial justice decided that a reasonable jury could have found that Badot's actions in badgering the plaintiff and then having him arrested were a pretext for retaliating against the plaintiff for having called in the Department of Health. The trial justice concluded that a reasonable jury certainly could have found that the confrontation between Badot and the plaintiff was designed by Badot to provoke a reaction from the plaintiff that would serve as Badot's excuse to fire him, even though that was merely a pretext for the real reason—the plaintiff's call to the Department of Health....

Although the plaintiff at trial did not specifically quantify his damages, he did testify that it took him eleven days to find employment after his being

---

*The Rhode Island Whistleblowers' Protection Act, G.L. 1956 28-50-4(a) provides that "A person who alleges a violation of this act may bring a civil action for appropriate injunctive relief, or actual damages, or both within three (3) years after the occurrence of the alleged violation of this chapter."

continued

terminated by the defendant. In addition to his economic damages, he claimed and testified that he suffered emotional distress and humiliation as a result of the defendant's wrongful conduct in initiating criminal proceedings against him that resulted in the loss of his National Guard security clearance and disqualification from an overseas National Guard mission. He offered no expert medical testimony in support of his claim for emotional distress....

On the particular case facts before us, we do not find the absence of expert medical testimony to support the plaintiff's claim for damages resulting from his alleged emotional distress and humiliation to be fatal to that portion of his claim for damages. Unlike the usual case where a claim for emotional distress and humiliation is oftentimes made without objective facts to substantiate such a claim, expert medical testimony is deemed necessary to assist the factfinder in determining not only the validity but also the casual relationship of any emotional distress. In this case, the trial jury had before it clear objective and uncontroverted evidence concerning the complaint to the Warwick police; his arrest by the Warwick police; the criminal charge for disorderly conduct made against him; his arraignment on that charge; the revocation of his military security clearance and the resulting loss of his opportunity to accompany his National Guard unit in an overseas mission to Germany.** From such objective and uncontradicted evidence, we believe that an ordinary lay person or trial juror would be capable of determining without the aid of expert medical testimony whether emotional distress and humiliation could ordinarily and naturally follow from such events. Trial jurors, we are satisfied, do not leave their common sense in the cloakroom when they come to sit in the courtroom....

In this case, the trial evidence clearly reveals that the plaintiff Adams was particularly troubled over his being arrested for disorderly conduct and the resulting loss of his security clearance as a National Guard reservist. That loss of security clearance subsequently

prevented him from participating with his National Guard unit in an overseas mission to Germany. The trial justice apparently noted the significance of those matters upon the plaintiff's emotional well-being, when in overruling defense counsel's objection to the plaintiff's testimony concerning those matters he noted: "I'll allow it. To him it's very important. Whether it is to you or the jury remains to be seen."

In passing upon and granting the defendant's motion to set aside the jury's damages award to the plaintiff, the trial justice pondered whether the proximate cause for any damages the plaintiff would otherwise have been entitled to recover had been interrupted when the plaintiff threatened Badot. However, he later acknowledged that the jury could have reasonably concluded from the plaintiff's testimony that he did suffer actual economic losses and mental anguish from his having been terminated and humiliated by Badot in the presence of the plaintiff's fellow employees as well as from embarrassment stemming from the police visit to his second employer inquiring about the threat made against Badot. He observed also that the jury could reasonably have concluded that the plaintiff's loss of his National Guard security clearance and subsequent inability to participate in overseas missions caused him emotional distress....

Conclusion

For the reasons set out above, the case papers are remanded to the court for entry of an amended final judgment that will include the trial jury's award of damages to the plaintiff in the amount of $7,500.

Questions

1. Is it illegal under state law for an employer to retaliate against an employee for calling the state Health Department about an unsafe or unsanitary kitchen condition?
2. What is a pretext? How did the pretext apply in this case?
3. Was Adams entitled to damages for emotional distress without supportive expert medical testimony?

**The plaintiff aptly summarized the scope of his damages at trial: "So now I'm still fighting through the momentum that they caused on me affecting my civil life, my military career, my standing in the job market."

CASE 16.2	HADDLE V. GARRISON
	SUPREME COURT OF THE UNITED STATES, 525 U.S. 121 (1998).

[Michael A. Haddle, an at-will employee, alleges that the defendants conspired to have him fired from his job in retaliation for obeying a federal grand jury subpoena and to deter him from testifying at a federal criminal trial. According to Haddle's complaint, a federal grand jury indictment in March 1995 charged Healthmaster, Inc., and defendants Jeanette Garrison and Dennis Kelly, officers of Healthmaster, with Medicare fraud. Haddle cooperated with the federal agents in the investigation that preceded the indictment. He also appeared to testify before the grand jury pursuant to a subpoena but did not testify because of the press of time. He was also expected to appear as a witness in the criminal trial resulting from the indictment. Although Garrison and Kelly were barred by the Bankruptcy Court from participating in the affairs of Healthmaster, Haddle contended that they conspired with G. Peter Molloy, Jr., one of the remaining officers of Healthmaster, to bring about Haddle's termination. They did this both to intimidate him and to retaliate against him for his attendance at the federal court proceedings. Haddle contends that their acts had "injured [him] in his person or property" in violation of 42 U.S.C. Section 1985(2). In dismissing the suit for failure to state a claim, the district court relied on circuit precedent holding that an at-will employee discharged pursuant to a conspiracy proscribed by Section 1985(2) has suffered no actual injury because he has no constitutionally protected interest in continued employment. The Eleventh Circuit affirmed.]

REHNQUIST, C. J....

The Eleventh Circuit held that an at-will employee who is dismissed pursuant to a conspiracy proscribed by § 1985(2) has no cause of action. The *Morast* court explained that "to make out a cause of action under § 1985(2) the plaintiff must have suffered an actual injury. Because Morast was an at will employee,... he had no constitutionally protected interest in continued employment. Therefore, Morast's discharge did not constitute an actual injury under this statute." *Id.*, at 930. Relying on its decision in

Morast, the Court of Appeals affirmed. Judgt. order reported at 132 F. 3d 46 (1997)....

Section 1985(2), in relevant part, proscribes conspiracies to "deter, by force, intimidation, or threat, any party or witness in any court of the United States from attending such court, or from testifying to any matter pending therein, freely, fully, and truthfully, or to injure such party or witness in his person or property on account of his having so attended or testified." The statute provides that if one or more persons engaged in such a conspiracy "do, or cause to be done, any act in furtherance of the object of such conspiracy, whereby another is injured in his person or property,... the party so injured... may have an action for the recovery of damages occasioned by such injury... against any one or more of the conspirators." § 1985(3)....

Our review in this case is accordingly confined to one question: Can petitioner state a claim for damages by alleging that a conspiracy proscribed by § 1985(2) induced his employer to terminate his at-will employment?

We disagree with the Eleventh Circuit's conclusion that petitioner must suffer an injury to a "constitutionally protected property interest" to state a claim for damages under § 1985(2). Nothing in the language or purpose of the proscriptions in the first clause of § 1985(2), nor in its attendant remedial provisions, establishes such a requirement. The gist of the wrong at which § 1985(2) is directed is not deprivation of property, but intimidation or retaliation against witnesses in federal-court proceedings. The terms "injured in his person or property" define the harm that the victim may suffer as a result of the conspiracy to intimidate or retaliate. Thus, the fact that employment at will is not "property" for purposes of the Due Process Clause, see *Bishop v. Wood*, 426 U.S. 341, 345–347 (1976), does not mean that loss of at-will employment may not "injur[e] [petitioner] in his person or property" for purposes of § 1985(2).

continued

We find that the sort of harm alleged by petitioner here—essentially third-party interference with at-will employment relationships—states a claim for relief under § 1985(2). Such harm has long been a compensable injury under tort law, and we see no reason to ignore this tradition in this case. As Thomas Cooley recognized:

> "One who maliciously and without justifiable cause, induces an employer to discharge an employee, by means of false statements, threats or putting in fear, or perhaps by means of malevolent advice and persuasion, is liable in an action of tort to the employee for the damages thereby sustained. *And it makes no difference whether the employment was for a fixed term not yet expired or is terminable at the will of the employer.*" 2 T. Cooley, Law of Torts 589-91 (3d ed. 1906) (emphasis added).

This Court also recognized in *Truax v. Raich*, 239 U.S. 33 (1915):

> "The fact that the employment is at the will of the parties, respectively, does not make it one at the will of others. The employee has manifest interest in the freedom of the employer to exercise his judgment without illegal interference or compulsion and, by the weight of authority, the unjustified interference of third persons is actionable although the employment is at will." Id., at 38 (citing cases).

The kind of interference with at-will employment relations alleged here is merely a species of the traditional torts of intentional interference with contractual relations and intentional interference with prospective contractual relations. See Restatement (Second) of Torts § 766, Comment g, pp.10–11 (1977); ... For example, the State of Georgia, where the acts underlying the complaint in this case took place, provides a cause of action against third parties for wrongful interference with employment relations. See *Georgia Power Co. v. Busbin*, 242 Ga. 612, 613, 250 S. E. 2d 442, 444 (1978) ("[E]ven though a person's employment contract is at will, he has a valuable contract right which may not be unlawfully interfered with by a third person"); ... Thus, to the extent that the terms "injured in his person or property" in § 1985 refer to principles of tort law, see 3 W. Blackstone, Commentaries on the Laws of England 118 (1768) (describing the universe of common law torts as "all private wrongs, or civil injuries, which may be offered to the rights of either a man's person or his property"), we find ample support for our holding that the harm occasioned by the conspiracy here may give rise to a claim for damages under § 1985(2).

The judgment of the Court of Appeals is reversed, and the case is remanded for further proceedings consistent with this opinion.

It is so ordered.

Case Questions

1. Explain the court of appeals' reasoning that Section 1985(2) did not provide a remedy for Haddle.
2. What is the flaw in the court of appeals' reasoning that Section 1985(2) did not provide a remedy for Haddle?
3. State the rule of the law.

CASE 16.3	SEMPLE V. FEDERAL EXPRESS CORP.
	UNITED STATES DISTRICT COURT, 2008 U.S. DIST. LEXIS 31744 (W.D.S.D. APR. 17, 2008).

[The plaintiff, John Semple, was terminated from his employment with FedEx for falsification of company documents. He appealed his termination through internal FedEx procedures without success and thereafter sued the employer in federal court, contending that his termination was in violation of the "public policy exception" to the employment at-will doctrine and that he was protected by the employee handbook exception to the at-will doctrine.]

BOGUE, S.D.J....
Plaintiff was hired by Federal Express Corporation (FedEx) in 1990. At that time, he signed an employment contract that included the following statement:

> I do hereby agree ... (11) That during the time of my employment, which term I understand is indefinite, I will comply with the guidelines set forth in the Company's policies, rules, regulations and procedures ... I ALSO AGREE THAT

continued

MY EMPLOYMENT AND COMPENSATION CAN BE TERMINATED WITH OR WITHOUT CAUSE AND WITHOUT NOTICE OR LIABILITY WHATSOEVER, AT ANY TIME, AT THE OPTION OF EITHER THE COMPANY OR MYSELF.

Plaintiff signed this contract below the statement: "I HAVE READ AND UNDERSTAND THIS AGREEMENT." Throughout his time at FedEx, Plaintiff verified by his signature that he received at least three different employee handbooks from his employer. Regarding the handbook he received in 1990, Plaintiff signed a record of receipt which stated: "I understand [the handbook] is not a contract and the information provided may need to be changed by the company from time to time." Plaintiff signed similar records of receipt in June 1997 and February 2002 certifying he had received a copy of the employee handbook. That same signature certifies that Plaintiff read and understood an accompanying statement which expresses that the handbook is not a contract of employment, that the handbook should not be read or implied to create a contract, that an employee's rights are governed by the employment contract and not the handbook, that the handbook "contains guidelines only," and that FedEx reserves the right to modify the publication and its policies at any time....

The handbook ... includes Section 4-90 "Termination," which is almost entirely made up of a subsections entitled "Guidelines" and "Employment Termination Chart." Within the Guidelines portion, a subsection labeled "Employment at Will" states the following:

> The employment relationship between the Company and any employee may be terminated at the will of either party as stated in the employment agreement signed upon application for employment. As described in that agreement, the policies and procedures set forth in this manual provide guidelines for management and employees during employment, but do not create contractual rights regarding termination or otherwise....

Public Policy Exception

The South Dakota Supreme Court recognized a "narrow" public policy exception to the employment-at-will doctrine in *Johnson v. Kreiser's, Inc.,* 433 N.W.2d 225, 227 (S.D. 1988). That court first defined this exception in this way:

> An employee has a cause of action for wrongful discharge when the employer discharges him in retaliation for his refusal to commit a criminal or unlawful act. It is repugnant to public policy to expect an employee to commit such acts in order to save his job. Consequently, we carve out this exception to the at-will doctrine codified at SDCL 60-4-4.... [W]e leave the statutory at-will doctrine intact, subject only to this narrow public policy exception and our holdings ... regarding employee handbooks and ... regarding an employer's oral representations....

With regard to the public policy exception, Defendant argues that even if Plaintiff's allegations are true—that he was fired for filing an internal grievance regarding harassment by his supervisors—this is not a clear violation of a substantial public policy and thus the public policy exception to the at-will doctrine does not apply. Plaintiff argues that South Dakota public policy prohibits a retaliatory firing for filing an internal grievance. Pointing to the FedEx employment manual, which prohibits any form of harassment—not just harassment which falls within the parameters of federal or state law—the Plaintiff seems to state that the public policy behind anti-retaliation laws in the context of Title VII harassment claims would be violated if retaliation were permitted in the context of non-Title VII harassment claims. "Therefore, if Semple can prove that his termination was in retaliation for his harassment complaint, in violation of the [employment manual's] stated policy, he will also prove that the retaliatory discharge violated South Dakota public policy."

The Court is not persuaded that a termination in retaliation for an internal complaint of harassment violates a "clear mandate of a substantial public policy," as required for the public policy exception to apply. The primary sources of public policy are constitutions, statutes, and judicial decisions. The Court does not believe that the public policy Plaintiff is claiming—anti-retaliation policy borrowed from employment discrimination statutes—is indeed a "clear mandate" but instead can only arise from a distorted interpretation of existing state law. Simply, South Dakota has not outlawed retaliatory firings for filing an internal grievance of general harassment, and this Court refuses to create such a public policy here....

Employee Handbook Exception

Plaintiff also claims that the Court should apply the employee handbook exception to the at-will doctrine and hold that FedEx's handbook created an implied contract that he would only be fired for cause.

continued

The Court does not believe that FedEx's employment manual includes a "a clear intention on the employer's part to surrender its statutory power to terminate its employees at will,"... First, Plaintiff's employment contract includes explicit language that his employment could be terminated "WITH OR WITHOUT CAUSE AND WITHOUT NOTICE OR LIABILITY WHATSOEVER, AT ANY TIME, AT THE OPTION OF EITHER THE COMPANY OR MYSELF." Second, Plaintiff signed a receipt form certifying that he received periodic copies of FedEx's employment manual; that receipt form stated that the handbook is not a contract and that the company reserves the right to change the information within the manual at its discretion. Two of such receipts signed by Plaintiff stated that the handbook should not be read or implied to create a contract and that the handbook "contains guidelines only," stating that "[y]our specific rights as an employee are governed by the Employment Agreement you signed in your employment application." Finally, the employment manual itself in policy 4-90 Termination states:

> The employment relationship between the Company and employee may be terminated at the will of either party as stated in the employment agreement signed upon application for employment. As described in that agreement, the

policies and procedures set forth in this manual provide guidelines for management and employees during employment, but do not create contractual rights regarding termination or otherwise.

Conclusion

As the Court finds that Defendant has not surrendered its statutory right to terminate employees at will through its employment handbook, nor does any public policy prevent FedEx from terminating Plaintiff's employment, Plaintiff is an at-will employee.... Thus, Plaintiff does not have a cause of action for wrongful discharge. Accordingly, summary judgment for Defendant is required.

Case Questions

1. Did the policies and procedures set forth in the employee handbook provide legally enforceable rights for the covered employees working under the handbook rules?

2. What are the primary sources of public policy under the state's public policy exception to the employment at-will doctrine? Is a firing for filing a general harassment grievance against supervisors a protected public policy under state law?

SECTION 134: WHISTLEBLOWER PROTECTION UNDER THE SARBANES-OXLEY ACT

The Sarbanes-Oxley Act (SOX) of 2002 was enacted to restore investor confidence in financial markets following the exposure in 2001–2002 of widespread misconduct by directors and officers of publicly held companies. The SOX contains reforms regarding corporate accountability, enhanced disclosure requirements, and enforcement and liability provisions. Title VIII of the Act contains protections for corporate whistleblowers.[22]

PROTECTIONS PROVIDED

The Act prohibits a publicly traded company or any agent of a publicly traded company from taking an adverse employment action against an employee who provides information, testifies, or "otherwise assists" in proceedings regarding (1) mail, wire, bank, or securities fraud; (2) any violation of an SEC

---

[22] 18 U.S.C. § 1514A (2005).

rule or regulation; or (3) any federal law protecting shareholders against fraud.[23] The Act sets forth the types of adverse employment actions that qualify for protection, specifically protecting employees from discharge, demotion, suspension, threats, harassment, failure to hire or rehire, blacklisting, or action otherwise discriminatory against employees in their terms and conditions of employment.[24]

While the Act directly applies to publicly traded companies, the Act also applies to any agents of the publicly traded companies. In *Kalkunte v. DVI Financial Services, Inc.*,[25] the ALJ found that a privately held company, AP Services, a turnaround specialist that helps bankrupt companies reorganize, was liable for the termination of an employee whistleblower under Sarbanes-Oxley based upon "agency" theory. That is, AP Services was acting as the employer's agent and was liable along with the employer for the termination of the employee who uncovered and reported financial improprieties.

An employee who provides information to the SEC may be incorrect in the belief that an activity by the employer is illegal. Nevertheless, the employee is considered involved in protected activity so long as the employee had an objectively "reasonable belief" that the reported activity was in violation of a federal law protecting shareholders from fraud. For example, where an employee reported to the Securities and Exchange Commission what he believed to be a financial impropriety regarding delays in payments owed by the company to a subsequent quarter and an SEC investigation exonerated the employer, an ALJ found the whistleblower to have been engaged in "protected activities" because he had a reasonable belief that the company action was illegal.[26]

PROCEDURES

An individual who believes that he or she has been subject to an adverse employment action because of whistleblowing activities must file a complaint with the Department of Labor's (DOL's) Occupational Safety & Health Administration (OSHA) within 90 days after the asserted adverse employment action. OSHA administers 13 other federal whistleblower laws and has experienced investigators to facilitate its responsibilities under the SOX. Investigations are conducted and a preliminary order is issued within 60 days.[27] If requested, a hearing is conducted by an Administrative Law Judge. Appeals from an ALJ's recommended decision may be taken to the Secretary of Labor's Administrative Review Board (ARB). Appeals from ARB decisions must be filed with the United States Circuit Court of Appeals within 60 days of the decision. A claimant may file a *de novo* action in a United States District Court if the DOL fails to act within 100 days of the filing of the complaint.

The burden of proof is on the complainant to demonstrate that the complainant's protected activity was a "contributing factor" in the adverse employment action. If this is established, the burden shifts to the employer to prove by "clear and

---

[23] 18 U.S.C. § 1514A(a)(1) (2005).

[24] 18 U.S.C. § 1514A(a).

[25] 2004-SOX-56 (ALJ July 18, 2005).

[26] *Halloum v. Intel Corp.*, 2003-SOX-7 (ALJ Mar. 4, 2004).

[27] An investigator may order reinstatement of an employee claiming protection of the SOA at this early stage.

convincing evidence," a heavy burden of proof, that it would have taken the same adverse action in the absence of the protected activity.[28]

Whistleblowers are entitled to make whole relief, including reinstatement with all rights unimpaired, and compensatory damages, including back pay with interest, and "special damages" such as reasonable attorney fees and expert witness fees.

Criminal penalties may be imposed against the employer or its agents for retaliating against an informant who has provided truthful information relating to a federal offense.[29]

DEVELOPING CASE LAW

Decisions by the DOL's Administrative Review Board (ARB) and the courts rely on precedents involving other OSHA-enforced whistleblower statutes and borrow from case law developed under Title VII and other discrimination statutes. To date, SOX whistleblowers have not fared very well in administrative proceedings and the courts.[30]

Claimants who proceed before the DOL are entitled to "interim reinstatement" under SOX.[31] In *Bechtel v. Competitive Technologies, Inc.*,[32] the complainant, John Bechtel, applied to the U.S. District Court for the enforcement of the investigator's preliminary order of reinstatement, which was made before the ALJ hearing. The court issued the requested injunction. On appeal, the Second Circuit determined that because the order of reinstatement was not a "final order" of the agency, the court lacked jurisdiction to enforce it. In his dissenting opinion, Judge Straub stated that the failure to enforce the preliminary reinstatement order negated congressional intent to provide a quick remedy for whistleblowers.[33]

In *Livingston v. Wyeth, Inc.*, presented in this section, the court dealt with the question of "reasonableness of belief" and "materiality" issues, deciding against the complainant. The court pointed out that the conduct disclosed could not have constituted a violation of federal laws regulating shareholder fraud or a plan to violate such laws. Case law cautions that SOX whistleblower protection provisions do not provide "whistleblower protection for all employee complaints about how a public company spends it money and pays its bills."[34]

---

[28] 18 U.S.C. § 1514A (b)(2)(C) and 29 C.F.R. § 1980.104.

[29] 18 U.S.C. § 1513(e) (2005).

[30] See V. Watnick, "Whistleblower Protections Under the Sarbanes-Oxley Act"; *12 Fordham J. of Corp. and Financial Law* 831, 862 (2007), where as of June 2005, only 4 out of 119 total whistleblower complaints under SOX had been successful at a hearing.

[31] See 18 U.S.C. § 1514A(b)(2)(A).

[32] 448 F.3d 469 (2d Cir. 2006).

[33] See also *Welch v. Cardinal Bankshares Corp.*, 445 F.Supp.2d 552 (W.D. VA. 2006), dismissing the complainant's case on the basis that the SOX statute did not grant judicial authority to enforce preliminary orders.

[34] *Platone v. Flyi, Inc.*, DOL ARB No. 04-154 (Sept. 29, 2006). See also *Welch v. Choa* 536 F.3d 269 (4th Cir. 2008), where CFO David Welch had refused to certify an SEC quarterly report as required by SOX because of accounting irregularities and he was fired. The Court of Appeals held that the conduct in question was not shown to be in violation of any fraud or securities laws listed in SOX; thus, Welch was not protected.

CASE 16.4	LIVINGSTON V. WYETH, INC.
	UNITED STATES DISTRICT COURT, 2006 U.S. DIST, LEXIS 52978 (M.D. N.C. 2006).

[Mark Livingston, a former manager of Training and Continuous Improvement at Wyeth's Sanford, North Carolina, facility, filed a complaint alleging violation of the employee protection provisions of Section 806 of the Sarbanes-Oxley Act. Livingston wrote a memo to his supervisors expressing concern about training deficiencies at the Sanford plant where components of a vaccine for infants and toddlers were manufactured. He stated in a July 10 memo that any attempt to verify compliance would be providing "false and misleading information to outside auditors, including the FDA." Mr. Livingston was terminated on December 19 for what the employer deemed insubordination resulting from a public confrontation Mr. Livingston had with the human resources director at an off-site holiday party.]

SHARP, M. J....

... Sarbanes-Oxley was enacted to address corporate fraud on shareholders. One way it does so is by protecting employees who report violations of laws that relate to shareholder fraud. It is clear from the plain language of the statute and its legislative history that fraud is an integral element of a whistleblower cause of action. To be protected, the whistleblower must not only subjectively believe that the reported conduct may constitute fraud on shareholders, there must also be a reasonable, objective basis for suspecting such fraud. The "reasonableness" test used under Sarbanes-Oxley is the same test as that generally used in a variety of legal contexts.

Livingston alleges that his protected activity consisted of his July 10, 2002 memorandum, his July 29, 2002 internal ethics and compliance complaint, his conversations with Babiarz and O'Brien in August 2002, and persistence through September 2002 in his complaints about training deficiencies and a perceived cover-up of those deficiencies. He claims that he had a reasonably objective basis for believing that if Sanford went forward with compliance verification as scheduled, it would be providing false and misleading information to compliance auditors, including the FDA, thereby potentially subjecting Wyeth to fines and penalties. According to Livingston, based on the history of FDA compliance issues at Wyeth, the gravity of the Consent Decree (as portrayed by management itself), and

management's stubborn refusals to heed his criticisms, it was reasonable for him to believe that Wyeth was "probably violating some SEC 'rule or regulation,' or some 'provision of Federal law relating to fraud against shareholders.'"...

Defendants argue that none of the evidence adduced by Livingston would have provided a reasonable basis for believing that Wyeth was about to commit some form of wrongdoing. Having reviewed the entire record on summary judgment, the Court agrees. To be protected under Sarbanes-Oxley, an employee's disclosures must be related to illegal activity that, at its core, involves shareholder fraud. It may be that the employee need not know precisely what securities law is about to be violated, but there must be some basis for an objectively reasonable belief, considering the employee's experience and knowledge, that the corporation is about to commit wrongdoing. There is nothing in the record—or in Livingston's allegations—indicating that Wyeth made false or misleading statements, or omitted relevant information, in any documents provided to its shareholders....

Nor was there an objectively reasonable basis, at the time of the allegedly protected activity, for Livingston to equate the perceived training deficiencies with imminent wrongdoing. On the record before the Court, it is entirely speculative to say that because Defendants disagreed with Livingston's belief that the facility could not meet the September 30, 2002 deadline, this meant that management planned to conceal critical information. Aside from Livingston's self-serving averments in his affidavit, on matters of which he does not have personal knowledge or which are contradicted by his deposition testimony, the record is insufficient to support a finding that Defendants appeared to be ready to commit wrongdoing. Livingston admits in his affidavit that "the Consent Decree did not specifically require [training compliance standards] to be implemented by a specific date." Although Defendants concede that Wyeth had committed to a September 30, 2002 target for implementing certain training guidelines, Livingston admits that even if compliance concerns persisted on that date, a legacy plan could be created for purposes of avoiding penalties under the Consent

continued

Decree. This concession is fatal to Plaintiff's claims. No reasonable employee in Plaintiff's position could have believed Wyeth was headed toward wrongly concealing training deficiencies. Any such deficiencies, as Livingston well knew, would be deemed by the FDA to be adequately addressed if a legacy plan were adopted by Wyeth to afford it additional time to close any compliance gaps.

Livingston contends that the potential financial impact of non-compliance was so significant that the concerns about training deficiencies should have been communicated to shareholders. Even if it were reasonable to believe that the FDA might, in the future, take some type of enforcement action based on GMP and/or training compliance issues at Sanford, it is not clear that Wyeth would have been obligated to report these alleged violations before the FDA took any action. Information must be sufficiently material to a company's financial picture before it will form the basis for securities fraud. Under Supreme Court authority, for information to be material, there must be "a substantial likelihood that a reasonable shareholder would consider [the matter] important to his decision to invest." *TSC Indus., Inc. v.*

Northway, Inc., 426 U.S. 438,449 (1976); *see also Basic, Inc. v. Levinson*, 485 U.S. 224, 231-32 (1988). Given the importance of "materiality" under the securities laws, Administrative Law Judges have rejected whistleblower retaliation claims where the information disclosed would not be sufficiently material to shareholders....

[*Defendant's motion for summary judgment is granted.*]

Case Questions

1. To come within the protection of SOX, must an employee's disclosures be related to illegal activity that at its core involves shareholder fraud?

2. Must an employee have precise knowledge of what securities law is about to be violated in order to be protected under the Act?

3. Was the information about the perceived training deficiencies disclosed by Livingston sufficiently "material" that a reasonable shareholder would consider the matter important in his or her decision to invest?

SECTION 135: NONCOMPETITION AGREEMENTS

A trade secret may consist of any formula, device, or compilation of information that is used in a business and is of such a nature that it provides an advantage over competitors who do not have this information. For example, a formula for a chemical compound or a process for manufacturing or, to a limited extent, certain customer lists may be trade secrets.[35] Employers commonly seek to restrict employees who have access to trade secrets or other confidential information from competing against them subsequent to leaving the employers' business. They do so by having their employees sign noncompetition agreements, sometimes called "covenants not to compete," as part of their employment contracts. As set forth in the *NIKE, Inc. v. McCarthy* decision, presented in this section, these covenants will be enforced as follows: (1) they are limited as to duration and geographic area; (2) they must be based on some good consideration; and (3)

---

[35] In *Innovative Techs Corp. v. Kenton Trace Techs*, 7 DLR A-7 (Jan. 11, 2008), a jury awarded $23 million in compensatory and punitive damages against three former employees and a competitor, AMTI. The three ex-employees were found to be "faithless servants" by the court because while still employed by ITC, over a 14-month period, they had formed their own company using ITC proprietary information for their own advantage in violation of state trade secrecy law and for the advantage of AMTI.

they must be reasonable, affording only fair protection to the employer in whose favor they are made, and not interfere with the interests of the public.

Our legal system generally disapproves of limitations on competition. Accordingly, the courts balance the aim of protecting the legitimate interests of the employer with the rights of the employee to follow gainful employment and provide services required by the public and other employers. Noncompetition agreements that are more than reasonably necessary to protect the employer will not be enforced. In *H&R Block v. Swenson*, Mary Swenson and five other former H&R Block employees in La Crosse, Wisconsin, started a tax and bookkeeping business there. Block sued for injunctive relief and damages under the noncompetition provision of each individual's employment contract. The provision required that each individual would not provide tax or bookkeeping services for any H&R Block clients for two years after termination of employment; the provisions further stated that the two-year provision would be "extended by any period(s) of violation" of the agreements. The court determined that there could be legitimate disputes about whether the former employees engaged in conduct prohibited by the employment contract. The court concluded that the extension provision made the restraints unreasonable because it made the duration not a fixed and definite time, but a period that was contingent upon outcomes the employees could not predict. The extension provision thus rendered the two-year clause unreasonable in its entirety.[36] However, when presented with an unreasonable agreement, the courts in some states will enforce only the reasonable restrictions in the agreement and will strike down unreasonable features.

When an employee subject to a noncompetition agreement separates from employment, the employer may well conduct an exit interview reminding the employee of its intent to enforce the noncompetition agreement. And should the employer believe that the agreement is being violated, it will seek a preliminary injunction against the former employee, seeking to restrain the individual from breaching the agreement.

CASE 16.5	NIKE, INC. v. MCCARTHY
	UNITED STATES COURT OF APPEALS, 379 F.3D 576 (9TH CIR. 2004).

[Eugene McCarthy left his position as director of sales for Nike's Brand Jordan division in June 2003 to become vice president of U.S. footwear sales and merchandising at Reebok, one of Nike's competitors. Nike sought a preliminary injunction to prevent McCarthy from working for Reebok for a year, invoking a noncompete agreement McCarthy had signed in 1997 when Nike had promoted him to his earlier position as a regional footwear sales manager. The agreement stated in pertinent part:

During EMPLOYEE'S employment by NIKE … and for one (1) year thereafter, (the "Restriction Period"), EMPLOYEE will not directly or indirectly … be employed by, consult for, or be connected in any manner with, any business engaged anywhere in the world in the athletic footwear, athletic apparel or sports equipment and accessories business, or any other business which directly competes with NIKE or any of its subsidiaries or affiliated corporations.

continued

---

[36] *H&R Block Eastern Enterprises, Inc. v. Swenson*, 745 N.W.2d 421 (Wis. Ct. App. 2007).

The U.S. District Court granted Nike's motion for a preliminary injunction, and McCarthy appealed.]

FISHER, C. J....

Protectible Interest

Even if the covenant not to compete is not void ... it is a contract in restraint of trade that must meet three requirements under Oregon common law to be enforceable:

> (1) it must be partial or restricted in its operation in respect either to time or place; (2) it must be on some good consideration; and (3) it must be reasonable, that is, it should afford only a fair protection to the interests of the party in whose favor it is made, and must not be so large in its operation as to interfere with the interests of the public.

Eldridge v. Johnston, 245 P.2d 239, 250 (Or. 1952). To satisfy the reasonableness requirement, the employer must show as a predicate "that [it] has a 'legitimate interest' entitled to protection."*North Pac. Lumber Co. v. Moore*, 551 P.2d 431, 434 (Or. 1976). McCarthy argues that Nike has failed to show such a legitimate interest in this case.* ...

Nike has shown that McCarthy acquired information pertaining especially to Nike's business during the course of his employment with Nike. As Brand Jordan's director of sales, McCarthy obtained knowledge of Nike's product launch dates, product allocation strategies, new product development, product orders six months in advance and strategic sales plans up to three years in the future. This information was not general knowledge in the industry. For instance, McCarthy was privy to information about launch dates—the date Nike plans to introduce a product in the marketplace— for Brand Jordan shoes up through the spring of 2004. According to the undisputed testimony of one of Nike's

---

*McCarthy does not contest the geographic or temporal scope of the noncompete agreement, nor does he claim that it lacked consideration....

executives, if a company knew its competitor's launch dates, it could time the launch dates of its own products to disrupt the sales of its competitor....

An employee's knowledge of confidential information is sufficient to justify enforcement of the noncompete if there is a "substantial risk" that the employee will be able to divert all or part of the employer's business given his knowledge. *See Volt Servs. Group v. Adecco Employment Servs., Inc.*, 35 P.3d 329, 334 (Or. Ct. App. 2001).... Given the nature of the confidential information that McCarthy acquired at Nike and his new position with Reebok, there is a substantial risk that Reebok would be able to divert a significant part of Nike's business given McCarthy's knowledge. McCarthy had the highest access to confidential information concerning Nike's product allocation, product development and sales strategies. As vice president of U.S. footwear sales and merchandising for Reebok, McCarthy would be responsible for developing strategic sales plans, providing overall direction for product allocation and shaping product lines, including how products are priced. Thus, McCarthy could help choose product allocation, sales and pricing strategies for Reebok that could divert a substantial part of Nike's footwear sales to Reebok based on his knowledge of information confidential to Nike without explicitly disclosing this information to any of Reebok's employees. Accordingly, the potential use of confidential information by McCarthy in his new position with Reebok is sufficient to justify enforcing the noncompete agreement. We conclude that Nike has demonstrated a likelihood of success as to the enforceability of its noncompete agreement with McCarthy....

[*Affirmed.*]

Case Questions

1. Review the wording of the noncompete agreement as to duration and territory. Is it unreasonably restrictive on McCarthy?
2. Was the restraint reasonably necessary to protect Nike's business?

SECTION 136: EMPLOYER LIABILITY FOR TORTS OF EMPLOYEES

The legal concept of imposing liability on an employer for the wrongs of its employees is known as vicarious liability and is sometimes called the doctrine of *respondeat superior*—let the master (employer) respond. It imposes liability, however, only when an employee is acting within the course of employment. The concept is justified on the grounds that the business should pay for the harm caused in the undertaking of the business, that the employer will be more careful in the selection of employees if made responsible for their actions, and that the employer is in a position to obtain liability insurance to protect against claims of third persons.

EMPLOYEE OR INDEPENDENT CONTRACTOR

If the work is done by an independent contractor rather than an employee, the owner is generally not liable for harm caused by the contractor to third persons or their property. An exception exists, however, when the work undertaken by the contractor is inherently dangerous.

In *Studebaker v. Nettie's Flower Garden, Inc.*, presented in this section, Judith Studebaker sued a florist for her injuries caused when a van driven by James Ferry collided with her car. The florist asserted that Ferry was an independent contractor; however, Studebaker established that the florist either controlled or had the right to control Ferry at the time of the accident, thus making the florist responsible for the harm caused by Ferry.

CASE 16.6	## STUDEBAKER V. NETTIE'S FLOWER GARDEN, INC. MISSOURI APPEALS COURT, 842 S.W.2D 227 (1992).

[Judith Studebaker was injured when a van driven by James Ferry collided with her vehicle. She brought an action against Nettie's Flower Garden, Inc. (Nettie's), on a *respondeat superior* theory in the belief that Ferry was Nettie's employee at the time of the accident. Nettie's defended that Ferry was an independent contractor, not an employee. From a judgment in favor of Studebaker for $125,000, Nettie's appealed.]

CRANDALL, P. J....

... Ferry delivered flowers for Nettie's from its main shop on Grand Avenue in the City of St. Louis. Ferry was paid, not by the hour, but at a rate of $2.50 to $3.00 per delivery. If there were no deliveries, he was not paid. He delivered only in an area of St. Louis which Nettie's designated as his territory. Nettie's required him to make two runs each day: one in the morning at 9:30 A.M.; one in the afternoon at 1:30 P.M. When he arrived at the shop, he set up his own route based upon the location of the deliveries in his area. He generally got to work at 8:00 A.M. to prepare for the morning run and at 12:00 P.M. to prepare for the afternoon run. Nettie's also required Ferry to stop by its shop in downtown St. Louis at St. Louis Centre

before noon each day to pick up items which needed to be transported to the Grand Avenue shop. After this stop, Ferry proceeded to the Grand Avenue shop for his afternoon run. Nettie's paid Ferry $5.00 for this stop, whether or not there was anything for him to take to the Grand Avenue shop.

Ferry used his own van for the deliveries; Nettie's required that it be heated and air-conditioned to protect the flowers and plants. Although he did not wear a uniform, Nettie's directed that Ferry be neat in appearance and that he conduct himself in a certain manner when on the job. If his behavior or appearance fell below its standards, Nettie's reprimanded Ferry. Ferry paid his own expenses and received no fringe benefits from Nettie's.

On August 9, 1989, the date of the accident in question, Ferry made his morning run and then his mid-day stop at the downtown shop at about 11:00 A.M. There was nothing for him to transport to the Grand Avenue shop. After Ferry left the downtown shop, he stopped at a pawn shop to conduct personal business. He then proceeded to the Grand Avenue shop to prepare for his afternoon run. On the way to the Grand Avenue shop, at approximately 11:45 A.M., Ferry's van collided with plaintiff's automobile....

continued

Under the doctrine of respondeat superior an employer is liable for those negligent acts or omissions of his employee which are committed within the scope of his employment....Liability based on respondeat superior requires some evidence that a master-servant relationship existed between the parties.... The test to determine if respondeat superior applies to a tort is whether the person sought to be charged as master had the right or power to control and direct the physical conduct of the other in the performance of the act.... If there was no right to control there is no liability; for those rendering services but retaining control over their own movements are not servants.... The master-servant relationship arises when the person charged as master has the right to direct the method by which the master's service is performed.... An additional inquiry is whether the person sought to be charged as the servant was engaged in the prosecution of his master's business and not simply whether the accident occurred during the time of employment.... Whether a party is liable under the doctrine of respondeat superior depends on the facts and circumstances in evidence in each particular case and no single test is conclusive of the issue of the party's interest in the activity and his right of control....

Nettie's first asserts that, when the accident in question occurred, Ferry was not driving his vehicle to serve Nettie's business interests. It argues that Ferry was on his own time, conducting his own business....

Ferry's slight detour prior to the accident to conduct personal business did not mean that he was using his van exclusively for his independent purposes.... The object of Ferry's trip was not just to go to the pawn shop. At the time of the accident, Ferry was doing Nettie's business because he was returning to the Grand Avenue shop after making his routine mid-day stop at the downtown shop. This stop was so encompassed within his daily routine that it would be difficult to segregate it from his morning and afternoon runs.

There was sufficient evidence for the jury to determine that at the time of the accident, Ferry was engaged primarily in advancing the business interests of Nettie's and thus was acting within the scope of his employment. Nettie's first point is denied.

Nettie's further contends that there was no substantial evidence that Nettie's controlled or had the right to control Ferry at the time of the collision. Whether or not the right of control existed in a particular case is ordinarily a question of fact for the jury....

In the instant action, Ferry furnished his own means of transportation; but it was mandatory that he have a vehicle to carry out his job responsibilities. Nettie's required that his vehicle be equipped with heating and air-conditioning systems. Nettie's also set standards for Ferry's dress and conduct while he was on the job, and monitored his compliance with these standards. In addition, although Ferry mapped out his own route to deliver the flowers, Nettie's gave him the list of customers and determined his territory. Nettie's directed Ferry to make the mid-day stop at its downtown shop on a daily basis and paid him for that stop. Ferry incorporated that stop into his route. The stop usually occurred after his morning run and prior to his return trip to the Grand Avenue shop for his afternoon run. In addition, Nettie's always paid him for this stop, whether or not he transported anything. There was substantial evidence from which a jury reasonably could have found that, at the time of the accident in question, Nettie's either controlled or had the right to control the manner in which Ferry performed the duties for which he was employed. Nettie's second point is denied.

[Judgment affirmed.]

Case Questions

1. Did Nettie's control or have the right to control Ferry at the time of the collision?
2. Is not the fact that Ferry, just prior to the accident, had gone to a pawn shop compelling evidence that he was using his van exclusively for his independent purposes and was not acting within the course of his employer's business?
3. Give your opinion on the ethics of businesses converting employees to independent contractors to reduce or eliminate costs, such as health and retirement benefits, vacations, overtime, and maintenance and proper insurance of motor vehicles.

SECTION 137: PROPER CLASSIFICATION OF WORKERS

In the *Studebaker* case, presented in the previous section, the employer did not consider its delivery person an employee; yet it turned out that the employer was held responsible for $125,000 in damages caused by the driver. It is critical therefore to properly assess whether an individual is an employee or independent contractor so the employer purchases appropriate liability insurance and exercises proper care in the selection and supervision of the individual(s) in question.

Other considerations exist as well. If the individual is an independent contractor who has earned over $600, the "employer" must supply an IRS 1099 Misc form to each contractor stating the amount of money paid the contractor during the year. If the employer hires "employees," the employer must have an IRS employer identification number; pay state and federal unemployment taxes; supply workers' compensation insurance; withhold payroll taxes, both federal and state, and submit payroll tax returns monthly or quarterly; and pay Social Security taxes equal to the amount withheld and paid by the employee. The employer may also provide benefits to employees, such as vacations, sick days, medical and dental plans, and a retirement plan. Benefits are not provided to independent contractors.[37]

Substantial penalties exist for employers who attempt to misclassify their employees as independent contractors to avoid paying taxes and benefits. For example, the penalty for an employer who does not provide a 1099 form and has misclassified an employee as an independent contractor is 40 percent of the Social Security (FICA) tax owed and 3 percent of wages paid. If overtime is not paid employees because they are willfully misclassified as independent contractors, it is a violation of the Fair Labor Standards Act and the employer is subject to a fine of $10,000 and imprisonment of up to six months. Figure16-1 (on the next page) provides questions that can be used to determine whether an individual is an independent contractor or an employee. You will note that the degree of control the employer exercises over the individual's work is pivotal in making the proper determination.[38]

---

[37] See *Vizcaino v. Microsoft Corp.*, 173 F.3d 713 (9th Cir. 1999), setting forth a fact pattern where the IRS reclassified a number of independent contractor positions of individuals doing work for Microsoft to the status of employees and thereafter Microsoft converted many independent contractor positions to temporary agency employees. The court of appeals ordered all individuals who meet the common law definition of employee to proceed with claims against Microsoft based on state law to participate in the company's employee stock purchase plan.

[38] In *Nationwide Mutual Insurance Co. v. Darden*, 503 U.S. 318 (1992), the U.S. Supreme Court set forth the factors to be considered in determining whether "temp" workers are common law employees of the company for which they perform services. The factors are recruitment, training, duration, right to assign additional work, and control over the relationship between workers and the employment agency.

FIGURE 16.1 | QUESTIONS FOR ASCERTAINING INDEPENDENT CONTRACTOR OR EMPLOYEE STATUS

	Independent Contractor	Employee
1. Does the employer control the manner and means of accomplishing the work? (A worker who is required to follow the employer's instruction on when, where, and how and with what tools is generally considered an employee.)	No	Yes
2. Does the employer set the hours of employment?	No	Yes
3. Does the employer provide substantial training or schooling?	No	Yes
4. Does the employer provide tools, supplies, and equipment?	No	Yes
5. Does the individual have a continuing relationship with the employer and maintain regular hours of work at the employer's business?	No	Yes
6. Is the employer the individual's sole source of income?	No	Yes
7. Does the employer have other "employees" on the payroll doing the same kind of work?	No	Yes
8. Does the individual have an office rented at fair value from a party unrelated to the employer?	Yes	No
9. Does the individual work as a professional or skilled technician?	Yes	No
10. Does the individual have business stationery, advertise, have a written contract, and send bills for work performed?	Yes	No

SECTION 138: NEGLIGENT HIRING AND RETENTION OF EMPLOYEES

In addition to a complaint against the employer based on the doctrine of *respondeat superior*, a lawsuit may often raise a second theory, that of negligent hiring or retention of an employee.[39] Unlike the *respondeat superior* theory by which the employer may be vicariously liable for the tort of an employee, the negligent hiring theory is based upon the negligence of the employer in the hiring process. Under the *respondeat superior* rule, the employer is liable for only those torts committed within the scope of employment or in the furtherance of the employer's interests. The negligent hiring theory has been used to impose liability in cases where an employee commits an intentional tort, almost invariably outside the scope of employment, against a customer or the general public where the employer knew or should have known that the employee was incompetent, violent, dangerous, or criminal. In *Harrison v. Tallahassee Furniture*

---

[39] *Medina v. Graham's Cowboys, Inc.*, 827 P.2d 859 (N.M. App. Ct. 1992).

Company,[40] the employer hired John Turner to deliver furniture to customers' houses without having him fill out a job application form and without conducting an interview and checking references. It turned out that Turner had a juvenile record for armed robbery and burglary, a conviction involving cutting his former wife's face with a knife, and a voluntary hospitalization for psychiatric problems. He was an intravenous drug user, and he had been fired from his former employment. Under a negligent hiring theory, the court held the employer liable for damages that resulted when Turner attacked a customer (Harrison) in her home.

NEED FOR DUE CARE IN HIRING

An employer may be liable on a theory of negligent hiring when it is shown that the employer knew, or in the exercise of ordinary care should have known, that the job applicant would create an undue risk of harm to others in carrying out job responsibilities. Moreover, it must also be shown that the employer could have reasonably foreseen injury to the third party. Thus, an employer who knows of an employee's preemployment drinking problems and violent behavior may be liable to customers assaulted by that employee.

Employers might protect themselves from liability for negligent hiring by having each prospective employee fill out an employment application form and then checking into the applicant's work experience, background, character, and qualifications. This would be evidence of due care in hiring. Generally, the scope of preemployment investigation should correlate to the degree of opportunity the prospective employee would have to do harm to third persons. A minimum investigation consisting of the filling out of an application form and a personal interview would be satisfactory for the hiring of an outside maintenance person, but a full background inquiry would be necessary for the hiring of a security guard.[41] However, such inquiry does not bar *respondeat superior* liability.

---

[40] 583 So.2d 744 (Fla. App. 1991). See also *Brimage v. City of Boston*, 2001 WL 69488 (Mass. Super.), where summary judgment for the City was disallowed where it had hired Pedro Rosario as a supervisor for a summer program known as the Boston Youth Cleanup Crew and Rosario raped and assaulted a 16-year-old summer employee. Had the City conducted a criminal background check, it would have discovered that Rosario had recently served time in prison for rape, but even without a criminal background check, Rosario's résumé reflected a long, unexplained gap in his employment history representing the time he served in prison, which should have put the City on notice to make reasonable inquiry.

[41] Often employers desire to evaluate a potential employee's credit standing when hiring for a responsible position. The federal Fair Credit Reporting Act (FCRA), 15 U.S.C. §§ 1681-1681(t), defines the employment context for creditworthiness reporting. If an applicant is denied employment because of a credit report, under the FCRA, the employer must notify the applicant and give the name of the consumer credit company making the report. The FCRA requirements are quite burdensome and complicated. It is therefore advisable to consult an attorney expert in this area of law before utilizing consumer credit reports for personnel purposes. Moreover, Congress explicitly established a private cause of action for negligent FCRA violations, including failure to use reasonable procedures as required by Section 1681e(b). For example, Derek Wilson's FCRA suit against CARCO Group, Inc., a background checking firm, was reinstated when CARCO failed to conduct a complete and timely background check, causing a job offer to be withdrawn. Prudential enclosed a copy of the CARCO report with the letter withdrawing the job offer, and the report stated "A criminal record search for convictions and arrests, where prosecution is pending, was [initiated] ... on the subject as follows." Below this statement, a chart listed "Pending" next to the Oklahoma entry for "Wilson, Derek." Wilson immediately demonstrated to CARCO that he had no criminal history. After CARCO had taken 36 days to complete its check, it agreed that Wilson had no criminal history. The job offer was not reinstated, and Wilson sued CARCO. See *Wilson v. CARCO Group, Inc.*, 518 F.3d 46 (D.C. Cir. 2008).

EMPLOYEES WITH CRIMINAL RECORDS

The hiring of an individual with a criminal record does not by itself establish the tort of negligent hiring.[42] An employer who knows that an applicant has a criminal record has a duty to investigate to determine whether the nature of the conviction in relationship to the job to be performed creates an unacceptable risk to third persons.

NEGLIGENT RETENTION

Courts assign liability under negligent retention on a basis similar to negligent hiring. That is, the employer knew or should have known that the employee would create an undue risk of harm to others in carrying out job responsibilities. The *Bryant v. Livigni* case, presented in this section, involves *respondeat superior* liability as well as negligent retention liability.

A hospital is liable for negligent retention when it continues the staff privileges of a physician that it knew or should have known had sexually assaulted a female patient in the past.[43]

CASE 16.7

BRYANT V. LIVIGNI
ILLINOIS COURT OF APPEALS, 250 ILL. APP. 3D 303 (1994).

[Mark Livigni was manager of the National Super Markets, Inc., store in Cahokia, Illinois. After drinking alcoholic beverages one evening, he stopped by the store to check the operation and observed a 10-year-old boy's unacceptable behavior outside the store. Livigni chased the boy to a car, where he then pulled a 4-year-old child named Farris Bryant from the car and threw him through the air. A multicount lawsuit was brought against National and Livigni. A verdict was rendered against National for $20,000 on a *respondeat superior* theory for the battery of Farris Bryant. A verdict was also rendered against National for $15,000 in negligent retention of Livigni and for $115,000 punitive damages for willful and wanton retention. National appealed the trial court's denial of its motions for directed verdicts on these counts.]

MAAG, J....

On March 18, 1987, while off duty, Livigni stopped by the Cahokia National store. As manager, he was authorized to check and supervise the operation of the store even during off-duty hours. He was intoxicated at the time of his visit, which was a violation of National rules.... Livigni observed a young man urinating on the store wall outside the east exit doors. He hollered at the young man and followed the fleeing youth to the parked vehicle of Diana Bryant.

Livigni pulled 4-year-old Farris Bryant from the automobile, ... throwing the child through the air.

Farris was taken to Centreville Township Hospital's emergency room for medical treatment. Farris was admitted to the hospital and was released after four days. He was released from all medical treatment approximately one month after the battery....

At trial, Livigni's supervisor testified that during Livigni's 17-year tenure with National, Livigni had been a good employee. This supervisor never received any reports from customers or employees that Livigni had "violent-related" problems, although he was aware of a report that Livigni threw an empty milk crate which struck a coworker.

continued

---

[42] *Connes v. Molalla Transportation Systems*, 831 P.2d 1316 (Colo. 1992).

[43] *Capithorne v. Framingham Union Hospital*, 401 Mass. 860, 520 N.E.2d 139 (1988).

Evidence was offered of two batteries committed by Livigni prior to his attack of Farris. In 1980, Livigni had a disagreement with a subordinate employee resulting in Livigni throwing an empty milk crate at the employee striking him on the arm and necessitating medical treatment. At the time of this battery, Livigni was an assistant store manager. A workers' compensation claim was filed against National by the injured employee. A short time after the workers' compensation claim was resolved, Livigni was promoted to store manager by National in spite of this incident.

The second battery occurred in 1985 when Livigni, while disciplining his 13-year-old son, threw the boy into a bed causing the boy to sustain a broken collar bone. In June 1986 Livigni pleaded guilty to aggravated battery to a child and was sentenced to two years' probation. He was still on probation at the time he attacked Farris.

Livigni testified at the trial that he had not told any of his supervisors at National about the battery of his son. He admitted to telling employees of equal or lesser positions than himself about the battery. He considered these people to be his friends....

According to National, there was no evidence that it knew or had reason to know that Livigni was anything other than "an excellent store manager, fit for his position." To support this argument, National claims that there was conflicting evidence regarding the 1980 incident where Livigni threw a milk crate at a coworker causing injury. It argues that the 1980 incident was of uncertain origin since differing versions of the incident and its cause were presented in the evidence. It asserts that due to this conflicting evidence the incident could not form the basis for a negligent retention claim....

Rather than disciplining Livigni after he injured a subordinate employee in an unprovoked attack, National promoted him following the resolution of the injured employee's workers' compensation claim.

National further argues that it had no knowledge of the incident involving Livigni's son that resulted in Livigni's felony conviction for aggravated battery of a child. Relying upon *Campen v. Executive House Hotel, Inc.* (1982), 105 Ill. App.3d 576, 61 Ill.Dec. 358, National points to the general rule which states that to impute knowledge of this occurrence to National a showing was required that an agent or employee of National had notice or knowledge of the incident and that the knowledge concerned a matter within the scope of the agent's authority. According to National, evidence of such knowledge was lacking....

National first admits that Livigni told employees of equal or lesser rank within the corporation about the battery involving his son. However, it claims that this is insufficient notice to the corporation. It argues that the people Livigni told were his "friends" and that as mere "coworkers" of equal or subordinate position no notice could legally be imputed to National. We disagree....

Viewing the evidence in the light most favorable to the plaintiff, we believe that a reasonable jury could have concluded that the information concerning the battery of Livigni's son, learned by these coworkers, was within the scope of their authority to act upon. Whether reported to higher authorities or not, the information still constitutes "corporate knowledge." (*Campen*, 105 Ill. App.3d at 586....) In such a case, their knowledge is chargeable to National....

We conclude that the circuit court did not err in denying National's motion for a directed verdict, nor did it err in refusing to grant a judgment *n.o.v.* on plaintiff's claim of negligent retention. Viewing the evidence in the light most favorable to the plaintiff, we cannot state that the evidence so overwhelmingly favored National that this verdict cannot stand.

National next claims that the circuit court should have directed a verdict in its favor or granted a judgment *n.o.v.* on the plaintiff's punitive damages claim. This count alleged that National's retention of Mark Livigni as a management employee constituted willful and wanton misconduct....

The Restatement (Second) of Torts, section 909, at 467 (1977) provides:

> "Punitive damages can properly be awarded against a master or other principal because of an act by an agent if, but only if,
>
> * * *
>
> (b) the agent was unfit and the principal or a managerial agent was reckless in ... retaining him."

This count did not seek to impose liability upon the defendant vicariously. Rather, the plaintiff's cause of action alleged wrongful conduct on the part of National itself. Section 909(b) of the Restatement (Second) of Torts speaks directly to the issue under discussion. So too does the case of *Easley v. Apollo Detective Agency, Inc.* (1979), 69 Ill.App.3d 920, 26 Ill.Dec. 313, 387 N.E.2d 1241.

continued

Easley recognized that it is settled law that a cause of action exists in Illinois for negligent hiring of an employee, and that if the defendant's conduct could properly be characterized as willful and wanton then punitive damages are recoverable. (*Easley*, 69 Ill.App.3d at 931, 26 Ill. Dec. at 320, 387 N.E.2d at 1248). We see little difference between a punitive damages claim for willfully and wantonly hiring an employee in the first instance and a claim for willfully and wantonly retaining an unfit employee after hiring. In both instances, the interest to be protected is the same. Employers that wrongfully (whether negligently or willfully and wantonly) hire or retain unfit employees expose the public to the acts of these employees. In such cases it is not unreasonable to hold the employer accountable when the employee causes injury or damage to another. The principle at issue is not *respondeat superior*, although that may also be implicated. Rather, the cause of action is premised upon the wrongful conduct of the employer itself. (*Easley*, 69 Ill.App.3d at 931, 26 Ill.Dec. at 320, 387 N.E.2d at 1248). For this reason, the cause of action is distinguishable from the situation in *Mattyasovszky v. West Towns Bus Co.* (1975), 61 Ill.2d 31, 330 N.E.2d 509, where the plaintiff sought to hold the employer responsible for an employee's acts based upon principles of vicarious liability.

The jury heard evidence that Livigni attacked a fellow employee in 1980 and was then promoted. He injured his own son, he was convicted of aggravated battery in a criminal proceeding, and members of National's management admittedly knew of that incident. National took no action. Then while a store manager, in an intoxicated state, he attacked a 4-year-old child and threw him through the air, resulting in his hospitalization. National itself characterizes this attack on young Farris as outrageous. We cannot say the jury was unjustified in concluding the same and also concluding that retaining this man as a managerial employee constituted willful and wanton misconduct....

...The circuit court did not err in refusing to grant a directed verdict, not did it err in refusing to grant a judgment *n.o.v.* on plaintiff's punitive damages claim.

Finally, National asks that a judgment *n.o.v.* be entered in its favor on the plaintiff's *respondeat superior* claims.

In order to impose liability upon National, it was not necessary that Livigni be motivated *solely* by a desire to further National's interest. It is sufficient if his actions were prompted only *in part* by a purpose to protect store property or further the employer's business. (*Wilson v. Clark Oil & Refining Corp.* (1985), 134 Ill.App.3d 1084, 1089, 90.) The evidence was sufficient to justify such a conclusion by the jury.

Finally, the actions of Livigni in attacking Farris were committed within the constraints of the authorized time and location of his employment, thus bolstering a finding that the battery occurred within the course and scope of his employment. *Sunseri v. Puccia* (1981), 97 Ill. App. 3d 488....

Conclusion

For the foregoing reasons, the judgment of the circuit court of St. Clair County is affirmed.

Affirmed.

JUSTICE WELCH, concurring in part and dissenting in part...

I concur with the majority's opinion with respect to, and would affirm the judgment of the circuit court on the jury verdict against National Food Stores on, the *respondeat superior* counts of plaintiff's complaint. With respect to the majority's opinion concerning the judgment against National on the negligent and willful and wanton retention counts of plaintiffs' complaint, however I must respectfully dissent....

From a practical standpoint, the majority's opinion sends a message to all employers that in order to insulate themselves from liability for negligent or willful and wanton retention any employee who has ever had an altercation on or off the workplace premises must be fired. Moreover, the majority opinion places an unreasonable investigative burden upon the employer by forcing the employer to discover, retain, and analyze the criminal records of its employees. Is not the majority's opinion then at cross-purposes with the established public policy and laws of Illinois protecting the privacy of citizens and promoting the education and rehabilitation of criminal offenders? See Ill. Rev. Stat. 1991, ch. 68, par. 2-103 (making it a civil rights violation to ask a job applicant about an arrest record); see also Ill. Rev.Stat.1991, ch. 38, par. 1003-12-1 *et seq.* (concerning correctional employment programs whose function is to teach marketable skills and work habits and responsibility to Illinois prisoners).

I would have granted defendant National Food Stores' motion for judgment *non obstante veredicto*....

continued

Case Questions

1. Was there *respondeat superior* liability in this case?
2. Should National have reasonably known about Livigni's "violent-related" problems? And if so, did it act negligently in retaining him as an employee?
3. From Judge Welch's dissent, will the *Livigni* case hurt the employment prospects of individuals with criminal records involving violence?

CHAPTER QUESTIONS AND PROBLEMS

1. List the four types of exceptions to the classic employment-at-will rule.

2. Five years after Kathy Small began her employment with Spring Industries, the company distributed an employee handbook to all employees setting forth the company's termination procedure. It outlined a four-step disciplinary process consisting of a verbal reprimand, a written warning, a final written warning, and discharge. Small was discharged after only one written warning and sued the company for breach of contract.

   Small contended that the company was bound by the plain language of the handbook and that it would be unjust for an employer to issue a handbook and not be held to its contents. Moreover, she contended that if company policies were not worth the paper on which they were printed, it would be better not to mislead employees by distributing them.

   The company contended that Small did not present evidence that the parties agreed that the handbook was to become part of her employment contract and that if Small were to succeed, it would result in the removal of employee handbooks from the workforce and stifle economic growth in the state.

   Did Small have an enforceable contract? Comment on whether handbooks will be removed from the workplace because of cases like this. What can an employer do to avoid liability under similar circumstances? [*Small v. Spring Industries, Inc.*, 357 S.E.2d 452. (S.C.).]

3. Under an oral contract of indefinite duration, Marlene S. Gates worked as a cashier for Life of Montana Insurance Company for over three years prior to October 19, 1979, when she was called in to meet with her supervisor, Roger Syverson. Without any prior warning, she was given the option of resigning or being fired. She testified that while in a distraught condition and under duress, she signed a letter of resignation that was handed to her by Syverson. Gates stated that she signed the letter of resignation because she thought it would be better for her record and because Syverson told her he would give her a letter of recommendation so that she could be reemployed. Gates went home and discussed the situation with her husband, who advised her to retrieve the letter of resignation and inform her supervisor that she was not resigning. Appellant stated that she immediately called Syverson and demanded the letter be returned and that he promised to do so. Syverson testified that she only requested a photocopy of the letter. Syverson testified that he offered to give Gates a letter of recommendation if she resigned. However, he testified that he planned to give her only a letter that would state that appellant was employed by Life of Montana Insurance Company; he never intended to provide appellant with a favorable letter of recommendation. There was evidence from which a jury might infer that Gates understood she was to receive a favorable letter of recommendation and that Syverson allowed her to resign on this basis. The company contended that Gates was discharged for incompetence and insubordination. The evidence indicated that a resignation rather than a discharge may protect an employer from immediately becoming

liable for unemployment compensation benefits in Montana and that by obtaining a letter of resignation, an employer may be insulating itself against a claim for wrongful discharge.

Montana law allows for the litigation of the question of whether there was a breach of an implied covenant of fair dealing where an employee is discharged without warning and an opportunity for a hearing. Montana law holds that a breach of the covenant of fair dealing is imposed by operation of law; therefore, its breach should find a remedy in tort for which punitive damages can be recovered if the defendant's conduct is sufficiently culpable, that is, if there was fraud, oppression, or malice.

The company contended that it was a legislative rather than a judicial function to create a cause of action that would apply a just-cause standard for the discharge of at-will employees and that, in any event, the company should not be liable for punitive damages if new legal rights are granted Gates, which rights could not have been known by the company at the time it terminated her.

Did the company breach its implied covenant of fair dealing to Gates when it terminated her? Should the company be held liable for punitive damages? Decide. [*Gates v. Life of Montana Insurance Co.*, 668 P.2d 213 Mont., DLR No. 162]

4. Michael Hauck claims that he was discharged by his employer, Sabine Pilot Service, Inc., because he refused his employer's direction to perform the illegal act of pumping the bilges of his employer's vessel into the waterways. Hauck was an employee at will, and Sabine contends that it therefore had the right to discharge him without having to show cause. Hauck brought a wrongful discharge action against Sabine. Decide. [*Sabine Pilot Service, Inc. v. Hauck*, 687 S.W.2d 733 (Tex)]

5. Steven Trujillo was told by the assistant door manager of Cowboys Bar "to show up to work tonight in case we need you as a doorman." He came to the bar that evening, wearing a jacket with the bar logo on it. Trujillo "attacked" Rocky Medina in the parking lot of the bar, causing Medina serious injury. Prior to working for Cowboys, Trujillo was involved in several fights at that bar and in its parking lot; and Cowboys knew of these matters. Medina sued Cowboys on two theories of liability: (1) *respondeat superior* and (2) negligent hiring of Trujillo. Cowboys defends that the *respondeat superior* theory should be dismissed because the assault was clearly not within the course of Trujillo's employment. Concerning the negligent hiring theory, Cowboys asserts that Trujillo was not on duty that night as a doorman. Decide. [*Medina v. Graham's Cowboys, Inc.*, 827 P.2d 859 (N.M.App.)]

6. Neal Rubin, while driving his car in Chicago, inadvertently blocked the path of a Yellow Cab Company taxi driven by Robert Ball, causing the taxi to swerve and hit Rubin's car. Angered by Rubin's driving, Ball got out of his cab and hit Rubin over the head and shoulders with a metal pipe. Rubin sued the Yellow Cab Company for the damages caused by this beating, contending that the employer was vicariously liable for the beating under the doctrine of *respondeat superior*, as the beating occurred in furtherance of the employer's business, which was to obtain fares without delay. The company defended that Ball's beating of Rubin was not an act undertaken to further the employer's business. Is the employer liable under *respondeat superior*? Decide. [*Rubin v. Yellow Cab Co.*, 154 Ill. App. 3d 336, 107 Ill. Dec. 450, 507 N.E.2d 114]

7. On July 11, Jose Padilla was working as a vacation-relief route salesperson for Frito-Lay. He testified that he made a route stop at Sal's Beverage Shop. He was told by Mrs. Ramos that she was dissatisfied with Frito-Lay service and no longer wanted their products in the store. He asked if there was anything he could do to change her mind. She said no and told him to pick up his

merchandise. He took one company-owned merchandise rack to his van and was about to pick up another rack when Mr. Ramos said that the rack had been given to him by the regular route salesperson. Padilla said the route salesperson had no authority to give away Frito-Lay racks. A confrontation occurred over the rack, and Padilla pushed Mr. Ramos against the cash register, injuring Ramos's back. Frito-Lay has a company policy, clearly communicated to all employees, that prohibits them from getting involved in any type of physical confrontation with a customer. Frito-Lay contended that Padilla was not acting within the course and scope of his employment when the pushing incident took place and that the company was therefore not liable to Ramos. Ramos contended that Frito-Lay was responsible for the acts of its employee Padilla. Decide. [*Frito-Lay Inc. v. Ramos*, 770 S.W.2d 887 (Tex. Civ. App.)]

8. Hewlett-Packard has an employee manual called *The H-P Way* that states the corporate philosophy of "belief in people." The manual stated the company goal "to provide job security based on their [employees'] performance." The manual stated on its first page that its contents do not present a contract and that it was intended only for distribution among managers. The manual described a discipline process.

The company did not follow the process set forth in the manual when it terminated Orbach, and the at-will employee sued H-P for wrongful termination. Did the discipline process set forth in the manual have a limiting effect on Orbach's at-will employment status and bar H-P from terminating him without following the procedures? Decide. [*Orbach v. Hewlett-Packard Co.*, 97 F.3d 429 (10th Cir.)]

9. Michael Paolella was employed as sales manager for Browning-Ferris (BFI) with responsibility for a district in Delaware. When the state's Solid Waste Authority announced plans to raise disposal rates 25 percent, the district manager, Ronald Hanley, devised a scheme to increase BFI's revenues by leading customers to believe that increased fees were the result of the 25 percent increase in disposal rates when, in fact, a significant portion of the increased charges to customers was based on an artificially inflated average weight per cubic yard. Paolella admitted that he did not object to the plan when it was proposed by Hanley. He testified that later he raised concern with Hanley at least twice weekly but nevertheless complied with instructions to send a letter to customers advising them of the 25 percent increase in June 1992. And he negotiated contracts with customers based on these rates. In late 1993, Paolella sent BFI a letter warning BFI to "cease all illegal activities." He was fired at 51 years of age, on January 17, 1994, for "poor performance." He sued BFI for wrongful discharge under the public policy exception to the employment-at-will doctrine based on the public policy set forth in the state law against theft by false pretenses. The jury returned a verdict of $732,000, representing $135,000 of back pay and $597,000 in front pay. The judge reduced the damages by $132,000 because of Paolella's participation. BFI appealed, contending that Paolella's participation should preclude him from relying on the public policy exception, and it contended that the front pay was excessive. Is BFI correct? Decide. [*Paolella v. Browning-Ferris, Inc.*, 158 F.3d 195 (3d Cir.)]

EMPLOYEE PRIVACY TOPICS

CHAPTER 17

SECTION 139: HISTORICAL BACKGROUND, INTRODUCTION TO EMPLOYEE PRIVACY

In *Robertson v. Rochester Folding Box Co.*,[1] a 1902 decision by New York State's highest court, the court, by a 4–3 margin, refused to grant injunctive relief based on an asserted violation of a young woman's right to privacy. The defendant had used a picture of Abigail Robertson on 25,000 posters advertising Franklin Mills' flour without her consent. The court majority indicated that the right to privacy was nonexistent at common law, because mention of it was "not to be found in Blackstone, Kent, or any of the great commentators on the law." The majority also stated:

> While most persons would much prefer to have a good likeness of themselves appear in a responsible periodical or leading newspaper, rather than upon an advertising card

---

[1] 171 N.Y. 538 (1902).

or sheet, the doctrine which the courts are asked to create for this case would apply to one publication as to the other, for the principle which a court of equity is asked to assert in support of recovery in this action is that the right of privacy exists and is enforceable in equity....

The dissenting opinion was less fearful of recognizing such a doctrine. It stated:

> Security of person is as necessary as the security of property; and for that complete personal security which will result in the peaceful and wholesome enjoyment of one's privileges as a member of society there should be afforded protection, not only against the scandalous portraiture and display of one's features and person, but against the display and use thereof for another's commercial purposes or gain. The proposition is to me, an inconceivable one that these defendants may, unauthorizedly, use the likeness of this young woman upon their advertisement as a method of attracting widespread public attention to their wares, and that she must submit to the mortifying notoriety without right to invoke the exercise of the preventive power of a court of equity.

Outraged by the decision and persuaded by the thought-provoking law review article written over a decade before by Samuel D. Warren and Louis D. Brandeis which concluded that a right to privacy existed in the common law,[2] the New York legislature passed a statutory right to privacy in 1903.[3]

The common law right of privacy goes beyond the mere unauthorized use of one's portrait. It extends to any unreasonable intrusion on one's private life. The Restatement of Torts provided that "any person who unreasonably and seriously interferes with another's interest in not having his affairs known to others or his likeness exhibited to the public is liable to the other."[4] Early applications of the doctrine provided recovery in situations ranging from eavesdropping by tapping a telephone line to barging into a woman's stateroom on a steamship. It should also be made clear that the common law right to privacy was never intended to interfere with the constitutional guarantees of freedom of speech and freedom of the press, including the public's right to know about matters of legitimate public interest and to be informed about the lives of public figures. Although not specifically spelled out in the U.S. Constitution, the Supreme Court has recognized that there is a federal constitutional right to personal privacy. The Court found in *Griswold v. Connecticut*[5] that the right to privacy is implicit in the Bill of Rights, which prohibits various types of unreasonable governmental intrusion upon personal freedom.

Employers may want to monitor employee telephone conversations in the ordinary course of their business in order to evaluate employee performance and customer service or document business transactions between employees and customers or meet special security, efficiency, or other needs. Employers may likewise want to monitor e-mail for what employers perceive to be sound business reasons.

---

[2] Warren & Brandeis, *The Right to Privacy*, 4 Harv. L. Rev. 193 (1890).

[3] Civil Rights Law of New York, §§ 50, 51; N.Y. Laws 1903, ch. 132 §§ I, 2.

[4] Restatement of Torts, § 867.

[5] 381 U.S. 479 (1965).

Or employers may seek to test employees for drug use or search employees' lockers for illicit drugs. Employers need to make personnel decisions based on medical reports by physicians about employees, and management needs to fully discuss the strengths and weaknesses of employees for hiring, promotion, and retention decisions. Employers are called upon to provide evaluations for their former employees. Litigation may result because employees may believe that such activities violate their right to privacy. The focus of this chapter will be on the extent of employee rights to privacy in the public and private sectors. Recommendations will be made for employers on reasonable steps to take to avoid violating employee privacy rights.

The Bill of Rights contained in the U.S. Constitution, including the First Amendment's protection of the freedom to associate and the Fourth Amendment's protection against unreasonable search and seizure, provides a philosophical and legal basis for individual privacy rights for federal employees. The Fourteenth Amendment applies this privacy protection to actions taken by state and local governments affecting their employees. The privacy rights of individuals working in the private sector are not directly controlled by the Bill of Rights, however, because challenged employer actions are not governmental actions. Limited employee privacy rights in the private sector are provided by state constitutions, statutes, case law, and collective bargaining agreements.[6]

SECTION 140: PUBLIC EMPLOYEES' PRIVACY RIGHTS

Federal employees have certain protections against disclosures under the Privacy Act of 1974. Federal and state employees have privacy protection against unreasonable searches under the federal Constitution.

THE PRIVACY ACT

The Privacy Act of 1974 provides federal employees limited protection from the dissemination of personal records without the prior written consent of the employee. Eleven exceptions exist, including use by officers or employees of the agency that maintains the records who have a need for the records in the performance of their agency duties and court orders for the records. The Privacy Act also bars disclosure of information about federal employees unless it would be

---

[6] An example of the establishment of privacy rights by a state constitution is found in Article 1, Section 1, of the Constitution of the state of California, which was amended in 1972 to provide as follows:

> All people are by nature free and independent and have inalienable rights. Among these are enjoying and defending life and liberty, acquiring, possessing, and protecting property, and pursuing and obtaining safety, happiness and *privacy*. [Emphasis added]

Two examples of ordinances protecting the privacy of employees in the private sector may be found on the Web at http://www.municode.com/database.html, Revised Municipal Code of Denver, Colorado, Title II, Chapter 28, Article IV, § 28-93 and Discriminatory Practices in Employment, Tucson Code, Part II, Chapter 17, Article III, § 17.

required under the Freedom of Information Act. In *U.S. Department of Defense v. FLRA*,[7] the Federal Labor Relations Authority directed federal agencies to provide unions with home addresses of all agency employees eligible to be represented by unions, including nonunion members. The Department of Defense refused to comply because it believed that such an order violated the Privacy Act. The U.S. Supreme Court, applying a balancing test between the privacy interests of employees and the relevant public interest, determined that the nonunion members who for whatever reason have chosen not to give unions their addresses had a nontrivial privacy interest in nondisclosure that outweighed any public interest in disclosure. The privacy interest of federal employees thus prevailed.

The Privacy Act prohibits federal agencies from disclosing any record "contained in a system of records." The Privacy Act does not prohibit disclosure of information independently acquired and does not cover personal knowledge and memories.[8] In *Olberding v. U.S. Department of Defense*, an army captain brought suit under the Privacy Act for disclosure that he had been evaluated by a psychiatrist for mental disorders. Although the communication in question in *Olberding* duplicated information in the agency's "system of records," the information had not been retrieved from a record covered by the Privacy Act. Rather, the disclosure arose from the personal knowledge of the discloser.[9]

PROPERTY SEARCHES IN THE PUBLIC SECTOR

As set forth previously, the Fourth Amendment's provision against unreasonable searches and seizures protects federal employees, and the Fourteenth Amendment extends this protection to state employees. In *O'Connor v. Ortega*, presented in this section, the Supreme Court set forth the parameters for property searches in the public sector. The case involved the search of a Dr. Ortega's office, desk, and files in connection with possible impropriety in the management of a residency program. The Court majority determined that Dr. Ortega had a reasonable expectation of privacy in his office desk and file cabinets but the state had a public interest in the supervision, control, and efficient operation of the workplace. The Court directed that searches conducted by public employers be evaluated under a "reasonableness" standard that balances the employee's expectation of privacy against the employer's legitimate business needs.[10]

---

[7] 510 U.S. 487 (1994).

[8] *Doe v. Department of Veterans Affairs*, 519 F.3d 456 (8th Cir. 2008).

[9] 709 F.2d 621 (8th Cir. 1983).

[10] The *O'Connor* principles apply as well to closed-circuit television monitoring of a public employer's workplace, with a critical inquiry being whether employees have a reasonable expectation of privacy in the areas under surveillance. If the employer uses cameras to detect wrongdoing in hallways, lunchrooms, or other public areas, there is no employee privacy violation because there is no reasonable expectation of privacy in such areas. However, surreptitious visual surveillance of restrooms or dressing rooms would be a privacy violation, absent a specific advisory of the surveillance program to employees. In *Thornton v. University Aire Services Board*, (9 IER Cases (BNA) 338 (Conn. 1994)), the use of a hidden video camera installed in a public university's police station was held not to be a privacy violation in a lawsuit over the discipline of a police officer shown on the video to be involved in unlawful gambling.

Some 17 years after Dr. Ortega's office was searched, the litigation concluded with a decision by the Ninth Circuit Court of Appeals affirming a jury award in his favor. That decision is also set forth in part in this section.

CASE 17.1	O'CONNOR V. ORTEGA
	SUPREME COURT OF THE UNITED STATES, 480 U.S. 710 (1987).

[The respondent, Dr. Magno Ortega, a physician and psychiatrist, was an employee of a state hospital and had primary responsibility for training physicians in the psychiatric residency program. Hospital officials, including the executive director of the hospital, Dr. Dennis O'Connor, became concerned about possible improprieties in Dr. Ortega's management of the program, particularly with respect to his acquisition of a computer and charges against him concerning sexual harassment of female hospital employees and inappropriate disciplinary action against a resident. In 1981, while Dr. Ortega was on administrative leave pending investigation of the charges, hospital officials, allegedly to inventory and secure state property, searched his office and seized personal items from his desk and file cabinets that were used in administrative proceedings resulting in his discharge. No formal inventory of property in the office was ever made, and all the other papers in the office were merely placed in boxes for storage. Dr. Ortega filed an action against the hospital officials under 42 U.S.C. Section 1983, alleging that the search of his office violated the Fourth Amendment. On cross-motions for summary judgment, the district court granted judgment for the hospital, concluding that the search was proper because there was a need to secure state property in the office. Affirming in part, reversing in part, and remanding the case, the court of appeals concluded that Dr. Ortega had a reasonable expectation of privacy in his office and that the search violated the Fourth Amendment. The court held that the record justified a grant of partial summary judgment for him on the issue of liability for the search, and it remanded the case to the district court for a determination of damages. The Supreme Court granted certiorari.]

O'CONNOR, J....

... We accept the conclusion of the Court of Appeals that Dr. Ortega had a reasonable expectation of privacy at least in his desk and file cabinets....

In our view, requiring an employer to obtain a warrant whenever the employer wished to enter an employee's office, desk, or file cabinets for a work-related purpose would seriously disrupt the routine conduct of business and would be unduly burdensome....

The governmental interest justifying work-related intrusions by public employers is the efficient and proper operation of the workplace. Government agencies provide myriad services to the public, and the work of these agencies would suffer if employers were required to have probable cause before they entered an employee's desk for the purpose of finding a file or piece of office correspondence. Indeed, it is difficult to give the concept of probable cause, rooted as it is in the criminal investigatory context, much meaning when the purpose of a search is to retrieve a file for work-related reasons. Similarly, the concept of probable cause has little meaning for a routine inventory conducted by public employers for the purpose of securing state property. ... To ensure the efficient and proper operation of the agency, therefore, public employers must be given wide latitude to enter employee offices for work-related, non-investigatory reasons.

We come to a similar conclusion for searches conducted pursuant to an investigation of work-related employee misconduct. Even when employers conduct an investigation, they have an interest substantially different from "the normal need for law enforcement." *New Jersey v. T.L.O., supra*, 469 U.S. at 351, 105 S. Ct., at 748 (BLACKMUN, J., concurring in judgment). Public employers have an interest in ensuring that their agencies operate in an effective and efficient manner, and the work of these agencies inevitably suffers from the inefficiency, incompetence, mismanagement, or other work-related misfeasance of its employees. Indeed, in many cases, public employees are entrusted with tremendous responsibility, and the consequences of their misconduct or incompetence to both the agency and the public interest can be severe. In contrast to law

continued

enforcement officials, therefore, public employers are not enforcers of the criminal law; instead, public employers have a direct and overriding interest in ensuring that the work of the agency is conducted in a proper and efficient manner. In our view, therefore, a probable cause requirement for searches of the type at issue here would impose intolerable burdens on public employers. The delay in correcting the employee misconduct caused by the need for probable cause rather than reasonable suspicion will be translated into tangible and often irreparable damage to the agency's work, and ultimately to the public interest....

Balanced against the substantial government interests in the efficient and proper operation of the workplace are the privacy interests of government employees in their place of work which, while not insubstantial, are far less than those found at home or in some other contexts. As with the building inspections at *Camara*, the employer intrusions at issue here "involve a relatively limited invasion" of employee privacy. 387 U.S., at 537, 87 S.Ct., at 1735. Government offices are provided to employees for the sole purpose of facilitating the work of an agency. The employee may avoid exposing personal belongings at work by simply leaving them at home.

In sum, we conclude that the "special needs, beyond the normal need for law enforcement make the ... probable-cause requirement impracticable," 469 U.S., at 351, 105 S.Ct., at 748 (BLACKMUN, J., concurring in judgment), for legitimate work-related, noninvestigatory intrusions as well as investigations of work-related misconduct. A standard of reasonableness will neither unduly burden the efforts of government employers to ensure the efficient and proper operation of the workplace, nor authorize arbitrary intrusions upon the privacy of public employees. We hold, therefore, that public employer intrusions on the constitutionally protected privacy interests of government employees for noninvestigatory, work-related purposes, as well as for investigations of work-related misconduct, should be judged by the standard of reasonableness under all circumstances. Under this reasonableness standard, both the inception and the scope of the intrusion must be reasonable:

"Determining the reasonableness of any search involves a twofold inquiry: first, one must consider 'whether the ... action was justified at its inception.' Terry v. Ohio, 392 U.S. [1], at 20 [88 S.Ct. 1868, 1879, 20 L.Ed.2d 889 (1968)]; second, one

must determine whether the search as actually conducted 'was reasonable related in scope to the circumstances which justified the interference in the first place,' ibid." New Jersey v. T.L.O., supra, at 341, 105 S.Ct., at 742–743.

Ordinarily, a search of an employee's office by a supervisor will be "justified at its inception" when there are reasonable grounds for suspecting that the search will turn up evidence that the employee is guilty of work-related misconduct, or that the search is necessary for a noninvestigatory work-related purpose such as to retrieve a needed file.... The search will be permissible in its scope when "the measures adopted are reasonably related to the objectives of the search and not excessively intrusive in light of ... the nature of the [misconduct]." 469 U.S., at 342.

In the procedural posture of this case, we do not attempt to determine whether the search of Dr. Ortega's office and the seizure of his personal belongings satisfy the standard of reasonableness we have articulated in this case. No evidentiary hearing was held in this case because the District Court acted on cross-motions for summary judgment, and granted petitioners summary judgment. The Court of Appeals, on the other hand, concluded that the record in this case justified granting partial summary judgment on liability to Dr. Ortega.

We believe that both the District Court and the Court of Appeals were in error because summary judgment was inappropriate....

... A search to secure state property is valid as long as petitioners had a reasonable belief that there was government property in Dr. Ortega's office which needed to be secured, and the scope of the intrusion was itself reasonable in light of this justification. Indeed, petitioners have put forward evidence that they had such a reasonable belief; at the time of the search, petitioners knew that Dr. Ortega had removed the computer from the Hospital. The removal of the computer—together with the allegations of mismanagement of the residency program and sexual harassment—may have made the search reasonable at its inception under the standard we have put forth in this case. As with the District Court order, therefore, the Court of Appeals conclusion that summary judgment was appropriate cannot stand.

On remand, therefore, the District Court must determine the justification for the search and seizure, and evaluate the reasonableness of both the inception of the search and its scope.

continued

Accordingly, the judgment of the Court of Appeals is reversed, and the case is remanded to that court for further proceedings consistent with this opinion.

It is so ordered.

JUSTICE SCALIA, Concurring in the judgment.

JUSTICE BLACKMUN, with whom JUSTICE BRENNAN, JUSTICE MARSHALL, and JUSTICE STEVENS join, Dissenting...

The facts of this case are simple and straightforward. Dr. Ortega had an expectation of privacy in his office, desk, and file cabinets, which were the target of a search by petitioners that can be characterized only as investigatory in nature. Because there was no "special need," see *New Jersey v. T.L.O.*, 469 U.S. 325, 351, 105 S.Ct. 733, 748, 83 L.Ed.2d 720

(1985) (opinion concurring in judgment), to dispense with the warrant and probable-cause requirements of the Fourth Amendment, I would evaluate the search by applying this traditional standard. Under that standard, this search clearly violated Dr. Ortega's Fourth Amendment rights.

Case Questions

1. Did Dr. Ortega have a reasonable expectation of privacy, at least as to his desk and file cabinets?
2. Why didn't the Supreme Court require that the employer have a warrant based on probable cause to search an employee's desk and files when investigating work-related misconduct?
3. What did the Court decide in this case?

CASE 17.2 | ORTEGA V. O'CONNOR
U.S. COURT OF APPEALS, 146 F.3D 1149 (9TH CIR. 1998).

[On remand after a trial and after an appeal, a retrial was held where the jury found for Dr. Ortega in all respects, awarding him $436,000 in compensatory and punitive damages and from which the defendants appealed.]

REINHARDT, C. J....

[T]he plaintiff and the defendants jointly proposed to the district court, and the court accepted, a jury instruction that applied a "reasonableness" test, not as the district court had suggested, to the search itself, but instead to the defendants' beliefs regarding the search. More important, that instruction stated that the reasonableness inquiry as to public officials' beliefs is determined under an objective standard— whether a reasonable officer would have believed he had a reasonable basis for the search. The instruction, as it was read to the jury, provided as follows:

[The Defendants] contend that any actions they took relative to the search of the Plaintiff's office were justified by their reasonable belief that these actions were permitted or required and, therefore, were lawful....

If a Defendant reasonably believed that a search or seizure was lawful, and acted on the basis of that belief, then his reasonable belief would constitute a complete defense to the

Plaintiff's claim even though, in fact, the search or seizure was not lawful. Put another way, even if you find that a Defendant violated Plaintiff's constitutional rights by an unlawful search or seizure, the Defendant cannot be liable if he reasonably believed at the time he acted that his actions were in accordance with the law.

But keep in mind that his reasonableness inquiry is an objective one. [The question is whether a] reasonable officer under those same circumstances would believe that he had a basis, a reasonable basis for searching consistent again with these instructions....

The instruction ... provided a classic qualified immunity instruction....

... In light of the clearly established law in 1981 and the parties' factual disputes regarding the justification for the search and the intended and actual scope of the search and seizure, the defendants were entitled to an instruction that told the jury two things: (1) that the law provided that they were entitled to search Dr. Ortega's office for work-related reasons, or to look for evidence of specific work-related misconduct, subject essentially to *Terry's* [*Terry v. Ohio* 392 U.S. 1 (1968)] minimum requirement that the search and seizure be "reasonable" in both its inception and scope; and (2) that if, given the facts as proved at trial,

continued

reasonable officials in the defendants' position could have believed that their conduct was in conformity with that law, the defendants could not be held liable. That is exactly what the district judge told the jury in the instructions she gave.

Because the jury found in Dr. Ortega's favor, we must assume that it accepted his version of the facts, which was supported by substantial evidence—i.e., (1) that the defendants, under the pretense of conducting an "inventory" of state property in order to separate personal from official materials, conducted instead a purely indiscriminate fishing expedition through his most personal belongings in hopes of discovering some evidence that might be useful at an adversary administrative hearing; (2) that the repeated intrusions and examinations of Dr. Ortega's private possessions, including his purely personal belongings, clearly exceeded the scope of a reasonable work-related search; (3) that the defendants retained all of the property that had been in his office, both personal and official, in one undivided mass; and (4) that when their first explanation was exposed as false, the defendants then offered other equally untruthful rationales for their conduct. A reasonable official in the defendants'

position could not have believed that a search and seizure conducted under the circumstances and in the manner described by Dr. Ortega was reasonably work-related or otherwise consistent with established law. The defendants, therefore, could not have prevailed on their qualified immunity defense under any set of lawful qualified immunity instructions....

It is now seventeen years since the search of Dr. Ortega's office occurred and his most personal letters and possessions were examined and seized. It is time to bring this matter to a conclusion. We have considered the defendants' remaining assertions regarding the district court's evidentiary rulings, the jury's damage awards, and the district court's award of attorney's fees, and we find them to be without merit. Accordingly, the judgment of the district court is
AFFIRMED.

Case Questions

1. What is a qualified privilege in the context of this case?
2. Did the court find that a qualified privilege existed in this case?

SECTION 141: PRIVATE SECTOR EMPLOYEES: PROPERTY SEARCHES

Private sector employers are not subject to the same restrictions imposed on public sector employers by the federal Constitution. Private employers, then, are generally less restricted in conducting searches on company property. However, some restrictions exist on employer searches in some states based on the state constitution, statutes, or the common law.

In *K-Mart Corp. v. Trotti*,[11] the court determined that a private sector employer may create a reasonable expectation of privacy in the workplace by providing an employee with a locker and allowing the employee to provide his or her own lock and key. A search of lockers under such circumstances could be an invasion of privacy. Or a search of lockers where the employer has a "respect of the privacy rights of employees" policy in effect could be an invasion of privacy. An employer may minimize the risk of liability for invasion of privacy if it formulates and disseminates a written company policy to all employees stating that due to security problems, concern for a drug-free environment, or other managerial concerns, it is company policy that it may search all lockers, desks, purses, briefcases, and lunch boxes as it deems necessary at any time. Employers should provide all

---

[11] 677 S.W.2d 632 (Tex. Civ. App. 1984).

locks used on company property and prohibit the use of employee-owned locks. Each employee should be required to acknowledge receipt of the company's search policy.

SECTION 142: INVASION OF PRIVACY

The right to privacy protects employees' interests in not disclosing personal matters. It may include protection of medical records as well as unreasonable disclosure of an employee's private facts and intrusion upon seclusion.

CONFIDENTIALITY OF MEDICAL RECORDS

Medical records, which may contain intimate facts of a personal nature, are well within the orbit of materials entitled to privacy protection. Indeed, disclosing a list of names with specific medications being used by the named employees may reveal the nature of the employee illnesses, where, for example, certain drugs are used exclusively to treat HIV infections.

The Americans with Disabilities Act (ADA) requires that any information relating to the medical conditions or history of a job applicant or employee be collected and maintained by employers on separate forms and kept in medical files separate and distinct from general personnel files. Disclosure of medical records or information is allowed only in three situations under the ADA: (1) when supervisors need to be informed regarding necessary restrictions on the duties of an employee or necessary accommodations, (2) when the employer's medical staff needs to be informed about a disability that might require emergency treatment, and (3) when government officials investigating compliance with the ADA request access to such records or information.[12]

State laws may also require employers and health care providers to establish and maintain appropriate procedures to ensure that employee medical information remains confidential, and such laws may prohibit disclosure of medical information with a signed authorization from the employee. Not only must the employer protect the confidentiality of employees' medical records in its possession, but providers paid by the employer to make medical evaluations of employees cannot divulge details of the employees' personal lives to the employer without the written consent of the employees and can report only on the functional limits of patients.

MOTOR VEHICLE INFORMATION

When a labor organization initiates a campaign to organize the employees of an employer, it obtains lists of names and addresses of employees from various sources, including telephone directories, Internet databases, and other employees. The union may also take down license plate numbers of cars parked in employee parking lots and obtain employees' names and addresses from motor vehicle records. The Union of Needletrades, Industrial and Textile Employees (UNITE) obtained some employee names and addresses from motor vehicle records in an

---

[12] 42 U.S.C. § 12112(c)(3)(B).

organizing campaign of Cintras Corp., a corporate uniform supplier, employing 28,000 employees at some 351 facilities in the United States. Using this information, it pursued home visits of employees to identify problematic working conditions at Cintras and to gauge employee interest in unionizing. In *Pichler v. UNITE*,[13] a group of Cintras employees were allowed to proceed with an employer-financed class action lawsuit alleging that the union had violated the federal Driver's Privacy Protection Act of 1994[14] (DPPA). The law provides in part those who knowingly obtain, disclose, or use personal information from a motor vehicle record are liable for actual damages, but not less than liquidated damages in the amount of $2,500. The union's assertion that it was unaware of the DPPA and has now stopped using license plate numbers as part of its organizing drives was held not to be a valid defense by the trial court judge.

UNREASONABLE DISCLOSURE OF PRIVATE FACTS

Invasion of privacy by the unreasonable publicity given to the private life of another is a recognized tort in some 30 jurisdictions that have considered this question.[15]

Thus, disclosure by an employer and publicity of the private facts of a private person's exposure to the HIV virus and his homosexual lifestyle may be an actionable tort in these jurisdictions. To prevail on a claim for unreasonable disclosure of private facts, a plaintiff must establish that (1) the fact disclosed was private in nature, (2) the disclosure was made to the public, (3) the disclosure was one that would be highly offensive to a reasonable person, (4) the disclosed fact was not of legitimate concern to the public, and (5) the one who disclosed the fact did so with reckless disregard of the private nature of the fact disclosed.

INTRUSION ON SECLUSION

To prevail on a claim for "intrusion upon seclusion" as a violation of one's privacy, a plaintiff-employee must show (1) intrusion into a private place, conversation, or matter (2) in a manner highly offensive to a reasonable person.[16] For the first element, the plaintiff must show that the defendant penetrated some zone of physical or sensory privacy surrounding the plaintiff or obtained unwanted access to data about the plaintiff. The tort is proven only if the plaintiff had an objectively reasonable expectation of seclusion or solitude in the place, conversation, or data source.[17]

---

[13] 339 F. Supp. 2d 665 (ED. PA 2005).

[14] 18 U.S.C §§ 2721–2725 (2005).

[15] *Borquez v. Ozer*, 923 P.2d 166 (Colo. App. 1995), *aff'd in part* and *rev'd in part*, 940 P.2d 371 (Colo. 1997).

[16] *Shulman v. Group W Productions, Inc.*, 18 Cal. 4th 200, 231 (1998). See also Restatement of Torts, § 652B and *Purrelli v. State Farm Fire and Casualty Co.*, 698 So. 2d 618 (Fla. Dist. Ct. App. 1997).

[17] *Shulman*, at 232. See *Ruzicka Electric v. IBEW, Local 1*, 427 F.3d 511 (8th Cir. 2005), where the U.S. Court of Appeals determined that the invasion of privacy issue should have been allowed to go to a jury, where a reasonable jury could conclude that IBEW Local 1's investigators trespassed on an electrical contractor's private residential property to conduct surveillance on him and his family.

There are degrees and nuances to societal recognition of expectations of privacy. Although the intrusion tort is often defined in terms of "seclusion," the seclusion need not be absolute. Like privacy, the concept of seclusion is relative. Privacy for the purposes of the intrusion tort must be evaluated with respect to the identity of the alleged intruder and the nature of the intrusion. In *Sanders v. American Broadcasting Cos., Inc.*, presented in this section, the California Supreme Court determined that the fact that a workplace interaction was witnessed by others on the premises does not defeat an employee's reasonable expectation of privacy for the purposes of the intrusion tort.

VIDEO SURVEILLANCE

Many businesses use overt or hidden video cameras as a means of security in the workplace to enhance worker safety and to prevent and/or detect theft or other criminal conduct. To avoid state constitutional or statutory claims for invasion of privacy, employers should not set up video cameras in areas where employees have a reasonable expectation of privacy. Utilizing signs to notify employees and members of the public that certain areas are under video surveillance is a common business practice and not likely to initiate privacy claims. Additionally, employers should prepare and disseminate their written policy on surveillance and obtain a consent form from employees acknowledging that they received this notice in order to preserve their consent defense.

As will be seen in the *Cramer v. Consolidated Freightways, Inc.* decision, presented in this section, surreptitiously placing video cameras in men's and women's restrooms at work is a state criminal law violation in California and will expose the employer to invasion of privacy litigation. In *Kline v. Security Guards, Inc.*, some 370 employees of Dana Corporation's Reading, Pennsylvania, facility sued the corporation and its security guard company after employees learned that a new audio and video surveillance system at the entryway of the facility allowed what was said in the area where employees "punch in" for work to be observed and heard in the guard booth. The Third Circuit Court of Appeals rejected the employer's preemption claims and remanded the matter to the state court to handle the invasion of privacy and other tort claims.[18]

CASE 17.3	SANDERS V. AMERICAN BROADCASTING COS., INC. SUPREME COURT OF CALIFORNIA, 20 CAL. 4TH 907 (1999).

[Defendant Stacy Lescht, a reporter employed by defendant American Broadcasting Companies, Inc. (ABC), obtained employment as a "telepsychic" with the Psychic Marketing Group (PMG), which also employed plaintiff Mark Sanders in that same capacity. While she worked in PMG's Los Angeles office, Lescht, who wore a small video camera in her hat, covertly videotaped her conversations with several coworkers, including Sanders. Sanders sued Lescht and ABC for, among other causes of action, the tort of invasion of privacy by intrusion. Although a jury found for Sanders on the intrusion cause of action, awarding

continued

---

[18] 386 F.3d 246 (3d Cir. 2004).

$335,000 in compensatory damages and $300,000 in punitive damages, the court of appeals reversed the resulting judgment in his favor because Sanders could have had no reasonable expectation of privacy in his workplace conversations as such conversations could be overheard by others in the shared office space. The California Supreme Court granted review to determine whether the fact that a workplace interaction might be witnessed by others on the premises necessarily defeats, for purposes of tort law, any reasonable expectation of privacy the participants have against covert videotaping by a journalist.]

WERDGAR, J....

Discussion

Question: May a person who lacks a reasonable expectation of complete privacy in a conversation because it could be seen and overheard by coworkers (but not the general public) nevertheless have a claim for invasion of privacy by intrusion based on a television reporter's covert videotaping of that conversation?
Answer: Yes.

Neither the trial court nor the Court of Appeal had the benefit of our recent decision in *Shulman v. Group W Productions, Inc., supra,* 18 Cal. 4th 200 (1998) (*Shulman*)....

This case squarely raises the question of an expectation of limited privacy. On further consideration, we adhere to the view suggested in *Shulman*: privacy, for purposes of the intrusion tort, is not a binary, all-or-nothing characteristic....

Defendants' claim, that a "complete expectation of privacy" is necessary to recover for intrusion, ... fails as inconsistent with case law as well as with the common understanding of privacy. Privacy for purposes of the intrusion tort must be evaluated with respect to the identity of the alleged intruder and the nature of the intrusion. As seen below, moreover, decisions on the common law and statutory protection of *workplace* privacy show that the same analysis applies in the workplace as in other settings; consequently, an employee may, under some circumstances, have a reasonable expectation of visual or aural privacy against electronic intrusion by a stranger to the workplace, despite the possibility the conversations and interactions

at issue could be witnessed by coworkers or the employer....

Doe by Doe v. B.P.S. Guard Services, Inc. (8th Cir. 1991) 945 F.2d 1422 illustrates the existence of limited, but reasonable, *visual* privacy in the workplace. A fashion show was being held at a convention center. The organizers had set up a curtained dressing area for the models, unaware that the area was visible on one of the convention center's security cameras. Guards in the security control room used the surveillance camera to watch and videotape the models changing clothes. (*Id.* at p. 1424.) Nothing in the opinion suggests the curtained changing area, used by all the models and presumably accessible to the show's director and assistants, was a place of complete seclusion for any of the models. Nonetheless, the appellate court, in an action for common law invasion of privacy, had no difficulty discerning a reasonable expectation of privacy on the models' part, violated in this circumstance by a visual "invasion by strangers." ...

We conclude that in the workplace, as elsewhere, the reasonableness of a person's expectation of visual and aural privacy depends not only on who might have been able to observe the subject interaction, but on the identity of the claimed intruder and the means of intrusion. (*Shulman, supra,* 18 Cal. 4th at pp. 233–235; *Dietemann v. Time, Inc. supra,* 449 F.2d at p. 249; *Huskey v. National Broadcasting Co., Inc., supra,* 632 F.Supp. at pp. 1287–1288; *Nader v. General Motors Corporation, supra,* 307 N.Y.S.2d at p. 655; *Pearson v. Dodd, supra,* 410 F.2d at p. 704; *Walker v. Darby, supra,* 911 F.2d at p. 1579.) For this reason, we answer the briefed question affirmatively: a person who lacks a reasonable expectation of complete privacy in a conversation, because it could be seen and overheard by coworkers (but not the general public), may nevertheless have a claim for invasion of privacy by intrusion based on a television reporter's covert videotaping of that conversation.

Defendants warn that "the adoption of a doctrine of *per se* workplace privacy would place a dangerous chill on the press' investigation of abusive activities in open work areas, implicating substantial First Amendment concerns." (Italics in original.) We adopt no such *per se* doctrine of privacy. We hold only that the possibility of being overheard by coworkers does not, as a matter of law, render unreasonable an employee's expectation that his or her interactions

continued

within a nonpublic workplace will not be videotaped in secret by a journalist. In other circumstances, where, for example, the workplace is regularly open to entry or observation by the public or press, or the interaction that was the subject of the alleged intrusion was between proprietor (or employee) and customer, any expectation of privacy against press recording is less likely to be deemed reasonable. Nothing we say here prevents a media defendant from attempting to show, in order to negate the offensiveness element of the intrusion tort, that the claimed intrusion, even if it infringed on a reasonable expectation of privacy, was "justified by the legitimate motive of gathering the news." (*Shulman, supra*, 18 Cal. 4th at pp. 236–237.) As for possible First Amendment defenses, any discussion must await a later case, as no constitutional issue was decided by the lower courts or presented for our review here....

Disposition

The judgment of the Court of Appeal is reversed, and the cause is remanded to that court for further proceedings consistent with our opinion.

WERDEGAR, J.
WE CONCUR:
GEORGE, C.J.
MOSK, J.
KENNARD, J.
BAXTER, J.
CHIN, J.
BROWN, J.

Case Questions

1. Identify the "intrusion on seclusion" in this case.
2. Was the court of appeal correct in setting aside the jury verdict in favor of the plaintiff because there must be a complete expectation of privacy to recover for intrusion and other employees could hear the conversations in question?
3. How does the court deal with ABC's argument that an adverse decision would have a chilling effect on the press's investigation of abusive activities in open work areas?

CASE 17.4	CRAMER V. CONSOLIDATED FREIGHTWAYS, INC.
	U.S. COURT OF APPEALS, 255 F.3D 683 (9TH CIR. 2001) (EN BANC).

[Consolidated Freightways ("Consolidated"), the defendant in this action, is a large trucking company. It concealed video cameras and audio listening devices behind two-way mirrors in the restrooms at its terminal in Mira Loma, California, ostensibly to detect and prevent drug use by its drivers. Employees at the terminal discovered the surveillance equipment when a mirror fell off the men's restroom wall, exposing a camera with a wire leading out through a hole in the wall behind it. Subsequent investigation revealed a similar hole in the wall behind the mirror in the adjoining women's restroom.

Under California Penal Code Section 653n, "any person who installs or who maintains ... any two-way mirror permitting observation of any restroom, toilet, bathroom, washroom, shower, locker room, fitting room, motel room, or hotel room, is guilty of a misdemeanor." Thus, Consolidated's installation of the two-way mirror was a direct violation of California criminal law.

Truck driver Lloyd Cramer and over 280 other employees brought an invasion of privacy lawsuit against Consolidated in state court. Consolidated removed the cases to federal court, contending that the state claims were preempted under Section 301 of the LMRA because of a provision of the collective bargaining agreement (CBA) that dealt with drug use and another provision that dealt with camera surveillance. The U.S. district court dismissed the invasion of privacy claims, and the matter was considered by the Ninth Circuit Court of Appeals en banc.]

continued

FISHER, J....

We now turn to the specifics of the case before us. In arguing in favor of dismissal, Consolidated cites provisions of the CBA it negotiated with the International Brotherhood of Teamsters, Local No. 63, claiming these provisions brought its covert surveillance within the purview of the CBA. Article 26, Section 2 of the agreement forbids the use of camera surveillance for disciplinary reasons except to prove a charge of property theft or dishonesty. The section also specifies the procedure to be employed for the use of videotapes in the context of theft or dishonesty allegations. Article 35, Section 3 discusses alcohol and drug use and the procedures to be employed for drug testing. Consolidated contends that any employee claim based on its covert restroom surveillance requires recourse to these provisions of the CBA to determine the employees' reasonable expectations of privacy. Without such an analysis, Consolidated argues, the court would be unable to determine whether these expectations were violated....

Consolidated's insistence that we must refer to the CBA because one provision mentions drug use and another contemplates the use of surveillance videotapes in certain specified circumstances does not change our analysis. Neither of these provisions purports to have any bearing on secret spying on Consolidated's employees in company rest-rooms—no matter how well-intentioned Consolidated's alleged purpose may have been in doing so. Indeed, the surreptitious nature of the violation of plaintiffs' privacy belies any notion of bargaining or consent to hidden cameras behind two-way mirrors. Consolidated cannot create a dispute as to the meaning of the terms of the CBA by picking out terms that refer to videotapes and drug use, particularly when a cursory examination of those provisions makes clear they apply to a completely different context and set of circumstances. In short, this is a classic example of a defendant's attempt to "inject[] a federal question into an action that asserts what is plainly a state-law claim [in order to] transform the action into one arising under federal law, thereby selecting the forum in which the claim shall be litigated." *Caterpillar*, 482 U.S. at 399, 107 S.Ct. 2425. The Supreme Court has instructed that we are not to reward defendants who engage in such hypothetical exercises....

Even if the CBA did expressly contemplate the use of two-way mirrors to facilitate detection of drug users, such a provision would be illegal under California law. Section 653n of the California Penal Code makes the installation and maintenance of two-way mirrors permitting the observation of restrooms illegal without reference to the reasonable expectations of those so viewed. Determination of guilt under the statute is not dependent on context or subjective factors; use of the mirrors is a per se violation of the penal code, and an assumption that the mirrors will not be used is per se reasonable....

Consolidated argues that, under California law, violation of a right to privacy is necessarily context-dependent; if an individual consents to a certain action, even an invasive one, she cannot then claim her privacy rights were violated by the action. *See Stikes*, 914 F.2d at 1270. It cannot substantiate this blanket proposition....

Conclusion

Section 301 does not preempt claims to vindicate nonnegotiable state law rights. Nor does it preempt claims for state law rights that, although potentially negotiable, do not reasonably require the court to interpret an existing provision of a CBA to resolve the dispute. Plaintiffs' privacy claims are therefore not preempted by § 301. The ... plaintiff's claim for intentional infliction of emotional distress is likewise not preempted.

Because the state law privacy claims in these cases were not preempted by § 301, the district court lacked removal jurisdiction over these actions. They must therefore be remanded to state court.

REVERSED and REMANDED.

Case Questions

1. Did the union and the company agree in their collective bargaining contract that the company could conduct surveillance of its employees with hidden cameras behind two-way mirrors?
2. Is the use of two-way mirrors permitting the observation of restrooms illegal *per se* under California criminal law?
3. How did the court of appeals decide the case?

SECTION 143: MONITORING EMPLOYEE TELEPHONE CONVERSATIONS AND E-MAIL

The Federal Wiretapping Act[19] makes it unlawful to intercept oral and electronic communications and provides for both criminal liability and civil damages against the violator. There are two major exceptions, however. The first allows an employer to monitor a firm's telephones in the "ordinary course of business" through the use of extension telephones; a second exception applies where there is prior consent to the interception. If monitoring by the employer results in intercepting a business call, it is within the ordinary course of business exception.[20] Personal calls can be monitored, however, only to the extent necessary to determine that the call is personal, and then the employer must cease listening. To illustrate, in the *Deal v. Spears* case presented in this section, Newell Spears taped all phone conversations at his store to try to find out if an employee was connected to a theft at the store. He listened to virtually all 22 hours of intercepted and recorded telephone conversations between his employee Sibbie Deal and her boyfriend Calvin Lucas without regard to the conversations' relation to Spears's business interest. While Spears might well have legitimately monitored Deal's calls to the extent necessary to determine that the calls were personal and made or received in violation of store policy, the scope of the interception in this case was well beyond the boundaries of the ordinary course of business exception and thus in violation of the Act.

Employer monitoring of employee phone calls can be accomplished without fear of violating the Act if consent is established. Consent may be established by prior written notice to employees of the employer's monitoring policy. It is prudent as well for the employer to give customers notice of the policy through a recorded message as part of the employer's phone answering system.

In *Diselets v. Wal-Mart Stores, Inc.,*[21] two store managers used a voice-activated tape recorder to secretly record and listen to its four night-shift employees at the Wal-Mart store in Claremont, New Hampshire. The employees were each awarded $10,000 in liquidated damages plus attorney fees.

E-MAIL MONITORING

Electronic mail (e-mail) network systems are a primary means of communication in many of today's businesses and are deemed alternatives to fax, telephone, or the Postal Service by some employers. With monitoring technology becoming more sophisticated and less expensive, employers seek to monitor the e-mail messages of their employees for the purpose of evaluating the productivity and effectiveness of the employees or for corporate security purposes, including the protection of trade secrets and other intangible property interests. When employees are disciplined or terminated for alleged wrongful activities discovered as a result of e-mail searches, the privacy issue may be raised.

---

[19] Title III of the Omnibus Crime Control and Safe Streets Act of 1968, 18 U.S.C. §§ 2510–2520.

[20] *Arias v. Mutual Central Alarm Services, Inc.*, 182 F.R.D. 407 (S.D.N.Y. 1998).

[21] 171 F.3d 711 (1st Cir. 1999).

The Electronic Communications Privacy Act (ECPA)[22] amended the Federal Wiretapping Act and was intended, in part, to apply to e-mail. However, "ordinary course of business" and "consent" exceptions apply to e-mail, and it would appear that employers have broad latitude to monitor employee e-mail use. Alana Shoars, an e-mail administrator for Epson America, Inc., was fired after complaining about her supervisor's reading of employee e-mail messages. Her state court invasion of privacy case was unsuccessful.[23] Very few cases involving e-mail issues have been adjudicated to date under the ECPA.[24]

An employer can place itself within the "consent" exception to the Act by issuing a policy statement to all employees, informing them of the monitoring program and its purposes and justification.

TEXT MESSAGES

Congress passed the Stored Communications Act (SCA) in 1986 as part of the Electronic Communications Privacy Act. The SCA distinguishes between two types of providers, **remote computing services (RCS)** and **electronic communication services (ECS)**. An RCS is defined in the SCA as "the provision to the public of computer storage or processing...." An RCS may disclose communications held in storage with the consent of the "account holder." An ECS is defined in the statute as "any service which provides to users thereof the ability to send or receive wire of electronic communications." The SCA prohibits an ECS from divulging the contents of stored communications except with the consent of the sender or intended recipient. Text messaging pager services are electronic communication services, ECS. In *Quon v. Arch Wireless Operating Co.*, presented in this section, Arch Wireless provided the city of Ontario Police Department with wireless services; and as part of the police department's assessment of police officers exceeding a per-month limit of 25,000 characters per pager, the department contacted Arch Wireless, which provided transcripts of text messages sent and received by certain pagers. The transcripts revealed that many of Sergeant Quon's messages were personal and sexually explicit. Quon sued Arch Wireless, alleging violation of the SCA. He also sued the city, alleging violation of the Fourth Amendment of the U.S. Constitution. The Ninth Circuit Court of Appeals determined that Arch Wireless violated the SCA when it turned over the text messaging transcripts to the city on the basis that the city was not the sender or intended recipient of the communications. Quon also was successful on the Fourth Amendment constitutional privacy claim against the police department.

---

[22] 18 U.S.C. §§ 2510–2520 (1988); the Act was amended in 1994 to apply to cellular phones.

[23] See *Shoars v. Epson America, Inc.*, 1994 Cal. LEXIS 3670 (Cal. June 29, 1994).

[24] See *Fraser v. Nationwide Mutual Insurance Co.*, 352 F.3d 107 (3d Cir. 2003), where the court held that the wiretap act was not violated because the employer did not "intercept" the e-mail, but retrieved it after it had been sent and received. See also *Konop v. Hawaiian Airlines, Inc.*, 302 F.3d 868 (9th Cir. 2002), where the Ninth Circuit originally determined that the airline violated the ECPA by accessing an employee's secure privately owned web site under false pretenses, but withdrew its opinion some seven months later and concluded that the employer did not "intercept" the web site's content in violation of the wiretap act. This unusual reversal came after federal and state prosecutors warned that the ruling would hamper investigations of child molesters who recruited victims online.

While the city did have an e-mail policy signed by each employee that warned that the use of the e-mail system was not confidential and could be monitored and that access to all web sites would be recorded and periodically reviewed, a "consent exception" was not applicable in this case because an informal policy was in place regarding the use of the pagers. The lieutenant administering the contract with Arch Wireless told the officers that he would not audit their text messages for personal messages as long as they paid the overage charges for exceeding the 25,000 characters per month. The court applied this informal policy.

CASE 17.5 | ## DEAL V. SPEARS
UNITED STATES COURT OF APPEALS, EIGHTH CIRCUIT 980 F.2D 1153 (1992).

[Sibbie Deal and Calvin Lucas brought a civil action for damages under the federal wiretapping statute against Deal's former employers, Newell and Juanita Spears, doing business as the White Oaks Package Store, for the intentional interception and disclosure of their telephone conversations. The district court awarded statutory damages to Deal and Lucas in the amount of $40,000 and granted their request for attorney fees. Newell and Juanita Spears appealed. Deal and Lucas cross-appealed the court's refusal to award punitive damages.]

BOWMAN, C. J....

Newell and Juanita Spears have owned and operated the White Oaks Package Store near Camden, Arkansas, for about twenty years. The Spearses live in a mobile home adjacent to the store. The telephone in the store has an extension in the home, and is the only phone line into either location. The same phone line thus is used for both the residential and the business phones.

Sibbie Deal was an employee at the store from December 1988 until she was fired in August 1990. The store was burglarized in April 1990 and approximately $16,000 was stolen. The Spearses believed that it was an inside job and suspected that Deal was involved. Hoping to catch the suspect in an unguarded admission, Newell Spears purchased and installed a recording device on the extension phone in the mobile home. When turned on, the machine would automatically record all conversations made or received on either phone, with no indication to the parties using the phone that their conversation was being recorded. Before purchasing the recorder, Newell Spears told a sheriff's department investigator that he was considering this surreptitious monitoring and the investigator

told Spears that he did not "see anything wrong with that."

Calls were taped from June 27, 1990, through August 13, 1990. During that period, Sibbie Deal, who was married to Mike Deal at the time, was having an extramarital affair with Calvin Lucas, then married to Pam Lucas. Deal and Lucas spoke on the telephone at the store frequently and for long periods of time while Deal was at work. (Lucas was on 100% disability so he was at home all day.) Based on the trial testimony, the District Court concluded that much of the conversation between the two was "sexually provocative." Deal also made or received numerous other personal telephone calls during her workday. Even before Newell Spears purchased the recorder, Deal was asked by her employers to cut down on her use of the phone for personal calls, and the Spearses told her they might resort to monitoring calls or installing a pay phone in order to curtail the abuse.

Newell Spears listened to virtually all twenty-two hours of the tapes he recorded, regardless of the nature of the calls or the content of the conversations, and Juanita Spears listened to some of them. Although there was nothing in the record to indicate that they learned anything about the burglary, they did learn, among other things, that Deal sold Lucas a keg of beer at cost, in violation of store policy. On August 13, 1990, when Deal came in to work the evening shift, Newell Spears played a few seconds of the incriminating tape for Deal and then fired her. Deal and Lucas filed this action on August 29, 1990, and the tapes and recorder were seized by a United States deputy marshal pursuant to court order on September 3, 1990....

The Spearses challenge the court's finding of liability. They admit the taping but contend that the facts

continued

here bring their actions under two statutory exceptions to civil liability....

The elements of a violation of the wire and electronic communications interception provisions (Title III) of the Omnibus Crime Control and Safe Streets Act of 1968 are set forth in the section that makes such interceptions a criminal offense. 18 U.S.C. § 2511 (1988). Under the relevant provisions of the statute, criminal liability attaches and a federal civil cause of action arises when a person intentionally intercepts a wire or electronic communication or intentionally discloses the contents of the interception. *Id.* §§ 2511(1)(a), (c), 2520(a). The successful civil plaintiff may recover actual damages plus any profits made by the violator. If statutory damages will result in a larger recovery than actual damages, the violator must pay the plaintiff "the greater of $100 a day for each day of violation or $10,000." *Id.* § 2520(c)(2)(B) (1988). Further, punitive damages, attorney fees, and "other litigation costs reasonably incurred" are allowed. *Id.* § 2520(b)(2), (3) (1988).

The Spearses first claim they are exempt from civil liability because Sibbie Deal consented to the interception of calls that she made from and received at the store. Under the statute, it is not unlawful "to intercept a wire, oral, or electronic communication ... where one of the parties to the communication has given prior consent to such interception," 18 U.S.C. § 2511(2)(d), and thus no civil liability is incurred. The Spearses contend that Deal's consent may be implied because Newell Spears had mentioned that he might be forced to monitor calls or restrict telephone privileges if abuse of the store's telephone for personal calls continued. They further argue that the extension in their home gave actual notice to Deal that her calls could be overheard, and that this notice resulted in her implied consent to interception. We find these arguments unpersuasive.

There is no evidence of express consent here. Although constructive consent is inadequate, actual consent may be implied from the circumstances. *See Griggs-Ryan v. Smith*, 904 F.2d 112, 116 (1st Cir. 1990). Nevertheless, "[c]onsent under Title III is not to be cavalierly implied.... [K]nowledge of the *capability* of monitoring alone cannot be considered implied consent." *Watkins v. L. M. Berry & Co.*, 704 F.2d 577, 581 (11th Cir. 1983) (citations omitted).

We do not believe that Deal's consent may be implied from the circumstances relied upon in the Spearses' arguments. The Spearses did not inform Deal that they were monitoring the phone, but only told her they might do so in order to cut down on personal calls. Moreover, it seems clear that the couple anticipated Deal would not suspect that they were intercepting her calls, since they hoped to catch her making an admission about the burglary, an outcome they would not expect if she knew her calls were being recorded. As for listening in via the extension, Deal testified that she knew when someone picked up the extension in the residence while she was on the store phone, as there was an audible "click" on the line.

Given these circumstances, we hold as a matter of law that the Spearses have failed to show Deal's consent to the interception and recording of her conversations.

The Spearses also argue that they are immune from liability under what has become known as an exemption for business use of a telephone extension....

We do not quarrel with the contention that the Spearses had a legitimate business reason for listening in: they suspected Deal's involvement in a burglary of the store and hoped she would incriminate herself in a conversation on the phone. Moreover, Deal was abusing her privileges by using the phone for numerous personal calls even, by her own admission, when there were customers in the store. The Spearses might legitimately have monitored Deal's calls to the extent necessary to determine that the calls were personal and made or received in violation of store policy.

But the Spearses recorded twenty-two hours of calls, and Newell Spears listened to all of them without regard to their relation to his business interests. Granted, Deal might have mentioned the burglary at any time during the conversations, but we do not believe that the Spearses' suspicions justified the extent of the intrusion. *See Watkins*, 704 F.2d at 583 ("We hold that a personal call may not be intercepted in the ordinary course of business under the exemption in section 2510(5)(a)(i), except to the extent necessary to guard against unauthorized use of the telephone or to determine whether a call is personal or not."); *Briggs v. American Air Filter Co.*, 630 F.2d 414, 420 n. 9 (5th Cir. 1980) ("A general practice of surreptitious monitoring would be more intrusive on employees' privacy than monitoring limited to specific occasions."). We conclude that the scope of the interception in this case takes us well beyond the boundaries of the ordinary course of business.

continued

For the reasons we have indicated, the Spearses cannot avail themselves of the telephone extension/business use exemption of Title III....

We agree with the District Court that defendants' conduct does not warrant the imposition of punitive damages.

The judgment of the District Court is affirmed in all respects.

Case Questions

1. It is not unlawful to monitor the telephone conversation of an employee if the employee has given prior consent. Did Deal give her employer consent in this case?

2. Because of the recent burglary of the store, did the employer have a legitimate business reason to record and review the employee's phone calls made or received while at work?

3. Under the *Watkins* precedent, what is the extent to which an employer can monitor personal phone calls to employees within the ordinary course of business exemption of the federal wiretapping law?

CASE 17.6

QUON V. ARCH WIRELESS OPERATING CO.
UNITED STATES COURT OF APPEALS, NINTH CIRCUIT 529 F.3D 892 (2008).

[This case arises from the Ontario Police Department's review of text messages sent and received by Jeff Quon, a sergeant and member of the city of Ontario's Police Department. Arch Wireless Operating Co. provided the city of Ontario, California Police Department with wireless services. The city did have an e-mail policy warning that the use of the e-mail system was not confidential and could be monitored and that access to all web sites would be recorded and periodically reviewed. An informal policy was in place at the police department regarding the use of its pagers. The lieutenant administering the purchasing contract with Arch Wireless, Lieutenant Duke, told the officers that he would not audit their text messages for personal messages as long as they paid the overage charges for exceeding the basic monthly fee based on 25,000 characters per month.

Quon went over the monthly character limit "three or four times" and paid the city for the overages. Each time Lieutenant Duke would tell Quon that he owed X amount of dollars because he went over his allotted characters, and each time Quon paid the city for the overages. In August 2002, Quon and another officer again exceeded the 25,000 character limit. Lieutenant Duke let it be known at a meeting that he was "tired of being a bill collector with guys going over the allotted amount of characters on their text pagers." In response, Chief Scharf ordered Lieutenant Duke to "request the transcripts of those pagers for auditing purposes." Chief Scharf asked Lieutenant Duke "to determine if the messages were exclusively work related, thereby requiring an increase in the number of characters officers were permitted, which had occurred in the past, or if they were using the pagers for personal matters." One of the officers whose transcripts he requested was plaintiff Jeff Quon.

City officials were not able to access the text messages themselves. Instead, the city e-mailed Jackie Deavers at Arch Wireless, requesting the transcripts. Deavers stated that she would deliver messages only to the "contact" on the account and that she would not deliver messages to the "user" unless he also was the contact on the account. In this case, the "contact" was the city. After receiving the transcripts, Lieutenant Duke conducted an initial audit and reported the results to Chief Scharf. Subsequently, Chief Scharf and Quon's supervisor, Lieutenant Tony Del Rio, reviewed the transcripts. Then in October 2002, Chief Scharf referred the matter to Internal Affairs "to determine if someone was wasting ... [c]ity time not doing work when they should be." Sergeant McMahon, who conducted this investigation on behalf of Internal Affairs, released the McMahon memorandum on July 2, 2003. According to the memorandum, the transcripts revealed that Quon "had exceeded his monthly allotted characters by 15,158 characters" and that many of the messages were personal in nature and were often sexually explicit. These messages were directed to and received from, among others, the other appellants.

The Stored Communications Act (SCA) distinguishes between two types of providers: "remote

continued

computing services" (RCS) and "electronic communication services (ECS). An RCS is defined in the SCA as "the provision to the public of computer storage or processing...." An RCS may disclose communications held in storage with the consent of the "account holder." An ECS is defined in the statute as "any service which provide to users thereof the ability to send or receive wire or electronic communications." The SCA prohibits an ECS from divulging the contents of stored communication except with the consent of the sender or intended recipient. The district court concluded that Arch Wireless was an RCS and found that the disclosure was permissible since it was at the request of the city. Quon and the others he "texted" appealed.]

WARDLAW, J....

Stored Communications Act

Congress passed the Stored Communications Act in 1986 as part of the Electronic Communications Privacy Act. The SCA was enacted because the advent of the Internet presented a host of potential privacy breaches that the Fourth Amendment does not address.... Appellants challenge the district court's finding that Arch Wireless is a "remote computing service" ("RCS") as opposed to an "electronic communication service" ("ECS") under the SCA, § § 2701-2711. The district court correctly concluded that if Arch Wireless is an ECS, it is liable as a matter of law, and that if it is an RCS, it is not liable. However, we disagree with the district court that Arch Wireless acted as an RCS for the City. Therefore, summary judgment in favor of Arch Wireless was error.

Section 2702 of the SCA governs liability for both ECS and RCS providers. 18 U.S.C. § 2702(a)(1)-(2). The nature of the services Arch Wireless offered to the City determines whether Arch Wireless is an ECS or an RCS. As the Niekamp Declaration makes clear, Arch Wireless provided to the City a service whereby it would facilitate communication between two pagers—"text messaging" over radio frequencies. As part of that service, Arch Wireless archived a copy of the message on its server. When Arch Wireless released to the City the transcripts of Appellants' messages, Arch Wireless potentially ran afoul of the SCA. This is because both an ECS and RCS can release private information to, or with the lawful consent of, "an addressee or intended recipient of such com-

munication," *id.* § 2702(b)(1), (b)(3), whereas only an RCS can release such information "with the lawful consent of ... the subscriber." *Id.* § 2702(b)(3). It is undisputed that the City was not an "addressee or intended recipient," and that the City was a "subscriber."...

An RCS is defined as "the provision to the public of computer storage or processing services by means of an electronic communications system." *Id.* § 2711(2).... The SCA prohibits an RCS from "knowingly divulg [ing] to any person or entity the contents of any communication which is carried or maintained on that service." Unlike an ECS, an RCS may release the contents of a communication with the lawful consent of a "subscriber."*Id.* § 2702(a)(2), (b)(3).

We turn to the plain language of the SCA, including its common-sense definitions, to properly categorize Arch Wireless. An ECS is defined as "any service which provides to users thereof the ability to send or receive wire or electronic communications." 18 U.S.C. § 2510(15). On its face, this describes the text-messaging pager services that Arch Wireless provided. Arch Wireless provided a "service" that enabled Quon and the other Appellants to "send or receive ... electronic communications," i.e., text messages. Contrast that definition with that for an RCS, which "means the provision to the public of computer storage or processing services by means of an electronic communications system."*Id.* § 2711(2). Arch Wireless did not provide to the City "computer storage"; nor did it provide processing services." By archiving the text messages on its server, Arch Wireless certainly was "storing" the messages. However, Congress contemplated this exact function could be performed by an ECS as well, stating that an ECS would provide (A) temporary storage incidental to the communication; and (B) storage for backup protection. *Id.* § 2510(17)....

[Under the Fourth Amendment of the U.S. Constitution, a public employee must demonstrate a reasonable expectation of privacy in the matter searched and demonstrate that the search was unreasonable. Because of the city's informal policy on allowing employees to pay for "overages," the court found that Quon had a reasonable expectation of privacy in the text messages stored at Arch Wireless. The court also determined that the search itself was unreasonable in scope since there were so many simple ways to verify the efficacy of the 25,000

continued

character limit without violating Quon's Fourth Amendment rights.]

Affirmed in part. Reversed in part, and remanded.

Case Questions

1. What is the legal significance of a determination that Arch Wireless was an "electronic communi-

cation service" rather than a "remote computing service"?

2. Is not a request from the subscriber (and bill payer) to the text message service provider to remit a transcript of certain text messages lawful and within an employer's prerogative?

SECTION 144: DRUG TESTING

It is estimated that some 6 million Americans currently use cocaine and that some 23 million Americans use marijuana. The outward signs of drug use and impairment are sometimes not as evident as is impairment due to the abuse of alcohol. Employee drug users often believe that they are not impaired while at work. For example, in a study of 10 experienced pilots who were trained for eight hours on a flight simulator for landing tasks, when each smoked a marijuana cigarette containing 19 milligrams of THC, 24 hours after smoking the cigarettes their mean performance on flight tasks showed trends toward impairment on all variables. Moreover, each experienced significant impairment in "distance off center" in landing and vertical and lateral deviation on approach to landing. Despite these deficiencies, the pilots reported no awareness of impaired performance. Such a study conducted by the Stanford University School of Medicine and other studies indicate a need for concern about the performance of those entrusted with complex behavioral and cognitive tasks within 24 hours after smoking marijuana.

GOVERNMENTAL TESTING

Employee drug use costs the United States government alone an estimated $33 billion per year. The seriousness of the problem at all levels of government has led public employers to combat drug use by drug testing. Constitutional challenges of the testing programs have been made in courts by individual employees and public-sector unions. Certain patterns have emerged as to the legality of various types of testing.

The most common challenge to government employers' drug testing programs is that the tests violate the Fourth Amendment prohibition against unreasonable searches and seizures. Courts uniformly have found that requiring an individual to submit urine samples for drug analysis constitutes a search and seizure within the meaning of the Fourth Amendment. The *Patchogue-Medford Congress of Teachers v. Board of Education* decision of New York State's highest court, made very clear that such testing constitutes a search.[25] The next question for a court is whether the search was reasonable under the Fourth Amendment. This question is answered on a case-by-case basis by balancing the social and governmental need for the testing in question against the invasion of personal privacy rights that the search entails.[26]

---

[25] 517 N.Y.2d 456 (1987).

[26] See *United Teachers of New Orleans v. Orleans Parish School Board*, 142 F.3d 853 (5th Cir. 1998), where a school board was not allowed to conduct urine drug tests without a showing of individualized suspicion of wrongdoing.

In *Skinner v. Railway Labor Executives' Ass'n*[27] and *National Treasury Employees Union v. Von Raab*,[28] the Supreme Court established a "special needs" exception to the Fourth Amendment's protections against warrantless and suspicionless drug testing of public employees or the testing of private railroad employees under a federal administrative agency's regulations.[29]

The *Jakubowicz v. Dittemore* decision involving a random, suspicionless drug testing policy by a state's Department of Mental Health, while a "symbol" that the agency did not approve illegal drug use, was not found to be a "special needs" exception. The case is presented in this section.

In the *Skinner* case, certain railroad unions challenged Federal Railway Administration (FRA) regulations that mandated warrantless, suspicionless breath, blood, and urinalysis testing of railroad employees involved in rail accidents resulting in deaths, injuries, or property damage. The FRA contended that the long history of drug and alcohol abuse in the railroad industry justified the random testing mandates. The Supreme Court recognized that to collect blood, urine, or breath for analysis is a search and seizure under the Fourth Amendment. But the Court stated that the Fourth Amendment does not prohibit all searches and seizures, only those that are unreasonable based upon a review of the surrounding circumstances. The Court determined that the special need for the protection of public safety in rail transportation made the typical prerequisites of search warrants or individualized suspicion impracticable.

Once the special need has been shown, the Supreme Court indicated, a balancing test must be used that weighs the intrusion on the individual's privacy rights against the promotion of legitimate governmental objectives. The Court determined that railroad employees holding safety-sensitive positions within a heavily regulated industry possess a diminished expectation of privacy. The Court also determined that there was only a minimum intrusion on individual privacy under the FRA regulations. Balanced against these considerations was the government interest in protecting the public from the immediate potential for catastrophic railway accidents. The Court determined that the government interest outweighed employee interests.

In the *Von Raab* case, presented in this section, the Supreme Court found special needs beyond mere law enforcement and, applying a balancing test, determined that the governmental interests of protecting national borders and the public safety outweighed employee privacy interests. The Court then justified the warrantless, suspicionless drug testing utilized by the Customs Service.

TESTING IN THE PRIVATE SECTOR

The federal constitutional protections of privacy, to whatever extent they exist, apply only to the actions of the state.[30] Thus, constitutional defenses may be raised

---

[27] 489 U.S. 602 (1989).

[28] 489 U.S. 656 (1989).

[29] See *Aeronautical Repair Station Assn., Inc. v. FAA*, 494 F.3d 161 (D.C. Cir. 2007) where the court upheld the FAA's regulation requiring that air carriers mandate drug and alcohol testing of all employees of its contractors and subcontractors who perform safety-related functions.

[30] *Jackson v. Metropolitan Edison Co.*, 419 U.S. 345 (1974).

against public employers, as set forth previously. Private-sector employers may have collective bargaining agreements that restrict employer testing to "reasonable cause" situations. These employers may have to meet just-cause standards in disciplinary matters. However, unless restricted or prohibited by collective bargaining contracts or state or local law, private employers have a right to require employees to submit to drug testing.[31]

It is common for private-sector employers to test applicants for employment for drug use as one of the numerous tests given in a preemployment physical examination. Past drug users may be protected from discrimination by certain state and federal laws; however, if they test positive for drugs in a preemployment drug test, they lose protection under the Americans with Disabilities Act of 1990 and the Rehabilitation Act of 1973. Job applicants ordinarily have no protection under collective bargaining contracts, and unions have no standing to bring suit against the employers as union members do not face the risk of exposure to the testing.[32] Government regulations may require notice of testing. However, private-sector employers generally have wide latitude in testing job applicants for drug use. Job applicants who test positive for drug use simply are not offered a position.

Private-sector employers have an obligation to bargain with their unions about new drug testing programs for their current employees unless the employers have expressly reserved rights to make changes in these programs in their current collective bargaining contracts.

TESTING PROCEDURES AND METHODS

Questions may be raised at an arbitration or in a wrongful discharge lawsuit as to the integrity of the chain of custody of the test sample, the accuracy of the type of test(s) performed, and the reliability of the testing laboratory. It is widely accepted that the gas chromatography/mass spectrometry (GC/MS) test is highly accurate. This expensive test is used as a second or confirmatory test if the EMIT (enzyme-multiplied immunoassay technique) test yields a positive result. Some employers and unions have reached agreements on testing protocols, which help eliminate testing issues. Thus, the Teamsters and a committee of employers have reached a reasonable-cause testing agreement as part of a Master Freight Agreement. The agreement designates the testing laboratory and procedures and covers such details as the amount of urine to be taken and the type of tests to be performed.

---

[31] In New Jersey, for example, where the New Jersey Constitution protects individuals' right to privacy, the state's supreme court approved random drug testing in the private sector. The court held that the right of privacy was outweighed by the competing public interest in safety, where an employee who attempts to perform his or her duties impaired by drugs would pose a threat to coworkers, the workplace, or the public at large. *Hennessey v. Costal Eagle Point Oil Co.*, 129 N.J. 81, 609 A.2d 611.

[32] *APWU v. Frank*, 968 F.2d 1373 (1st Cir. 1992).

CASE 17.7	JAKUBOWICZ V. DITTEMORE
	UNITED STATES DISTRICT COURT, 25 IER 312 (W.D. MO. 2006).

[On April 6, 2005, the director of the Missouri Department of Mental Health (DMH) notified employees about the DMH's new drug testing plan in part as follows:

> In order to provide a safe and secure living environment for the people we serve and for those whom we work with on a daily basis, the [DMH] is implementing random drug testing in May 2005. All employees will be subject to random selection.

Chester Jakubowicz and other employees brought suit against the director of DMH, Ron Dittemore, in federal district court, claiming that the random, suspicionless drug testing policy was unconstitutional on its face and should be permanently enjoined.]

LAUGHREY, D. J....

Discussion

The Fourth Amendment to the United States Constitution protects citizens from unreasonable searches. U.S. Const. amend. IV. The purpose of the Amendment is to protect "the privacy, dignity, and security of persons against certain arbitrary and invasive acts by officers of the Government or those acting at their direction," *Skinner v. Ry. Labor Executives' Ass'n*, 489 U.S. 602.

When a governmental entity conducts urinary drug tests, those tests are considered searches under the Fourth Amendment that ordinarily would require a search warrant based on probable cause. *Skinner*, 489 U.S. at 616. Individualized suspicion and probable cause, however, are not necessary when a government's search is based on special needs, beyond the normal need for law enforcement. *Chandler v. Miller*, 520 U.S. 305, 313....

When a governmental entity alleges a "special need"—as DMH alleges here—"courts must undertake a context-specific inquiry, examining closely the competing private and public interests advanced by the parties." *Chandler*, 520 U.S. at 314. "The special need for drug testing must be substantial—important enough to override the individual's acknowledged privacy interest, sufficiently vital to suppress the Fourth Amendment's normal requirement of individualized suspicion." *Id*. at 318. In special needs cases, courts employ a balancing test that considers the

nature of the privacy interest, the character of the intrusion, and the nature and immediacy of the government's interest. *Bd. of Educ. of Indep. Sch. Dist. No. 92 of Pottawatomie County v. Earls*, 536 U.S. 822, 829-33 (2002).

The burden of proving whether an employee falls within this special needs exception to the Fourth Amendment falls on the governmental agency seeking to conduct the testing. "The government must prove ... that its search meets a general test of 'reasonableness." *Joy v. Penn-Harris-Madison Sch. Corp.*, 212 F.3d 1052, 1058 (7th Cir. 2000)....

Role Model

DMH's drug testing policy applies, on its face, to every person employed by DMH, from the Director to an accountant to a receptionist, both in and outside residential treatment centers.

Defendant Dittemore justifies including all DMH employees in its drug testing program because, according to the Department, every employee is a role model for DMH's clients. Dittemore argues that some or most of DMH's clients participate in vocational programs which require them to work in DMH facilities. He also contends that drug addicts being treated by DMH can spot a drug user better than the professional staff of DMH. Dittemore then reasons that if a client sees that a drug using employee is not punished by DMH, the client will conclude that DMH is duplicitous when it expects its clients to live a drug free life....

Dr. Vincenz did not identify a single DMH patient who had special skills at detecting prior drug use, making it impossible to test his hypothesis. Nor has Dr. Vincenz identified any testing or professional literature to support a conclusion generally that drug users are better than trained staff at identifying drug users. Dr. Vincenz's conclusions on this subject are particularly puzzling because he suggests that the special ability to discern the subtle evidence of prior drug use is possessed by family members of the addicted person as well. Vincenz Dep. at p. 43. Yet, he does not explain how an untrained family member is better able to detect this subtle behavior but a trained DMH supervisor who is around drug addicts regularly is not able to discern that DMH employees are using

continued

drugs outside the workplace. Because the Court does not find persuasive Dr. Vincenz's testimony that DMH clients are better than trained staff at identifying off duty drug use by DMH employees, it rejects DMH's argument that there is a special need to randomly drug test all DMH employees, even those that do not provide patient care. If DMH's staff is as able as DMH's clients to see that a DMH employee is engaged in off duty drug use, there is no need for random testing of employees. Drug testing can be done based on an actual suspicion that an employee's drug use is changing cognition, response time, ability to make appropriate judgments; i.e., things that affect the quality of the employee's job performance.

The weight to be given to DMH's role model argument is also diminished by the fact that DMH has not instituted any screening mechanism to address other employee behaviors that might undermine DMH's treatment plan. There are no special testing measures for alcohol use. There is no evidence that people with eating disorders are investigated even if they physically exhibit their disease. It does not make sense that the role model argument would apply only to drug users.

DMH's role model argument is also undermined by its own admission that if an employee tests positive for drugs, they are not disciplined unless they refuse treatment. If no discipline is imposed, the employee would continue to work at DMH and a patient with the sixth sense to detect prior drug use would not know that DMH had taken corrective procedures. Thus, under Defendant's theory, the DMH client would continue to believe that DMH was condoning drug use....

Conclusion

In the end, DMH's decision to subject the Plaintiffs to random drug tests is nothing more than a "gesture or symbol" that DMH does not approve illegal drug use. The Court is unaware of any government agency that approves illegal drug use. If DMH's role model justification for agency-wide drug testing is Constitutional, then the Supreme Court has indeed wasted its time identifying the many factors that must be present before Fourth Amendment protections will be sacrificed for the special needs of the government. Every public employer has an interest in ensuring that its employees are not under the influence of illicit drugs and that they are role models for the community. Because this interest is so pervasive, if it alone were enough to justify warrantless drug testing, the Fourth Amendment's protection for public employees would be meaningless. The exception would, in the end, swallow the rule.

In *Chandler*, Georgia enacted a statute that required candidates for public office submit to drug testing before their names could be placed on the ballot. The Supreme Court struck down the provision because Georgia's only articulated basis for having the policy was the need for its public officials to serve as role models. The Court stated, "The need revealed, in short, is symbolic, not 'special,' as that term draws meaning from our case law." 520 U.S. at 322.

ORDERED ... DMH is permanently enjoined from randomly drug testing the Plaintiffs.

Case Questions

1. When a governmental agency such as DMH conducts urinary drug tests, are they considered "searches" under the Fourth Amendment?
2. Did the DMH establish that it had a "special need" for the mandatory drug testing of all department employees?

CASE 17.8	EMPLOYEES UNION v. VON RAAB
	SUPREME COURT OF THE UNITED STATES, 489 U.S. 656 (1989).

[The U.S. Customs Service, which has as a primary enforcement mission the interdiction and seizure of illegal drugs smuggled into the country, has implemented a drug screening program requiring urinalysis tests from Service employees seeking transfer or promotion to positions having a direct involvement in drug interdiction or requiring the incumbent to carry firearms or to handle "classified" material. Among other things,

continued

the program requires that an applicant be notified that selection is contingent upon successful completion of drug screening. Petitioners, a federal employees union, filed suit on behalf of Service employees, alleging that the drug testing program violated the Fourth Amendment. The district court agreed and enjoined the program. The court of appeals vacated the injunction, holding that although the program effects a search within the meaning of the Fourth Amendment, such searches are reasonable in light of their limited scope and the Service's strong interest in detecting drug use among employees in covered positions. The Supreme Court granted certiorari.]

KENNEDY, J....

I.

... After an employee qualifies for a position covered by the Customs testing program, the Service advises him by letter that his final selection is contingent upon successful completion of drug screening. An independent contractor contacts the employee to fix the time and place for collecting the sample. On reporting for the test, the employee must produce photographic identification and remove any outer garments, such as a coat or a jacket, and personal belongings. The employee may produce the sample behind a partition, or in the privacy of a bathroom stall if he so chooses. To ensure against adulteration of the specimen, or substitution of a sample from another person, a monitor of the same sex as the employee remains close at hand to listen for the normal sounds of urination. Dye is added to toilet water to prevent the employee from using the water to adulterate the sample.

Upon receiving the specimen, the monitor inspects it to ensure its proper temperature and color, places a tamper-proof custody seal over the container, and affixes an identification label indicating the date and the individual's specimen number. The employee signs a chain-of-custody form, which is initialed by the monitor, and the urine sample is placed in a plastic bag, sealed, and submitted to a laboratory.

The laboratory tests the sample for the presence of marijuana, cocaine, opiates, amphetamines, and phencyclidine. Two tests are used. An initial screening test uses the enzyme-multiplied-immunoassay technique (EMIT). Any specimen that is identified as positive on this initial test must then be confirmed using gas chromatography/mass spectrometry (GC/MS).

Confirmed positive results are reported to a "Medical Review Officer," "[a] licensed physician ... who has knowledge of substance abuse disorders and has appropriate medical training to interpret and evaluate the individual's positive test result together with his or her medical history and any other relevant biomedical information." HHS Reg. § 1.2, 53 Fed.Reg. 11980 (1988); HHS Reg. § 2.4(g), *id.*, at 11983. After verifying the positive result, the Medical Review Officer transmits it to the agency.

Customs employees who test positive for drugs and who can offer no satisfactory explanation are subject to dismissal from the Service. Test results may not, however, be turned over to any other agency, including criminal prosecutors, without the employee's written consent.

II.

In *Skinner v. Railway Labor Executives Assn.*, 109 S.Ct. 1402, 1412–1413, decided today, we hold that federal regulations requiring employees of private railroads to produce urine samples for chemical testing implicate the Fourth Amendment, as those tests invade reasonable expectations of privacy. Our earlier cases have settled that the Fourth Amendment protects individuals from unreasonable searches conducted by the Government, even when the Government acts as an employer, and, in view of our holding in *Railway Labor Executives* that urine tests are searches, it follows that the Customs Service's drug testing program must meet the reasonableness requirement of the Fourth Amendment.

While we have often emphasized, and reiterate today, that a search must be supported, as a general matter, by a warrant issued upon probable cause, our decision in *Railway Labor Executives* reaffirms the long-standing principle that neither a warrant nor probable cause, nor, indeed, any measure of individualized suspicion, is an indispensable component of reasonableness in every circumstance.

As we note in *Railway Labor Executives*, our cases establish that where a Fourth Amendment intrusion serves special governmental needs, beyond the normal need for law enforcement, it is necessary to balance the individual's privacy expectations against the Government's interest to determine whether it is impractical to require a warrant or some level of individualized suspicion in the particular context. *Ante,* at 1413–1414.

continued

It is clear that the Customs Service's drug testing program is not designed to serve the ordinary needs of law enforcement. Test results may not be used in a criminal prosecution of the employee without the employee's consent. The purposes of the program are to deter drug use among those eligible for promotion to sensitive positions within the Service and to prevent the promotion of drug users to those positions. These substantial interests, no less than the Government's concern for safe rail transportation at issue in *Railway Labor Executives*, present a special need that may justify departure from the ordinary warrant and probable cause requirements....

Even where it is reasonable to dispense with the warrant requirement in the particular circumstances, a search ordinarily must be based on probable cause. *Ante*, at 1416. Our cases teach, however, that the probable-cause standard "'is peculiarly related to criminal investigations.'" *Colorado v. Bertine*, 479 U.S. 367, 371, 107 S.Ct. 738, 741, 93 L.Ed.2d 739 (1987). In particular, the traditional probable-cause standard may be unhelpful in analyzing the reasonableness of routine administrative functions, *Colorado v. Bertine, supra*, 479 U.S., at 371.

... The Customs Service is our Nation's first line of defense against one of the greatest problems affecting the health and welfare of our population. We have adverted before to "the veritable national crisis in law enforcement caused by smuggling of illicit narcotics." *United States v. Montoya de Hernandez*, 473 U.S. 531, 538, 105 S.Ct. 3304, 3309, 87 L.Ed.2d 381 (1985). Our cases also reflect the traffickers' seemingly inexhaustible repertoire of deceptive practices and elaborate schemes for importing narcotics....

It is readily apparent that the Government has a compelling interest in ensuring that frontline interdiction personnel are physically fit, and have unimpeachable integrity and judgment....

A drug user's indifference to the Service's basic mission or, even worse, his active complicity with the malefactors, can facilitate importation of sizable drug shipments or block apprehension of dangerous criminals. The public interest demands effective measures to bar drug users from positions directly involving the interdiction of illegal drugs.

The public interest likewise demands effective measures to prevent the promotion of drug users to positions that require the incumbent to carry a firearm, even if the incumbent is not engaged directly in the interdiction of drugs. Customs employees who may use deadly force plainly "discharge duties fraught with such risks of injury to others that even a momentary lapse of attention can have disastrous consequences." *Ante*, at 1419. We agree with the Government that the public should not bear the risk that employees who may suffer from impaired perception and judgment will be promoted to positions where they may need to employ deadly force. Indeed, ensuring against the creation of this dangerous risk will itself further Fourth Amendment values, as the use of deadly force may violate the Fourth Amendment in certain circumstances.

Against these valid public interests we must weight the interference with individual liberty that results from requiring these classes of employees to undergo a urine test. The interference with individual privacy that results from the collection of a urine sample for subsequent chemical analysis could be substantial in some circumstances. *Ante*, at 1418. We have recognized, however, that the "operational realities of the workplace" may render entirely reasonable certain work-related intrusions by supervisors and co-workers that might be viewed as unreasonable in other contexts. While these operational realities will rarely affect an employee's expectations of privacy with respect to searches of his person, or of personal effects that the employee may bring to the workplace, *id.*, at 716, 725, 107 S.Ct., at 1498, 1502, it is plain that certain forms of public employment may diminish privacy expectations even with respect to such personal searches. Employees of the United States Mint, for example, should expect to be subject to certain routine personal searches when they leave the workplace every day....

We think Customs employees who are directly involved in the interdiction of illegal drugs or who are required to carry firearms in the line of duty likewise have a diminished expectation of privacy in respect to the intrusions occasioned by a urine test. Unlike most private citizens or government employees in general, employees involved in drug interdiction reasonably should expect effective inquiry into their fitness and probity. Much the same is true of employees who are required to carry firearms. Because successful performance of their duties depends uniquely on their judgment and dexterity, these employees cannot reasonably expect to keep from the Service personal information that bears directly on their fitness. Cf. In re *Caruso v.*

continued

Ward, 72 N.Y.2d 433, 441, 534 N.Y.S.2d 142, 146–148, 530 N.E.2d 850, 854-855 (1988). While reasonable tests designed to elicit this information doubtless infringe some privacy expectations, we do not believe these expectations outweigh the Government's compelling interests in safety and in the integrity of our borders.*

III.

Where the Government requires its employees to produce urine samples to be analyzed for evidence of illegal drug use, the collection and subsequent chemical analysis of such samples are searches that must meet the reasonableness requirement of the Fourth Amendment. Because the testing program adopted by the Customs Service is not designed to serve the

---

*The procedures prescribed by the Customs Service for the collection and analysis of the requisite samples do not carry the grave potential for "arbitrary and oppressive interference with the privacy and personal security of individuals," *United States v. Martinez-Fuerte*, 428 U.S. 543, 554, 96 S.Ct. 3074, 3081, 49 L.Ed.2d 1116 (1976), that the Fourth Amendment was designed to prevent. Indeed, these procedures significantly minimize the program's intrusion on privacy interests. Only employees who have been tentatively accepted for promotion or transfer to one of the three categories of covered positions are tested, and applicants know at the outset that a drug test is a requirement of those positions. Employees are also notified in advance of the scheduled sample collection, thus reducing to a minimum any "unsettling show of authority." *Delaware v. Prouse*, 440 U.S. 648, 657, 99 S.Ct. 1391, 1398, 59 L.Ed.2d 660 (1979), that may be associated with unexpected intrusions on privacy. Cf. *United States v. Martinez-Fuerte, supra*, 428 U.S., at 559, 96 S.Ct. at 3083 (noting that the intrusion on privacy occasioned by routine highway checkpoints is minimized by the fact that motorists "are not taken by surprise as they know, or may obtain knowledge of, the location of the checkpoints and will not be stopped elsewhere"); *Wyman v. James*, 400 U.S. 309, 320–321, 91 S.Ct. 381, 387-388, 27 L.Ed.2d 408 (1971) (providing a welfare recipient with advance notice that she would be visited by a welfare caseworker minimized the intrusion on privacy occasioned by the visit). There is no direct observation of the act of urination, as the employee may provide a specimen in the privacy of a stall.

Further, urine samples may be examined only for the specified drugs. The use of samples to test for any other substances is prohibited. See HHS Reg. § 2.1(c), 53 Fed. Reg. 11980 (1988). And, as the court of appeals noted, the combination of EMIT and GC/MS tests required by the Service is highly accurate, assuming proper storage, handling, and measurement techniques. 816 F.2d at 181. Finally, an employee need not disclose personal medical information to the Government unless his test result is positive, and even then any such information is reported to a licensed physician. Taken together, these procedures significantly minimize the intrusiveness of the Service's drug screening program.

ordinary needs of law enforcement, we have balanced the public interest in the Service's testing program against the privacy concerns implicated by the tests, without reference to our usual presumption in favor of the procedures specified in the Warrant Clause, to assess whether the tests required by Customs are reasonable.

We hold that the suspicionless testing of employees who apply for promotion to positions directly involving the interdiction of illegal drugs, or to positions which require the incumbent to carry a firearm, is reasonable. The Government's compelling interests in preventing the promotion of drug users to positions where they might endanger the integrity of our Nation's borders or the life of the citizenry outweigh the privacy interests of those who seek promotion to these positions, who enjoy a diminished expectation of privacy by virtue of the special, and obvious, physical and ethical demands of those positions. We do not decide whether testing those who apply for promotion to positions where they would handle "classified" information is reasonable because we find the record inadequate for this purpose.

The judgment of the Court of Appeals for the Fifth Circuit is affirmed in part and vacated in part, and the case is remanded for further proceedings consistent with this opinion.

It is so ordered.

JUSTICE MARSHALL, with whom JUSTICE BRENNAN joins, Dissenting...

For the reasons stated in my dissenting opinion in *Skinner v. Railway Labor Executives Association*, I also dissent from the Court's decision in this case. Here, as in *Skinner*, the Court's abandonment of the Fourth Amendment's express requirement that searches of the person rest on probable cause is unprincipled and unjustifiable....

JUSTICE SCALIA, with whom JUSTICE STEVENS joins, Dissenting...

The issue in this case is not whether Customs Service employees can constitutionally be denied promotion, or even dismissed, for a single instance of unlawful drug use, at home or at work. They assuredly can. The issue here is what steps can constitutionally be taken to *detect* such drug use. The Government asserts it can demand that employees perform "an excretory function traditionally shielded by great privacy,"

continued

Skinner v. Railway Labor Executives' Assn., 109 S.Ct., at 1418, while "a monitor of the same sex ... remains close at hand to listen for the normal sounds," *ante*, at 1388, and that the excretion thus produced be turned over to the Government for chemical analysis. The Court agrees that this constitutes a search for purposes of the Fourth Amendment—and I think it obvious that it is a type of search particularly destructive of privacy and offensive to personal dignity.

Until today this Court had upheld a bodily search separate from arrest and without individualized suspicion of wrongdoing only with respect to prison inmates, relying upon the uniquely dangerous nature of that environment. Today, in *Skinner*, we allow a less intrusive bodily search of railroad employees involved in train accidents. I joined the Court's opinion there because the demonstrated frequency of drug and alcohol use by the targeted class of employees, and the demonstrated connection between such use and grave harm, rendered the search a reasonable means of protecting society. I decline to join the Court's opinion in the present case because neither frequency of use nor connection to harm is demonstrated or even likely. In my view the Customs Service rules are a kind of immolation of privacy and human dignity in symbolic opposition to drug use....

Those who lose because of the lack of understanding that begot the present exercise in symbolism are not just the Customs Service employees, whose dignity is thus offended, but all of us—who suffer a coarsening of our national manners that ultimately give the Fourth Amendment its content, and who become subject to the administration of federal officials whose respect for our privacy can hardly be greater than the small respect they have been taught to have for their own.

Case Questions

1. Summarize the testing procedures utilized by the Customs Service.
2. Is the GC/MS test usually accurate?
3. What "special needs" were identified by the Court that could justify departure from the ordinary warrant and probable cause requirements?
4. In your own words, explain Justice Scalia's concern about those "who lose because of the lack of understanding that begot the present exercise in symbolism."

SECTION 145: ALCOHOL ABUSE AND EMPLOYEE ASSISTANCE PROGRAMS

Alcohol abuse in the workplace is the cause of many deaths, injuries, and lost workdays and much unsatisfactory worker performance. The economic costs to employers are significant. Most employers publicize and enforce plant or company rules prohibiting the use or possession of alcoholic beverages (and drugs) while on duty or subject to duty. Through the observations of an employee, such as an unsteady or staggering walk, slurred speech, bloodshot eyes, and the odor of alcohol on the breath, supervisors are often able to identify an employee who has been apparently violating the employer's no-alcohol rule. Commonly, employers require two supervisors to observe the employee, and where their observations indicate a rule violation, the supervisors will confront the employee and offer the employee the opportunity to vindicate himself or herself by taking a blood-alcohol test. Employees who violate an employer's no-alcohol rule are subject to major discipline up to and including discharge.

Most employers have made major investments in the selection and training of their employees. It is in the employer's best interest to retain valuable employees by providing a rehabilitation program for those employees who suffer from alcohol abuse. Employee assistance programs (EAPs) exist in most major companies to help troubled employees overcome difficulties such as drug and alcohol abuse, work and family tensions, eating disorders, gambling addictions, and financial and other problems.

The recovery rate from alcohol abuse under EAPs has been determined to be as high as 80 percent. Employers, cooperating unions, and the individual participants are pleased with the success of the EAPs in dealing with alcohol problems. Instead of disciplining or discharging employees for the no-alcohol rule violation on a first offense, the matter is commonly handled through the EAP, with the employee signing a conditional reinstatement agreement under which the employee, after a period of hospitalization at a rehabilitation facility, promises to abide by the rehabilitation program. Should the employee fail to do so, the employee agrees and acknowledges that she or he may be subject to termination.

Where an employee is unwilling to participate in an employee assistance program and where there is a collective bargaining agreement with a just-cause provision restricting the employer's right to discharge, the employee may be discharged for the no-alcohol rule violation. If the observations of two supervisors indicate a problem concerning the demeanor of an employee and if the odor of alcohol is present on the employee's breath, as just discussed, there is probable cause for the employer to seek a blood-alcohol test. Under such circumstances, no serious challenge to the decision to test can be raised at an arbitration hearing. Absent mitigating or unusual circumstances, the discharge of the employee will likely be upheld in arbitration.

Incidents such as accidents or major safety rule violations may also trigger an employer's testing program, and where impairment due to alcohol is found through a test, the EAP procedures may also be followed. In the case of serious accidents or injuries caused by alcohol or drug impairment, reinstatement to employment may not be offered, absent an agreement to the contrary.

The misconduct involved in the *Brotherhood of Locomotive Engineers* arbitration decision, presented in this section, led to the criminal conviction of the engineer. The misconduct stirred a national dialogue on the issue of alcohol and drug testing for operating employees in the transportation industries.

CASE 17.9	BROTHERHOOD OF LOCOMOTIVE ENGINEERS AND ILLINOIS CENTRAL GULF RAILROAD

PLB 3538, No. 2 (NMB, July 3, 1984).

FROM THE FINDINGS OF THE ARBITRATION BOARD...

The record before the Board indicates that on September 27, 1982, the Claimant, Engineer E. P. Robertson and crew went on duty about 7:00 P.M. at McComb, Mississippi, to take a train to Baton Rouge, Louisiana. They went off duty at 10:40 P.M. at Baton Rouge and were immediately transported to their designated lodging at the Prince Murat Inn to rest because, according to the usual routine of their assignment, they would be required after the rest period to work the return assignment back to McComb. The

crew was thereafter called at 2:30 A.M., September 28, and listed for work at 3:30 A.M.

The testimony indicates that Mr. Robertson did not take his rest when he arrived at the motel; and that he and Brakeman Reeves went to the motel bar and stayed until midnight. He drank at least one drink and ordered a drink to go in a plastic cup, according to the testimony of the bartender Mr. J. D. Morales and the waitress Ms. K. M. Sword. Sometime after midnight, he and Mr. Reeves met with Clerk Janet Byrd, and it developed that he, Brakeman Reeves, and Ms. Byrd boarded the cab of the locomotive

continued

together. The crew had been called at 2:30 A.M., listed for work at 3:30 A.M., and departed Baton Rouge at 4:15 A.M. Ms. Byrd later told company officials that Mr. Robertson invited Ms. Byrd to "run" the engine.

At approximately 5:05 A.M. on September 28, 1982, the train Extra 9629 East (GS-2-28) derailed 43 cars on the single main track of the Hammond District in Livingston, Louisiana. Of the derailed cars, 36 were tank cars; 27 of these cars contained various regulated hazardous materials, and 5 contained flammable petroleum products. Fires broke out in the wreckage, and smoke and toxic gases were released into the atmosphere. Explosions of two tank cars that had not been punctured caused them to rocket violently. Some 3000 persons living within a five-mile radius of the derailment site were evacuated for as long as two weeks. Nineteen residences and other buildings in Livingston were destroyed or severely damaged. Toxic chemical products were spilled and absorbed into the ground requiring extensive excavation of contaminated soil and its transportation to a distant dump site. This caused the closing of the track for a year; and the derailment costs to the Carrier are presently over $25,000,000, with several lawsuits pending.

The Carrier does not hold that Mr. Robertson caused the derailment, for its experts determined that the derailment was caused by equipment failure. The Carrier did, however, find that Mr. Robertson was responsible for three serious rule violations: (1) drinking while subject to duty [Rule G], (2) speeding at several locations during his trip, and (3) allowing an unauthorized passenger to ride in the locomotive. We find that substantial evidence of record exists to support the Carrier's findings in this case.

Two employees from the Prince Murat Inn, J. D. Morales and Kelly M. Sword, testified that two drinks were served to Mr. Robertson containing one and one-half ounces of alcohol, one he drank at the bar and the other was put in a plastic glass to go. Mr. Robertson knew full well that he was on a short layover and that he was subject to duty, after a limited

rest period. When an engineer, entrusted with the responsibility for a train, and particularly when entrusted with responsibility for a train containing hazardous chemicals, spends a portion of his short layover in a bar drinking any amount of alcohol, he is guilty of the highest degree of irresponsibility. Such is a clear violation of Rule G, for that employee is "subject to duty" within the explicit language of that rule. Clearly one drink by an employee subject to duty causes some impairment of that individual, and the Carrier and the public have a right not to have a train operated by an individual impaired to any degree. Mr. Robertson acted in a most irresponsible manner by purchasing alcoholic beverages while subject to duty and he was clearly in violation of Rule G.

The evidence of record, including the testimony of Supervisor of Communications R. L. Mont and Supervisor Instructor A. J. Puth, make it evident that Mr. Robertson's train was operated well beyond the time-table authorized at several locations during the trip....

... Mr. Robertson's widely publicized misconduct not only caused a national embarrassment to the Illinois Central Gulf Railroad, but tarnished the high professional reputation of locomotive engineers throughout the Country. The discipline of dismissal is appropriate.

Claim denied.

Case Questions

1. Company Rule G prohibits the use of alcohol or drugs not only while on duty but also while "subject to duty." Give your opinion as to whether an employer can properly regulate the actions of its employees when they are off duty and not being paid.

2. Should Engineer Robertson be returned to service upon successful completion of the EAP alcohol rehabilitation program? See Section 104 of the ADA in the Appendixes.

SECTION 146: POLYGRAPH EXAMINATIONS

Law enforcement and security agencies do not want to hire individuals who have sold or who use illegal drugs because drug-impaired judgment would adversely affect law enforcement duties and may lead to compromised operations. A large segment of society believes that there is an inherent contradiction in lawbreakers being hired to enforce the law. Some law enforcement and security agencies believe that preemployment polygraph testing is an effective tool in finding out whether certain applicants should be disqualified for employment. The applicants may truthfully admit drug sales or drug use during the polygraph examination, or where no admissions are made during the examination, the polygraph examiners may find that certain applicants are "deceptive."

Employers believe that polygraph examinations are one of the best tools that management has at its disposal to investigate thefts and related workplace misconduct. The problem is that there is no widely accepted evidence establishing the scientific validity of polygraph testing, and the utility of such testing is debatable and, indeed, is much debated.[33] In a polygraph examination, a relative increase in heart rate, respiration, and perspiration when questions related to theft or economic loss are asked is interpreted as a sign of guilt. Opponents of polygraph testing point out that errors may result when an innocent person, who believes that the test could be wrong, out of fear exhibits an increase in heart rate, respiration, and perspiration when asked such incident-related questions.[34]

STATE LAWS

Some 25 states and the District of Columbia either prohibit or restrict the use of polygraphs in employment matters. In the *Anderson v. Philadelphia* decision, presented in this section, the U.S. Court of Appeals for the Third Circuit rejected employment applicants' constitutional challenges to a state law that forbade preemployment polygraph testing except for public law enforcement agencies. The court deferred to the state legislature's judgment to allow polygraph testing in the limited circumstances of law enforcement. Where a state statute prohibits requiring a polygraph as a condition of employment, an employer who terminates or adversely affects employees who refuse to take such examinations may be found liable under a "public policy" tort theory for back pay, damages for emotional distress, and punitive damages.[35]

POLYGRAPH EXAMINATIONS AND THE RIGHT TO PRIVACY

In *Thorne v. City of El Segundo*,[36] the Ninth Circuit Court of Appeals held that Thorne's First Amendment rights to privacy and free association were abridged when she was denied the opportunity to become a city police officer after she was required to disclose information regarding personal sexual matters during a polygraph examination.

---

[33] See *Anderson v. Philadelphia*, 845 F.2d 1216 (3d Cir. 1988).

[34] P. Ekman, Telling Lies (New York: Berkley, 1985), 201–206. A new lie detection technology exists that detects neurological evidence of the decision to lie. It is called fMRI. Columbia University has an fMRI Research Center, and commercial applications exist. While it is unlawful for private employers to use lie detectors for personal screening, military and governmental markets exist for this technology. Retrieved June 30, 2008, from http://www.wired.com/wired/archive/14.01/lying_pr.html

[35] *Moniodis v. Cook*, 1 ITER Cases 441 (Md. Ct. Spec. App. 1985).

[36] 726 F.2d 459 (9th Cir. 1983).

FEDERAL LAWS

The federal Employee Polygraph Protection Act of 1988 (EPPA)[37] makes it unlawful for private employers to use preemployment lie detector (polygraph) tests while screening applicants for employment or to take any disciplinary action or deny employment or promotion to any individual who refuses to take a polygraph test. However, federal, state, and local government employers are exempt from any restrictions on the use of polygraph tests, and the federal government may also test private consultants under contract to the Defense Department, CIA, FBI, the National Security Agency, or the Department of Energy. The law also permits private security firms and drug companies to administer polygraph tests to job applicants and employees.

Under the law, a limited exemption allows employers to request an employee to submit to a polygraph test if (1) the test is administered in connection with an ongoing investigation involving economic loss or injury to an employer's business, such as theft or embezzlement; (2) the employee had access to the property in question; (3) the employer has "reasonable suspicion" of the employee; and (4) the employer gives a written statement to the employee of the basis for its reasonable suspicion. In *Polkey v. Transtecs Corp.*, a supervisor for a defense contractor providing mailroom services at the Pensacola Naval Air Station in Florida was successful in her EPPA lawsuit against her employer, Transtecs. The Court of Appeals decided that the employer did not meet its burden of proof regarding "reasonable suspicion" of the employee that she was responsible for the improper mail handling incident in question. As a result, it violated the Act by "requesting" that she take a polygraph exam.[38]

The EPPA also deals with a number of objections to the testing process itself. To avoid short, incomplete, and unfair tests, the law requires that tests last at least 90 minutes.[39] Because examiners have sometimes asked offensive questions about sexual preferences and practices, racial matters, religious beliefs, or political or union affiliations or beliefs, the law prohibits questions on such topics.[40] Section 8 of the EPPA sets forth detailed procedures that must be followed prior to, during, and following any lie detector test permitted under the limited exception for "ongoing investigations."

The law authorizes civil suits to enforce the Act and to make whole adversely affected individuals, including the payment of lost wages and benefits. For example, in *Veazey v. Communications and Cable of Chicago, Inc.,*[41] the Seventh Circuit Court of Appeals determined that an employee's refusal to provide a tape-recorded voice sample that could be subjected to a stress analyzer was within the definition of a lie detector, since in combination with other devices, it would enable the employer to determine whether the employee was telling the truth about not

---

[37] Pub. L. 100–347, signed into law on June 27, 1988.

[38] 404 F. 3d 1264 (11th Cir. 2005).

[39] § 8(b)(5).

[40] § 8(b)11(c).

[41] 194 F.3d 850 (1999).

sending a threatening voice mail message. The matter was returned to the district court for trial. An employer who violates the Act may also be assessed a civil penalty of up to $10,000 as determined by the Secretary of Labor.[42]

The law does not preempt any state or local law or collective bargaining agreement that prohibits lie detector tests or is more restrictive than the federal law.

CASE 17.10	ANDERSON V. PHILADELPHIA U.S. COURT OF APPEALS, 845 F.2D 1216 (3D CIR. 1988).

[Pennsylvania law forbids the use of polygraph testing for preemployment screening by any private or public employer. An exception exists, however, for public law enforcement agencies. The city of Philadelphia police and prison departments base their hiring on the results of a competitive civil service examination, with individuals passing this test being placed on a certified eligibility list. As openings occur, individuals ranked high on the eligibility lists are notified and must then pass a number of additional tests before being found qualified for employment. These additional tests include a medical examination; a psychiatric examination; a background investigation; and, usually last in the process, a polygraph test. As part of the background investigation, candidates must fill out a Personal Data Questionnaire (PDQ), which includes questions about family and financial status; driving record; educational and employment history; criminal record; use of alcoholic beverages; and the use, sale, and possession of illicit drugs. Candidates are given prior notification of the content of the PDQ, including the questions relating to illicit drugs. Candidates are also informed that deception or falsification in answering PDQ/polygraph questions may result in rejection. The police and prison departments will hire otherwise qualified individuals who admit that they have used or possessed drugs over six months before completing the PDQ and taking the polygraph. The plaintiffs claim that the use of the polygraph test results in order to deny them employment deprives them of their constitutional rights to procedural and substantive due process and equal protection of the law. After a bench trial, the district court held in favor of the plaintiffs and the city appealed.]

STAPLETON, C. J....

I.

... The polygraph testing procedures currently used by both the police and prison departments were developed in 1983 in the course of settling class actions by blacks and Hispanics who had brought suit alleging that the Philadelphia Police Department's hiring and promotion policies were discriminatory. These settlements require the above-described prior notification concerning the PDQ/polygraph questions, and require that if during the test the polygraph examiner finds the applicant "deceptive," the applicant must be told immediately and given a chance to explain, deny, or admit the deception. If the applicant denies being deceptive, or if the explanation is found unsatisfactory by the examiner, the applicant must have the opportunity to retake the test with a second examiner. The second examiner does not review the results of the first prior to readministering the polygraph. If the second examiner finds no deception, the applicant is considered to have passed; if the second examiner also finds the applicant deceptive, that finding is ordinarily final and preclusive of employment. The applicant may, however, appeal to either the Police Department's Review Panel or to the Superintendent of Prisons or the prison review panel, and the reviewers may decide to give the applicant the opportunity to take a third test. If the applicant is found deceptive on a third test, he or she will not be hired. Deception is found on about half of all the tests given.

During a pre-test interview, applicants are asked if there is any other information they would like to

continued

---

[42] § 6(a).

provide. During a post-test review, if deception is indicated, they are asked again if there is any information they are withholding. Admissions to disqualifying information were made during these interviews by 315 of the 1028 applicants for positions with the Police Department in 1985, and 251 of the 619 applicants in 1986.

... The results of the tests are not made public, but are used only within the departments for evaluating the suitability of the applicant for employment.

There is considerable controversy about the validity and reliability of polygraph testing. The polygraph measures stress or anxiety, which in many cases may not correlate very well with deception. In 1983, Congress' Office of Technology Assessment put out a Technical Memorandum on polygraph testing, which read in part as follows:

> There are two major reasons why an overall measure of validity is not possible. First, the polygraph test is, in reality, a very complex process that is much more than the instrument. Although the instrument is essentially the same for all applications, the types of individuals tested, training of the examiner, purpose of the test, and types of questions asked, among other factors, can differ substantially. A polygraph test requires that the examiner infer deception or truthfulness based on a comparison of the person's physiological responses to various questions.... Second, the research on polygraph validity varies widely in terms of not only results, but also in the quality of research design and methodology. Thus, conclusions about scientific validity can be made only in the context of specific applications and even then must be tempered by the limitations of available research evidence.
>
> ... OTA concluded that the available research evidence does not establish the scientific validity of the polygraph test for personnel security screening.
>
> ... [D]espite many decades of judicial, legislative, and scientific discussion, no consensus has emerged about the accuracy of polygraph tests.

App. at 618, 652, Professor Leonard Saxe, who headed the OTA group, testified as an expert witness for the plaintiffs. According to Professor Saxe, polygraph tests are likely to find many truthful applicants deceptive (false positives) and some unknown lesser, though "potentially large," number of deceptive applicants truthful (false negatives). App. at 344. When polygraphs are used for pre-employment screening, the risk of false positive results is generally thought to be higher than that of false negative results.

The City's law enforcement departments consider polygraph tests reliable and valid. An additional advantage of using the polygraph test, in the department's view, is that it encourages applicants to be candid in responding to questions on the PDQ. The departments do not believe that this secondary advantage can be separated from the trustworthiness that they consider to be the main advantage of the polygraph. Both advantages, the departments believe, enable them to acquire necessary information about potential employees.

The department's experts do admit that polygraph testing is not perfect. While they recognize the impossibility of conducting error-free polygraph testing, however, they correctly point out that there is no evidence establishing that the polygraph is not valid. Moreover, they point out that there must be some method of acquiring the information necessary to make choices among applicants and stress that the decision to utilize a polygraph examination must be evaluated in light of the available alternatives. One of the department's experts, Dr. Frank Horvath, noted that

> there is also little scientific support for many of the procedures which are used in employment screening. There is little "scientific" evidence, for instance, to show that background investigations actually yield accurate information or that psychiatric interviews accurately discriminate between "good" and "bad" candidates. On the other hand, there is considerable scientific data to show that personal interviews as generally used in employment screening are unreliable; yet, employers continue to carry out such interviews. Written psychological tests, moreover, have received considerable research attention which, according to many, shows little scientific support for their use.

App. at 398....

II.

... In *Board of Regents v. Roth*, the Supreme Court made it clear that "[t]he requirements of procedural due process apply only to the deprivation of interests encompassed by the Fourteenth Amendment's protection of liberty and property." 408 U.S. 564, 569 (1972). According to the Court, "to determine whether due process requirements apply in the first place, we must look

continued

... to the *nature* of the interest at stake." *Id.* at 571. In this case, the plaintiffs have alleged that they have been deprived of both property and liberty interests by the City departments' use of the polygraph test to disqualify them from employment.

Property Interest

... While the departments were bound to consider the plaintiffs for employment, they were by no means bound to hire the plaintiffs. The plaintiffs can cite to no section of the Pennsylvania statutes which sets an objective standard for the hiring or rejection of applicants from the eligibility lists, and which might thereby create a legitimate claim of entitlement to employment. On the contrary, under the state law applicable here, agencies such as the defendant departments may and do exercise broad discretion in hiring....

[W]e find nothing in the departmental hiring practices or in Pennsylvania law that establishes a legitimate claim of entitlement to employment in applicants like the plaintiffs. We therefore conclude that the plaintiffs' interest in the civil service positions they sought did not rise to the level of a property interest protected by the Constitution.

Liberty Interest

On the subject of liberty interests in employment, this court has stated that

> [a]n employment action implicates a fourteenth amendment liberty interest only if it (1) is based on a "charge against [the individual] that might seriously damage his standing and associations in the community ... for example, [by implying] that he had been guilty of dishonesty, or immorality," or (2) "impose[s] on him a stigma or other disability that forecloses his freedom to take advantage of other employment opportunities."

Robb, 733 F.2d at 294 (citing *Roth,* 408 U.S. at 573)....

In this case, plaintiffs assert that they have been "branded as liars" on account of their failure to pass the polygraph examination. While the polygraph results might conceivably be viewed as stigmatizing the plaintiffs or damaging their reputations, the plaintiffs have not alleged that any of their polygraph test results were made public. Rather, the departments' assertion that the polygraph results are kept confidential and undisclosed stands unchallenged. Given that, we find untenable the plaintiffs' claim that they have been deprived of a liberty interest.

We conclude that the City's polygraph requirement does not violate the plaintiffs' right to procedural due process, since no protected property or liberty interest of the plaintiffs is at stake.

III.

We next address the plaintiff's argument that they have been denied equal protection of the law.... The plaintiffs bear the burden of proof on this issue, and so must show that the requirements imposed by law or regulation "so lack rationality that they constitute a constitutionally impermissible denial of equal protection." *Rogin v. Bensalem Township,* 616 F.2d 680, 688 (3d Cir. 1980). In considering this issue, we bear in mind the Court's statement that a statute or regulation should not be overturned on equal protection grounds "unless the varying treatment of different groups or persons is so unrelated to the achievement of any combination of legitimate purposes that we can only conclude that the legislature's actions were irrational." *Vance v. Bradley,* 440 U.S. 93, 97 (1979).

The defendants stress, and the plaintiffs acknowledge, that the public has a legitimate and, indeed, compelling interest in hiring applicants who are qualified for employment as public law enforcement officers. It is this interest that the polygraph requirement is said to serve. The key question we confront here, therefore, is whether the requirement that applicants pass a polygraph test can arguably be said to result in a better-qualified group of new employees. The defendant City departments need not show that the polygraph requirement does in fact result in the selection of a better-qualified group of new employees. Rather, the burden is on the plaintiff applicants to show that the department's use of the polygraph could not reasonably be believed to produce a better-qualified group of new hires than would be chosen absent the polygraph requirement.

It is clear that the district court placed the burden on the wrong party in this case, since a necessary stepping-stone to that court's holding was its conclusion that "[t]he testimony, exhibits and evidence presented at the trial failed to prove the reliability of polygraph tests in general." App. at 706, 709....

Professor Saxe's testimony supports the proposition that the validity and reliability of polygraph testing as a device to screen prospective employees have not been scientifically established. It does not demonstrate, however, that it is irrational to believe that the

continued

polygraph has utility in connection with the selection of law enforcement officers. First, Professor Saxe acknowledges that "virtually no research has been conducted on the validity of polygraph tests to screen prospective employees." App. at 354, and it is, accordingly, apparent that such testing has not been empirically established as invalid or unreliable. Moreover, Professor Saxe does not dispute that preemployment polygraph screening is widely used by intelligence and law enforcement agencies which consider it useful in eliminating unqualified candidates. The record indicates that such screening is used by the National Security Administration, the Central Intelligence Agency, and approximately 50% of police departments throughout the nation. Finally, Professor Saxe does not dispute Dr. Horvath's assertion that "both proponents and opponents maintain that such testing can distinguish between truthful and deceptive persons with an accuracy greater than chance." App. at 394....

... As Dr. Horvath put it,

> the important practical issue is not whether polygraph testing is 95% or 90% or even 70% accurate but whether relative to other methods it yields a reasonable degree of accuracy and whether there is another more suitable method of accomplishing the same objective.

App. at 397. The record in this case provides no basis for concluding that superior alternatives are available.

... [W]e think it rational for the departments to believe that the polygraph requirement results in fuller, more candid disclosures on the PDQ and thus provides additional information that is helpful in selecting qualified law enforcement officers.

In sum, from the plaintiffs' perspective, the most that can be said on the basis of this record is that the utility of polygraph testing in the preemployment screening of candidates for law enforcement positions is a debatable and much-debated issue. In such situations, legislators and administrators are free to exercise their judgment regarding the manner in which the public interest will best be served. *Ginsberg v. New York*, 390 U.S. 629, 642–43 (1967) (where causal link between pornography and impaired ethical and moral development of youth is debatable, courts "do not demand of legislatures 'scientifically certain criteria of legislation'" and will not overturn the legislative judgment). Accordingly, we conclude that in the absence of a scientific consensus, reasonable law enforcement administrators may choose to include a polygraph requirement in their hiring process without offending the equal protection clause....

IV.

For the foregoing reasons, we reverse the judgment of the district court and remand with instructions that judgment be entered for the defendants.

Case Questions

1. Did the congressional Office of Technology Assessment (OTA) Memorandum conclude that the evidence established the scientific validity of polygraph tests for personnel security screening?
2. Does the city believe that polygraph tests encourage applicants to be candid in responding to questions on the PDQ?
3. Did the court conclude that the city's polygraph test requirement violated the plaintiff's right to procedural due process having been deprived of a "liberty interest"?
4. Was it important to the outcome of this case that the plaintiffs had the burden of proof?

SECTION 147: EMPLOYEE DEFAMATION CLAIMS

Individuals whose employment is terminated by their employers may join claims based on exceptions to the employment-at-will doctrine and a claim based on Title VII, the ADEA, or a violation of their constitutional right to privacy. In addition, such individuals may also pursue a claim based on "defamation." Employee defamation claims commonly stem from unfavorable evaluations, investigations of workplace misconduct, and negative references.

Defamation consists of a false statement about the plaintiff that is communicated—"published"—to a third party and that tends to harm the plaintiff's reputation or standing in the community. Thus, falsely accusing an employee in front of others of improper conduct such as theft or dishonesty on the job is defamatory per se. While heavily veiled references to "certain parties" stealing from the company may not be actionable because a specific individual is not reasonably identifiable in such a statement, the statement that "a certain head of the accounting department is skimming from the till" is clearly actionable.[43]

ABSOLUTE AND CONDITIONAL PRIVILEGES

An **absolute privilege** provides a complete defense against a defamation suit, even though the statement turns out to be false or is in reckless disregard for the rights of the defamed person. This privilege is ordinarily limited to statements made in the course of litigation, legislative proceedings, or administrative agency hearings.

A **conditional** or **qualified privilege** exists in situations where the publisher of the statement and the recipient share a legitimate business interest in the information exchanged, provided it is made in good faith and without a willful design to defame. Employers have a conditional privilege concerning employee evaluations, investigations of misconduct, and references. For example, when the plaintiff, a former University of New Haven police officer, sued the university and a university police sergeant for defamation regarding the sergeant's reference to the Glastonbury Police Department concerning her qualifications for employment in Glastonbury, the sergeant's statements that the plaintiff's skills were "marginal at best," her leadership ability was "poor," and at times she had been "negative and uncaring" were subject to a qualified privilege.[44]

EMPLOYEE EVALUATIONS

Employers and their managers are conditionally privileged to communicate frankly about the skills, performance, and qualifications of their employees. The employer is entitled to appraisals of employees' character, as well. However, sound business judgment dictates that sensitive communications should be strictly confined to those who need to know. The burden of proof is on the employee to show that the defamatory statements were made recklessly or that they were excessively published.

INVESTIGATION OF MISCONDUCT IN THE WORKFORCE

Employers have a duty to maintain safe and healthful working conditions under OSHA. They also have a duty to maintain a workforce free of sexual harassment. Employers thus have a duty to conduct investigations into safety and sexual harassment matters. Numerous other circumstances arise where either the employer has a duty to investigate or sound business judgment requires an investigation into

---

[43] *McCallum v. Lambie*, 145 Mass. 234, 238 (1887).

[44] *Miron v. University of New Haven Police Department*, 931 A.2d 847 (Conn. 2007).

possible workplace wrongdoing. The employer has a conditional privilege to conduct prudent, discreet, and well-meaning investigations into such matters. Where defamatory facts result, the publisher-employer's actual belief in their truth or the absence of recklessness in holding and expressing the belief will generally preserve the conditional privilege.

REFERENCES

Where prospective employers make inquiries to a former employer about the character and capabilities of a former employee, the former employer has a conditional privilege to communicate this information. When the former employer discloses defamatory information in such a privileged situation, the statement may turn out not to be true, but truth or falsehood is not material if there is no abuse of the privilege or if no actual malice is shown. Employers' false accusations are not privileged, however, if they did not act on their honest belief that the statements were true. While frank opinions about a former employee's work habits, competence, and character are well protected by the employer's conditional privilege, many employers desiring to steer clear of possible litigation give very limited reference information, such as the former employee's job title, a job description, and rates of pay and employment dates.

As seen in the *Gibson v. Overnight Transportation Co.* decision, a Wisconsin case presented in this section that follows the common law rule, employers are liable for defamation where there is "actual malice," which requires a finding that the statements were made knowing they were false or with reckless disregard for the truth. Employers are also liable for defamation where there is "express malice," under the common law rule where the defamatory statements are made solely from spite or ill will. The plaintiffs have a heavy burden of proof and must prove their case by clear and convincing evidence.

Where employers obtain the applicant's written consent to obtain references and release from liability of the persons providing the reference, such a written release may lead to a more complete and candid reference.

| **CASE 17.11** | GIBSON V. OVERNIGHT TRANSPORTATION CO.
 COURT OF APPEALS OF WISCONSIN, 671 N.W. 2D 388 (WIS. APP. 2003). |

[Overnite Transportation Co. (OTC) is a nationwide trucking company. James Gibson worked for OTC out of the Kaukauna, Wisconsin, terminal, a nonunion facility. Gibson began working for OTC in May 1999. In October 1999, the Teamsters went on strike and established a picket line at OTC's Milwaukee terminal, a union facility. Due to the strike, the Milwaukee terminal was essentially shut down. OTC therefore ran some of the Milwaukee freight through Kaukauna. Because Gibson had previously worked in Milwaukee and was

familiar with the area, he was temporarily assigned to pick up freight at the Milwaukee facility. When he was there, Teamster supporters harassed him. Gibson decided to resign from Overnite, telling Tim Behling, the terminal manager in Kaukauna, that he had to quit immediately to help his ailing grandfather's company. In fact, Gibson went to work for another trucking company, USF Holland, the next day. Gibson testified at trial that he lied because he was afraid Behling would retaliate against him for quitting to avoid confrontation with the

continued

Teamsters in Milwaukee and for going to work for a union company. He started at USF Holland as a probationary employee. In January 2000, USF Holland hired Robert Arden & Associates to check Gibson's background. An Arden representative called Behling for an employment reference. The report Arden generated indicated that Behling made the following comments regarding Gibson: "He was way below average. He needed to improve his work ethic and attitude." "He was late most of the time and he missed anywhere from two to three days a week." "He had a real problem with authority." "He has a very negative attitude." "He's everybody's best friend—so he thinks. He did get along with some people, but most saw through him." "His paperwork was fair. It needed help like you wouldn't believe." Behling also indicated that Gibson's trustworthiness was "borderline" and that he would "never" rehire Gibson. OTC was the only one of Gibson's former employers to give a negative report to Arden. Based on the report, USF Holland terminated Gibson's employment and Gibson sued for defamation. Gibson testified that people in the trucking industry were aware of Arden's report, and as a result, it took a year and a half to find another job. The jury found that Behling's statements were defamatory and it awarded him $33,000 in compensatory damages and $250,000 in punitive damages. The court entered judgment on the jury's verdict and OTC appealed.]

PETERSON, J....

An employer has a conditional privilege under WIS. STAT. § 895.487 to make statements about a former employee. Overnite argues that, to abuse the privilege, statements must be made with actual malice, that is, with knowledge of falsity or with reckless disregard for the truth. *Torgerson v. Journal/Sentinel. Inc.*, 210 Wis.2d 524, 528, 563 N.W.2d 472 (1997). Express malice, however, requires only a showing of ill will, bad intent, envy, spite, hatred, revenge, or other bad motives against the person defamed. *Polzin v. Helmbrecht*, 54 Wis.2d 578, 587–88, 196 N.W.2d 685 (1972). Because the jury found express malice, and not actual malice, Overnite contends it cannot be held liable....

An employer who, on the request of an employee or a prospective employer of the employee, provides a reference to that prospective employer is presumed to be acting in good faith and, unless lack of good faith is shown by clear and convincing evidence, is immune from all civil liability that may result from providing that reference. The presumption of good faith under this subsection may be rebutted only upon a showing by clear and convincing evidence that the employer knowingly provided false information in the reference or *that the employer made the reference maliciously*. ... (Emphasis added.)

The statute is silent as to whether actual or express malice is required.

... At the time the statute was enacted, the common law simply required express malice to rebut the conditional privilege.... ("The proper test to apply to determine whether the nonconstitutional conditional privilege was abused is a question of express malice. This is what is termed 'common law malice,' by the United States Supreme Court." (Citation omitted.)). The Legislative Reference Bureau encouraged the legislature to specifically require express malice in the statute as well in order to clarify the standard. However, the legislature made no change.

Overnite interprets the legislature's failure to make the suggested change to mean it intended the standard to be actual malice. Gibson's interpretation is that the legislature intended to retain the common law standard of express malice. We agree with Gibson.

WISCONSIN STAT. § 895.487(2) provides [the] ways in which the presumption of good faith may be rebutted: (1) "the employer knowingly provided false information in the reference," [or] (2) "the employer made the reference maliciously," ... The first option could arguably require actual malice because it requires that the employer act "knowingly." ... The second option simply requires malice. The legislature was alerted to the ambiguity of the word "maliciously" but did not make any change. Common law prevails in Wisconsin until changed by statute. To abrogate the common law, the intent of the legislature must be clearly expressed, either in specific language or in a manner that leaves no reasonable doubt of the legislature's purpose. We therefore conclude that the legislature intended to keep the same standard of malice as existed in the common law—express malice.

Our conclusion is further supported by the jury instructions. Like WIS. STAT § 895.487(2), WIS JI—CIVIL 2507 lists ways in which the jury can find that an employer abused its privilege to make statements about former employees. First, the jury may find that the defendant made the statements knowing that they were false or in reckless disregard as to the truth or falsity of them. This is actual malice. However, the jury may also find defamation where the defendant

continued

made statements solely from spite or ill will. This is express malice, which is what the jury found here. Actual malice is not required....

[*Affirmed.*]

Case Questions

1. Are employers who provide references to prospective employees presumed to be acting in good faith unless a lack of good faith is shown by clear and convincing evidence?

2. What is the difference between "actual malice" and "express malice"? Was the employer liable for defamation in this case even though the jury found express malice and not actual malice?

CHAPTER QUESTIONS AND PROBLEMS

1. Why does the law differ between public sector employers and private sector employers in their testing of employees for drug use?

2. Local 1 of the Association of Western Pulp and Paper Workers was the bargaining representative for employees at Boise-Cascade Corporation's paper mill in St. Helen's, Oregon. Workers at the mill worked with heavy equipment, pressurized vessels, and hazardous chemicals. As a result, injuries were common.

   The labor agreement in effect between Local 1 and Boise-Cascade allowed the company unilaterally to introduce work rules that were consistent with the agreement. The union could challenge the reasonableness of a rule through grievance arbitration. In an effort to combat on-the-job injuries, Boise-Cascade unilaterally implemented a drug and alcohol testing program. The company announced that the testing program would apply to employees suspected by their supervisor of being under the influence of drugs or alcohol, employees who suffered on-the-job injuries that required more than first aid, and all employees involved in accidents at the mill. A positive result could result in discipline or discharge. In addition, refusal to submit to a test under the circumstances outlined above would result in discipline.

   The union objected to the drug and alcohol testing program as "illegal" and "unconstitutional." The union has asked you for advice on how to challenge the testing program.

   Should the union bring the issue to arbitration? The NLRB? The courts? Advise the union and explain. [*Paper Workers v. Boise-Cascade Corp.*, 1 ITER Cases 1072 (D. Ore.)]

3. The Nebraska Public Power District (NPPD) operated the Cooper Nuclear Station and instituted a "fitness for duty" program that required all employees who had access to protected areas at the Cooper plant to undergo random annual urine tests for drugs.

   The employees challenged the testing program on the grounds that it was contrary to the Fourth Amendment's ban on unreasonable searches and seizures as there was no individualized suspicion. They also argued that through tampering or mistakes in the testing process, employees could be wrongly accused of drug use.

   The NPPD stated that its testing program was "reasonable" and that its "chain of custody" rules and confirmatory tests protected employees from mistakes in the test results. Decide. [*Rushton v. Nebraska Public Power District*, 653 F. Supp. 1513 (D. Neb)]

4. Prior to 1988, Marguerite Cook and other former employees of Rite Aid of Maryland, Inc., were directed to submit to polygraph examinations regarding inventory shortages or "shrinkage" at certain Rite Aid stores. Cook and others refused to take the examination. After her refusal, Cook had her hours cut, had her store keys taken away, and was transferred to a distant store.

When Cook refused to comply with the transfer and schedule changes, she was terminated for refusing the directives of management. The state polygraph statute prohibits employers from requiring individuals or employees to take polygraph examinations and authorizes the attorney general to bring suit on behalf of "any aggrieved applicant for employment."

Cook brought a common law tort action for "discharge contrary to public policy" against Rite Aid, seeking compensatory and punitive damages from Rite Aid. Cook contended that Rite Aid improperly challenged her trustworthiness by ordering her to take a polygraph test and then aggravated the injury by attempting to force her to resign by giving her undesirable work hours at an undesirable work location. She stated that when she refused the new assignment, she was wrongfully discharged.

Rite Aid contended that the common law action must be dismissed because the polygraph statute includes a civil remedy, and such is Cook's exclusive remedy. Rite Aid contended that while the polygraph statute prohibits the discharge of employees who refuse to take a polygraph test, it did not prohibit a transfer or a reduction in hours for an employee who refused to take such an examination. Rite Aid contended that it terminated Cook because she failed to follow a proper directive of management, which was its right, and that chaos would result if an employer were not allowed to terminate insubordinate employees.

Was Cook precluded from bringing a wrongful discharge case on her own rather than seeking a remedy under the polygraph statute? Will the EPPA of 1988 preclude similar public policy wrongful discharge actions? Did the employer have a right to terminate Cook for failure to comply with the assignment and hours given to her? Decide. [*Moniodis v. Cook*, 64 Md. App. 1]

5. Ms. Gay, a nurse's aide at the William Hill Manor Nursing Home, was discharged by her employer for placing a pillow on a resident's face to keep her from shouting. Following her termination, she was escorted through the facility to her car by three managers. Gay filed a defamation claim alleging her reputation was severely harmed by being publicly escorted out of the home. She also contended that a report submitted to the state unemployment agency, which gave "physical mistreatment of a resident" as the reason for termination, was defamatory publication that fell outside the scope of the home's qualified privilege.

Was defamatory information about Gay disseminated to employees and patients by the fact that three supervisors had escorted her to her car? If it is established that Gay had applied minimum pressure to the resident to stop her from shouting and disrupting the peace and quiet of the home, will she succeed in her defamation suit based on the employer's published reason for termination of "physical mistreatment of a resident?" Decide. [*Gay v. William Hill Manor, Inc.*, 3 IER Cases 744]

6. From June 25, 1982, to February 5, 1987, Brent Jennings was employed as a police officer/dispatcher for the city of Warrensville Heights. As a dispatcher, Jennings was required to answer incoming phone calls requesting police or fire department assistance and to dispatch the proper persons to meet those requests. On February 5, 1987, Jennings was called into the office of Warrensville Heights Police Chief Craig Merchant. Merchant was concerned about Jennings's involvement in "some drug incident in another community." In October 1986, Jennings had been arrested by Highland Heights police after he was found with two friends in a restroom stall at a theater, with cocaine and marijuana in the stall's toilet bowl. Jennings stated that he was not formally charged in the incident and that the record of his arrest in the incident was eventually expunged. At the meeting on February 5, Jennings gave Merchant his

account of the incident. However, Merchant was not satisfied, particularly in light of Jennings's admissions during a preemployment polygraph test that he had previously used marijuana. Merchant testified that he told Jennings it was necessary for Jennings to take a polygraph test to confirm his account and to make certain he was not involved in the drug incident. Jennings testified that he knew the sole purpose of the polygraph test was to determine whether he had been involved with any drugs. Merchant told Jennings that he was not "after any criminal prosecution" and that the results of the polygraph test would not be used in any criminal proceeding. He also told Jennings that he must take the polygraph test or otherwise be discharged. Jennings refused to take the polygraph test. To avoid being discharged, Jennings submitted his resignation. Jennings later submitted an application for unemployment compensation. Under state law, individuals can be denied unemployment benefits if terminated for "just cause in connection with their work." A department rule prohibited any member from illegally taking, possessing, or using any controlled substances both on and off duty. Jennings argued that polygraph tests are unreliable and thus a refusal to take one cannot serve as a basis for a "just-cause" discharge. Moreover, the conduct being questioned was off-duty, not work-related, conduct. The city responded that a police dispatcher is the "hub" of the department, and an impaired dispatcher could undermine the public safety. It states that polygraph tests, while not admissible in evidence at court, can be a useful internal investigative device; and failure to take the test was insubordination.

Decide, answering the contentions of the parties. [*City of Warrensville Heights v. Jennings,* 569 N.E.2d 489 (Ohio)]

7. John Doe, an employee at a Veterans Administration hospital, saw VA physician Dr. Hall as a patient at the hospital's Employee Health Center (EHC) on two occasions. On September 30, 2002, Doe saw Dr. Hall for chills and mentioned his HIV infection and Dr. Hall recorded that information in John Doe's file. At a February 3, 2003 visit, Doe again mentioned to Dr. Hall his HIV status and revealed that he smoked marijuana to increase his appetite. Dr. Hall made a note of the information, which was recorded in Doe's medical file. On February 26, 2003, a meeting had been set up by Doe's supervisor with Dr. Hall to try to address any medical problems that might be contributing to Doe's poor attendance record. Doe felt apprehensive about the meeting and asked his union representative, George Rankin, to attend with him. Rankin arrived at Dr. Hall's office shortly after the doctor, and Doe began to talk. Doe does not dispute that he invited Rankin into the room, but he claims he first told Dr. Hall not to reveal any of his medical information to Rankin. Dr. Hall denies that Doe told him that, and during the meeting, Dr. Hall mentioned Doe's HIV positive status and his use of marijuana. Doe became upset, objected to the comments, and left the room with Rankin. Doe sued the VA and Dr. Hall for improperly revealing private medical and personal information to Rankin in violation of the Privacy Act. Doe asserts that revealing information as was done in this case chills dialogue between doctors and patients and leads to irrational results. The VA argues that no disclosure forbidden under the Privacy Act occurred. Decide. [*Doe v. Department of Veterans Affairs,* 519 F.3d 456 (8th Cir. 2008)]

8. Louis Pettus was employed by the DuPont Company for some 22 years. He sought time off from work under the company's short-term disability leave policy due to work-related stress. As required by the company policy, in order to qualify for the leave, Pettus had to submit to a DuPont-selected doctor to confirm the necessity for the leave. This company-selected doctor recommended that Pettus be evaluated by a psychiatrist,

Dr. Cole; and Dr. Cole recommended that Pettus see a chemical dependency specialist, Dr. Unger. Drs. Cole and Unger submitted reports to DuPont stating that Pettus's stress condition might be caused by misuse of alcohol. Dr. Cole telephoned Pettus's supervisor after his evaluation of Pettus, and Dr. Unger prepared a written report that was sent to DuPont's employee relations manager containing information about Pettus's family and work histories, his drinking habit, and his emotional condition. When Pettus refused to enter a 30-day inpatient alcohol rehabilitation program, DuPont terminated him. Pettus sued DuPont and the doctors for violation of California's Confidentiality of Medical Information Act. He believed that the doctors would only report their medical conclusions on whether or not he was entitled to the unpaid short-term leave, as he did not authorize the doctors to disclose full details. The company believes that it acted in good faith and for Mr. Pettus's own good and for the safety of coworkers by providing and paying for a full medical evaluation of his problems. The company asserts that once the alcohol problem was ascertained, its insistence that it be corrected before the company could safely allow him to return to work was a sound business judgment. Decide. [*Pettus v. Cole*, 57 Cal. Rptr. 2d 46]

9. Michael Smyth was an operations manager at the Pillsbury Company, and his employment status was that of an employee at will. Smyth received certain e-mail messages at home, and he replied to his supervisor by e-mail. His e-mail messages contained some provocative language, including a reference to "kill the backstabbing bastards" and a reference to an upcoming company party as the "Jim Jones Koolaid affair." Later Smyth was given two weeks' notice of his termination, and he was told that his e-mail remarks were inappropriate and unprofessional. Smyth believes that he is the victim of invasion of privacy because the e-mail

messages caused his termination and the company had promised that e-mail communications would not be intercepted and used as a basis for discipline or discharge. The company denies that it intercepted the e-mail messages and points out that Smyth himself sent the unprofessional comments to his supervisor. Is Smyth entitled to reinstatement and back pay because of the invasion of privacy? Decide. [*Smyth v. Pillsbury Co.*, 914 F. Supp. 97 (E.D.Pa.)]

10. Walter Finley is an engineer employed at Generic Engineering Corporation. Randomly teamed with Erin Cronin in a company golf tournament, the two exchanged stories about each other's department and work. Erin works for the information technology manager, Arch Woodside, and she told Walter of his monitoring activities of employee computer use. Erin said, "He doesn't apologize for it. He tells people, 'You live in a democracy; you don't work in one.' He uses web surveillance software that churns out reports identifying the busiest web sites and all kinds of other data." "That's nuts," Walter exclaimed as Erin finished her discourse on her boss. "They can't do that!" Erin replied, "Now don't get upset. The company has a policy restricting personal use of the Web to lunchtime or before or after work, and the policy states that the company has the ability to monitor *all* Internet usage." Walter was upset. "I use ETrade and BigCharts.com all the time. That's *my* business, not the company's. They had better not have invaded my privacy ... the bastards." Erin replied soothingly, "The company has called up data logs on ETrade activity of engineers, but they have not taken any action." Walter objected, "That's wiretapping and an invasion of my privacy–intrusion on seclusion, it's called. I may sue the bastards."

Advise Walter as to his rights, if any, against Woodside and the company to bring an action under the Electronic Communications

Privacy Act and the common law tort theory of invasion of privacy by intrusion on seclusion. (See M. J. McCarthy, "Websurfers Beware: The Company Tech May Be a Secret Agent," *Wall Street Journal*, Jan. 10, 2000, pp. 1-A12.)

11. Officers John Bohach and Jon Catalono of the Reno, Nevada, Police Department communicated with each other on the Alphapage computer system, typing messages on a keyboard and sending them to each other by use of a "send" key. The computer dials a commercial paging company that receives the message by modem, and the message is sent to the pager by radio broadcast. When the system was installed, the police chief warned that every Alphapage message is logged on the network. The chief barred messages critical of department policy and messages that were discriminatory in nature. The two police officers sought to block a department investigation into their messages and to prevent disclosure of the content of the messages. The officers claimed the messages should be treated the same as telephone calls under federal wiretap laws. The department contended that the system is essentially a form of e-mail, whose messages are, by definition, stored in a computer, and the storage itself is not part of the communication. Were the federal wiretap laws violated? Decide. [*Bohach v. City of Reno*, 932 F. Supp. 1772 (D. Nev.)]

WAGE AND HOUR LAW— PLANT CLOSINGS AND UNEMPLOYMENT—FOREIGN WORKERS

SECTION 148: DEVELOPING LAW REGULATING WAGES AND HOURS

On January 3, 1938, President Franklin Roosevelt declared in his annual message to Congress:

> The people of this country by an overwhelming vote are in favor of having Congress—this Congress—put a floor below which individual wages shall not fall, and a ceiling beyond which the hours of individual labor shall not rise.

Within six months of the president's message, Congress passed a federal wage and hour law called the Fair Labor Standards Act (FLSA). It was signed into law on June 25, 1938.[1] The FLSA has three broad objectives:

1. The establishment of minimum wages, a floor that would provide a basic minimum standard of living for workers under which wages would not fall.[2]
2. The encouragement of a ceiling on the number of hours of labor for individual workers in a workweek, the ultimate purpose of which was to put financial pressure on employers to spread employment opportunities and hire additional workers to avoid the extra pay required for overtime hours (time worked in excess of 40 hours per week).[3]
3. The discouragement of "oppressive child labor."[4]

COVERAGE AND EXEMPTIONS

Workers at enterprises engaged in interstate commerce are covered by the FLSA. Moreover, the Act has been amended to cover domestic service workers, including day workers such as housekeepers, chauffeurs, cooks, and full-time babysitters. The FLSA applies to most federal employees as well as to state and local government workers.[5]

Workers exempt from both the minimum wage and overtime provisions of the law include executive, administrative, and professional employees and outside salespersons. Also exempt are employees of certain small farmers and casual babysitters.

Certain highly paid commissioned employees of retail and service businesses are exempt from the overtime pay provision, as are farm workers and domestic service workers residing in their employer's homes.

The Wage and Hour Division (Wage-Hour Office) of the U.S. Department of Labor (DOL) administers and enforces the FLSA. Detailed information about coverage and exemptions is beyond the scope of this section but is available at local Wage-Hour Offices.

The *Singh v. Jutla* decision, presented in this section, shows the far-reaching scope of coverage of the FLSA. It upheld an undocumented alien's right to sue an employer for certain violations of the FLSA.

SUBMINIMUM WAGE PROVISIONS

The FLSA provides for the employment of certain individuals at wage rates below the statutory minimum, including full-time students at institutions of higher education. Under the 1996 amendments to the FLSA, a special youth subminimum wage can be paid to employees under 20 years of age for their first 90 consecutive calendar days of employment with an employer.

---

[1] Pub. L. 718, 75th Cong., 52 Stat. 1060.

[2] The federal minimum wage as of July 1, 2009, is $7.25 per hour.

[3] See § 7(a) of the FLSA and *Overnight Motor Transportation Co. v. Missel*, 316 U.S. 572 (1942).

[4] See § 12(a) of the FLSA.

[5] See *Garcia v. San Antonio Metropolitan Transit Authority*, 469 U.S. 528 (1985); see also *Alden v. Maine*, 527 U.S. 706 (1999).

Individuals whose productive capacity is impaired by age or physical or mental deficiency or injury may also be employed at less than the minimum wage in order to prevent the curtailment of work opportunities for these individuals. However, such employment is permitted only under certificates issued by the appropriate Wage-Hour Office. Compliance officers closely scrutinize practices in regard to the issuance and reissuance of certificates allowing subminimum wages.

BASIC WAGE STANDARDS

Wages required by the FLSA are due on the regular payday for the period covered. Deductions made from wages for such items as cash or merchandise shortages, employer-required uniforms, and tools of a trade are not legal if they reduce wages below the minimum wage or reduce the amount of overtime pay due under the FLSA. Moreover, should an employer require employees to provide uniforms or tools on their own, it is also a violation of the law to the extent that they reduce wages below the minimum wage. Thus, nursing homes that require their nurse's aides to wear white dresses or white pantsuits to work each day but pay these individuals the minimum wage are in violation of the FLSA. The employer nursing homes must, in addition to the minimum wage, compensate these employees for the value of such uniforms. Likewise, an employer may not deduct from the wages of migrant farm workers from Mexico working on H-2A immigration visas the costs of "facilities" that primarily benefit the employer if such deductions drive wages below the minimum wage rate. Thus, employers must reimburse the workers up to the level of meeting the minimum wage rate for visa costs, visa applications, and immigration fees.[6] In *Rivera v. Brickman Group, Ltd.*, presented in this section, costs paid by H-2B workers brought them below the FLSA minimum wage.

Job-related training generally is compensable under the FLSA. However, an exception exists for voluntary training not directly related to an employee's job where the employee does not perform productive work. For example, Hogar, Inc., operates a nursing home and required new employees to undergo two days of unpaid training before assuming paid duties as nurses' aids, maintenance/laundry workers, and kitchen workers. Little or no instruction was offered to these "trainees," and each individual would perform the regular duties of the position for the two-day period. Hogar's practices did not fall within the training exception since the trainees performed productive work with little or no actual training during a regular shift. In a lawsuit brought by the Secretary of Labor, Hogar was ordered by the court to pay 14 hours' pay (two days' pay) for each employee so "trained," plus liquidated damages of an additional 14 hours' pay.[7]

OVERTIME PAY

Overtime must be paid at a rate of at least 1½ times the employee's regular rate of pay for each hour worked in a workweek in excess of 40 hours. Thus, an employee whose regular rate of pay is $10 per hour and who works 44 hours in a workweek

---

[6] *Arriaga v. Florida Pacific Farming, LLC*, 305 F.3d 1228 (11th Cir. 2002).

[7] *Herman v. Hogar Praderas De Amor, Inc.*, 130 F. Supp. 2d 257 (S.D.P.R. 2001).

is entitled to $400 for the first 40 hours plus $15 for each of the four hours over 40—the overtime hours—for a total of $460 pay for the workweek.

The Wage and Hour Division provides regulations for employers to guide them in the calculation of overtime for piecework and salaried workers. Special occasion and discretionary bonuses and profit-sharing plans are excluded from the calculation of each covered worker's regular rate of pay. Performance bonuses, however, must be considered part of an employee's regular rate of pay for purposes of calculating overtime pay.

EXEMPTIONS. New DOL regulations, referred to as the "White Collar" exemptions from the overtime requirements of the FLSA, took effect on August 23, 2004.[8] Generally, executive, administrative, professional, outside sales, computer professionals, and certain "highly compensated employees" are exempt from the overtime requirements if they meet the "tests" set forth in the new regulations.[9]

Under the "salary level test," regardless of duties, including executive, administrative, and certain professional duties, employees earning less than $455 per week will not be exempt from the overtime requirements, nor will computer professionals earning less than $27.63 per hour be exempt. Highly compensated employees are exempt under the new regulations if they earn total compensation of $100,000 or more per year, provided the individual receives at least $455 per week on a salary or fee basis and customarily and regularly perform any one or more exempt duties and perform office or non-manual work. Thus, a highly skilled mechanic earning $55 per hour and over $100,000 per year would not be exempt from the overtime provisions because of not performing office or non-manual work or not performing one or more exempt duties, either executive or administrative. The $455 minimum salary level requirement does not apply to the exemption of teachers, lawyers, or physicians from the overtime requirement, nor is there a minimum salary requirement for the outside sales exemption.

The regulations set forth "duties tests" for executive, administrative, or professional exemptions. "Executive employees" in their duties must customarily and regularly direct work of two or more other employees and have authority to hire or fire other employees or their recommendations on personnel issues are given particular weight.[10] An administrative employee's primary duty must be the performance of office or non-manual work directly related to "management or general business operations," and the primary duty must include the exercise of discretion and

---

[8] The Secretary of Labor's new regulations are set forth in 29 C.F.R. Part 541. The U.S. Department of Labor's fact sheets on the new rule are available at http://www.dol.gov/era/regs/compliance/whd/fairpay/main.htm.

[9] Employees working in executive, administrative, or professional capacities are exempt from the requirements of being paid time and one half of their regular rate of pay for all hours worked in excess of 40 hours, 29 U.S.C. § 207(a)(1). The employer has the burden of proof to establish that its employees are exempt.

[10] In *Williams v. Staples*, Cal. Super. Ct., 214 DLR A-1, (Nov. 6, 2007), the parties settled overtime claims for California-based Staples assistant managers under state law for $38 million. The assistant managers had argued that they were misclassified as exempt executive employees even though they spent most of their time performing nonexempt work such as stacking shelves and waiting on customers and had limited discretion and limited independent judgment.

independent judgment with respect to "matters of significance." Examples of exempt administrative employees include human resources managers, insurance claims adjusters and purchasing agents.

Tests exist for "learned professionals" and "creative professionals." Learned professionals, who have advanced knowledge in a field of science or learning customarily acquired by a prolonged course of specialized intellectual instruction, include registered nurses (but not licensed practical nurses), accountants, funeral directors, and certain athletic trainers.[11] Paralegals generally do not qualify as learned professionals. Creative or artistic professionals are individuals whose work requires invention, originality, or talent in a recognized field of artistic or creative endeavor. An example is found in the *Freeman v. NBC Inc.*[12] case. In the *Freeman* case, Jacob Freeman was the domestic newswriter for *NBC Nightly News with Tom Brokaw.* He wrote headlines, teasers, transitions, voice-overs, lead-ins, and stories to be read by the news anchor and was one of only two newswriters assigned to *Nightly News.* Under a collective bargaining agreement, NBC paid him overtime at 1½ times his hourly rate for time worked in excess of 40 hours. Under the FLSA, overtime pay is based on one's hourly rate and fees paid per hour. Freeman and others sued NBC for the difference in overtime pay calculated by inclusion of fees in the rate. NBC responded that Congress had expressly exempted persons employed in a "professional" capacity from the FLSA's overtime provisions. The Second Circuit Court of Appeals rejected the application of the Department of Labor's guidelines that the reporting of news must be considered nonexempt work and concluded that Freeman and certain others at NBC who hold some of the most coveted jobs in broadcast journalism were "artistic professionals," exempt from the FLSA's overtime provisions.

In *Auer v. Robbins,*[13] the Supreme Court upheld the Secretary of Labor's determination that certain police sergeants and a lieutenant were not entitled to overtime pay because they were within the "executive, administrative or professional" employees' exemption from the overtime provisions.

Details on "salary level tests" are beyond the scope of this section and are available at local DOL Wage-Hour offices.

SELECTED PAY FOR "WORK" ISSUES

When does an employee's working time begin for compensation purposes and what pay, if any, is an employee entitled to when "on call" are two of the many pay-for-work issues addressed by the DOL's Wage-Hour Office and ultimately the courts.

---

[11] In *DeJesús-Rentas v. Baxter Pharmacy Services Corp.*, 400 F.3d 72 (1st Cir. 2005), Eilliam DeJesús-Rentas and four other licensed pharmacists challenged their employer's determination not to pay them overtime because it believed they were exempt professionals. On appeal from a summary judgment for the employer, the court of appeals held that their duties required "consistent exercise of discretion and judgment," thus establishing exempt status. Under the new regulations, 29 C.F.R. § 541. 300, the "consistently exercise discretion and judgment" language has been eliminated.

[12] 3 WH2d 289 (2d Cir. 1996).

[13] 519 U.S. 452 (1997).

Under the Portal-to-Portal Act of 1947,[14] which amended the FSLA, preliminary activities of employees that take place before an employee begins or after the employee completes the "principal activities" for which the employee was hired are not to be included in "working time" for compensation purposes unless required by a collective bargaining contract or by past practice. Examples of nonproductive activities for which no pay is due under the FLSA are walking from the plant gate to the work site and changing clothes for the employees' convenience. In *Singh v. City of New York*,[15] the city's fire inspectors were required to carry 15 to 20 pounds of files with them every week as they traveled to and from work and around the city. The inspectors testified that carrying a heavy briefcase slowed them down during commutes and that at the end of the workday, they had to travel directly to their homes to secure the files. The court noted that commuting time has generally been considered noncompensable. It held that carrying a briefcase during a commute without any other employment-related activity does not transform the entire commute into work for purposes of the FLSA.

In *IBP, Inc. v. Alvarez*,[16] the U.S. Supreme Court was called upon to decide when production workers engaged in the meatpacking industry start their workday for pay purposes under the FLSA, as amended by the Portal-to-Portal Act. Production workers in this industry commonly wear a variety of protective equipment for their hands, arms, torsos, and legs, along with protective outer garments and other gear. The Court decided that donning and doffing of clothing and equipment required by the companies or government regulation, as opposed to clothing an employee chooses to wear, are an integral part of the employee's work and a "principal activity" and are thus not excluded from FLSA compensation under the Portal-to-Portal Act as "preliminary or postliminary activities." And relying upon the DOL's "continuous workday rule,"[17] the Court determined that the time spent walking to and from the production floor, as well as the time spent waiting to doff, is compensable time under the FLSA. The Court, however, rejected the employees' contention that they should be paid for the time spent waiting in line to obtain the protective equipment prior to donning the first piece of gear that marks the beginning of the "continuous workday," classifying this as a preliminary activity.

In the Supreme Court's *Armour & Co. v. Wantock* case, decided soon after the FLSA became law, the Court broadly determined that "exertion" was not a necessary activity to constitute "work" and that "an employer, if he chooses, may hire a man to do nothing or do nothing but wait for something to happen."[18] Pay for time "on call" is a current issue before the courts under a broad definition of the term **work**. In the *Dinges v. Sacred Heart St. Mary's Hospitals* decision, presented in this section, the Seventh Circuit Court of Appeals applied a "what can the employee do during the on-call period" test in deciding whether hours spent on call should be treated as work under the FLSA. The court determined that the on-call

---

[14] 29 U.S.C. §§ 251-263 (1947).

[15] 524 F.3d 361 (2d Cir. 2008).

[16] 126 S.Ct. 514 (2005).

[17] 29 C.F.R. 790.6(a) (2005); see also *Andrako v. U.S. Steel Corp.*, 2008 WL 2020176 (W.D.Pa. 2008).

[18] 323 U.S. 126, 133 (1944).

hours for two emergency medical technicians (EMTs) were not work under the Act because they could devote this time to ordinary activities of everyday life.

CHILD LABOR PROVISIONS

The FLSA child labor provisions are designed to protect the educational opportunities of minors and prohibit their employment in occupations detrimental to their health and well-being. The FLSA restricts hours of work for minors under 16 and lists hazardous occupations too dangerous for minors to perform.

RECORDKEEPING

Employers are required by the Act to keep records on wages and hours for each employee for three years from the date of last entry.[19] Should an employer have to defend a wage or overtime suit under the FLSA, adequate records are essential for the employer's defense.

ENFORCEMENT

Enforcement of the FLSA is carried out by wage-hour compliance officers. Wage-hour officers may supervise the recovery and payment of back wages. Either the Secretary of Labor or an employee may file suit for back wages plus an equal amount as liquidated damages against employers who violate the FLSA. A two-year statute of limitations applies to the recovery of back pay except in the case of willful violations, in which a three-year statute applies.

In *McLaughlin v. Richland Shoe Co.*,[20] the Supreme Court held that a violation of the FLSA is "willful" for purposes of triggering the three-year statute of limitations if the employer knew or showed reckless disregard for whether the employer's conduct was prohibited by the FLSA.

CASE 18.1	SINGH V. JUTLA & C.D. & R'S OIL, INC.
	U.S. DISTRICT COURT, 214 F. SUPP. 2D 1056 (N.D. CAL. 2002).

[Macan Singh was recruited by the defendant Jutla to come work for him in the United States. Jutla promised that he would have him a place to live and tuition for education and that he would eventually become Jutla's business partner in his corporation, C.D. & R's Oil, Inc. Singh worked for Jutla in the United States illegally from approximately May 1995 to February 1998 and received no pay. On January 6, 1999, Singh filed a wage claim against the defendant. He sought unpaid wages and overtime pay for work actually performed. Thereafter, Jutla

threatened to report him to the INS, but Singh refused to submit to Jutla. The Labor Commissioner awarded Singh $69,633.73 and Jutla appealed. Ultimately, on May 3, 2001, Jutla agreed to make the payments to Singh. The following day, May 4, 2001, the INS arrested and detained Singh, and he remained in INS custody for 14 months. He alleged that defendant Jutla contacted the INS and provided them with information on his status in an act of retaliation. On March 7, 2002, Singh filed a complaint with the district court against defendant for

continued

---

[19] § 11(c) of the FLSA and regulations 29 C.F.R., ch. V, § 516.5.
[20] 486 U.S. 128 (1988).

retaliation under the FLSA, requesting declaratory, injunctive, and monetary relief. Jutla filed a motion to dismiss, claiming under the Supreme Court's *Hoffman Plastic Compounds, Inc. v. NLRB* decision that plaintiff had no cause of action.]

BREYER, D. J....

The FLSA's anti-retaliation provision

The FLSA's anti-retaliation provision, 29 U.S.C. § 215(a)(3), provides that it shall be unlawful for "any person" to "discharge or in any other manner discriminate against any employee because such employee has filed any compliant or instituted or caused to be instituted any proceeding under or related to this Act ..."

... The most common retaliatory act is discharge, however certain post-employment misconduct has also been found to violate section 215(a)(3). Post-employment misconduct that has been found to violate the anti-retaliation provision includes: informing a prospective employer that an employee had filed a complaint with the Department of Labor ("DOL"), *Dunlop v. Carriage Carpet Co.*, 548 F.2d 139 (6th Cir. 1977); interfering with a former employee's subsequent employment opportunities by speaking to the landlord of the new employer, *Bonham v. Copper Cellar Corp.*, 476 F.Supp. 98 (E.D. Tenn. 1979)....

Defendant in this case was not just a knowing employer, but allegedly, actively recruited plaintiff to come to work in the United States. Defendants continued to employ him for approximately three years, throughout which they were aware of his illegal status.

Plaintiff is not seeking back pay

Hoffman [Plastic Compounds, Inc. v. NLRB, 122 S. Ct. 1275 (2002)] eliminated back pay as a remedy available to undocumented workers, thus the decision precludes illegal aliens from a very specific remedy. "*Hoffman* does not establish that an award of unpaid wages to undocumented workers for work actually performed runs counter to IRCA." *Flores v. Albertsons, Inc.*, 2002 WL 1163623 (C.D.Cal.2002). [FN3]

Including undocumented workers in the FLSA's coverage is consistent with immigration policy.

Allowing an undocumented worker to bring an anti-retaliation claim under the FLSA is consistent with the immigration policies underlying the IRCA. Congress enacted the FLSA to eliminate substandard working conditions by requiring employers to pay their employees a statutorily prescribed minimum wage and prohibiting employers from requiring their employees to work more than forty hours per week unless the employees are compensated at one and one half times their regular hourly rate. *See* 29 U.S.C. § 202; § 206, and § 207(a)(1). Congress enacted the IRCA to reduce the illegal immigration not only to eliminate the economic incentive for illegal workers to come to this country, but also to eliminate employers' incentive to hire undocumented workers by imposing sanctions on employers who hire such workers. *See* U.S.C. § 1324a. Though the FLSA does not impose sanctions, it also discourages employers from hiring such workers because it eliminates employers' ability to pay them less than minimum wage or otherwise take advantage of their status. As the *Patel [v. Quality Inn South*, 846 F.2d 700 (11th Cir. 1988)] court noted, "[i]f the FLSA did not cover undocumented aliens, employers would have an incentive to hire them. Employers might find it economically advantageous to hire and underpay undocumented workers and run the risk of sanctions under the IRCA." 846 F.2d at 704. If the employers know they have to pay illegal aliens the same wage as legal workers, they are far less likely to hire an illegal worker and run the risk of subjecting themselves to sanctions under the IRCA. As a result, there are fewer employment opportunities and therefore fewer incentives to enter this country illegally.

Admittedly, similar arguments could be used to support the award of back pay, which was rejected in *Hoffman*. Indeed, every remedy extended to undocumented workers under the federal labor laws provides a marginal incentive for those workers to come to the United States. It is just as true, however, that every remedy denied to undocumented workers provides a marginal incentive for employers to hire those workers. The economic incentives are in tension. Given this tension, the courts must attempt to sensibly balance competing considerations. In this case, the balance tips sharply in favor of permitting this cause of action, and the remedies it seeks, to go forward. Prohibiting plaintiff from bringing this claim under the FLSA would provide a perverse economic incentive to employers to seek out and knowingly hire illegal workers, as defendant did here, in direct contravention of immigration laws. Though employers that succumbed to these incentives would run the

continued

risk of sanctions under the IRCA, that risk may be worth taking. National labor and immigration policy is most appropriately balanced by permitting this case to go forward.

Conclusion

Because this Court finds that plaintiff's action under the FLSA is not barred for the aforementioned reasons, defendant's motion to dismiss is *DENIED*.

Case Questions

1. Did the Court agree with Jutla's contention that the Supreme Court's *Hoffman Plastics* decision precluded the plaintiff from bringing the FLSA anti-retaliation lawsuit against it?
2. How does the FLSA coverage of undocumented workers go hand in hand with the policies behind the IRCA?
3. Explain the court's ruling in this case.

CASE 18.2	RIVERA V. BRICKMAN GROUP, LTD. UNITED STATES DISTRICT COURT, 2008 U.S. DIST. LEXIS 1167 (E.D. PA. 2008).

[Rivera and the other plaintiffs are citizens of Guatemala and Mexico who worked as seasonal landscapers for defendant the Brickman Group between 2003 and 2005. Brickman petitioned for and was granted temporary work visas for the plaintiffs under 8 U.S.C. § 1101 (a)(15) (H)(ii)(b) and 8 C.F.R. § 214.2(h)(6). That program (commonly known as the "H-2B program") allows U.S. employers to petition the Department of Labor for permission to employ nonagricultural foreign workers for periods of less than one year.

Although plaintiffs' cash wages appeared to comply with all applicable laws, plaintiffs claim that Brickman forced them to pay for employment-related costs out of pocket. These costs, they contend, operated as *de facto* deductions that reduced their real wages below the applicable minimum wage.]

POLLAK, J....

Having concluded that neither the INA nor the Portal-to-Portal Act has any bearing on this case, I turn to how the FLSA treats the three categories of expenses at issue here. The FLSA defines "wage" to include both cash wages and "the reasonable cost ... to the employer of furnishing such employee with board, lodging, or other facilities, if such board, lodging, or other facilities are customarily furnished by such employer to his employees." 29 U.S.C. § 203(m). In other words, when the employer pays for "board, lodging, or other facilities," it may add the costs of those facilities to the cash wage for purposes of complying with the FLSA minimum. The Department of Labor has stipulated that an employer may not count as "other facilities" goods or services that are "primarily

for the benefit or convenience of the employer," 29 C.F.R. § 531,3(d)(1), and, as a corollary, has provided that employers may not pass along to employees expenses for such goods or services, 29 C.F.R. § 531.35. If an employer does pass along such an expense, then the expense is deducted from the cash wage to determine compliance with the FLSA minimum....

1. Transportation costs

...Rivera emphasizes the fact that, unlike an employer generally advertising a job opening, Brickman specifically directed its recruiting efforts to workers in Mexico and Guatemala by (1) participating in the H-2B program, and (2) hiring third-party recruiters based in Mexico and Guatemala to hire potential workers. To participate in the H-2B program, Brickman had to demonstrate to the Department of Labor that it was unable to find a sufficient number of suitable workers in the United States. Rivera argues that, under circumstances like these, in which an employer specifically directs its recruiting to remote points-of-hire because it cannot find suitable labor in its area, transportation is an expense that primarily benefits the employer. Indeed, assuming that Brickman and the Department of Labor correctly determined that there were not enough suitable workers in the United States, Brickman would have been unable to staff its operations had it not participated in the H-2B program and hired foreign workers....

I conclude that, in the context of this case, the cost of transportation from remote points-of-hire is "primarily for the benefit of the employer." That means that it was

continued

not permissible for Brickman to pass along to plaintiffs the costs of travel between the points-of-hire in the workers' home countries and the Brickman worksites to the extent that doing so reduced the plaintiffs' wages below the FLSA minimum.

2. Visa-related costs

The visa-related costs at issue here are various fees associated with obtaining a valid H-2B work visa. The *Arriaga* court also considered this issue and concluded that because the visa costs arise directly and necessarily from the employer's decision to recruit guest workers, and because visa costs are not ordinary living expenses, the visa costs are primarily for the benefit of the employer. 305 F.3d at 1244....

Passport costs, however, are different. Unlike the cost of an employer-specific visa, which has but one use, a passport has more general use, and seems more like an ordinary living expense (similar to the cost of obtaining a non-commercial driver's license). Therefore, while I conclude that plaintiffs' expenses related to obtaining work visas were "primarily for the benefit of the employer," I exclude costs associated with obtaining passports of general use from that category.

3. Workers' representatives' fees

To recruit H-2B workers, Brickman hired third-party recruiters in Mexico and Guatemala to secure for them a suitable workforce. These recruiters found prospective employees by consulting firms that specialized in bringing together large cohorts of able-bodied workers and representing them in finding suitable foreign employment. These firms acted as the prospective workers' representatives in connecting the workers with Brickman. To prevent fraud, the government requires that H-2B employers designate which workers' representatives are authorized to represent their employees. According to Brickman's paperwork and responses to Rivera's statement of undisputed facts, Brickman authorized no more than one workers' representative per country in each year. Thus, it appears that prospective employees wishing to work for Brickman had little choice but to go through the Brickman-designated workers' representative.

These workers' representatives charged fees to Brickman's prospective employees, and plaintiffs argue that these fees were primarily for Brickman's benefit, as employees wishing to work for Brickman had no choice but to pay them. The *Arriaga* court rejected a similar argument on the ground that the employees had not shown that the designated recruiter was the employer's agent. *Arriaga*, 305 F.3d at 1244–45. In that case, however, there was no indication that going through a workers' representative was mandatory. Moreover, I do not believe that the law of agency affects the decision. It seems, rather, that if Brickman has structured the process in such a way that a prospective employee cannot but pay a recruiting fee in order to work for Brickman, then the cost of the recruiting fee is primarily for Brickman's benefit as a cost associated with Brickman's business decision to utilize an exclusive workers' representative. Agency law would seem as irrelevant here as it was to the questions of visa and transportation costs (in neither case did the lack of an agency relationship between the person to whom the expense was paid and the employer matter).

The real question is a factual one. If it was the case that a worker had to go through a Brickman-designated workers' representative in order to be employed, then it would seem that any costs associated with that process were incurred primarily for Brickman's benefit.... At the end of each season, Brickman handed out instructions to workers wishing to return the following season. In one iteration of those instructions, the following statement appeared:

> **IF YOU WANT TO RETURN TO YOUR JOB WITH BRICKMAN IN 2004 YOU WILL NEED TO CONTACT [Brickman's designated workers' representative] LLS. PLEASE FOLLOW THE INSTRUCTIONS PRINTED ON THE BACK OF THIS PAGE....**

... I conclude that fees associated with Brickman-designated workers' representatives are costs "primarily for the benefit of the employer," and that Brickman, therefore, was not allowed to pass those costs along to the extent that doing so reduced their wages below the FLSA minimum.

Conclusion

Plaintiffs have incurred a range of costs associated with becoming seasonal employees of the defendant Brickman Group. That these costs were incurred is not disputed. I have determined that plaintiffs' point-of-hire transportation costs, their visa costs, and the fees paid to workers' representatives, were primarily for Brickman's benefit. Under this interpretation of the FLSA, Brickman acknowledges that these costs reduced plaintiffs' wages below the FLSA minimum.

continued

As to these costs, partial summary judgment in plaintiffs' favor is warranted. Plaintiffs' passport costs, however, were not incurred primarily for Brickman's benefit, and so summary judgment in Brickman's favor on that issue is appropriate.

[*It is so ORDERED.*]

Case Questions

1. What is the purpose of the H-2B visa program?
2. May an employer pass along to employees expenses for goods and services that are "primarily for the benefit or convenience of the employer" and be in compliance with the FLSA minimum wage if the expenses reduce real wages below the minimum wage? Or must the employer deduct those expenses from the cash wage to determine compliance with the FLSA minimum?
3. Did the court find that out-of-the-ordinary expenses the employees incurred because of the business decisions of the employer, such as travel from remote points of hire, costs of passports and work visas, and fees paid to mandatory recruiters, should be deducted from cash wages to determine the FLSA wage rate?

| CASE 18.3 | DINGES V. SACRED HEART ST. MARY'S HOSPITALS, INC. |
| | U.S. COURT OF APPEALS, 164 F.3D 1056 (7TH CIR. 1999). |

[Sacred Heart St. Mary's Hospitals operate a hospital in rural Tomahawk, Wisconsin. The hospital's ambulance department has two emergency medical technicians (EMTs) in-house during the day, but after hours, the hospital relies on standby crews. Two EMTs serve as the "first-out" crew and two more as the "second-out" crew. An EMT on first-out status must arrive at the hospital within seven minutes of receiving a page. Members of the first-out crew receive $2.25 per hour of on-call time, plus pay at time-and-a-half for all hours devoted to handling a medical emergency. The hospital credits them with at least two hours' work for each emergency call even if they are back home in less time, as they usually are. Garret Dinges and Christine Foster asked for and were assigned first-out status. Now, in this suit, they contend that the rewards should have been even greater than those the hospital promised and delivered—that the entire 14- to 16-hour on-call period should be treated as working time, so it would produce 21 to 24 hours' wages even if they did not receive an emergency call. Both Dinges and Foster live within seven minutes' drive from the hospital; indeed, the entire city of Tomahawk is within the seven-minute radius, so they can and do pass the on-call time at home or at other activities in or near the city. Mr. Dinges and Ms. Foster can't travel outside Tomahawk. Each has spent holidays at home rather than with relatives and has been unable to attend weddings, family reunions, parties, and other events. While on call, Dinges cannot assist in operation of the family business, located 20 miles from the hospital. Hunting, fishing, boating, camping, and other recreational activities are restricted to what is possible near the hospital.

The hospital responds by emphasizing what EMTs can do during on-call hours: cook; eat; sleep; read; exercise; watch TV and movies; do housework; and care for pets, family, and loved ones at home. Many things in the vicinity of home also are compatible with first-out status. For example, Foster watches her children participate in sports, attends dance recitals, and goes to restaurants and parties. From a judgment for the hospital, the plaintiffs appealed.]

EASTERBROOK, C. J....

Working more than 40 hours per week draws premium pay under the Fair Labor Standards Act, 29 U.S.C. sec. 207. Should hours spent "on call" be treated as work? According to the Supreme Court, the answer depends on whether one has been "engaged to wait" or is "waiting to be engaged." Compare *Armour & Co. v. Wantock*, 323 U.S. 126 (1944), with *Skidmore v. Swift & Co.*, 323 U.S. 134 (1944). That evocative distinction rarely decides a concrete case; on-call time readily can be characterized either way. For most purposes it is best to ask what the employee can do during on-call periods. Can the time be devoted to the ordinary activities of private life? If so, it is not "work."

continued

Even a functional approach produces close calls, however; this is one.

An employee who is not required to remain on the employer's premises but is merely required to leave word at home or with company officials where he or she may be reached is not working while on call. Time spent at home on call may or may not be compensable depending on whether the restrictions placed on the employee preclude using the time for personal pursuits. Where, for example, a firefighter has returned home after the shift, with the understanding that he or she is expected to return to work in the event of an emergency in the night, such time spent at home is normally not compensable. On the other hand, where the conditions placed on the employee's activities are so restrictive that the employee cannot use the time effectively for personal pursuits, such time spent on call is compensable.

29 C.F.R. sec. 553.221 (d). See *Auer v. Robbins*, 117 S. Ct. 905 (1997) (courts should defer to the Secretary's definitions of terms). The regulatory question is whether the employee can "use the time effectively for personal pursuits"—not for all personal pursuits, but for many. But then there is that weasel word "effectively." An employee who can remain at home while on call, but is called away every few hours, can't use the time "effectively" for sleeping, and probably not for many other activities. Plaintiffs, however, experience less than a 50% chance that there will be any call in a 14- to 16-hour period, so their time may be used effectively for sleeping, eating, and many other activities at home and around Tomahawk. (Over 338 on-call periods, Dinges had 184 pass without a call. Thus Dinges responded to at least one call only 46% of the time. Foster's experience was similar.)...

... Although the FLSA overrides contracts, in close cases it makes sense to let private arrangements endure—for the less flexible statutory approach has the potential to make everyone worse off. Suppose we were to hold that time the EMTs spend on call counts as "work." That would produce a windfall for Dinges and Foster today, but it would lead the Hospital to modify its practices tomorrow. If the EMTs are "working" 24 hours a day, then the Hospital will abolish the on-call system and have EMTs on its premises 24 hours a day, likely hiring additional EMTs so that it can limit the premium pay for overtime. This is what St. Mary's already has done at its hospital in Rhinelander, Wisconsin. The Hospital will pay more in the process, but EMTs such as Dinges and Foster will receive less, spend more time at the Hospital (and less at home), or both. Ambulatory statutory and regulatory language permits labor and management to structure their regulations so that each side gains. That is what the Hospital has done in Tomahawk, and we do not think the FLSA compels a different arrangement.

Affirmed.

Case Questions

1. What test does the Secretary of Labor's regulations apply in determining whether on-call status is compensable work time?
2. Explain what the court means when it refers to "that weasel word 'effectively.'"
3. Does the court speculate on a possible management response should the on-call period be deemed "work" under the FLSA?

SECTION 149: PLANT CLOSING LAWS: THE WARN ACT

All areas of the United States have experienced the closing of manufacturing facilities in recent years. Often these closings were the result of decisions made by large corporations who believed the benefits of moving to new facilities in other areas of the country or moving to foreign countries were more economically advantageous than remaining in their older unprofitable or less profitable facilities.

Some argue that such decisions, which were made solely by looking at "private" costs and benefits to the firms, ignored the "external" costs to the community and industry, worker unemployment, economic hardships on community businesses and others, decreases in tax revenues of the community, the loss of real estate values in the community, and numerous significant social costs. These individuals advocate laws to restrict plant closings. Others argue that to impose restrictions on plant closings would inhibit the economy's ability to grow and apply new manufacturing technology and would inhibit businesses' ability to be efficient producers in today's worldwide marketplace.

Through collective bargaining, unions and employers have often agreed in their labor agreements to provide limited notice to their employees of layoffs at their plants, and they have agreed to pay severance pay to employees who are permanently laid off. Where no plant closing language exists in a collective bargaining contract, the employer has an obligation to bargain over the "effects" of its decision to close the plant under *First National Maintenance Corp. v. NLRB*,[21] as discussed in Chapter 5.

In 1988, Congress enacted the first federal plant closing law, the Worker Adjustment and Retraining Notification Act (WARN Act).[22] It requires employers who have 100 or more employees to give a 60-day notice of a plant closing if 50 or more workers at one site are to lose their jobs. A "mass layoff" provision of the law requires a 60-day notice of layoffs to affected workers if the affected workers make up at least 33 percent of the workforce at the site (with a minimum of 50 affected workers).[23] In *OCAWIU, Local 7-629 v. RMI Titanium Co.*,[24] the company laid off 87 workers, or some 32.34 percent of the total number of employees at this facility, 2 workers short of the number needed to make this action a "mass layoff" requiring a 60-day notice under the "33 percent of the workforce" rule set forth in the WARN Act. Around the same time, three workers were laid off from a research and development project, called the ETP project, which was a joint effort with an Italian company, SIT. SIT had not paid its share of the project's expenses for over 60 days, and it was for this specific reason that the company shut the project down and laid off the three ETP project workers. The union argued that the three ETP workers should be counted with the 87 other layoffs so as to bring about WARN Act liability. The court noted that an employer is not held to WARN Act liability if it can show that the layoffs had separate causes and were separate actions not intended to evade the WARN Act requirements. As such, the court did not add the 3 ETP workers to the 87, creating WARN Act liability. If 500 or more employees are to be laid off, notice is required regardless of the percentage of the workforce to be laid off at the site.

In the *UPIU v. Alden Corrugated Container Corp.* decision, reported in this section, two different corporations with common ownership and management were considered a "single business entity" under federal law standards, thus bringing them within the 100-employee requirement triggering the WARN Act notice requirements. Factors utilized to determine if an affiliated company or lender constitute a "single employer" under the WARN Act are (1) common ownership, (2) common directors and/or officers, (3) de facto exercise of control, (4) unity of personnel

---

[21] 452 U.S. 666 (1981).

[22] 29 U.S.C. §§ 2101–2109.

[23] In *Campbell v. PMI Food Equipment Co.*, 52 eligible workers accepted PMI's $325,275 offer of judgment on WARN Act claims, 243 DLR AA-1 (Dec. 19, 2007).

[24] *Oil Chemical and Atomic Workers International Union (OCAWIU), Local 7-629 v. RMI Titanium Co.*, 2000 U.S. LEXIS 363 (6th Cir. 2000).

policies emanating from a common source, and (5) dependency of operations.[25] The remedy for the notice violation in the *Alden* case was back pay and benefits for each of the 60-day notice periods.[26] However, a majority of the federal appeals courts that have interpreted the WARN Act's reference to back pay "for each day of violation" regard this language as requiring payment for each working day during the 60-day period, not back pay for the entire 60-calendar-day period.[27]

Exceptions to the notice requirement exist for unforeseen business circumstances, faltering companies, closures or layoffs from temporary projects, and closures due to legitimate strike and lockout activity. The sale of a manufacturing facility as a going concern to a new owner does not entitle employees to WARN Act notice, because the new owner is likely to retain most employees in order to continue the ongoing business, and thus no mass layoff should occur.[28]

Congress did not set a time limit for filing WARN Act lawsuits. In *North Star Steel Co. v. Thomas*,[29] the U.S. Supreme Court determined that the appropriate time limit for filing a lawsuit for failure to give proper notice of a plant closing or a mass layoff under the Act is to be determined by borrowing a time limit from an analogous state law, such as the two-year limitation period for civil penalties and a three-year period for state wage payment actions. Certain employers believed that the time limit should have been the six-month deadline of the NLRA. The Court's ruling allowed a lawsuit to proceed that would have been untimely if the NLRA time limits applied. The suit was on behalf of workers at a plant in Pennsylvania who claimed that the steel company had laid off 270 workers without giving 60 days' advance notice.

In *United Food Commercial Workers v. Brown Shoe Co.*,[30] the U.S. Supreme Court held that a union has standing to bring a WARN Act lawsuit against an employer on behalf of its workers. This decision revived a lawsuit against the shoe company based on the union's belief that the employer had already begun the layoff of workers at a plant it was closing before giving the union the closing notice required by the Act.

A small number of states have passed laws regulating plant closings. A state plant-closing law may require that the employer give advance notice to employees that the plant will be closing.[31] This would allow employees to have a reasonable period of time, while still employed, to find another job. The law may also require that notice be given to a designated state agency, whereby a program to provide

---

[25] See Department of Labor Regulations 20 C.F.R. § 639.3 (a)(2) (2002). See also *Pearson v. Component Tech. Corp.*, 247 F.3d 471 (3d Cir. 2001), and *UAW Local 157 v. OEM/Eire Westland, LLC*, 203 F. Supp 2d 825, 832 (E.D. Mich. 2002).

[26] In *UMW v. Eighty-Four Mining Co.*, 2005 WL 3099643 (3d Cir. 2005), the Third Circuit follows this view on damages, concluding that back pay includes as well compensation for overtime that was normally or regularly available.

[27] *Breedlove v. Earthgrains Baking Co. Inc.*, 140 F.2d 797 (8th Cir. 1998).

[28] *Smullin v. Mity Enterprises Inc.*, 420 F.3d 836 (8th Cir. 2005).

[29] 515 U.S. 29 (1995).

[30] 517 U.S. 544 (1996).

[31] Wis. Stat. Ann. § 109.07.

placement counseling, retraining, and other services could be set up for the benefit of employees.[32] Moreover, a state may enact laws that provide severance pay for qualifying employees[33] or provide for the continuation of employer-provided health insurance benefits for a certain number of months after the closing.[34] Under COBRA, former workers can stay in group health care plans commonly for up to 18 months, but they can be required to pay the full cost of their coverage.

In *Fort Halifax Packing Co. v. Coyne*,[35] the U.S. Supreme Court upheld Maine's law requiring employers to pay severance pay to employees who lose their jobs because of a plant closing.

CASE 18.4	UPIU v. Alden Corrugated Container Corp.
	U.S. District Court, 10 IER Cases 1700 (D.C. Mass. 1995).

[Sixty days prior to the plant closing at Alden Corrugated Container Corporation, the plant employed some 51 workers and Bates Corrugated Box Corporation employed some 93 workers 60 days prior to the Bates plant closing. The companies were interconnected, sharing certain officers and directors, and stock of both companies was owned by a common holding company, Alden Holdings Corporation. The companies did not believe that a WARN Act notice was required because neither company employed 100 employees 60 days prior to the plant closings. The United Paperworkers International Union (UPIU) believed that collectively the companies formed a "single business enterprise" under the Act and that notice was required.]

COLLINGS, U.S.M.J....

There is no dispute that the closings of the Alden and Bates Plants constitute plant closings under § 2101 (a)(2) of the Act in that each was a permanent shutdown of a single site as a consequence of which over fifty employees suffered the loss of employment. However, in order to establish both the applicability of the WARN Act and the defendants' liability thereunder, the plaintiffs must prove that Alden and Bates were "employers" as defined by § 2101 (a)(1) of the statute, i.e., that they were business enterprises that employed one hundred (100) or more employees.

According to the regulations, "[t]he point in time at which the number of employees is to be measured for the purpose of determining coverage is the date the first notice is required to be given." 20 C.F.R. § 639.5 (a)(3). Thus, the relevant date for determining whether Alden was an employer is December 25, 1990, sixty days prior to the Alden Plant closing on February 22, 1991. At that time, Alden employed at least fifty-one (51) full time workers. On November 18, 1990, sixty days before the Bates Plant closing on January 18, 1991, ninety-three (93) employees were working for Bates. *See, e.g., United Electrical, Radio and Machine Workers of America (UE) and UE Local 291 v. Maxim, Inc.* 1990 WL 66578, *1–*2 (D. Mass.).

Although neither Alden nor Bates per se had the requisite number of employees working at their respective plants on the relevant dates, the plaintiffs advance several theories pursuant to which they contend that the corporations could be considered employers within the meaning of the WARN Act. The plaintiffs' primary argument is that the defendants are so interconnected that, collectively, they constituted a single business enterprise. There is no dispute that if the Alden and Bates workers were aggregated, the threshold number of one hundred (100) employees on the relevant dates would be met.

continued

---

[32] Mass. Stat. Ann. 151 A § 71 B(a).

[33] Me. Rev. Stat. Ann., Tit. 26 § 625 B-2-3.

[34] Mass. Stat. Ann. 151 A § 71 G.

[35] 482 U.S. 1 (1987).

The term "business enterprise" is not defined in the statute. The pertinent regulation provides:

Under existing legal rules, independent contractors and subsidiaries which are wholly or partially owned by a parent company are treated as separate employers or as a part of the parent or contracting company depending upon the degree of their independence from the parent. Some of the factors to be considered in making this determination are (i) common ownership, (ii) common directors and/or officers, (iii) de facto exercise of control, (iv) unity of personnel policies emanating from a common source, and (v) the dependency of operations.

20 C.F.R. § 639.3 (a)(2).

To further clarify the definition of "independent contractors and subsidiaries" as used in § 639.3 (a)(2), the Department of Labor has stated:

The intent of the regulatory provision relating to independent contractors and subsidiaries is not to create a special definition of these terms for WARN purposes; the definition is intended only to summarize existing law that has developed under State Corporations laws and such statutes as the NLRA, the Fair Labor Standards Act (FLSA) and the Employee Retirement Income Security Act (ERISA). The Department does not believe that there is any reason to attempt to create new law in this area especially for WARN purposes when relevant concepts of State and federal law adequately cover the issue. Thus, no change has been made in the definition. Similarly, the regulation is not intended to foreclose any application of existing law or to identify the source of legal authority for determinations of whether related entities are separate. To the extent that existing law recognizes the joint employer doctrine or the special situation of the garment industry, nothing in the regulation prevents application of that law. Nor does the regulation preclude recognition of the National Mediation Board as an authoritative decision maker for entities covered by the RLA. Neither does the regulation preclude treatment of operating divisions as separate entities if such divisions could be so defined under existing law.

54 Fed. Reg. 16045 (April 10, 1989) ...

The factors suggested to be weighed in the WARN regulations are quite similar to those in the single employer analysis. The facts of common ownership

and management of the corporate defendants have already been established, and need not be repeated. Similarly, the centralized control of labor negotiations has been discussed, as has the interdependency of the Alden and Bates operations. The final factor to be examined is de facto control.

A number of facts underscore the control that Alden Holdings had, and exercised, over Alden and Bates. Alden Holdings owned all the stock of Alden and ninety-one percent (91%) of the stock of Bates. The primary stockholders of Alden Holdings, Walter Zuckerman, Benjamin Gottlieb and Frederic M. Gottlieb, with one exception, were each officers and directors of Alden Holdings, Alden and Bates. Three of the four directors of Alden Holdings supervised the labor negotiations of Alden and Bates. Alden Holdings secured financing for Alden and Bates. Two of the officers/directors of Alden Holdings determined the allocation of Stanley Jacobson's salary between Alden and Bates. Representatives of Alden Holdings attended the meeting of Alden's and Bates' paper suppliers. De facto control of Alden and Bates by Alden Holdings is amply supported by the record.

Considering the factors set forth in the WARN regulations, the plaintiffs have proven that defendants Alden Holdings, Alden and Bates were a single business enterprise.

To summarize, a conclusion in favor of the separateness of defendants is reached under state common law. However, when the tests predicated on federal law are applied, Alden Holdings, Alden and Bates must be deemed to be a single business enterprise. Given these disparate results, it is important to bear in mind that the WARN Act,

... like other federal labor statues, has as its goal the protection of workers, and therefore, the single employer test and the factors enumerated in the D.O.L. regulations, which echo and expand the single employer test, are persuasive.

Local 397 II, 779 F.Supp. at 800.

Consequently, Alden Holdings, Alden and Bates are found to be a single business enterprise. Together, their aggregate number of workers surpasses the minimum number of employees required for the provisions of the WARN Act to apply. As a matter of law, Alden Holdings, Alden and Bates were a single employer and, as such, are liable for the established violations of the WARN Act.

continued

Title 29 U.S.C. § 2102(b)(1) provides for a reduction in the notification period as follows:

> An employer may order the shutdown of a single site of employment before the conclusion of the 60-day period if as of the time that notice would have been required the employer was actively seeking capital or business which, if obtained, would have enabled the employer to avoid or postpone the shutdown and the employer reasonably and in good faith believed that giving the notice required would have precluded the employer from obtaining the needed capital or business.

From and after the business reorganization in May of 1990, its financial losses continued to mount as Bates proved unable to manage effectively the finished box business transferred from Alden. Although a decision was made to attempt to sell the Bates operation in November, 1990, no interested buyers could be found. There is absolutely no evidence in the record with regard to what specific steps Bates took to sell its business.

After receipt of Bates' 1990 year-end figures, the Bank of Boston called the company's loan effective January 18, 1991. Again, there is no objective proof in the record to demonstrate that Bates' expectation that its operation could be maintained was held reasonably and in good faith.

Based on this record, the Court finds that Bates has failed to carry its burden of proof that the conditions for the "faltering company" exception have been met.

2. The Unforeseeable Business Circumstances Exception

As a second exception to the notification requirement, the WARN Act provides:

> An employer may order a plant closing or mass layoff before the conclusion of the 60-day period if the closing or mass layoff is caused by business circumstances that were not reasonably foreseeable as of the time that notice would have been required.

29 U.S.C. § 2102 (b) (2) (A)....

The regulations are instructive in interpreting and applying this exception, stating in relevant part:

> An important indicator of a business circumstance that is not reasonably foreseeable is that the circumstance is caused by some sudden, dramatic, and unexpected action or condition outside the employer's control.

The test for determining when business circumstances are not reasonably forseeable focuses on an employer's business judgment. The employer must exercise such commercially reasonable business judgment as would a similarly situated employer i[n] predicting the demands of its particular market....

20 C.F.R. §§ 639.9(b)(1) and (2).

Both Alden and Bates contend that the decision by the Bank of Boston to call their loans and order that they cease operations was an unforeseen business circumstance.

The fiscal misfortunes of both companies were apparent even before May of 1990, as evidenced by the ever increasing losses they sustained beginning in 1988 as well as the fact that their loans were in a workout mode with the Bank of Boston. The slide continued unabated after the business reorganization as reflected by the C.O.D. decision of their paper suppliers in September, 1990. The extremely poor year end figures demonstrate that both Alden's and Bates' financial decline accelerated dramatically in the latter part of 1990.

In light of this deepening downward fiscal spiral, the Bank of Boston's ultimate order to cease operations cannot be viewed as an unforeseen business circumstance within the meaning of the WARN Act. While certainly dramatic, the decision was neither unforeseen or sudden, but rather the culmination of the continuing, and admittedly worsening, financial devastation of Alden and Bates. In the exercise of commercially reasonable business judgment, Alden and Bates could have anticipated by the end of 1990 that their plants would be forced to close, and, therefore, could have given the notification required by the WARN Act.

An employer found to have violated the WARN Act shall be liable to each aggrieved employee for back pay for each day of violation as well as benefits under an employee benefit plan. 29 U.S.C. § 2104(1). Given that no notices were provided in these cases, liability is calculated based on the maximum allowable period of violation, i.e., sixty days. *Id.*

The amounts of back pay and benefits are the subject of stipulation by the parties. Based on an eight hour day, the collective daily pay of the twenty-four Union members who were terminated by Alden in the Alden Plant closing was one thousand eight hundred seventy-six dollars and fifty-six cents ($1,876.56) (Stip. [f]) The collective daily pay multiplied by the sixty-day period of violation equals one hundred

continued

twelve thousand five hundred ninety-three dollars and sixty cents ($112,593.60). The value of sixty days of benefits for these same Union members is twelve thousand eight hundred ninety-six dollars and eighty-eight cents ($12,896.88).

The total amount of collective daily pay and employee benefits for the members of Local 996 laid off and/or terminated at Bates for a sixty-day period is four hundred eighty-six thousand, three hundred ninety-six dollars and ninety-two cents ($486,396.92). The value of sixty days collective pay and employee benefits for the eleven nonunion Bates employees terminated when the Bates Plant closed is ninety-five thousand eight hundred fifty dollars and thirty-eight cents ($95,850.38).

Case Questions

1. Did either Alden or Bates have the 100 employees necessary for the WARN Act to apply?
2. Were the shutdowns caused by "business circumstances that were not reasonably foreseeable" as of the time that notice would have been required?
3. What are the damages owed the employees who did not receive notice?

SECTION 150: UNEMPLOYMENT COMPENSATION

As set forth in the previous section, federal and state laws require notice to workers of impending unemployment due to plant shutdowns, in some situations. A federally mandated unemployment compensation system exists for the benefit of unemployed workers. Over 96 percent of wage and salary workers in the United States may qualify for unemployment benefits.

Unemployment compensation is provided primarily through a federal-state system under the unemployment insurance provisions of the Social Security Act of 1935. All states have laws that provide benefits under the broad federal standards of the 1935 law. The states are largely free to prescribe the amount and durations of benefits and the conditions for eligibility. Weekly benefits are paid at approximately 50 percent of the worker's wage up to set maximums, and "regular benefits" commonly continue for a period of up to 26 weeks. The unemployed person must be available for placement in a similar position at comparable pay. Individuals may be disqualified from receiving benefits if the individual quits a job without good cause or is fired for misconduct.

Employers are taxed for unemployment benefits based on each employer's "experience rating" account. Thus, employers with a stable workforce with no layoffs, who therefore do not draw upon the state unemployment insurance fund, pay favorable tax rates. Employers whose experience ratings are higher pay higher rates. Motivated by the desire to avoid higher unemployment taxes, employers may challenge the state's payment of unemployment benefits to individuals whom they believe are not properly entitled to benefits.

MISCONDUCT

Like workers' compensation statutes, unemployment compensation statutes are humanitarian in nature and are liberally construed. In determining an individual's entitlement to unemployment compensation benefits, the issue is not whether the employer was justified in discharging the employee, but, rather, whether the employee committed "misconduct." Misconduct resulting in disqualification for unemployment benefits is conduct resulting in a willful or wanton substantial disregard of the employer's interests. Mere negligence or incompetence will not suffice. For example, in *Lyster v. Florida Unemployment Appeals Commission*,[36] an over-the-road truck driver was fired by Southern Refrigerated Transportation (SRT) due to his involvement in five nonserious accidents in a 10-month period and was denied unemployment benefits by the state unemployment commission on the basis of "misconduct connected with ... work." The decision was overturned by the district court of appeals because the driver's carelessness did not "manifest culpability, wrongful intent, or evil design" and thus did not constitute "misconduct" within the meaning of the law.

In *McCourtney v. Imprimis Technology, Inc.*,[37] an individual who was discharged for frequent absences from work, while properly dismissed by her employer, nevertheless was not disqualified from unemployment benefits because her absences did not amount to "misconduct" under the Act. The dismissed individual was unable to obtain child care for her sick infant and her missing of work was thus not "in wanton disregard of her employer's interests" but motivated by her child's interests.

In *Hill v. Commissioner of Labor*,[38] Hill had been returned to work under a "last chance" drug treatment agreement. The evidence established that he had failed to follow through with the drug treatment program and tested positive for drugs. As a result, the employer dismissed him. The court ruled that Hill was disqualified from receiving unemployment benefits because of his "misconduct."

In some states, an employee's off-duty use of illegal drugs is not considered work-connected misconduct. Such decisions are narrow, however, and there must not be work-connected rules violations that result from the off-duty use of drugs. In *Weyerhauser Co. v. Employment Division*,[39] the Oregon Court of Appeals held that a worker's poor attendance record, related to his off-duty use of alcohol and drugs, was willful misconduct making him ineligible for unemployment compensation.

Voluntary Quits

Every state disqualifies individuals from receiving benefits when they voluntarily leave their job without good cause. Exceptions to this voluntary quit rule exist in some states for employees who elect voluntary termination under a voluntary termination plan (VTP) adopted by the employer, whereby an employer purchases employees' employment and seniority rights in exchange for separation packages. In *Ford Motor Co. v. Ohio Bureau of Employment Services*,[40] the Supreme Court of Ohio ruled that an employee who was voluntarily terminated under a VTP, even

---

[36] 826 So. 2d 482 (1st Dist.Ct. App. 2002).

[37] *McCourtney v. Imprimis Technology, Inc.* (Minn. App.), 465 N.W.2d 74 (1991).

[38] *Hill v. Commissioner of Labor*, 172 A.D.2d 954, 568 N.Y.S.2d 235 (1991).

[39] 107 Or. App. 505, 812 P.2d 44 (1991). See also *Leibbrand v. Employment Security Dept. of State of Washington*, 107 Wash. App. 411 (2001).

[40] 571 N.E.2d 727 (Ohio 1991). See also *Verizon North Inc. v. Ohio Department of Job and Family Service*, 865 N.E.2d 956 (Ohio App. 2007), where the Appeals Court upheld the Commission's findings that the employees were entitled to receive benefits because they quit pursuant to an established employer plan that permitted them to separate from employment due to a lack of work.

though she had sufficient seniority to avoid the layoff in question, was entitled to unemployment compensation benefits.[41]

A voluntary quit because of sex discrimination or sexual harassment constitutes "good cause" for leaving employment where the victim makes reasonable efforts to resolve the matter before leaving the employment.[42] In *Umbarger v. Virginia Employment Comm'n*, presented in this section, the court held that an employee who reasonably believed that she was the victim of sexual discrimination, and had exhausted all reasonable alternatives for redress, was not disqualified from receiving unemployment benefits.

AVAILABILITY

In most states the unemployed person must be available for placement in a similar job and be willing to take such employment at a comparable rate of pay.[43] Full-time students generally have difficulty proving that they are "available" for work once they become unemployed. In *Evjen v. Employment Agency*,[44] full-time student Robert Evjen was laid off from his full-time employment at Boise Cascade Company. The court decided that Evjen was entitled to benefits because he had overcome the inference of nonavailability that exists for full-time students by his uncontroverted testimony that he never missed work in order to go to classes and that his education was secondary to his employment.

CASE 18.5	UMBARGER V. VIRGINIA EMPLOYMENT COMMISSION
	COURT OF APPEALS OF VIRGINIA, 404 S.E.2D 380 (VA APP. 1991).

[Kathy Umbarger was disqualified from receiving unemployment benefits based on her separation from Glenn Roberts Tire and Recapping, Inc., and she appealed the decision ultimately to the Court of Appeals.]

KOONTZ, C. J....

From November 28, 1978 until her resignation on August 8, 1988, Ms. Umbarger worked as a bookkeeper for Glenn Roberts Tire and Recapping, ultimately earning $5.10 per hour. Glenn Roberts Tire

continued

---

[41] But see *Mansberger v. Unemployment Compensation Board of Review*, 785 A.2d 126 (Pa. Comm. Ct. 2001), where an individual who accepted early retirement incentive was not entitled to unemployment benefits.

[42] See *Spain v. The Employment Security Department*, 185 P.3d 1188 (Wash. 2008), where in addition to the broad undefined category of "good cause," nondisqualifying reasons include separation necessary because of the illness or disability of the claimant or the death, illness, or disability of a member of the claimant's immediate family. The remaining nondisciplinary reasons are, in essence, relocation of a military spouse, protection of the claimant or immediate family member from domestic violence or stalking, a 25 percent or more reduction in pay, a 25 percent or more reduction in hours, a change in the worksite resulting in increased distance or difficulty in travel, an unsafe workplace, illegal activities on the worksite, and a change in work that violates the claimant's religious or moral beliefs.

[43] *Laurel Racing Assn. Ltd. v. Barbendreier*, 806 A.2d 357 (Md. Ct. Sp. App. 2002).

[44] 22 Or. App. 372, 539 P.2d 662 (1975).

and Recapping has two stores, one in Big Stone Gap and one in Norton, and is owned by Appalachian Tire Products in Charleston, West Virginia. During the latter part of her employment, Ms. Umbarger became increasingly anxious about the future of her job since the business was doing poorly. On July 1, 1988, the manager of the Big Stone Gap store retired. Shortly thereafter, the service manager of this store resigned, and with three male employees from the service department, started his own business. In an unsuccessful attempt to retain some of those employees, Glenn Roberts offered them raises but they declined the offers. As a result of those departures, the Glenn Roberts store in Big Stone Gap was left with one male employee in the service department and Ms. Umbarger in the office.

Subsequently, a salesman from the Norton store was made manager of the Big Stone Gap store. The new manager retained sales responsibilities that required him to be away from the Big Stone Gap store on a regular basis. During the latter part of July and without notice to Ms. Umbarger, Glenn Roberts hired Tim Mack to oversee inventory at the Big Stone Gap store and potentially become a store manager. Mack was paid $5.50 per hour for this newly created position titled "Supervisor in Inventory Control." Mack had prior inventory control experience at Westmoreland Coal Company where he recently had been laid off, but no prior experience in the tire business.

Ms. Umbarger was displeased with the fact that Mack was doing some of the work that she had performed for Glenn Roberts for nearly the ten previous years. On August 8, 1988, she discovered Mack was earning forty cents per hour more than she was earning. Upon returning from lunch that day, Ms. Umbarger approached Leonard Canfield, Glenn Roberts' operations manager for the two stores. She demanded an explanation of the pay differential. Canfield told her that Mack was in a different classification than her and would possibly become store manager someday. She responded that she did not think it was fair and demanded a pay raise, which Canfield told her conditions would simply not permit. At that point, Ms. Umbarger told Canfield she felt she was the victim of sex discrimination and left the store. The next day she removed her personal belongings and filed her claim for unemployment compensation....

An individual is disqualified from receiving unemployment benefits if the commission finds that individual voluntarily left work without good cause. The corollary to that rule is that an individual may receive unemployment benefits if the commission finds that individual voluntarily left work with good cause. The determination of what constitutes "good cause" is a mixed question of law and fact, and therefore is subject to review on appeal. In *Lee v. Virginia Employment Comm'n*, 335 S.E.2d 104, 106 (1985), we considered the requirement of "good cause" in the context of an employee who voluntarily leaves employment and stated: "[B]efore relinquishing his employment ... the claimant must have made every effort to eliminate or adjust with his employer the differences or conditions of which he complains. He must take those steps that could be reasonably expected of a person desirous of retaining his employment before hazarding the risks of unemployment." *Id.* In other words, a claimant must take all reasonable steps to resolve his conflicts with his employer and retain his employment before voluntarily leaving that employment.

... [W]hen determining whether good cause existed for a claimant to voluntarily leave employment, the commission and the reviewing courts must first apply an objective standard to the reasonableness of the employment dispute and then to the reasonableness of the employee's efforts to resolve that dispute before leaving the employment. In making this two-part analysis, the claimant's claim must be viewed from the standpoint of a reasonable employee. "Factors that ... are peculiar to the employee and her situation are factors which are appropriately considered as to whether good cause existed...." *Id.* 382 S.E.2d at 481.

In the present case, the commission and Glenn Roberts contend Ms. Umbarger's evidence fails to show she had no reasonable alternative except to quit her job....

We interpret the circuit court's finding that Ms. Umbarger "felt she was ... discriminated against in view of the recently hired higher paid male employee" as a determination that she reasonably believed she was a victim of sexual discrimination. The record supports such a determination. Without notifying her or allowing her to apply, Glenn Roberts hired a male, Tim Mack, who lacked any apparent experience in the tire business, to fill a newly created position that entailed performing many of her current duties. Mack's starting salary was forty cents per hour more than Ms. Umbarger's salary even though she had been employed at Glenn Roberts for nearly ten years.

continued

Finally, she was denied a raise after Glenn Roberts recently had offered several male employees raises. The combination of these factors demonstrates the reasonableness of Ms. Umbarger's belief that she was the victim of sexual discrimination. The determination that Ms. Umbarger reasonably believed that she was a victim of sexual discrimination negates an assertion that her belief was a purely subjective perception on her part, even though she may have erroneously held this belief. Consequently, the commission's finding in this case that Ms. Umbarger did not demonstrate she was in fact discriminated against is immaterial.

Based upon the initial determination that Ms. Umbarger reasonably believed she was being discriminated against, we also must decide whether she took those steps that could be reasonably expected of a person desirous of retaining her employment. Unlike *Lee*, there is no evidence that Ms. Umbarger had the benefit of an established, designated procedure for addressing employee grievances. The evidence shows that Glenn Roberts was owned by an out-of-state corporation, Appalachian Tire Products, and that Mr. Canfield, the operations manager in charge of the two Glenn Roberts stores, was one of the top officers, if not the top officer, in Glenn Roberts available to review Ms. Umbarger's complaint. Nothing in the record indicates or suggests that Appalachian Tire

Products took an active role in the management of Glenn Roberts or in any way oversaw employee affairs. In a situation such as this, we find, as a matter of law, that Ms. Umbarger exhausted all reasonable alternatives within Glenn Roberts to resolve her complaint of discrimination when she confronted Mr. Canfield and he failed to respond to that complaint.

Based on our findings, we hold Ms. Umbarger is not disqualified from receiving unemployment benefits. Accordingly, the decision of the circuit court is reversed and the case is remanded for entry of an order consistent with this opinion.

Reversed and remanded.

Case Questions

1. May an individual receive unemployment benefits if that individual voluntarily left work with good cause?
2. What analysis must the commission and reviewing courts pursue in order to determine if a claimant who voluntarily leaves employment does so for "good cause"?
3. Did Umbarger have a reasonable basis to believe she was the victim of sex discrimination?
4. Did Umbarger make a sufficient effort to resolve the dispute before leaving the job?

SECTION 151: EMPLOYMENT-RELATED IMMIGRATION LAWS: INTRODUCTION

The Immigration Reform and Control Act of 1986[45] (IRCA) addressed problems associated with illegal immigration to the United States through a broad amnesty program and the initiation of both criminal and civil sanctions against employers who employ undocumented aliens.

The Immigration Act of 1990[46] reformed legal immigration to the United States. The 1990 Act provides for 140,000 visas annually for employer-sponsored immigrants. The Act includes aliens with extraordinary ability such as outstanding professors and researchers, as well as aliens who are members of the professions holding advanced degrees. Some 10,000 annual visas will be available for entrepreneurs who invest at least $1 million and create at least 10 new jobs. Congress provided the

---

[45] Pub. L. 99-603, 100 Stat. 3359, 8 U.S.C. § 1324a.

[46] Pub. L. 101-949, 101 Stat. 4978. A 1996 immigration law doubled the size of the Border Patrol and introduced procedures to speed up the deportation of immigrants without proper travel documents in an effort to reduce illegal immigration.

largest increase in visas for those aliens with the greatest skills who could stimulate the American economy through their employment and job-creating investment.[47]

SECTION 152: EMPLOYER SANCTIONS AND VERIFICATION RESPONSIBILITIES

The availability of jobs and the higher pay scales in the United States have been a principal factor in drawing illegal immigrants to the country. The IRCA is structured on the premise that if employer sanctions are applied and employers are enlisted to help enforce the immigration laws, employment opportunities for illegal immigrants will be drastically diminished and so will illegal immigration. The employer sanctions and verification responsibilities under the law are covered below.

EMPLOYER SANCTIONS

Section 101 of the IRCA makes it illegal to hire, recruit, or refer for a fee unauthorized aliens. The law also makes it illegal for an employer to employ an alien in the United States knowing that the alien is (or has become) an unauthorized alien with respect to employment. An employer who violates the law is subject to civil penalties of $250 to $2,000 for each unauthorized alien. This penalty is increased to $2,000 to $5,000 for each alien for a second violation.[48] Criminal penalties where a "pattern or practice" of unlawful hiring exists can include a fine of not more than $3,000 for each unauthorized alien and imprisonment for up to six months.[49]

EMPLOYER VERIFICATION

The law requires employers to verify that each new employee hired after November 6, 1986, is authorized to work in the United States. The Immigration and Naturalization Service (INS) has designated Form I-9, Immigration Eligibility Verification Form, as the official verification form to comply with the IRCA.

The prospective employee must complete the initial portion of Form I-9 attesting under the penalty of perjury that he or she is a U.S. citizen or is authorized by the INS to work in the United States and that the verification document(s) presented to the employer are genuine and relate to the signer. The employer must then review the documents that support the individual's right to work in the

---

[47] In a report released by the Fiscal Policy Institute of Albany, New York, on November 26, 2007, entitled "Working for a Better Life: A Profile of Immigrants in the New York State Economy," the whole range of immigrants in the state, both documented and undocumented, was studied. The report found that immigrants comprise 37 percent of the population of New York City and 46 percent of its labor force. They make up 25 percent of the city's CEOs; 50 percent of accountants; and 33 percent of clerks, receptionists, and cleaners. In upstate areas, immigrants comprise 5 percent of the population and labor force, 20 percent of professors, 35 percent of physicians, 20 percent of software engineers, and 80 percent of seasonal farm workers. All told, they contributed an estimated $229 billion in economic output in the state in 2006. Basically, there are rich, poor, and middle class immigrants, like everyone else. See 227 DLR A-9 (Nov. 27, 2007).

[48] IRCA § 101(a)(1), 8 U.S.C. § 1324 A(e)(4).

[49] IRCA § 101(a)(1), 8 U.S.C. § 1324 A(f).

United States. Documents that both identify and support an individual's eligibility to work are a U.S. passport, a certificate of U.S. citizenship, a certificate of naturalization, an unexpired foreign passport with attached visa authorizing U.S. employment, or an Alien Registration Card with photograph. Where the individual does not have one of the above documents, the individual may provide a document evidencing his or her identity and another document evidencing the right to employment. Thus, a state-issued driver's license is sufficient to provide identity and a Social Security card or official birth certificate issued by a municipal authority is sufficient to prove employment eligibility. Numerous other documents exist that will satisfy the identity and employment eligibility documentation requirements.

The employer has three days to complete the I-9s. I-9s must be completed for all employees hired after November 6, 1986, including employees who are U.S. citizens. I-9s must be kept for three years after the date of hire. Fines of between $100 and $1,000 may be assessed for each individual employee for failure to comply with the paperwork verification requirements.

Employers may verify new employee worker status through the federal government's voluntary employment verifications program called E-Verify. The E-Verify system is an Internet-based voluntary system that electronically compares information on the employment authorization forms, commonly known as I-9 forms, with records at the Social Security Administration and the Department of Homeland Security.

Executive Order 12989 was amended on June 6, 2008, to *require* federal government contractors to utilize an electronic verification system designated by the Secretary of Homeland Security (DHS) to confirm the employment eligibility of their workforces. DHS designated E-Verify as the system to be used under the Executive Order.[50]

Some states have mandated the use of E-Verify to verify the work eligibility of new hires.[51]

BURDEN OF PROOF AND AFFIRMATIVE DEFENSES

In an action against the employer under the IRCA, the government must establish that the employer had "actual knowledge" that the employee was unauthorized to work in the United States. This standard is one of the highest standards of proof under law.

The IRCA provides an affirmative defense for an employer if the employer, in good faith, simply complies with the verification requirements of the Act. This is accomplished "if the document reasonably appears on its face to be genuine."[52] However, an employer who is informed by the INS that named employees may have used fraudulent green cards, but takes no investigative or corrective action whatsoever, cannot avail itself of the good faith defense.[53]

---

[50] 111 DLR A-1 (June 10, 2008).

[51] See for example the Mississippi Employment Protection Act (S.B. 2988) signed into law March 17, 2008. 53 DLR A-2 (Mar. 19, 2008).

[52] IRCA § 101(a)(1) and 8 U.S.C. § 1324 A(b)(1)(A).

[53] *Mester Manufacturing Co. v. INS*, 879 F.2d 561 (9th Cir. 1989).

SECTION 153: EMPLOYER DISCRIMINATION

Under Section 102 of the IRCA and Title VII of the Civil Rights Act, it is an unfair practice to discriminate against a person in employment situations on the basis of national origin. Additionally, Section 102 of the IRCA makes it an unfair immigration-related practice to discriminate against an individual in hiring, discharging, recruiting, or referring for a fee because of an individual's national origin or, in the case of a citizen or intending citizen, because of that individual's citizenship status.

Since the IRCA imposes employer sanctions for violations of the Act, Congress was concerned that the IRCA might lead to employment discrimination against "foreign-looking" or "foreign-sounding" persons or against persons who, although not citizens, reside legally in the United States. In order to prevent the occurrence of such practices, Congress enacted Section 102 and established enforcement measures including the creation of a "Special Counsel for Immigration-Related Unfair Employment Practices" within the Department of Justice. Among the special counsel's statutory responsibilities is the investigation of unfair immigration-related employment practices either on the counsel's own initiative or in response to charges filed with the Office of Special Counsel by aggrieved individuals, their representatives, or officers of the Immigration and Naturalization Service.

The Immigration Act of 1990 strengthened the antidiscrimination provisions of the IRCA by prohibiting employers from demanding overdocumentation. Section 535(a) of the 1990 Act provides that employers' requests for more or different documents than required under the IRCA or refusal to honor documents that on their face reasonably appear to be genuine shall be treated as an unfair immigration-related employment practice.[54]

In *Jones v. DeWitt Nursing Home*,[55] Jones, a newly hired employee, gave DeWitt Nursing Home a Social Security card and a driver's license to show work authorization in conjunction with the I-9 form requirements. The employer asked to see Jones's birth certificate. Jones, a U.S. citizen, refused to provide the additional document, and the employer fired him. The employer was found to have violated the IRCA and was ordered to reinstate Jones with back pay.

SECTION 154: BUSINESS VISAS

Nonimmigrant B-1 business visas are issued by a U.S. consular office abroad after it has been shown that the visitor (1) has an unabandoned foreign residence, (2) intends to enter the United States for a limited period of time, and (3) will engage solely in legitimate business activities for which the visitor will not be paid in the United States.[56]

Certain investors qualify for E-2 business visas. Principal foreign investors responsible for development and direction of an enterprise in the United States

---

[54] 8 U.S.C. § 1324 B(a)(6).

[55] 67 Interpreter Releases, 88-86 (Aug. 13, 1990).

[56] Department of State, *9 Foreign Affairs Manual*, § 41.25.

are granted such a visa. An E visa is very desirable because it is issued for extended periods of time, usually four to five years, and may be renewed indefinitely so long as the alien maintains her or his role with respect to the investment. An E-2 visa will not be issued to an applicant who has invested "a relatively small amount of capital in a marginal enterprise solely for the purpose of earning a living."[57]

L-1 visas allow qualifying multinational businesses to make intracompany transfers of foreign persons to the United States when the individuals are employed in management or have "specialized knowledge." L-1 visas are good for up to seven years for executives and managers. "Specialized knowledge" personnel may stay for five years.[58] There are no annual caps on the number of L-1 visas issued, and the employer is not required to attest that no American worker will be laid off.

H-1 classification visas allow aliens of "distinguished merit and ability" to enter and work in the United States on a temporary basis. These people include architects, engineers, lawyers, physicians, and teachers. An annual cap of 65,000 visas is applied to the H-1B visa classification. The hiring employer must attest that it will not lay off an American employee 90 days before or after filing a petition to employ a foreign worker regarding any position to be filled by the foreign worker. H-1B professionals must be paid the higher of the actual or prevailing wage for each position in order to eliminate economic incentives to use this foreign workers program. The demand for the 65,000 visas far exceeded the supply in 2008 and prior years. Many technology companies are utilizing the L-1 visas as an alternative to the H-1B visas.[59] While the H-1B visa program requires employers to pay foreign workers the prevailing U.S. wage for a particular job, the L-1 visa has no such requirement. For example, an engineer on a L-1 visa from India may be paid the same wage rate as that paid in India rather than the much higher prevailing rate for U.S. engineers.

The TN (Trade NAFTA) visa category is part of the North American Free Trade Agreement of 1994 (NAFTA) that enables Canadian and Mexican citizens to enter the United States to engage in professional business activities on a temporary basis up to a year at a time. The TN status may be renewed indefinitely in one-year increments. The most common minimum requirement is a baccalaureate degree and licensure if required for the profession.[60]

In the *Brazil Quality Stones, Inc. v. Chertoff* case, the director of the United States Bureau of Citizenship and Immigration Services (USCIS) within the Department of Homeland Security (DHS) denied an L-1 visa to the Brazilian president and CEO of a small granite company because the record failed to establish that he was employed in a "managerial or executive" capacity.

---

[57] 22 C.F.R. § 41:51 (b)(1) (1996).

[58] Pub. L. 101-649, § 206(b)(2) (1990).

[59] The United States granted 53,000 L-1 visas in 2006, up 33 percent from the year 2000.

[60] For additional information, see University of Michigan's International Center, http://www.internationalcenter.umich.edu/immig/tnvisa.

Temporary agricultural workers are admissible to the United States under the H-2A category of the 1990 Act.[61] An H-2B nonagricultural worker is an alien who is coming to the United States temporarily to perform services or labor, is not displacing U.S. workers capable of performing such services or labor, and whose employment is not adversely affecting the wages and working conditions of a U.S. worker.[62] The 1990 Act places an annual limit on the number of H-2B visas at 66,000.

The 1990 Act created new categories of visas. The R visa facilitates the temporary entry of religious workers into the United States. The Q visa allows private businesses to bring individuals into the country for cultural events. The O and P visas apply to professional entertainers and athletes.

In the *Shanti, Inc.* decision, presented in this section, the court determined that a manager's position at a 14-employee fine Indian cuisine restaurant was not a "specialty occupation" or profession entitling a nonimmigrant temporary worker to an H-1B visa.

CASE 18.6	BRAZIL QUALITY STONES, INC. V. CHERTOFF
	UNITED STATES COURTS OF APPEALS, 531 F.3D 1063 (9TH CIR. 2008).

[The Citizenship and Immigration Services determined that the transferee was not entitled to an L-1A visa. The employer appealed the decision to the Department of Homeland Security's Administrative Appeals Office (AAO), which dismissed the appeal. The matter was next considered by the United States District Court.]

O'SCANNLAIN, J....

Eugene Tavares dos Santos is a Brazilian citizen who has served as the President and Chief Executive Officer ("CEO") of a Brazilian corporation known as Granite Ebenezer since the corporation's founding in 1998. Granite Ebenezer sells and exports Brazilian granite and other decorative stones for use in residential and commercial construction....

In 2002, in an effort to improve its ability to import its wares into the United States, Granite Ebenezer established a U.S.-based affiliate, Brazil Quality Stones,

Inc. ("BQS"), as a California corporation. Like Granite Ebenezer, dos Santos owns 99% of the corporation's stock, while his wife owns the remaining 1%.

Once established, BQS and dos Santos (collectively "Petitioners") sought to transfer dos Santos from Brazil to the United States so that he could operate BQS as its President and CEO. Thus, BQS filed a petition for an L-1A nonimmigrant visa on dos Santos's behalf. The L visa is designed to allow multinational firms to transfer employees from the firm's overseas operations to its operations in the United States. The Immigration and Nationality Act ("INA") requires an alien granted such a visa (referred to as an "intra-company transferee") to be employed by the entity sponsoring his or her petition for a continuous period of at least one year within the three years preceding the petition. In addition, the noncitizen must "seek to enter the United States temporarily in order to

continued

---

[61] *Arriaga v. Florida Pacific Farming*, LLC, 305 F.3d 1228 (11th Cir. 2002). In February 2008, the DOL proposed new H-2A regulations to streamline processing and to encourage more employers to hire legal workers. U.S. workers would receive accurate notice of available job opportunities in advance of the hiring of immigrant workers. Employers would be prohibited from shifting the costs of the H-2A application process to workers. Violation penalties would increase from $1,000 to $5,000. Fines for injuries resulting from unsafe working conditions could total up to $50,000. The proposed regulations were published in the *Federal Register* in February 2008 and are posted at http://www.doleta.gov.

[62] 8 C.F.R. § 214.2(h)(5)(i) (2000). See DLR No. 99 (5-24-05) for information on new exemptions allowing 35,000 new H-2B visas for "returning workers" with certain fee increases for employers, with a new $150 "fraud and detection" fee per petition.

continue to render his services to the same employer ... in a capacity that is managerial, executive, or involves specialized knowledge." *Id.* A noncitizen employed in a "managerial" or "executive capacity" is eligible for an L-1A classification, while a noncitizen employed in a position of "specialized knowledge" is eligible for L-1B status. The two classifications impose different limitations upon the noncitizen's stay.

On August 29, 2002, the Immigration and Naturalization Service ("INS") granted dos Santos the L1-A visa Petitioners had requested. Dos Santos arrived in the United States and began operating BQS the next month. Because the applicable regulations classified BQS as a "new office," however, dos Santos's L-1A classification was approved for only one year, subject to extension by a later application. Thus, as the end of dos Santos's first year in the United States drew near, BQS filed a second petition seeking to extend his L-1A classification for an additional three years. To obtain such extension, the INA and applicable regulations required BQS to demonstrate that it was "doing business" in the United States for the year preceding dos Santos's petition and that dos Santos was employed in a "managerial" or "executive capacity," 8 U.S.C. §§ 1101(a)(15)(L), 1101(a)(44).

The United States Bureau of Citizenship and Immigration Services ("USCIS"), as the successor to the INS, received the petition and soon thereafter requested additional evidence from BQS, explaining that the petition failed to establish that dos Santos was employed in a managerial or executive capacity. BQS timely responded with additional documentation.

The evidence submitted by BQS included an organizational chart of the corporation listing dos Santos, at the top, supervising five employees: an International Budget Analyst, an Accounting Clerk, and a three-person sales team. Yet payroll records indicated that BQS had paid only three employees other than dos Santos during the quarter preceding the petition.

BQS also set forth dos Santos's duties, explaining that he was responsible for (1) supervising and managing BQS's "office and business affairs"; (2) "overseeing capital investment opportunities"; (3) developing "plans to further channels of distribution"; (4) "hiring and firing all employees and supervising managers"; (5) overseeing "domestic and international sales"; and (6) managing "outsourced relationships" with BQS's accounting firm and warehouse.

To document dos Santos's performance of these tasks, BQS submitted, among other things, a letter dos Santos sent to the INS seeking an H-1B visa on behalf

of the International Budget Analyst, letters from BQS's accounting and warehousing firms indicating that dos Santos managed BQS's relations with them, and a brochure for a $35,000 piece of granite-cutting equipment that dos Santos had proposed for purchase by BQS.

After reviewing this evidence, the Director of the USCIS California Civil Service Center denied the petition to extend dos Santos's L-1A classification, concluding that the record failed to establish that dos Santos was employed in a managerial or executive capacity and that the record did not prove that BQS was doing business in the United States.

BQS appealed the Director's decision to the DHS Administrative Appeals Office ("AAO").... The AAO ... dismissed the appeal, affirming the Director's conclusion that the record failed to show that dos Santos was a qualifying employee or that BQS was a qualifying organization....

In 1970, Congress created the L nonimmigrant visa for a multinational firm's intra-company transferees by providing for the temporary admission of such noncitizens if, among other things, the noncitizen sought to render services in the United States to the firm or its subsidiary or affiliate "in a capacity that is managerial, executive, or involves specialized knowledge." 8 U.S.C. § 1101(a)(15)(L). Years later, in 1987, the INS in a set of regulations defined the terms "managerial" and "executive capacity." *See* 8 C.F.R. § 214.2(*l*)(1)(ii)(B), (C)(198). Although nothing in the express language of the INA limited the availability of L visas to employees of multinational firms of a certain size, the INS comments accompanying the final rule expressed concern that sole proprietors were taking improper advantage of this classification. As the INS explained,

> self-employed person ... will frequently attempt to qualify under the L category by setting up a corporation in the United States, giving himself an executive title (e.g., "president") and continuing his self-employment in the U.S., often with a minimal "investment," with no foreign operations abroad and no intent to return abroad .... We do not believe that Congress intended the L classification to be used in this manner, and the regulations are intended to control this abuse.

Temporary Alien Workers Seeking Classification Under the Immigration and Nationality Act, 52 Fed. Reg. 5738, 510 (Feb, 26, 1987)....

In the Immigration Act of 1990, Congress availed the L-1A classification to a wider group of

continued

noncitizens by amending the INA to define the term "managerial capacity" more broadly than in the preceding regulation. Specifically, the Act provided that an intra-company transferee would qualify as an employee acting in a "managerial capacity" if he or she "primarily... supervises and controls the work of her supervisory, professional, or managerial employees, *or manages an essential function within the organization,* or a department or subdivision of the organization." 8 U.S.C. § 1101(a)(44)(A) (ii) (emphasis added)....

...[R]egardless of an intra-company transferee's position in the organizational hierarchy of his employer, the INA imposes the burden on the transferee and his or her employer to demonstrate that the transferee's responsibilities are "primarily" managerial. *Id.* § 1101(a)(44)(A).

The Director held, and the AAO affirmed, that BQS failed to satisfy this burden. First, while BQS suggested that dos Santos was responsible for overseeing capital investment opportunities at BQS, the AAO pointed out that the only evidence to support such assertion was the fact that dos Santos proposed the purchase of a single piece of granite-cutting equipment. The AAO reasoned that this purchase, even if consummated, indicated only that dos Santos had authority to invest in equipment on BQS's behalf, but did not indicate that such investments were made on a regular basis or that their oversight constituted a significant portion of dos Santos's responsibilities.

Petitioners also maintain that dos Santos was responsible for overseeing BQS's domestic and international sales and its distribution chains. Yet the documents submitted to the agency do not describe with particularity what such duties entailed. In summarizing the evidence, the AAO acknowledged dos Santos's leadership role at the top of BQS's hierarchy, but also concluded that dos Santos's direct involvement in the corporation's daily operations was necessary for its success and that such fact precluded dos Santos from qualifying as a managerial employee. In other words, the AAO determined that BQS has not yet reached the level of organizational sophistication in which dos Santos could devote his primary attention to managerial duties as opposed to operational ones, even though he held a position at the head of BQS's corporate structure....

BQS bore the burden of demonstrating that dos Santos was primarily engaged in overseeing essential functions of BQS's business rather than performing them himself. While the record contains evidence that dos Santos performed managerial tasks, it does not compel the conclusion that such tasks comprised his primary responsibilities at BQS.

Petitioners argue that requiring such a showing will impose an onerous burden on small businesses seeking to gain visas for their executive and managerial employees. Yet whatever policy Petitioners' argument might advance, we are bound by the plain terms of the INA and confined by the deferential standard with which we review agency decisions. Accordingly, based on the record before us, we conclude that the agency's determination that dos Santos was not acting in a managerial capacity at the time of BQS's petition to extend his visa was not an abuse of discretion....

Affirmed.

Case Questions

1. What business purpose is served by the L-1 visa program?
2. Does the INA impose the burden of proof on the transferee and his or her employer to demonstrate that the transferee's responsibilities are "primarily managerial"?
3. Why did the USCIS deny Mr. dos Santos's petition for an L-1A visa?

CASE 18.7	SHANTI, INC. v. JANET RENO
	UNITED STATES DISTRICT COURT, 36 F. SUPP. 2D 1151 (D. MINN. 1999).

[The plaintiff, Shanti, Inc., d/b/a Moghals Fine Indian Cuisine Restaurant, sought to compel the INS to approve its petition to classify Nancy James as a nonimmigrant temporary worker and accord her H-1B status under the INA. Moghals employs 14 individuals and grosses $185,000 in annual income. James, a citizen of Bangladesh, was to perform services as the restaurant manager. She has a bachelor of arts degree in economics from the University of Dhaka. The Attorney General of the United States sought a motion for summary judgment based on the INS Administrative Appeals Unit (AAU) decision refusing to grant James H-1B status.]

continued

DAVIS. D.C....

Background

I. Legal Standards for H-1B Status

8 U.S.C. § 1101(a)(15)(H)(i)(b) provides for the temporary admission of a nonimmigrant alien:

> to perform services ... in a specialty occupation described in section 1184(i)(1) of this title ... who meets the requirements for the occupation specified in section 1184(i)(2) of this title ... and with respect to whom the Secretary of Labor determines and certifies to the Attorney General that the intending employer has filed with the Secretary an application under section 1182(n)(1) of this title.

8 C.F.R. § 214.2(h)(4)(i)(A)(1) provides that an H-1B classification may be granted to an alien who:

> [w]ill perform services in a specialty occupation which requires theoretical and practical application of a body of highly specialized knowledge and attainment of a baccalaureate or higher degree or its equivalent as a minimum requirement for entry into the occupation in the United States, and who is qualified to perform services in the specialty occupation because he or she has attained a baccalaureate or higher degree or its equivalent in the specialty occupation.

To qualify for a nonimmigrant H-1B visa, an alien must satisfy a two-prong test: (1) the position that the alien seeks to occupy must qualify as a "specialty occupation"; and (2) the alien must herself be qualified to perform services in said occupation....

... 8 C.F.R. § 214.2(h)(4)(ii) provides that:

> Specialty occupation means an occupation which requires theoretical and practical application of a body of highly specialized knowledge in fields of human endeavor including, but not limited to, architecture, engineering, mathematics, physical sciences, social sciences, medicine and health, education, business specialties, accounting, law, theology, and the arts, and which requires the attainment of a bachelor's degree or higher in a specific specialty, or its equivalent, as a minimum for entry into the occupation in the United States....

...[T]he INS has consistently refused to hold that managerial positions require a "member of the professions" or qualify as "specialty occupations." *See, e.g. matter of Caron International, Inc.*, 19 I. & N. Dec. at 794 (finding that "general managerial occupations ... are normally not considered to be professional endeavors requiring specific academic degrees"). In *China Chef*, the Sixth Circuit upheld a district court's determination that "an academic degree is not a minimum requirement for entry into that occupation [restaurant manager]" *China Chef*, 1993 WL 524276 at *1, and that "general manager positions are usually not considered 'professional' positions requiring a degree." *Id.* at *1. In addition, in the present case, the baccalaureate degree allegedly required for Shanti's position of restaurant manager is one in business administration. As discussed above, a specialty occupation "must require a degree that involved a 'precise and specific course of study which relates directly and closely to the position in question' (citation omitted). An occupation that requires a general degree such as business administration ... therefore, is not a 'profession'." *Hird/Blaker*, 764 F. Supp. at 875; *see also Central Indonesian Trading Company* 1990 Wl 161020 at *4.

The Court therefore finds that the INS did not abuse its discretion by denying Moghals' petition for an H-1B visa for the alien beneficiary, James.

Case Questions

1. Is an occupation that requires a general degree such as business administration a "profession" according to the INS?
2. Are managerial positions such as restaurant manager considered "specialty occupations" by the INS?

CHAPTER QUESTIONS AND PROBLEMS

1. A plant closing law entitles employees to a 60-day notice of the closing of the plant. Present an employer's view of such a law. Present an employee's view of such a law.

2. Under IRCA verification procedures, may an employer insist that a prospective employee with a foreign accent produce either a certificate of naturalization or an Alien Registration Card?

3. Knifepersons performed butchering operations at King Packing Company. Various knives and three types of electric saws were used in the butchering operation. Some of the knives were furnished by the employees. The saws and the more expensive knives were furnished by the employer. All of the knives as well as the saws had to be razor-sharp for the proper performance of work. A dull knife slowed down production, which was conducted on an assembly line basis, affected the appearance of the meat as well as the quality of the hides, and caused waste and accidents. The knifepersons were required to sharpen their own knives outside the scheduled shift of eight hours, and they were not paid for the time so spent.

   The Secretary of Labor contended that the time spent sharpening knives was compensable working time under the FLSA. King Packing Company contended that such time spent is noncompensable preliminary activity under the Portal-to-Portal Act. Decide. [*Mitchell v. King Packing Co.*, 350 U.S. 260]

4. Mester Manufacturing Company makes furniture at facilities in San Diego, California. INS Agent Shanks made an educational visit to the facilities in July 1987. On September 2, 1987, INS agents inspected I-9s on file at the facility. The INS then made a computer search of its records, which showed that the numbers on the green cards used by three employees belonged to other aliens. On September 3, 1987, Shanks gave Barry Mester, the company president, a handwritten list identifying the three employees in question. Mester took no investigative or corrective actions. On September 25, INS agents returned to again inspect Mester's I-9s and found that the three named individuals suspected of using false green cards were still employed by Mester. Mester was penalized a total of $1,500 for continuing to employ the three individuals. Mester appealed, contending that INS did not give it proper notice that it suspected green card fraud and that the evidence did not support a finding of green

card fraud. Which party has the burden of proof? Decide. [*Mester Manufacturing Co. v. INS*, 879 F.2d. 561 (9ᵗʰ Cir.)]

5. Workers at the Greeley, Colorado, beef processing plant of Monfort, Inc., are required to spend time before and after their shift putting on and removing special safety equipment and at the end of the shift cleaning the special gear worn by these knifepersons. The workers believe that they are entitled to be paid for this "work." The employer believes that it is not "work" for which they should be paid. Is there a government agency that employees may turn to that has the power to evaluate their claim for additional pay and, if appropriate, seek a remedy on their behalf? Are the employees entitled to pay for the functions performed before and after their shifts? And if so, at what rate? [*Reich v. Montfort*, No. 92-M-2456 11/15/96 D. Colo.]

6. The American Friends Service Committee (AFSC) is a Quaker organization that employs some 400 individuals in charitable and relief work. The Immigration Reform and Control Act prohibits employers from hiring aliens not authorized to work in the United States and requires examination of documents evidencing identity and work authorization. The AFSC seeks declaratory relief, alleging that the IRCA violates its free exercise of religion, a religion that requires its members to welcome and not show hostility to strangers, the poor, and the dispossessed. The U.S. Attorney General contends that the law is neutral and not directed at religious beliefs. Should the injunction be issued? Decide. [*American Friends Service Committee v. Thornburg*, 941 F.2d 808 (9ᵗʰ Cir.)]

7. The Fort Halifax Packing Company closed its poultry packaging and processing plant and laid off its employees. The director of Maine's Bureau of Labor Standards, Daniel Coyne, filed suit to enforce the provisions of a state statute. This statute provided that any employer that terminates operations at a plant with 100 or more employees or

relocates those operations more than 100 miles away must provide one week's pay for each year of employment to all employees who have worked in the plant at least three years. The employer has no such liability if the employee accepts employment at the new location or if the employee is covered by a contract that deals with the issue of severance pay. The employer contended that the state statute was preempted by the Employee Retirement Income Security Act of 1974 (ERISA) and by the National Labor Relations Act (NLRA). Decide. [*Fort Halifax Packing Co. v. Coyne*, 107 S. Ct. 2211]

8. Noreen Nee began working for the New Life Mission (New Life) in August 2000 as a behavioral specialist. She worked with students who had behavioral and emotional problems, transported them to and from school, and spent time with them one-on-one. Nee, an attorney, had some background in special education but had not worked as a counselor before starting this position. Nee attended mandatory training and received her certification as a counselor. New Life did not provide a manual, a handbook, or additional training.

Nee had an admitted problem with establishing and maintaining professional "boundaries." At one point, she drove a client to her house to make him lunch because he had not yet eaten, she approached a client's parent in public to discuss being removed from his case, and she allowed her husband to transport her and her client to a sledding trip. Although New Life provided no ethics training, they did inform her, after the fact, that her conduct violated their rules. After receiving the instruction, she did not engage in the prohibited conduct.

At some point during the fall of 2000, Nee was taking the prescription pain medication Oxycontin for pain due to an eye condition. Nee apparently discussed this medication with a client's parent, and the parent alleged that Nee attempted to purchase some Oxycontin from him. The parent was concerned that Nee was taking the medication while driving with his child and reported the situation to New Life. Based on this report, New Life's own suspicions regarding Nee's sobriety at work, and concern for the safety of the children in Nee's care, New Life required a note from Nee's doctor detailing the medications she was currently taking. Nee produced the note, but it did not mention Oxycontin. Nee claims this was because she was no longer taking the medication. New Life requested an additional note documenting the time period Nee used Oxycontin. Despite requests from Nee, the doctor never supplied the note.

On March 4, 2001, New Life terminated Nee's employment for misconduct, specifically for her problems relating to professional boundaries and her failure to satisfy its request for documentation relating to Oxycontin. Nee applied for unemployment benefits, and the employer objected to payment of benefits, contending she was terminated for misconduct. Under state law, misconduct is defined as "A culpable breach of the employee's duties or obligations to the employer or a pattern of irresponsible behavior, which in either case manifests a disregard for a material interest of the employer." Did the employer New Life Mission meet the burden of proof establishing that Ms. Nee was discharged for misconduct connected to her work? Was Ms. Nee entitled to unemployment compensation benefits? Decide. [*New Life Mission v. Maine Unemployment Insurance Commission*, 2002 WL31546088 (Me. Super.)]

APPENDICES

Types of Cases Before the National Labor Relations Board

1. CHARGES OF UNFAIR LABOR PRACTICES (C CASES)

CHARGE AGAINST LABOR ORGANIZATION

SECTION OF THE ACT CB	SECTION OF THE ACT CC	SECTION OF THE ACT CD
8(b)(1)(A) To restrain or coerce employees in exercise of their rights under Section 7 (to join or assist a labor organization or to refrain).	*8(b)(4)(i)* To engage in, or induce or encourage any individual employed by any person engaged in commerce or in an industry affecting commerce, to engage in a strike, work stoppage, or boycott, or (ii) to threaten, coerce, or restrain any person engaged in commerce or in an industry affecting commerce, where in either case an object is:	(D) To force or require any employer to assign particular work to employees in a particular labor organization or in a particular trade, craft, or class rather than to employees in another trade, craft, or class, unless such employer is failing to conform to an appropriate Board order or certification.
8(b)(1)(B) To restrain or coerce an employer in the selection of its representatives for collective bargaining or adjustment of grievances.	(A) to force or require any employer or self-employed or person to join any labor employer organization or to enter into any agreement prohibited by Sec. 8(e).	
8(b)(2) To cause or attempt to cause an employer to discriminate against an employee.	(B) To force or require any person to cease using, selling, handling, transporting, or otherwise dealing in the products of any other producer, processor, or manufacturer, or to cease doing business with any other person, or force or require any other employer to recognize or bargain with a labor organization as the representative of its employees unless such labor organization has been so certified.	**SECTION OF THE ACT CG**
8(b)(3) To refuse to bargain collectively with employer.		*8(g)* To strike, picket, or otherwise concertedly refuse to work at any health care institution without notifying the institution and the Federal Mediation and Conciliation Service in writing 10 days prior to such action.
8(b)(5) To require of employees the payment of excessive or discriminatory fees for membership.		
8(b)(6) To cause or attempt to cause an employer to pay or agree to pay money or other thing of value for services which are not performed or not to be performed.	(C) To force or require any employer to recognize or bargain with a particular labor organization as the representative of its employees if another labor organization has been certified as the representative.	

CHARGE AGAINST LABOR ORGANIZATION	CHARGE AGAINST EMPLOYER	CHARGE AGAINST LABOR ORGANIZATION AND EMPLOYER
SECTION OF THE ACT CP	**SECTION OF THE ACT** CA	**SECTION OF THE ACT** CE
8(b)(7) To picket, cause, or threaten the picketing of any employer where an object is to force or require an employer to recognize or bargain with a labor organization as the representative of its employees, or to force or require the employees of an employer to select such labor organization as their collective-bargaining representative, unless such labor organization is currently certified as the representative of such employees:	*8(a)(1)* To interfere with, restrain, or coerce employees in exercise of their rights under Section 7 (to join or assist a labor organization or to refrain).	*8(e)* To enter into any contract or agreement (*any* labor organization and any employer) whereby such employer ceases or refrains or agrees to cease or refrain from handling or dealing in any product of any other employer, or to cease doing business with any other person.

8(b)(7) To picket, cause, or threaten the picketing of any employer where an object is to force or require an employer to recognize or bargain with a labor organization as the representative of its employees, or to force or require the employees of an employer to select such labor organization as their collective-bargaining representative, unless such labor organization is currently certified as the representative of such employees:

(A) where the employer has lawfully recognized any other labor organization and a question concerning representation may not appropriately be raised under Section 9(c).

(B) where within the preceding 12 months a valid election under Section 9(c) has been conducted, or

(C) where picketing has been conducted without a petition under 9(c) being filed within a reasonable period of time not to exceed 30 days from the commencement of the picketing; except where the picketing is for the purpose of truthfully advising the public (including consumers) that an employer does not employ members of, or have a contract with, a labor organization, and it does not have an effect of interference with deliveries or services.

8(a)(2) To dominate or interfere with the formation or administration of a labor organization or contribute financial or other support to it.

8(a)(3) By discrimination in regard to hire or tenure of employment or any term or condition of employment to encourage or discourage membership in any labor organization.

8(a)(4) To discharge or otherwise discriminate against employees because they have given testimony under the Act.

8(a)(5) To refuse to bargain collectively with representatives of its employees.

[Charges filed with the National Labor Relations Board are letter-coded and numbered. Unfair labor practice charges are classified as "C" cases and petitions for certification or decertification of representatives as "R" cases. This chart indicates the letter codes used for "C" cases above and on next page, and "R" ?cases on page 700, and also presents a summary of each section involved.]

2. PETITIONS FOR CERTIFICATION OR DECERTIFICATION OF REPRESENTATIVES (R CASES)	3. OTHER PETITIONS
BY OR IN BEHALF OF EMPLOYEES	**BY OR IN BEHALF OF EMPLOYEES**
SECTION OF THE ACT RC	**SECTION OF THE ACT** UD
9(c)(1)(A)(i) Alleging that a substantial number of employees wish to be represented for collective bargaining and their employer declines to recognize their representative.*	*9(e)(1)* Alleging that employees (30 percent or more of an appropriate unit) wish to rescind an existing union-security agreement.
SECTION OF THE ACT RD	**BY A LABOR ORGANIZATION OR AN EMPLOYER**
9(c)(1)(A)(ii) Alleging that a substantial number of employees assert that the certified or currently recognized bargaining representative is no longer their representative.*	**BOARD RULES** UC *Subpart* C Seeking clarification of an existing bargaining unit.
BY AN EMPLOYER	**BOARD RULES** AC
SECTION OF THE ACT RM	*Subpart* C Seeking amendment of an outstanding certification of bargaining representative.
9(c)(1)(B) Alleging that one or more claims for recognition as exclusive bargaining representative have been received by the employer.*	

---

*If an 8(b)(7) charge has been filed involving the same employer, these statements in RC, RD, and RM petitions are not required.

LABOR MANAGEMENT RELATIONS ACT, 1947, AS AMENDED BY PUBLIC LAWS 86-257, 1959[*] AND 93-360, 1974

[Public Law 101—80th Congress]

An Act To amend the National Labor Relations Act, to provide additional facilities for the mediation of labor disputes affecting commerce, to equalize legal responsibilities of labor organizations and employers, and for other purposes.

Be it enacted by the Senate and House of Representatives of the United States of America in Congress assembled,

SHORT TITLE AND DECLARATION OF POLICY

SECTION 1. (a) This Act may be cited as the "Labor Management Relations Act, 1947."

(b) Industrial strife which interferes with the normal flow of commerce and with the full production of articles and commodities for commerce, can be avoided or substantially minimized if employers, employees, and labor organizations each recognize under law one another's legitimate rights in their relations with each other, and above all recognize under law that neither

---

[*]Sec. 201(d) and (e) of the Labor-Management Reporting and Disclosure Act of 1959 which repealed Sec. 9(f), (g), and (h) of the Labor Management Relations Act, 1947, and Sec. 505, amending Sec. 302(a), (b), and (c) of the Labor Management Relations Act, 1947, took effect upon enactment of Public Law 86-257, Sept. 14, 1959. As to the other amendments of the Labor Management Relations Act, 1947, Sec. 707 of the Labor-Management Reporting and Disclosure Act provides:

The amendments made by this title shall take effect sixty days after the date of the enactment of this Act and no provision of this title shall be deemed to make an unfair labor practice, any act which is performed prior to such effective date which did not constitute an unfair labor practice prior thereto.

party has any right in its relations with any other to engage in acts or practices which jeopardize the public health, safety, or interest.

It is the purpose and policy of this Act, in order to promote the full flow of commerce, to prescribe the legitimate rights of both employees and employers in their relations affecting commerce, to provide orderly and peaceful procedures for preventing the interference by either with the legitimate rights of the other, to protect the rights of individual employees in their relations with labor organizations whose activities affect commerce, to define and proscribe practices on the part of labor and management, which affect commerce and are inimical to the general welfare, and to protect the rights of the public in connection with labor disputes affecting commerce.

TITLE I—AMENDMENT OF NATIONAL LABOR RELATIONS ACT

SECTION 101. The National Labor Relations Act is hereby amended to read as follows:

FINDINGS AND POLICIES

SECTION 1. The denial by some employers of the right of employees to organize and the refusal by some employers to accept the procedure of collective bargaining lead to strikes and other forms of industrial strife or unrest, which have the intent or the necessary effect of burdening or obstructing commerce by (a) impairing the efficiency, safety, or operation of the instrumentalities of commerce; (b) occurring in the current of commerce; (c) materially affecting, restraining, or controlling the flow of raw materials or manufactured or processed goods from or into the channels of commerce, or the prices of such materials or goods in commerce; or (d) causing diminution of employment and wages in such volume as substantially to impair or disrupt the market for goods flowing from or into the channels of commerce.

The inequality of bargaining power between employees who do not possess full freedom of association or actual liberty of contract, and employers who are organized in the corporate or other forms of ownership association substantially burdens and affects the flow of commerce, and tends to aggravate recurrent business depressions, by depressing wage rates and the purchasing power of wage earners in industry and by preventing the stabilization of competitive wage rates and working conditions within and between industries.

Experience has proved that protection by law of the right of employees to organize and bargain collectively safeguards commerce from injury, impairment, or interruption, and promotes the flow of commerce by removing certain recognized sources of industrial strife and unrest, by encouraging practices fundamental to the friendly adjustment of industrial disputes arising out of differences as to wages, hours, or other working conditions, and by restoring equality of bargaining power between employers and employees.

Experience has further demonstrated that certain practices by some labor organizations, their officers, and members have the intent or the necessary effect of burdening or obstructing commerce by preventing the free flow of goods in such commerce through strikes and other forms of industrial unrest or through concerted activities which impair the interest of the public in the free flow of such commerce. The elimination of such practices is a necessary condition to the assurance of the rights herein guaranteed.

It is hereby declared to be the policy of the United States to eliminate the causes of certain substantial obstructions to the free flow of commerce and to mitigate and eliminate these obstructions when they have occurred by encouraging the practice and procedure of collective bargaining and by protecting the exercise by workers of full freedom of association, self-organization, and designation of representatives of their own choosing, for the purpose of negotiating the terms and conditions of their employment or other mutual aid or protection.

DEFINITIONS

SECTION 2. When used in this Act—

(1) The term "person" includes one or more individuals, labor organizations, partnerships, associations, corporations, legal representatives, trustees, trustees in bankruptcy, or receivers.

(2) The term "employer" includes any person acting as an agent of an employer, directly or indirectly, but shall not include the United States or any wholly owned Government corporation, or any Federal Reserve Bank, or any State or political subdivision thereof, or any person subject to the Railway Labor Act, as amended from time to time, or any labor organization (other than when acting as an employer), or anyone acting in the capacity of officer or agent of such labor organization.

(3) The term "employee" shall include any employee, and shall not be limited to the employees of a particular employer, unless the Act explicitly states otherwise, and shall include any individual whose work has ceased as a consequence of, or in connection with, any current labor dispute or because of any unfair labor practice, and who has not obtained any other regular and substantially equivalent employment, but shall not include any individual employed as an agricultural laborer, or in the domestic service of any family or person at his home, or any individual employed by his parent or spouse, or any individual having the status of an independent contractor, or any individual employed as a supervisor, or any individual employed by an employer subject to the Railway Labor Act, as amended from time to time, or by any other person who is not an employer as herein defined.

(4) The term "representatives" includes any individual or labor organization.

(5) The term "labor organization" means any organization of any kind, or any agency or employee representation committee or plan, in which employees participate and which exists for the purpose, in whole or in part, of dealing with employers concerning grievances, labor disputes, wages, rates of pay, hours of employment, or conditions of work.

(6) The term "commerce" means trade, traffic, commerce, transportation, or communication among the several States, or between the District of Columbia or any Territory of the United States and any State or other Territory, or between any foreign country and any State, Territory, or the District of Columbia, or within the District of Columbia or any Territory, or between points in the same State but through any other State or any Territory or the District of Columbia or any foreign country.

(7) The term "affecting commerce" means in commerce, or burdening or obstructing commerce or the free flow of commerce, or having led or tending to lead to a labor dispute burdening or obstructing commerce or the free flow of commerce.

(8) The term "unfair labor practice" means any unfair labor practice listed in Section 8.

(9) The term "labor dispute" includes any controversy concerning terms, tenure or conditions of employment, or concerning the association or representation of persons in negotiating, fixing, maintaining, changing, or seeking to arrange terms or conditions of employment, regardless of whether the disputants stand in the proximate relation of employer and employee.

(10) The term "National Labor Relations Board" means the National Labor Relations Board provided for in Section 3 of this Act.

(11) The term "supervisor" means any individual having authority, in the interest of the employer, to hire, transfer, suspend, lay off, recall, promote, discharge, assign, reward, or discipline other employees, or responsibly to direct them, or to adjust their grievances, or effectively to recommend such action, if in connection with the foregoing the exercise of such authority is not of a merely routine or clerical nature, but requires the use of independent judgment.

(12) The term "professional employee" means—

> (a) any employee engaged in work (i) predominantly intellectual and varied in character as opposed to routine mental, manual, mechanical, or physical work; (ii)

involving the consistent exercise of discretion and judgment in its performance; (iii) of such a character that the output produced or the result accomplished cannot be standardized in relation to a given period of time; (iv) requiring knowledge of an advanced type in a field of science or learning customarily acquired by a prolonged course of specialized intellectual instruction and study in an institution of higher learning or a hospital, as distinguished from a general academic education or from an apprenticeship or from training in the performance of routine mental, manual, or physical processes; or

(b) any employee, who (i) has completed the courses of specialized intellectual instruction and study described in clause (iv) of paragraph (a), and (ii) is performing related work under the supervision of a professional person to qualify himself to become a professional employee as defined in paragraph (a).

(13) In determining whether any person is acting as an "agent" of another person so as to make such other person responsible for his acts, the question of whether the specific acts performed were actually authorized or subsequently ratified shall not be controlling.

(14) The term "health care institution" shall include any hospital, convalescent hospital, health maintenance organization, health clinic, nursing home, extended care facility, or other institution devoted to the care of sick, infirm, or aged persons.

NATIONAL LABOR RELATIONS BOARD

SECTION 3. (a) The National Labor Relations Board (hereinafter called the "Board") created by this Act prior to its amendment by the Labor Management Relations Act, 1947, is hereby continued as an agency of the United States, except that the Board shall consist of five instead of three members, appointed by the President by and with the advice and consent of the Senate. Of the two additional members so provided for, one shall be appointed for a term of five years and the other for a term of two years. Their successors, and the successors of the other members, shall be appointed for terms of five years each, excepting that any individual chosen to fill a vacancy shall be appointed only for the unexpired term of the member whom he shall succeed. The President shall designate one member to serve as Chairman of the Board. Any member of the Board may be removed by the President, upon notice and hearing, for neglect of duty or malfeasance in office, but for no other cause.

(b) The Board is authorized to delegate to any group of three or more members any or all of the powers which it may itself exercise. The Board is also authorized to delegate to its regional directors its powers under Section 9 to determine the unit appropriate for the purpose of collective bargaining, to investigate and provide for hearings, and determine whether a question of representation exists, and to direct an election or take a secret ballot under subsection (c) or (e) of Section 9 and certify the results thereof, except that upon the filing of a request therefore with the Board by any interested person, the Board may review any action of a regional director delegated to him under this paragraph, but such a review shall not, unless specifically ordered by the Board, operate as a stay of any action taken by the regional director. A vacancy in the Board shall not impair the right of the remaining members to exercise all of the powers of the Board, and three members of the Board shall, at all times, constitute a quorum of the Board, except that two members shall constitute a quorum of any group designated pursuant to the first sentence hereof. The Board shall have an official seal which shall be judicially noticed.

(c) The Board shall at the close of each fiscal year make a report in writing to Congress to the President stating in detail the cases it has heard, the decisions it has rendered, and an account of all moneys it has disbursed.

(d) There shall be a General Counsel of the Board who shall be appointed by the President, by and with the advice and consent of the Senate, for a term of four years. The General Counsel of the Board shall exercise general supervision over all attorneys employed by the Board (other than trial examiners and legal assistants to Board members) and over the officers and employees in the regional offices. He shall have final authority, on behalf of the Board, in respect of the investigation of charges and issuance of complaints under Section 10, and in respect of the prosecution of such complaints before the Board, and shall have such other duties as the Board may prescribe or as may be provided by law. In case of a vacancy in the office of the General Counsel the President is authorized to designate the officer or employee who shall act as General Counsel during such vacancy, but no person or persons so designated shall so act (1) for more than forty days when the Congress is in session unless a nomination to fill such vacancy shall have been submitted to the Senate, or (2) after the adjournment *sine die* of the session of the Senate in which such nomination was submitted.

SECTION 4. (a) Each member of the Board and the General Counsel of the Board shall receive a salary of $12,000[*] a year, shall be eligible for reappointment, and shall not engage in any other business, vocation, or employment. The Board shall appoint an executive secretary, and such attorneys, examiners, and regional directors, and such other employees as it may from time to time find necessary fro the proper performance of its duties. The Board may not employ any attorneys for the purpose of reviewing transcripts of hearings or preparing drafts of opinions except that any attorney employed for assignment as a legal assistant to any Board member may for such Board member review such transcripts and prepare such drafts. No trial examiner's report shall be reviewed, either before or

after its publication, by any person other than a member of the Board or his legal assistant, and no trial examiner shall advise or consult with the Board with respect to exceptions taken to his findings, rulings, or recommendations. The Board may establish or utilize such regional, local, or other agencies, and utilize such voluntary and uncompensated ser-vices, as may from time to time be needed. Attorneys appointed under this section may, at the direction of the Board, appear for and represent the Board in any case in court. Nothing in this Act shall be construed to authorize the Board to appoint individuals for the purpose of conciliation or mediation, or for economic analysis.

(b) All of the expenses of the Board, including all necessary traveling and subsistence expenses outside the District of Columbia incurred by the members or employees of the Board under its orders, shall be allowed and paid on the presentation of itemized vouchers therefor approved by the Board or by any individual it designates for that purpose.

SECTION 5. The principal office of the Board shall be in the District of Columbia, but it may meet and exercise any or all of its powers at any other place. The Board may, by one or more of its members or by such agents or agencies as it may designate, prosecute any inquiry necessary to its functions in any part of the United States. A member who participates in such an inquiry shall not be disqualified from subsequently participating in a decision of the Board in the same case.

SECTION 6. The Board shall have authority from time to time to make, amend, and rescind, in the manner prescribed by the Administrative Procedure Act, such rules and regulations as may be necessary to carry out the provisions of this Act.

---

[*]Pursuant to Public Law 9-206, 90th Cong. 81 Stat. 644, approved Dec. 16, 1967, and in accordance with Sec. 225 (f)(ii) thereof, effective in 1969, the salary of the Chairman of the Board shall be $40,000 per year and the salaries of the General Counsel and each Board member shall be $38,000 per year.

RIGHTS OF EMPLOYEES

SECTION 7. Employees shall have the right to self-organization, to form, join, or assist labor organizations, to bargain collectively through representatives of their own choosing, and to engage in other concerted activities for the purpose of collective bargaining or other mutual aid or protection, and shall also have the right to refrain from any or all of such activities except to the extent that such right may be affected by an agreement requiring membership in a labor organization as a condition of employment as authorized in Section 8(a) (3).

UNFAIR LABOR PRACTICES

SECTION 8. (a) It shall be an unfair labor practice for an employer—

(1) to interfere with, restrain, or coerce employees in the exercise of the rights guaranteed in Section 7;

(2) to dominate or interfere with the formation or administration of any labor organization or contribute financial or other support to it: *Provided*, That subject to rules and regulations made and published by the Board pursuant to Section 6, an employer shall not be prohibited from permitting employees to confer with him during working hours without loss of time or pay;

(3) by discrimination in regard to hire or tenure of employment or any term or condition of employment to encourage or discourage membership in any labor organization: *Provided*, That nothing in this Act, or in any other statute of the United States, shall preclude an employer from making an agreement with a labor organization (not established, maintained, or assisted by any action defined in Section 8(a) of this Act as an unfair labor practice) to require as a condition of employment membership therein on or after the thirtieth day following the beginning of such employment or the effective date of such agreement, whichever is the later, (i) if such labor organization is the representative of the employees as provided in Section 9(a), in the

appropriate collective-bargaining unit covered by such agreement when made, and (ii) unless following an election held as provided in Section 9(e) within one year preceding the effective date of such agreement, the Board shall have certified that at least a majority of the employees eligible to vote in such election have voted to rescind the authority of such labor organization to make such an agreement: *Provided further*, That no employer shall justify any discrimination against an employee for nonmembership in a labor organization (A) if he has reasonable grounds for believing that such membership was not available to the employee on the same terms and conditions generally applicable to other members, or (B) if he has reasonable grounds for believing that membership was denied or terminated for reasons other than the failure of the employee to tender the periodic dues and the initiation fees uniformly required as a condition of acquiring or retaining membership;

(4) to discharge or otherwise discriminate against an employee because he has filed charges or given testimony under this Act;

(5) to refuse to bargain collectively with the representatives of his employees, subject to the provisions of Section 9(a).

(b) It shall be an unfair labor practice for a labor organization or its agents—

(1) to restrain or coerce (A) employees in the exercise of the rights guaranteed in Section 7: *Provided*, That this paragraph shall not impair the right of a labor organization to prescribe its own rules with respect to the acquisition or retention of membership therein; or (B) an employer in the selection of his representatives for the purposes of collective bargaining of the adjustment of grievances;

(2) to cause or attempt to cause an employer to discriminate against an employee in violation of subsection (a)(3) or to discriminate against an employee with respect to whom membership in such organization has been denied or terminated on some ground other than his failure to tender the periodic dues and the initiation fees

uniformly required as a condition of acquiring or retaining membership:

(3) to refuse to bargain collectively with an employer, provided it is the representative of his employees subject to the provisions of Section 9(a);

(4)(i) to engage in, or to induce or encourage any individual employed by any person engaged in commerce or in an industry affecting commerce to engage in, a strike or a refusal in the course of his employment to use, manufacture, process, transport, or otherwise handle or work on any goods, articles, materials, or commodities or to perform any services; or (ii) to threaten, coerce, or restrain any person engaged in commerce or in an industry affecting commerce, where in either case an object thereof is:

(A) forcing or requiring any employer or self-employed person to join any labor or employer organization or to enter into any agreement which is prohibited by Section 8(e);

(B) forcing or requiring any person to cease using, selling, handling, transporting, or otherwise dealing in the products of any other producer, processor, or manufacturer, or to cease doing business with any other person, or forcing or requiring any other employer to recognize or bargain with a labor organization as the representative of his employees unless such labor organization has been certified as the representative of such employees under the provisions of Section 9: *Provided*, That nothing contained in this clause (B) shall be construed to make unlawful, where not otherwise unlawful, any primary strike or primary picketing;

(C) forcing or requiring any employer to recognize or bargain with a particular labor organization as the representative of his employees if another labor organization has been certified as the representative of such employees under the provisions of Section 9;

(D) forcing or requiring any employer to assign particular work to employees in a particular labor organization or in a particular trade, craft, or class rather than to employees in another labor organization or in another trade, craft, or class, unless such employer is failing to conform to an order or certification of the Board, determining the bargaining representative for employees performing such work:

Provided, That nothing contained in this subsection (b) shall be construed to make unlawful a refusal by any person to enter upon the premises of any employer (other than his own employer), if the employees of such employer are engaged in a strike ratified or approved by a representative of such employees whom such employer is required to recognize under this Act: *Provided further*, That for the purposes of this paragraph (4) only, nothing contained in such paragraph shall be construed to prohibit publicity, other than picketing, for the purpose of truthfully advising the public, including consumers and members of a labor organization, that a product or products are produced by an employer with whom the labor organization has a primary dispute and are distributed by another employer, as long as such publicity does not have an effect of inducing any individual employed by any person other than the primary employer in the course of his employment to refuse to pick up, deliver, or transport any goods, or not to perform any services, at the establishment of the employer engaged in such distribution:

(5) to require of employees covered by an agreement authorized under subsection (a)(3) the payment, as a condition precedent to becoming a member of such organization, of a fee in an amount which the Board finds excessive or discriminatory under all the circumstances. In making such a finding, the Board shall consider among other relevant factors, the practices and customs of labor organizations in the particular industry, and the wages currently paid to the employees affected;

(6) to cause or attempt to cause an employer to pay or deliver or agree to pay or deliver any money or other thing of value, in the nature of an exaction, for services which are not performed or not to be performed; and

(7) to picket or cause to be picketed, or threaten to picket or cause to be picketed, any employer where an object thereof is forcing or requiring an employer to recognize or bargain with a labor organization as the representative of his employees, or forcing or requiring the employees of an employer to accept or select such labor organization as their collective bargaining representative, unless such labor organization is currently certified as the representative of such employees:

(A) where the employer has lawfully recognized in accordance with this Act any other labor organization and a question concerning representation may not appropriately be raised under Section 9(c) of this Act,

(B) where within the preceding twelve months a valid election under Section 9(c) of this Act has been conducted, or

(C) where such picketing has been conducted without a petition under Section 9(c) being filed within a reasonable period of time not to exceed thirty days from the commencement of such picketing: *Provided*, That when such a petition has been filed the Board shall forthwith, without regard to the provisions of Section 9(c)(1) or the absence of a showing of a substantial interest on the part of the labor organization, direct an election in such unit as the Board finds to be appropriate and shall certify the results thereof: *Provided further*, That nothing in this sub-paragraph (C) shall be construed to prohibit any picketing or other publicity for the purpose of truthfully advising the public (including consumers) that an employer does not employ members of, or have a contract with, a labor organization, unless an effect of such picketing is to induce any individual employed by any other person in the course of his employment, not to pick up, deliver or transport any goods or not to perform any services. Nothing in this paragraph (7) shall be construed to permit any act which would otherwise be an unfair labor practice under this Section 8(b).

(c) The expressing of any views, argument, or opinion, or the dissemination thereof, whether in written, printed, graphic, or visual form, shall not constitute or be evidence of an unfair labor practice under any of the provisions of this Act, if such expression contains no threat of reprisal or force or promise of benefit.

(d) For the purposes of this section, to bargain collectively is the performance of the mutual obligation of the employer and the representative of the employees to meet at reasonable times and confer in good faith with respect to wages, hours, and other terms and conditions of employment, or the negotiation of an agreement, or any question arising thereunder, and the execution of a written contract incorporating any agreement reached if requested by either party, but such obligation does not compel either party to agree to a proposal or require the making of a concession: *Provided*, That where there is in effect a collective-bargaining contract covering employees in an industry affecting commerce, the duty to bargain collectively shall also mean that no party to such contract shall terminate or modify such contract, unless the party desiring such termination or modification—

(1) serves a written notice upon the other party to the contract of the proposed termination or modification sixty days prior to the expiration date thereof, or in the event such contract contains no expiration date, sixty days prior to the time it is proposed to make such termination or modification;

(2) offers to meet and confer with the other party for the purpose of negotiating a new contract or a contract containing the proposed modifications;

(3) notifies the Federal Mediation and Conciliation Service within thirty days after such notice of the existence of a dispute, and simultaneously therewith notifies any State or Territorial agency established to mediate and conciliate disputes within the State or Territory where the dispute occurred, provided no agreement has been reached by that time; and

(4) continues in full force and effect, without resorting to strike or lockout, all the terms and conditions of the existing contract for a period of sixty days after such notice is given or until the expiration date of such contract, whichever occurs later.

The duties imposed upon employers, employees, and labor organizations by paragraphs (2), (3), and (4) shall become inapplicable upon an intervening certification of the Board, under which the labor organization or individual, which is a party to the contract, has been superseded as or ceased to be the representative of the employees subject to the provisions of Section 9(a), and the duties so imposed shall not be construed as requiring either party to discuss or agree to any modification of the terms and conditions contained in a contract for a fixed period, if such modification is to become effective before such terms and conditions can be reopened under the provisions of the contract. Any employee who engages in a strike within any notice period specified in this subsection, or who engages in any strike within the appropriate period specified in subsection (g) of this section shall lose his status as an employee of the employer engaged in the particular labor disputes, for the purposes of Sections 8, 9, and 10 of this Act, as amended, but such loss of status for such employee shall terminate if and when he is reemployed by such employer. Whenever the collective bargaining involves employees of a health care institution, the provisions of this Section 8(d) shall be modified as follows:

(A) The notice of Section 8(d)(1) shall be ninety days; the notice of Section 8(d)(3) shall be sixty days; and the contract period of Section (8)(d)(4) shall be ninety days;

(B) Where the bargaining is for an initial agreement following certification or recognition, at least thirty days' notice of the existence of a dispute shall be given by the labor organization to the agencies set forth in Section 8(d)(3).

(C) After notice is given to the Federal Mediation and Conciliation Service under either clause (A) or (B) of this sentence, the Service shall promptly communicate with the parties and use its best efforts, by mediation and conciliation, to bring them to agreement. The parties shall participate fully and promptly in such meetings as may be undertaken by the Service for the purpose of aiding in a settlement of the dispute.

(e) It shall be an unfair labor practice for any labor organization and any employer to enter into any contract or agreement, express or implied, whereby such employer ceases or refrains or agrees to cease or refrain from handling, using, selling, transporting or otherwise dealing in any of the products of any other employer, or to cease doing business with any other person, and any contract or agreement entered into heretofore or hereafter containing such an agreement shall be to such extent unenforceable and void: *Provided*, That nothing in this subjection (e) shall apply to an agreement between a labor organization and an employer in the construction industry relating to the contracting or subcontracting of work to be done at the site of the construction, alteration, painting, or repair of a building, structure, or other work: *Provided further*, That for the purposes of this subjection (e) and Section 8(b)(4)(B) the terms "any employer", "any person engaged in commerce or in industry affecting commerce", and "any person" when used in relation to the terms "any other producer, processor, or manufacturer", "any other employer", or "any other person" shall not include persons in the relation of a jobber, manufacturer, contractor, or subcontractor working on the goods or premises of the jobber or manufacturer or performing parts of an integrated process of production in the apparel and clothing industry: *Provided further*, That nothing in this Act shall prohibit the enforcement of any agreement which is within the foregoing exception.

(f) It shall not be an unfair labor practice under subsections (a) and (b) of this section for an employer engaged primarily in the building and construction industry to make an agreement covering employees engaged (or who, upon their employment, will be engaged) in the building and construction industry with a labor organization of which building and construction employees are members (not established, maintained, or assisted by any action defined in Section 8(a) of this Act as an unfair labor practice) because (1) the majority status of such labor organization has not been established under the provisions of Section 9 of this Act prior to the making of such agreement, or (2) such agreement requires as a condition of employment, membership in such labor organization after the seventh day following the beginning of such employment or the effective date of the agreement, whichever is later, or (3) such agreement requires the employer to notify such labor organization of opportunities for employment with such employer, or gives such labor organization an opportunity to refer qualified applicants for such employment, or (4) such agreement specifies minimum training or experience qualifications for employment or provides for priority in opportunities for employment based upon length of service with such employer, in the industry or in the particular geographical area: *Provided*, That nothing in this subsection shall set aside the final proviso to Section 8(a)(3) of this Act: *Provided further*, That any agreement which would be invalid, but for clause (1) of this subsection, shall not be a bar to a petition filed pursuant to Section 9(c) or 9(e).*

(g) A labor organization before engaging in any strike, picketing, or other concerted refusal to work at any health care institution shall, not less than ten days prior to such action, notify the institution in writing and the Federal Mediation and Conciliation Service of that intention, except that in the case of bargaining for an initial agreement following certification or recognition the notice required by this subsection shall not be given until the expiration of the period specified in clause (B) of the last sentence of Section 8(d) of this Act. The notice shall state the date and time that such action will commerce. The notice, once given, may be extended by the written agreement of both parties.

REPRESENTATIVES AND ELECTIONS

SECTION 9. (a) Representatives designated or selected for the purposes of collective bargaining by the majority of the employees in a unit appropriate for such purposes, shall be the exclusive representatives of all the employees in such unit for the purposes of collective bargaining in respect to rates of pay, wages, hours of employment, or other conditions of employment: *Provided*, That any individual employee or a group of employees shall have the right at any time to present grievances to their employer and to have such grievances adjusted, without the intervention of the bargaining representative, as long as the adjustment is not inconsistent with the terms of a collective-bargaining contract or agreement then in effect: *Provided further*, That the bargaining representative has been given opportunity to be present at such adjustment.

(b) The Board shall decide in each case whether, in order to assure to employees the fullest freedom in exercising the rights guaranteed by this Act, the unit appropriate for the purposes of collective bargaining shall be the employer unit, craft unit, plant unit, or subdivision thereof: *Provided*, That the Board shall not (1) decide that any unit is appropriate for such purposes if such unit includes both professional employees and employees who are not professional

---

*Sec. 8(f) is inserted in the Act by subsec. (a) of Sec. 705 of Public Law 86-257. Sec. 705(b) provides:

Nothing contained in the amendment made by sub-section (a) shall be construed as authorizing the execution or application of agreements requiring membership in a labor organization as a condition of employment in any State or Territory in which such execution or application is prohibited by State or Territorial law.

employees unless a majority of such professional employees vote for inclusion in such unit; or (2) decide that any craft unit is inappropriate for such purposes on the ground that a different unit has been established by a prior Board determination, unless a majority of the employees in the proposed craft unit vote against separate representation or (3) decide that any unit is appropriate for such purposes if it includes, together with other employees, any individual employed as a guard to enforce against employees and other persons rules to protect property of the employer or to protect the safety of persons on the employer's premises; but no labor organization shall be certified as the representative of employees in a bargaining unit of guards if such organization admits to membership, or is affiliated directly or indirectly with an organization which admits to membership, employees other than guards.

(c)(1) Wherever a petition shall have been filed, in accordance with such regulations as may be prescribed by the Board—

(A) by an employee or group of employees or any individual or labor organization acting in their behalf alleging that a substantial number of employees (i) wish to be represented for collective bargaining and that their employer declines to recognize their representative as the representative defined in Section 9(a), or (ii) assert that the individual or labor organization, which has been certified or is being currently recognized by their employer as the bargaining representative, is no longer a representative as defined in Section 9(a); or

(B) by an employer, alleging that one or more individuals or labor organizations have presented to him a claim to be recognized as the representative defined in Section 9(a);

the Board shall investigate such petition and if it has reasonable cause to believe that a question of representation affecting commerce exists shall provide for an appropriate hearing upon due notice. Such hearing may be conducted by an officer or employee of the regional office, who shall not make any recommendations with respect thereto.

If the Board finds upon the record of such hearing that such a question of representation exists, it shall direct an election by secret ballot and shall certify the results thereof.

(2) In determining whether or not a question of representation affecting commerce exists, the same regulations and rules of decision shall apply irrespective of the identity of the persons filing the petition or the kind of relief sought and in no case shall the Board deny a labor organization a place on the ballot by reason of an order with respect to such labor organization or its predecessor not issued in conformity with Section 10(c).

(3) No election shall be directed in any bargaining unit or any subdivision within which, in the preceding twelve-month period, a valid election shall have been held. Employees engaged in an economic strike who are not entitled to reinstatement shall be eligible to vote under such regulations as the Board shall find are consistent with the purposes and provisions of this Act in any election conducted within twelve months after the commencement of the strike. In any election where none of the choice on the ballot receives a majority, a run-off shall be conducted, the ballot providing for a selection between the two choices receiving the largest and second largest number of valid votes cast in the election.

(4) Nothing in this section shall be construed to prohibit the waiving of hearings by stipulation for the purpose of a consent election in conformity with regulations and rules of decision of the Board.

(5) In determining whether a unit is appropriate for the purposes specified in subsection (b) the extent to which the employees have organized shall not be controlling.

(d) Whenever an order of the Board made pursuant to Section 10(c) is based in whole or in part upon facts certified following an investigation pursuant to subsection (c) of this section and there is a petition for the enforcement or review of such order, such certification and the record of such investigation shall be included in the transcript of the entire record required to be filed under Section 10(e) or 10(f), and thereupon the decree of the court- enforcing, modifying, or setting aside in whole or in part the order of the Board shall be made and entered upon the pleadings, testimony, and proceedings set forth in such transcript.

(e)(1) Upon the filing with the Board, by 30 per centum or more of the employees in a bargaining unit covered by an agreement between their employer and a labor organization made pursuant to Section 8(a)(3), of a petition alleging they desire that such authority be rescinded, the Board shall take a secret ballot of the employees in such unit and certify the results thereof to such labor organization and to the employer.

(2) No election shall be conducted pursuant to this subsection in any bargaining unit or any subdivision within which, in the preceding twelve-month period, a valid election shall have been held.

PREVENTION OF UNFAIR LABOR PRACTICES

SECTION 10. (a) The Board is empowered, as hereinafter provided, to prevent any person from engaging in any unfair labor practice (listed in Section 8) affecting commerce. This power shall not be affected by any other means of adjustment or prevention that has been or may be established by agreement, law, or otherwise: *Provided,* That the Board is empowered by agreement with any agency of any State or Territory to cede to such agency jurisdiction over any cases in any industry (other than mining, manufacturing, communications, and transportation except where predominantly local in character) even though such cases may involve labor disputes affecting commerce, unless the provision of the State or Territorial statute applicable to the determination of such cases by such agency is inconsistent with the corresponding provision of this Act or has received a construction inconsistent therewith.

(b) Whenever it is charged that any person has engaged in or is engaging in any such unfair labor practice, the Board, or any agent or agency designated by the Board for such purposes, shall have power to issue and cause to be served upon such person a complaint stating the charges in that respect, and containing a notice of hearing before the Board or a member thereof, or before a designated agent or agency, at a place therein fixed, not less than five days after the serving of said complaint: *Provided,* That no complaint shall issue based upon any unfair labor practice occurring more than six months prior to the filing of the charge with the Board and the service of a copy thereof upon the person against whom such charge is made, unless the person aggrieved thereby was prevented from filing such charge by reason of service in the armed forces, in which event the six-month period shall be computed from the day of his discharge. Any such complaint may be amended by the member, agent, or agency conducting the hearing or the Board in its discretion at any time prior to the issuance of an order based thereon. The person so complained of shall have the right to file an answer to the original or amended complaint and to appear in person or otherwise and give testimony at the place and time fixed in the complaint. In the discretion of the member, agent, or agency conducting the hearing or the Board, any other person may be allowed to intervene in the said proceeding and to present testimony. Any such proceeding shall, so far as practicable, be conducted in accordance with the rules of evidence applicable in the district courts of the United States under the rules of civil procedure for the district courts of the United States, adopted by the Supreme Court of the United States pursuant to the Act of June 19, 1934 (U.S.C. Title 28, Secs. 723-B, 723-C).

(c) The testimony taken by such member, agent, or agency or the Board shall be reduced to writing and filed with the Board. Thereafter, in its discretion, the Board upon notice may take further testimony or hear argument. If upon the preponderance of the testimony taken the Board shall be of the opinion that any person named in the complaint has engaged in or is engaging in any such unfair labor practice, then the Board shall state its findings of fact and shall issue and cause to be served on such person an order requiring such person to cease and desist from such unfair labor practice, and to take such affirmative action including reinstatement of employees with or without back pay, as will effectuate the policies of this Act: *Provided*, That where an order directs reinstatement of an employee, back pay may be required of the employer or labor organization, as the case may be, responsible for the discrimination suffered by him: *And provided further*, That in determining whether a complaint shall issue alleging a violation of Section 8(a)(1) or Section 8(a)(2), and in deciding such cases, the same regulations and rules of decision shall apply irrespective of whether or not the labor organization affected is affiliated with a labor organization national or international in scope. Such order may further require such person to make reports from time to time showing the extent to which it has complied with the order. If upon the preponderance of the testimony taken the Board shall not be of the opinion that the person named in the complaint has engaged in or is engaging in any such unfair labor practice, then the Board shall state its findings of fact and shall issue an order dismissing the said complaint. No order of the Board shall require the reinstatement of any individual as an employee who has been suspended or discharged, or the payment to him of any back pay, if such individual was suspended or discharged for cause. In case the evidence is presented before a member of the Board, or before an examiner or examiners thereof, such member, or such examiner or examiners, as the case may be, shall issue and cause to be served on the parties to the proceeding a proposed report, together with a recommended order, which shall be filed with the Board, and if no exceptions are filed within twenty days after service thereof upon such parties, or within such further period as the Board may authorize, such recommended order shall become the order of the Board and become effective as therein prescribed.

(d) Until the record in a case shall have been filed in a court, as hereinafter provided, the Board may at any time, upon reasonable notice and in such manner as it shall deem proper, modify or set aside, in whole or in part, any finding or order made or issued by it.

(e) The Board shall have power to petition any court of appeals of the United States, or if all the courts of appeals to which application may be made are in vacation, any district court of the United States, within any circuit or district, respectively, wherein the unfair labor practice in question occurred or wherein such person resides or transacts business, for the enforcement of such order and for appropriate temporary relief or restraining order, and shall file in the court the record in the proceedings, as provided in Section 2112 of Title 28, United States Code. Upon the filing of such petition, the court shall cause notice thereof to be served upon such person, and thereupon shall have jurisdiction of the proceeding and of the question determining therein, and shall have power to grant such temporary relief or restraining order as it deems just and proper, and to make and enter a decree enforcing, modifying, and enforcing as so modified, or setting aside in whole or in part the order of the Board. No objection that has not been urged before the Board, its member, agent, or agency, shall be considered by the court, unless the failure or neglect to urge such objection shall be excused because of extraordinary circumstances. The findings of the Board with respect to questions of fact if supported by substantial evidence on the record considered as a whole shall be conclusive. If either party shall apply to the court for leave to adduce additional evidence and shall show to the satisfaction of the court that such additional evidence is material and that there were reasonable grounds for the failure to adduce such evidence in the hearing before the Board, its member, agent, or agency, the court may order such additional evidence to be taken before the Board, its member, agent, or agency, and to be made a part of the record. The Board may modify its findings as to the facts, or make new findings, by reason of additional evidence so taken and filed, and it shall file such modified or new findings, which findings with respect to questions of fact if supported by substantial evidence on the record considered as a whole shall be conclusive, and shall file its recommendations, if any, for the modification or setting aside of its original order.

Upon the filing of the record with it the jurisdiction of the court shall be exclusive and its judgment and decree shall be final, except that the same shall be subject to review by the appropriate United States court of appeals if application was made to the district court as hereinabove provided, and by the Supreme Court of the United States upon writ of certiorari or certification as provided in Section 1254 of Title 28.

(f) Any person aggrieved by a final order of the Board granting or denying in whole or in part the relief sought may obtain a review of such order in any circuit court of appeals of the United States in the circuit of appeals of the United States in the circuit wherein the unfair labor practice in question was alleged to have been engaged in or wherein such person resides or transacts business, or in the United States Court of Appeals for the District of Columbia, by filing in such court a written petition praying that the order of the Board be modified or set aside. A copy of such petition shall be forthwith transmitted by the clerk of the court to the Board, and thereupon the aggrieved party shall file in the court the record in the proceeding, certified by the Board, as provided in Section 2112 of Title 28, United States Code. Upon the filing of such petition, the court shall proceed in the same manner as in the case of an application by the Board under subsection (e) of this section, and shall have the same jurisdiction to grant to the Board such temporary relief or restraining order as it deems just and proper, and in like manner to make and enter a decree enforcing, modifying, and enforcing as so modified, or setting aside in whole or in part the order of the Board; the findings of the Board with respect to questions of fact if supported by substantial evidence on the record considered as a whole shall be conclusive.

(g) The commencement of proceedings under subsection (e) or (f) of this section shall not, unless specifically ordered by the court, operate as a stay of the Board's order.

(h) When granting appropriate temporary relief or a restraining order, or making and entering a decree enforcing, modifying, and enforcing as so modified, or setting aside in whole or in part an order of the Board, as provided in this section, the jurisdiction of courts sitting in equity shall not be limited by the Act entitled "An Act to amend the Judicial Code and to define and limit the jurisdiction of courts sitting in equity, and for other purposes," approved March 23, 1932 (U.S.C. Supp. VII, Title 29, Secs. 101–115).

(i) Petitions filed under this Act shall be heard expeditiously, and if possible within ten days after they have been docketed.

(j) The Board shall have power, upon issuance of a complaint as provided in subsection (b) charging that any person has engaged in or is engaging in an unfair labor practice, to petition any district court of the United States (including the District Court of the United States for the District of Columbia), within any district wherein the unfair labor practice in question is alleged to have occurred or wherein such person resides or transacts business, for appropriate temporary relief or restraining order. Upon the filing of any such petition the court shall cause notice thereof to be served upon such person, and thereupon shall have jurisdiction to grant to the Board such temporary relief or restraining order as it deems just and proper.

(k) Whenever it is charged that any person has engaged in an unfair labor practice within the meaning of paragraph (4)(D) of Section 8(b), the Board is empowered and directed to hear and determine the dispute out of which such unfair labor practice shall have arisen, unless, within ten days after notice that such charge has been filed, the parties to such dispute submit to the Board satisfactory evidence that they have adjusted, or agreed upon methods for the voluntary adjustment of, the dispute. Upon compliance by the parties to the dispute with the decision of the Board or upon such voluntary adjustment of the dispute, such charge shall be dismissed.

(l) Whenever it is charged that any person has engaged in an unfair labor practice within the meaning of paragraph (4)(A), (B), or (C) of Section 8(b), or Section 8(e) or section 8(b)(7), the preliminary investigation of such charge shall be made forthwith and given priority over all other cases except cases of like character in the office where it is filed or to which it is referred. If, after such investigation, the officer or regional attorney to whom the matter may be referred has reasonable cause to believe such charge is true and that a complaint should issue, he shall, on behalf of the Board, petition any district court of the United States (including the District Court of the United States for the District of Columbia) within any district where the unfair labor practice in question has occurred, is alleged to have occurred, or wherein such person resides or transacts business, for appropriate injunctive relief pending the final adjudication of the Board with respect to such matter. Upon the filing of any such petition the district court shall have jurisdiction to grant such injunctive relief or temporary restraining order as it deems just and proper, notwithstanding any other provision of law: *Provided further*, That no temporary restraining order shall be issued without notice unless a petition alleges that substantial and irreparable injury to the charging party will be unavoidable and such temporary restraining order shall be effective for no longer than five days and will become void at the expiration of such period: *Provided further*, That such officer or regional attorney shall not apply for any restraining order under Section 8(b)(7) if a charge against the employer under Section 8(a)(2) has been filed and after the preliminary investigation, he has reasonable cause to believe that such charge is true and that a complaint should issue. Upon filing of any such petition the courts shall cause notice thereof to be served upon any person involved in the charge and such person, including the charging party, shall be given an opportunity to appear by counsel and present any relevant testimony: *Provided further*, That for the purposes of this subsection district courts shall be deemed to have jurisdiction of a labor organization (1) in the district in which such organization maintains its principal office, or (2) in any district in which its duly authorized officers or agents are engaged in promoting or protecting the interests of employee members. The service of legal process upon such officer or agent shall constitute service upon the labor organization and make such organizations a party to the suit. In situations

where such relief is appropriate the procedure specified herein shall apply to charges with respect to Section 8(b)(4)(D).

(m) Whenever it is charged that any person has engaged in an unfair labor practice within the meaning of subsection (a)(3) or (b)(2) of Section 8, such charge shall be given priority over all other cases except cases of like character in the office where it is filed or to which it is referred and cases given priority under subsection (1).

INVESTIGATORY POWERS

SECTION 11. For the purpose of all hearings and investigations, which, in the opinion of the Board, are necessary and proper for the exercise of the powers vested in it by Section 9 and Section 10—

(1) The Board, or its duly authorized agents or agencies, shall at all reasonable times have access to, for the purpose of examination, and the right to copy any evidence of any person being investigated or proceeded against that relates to any matter under investigation or in question. The Board, or any member thereof, shall upon application of any party to such proceedings, forthwith issue to such party subpoenas requiring the attendance and testimony of witnesses or the production of any evidence in such proceeding or investigation requested in such application. Within five days after the ser-vice of a subpoena on any person requiring the production of any evidence in his possession or under his control, such person may petition the Board to revoke, and the Board shall revoke, such subpoena if in its opinion the evidence whose production is required does not relate to any matter under investigation, or any matter in question in such proceedings, or if in its opinion such subpoena does not describe with sufficient particularity the evidence whose production is required. Any member of the Board, or any agent or agency designated by the Board for such purposes, may administer oaths and affirmations, examine witnesses, and receive evidence. Such attendance of witnesses and the production of such evidence may be required from any place in the United

States or any Territory or possession thereof, at any designated place of hearing.

(2) In case of contumacy or refusal to obey a subpoena issued to any person, any district court of the United States or the United States courts of any Territory or possession, or the District Court of the United States for the District of Columbia, within the jurisdiction of which the inquiry is carried on or within the jurisdiction of which said person guilty of contumacy or refusal to obey is found or resides or transacts business, upon application by the Board shall have jurisdiction to issue to such person an order requiring such person to appear before the Board, its member, agent, or agency, there to produce evidence if so ordered, or there to give testimony touching the matter under investigation or in question; and any failure to obey such order of the court may be punished by said court as a contempt thereof.

(3)*

(4) Complaints, order, and other process and papers of the Board, its member, agent, or agency, may be served either personally or by registered mail or by telegraph or by leaving a copy thereof at the principal office or place of business of the person required to be served. The verified return by the individual so serving the same setting forth the manner of such service shall be proof of the same, and the return post office receipt or telegraph receipt therefor when registered and mailed or telegraphed as aforesaid shall be proof of service of the same. Witnesses summoned before the Board, its member, agent, or agency, shall be paid the same fees and mileage that are paid witnesses in the courts of the United States, and witnesses whose depositions are taken and the persons taking the same shall severally be entitled to the same fees as are paid for like services in the courts of the United States.

(5) All process of any court to which application may be made under this Act may be served in the judicial district wherein the defendant or other person required to be served resides or may be found.

(6) The several departments and agencies of the Government, when directed by the President, shall furnish the Board, upon its request, all records, papers, and information in their possession relating to any matter before the Board.

SECTION 12. Any person who shall willfully resist, prevent, impede, or interfere with any member of the Board or any of its agents or agencies in the performance of duties pursuant to this Act shall be punished by a fine of not more than $5,000 or by imprisonment for not more than one year, or both.

LIMITATIONS

SECTION 13. Nothing in this Act, except as specifically provided for herein, shall be construed so as either to interfere with or impede or diminish in any way the right to strike, or to affect the limitations or qualifications on that right.

SECTION 14. (a) Nothing herein shall prohibit any individual employed as a supervisor from becoming or remaining a member of a labor organization, but no employer subject to this Act shall be compelled to deem individuals defined herein as supervisors as employees for the purpose of any law, either national or local, relating to collective bargaining.

(b) Nothing in this Act shall be construed as authorizing the execution or application of agreements requiring membership in a labor organization as a condition of employment in any State or Territory in which such execution or application is prohibited by State or Territorial law.

(c)(1) The Board, in its discretion, may, by rule of decision or by published rules adopted pursuant to the Administrative Procedure Act, decline to assert jurisdiction over any labor dispute involving any class or category of employers, where, in the opinion of the Board, the effect of such labor dispute on commerce is not sufficiently

---

*Sec. 11(3) is repealed by Sec. 234, Public Law 91-452, 91st Cong., S. 30, 84 Stat. 926, Oct. 15, 1970. See Title 18, U.S.C. Sec. 6001, *et seq.*

substantial to warrant the exercise of its jurisdiction: *Provided*, That the Board shall not decline to assert jurisdiction over any labor dispute over which it would assert jurisdiction under the standards prevailing upon August 1, 1959.

(2) Nothing in this Act shall be deemed to prevent or bar any agency or the courts of any State or Territory (including the Commonwealth of Puerto Rico, Guam, and the Virgin Islands), from assuming and asserting jurisdiction over labor disputes over which the Board declines, pursuant to paragraph (1) of this subsection, to assert jurisdiction.

SECTION 15. Wherever the application of the provisions of Section 272 of chapter 10 of the Act entitled "An Act to establish a uniform system of bankruptcy throughout the United States," approved July 1, 1898, and Acts amendatory thereof and supplementary thereto (U.S.C., Title 11, Sec. 672), conflicts with the application of the provisions of this Act, this Act shall prevail: *Provided*, That in any situation where the provisions of this Act cannot be validly enforced, the provisions of such other Acts shall remain in full force and effect.

SECTION 16. If any provision of this Act, or the application of such provision to any person or circumstances, shall be held invalid, the remainder of this Act, or the application of such provision to persons or circumstances other than those as to which it is held invalid, shall not be affected thereby.

SECTION 17. This Act may be cited as the "National Labor Relations Act."

SECTION 18. No petition entertained, no investigation made, no election held, and no certification issued by the National Labor Relations Board, under any of the provisions of Section 9 of the National Labor Relations Act, as amended, shall be invalid by reason of the failure of the Congress of Industrial Organizations to have complied with the requirements of Section 9(f), (g), or (h) of the aforesaid Act prior to December 22,

1949, or by reason of the failure of the American Federation of Labor to have complied with the provisions of Section 9(f), (g), or (h) of the aforesaid Act prior to November 7, 1947: *Provided*, That no liability shall be imposed under any provision of this Act upon any person for failure to honor any election or certificate referred to above, prior to the effective date of this amendment: *Provided, however*, That this proviso shall not have the effect of setting aside or in any way affecting judgments or decrees heretofore entered under Section 10(e) or (f) and which have become final.

INDIVIDUALS WITH RELIGIOUS CONVICTIONS

SECTION 19. Any employee who is a member of and adheres to established and traditional tenets or teachings of a bona fide religion, body, or sect which has historically held conscientious objections to joining or financially supporting labor organizations shall not be required to join or financially support any labor organization as a condition of employment; except that such employee may be required, in a contract between such employees' employer and a labor organization in lieu of periodic dues and initiation feeds, to pay sums equal to such dues and initiation fees to a nonreligious charitable fund exempt from taxation under Section 501(c)(3) of the Internal Revenue Code, chosen by such employee from a list of at least three such funds, designated in such or if the contract fails to designate such funds, then to any such fund chosen by the employee. If such employee who holds conscientious objections pursuant to this section requests the labor organization to use the grievance-arbitration procedure on the employee's behalf, the labor organization is authorized to charge the employee for the reasonable cost of using such procedure.

EFFECTIVE DATE OF CERTAIN CHANGES

SECTION 102. No provision of this title shall be deemed to make an unfair labor practice any act which was performed prior to the date of the enactment of this Act which did not constitute an unfair labor practice prior hereto, and the provisions of Section 8(a)(3) and Section 8(b)(2) of the National Labor Relations Act as amended by this title shall not make an unfair labor practice the performance of any obligation under a collective-bargaining agreement entered into prior to the date of the enactment of this Act, or (in the case of an agreement for a period of not more than one year) entered into on or after such date of this title, if the performance of such obligation would not have constituted an unfair labor practice under Section 8(3) of the National Labor Relations Act prior to the effective date of this title, unless such agreement was renewed or extended subsequent-thereto.

SECTION 103.   No provisions of this title shall affect any certification of representatives or any determination as to the appropriate collective-bargaining unit, which was made under Section 9 of the National Labor Relations Act prior to the effective date of this title until one year after the date of such certification or if, in respect of any such certification, a collective-bargaining contract was entered into prior to the effective date of this title, until the end of the contract period or until one year after such date, whichever first occurs.

SECTION 104.   The amendments made by this title shall take effect sixty days after the date of the enactment of this Act, except that the authority of the President to appoint certain officers conferred upon him by Section 3 of the National Labor Relations Act as amended by this title may be exercised forthwith.

TITLE II—CONCILIATION OF LABOR DISPUTES IN INDUSTRIES AFFECTING COMMERCE: NATIONAL EMERGENCIES

SECTION 201.   That it is the policy of the United States that—

(a) sound and stable industrial peace and the advancement of the general welfare,

health, and safety of the Nation and of the best interest of employers and employees can most satisfactorily be secured by the settlement of issues between employers and employees through the processes of conference and collective bargaining between employers and the representatives of their employees;

(b) the settlement of issues between employers and employees through collective bargaining may be advanced by making available full and adequate governmental facilities for conciliation, mediation, and voluntary arbitration to aid and encourage employers and the representatives of their employees to reach and maintain agreements concerning rates of pay, hours, and working conditions, and to make all reasonable efforts to settle their differences by mutual agreement reached through conferences and collective bargaining or by such methods as may be provided for in any applicable agreement for the settlement of disputes; and

(c) certain controversies which arise between parties to collective-bargaining agreements may be avoided or minimized by making available full and adequate governmental facilities for furnishing assistance to employers and the representatives of their employees in formulating for inclusion within such agreements provision for adequate notice of any proposed changes in the terms of such agreements, for the final adjustment of grievances or questions regarding the application or interpretation of such agreements, and other provisions designed to prevent the subsequent arising of such controversies.

SECTION 202.   (a) There is hereby created an independent agency to be known as the Federal Mediation and Conciliation Service (herein referred to as the "Service," except that for sixty days after the date of the enactment of this Act such term shall refer to the Conciliation Service of the Department of Labor). The Service shall be under the direction of a Federal Mediation and Conciliation Director (hereinafter referred to as the "Director") who shall be appointed by the

President by and with the advice and consent of the Senate. The Director shall receive compensation at the rate of $12,000* per annum. The Director shall not engage in any other business, vocation, or employment.

(b) The Director is authorized, subject to the civil-service laws, to appoint such clerical and other personnel as may be necessary for the execution of the functions of the Service, and shall fix their compensation in accordance with the Classification Act of 1923, as amended, and may, without regard to the provisions of the civil-service laws and the Classification Act of 1923, as amended, appoint and fix the compensation of such conciliators and mediators as may be necessary to carry out the functions of the Service. The Director is authorized to make such expenditures for suppliers, facilities, and services as he deems necessary. Such expenditures shall be allowed and paid upon presentation of itemized vouchers therefor approved by the Director or by any employee designated by him for that purpose.

(c) The principal office of the Service shall be in the District of Columbia, but the Director may establish regional offices convenient to localities in which labor controversies are likely to arise. The Director may by order, subject to revocation at any time, delegate any authority and discretion conferred upon him by this Act to any regional director, or other officer or employee of the Service. The Director may establish suitable procedures for cooperation with State and local mediation agencies. The Director shall make an annual report in writing to Congress at the end of the fiscal year.

(d) All mediation and conciliation functions of the Secretary of Labor or the United States Conciliation Service under Section 8 of the Act entitled "An Act to create a Department of Labor," approved March 4, 1913 (U.S.C., Title 29, Sec. 51), and all functions of the United States Conciliation Service under any other law are hereby transferred to the Federal mediation and Conciliation Service, together with the personnel and records of the United States Conciliation Service. Such transfer shall take effect upon the sixtieth day after the date of enactment of this Act. Such transfer shall not affect any proceedings pending before the United States Conciliation Service or any certification, order, rule, or regulation theretofore made by it or by the Secretary of Labor. The Director and the Service shall not be subject in any way to the jurisdiction or authority of the Secretary of Labor or any official or division of the Department of Labor.

FUNCTIONS OF THE SERVICE

SECTION 203. (a) It shall be the duty of the Service, in order to prevent or minimize interruptions of the free flow of commerce growing out of labor disputes to assist parties to labor disputes in industries affecting commerce to settle such disputes through conciliation and mediation.

(b) The Service may proffer its services in any labor dispute in any industry affecting commerce, either upon its own motion or upon the request of one or more of the parties to the dispute, whenever in its judgment such dispute threatens to cause a substantial interruption of commerce. The Director and the Service are directed to avoid attempting to mediate disputes which would have only a minor effect on interstate commerce if State or other conciliation services are available to the parties. Whenever the Service does proffer its services in any dispute, it shall be the duty of the Service promptly to put itself in communication with the parties and to use its best efforts, by mediation and conciliation, to bring them to agreement.

(c) If the Director is not able to bring the parties to agreement by conciliation within a reasonable time, he shall seek to induce the parties voluntarily to seek other means of settling the dispute without resort to strike, lock-out, or

---

*Pursuant to Public Law 9-206, 90th Cong. 81 Stat. 644, approved Dec. 16, 1967, and in accordance with Sec. 225 (f)(ii) thereof, effective in 1969, the salary of the Director shall be $40,000 per year.

other coercion, including submission to the employees in the bargaining unit of the employer's last offer of settlement for approval or rejection in a secret ballot. The failure or refusal of either party to agree to any procedure suggested by the Director shall not be deemed a violation of any duty or obligation imposed by this Act.

(d) Final adjustment by a method agreed upon by the parties is hereby declared to be the desirable method for settlement of grievance disputes arising over the application or interpretation of an existing collective-bargaining agreement. The Service is directed to make its conciliation and mediation services available in the settlement of such grievance disputes only as a last resort and in exceptional cases.

SECTION 204.   (a) In order to prevent or minimize interruptions of the free flow of commerce growing out of labor disputes, employers and employees and their representatives, in any industry affecting commerce, shall—

(1) exert every reasonable effort to make and maintain agreements concerning rates of pay, hours, and working conditions, including provision for adequate notice of any proposed changed in the terms of such agreements;

(2) whenever a dispute arises over the terms or application of a collective-bargaining agreement and a conference is requested by a party or prospective party thereto, arrange promptly for such a conference to be held and endeavor in such conference to settle such dispute expeditiously; and

(3) in case such dispute is not settled by conference, participate fully and promptly in such meetings as may be undertaken by the Service under this Act for the purpose of aiding in a settlement of the dispute.

SECTION 205.   (a) There is hereby created a National Labor-Management Panel which shall be composed of twelve members appointed by the President, six of whom shall be selected from among persons outstanding in the field of management and six of whom shall be selected from among persons outstanding in the field of labor. Each member shall hold office for a term of three years, except that any member appointed to fill a vacancy occurring prior to the expiration of the term for which his predecessor was appointed shall be appointed for the remainder of such term, and the terms of office of the members first taking office shall expire, as designated by the President at the time of appointment, four at the end of the first year, four at the end of the second year, and four at the end of the third year after the date of appointment. Members of the panel, when serving on business of the panel, shall be paid compensation at the rate of $25 per day, and shall also be entitled to receive an allowance for actual and necessary travel and subsistence expenses while so serving away from their places of residence.

(b) It shall be the duty of the panel, at the request of the Director, to advise in the avoidance of industrial controversies and the manner in which mediation and voluntary adjustment shall be administered, particularly with reference to controversies affecting the general welfare of the country.

NATIONAL EMERGENCIES

SECTION 206.   Whenever in the opinion of the President of the United States, a threatened or actual strike or lock-out affecting an entire industry or a substantial part thereof engaged in trade, commerce, transportation, transmission, or communication among the several States or with foreign nations, or engaged in the production of goods for commerce, will, if permitted to occur or to continue, imperil the national health or safety, he may appoint a board of inquiry to inquire into the issues involved in the dispute and to make a written report to him within such time as he shall prescribe. Such report shall include a statement of the facts with respect to the dispute, including each party's statement of its position but shall not contain any recommendations. The President shall file a copy of such report with the Service and shall make its contents available to the public.

SECTION 207. (a) A board of inquiry shall be composed of a chairman and such other members as the President shall determine, and shall have power to sit and act in any place within the United States and to conduct such hearings either in public or in private, as it may deem necessary or proper, to ascertain the facts with respect to the causes and circumstances of the dispute.

(b) Members of a board of inquiry shall receive compensation at the rate of $50 for each day actually spent by them in the work of the board, together with necessary travel and subsistence expenses.

(c) For the purpose of any hearing or inquiry conducted by any board appointed under this title, the provisions of Sections 9 and 10 (relating to the attendance of witnesses and the production of books, papers, and documents) of the Federal Trade Commission Act of September 16, 1914, as amended (U.S.C. 19, Title 15, Secs. 49 and 50, as amended), are hereby made applicable to the powers and duties of such board.

SECTION 208. (a) Upon receiving a report from a board of inquiry the President may direct the Attorney General to petition any district court of the United States having jurisdiction of the parties to enjoin such strike or lock-out or the continuing thereof, and if the court finds that such threatened or actual strike or lock-out—

(i) affects a entire industry or a substantial part thereof engaged in trade, commerce, transportation, transmission, or communication among the several States or with foreign nations, or engaged in the production of goods for commerce; and

(ii) if permitted to occur or to continue, will imperil the national health or safety, it shall have jurisdiction to enjoin any such strike or lock-out, or the continuing thereof, and to make such other orders as may be appropriate.

(b) In any case, the provisions of the Act of March 23, 1932, entitled "An Act to amend the Judicial Code and to define and limit the jurisdiction of courts sitting in equity, and for other purposes," shall not be applicable.

(c) The order or orders of the court shall be subject to review by the appropriate circuit court of appeals and by the Supreme Court upon writ of certiorari or certification as provided in Sections 239 and 240 of the Judicial Code, as amended (U.S.C., Title 29, Secs. 346 and 347).

SECTION 209. (a) Whenever a district court has issued an ordered under Section 208 enjoining acts or practices which imperil or threaten to imperil the national health or safety, it shall be the duty of the parties to the labor dispute giving rise to such order to make every effort to adjust and settle their differences, with the assistance of the Service created by this Act. Neither party shall be under any duty to accept, in whole or in part, any proposal of settlement made by the Service.

(b) Upon the issuance of such order, the President shall reconvene the board of inquiry which has previously reported with respect to the dispute. At the end of a sixty-day period (unless the dispute has been settled by that time), the board of inquiry shall report to the President the current position of the parties and the efforts which have been made for settlement, and shall include a statement by each party of its position and a statement of the employer's last offer of settlement. The President shall make such report available to the public. The National Labor Relations Board, within the succeeding fifteen days, shall take a secret ballot of the employees of each employer involved in the dispute on the question of whether they wish to accept the final offer of settlement made by their employer as stated by him and shall certify the results thereof to the Attorney General within five days thereafter.

SECTION 210. Upon the certification of the results of such ballot or upon a settlement being reached, whichever happens sooner, the Attorney General shall move the court to discharge the injunction, which motion shall then be granted and the injunction discharged. When such motion is granted, the President shall submit to the Congress a full and comprehensive report of the proceedings, including the findings of the board of inquiry and the ballot taken by the National

Labor Relations Board, together with such recommendations as he may see fit to make for consideration and appropriate action.

COMPILATION OF COLLECTIVE-BARGAINING AGREEMENTS, ETC.

SECTION 211. (a) For the guidance and information of interested representatives of employers, employees, and the general public, the Bureau of Labor Statistics of the Department of Labor shall maintain a file of copies of all available collective-bargaining agreements and other available agreements and actions thereunder settling or adjusting labor disputes. Such file shall be open to inspection under appropriate conditions prescribed by the Secretary of Labor, except that no specific information submitted in confidence shall be disclosed.

(b) The Bureau of Labor Statistics in the Department of Labor is authorized to furnish upon request of the Service, or employers, employees, or their representatives, all available data and factual information which may aid in the settlement of any labor dispute, except that no specific information submitted in confidence shall be disclosed.

EXEMPTION OF RAILWAY LABOR ACT

SECTION 212. (a) The provisions of this title shall not be applicable with respect to any matter which is subject to the provisions of the Railway Labor Act, as amended from time to time.

CONCILIATION OF LABOR DISPUTES IN THE HEALTH CARE INDUSTRY

SECTION 213. (a) If, in the opinion of the Director of the Federal Mediation and Conciliation Service a threatened or actual strike or lockout affecting a health care institution will, if permitted to occur or to continue, substantially interrupt the delivery of health care in the locality

concerned, the Director may further assist in the resolution of the impasse by establishing within 30 days after the notice to the Federal Mediation and Conciliation Service under clause (A) of the last sentence of Section 8(d) (which is required by clause (3) of such Section 8(d))., or within 10 days after the notice under clause (B), an impartial Board of Inquiry to investigate the issues involved in the dispute and to make a written report thereon to the parties within fifteen (15) days after the establishment of such a Board. The written report shall contain the findings of act together with the Board's recommendations for settling the dispute, with the objective of achieving a prompt, peaceful and just settlement of the dispute. Each such Board shall be composed of such number of individuals as the Director may deem desirable. No member appointed under this section shall have any interest or involvement in the health care institutions or the employee organizations involved in the dispute.

(b)(1) Members of any board established under this section who are otherwise employed by the Federal Government shall serve without compensation but shall be reimbursed for travel, subsistence, and other necessary expenses incurred by them in carrying out its duties under this section.

(2) Members of any board established under this section who are not subject to paragraph (1) shall receive compensation at a rate prescribed by the Director but not to exceed the daily rate prescribed for GS-18 of the General Schedule under Section 5332 of Title 5, United States Code, including travel for each day they are engaged in the performance of their duties under this section and shall be entitled to reimbursement for travel, subsistence, and other necessary expenses incurred by them in carrying out their duties under this section.

(c) After the establishment of a board under subsection (a) of this section and for 15 days after any such board has issued its report, no change in the status quo in effect prior to the expiration of the contract in the case of negotiations for a contract renewal, or in effect prior to the time of the impasse in the case of an initial bargaining negotiation, except by agreement, shall be made by the parties to the controversy.

(d) There are authorized to be appropriated such sums as may be necessary to carry out the provisions of this section.

TITLE III—SUITS BY AND AGAINST LABOR ORGANIZATIONS

SECTION 301. (a) Suits for violation of contracts between an employer and a labor organization representing employees in an industry affecting commerce as defined in this Act, or between any such labor organizations, may be brought in any district court of the United States having jurisdiction of the parties, without respect to the amount in controversy or without respect to the amount in controversy or without regard to the citizenship of the parties.

(b) Any labor organization which represents employees in an industry affecting commerce as defined in this Act and any employer whose activities affect commerce as defined in this Act shall be bound by the acts of its agents. Any such labor organization may sue or be sued as an entity and in behalf of the employees whom it represents in the courts of the United States. Any money judgment against a labor organization in a district court of the United States shall be enforceable only against the organization as an entity and against its assets, and shall not be enforceable against any individual member or his assets.

(c) For the purposes of actions and proceedings by or against labor organizations in the district courts of the United States, district courts shall be deemed to have jurisdiction of a labor organization (1) in the district in which such organization maintains its principal offices, or (2) in any district in which its duly authorized officers or agents are engaged in representing or acting for employee members.

(d) The service of summons, subpoena, or other legal process of any court of the United States upon an officer or agent of a labor organization, in his capacity as such, shall constitute service upon the labor organization.

(e) For the purposes of this section, in determining whether any person is acting as an "agent" of another person so as to make such other person responsible for his acts, the question of whether the specific acts performed were actually authorized or subsequently ratified shall not be controlling.

RESTRICTIONS ON PAYMENTS TO EMPLOYEE REPRESENTATIVES

SECTION 302. (a) It shall be unlawful for any employer or association of employers or any person who acts as a labor relations expert, adviser, or consultant to an employer or who acts in the interest of an employer to pay, lend, or deliver, or agree to pay, lend, or deliver, any money or other thing of value—

(1) to any representative of any of his employees who are employed in an industry affecting commerce; or

(2) to any labor organization, or any officer or employee thereof, which represents, seeks to represent, or would admit to membership, any of the employees of such employer who are employed in an industry affecting commerce; or

(3) to any employee or group or committee of employees of such employer employed in an industry affecting commerce in excess of their normal compensation for the purpose of causing such employee or group or committee directly or indirectly to influence any other employees in the exercise of the right to organize and bargain collectively through representatives of their own choosing; or

(4) to any officer or employee of a labor organization engaged in an industry affecting commerce with intent to influence him in respect to any of his actions, decisions, or duties as a representative of employees or as such officer or employee of such labor organization.

(b)(1) It shall be unlawful for any person to request, demand, receive, or accept, or agree to receive or accept any payment, loan, or delivery of any money or other thing of value prohibited by subsection (a).

(2) It shall be unlawful for any labor organization, or for any person acting as an officer, agent, representative, or employee of such labor organization, to demand or accept from the operator of any motor vehicle (as defined in part II of the Interstate Commerce Act) employed in the transportation of property in commerce, or the employer of any such operator, any money or other thing of value payable to such organization or to an officer, agent, representative or employee thereof as a fee or charge for unloading, or the connection with the unloading, of the cargo of such vehicle: *Provided,* That nothing in this paragraph shall be construed to make unlawful any payment by an employer to any of his employees as compensation for their services as employees.

(c) The provisions of this section shall not be applicable (1) in respect to any money or other thing of value payable by an employer to any of his employees whose established duties include acting openly for such employer in matters of labor relations or personnel administration or to any representative of his employees, or to any officer or employee or former employee of such employer, as compensation for, or by reason of, his service as an employee of such employer; (2) with respect to the payment or delivery of any money or other thing of value in satisfaction of a judgment of any court or a decision or award of an arbitrator or impartial chairman or in compromise, adjustment, settlement, or release of any claim, complaint, grievance, or dispute in the absence of fraud or duress; (3) with respect to the sale or purchase of an article or commodity at the prevailing market price in the regular course of business; (4) with respect to money deducted from the wages of employees in payment of membership dues in a labor organization: *Provided,* That the employer has received from each employee, on whose account such deductions are made, a written assignment which shall not be irrevocable for a period of more than one year, or beyond the termination date of the applicable collective agreement, whichever occurs sooner;

(5) with respect to money or other thing of value paid to a trust fund established by such representative, for the sole and exclusive benefit of the employees of such employer, and their families and dependents (or of such employees, families, and dependents jointly with the employees of other employers making similar payments, and their families and dependents): *Provided,* That (A) such payments are held in trust for the purpose of paying, either from principal or income or both, for the benefit of employees, their families and dependents, for medical or hospital care, pensions on retirement or death of employees, compensation for injuries or illness resulting from occupational activity or insurance to provide any of the foregoing, or unemployment benefits or life insurance, disability and sickness insurance, or accident insurance; (B) the detailed basis on which such payments are to be made is specified in a written agreement with the employer, and employees and employers are equally represented in the administration of such fund, together with such neutral persons as the representatives of the employers and the representatives of employees may agree upon and in the event the employer and employee groups deadlock on the administration of such fund and there are no neutral persons empowered to break such deadlock, such agreement provides that the two groups shall agree on an impartial umpire to decide such dispute, or in event of their failure to agree within a reasonable length of time, an impartial umpire to decide such dispute shall, on petition of either group, be appointed by the district court of the United States for the district where the trust fund has its principal office, and shall also contain provisions for an annual audit of the trust fund, a statement of the results of which shall be available for inspection by interested persons at the principal office of the trust fund and at such other places as may be designated in such written agreement; and (C) such payments as are intended to be used for the purpose of providing pensions or annuities for employees are made to a separate trust which provides that the funds held therein cannot be used for any purpose other than paying such pensions or annuities;

(6) with respect to money or other thing of value paid by any employer to a trust fund established by such representative for the purpose of pooled vacation, holiday, severance or similar benefits, or defraying costs of apprenticeship or other training program: *Provided*, That the requirements of clause (B) of the proviso to clause (5) of this subsection shall apply to such trust funds; or (7) with respect to money or other thing of value paid by any employer to a pooled or individual trust fund established by such representative for the purpose of (A) scholarships for the benefit of employees, their families, and dependents for study at educational institutions, or (B) child care centers for preschool and school age dependents of employees: *Provided*, That no labor organization or employer shall be required to bargain on the establishment of any such trust fund, and refusal to do so shall not constitute an unfair labor practice: *Provided further*, That the requirements of clause (B) of the proviso to clause (5) of this subsection shall apply to such trust funds; or (8) with respect to money or any other thing of value paid by any employer to a trust fund established by such representative for the purpose of defraying the costs of legal services for employees, their families, and dependents for counsel or plan of their choice: *Provided*, That the requirements of clause (B) of the proviso to clause (5) of this subsection shall apply to such trust funds: *Provided further*, That no such legal services shall be furnished: (A) to initiate any proceeding directed (i) against any such employer or its officers or agents except in workman's compensation cases, or (ii) against such labor organization, or its parent or subordinate bodies, or their officers, or agents, or (iii) against any other employer or labor organization, or their officers or agents, in any matter arising under the National Labor Relations Act, as amended, or this Act; and (B) in any proceeding where a labor organization would be prohibited from defraying the costs of legal services by the provisions of the Labor-Management Reporting and Disclosure Act of 1959.

(d) Any person who willfully violates any of the provisions of this section shall, upon conviction

thereof, be guilty of a misdemeanor and be subject to a fine of not more than $10,000 or to imprisonment for not more than one year, or both.

(e) The district courts of the United States and the United States courts of the Territories and possessions shall have jurisdiction, for cause shown, and subject to the provisions of Section 17 (relating to notice to opposite party) of the Act entitled "An Act to supplement existing laws against unlawful restraints and monopolies, and for other purposes," approved October 15, 1914, as amended (U.S.C., Title 28, Sec. 381), to restrain violations of this section, without regard to the provisions of Sections 6 and 20 of such Act of October 15, 1914, as amended (U.S.C., Title 15, Sec. 17, and Title 29, Sec. 52), and the provisions of the Act entitled "An Act to amend the Judicial Code and to define and limit the jurisdiction of courts sitting in equity, and for other purposes," approved March 23, 1932 (U.S.C., Title, 29, Secs. 101–115).

(f) This section shall not apply to any contract in force on the date of enactment of this Act, until the expiration of such contract, or until July 1, 1948, whichever first occurs.

(g) Compliance with the restrictions contained in subsection (c)(5)(B) upon contributions to trust funds, otherwise lawful, shall not be applicable to contributions to such trust funds established by collective agreement prior to January 1, 1946, nor shall subsection (c)(5)(A) be construed as prohibiting contributions to such trust funds if prior to January 1, 1947, such funds contained provisions for pooled vacation benefits.

BOYCOTTS AND OTHER UNLAWFUL COMBINATIONS

SECTION 303. (a) It shall be unlawful, for the purpose of this section only, in an industry or activity affecting commerce, for any labor organization to engage in any activity or conduct defined as an unfair labor practice in Section 8(b)(4) of the National Labor Relations Act, as amended.

(b) Whoever shall be injured in his business or property by reason of any violation of subsection (a) may sue therefore in any district court of the United States subject to the limitations and provisions of Section 301 hereof without respect to the amount in controversy, or in any other court having jurisdiction of the parties, and shall recover the damages by him sustained and the cost of the suit.

RESTRICTION ON POLITICAL CONTRIBUTIONS

SECTION 304. Section 313 of the Federal Corrupt Practices Act, 1925 (U.S.C., 1940 edition, Title 2, Sec. 251; Supp. V, Title 50, App., Sec. 1509), as amended, is amended to read as follows:

> **SECTION 313.** (a) It is unlawful for any national bank, or any corporation organized by authority of any law of Congress to make a contribution or expenditure in connection with any election to any political office, or in connection with any primary election or political convention or caucus held to select candidates for any political office, or for any corporation whatever, or any labor organization to make a contribution or expenditure in connection with any election at which Presidential and Vice Presidential electors or a Senator or Representative in, or a Delegate or Resident Commissioner to Congress are to be voted for, or in connection with any primary election or political convention or caucus held to select candidates for any of the foregoing offices, or for any candidate, political committee, or other person to accept or receive any contribution prohibited by this section. Every corporation or labor organization which makes any contribution or expenditure in violation of this section shall be fined not more than $5,000; and every office or director of any corporation, or officer of any labor organization, who consents to any contribution or expenditure by the corporation or labor organization, as the case may be, in violation of this section shall be fined not more than $1,000 or imprisoned for not more than one year, or both. For the purposes of this section "labor organization" means any organization of any kind, or any agency or employee representation committee or plan, in which employees participate and which exists for the purpose, in whole or in part, of dealing with employers concerning grievances, labor disputes, wages, rates of pay, hours of employment, or conditions of work.

EXCERPTS FROM THE LABOR-MANAGEMENT REPORTING AND DISCLOSURE ACT OF 1959

[Public Law 86-257—86th Congress, S. 1555 September 14, 1959]

An Act to provide for the reporting and disclosure of certain financial transactions and administrative practices of labor organizations and employers, to prevent abuses in the administration of trusteeships by labor organizations, to provide standards with respect to the election of officers of labor organizations, and for other purposes.

Be it enacted by the Senate and House of Representatives of the United States of America in Congress assembled,

SHORT TITLE

SECTION 1. This Act may be cited as the "Labor-Management Reporting and Disclosure Act of 1959."

DECLARATION OF FINDINGS, PURPOSES, AND POLICY

SECTION 2. (a) The Congress finds that, in the public interest, it continues to be the responsibility of the Federal Government to protect employees' rights to organize, choose their own representatives, bargain collectively, and otherwise engage in concerted activities for their mutual aid or protection; that the relations between employers and labor organizations and the millions of workers they represent have a substantial impact on the commerce of the Nation; and that in order to accomplish the objective of a free flow of commerce it is essential that labor organizations, employers, and their officials adhere to the highest standards of responsibility and ethical conduct in administering the affairs of their organizations, particularly as they affect labor-management relations.

(b) The Congress further finds, from recent investigations in the labor and management fields, that there have been a number of instances of breach of trust, corruption, disregard of the rights of individual employees, and other failures to observe high standards of responsibility and ethical conduct which require further and supplementary legislation that will afford necessary protection of the rights and interests of employees and the public generally as they relate to the activities of labor organizations, employers, labor relations consultants, and their officers and representatives.

(c) The Congress, therefore, further finds and declares that the enactment of this Act is necessary to eliminate or prevent improper practices on the part of labor organizations, employers, labor relations consultants, and their officers and representatives which distort and defeat the policies of the Labor Management Relations Act, 1947, as amended, and the Railway Labor Act, as amended, and have the tendency or necessary effect of burdening or obstructing commerce by (1) impairing the efficiency, safety, or operation of the instrumentalities of commerce; (2) occurring in the current of commerce; (3) materially affecting, restraining, or controlling the flow of raw materials or manufactured or processed goods into or from the channels of commerce, or the prices of such materials or goods in commerce; or (4) causing diminution of employment and wages in such volume as substantially to impair or disrupt the market for goods flowing into or from the channels of commerce.

...

TITLE I—BILL OF RIGHTS OF MEMBERS OF LABOR ORGANIZATIONS

BILL OF RIGHTS

SECTION 101. (a)(1) EQUAL RIGHTS.— Every member of a labor organization shall have equal rights and privileges within such organization to nominate candidates, to vote in elections or referendums of the labor organization, to attend membership meetings, and to participate in the deliberations and voting upon the business of such meetings, subject to reasonable rules and regulations in such organization's constitution and bylaws.

(2) FREEDOM OF SPEECH AND ASSEMBLY.—Every member of any labor organization shall have the right to meet and assemble freely with other members; and to express any views, arguments, or opinions; and to express at meetings of the labor organization his views, upon candidates in an election of the labor organization or upon any business properly before the meeting, subject to the organization's established and reasonable rules pertaining to the conduct of meetings: *Provided*, That nothing herein shall be construed to impair the right of a labor organization to adopt and enforce reasonable rules as to the responsibility of every member toward the organization as an institution and to his refraining from conduct that would interfere with its performance of its legal or contractual obligations.

(3) DUES, INITIATION FEES, AND ASSESSMENTS.—Except in the case of a federation of national or international labor organizations, the rates of dues and initiation fees payable by members of any labor organization in effect on the date of enactment of this Act shall not be increased, and no general or special assessment shall be levied upon such members, except—

(A) in the case of a local labor organization, (i) by majority vote by secret ballot of the members in good standing voting at a general or special membership meeting, after reasonable notice of the intention to vote upon such question, or (ii) by majority vote of the members in good standing voting in a membership referendum conducted by secret ballot; or

(B) in the case of a labor organization, other than a local labor organization or a federation of national or international labor organizations, (i) by majority vote of the delegates voting at a regular convention, or at a special convention of such labor organization held upon not less than thirty days' written notice to the principal office of each local or constituent labor organization entitled to such notice, of (ii) by majority vote of the members in good standing of such labor organization voting in a membership referendum conducted by secret ballot, or (iii) by majority vote of the members of the executive board or similar governing body of such labor organization, pursuant to express authority contained in the constitution and bylaws of such labor organization: *Provided*, That such action on the part of the executive board or similar governing body shall be effective only until the next regular convention of such labor organization.

(4) PROTECTION OF THE RIGHT TO SUE.—No labor organization shall limit the right of any member thereof to institute an action in any court, or in a proceeding before any administrative agency, irrespective of whether or not the labor organization or its officers are named as defendants or respondents in such action or proceeding, or the right of any member of a labor organization to appear as a witness in any judicial, administrative, or legislative proceeding, or to petition any legislature or to communicate with any legislator: *Provided*, That any such member may be required to exhaust reasonable hearing procedures (but not to exceed a four-month lapse of time) within such organization, before instituting legal or administrative proceedings against such organizations or any officer thereof: *And provided further*, That no interested employer or employer association shall directly or indirectly finance, encourage, or participate in, except as a party, any such action, proceeding, appearance, or petition.

(5) SAFEGUARDS AGAINST IMPROPER DISCIPLINARY ACTION.—No member of any labor organization may be fined, suspended, expelled, or otherwise disciplined except for nonpayment of dues by such organization or by any officer thereof unless such member has been (A) served with written specific charges; (B) given a reasonable time to prepare his defense; (C) afforded a full and fair hearing.

(b) Any provision of the constitution and bylaws of any labor organization which is inconsistent with the provisions of this section shall be of no force or effect.

...

TITLE II—REPORTING BY LABOR ORGANIZATIONS, OFFICERS AND EMPLOYEES OF LABOR ORGANIZATIONS, AND EMPLOYERS

REPORT OF LABOR ORGANIZATIONS

SECTION 201. (a) Every labor organization shall adopt a constitution and bylaws and shall file a copy thereof with the Secretary, together with a report, signed by its president and secretary or corresponding principal officers, containing the following information—

(1) the name of the labor organizations, its mailing address, and any other address at which it maintains its principal office or at which it keeps the records referred to in this title;

(2) the name and title of each of its officers;

(3) the initiation fee or fees required from a new or transferred member and fees for work permits required by the reporting labor organization;

(4) the regular dues or fees or other periodic payments required to remain a member of the reporting labor organization; and

(5) detailed statements, or references to specific provisions of documents filed under this subsection which contain such statements, showing the provision made and procedures followed with respect to each of the following: (A) qualifications for or restrictions on membership, (B) levying of assessments, (C) participation in insurance or other benefit plans, (D) authorization for disbursement of funds of the labor organization, (E) audit of financial transactions of the labor organization, (F) the calling of regular and special meetings, (G) the selection of officers and stewards and of any representatives to other bodies composed of labor organizations' representatives, with a specific statement of the manner in which each officer was elected, appointed, or otherwise selected, (H) discipline

or removal of officers or agents for breaches of their trust, (I) imposition of fines, suspensions, and expulsions of members, including the grounds for such action and any provision made for notice, hearing, judgment on the evidence, and appeal procedures, (J) authorization for bargaining demands, (K) ratification of con-tract terms, (L) authorization for strikes, and (M) issuance of work permits. Any change in the information required by this subsection shall be reported to the Secretary at the time the reporting labor organization files with the Secretary the annual financial report required by subsection (b).

(b) Every labor organization shall file annually with the Secretary a financial report signed by its president and treasurer or corresponding principal officers containing the following information in such detail as may be necessary accurately to disclose its financial condition and operations for its preceding fiscal year—

(1) assets and liabilities at the beginning and end of the fiscal year;

(2) receipts of any kind and the sources thereof;

(3) salary, allowances, and other direct or indirect disbursements (including reimbursed expenses) to each officer and also to each employee who, during such fiscal year, received more than $10,000 in the aggregate from such labor organization and any other labor organization affiliated with it or with which it is affiliated, or which if affiliated with the same national or international labor organization;

(4) direct and indirect loans made to any officer, employee, or member, which aggregated more than $250 during the fiscal year, together with a statement of the purpose, security, if any, and arrangements for repayment;

(5) direct or indirect loans to any business enterprise, together with a statement of the purpose, security, if any, and arrangements for repayment; and

(6) other disbursements made by it including the purposes thereof; all in such categories as the Secretary may prescribe.

(c) Every labor organization required to submit a report under this title shall make available the information required to be contained in such report to all of its members, and every such labor organization and its officers shall be under a duty enforceable at the suit of any member of such organization in any State court of competent jurisdiction or in the district court of the United States for the district in which such labor organization maintains its principal officer to permit such member for just cause to examine any books, records, and accounts necessary to verify such report. The court in such action may, in its discretion, in addition to any judgment awarded to the plaintiff or plaintiffs, allow a reasonable attorney's fee to be paid by the defendant, and cost of the action.

...

TITLE IV—ELECTIONS

TERMS OF OFFICE; ELECTION PROCEDURES

SECTION 401. (a) Every national or international labor organization, except a federation of national or international labor organizations, shall elect its officers not less often than once every five years either by secret ballot among the members in good standing or at a convention of delegates chosen by secret ballot.

(b) Every local labor organization shall elect its officers not less often than once every three years by secret ballot among the members in good standing.

(c) Every national or international labor organization, except a federation of national or international labor organizations, and every local labor organization, and its officers, shall be under a duty, enforceable at the suit of any bona fide candidate for office in such labor organization in the district court of the United States in which such labor organization maintains its principal office, to comply with all reasonable requests of any candidate to distribute by mail or otherwise at the candidate's expense campaign literature in aid of such person's candidacy to all members in good standing of such labor organization and to refrain from discrimination in favor of or against any candidate with respect to the use of lists or members, and whenever such labor organization is or its officers authorize the distribution by mail or otherwise to members of campaign literature on behalf of any candidate or of the labor organization itself with reference to such election, similar distribution at the request of any other bona fide candidate shall be made by such labor organization and its officers, with equal treatment as to the expense of such distribution. Every bona fide candidate shall have the right, once within 30 days prior to an election of a labor organization in which he is a candidate, to inspect a list containing the names and last known addresses of all members of the labor organization who are subject to a collective bargaining agreement requiring membership therein as a condition of employment, which list shall be maintained and kept at the principal office of such labor organization by a designated official thereof. Adequate safeguards to insure a fair election shall be provided, including the right of any candidate to have an observer at the polls and at the counting of the ballots.

(d) Officers of intermediate bodies, such as general committee, system boards, joint boards, or joint councils, shall be elected not less often than once every four years by secret ballot among the members in good standing or by labor organization officers representative of such members who have been elected by secret ballot.

(e) In any election required by this section which is to be held by secret ballot a reasonable opportunity shall be given for the nomination of candidates and every member in good standing shall be eligible to be a candidate and to hold office (subject to Section 504 and to reasonable qualifications uniformly imposed) and shall have the right to vote for or otherwise support the candidate or candidates of his choice, without being subject to penalty, discipline, or improper interference or reprisal of any kind by such organization or any member thereof. Not less than fifteen days prior to the election notice thereof shall be mailed to each member at his last known home address. Each member in good standing shall be entitled to one vote. No member whose dues have been withheld by his employer for payment to such organization pursuant to his voluntary authorization provided for in a collective bargaining agreement shall be declared ineligible to vote or be a candidate for office in such organization by reason of alleged delay or default in the payment of dues. The votes cast by members of each local labor organization shall be counted, and the results published, separately. The election officials designated in the constitution and bylaws or the secretary, if no other official is designated, shall preserve for one year the ballots and all other records pertaining to the election. The election shall be conducted in accordance with the constitution and bylaws of such organization insofar as they are not inconsistent with the provisions of this title.

(f) When officers are chosen by a convention of delegates elected by secret ballot, the convention shall be conducted in accordance with the constitution and bylaws of the labor organization insofar as they are not inconsistent with the provisions of this title. The officials designated in the constitution and bylaws or the secretary, if no other is designated, shall preserve for one year the credentials of the delegates and all minutes and other records of the convention pertaining to the election of officers.

(g) No moneys received by any labor organization by way of dues, assessment, or similar levy, and no moneys of an employer shall be contributed or applied to promote the candidacy of any person in an election subject to the provisions of this title. Such moneys of a labor organization may be utilized for notices, factual statements of issues not involving candidates, and other expenses necessary for the holding of an election.

(h) If the Secretary, upon application of any member of a local labor organization, finds after hearing in accordance with the Administrative Procedure Act that the constitution and bylaws of such labor organization do not provide an adequate procedure for the removal of an elected officer guilty of serious misconduct, such officer may be removed, for cause shown and after notice and hearing, by the members in good standing voting in a secret ballot conducted by the officers of such labor organization in accordance with its constitution and bylaws insofar as they are not inconsistent with the provisions of this title.

(i) The Secretary shall promulgate rules and regulations prescribing minimum standards and procedures for determining the adequacy of the removal procedures to which reference is made in subsection (h).

ENFORCEMENT

SECTION 402. (a) A member of a labor organization—

(1) who has exhausted the remedies available under the constitution and bylaws of such organization and of any parent body, or

(2) who had invoked such available remedies without obtaining a final decision within three calendar months after their invocation.

may file a complaint with the Secretary within one calendar month thereafter alleging the violation of any provision of Section 401 (including violation of the constitution and bylaws of the labor organization pertaining to the election and removal of officers). The challenged election shall be presumed valid pending a final decision thereon (as hereinafter provided) and in the interim the affairs of the organization shall be conducted by the officers elected or in such other manner as its constitution and bylaws may provide.

(b) The Secretary shall investigate such complaint and, if he finds probable cause to believe that a violation of this title has occurred and has not been remedied, he shall, within sixty days after the filing of such complaint, bring a civil action against the labor organization as an entity in the district court of the United States in which such labor organization maintains its principal office to set aside the invalid election, if any, and to direct the conduct of an election or hearing and vote upon the removal of officers under the supervision of the Secretary and in accordance

with the provisions of this title and such rules and regulations as the Secretary may prescribe. The court shall have power to take such action as it deems proper to preserve the assets of the labor organization.

(c) If, upon a preponderance of the evidence after a trial upon the merits, the court finds—

(1) that an election has not been held within the time prescribed by Section 401, or

(2) that the violation of Section 401 may have affected the outcome of an election,

the court shall declare the election, if any, to be void and direct the conduct of a new election under supervision of the Secretary and, so far as lawful and practicable, in conformity with the constitution and bylaws of the labor organization. The Secretary shall promptly certify to the court the names of the persons elected, and the court shall thereupon enter a decree declaring such persons to be the officers of the labor organization. If the proceeding is for the removal of officers pursuant to the subsection (h) of Section 401, the Secretary shall certify the results of the vote and the court shall enter a decree declaring whether such persons have been removed as officers of the labor organization.

(d) An order directing an election, dismissing a complaint, or designating elected officers or a labor organization shall be appealable in the same manner as the final judgment in a civil action, but an order directing an election shall not be stayed pending appeal.

TITLE V—SAFEGUARDS FOR LABOR ORGANIZATIONS

FIDUCIARY RESPONSIBILITY OF OFFICERS OF LABOR ORGANIZATIONS

SECTION 501. (a) The officers, agents, shop stewards, and other representatives of a labor organization occupy positions of trust in relation to such organization and its members as a group. It is, therefore, the duty of each such person, taking into account the special problems and functions of a labor organization, to hold its money and property solely for the benefit of the organization and its members and to manage, invest, and expend the same in accordance with its constitution and bylaws and any resolutions of the governing bodies adopted thereunder, to refrain from dealing with such organization as an adverse party or in behalf of an adverse party in any matter connected with his duties and from holding or acquiring any pecuniary or personal interest which conflicts with the interests of such organization, and to account to the organization for any profit received by him in whatever capacity in connection with transactions conducted by him or under his direction on behalf of the organization. A general exculpatory provision in the constitution and bylaws of such a labor organization or a general exculpatory resolution of a governing body purporting to relieve any such person of liability for breach of the duties declared by this section shall be void as against public policy....

EXCERPTS FROM TITLE VII OF THE CIVIL RIGHTS ACT OF 1964 AS AMENDED BY THE EQUAL EMPLOYMENT OPPORTUNITY ACT OF 1972

DISCRIMINATION BECAUSE OF RACE, COLOR, RELIGION, SEX, OR NATIONAL ORIGIN

SECTION 703. (a) It shall be an unlawful employment practice for an employer—

(1) to fail or refuse to hire or to discharge any individual, or otherwise to discriminate against any individual with respect to his compensation, terms, conditions, or privileges of employment, because of such individual's race, color, religion, sex, or national origin; or

(2) to limit, segregate, or classify his employees or applicants for employment in any way which would deprive any individual of employment opportunities or otherwise adversely affect his status as an employee, because of such individual's race, color, religion, sex, or national origin. (As amended by P.L. 92-261, eff. March 24, 1972.)

(b) It shall be an unlawful employment practice for an employment agency to fail or refuse to refer for employment, or otherwise to discriminate against, any individual because of his race, color, religion, sex, or national origin, or to classify or refer for employment any individual on the basis of his race, color, religion, sex, or national origin.

(c) It shall be an unlawful employment practice or a labor organization—

(1) to exclude or to expel from its membership, or otherwise to discriminate against, any individual because of his race, color, religion, sex, or national origin;

(2) to limit, segregate, or classify its membership or applicants for membership or to classify or fail or refuse to refer for employment any individual, in any way which would deprive or tend to deprive any individual of employment opportunities, or would limit such employment opportunities

or otherwise adversely affect his status as an employee or as an applicant for employment, because of such individual's race, color, religion, sex, or national origin; or

(3) to cause or attempt to cause an employer to discriminate against an individual in violation of this section.

(d) It shall be an unlawful employment practice for any employer, labor organization, or joint labor-management committee controlling apprenticeship or other training or retraining, including on-the-job training programs to discriminate against any individual because of his race, color, religion, sex, or national origin in admission to, or employment in, any program established to provide apprenticeship or other training.

(e) Notwithstanding any other provision of this title, (1) it shall not be an unlawful employment practice for an employer to hire and employ employees, for an employment agency to classify, or refer for employment any individual, for a labor organization to classify its membership or to classify or refer for employment any individual, or for an employer, labor organization, or joint labor-management committee controlling apprenticeship or other training or retraining programs to admit or employ any individual in any such program, on the basis of his religion, sex, or national origin in those certain instances where religion, sex, or national origin is a bona fide occupational qualification reasonably necessary to the normal operation of that particular business or enterprise, and (2) it shall not be an unlawful employment practice for a school, college, university, or other educational institution or institution of learning to hire and employ employees of a particular religion if such school, college, university or other educational institution or institution of learning is, in whole or in substantial part, owned, supported, controlled, or managed, by a particular religion or by a particular religious corporation, association, or society, or if the curriculum of such school, college, university, or other educational institution or institution of learning is directed toward the propagation of a particular religion.

(f) As used in this title, the phrase "unlawful employment practice" shall not be deemed to include any action or measure taken by an employer, labor organization, join labor-management committee or employment agency with respect to an individual who is a member of the Communist Party of the United States or of any other organization required to register as a Communist-action or Communist-front organization by final order of the Subversive Activities Control Board pursuant to the Subversive Activities Control Act of 1950.

(g) Notwithstanding any other provision of this title, it shall not be an unlawful employment practice for an employer to fail or refuse to hire and employ any individual for any position, for an employer to discharge an individual from any position, or for an employment agency to fail or refuse to refer any individual for employment in any position, or for a labor organization to fail or refuse to refer any individual for employment in any position, if—

(1) the occupancy of such position, or access to the premises in or upon which any part of the duties of such position is performed or is to be performed, is subject to any requirement imposed in the interest of the national security of the United States under any security program in effect pursuant to or administered under any statute of the United States or any Executive order of the President; and

(2) such individual has not fulfilled or has ceased to fulfill that requirement.

(h) Notwithstanding any other provision of this title, it shall not be an unlawful employment practice for an employer to apply different standards of compensation, or different terms, conditions, or privileges of employment pursuant to a bona fide seniority or merit system, or a system which measures earnings by quantity or quality of production or to employees who work in different locations, provided that such differences are not the result of an intention to discriminate because of race, color, religion, sex, or national origin; nor shall it be an unlawful employment practice for an employer to give and to act upon the results of any professionally developed ability test provided that such test, its administration or action upon the results is not designed, intended, or used to discriminate because of race, color, religion, sex, or national origin. It shall not be an unlawful employment practice under this title for any employer to differentiate upon the basis of sex in determining the amount of the wages or compensation paid to employees of such employer if such differentiation is authorized by the provisions of Section 6(d) of the Fair Labor Standards Act of 1938 as amended (29 USC 206(d)).

(i) Nothing contained in this title shall apply to any business or enterprise on or near an Indian reservation with respect to any publicly announced employment practice of such business or enterprise under which a preferential treatment is given to any individual because he is an Indian living on or near a reservation.

(j) Nothing contained in this title shall be interpreted to require any employer, employment agency, labor organization, or joint labor-management committee subject to this title to grant preferential treatment to any individual or to any group because of the race, color, religion, sex, or national origin of such individual or group on account of an imbalance which may exist with respect to the total number or percentage of persons of any race, color, religion, sex, or national origin employed by any employer, referred or classified for employment by any employment agency or labor organization, admitted to membership or classified by any labor organization, or admitted to, or employed in, any apprenticeship or other training program, in comparison with the total number or percentage of persons of such race, color, religion, sex, or national origin in any community, State, section, or other area, or in the available work force in any community, State, section, or other area. (As amended by P.L. 92-261, eff. March 24, 1972.)

OTHER UNLAWFUL EMPLOYMENT PRACTICES

SECTION 704. (a) It shall be an unlawful employment practice for an employer to discriminate against any of his employees or applicants for employment, for an employment agency or joint labor-management committee controlling apprenticeship or other training or retraining, including on-the-job training programs, to discriminate against any individual, or for a labor organization to discriminate against any member thereof or applicant for membership, because he has opposed any practice, made an unlawful employment practice by this title, or because he has made a charge, testified, assisted, or participated in any manner in an investigation, proceeding, or hearing under this title. (As amended by P.L. No. 92-261, eff. March 24, 1972.) ...

Excerpts from the Civil Rights Act of 1991

Public Law 102–166, 105 Stat. 1071, 42 U.S.C. 1981

November 21, 1991

Be it enacted by the Senate and House of Representatives of the United States of America in Congress assembled,

SHORT TITLE

SECTION 1. This Act may be cited as the "Civil Rights Act of 1991".

FINDINGS

SECTION 2. The Congress finds that—

(1) additional remedies under Federal law are needed to deter unlawful harassment and intentional discrimination in the workplace;

(2) the decision of the Supreme Court in *Wards Cove Packing Co. v. Atonio,* 490 U.S. 642 (1989) has weakened the scope and effectiveness of Federal civil rights protections; and

(3) legislation is necessary to provide additional protections against unlawful discrimination in employment.

PURPOSES

SECTION 3. The purposes of this Act are—

(1) to provide appropriate remedies for intentional discrimination and unlawful harassment in the workplace;

(2) to codify the concepts of "business necessity" and "job related" enunciated by the Supreme Court in *Griggs v. Duke Power Co.,* 401 U.S. 424 (1971), and in the other Supreme Court decisions prior to *Wards Cove Packing Co. v. Atonio,* 490 U.S. 642 (1989);

(3) to confirm statutory authority and provide statutory guidelines for the adjudication of disparate impact suits under Title VII of the Civil Rights Act of 1964 (42 U.S.C. 2000e *et seq.*); and

(4) to respond to recent decisions of the Supreme Court by expanding the scope of relevant

civil rights statutes in order to provide adequate protection to victims of discrimination. Title I—Federal Civil Rights Remedies.

PROHIBITION AGAINST ALL RACIAL DISCRIMINATION IN THE MAKING AND ENFORCEMENT OF CONTRACTS

SECTION 101. Section 1977 of the Revised Statutes (42 U.S.C. 1981) is amended—

(1) by inserting "(a)" before "All persons within"; and

(2) by adding at the end the following new subsections:

(b) For purposes of this section, the term 'make and enforce contracts' includes the making, performance, modification, and termination of contracts, and the enjoyment of all benefits, privileges, terms, and conditions of the contractual relationship.

(c) The rights protected by this section are protected against impairment by nongovernmental discrimination and impairment under color of State law.

DAMAGES IN CASES OF INTENTIONAL DISCRIMINATION

SECTION 102. The Revised Statutes are amended by inserting after Section 1977 (42 U.S.C. 1981) the following new section:

DAMAGES IN CASES OF INTENTIONAL DISCRIMINATION IN EMPLOYMENT SECTION 1977A. (a) Right of Recovery.—

(1) Civil rights.—In an action brought by a complaining party under Section 706 or 717 of the Civil Rights Act of 1964 (42 U.S.C. 2000e-5) against a respondent who engaged in unlawful intentional discrimination (not an employment practice that is unlawful because of its disparate impact) prohibited under Section 703, 704, or 717 of the Act (42 U.S.C. 2000e-2 or 2000e-3), and provided that the complaining party cannot recover under Section 1977 of the Revised Statutes (42 U.S.C. 1981), the complaining party may

recover compensatory and punitive damages as allowed in subsection (b), in addition to any relief authorized by Section 706(g) of the Civil Rights Act of 1964, from the respondent.

(2) Disability.—In an action brought by a complaining party under the powers, remedies, and procedures set forth in Section 706 or 717 of the Civil Rights Act of 1964 (as provided in Section 107(a) of the Americans with Disabilities Act of 1990 (42 U.S.C. 12117(a)), and Section 505(a)(1) of the Rehabilitation Act of 1973 (29 U.S.C. 794a(a)(1)), respectively) against a respondent who engaged in unlawful intentional discrimination (not an employment practice that is unlawful because of its disparate impact) under Section 501 of the Rehabilitation Act of 1973 (29 U.S.C. 791) and the regulations implementing Section 501, or who violated the requirements of Section 501 of the Act or the regulations implementing Section 501 concerning the provision of a reasonable accommodation, or Section 102 of the Americans with Disabilities Act of 1990 (42 U.S.C. 12112), or committed a violation of Section 102(b)(5) of the Act, against an individual, the complaining party may recover compensatory and punitive damages as allowed in subsection (b), in addition to any relief authorized by Section 706(g) of the Civil Rights Act of 1964, from the respondent.

(3) Reasonable accommodation and good faith effort.—In cases where a discriminatory practice involves the provision of a reasonable accommodation pursuant to Section 102(b)(5) of the Americans with Disabilities Act of 1990 or regulations implementing Section 501 of the Rehabilitation Act of 1973, damages may not be awarded under this section where the covered entity demonstrates good faith efforts, in consultation with the person with the disability who has informed the covered entity that accommodation is needed, to identify and make a reasonable accommodation that would provide such individual with an equally effective opportunity and would not cause an undue hardship on the operation of the business.

(b) Compensatory and Punitive Damages.—

(1) Determination of punitive damages.—A complaining party may recover punitive damages under this section against a respondent (other than a government, government agency or political subdivision) if the complaining party demonstrates

that the respondent engaged in a discriminatory practice or discriminatory practices with malice or with reckless indifference to the federally protected rights of an aggrieved individual.

(2) Exclusions from compensatory damages.—Compensatory damages awarded under this section shall not include backpay, interest on backpay, or any other type of relief authorized under Section 706(g) of the Civil Rights Act of 1964.

(3) Limitations.—The sum of the amount of compensatory damages awarded under this section for future pecuniary losses, emotional pain, suffering, inconvenience, mental anguish, loss of enjoyment of life, and other nonpecuniary losses, and the amount of punitive damages awarded under this section, shall not exceed, for each complaining party—

(A) in the case of a respondent who has more than 14 and fewer than 101 employees in each of 20 or more calendar weeks in the current or preceding calendar year, $50,000;

(B) in the case of a respondent who has more than 100 and fewer than 201 employees in each of 20 or more calendar weeks in the current or preceding calendar year, $100,000; and

(C) in the case of a respondent who has more than 200 and fewer than 501 employees in each of 20 or more calendar weeks in the current or preceding calendar year, $200,000; and

(D) in the case of a respondent who has more than 500 employees in each of 20 or more calendar weeks in the current or preceding calendar year, $300,000.

(4) Construction.—Nothing in this section shall be construed to limit the scope of, or the relief available under, Section 1977 of the Revised Statutes (42 U.S.C. 1981).

(c) Jury Trial.—If a complaining party seeks compensatory or punitive damages under this section —

(1) any party may demand a trial by jury; and

(2) the court shall not inform the jury of the limitations described in subsection (b)(3).

(d) Definitions.—As used in this section:

(1) Complaining party.—The term 'complaining party' means—

(A) in the case of a person seeking to bring an action under subsection (a)(I), the Equal Employment Opportunity Commission, the Attorney General, or a person who may bring an action

or proceeding under Title VII of the Civil Rights Act of 1964 (42 U.S.C. 2000e *et seq.*).; or

(B) in the case of a person seeking to bring an action under subsection (a)(2), the Equal Employment Opportunity Commission, the Attorney General, a person who may bring an action or proceeding under Section 505(a)(1) of the Rehabilitation Act of 1973 (29 U.S.C. 794a(a)(1), or a person who may bring an action or proceeding under Title I of the Americans with Disabilities Act of 1990 (42 U.S.C. 12101 *et seq.*)

(2) Discriminatory practice.—The term 'discriminatory practice' means the discrimination described in paragraph (1), or the discrimination or the violation described in paragraph (2), of subsection (a).

ATTORNEY'S FEES

SECTION 103.   The last sentence of Section 722 of the Revised Statutes (42 U.S.C. 1988) is amended by inserting, "1977A" after "1977".

DEFINITIONS

SECTION 104.   Section 701 of the Civil Rights Act of 1964 (42 U.S.C. 2000e) is amended by adding at the end the following new subsections:

(1) The term 'complaining party' means the Commission, the Attorney General, or a person who may bring an action or proceeding under this title.

(m) The term 'demonstrates' means meets the burdens of production and persuasion.

(n) The term 'respondent' means an employer, employment agency, labor organization, joint labor-management committee controlling apprenticeship or other training or retraining program, including an on-the-job training program, or Federal entity subject to Section 717.

BURDEN OF PROOF IN DISPARATE IMPACT CASES

SECTION 105.   (a) Section 703 of the Civil Rights Act of 1964 (U.S.C. 2000e-2) is amended by adding at the end the following new sub-section:

(k)(1)(A) An unlawful employment practice based on disparate impact is established under this title only if—

(i) a complaining party demonstrates that a respondent uses a particular employment practice that causes a disparate impact on the basis of race, color, religion, sex, or national origin and the respondent fails to demonstrate that the challenged practice is job related for the position in question and consistent with business necessity; or

(ii) the complaining party makes the demonstration described in subparagraph (C) with respect to an alternative employment practice and the respondent refuses to adopt such alternative employment practice.

(B)(i) With respect to demonstrating that a particular employment practice causes a disparate impact as described in subparagraph (A)(i), the complaining party shall demonstrate that each particular challenged employment practice causes a disparate impact, except that if the complaining party can demonstrate to the court that the elements of a respondent's decisionmaking process are not capable of separation for analysis, the decisionmaking process may be analyzed as one employment practice.

(ii) If the respondent demonstrates that a specific employment practice does not cause the disparate impact, the respondent shall not be required to demonstrate that such practice is required by business necessity.

(C) The demonstration referred to by subparagraph (A)(ii) shall be in accordance with the law as it existed on June 4, 1989, with respect to the concept of 'alternative employment practice'.

(2) A demonstration that an employment practice is required by business necessity may not be used as a defense against a claim of intentional discrimination under this title.

(3) Notwithstanding any other provision of this title, a rule barring the employment of an individual who currently and knowingly uses or possesses a controlled substance, as defined in schedules I and II of Section 102(6) of the Controlled Substances Act (21 U.S.C. 802(6)), other than the use or possession of a drug taken under the supervision of a licensed health care professional, or any other use or possession authorized by the Controlled Substances Act or any other provision of Federal law, shall be considered an unlawful employment practice under this title only if such rule is adopted or applied with an intent to discriminate because of race, color, religion, sex, or national origin.

(b) No statements other than the interpretive memorandum appearing at Vol. 137 Congressional Record S 15276 (daily ed. Oct. 25, 1991) shall be considered legislative history of, or relied upon in any way as legislative history in construing or applying, any provision of this Act that relates *Wards Cove*-Business necessity/cumulation/ alternative business practice.

PROHIBITION AGAINST DISCRIMINATORY USE OF TEST SCORES

SECTION 106. Section 703 of the Civil Rights of 1964 (42 U.S.C. 2000e-2) (as amended by Section 105) is further amended by adding at the end the following new subsection:

(1) It shall be an unlawful employment practice for a respondent, in connection with the selection or referral of applicants or candidates for employment or promotion, to adjust the scores of, use different cutoff scores for, or otherwise alter the results of, employment related tests on the basis of race, color, religion, sex, or national origin.

CLARIFYING PROHIBITION AGAINST IMPERMISSIBLE CONSIDERATION OF RACE, COLOR, RELIGION, SEX, OR NATIONAL ORIGIN IN EMPLOYMENT PRACTICES

SECTION 107. (a) In General.—Section 703 of the Civil Rights Act of 1964 (42 U.S.C. 2000e-2) (as amended by Sections 105 and 106) is further amended by adding at the end the following new subsection:

(m) Except as otherwise provided in this title, an unlawful employment practice is established when the complaining party demonstrates that race, color, religion, sex, or national origin was a motivating factor for any employment practice, even though other factors also motivated the practice.

(b) Enforcement Provisions.—Section 706(g) of such Act (42 U.S.C. 2000e-5(g)) is amended—

(1) by designating the first through third sentences as paragraph (1);

(2) by designating the fourth sentence as paragraph (2)(A) and indenting accord-ingly; and

(3) by adding at the end the following new subparagraph:

(B) On a claim in which an individual proves a violation under Section 703(m) and a respondent demonstrates that the respondent would have taken the same action in the absence of the impermissible motivating factor, the court—

(i) may grant declaratory relief, injunctive relief (except as provided in clause (ii)), and attorney's fees and costs demonstrated to be directly attributable only to the pursuit of a claim under Section 703(m); and

(ii) shall not award damages or issue an order requiring any admission, reinstatement, hiring, promotion, or payment, described in subparagraph (A).

FACILITATING PROMPT AND ORDERLY RESOLUTION OF CHALLENGES TO EMPLOYMENT PRACTICES IMPLEMENTING LITIGATED OR CONSENT JUDGMENTS OR ORDERS

SECTION 108. Section 703 of the Civil Rights Act of 1964 (42 U.S.C. 2000e-2) (as amended by Sections 105, 106, and 107 of this title) is further amended by adding at the end the following new subsection:

(n)(1)(A) Notwithstanding any other provision of law, and except as provided in paragraph (2), an employment practice that implements and is within the scope of a litigated or consent judgmentor order that resolves a claim of employment discrimination under the Constitution or Federal civil rights laws may not be challenged under the circumstances described in subparagraph (B).

(B) A practice described in subparagraph (A) may not be challenged in a claim under the Constitution or Federal civil rights laws—

(i) by a person who, prior to the entry of the judgment or order described in subparagraph (A), had—

(I) actual notice of the proposed judgment or order sufficient to apprise such person that such judgment or order might adversely affect the interests and legal rights of such person and that an opportunity was available to present objections to such judgment or order by a future date certain; and

(II) a reasonable opportunity to present objections to such judgment or order; or

(ii) by a person whose interests were adequately represented by another person who had previously challenged the judgment or order on the same legal grounds and with a similar factual situation, unless there has been an intervening change in law or fact.

(2) Nothing in this subsection shall be construed to—

(A) alter the standards for intervention under rule 24 of the Federal Rules of Civil Procedure or apply to the rights of parties who have successfully intervened pursuant to such rule in the proceeding in which the parties intervened;

(B) apply to the rights of parties to the action in which a litigated or consent judgment or order was entered, or of members of a class represented or sought to be represented in such action, or of members of a group on whose behalf relief was sought in such action by the Federal Government;

(C) prevent challenges to a litigated or consent judgment or order on the ground that such judgment or order was obtained through collusion or fraud, or is transparently invalid or was entered by a court lacking subject matter jurisdiction; or

(D) authorize or permit the denial to any person of the due process of law required by the Constitution.

(3) Any action not precluded under this subsection that challenges an employment consent judgment or order described in paragraph (1) shall be brought in the court, and if possible before the judge, that entered such judgment or order. Nothing in this subsection shall preclude a transfer of such action pursuant to Section 1404 of Title 28, United States Code.

PROTECTION OF EXTRA-TERRITORIAL EMPLOYMENT

SECTION 109. (a) Definition of Employee.—Section 701(f) of the Civil Rights Act of 1964 (42 U.S.C. 2000e(f)) and Section 101(4) of the Americans with Disabilities Act of 1990 (42 U.S.C. 12111(4)) are each amended by adding at the end the following 'With respect to employment in a foreign country, such term includes an individual who is a citizen of the United States.'

(b) Exemption.—

(1) Civil rights act of 1964.—Section 702 of the Civil Rights Act of 1964 (42 U.S.C. 2000e-1) is amended—

(A) by inserting "(a)" after "Sec. 702"; and (B) by adding at the end of the following:

(b) It shall not be unlawful under Section 703 or 704 for an employer (or a corporation controlled by an employer), labor organization, employment agency, or joint labor-management committee controlling apprenticeship or other training or retraining (including on-the-job training programs) to take any action otherwise prohibited by such section, with respect to an employee in a workplace in a foreign country if compliance with such section would cause such employer (or such corporation), such organization, such agency, or such committee to violate the law of the foreign country in which such workplace is located.

(c)(1) If an employer controls a corporation whose place of incorporation is a foreign country, any practice prohibited by Section 703 or 704 engaged in by such corporation shall be presumed to be engaged in by such employer.

(2) Sections 703 and 704 shall not apply with respect to the foreign operations of an employer that is a foreign person not controlled by an American employer.

(3) For purposes of this subsection, the determination of whether an employer controls a corporation shall be based on—

(A) the interrelation of operations;

(B) the common management;

(C) the centralized control of labor relations; and

(D) the common ownership or financial control, of the employer and the corporation.

(2) Americans with Disabilities Act of 1990.—Section 102 of the Americans with Disabilities Act of 1990 (42 U.S.C. 12112) is amended—

(A) by redesignating subsection (c) as subsection (d); and

(B) by inserting after subsection (b) the following new subsection:

(c) Covered Entities in Foreign Countries.—

(1) In general.—It shall not be unlawful under this section for a covered entity to take any action that constitutes discrimination under this section with respect to an employee in a workplace in a foreign country if compliance with this section would cause such covered entity to violate the law of the foreign country in which such workplace is located.

(2) Control of corporation.—

(A) Presumption.—If an employer controls a corporation whose place of incorporation is a foreign country, any practice that constitutes discrimination under this section and is engaged in by such corporation shall be presumed to be engaged in by such employer.

(B) Exception.—This section shall not apply with respect to the foreign operations of an employer that is a foreign person not controlled by an American employer.

(C) Determination.—For purposes of this paragraph, the determination of whether an employer controls a corporation shall be based on—

(i) the interrelation of operations;

(ii) the common management;

(iii) the centralized control of labor relations; and

(iv) the common ownership or financial control, of the employer and the corporation.

(c) Application of Amendments.—The amendments made by this section shall not apply with respect to conduct occurring before the date of the enactment of this Act.

TECHNICAL ASSISTANCE TRAINING INSTITUTE

SECTION 110. (a) Technical Assistance.— Section 705 of the Civil Rights Act of 1964 (42 U.S.C. 2000e-4) is amended by adding at the end the following new subsection.

(j)(1) The Commission shall establish a Technical Assistance training Institute, through which the Commission shall provide technical assistance and training regarding the laws and regulations enforced by the Commission.

(2) An employer or other entity covered under this title shall not be excused from compliance with the requirements of this title because of any failure to receive technical assistance under this subsection.

(3) There are authorized to be appropriated to carry out this subsection such sums as may be necessary for fiscal year 1992.

(b) Effective Date.—The amendment made by this section shall take effect on the date of the enactment of this Act.

EDUCATION AND OUTREACH

SECTION 111. Section 705(h) of the Civil Rights Act of 1964 (42 U.S.C. 2000e-4(h)) is amended—
(1) by inserting "(1)" after "(h)"; and
(2) by adding at the end the following new paragraph:

(2) In exercising its powers under this title, the Commission shall carry out educational and outreach activities (including dissemination of information in languages other than English) targeted to—
(A) individuals who historically have been victims of employment discrimination and have not been equitably served by the Commission; and
(B) individuals on whose behalf the Commission has authority to enforce any other

law prohibiting employment discrimination, concerning rights and obligations under this title or such law, as the case may be.

EXPANSION OF RIGHT TO CHALLENGE DISCRIMINATORY SENIORITY SYSTEMS

SECTION 112. Section 706(e) of the Civil Rights Act of 1964 (42 U.S.C. 2000e-5(e)) is amended—
(1) by inserting "(1)" before "A charge under this section"; and
(2) by adding at the end the following new paragraph:

(2) For purposes of this section , an unlawful employment practice occurs, with respect to a seniority system that has been adopted for an intentionally discriminatory purpose in violation of this title (whether or not that discriminatory purpose is apparent on the face of the seniority provision), when the seniority system is adopted, when an individual becomes subject to the seniority system, or when a person aggrieved is injured by the application of the seniority system or provision of the system.

AUTHORIZING AWARD OF EXPERT FEES

SECTION 113. (a) Revised Statutes.—Section 722 of the Revised Statutes is amended—
(1) by designating the first and second sentences as subsections (a) and (b), respectively, and indenting accordingly; and
(2) by adding at the end the following new subsection:

(c) In awarding an attorney's fee under subsection (b) in any action or proceeding to enforce a provision of Sections 1977 or 1977A of the Revised Statutes, the court, in its discretion, may include expert fees as part of the attorney's fee.

(b) Civil Rights Act of 1964.—Section 706(k) of the Civil Rights Act of 1964 (42 U.S.C. 2000e-5(k)) is amended by inserting, '(including expert fees),' after 'attorney's fee'.

PROVIDING FOR INTEREST AND EXTENDING THE STATUTE OF LIMITATIONS IN ACTIONS AGAINST THE FEDERAL GOVERNMENT

SECTION 114.　Section 717 of the Civil Rights Act of 1964 (42 U.S.C. 2000e-16) is amended—

(1) in subsection (c), by striking, 'thirty days' and inserting '90 days'; and

(2) in subsection (d), by inserting before the period, 'and the same interest to compensate for delay in payment shall be available as in cases involving nonpublic parties.'

NOTICE OF LIMITATIONS PERIOD UNDER THE AGE DISCRIMINATION IN EMPLOYMENT ACT OF 1967

SECTION 115.　Section 7(e) of the Age Discrimination in Employment Act of 1967 (29 U.S.C. 626(e)) is amended—

(1) by striking paragraph (2);

(2) by striking the paragraph designation in paragraph (1);

(3) by striking, 'Sections 6 and' and inserting, 'section'; and

(4) by adding at the end the following: 'If a charge filed with the Commission under this Act is dismissed or the proceedings of the Commission are otherwise terminated by the Commission, the Commission shall notify the person aggrieved. A civil action may be brought under this section by a person defined in Section 11(a) against the respondent named in the charge within 90 days after the date of the receipt of such notice.'

LAWFUL COURT-ORDERED REMEDIES, AFFIRMATIVE ACTION, AND CONCILIATION AGREEMENTS NOT AFFECTED

SECTION 116.　Nothing in the amendments made by this title shall be construed to affect court-ordered remedies, affirmative action, or conciliation agreements, that are in accordance with the law....

EXCERPTS FROM THE EEOC'S UNIFORM GUIDELINES ON EMPLOYEE SELECTION PROCEDURES (1978)

ADVERSE IMPACT

The fundamental principle underlying the guidelines is that employer policies or practices which have an adverse impact on employment opportunities of any race, sex, or ethnic group are illegal under Title VII and the Executive order unless justified by business necessity.

If adverse impact exists, it must be justified on grounds of business necessity. Normally, this means by validation which demonstrates the relation between the selection procedure and performance on the job.

The guidelines adopt a "rule of thumb" as a practical means of determining adverse impact for use in enforcement proceedings. This rule is known as the "4/5ths" or "80 percent" rule.

WHERE ADVERSE IMPACT EXISTS: THE BASIC OPTIONS

Once an employer has established that there is adverse impact, what steps are required by the guidelines? As previously noted, the employer can modify or eliminate the procedure which produces the adverse impact, thus taking the selection procedure from the coverage of these guidelines. If the employer does not do that, then it must justify the use of the procedure on grounds of "business necessity." This normally means that it must show a clear relation between performance on the selection procedure and performance on the job.

GENERAL PRINCIPLES

1. Relationship between validation and elimination of adverse impact, and affirmative action. Federal equal employment opportunity law generally does not require evidence of validity for a selection procedure if there is not adverse impact: e.g., *Griggs v. Duke Power Co.* Therefore, a user has the choice of complying either by providing evidence of validity (or otherwise justifying use in accord with

Federal law), or by eliminating the adverse impact. These options have always been present under Federal law and the Federal Executive Agency Guidelines. The December 30 draft guidelines, however, clarified the nature of the two options open to users.

2. The "*bottom line*" (Section 4C). The guidelines provide that when the overall selection process does not have an adverse impact the Government will usually not examine the individual components of that process for adverse impact or evidence of validity. The concept is based upon the view that the Federal Gover nment should not generally concern itself with individual components of a selection process, if the overall effect of that process is nonexclusionary. Many commenters criticized the ambiguity caused by the word "generally" in the December 30 draft of Section 4C which provided, "the Federal enforcement agencies generally will not take enforcement action based upon adverse impact of any component" of a process that does not have an overall adverse impact. Employer groups stated the position that the "bottom line" should be a rule prohibiting enforcement action by Federal agencies with respect to all or part of a selection process where the bottom line does not show adverse impact. Civil rights and some labor union representatives expressed the opposing concerns that the concept may be too restrictive, that it may be interpreted as a matter of law, and that it might allow certain discriminatory conditions to go unremedied.

SECTION 5. *General Standards for validity studies.*

A. Acceptable types of validity studies. For the purposes of satisfying these guidelines, users may rely upon criterion-related validity studies, content validity studies or construct validity studies, in accordance with the standards set forth in the technical standards of the guidelines. New strategies procedures will be evaluated as they become accepted by the psychological profession.

B. *Criterion-related content, and construct validity.* Evidence of the validity of a test or other selection procedure by a criterion-related validity study should consist of empirical data demonstrating that the selection procedure is predictive of or significantly correlated with important elements of job performance. Evidence of the validity of a test or other selection procedure by a content validity study should consist of data showing that the content of the selection procedure is representative of important aspects of performance on the job for which the candidates are to be evaluated. Evidence of the validity of a test or other selection procedure through a construct validity study should consist of data showing that the procedure measures the degree to which candidates have identifiable characteristics which have been determined to be important in successful performance in the job for which the candidates are to be evaluated.

C. *Guidelines are consistent with professional standards.* The provisions of these guidelines relating to validation of selection procedures are intended to be consistent with generally accepted professional standards for evaluating standardized tests and other selection procedures, such as those described in the Standards for Educational and Psychological Tests prepared by a joint committee of the American Psychological Association, the American Educational Research Association, and the National Council on Measurement in Education (American Psychological Association, Washington, D.C., 1974) (hereinafter "A.P.A. Standards") and standard textbooks and journals in the field of personnel selection.

D. *Need for documentation of validity.* For any selection procedure which is part of a selection process which has an adverse impact and which selection procedure has an adverse impact, each user should maintain and have available such documentation as is described in Section 15 below.

E. *Accuracy and standardization.* Validity studies should be carried out under conditions which assure insofar as possible the adequacy and accuracy of the research and the report. Selection procedure should be administered and scored under standardized conditions.

F. *Caution against selection on basis of knowledges, skills, or ability learned in brief orientation period.* In general, users should avoid making employment decisions on the basis of measures of knowledges, skills, or abilities which are normally learned in a brief orientation period, and which have an adverse impact.

G. *Method of use of selection procedures.* The evidence of both the validity and utility of a selection procedure should support the method the user chooses for operational use of the procedure, if that method of use has a greater adverse impact than another method of use. Evidence which may be sufficient to support the use of a selection procedure on a pass/fail (screening) basis may be insufficient to support the use of the same procedure on a ranking basis under these guidelines. Thus if user decides to use a selection procedure on a ranking basis, and that method of use has a greater adverse impact than use on an appropriate pass/fail basis (see Section 5H below), the user should have sufficient evidence of validity and utility to support the use on a ranking basis.

H. *Cutoff scores.* Where cutoff scores are used, they should normally be set so as to be reasonable and consistent with normal expectations of acceptable proficiency within the work force. Where applicants are ranked on the basis of properly validated selection procedures and those applicants scoring below a higher cutoff score than appropriate in light or no chance of being selected for employment, the higher cutoff score may be appropriate, but the degree of adverse impact should be considered.

Documentation of Impact and Validity Evidence

SECTION 15. *Documentation of impact and validity evidence.*

A. *Required information.* Users of selection procedures other than those users complying with Section 15 A(1) below should maintain and have available for each job information on adverse impact of the selection process for that job and, where it is determined a selection process has an adverse impact, evidence of validity as set forth below.

(1) *Simplified recordkeeping for users with less than 100 employees.* In order to minimize recordkeeping burdens on employers who employ one hundred (100) or fewer employees and other users not required to file EEO-1. et seq., reports, such users may satisfy the requirements of this Section 15 if they maintain and have available records showing, for each year:

(a) The number of persons hired, promoted, and terminated for each job, by sex, and where appropriate by race and national origins;

(b) The number of applicants for hire and promotion by sex and where appropriate by race and national origin: and

(c) The selection procedures utilized (either standardized or not standardized).

These records should be maintained for each race or national group constituting more than two percent (2%) of the labor force in the relevant labor area. However, it is necessary to maintain records by race and/or national origin if one race or national origin group in the relevant labor area constitutes more than ninety-eight percent (98%) of the labor force in the area. If the user has reason to believe that a selection procedure has an adverse impact, the user should maintain any available evidence of validity for that procedure.

Definitions

SECTION 16. *Definitions.* The following definitions shall apply throughout these guidelines:

A. *Ability.* A present competence to perform an observable behavior or a behavior whi[ch] results in an observable product.

B. *Adverse impact.* A substantially different rate of selection in hiring, promotion, or other employment decisions which work to the disadvantage of members of a race, sex, or ethnic group.

C. *Compliance with these guidelines.* Use of a selection procedure is in compliance with these guidelines if such use has been validated in accord with these guidelines, or if such use does not result in adverse impact on any race, sex, or ethnic group, or, in unusual circumstances, if use of the procedure is otherwise justified in accord with Federal law.

D. *Content validity.* Demonstrated by data showing that the content of a selection procedure is representative of important aspects of performance on the job.

E. *Construct validity.* Demonstrated by data showing that the selection procedure measures the degree to which candidates have identifiable characteristics which have been determined to be important for successful job performance.

F. *Criterion-related validity.* Demonstrated by empirical data showing that the selection procedure is predictive of or significantly correlated with important elements of work behavior.

G. *Employer.* Any employer subject to the provisions of the Civil Rights Act of 1964, as amended, including State or local governments and any Federal agency subject to the provisions of Section 717 of the Civil Rights Act of 1964, as amended, and any Federal contractor or subcontractor or federally assisted construction contractor or subcontractor by Executive Order 11246, as amended.

H. *Employment agency.* Any employment agency subject to the provisions of the Civil Rights Acts of 1964, as amended.

I. *Enforcement action.* A proceeding by a Federal enforcement agency such as a lawsuit or an administrative proceeding leading to debarment from withholding, suspension, or termination of Federal Government funds; but not a finding of reasonable cause or a conciliation process or the issuance of right to sue letters under Title VII or under Executive Order 11246 where such finding, conciliation, or issuance of notice of right to sue is based upon an individual complaint.

J. *Enforcement agency.* Any agency of the executive branch of the Federal Government which adopts these guidelines for purposes of the enforcement of the equal employment opportunity laws or which has responsibility for securing compliance with them.

K. *Job analysis.* A detailed statement of work behaviors and other information relevant to the job.

L. *Job descriptions.* A general statement of job duties and responsibilities.

M. *Knowledge.* A body of information applied directly to the performance of a function. Evidence for intermittent leave, or leave on a reduced leave schedule, for planned medical treatment, the dates on which such treatment is expected to be given and the duration of such treatment.

Excerpts from the EEOC's Guidance on Vicarious Employer Liability for Harassment by Supervisors

EEOC
NOTICE
Number
915.002
Date
6/18/99

ENFORCEMENT GUIDANCE ON VICARIOUS EMPLOYER LIABILITY FOR UNLAWFUL HARASSMENT BY SUPERVISORS

INTRODUCTION

In *Burlington Industries, Inc. v. Ellerth*, 118 S. Ct. 2257 (1998), and *Faragher v. City of Boca Raton*, 118 S. Ct. 2275 (1998), the Supreme Court made clear that employers are subject to vicarious liability for unlawful harassment by supervisors. The standard of liability set forth in these decisions is premised on two principles: 1) an employer is responsible for the acts of its supervisors, and 2) employers should be encouraged to prevent harassment and employees should be encouraged to avoid or limit the harm from harassment. In order to accommodate these principles, the Court held that an employer is always liable for a supervisor's harassment if it culminates in a tangible employment action. However, if it does not, the employer may be able to avoid liability or limit damages by establishing an affirmative defense that includes two necessary elements:

a) the employer exercised reasonable care to prevent and correct promptly any harassing behavior, and

b) the employee unreasonably failed to take advantage of any preventive or corrective opportunities provided by the employer or to avoid harm otherwise.

While the *Faragher* and *Ellerth* decisions addressed sexual harassment, the Court's analysis drew upon standards set forth in cases involving harassment on other protected bases. Moreover, the Commission has always taken the position that the same basic standards apply to all types of prohibited harassment.[1] Thus, the standard of liability set forth in the decisions applies to all forms of unlawful harassment. (See Section II, below).

HARASSMENT BY SUPERVISOR THAT RESULTS IN A TANGIBLE EMPLOYMENT ACTION

A. STANDARD OF LIABILITY

An employer is always liable for harassment by a supervisor on a prohibited basis that culminates in a tangible employment actin. No affirmative defense is available in such cases. The Supreme Court recognized that this result is appropriate because an employer acts through its supervisors, and a supervisor's undertaking of a tangible employment action constitutes an act of the employer.

B. DEFINITION OF "TANGIBLE EMPLOYMENT ACTION"

A tangible employment action is "a significant change in employment status." Unfulfilled threats are insufficient. Characteristics of a tangible employment action are:

1. A tangible employment action is the means by which the supervisor brings the official power of the enterprise to bear on subordinates, as demonstrated by the following:
   —it requires an official act of the enterprise;
   —it usually is documented in official company records;
   —it may be subject to review by higher level supervisors; and
   —it often requires the formal approval of the enterprise and use of it internal processes.
2. A tangible employment action usually inflicts direct economic harm.

3. A tangible employment action, in most instances, can only be caused by a supervisor or other person acting with the authority of the company. Examples of tangible employment actions include:

- hiring and firing;
- promotion and failure to promote;
- demotion;
- undesirable reassignment;
- compensation decisions; and
- work assignment.

Any employment action qualifies as "tangible" if it results in a significant change in employment status. For example, significantly changing an individual's duties in his or her existing job constitutes a tangible employment action regardless of whether the individual retains the same salary and benefits. Similarly, altering an individual's duties in a way that blocks his or her opportunity for promotion or salary increases also constitutes a tangible employment action.

On the other hand, an employment action does not reach the threshold of "tangible" if it results in only an insignificant change in the complainant's employment status. For example, altering an individual's job title does not qualify as a tangible employment action if there is no change in salary, benefits, duties, or prestige, and the only effect is a bruised ego. However, if there is a significant change in the status of the position because the new title is less prestigious and thereby effectively constitutes a demotion, a tangible employment action would be found.

If a supervisor undertakes or recommend a tangible job action based on a subordinate's response to unwelcome sexual demands, the employer is liable and cannot raise the affirmative defense. The result is the same whether the employee rejects the demands and is subjected to an adverse tangible employment action or

[1]See, *e.g.*, 29 C.F.R. § 1604.11 n. 1 ("The principles involved here continue to apply to race, color, religion or national origin."); EEOC Compliance Manual Section 615.11 (a) (BNA) 615:0025 ("Title VII law and agency principles will guide the determination of whether an employer is liable for age harassment by its supervisors, employees, or non-employees").

submits to the demands and consequently obtains a tangible job benefit. Such harassment previously would have been characterized as "quid pro quo." It would be a perverse result if the employer is foreclosed from raising the affirmative defense if its supervisor denies a tangible job benefit based on an employee's rejection of unwelcome sexual demands, but can raise the defense if its supervisor grants a tangible job benefit based on submission to such demands. The Commission rejects such an analysis. In both those situations the supervisor undertakes a tangible employment action on a discriminatory basis. The Supreme Court stated that there must be a significant change in employment status; it did not require that the change be adverse in order to qualify as tangible.

If a challenged employment action is not "tangible," it may still be considered, along with other evidence, as part of a hostile environment claim that is subject to the affirmative defense. In *Ellerth*, the Court concluded that there was no tangible employment action because the supervisor never carried out his threats of job harm. Ellerth could still proceed with her claim of harassment, but the claim was properly "categorized as a hostile work environment claim which requires a showing of severe or pervasive conduct." 118 S. Ct. at 2265...

H | Excerpts from the Americans with Disabilities Act of 1990

Public Law 101-336; 42 U.S.C. 12101; July 26, 1990

An Act to establish a clear and comprehensive prohibition of discrimination on the basis of disability.

Be it enacted by the Senate and House of Representatives of the United States of America in Congress assembled,

FINDINGS AND PURPOSES

SECTION 2. (a) FINDINGS. The Congress find that:

(1) some 43,000,000 Americans have one or more physical or mental disabilities, and this number is increasing as the population as a whole is growing older;

(2) historically, society has tended to isolate and segregate individuals with disabilities, and, despite some improvements, such forms of discrimination against individuals with disabilities continue to be a serious and pervasive social problem;

(3) discrimination against individuals with disabilities persists in such critical areas as employment, housing, public accommodations, education, transportation, communication, recreation, institutionalization, health services, voting, and access to public services;

(4) unlike individuals who have experienced discrimination on the basis of race, color, sex, national origin, religion, or age, individuals who have experienced discrimination on the basis of disability have often had no legal recourse to redress such discrimination;

(5) individuals with disabilities continually encounter various forms of discrimination, including outright intentional exclusion, the discriminatory effects of architectural, transportation, and communication barriers, overprotective rules and policies, failure to make modifications to existing facilities and practices, exclusionary qualification standards and criteria, segregation, and relegation to lesser services, programs, activities, benefits, jobs, or other opportunities;

(6) census data, national polls, and other studies have documented that people with disabilities, as a group, occupy an inferior status in our society, and are severely disadvantaged socially, vocationally, economically, and educationally;

(7) individuals with disabilities are a discrete and insular minority who have been faced with

restrictions and limitations, subjected to a history of purposeful unequal treatment, and relegated to a position of political powerlessness in our society, based on characteristics that are beyond the control of such individuals and resulting from stereotypic assumptions not truly indicative of the individual ability of such individuals to participate in, and contribute to, society;

(8) the Nation's proper goals regarding individuals with disabilities are to assure equality of opportunity, full participation, independent living, and economic self-sufficiency for such individuals; and

(9) the continuing existence of unfair and unnecessary discrimination and prejudice denies people with disabilities the opportunity to compete on an equal basis and to pursue those opportunities for which our free society is justifiably famous, and costs the United States billions of dollars in unnecessary expenses resulting from dependency and nonproductivity.

(b) PURPOSE. It is the purpose of this Act:

(1) to provide a clear and comprehensive national mandate for the elimination of discrimination against individuals with disabilities;

(2) to provide clear, strong, consistent, enforceable standards addressing discrimination against individuals with disabilities;

(3) to ensure that the Federal Government plays a central role in enforcing the standards established in this Act on behalf of individuals with disabilities; and

(4) to invoke the sweep of congressional authority, including the power to enforce the fourteenth amendment and to regulate commerce, in order to address the major areas of discrimination faced day-to-day by people with disabilities.

DEFINITIONS

...(8) QUALIFIED INDIVIDUAL WITH A DISABILITY. The term "qualified individual with a disability" means an individual with a disability who, with or without reasonable accommodation, can perform the essential functions of the employment position that such individual holds or desires. For the purposes of this title,

consideration shall be given to the employer's judgment as to what functions of a job are essential, and if an employer has prepared a written description before advertising or interviewing applicants for the job, this description shall be considered evidence of the essential functions of the job.

(9) REASONABLE ACCOMMODATION. The term "reasonable accommodation" may include:

(A) making existing facilities used by employees readily accessible to and usable by individuals with disabilities; and

(B) job restructuring, part-time or modified work schedules, reassignment to a vacant position, acquisition or modification of equipment or devices, appropriate adjustment or modifications of examinations, training materials or policies, the provision of qualified readers or interpreters, and other similar accommodations for individuals with disabilities.

(10) UNDUE HARDSHIP.

(A) IN GENERAL. The term "undue hardship" means an action requiring significant difficulty or expense, when considered in light of the factors set forth in subparagraph (B).

(B) FACTORS TO BE CONSIDERED. In determining whether an accommodation would impose an undue hardship on a covered entity, factors to be considered include:

(i) the nature and cost of the accommodation needed under this Act;

(ii) the overall financial resources of the facility or facilities involved in the provision of the reasonable accommodation; the number of persons employed at such facility; the effect on expenses and resources, or the impact otherwise of such accommodation upon the operation of the facility;

(iii) the overall financial resources of the covered entity; the overall size of the business of a covered entity with respect to the number of its employees; the number, type, and location of its facilities; and

(iv) the type of operation or operations of the covered entity, including the composition, structure, and functions of the workforce of such entity; the geographic separateness, administrative, or fiscal relationship of the facility or facilities in question to the covered entity.

DISCRIMINATION

SECTION 102. (a) GENERAL RULE. No covered entity shall discriminate against a qualified individual with a disability because of the disability of such individual in regard to job application procedures, the hiring, advancement, or discharge of employees, employee compensation, job training, and other terms, conditions, and privileges of employment.

(b) CONSTRUCTION. As used in subsection (a), the term "discriminate" includes:

(1) limiting, segregating, or classifying a job applicant or employee in a way that adversely affects the opportunities or status of such applicant or employee because of the disability of such applicant or employee;

(2) participating in a contractual or other arrangement or relationship that has the effect of subjecting a covered entity's qualified applicant or employee with a disability to the discrimination prohibited by this title (such relationship includes a relationship with an employment or referral agency, labor union, an organization providing fringe benefits to an employee of the covered entity, or an organization providing training and apprenticeship programs);

(3) utilizing standards, criteria, or methods of administration;

(A) that have the effect of discrimination on the basis of disability; or

(B) that perpetuate the discrimination of others who are subject to common administrative control;

(4) excluding or otherwise denying equal jobs or benefits to a qualified individual because of the known disability of an individual with whom the qualified individual is known to have a relationship or association;

(5) (A) not making reasonable accommodations to the known physical or mental limitations of an otherwise qualified individual with a disability who is an applicant or employee, unless

such covered entity can demonstrate that the accommodation would impose an undue hardship on the operation of the business of such covered entity; or

(B) denying employment opportunities to a job applicant or employee who is an otherwise qualified individual with a disability, if such denial is based on the need of such covered entity to make reasonable accommodation to the physical or mental impairments of the employee or applicant;

(6) using qualification standards, employment tests or other selection criteria that screen out or tend to screen out an individual with a disability or a class of individuals with disabilities unless the standard, test or other selection criteria, as used by the covered entity, is shown to be job-related for the position in question and is consistent with business necessity; and

(7) failing to select and administer tests concerning employment in the most effective manner to ensure that, when such test is administered to a job applicant or employee who has a disability that impairs sensory, manual, or speaking skills, such test results accurately reflect the skills, aptitude, or whatever other factor of such applicant or employee that such test purports to measure, rather than reflecting the impaired sensory, manual, or speaking skills of such employee or applicant (except where such skills are the factors that the test purports to measure).

(c) MEDICAL EXAMINATIONS AND INQUIRIES.

(1) IN GENERAL. The prohibition against discrimination as referred to in subsection (a) shall include medical examinations and inquiries.

(2) PREEMPLOYMENT.

(A) PROHIBITED EXAMINATION OR INQUIRY. Except as provided in paragraph (3), a covered entity shall not conduct a medical examination or make inquiries of a job applicant as to whether such applicant is an individual with a disability or as to the nature or severity of such disability.

(B) ACCEPTABLE INQUIRY. A covered entity may make preemployment inquiries into the ability of an applicant to perform job-related functions.

(3) EMPLOYMENT ENTRANCE EXAMI-NATION. A covered entity may require a medical examination after an offer of employment has been made to a job applicant and prior to the commencement of the employment duties of such applicant, and may condition an offer of employment on the results of such examination, if:

(A) all entering employees are subjected to such an examination regardless of disability;

(B) information obtained regarding the medical condition or history of the applicant is collected and maintained on separate forms and in separate medical files is treated as a confidential medical record, except that

(i) supervisors and managers may be informed regarding necessary restrictions on the work or duties of the employee and necessary accommodations;

(ii) first aid and safety personnel may be informed, when appropriate, if the disability might require emergency treatment; and

(iii) government officials investigating compliance with this Act shall be provided relevant information on request; and

(C) the results of such examination are used only in accordance with this title.

(4) EXAMINATION AND INQUIRY.

(A) PROHIBITED EXAMINATIONS AND INQUIRIES. A covered entity shall not require a medical examination and shall not make inquiries of an employee as to whether such employee is an individual with a disability or as to the nature or severity of the disability, unless such examination or inquiry is shown to be job-related and consistent with business necessity.

(B) ACCEPTABLE EXAMINATIONS AND INQUIRIES. A covered entity may conduct voluntary medical examinations, including voluntary medical histories, which are part of an employee health program available to employees at that work site. A covered entity may make inquiries into the ability of an employee to perform job-related functions.

(C) REQUIREMENT. Information obtained under subparagraph (B) regarding the medical condition or history of any employee are subject to the requirements of subparagraphs (B) and (C) of paragraph (3)....

ILLEGAL USE OF DRUGS AND ALCOHOL

SECTION 104. (a) QUALIFIED INDIVIDUAL WITH A DISABILITY. For purposes of this title, the term "qualified individual with a disability" shall not include any employee or applicant who is currently engaging in the illegal use of drugs, when the covered entity acts on the basis of such use.

(b) RULES OF CONSTRUCTION. Nothing in subsection (a) shall be construed to exclude as a qualified individual with a disability an individual who:

(1) has successfully completed a supervised drug rehabilitation program and is no longer engaging in the illegal use of drugs, or has otherwise been rehabilitated successfully and is no longer engaging in such use;

(2) is participating in a supervised rehabilitation program and is no longer engaging in such use; or

(3) is erroneously regarded as engaging in such use, but is not engaging in such use;

except that it shall not be a violation of this Act for a covered entity to adopt or administer reasonable policies or procedures, including but not limited to drug testing, designed to ensure that an individual described in paragraph (1) or (2) is no longer engaging in the illegal use of drugs....

EXCERPTS FROM THE ADA AMENDMENTS ACT OF 2008 (S.3406, P.L. 110-325)

SECTION 1. SHORT TITLE

This Act may be cited as the "ADA Amendments Act of 2008".

SECTION 2. FINDINGS AND PURPOSES

(a) Findings—Congress finds that—

(1) in enacting the Americans with Disabilities Act of 1990 (ADA), Congress intended that the Act "provide a clear and comprehensive national mandate for the elimination of discrimination against individuals with disabilities" and provide broad coverage;

(2) in enacting the ADA, Congress recognized that physical and mental disabilities in no way diminish a person's right to fully participate in all aspects of society, but that people with physical or mental disabilities are frequently precluded from doing so because of prejudice, antiquated attitudes, or the failure to remove societal and institutional barriers;

(3) while Congress expected that the definition of disability under the ADA would be interpreted consistently with how courts had applied the definition of a handicapped individual under the Rehabilitation Act of 1973, that expectation has not been fulfilled;

(4) the holdings of the Supreme Court in *Sutton v. United Air Lines, Inc.*, 527 U.S. 471 (1999) and its companion cases have narrowed the broad scope of protection intended to be afforded by the ADA, thus eliminating protection for many individuals whom Congress intended to protect;

(5) the holding of the Supreme Court in *Toyota Motor Manufacturing, Kentucky, Inc. v. Williams*, 534 U.S. 184 (2002) further narrowed the broad scope of protection intended to be afforded by the ADA;

(6) as a result of these Supreme Court cases, lower courts have incorrectly found in individual cases that people with a range of substantially limiting impairments are not people with disabilities;

(7) in particular, the Supreme Court, in the case of *Toyota Motor Manufacturing, Kentucky, Inc. v. Williams*, 534 U.S. 184 (2002), interpreted the term "substantially limits" to require a greater degree of limitation than was intended by Congress; and

(8) Congress finds that the current Equal Employment Opportunity Commission ADA regulations defining the term "substantially limits" as "significantly restricted" are inconsistent with congressional intent, by expressing too high a standard.

(b) Purposes—The purposes of this Act are—

(1) to carry out the ADA's objectives of providing "a clear and comprehensive national mandate for the elimination of discrimination" and "clear, strong, consistent, enforceable standards addressing discrimination" by reinstating a broad scope of protection to be available under the ADA;

(2) to reject the requirement enunciated by the Supreme Court in *Sutton v. United Air Lines, Inc.*, 527 U.S. 471 (1999) and its companion cases that whether an impairment substantially limits a major life activity is to be determined with reference to the ameliorative effects of mitigating measures;

(3) to reject the Supreme Court's reasoning in *Sutton v. United Air Lines, Inc.*, 527 U.S. 471 (1999) with regard to coverage under the third prong of the definition of disability and to reinstate the reasoning of the Supreme Court in *School Board of Nassau County v. Arline*, 480 U.S. 273 (1987) which set forth a broad view of the third prong of the definition of handicap under the Rehabilitation Act of 1973;

(4) to reject the standards enunciated by the Supreme Court in *Toyota Motor Manufacturing, Kentucky, Inc. v. Williams*, 534 U.S. 184 (2002), that the terms "substantially" and "major" in the definition of disability under the ADA "need to be interpreted strictly to create a demanding standard for qualifying as disabled," and that to be substantially limited in performing a major life activity under the ADA "an individual must have an impairment that prevents or severely restricts the individual from doing activities that are of central importance to most people's daily lives";

(5) to convey congressional intent that the standard created by the Supreme Court in the case of *Toyota Motor Manufacturing, Kentucky, Inc. v. Williams*, 534 U.S. 184 (2002) for "substantially limits", and applied by lower courts in numerous decisions, has created an inappropriately high level of limitation necessary to obtain coverage under the ADA, to convey that it is the intent of Congress that the primary object of attention in cases brought under the ADA should be whether entities covered under the ADA have complied with their obligations, and to convey that the question of whether an individual's impairment is a disability under the ADA should not demand extensive analysis; and

(6) to express Congress' expectation that the Equal Employment Opportunity Commission will revise that portion of its current regulations that defines the term "substantially limits" as "significantly restricted" to be consistent with this Act, including the amendments made by this Act.

SECTION 3. CODIFIED FINDINGS

Section 2(a) of the Americans with Disabilities Act of 1990 (42 U.S.C. 12101) is amended—

(1) by amending paragraph (1) to read as follows:

(1) physical or mental disabilities in no way diminish a person's right to fully participate in all aspects of society, yet many people with physical or mental disabilities have been precluded from doing so because of discrimination; others who have a record of a disability or are regarded as having a disability also have been subjected to discrimination;

(2) by striking paragraph (7); and

(3) by redesignating paragraphs (8) and (9) as paragraphs (7) and (8), respectively.

SECTION 4. DISABILITY DEFINED AND RULES OF CONSTRUCTION

(a) Definition of Disability—Section 3 of the Americans with Disabilities Act of 1990 (42 U.S.C. 12102) is amended to read as follows:

Section 3. Definition of Disability

As used in this Act:

(1) DISABILITY— The term 'disability' means, with respect to an individual—

(A) a physical or mental impairment that substantially limits one or more major life activities of such individual;

(B) a record of such an impairment; or

(C) being regarded as having such an impairment (as described in paragraph (3)).

(2) MAJOR LIFE ACTIVITIES—

(A) IN GENERAL— For purposes of paragraph (1), major life activities include, but are not limited to, caring for oneself, performing manual tasks, seeing, hearing, eating, sleeping, walking, standing, lifting, bending, speaking, breathing, learning, reading, concentrating, thinking, communicating, and working.

(B) MAJOR BODILY FUNCTIONS— For purposes of paragraph (1), a major life activity also includes the operation of a major bodily function, including but not limited to, functions of the immune system, normal cell growth, digestive, bowel, bladder, neurological, brain, respiratory, circulatory, endocrine, and reproductive functions.

(3) REGARDED AS HAVING SUCH AN IMPAIRMENT— For purposes of paragraph (1)(C):

(A) An individual meets the requirement of 'being regarded as having such an impairment' if the individual establishes that he or she has been subjected to an action prohibited under this Act because of an actual or perceived physical or mental impairment whether or not the impairment limits or is perceived to limit a major life activity.

(B) Paragraph (1)(C) shall not apply to impairments that are transitory and minor. A transitory impairment is an impairment with an actual or expected duration of 6 months or less.

(4) RULES OF CONSTRUCTION REGARDING THE DEFINITION OF DISABILITY— The definition of 'disability' in paragraph (1) shall be construed in accordance with the following:

(A) The definition of disability in this Act shall be construed in favor of broad coverage of individuals under this Act, to the maximum extent permitted by the terms of this Act.

(B) The term 'substantially limits' shall be interpreted consistently with the findings and purposes of the ADA Amendments Act of 2008.

(C) An impairment that substantially limits one major life activity need not limit other major life activities in order to be considered a disability.

(D) An impairment that is episodic or in remission is a disability if it would substantially limit a major life activity when active.

(E)(i) The determination of whether an impairment substantially limits a major life activity shall be made without regard to the ameliorative effects of mitigating measures such as—

(I) medication, medical supplies, equipment, or appliances, low-vision devices (which do not include ordinary eyeglasses or contact lenses), prosthetics including limbs and devices, hearing aids and cochlear implants or other implantable hearing devices, mobility devices, or oxygen therapy equipment and supplies;

(II) use of assistive technology;

(III) reasonable accommodations or auxiliary aids or services; or

(IV) learned behavioral or adaptive neurological modifications.

(ii) The ameliorative effects of the mitigating measures of ordinary eyeglasses or contact lenses shall be considered in determining whether an impairment substantially limits a major life activity.

(iii) As used in this subparagraph—

(I) the term 'ordinary eyeglasses or contact lenses' means lenses that are intended to fully correct visual acuity or eliminate refractive error; and

(II) the term 'low-vision devices' means devices that magnify, enhance, or otherwise augment a visual image. . . .

SECTION 5. DISCRIMINATION ON THE BASIS OF DISABILITY

(a) On the Basis of Disability— Section 102 of the Americans with Disabilities Act of 1990 (42 U.S.C. 12112) is amended—

(1) in subsection (a), by striking "with a disability because of the disability of

such individual" and inserting "on the basis of disability"; and

(2) in subsection (b) in the matter preceding paragraph (1), by striking "discriminate" and inserting "discriminate against a qualified individual on the basis of disability". . . .

SECTION 6. RULES OF CONSTRUCTION.

(a) Title V of the Americans with Disabilities Act of 1990 (42 U.S.C. 12201 *et seq.*) is amended—

(1) by adding at the end of Section 501 the following: . . .

(h) Reasonable Accommodations and Modifications. A covered entity under Title I, a public entity under Title II, and any person who owns, leases (or leases to), or operates a place of public accommodation under Title III, need not provide a reasonable accommodation or a reasonable modification to policies, practices, or procedures to an individual who meets the definition of disability in Section 3(1) solely under subparagraph (C) of such section.

EXCERPTS FROM THE EEOC's ADA ENFORCEMENT GUIDANCE: PREEMPLOYMENT DISABILITY-RELATED QUESTIONS AND MEDICAL EXAMINATIONS

INTRODUCTION

Under the Americans with Disabilities Act of 1990 (the "ADA"), an employer may ask disability-related questions and require medical examinations of an applicant only after the applicant has been given a conditional job offer. This Enforcement Guidance explains these ADA provisions.

BACKGROUND

In the past, some employment applications and interviews requested information about an applicant's physical and/or mental condition. This information was often used to exclude applicants with disabilities before their ability to perform the job was even evaluated.

For example, applicants may have been asked about their medical conditions at the same time that they were engaging in other parts of the application process, such as completing a written job application or having references checked. If an applicant was then rejected, s/he did not necessarily know whether s/he was rejected because of disability, or because of insufficient skills or experience or a bad report from a reference.

As a result, Congress established a process within the ADA to isolate an employer's consideration of an applicant's non-medical qualifications from any consideration of the applicant's medical condition.

THE STATUTORY AND REGULATORY FRAMEWORK

Under the law, an employer may not ask disability-related questions and may not conduct medical examinations until *after* it makes a conditional job offer to the applicant. This helps ensure that an applicant's possible hidden disability (including a prior history of a disability) is not considered before the employer evaluates an applicant's non-medical qualifications. An employer may not ask disability-related questions or require a medical examination pre-offer even if it intends to look at the answers or results only at the post-offer stage.

Although employers may not ask disability-related questions or require medical examinations at the pre-offer stage, they *may* do a wide variety of things to evaluate whether an applicant is qualified for the job, including the following:

- Employers *may* ask about an applicant's ability to perform specific job functions. For example, an employer may state the physical requirements of a job (such as the ability to lift a certain amount of weight, or the ability to climb ladders), and ask if an applicant can satisfy these requirements.
- Employers *may* ask about an applicant's non-medical qualifications and skills, such as the applicant's education, work history, and required certifications and licenses.
- Employers *may* ask applicants to describe or demonstrate how they would perform job tasks.

Once a conditional job offer is made, the employer may ask disability-related questions and require medical examinations as long as this is done for all entering employees in that job category. If the employer rejects the applicant after a disability-related question or medical examination, investigators will closely scrutinize whether the rejection was based on the results of that question or examination.

If the question or examination screens out an individual because of a disability, the employer must demonstrate that the reason for the rejection is "job-related and consistent with business necessity."

In addition, if the individual is screened out for safety reasons, the employer must demonstrate that the individual poses a "direct threat." This means that the individual poses a significant risk of substantial harm to him/herself or others, and that the risk cannot be reduced below the direct threat level through reasonable accommodation.

Medical information must be kept confidential. The ADA contains narrow exceptions for disclosing specific, limited information to supervisors and managers, first aid and safety personnel, and government officials investigating compliance with the ADA. Employers may also disclose medical information to state workers' compensation offices, state second injury funds, or workers' compensation insurance carriers in accordance with state workers' compensation laws and may use the medical information for insurance purposes.

THE PRE-OFFER STAGE

What is a Disability-Related Question? Definition: "Disability-Related Question" means a question that is *likely* to *elicit* information about a disability.

At the pre-offer stage, an employer cannot ask questions that are *likely* to *elicit* information about a disability. This includes directly asking whether an applicant has a particular disability. It also means that an employer cannot ask questions that are *closely related* to disability.

On the other hand, if there are many possible answers to a question and only some of those answers would contain disability-related information, that question is not "disability-related."

Below are some commonly asked questions about this area of the law.

- May an employer ask **whether an applicant can perform the job?**

  Yes. An employer may ask whether applicants can perform any or all job functions, including whether applicants can perform job functions "with or without reasonable accommodation."

- May an employer ask applicants to **describe or demonstrate how they would perform the job** (including any needed reasonable accommodations)?

  Yes. An employer may ask applicants to describe how they would perform any or all job functions, as long as all applicants in the job category are asked to do this.

Employers should remember that, if an applicant says that s/he will need a reasonable accommodation to do a job demonstration, the employer must either:

- provide a reasonable accommodation that does not create an undue hardship; or
- allow the applicant to simply describe how s/he would perform the job function.

- May an employer ask a **particular applicant to describe or demonstrate how s/he would perform the job**, if other applicants aren't asked to do this?

When an employer could reasonably believe that an applicant will not be able to perform a job function because of a known disability, the employer may ask that particular applicant to describe or demonstrate how s/he would perform the function. An applicant's disability would be a "known disability" either because it is obvious (for example, the applicant uses a wheelchair), or because the applicant has voluntarily disclosed that s/he has a hidden disability.

- May an employer ask applicants **whether they will need reasonable accommodation for the hiring process?**

Yes. An employer may tell applicants what the hiring process involves (for example, an interview, timed written test, or job demonstration), and may ask applicants whether they will need a reasonable accommodation for this process....

- May an employer ask applicants **whether they will need reasonable accommodation to perform the functions of the job?**

In general, an employer may not ask questions on an application or in an interview about whether an applicant will need reasonable accommodation for a job. This is because these questions are likely to elicit whether the applicant has a disability (generally, only people who have disabilities will need reasonable accommodations).

Example: An employment application may not ask, "Do you need reasonable accommodation to perform this job?"

Example: An employment application may not ask, "Can you do these functions with—without reasonable accommodations? (Check One)"

Example: An applicant with no known disability is being interviewed for a job. He has not asked for any reasonable accommodation, either for the application process or for the job. The employer may not ask him, "Will you need reasonable accommodation to perform this job?"

However, when an employer could reasonably believe that an applicant will need reasonable accommodation to perform the functions of the job, the employer may ask that applicant certain limited questions. Specifically, the employer may ask *whether s/he needs reasonable accommodation and what type of reasonable accommodation* would be needed to perform the functions of the job. The employer could ask these questions if:

- the employer reasonably believes the applicant will need reasonable accommodation because of an obvious disability;
- the employer reasonably believes the applicant will need reasonable accommodation because of a hidden disability that the applicant has voluntarily disclosed to the employer; or
- an applicant has voluntarily disclosed to the employer that s/he needs reasonable accommodation to perform the job.

Example: An individual with diabetes applying for a receptionist position voluntarily discloses that she will need periodic breaks to take medication. The employer may ask the applicant questions about the reasonable accommodation such as how often she will need breaks, and how long the breaks must be. Of course, the employer may not ask any questions about the underlying physical condition.

Example: An applicant with a severe visual impairment applies for a job involving computer work. The employer may ask whether he will need reasonable accommodation to perform the functions of the job. If the applicant answers "no," the employer may not ask additional questions about reasonable accommodation (although, of course, the employer could ask the applicant to describe or demonstrate performance). If the applicant says that he *will* need accommodation, the employer may ask questions about the type of required accommodation such as, "What will you need?" If the applicant says he needs software that increases the size of text on the computer screen, the employer may ask questions such as, "Who makes that software?" "Do you need a particular brand?" or "Is that software compatible with our computers?" However, the employer may not ask questions about the applicant's underlying condition. In addition, the employer may not ask reasonable accommodation questions that are unrelated to job functions such as, "Will you need reasonable accommodation to get to the cafeteria?"

An employer may only ask about reasonable accommodation that is needed now or in the near future. An applicant is not required to disclose reasonable accommodations that may be needed in the more distant future.

- May an employer ask **whether an applicant can meet the employer's attendance requirements?**

  Yes. An employer may state its attendance requirements and ask whether an applicant can meet them. An employer also may ask about an applicant's prior attendance record (for example, how many days the applicant was absent from his/her last job). These questions are not likely to elicit information about a disability because there may be many reasons unrelated to disability why someone cannot meet attendance requirements or was frequently absent from a previous job (for example, an applicant may have had day-care problems).

An employer also may ask questions designed to detect whether an applicant abused his/her leave because these questions are not likely to elicit information about a disability.

Example: An employer may ask an applicant, "How many Mondays or Fridays were you absent last year on leave other than approved vacation leave?"

However, at the pre-offer stage, an employer may not ask how many days an applicant was *sick*, because these questions relate directly to the *severity of an individual's impairments*. Therefore, these questions are likely to elicit information about a disability.

THE POST-OFFER STAGE

After giving a job offer to an applicant, an employer may ask disability-related questions and perform medical examinations. The job offer may be conditioned on the results of post-offer disability-related questions or medical examinations.

At the "post-offer" stage, an employer may ask about an individual's workers' compensation history, prior sick leave usage, illnesses/diseases/impairments, and general physical and mental health. Disability-related questions and medical examinations at the post-offer stage do not have to be related to the job.

If an employer asks post-offer disability-related questions, or requires post-offer medical examinations, it must make sure that it follows certain procedures:

- all entering employees in the same job category must be subjected to the examination/inquiry, regardless of disability, and
- medical information obtained must be kept confidential.

Below are some commonly asked questions about the post-offer stage.

- What is considered a *real* job offer?

  Since an employer can ask disability-related questions and require medical examinations after a job offer, it is important that the job offer be *real*. A job offer is real if the employer has evaluated all relevant non-medical information which it reasonably could have obtained and analyzed prior to giving the offer. Of course, there are times when an employer cannot reasonably obtain and evaluate *all* non-medical information at the pre-offer stage. If an employer can show that is the case, the offer would still be considered a real offer.

Example: It may be too costly for a law enforcement employer wishing to administer a polygraph examination to administer a pre-offer examination asking non-disability-related questions, and a post-offer examination asking disability-related questions. In this case, the employer may be able to demonstrate that it could not reasonably obtain and evaluate the non-medical polygraph information at the pre-offer stage.

Example: An applicant might state that his current employer should not be asked for a reference check until the potential employer makes a confidential job offer. In this case, the potential employer could not reasonably obtain and evaluate the non-medical information from the reference at the pre-offer stage.

- Do offers have to be limited to **current vacancies?**

  No. An employer may give offers to fill current vacancies or reasonably anticipated openings....

- After an employer has obtained basic medical information from all individuals who have been given conditional offers in a job category, may it ask **specific individuals for more medical information?**

  Yes, if the follow-up examinations or questions are medically related to the previously obtained medical information.

  Example: At the post-offer stage, an employer asks new hires whether they have had back injuries, and learns that some of the individuals have had such injuries. The employer may give medical examinations designed to diagnose back impairments to persons who stated that they had prior back injuries, as long as these examinations are medically related to those injuries.

- At the post-offer stage, may an employer ask all individuals **whether they need reasonable accommodation to perform the job?**

  Yes.

- If, at the post-offer stage, someone requests **reasonable accommodation to perform the job,** may the employer ask him/her for **documentation of his/her disability?**

  Yes. If someone requests reasonable accommodation so s/he will be able to perform a job and the need for the accommodation is not obvious, the employer may require reasonable documentation of the individual's entitlement to reasonable accommodation. So, the employer may require documentation showing that the individual has a *covered disability*, and stating his/her *functional limitations*.

  Example: An entering employee states that she will need a 15-minute break every two hours to eat a snack in order to maintain her blood sugar level. The employer may ask her to provide documentation from her doctor showing that: (1) she has an impairment that substantially limits a major life activity; and (2) she actually needs the requested breaks because of the impairment.

CONFIDENTIALITY

An employer must keep any medical information on applicants or employees confidential, with the following limited exceptions:

- supervisors and managers may be told about necessary restrictions on the work or duties of the employee and about necessary accommodations;

- first aid and safety personnel may be told if the disability might require emergency treatment;
- government officials investigating compliance with the ADA must be given relevant information on request;
- employers may give information to state workers' compensation offices, state second injury funds or workers' compensation insurance carriers in accordance with state workers' compensation laws; and
- employers may use the information for insurance purposes.

Below are some commonly asked questions about the ADA's confidentiality requirements.

- May **medical information** be given to **decision-makers involved in the hiring process?**

  Yes. Medical information may be given to—and used by—appropriate decision-makers involved in the hiring process so they can make employment decisions consistent with the ADA. In addition, the employer may use the information to determine reasonable accommodations for the individual. For example, the employer may share the information with a third party, such as a health care professional, to determine whether a reasonable accommodation is possible for a particular individual. The information certainly must be kept confidential.

  Of course, the employer may only share the medical information with individuals involved in the hiring process (or in implementing an affirmative action program) who *need to know* the information. For example, in some cases, a number of people may be involved in evaluating an applicant. Some individuals may simply be responsible for evaluating an applicant's references; these individuals may have no need to know an applicant's medical condition and therefore should not have access to the medical information.

- Can an individual **voluntarily disclose his/her own medical information** to persons beyond those to whom an employer can disclose such information?

  Yes, as long as it's *really* voluntary. The employer cannot request, persuade, coerce, or otherwise pressure the individual to get him/her to disclose medical information.

- Does the employer's confidentiality obligation extend to **medical information that an individual voluntarily tells the employer?**

  Yes. For example, if an applicant voluntarily discloses bipolar disorder and the need for reasonable accommodation, the employer may not disclose the condition or the applicant's need for accommodation to the applicant's references.

- Can **medical information be kept in an employee's regular personnel file?**

  No. Medical information must be collected and maintained on separate forms and in separate medical files. An employer should not place any medical-related material in an employee's non-medical personnel file. If an employer wants to put a document in a personnel file, and that document happens to contain some medical information, the employer must simply remove the medical information from the document before putting it in the personnel file.

- Does the **confidentiality obligation end when the person is no longer an applicant or employee?**

  No, an employer must keep medical information confidential *even* if someone is no longer an applicant (for example, s/he wasn't hired) or is no longer an employee.

- Is an employer required to **remove from its personnel files medical information obtained before the ADA's effective date?**

  No.

Excerpts from the EEOC's Enforcement Guidance: Workers' Compensation and the ADA

INTRODUCTION

This enforcement guidance concerns the interaction between Title I of the Americans with Disabilities Act of 1990 (ADA) and state workers' compensation laws. The purpose of Title I of the ADA is to prohibit employers from discriminating against qualified individuals because of disability in all aspects of employment. On the other hand, the purpose of a workers' compensation law is to provide a system for securing prompt and fair settlement of employees' claims against employers for occupational injury and illness. While the purposes of the two laws are not in conflict, the simultaneous application of the laws has raised questions for EEOC investigators, for employers, and for individuals with disabilities in a number of areas. In this document, the Commission provides guidance concerning the following issues:

- whether a person with an occupational injury has a disability as defined by the ADA;

- disability-related questions and medical examinations relating to occupational injury and workers' compensation claims;
- hiring of persons with a history of occupational injury, return to work of persons with occupational injury, and application of the direct threat standard;
- reasonable accommodation for persons with disability-related occupational injuries;
- light duty issues; and
- exclusive remedy provisions in workers' compensation laws.

REASONABLE ACCOMMODATION

The ADA requires that an employer make reasonable accommodation to the known physical or mental limitations of an otherwise qualified individual with a disability, unless the employer can demonstrate that the accommodation would impose an undue hardship.... This section provides specific guidance regarding reasonable accommodation in the context of workers' compensation.

17. Does the ADA require an employer to provide reasonable accommodation for an employee with an occupational injury who does not have a disability as defined by the ADA?

> No. The ADA does not require an employer to provide a reasonable accommodation for an employee with an occupational injury who does not have a disability as defined by the ADA.

18. May an employer discharge an employee who is temporarily unable to work because of a disability-related occupational injury?

> No. An employer may not discharge an employee who is temporarily unable to work because of a disability-related occupational injury where it would not impose an undue hardship to provide leave as a reasonable accommodation.

19. What are the reinstatement rights of an employee with a disability-related occupational injury?

> An employee with a disability-related occupational injury is entitled to return to his/her same position unless the employer demonstrates that holding open the position would impose an undue hardship.
>
> In some instances, an employee may request more leave even after the employer has communicated that it would impose an undue hardship to hold open the employee's position any longer. In this situation, the employer must consider whether it has a vacant, equivalent position for which the employee is qualified and to which the employee can be reassigned without undue hardship to continue his/her leave for a specific period of time. For example, suppose that an employee needs six months to recover from a disability-related occupational injury, but holding his/her original position open for more than four months will

impose an undue hardship. The employer must consider whether it has a vacant equivalent position to which the employee can be reassigned for the remaining two months of leave. If an equivalent position is not available, the employer must look for a vacant position at a lower level. Continued leave is not required as a reasonable accommodation if a vacant position at a lower level is also unavailable.

20. Must an employer, as a reasonable accommodation, reallocate job duties of an employee with a disability-related occupational injury?

> Yes, if the duties to be reallocated are marginal functions of the position that the employee cannot perform because of the disability. Reasonable accommodation includes restructuring a position by reallocating or redistributing the marginal functions that the employee cannot perform because of the disability. However, an employer need not eliminate essential functions of the position.

21. May an employer unilaterally reassign an employee with a disability-related occupational injury to a different position instead of first trying to accommodate the employee in the position s/he held at the time the injury occurred?

> No. An employer must first assess whether the employee can perform the essential functions of his/her original position, with or without a reasonable accommodation. Examples of reasonable accommodation include job restructuring, modification of equipment, or a part-time work schedule. Reassignment should be considered only when accommodation within the employee's original position is not possible or would impose an undue hardship.

22. Must an employer reassign an employee who is no longer able to perform the essential functions of his/her original position, with or without a reasonable accommodation,

because of a disability-related occupational injury?

Yes. Where an employee can no longer perform the essential functions of his/her original position, with or without a reasonable accommodation, because of a disability-related occupational injury, an employer must reassign him/her to an equivalent vacant position for which s/he is qualified, absent undue hardship. If no equivalent vacant position (in terms of pay, status, etc.) exists, then the employee must be reassigned to a lower graded position for which s/he is qualified, absent undue hardship.

23. If there is no vacancy for an employee who can no longer perform his/her original position because of a disability-related occupational injury, must an employer create a new position or "bump" another employee from his/her position?

No. The ADA does not require an employer to create a new position or to bump another employee from his/her position in order to reassign an employee who can no longer perform the essential functions of his/her original position, with or without a reasonable accommodation.

24. When an employee requests leave as a reasonable accommodation under the ADA because of a disability-related occupational injury, may an employer provide an accommodation that requires him/her to remain on the job instead?

Yes. An employer need not provide an employee's preferred accommodation as long as the employer provides an effective accommodation—one that is sufficient to meet the employee's job-related needs.

Accordingly, an employer may provide a reasonable accommodation that requires an employee to remain on the job, in lieu of providing leave (e.g., reallocating marginal functions, or providing temporary reassignment).

The employer is obligated, however, to restore the employee's full duties or to return the employee to his/her original position once s/he has recovered sufficiently to perform its essential functions, with or without a reasonable accommodation.

25. May an employer make a workplace modification that is not a required form of reasonable accommodation under the ADA in order to offset workers' compensation costs?

Yes. Nothing in the ADA prohibits an employer from making a workplace modification that is not a required form of reasonable accommodation under the ADA for an employee with an occupational injury in order to offset workers' compensation costs. For example, the ADA does not require employers to lower production standards to accommodate individuals with disabilities. However, an employer is clearly permitted to lower production standards for an occupationally injured employee as a way of returning him/her to work more quickly.

LIGHT DUTY

The term "light duty" has a number of different meanings in the employment setting. Generally, "light duty" refers to temporary or permanent work that is physically or mentally less demanding than normal job duties. Some employers use the term "light duty" to mean simply excusing an employee from performing those job functions that s/he is unable to perform because of an impairment. "Light duty" also may consist of particular positions with duties that are less physically or mentally demanding created specifically for the purpose of providing alternative work for employees who are unable to perform some or all of their normal duties. Further, an employer may refer to any position that is sedentary or is less physically or mentally demanding as "light duty."

In the following questions and answers, the term "light duty" refers only to particular positions created specifically for the purpose of providing work for employees who are unable to perform some or all of their normal duties.

27. Does the ADA prohibit an employer from creating a light duty position for an employee when s/he is injured on the job?

No, in most instances. An employer may recognize a special obligation arising out of the employment relationship to create a light duty position for an employee when s/he has been injured while performing work for the employer and, as a consequence, is unable to perform his/her regular job duties. Such a policy, on its face, does not treat an individual with a disability less favorably than an individual without a disability; nor does it screen out an individual on the basis of disability.

Of course, an employer must apply its policy of creating a light duty position for an employee when s/he is occupationally injured on a non-discriminatory basis. In other words, an employer may not use disability as a reason to refuse to create a light duty position when an employee is occupationally injured.

An employer need not create a light duty position for a non-occupationally injured employee with a disability as a reasonable accommodation. The principle that the ADA does not require employers to create positions as a form of reasonable accommodation applies equally to the creation of light duty positions. However, an employer must provide other forms of reasonable accommodation required under the ADA....

Example: R creates light duty positions for employees when they are occupationally injured if they are unable to perform one or more of their regular job duties. CP can no longer perform functions of her position because of a disability caused by an off-the-job accident. She requests that R create a light duty position for her as a reasonable accommodation. R denies CP's request because she has not been injured on the job. R has not violated the ADA. However, R must provide another reasonable accommodation, absent undue hardship. If it is determined that the only effective accommodation is to restructure CP's position by redistributing the marginal functions, and the restructured position resembles a light duty position, R must provide the reasonable accommodation unless it can prove that it imposes an undue hardship....

L | Excerpts from the EEOC's Compliance Manual Section on Religious Discrimination (2008)

[On July 22, 2008 the EEOC approved a new Compliance Manual section on religious discrimination under Title VII of the 1964 Civil Rights Act. The EEOC's Associate Legal Counsel expressed the view that the increase in religious diversity in the workplace may be contributing to the rise in religious bias charges over the past 15 years, with the increasing numbers of Muslims, Hindu and Buddhist employees in the U.S. workforce. Selected Questions and Answers follow:]

...WHEN IS AN EMPLOYER LIABLE FOR RELIGIOUS HARASSMENT?

An employer is always liable for a supervisor's harassment if it results in a tangible employment action. However, if it does not, the employer may be able to avoid liability or limit damages by showing that: (a) the employer exercised reasonable care to prevent and correct promptly any harassing behavior, and (b) the employee unreasonably failed to take advantage of any preventive or corrective opportunities provided by the employer or to avoid harm otherwise. An employer is liable for harassment by co-workers where it knew or should have known about the harassment, and failed to take prompt and appropriate corrective action. An employer is liable for harassment by non-employees where it knew or should have known about the harassment, could control the harasser's conduct or otherwise protect the employee, and failed to take prompt and appropriate corrective action.

...WHEN DOES AN ACCOMMODATION POSE AN "UNDUE HARDSHIP"?

An accommodation would pose an undue hardship if it—would cause more than de minimis cost on the operation of the employer's business. Factors relevant to undue hardship may include the type of workplace, the nature of the employee's duties, the identifiable cost of the accommodation in relation to the size and operating costs of the employer, and the number of employees who will in fact need a particular accommodation.

Costs to be considered include not only direct monetary costs but also the burden on the conduct of the employer's business. For example, courts have found undue hardship where the accommodation diminishes efficiency in other jobs, infringes on the employees' job rights or benefits, impairs workplace safety, or causes co-workers to carry the accommodated employee's share of potentially hazardous or burdensome work. Whether the proposed accommodation conflicts with another law will also be considered.

To prove undue hardship, the employer will need to demonstrate how much cost or disruption a proposed accommodation would involve. An employer cannot rely on potential or hypothetical hardship when faced with a religious obligation that conflicts with scheduled work, but rather should rely on objective information.

A mere assumption that many more people with the same religious practices as the individual being accommodated may also seek accommodation is not evidence of undue hardship.

If an employee's proposed accommodation would pose an undue hardship, the employer should explore alternative accommodations.

...DO NATIONAL ORIGIN, RACE, COLOR, AND RELIGIOUS DISCRIMINATION INTERSECT IN SOME CASES?

Yes. Title VII's prohibition against religious discrimination may overlap with the Title VII prohibitions against discrimination based on national origin, race, and color. Where a given religion is strongly associated—or perceived to be associated—with a certain national origin, the same facts may state a claim of both religious and national origin discrimination. All four bases might be implicated where, for example, co-workers target a dark-skinned Muslim employee from Saudi Arabia for harassment because of his religion, national origin, race, and/or color.

GLOSSARY

A

administrative law judge a government official who presides at hearings of the NLRB or other government agencies. In the absence of objections by a party, the NLRB routinely endorses the administrative law judge's findings of fact and recommendations.

affidavit a statement of facts set forth in written form and supported by the oath or affirmation of the person making the statement that such facts are true to the person's knowledge, information, and belief. The affidavit is executed before a notary public or other person authorized to administer oaths.

agency a situation in which one person acts for or represents another by the latter's authority.

agency shop a union contract provision requiring that nonunion employees pay to the union the equivalent of union dues in order to retain their employment.

agent one who is acting for an employer or union. An agent's actions may subject a principal to liability with respect to unfair labor practices even in the absence of specific authorization.

amici a person or organization that has no right to appear in a suit but is allowed to introduce argument, authority, or evidence to protect the individual's or group's interests.

amicus curiae literally, a friend of the court; one who is allowed to volunteer information or argument to protect his or her interest.

animus mind or intention. In labor law, animus is used as a shortened form of "antiunion animus" or antiunion mind set or intent.

anti-injunction acts statutes prohibiting the use of injunctions in labor disputes except under exceptional circumstances, notably the federal Norris-LaGuardia Act of 1932.

antitrust act statute prohibiting combinations and contracts in restraint of trade, notably the federal Sherman Antitrust Act of 1890.

arbitration the settlement of disputed questions, whether concerning contractual language or fact, by one or more arbitrators by whose decision the parties agreed to be bound. Increasingly used as a procedure for labor dispute settlement.

authorization card a signed statement authorizing a union to act as an agent for an employee for collective bargaining purposes.

B

back pay wages required to be paid to an employee upon a finding of discharge or layoff of the employee in violation of a contractual or statutory right.

bail variously used in connection with the release of a person or property from the custody of the law, referring (a) to the act of releasing or bailing, (b) to the persons who assume liability in the event that the released person does not appear at a time and place certain or it is held that the property should not be released, and (c) to the bond or sum of money that is furnished the court or other official as indemnity for nonperformance of the obligation.

bargaining unit a group of employees performing jobs in a plant or industry with sufficient community of interests to constitute a unit to be represented in collective bargaining with an employer or employer-group by a bargaining agent.

bilateral agreement an agreement under which each party promises or undertakes performance, the promise or the undertaking by the one

769

furnishing the consideration for the promise or undertaking of the other.

bond a written obligation or evidence of debt.

boycott a refusal to deal with, purchase goods from, or work for an employer; a conspiracy to inhibit the carrying on of business to exert pressure on a party to a labor dispute.

bumping a right granted by a collective bargaining contract allowing a worker laid off from a job that has been discontinued by the employer to displace a less senior employee in the same facility.

burden of proof the requirement that a certain party to a legal dispute prove a fact or facts in question.

business agent local union officer who is paid to administer the union's affairs, enroll new members, handle grievances, and negotiate with the employer.

bylaws regulations or provisions supplementing the constitution or charter of a labor union (or corporation).

C

case law the law as laid down in the decisions of the courts as distinct from statutes and other sources of law.

cause of action the right to damages or other judicial relief when a legally protected right of the plaintiff is violated by an unlawful act of the defendant.

cease and desist order an order by the National Labor Relations Board that requires an employer or union to cease an unfair labor practice.

certification formal recognition of a union as exclusive bargaining representative for a unit of employees.

certiorari an appellate proceeding for reexamination of an action or judgment of a lower court. It usually requires the lower court to certify and return its records to the reviewing court.

charge a written statement alleging violation of a labor relations statute.

charging party the person initiating unfair labor practice procedures before the National Labor Relations Board or the person initiating

unlawful employment practice procedures before the Equal Employment Opportunity Commission.

checkoff a system by which an employer deducts union dues from the employees' paychecks and transfers the funds to the union.

civil action in many states a simplified form of action combining all or many of the former common law actions.

class action suit an action in which one or more members of a numerous class having a common interest sue on behalf of themselves and all other members of that class.

closed shop a union security agreement by which only union members may be hired. Now generally prohibited under federal labor statutes.

coercion pressure exerted by an employer to prevent employees from engaging in concerted activities or activities by a union to compel employees to become members.

collective bargaining agreement a contract governing wages, hours, and conditions of employment between an employer and a union that is the product of the collective bargaining process.

common carrier a carrier that holds out its facilities to serve the general public for compensation without discrimination.

common law the body of unwritten principles originally based on the usages and customs of the community which were recognized and enforced by the courts.

complaint the initial pleading filed by the plaintiff in a civil action; also a formal statement by the NLRB, after investigating a charge, that the Board has jurisdiction and *prima facie* evidence that an unfair labor practice exists.

concerted activities activities engaged in by employees for their mutual aid or protection allowing employees to organize and to form, join, or assist a labor union, as protected under Section 7 of the National Labor Relations Act.

conciliation process where a third party acts as intermediary between the

parties to a labor dispute, helping them to reach a settlement.

conclusive presumption also called an irrebuttable presumption; a legal rule that a certain amount of evidence determines that a fact is true and not subject to contradiction.

consent decree an agreement reached by parties to a case after careful negotiation which is then entered as a judgment by a court.

consumer picketing picketing to discourage consumers from patronizing a retail store or from buying a particular product.

contract a binding agreement based upon the genuine assent of competent parities, made for a lawful object, in the form required by law, and generally supported by consideration; a collective bargaining agreement.

corporation an artificial legal person or being created by government grant, which for many purposes is treated as a natural person.

crime a violation of the law that is punished as an offense against the state or government.

cross-examination the questioning of a witness by the attorney for the adverse party.

D

damages a sum of money recovered to redress or make amends for the legal wrong or injury done.

d.b.a. abbreviation for "doing business as."

decertification removal of a union's certification as exclusive bargaining representative upon ascertainment of a loss of a majority favoring the union pursuant to an election that is requested by a petitioner.

declaratory judgment an accelerated procedure for obtaining the decision of a court on a question before any action has been taken or loss sustained. It differs from an advisory opinion in that there must be an actual, imminent controversy. The judgment declares the legal rights of the parties.

de facto existing in fact as distinguished from existing by lawful right.

deposition the testimony of a witness taken out of court before a person authorized to administer oaths.

discovery procedures for ascertaining facts prior to the time of trial in order to eliminate the element of surprise in litigation.

discrimination unequal treatment of workers. The National Labor Relations Act prohibits discrimination with respect to hire or tenure of employment as a means of encouraging or discouraging membership in a labor organization.

dismiss, motion to a procedure to terminate an action by requesting dismissal on the ground that the plaintiff has not pleaded a cause entitling the plaintiff to relief.

domicile the home of a person or the state of incorporation. To be distinguished from a place where a person lives but which the person does not regard as home or a state in which a corporation does business but in which it was not incorporated.

due process of law the guarantee by the Fifth and Fourteenth Amendments of the federal Constitution and of many state constitutions that no person shall be deprived of life, liberty, or property without due process of law. As presently interpreted, this prohibits any law, either state or federal, that sets up an unfair procedure. Due process requires that a defendant be given notice of the charges and an opportunity to defend against the charges.

E

economic strike a strike to induce changes in wages, hours, and working conditions. The employer is free to hire replacements in an economic strike in contrast to a strike in response to an employer unfair labor practice.

election, consent An election conducted by a Regional Director of the NLRB pursuant to an agreement signed by all parties concerned. The agreement provides for the waiving of a hearing, the establishment of the appropriate unit by mutual consent, and the final determination of all postelection issues by the Regional Director.

election, runoff An election conducted by a Regional Director of the NLRB after an initial election, having three or more choices on the ballot, has turned out to be inconclusive (none of the choices receiving a majority of the valid votes cast). The Regional Director conducts the runoff election between the choices on the original ballot which received the highest and the next highest number of votes.

election, stipulated An election held by a Regional Director of the NLRB pursuant to an agreement signed by all the parties concerned. The agreement provides for the waiving of a hearing and the establishment of the appropriate unit by mutual consent. Final postelection rulings are made by the Board, after the Regional Director has made interim rulings.

employee one who performs services under the direction and control of another.

employer one who employs the services of others in exchange for wages.

employer association an organization formed by employers usually engaged in the same industry that often bargains as a unit with the union(s) or promulgates uniform labor practices.

equity the body of principles that originally developed because of the inadequacy of the rules then applied by the common law courts of England. Equity embodies notions of natural rights, justice, ethics, and conscience.

estoppel the principle by which a person is barred from pursuing a certain course of action or of disputing the truth of certain matters when that person's conduct has been such that it would be unjust to permit the person to do so.

evidence that which is presented to the trier of fact as the basis on which the trier is to determine what happened.

F

fair employment practice for hiring, promotion, and tenure of employees without discrimination due to race, color, national origin, religion, or sex.

featherbedding the exaction of money for services not performed or the union practice of making work for union members that is inconsistent with efficiency; an unfair labor practice under the National Labor Relations Act, Section 8(a)(6).

fiduciary a person in a position of trust, such as an administrator or manager of a pension plan.

fraud the making of a false statement of a past or existing fact with knowledge of its falsity or with reckless indifference as to its truth with the intent to cause another to rely thereon, and the other does rely thereon to the other's injury.

free speech the constitutional protection that is a basis for the right of a union to picket. Employers are entitled to express views hostile to unionization under the same auspices.

front pay an amount of money awarded a victim of discrimination to make the victim whole for the loss of future work opportunities with an employer due to the employer's wrongful discrimination.

G

good faith bargaining the National Labor Relations Act obligates the union and employer to meet at reasonable times and bargain in good faith concerning terms and conditions of employment. Good faith does not require the parties to make concessions.

grievance a complaint by the union, employer, or employees usually alleging a violation of the collective bargaining agreement.

grievance procedure a procedure for settling disputes set forth in the collective bargaining agreement. It usually involves several steps, with the aggrieved worker and representative meeting with the supervisor involved, followed by an appeal system with strict time limits and ultimately ending in binding arbitration.

H

hiring halls a place that refers workers to employment opportunities; often used in casual and seasonal industries.

hot cargo clauses a contract clause granting union members the right to refuse to handle goods from a plant that is on strike or is nonunion, etc. Such clauses are illegal under the Taft-Hartley Act.

I

impasse a situation arising in negotiating a collective bargaining agreement where the parties are unable to make further progress towards reaching agreement.

informational picketing picketing designed to apprise the public that an employer either is selling nonunion goods or is operating without a contract with the union. Picketing to publicize information concerning such labor disputes must conform with the Taft-Hartley Act.

initiation fees fees necessary to becoming a union member, which may not legally be excessive or discriminatory.

injunction an order of a court of equity to refrain from doing (negative injunction) or to do (affirmative or mandatory injunction) a specified act. Its use in labor disputes has been greatly restricted by the Norris-LaGuardia Act.

interest arbitration when the parties are unable to reach an agreement on a new collective bargaining agreement, the parties select an arbitrator to resolve the impasse, agreeing to be bound by the arbitrator's decisions on the terms of the new contract. Infrequently used in the private sector. Sometimes used in Railway Labor Act disputes and public sector disputes.

international union many unions have affiliates in Canada, such as the United Auto Workers, the Sheet Metal Workers International Union and the International Association of Machinists and Aerospace Workers, thus making these organizations "international" labor unions.

J

joint council a group consisting of management and union representatives that attempts to resolve disputes arising under the contract and to facilitate the collective bargaining process.

journeyman a worker who has successfully completed an apprenticeship and is entirely skilled at a craft.

judgment the final sentence, order, or decision entered into at the conclusion of an action which determines the rights of the parties.

jurisdiction the power of a court or agency to hear and to determine a given class of cases; the power to act over a particular defendant. Also, a right sought by a union to bargain for a certain group or class of employees to the exclusion of another union.

jurisdictional dispute a dispute between rival labor unions that may take the form of each claiming that particular work should be assigned to it or claiming the right to organize a class of employees.

L

layoff separation of employees from their jobs due to lack of work or other commercial reasons not caused by the fault of the employees. It is also referred to as a "reduction in force".

local union the primary unit of union organization, often limited to one plant or to a small geographic area. The local is chartered by an international or national union but has its own constitution, bylaws, and government.

lockout economic pressure tactic of an employer during negotiations which consists of the withholding of work; it also may be an illegal attempt to discourage union activity.

M

maintenance of membership a mild form of union security that imposes no obligation on an employee to join a union but merely the obligation to remain a member in good standing for the duration of the collective bargaining agreement if an employee has already joined a union.

mandatory injunction an injunction that commands a defendant to do an act.

mediation a method of resolving labor disputes whereby a disinterested third party listens to the arguments of both

the employer and the union and then suggests methods of reconciling the dispute. Unlike arbitration, the solutions proposed as a result of mediation are not binding on either party.

N

National Labor Relations Act the federal statute designed to protect the organization rights of labor and to prevent unfair labor practices by management or labor.

negotiation the process by which representatives of labor and management bargain to reach a contract regarding wages, hours and working conditions for an appropriate bargaining unit.

Norris-LaGuardia Anti-Injunction Act a federal statute prohibiting the use of the injunction in labor disputes, except in particular cases.

no-solicitation rules by banning all solicitation and literature distribution on its private property employers are able to ban non-employee union organizers from their property in most states.

no-strike clause a contract provision in which the union agrees not to call a work stoppage during the term of the collective bargaining agreement.

O

Occupational Safety and Health Act a federal statute enabling the government to set safety and health standards in industries and to enforce those standards.

operation of law the attaching of certain consequences to certain facts because of legal principles that operate automatically, as contrasted with consequences that arise because of the voluntary action of a party designed to create those consequences.

organizational picketing picketing to encourage employees to join or endorse a particular union.

P

pattern bargaining after the first contract in an industry is reached by an employer and a union, subsequent contract settlements by other employers in the industry with the union in question will contain many of the essential terms of the first contract.

petitioner the party initiating an appeal from an adverse decision by a lower court or administrative agency.

picketing the placing of persons outside of places of employment or distribution so that by words or banners they may inform the public of the existence of a labor dispute.

PL Boards public law boards. Special boards of adjustment created under the 1966 amendments to the Railway Labor Act (Public Law No. 89-456) to resolve disputes between carriers and unions that have been pending before the NRAB for a year or more.

pleadings the papers filed by the parties in an action which set forth the facts and the nature of the issues to be tried.

preponderance of evidence the degree or quantum of evidence in favor of the existence of a certain fact when from a review of all the evidence it appears more probable than not that the fact exists. The margin of probability required is a greater than 50 percent likelihood of the fact's existence.

Presidential Emergency Board A 3 person board appointed by the President of the United States under the Railway Labor Act to submit a report the President with recommendations for the fair and equitable resolution of a labor dispute in the railroad or airline industry.

prima facie such evidence as by itself would establish the claim or defense of the party if the evidence were believed.

prima facie case a case that will be sufficient if not contradicted by rebutting evidence.

proof the probative effect of the evidence; the conclusion drawn from the evidence as to the existence of particular facts.

public policy certain objectives relating to health, morals, and integrity of government that the law seeks to advance.

punitive damages damages in excess of those required to compensate the plaintiff for the wrong done, which are imposed in view of the wanton or willful character of the defendant's wrongdoing; also called exemplary damages.

Q

quasi as if, as though it were, having the characteristics of; a modifier employed to indicate that the subject is to be treated as an analogy to the noun that follows the word *quasi,* as in quasi contract, quasi corporation.

R

ratification the process of approval of a newly negotiated collective bargaining agreement by the full union membership.

RICO an acronym for Racketeer Influenced and Corrupt Organizations Act, a federal statute designed to stop organized criminal activity from infiltrating legitimate businesses.

recognition an employer's acknowledgment and acceptance of a union as the exclusive representative of employees in a unit for purposes of collective bargaining.

recognition picketing picketing to induce an employer to recognize a union as bargaining representative for a unit for employees. Such picketing is restricted under the National Labor Relations Act, under the National Labor Relations Act, Section 8(b)(7).

referee an impartial person selected by the parties or appointed by a court to determine various matters relating to arbitration proceedings.

remedy the action or procedure that is followed in order to enforce a right or obtain damages for injury to a right.

respondeat superior let the master answer. This maxim means that an employer is liable in certain cases for the wrongful acts of its employees.

respondent one who is called upon to answer a charge before the NLRB. Also a party against whom an appeal is brought in a federal appeals court.

reverse discrimination preferential treatment with regard to hire or tenure of employment that attempts to remedy past discrimination by means of quotas in hiring or immunity from layoff despite low seniority.

right-to-work law a state law that prohibits employment arrangements which mandate union membership as a condition of employment.

S

sanction that part of a law which signifies the penalty that will be exacted for its breach.

scab a slang expression used to describe workers who do not comply with a strike, analogous to the term *traitor.*

scienter knowledge, referring to those wrongs or crimes that require a knowledge of wrong in order to constitute the offense.

secondary activities strike, picketing, or boycott activities upon an employer with whom a union has no dispute to persuade the employer to cease doing business with a party to a dispute.

secondary boycott a refusal to do business with a neutral party to coerce the neutral party to exert pressure on a party to a labor dispute to comply with the union's dispute to comply with the union's demands.

seniority system a system that grants employees employment preferences according to the employee's length of service.

Sherman Antitrust Act a federal statute prohibiting combinations and contracts in restraint of interstate trade.

shop steward union person who handles union matters in a particular department or shop. A steward processes employee grievances and may be responsible for the collection of dues.

slowdown a slowing down of production by employees without actually stopping work; a means of exerting pressure on the employer.

stare decisis the principle that the decision of a court should serve as a guide or precedent and control the decision of a similar case in the future.

statute of limitations a statute that restricts the period of time within which an action may be brought under the National Labor Relations Act; an unfair labor charge must be filed within six months of the events.

stranger picketing picketing by persons who are not employees of the picketed company.

struck-work clause a contract clause that allows employees to refuse to perform work which would have been performed by employees of another company or employer if the latter company were not on strike.

subpoena a court order directing a person to appear as a witness.

summons a writ by which a defendant is notified that an action was commenced against the defendant and must be answered.

sympathy strike a strike by workers not directly involved in a labor dispute who refuse to cross a picket line of another bargaining unit that is on strike against its employer.

T

Taft-Hartley Act popular name for the National Labor Relations Act as amended in 1947.

testimony the answers of witnesses under oath to questions given at the time of trial in the presence of the trier of fact.

trespass an unlawful act causing injury to the person, property, or rights of another.

trial examiner a National Labor Relations Board official who formerly conducted hearings to ascertain the facts surrounding a petition for representation or an unfair labor practice charge; such a person is called an administrative law judge.

U

unfair employment practice employment discrimination with respect to race, color, religion, sex, or national origin.

unfair labor practices practices of employers or unions that are prohibited under Section 8 of the National Labor Relations Act or under state labor statutes.

unfair labor practice strike a strike in protest of an employer's unfair labor practice(s). The employer is required to reinstate such strikers.

union security clause a provision in a collective bargaining agreement that is designed to expand the membership and treasury of the union. Such clauses include maintenance of membership, dues checkoff, and an agency or union shop clause.

union shop a form of union security under which an employer may hire a nonunion employee, but the employee must become a union member within a specified period of time and remain a member in good standing as a condition of employment.

V

validation study a study of a personnel test to determine the test's validity as an accurate predictor of successful work behavior. A method for validating a test is to administer it to all applicants while making selections for hiring without regard to test scores. After an appropriate period of time on the job, work performance can be compared with test scores.

W

whipsaw strike one of a pattern of successive strikes against one after another of the various members of an employers' association. The object is to enhance the union's bargaining position by threatening the employer with a decrease in market share as customers turn to competitors that have not been struck.

writ a writing issued from a court in the name of a state or the United States and addressed to an officer of the law or an individual whose action the court desires to command, requiring the performance of specified act or giving authority to have it done, such as the commencement of a lawsuit.

Index of Cases

Index of Subjects